INSTRUCTOR EDITION

WELCOME

At Course Technology our mission is to help people teach and learn about technology. This special Instructor Edition is all about helping YOU teach. We know you have a great deal to manage, and for this reason, we provide you with great tools and resources with every book. This Instructor Edition will save you time by helping you sort through all of this material, and choose the right combination of tools to help you teach the way you want to teach.

CONTENTS AT A GLANCE

Page IE 2: **CoursePort**

The powerful, new CoursePort site provides a central location from which you can access Thomson Course Technology's online learning solutions with convenience and flexibility. Centralized access to online activities for all of your classes will increase your productivity and save you time. Use CoursePort to gain access to robust online resources including Instructor Resources, Student Online Companion Web sites, and more.

Page IE 3: **About *New Perspectives on Computer Concepts 8th Edition***

This section describes the new 8th Edition features that you can take advantage of in your course, as well as the major content updates on a chapter-by-chapter basis.

Page IE 5: **Anatomy of a New Perspectives on Computer Concepts Chapter**

This section describes the pedagogical and design elements you'll find in every New Perspectives on Computer Concepts 8th edition chapter—including both the time-tested features you are already familiar with, plus the enhancements we've made with this edition.

Page IE 11: **Anatomy of the NP8 Web Site**

Increase your options for assignments with Pre-Assessments, Online Games and Student Edition Labs, all available through the NP8 Web site.

Page IE 14: **Anatomy of the New Perspectives Computer Concepts BookOnCD**

If you want to add an interactive element to your student's classroom experience, take advantage of the multimedia elements on the New Perspectives BookOnCD and WebTrack software.

Page IE 16: **Anatomy of the New Perspectives Computer Concepts Instructor Resources**

An in-depth description of everything this textbook has to offer to help you teach, so you can choose what makes the most sense for your classroom.

Page IE 19: **Making the New Perspectives on Computer Concepts Learning System Work for You**

Course Technology has some incredible tools for you. We'd like to help you incorporate all of our resources into your day-to-day teaching to enhance the classroom learning experience. This section provides a table summarizing all of the resources and their benefits, as well as suggestions on how you can implement these materials in your classroom.

//COURSE**PORT**

HARNESS THE POWER OF THOMSON COURSE TECHNOLOGY'S ONLINE TEACHING AND LEARNING SOLUTIONS WITH COURSEPORT.

The powerful, new CoursePort site provides a central location from which you can access Thomson Course Technology's online learning solutions with convenience and flexibility. Centralized access to online activities for all of your classes will increase your productivity and save you time. Use CoursePort to gain access to robust online resources including Instructor Resources, Student Online Companion Web sites, and more.

- A single password allows you to utilize our Universal Gradebook to track the work your students complete in the Student Online Companion that accompanies this text. Within the Universal Gradebook, you can easily link each student to your class and view results for the individuals or the class as a whole.
- Customized reporting reveals exactly what content is engaging your students and what is challenging them.
- CoursePort's personalized services add value and convenience to Thomson Course Technology's Web sites including personalized homepages for you and your students.
- An easy transition allows you to use your current Thomson Course Technology username and password to launch CoursePort. If you do not currently have a username and password, see the simple instructions at the bottom of this page.

THE COURSEPORT STUDENT EXPERIENCE

Your students will receive a key code bound into each textbook with clear instructions on how to create a CoursePort account.

To create a CoursePort account, your students should do the following:
1. Visit login.course.com
2. Click the New User Registration link
3. Enter the key code found on the card bound into their text.
4. Follow the onscreen instructions to complete their registration.

OBTAIN AN INSTRUCTOR USERNAME AND PASSWORD

If you do not currently have a Thomson Course Technology username and password for www.course.com, contact us:

For colleges and universities and private career colleges in the US: Call Thomson Course Technology at **1.800.648.7450** and select option 3 for Support Services.

For High Schools: Call Thomson Learning-School at: **1.800.824.5179**

For Corporations, IT Training Centers, and Federal Government Agencies: Call Thomson Course Technology at **1.800.648.7450**

Ensuring students don't get their hands on the answers, test banks, or other resources that we provide you through our Instructor Resources, password protection is at the forefront of our minds at all times. Each and every time a caller requests a password, we verify the caller's affiliation with the school that he/she indicates.

Username: _____

Password: _____

ABOUT NEW PERSPECTIVES ON COMPUTER CONCEPTS 8ᵀᴴ EDITION

To ensure that this 8ᵗʰ Edition of *New Perspectives on Computer Concepts* contains the most current content and resources for learning about computers, we enlisted the help of our New Perspectives Computer Concepts Advisory Committee, which was made up of over 20 instructors who gave us invaluable feedback on their courses and needs. Based on their user input and feedback from instructors like you, we focused our revisions in two distinct areas:

- Making the chapter content **approachable** and **relevant** to students of all levels and backgrounds.

- Ensuring that our NP8 Learning System with the NP8 Web site and accompanying BookOnCD is fully **integrated** and **easy to use**.

APPROACHABLE AND RELEVANT CONTENT

TechBuzz

Some new technologies make a lasting impact, while others are just a flash in the pan. The new 8-page magazine-like TechBuzz section at the end of the book helps students follow tech trends, cutting-edge products, and emerging technologies, such as BitTorrent networks, Wi-Fi technology, and voice over IP.

Expanded Web Activities

A two-page Review on the Web section includes Student Edition Lab Assignments that challenge students to apply the skills learned in the Student Edition Labs, as well as TechTV Projects, which feature TechTV news clips that explore technology-related issues and trends.

Revised Chapter Openers

In the 8ᵗʰ Edition, the Chapter Openers have been revised to focus more on the Preview Activities, available on the NP8 Web Site, including an Interactive Overview, revised Pre-Assessments that now incorporate adaptive testing, and Detailed Learning Objectives.

Focus on Online Security

With Internet transactions becoming more prevalent in our daily lives and computer crime on the rise, students need practical information and tips on how to protect their data and privacy online. The Orientation chapter's new section on Security and Privacy provides students with guidelines and tips on how to avoid viruses and intrusions and protect their privacy and e-commerce transactions online. Additionally, the new Chapter 5 TechTalk on Online Access Security explains the most important steps to take to protect Windows-based computers from intrusions.

EASE-OF-USE TECHNOLOGY

New CoursePort Personalized Homepage and the NP8 Web Site

The new CoursePort site allows you and your students to use a single user name and password to access all of Thomson Course Technology's online resources, including the NP8 Web site and, instructor files. CoursePort also offers access to our Universal Gradebook, which allows robust tracking within the NP8 Web Site so that you can record your students' progress on the NP8 Online Games and Practice Tests.

Online Interactive Practice Tests

In order to give you and your students more flexibility, we have made the Interactive Practice Tests (previously only available on the BookOnCD) also available online through the NP8 Web site. With the new Universal Gradebook, you can also track your students progress and scores on the online Interactive Practice Tests.

Save BookOnCD Tracking Results to Any Location

To better support students who cannot save their tracking data from the BookOnCD to either the A: or C: drives, we have now built in the flexibility of allowing students to select any drive/folder for their BookOnCD tracking data.

CHAPTER-BY-CHAPTER UPDATES

In addition to the new features we added for the 8th Edition, we have made numerous currency updates and changes to the content. In order to get you up-to-speed on the major content changes, they are outlined below on a chapter-by-chapter basis.

Orientation chapter

■ New design of Try It activities and Explore NP8 Learning Tools activities help students to differentiate between sections that teach basic computer skills, such as using a mouse, and sections that teach how to use the NP8 learning system and technologies, such as the BookOnCD and NP8 Web site.

■ New Section E on Security and Privacy offers timely tips on preventing viruses, blocking spyware and pop-up ads, securing e-commerce transactions, and protecting privacy online.

Chapter 1

■ New coverage on convergence of PDAs and cell phones with focus on special features, such as address books, built-in cameras, cell phone communications, instant messaging, e-mail access, Web access, games, and personal scheduling software.

■ New coverage on spam and anti-spam legislation.

■ New Computers in Context on homeland security covers how computer systems are being used to identify terrorists entering the U.S. and to conduct electronic surveillance and analyze data.

Chapter 2

■ New coverage of miniature hard disk drives, using the Apple iPod as an example.

■ New focus on adding storage space with additional hard drives, rather than making backups.

■ New focus on tape backups for use in business applications.

■ Introduces the new key term "double layer DVD."

Chapter 3

■ New coverage of DVD authoring software.

■ New coverage of software patches and service packs.

Chapter 4

■ New coverage in Section C on Computer Viruses including "social engineering" to make malicious code seem legitimate; spoofed addresses and the difficulty they cause when trying to track the sources of infections; the latest information about worms, like Sasser, that spread without user intervention; and worms that spread by instant messaging and over handheld devices.

■ Also includes new screenshots of an infected HTML link in an email message and a credit card number-stealing Trojan horse.

Chapter 5

■ New coverage of analog and digital signals and LAN Internet Access.

■ Expanded Mobile Internet Access coverage, including new coverage of Internet services available from handheld devices and cellular network technologies.

■ New TechTalk on Internet Access Security.

Chapter 6

■ Revised Issue on Internet hoaxes with updated examples, such as the recent Internet rumor on an impending military draft.

■ New Computers in Context on the fashion industry covers technology applications, such as RFID tags, Quick Response (QR) models, and wearable computers.

Chapter 7

■ New focus in Section C from Desktop Video to Digital Video, with new coverage of DVD and PDA video; TiVo; explanation about DVD-video formats and how to transfer digital videos to DVDs; and a new figure (Figure 7-35) showing how to generate clips in Windows Movie Maker.

■ New coverage of portable audio players, including iPod and its versatile use as a mass storage device.

■ Heavily revised Issue on Digital Rights Management includes new coverage of remixing and the gray album controversy, and legal music download sites such as the new Napster, Wal-Mart, iTunes, and RealNetworks Music Store.

Chapter 8

■ New coverage of outsourcing and offshoring.

■ New Issue about offshoring includes coverage of the pros and cons of offshoring and the effects of it on the U.S. unemployment rate.

Chapter 9

■ New coverage of project management software as a tool to use in the planning phase for an information systems project.

■ Issue on Professional Ethics originally in Chapter 8 in previous editions moved to Chapter 9.

Chapter 10

■ New coverage in TechTalk on how data analysis is used today.

■ Updated Issue section with current examples, including new privacy concerns with Google's Gmail service.

Chapter 11

■ Updated Issue section with new example of usability issues with using cell phone keypads for entering text messages.

Chapter 12

■ New coverage of flash mob supercomputers.

■ New Computers in Context on the banking industry includes coverage of the history of technology in banking from automated check clearing to ATMs and online banking services.

ANATOMY OF A NEW PERSPECTIVES ON COMPUTER CONCEPTS CHAPTER

Each chapter is organized into manageable **sections**. This allows you to pick and choose the sections to cover that are the most relevant to your course.

1

COMPUTER, INTERNET, WEB, AND E-MAIL BASICS

CONTENTS

TIP

When using the BookOnCD, the ✳ icons are "clickable" to access resources on the CD. The ⊥ icons are clickable to access resources on the Web. You can also access Web resources by using your browser to connect directly to the NP8 New Perspectives Web site at:

www.course.com/np/concepts8/ch01

LABS

Students can access **New Perspectives Labs** for each chapter through the BookOnCD. Each lab has a corresponding Lab Assignment in the book, which gives the student a more structured framework in which to complete the lab, and submit their work to you for grading.

The ✳ icon helps students easily identify interactive elements that are clickable on the **BookOnCD**. When using the BookOnCD, links on the chapter contents page allow students to quickly jump to a specific section or end-of-chapter activity.

The ⊥ icon helps students to easily identify interactive elements that are accessible through the **NP8 Web site**. Web Activities offer a wealth of resources and interactive games specific to each chapter that help students learn and reinforce the concepts presented in the book.

INSTRUCTOR EDITION

Chapter Preview Activities, available through the NP8 Website, allow students to tailor their study plans for each chapter.

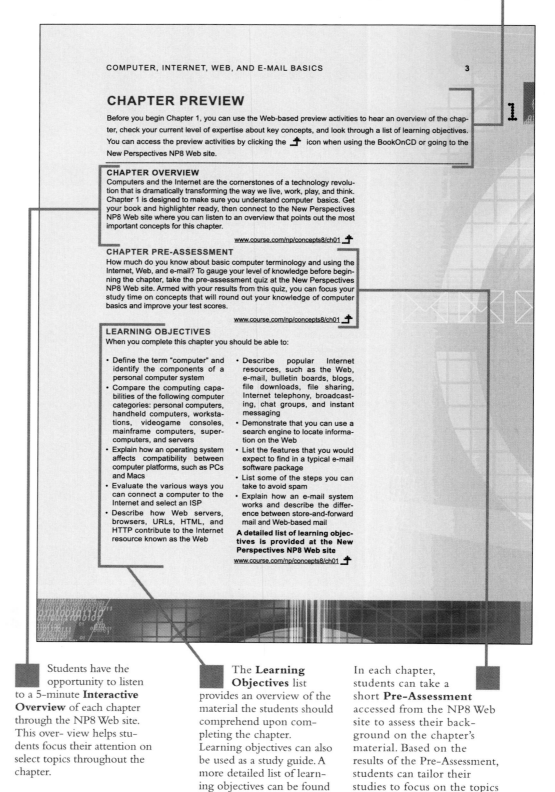

CHAPTER PREVIEW

Before you begin Chapter 1, you can use the Web-based preview activities to hear an overview of the chapter, check your current level of expertise about key concepts, and look through a list of learning objectives. You can access the preview activities by clicking the ⌖ icon when using the BookOnCD or going to the New Perspectives NP8 Web site.

CHAPTER OVERVIEW
Computers and the Internet are the cornerstones of a technology revolution that is dramatically transforming the way we live, work, play, and think. Chapter 1 is designed to make sure you understand computer basics. Get your book and highlighter ready, then connect to the New Perspectives NP8 Web site where you can listen to an overview that points out the most important concepts for this chapter.

www.course.com/np/concepts8/ch01 ⌖

CHAPTER PRE-ASSESSMENT
How much do you know about basic computer terminology and using the Internet, Web, and e-mail? To gauge your level of knowledge before beginning the chapter, take the pre-assessment quiz at the New Perspectives NP8 Web site. Armed with your results from this quiz, you can focus your study time on concepts that will round out your knowledge of computer basics and improve your test scores.

www.course.com/np/concepts8/ch01 ⌖

LEARNING OBJECTIVES
When you complete this chapter you should be able to:

- Define the term "computer" and identify the components of a personal computer system
- Compare the computing capabilities of the following computer categories: personal computers, handheld computers, workstations, videogame consoles, mainframe computers, supercomputers, and servers
- Explain how an operating system affects compatibility between computer platforms, such as PCs and Macs
- Evaluate the various ways you can connect a computer to the Internet and select an ISP
- Describe how Web servers, browsers, URLs, HTML, and HTTP contribute to the Internet resource known as the Web

- Describe popular Internet resources, such as the Web, e-mail, bulletin boards, blogs, file downloads, file sharing, Internet telephony, broadcasting, chat groups, and instant messaging
- Demonstrate that you can use a search engine to locate information on the Web
- List the features that you would expect to find in a typical e-mail software package
- List some of the steps you can take to avoid spam
- Explain how an e-mail system works and describe the difference between store-and-forward mail and Web-based mail

A detailed list of learning objectives is provided at the New Perspectives NP8 Web site

www.course.com/np/concepts8/ch01 ⌖

Students have the opportunity to listen to a 5-minute **Interactive Overview** of each chapter through the NP8 Web site. This over- view helps students focus their attention on select topics throughout the chapter.

The **Learning Objectives** list provides an overview of the material the students should comprehend upon completing the chapter. Learning objectives can also be used as a study guide. A more detailed list of learning objectives can be found on the NP8 Web site.

In each chapter, students can take a short **Pre-Assessment** accessed from the NP8 Web site to assess their background on the chapter's material. Based on the results of the Pre-Assessment, students can tailor their studies to focus on the topics and skills they have not yet mastered.

InfoWebLinks provide access to Web-based material that supplements the text. Students can use InfoWebLinks as a starting point for research projects or simply to gather additional information about an interesting subject. You can use InfoWebLinks to find additional lecture material, or to increase your own understanding about a particular subject.

Is Windows software the same as the Windows operating system?
No. The term "Windows software" refers to any application software designed to run on computers that use the Microsoft Windows operating system. A program called Microsoft Word for Windows is an example of a word processing program—application software—that is referred to as "Windows software."

How does an operating system affect compatibility? Computers that operate in essentially the same way are said to be "compatible." Two of the most important factors that influence compatibility and define a computer's **platform** are the microprocessor and the operating system. Today, two of the most popular personal computer platforms are PCs and Macs.

PCs are based on the design for one of the first personal computer "superstars"—the IBM PC. The "great grandchildren" of the IBM PC are on computer store shelves today—a huge selection of personal computer brands and models manufactured by companies such as IBM, Hewlett-Packard, Toshiba, Dell, and Gateway. The Windows operating system was designed specifically for these personal computers and, therefore, the PC platform is sometimes called the "Windows platform." Most of the examples in this book pertain to PCs because they are so popular.

Macs are based on a proprietary design for a personal computer called the Macintosh, manufactured almost exclusively by Apple Computer, Inc. The stylish iMac is one of Apple's most popular computers, and like other computers in the Mac platform, it uses Mac OS as its operating system.

The PC and Mac platforms are not compatible because their microprocessors and operating systems differ. Consequently, application software designed for Macs does not typically work with PCs and vice versa. When shopping for new software, it is important to read the package to make sure it is designed to work with your computer platform.

INFOWEBLINKS

Apple Computer, Inc. is known for its innovative computer designs. You can learn about its newest computers by connecting to the **Apple Computers InfoWeb.**

www.course.com/np/concepts8/ch01

QUICKCHECK......SECTION A

1. A computer accepts input, processes data, stores data, and produces [   ] according to a series of instructions.

2. The term "microprocessor" is a synonym for the term "microcomputer." True or false? [   ]

3. A(n) [   ] computer is also referred to as a laptop.

4. Most computers include a network card designed to connect a computer to the Internet using standard telephone service. True or false? [   ]

5. Eight [   ] form a byte.

6. PCs and Macs are not considered [   ] because their microprocessors and operating systems differ.

CHECK ANSWERS

Each section has several **FAQ** questions that provide a framework for the section's topics in a format that students can relate to. FAQ questions are worded as if they are being asked by the student, himself/herself.

Each section of a chapter ends with a **QuickCheck**—a series of questions highlighting the most important concepts. The Quick Check questions have been updated for the 8th Edition. On the BookOnCD, QuickCheck questions are interactive and may be tracked and graded.

INSTRUCTOR EDITION

Each chapter includes a **TechTalk** section, which allows advanced students to learn more technical concepts. The TechTalk section incorporates the same pedagogy as the chapter's sections, such as the FAQ format, InfoWebLinks, and QuickCheck.

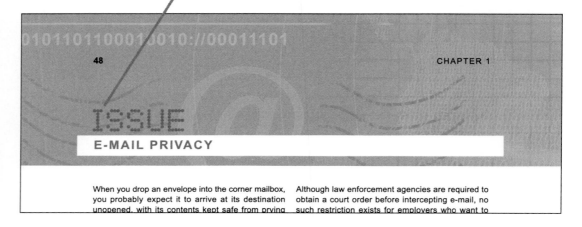

44   TECHTALK, CHAPTER 1

TECHTALK
THE BOOT PROCESS

The sequence of events that occurs between the time that you turn on a computer and the time that it is ready for you to issue commands is referred to as the boot process or "booting" your computer. The term "boot" comes from the word "bootstrap," which describes a small loop on the back of a boot. Just as you can pull on a big boot using a small bootstrap, your computer boots up by first loading a small program into memory, and then it uses that small program to load a large operating system. Your computer's small bootstrap program is built into special

The **Issue** section presents a social or ethical issue that relates to the topics in the chapter. It features InfoWebLinks and "What Do You Think?" questions that pose thought-provoking questions to students. Student responses to the "What Do You Think?" questions can be saved and tracked.

48   CHAPTER 1

ISSUE
E-MAIL PRIVACY

When you drop an envelope into the corner mailbox, you probably expect it to arrive at its destination unopened, with its contents kept safe from prying | Although law enforcement agencies are required to obtain a court order before intercepting e-mail, no such restriction exists for employers who want to

Each chapter also includes a **Computers in Context** section. The Computers in Context section highlights how computer technology is used in various fields, such as medicine, entertainment, and banking.

50   CHAPTER 1

COMPUTERS IN CONTEXT
HOMELAND SECURITY

Once a localized problem affecting the Middle East and South Asia, terrorism is now spreading around the globe. Governments in many countries are devoting significant resources to

Each chapter concludes with a set of **Review Activities** which are printed in the book and also accessible in an interactive format on the BookOnCD. The Review Activities include the Interactive Summary, Interactive Situation Questions, Interactive Key Terms, Interactive Practice Tests, and Review on the Web. Students can use all of the Review Activities as study aides. Additionally, student work on the Interactive Summary, Interactive Situation Questions, and the Interactive Practice Tests can be tracked and submitted for grading.

INTERACTIVE SUMMARY

To review important concepts from this chapter, fill in the blanks to best complete each sentence. When using the NP8 BookOnCD, click the Check Answers buttons to automatically score your answers. Place your Tracking Disk in the floppy disk drive if you want to save your scores.

A computer is a device that accepts input, [ ] data, stores data, and produces output according to a series of stored instructions. Before a computer processes data, it is temporarily held in [ ]. This data is then processed in the [ ] (CPU). The idea of a [ ] program means that a series of instructions for a computing task can be loaded into a computer's memory.

Computers are grouped into categories, such as personal computers, handhelds, mainframes, supercomputers, servers, workstations, and videogame consoles. A [ ] computer is a type of microcomputer designed to meet the needs of an individual. Computers process, store, and transmit data

in [ ] format as a series of 1s and 0s. Each 1 or 0 is called a [ ]. Eight bits, called a [ ], represent one character—a letter, number, or punctuation mark. Data becomes [ ] when it is presented in a format that people can understand and use.

An [ ] system, such as Windows, UNIX, or Mac OS, is essentially the master controller for all activities that take place within a computer. [ ] software is any set of computer programs that helps a person carry out a task. Although "Windows" is the name of an operating system, the term "Windows software" refers to application software designed for computers that run the Windows operating system.

✳ CHECK ANSWERS

The Internet is a collection of local, regional, national, and international computer [ ] that are linked together to exchange data and distribute processing tasks. The main routes of the Internet are referred to as the Internet [ ]. Communication between all the devices on the Internet is made possible by a standard set of rules called [ ]. The Internet hosts a wide variety of activities, such as Web browsing, e-commerce, e-mail, bulletin boards, chat groups, instant messaging, Internet telephony, digital broadcasts, remote access, downloads, uploads, and peer-to-peer file sharing.

Many people access the Internet using a dial-up connection that simply requires a telephone line and a

Students must complete the **Interactive Summary** narrative by filling in the blanks. Like the other Review Activities, the Interactive Summary makes an excellent study guide for students or it can also be assigned and turned in for credit.

Interactive Situation Questions challenge students to apply what they have learned in the chapter to typical computing situations.

INTERACTIVE SITUATION QUESTIONS

Apply what you've learned to some typical computing situations. When using the NP8 BookOnCD, you can type your answers, and then use the Check Answers button to automatically score your responses. Place your Tracking Disk in the floppy disk drive if you want to save your scores.

1. Suppose that you walk into an office and see the devices pictured to the right. You would probably assume that they are the screen and keyboard for a [ ] personal computer, [ ], or server.

2. You receive a CD from a friend. It contains a file called EverQuest.exe. Because of the file extension, you assume that the disk contains a(n) [ ] file that is some type of computer program, rather than a data file.

3. You are a musician and you use your Gateway PC to compose music. Your friend, who has an iMac computer, wants you to try the software she uses. If she loans you her composition software, can you use it on your PC? Yes or no? [ ]

4. You are a computer technician hired by Ben and Jerry's Ice Cream to set up a Web site. You know that your site requires a unique [ ] that pinpoints its location on the Internet, and your server will have to use [ ], the standard Internet protocol that transports data between all sorts of computer platforms over the Internet.

5. You want the cheapest Internet connection. You don't mind if the connection is limited to speeds under 56 Kbps and doesn't provide very good video performance. You would probably select an ISP that provides a(n) [ ] connection.

6. You need to select a password for your online bank account. Which of the following passwords

would be the LEAST secure: jeff683, hddtmrutc, gargantuan, brickcloset, fanhotshot, or high348? [ ]

7. You want to look at the latest Nike athletic shoes. The URL that will probably get you to Nike's home page is [ ].

8. You want to find some Web pages that contain information about snowboarding competitions. You know that your [ ] can only fetch and display Web pages, so you'll need to connect to a(n) [ ] and enter a query, such as "snowboard competition."

9. If your ISP does not supply you with an e-mail account, you can get a free [ ] e-mail account from a site such as Hotmail or Yahoo!.

10. You receive an e-mail message that contains colored text and underlining. You assume that the person who sent the message had his mail software set for [ ] format.

✳ CHECK ANSWERS

INTERACTIVE PRACTICE TESTS

Practice tests that consist of 10 multiple-choice, true/false, and fill-in-the-blank questions are available on both the NP8 BookOnCD and the NP8 Web site. The questions are selected at random from a large test bank, so each time you take a test, you'll receive a different set of questions. Your tests are scored immediately, and you can print study guides that help you find the correct answers for any questions that you missed.

www.course.com/np/concepts8/ch01

CLICK ✳ TO START

Students can test their comprehension of the concepts in each chapter with the **Interactive Practice Tests,** which are available both through the BookOnCD and the NP8 Web site.

Students can take their knowledge of the concepts one step further with the **Review on the Web** activities available on the NP8 Web site. These activities reinforce the concepts learned in each chapter. Additionally, student scores from the Review on the Web activities can be saved and made accessible to you through the Universal Gradebook.

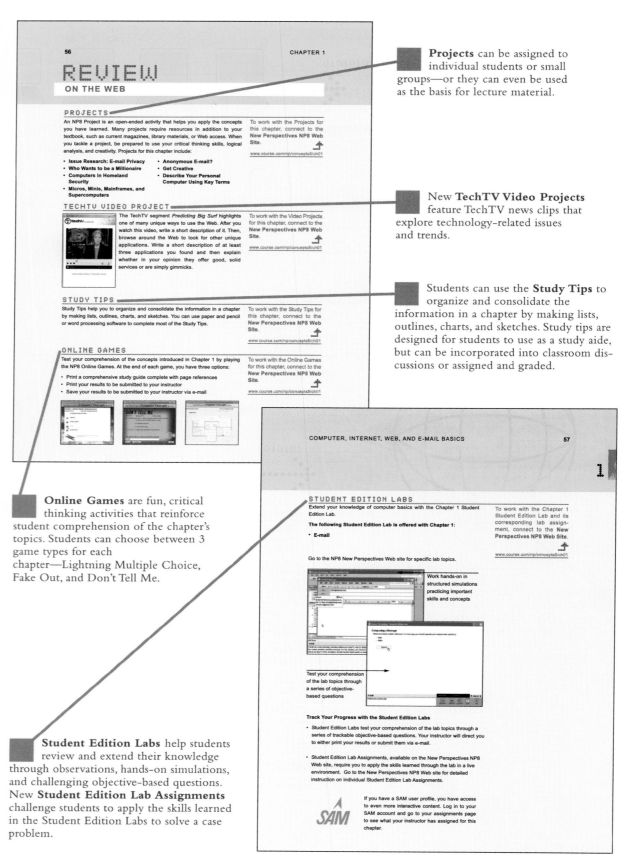

Projects can be assigned to individual students or small groups—or they can even be used as the basis for lecture material.

New **TechTV Video Projects** feature TechTV news clips that explore technology-related issues and trends.

Students can use the **Study Tips** to organize and consolidate the information in a chapter by making lists, outlines, charts, and sketches. Study tips are designed for students to use as a study aide, but can be incorporated into classroom discussions or assigned and graded.

Online Games are fun, critical thinking activities that reinforce student comprehension of the chapter's topics. Students can choose between 3 game types for each chapter—Lightning Multiple Choice, Fake Out, and Don't Tell Me.

Student Edition Labs help students review and extend their knowledge through observations, hands-on simulations, and challenging objective-based questions. New **Student Edition Lab Assignments** challenge students to apply the skills learned in the Student Edition Labs to solve a case problem.

ANATOMY OF THE NEW PERSPECTIVES NP8 WEB SITE

Students deserve a wealth of resources to reinforce their studies. This text's Web site, available at www.course.com/np/concepts8, features the following:

- Interactive Overviews
- Pre-Assessments
- Detailed Chapter Objectives
- Online Games
- Projects
- TechTV Video Projects
- InfoWebLinks
- Study Tips
- Student Edition Labs and Lab Assignments
- Interactive Practice Tests

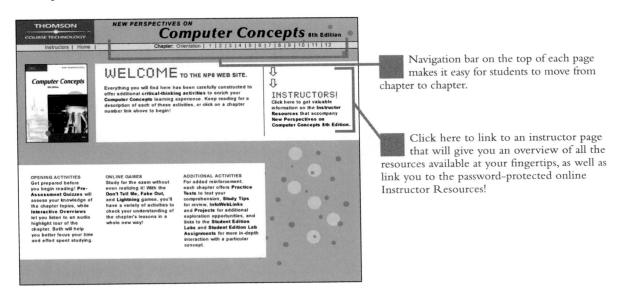

Navigation bar on the top of each page makes it easy for students to move from chapter to chapter.

Click here to link to an instructor page that will give you an overview of all the resources available at your fingertips, as well as link you to the password-protected online Instructor Resources!

Preview Activities offer students a great way to prepare for each chapter through listening to an Interactive Overview audio clip, testing their knowledge with a Pre-Assessment and reviewing a list of Detailed Chapter Objectives.

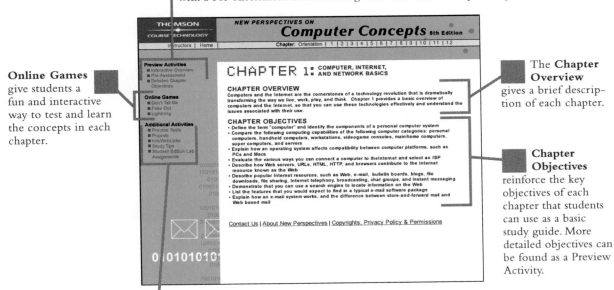

Online Games give students a fun and interactive way to test and learn the concepts in each chapter.

The **Chapter Overview** gives a brief description of each chapter.

Chapter Objectives reinforce the key objectives of each chapter that students can use as a basic study guide. More detailed objectives can be found as a Preview Activity.

The NP8 Web site offers various **Additional Activities** such as Practice Tests, Projects, TechTV Video Projects, InfoWebLinks, Study Tips and Student Edition Labs. These activities can be used by the students on their own time or assigned as homework or extra-credit.

USE THE UNIVERSAL GRADEBOOK TO TRACK YOUR STUDENTS' PROGRESS ON THE NP8 WEB SITE

The **Pre-Assessment**, **Online Games**, and **Interactive Practice Tests** all give students a rewarding, interactive way to reinforce and test their knowledge of the concepts in each chapter. Remediation at the end of each one can be used as a study guide or submitted as homework or an extra-credit assignment. Student scores on the Pre-Assessment, Online Games, and Interactive Practice Tests can also be saved automatically into your Universal Gradebook, allowing you to track your students' progress and run grading reports for all of your students.

PRE-ASSESSMENT

The Pre-Assessments have been updated for the 8th Edition to use an adaptive testing model. This new testing model will help your students more effectively gauge their understanding of the concepts before they start the chapter so that they can focus their study time appropriately.

ONLINE GAMES

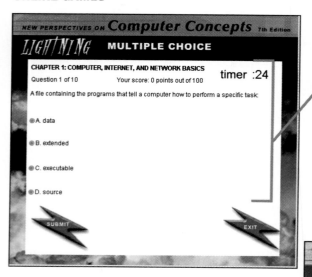

Lightning Multiple Choice tests students' ability to handle pressure and answer a series of 10 randomly selected multiple choice questions correctly in a timed lightning round.

In the **Don't Tell Me** game, students can use a series of hints to correctly answer the question. The fewer hints needed, the more points earned.

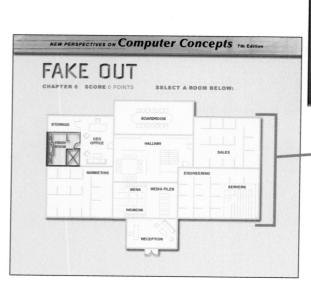

The **Fake Out** game is a detective game where students are trying to find a stolen zip disk full of valuable information. Students look through a building room by room for the disk, and for each room they look in they are given three statements about the concepts learned in the chapter and they must determine which one is true without being "Faked Out."

INTERACTIVE PRACTICE TESTS

The NP8 **Interactive Practice Tests** are now available both on the BookOnCD and the NP8 Web site. These Practice Tests on the NP8 Web site offer students the opportunity to test their comprehension of the topics by answering a series of 10 randomly selected objective-based questions online and save their scores through the Universal Gradebook.

STUDENT EDITION LABS

Student Edition Labs allow your students to master hundreds of computer concepts, including input and output devices, file management and desktop applications, computer privacy, virus protection, and much more. These interactive labs help students learn through dynamic observation, step-by-step practice, and challenging review questions. You can also use the new **Student Edition Lab Assignments** to further challenge your students to apply the skills learned in the labs to realistic case problems.

Hands-on practice reinforces important topics.

Feedback on each step guides you through the simulations

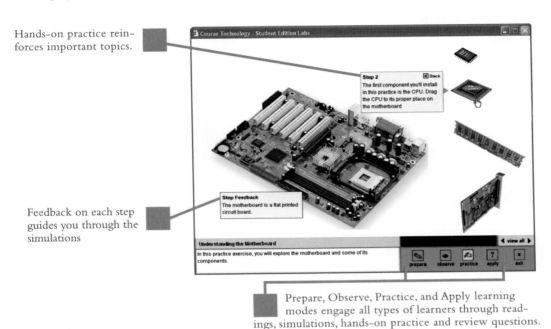

Prepare, Observe, Practice, and Apply learning modes engage all types of learners through readings, simulations, hands-on practice and review questions.

Student Edition Labs currently include

- Using Input Devices
- Peripheral Devices
- Using Windows
- Working with Graphics
- Working with Audio
- Working with Video
- Binary Numbers
- Understanding the Motherboard
- Installing and Uninstalling Software
- Protecting your Privacy Online
- Keeping your Computer Virus Free
- E-mail
- Creating Web Pages
- Connecting to the Internet
- Getting the Most out of the Internet

- Word Processing
- Spreadsheets
- Databases
- Presentation Software
- Maintaining a Hard Drive
- Managing Files and Folders
- Backing up Your Computer
- Visual Programming
- Advanced Spreadsheets
- Advanced Databases
- Networking Basics
- E-Commerce
- Web Design Principles
- Project Management
- Wireless Networking

ANATOMY OF THE NEW PERSPECTIVES COMPUTER CONCEPTS BOOKONCD

Since the 3rd edition of *New Perspectives on Computer Concepts*, we've been the only book on the market to feature the entire BookOnCD. The BookOnCD is an electronic version of each page of the printed textbook that's loaded with features, such as videos, screentours, Interactive QuickChecks, and Practice Tests, to create a highly interactive learning experience.

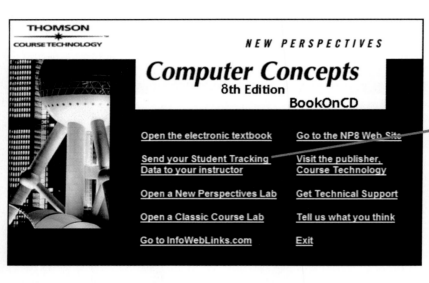

Students can save their scores on the New Perspectives Labs or Practice Tests and send the results to their instructor. New to this edition, student scores can be saved to any location.

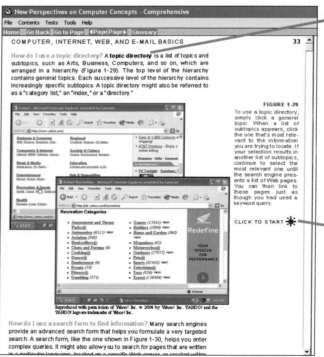

To become more familiar with new terminology, students can click on bold-faced **key terms** to access definitions.

Specially marked screenshots morph into guided software tours, photos come to life as videos, and labs launch step–by step conceptual and skills-based tutorials.

THE NEW PERSPECTIVES LABS

Directly from the BookOnCD, students can access the New Perspectives Labs. These labs are considered one of the most valuable resources on the BookOnCD by instructors globally, and can be used in a variety of different ways in your classroom:

- Assign labs as out-of-classroom homework, or as student-choice extra credit assignments. Collect the scores from the Tracking Disks.
- Use labs as in-class activities in computer-equipped classrooms.
- Use labs to enhance your lectures.

Through the **New Perspectives Labs** students have the chance to engage with concepts through reading hands-on steps. Each section of a lab concludes with its own trackable QuickCheck questions. The BookOnCD also features the 27 **Classic Course Labs** that you can assign to your students for additional practice.

Yellow highlighted boxes give students hints about where to click with their mouse

Step-by-step instructions help students learn the activity in a simulated environment.

Each lab is divided into five easy to follow topics.

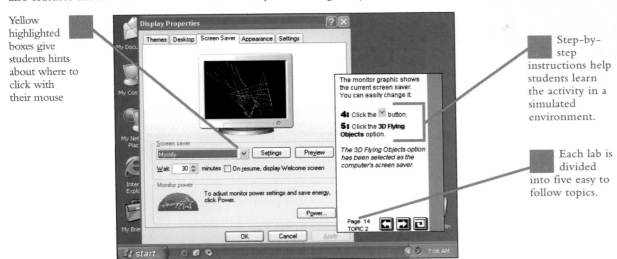

USE WEBTRACK TO TRACK STUDENTS' PROGRESS USING THE BOOKONCD

WebTrack is application software that takes advantage of Internet technology to collect and transport data pertaining to students' progress. When students complete practice tests, labs, and other activities on the BookOnCD, the results are stored in their Tracking Location (a floppy disk, a hard disk drive, or a removable storage device). These results can be uploaded directly to the WebTrack server through the BookOnCD menu, where they are held until you download them. WebTrack data is stored on your local computer, so you don't have to worry about security issues—it's available only to you, the instructor.

Once you obtain student results through WebTrack, you can use the scores in a variety of ways, such as:

- Collect student scores and assign them as a percentage of the final grade.
- Collect student scores, but use them as pass/fail milestones.
- Use scores as a way to keep track of student progress and identify students who are falling behind.

See the WebTrack Instructions available on the Instructor Resources CD for more information on how you can use WebTrack in your classroom.

NOTE: *These labs are available only on the BookOnCD. For more information on our Web accessible Student Edition Labs, see page IE 13.*

ANATOMY OF THE NEW PERSPECTIVES COMPUTER CONCEPTS INSTRUCTOR RESOURCES

We know you need more than great textbooks to effectively teach your class. That's why we take the next step in providing you with outstanding Instructor Resources—developed by educators and tested through our rigorous Quality Assurance process. Our goal is to make the teaching and learning experience in your classroom the best it can be. With Course Technology's resources, you'll spend less time prepping, and more time teaching.

INSTRUCTOR RESOURCES CD AND WEB SITE: The first place to go when preparing for your next class. Both the CD (ISBN: 0-619-26763-1) and the Web site (www.course.com/np/concepts8) contain everything you need to get started. Check the site before each semester for updates to the Instructor Resources for this title.

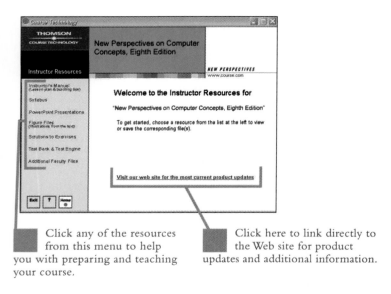

Click any of the resources from this menu to help you with preparing and teaching your course.

Click here to link directly to the Web site for product updates and additional information.

COURSE PRESENTER: Delivering engaging and visually impressive lectures is easy with the professionally-designed Course Presenter available for each chapter in this book. The Course Presenter is a PowerPoint presentation multimedia-enhanced with screentours, animations, and videos! The Course Presenter comes packaged together with the Instructor Resources CD, so you have fewer ISBNs to order! We also offer the editable PowerPoint presentations, without any of the multimedia enhancements, on the Instructors Resources CD.

INSTRUCTOR'S MANUAL: Need to compile a lecture on file sharing for your class that's starting in an hour? Need a Quick Quiz to test your students' understanding of the material? Or looking for ways to challenge your students with group projects? The electronic Instructor's Manual is a great place to look for solutions to all of these dilemmas. Each chapter in the Instructor's Manual is a Microsoft Word document that you can customize easily with your own notes, but it is also filled with great ideas from instructors like you.

SYLLABUS: Need to keep your students on track with assignments, class policies, and due dates? Our sample syllabi provide a great place to start! The syllabi come with laboratory instructions, class and school policies, sample weekly assignments, and are fully customizable by you.

FIGURE FILES: Looking for figures in the book that are not incuded in the Course Presenter? Files for every figure in the textbook are available in electronic form.

SOLUTIONS: Solutions to activities in the book are provided in an easy to read Word document. Included in this document are solutions for:

- Chapter QuickChecks
- TechTalk QuickChecks
- Lab Assignments
- Interactive Summaries
- Interactive Situation Questions
- Study Tips
- Projects
- TechTV Video Projects
- Student Edition Lab Assignments

EXAMVIEW TEST BANK: ExamView features a user-friendly testing environment that allows you to not only publish traditional paper and LAN-based tests, but also Web-deliverable exams. Utilize the ultra-efficient Quick Test Wizard to create an exam in less than five minutes; or take advantage of the Course Technology question banks; or even customize your own exams from scratch. New to this edition, we've enhanced our testbanks with scenario-based critical thinking questions to help you better assess total student comprehension of key concepts.

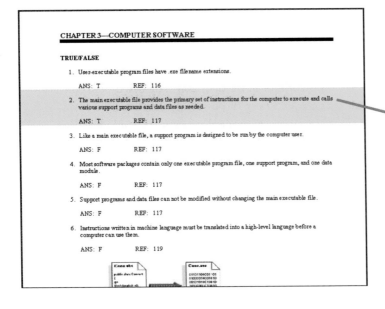

With over 200 questions provided for each chapter in NP8 you can create the perfect Practice Test, Pop Quiz, Test, and Final Exam.

ADDITIONAL FACULTY FILES: Also available on the Instructor's Resources CD, you can find the Instructor's Edition material as well as WebTrack instructions. The WebTrack Instructions are designed to help you use the WebTrack software to effectively track your students' progress on the BookOnCD and communicate with students via WebTrack's Online Annotation and Syllabus tools.

WEBCT AND BLACKBOARD WebCT and Blackboard are the leading distance learning solutions available today. In the past few years, they've also become popular class management platforms. Course Technology has partnered with WebCT and Blackboard to bring you online content that fits into both platforms. *New Perspectives on Computer Concepts, 8th Edition* is available with online content in WebCT e-Pack and Blackboard Course Cartridge-format, which includes the following components:

- Topic Reviews
- Review Questions
- Case Projects
- PowerPoint Presentations

- Test Banks
- Crossword Puzzles
- Custom Syllabus
- And more!

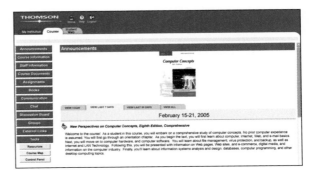

Add more muscle and flexibility to your Student Edition Labs with SAM (Skills Assessment Manager) Computer Concepts! SAM Computer Concepts adds the power of skill-based assessment and the award-winning SAM classroom administration system to your Student Edition Labs, putting you in control of how you deliver exams and training in your course.

By adding SAM Computer Concepts to your curriculum, you can:

- Reinforce your students' knowledge of key computer concepts with hands-on application exercises.
- Allow your students to "learn by listening," with access to rich audio in their Student Edition Labs.
- Build hands-on computer concepts exams from a test bank of more than 200 skill-based concepts tasks.
- Schedule your students' concepts training and testing exercises with powerful administrative tools.
- Track student exam grades and training progress using more than one dozen student and classroom reports.

Teach your introductory course with the simplicity of a single system! You can now administer your entire Computer Concepts and Microsoft Office course through the SAM platform. For more information on the SAM administration system, SAM Computer Concepts and other SAM products, please visit http://www.course.com/sam.

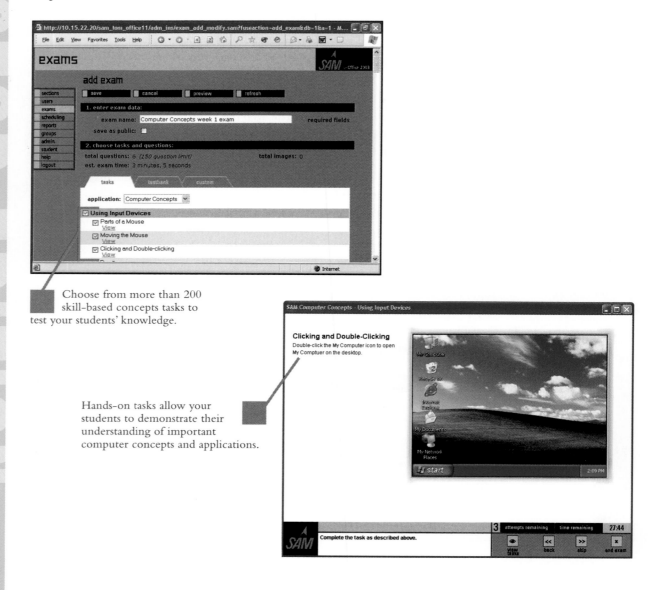

Choose from more than 200 skill-based concepts tasks to test your students' knowledge.

Hands-on tasks allow your students to demonstrate their understanding of important computer concepts and applications.

MAKING THE NEW PERSPECTIVES ON COMPUTER CONCEPTS LEARNING SYSTEM WORK FOR YOU

Now that you have a better understanding of all the tools that come with *New Perspectives on Computer Concepts 8th Edition*, how do you fit them all together? More importantly, how do you make these tools work for your specific classroom needs? This section will help you sort through the available tools and determine which ones may be appropriate to use for your class.

Resource	Student Benefit	Instructor Benefit	How do I access it?	Is it trackable?
NP8 Web Site	• The NP8 Web site provides students with an interactive way to reinforce the concepts and topics they learn in each chapter. • Students can use the Chapter Preview Activities, such as the Interactive Overview and Pre-Assessment, to develop a tailored study plan for each chapter. • Students have the opportunity to further research special topics of interest through the InfoWebLinks. • The Student Edition Labs give students hands-on interaction with topics and skills beyond those covered in the textbook.	• The NP8 Web site gives instructors flexibility to assign additional projects and activities to their students beyond what is offered in the textbook. • Use the Universal Gradebook to measure students progress on the NP8 Web site.	*www.course.com/np/concepts8* To find out what Web resources are available with each chapter, see the chapter opener and the Review on the Web pages of each chapter. Each time you see a [⏏] icon, there is a related Web activity available.	Yes, Students can save their scores on the Pre-Assessments, Online Games and Interactive Practice Tests. Saved scores are available through the Universal Gradebook.
BookOnCD	• The BookOnCD brings concepts to life for students through animations, screen tours, labs and interactive review activities.	• You can assign CD resources such as the Interactive Summaries, Interactive Situation Questions, Interactive Practice Tests, and Labs as homework. • Use the WebTrack software to measure student progress and manage grading. • You can use the screen tours, animations, and labs on the BookOnCD during lectures.	• All BookOnCD resources are available on the BookOnCD that is affixed to the back inside cover of every *New Perspectives on Computer Concepts 8th Edition* textbook. • WebTrack can be downloaded from the Instructor's Resources CD or from the Instructor's Resources Web site at *www.course.com/np/concepts8*	Yes. Students can save their scores on the QuickChecks, Lab QuickChecks, Interactive Summaries, Interactive Situation Questions, and Interactive Practice Tests. Saved scores can be submitted to you via the WebTrack software.
Distance Learning	• Distance Learning offers students a self paced way to learn the material. Even in a face-to-face class they can use it as an additional study tool.	• Distance Learning content provides instructors in a DL environment with a ready to use course. You can even set up a course for your normal classes to give students additional study tools and activities.	*www.course.com* or talk to your sales representative	No.
SAM	• Students get to take in depth training on the concepts taught in the book. SAM also offers realistic assessments to test what they know.	• You can reinforce the lessons presented in this text and create realistic hands-on exams with SAM for Computer Concepts.	*www.course.com/sam* or talk to your sales representative	Yes. SAM has a powerful Web-based reporting and administrative system for both students and instructors.
IR Resources	• Students benefit from great instruction!	• The Instructor Resources give instructors valuable tools and teaching tips that make preparing and teaching a course easier.	Can be accessed on the Instructor Resources CD or on *www.course.com/np/concepts8*.	No.
Presenter	• The Course Presenter gives students a stimulating addition to their lecture.	• The Course Presenter offers instructors a visual and interactive way to spice up their lecture.	• The Course Presenter is available as part of the Instructor Resources CD package	No.

COURSE FORMAT: TIPS FOR LAB-BASED, DISTANCE EDUCATION, SELF-PACED, AND TRADITIONAL LECTURE COURSES

Different types of courses require different approaches. A distance learning course is different from a traditional class-room-based course. A lab-based course requires a different approach from a "chalk-talk" course. Self-paced courses offer yet another set of challenges. *New Perspectives on Computer Concepts* offers resources for each of these course formats. The following tips are meant to help you determine which resources work best for your course's format.

Lab-Based Courses

- If you require students to remain in the lab for the entire session, you might need to devise some "filler" or extra-credit activity for students who complete work early. Extra credit activity could include assigning the Online Games, Projects, or TechTV Video Projects from the NP8 Web site.

- An obvious choice of activities for lab sessions is one of the New Perspectives or Student Edition Labs referred to within each chapter. Students can be "let loose" in a lab setting to do all or some of the labs included in a chapter.

- Practice Tests may also be assigned as a lab activity. Each chapter includes Interactive Practice Tests, available both on the BookonCD and NP8 Web site, that are generated on-the-fly. These tests may be taken multiple times because each test is generated when the student begins the test. Results are stored either on the student's Tracking Location or through the Universal Gradebook.

- Interactive Summaries are also great lab activities. Because the interactive summary is a static resource (as opposed to the practice tests, which are designed to be generated on-the-fly and as such, are different every time a student takes one) they are excellent choices for proctored quizzes or tests. As with all BookOnCD resources, the results are stored on the student's Tracking Location, so no manual grading is required.

- Lab sessions are an ideal setting for proctored tests and exams, such as those provided by ExamView. To learn more about using this tool to select questions, create your own questions, and administer tests, refer to page IE 17.

- You may want to generate a competitive spirit in your students by holding a "game day" with one of the online games on the NP8 Web site.

Distance Education Courses

- Both the NP8 Web site and the WebTrack software provide tools that allow you to keep track of student progress and identify students who have fallen behind in assignments. The Universal Gradebook, available through the NP8 Web site, saves student results on the Pre-Assessments, Online Games, and Interactive Practice Tests. Instructors can view their students' grades and run a variety of reports to track student progress.

- Distance education students often lack the face-to-face interaction a student typically receives in a traditional classroom. WebTrack provides tools that allow you to personalize your distance education course by adding online annotations to the textbook. You can create annotations for any page of the text to point out key concepts, add your own examples, and offer alternative explanations for particularly difficult concepts. Your annotations can include text, photos, diagrams, sound files, and even videos. You can also link to Web sites that contain relevant information and diagrams. For specific information about creating annotations, see the WebTrack Instructions that are in the accompanying Instructor Resource CD.

- WebTrack also provides you with an online syllabus feature that you can use to focus student interest. Revise your online syllabus weekly by adding hints and study tips for the currently assigned chapter. If you color-code your current set of hints and tips (use your HTML editor to quickly alter the text color), your students can easily see what's new.

- Your distance students could use the BookOnCD interactive exercises and store results to their Tracking Location. Periodically, you can require students to submit tracking data. After using WebTrack to consolidate the data submitted by your students, refer to the Last Results report. This report tells you at a glance which students are falling behind.

- Use SAM, the Interactive Practice Tests, or ExamView to administer open-book tests. With both SAM and ExamView, it is possible to impose a time limit which would effectively prevent students from looking up every answer.

- Require students to sit for exams in a proctored environment, such as a library near their homes. Students can use SAM, ExamView, the NP8 Web site or BookOnCD to take practice tests on a library computer. SAM even has password capabilities, so you can further ensure that only students in your course are gaining entrance to the exam. Students can then submit their scores to you via ExamView, WebTrack, or the Universal Gradebook, as appropriate.

- Another idea is to require students to take the Interactive Practice Tests on the NP8 Web site or BookOnCD until they score 100% on at least five tests.

Self-Paced Courses

- Self-paced courses often require a learning contract, in which a student commits to due dates for certain course milestones. These milestones are often exams, but can include other deliverables. For students using *New Perspectives on Computer Concepts*, those deliverables might include SAM reports, QuickCheck answers, Interactive Chapter Summaries, Interactive Situation Question answers, Projects, Lab QuickCheck answers, Pre-Assessments, Interactive Practive Tests or Online Games results. As part of the syllabus, you can provide students with a learning contract form that lists deliverables and milestones. Allow students to fill in a date for each milestone, then submit the learning contract. You can use this form as a checklist when milestones are completed.

- Self-paced students need plenty of feedback in order to determine when they have mastered course material and are ready to take tests. The Web Activities, such as the Pre-Assessments, Online Games, and Interactive Practice Tests found on the NP8 Web site, provide students with immediate feedback and results. Students' computers do the grading, so feedback is immediate. New Perspectives interactive tools found on the BookOnCD, such as Interactive Chapter Summaries, QuickChecks, Interactive Situation Questions, Interactive Practice Tests, and Lab QuickChecks, provide students with lots of feedback, as well.

- Without tracking tools, it can be difficult for instructors to gauge which students are on track and which have fallen behind. The NP8 Web site has powerful tracking and reporting tools available through the Universal Gradebook. With the BookOnCD's WebTrack, you can use the data on the Last Results report to quickly check off milestones on student learning contracts.

- In a self-paced environment, students can usually take exams whenever they believe they are ready. In order to proctor exams, they are often administered on campus in a computer lab. ExamView allows you to create tests from the New Perspectives test bank and post them online. Online tests can be configured to allow students to take them at any time or during a specific time period. You can also configure a time limit for online tests, which can effectively prevent students from looking up each answer in the text as the test progresses.

Traditional Lecture-Based Courses

- Start a class session by using the Pre-Assessment questions on the NP8 Web site. Students can "grade" each other's answers based on the lecture that you present. You can also use the QuickChecks, Interactive Summaries, and Interactive Practice Tests as a post-test at the end of a lecture.

- Use the New Perspectives and Student Edition Labs as the basis for lectures. Walk through the lab, adding your own comments and explanations to those provided by the lab.

- Use the ready-made presentations on the Course Presenter CD. Designed by experienced instructors, each chapter presentation includes bulleted highlights from the chapter, plus key terms, illustrations, screen tours, animations, and other multimedia resources. You can also create your own customized presentations using the software of your choice and the figure files, which are available on the Instructor Resources CD.

- Use the figures, screen tours, and videos from the BookOnCD that pertain to your lecture. The advantage of using media elements from the BookOnCD is that they are simulated, and enable you to display screens from software that is not even installed on your presentation system.

- Use the FAQs to start discussions or to test students' knowledge.

- Assign TechTV Video Projects to individual or small groups of students for completion inside or outside of class. Once completed, the projects can be shared with all students to hold classroom discussion.

- Assign Study Tips from the NP8 Web site to individual or small groups of students for completion inside or outside of class. Once completed, the answers can be shared with all students.

- Use the Issue and "What Do You Think?" questions as a springboard for the chapter. After students read the chapter, find out if their opinions have changed.

COMPUTER LABS: USING CAMPUS RESOURCES

Your school's on-campus computer lab can provide an excellent resource for students who do not own their own computers. The "install-free" BookOnCD places only temporary files on a computer's hard disk, which allows students to simply insert the CD to access all of the media and electronic elements that accompany the *New Perspectives on Computer Concepts* textbook.

If lab computers have Internet access, students can also access the NP8 Web site and submit their tracking results from the BookOnCD via e-mail or WebTrack. The following are some hints for making sure that your students' lab experience is trouble free:

- Carefully read the system requirements, located on the BookOnCD, to make sure that your lab computers are sufficiently equipped and configured to run the BookOnCD. Security measures designed to protect lab machines from viruses, intrusion, and student misuse, sometimes prevent legitimate software from running. The BookOnCD does require that students have write access to the hard drive.

- Take time before the beginning of the semester to test the BookOnCD on your lab computers. If your school provides more than one lab facility, test the CD at all venues.

- Communicate with lab managers and workers about your choice of software and the type of activities you expect your students to undertake.

- If you want your students to communicate with you via e-mail, make sure that you have taken the necessary steps to activate e-mail accounts and collect e-mail addresses. If you want your students to submit results to WebTrack, make sure that they have Internet access.

- Provide your students with an orientation to lab facilities and policies. Make sure that they know how to do the following:
  - Start the computer, log in (if necessary), log out (if necessary), and shut down (if necessary).
  - Insert and eject the BookOnCD from the CD drive.
  - Navigate to a chapter or page of the BookOnCD.
  - Format a floppy disk to use as a Tracking Disk.
  - Make a backup copy of the Tracking Disk.
  - Save results on a Tracking Disk or hard disk.
  - Submit results via e-mail or WebTrack.
  - Start the labs.
  - Access the NP8 Web site and return to the BookOnCD.
  - Access the Student Edition Labs.

ACCESS TO TECHNOLOGY: HOW CAN YOU GIVE TECHNOLOGY-BASED ASSIGNMENTS IF SOME OF YOUR STUDENTS DON'T HAVE ACCESS TO COMPUTERS?

Your students invariably have access to many different levels of computer technology. Some might have the latest-and-greatest computer on their dorm room desks; others have to trudge to the nearest computer lab. Others might not have access to any computer at all, or the lab computers may not be equipped with Web access or CD-ROM players.

You don't want to restrict students with computer access from using the multimedia features provided in the New Perspectives on Computer Concepts Learning System, but at the same time, you can't penalize the students without computer access. New Perspectives supports a variety of pencil-and-paper options. Experienced instructors have provided the following tips:

- Complete the Interactive Summary at the end of each chapter. Students can simply write their answers in the blank boxes.

- Write definitions of key terms. Using the Interactive Key Terms list as a guide, students should write a definition of each term using their own words. Note that the Glossary in the back of the book contains definitions. Make sure that you are familiar with this wording if you require students to use their own words.

- Answer the Interactive Situation Questions. Students should list the question number and the answer. To extend this assignment, ask students to explain their answers, citing page references in the textbook.

- Take a Practice Test. If your classroom is equipped with a presentation device, you can open the BookOnCD, jump to the end of the chapter, and display a Practice Test. Students should write their answers on paper to be graded by you, exchanged and graded by another student, or simply discussed and then discarded.

- Complete one or more projects. Projects can be assigned to individual students or to small groups.

CHAPTER ASSIGNMENTS: ALTERNATIVES TO ONE CHAPTER PER WEEK

New Perspectives chapters are all about flexibility. Although one chapter per week is a good rule of thumb, chapters can be abbreviated, extended, or rearranged to fit many different course schedules. Each chapter includes supplementary material such as Labs, TechTalks, Issues, and Computers in Context sections, InfoWebLinks, Projects, and Web Activities that can be assigned or skipped as your course requires.

Too many chapters?

- Omit one or more chapters.
- Consolidate the less technical chapters.

Not enough chapters?

- Reserve all of the TechTalk sections for the end of the course, then tackle them as if they were combined into a single chapter (or two chapters as time permits). You'll find this option especially effective for less technical students because they will not be required to tackle technical topics until they have covered all of the basics in the main chapters.
- Reserve the Issue and Computers in Context sections for the end of the semester, then select one for class discussion each day during the last week or two of the semester. This strategy uses the issues as a capstone experience, and allows students to integrate and apply their technical understanding to technology-related social and ethical issues.
- Chapter 2, Computer Hardware, includes enough material for two weeks. You might want to assign Sections A and B for one week, and Sections C and D for another week.
- Chapter 4, File Management, Virus Protection, and Backup, also lends itself well to a two-week format. Section C on Computer Viruses provides a topic that is very interesting to students, and supplemental lectures such as the following would provide your students with some practical information:
  - Details on current virus threats, such as Sasser and MyDoom
  - How to select, configure, use, and update anti-virus software
  - How to set e-mail and browser security in Windows
  - How to locate information about viruses at various Web sites and when to use their instructions for manually eradicating viruses
- A third chapter that works well in a two-week format is Chapter 5, Internet and LAN Technology.
- Many of the projects are easily converted to classroom activities. Some projects are designed to be discussion topics; others, such as projects that result in research papers or research projects, are easily converted to class discussions or in-class research projects.

Chapters too short?

- Extend the chapter by assigning InfoWebLinks.
- Make sure that you cover the TechTalk, Issue, and Computers in Context sections.
- Assign all of the labs.
- Consider assigning Student Edition Labs in addition to the New Perspectives Labs.
- Require at least one project per chapter as an individual or small group assignment.
- Use the Issue section to start discussions and pose "what-if" scenarios. The Issue section works as either a traditional reading assignment, or as a lecture-only presentation. You can also assign the Issue section as a reading assignment, and use the "What Do You Think" questions as the basis for a class discussion instead of a traditional lecture.
- Study tips can be used as classroom reviews, discussion topics, or written assignments.

Chapters too long?

- Assign only relevant sections. In general, the first sections of each chapter contain general information about the chapter topics, and the later sections introduce more technical information. Overview or non-technical courses can often shorten chapters by concentrating on Sections A and B.
- Skip the TechTalk, Issue, and Computers in Context sections of each chapter.
- Assign only one New Perspectives lab or Student Edition Lab per chapter.
- Use the Interactive Summary in each chapter to help design lectures that comment on the most relevant topics in the chapter. The Interactive Summary paraphrases each section, and highlights key terms and definitions. Multiple sections can be introduced in one lecture period by concentrating only on the most important topics.

SPECIAL TOPICS COURSES: TAKE ADVANTAGE OF NEW PERSPECTIVES FLEXIBILITY

Is it a challenge or a nightmare to teach a special topics course? The "Intro to Computer Applications, History, and the Internet" course that somehow dropped into your lap, or the "Computer Issues and Ethics" elective that's offered every two years can mean many late nights spent searching for textbooks and writing syllabi. Happily, *New Perspectives on Computer Concepts* can be customized and adapted to suit a variety of computer-related courses.

The following tips can help you design special topics courses:

- Use *New Perspectives on Computer Concepts Brief* as a quick overview of computer concepts and terminology before tackling the crux of special topics with an additional textbook or assigned readings.
- Construct reading assignments based on New Perspectives sections, rather than whole chapters. Assign only sections that are relevant to your course and skip the others.
- Labs and screen tours can be used as standalone topics. Browse through the New Perspectives Table of Contents for lab and screen tour topics that fit your special topics course.
- Use material from the InfoWebLinks to extend the topics that are most relevant to your special topics course.
- Use the new TechBuzz section to provide students with information on the latest technology trends and products.

Course: Web Basics

Assign the following:

- Orientation Chapter, Section E: Computers and Security
- Chapter 1: Computer, Internet, and Network Basics, including the New Perspectives Labs on Internet basics, Web basics, and E-mail basics and the Student Edition Lab on Using E-mail
- Chapter 5: Internet and LAN Technology, including the New Perspectives Labs on tracking packets and securing your connection and the Student Edition Lab on Connection to the Internet, Networking Basics, and Wireless Technology
- Chapter 6: Web Pages, Web Sites, and E-Commerce, including the New Perspectives Labs on working with cookies and browser security settings and the Student Edition Labs on Protecting Your Privacy, Creating Web Pages, Getting the Most Out of the Internet, Electronic Commerce, and Web Design Principles.

Course: Technical Issues and Ethics

Assign the following:

- Orientation Chapter, Section E: Computers and Security
- Chapter 1: Computer, Internet, and Network Basics, plus Issues and corresponding background material from the Comprehensive edition. Choose as many Issues as your schedule permits. Also include InfoWebLinks on Netiquette, E-mail privacy, Software Copyright, Copyright and Piracy, Hoax, Computer Crime, Intellectual Property, Ethics in Computing, and Privacy.

Course: The Computer Industry

Assign the following:

- Chapter 6: Web Pages, Web Sites, and E-Commerce; Chapter 8: The Computer Industry, including the Online Job Hunting lab
- Chapter 12: Beyond Desktop Computing, including the SETI lab. Include InfoWebLinks as appropriate.
- TechBuzz

Course: Programming Basics

Assign the following:

- Chapter 1, Section A: Computer Basics
- Chapter 2: Computer Hardware
- Chapter 3: Computer Software
- Chapter 6, Section C: Web Page Extensions, Scripts, and Programs
- Chapter 9: Information Systems Analysis and Design
- Chapter 10, Section D: SQL
- Chapter 11: Computer Programming. Include the New Perspectives Labs, Student Edition Labs, and InfoWebLinks as appropriate.

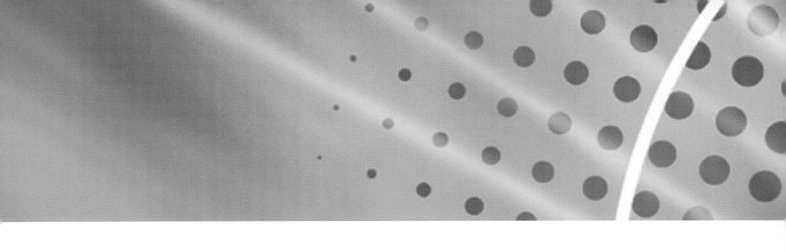

NEW PERSPECTIVES ON
COMPUTER CONCEPTS

8 EDITION

by June Jamrich Parsons and Dan Oja

COMPREHENSIVE

Includes access to an integrated companion Web site and an interactive BookOnCD. The companion Web site offers audio clips, labs, games, relevant links, practice tests, and more. The BookOnCD contains the entire contents of the textbook with figures that come to life as videos, software tours, and animations. See the inside back cover!

THOMSON

COURSE TECHNOLOGY™

Australia • Canada • Denmark • Japan • Mexico • New Zealand • Philippines • Puerto Rico • Singapore • South Africa • Spain • United Kingdom • United States

MANAGING EDITOR
Rachel Goldberg

SENIOR PRODUCT MANAGER
Kathy Finnegan

SENIOR PRODUCT MANAGER
Amanda Young Shelton

PRODUCT MANAGER
Karen Stevens

PRODUCT MANAGER
Brianna Hawes

ASSOCIATE PRODUCT MANAGER
Emilie Perreault

EDITORIAL ASSISTANT
Shana Rosenthal

MARKETING MANAGER
Joy Stark

DEVELOPMENTAL EDITOR
Lisa M. Lord

PRODUCTION EDITOR
Jennifer Goguen

TEXT DESIGN
Steve Deschene

DTP AND COMPOSITION
Tensi Parsons

PREPRESS PRODUCTION
GEX Publishing Services

MEDIA DEVELOPERS
Donna Mulder, Fatima Lockhart,
Keefe Crowley, Tensi Parsons

PHOTO RESEARCHER
Christina Micek

PHOTOGRAPHERS
Greg Manis, Joe Bush

ILLUSTRATOR
Eric Murphy, GEX Publishing Services

NARRATORS
Chris Robbert and Michele Martinez

BOOKONCD DEVELOPMENT
MediaTechnics Corporation

CONTENTS AT A GLANCE

TABLE OF CONTENTS

CHAPTER 1
COMPUTER, INTERNET, WEB, AND E-MAIL BASICS

ON THE BOOKONCD

ON THE WEB

CHAPTER 3

COMPUTER SOFTWARE

CHAPTER 4

FILE MANAGEMENT, VIRUS PROTECTION, AND BACKUP

CHAPTER 5

INTERNET AND LAN TECHNOLOGY

ON THE BOOKONCD

ON THE WEB

CHAPTER 6
WEB PAGES, WEB SITES, AND E-COMMERCE

ON THE BOOKONCD

ON THE WEB

CHAPTER 10

DATABASES

CHAPTER 11

COMPUTER PROGRAMMING

ON THE BookOnCD

ON THE WEB

CHAPTER 12
BEYOND DESKTOP COMPUTING

NEW PERSPECTIVES ON COMPUTER CONCEPTS 8TH EDITION

Whether you're a complete novice or computer-savvy, *New Perspectives on Computer Concepts 8th Edition* offers an engaging hands-on approach to computers backed by innovative learning technology. The 8th Edition incorporates invaluable feedback from the New Perspectives on Computer Concepts Advisory Committee, made up of over twenty instructors, to ensure that this book contains the most current information and resources for learning about computers.

THE NP8 LEARNING SYSTEM

You have purchased more than just a book. *New Perspectives on Computer Concepts 8th Edition* includes a printed book, an integrated Web site, and an interactive BookOnCD designed to be used together to provide a cutting-edge learning experience.

Want to study smarter? The NP8 Web site offers tools to help you understand the material from all angles and to thoroughly prepare you for exams. Want to see the concepts in the book in action? The BookOnCD brings concepts to life by directly linking to videos and animations.

Throughout this book you'll see CD ✳ and Web Activities ♣ icons. These tell you that there's more to explore beyond the surface of your textbook.

NP8 BOOK FEATURES

ORIENTATION CHAPTER

If you have little or no experience with computers, this chapter will put you at ease with the essential computer concepts you need to get up and running quickly. Even if you already know how to use computers, the Orientation offers helpful tips about how to most effectively use NP8's technology-based learning tools.

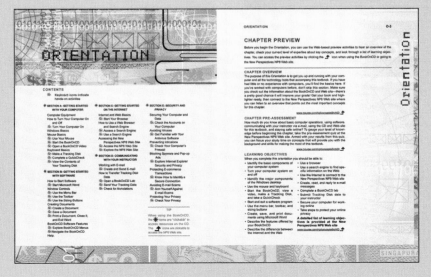

CHAPTER OPENER

The Chapter Openers serve as guides to everything you'll learn and do in each chapter.

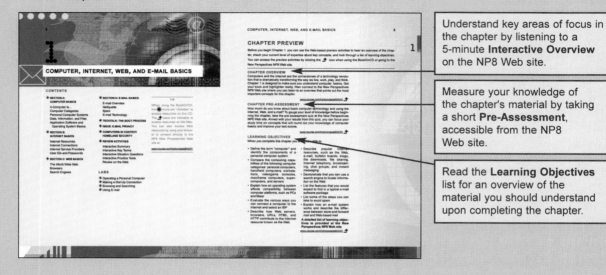

Understand key areas of focus in the chapter by listening to a 5-minute **Interactive Overview** on the NP8 Web site.

Measure your knowledge of the chapter's material by taking a short **Pre-Assessment**, accessible from the NP8 Web site.

Read the **Learning Objectives** list for an overview of the material you should understand upon completing the chapter.

CHAPTER FEATURES

Chapter features, such as **FAQs**, **InfoWebLinks**, and **QuickChecks**, help you understand concepts, put information in context, and explore topics beyond those presented in the text.

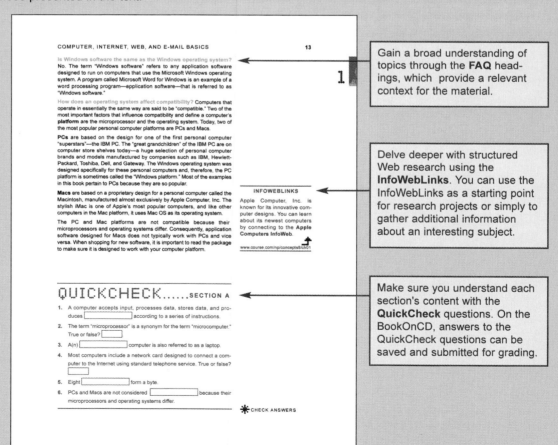

Gain a broad understanding of topics through the **FAQ** headings, which provide a relevant context for the material.

Delve deeper with structured Web research using the **InfoWebLinks**. You can use the InfoWebLinks as a starting point for research projects or simply to gather additional information about an interesting subject.

Make sure you understand each section's content with the **QuickCheck** questions. On the BookOnCD, answers to the QuickCheck questions can be saved and submitted for grading.

TECHTALK

Each chapter includes a **TechTalk** section that presents challenging technical information in a easy-to-understand way. TechTalk helps you delve deeper into the mechanics of how computers and computer technologies work.

ISSUE

Controversy and technology seem to go hand and hand. It's no longer enough to study what computers are, but rather how they shape our world. Each chapter explores a contemporary **Issue** and gives you the opportunity to express your opinion through What Do You Think questions.

COMPUTERS IN CONTEXT

So you're not a computer major? There are still a number of ways technology will affect you in your future career. In the **Computers in Context** section, you'll discover how technology plays a role in careers such as film-making, architecture, banking, and fashion.

REVIEW ACTIVITIES

Prove your mastery of the concepts in each chapter with the **Review Activities**, which are printed in the book and also accessible in an interactive format on the BookOnCD. The Review Activities include the Interactive Summary, Interactive Situation Questions, Interactive Key Terms, and Interactive Practice Tests. When you work on the Review Activities using the BookOnCD, you can save and submit your scores to your instructor. The Interactive Practice Tests are also available through the NP8 Web site.

REVIEW ON THE WEB

Take your knowledge of the concepts one step further with the **Review on the Web** activities available on the New Perspectives NP8 Web site. These activities, which include **Projects**, **Study Tips**, and **Online Games**, reinforce the concepts that you have learned in the chapter.

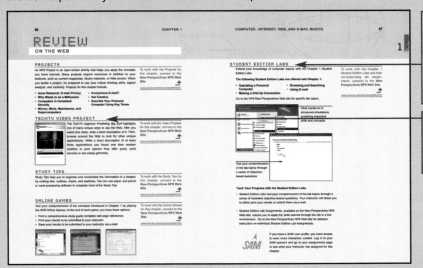

Student Edition Labs help you review and extend your knowledge through observations, hands-on simulations, and challenging objective-based questions.

TechTV Video Projects feature TechTV news clips that explore technology-related issues and trends.

TECHBUZZ

Some new technologies make a lasting impact, while others are just a flash in the pan. The new magazine-like **TechBuzz** section at the end of the book helps you follow tech trends, cutting-edge products, and emerging technologies.

NP8 WEB SITE

Use Course Technology's centralized login page, CoursePort, to gain access to the NP8 Web site. Web Activity icons ✚ in each chapter direct you to the NP8 Web site, which offers a wealth of online resources and study tools.

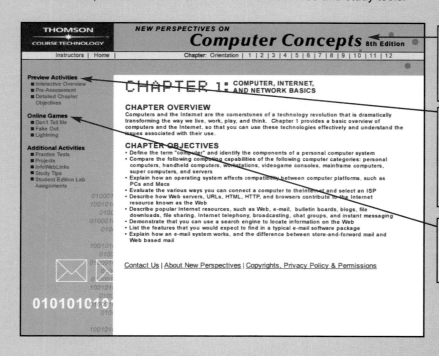

Use the NP8 Web site to access valuable resources, including the **InfoWebLinks, TechTV Library, Study Tips,** and **Student Edition Labs.**

Tailor your study plans for the chapter by using the **Chapter Preview Activities**. Listen to an interactive overview, take a pre-assessment quiz, and read through the detailed chapter objectives.

Test your comprehension with the **Online Games**, which challenge you with different interactive scenarios.

AUDIO INTERACTIVE OVERVIEW

Get your book and highlighter ready, and listen to a 5-minute **Interactive Overview,** which points out key concepts and topics in each chapter.

PRE-ASSESSMENT QUESTIONS

Use the **Pre-Assessment** to gauge your level of knowledge of the concepts in each chapter. Upon completing the Pre-Assessment, you can view and print a study guide that helps focus your study time in your weakest areas of knowledge.

ONLINE GAMES

The **Online Games** give you a rewarding interactive way to reinforce concepts taught in each chapter. Each game offers a printable study guide that points you back to specific pages in the text for review. You can also save your results from the Online Games and submit them electronically to your instructor for grading.

INTERACTIVE PRACTICE TESTS

Interactive Practice Tests, also available on the BookOnCD, consist of 10 multiple-choice, true/false, and fill-in-the-blank questions chosen at random from a large test bank. Each test offers a printable study guide with page references. Your test scores can be saved and submitted to your instructor electronically.

TECHTV VIDEO CLIPS LIBRARY

Ever wondered what it is like to program your own video game? What are the social implications of a digital system that tracks patrons at a neighborhood bar? Stay on top of emerging technologies and technology-related issues with our library of **TechTV Video Clips**. TechTV Video Projects, included in every chapter, challenge you to further investigate the issues and topics raised in the video clips.

PROJECTS

Work with the NP8 **Projects** to apply the concepts you have learned from reading and lab activities. NP8 Projects are open-ended assignments that require you to research topics, apply critical-thinking skills, and produce reports, summaries, graphics, or other creative deliverables.

STUDY TIPS

Study Tips help you organize and consolidate the information in a chapter by making lists, outlines, charts, and sketches.

STUDENT EDITION LABS

You can master hundreds of computer concepts including input and output devices, file management and desktop applications, computer privacy, virus protection, and much more using the **Student Edition Labs**. The interactive Student Edition Labs help you learn through dynamic observation, step-by-step practice, and challenging review questions. Student Edition Lab Assignments challenge you to apply the skills learned in the labs to realistic case problems.

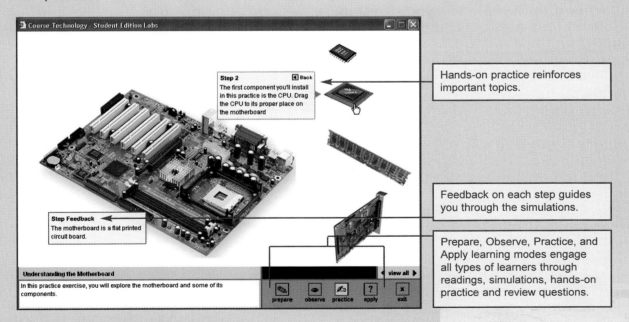

NP8 BOOKONCD

The interactive BookOnCD includes the entire contents of the printed book and brings the concepts to life with the following interactive features:

- **Interactive Review Activities** test your understanding of the concepts presented in each chapter.
- **Interactive QuickCheck** questions check your comprehension of each section.
- **Videos**, **animations** and **screentours** throughout each chapter bring the figures to life.
- **New Perspectives Labs** give you hands-on experience applying concepts and using software.

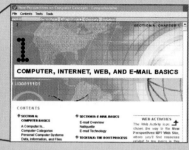

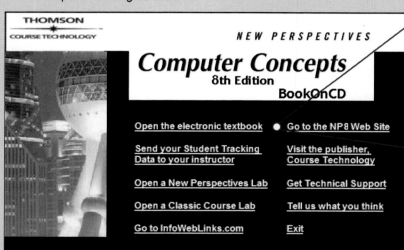

You can save or print your results from the BookOnCD Interactive Review Activities, QuickCheck questions, and New Perspectives Labs to submit to your instructor.

SAM COMPUTER CONCEPTS

If your instructor has chosen to use SAM Training and Assessment Software in your course, you will have access to interactive training simulations that reinforce the lessons presented in this text, as well as realistic hands-on exams.

Hands-on tasks allow you to demonstrate your understanding of important computer concepts and applications.

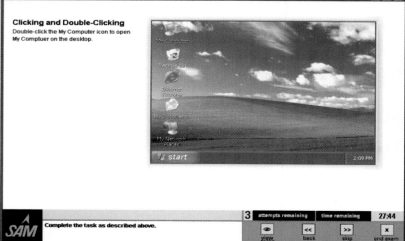

NP8 INSTRUCTOR RESOURCES

New Perspectives instructional resources and technology provide instructors with a wide range of tools that enhance teaching and learning. These tools can be accessed from the Instructor Resources CD or at *www.course.com*.

INSTRUCTOR'S MANUAL: HELP IS ONLY A FEW KEYSTROKES AWAY

An enhanced Instructor's Manual offers an outline for each chapter, plus instructional suggestions and teaching tips, including how to effectively use and integrate the Web site content, CD content, and labs.

EXAMVIEW: OUR POWERFUL TESTING SOFTWARE PACKAGE

With ExamView, instructors can generate printed tests, create LAN-based tests, or test over the Internet.

COURSE PRESENTER

Instructors can deliver engaging and visually impressive lectures for each chapter with the professionally-designed Course Presenter. The Course Presenter is a PowerPoint presentation that is multimedia-enhanced with screentours, animations, and videos.

INSTRUCTOR'S EDITION

The Instructor's Edition content explains in depth the New Perspectives Computer Concepts pedagogy and technology resources. It also provides suggestions on how to use New Perspectives on Computer Concepts technology in the classroom.

BLACKBOARD AND WEBCT CONTENT

Course Technology offers a full range of content for use with BlackBoard and WebCT to simplify the use of New Perspectives in distance education settings.

FROM THE AUTHORS

Technology continues to move forward at a rapid pace. To help instructors and students stay in step with the march of technology, we produced this media-rich and Web-enhanced 8th Edition of New Perspectives on Computer Concepts. An expanded Orientation section at the beginning of the book now includes a hands-on introduction to computer security and privacy—essential information for both beginning students and those who are computer savvy. A new TechBuzz section at the end of the book gets students thinking about technology trends and the potential of new products to become the next "killer apps" or "tech turkeys."

We retained the same basic organization for Chapters 1 through 12 and updated their content to reflect current developments. Based on feedback from students, instructors, and reviewers, we focused on making technology concepts even more understandable by streamlining explanations and honing figures for the clearest presentation possible. We logged countless hours of research to bring you the most up-to-date information about new products and trends in computers, software, and the Internet. Please make sure to check the InfoWebLinks for important updates on post-publication events.

Many of today's students have substantially more practical experience with computers than their counterparts of 10 years ago, and yet other students enter college with inadequate technology preparation. The goal of New Perspectives on Computer Concepts is to bring every student up to speed with computer basics, and then go beyond basic computer literacy to provide students with technical information that every college-educated person would be expected to know. Whether you are an instructor or a student, we hope that you enjoy the learning experience provided by our text-based and technology-based materials.

ACKNOWLEDGEMENTS

The book would not exist—and certainly wouldn't arrive on schedule—were it not for the efforts of our media, editorial, and production teams. We thank Amanda Young Shelton and Emilie Perreault for tireless work on every detail of the project; Rachel Goldberg for her leadership for the entire New Perspectives series; Jennifer Goguen for managing production; Fatima Lockhart, Donna Mulder, Tensi Parsons, Keefe Crowley, Greg Manis, Joe Bush, and Eric Murphy for creating videos, screentours, interactive tests, photos, illustrations, and animations; Rebekah Tidwell for her work on the Pre-Assessments; Dave Nuscher for his work on updating the Online Games; Chris Robbert for his clear narrations; Sue Oja, Debora Elam, Deana Martinson, Karen Kangas, Jaclyn Kangas, and Kevin Lappi for checking and double-checking the alpha and beta CDs; Lisa Lord for her insightful developmental edit; Robin K. Flynn for making sure that every comma is in the right place; Keefe Crowley for designing and maintaining our InfoWebLinks site; artist Steve Deschene for a stunning interior design; and Christina Micek for her photo research. We want to thank you all!

-June Parsons and Dan Oja

NEW PERSPECTIVES ON COMPUTER CONCEPTS
ADVISORY COMMITTEE

Dr. Nazih Abdallah
University of Central Florida

Paula F. Bell
Lock Haven University of
Pennsylvania

Wendy Chisholm
Barstow College

David Courtaway
Devry University, Pomona

Sallie B. Dodson
Radford University

Philip Funk
Southern New Hampshire University

Michael Gaffney
Century College

Ernest Gines
Tarrant County College Southeast

Ione Good
Southeastern Community College

Thomas E. Gorecki
College of Southern Maryland

Steven Gramlich
Pasco-Hernando Community
College

Michael J. Hanna
Colorado State University

Stan Leja
Del Mar College

Martha Lindberg
Minnesota State University, Mankato

Teresa C. Long
Valencia Community College

Dr. W. Benjamin Martz
University of Colorado,
Colorado Springs

DeAnn McMullen
West Kentucky Community
and Technical College

Robert P. Moore
Laredo Community College

Dr. Rodney Pearson
Mississippi State University

Lana Shryock
Monroe County Community College

Betty Sinowitz
SUNY Rockland Community
College

Martin Skolnik
Florida Atlantic University

Jerome Spencer
Rowan University

We would also like to thank the reviewers from the recent past editions who helped provide valuable feedback that is still an influence on the 8th Edition:

ACADEMIC REVIEWERS
Dr. Nazih Abdallah
University of Central Florida

Beverly Amer
Northern Arizona University

Ken Baldauf
Florida State University

Mary Caldwell
Rollins College

Chuck Calvin
Computer Learning Centers

Becky Curtin
William Rainey Harper College

Eric Daley
University of New Brunswick

Robert Erickson
University of Vermont

Mike Feiler
Merritt College

Ed Mott
Central Texas College

Catherine Perlich
MediaTechnics

David Primeaux
Virginia Commonwealth University

Gregory Stefanelli
Carroll Community College

Martha J. Tilmann
College of San Mateo

Mary Zayac
University of the Virgin Islands

STUDENT REVIEWERS
Kitty Edwards

Heather House

TECHNICAL REVIEWERS
Ramachandran Bharath

Jeff Harrow

Barbra D. Letts

John Lucas

Karl Mulder

ORIENTATION

CONTENTS

TIP

⌨ Keyboard icons indicate hands-on activities.

When using the BookOnCD, the ❋ icons are "clickable" to access resources on the CD. The ✛ icons are clickable to access the NP8 Web site.

CHAPTER PREVIEW

Before you begin the Orientation, you can use the Web-based preview activities to hear an overview of the chapter, check your current level of expertise about key concepts, and look through a list of learning objectives. You can access the preview activities by clicking the ✝ icon when using the BookOnCD or going to the New Perspectives NP8 Web site.

CHAPTER OVERVIEW

The purpose of this Orientation is to get you up and running with your computer and all the technology tools that accompany this textbook. If you have had little or no experience with computers, you'll find the basics here. If you've worked with computers before, don't skip this section. Make sure you check out the information about the BookOnCD and Web site—there's a pretty good chance it will improve your grade! Get your book and highlighter ready, then connect to the New Perspectives NP8 Web site where you can listen to an overview that points out the most important concepts for this chapter.

www.course.com/np/concepts8/ch00 ✝

CHAPTER PRE-ASSESSMENT

How much do you know about basic computer operations, using software, communicating with your instructor via e-mail, using the CD and Web site for this textbook, and staying safe online? To gauge your level of knowledge before beginning the chapter, take the pre-assessment quiz at the New Perspectives NP8 Web site. Armed with your results from this quiz, you can focus your study time on concepts that will provide you with the background and skills for making the most of this textbook.

www.course.com/np/concepts8/ch00 ✝

LEARNING OBJECTIVES

When you complete this orientation you should be able to:

- Identify the basic components of your computer system
- Turn your computer system on and off
- Identify the major components of the Windows desktop
- Use the mouse and keyboard
- Start the BookOnCD, view a video, make a Tracking Disk, and take a QuickCheck
- Start and exit a software program
- Use the menu bar, toolbar, and sizing buttons
- Create, save, and print documents using Microsoft Word
- Describe the features offered by your BookOnCD
- Describe the difference between the Internet and the Web

- Use a browser
- Use a search engine to find specific information on the Web
- Use the Internet to connect to the New Perspectives NP8 Web site
- Create, read, and reply to e-mail messages
- Complete a BookOnCD lab
- Submit Tracking Disk data to your instructor
- Secure your computer for working online
- Take steps to protect your online privacy

A detailed list of learning objectives is provided at the New Perspectives NP8 Web site

www.course.com/np/concepts8/ch00 ✝

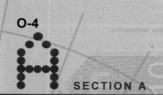

SECTION A

GETTING STARTED WITH YOUR COMPUTER

When you use the *New Perspectives on Computer Concepts* textbook, you not only learn about computers, you also use computers as learning tools. You can read your textbook on-screen where many of the photos come alive as videos, where screen shots open into guided tours of popular software, and where you can take interactive quizzes to make sure you understand chapter material before encountering it on a test. In Section A you'll learn how to turn on your computer, start the on-screen version of your textbook, use your computer's mouse, start a BookOnCD video, use a computer keyboard, and take an interactive quiz.

COMPUTER EQUIPMENT

What do I need to know about my computer? Your computer—the one you own, the one you use in a school lab, or the one provided to you at work—is technically classified as a microcomputer and sometimes referred to as a personal computer. A computer runs software (or "programs") that help you accomplish a variety of tasks. A typical computer system consists of several devices—you must be able to identify these devices to use them.

What are the important components of my computer system? The system unit contains your computer's circuitry, such as the microprocessor that is the "brain" of your computer and memory chips that temporarily store information. It also contains storage devices, such as a hard disk drive.

Your computer system also includes basic hardware devices that allow you to enter information and commands, view work, and store information for later retrieval. Devices for entering information include a keyboard and mouse. A display device, such as a TV-like monitor, allows you to view your work, a printer produces "hard copy" on paper, and speakers produce beeps and chimes that help you pay attention to what happens on the screen.

Where are the important components of a desktop computer system? A desktop computer is designed for stationary use on a desk or table. Figure 1 shows the key components of a desktop computer system.

PC or Mac?

Microcomputers can be divided into two camps: PCs and Macs. The CD that comes with this book is designed for use with PCs, and the Orientation instructions apply specifically to PCs.

You can usually determine whether you have a PC or Mac by noting your computer's brand name. PC brands include Dell, IBM, Hewlett-Packard, Compaq, Gateway, and Sony. You can use the software that accompanies your textbook with these and other PC brands.

Macintosh computers are manufactured by Apple Computers, Inc. and sport a rainbow-colored logo of an apple. If you have a Mac, check with your instructor for the location of your school's PC lab.

FIGURE 1
A desktop computer system includes several components, usually connected by cables.

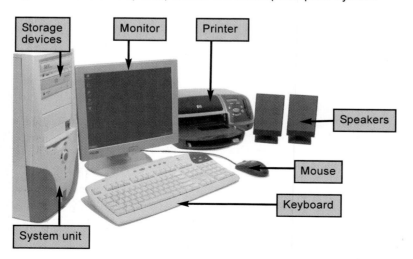

Storage devices
Monitor
Printer
Speakers
Mouse
Keyboard
System unit

Where are the important components of a notebook computer system? Notebook computers (sometimes called "laptops") are small, lightweight computers designed to be carried from place to place. The components of a notebook computer system, except the printer, are housed in a single unit, as shown in Figure 2.

LCD screen

Speakers

Keyboard

Touchpad

Storage devices

FIGURE 2

A notebook computer includes a flat-panel LCD screen, keyboard, speakers, and touchpad in the same unit that contains the microprocessor, memory, and storage devices. An external mouse is sometimes used instead of the touchpad.

FIGURE 3

You should use the hard disk to store most of your data, but to transport or back up data, you can use floppy disks, CDs, DVDs, or USB flash drives.

How do I identify my computer's storage devices? Your computer contains a hard disk, housed inside the system unit. It is also likely to have a floppy disk drive and some type of drive that works with CDs. Figure 3 can help you identify your computer's storage devices and their uses.

Floppy disk drive

Capacity: 1.44 million characters

Low-capacity storage, but handy for transferring work between home and school labs.

CD drive

Capacity: 640 million characters

A CD-ROM drive reads CDs, but does not allow you to store your own data on them. CD-R or CD-RW drives allow you to store data.

DVD drive

Capacity: 4.7 billion characters

DVD-ROM drives read CDs and DVDs, but do not let you store your own data. The R or RW versions allow you to store data.

USB flash drive

Capacity: 32 million–2 billion characters

A USB flash drive is about the size of a highlighter and plugs directly into the computer system unit.

HOW TO TURN YOUR COMPUTER ON AND OFF

How do I turn it on? A notebook computer typically has one switch that turns on the entire system. Look for the switch along the sides of the computer or on the top above the keyboard. When using a desktop computer, turn on the monitor, printer, and speakers before you flip the switch on the system unit.

Most computers take a minute or two to power up, and you might be required to log in by entering a user ID and password. Your computer is ready to use when the Windows desktop (Figure 4 on the next page) appears on the computer screen and you can move the arrow-shaped pointer with your mouse.

How do I turn it off? Your computer is designed to turn itself off after you initiate a shutdown sequence by clicking the Start button, selecting "Shut Down" or "Turn Off Computer," and following the instructions on the screen. After the computer shuts itself off, you can turn off the monitor, speakers, and printer. When using computers in a school lab, ask about the shutdown procedure. Your lab manager might ask that you log out but do not turn the computer off.

TRY IT

Turn your computer on

1. Locate the power switch for any devices connected to your computer and turn them on.

2. Locate the power switch for your computer and turn it on.

3. If a message asks for your user ID and/or password, type them in, and then press the Enter key on your computer's keyboard.

4. Wait for the Windows desktop to appear.

WINDOWS BASICS

What is Windows? Microsoft Windows is an example of a type of software called an operating system. The operating system controls all the basic tasks your computer performs, such as running application software, manipulating files on storage devices, and transferring data to and from printers, digital cameras, and other devices. The operating system also controls the user interface—the way software appears on the screen and the way you control what it does.

What is the Windows desktop? The Windows desktop is your base of operations for using your computer. It displays small pictures called "icons" that help you access software, documents, and the components of your computer system. The desktop is divided into several areas, as shown in Figure 4.

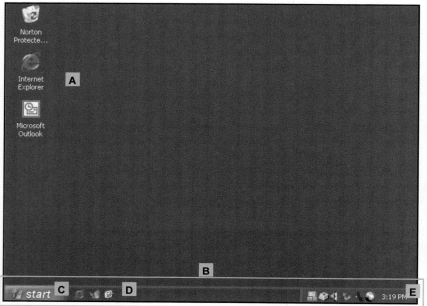

FIGURE 4
The Windows Desktop

A The main part of the desktop displays icons that represent software, files, and folders containing documents, graphics, and other data.

B The taskbar contains the Start button, Quick Start bar, and Notification area.

C The Start button is used to display the Start menu, which lists all the programs installed on your computer.

D The Quick Start bar is always visible, making it a good place for icons that represent the programs you frequently use.

E The Notification area displays the current time and the status of programs, devices, and Internet connections.

When working with your computer, you'll frequently use the Start button in the lower-left corner of the screen to display the Start menu that provides options for accessing software, finding data, configuring hardware, and finding answers to your questions about using Windows (Figure 5).

How do I manipulate icons and other Windows controls? To use the Start button and other desktop controls, you'll need to become familiar with how to use a mouse to control an on-screen pointer. The pointer is usually shaped like an arrow ⇧, but you can change to a different shape, depending on the task you're doing. For example, when the computer is busy, the arrow shape turns into an hourglass, signifying that you should wait for the computer to finish its current task before attempting to start a new task.

FIGURE 5
The Start Menu

MOUSE BASICS

What is a mouse? A mouse is a device used to manipulate items on the screen, such as the controls displayed on the Windows desktop. PC compatible mice have at least two buttons, typically located on top of the mouse. Some mice also include a scroll wheel mounted between the left and right mouse buttons. Other mice include additional buttons on the top or sides (Figure 6).

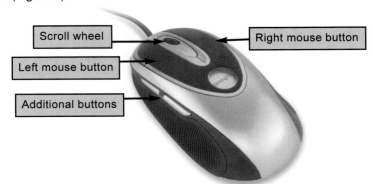

FIGURE 6
For basic mousing, you need use only the left and right mouse buttons.

How do I use a mouse? Hold the mouse in your right hand as shown in Figure 7. When you drag the mouse from left to right over your mousepad or desk, the arrow-shaped pointer on the screen moves from left to right. If you run out of room to move the mouse, simply pick it up and reposition it. The pointer does not move when the mouse is not in contact with a flat surface.

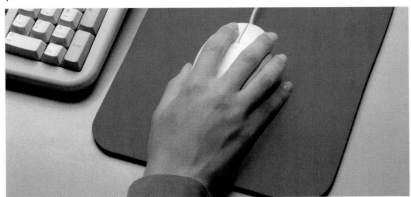

FIGURE 7
Rest the palm of your right hand on the mouse. Position your index finger over the left mouse button and your middle finger over the right mouse button.

There are several ways you can manipulate on-screen objects. Although you might not be able to manipulate every object in all possible ways, you'll soon learn which mouse actions are allowed for each type of control. The following list describes your repertoire of mouse actions.

Action	How to	Result
Click	Press the left mouse button once, and then immediately release it.	Select an object
Double-click	Press the left mouse button twice in rapid succession without moving the body of the mouse.	Activate an object
Right-click	Press the right mouse button once, and then immediately release it.	Display a shortcut menu
Drag	Hold the left mouse button down while you move the mouse.	Move an object

⌨**TRY IT**

Use your mouse

1. With your computer on and the Windows desktop showing on the screen, move your mouse around on the desk and notice how the mouse movements correspond to the movement of the arrow-shaped pointer.

2. Move the mouse to position the pointer on the Start button.

3. Click the left mouse button to open the Start menu.

4. Click the **Start** button again to close the Start menu.

You can find out more about using a mouse by watching a video from the CD version of your textbook. The BookOnCD supplied with your textbook includes many photos like the one in Figure 8 that come to life as videos. The BookOnCD also includes diagrams that become animations and screen shots that open to guided software tours. Any figure in your textbook that displays the ✳ symbol has a corresponding video, animation, or software tour.

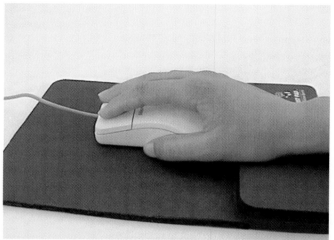

FIGURE 8

Use your palm to move the mouse in the direction you want the on-screen pointer to move. Use your fingers to click the mouse buttons to choose an action.

CLICK TO START ✳

How do I start the BookOnCD? Now that you know how to use a mouse, you can work with the CD supplied with your textbook. To learn how to start the BookOnCD and take advantage of its interactive features, you can follow the instructions in the box below.

EXPLORE NP8 LEARNING TOOLS

Start the BookOnCD

1. Locate the button on your computer's CD or DVD drive and push it to open the tray.

2. Insert the BookOnCD into the tray, label side up.

3. Push the button on the drive to close it.

4. Wait a few seconds until the BookOnCD main menu appears.

5. Position the arrow-shaped pointer over the option **Open the electronic textbook** and click the left mouse button one time. Click the **No** button when you see the Tracking Disk message.

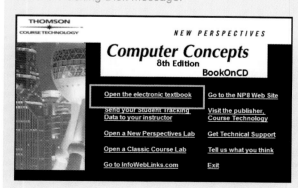

Open a BookOnCD video

1. When the first page appears, click the **Go to Page** button, then type **O-8**. Hint: Use an uppercase "O," not a zero!

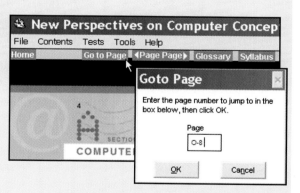

2. When the mouse photo appears, click ✳ to start the screen tour.

3. Watch the video to learn more about using your mouse. When the video is finished, click the **Exit** button.

4. You could leave the CD in the drive and continue to read the book on your computer screen, but for now, click the ⊠ Close button in the upper-right corner of the screen to close the electronic textbook. From the main BookOnCD menu, click **Exit** before removing the CD from the drive.

KEYBOARD BASICS

What are the important features of a computer keyboard? You use the computer keyboard to input commands, respond to prompts, and type the text of documents. An insertion point that looks like a flashing vertical bar indicates where the characters you type will appear. You can change the location of the insertion point by using the mouse or the arrow keys. Study Figure 9 for an overview of important computer keys and their functions.

FIGURE 9
Computer Keyboard

A The **Esc** or "escape" key cancels an operation.

B **Function keys** activate commands, such as Save, Help, and Print. The command associated with each key depends on the software you are using.

C The **Print Screen** key prints the contents of the screen or stores a copy of the screen in memory that you can print or manipulate with graphics software.

D The **Scroll Lock** key's function depends on the software you're using. This key is rarely used with today's software.

E **Indicator Lights** show you the status of three toggle keys: Num Lock, Caps Lock, and Scroll Lock. The Power light indicates whether the computer is on or off.

F The **Backspace** key deletes one character to the left of the insertion point.

G The **Insert** key switches between insert mode and typeover mode.

H The **Home** key takes you to the beginning of a line or the beginning of a document, depending on the software you are using.

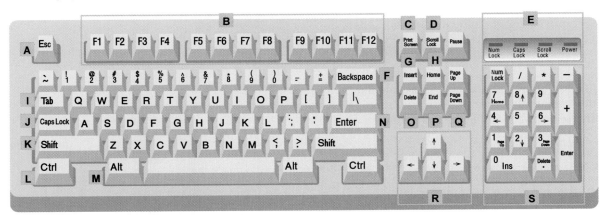

I The **Tab** key can move your current typing location to the next tab stop or the next text-entry box.

J The **Caps Lock** key capitalizes all the letters you type when it is engaged, but does not produce the top symbol on keys that contain two symbols. This key is a toggle key, which means that each time you press it, you switch between uppercase and lowercase modes.

K The **Shift** key capitalizes letters and produces the top symbol on keys that contain two symbols.

L You hold down the **Ctrl** key while pressing another key. The result of Ctrl or Alt key combinations depends on the software you are using.

M You hold down the **Alt** key while you press another key.

N The **Enter** key is used to indicate that you have completed a command or want to move your typing position down to the next line.

O The **Delete** key deletes the character to the right of the insertion point.

P The **End** key takes you to the end of a line or the end of a document, depending on the software you are using.

Q The **Page Up** key displays the previous screen of information. The **Page Down** key displays the next screen of information.

R The up, down, right, and left **arrow keys** move the insertion point.

S The **numeric keypad** produces numbers or moves the insertion point, depending on the status of the Num Lock key shown by the status lights.

What do Alt and Ctrl mean? The Alt and Ctrl keys work with the letter keys. If you see <Ctrl X>, Ctrl+X, [Ctrl X], Ctrl-X, or Ctrl X on the screen or in an instruction manual, it means to hold down the Ctrl key while you press X. For example, Ctrl+X is a keyboard shortcut for clicking the Edit menu, and then clicking the Cut option. A keyboard shortcut allows you to use the keyboard rather than the mouse to select menu commands. For more tips on using your computer keyboard, start the video for Figure 10.

FIGURE 10
Using a computer keyboard is similar to using a typewriter. Unlike typewriters, computer keyboards include many special keys designed to simplify common tasks.

CLICK TO START

What if I make a mistake? Everyone makes mistakes. The first rule is don't panic! Most mistakes are reversible. The hints and tips in Figure 11 should help you recover from mistakes.

FIGURE 11
Most mistakes are easy to fix.

What Happened	What To Do
Typed the wrong thing	Use the Backspace key to delete the last characters you typed.
Selected the wrong menu	Press the Esc key to close the menu.
Opened something you didn't mean to	Click the X button in the upper-right corner of the screen.
Computer has "hung up" and no longer responds to mouse clicks or typed commands	Hold down the Ctrl, Alt, and Delete keys, and then follow instructions to close the program.
Pressed the Enter key in the middle of a sentence	Press the Backspace key to paste the sentence back together.

You can practice using the keyboard when you type your answers for the QuickCheck questions at the bottom of the next page.

What is a QuickCheck? Each chapter of your textbook is divided into four main sections: A, B, C, and D. Each section ends with a series of QuickCheck questions that help you assess your understanding of material you've read. You can fill in the answers on the page, and then check your answers by referring to the end of the book. If you are using the BookOnCD, you can type your answers into the boxes and your computer automatically corrects them. You can save your score on a Tracking Disk for later reference or to submit to your instructor. Follow the instructions on the next page to make a Tracking Disk, complete the QuickCheck at the end of this section, and access your Tracking Disk summary.

TIP

Whether reading from your printed textbook or working with the BookOnCD, you might get a better grasp of the material if you take a break between sections rather than attempt to complete the entire chapter in one sitting.

EXPLORE NP8 LEARNING TOOLS

Make a Tracking Disk

1. Place the BookOnCD in your computer's CD or DVD drive, and then close the tray.

2. From the main menu, click **Open the electronic textbook**.

3. When you see the message, "Do you want to check for a Tracking Disk to load Annotation and Syllabus Links?" click the **Yes** button.

4. A box titled Tracking Disk Not Found appears. Click the **Create** button.

5. Fill in the information requested (shown at right).

6. Insert a floppy disk into the drive, silver part first.

7. Click the **OK** button. Your Tracking Disk is ready when you see the first page of the textbook.

Tracking Data

First name: [ ]

Last name: [ ]

User ID: [ ]

Section: [ ]

Insert a formatted disk in drive A, then click OK to create your Tracking File.

[OK] [Cancel]

In the User ID box, enter a unique identification, such as your student ID number.

Tracking Disk Location

Tracking data is currently being stored in:

A:\TRACKING.TK2

● 1. **Store data on drive a: (default)**
○ 2. **Store data on drive c:**
○ 3. Data is stored on drive w via manual .INI file entry
○ 4. **Store data in custom location**

1. Use the default a: floppy location to save your data on a floppy disk for easy transport between computers.
2. Use drive c: if you are the only person using your computer.
3. The drive w: option is intended for use by Computer Lab managers as documented in the Readme.doc file on the CD.
4. You can save your data in a custom location, such as a removable USB device. IMPORTANT: If someone changes the data location, you must remember where you stored your data so you can set it back to your custom location the next time you use this computer.

[Save and Exit] [Cancel]

If you'd rather store tracking data on your computer's hard disk or on a flash drive that plugs into the USB port, click **Tools**, and then click **Change Tracking Location**. Select a storage location from the list shown above.

Complete a QuickCheck

1. Use the **Go To Page** button to jump to page O-11. Click the ▼ scroll button in the lower-right corner of your screen several times until you can see the entire set of QuickCheck questions.

2. Click the answer box for question 1, and then type your answer. Remember that you can use the Backspace key if you make a typing error.

3. Press the **Enter** key to jump to question 2, and then type your answer.

4. When you have answered all the questions, click the **Check Answers** icon. The computer will indicate if your first answer is correct. Click **OK** to check the rest of your answers.

5. When you've reviewed all your answers, the computer presents a summary of your score and asks if you want to save your score on a Tracking Disk. Click **OK**. When you see the Responses Saved message, click **OK** again.

View the contents of your Tracking Disk

1. Click the **Tools** menu at the top of your screen.

2. Click **Tracking Disk**. Your computer displays a summary score for the QuickCheck you completed. The list of summary scores grows as you save additional QuickChecks, end-of-chapter Interactive Summaries, Interactive Situation Questions, and Lab QuickChecks.

3. Click **Exit** to return to the electronic textbook pages. You can then exit the BookOnCD and remove the CD from the drive.

QUICKCHECK......SECTION A

1. When turning on the components of a desktop computer system, the computer's system [ ] should be switched on last.

2. Instead of using the on/off switch to turn off your computer, you should use the [ ] button to initiate a shutdown.

3. Windows icons and controls are designed to be manipulated by a device called a(n) [ ].

4. Ctrl+X means to hold down the Ctrl key, then press +, then press X. True or false? [ ]

5. The [ ] key can be used to delete the last character you typed.

 CHECK ANSWERS

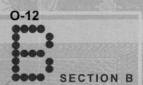

SECTION B

GETTING STARTED WITH SOFTWARE

Software helps you accomplish a variety of tasks, such as creating documents, generating graphs, maintaining to-do lists, and repairing old photographs. Section B begins with a quick overview of using word processing software called Microsoft Word. You might find this software handy for completing assignments and projects at the end of each chapter. This section also provides tips on using the menus and options included with your BookOnCD software.

HOW TO START SOFTWARE

How do I start a software program? You can use the Start button to launch just about any software that's installed on your computer. Clicking the Start menu displays a list of recently accessed software. Clicking the All Programs option displays a list of every software program installed on your computer. You can run a program from this list simply by clicking it. Follow the instructions in the TRY IT box to start Microsoft Word (assuming it is installed on your computer).

⌨ TRY IT

Start Microsoft Word

1. Make sure your computer is on and it is displaying the Windows desktop.

2. Click the **Start** button to display the Start menu.

3. Click **All Programs** to display a list of all software installed on your computer.

4. Click **Microsoft Word**.

5. Wait a few seconds for your computer to display the main screen for Microsoft Word, shown below. Leave Word open for use with the next TRY IT.

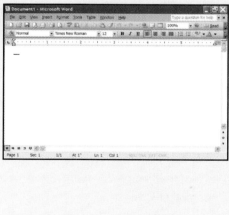

WINDOW CONTROLS

How do I tell the software what I want to do? Word processing, photo editing, and other software designed for use on computers running the Microsoft Windows operating system is referred to as "Windows software." Most Windows software works in a fairly uniform way and uses a similar set of controls.

Each software application appears in a rectangular area called a "window," which includes a title bar, a menu bar, and various controls shown in Figure 12.

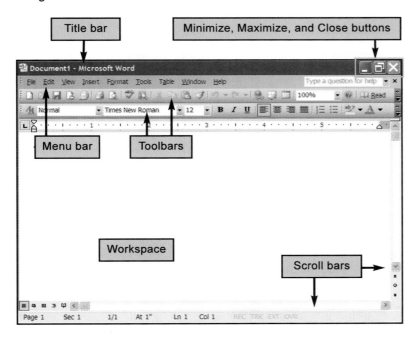

FIGURE 12

The **title bar** displays the title of the software, the name of the current data file, and the window sizing buttons.

The **Minimize button** shrinks the window to a button at the bottom of the screen.

The **Maximize button** stretches the window to fill the screen.

The **Close button** closes the window and exits the program.

The **menu bar** displays the titles of menus you can click to select commands.

The **toolbar** displays a series of tools for accomplishing various tasks.

The **scroll bar** can be clicked or dragged to see any material that does not fit in the displayed window.

The **workspace** is the area in which your document is displayed.

If you're unfamiliar with Windows controls, take a few minutes to complete the steps in the TRY IT box below.

⌨TRY IT

Use the menu bar

1. Click **Insert** on the menu bar.

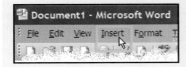

2. Click **Date and Time**.

3. Select the first option.

4. Click the **OK** button. The current date is inserted at the top of the workspace.

Use the toolbar

1. As shown below, click the **Spelling and Grammar** button on the Word toolbar.

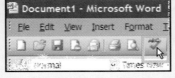

2. The computer checks the spelling in your document.

3. You didn't have any misspelled words, so click the **OK** button to end the spell check.

Use the sizing buttons

1. Click the 🔲 Minimize button.

2. The Microsoft Word window shrinks down to a button on the taskbar at the bottom of the screen.

3. Click the taskbar button to make the Word window appear again. Leave Word open for the next TRY IT.

CREATING DOCUMENTS

How do I create a document? To create a document, simply type the text in the workspace provided by the Microsoft Word window. The flashing vertical insertion point indicates your place in the document (Figure 13).

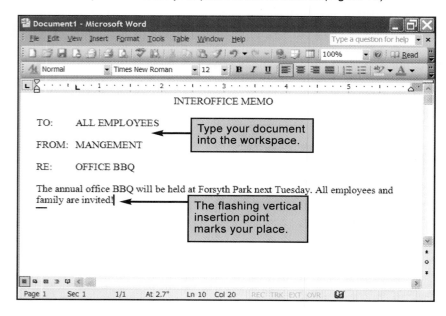

FIGURE 13

When typing text, you can use the following keys to move within the document and make revisions:

■ **Backspace**: Delete the character to the left of the insertion point.

■ **Delete:** Delete the character to the right of the insertion point.

■ **Enter:** End a paragraph and begin a new line.

■ **Arrow keys:** Move the insertion point up, down, right, or left.

How do I save a document? It is a good idea to save your work every few minutes, even if it is not finished. To save a document, use the Save option on the File menu, specify a storage location, and provide a name for the document, as shown in Figure 14.

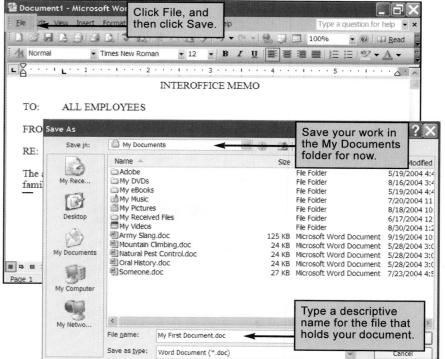

FIGURE 14

When you save a document, use the Save option on the File menu.

Your computer is probably configured to save documents in the My Documents folder on the hard disk. No need to change that until you gain more experience.

Make sure you enter a descriptive name for the document in the *File name* box. File names can be several words long; just do not use the * / \ " ' : symbols in the file name.

How do I print a document? To print a document, you simply click the File menu, and then select Print. Your computer displays a window containing a series of print options. If you want to print a single copy of your document, these settings should be correct, so you can click the OK button at the bottom of the window to send your document to the printer.

Can I send a document to my instructor? You can send a document via e-mail by using the Send To option on the File menu (Figure 15). To do so, you must know your instructor's e-mail address. You'll learn more about e-mail later in the Orientation, but keep this option in mind because it is a handy way to submit assignments, such as projects and term papers.

How do I find my documents again in the future? If you want to revise a document sometime in the future, simply start Microsoft Word, click File on the menu bar, and then click Open. Your computer should display a list of documents stored in the My Documents folder. Locate the one you want to revise and click it.

FIGURE 15

The File menu's Send To option produces a sub-menu of choices for sending mail.

Choose *Mail Recipient* to insert your document directly into the body of an e-mail message.

Choose *Mail Recipient (as Attachment)* to send the document as a file attached to the e-mail message.

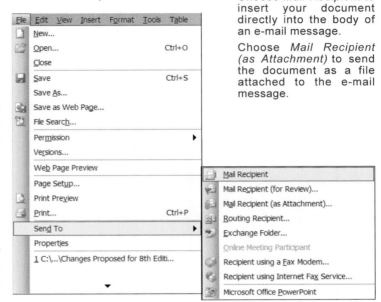

What should I do when I'm done? When you're ready to quit, you can close the document by clicking the Close option from the File menu. When you want to close Microsoft Word, you can click the ☒ Close button in the upper-right corner of the screen.

If you have not yet had an opportunity to use Microsoft Word to create, save, and print a document, complete the steps in the TRY IT box below.

⌨**TRY IT**

Create a document

1. Make sure that Microsoft Word is open.

2. Click the workspace to position the insertion point in the upper-left corner, just under the date.

3. Type a paragraph. Refer to Figure 13 for keys to use while typing and revising your work.

4. When the first paragraph is complete, press the **Enter** key to begin a new paragraph.

5. Type a second paragraph of text.

Save a document

1. Click **File** on the Word menu bar.

2. Click **Save**.

3. Make sure the *Save in* box lists My Documents. If not, click the ⏷ button and then click My Documents from the list.

4. In the File name box, type a name for your document.

5. Click the **Save** button.

6. When the Save As dialog box closes, your document is saved.

Print a document, close it, and exit Word

1. Click **File** on the Word menu bar, and then click **Print**.

2. Make sure the Print Range button is set to **All**.

3. Make sure Number of Copies is set to **1**.

4. Click the **OK** button and wait a few seconds for the printer to produce your document.

5. Close the document by clicking **File**, then clicking **Close**. The workspace should become blank.

6. Exit Microsoft Word by clicking the ☒ Close button. The Word window should close and your screen should display the Windows desktop.

BOOKONCD SOFTWARE FEATURES

How do I use the features of the BookOnCD software? The BookOnCD offers you a unique learning environment full of media presentations and interactive assessment opportunities (Figure 16). To make effective use of this learning tool, you can complete the steps below to become familiar with BookOnCD menus and toolbar options.

EXPLORE NP8 LEARNING TOOLS

Explore BookOnCD menus

1. Start the BookOnCD and use the main menu to open the electronic textbook. Click **No** when asked about downloading Tracking Data.

2. Click **File** on the menu bar. The only option on this menu is Exit, which closes the electronic textbook. Do not use this option yet.

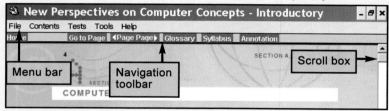

3. Click **Contents** on the menu bar. This menu lists the major sections of the textbook—preface, chapters, QuickCheck answers, Glossary, and Index. This option is most handy when you want to jump to a specific chapter.

4. Click **Tests** on the menu bar. Click **Chapter 1**. If you have a Tracking Disk, put it in; otherwise, click the **Continue** button. Your computer displays the first of 10 questions selected at random from a 150-question test bank. As you've not read Chapter 1 yet, click **Exit**.

5. Click **Tools** on the menu bar, which contains these options:

- Sound Settings: Turn off the volume when you are in a computer lab and have no earphones.

- Select Browser: Allows you to select Internet Explorer if you have multiple browsers installed on your computer.

- Tracking Disk: Displays scores stored on your Tracking Disk.

- Change Tracking Location: Stores your scores on the hard disk instead of a floppy disk.

Navigate the BookOnCD

1. Position the pointer over the scroll box on the right side of the BookOnCD page. (See diagram above.) Hold the mouse button down while dragging the mouse toward you. The BookOnCD page should scroll down. You can also click the ▼ or ▲ buttons several times to scroll the page.

2. Click the **Go to Page** button. Type **45**, and then click the **OK** button. Your computer displays page 45 of the textbook.

3. Click the **<Page** button. Your computer backs up and displays page 44.

4. Click the **Page>** button. Your computer displays page 45.

5. Click the **Glossary** button. Suppose you want to know the definition of MP3. Type **MP3** in the box and press the **Enter** key to see the definition, as shown to the right. Click the **Close** button to close the Glossary window.

6. The Syllabus and Annotation buttons appear only if your instructor has posted material for your class. You'll learn more about these features in Section D.

FIGURE 16
BookOnCD Resources

Entire Textbook

Carrying a notebook computer? Take the BookOnCD along. It's lighter than the printed book and contains every page.

Animated Figures

Specially marked figures come to life as animations, videos, and guided software tours.

Interactive Key Terms, Summaries, and Situation Questions

Help you assess your grasp of chapter material and study for tests.

Practice Tests

Take computer-graded tests with questions similar to those you'll find on in-class exams.

WebTrack

Keep a record of your scores and submit them electronically to your instructor.

New Perspectives Labs

Hands-on activities that help you explore chapter topics and apply what you've learned.

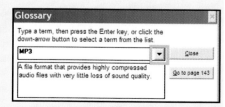

If you are unsure about the spelling of a term, click the ▼ button to see a list of terms.

HELP

How can I get help using software? If you've had problems using software, you're not alone! Everyone has questions at one time or another. Most software offers several sources of help, such as the following:

- **Message boxes.** When using software, it is important to pay attention to any message boxes displayed on the screen. Make sure you carefully read the options they present. If the box doesn't seem to apply to what you want to do, click its Cancel button to close it. Otherwise, set the options the way you want them, and then click the OK button to continue.

- **User manual.** Whether you're a beginner or a power user, the manual that comes with software can be an excellent resource. User manuals can contain quick-start guides, tutorials, detailed descriptions of menu options, and tips for using features effectively.

- **Help menu.** The Help menu provides access to on-screen documentation. Most Windows software offers a standard method for searching through its Help files. Documentation can be accessed through a table of contents, by consulting the index, or by searching for particular words or phrases (Figure 17 top).

- **Office Assistant.** Some software includes animated "assistants" that prompt you to type in simple questions (Figure 17 bottom). After you've entered a question, the assistant might ask you additional questions to refine your search, or it might display a list of documents that answer your question.

FIGURE 17

Clicking Help on the software menu bar usually produces a window, such as this one, where you can use the Contents, Index, or Find tabs to search the Help file for information.

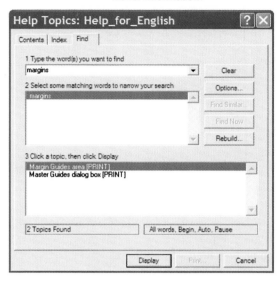

QUICKCHECK......SECTION B

1. The [   ] button on the Windows desktop can be used to launch just about any software installed on your computer.

2. It is a good idea to [   ] your work every few minutes, even if you are not finished with it.

3. When you have completed work on a document, you can close it by using an option on the [   ] menu.

4. If you've forgotten the definition of a key term in your textbook, you can use the [   ] button on the BookOnCD.

5. The [   ] menu provides access to on-screen documentation detailing the software's features and functions.

 CHECK ANSWERS

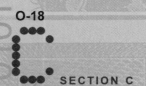

SECTION C

GETTING STARTED ON THE INTERNET

The Internet provides access to a vast collection of resources and information. As a student, you'll find it handy for research pertaining to many of your classes. You can also access information and activities designed to enhance the introductory computer material in this textbook. Section C shows you how to access these useful resources.

INTERNET AND WEB BASICS

What is the Internet? The Internet is the largest computer network in the world (Figure 18), carrying information from one continent to another in the blink of an eye. The computers connected to this network offer many types of resources, such as e-mail, instant messaging, popular music downloads, and online shopping.

What is the Web? Although some people use the terms "Internet" and "Web" interchangeably, the two are not the same. The Internet refers to a communications network that connects computers in every country in the world. The Web—short for World Wide Web—is just one of the many resources available over this communications network.

The World Wide Web is a collection of linked and cross-referenced information available for public access. This information is accessible from Web sites located on various computers. The information is displayed as a series of screens called Web pages. You'll use the Web for general research and for specific activities designed to accompany this textbook. To use the Web, your computer must have access to the Internet.

How do I access the Internet? Most computers can be configured to connect to the Internet by using telephone or cable television systems. Internet access can be obtained from school computer labs, local service providers, such as your cable television company, and national Internet service providers, such as AOL (America Online), AT&T, and MSN (Microsoft Network).

To expedite your orientation, it is assumed that your computer has Internet access. If it does not, refer to Chapters 5 and 6, consult your instructor, or ask an experienced computer user to help you get set up.

How do I know if my computer has Internet access? The easiest way to find out if your computer can access the Internet is to try it. You can quickly find out if you have Internet access by starting software called a browser that's designed to display Web pages.

Browser software called Internet Explorer is supplied with Microsoft Windows. Other browsers, such as Netscape, Mozilla, FireFox, and Opera, are also available. The NP8 Web site is optimized for Internet Explorer, so you should use it, if possible. Follow the steps in the TRY IT box to start Internet Explorer.

HOW TO USE A WEB BROWSER AND SEARCH ENGINE

How do I use a browser? A browser lets you type in a unique Web page address called a URL and jump from that page to other Web pages by

FIGURE 18
The Internet communications network stretches around the globe.

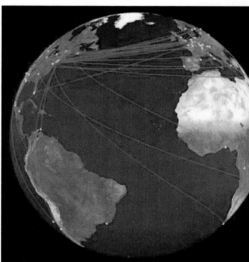

TRY IT

Start your browser

1. Click the ▢ icon located near the Start button.

2. Your computer should soon display a window containing "Microsoft Internet Explorer" in the title bar. (Refer to the next page.)

If your computer displays a *Connect to* box, click the **Dial** button to establish a dial-up connection via your telephone.

You'll need to cancel the browser command and consult an experienced computer user if:

■ Your computer displays a "working off line" message.

■ Your computer displays an Internet Connection Wizard box.

using links. Links are usually underlined, and when you position the arrow-shaped mouse pointer over a link, it changes to a hand shape.

You'll learn much more about browsers in Chapter 1. Until you read that material, you can get along quite well using the basic controls shown in Figure 19.

FIGURE 19
Using a Browser

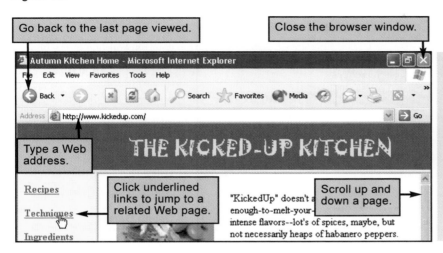

A full Web address might look like this:

http://www.kickedup.com

It is not necessary to type the http://, so to access the Kicked-Up Kitchen page shown here, you would type:

www.kickedup.com

When typing a Web address, do not use any spaces and copy upper- and lowercase letters exactly.

How do I find specific information on the Web? If you're looking for information and don't know the Web site where it might be located, you can use a search engine to find it. Follow the steps in the TRY IT box to "go "Googling" by using the Google search engine.

TRY IT

Access a search engine

1. Make sure the Internet Explorer browser window is open.

2. Click the Address box and type:

3. Press the **Enter** key. Your browser displays the Web page for the Google search engine.

Use a search engine

1. Click the blank search box and then type **national parks**.

2. Press the **Enter** key. Google displays a list of Web pages that relate to national parks.

3. Click the underlined **National Park Service** link. Your browser displays the ParkNet home page.

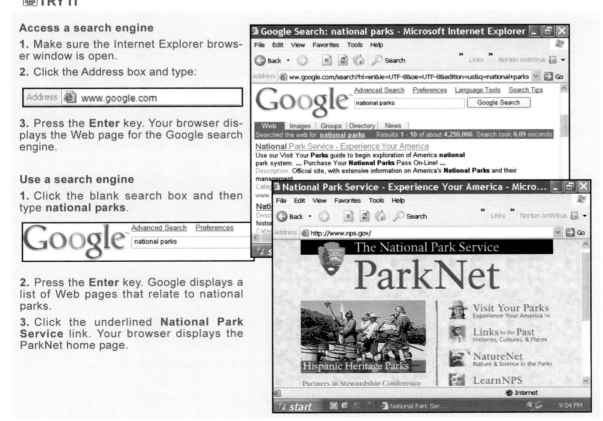

ACCESSING THE NEW PERSPECTIVES NP8 WEB SITE

FIGURE 20
NP8 Web Site Resources

What kinds of Web resources accompany my textbook? The New Perspectives NP8 Web site—NP8 Web site, for short—includes all sorts of activities and information to help you learn about computers. Figure 20 lists the resources you'll find at the site.

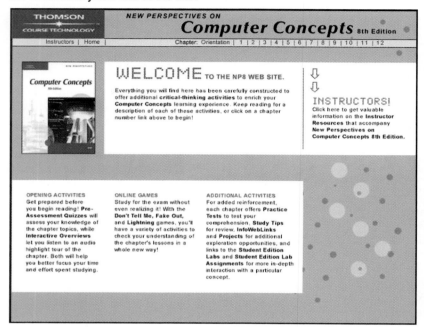

How do I access the NP8 Web site? You can get to the Web site in several ways:

- Open your browser and type *www.course.com/np/concepts8*. Your browser will display the main page of the NP8 Web site. From there, you can click links to various activities and information.

- Open your BookOnCD and click any ⚓ link. These links take you directly to the information or activity specified along with the link.

Follow the steps in the box below to access the NP8 Web site.

EXPLORE NP8 LEARNING TOOLS

Access the NP8 Web Site

1. Make sure the Internet Explorer browser window is open.

2. Click the address box and type:

Address www.course.com/np/concepts8

Make sure to use all lowercase letters, insert no spaces, and use the / slash, not the \ slash.

3. Press the **Enter** key. Your browser displays the Computer Concepts main page.

4. Read the Welcome message and scroll, if necessary, to get a look at the entire page.

5. Click **Chapter 1** at the top of the screen. Your browser displays links to activities for the first chapter in your textbook.

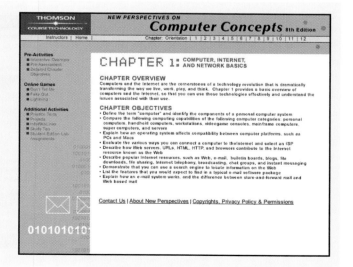

Interactive Overview (audio)

Listen to a 5-minute audio presentation of chapter highlights.

Pre-assessment

Take a short quiz to assess your background in the chapter material.

InfoWebLinks

Follow Web links to find the most current information on equipment and software you read about in a chapter.

Study Tips

When test time rolls around, try these tips for a complete review of chapter material.

Online Games

Have some fun while refreshing your memory about key concepts that might appear on the next exam.

Student Edition Labs

Get hands-on practice with some of the concepts presented in a chapter.

Projects

Find lots of topics for term papers and extra-credit projects here.

TechTV Video Project

Watch a video clip from a recent TechTV show and explore new tech trends.

How do I use the Interactive Overview and other resources? Follow
the steps in the box below to explore the NP8 Web site.

⌨EXPLORE NP8 LEARNING TOOLS

Explore the NP8 Web site

1. Make sure your browser is displaying the activities page for
Chapter 1 (*www.course.com/np/concepts8/ch01.htm*).

2. Click the **Interactive Overview** link. Listen to the chapter
overview for a few seconds, and then use the on-screen buttons
to return to the Chapter 1 page.

3. Click the **Pre-assessment** link. You might want to complete
the quiz to see how much of the material in Chapter 1 you already
know. Use the on-screen buttons when you are ready to return to
the Chapter 1 page and continue your exploration.

4. Click the **InfoWeb** link. When you see a list of InfoWebLinks
for Chapter 1, click the **Netiquette** link. Read the short overview,
and then click the first blue underlined link. Use the **Back** button
to get back to the Chapter 1 main page.

5. Click the **Study Tips** link and read through a few to get an idea
of the activities recommended to help you study for a test on the
material in Chapter 1. When you are ready, return to the main
Chapter 1 Web page.

6. Click the link to the **Lightning** game. Try your hand at a few
questions, and then go back to the main Chapter 1 Web page.

7. Click the **Student Edition Lab** link. Try this interactive lab to
get an idea of how it works. After exploring this activity, return to
the main Chapter 1 Web page.

8. Click the **TechTV Video Project** link. Take a few minutes to
watch the video, then return to the main page for Chapter 1.

9. Use your browser's ⊠ Close button to exit the NP8 Web site
when your exploration is complete. If you are using a dial-up connection, you might have to manually disconnect from the Internet
by double-clicking the 🖧 icon in the lower-right corner of your
screen, and then clicking **Disconnect**.

InfoWebLinks provide lots of information to supplement what you've read in
the textbook.

Online games, such as LIghtning, Don't
Tell Me, and Fake Out provide a fun
way to review chapter material.

Student Edition labs give you an in-
depth, hands-on look into one or more
chapter topics.

QUICKCHECK......SECTION C

1. The [_____] is a communications network that connects
   computers all over the world.

2. The World Wide [_____] is one of the many resources
   available on the Internet communications network.

3. Software called a(n) [_____] helps you access Web
   pages.

4. If you don't know where to find information, you can use a(n)
   [_____] engine to produce a list of links to Web pages
   that might contain the information you seek.

◈ CHECK ANSWERS

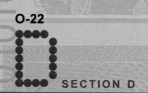

SECTION D

COMMUNICATING WITH YOUR INSTRUCTOR

Staying in contact with your instructor is important whether you attend classes on campus or online. Section D provides a quick overview of e-mail. It introduces you to your textbook's lab, annotation, WebTrack, and syllabus features. Plus, it shows you how to send your Tracking Disk scores to your instructor.

WORKING WITH E-MAIL

What is e-mail? E-mail is a form of communication that relies on computer networks, such as the Internet, to transmit messages from one computer to another. Like regular mail, e-mail messages are sent to a mailbox where they are kept until the recipient retrieves the message. Messages might arrive at their destination within minutes, or might not arrive for a few hours. Once sent, e-mail messages cannot be retrieved.

What do I need to use e-mail? To send and receive e-mail, you need an Internet connection, an e-mail account, and software that enables you to compose, read, and delete e-mail messages. An e-mail account consists of an e-mail address (Figure 21), a password, and a mailbox. You can usually obtain an e-mail account from your Internet service provider, your school, or a Web-based e-mail provider, such as Hotmail, Yahoo! Mail, or GMail.

How do I create and send an e-mail message? Many e-mail systems are available, and each uses slightly different software, making it impossible to cover all options in this short orientation. You might want to enlist the aid of an experienced computer user to help you get started. Chapter 1 provides more detail about e-mail, too. The steps in the TRY IT box are designed for students who use e-mail software called Outlook Express, which is supplied with Microsoft Windows.

FIGURE 21
E-mail Addresses

An e-mail address consists of a user ID followed by an @ symbol and the name of a computer that handles e-mail accounts. Ask your instructor for his or her e-mail address. It is likely similar to the following:

instructor@school.edu

When typing an e-mail address, use all lowercase letters and do not use any spaces.

TRY IT

Create and send e-mail

1. Click the icon located at the bottom of your screen. The Outlook Express window opens.

2. Click the **Create** button to display a form like the one at right.

3. Follow steps 4-6 as shown at right.

4. When your message is complete, click the **Send** button. With most computers, this button places the e-mail in your Outbox.

5. Click the **Send/Recv** button on the toolbar to ship the message from your Outbox over the network to your instructor.

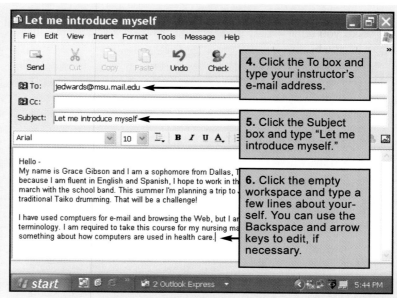

4. Click the To box and type your instructor's e-mail address.

5. Click the Subject box and type "Let me introduce myself."

6. Click the empty workspace and type a few lines about yourself. You can use the Backspace and arrow keys to edit, if necessary.

How do I get my mail? As with sending mail, the way you get mail depends on your mail system. In general, clicking the Send/Recv button collects your mail from the network and stores it in your Inbox. Your mail software displays a list of your messages. The new ones are usually shown in bold type. You can click any message to open it, read it, and reply to it, as shown in Figure 22.

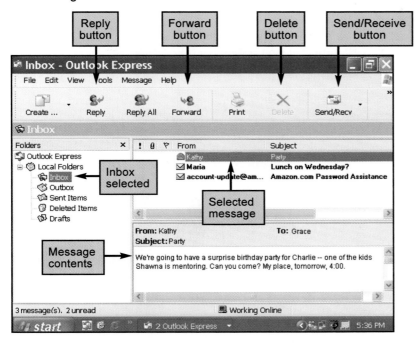

FIGURE 22

Most e-mail software displays a list of your messages. You can:

■ Open a message and read it.

■ Reply to a message.

■ Delete unwanted messages (a good idea to minimize the size of your mailbox).

■ Forward a message to someone else.

HOW TO TRANSFER TRACKING DISK DATA

What has my Tracking Disk got to do with communication? A feature of your textbook's technology called WebTrack allows your instructor to send you an updated syllabus and notes, called annotations, that supplement the pages in your textbook. It also enables you to transfer scores to your instructor. You can transfer QuickCheck, Practice Tests, Interactive Summary, Interactive Situation Questions, and Lab scores, as well as your opinions on the Issue questions.

Whenever you submit scores, your Tracking Disk collects any material posted for you by your instructor. For example, if your instructor has posted some annotations for Chapter 1, you'll automatically receive links to them when you send in your first QuickCheck score. The next time you use the BookOnCD with your Tracking Disk in the drive, the Annotation button will appear on the pages specified by your instructor, as shown in Figure 23. When you click the Annotation button, your computer accesses your instructor's annotation Web pages.

FIGURE 23

If your instructor has created annotations, the Annotation button will appear on your BookOnCD pages.

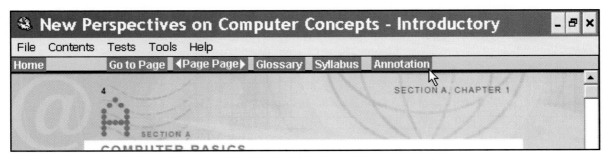

How do I submit Tracking Disk scores? Suppose you want to work on a BookOnCD lab, take the lab QuickChecks, and submit your score to your instructor. Follow the instructions below to find out how. Before you begin, make sure your instructor has posted some annotations for Chapter 1 and you have the following:

- An Internet connection
- Your instructor's e-mail address
- Tracking data stored on a Tracking Disk or drive C (you made a Tracking Disk or specified drive C as your tracking location in Section A)

EXPLORE NP8 LEARNING TOOLS

Open a BookOnCD lab

1. Make sure your Tracking Disk is in the drive (or you specified drive C for your tracking location) and start the BookOnCD.

2. When you see the main menu, click **Open a New Perspectives Lab** (shown at right).

3. Click the lab title **Operating a Personal Computer**.

4. Click the ▶ Continue button to view the objectives for Topic 1.

5. Click the ▶ button again to view page 1 of the lab. Read the information on the page, and then continue through the lab, making sure to follow any numbered instructions such as those shown at right.

6. After page 8, you will encounter the first QuickCheck question. Click the correct answer, and then click the Continue button. Complete all the QuickCheck Questions for Topic 1.

7. Complete the entire lab and answer all the QuickCheck questions.

8. When you complete the lab, follow the instructions to exit. Your QuickCheck Tracking Report is displayed and saved. For future reference, notice that you can print the report by using the Print button. After reviewing the report, click **Exit**.

9. From the NP Labs screen, click **Exit** to return to the main BookOnCD menu. Leave the main menu open in preparation for the next TRY IT.

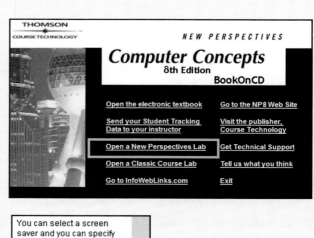

THOMSON
COURSE TECHNOLOGY

NEW PERSPECTIVES

Computer Concepts
8th Edition
BookOnCD

Open the electronic textbook | Go to the NP8 Web Site

Send your Student Tracking Data to your instructor | Visit the publisher, Course Technology

Open a New Perspectives Lab | Get Technical Support

Open a Classic Course Lab | Tell us what you think

Go to InfoWebLinks.com | Exit

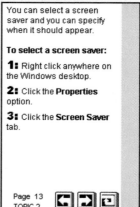

You can select a screen saver and you can specify when it should appear.

To select a screen saver:

1: Right click anywhere on the Windows desktop.

2: Click the **Properties** option.

3: Click the **Screen Saver** tab.

Page 13
TOPIC 2

In addition to Lab QuickChecks, each BookOnCD lab also includes a set of assignments located at the end of corresponding sections of your textbook. Your instructor might require you to complete these written online assignments. You can submit them on paper, on disk, or as an e-mail message, according to your instructor's directions.

Now you've completed a lab and your score has been automatically saved on your Tracking Disk. The steps on the next page guide you through the process of sending your tracking data to your instructor.

EXPLORE NP8 LEARNING TOOLS

Send your tracking data

1. Make sure your Tracking Disk is in the drive (or you specified drive C for your tracking location) and the BookOnCD main menu is displayed on your computer's screen.

2. Click the option **Send your Student Tracking Data to your instructor** (shown at right). Your computer makes an Internet connection, opens your browser, and displays the WebTrack site.

3. Click the underlined link **Click here to send your Tracking files to your instructor now**.

4. If this is the first time you have sent data, you might see a Security Warning window. Click **Yes** to download the MediaTechnics component that sends your tracking data. This operation takes a few seconds.

5. When you see the WebTrack Student Module window (shown at right), enter your instructor's e-mail address, and then click the **Submit TK2 Data** button.

6. On the next screen, confirm that your student ID is correct and then click the **Send Data** button.

7. Follow the instructions displayed on the screen to return to the main BookOnCD menu.

Check for annotations

1. If your instructor has posted annotations for Chapter 1, the Annotation button should now appear when you read the BookOnCD. Click to open the electronic textbook, and page through Chapter 1 to find your instructor's annotations.

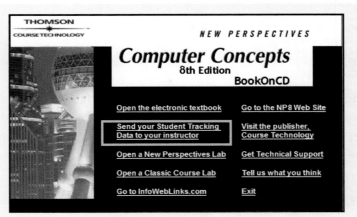

THOMSON
COURSE TECHNOLOGY

NEW PERSPECTIVES

Computer Concepts
8th Edition
BookOnCD

Open the electronic textbook	Go to the NP8 Web Site
Send your Student Tracking Data to your instructor	Visit the publisher, Course Technology
Open a New Perspectives Lab	Get Technical Support
Open a Classic Course Lab	Tell us what you think
Go to InfoWebLinks.com	Exit

WebTrack

Powered by MediaTechnics Corporation's BookOnWeb Technology

WebTrack Student Module

Use this page to send in data from Tracking Disks created with any BookOnWeb or BookOnCD product. It's as easy as 1, 2, 3!

1. Place your Tracking Disk in drive

2. Enter your instructor's e-mail   vglass@school.edu

3. Click the Submit button.   Submit .TK2 Data
                                From Concepts
                                Cancel

QUICKCHECK......SECTION D

1. The special symbol used in e-mail addresses is [＿＿＿＿＿＿].

2. An e-mail account consists of an e-mail address, a password, and a(n) [＿＿＿＿＿＿].

3. In general, clicking the Send/Receive button collects your mail from the network and stores it in your [＿＿＿＿＿＿].

4. It is a good idea to [＿＿＿＿＿＿] unwanted mail to minimize the size of your mailbox.

 CHECK ANSWERS

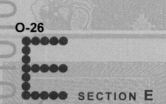

SECTION E

SECURITY AND PRIVACY

Today's digital landscape is dotted with a few obstacles that can trip up unwary computer users. As with most other facets of modern life, computing has its share of troublemakers, scam artists, and identity thieves. Section E offers some tips on navigating through the sometimes rough neighborhoods of cyberspace, while keeping your data safe and your identity private.

SECURING YOUR COMPUTER AND DATA

What's at risk if my computer is stolen? A computer can be an attractive target for thieves, but the value of a stolen computer is not so much in the hardware as in the data it contains. With stolen data such as your bank account numbers and PINs, a thief can wipe out your checking and savings accounts. With your credit card numbers, a thief can go on a spending spree. Even worse, a criminal can use stolen data to assume your identity, run up debts, get into legal trouble, ruin your credit rating, and cause you no end of trouble.

How can I protect my computer data from theft? When you carry a notebook computer, never leave it unattended. To thwart a thief who breaks into your home or dorm room, anchor your computer to your desk with a specially designed lock you can buy at most electronics stores.

If a thief steals your computer, you can make it difficult to access your data by setting up a password. Until the password is entered, your data is off limits. A thief might be able to boot up the Windows desktop, but should not be able to easily look at the data in your folders.

Many new computers are shipped with a standard administrator password that everyone knows. Create a secure password (Figure 24) for this account as soon as you can. If you are the only person using your computer, you can use the administrator account for your day-to-day computing.

Your computer might also include a preset guest account with an unsecure password such as "guest." You should disable this guest account or assign it a secure password.

FIGURE 24

To create a secure password:

■ Use at least five characters, mixing numbers with letters, as in 2by4s.

■ Do not use your name, the name of a family member, or pet's name.

■ Do not use a word that can be found in the dictionary.

■ Do not forget your password!

⌨ TRY IT

Check the accounts on your computer

1. Click the **Start** button, then select **Control Panel**.

2. Select **User Accounts**. The User Accounts window shown at right displays a list of accounts.

3. If you are working on a school lab computer, close the User Accounts window without making any changes. If you are using your own computer, click the Administrator account and make sure it has a secure password.

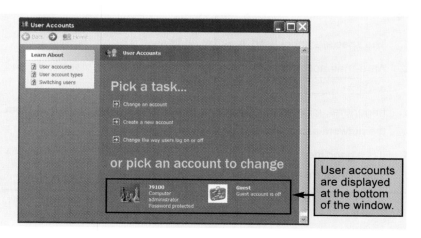

User accounts are displayed at the bottom of the window.

AVOIDING VIRUSES

What's so bad about computer viruses? The term "virus" has a technical meaning that you'll learn in Chapter 4, but many people use the term loosely when referring to malicious programs that circulate on disks, in e-mail attachments, and on the Internet. This malware, as it is sometimes called, can steal your data, destroy files, or create network traffic jams. It might display an irritating message to announce its presence, or it might work quietly behind the scenes to spread itself to various files on your computer or mail itself out to everyone in your e-mail address book.

After a virus takes up residence in your computer, it is often difficult to disinfect all your files and make sure it is eliminated. Rather than wait for a virus attack, you should take steps to keep your computer virus free.

How can I keep viruses out of my computer? Back when viruses were less sophisticated, computer users were commonly warned not to download pirated software or open e-mail attachments from unknown senders. These two common sources of viruses still exist, but virus creators have found ways to make pirated software look legitimate and to affix your friends' names to e-mails that carry infected attachments.

Although it is a good idea to avoid pirated software and stay alert when opening e-mail attachments, the best defense against viruses is to install antivirus software and configure it to run continuously whenever your computer is on. At least once a week your antivirus software should also run a full system check to make sure every file on your computer is virus free.

You should make sure your antivirus software is set up to scan for viruses in incoming files and e-mail messages. As new viruses emerge, your antivirus software needs to update its virus definition file. It gets this update as a Web download. If you've selected the auto update option, your computer should automatically receive updates as they become available.

FIGURE 25
Popular Antivirus Software

Norton AntiVirus
McAfee VirusScan
Kaspersky Anti-Virus
F-Prot
Softwin BitDefender
Panda Antivirus
Trend Micro PC-cillin

TRY IT

Get familiar with your antivirus software

1. Click the **Start** button, and then select **All Programs**. Look for antivirus software (refer to Figure 25 for a list). Open your antivirus software by clicking it.

Can't find any? If you are using your own computer and it doesn't seem to have antivirus software, you can connect to an antivirus Web site and download it.

2. Each antivirus program has unique features. The figure on the right shows the main screen for Norton AntiVirus software. Explore your antivirus software to make sure it is configured to do the following:

- Scan incoming e-mail
- Run continuously in the background—a feature sometimes called Auto Protect
- Block malicious scripts

3. Check the date of your last full system scan. If it was more than one week ago, you should check the settings that schedule antivirus scans.

4. Check the date when your computer last received virus definitions. If it was more than two weeks ago, you should make sure your antivirus software is configured to receive automatic live updates.

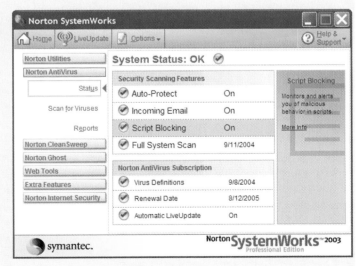

PREVENTING INTRUSIONS

Is it risky to go online? The Internet offers lots of cool stuff—music downloads, movie reviews and trailers, online shopping and banking, consumer information, chat groups, news, sports, weather, and much more. Most Internet offerings are legitimate, but some downloads contain viruses, and shady characters called "hackers" control programs that lurk about waiting to snatch your personal data or infiltrate your computer. The longer your computer remains connected to the Internet, the more vulnerable it is to a hacker's infiltration attempts.

If a hacker gains access to your computer, he or she can look through your files, use your computer as a launching platform for viruses and network-jamming attacks, or turn your computer into a server for pornography and other unsavory material. Hackers have even found ways to turn thousands of infiltrated computers into "zombies," link them together, and carry out coordinated attacks to disrupt online access to Microsoft, Bank of America, and other Internet businesses.

How do hackers gain access to my computer? Intruders gain access by exploiting security flaws in your computer's operating system, browser, and e-mail software. Software publishers are constantly creating patches to fix these flaws. As part of your overall security plan, you should download and install security patches as they become available.

How can I block hackers from infiltrating my computer? Firewall software (Figure 26) provides a protective barrier between a computer and the Internet. If your computer is directly connected to the Internet, it should have active firewall software. If your computer connects to a local area network for Internet access, the network should have a device called a router to block infiltration attempts.

When a firewall is active, it watches for potentially disruptive incoming data called "probes." When a probe is discovered, your firewall displays a warning and asks what to do. If the source looks legitimate, you can let it through; if not, you should block it (Figure 27).

Where do I get a firewall? Windows XP includes a built-in firewall called Windows Internet Connection Firewall (ICF) or Windows Firewall. If your computer uses an earlier version of Windows, you can download a third-party firewall.

FIGURE 26
Popular Firewall Software

Tiny Personal Firewall

McAfee Firewall Plus

Zone Alarm Pro

Sygate Firewall Pro

Norton Firewall

Black Ice Defender

Mac OS Firewall

Outpost Firewall

FIGURE 27
When your firewall software encounters new or unusual activity, it asks you what to do.

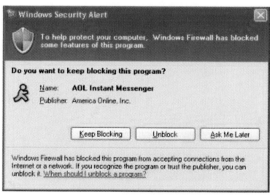

TRY IT

Check your computer's firewall

Finding out if your computer has an active firewall requires a little detective work. Try one or more of these three methods. If your computer doesn't seem to have a firewall, you might want to download one and install it.

For non-XP users:

Click the **Start** button, click **All Programs,** and then look through the program list for firewalls such as those in Figure 26. If you find a firewall listed, start it and explore to see if it has been activated.

For Windows XP Service Pack 2 users:

Click the **Start** button, then click **Control Panel**. Double-click the **Security Center** icon and then make sure the Firewall is on.

For Windows XP users:

Click the **Start** button, then click **Control Panel**. Click **Network Connections.** Click the connection you use for Internet access. Under Network Tasks, click **Change Settings for this connection**. Click the **Advanced** tab and look for a check mark in front of *Protect my computer and network by limiting or preventing access to this computer from the Internet.*

BLOCKING SPYWARE AND POP-UP ADS

Are some Web sites dangerous? When you access Web sites, data is transferred to your computer and displayed by your browser. Most of this data is harmless, but malicious HTML scripts, rogue ActiveX components, and spyware have the potential to search your computer for passwords and credit card numbers, install viruses, block your access to legitimate Web sites, or surreptitiously use your computer as a staging area for illicit activities.

Spyware is the most insidious threat. It often piggybacks on pop-up ads and activates if you click the ad window. Some spyware can begin its dirty work when you try to click the Close button to get rid of an ad.

How can I block spyware? The first line of defense is to never click pop-up ads—especially those that carry dire warnings about your computer being infected by a virus or spyware! (See Figure 28.) To close an ad, right-click its button on the taskbar at the bottom of your screen, and then select the Close option from the menu that appears. Some browsers can be configured to block spyware and pop-up ads. Your antivirus software might offer similar options. You can also install software specially designed to block spyware and pop-up ads. Figure 29 lists some popular titles.

What other steps can I take to browse the Web safely? Most browsers include security features. You should take some time to become familiar with them. For example, Internet Explorer allows you to specify how you want it to deal with ActiveX components. You can also specify how to deal with HTML scripts, cookies, security certificates, and other Web-based data. If you don't want to be bothered by these details, however, Internet Explorer offers several predefined configurations for Low, Medium, and High security. Most Internet Explorer users set security and privacy options to Medium.

FIGURE 28
Some pop-up ads contain fake warnings about viruses, spyware, and intrusion attempts.

FIGURE 29
Popular Antispyware and Ad-Blocking Software

Webroot SpySweeper

Ad-Aware

Spybot S&D

SpyHunter

SpyRemover

Pest Patrol

Spykiller

Pop-up Defender

TRY IT

Explore Internet Explorer security and privacy options

1. Start Internet Explorer. Click **Tools** on the menu bar, then select **Internet Options**.

2. Click the **Security** tab. Typically, your security setting should be Medium.

3. Click the **Privacy** tab. Typically, your privacy setting should be Medium.

4. Check the bottom of the window for a Pop-up Blocker option. If your version of Internet Explorer offers this feature, make sure its box contains a check mark so that it is activated.

5. If your version of Internet Explorer does not offer a pop-up blocker, check your antivirus software to see if it can provide protection. Otherwise, you can use the Start button to see if the software listed in Figure 29 has been installed. If your computer seems to have no antispyware or ad-blocking software, you might want to download some and install it.

PROTECTING E-COMMERCE TRANSACTIONS

Is online shopping safe? Online shopping is generally safe. From time to time, shoppers encounter fake storefronts designed to look like legitimate merchants, but that are actually set up to steal credit card information. You can avoid these fakes by making sure you enter correctly spelled URLs when connecting to your favorite shopping sites.

How safe is my credit card information when I shop online? Online shopping is no more dangerous than using your credit card for a telephone order or giving it to a server when you've finished eating in a restaurant. Anyone who handles your card can copy the card number, jot down the expiration date, and try to make unauthorized charges.

That's not to say that credit cards are risk free. Credit cards are surprisingly vulnerable both online and off. Thieves can break into merchant computers that store order information. Thieves might even pick up your credit card information from discarded order forms. Despite these risks, we continue to use credit cards.

Many people are concerned about their credit card data getting intercepted as it travels over the Internet. When you wrap up an online purchase and submit your credit card information, it is transmitted from your computer to the merchant's computer. Software called a packet sniffer, designed for legitimately monitoring network traffic, is occasionally used by unscrupulous hackers to intercept credit card numbers and other data traveling over the Internet.

How can I keep my credit card number confidential? When you submit credit card information, make sure the merchant provides a secure connection for transporting data. Typically, a secure connection is activated when you're in the final phases of checking out—as you enter your shipping and credit card information into a form and click a Submit button to send it. A secure connection encrypts your data. Even if your credit card number is intercepted, it cannot be deciphered and used. To make sure you have a secure connection, look for the lock icon in the lower-right corner of your screen. The Address box should also display a URL that begins with shttp:// or https:// (Secure HTTP), or contains ssl (Secure Sockets Layer).

🖮 TRY IT

Know how to identify a secure connection

1. Start your browser and connect to the site: **www.walmart.com**.

2. Select any item and use the **Add to Cart** option to place it in your online shopping cart.

3. Click the **Proceed to Checkout** button.

4. At the checkout screen, do you see any evidence that you're using a secure connection?

5. Close your browser so that you don't complete the transaction.

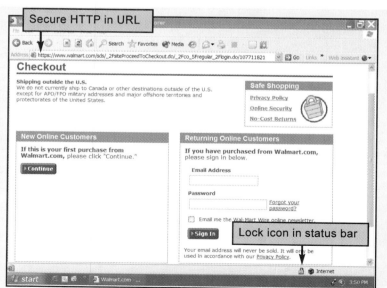

AVOIDING E-MAIL SCAMS

What are e-mail scams? From time to time, you hear about con artists who have bilked innocent consumers out of their life savings. The Internet has its share of con artists, too, who run e-mail scams designed to collect money and confidential information from unsuspecting "marks." E-mail scams are usually distributed in mass mailings called spam.

What do I need to know about spam? The Internet makes it easy and cheap to send out millions of e-mail solicitations. In the United States, the CAN-Spam law requires mass-mail messages to be labeled [SPAM] in the subject line. Recipients are supposed to be provided with a way to opt out of receiving future messages. Legitimate merchants and organizations comply with the law when sending product announcements, newsletters, and other messages. Unscrupulous spammers ignore the law and try to disguise their solicitations as messages from your friends, chat room participants, or co-workers (Figure 30).

		From	Subject
		FlyKelAir.com	[SPAM] Charter Specials
		Datamation IT Management Update	[SPAM] Conference Focuses on IT Service Management
		WDVL	[SPAM] Connect with Your Web Site Visitors Via TheGuestbook.com
		InfoWorld	[SPAM] Reminder! Take the InfoWorld Survey and Enter to Win a $...
		Datamation IT Management Update	[SPAM] Not Just Another Audit
		Sonja Crowder	Receive your Viagr&a order in 24 to 48 hours
		Dwayne Thurman	It's new and succsefull

FIGURE 30
Some spam is clearly labeled, whereas others are not.

Is spam dangerous? Many spam messages contain legitimate information, including daily or weekly newsletters to which you've subscribed. Some spam messages, however, advertise illegal products. Others are outright scams to get you to download a virus, divulge your bank account numbers, or send in money for products you'll never receive.

Beware of spam containing offers that seem just too good to be true. For example, you might receive a message from an African businessman who is seeking your help to transfer a large sum of money from his country to yours (Figure 31). These messages are frauds.

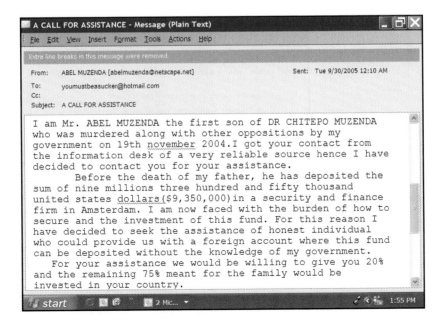

FIGURE 31
Many variations of this African money-transfer fraud—complete with deliberate grammatical errors—have circulated on the Internet for years. Victims who responded to these preposterous e-mails have found their bank accounts raided, their credit ratings destroyed, and their reputations ruined. According to the FBI, some victims have even been kidnapped!

What's phishing? Phishing (pronounced "fishing") is a scam that arrives in your e-mailbox looking like official correspondence from a major company, such as Microsoft, PayPal, eBay, MSN, Yahoo!, or America Online. The e-mail message is actually from an illegitimate source and is designed to trick you into divulging confidential information or downloading a virus. Links in the e-mail message often lead to a Web site that looks official, where you are asked to enter confidential information such as your credit card number, social security number, or bank account number.

The following are examples of phishing scams you should be aware of:

■ A message from Microsoft with an attachment that supposedly contains a security update for Microsoft Windows. Downloading the attachment infects your computer with a virus.

■ A message from America Online, complete with official-looking logos, that alerts you to a problem with your account. When you click the AOL Billing Center link and enter your account information, it is transmitted to a hacker's computer.

■ A message that's obviously spam, but contains a convenient opt-out link. If you click the link believing that it will prevent future spam from this source, you'll actually be downloading a program that hackers can use to remotely control your computer for illegal activities.

How do I avoid e-mail scams? If your e-mail software provides spam filters, you can use them to block some unsolicited mail from your e-mailbox. Spam filters are far from perfect, however, so don't assume everything that gets through is legitimate. Use your judgment before opening any e-mail message or attachment.

Never reply to a message that you suspect to be fraudulent. If you have a question about its legitimacy, check whether it's on a list of known scams. Never click a link provided in an e-mail message to manage your account information. Instead, go directly to the Web site and access your account as usual. Microsoft never sends updates as attachments. To obtain Microsoft updates, go to *www.microsoft.com* and click Windows Update or Office Update.

TRY IT

Arm yourself against e-mail scams

1. Start your browser and connect to the site **www.antiphishing.org**. Scroll down the page and become familiar with the list of recent phishing attacks.

2. Open your e-mail software and find out if it incudes spam filters. You can usually find this information by clicking Help on the menu bar and then typing "spam filter" in the search box.

3. Explore your options for configuring spam filters. If you use Microsoft Outlook for e-mail (shown at right), you can find these settings by clicking **Actions** on the menu bar, pointing to **Junk E-Mail**, then clicking **Junk E-mail Options**.

Spam filters sometimes catch legitimate mail and group it with junk mail. You might want to keep tabs on your spam filters when they are first activated to make sure they are set to a level that eliminates most unwanted spam without catching too much legitimate mail.

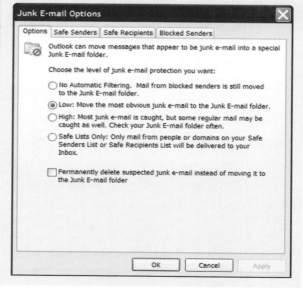

PROTECTING YOUR PRIVACY

How much information has been collected about me? No matter what steps you take to protect your privacy, information about you is stored in many places and has the potential to be consolidated by government agencies, private businesses, and criminals.

Some databases are legitimate—those maintained by credit bureaus and medical insurance companies, for example. By law, you have the right to ask for a copy of these records and correct any errors you find. Many other databases, such as those maintained at e-commerce sites and those illegally acquired by hackers, are not accessible, and you have no way of checking the data they contain.

Can I control who collects information about me? To some extent, you can limit your exposure to future data collection by supplying personal data only when absolutely necessary. When filling out online forms, consider whether you want to or need to provide your real name and address.

You should also be careful about revealing personal information in chat rooms and other online forums. Many chat room participants are not who they appear to be. Some people are just having fun with fantasy identities, but others are trying to con people by telling hard luck stories and faking illnesses. Never reveal personal information, such as your full name, address, or phone number. Resist the temptation to meet face to face with chat room participants. Taking these simple steps to protect your privacy is an important part of your overall security plan.

▧ TRY IT

Check your privacy

1. Start your browser and go Googling by connecting to **www.google.com**. Enter your name in the Search box. What turns up?

2. Connect to **www.peopledata.com** and click the **People Search** option. Enter your name and state of residence. Click the **Search** button. Notice all the information that's offered.

3. Connect to **www.ciadata.com** and scroll down the page to view the kind of information anyone can obtain about you for less than $100.

4. Connect to the Federal Trade Commission site:

http://www.ftc.gov/bcp/conline/pubs/credit/crdright.htm

At this site, you can read about your rights to view credit reports.

FIGURE 32
Security Checklist

- Use a password to protect your data in case your computer is stolen.
- Don't leave your computer unattended in public places.
- Run antivirus software and keep it updated.
- Install software service packs and security patches as they become available, but make sure they are legitimate.
- Install and activate firewall software, especially if your computer is directly connected to the Internet by an ISDN, DSL, satellite, or cable connection.
- Do not publish or post personal information, such as your physical address, passwords, social security number, and account numbers, on your Web site, your online resume, or other online documents.
- Be wary of contacts you make in public chat rooms.
- Don't click pop-up ads.
- Install and activate anti-spyware and ad-blocking software.
- Do not reply to spam.
- Ignore e-mail offers that seem too good to be true.

QUICKCHECK......SECTION E

1. The best defense against viruses is to use a phishing filter before opening e-mail attachments. True or false? [ ] .

2. Intruders can access your computer by exploiting [ ] flaws in a computer's operating system, browser, or e-mail software.

3. [ ] is an online threat that compromises your privacy by piggybacking on pop-up ads and collecting personal information.

4. E-mail scams are usually distributed in mass mailings called [ ] .

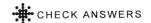 CHECK ANSWERS

Computer Concepts

8th Edition

COMPUTER, INTERNET, WEB, AND E-MAIL BASICS

CONTENTS

TIP

When using the BookOnCD, the ❖ icons are "clickable" to access resources on the CD. The ✚ icons are clickable to access resources on the Web. You can also access Web resources by using your browser to connect directly to the NP8 New Perspectives Web site at:

www.course.com/np/concepts8/ch01

CHAPTER PREVIEW

Before you begin Chapter 1, you can use the Web-based preview activities to hear an overview of the chapter, check your current level of expertise about key concepts, and look through a list of learning objectives. You can access the preview activities by clicking the ⚓ icon when using the BookOnCD or going to the New Perspectives NP8 Web site.

CHAPTER OVERVIEW

Computers and the Internet are the cornerstones of a technology revolution that is dramatically transforming the way we live, work, play, and think. Chapter 1 is designed to make sure you understand computer basics. Get your book and highlighter ready, then connect to the New Perspectives NP8 Web site where you can listen to an overview that points out the most important concepts for this chapter.

www.course.com/np/concepts8/ch01 ⚓

CHAPTER PRE-ASSESSMENT

How much do you know about basic computer terminology and using the Internet, Web, and e-mail? To gauge your level of knowledge before beginning the chapter, take the pre-assessment quiz at the New Perspectives NP8 Web site. Armed with your results from this quiz, you can focus your study time on concepts that will round out your knowledge of computer basics and improve your test scores.

www.course.com/np/concepts8/ch01 ⚓

LEARNING OBJECTIVES

When you complete this chapter you should be able to:

- Define the term "computer" and identify the components of a personal computer system
- Compare the computing capabilities of the following computer categories: personal computers, handheld computers, workstations, videogame consoles, mainframe computers, supercomputers, and servers
- Explain how an operating system affects compatibility between computer platforms, such as PCs and Macs
- Evaluate the various ways you can connect a computer to the Internet and select an ISP
- Describe how Web servers, browsers, URLs, HTML, and HTTP contribute to the Internet resource known as the Web

- Describe popular Internet resources, such as the Web, e-mail, bulletin boards, blogs, file downloads, file sharing, Internet telephony, broadcasting, chat groups, and instant messaging
- Demonstrate that you can use a search engine to locate information on the Web
- List the features that you would expect to find in a typical e-mail software package
- List some of the steps you can take to avoid spam
- Explain how an e-mail system works and describe the difference between store-and-forward mail and Web-based mail

A detailed list of learning objectives is provided at the New Perspectives NP8 Web site

www.course.com/np/concepts8/ch01

SECTION A

COMPUTER BASICS

Whether you realize it or not, you already know a lot about computers. You've picked up information from commercials and magazine articles, from books and movies, from conversations and correspondence—perhaps even from using your own computer and trying to figure out why it doesn't always work!

Section A provides an overview that's designed to help you start organizing what you know about computers, give you a basic understanding of how computers work, and get you up to speed with a basic computer vocabulary.

A COMPUTER IS...

How old is the word "computer"? The word "computer" has been part of the English language since 1646, but if you look in a dictionary printed before 1940, you might be surprised to find a computer defined as a person who performs calculations! Prior to 1940, machines designed to perform calculations were referred to as calculators and tabulators, not computers. The modern definition and use of the term "computer" emerged in the 1940s, when the first electronic computing devices were developed.

What is a computer? Most people can formulate a mental picture of a computer, but computers do so many things and come in such a variety of shapes and sizes that it might seem difficult to distill their common characteristics into an all-purpose definition. At its core, a **computer** is a device that accepts input, processes data, stores data, and produces output, all according to a series of stored instructions.

Computer **input** is whatever is typed, submitted, or transmitted to a computer system. Input can be supplied by a person, by the environment, or by another computer. Examples of the kinds of input that a computer can accept include words and symbols in a document, numbers for a calculation, pictures, temperatures from a thermostat, audio signals from a microphone, and instructions from a computer program. An input device, such as a keyboard or mouse, gathers input and transforms it into a series of electronic signals for the computer to store and manipulate.

In the context of computing, **data** refers to the symbols that represent facts, objects, and ideas. Computers manipulate data in many ways, and this manipulation is called **processing**. The series of instructions that tell a computer how to carry out processing tasks is referred to as a **computer program**, or simply a "program." These programs form the **software** that sets up a computer to do a specific task. Some of the ways that a computer can process data include performing calculations, sorting lists of words or numbers, modifying documents and pictures, and drawing graphs. In a computer, most processing takes place in a component called the **central processing unit** (CPU), which is sometimes described as the computer's "brain."

A computer stores data so that it will be available for processing. Most computers have more than one location for storing data, depending on how the data is being used. **Memory** is an area of a computer that temporarily holds data waiting to be processed, stored, or output. **Storage** is the area where data can be left on a permanent basis when it is not immediately needed for processing.

Output is the result produced by a computer. Some examples of computer output include reports, documents, music, graphs, and pictures. An output device displays, prints, or transmits the results of processing. Figure 1-1 helps you visualize the input, processing, storage, and output activities of a computer.

FIGURE 1-1

A computer can be defined by its ability to accept input, process data, store data, and produce output, all according to a set of instructions from a computer program.

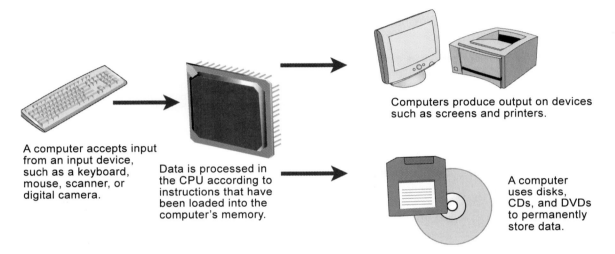

A computer accepts input from an input device, such as a keyboard, mouse, scanner, or digital camera.

Data is processed in the CPU according to instructions that have been loaded into the computer's memory.

Computers produce output on devices such as screens and printers.

A computer uses disks, CDs, and DVDs to permanently store data.

What's so significant about a computer's ability to store instructions? Take a moment to think about the way you use a simple handheld calculator to balance your checkbook each month. You're forced to do the calculations in stages. Although you can store data from one stage and use it in the next stage, you cannot store the sequence of formulas—the program—required to balance your checkbook. Every month, therefore, you have to perform a similar set of calculations. The process would be much simpler if your calculator remembered the set of calculations you needed to perform, and simply asked you for this month's checkbook entries.

Early "computers" were really no more than calculating devices, designed to carry out a specific mathematical task. To use one of these devices for a different task, it was necessary to rewire its circuits—a job best left to an engineer. In a modern computer, the idea of a **stored program** means that a series of instructions for a computing task can be loaded into a computer's memory. These instructions can easily be replaced by a different set of instructions when it is time for the computer to perform another task.

The stored program concept allows you to use your computer for one task, such as word processing, and then easily switch to a different type of computing task, such as editing a photo or sending an e-mail message. It is the single most important characteristic that distinguishes a computer from other simpler and less versatile devices, such as calculators and pocket-sized electronic dictionaries.

COMPUTER CATEGORIES

Why is it useful to categorize computers? Computers are versatile machines that are able to perform a truly amazing assortment of tasks, but some types of computers are better suited to certain tasks than other types of computers. Categorizing computers is a way of grouping them according to criteria such as usage, cost, size, and capability. Knowing how a computer has been categorized provides an indication of its best potential use.

During the 1940s and 1950s, very few computers existed, and there was really no need to categorize them. Because the main circuitry was usually housed in a closet-sized metal frame, computer techies called these computers "mainframes." The term soon became synonymous with a category of large, expensive computers that were sold to big corporations and government agencies.

In 1968, the term "minicomputer" was used to describe a second computer category. These computers were smaller, less expensive, and less powerful than mainframes, but were, nevertheless, able to provide adequate computing power for small businesses. In 1971, the first microcomputer appeared. A **microcomputer** could be clearly differentiated from computers in other categories because its CPU consisted of a single "chip" called a **microprocessor**.

At one time, then, it was possible to define three distinct categories of computers: mainframes, minicomputers, and microcomputers. Technology has advanced rapidly since then. Today, just about every computer—no matter how large or small—uses one or more microprocessors as its CPU. Therefore, the use of a microprocessor is no longer a distinction between microcomputers and other computer categories. Furthermore, the term "minicomputer" has fallen into disuse. To reflect today's computer technology, the following categories might be more appropriate: personal computers, handheld computers, workstations, videogame consoles, mainframes, supercomputers, and servers.

What is a personal computer? A **personal computer** is a type of microcomputer designed to meet the computing needs of an individual. It typically provides access to a wide variety of computing applications, such as word processing, photo editing, e-mail, and Internet access. Personal computers are available as desktop computers, notebook computers, or tablet computers, as shown in Figure 1-2.

What are the characteristics of desktop computers? A **desktop computer** fits on a desk and runs on power from an electrical wall outlet. A desktop computer's keyboard is typically a separate component, connected to the main unit by a cable. The main unit can be housed in a vertical case (like the one shown in Figure 1-2, top) or a horizontal case. The vertical case is sometimes placed on the floor or in a cubbyhole beneath the desk. The horizontal case can be placed under the display screen to reduce the computer's "footprint" on the desk. The first personal computers were desktop models, and this style remains popular for offices, schools, and homes. Because their components can be manufactured economically, desktop computers typically provide the most computing power for your dollar. The price of an entry-level desktop computer starts at $500 or a bit less, but most consumers select more powerful models that cost between $1,000 and $1,200.

How do notebook computers differ from desktops? A **notebook computer** (also referred to as a "laptop"), is a small, lightweight personal

FIGURE 1-2

Personal computers are available in desktop, notebook, and tablet configurations.

A desktop computer fits on a desk and features a vertical case (like the one shown) or a horizontal case.

A notebook computer is small and lightweight, giving it the advantage of portability. It can be plugged into an electrical outlet, or it can run on battery power.

A tablet computer is similar in size to a notebook computer, but features a touch-sensitive screen that can be used for input instead of a keyboard.

computer that incorporates screen, keyboard, storage, and processing components into a single portable unit. Notebook computers can run on power supplied by an electrical outlet or a battery. These portable computers are ideal for mobile uses because they are easy to carry and can be used outdoors, in airports, and in classrooms without the need for a nearby electrical outlet. Notebook computers cost a bit more than a desktop computer with similar computing power and storage capacity. The price of an entry-level notebook computer starts at about $700, but consumers often spend between $1,000 and $1,500 to get the performance they want.

What is a tablet computer? A **tablet computer** is a portable computing device featuring a touch-sensitive screen that can be used as a writing or drawing pad. A "slate" tablet configuration, like the one in Figure 1-2, lacks a keyboard (although one can be attached) and resembles a high-tech clipboard. A "convertible" tablet computer is constructed like a notebook computer, but the screen folds face up over the keyboard to provide a horizontal writing surface. Tablet computers shine for applications that involve handwritten input, and many experts believe they might replace notebook computers when prices fall to equivalent levels. Since tablet computers were first introduced in 2002, their price has remained high, starting at about $1,200, but more typically costing $2,000 to $2,500.

What is a handheld? A **handheld computer**, such as a Palm, an iPAQ, or a PocketPC, features a small keyboard or touch-sensitive screen and is designed to fit into a pocket, run on batteries, and be used while you are holding it. Also called a **PDA** (personal digital assistant), a computer in this category can be used as an electronic appointment book, address book, calculator, and notepad. Inexpensive add-ons make it possible to send and receive e-mail, use maps and global positioning to get directions, and synchronize information with a personal computer.

PDAs and "smart" cell phones are converging into a single handheld technology that provides keypad input, color screen, digital camera, PDA software, voice communications, text messaging, Web browsing, and e-mail. PDA and smartphone prices start below $100 and range up to $700 for a model with a color screen and integrated cellular phone (Figure 1-3).

With its slow processing speed and small screen, a handheld computer is not powerful enough to handle many of the tasks that can be accomplished by desktop, notebook, or tablet personal computers. Yet handhelds provide important computing and communications functions in a mobile package.

TERMINOLOGY NOTE

The term "personal computer" is sometimes abbreviated as "PC." However, the abbreviation "PC" can also refer to a specific type of personal computer that descended from the original IBM PC and runs Windows software. In this book, "PC" refers to IBM PC descendants. It is not used as an abbreviation for the term "personal computer."

INFOWEBLINKS

Learn more about the latest PDA models, prices, software, and accessories by visiting the **PDA InfoWeb**.

www.course.com/np/concepts8/ch01

FIGURE 1-3
Many handheld computers feature a small keyboard, while others accept handwriting input.

What types of computers can be classified as workstations? The term "**workstation**" has two meanings. Computers advertised as workstations are usually powerful desktop computers designed for specialized tasks. A workstation can tackle tasks that require a lot of processing speed, such as medical imaging and computer-aided design. Some workstations contain more than one microprocessor, and most have circuitry specially designed for creating and displaying three-dimensional and animated graphics. Workstation prices range from $3,000 to $20,000. Because of its cost, a workstation, like the one in Figure 1-4, is often dedicated to design tasks, but is not used for typical microcomputer applications, such as word processing, photo editing, and accessing the Web.

A second meaning of the term "workstation" applies to an ordinary personal computer that is connected to a network. A **computer network** is two or more computers and other devices connected for the purpose of sharing data, programs, and hardware. A **LAN** (local area network) is simply a computer network located within a limited geographical area, such as a school computer lab or a small business.

Is a PlayStation a computer? A **videogame console**, such as Nintendo's GameCube, Sony's PlayStation, or Microsoft's Xbox, *is* a computer, but videogame consoles have not been considered a computer category because of their history as dedicated game devices that connect to a TV set and provide only a pair of joysticks for input. Today's videogame consoles, however, contain microprocessors that are equivalent to any found in a fast personal computer, and they are equipped to produce graphics that rival those on sophisticated workstations. Add-ons, such as keyboards, DVD players, and Internet access, make it possible to use a videogame console to watch DVD movies, send and receive e-mail, and participate in online activities, such as multiplayer games. As with handheld computers, videogame consoles like the one in Figure 1-5 fill a specialized niche and are not considered a replacement for a personal computer.

What's so special about a mainframe computer? A **mainframe computer** (or simply a "mainframe") is a large and expensive computer capable of simultaneously processing data for hundreds or thousands of users. Mainframes are generally used by businesses or governments to provide centralized storage, processing, and management for large amounts of data. Mainframes remain the computer of choice in situations where reliability, data security, and centralized control are necessary.

The price of a mainframe computer typically starts at several hundred thousand dollars and can easily exceed $1 million. Its main processing circuitry is housed in a closet-sized cabinet (Figure 1-6), but after large components are added for storage and output, a mainframe can fill a good-sized room.

How powerful is a supercomputer? A computer falls into the **supercomputer** category if it is, at the time of construction, one of the fastest computers in the world. Because of their speed, supercomputers can tackle complex tasks that just would not be practical for other computers. Common uses for supercomputers include breaking codes, modeling worldwide weather systems, and simulating nuclear explosions. One impressive simulation designed to run on a supercomputer tracked the movement of thousands of dust particles as they were tossed about by a tornado.

FIGURE 1-4

A workstation resembles a desktop computer, but typically features more processing power and storage capacity.

FIGURE 1-5

A videogame console includes circuitry similar to a personal computer's, but its input and output devices are optimized for gaming.

FIGURE 1-6

This IBM S/390 zSeries 990 mainframe computer weighs about 1,400 pounds and is about 6.5 feet tall.

At one time, supercomputer designers focused on building specialized, very fast, and very large CPUs. Today, a supercomputer CPU is constructed from thousands of microprocessors. Approximately 300 of the 500 fastest supercomputers in the world use microcomputer technology.

What makes a computer a "server"? In the computer industry, the term "server" has several meanings. It can refer to computer hardware, to a specific type of software, or to a combination of hardware and software. In any case, the purpose of a **server** is to "serve" computers on a network (such as the Internet or a LAN) by supplying them with data. A personal computer, workstation, or software that requests data from a server is referred to as a **client**. For example, on a network, a server might respond to a client's request for a Web page. Another server might handle the steady stream of e-mail that travels among clients from all over the Internet. A server might also allow clients within a LAN to share files or access a centralized printer.

Remarkably, just about any personal computer, workstation, mainframe, or supercomputer can be configured to perform the work of a server. That fact should emphasize the concept that a server does not require a specific type of hardware. Nonetheless, computer manufacturers categorize some of their computers as "servers" because they are especially suited for storing and distributing data on a network. Despite impressive performance on server-related tasks, these machines do not include features, such as sound cards, DVD players, and other fun accessories, that consumers expect on their desktop computers. Most consumers would not want to buy a server to replace a desktop computer.

PERSONAL COMPUTER SYSTEMS

What's a personal computer system? The term "computer system" usually refers to a computer and all the input, output, and storage devices that are connected to it. At the core of a personal computer system is a desktop, notebook, or tablet computer, which probably looks like one of those in Figure 1-7.

INFOWEBLINKS

What's the latest news about supercomputers? Visit the **Supercomputer InfoWeb** to learn more about these amazing machines.

www.course.com/np/concepts8/ch01

FIGURE 1-7
Personal computer designs run the gamut from drab gray boxes to colorful curvy cases.

Despite cosmetic differences among personal computers, a personal computer system usually includes the following equipment:

■ **System unit.** The **system unit** is the case that holds the main circuit boards, microprocessor, power supply, and storage devices. The system unit for notebook computers holds a built-in keyboard and speakers, too.

■ **Display device.** Most desktop computers use a separate **monitor** as a display device, whereas notebook computers use a flat panel **LCD screen** (liquid crystal display screen) attached to the system unit.

■ **Keyboard.** Most computers are equipped with a keyboard as the primary input device.

■ **Mouse.** A **mouse** is an input device designed to manipulate on-screen graphical objects and controls.

■ **Hard disk drive.** A **hard disk drive** can store billions of characters of data. It is usually mounted inside the computer's system unit. A small external light indicates when the drive is reading or writing data.

■ **CD and DVD drives.** A **CD drive** is a storage device that uses laser technology to work with data on computer or audio CDs. A **DVD drive** can work with data on computer CDs, audio CDs, computer DVDs, or DVD movie disks. Some CD and DVD drives are classified as "read only" devices that cannot be used to write data onto disks. They are typically used to access data from commercial software, music, and movie CDs or DVDs. "Writable" CD and DVD drives, however, can be used to store and access data.

■ **Floppy disk drive.** A **floppy disk drive** is a storage device that reads and writes data on floppy disks.

■ **Sound card and speakers.** Desktop computers have a rudimentary built-in speaker that's mostly limited to playing beeps. A small circuit board, called a **sound card**, is required for high-quality music, narration, and sound effects. A desktop computer's sound card sends signals to external speakers. A notebook's sound card sends signals to speakers that are built into the notebook system unit.

■ **Modem and network cards.** Many personal computer systems include a built-in **modem** that can be used to establish an Internet connection using a standard telephone line. A **network card** is used to connect a computer to a network or cable Internet connection.

■ **Printer.** A computer printer is an output device that produces computer-generated text or graphical images on paper.

FIGURE 1-8

Computer storage media include floppy disks, DVDs and CDs .

FIGURE 1-9

A typical personal computer system includes the system unit and a variety of storage, input, and output devices.

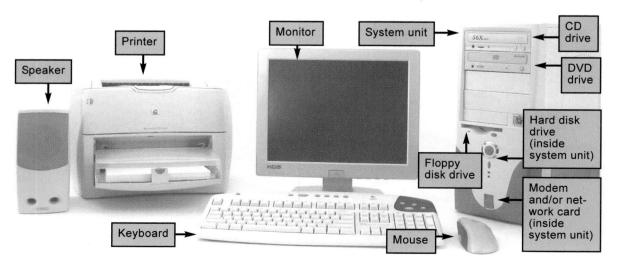

What's a peripheral device? The term **peripheral device** designates equipment that might be added to a computer system to enhance its functionality. Popular peripheral devices, such as those in Figure 1-10, include printers, digital cameras, scanners, joysticks, and graphics tablets.

Is a hard disk drive a peripheral device? The word "peripheral" is a relatively old part of computer jargon that dates back to the days of mainframes when the CPU was housed in a giant box and all input, output, and storage devices were housed separately. Technically, a peripheral is any device that is not housed within the CPU.

Although a hard disk drive seems to be an integral part of a computer, by the strictest technical definition, a hard disk drive would be classified as a peripheral device. The same goes for other storage devices and the keyboard, monitor, LCD screen, sound card, speakers, and modem. In the world of personal computers, however, the use of the term "peripheral" varies and is often used to refer to any components that are not housed inside the system unit.

DATA, INFORMATION, AND FILES

Is there a difference between data and information? In everyday conversation, people use the terms "data" and "information" interchangeably. Nevertheless, some computer professionals make a distinction between the two terms. They define data as the symbols that represent people, events, things, and ideas. Data becomes **information** when it is presented in a format that people can understand and use. Most computers store data in a **digital** format as a series of 1s and 0s. Each 1 or 0 is called a **bit**. Eight bits, called a **byte**, are used to represent one character—a letter, number, or punctuation mark.

As a rule of thumb, remember that (technically speaking) data is used by computers; information is used by humans. The bits and bytes that a computer stores are referred to as data. The words, numbers, and graphics displayed for people are referred to as information.

What is a file? A computer file, usually referred to simply as a **file**, is a named collection of data that exists on a storage medium, such as a hard disk, floppy disk, or CD. Although all files contain data, some files are classified as "data files," whereas other files are classified as "executable files." A **data file** contains data that can be processed—the text for a document, the numbers for a calculation, the specifications for a graph, the frames of a video, the contents of a Web page, or the notes of a musical passage. An **executable file** contains the programs or instructions that tell a computer how to perform a specific task. For example, the word processing program that tells your computer how to display and print text is stored as an executable file.

You can think of data files as passive—the data does not instruct the computer to do anything. Executable files, on the other hand, are active—the instructions stored in the file cause the computer to carry out some action.

How can I tell what's in a file? Every file has a **file name**, which often provides a clue to its contents. A file might also have a **file extension**—sometimes referred to as a "filename extension"—that further describes a file's contents. For example, in Pbrush.exe, "Pbrush" is the file name and "exe" is the file extension. As you can see, the file name is separated from the extension by a period called a "dot." To tell someone the name of the file Pbrush.exe, you would say, "Pbrush dot e-x-e."

FIGURE 1-10

Peripheral devices add to a computer's versatility.

Printer

Digital camera

Scanner

Graphics tablet

Executable files typically have .exe extensions. Data files have a variety of extensions, such as .bmp or .tif for a graphic, .mid for synthesized music, or .htm for a Web page. Chapter 4 provides additional information on file names and file types.

APPLICATION SOFTWARE AND OPERATING SYSTEM BASICS

What is application software? A computer can be "applied" to many tasks, such as writing, number crunching, video editing, and online shopping. **Application software** is a set of computer programs that helps a person carry out a task. Word processing software, for example, helps people create, edit, and print documents. Personal finance software helps people keep track of their money and investments. Video editing software helps people create and edit home movies—and even some professional films.

Is an operating system some type of application software? No. An **operating system** (OS) is essentially the master controller for all the activities that take place within a computer. Operating systems are classified as **system software**, not application software, because their primary purpose is to help the computer system monitor itself in order to function efficiently.

Unlike application software, an operating system does not directly help people perform application-specific tasks, such as word processing. People do, however, interact with the operating system for certain operational and storage tasks, such as starting programs and locating data files.

What are the most popular operating systems? Popular personal computer operating systems include Microsoft Windows and Mac OS. Microsoft Windows Mobile and Palm OS control most handheld computers. Linux and UNIX are popular operating systems for servers.

Microsoft Windows (usually referred to simply as "Windows") is the most widely used operating system for personal computers. As shown in Figure 1-11, the Windows operating system displays on-screen controls designed to be manipulated by a mouse.

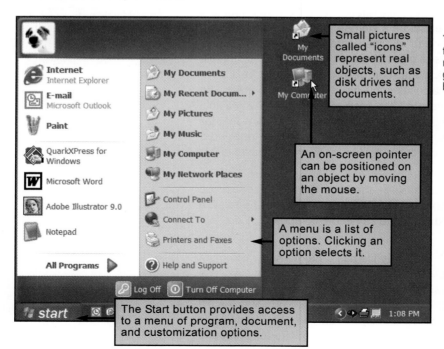

FIGURE 1-11
The Windows operating system displays on-screen icons, menus, buttons, and other graphical controls designed to be manipulated by a mouse.

Is Windows software the same as the Windows operating system?
No. The term "Windows software" refers to any application software designed to run on computers that use the Microsoft Windows operating system. A program called Microsoft Word for Windows is an example of a word processing program—application software—that is referred to as "Windows software."

How does an operating system affect compatibility? Computers that operate in essentially the same way are said to be "compatible." Two of the most important factors that influence compatibility and define a computer's **platform** are the microprocessor and the operating system. Today, two of the most popular personal computer platforms are PCs and Macs.

PCs are based on the design for one of the first personal computer "superstars"—the IBM PC. The "great grandchildren" of the IBM PC are on computer store shelves today—a huge selection of personal computer brands and models manufactured by companies such as IBM, Hewlett-Packard, Toshiba, Dell, and Gateway. The Windows operating system was designed specifically for these personal computers and, therefore, the PC platform is sometimes called the "Windows platform." Most of the examples in this book pertain to PCs because they are so popular.

Macs are based on a proprietary design for a personal computer called the Macintosh, manufactured almost exclusively by Apple Computer, Inc. The stylish iMac is one of Apple's most popular computers, and like other computers in the Mac platform, it uses Mac OS as its operating system.

The PC and Mac platforms are not compatible because their microprocessors and operating systems differ. Consequently, application software designed for Macs does not typically work with PCs and vice versa. When shopping for new software, it is important to read the package to make sure it is designed to work with your computer platform.

INFOWEBLINKS

Apple Computer, Inc. is known for its innovative computer designs. You can learn about its newest computers by connecting to the **Apple Computers InfoWeb**.

www.course.com/np/concepts8/ch01

QUICKCHECK......SECTION A

1. A computer accepts input, processes data, stores data, and produces [＿＿＿＿＿＿] according to a series of instructions.

2. The term "microprocessor" is a synonym for the term "microcomputer." True or false? [＿＿＿＿]

3. A(n) [＿＿＿＿＿] computer is also referred to as a laptop.

4. Most computers include a network card designed to connect a computer to the Internet using standard telephone service. True or false? [＿＿＿＿]

5. Eight [＿＿＿＿＿] form a byte.

6. PCs and Macs are not considered [＿＿＿＿＿＿] because their microprocessors and operating systems differ.

 CHECK ANSWERS

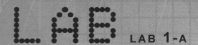
LAB 1-A

OPERATING A PERSONAL COMPUTER

In this lab, you'll learn:

- How to start a Windows computer
- What to do when a computer is in sleep mode
- How to deactivate a screen saver
- How to select a different screen saver
- The terminology used for the four sections of a computer keyboard
- How to use the Alt, Ctrl, Esc, Num Lock, Caps Lock, Windows, Fn, Backspace, Delete, and arrow keys
- The difference between forward and backward slashes
- The location of the tilde
- How to start and exit a program
- How to close a program that is not responding
- When to use the reset button
- How to shut down Windows

INTERACTIVE LAB

CLICK TO START THE LAB ✦

LAB ASSIGNMENTS

1. Start the interactive part of the lab. Insert your Tracking Disk if you want to save your QuickCheck results. Perform each lab step as directed, and answer all the lab QuickCheck questions. When you exit the lab, your answers are automatically graded and your results are displayed.

2. Make a note of the brand and location of the computer you're using to complete these lab assignments.

3. Use the Start button to access your computer's Control Panel folder. Describe the status of your computer's power saver settings.

4. Preview the available screen savers on the computer you use most frequently. Select the screen saver you like the best and describe it in a few sentences.

5. What is the purpose of an Fn key? Does your computer keyboard include an Fn key? Explain why or why not.

6. In your own words, describe what happens when you (a) click the Close button, (b) hold down the Ctrl, Alt, and Del keys, (c) press the reset button, and (d) select the Shut Down option.

SECTION B

INTERNET BASICS

The Internet has changed society. E-mail and instant messaging have caused a major shift in the way people communicate. Online stores have changed our shopping habits. The ability to easily download music has stirred up controversy about intellectual property. The possibility of unauthorized access to online databases has made us more aware of our privacy and safety. Section B provides a basic overview of the Internet, with an emphasis on how you can connect to it and use it.

INTERNET RESOURCES

How does the Internet work? The **Internet** is a collection of local, regional, national, and international computer networks linked together to exchange data and distribute processing tasks. You can think of the Internet as a network of interconnected communications lines creating a sort of highway system for transporting data. The main routes of the Internet—analogous to interstate highways—are referred to as the **Internet backbone**. Constructed and maintained by major telecommunications companies, such as AT&T and Sprint, these telecommunications links can move huge amounts of data at incredible speeds. Data traveling from the United States can arrive in England in less than 60 ms—60 thousandths of a second.

In addition to the backbone, the Internet encompasses an intricate collection of regional and local communications links. These links can include local telephone systems, cable television lines, cellular telephone systems, and personal satellite dishes.

Internet communications links (Figure 1-12) transport data to and from millions of computers and other electronic devices. Amazingly, this data transport works seamlessly between all kinds of platforms—between PCs and Macs and even between personal computers and mainframes. Communication between all the different devices on the Internet is made possible by **TCP/IP** (Transmission Control Protocol/Internet Protocol), a standard set of rules for electronically addressing and transmitting data.

INFOWEBLINKS

Sometimes used as a synonym for the Internet, the term "cyberspace" was coined by science-fiction writer William Gibson. Visit the **Cyberspace InfoWeb** for additional background and links to books for sci-fi aficionados.

www.course.com/np/concepts8/ch01

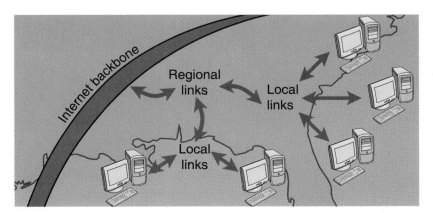

FIGURE 1-12
The Internet backbone connects to regional and local communications links, which provide Internet access to individuals working at their personal computers.

Where is all the Internet data stored? The Internet provides access to an amazing volume of data, including corporate Web pages, merchandise catalogs, software, music, tutorials on all manner of subjects, school science projects, telephone directories, library card catalogs, and so on. Although difficult to pin down exact figures, it is estimated that the Internet provides access to more data than is stored in all the academic research libraries in the United States.

Most of the "stuff" that's accessible on the Internet is stored on servers, which are owned and maintained by government agencies, corporations, small businesses, schools, organizations, and even individuals. These servers use special server software to locate and distribute data requested by Internet users.

What kind of resources are available on the Internet? If you're looking for information, if you want to communicate with someone, or if you want to buy something, the Internet offers a good set of resources. Here is a quick overview of Internet resources:

■ **Web sites.** Most people envision Web sites as various locations on the Internet that correspond to a corporation's headquarters, a store, a magazine, or a library. A Web site can provide information or access to other resources, such as search engines and e-mail.

■ **Search engines.** Without search engines, using the Internet would be like trying to find a book in the Library of Congress by wandering around the stacks. Search engines, such as Google and Yahoo!, help catalog a huge portion of the data stored at Web sites.

■ **Downloads and uploads.** Internet servers store all sorts of useful files containing documents, music, software, videos, animations, and photos. The process of transferring one of these files from a remote computer, such as a server, to a local computer, such as your personal computer, is called **downloading**. Sending a file from a local computer to a remote computer is called **uploading** (Figure 1-13).

INFOWEBLINKS

If you'd like to check out some of the resources described in this section, connect to the **Internet Resources InfoWeb**. There you'll find links to examples and to the software that you need to access these useful Internet resources. ✦

www.course.com/np/concepts8/ch01

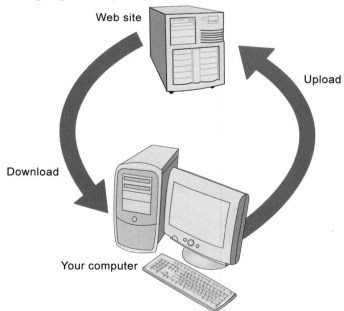

Web site

Upload

Download

Your computer

FIGURE 1-13

Many Web sites provide files that the public can download to personal computers. Uploads, on the other hand, are limited to people who have password access to the site.

For a demonstration of how to download a file, click the Start icon.

CLICK TO START ✦

■ **P2P file sharing.** A technology known as **peer-to-peer** (P2P) file sharing makes it possible to access files stored on another Internet user's hard disk—with permission, of course. This technology is the basis for popular music and file exchange Web sites, such as Morpheus and Kazaa.

■ **E-mail.** Also known as "electronic mail," **e-mail** allows one person to send an electronic message to another person or to a group of people listed in a personal address book. A variation of e-mail called a **mailing list server**, or "listserv," maintains a public list of people who are interested in a particular topic. Messages sent to the list server are automatically distributed to everyone on the mailing list.

■ **Bulletin boards. Usenet** is a worldwide bulletin board system that contains more than 15,000 discussion forums called **newsgroups**. Newsgroup members post messages to the bulletin board, which can be read and responded to by other group members.

■ **Blogs.** The term **blog**, derived from the phrase "WeB LOG," refers to a personal journal posted on the Web for access by the general public. Blogs can focus on a single topic or cover a variety of issues. A typical blog includes commentary by the author as well as links to additional information. To find blogs, you can use a blog directory, like the one in Figure 1-14.

FIGURE 1-14

Blogs have become a popular way of disseminating information over the Internet. Blog directories, such as this one, provide links to blogs on all sorts of topics.

■ **Chat groups and instant messaging.** A **chat group** consists of several people who connect to the Internet and communicate in a virtual "room" by typing comments to each other. A private version of a chat room, called **instant messaging**, allows two or more people to send typed messages back and forth.

■ **Internet telephony.** Although it is not as simple as picking up the telephone, **Internet telephony** allows telephone-style conversations to travel over the Internet to virtually anywhere in the world. When using Internet telephony, the sound quality is sometimes worse than a cellular phone, but the cost is much less than conventional long distance service.

■ **E-commerce.** The Internet is revolutionizing business by directly linking consumers with retailers, manufacturers, and distributors. **E-commerce**, or "electronic commerce," includes activities such as online shopping, electronic auctions, and online stock trading.

■ **Broadcasting.** The Internet carries radio shows and teleconferences that can be broadcast worldwide. Internet radio is popular because broadcasts aren't limited to a small local region. Internet broadcasting technology, referred to as "multicasting," has the potential to increase the use and popularity of Internet broadcasts.

■ **Remote access and control.** Using software, such as Telnet or SSH, and a valid password, it is possible to link two computers so that commands entered on one computer are executed remotely on the other computer. This capability of the Internet and other networks is handy, for example, when a technical support person located in a manufacturer's service center takes remote control of your computer to fix a problem.

INTERNET CONNECTIONS

What are my options for Internet connections? To take advantage of everything the Internet has to offer, you have to establish some sort of communications link between your computer and the Internet. Possibilities include using your existing telephone line, a cable television line, a personal satellite link, wireless or cell phone service, or special high-speed telephone services.

What's the easiest, cheapest way to access the Internet? Many people literally dial up the Internet using an existing telephone line. This type of connection—often referred to as a **dial-up connection**—is relatively simple and inexpensive because the necessary equipment and software are preinstalled on most new computers. A dial-up connection requires a device called a **voiceband modem** (often simply called a "modem"), which converts your computer's digital signals into a type of signal that can travel over telephone lines. Figure 1-15 can help you determine whether a computer has a modem.

FIGURE 1-15

The photo below shows three kinds of modems. An external modem (at the top left of this photo) connects to the computer with a cable. An internal modem (top right) is installed inside the computer's system unit. A PC card modem (bottom center) is typically used in notebook computers without built-in phone jacks.

CLICK TO START

To determine whether a computer has a modem, look for a place to plug in a standard phone cable.

Notebook computers without built-in modems require a PC card modem that slides into a small slot on the side of the case.

To establish a dial-up connection, your computer's modem dials a special access number, which is answered by an Internet modem. Once the connection is established, your computer is "on the Internet." When you complete an Internet session and log off, your modem "hangs up" and the connection is discontinued until the next time you dial in.

Theoretically, the top speed of a dial-up connection is 56 Kbps, meaning that 56,000 bits of data are transmitted per second. Actual speed is usually reduced by distance, interference, and other technical problems, however, so the speed of most 56 Kbps dial-up connections is more like 45 Kbps. This speed is usable for e-mail, e-commerce, and chat. It is not, however, optimal for applications that require large amounts of data to be quickly transferred over the Internet. Watching an Internet-based video or participating in a teleconference over a 56 Kbps dial-up connection can be like watching a badly organized parade—the sound can be out of sync with the image, and the "show" can be interrupted by lengthy pauses as your computer waits for the next set of video frames to arrive.

Does a cable modem provide a faster Internet connection? Many cable TV companies offer Internet access in addition to the traditional roster of movie channels, network television, and specialty channels. This type of Internet access, often referred to as "cable modem service," is offered to a cable company's customers for an additional monthly charge. Cable modem service usually requires two pieces of equipment: a network card and a cable modem. A network card is a device that's designed to connect a personal computer to a local area network—when you get cable modem service, this card allows you to join a computer network that provides Internet access. Many of today's computers come equipped with a preinstalled network card. If not, one can be added for less than $50. A **cable modem** (Figure 1-16) is a device that changes a computer's signals into a form that can travel over cable TV links. Cable modems can be installed by consumers or installed (sometimes for a fee) by the "cable guy" and typically remain the property of the cable company.

FIGURE 1-16
A cable modem can be a standalone device set up close to a computer, or it can be integrated with other electronic components in a "set-top box" on top of a television.

Cable modem service is referred to as an **always-on connection** because your computer is, in effect, always connected to the Internet, unlike a dial-up connection that is established only when the dialing sequence is completed. An always-on connection is convenient because you don't have to wait 30–40 seconds for the dial-answer sequence to be completed. A cable modem receives data at about 1.5 Mbps (1.5 million bits per second), which is more than 25 times faster than a dial-up connection. This speed is suitable for most Internet activities, including real-time video and teleconferencing.

What about access provided by a school or business network? The computers in a school lab or business are usually connected to a LAN that is linked to the Internet. These networked computers offer an always-on connection, similar to cable modem service. School and business networks do not, however, typically access the Internet via a cable company. Instead they use a high-speed telecommunications link dedicated solely to Internet access.

What other high-speed Internet access options are available? Many telephone and independent telecommunications companies offer high-speed Internet access over ISDN and DSL lines. **ISDN** (Integrated Services Digital Network) provides data transfer speeds of 64 Kbps or 128 Kbps. With substantial monthly fees and data transfer speeds that are only marginally better than a free 56 Kbps dial-up connection, ISDN ranks low on the list of high-speed Internet options for most consumers.

DSL (Digital Subscriber Line) is a generic name for a family of high-speed Internet links, including ADSL, SDSL, and DSL lite. Each type of DSL provides different maximum speeds—from twice as fast to approximately 125 times faster than a 56 Kbps dial-up connection. The faster types of DSL require professional installation, but DSL lite can be installed by consumers.

Both ISDN and DSL connections require proximity to a telephone switching station, which can be a problem for speed-hungry consumers in rural areas. Satellite dishes to the rescue! **DSS** (Digital Satellite Service) offers Internet access at an average speed of about 500 Kbps. Monthly fees for a DSS connection are typically more than DSL or cable modem service. DSS customers are also required to rent or purchase a satellite dish and pay for its installation.

INTERNET SERVICE PROVIDERS

What's an ISP? To access the Internet, you do not typically connect your computer directly to the backbone. Instead, you connect it to an ISP such as AOL (America Online), which in turn connects to the backbone. An **ISP** (Internet service provider) is a company that maintains Internet computers and telecommunications equipment in order to provide Internet access to businesses, organizations, and individuals. An ISP that offers dial-up connections, for example, maintains a bank of modems, which communicate with modems in customers' computers.

An ISP works in much the same way as a local telephone company. Just as a telephone company provides a point of access to telephones all over the world, an ISP is a point of access to the Internet. ISP customers arrange for service—in this case, for Internet access—for which they pay a monthly fee. In addition to a monthly fee, an ISP might also charge an installation fee. Dial-up subscribers might also be required to pay per-minute fees for long-distance access.

What's the difference between a local ISP and a national ISP? A local ISP usually supplies Internet access within a limited geographical area, such as within a particular city. Local ISPs typically provide dial-up service through a local telephone number.

A national ISP supplies access for customers spread throughout a large geographical area. AT&T WorldNet, for example, offers dial-up access numbers in more than 500 cities. Customers who live in or travel to any of these cities can use the access numbers without additional long-distance fees. Figure 1-17 lists some popular national ISPs.

FIGURE 1-17
Popular ISPs

ISP	SPECIALTY
AOL	Dial-up, cable
AOL Canada	Dial-up
AT&T WorldNet	Dial-up
AT&T Canada	Dial-up
Charter	Cable
Comcast	Cable
Cox	Cable
DirecWay	DSS
Earthlink	Dial-up, DSS
MSN	Dial-up, cable

How can I find a list of ISPs that provide service in my area? The Yellow Pages typically list ISPs under "Internet." Also, check newspaper ads for new services that are being offered in your area. Your computer might include a directory of national ISPs. Look for an Internet Connection icon on your desktop, or browse through the options on the Start menu to find the Internet Connection Wizard.

How do I choose an ISP? Selecting an ISP depends on a variety of factors, such as where service is provided; the speed of data transfer; and the cost of equipment, installation, and monthly service (Figure 1-18).

FIGURE 1-18

Choosing an ISP

Geographical Coverage	The ISP you select should provide service in the places that you typically use your computer. If your work takes you on the road a lot, you'll want to consider a national ISP that provides local access numbers in the cities you visit. Retirees and students who migrate between locations might also consider a national ISP. For homebodies, a local ISP is usually a very acceptable option. With cable modem or DSL service, your computer must remain tethered to your service provider's network, which does not provide Internet access while traveling.
Type of Service	Some ISPs specialize in one type of service. A company that offers dial-up connections might not also offer cable connections. If you want a particular type of service—cable modem service, for example—you might not have a choice of providers.
Quality of Service	The quality of dial-up and cable modem services tends to decrease as the number of customers increases. In the case of dial-up connections, too many customers clamoring for modem connections can result in busy signals when you try to connect to your ISP. Cable modem service works sort of like a lawn sprinkler system that's connected to a small water pump. With only one sprinkler, the water gushes out. Connect 100 sprinklers to the system and the gushing turns into a trickle. Because all the subscribers in your neighborhood use the same data "pipe," as more and more of your neighbors go online, the effective speed of your cable connection can deteriorate. Ask an ISP's current customers what they think of the access speed. Is it consistent, or does it deteriorate during peak usage hours?
Cost of Monthly Service	In the United States and Canada, monthly service fees vary from about $15–$20 per month for dial-up service to $50–$60 per month for basic cable service. ISP rate plans might offer unlimited access for a flat monthly fee. Other rate plans include a limited number of hours; if you're online for additional hours, you'll pay by the hour. Outside the United States and Canada, many ISPs charge by the minute for Internet access.
Cost of Equipment and Installation	When considering the cost of Internet service, it is important to factor in the cost of equipment and installation. Whereas a modem is relatively inexpensive, a satellite dish costs several hundred dollars. Installation can also be costly—sometimes exceeding $100.
Extra Services	An ISP typically provides a connection to the Internet and an e-mail account. It might also offer useful extra services, such as multiple e-mail accounts so that all members of your family can send and receive their own e-mail messages. Some ISPs, such as AOL, offer a host of proprietary services that are available only to subscribers. These services might include content channels with substantive articles on health, hobbies, investing, and sports; activities specially designed for kids and teens; online shops that comply with high standards for security and customer satisfaction; a variety of voice and text messaging services; and collections of free (and virus-free) software. To find out if proprietary features should influence your ISP choice, talk to subscribers who have similar computer experience; ask them if these features are useful.
Customer Service	Most ISPs are prepared to answer customers' questions over the phone or via e-mail. The critical customer service question is "How long will it take to get a response?" Some national ISPs are notorious for keeping customers on hold for hours, and an e-mail reply can take days. Given a choice, most customers prefer an ISP that can respond quickly. To get an idea of an ISP's response time and expertise, talk to current customers.

USER IDS AND PASSWORDS

Is access to the Internet restricted in any way? Although the Internet is a public network, access to the Internet, or to some parts of the Internet, can be restricted in various ways. For example, an ISP usually limits Internet access to its subscribers. Some parts of the Internet—such as military computers—are off limits to the general public. In addition, some parts of Web sites—such as the *New York Times* archives—limit access to paid members. Many parts of the Internet encourage memberships and offer additional perks if you sign up.

User IDs and passwords are designed to provide access for authorized users and to prevent unauthorized access. A **user ID** is a series of characters—letters and possibly numbers—that becomes a person's unique identifier, similar to a social security number. A **password** is a different series of characters that verifies the user ID, similar to the way a PIN (personal identification number) verifies your identity at an ATM machine. Typically, your ISP supplies a user ID and password that you use to connect to the Internet. You will accumulate additional user IDs and passwords from other sources for specific Internet activities, such as reading *New York Times* articles or participating in an online auction. The process of entering a user ID and password is usually referred to as "logging in" or "logging on" (Figure 1-19).

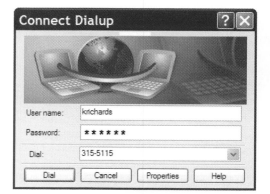

FIGURE 1-19
Typically, when you log in and enter your password, a series of asterisks appears on the screen to prevent someone from looking over your shoulder to discover your password.

Can I choose my own user ID? In some cases, you are allowed to select your user ID, but in other cases, it might be assigned by your service provider. Often a user ID is a variation of your name. Brunhilde Jefferson's user ID might be bjeffe, bjefferson, brunhilde_jefferson, or bjeff0918445.

The rules for creating a user ID are not consistent throughout the Internet, so it is important to read all the instructions carefully before finalizing your ID. For example, spaces might not be allowed in a user ID. Hence, the underline in brunhilde_jefferson is used instead of a space. There might be a length limitation, so Ms. Jefferson might have to choose a short user ID, such as bjeffe.

Some Internet computers don't differentiate between uppercase and lowercase letters, and would consider the user IDs B_Jefferson and b_jefferson to be the same. Other computers are **case sensitive** and differentiate between uppercase and lowercase. On such computers, if Ms. Jefferson selected Brun_Jeff as her user ID, she would not be able to gain access by typing brun_jeff. To avoid such problems, most people stick to lowercase letters for their user IDs.

How do I choose a secure password? Even when you are assigned a "starter" password, you should select a new password immediately, and then change it periodically. Don't share your password with anyone or write it down where it could be found. If your password is discovered, someone could log on and pretend to be you—sending inflammatory e-mail under your name and signing up for memberships at unsavory Web sites.

Your password should be a sequence of characters that is easy for you to remember, but would be difficult for someone else to guess. After all, your password provides protection only if it is secret (Figure 1-20).

 Do select a password that is at least five characters long

 Do try to use both numbers and letters in your password

 Do select a password that you can remember

 Do consider making a password by combining two or more words or the first letters of a poem or phrase

 Do change your password if you think that someone discovered it

 Don't select a password that can be found in a dictionary

 Don't use your name, nickname, social security number, birth date, or name of a close relative

 Don't write your password where it is easy to find—under the keyboard is the first place that a password thief will look

 Don't let anyone use your password "temporarily" to access Web sites or log on to your ISP

FIGURE 1-20
Use these tips to select a secure password.

How do I remember my passwords? When you use the Internet, you accumulate a batch of passwords—from your ISP, from online shopping sites, from your online travel agent, and maybe even from your favorite news and information sites. The problem is not remembering *one* password; it's remembering lots of different passwords and their corresponding user IDs.

Your passwords provide the most protection if they are unique, but if you want access to 40 different Internet sites that require passwords, you'll need a really good memory to remember 40 unique passwords and 40 user IDs. You can, of course, resort to writing them down. That practice, however, makes them much more susceptible to thievery.

Instead of using 40 different user IDs and passwords, you need some way to reduce the number of things you have to memorize. First, strive to select a unique user ID that you can use for more than one site. Remember that people with the same name who selected user IDs before you might have already taken the obvious user IDs. For example, when John Smith selects a user ID, you can bet that other people have already used johnsmith, jsmith, and john_smith. To keep his user ID unique, John might instead select jsl2wm (the first letters in "John Smith loves 2 watch movies").

Next, select two passwords—one for high security and one for low security. Use your high-security password to protect critical data—for online banking, for managing an online stock portfolio, or for your account at an online bookstore that stores a copy of your billing and credit card information. Change your high-security password periodically in all the places that you use it.

Use your low-security password in situations where you don't really care if your security is compromised. Some places on the Internet want you to establish an account with a user ID and password just to collect basic contact information and put your name on a mailing list. At other sites, your user ID and password provide access to information, but none of your own data (a credit card number, for example) is stored there. It is not necessary to change your low-security password very often.

QUICKCHECK......SECTION B

1. The main routes of the Internet are referred to as the Internet [_____].

2. Communication between all the different devices on the Internet is made possible by TCP/[_____].

3. The process of transferring a file from a remote computer to a local computer is referred to as [_____].

4. A(n) [_____] is a personal journal posted on the Web for access by the general public.

5. A(n) [_____] modem converts your computer's digital data into signals that can travel over telephone lines.

6. Dial-up, cable modem, and DSL service are examples of always-on connections. True or false? [_____]

7. ISDN and [_____] service require proximity to a telephone switching station, so they might not be available to rural customers.

8. Quality of [_____] from an Internet service provider can deteriorate as the number of customers increases.

9. [_____] sensitive computers distinguish between uppercase and lowercase letters.

10. When logging on to a computer or network, your [_____] verifies your user ID.

 CHECK ANSWERS

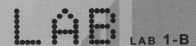

LAB 1-B
MAKING A DIAL-UP CONNECTION

In this lab, you'll learn:

- How to connect a computer to your telephone line
- How to connect your computer and your phone to the same wall plug
- The general procedure for subscribing to an ISP
- How to connect to the Internet using ISP-provided software
- Why you might need to manually create a dial-up connection
- What information is necessary to create a dial-up connection
- How to create your own customized dial-up icon
- How to use a dial-up icon to connect to your ISP
- How to disconnect at the end of an Internet session

INTERACTIVE LAB

CLICK TO START THE LAB

LAB ASSIGNMENTS

1. Start the interactive part of the lab. Insert your Tracking Disk if you want to save your QuickCheck results. Perform each lab step as directed, and answer all the lab QuickCheck questions. When you exit the lab, your answers are automatically graded and your results are displayed.

2. Make a list of at least five ISPs that are available in your area. If possible, include both local and national ISPs in your list.

3. Suppose that you intend to manually create a dial-up connection icon for AT&T WorldNet. What information do you need, in addition to the following, to create this dial-up connection?

   - AT&T's dial-in telephone number
   - AT&T's IP address
   - Your password

4. List the following information about the Internet connection you typically use: name of ISP, type of Internet connection (dial-up, DSL, cable modem, ISDN, DSS, school network, or business network), connection speed, and monthly fee. (If you don't currently have Internet access, describe the type of connection you would like to use.)

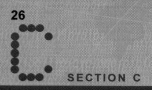
SECTION C

WEB BASICS

Once you have Internet access, you can begin to explore its many resources. The Web is one of the Internet's top attractions, used by millions of people every day. It is simple to use, yet provides access to a huge collection of information, including online stores, health information, stock quotes, genealogy data, dictionaries, online courses, music, photos, and videos.

Section C provides a basic introduction to the Web. If you're familiar with the Web, this section gives you a better understanding of how it works. For those of you just embarking onto the Web, this section describes the tools and techniques you need to get started. The Browsing and Searching lab at the end of this section provides hands-on experience with two important Web tools—browsers and search engines.

THE WORLD WIDE WEB

What is the Web? One of the Internet's most captivating attractions, the **Web** (short for "World Wide Web") is a collection of files that can be linked and accessed using HTTP. **HTTP** (Hypertext Transfer Protocol) is the communications standard that's instrumental in ferrying Web documents to all corners of the Internet.

Many Web-based files produce documents called **Web pages**. Other files contain photos, videos, animations, and sounds that can be incorporated into specific Web pages. Most Web pages contain **links** (sometimes called "hyperlinks") to related documents and media files (Figure 1-21).

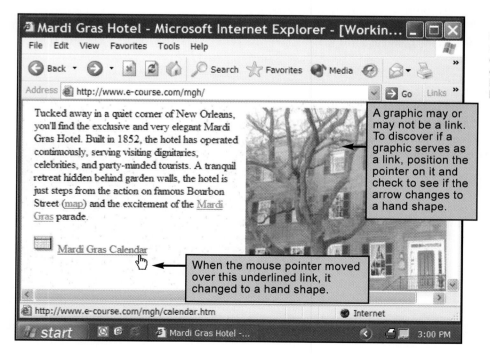

FIGURE 1-21
On most Web pages, underlined text indicates a link, but other objects can serve as links. To activate a link, simply click it.

What is a Web site? A series of Web pages can be grouped into a **Web site**—a sort of virtual "place" in cyberspace. Every day, thousands of people shop at Nordstrom's Web site, an online department store featuring clothing, shoes, and jewelry. Thousands of people visit the Webopedia Web site to look up the meaning of computer terms. At the ABC News Web site, people not only read about the latest news, sports, and weather, but also discuss current issues with other readers. The Web encompasses these and hundreds of thousands of other sites.

Web sites are hosted by corporate, government, college, and private computers all over the world. The computers and software that store and distribute Web pages are called **Web servers**.

What is a URL? Every Web page has a unique address called a **URL** (Uniform Resource Locator, pronounced "You Are ELL"). For example, the URL for the Cable News Network Web site is *http://www.cnn.com*. Most URLs begin with http:// to indicate the Web's standard communications protocol. When typing a URL, the http:// can usually be omitted, so *www.cnn.com* works just as well as *http://www.cnn.com*.

Most Web sites have a main page that acts as a "doorway" to the rest of the pages at the site. This main page is sometimes referred to as a "home page," although this term has another meaning that's discussed later in this chapter. The URL for a Web site's main page is typically short and to the point, like *www.cnn.com*.

The pages for a Web site are typically stored in topic area folders, which are reflected in the URL. For example, the CNN site might include a weather center at *www.cnn.com/weather/* and an entertainment desk at *www.cnn.com/showbiz/*. A series of Web pages are then grouped under the appropriate topic. For example, you might find a page about hurricanes at the URL *www.cnn.com/weather/hurricanes.html,* and you could find a page about El Niño at *www.cnn.com/weather/elnino.html*. The file name of a specific Web page always appears last in the URL—*hurricanes.html* and *elnino.html* are the names of two Web pages. Web page file names usually have an .htm or .html extension, indicating that the page was created with **HTML** (Hypertext Markup Language), a standard format for Web documents. Figure 1-22 identifies the parts of a URL.

FIGURE 1-22

The URL for a Web page indicates the computer on which it is stored, its location on the Web server, its file name, and its extension.

http://www.cnn.com/showbiz/movies.htm

| Web protocol standard | Web server name | Folder name | Document name and file extension |

What are the rules for correctly typing a URL? A URL never contains a space, even after a punctuation mark, so do not type any spaces within a URL. An underline character is sometimes used to give the appearance of a space between words, as in the URL *www.detroit.com/top_10.html*. Be sure to use the correct type of slash—always a forward slash (/)—and duplicate the URL's capitalization exactly. The servers that run some Web sites are case sensitive, which means that an uppercase letter is not the same as a lowercase letter. On these servers, typing *www.cmu.edu/Overview.html* (with an uppercase "O") will not locate the page that's actually stored as *www.cmu.edu/overview.html* (with a lower-case "o").

BROWSERS

What is a browser? A Web browser—usually referred to simply as a **browser**—is a software program that runs on your computer and helps you access Web pages. Two of today's most popular browsers are Microsoft Internet Explorer (IE) and Netscape Navigator (Navigator). A browser window is typically divided into the sections shown in Figure 1-23.

INFOWEBLINKS

The best-selling browsers are updated on a regular basis, and occasionally new browsers challenge the old standbys. For up-to-the-minute information on these impor-tant Web tools, tune into the **Browser InfoWeb**.

www.course.com/np/concepts8/ch01

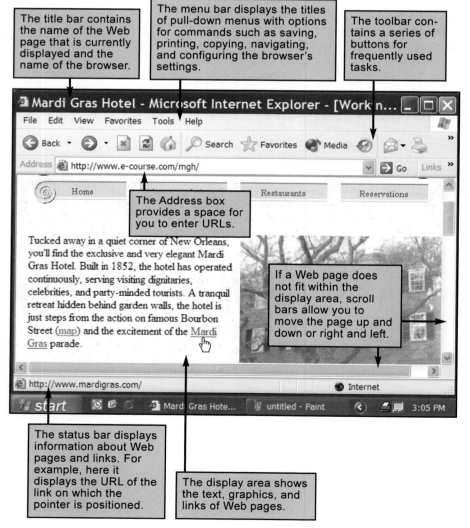

The title bar contains the name of the Web page that is currently displayed and the name of the browser.

The menu bar displays the titles of pull-down menus with options for commands such as saving, printing, copying, navigating, and configuring the browser's settings.

The toolbar con-tains a series of buttons for frequently used tasks.

The Address box provides a space for you to enter URLs.

If a Web page does not fit within the display area, scroll bars allow you to move the page up and down or right and left.

The status bar displays information about Web pages and links. For example, here it displays the URL of the link on which the pointer is positioned.

The display area shows the text, graphics, and links of Web pages.

FIGURE 1-23

A browser provides a sort of "window" in which it displays a Web page. The borders of the window contain a set of menus and controls to help you navigate from one Web page to another.

Which features are common to most browsers? Despite small cosmetic differences and some variations in terminology, Web browsers offer a remarkably similar set of features and capabilities. Figure 1-24 provides a quick overview of browser features, and Lab 1-C shows you how to use them.

FIGURE 1-24
Most browsers provide a standard set of features that allow you to work with Web pages.

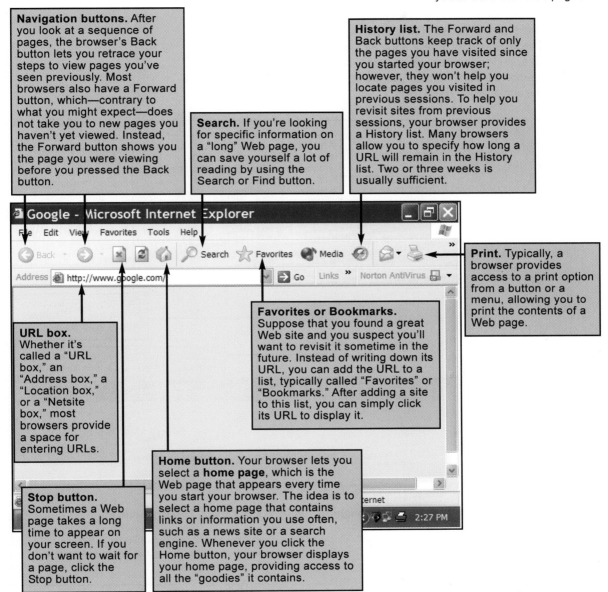

Navigation buttons. After you look at a sequence of pages, the browser's Back button lets you retrace your steps to view pages you've seen previously. Most browsers also have a Forward button, which—contrary to what you might expect—does not take you to new pages you haven't yet viewed. Instead, the Forward button shows you the page you were viewing before you pressed the Back button.

Search. If you're looking for specific information on a "long" Web page, you can save yourself a lot of reading by using the Search or Find button.

History list. The Forward and Back buttons keep track of only the pages you have visited since you started your browser; however, they won't help you locate pages you visited in previous sessions. To help you revisit sites from previous sessions, your browser provides a History list. Many browsers allow you to specify how long a URL will remain in the History list. Two or three weeks is usually sufficient.

Print. Typically, a browser provides access to a print option from a button or a menu, allowing you to print the contents of a Web page.

URL box. Whether it's called a "URL box," an "Address box," a "Location box," or a "Netsite box," most browsers provide a space for entering URLs.

Favorites or Bookmarks. Suppose that you found a great Web site and you suspect you'll want to revisit it sometime in the future. Instead of writing down its URL, you can add the URL to a list, typically called "Favorites" or "Bookmarks." After adding a site to this list, you can simply click its URL to display it.

Stop button. Sometimes a Web page takes a long time to appear on your screen. If you don't want to wait for a page, click the Stop button.

Home button. Your browser lets you select a **home page**, which is the Web page that appears every time you start your browser. The idea is to select a home page that contains links or information you use often, such as a news site or a search engine. Whenever you click the Home button, your browser displays your home page, providing access to all the "goodies" it contains.

Exactly what does a browser do? A browser fetches and displays Web pages. Suppose that you want to view the Web page located at *www.e-course.com/boxer.html.* You enter the URL into a special Address box that's provided by your browser. When you press the Enter key, the browser contacts the Web server at *www.e-course.com* and requests the *boxer.html* page. The server sends your computer the data stored in *boxer.html.* This data includes two things: the information you want to view, and embedded codes, called **HTML tags**, that tell your browser how to display it. The tags specify details such as the background color, the text color and size, and the placement of graphics. Figure 1-25 shows that a browser assembles a document on your computer screen according to the specifications contained in HTML tags.

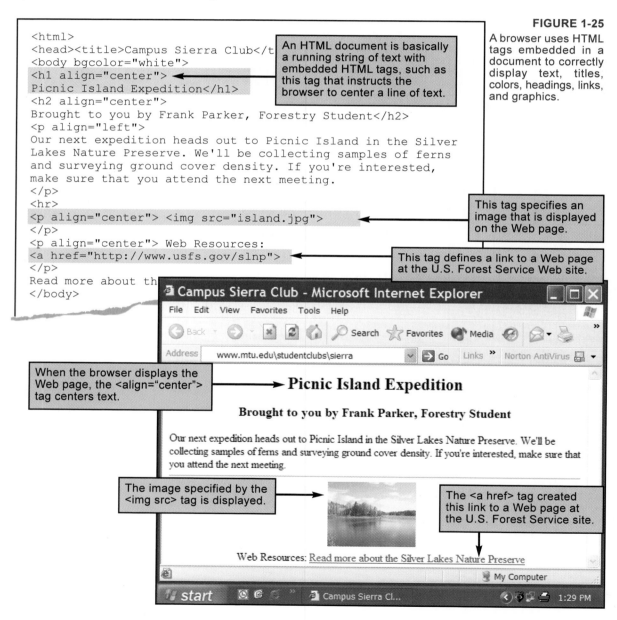

FIGURE 1-25

A browser uses HTML tags embedded in a document to correctly display text, titles, colors, headings, links, and graphics.

Can I copy and save information from a Web page? Most browsers provide a Copy command that allows you to copy a section of text from a Web page, which you can then paste into one of your own documents. To keep track of the source for each text section, you can use the Copy command to record the Web page's URL from the Address box, and then paste the URL into your document (Figure 1-26).

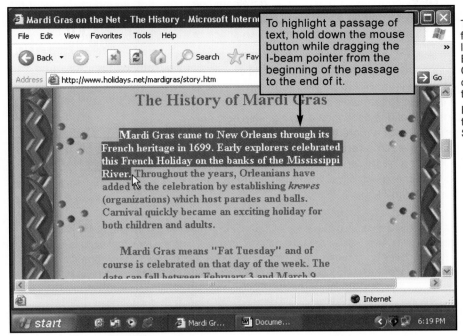

FIGURE 1-26

To copy a passage of text from a Web page, high-light the text, click the Edit menu, then select Copy. Next, switch to your own document and use the Paste option.

For a demonstration of this process, click the Start icon.

CLICK TO START ⁂

SEARCH ENGINES

What is a search engine? The term **search engine** popularly refers to a Web site that provides a variety of tools to help you find information. Search engines such as Google and Yahoo! are indispensable tools when it comes to finding information on the Web. Depending on the search engine you use, you can find information by entering a description, filling out a form, or clicking a series of links to drill down through a list of topics and subtopics. Based on your input, the search engine displays a list of Web pages like the one shown in Figure 1-27.

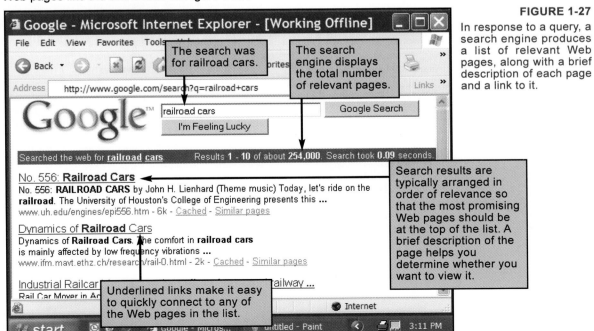

FIGURE 1-27

In response to a query, a search engine produces a list of relevant Web pages, along with a brief description of each page and a link to it.

Exactly what is a query? A **query** describes the information you want to find. It includes one or more keywords and can also include search operators. A **keyword** (sometimes called a "search term") is any word that describes the information you're trying to find. For example, *gorp* could be used as a keyword in a query for information about tasty trail mixes. You can enter more than one search term. Separate each term with a space or a search operator.

Search engines have a tendency to inundate you with possibilities—often finding thousands of potentially relevant Web pages. To receive a more manageable list of results, you need to formulate a more specific search. A **search operator** is a word or symbol that describes a relationship between keywords and thereby helps you create a more focused query. The search operators that you can use with each search engine vary slightly. To discover exactly how to formulate a query for a particular search engine, refer to its Help pages. Most search engines allow you to formulate queries with the search operators described in Figure 1-28.

INFOWEBLINKS

Search engines change at an astonishing rate. Visit the **Search Engine InfoWeb** for a list of popular search engines and their URLs, some comparative statistics, and tips on finding the search engine that's right for you.

www.course.com/np/concepts8/ch01

FIGURE 1-28
Search Operators

AND	When two search terms are joined by AND, both terms must appear on a Web page before it can be included in the search results. The query *railroad AND cars* will locate pages that contain both the words "railroad" and "cars." Your search results might include pages containing information about old railroad cars, about railroad car construction, and even about railroads that haul automobiles ("cars"). Some search engines use the plus symbol (+) instead of the word AND.
OR	When two search terms are joined by OR, either one or both of the search words could appear on a page. Entering the query *railroad OR cars* produces information about railroad fares, railroad routes, railroad cars, automobile safety records, and even car ferries.
NOT	The keyword following NOT must not appear on any of the pages found by the search engine. Entering *railroad NOT cars* would tell the search engine to look for pages that include "railroad" but not the keyword "cars." In some search engines, the minus sign (-) can be used instead of the word NOT.
Quotation Marks	Surrounding a series of keywords with quotation marks indicates that the search engine must treat the words as a phrase. The complete phrase must exist on a Web page for it to be included in the list of results. Entering *"green card"* would indicate that you are looking for information on immigration, not information on the color green, golf greens, or greeting cards.
NEAR	The NEAR operator tells a search engine that you want documents in which one of the keywords is located close to but not necessarily next to the other keyword. The query *library NEAR/15 congress* means that the words "library" and "congress" must appear within 15 words of each other. Successful searches could include documents containing phrases such as "Library of Congress" or "Congress funds special library research."
Wildcards	The asterisk (*) is sometimes referred to as a "wildcard character." It allows a search engine to find pages with any derivation of a basic word. For example, the query *medic** would not only produce pages containing the word "medic," but also "medics," "medicine," "medical," "medication," and "medicinal."
Field Searches	Some search engines allow you to search for a Web page by its title or by any part of its URL. The query *T:Backcountry Recipe Book* indicates that you want to find a specific Web page titled "Backcountry Recipe Book." In this search, the *T:* tells the search engine to look at Web page titles, and the information following the colon identifies the name of the title.

How do I use a topic directory? A **topic directory** is a list of topics and subtopics, such as Arts, Business, Computers, and so on, which are arranged in a hierarchy (Figure 1-29). The top level of the hierarchy contains general topics. Each successive level of the hierarchy contains increasingly specific subtopics. A topic directory might also be referred to as a "category list," an "index," or a "directory."

FIGURE 1-29

To use a topic directory, simply click a general topic. When a list of subtopics appears, click the one that's most relevant to the information you are trying to locate. If your selection results in another list of subtopics, continue to select the most relevant one until the search engine presents a list of Web pages. You can then link to these pages just as though you had used a keyword query.

CLICK TO START

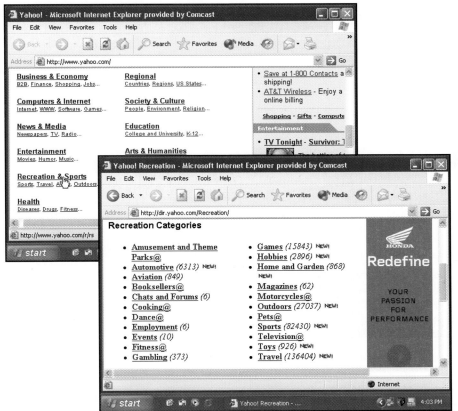

Reproduced with permission of Yahoo! Inc. © 2004 by Yahoo! Inc. YAHOO! and the YAHOO! logo are trademarks of Yahoo! Inc.

How do I use a search form to find information? Many search engines provide an advanced search form that helps you formulate a very targeted search. A search form, like the one shown in Figure 1-30, helps you enter complex queries. It might also allow you to search for pages that are written in a particular language, located on a specific Web server, or created within a limited range of dates.

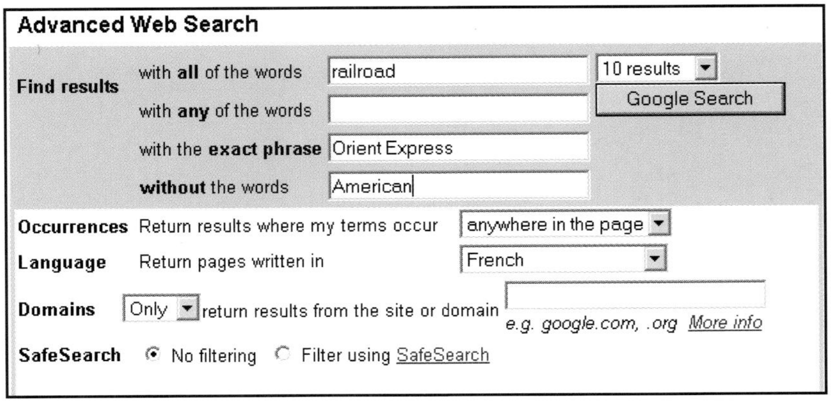

FIGURE 1-30

Many search engines provide forms that are designed to simplify the search process. These forms are usually accessible by clicking an Advanced Search link, which often is located on the main page of the search engine Web site.

Can't I just ask a simple question and get an answer? Instead of entering a cryptic query such as *movie+review+"The Producers"*, wouldn't it be nice to enter a more straightforward question like *Where can I find a review of The Producers?* A few search engines specialize in natural language queries, which accept questions written in plain English (Figure 1-31).

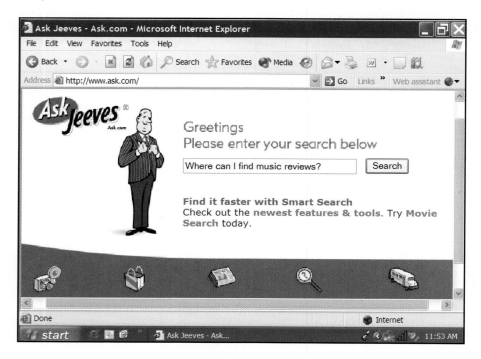

FIGURE 1-31
Some search engines accept natural language queries.

QUICKCHECK......SECTION C

1. HTTP ([   ] Transfer Protocol) is the communications standard for the Web.

2. Every Web page has a unique address called a(n) [   ]. Hint: Use the abbreviation.

3. A browser assembles a Web page on your computer screen according to the specifications contained in [   ] tags.

4. Google and Yahoo! are examples of [   ] engines.

5. The [   ] *railroad AND cars* will locate pages that contain both the words "railroad" and "cars."

6. Search [   ], such as AND and OR, help you create targeted searches.

7. A natural [   ] search engine accepts questions written in plain English.

✦ CHECK ANSWERS

LAB
LAB 1-C
BROWSING AND SEARCHING

1

In this lab, you'll learn:

- How to work with the URL box, site list, and History list
- How to use links and navigation buttons
- How to work with Bookmarks and Favorites lists
- What to do if you encounter a "page not found" message
- How to change your home page
- How to access a search engine
- Where to get help about using a search engine
- How to enter a keyword search query
- How to use a topic directory
- How to use the results list provided by a search engine

LAB ASSIGNMENTS

1. Start the interactive part of the lab. Insert your Tracking Disk if you want to save your QuickCheck results. Perform each lab step as directed, and answer all the lab QuickCheck questions. When you exit the lab, your answers are automatically graded and your results are displayed.

2. Make a note of the brand and location of the computer you're using to complete these lab assignments.

3. Examine the Favorites or Bookmarks list. How many pages are included in this list? Link to three of the pages, indicate their URLs, and provide a brief description of their contents.

4. Suppose that you want to make your own trail mix, but you need a recipe. Enter the query *"trail mix" AND recipe* in three different search engines. (Refer to the Search Engine InfoWeb for a list of popular search engines.) Describe the similarities and differences in the results lists the three search engines produce.

5. Use the search engine of your choice to determine whether the query

   "Blue book price" Taurus -"used car"

   produces the same results as the query

   Blue book price Taurus -"used car"

   Make sure you enter each query exactly as specified, including the quotation marks (no space after the hyphen). Explain the similarities and differences in the query results.

SECTION D
E-MAIL BASICS

The Internet really took off when people discovered electronic mail. More than 15 billion e-mail messages speed over the Internet each year. E-mail, which is derived from the term "electronic mail," can refer to a single message or to the entire system of computers and software that transmits, receives, and stores e-mail messages. In this section of the chapter, you get some background information about how e-mail works—in particular, the difference between "free" Web-based e-mail and "traditional" store-and-forward e-mail. The lab for this section provides a hands-on overview of how to read, compose, send, and reply to e-mail messages.

E-MAIL OVERVIEW

Who can use e-mail? Any person with an e-mail account can send and receive e-mail. An **e-mail account** provides the rights to a storage area, or "mailbox," supplied by an e-mail provider, such as an ISP. Each mailbox has a unique address, which typically consists of a user ID, an @ symbol, and the name of the computer that maintains the mailbox. For example, suppose that a university student named Dee Greene has an electronic mailbox on a computer called rutgers.edu. If her user ID is "dee_greene," her e-mail address would be *dee_greene@rutgers.edu*.

Exactly what is an e-mail message? An **e-mail message** is a document that is composed on a computer and remains in digital, or "electronic," form so that it can be transmitted to another computer. The **message header** includes the recipient's e-mail address, message subject, and attachment file name. The body of the e-mail contains your message. The message header and body are usually displayed in a form, as shown in Figure 1-32.

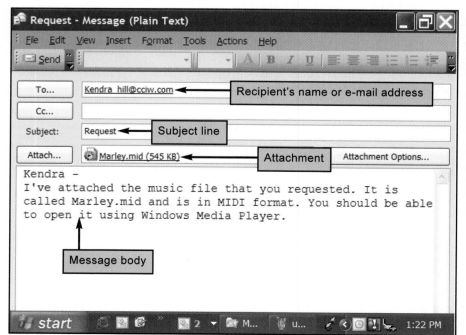

FIGURE 1-32

When you compose an e-mail message, you can begin by entering the address of one or more recipients and the subject of the message. You can also specify one or more files to attach to the message. The body of the e-mail message contains the message itself.

When the message is sent, your e-mail software adds the date and your e-mail address to identify you as the sender.

What can I do with basic e-mail? Basic e-mail activities consist of writing, reading, replying to (Figure 1-33), and forwarding messages. Messages can be printed, kept for later reference, or deleted.

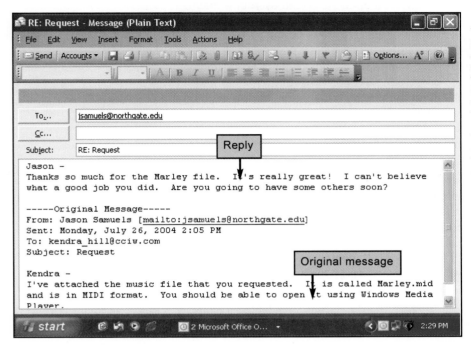

FIGURE 1-33

Your e-mail client's Reply button creates a new e-mail message and auto-matically addresses it to the person who sent the original message. Most e-mail systems also copy the text of the original message into the reply so that everyone has a complete transcript of the messages that were exchanged.

How does forwarding work? After you receive an e-mail message, you can use the Forward feature to pass it on to other people. You might, for example, forward a message that was sent to you but that should be handled by someone else. When you initiate the forwarding process, the original e-mail message is copied into a new message window, complete with the address of the original sender. You can then enter the address of the person to whom you are forwarding the message. You can also add a note about why you are passing the message along.

Some e-mail systems allow you to alter the text of the original message before you forward it. If you do so, include a note explaining your changes, especially if they alter the intent of the original message. You should not forward messages that were intended to be confidential. If you think that such a message needs to be shared with other people, obtain permission from the author of the original message.

What's an e-mail attachment? Originally, e-mail messages were stored in a plain and simple format called "ASCII text." No fancy formatting was allowed—no variation in font type or color, no underlining or boldface, and, of course, no pictures or sounds. Although you cannot insert a digital photo or sound file into a plain ASCII e-mail message, you can send these kinds of files as e-mail attachments. Any file that travels with an e-mail message is called an **e-mail attachment**. A conversion process called **MIME** (Multi-Purpose Internet Mail Extensions) provides a clever way of disguising digital photos, sounds, and other media as plain ASCII text that can travel over the Internet as e-mail attachments. An electronic message incorporated in the e-mail header provides your e-mail software with the information that allows it to reconstruct the attachment into its original form.

Suppose you want to e-mail a photo of your high school reunion to a friend. The photo is stored in a file called Reunion.gif. You can address an e-mail message to your friend, write a short note ("You missed a really fun reunion!"), and then use the Attachment option provided by your e-mail software to specify that the file Reunion.gif should accompany the e-mail. Your e-mail software converts Reunion.gif into a MIME format and sends it along with your message. When your friend receives the message, her e-mail software reconstitutes the file into your reunion photo. The way that the attachment is displayed on screen depends on your friend's e-mail software. The photo might appear at the end of the e-mail, or she might have to double-click an attachment icon to see it. With some e-mail systems, she might have to download the attachment file, and then open it using the same software with which it was created.

How does HTML relate to e-mail? Most e-mail software allows you to create e-mail messages in HTML format. Why use HTML format for your mail? HTML messages can contain lots of fancy formatting that's just not possible with plain ASCII text. By selecting your e-mail software's HTML option, you enter a world of colored, bold, italic, and underlined text; fancy fonts; embedded graphics; and various font sizes. The only limitation is that your e-mail recipients must have HTML-compliant e-mail software. Otherwise, your message will be delivered as plain, unformatted ASCII text.

What other e-mail features are available? In addition to attachments and HTML formatting, today's sophisticated e-mail systems typically offer features that help you perform the tasks listed in Figure 1-34.

FIGURE 1-34
E-mail features provide flexibility for sending and receiving messages.

- Maintain an address book and use it to select e-mail addresses instead of entering them every time you compose a message.
- Use the address book to send mail to a "group" that consists of several e-mail addresses.
- Send a "carbon copy" (Cc:) of a message to one or more recipients.
- Send a "blind carbon copy" (Bcc:), which hides the addresses in the Bcc: field from other recipients of the message.
- Assign a priority to a message—high priority is usually indicated by an exclamation point or red text.
- Find a particular message in your list of old mail.
- Enlarge text size for easier reading.
- Sort messages by date received, sender's name, subject, or priority.
- Refuse to accept messages that arrive from a particular e-mail address.
- Automate replies to messages that you receive while on vacation or when you will not be responding to e-mail messages for a few days.
- Automatically fetch mail at specified intervals.
- Check spelling before sending a message.

NETIQUETTE

Is e-mail different from other types of communication? In some respects, e-mail is similar to an old-fashioned letter because its message is conveyed without benefit of the facial expressions, voice inflections, and body gestures that accompany face-to-face conversations. When composing a message, it is important to carefully consider your audience and the message you want to convey.

For example, you might have gotten into the habit of using text messaging shorthand to write messages such as "thnq 4 spking w me 2day. c u 2moro at 10." (Translation: Thank you for speaking with me today. See you tomorrow at 10:00.) Text messaging shorthand recently emerged as a quick and convenient way to communicate when using e-mail, instant messaging, and cell phone text messaging. Although text messaging shorthand works among your friends, it would not be appropriate in other situations, such as confirming the time for a job interview.

By understanding netiquette, you can avoid some of the pitfalls and problems of e-mail communications. **Netiquette** is online jargon for "Internet etiquette." It is a series of customs or guidelines for maintaining civilized and effective communications in online discussions and e-mail exchanges.

■ **Put a meaningful title on the subject line.** The subject line of your message should clearly describe the content of your e-mail message.

■ **Use uppercase and lowercase letters.** An e-mail message that's typed in all uppercase means that you're "shouting."

■ **Check spelling.** Most e-mail software offers a Check Spelling command. Use it.

■ **Be careful what you send.** E-mail is not private, nor is it secure. Treat your messages as though they are postcards that can be read by anyone. Remember that all laws governing copyright, slander, and discrimination apply to e-mail.

■ **Be polite.** Avoid wording that could sound inflammatory or argumentative. If you would not say it face-to-face, don't say it in e-mail.

■ **Be cautious when using sarcasm and humor.** The words in your e-mail arrive without facial expressions or voice intonations, so a sarcastic comment can easily be misinterpreted.

■ **Use smileys and text messaging shorthand cautiously. Smileys** are symbols that represent emotions (Figure 1-35). They can help convey the intent behind your words. Smileys and text messaging shorthand should be used only in correspondence with people who understand them.

■ **Use the Bcc function for group mailings.** By placing your list of e-mail addresses in the Bcc box, the recipients of your message won't have to scroll through a long list of addresses before reaching the "meat" of your message.

■ **Don't send replies to "all recipients."** Use the Reply All command only when there is a very specific need for everyone listed in the To, Cc, and Bcc boxes to receive the message.

■ **Don't send huge attachments.** Try to limit the size of attachments to 50 KB or less. If necessary, use a compression program, such as WinZip, to shrink the attachment.

■ **Explain all attachments.** Attachments can harbor computer viruses. To determine whether an attachment is legitimate, your correspondents will want to know the file name of the attachment, what the attachment contains, and the name of the software you used to create it.

■ **Stay alert for viruses.** Because viruses can tag along with e-mail attachments, don't open an attachment unless it was sent from a reliable source, its purpose is clearly explained in the body of the e-mail, and it was scanned using antivirus software (see Chapter 4).

■ **Notify recipients of viruses.** If you discover that your computer sent out infected attachments, use antivirus software to remove the virus, and then notify anyone to whom you recently sent mail.

INFOWEBLINKS

You can read more about netiquette, smileys, and text messaging shorthand at the **Netiquette InfoWeb**.

www.course.com/np/concepts8/ch01

FIGURE 1-35

Smileys, which are sometimes called "emoticons," are clever symbols that can be added to e-mail messages to convey emotions and take the edge off potentially inflammatory remarks.

"Don't take offense."

"Just kidding!"

"I'm not happy about that."

"I'm perplexed."

"I'm amazed."

SPAM

What is all this junk in my mailbox? One of e-mail's main disadvantages is **spam**—unwanted electronic junk mail about medical products, low-cost loans, and fake software upgrades that arrives in your online mailbox. Today's proliferation of spam is generated by marketing firms that harvest e-mail addresses from mailing lists, membership applications, and Web sites.

Globally, spam accounts for about 75% of all e-mail messages. Legislation to minimize spam has not met expectations. Although it is impossible to avoid spam, you can reduce it by following these guidelines:

- **Don't reply.** Never reply to spam when you receive it.

- **Guard your e-mail address.** Provide your e-mail address only to people from whom you want to receive e-mail. Be wary of providing your e-mail address at Web sites, entering it on application forms, or posting it in public places such as online discussion groups.

- **Use spam filters.** If your e-mail client offers a spam filter to block unwanted messages, put it to use. If your e-mail client does not provide a spam filter, you can download and install one from a shareware site on the Web. A **spam filter** automatically routes advertisements and other junk mail to the Deleted Items folder maintained by your e-mail client. Although spam filters can be effective for blocking spam and other unwanted e-mails, it sometimes blocks e-mail messages you want. After activating spam filters, periodically examine your Deleted Items folder to make sure the filters are not overly aggressive.

- **Report spam.** If your e-mail provider offers a way to report spam, use it.

- **Change your e-mail address.** When spam gets out of hand, you might have to consider changing your e-mail account so that you have a different e-mail address.

E-MAIL TECHNOLOGY

What is an e-mail system? An **e-mail system** is the equipment and software that carries and manipulates e-mail messages. It includes computers and software called **e-mail servers** that sort, store, and route mail. An e-mail system also includes the personal computers that belong to individuals who send and receive mail. E-mail is based on **store-and-forward technology**—a communications method in which data that cannot be sent directly to its destination is temporarily stored until transmission is possible. This technology allows e-mail messages to be routed to a server and held until they are forwarded to the next server or to a personal mailbox.

Three types of e-mail systems are widely used today: POP, IMAP, and Web-based mail. **POP** (Post Office Protocol) temporarily stores new messages in your mailbox on an e-mail server. When you connect to your ISP and request your mail, it is downloaded and stored on your computer. **IMAP** (Internet Messaging Access Protocol) is similar to POP, except that you have the option of downloading your mail or leaving it on the server. **Web-based e-mail** keeps your mail at a Web site, instead of transferring it to your computer.

How do I use Web-based e-mail? Before you can use Web-based e-mail, you need an e-mail account with a Web-based e-mail provider. To obtain one, simply connect to the Web-based e-mail provider's Web site and enter the information required to obtain an e-mail address, a user ID, and a password. Armed with these identifiers, you can connect to the e-mail Web site from any computer that has access to the Internet (Figure 1-36). At the Web site, you can write, read, reply to, and delete e-mail messages. Because most Web-based e-mail providers allocate a limited amount of space to each account, it is important to delete messages when you no longer need them. You don't want your electronic mailbox to overflow and cause some messages to be returned to the senders.

FIGURE 1-36

If you have a Web-based e-mail account, you can use a browser to access your e-mail messages. Writing, reading, replying to, forwarding, and deleting messages can be accomplished by interacting with a series of Web pages that lists your mail.

How do POP and IMAP work? Although you can choose to use Web-based mail, you usually don't have much choice about whether you'll use POP or IMAP—you use the one offered by your ISP. Of the two, POP is currently the most typical. Most people who use POP have obtained an e-mail account from an ISP. Such an account provides a mailbox on the ISP's **POP server**—a computer that stores your incoming messages until they can be transferred to your hard disk. Using POP requires **e-mail client software**, such as Microsoft Outlook or QUALCOMM Eudora. This software, which is installed on your computer, provides an Inbox and an Outbox that allow you to work with your mail, even when your computer is not online.

An Inbox holds incoming messages. When you ask the e-mail server to deliver your mail, all messages stored in your mailbox on the server are transferred to your computer, stored on your computer's disk drive, and listed as new mail in your Inbox. You can then disconnect from the Internet, if you like, and read the new mail at your leisure.

As shown in Figure 1-37, an Outbox temporarily holds messages you have composed and completed, but haven't transmitted over the Internet. Suppose you want to compose several e-mail messages. You can fire up your e-mail client software, but remain offline while you work on the messages. The ability to compose mail offline is especially useful if you access the Internet over a dial-up connection because the phone line isn't tied up while you compose mail. As you complete a message, it is stored on your computer and listed in the Outbox. When you go online, you

FIGURE 1-37

Outgoing mail can be stored in your Outbox until you connect to the Internet and send it. Incoming mail can be stored on a POP server until it is downloaded to the Inbox on your hard disk.

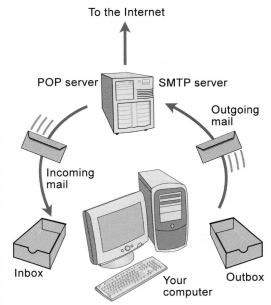

To the Internet

POP server   SMTP server

Outgoing mail

Incoming mail

Inbox   Your computer   Outbox

can send all the mail being held in your Outbox. Outgoing mail is routed by an **SMTP server** (Simple Mail Transfer Protocol server) instead of a POP server, as Figure 1-37 illustrates.

Does e-mail client software work only for offline e-mail tasks? No. Although you can use your e-mail client software to compose, read, and reply to messages while you're offline, you can also use it while you are online. In fact, this software often provides a setting that bypasses the Outbox and immediately sends messages out over the Internet.

Is POP mail better than Web-based e-mail? Before answering this question, let's review the important distinctions between the two types of e-mail. First, POP mail requires you to install and use e-mail client software, whereas Web-based e-mail allows you to use a browser as e-mail client software. Second, POP transfers messages to your computer's hard disk, whereas a Web-based e-mail system retains your messages on its server. Both e-mail systems have similar features, allowing you to read, compose, reply to, delete, and forward e-mail messages; maintain an address book; and send attachments. Each system does, however, have unique advantages. Your needs determine which system is better.

■ **Control.** POP mail gives you more control over your messages because they are transferred to your computer's hard disk, where you can control access to them. Web-based e-mail maintains your messages on its server, where you have less control over who can access them.

■ **Security.** When messages are stored on your computer, a hard disk drive malfunction could wipe out all your correspondence (along with the rest of your files). Your Web-based e-mail provider is rigorous about safeguarding its data, so your mail might be safer than if it was stored on your hard disk.

■ **Travel.** The major advantage of Web-based e-mail is that you can access your messages from any computer connected to the Internet. Therefore, you can get your e-mail when you travel without taking your computer. In contrast, with POP, your computer contains your old mail, your address book, and your e-mail software. Therefore, to use your familiar e-mail tools on the road, you really have to carry your computer with you.

INFOWEBLINKS

What's the latest news about e-mail client software? You'll find descriptions, reviews, and links at the **E-mail Client Software InfoWeb**.

www.course.com/np/concepts8/ch01

QUICKCHECK......SECTION D

1. In an e-mail address, the [＿＿＿＿＿＿] symbol separates the user ID from the name of the e-mail server.

2. E-mail attachments are typically converted using [＿＿＿＿＿＿], which disguises media and other files as plain ASCII text. Hint: Use the abbreviation.

3. Unwanted e-mail messages are called [＿＿＿＿＿＿].

4. Store-and-[＿＿＿＿＿＿] technology stores messages on an e-mail server until they are forwarded to an individual's computer.

5. For many e-mail systems, a(n) [＿＿＿＿＿＿] server handles outgoing mail, and a(n) [＿＿＿＿＿＿] server handles incoming mail.

✦ CHECK ANSWERS

LAB   LAB 1-D

USING E-MAIL

1

In this lab, you'll learn:

- How to open a Web-based e-mail account
- How to compose an e-mail message
- How to reply to a message
- How to intersperse your reply within the text of the original message
- How to delete a message
- How to print a message
- How to add a name to your address book
- How to create a group in your address book
- How to use your address book
- How to add an attachment to an e-mail message
- How to view an e-mail attachment

INTERACTIVE LAB

CLICK TO START THE LAB ✶

LAB ASSIGNMENTS

1. Start the interactive part of the lab. Insert your Tracking Disk if you want to save your QuickCheck results. Perform each lab step as directed, and answer all the lab QuickCheck questions. When you exit the lab, your answers are automatically graded and your results are displayed.

2. Using the e-mail software of your choice, send an e-mail message to *kendra_hill@cciw.com*. In the body of your message, ask for a copy of the "Most Influential Person Survey."

3. Wait a few minutes after sending the message to Kendra Hill, and then check your mail. You should receive a survey from Kendra Hill. Reply to this message and Cc: your instructor. In your reply, answer each question in the survey, interspersing your answers with the original text. Send the reply, following the procedures required by your e-mail provider.

4. Examine the address book offered by your e-mail software. Describe how much information (name, home address, business address, birth date, telephone number, fax number, and so on) you can enter for each person. In your opinion, would this address book be suitable for a business person to use for storing contact information? Why or why not? Send the descriptions and answers to these questions to your instructor in an e-mail.

TECHTALK

THE BOOT PROCESS

The sequence of events that occurs between the time that you turn on a computer and the time that it is ready for you to issue commands is referred to as the boot process or "booting" your computer. The term "boot" comes from the word "bootstrap," which describes a small loop on the back of a boot. Just as you can pull on a big boot using a small bootstrap, your computer boots up by first loading a small program into memory, and then it uses that small program to load a large operating system. Your computer's small bootstrap program is built into special ROM (read-only memory) circuitry housed in the computer's system unit. When you turn on a computer, the ROM circuitry receives power and begins the boot process.

With a Windows computer, the boot process usually proceeds smoothly and, in a short time, you can begin working with your application software. Sometimes, however, the boot process encounters a problem that must be fixed before you can begin a computing session. You can fix many of the problems a computer might encounter during the boot process. Make sure, however, that you follow the guidelines provided by your school or employer if you encounter equipment problems with computers in school labs or your workplace.

What's the purpose of the boot process? The **boot process** involves a lot of flashing lights, whirring noises, and beeping as your computer performs a set of diagnostic tests called the **power-on self-test** (POST). The good news is that these tests can warn you if certain crucial components of your computer system are out of whack. The bad news is that these tests cannot warn you of impending failures. Also, problems identified during the boot process usually must be fixed before you can start a computing session.

The boot process serves an additional purpose—loading the operating system from the hard disk into memory. Without the operating system, a computer's CPU is pretty much unable to communicate with any input, output, or storage devices. It can't display information, accept commands, store data, or run any application software. Therefore, loading the operating system is a crucial step in the boot process.

Why doesn't a computer simply leave the operating system in memory? Most of a computer's memory is "volatile" random access memory (RAM), which cannot hold any data when the power is off. Although a copy of the operating system is housed in RAM while the computer is in operation, this copy is erased as soon as the power is turned off.

In addition to RAM, computers have non-volatile memory circuitry, such as ROM and CMOS, which can store data even when the power is off. Typically, ROM and CMOS are not nearly large enough to store an entire operating system.

Given the volatility of RAM and the insufficient size of ROM and CMOS, computer designers decided to store the operating system on a computer's hard disk. During the boot process, a copy of the operating system is copied into RAM where it can be accessed quickly whenever the computer needs to carry out an input, output, or storage operation. The operating system remains in RAM until the computer is turned off (Figure 1-38).

FIGURE 1-38

The bootstrap program copies the operating system into RAM, where it can be directly accessed by the processor to carry out input, output, or storage operations.

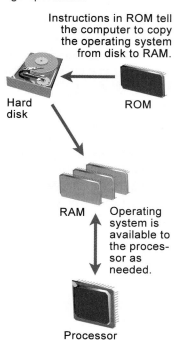

Instructions in ROM tell the computer to copy the operating system from disk to RAM.

Hard disk   ROM

RAM   Operating system is available to the processor as needed.

Processor

What is the order of events during the boot process? Six major events happen during the boot process:

1. Power up. When you turn on the power switch, the power light is illuminated, and power is distributed to the computer circuitry.

2. Start boot program. The microprocessor begins to execute the bootstrap program that is stored in ROM.

3. Power-on self-test. The computer performs diagnostic tests of several crucial system components.

4. Identify peripheral devices. The operating system identifies the peripheral devices that are connected to the computer and checks their settings.

5. Load operating system. The operating system is copied from the hard disk to RAM.

6. Check configuration and customization. The microprocessor reads configuration data and executes any customized startup routines specified by the user.

What if I turn on a computer and nothing happens? The first step in the boot process is the power-up stage. Power from a wall outlet or battery activates a small power light. If the power light does not come on when you flip the "on" switch, refer to the checklist in Figure 1-39.

What problems are likely to show up during the power-on self-test? The POST checks your computer's main circuitry, screen display, memory, and keyboard. It can identify when one of these devices has failed, but it cannot identify intermittent problems or impending failures.

The POST notifies you of a hardware problem by displaying an error message on the screen or by emitting a series of beeps. These error messages can help you pinpoint the source of a problem. Unfortunately, many computers display these error messages as numeric codes, such as "1790 Disk 0 Error." You can check the documentation or Web site for your computer to find the specific meaning of numeric error codes.

A **beep code** provides your computer with a way to signal a problem, even if the screen is not functioning. Two short beeps might mean a problem with the keyboard. Three long beeps might mean a problem with the screen display. Beep codes differ from one computer to another, depending on the ROM bootstrap program. The printed or online reference manual for a computer usually explains the meaning of each beep code.

Should I try to fix these problems myself? If a computer displays error messages, emits beep codes, or seems to "freeze up" during the boot process, you can take some simple steps that might fix it. First, turn the computer off. After the computer has powered off, wait five seconds, and then try to start the computer again and hope that the boot process proceeds smoothly. If the boot problem reoccurs, turn the computer off again and check all the cables that run between your computer and peripheral devices, such as the keyboard, mouse, and monitor. After checking the cables, try to boot again. If you still encounter a boot error, contact a technical support person.

FIGURE 1-39
Power-up Checklist

⏏ Make sure the power cable is plugged into the wall and into the back of the computer.

⎙ If you're using a notebook or tablet computer, check batteries or plug into a wall outlet.

⌨ Make sure the wall outlet is supplying power (plug in a lamp and make sure you can turn it on).

⏏ If the computer is plugged into a surge strip, extension cord, or uninterruptible power supply, make sure it is turned on and functioning correctly.

🔄 Can you hear the fan in your desktop computer? If not, the computer's power supply mechanism might have failed.

What's the long list of stuff that appears on my screen during the boot process? After the POST, the bootstrap program tries to identify all devices connected to the computer. On some computers, the settings for each device appear on the screen during the boot process, creating a list of rather esoteric information, as shown in Figure 1-40.

FIGURE 1-40
During the boot process, a computer attempts to identify storage devices, display devices, and other peripheral devices.

On occasion, a device gets skipped or misidentified during the boot process. An error message is not produced, but the device won't seem to work properly. To solve this problem, shut down the computer and reboot. If a device causes persistent problems, check the manufacturer's Web site to see if a new software "patch" will improve its operation.

Do computers have trouble loading the operating system? Problems during the last stages of the boot process are rare, except when a disk has been inadvertently left in the floppy disk drive. Before computers were equipped with hard disk drives, floppy disks were used to store the operating system and application software. As a legacy from these early machines, today's computers first check the floppy disk drive for a disk containing the operating system. If it doesn't find a disk in the drive, it merrily proceeds to look for the operating system on the hard disk. However, if a floppy disk happens to be hanging around in drive A, the computer assumes that you want to boot from it and looks for the operating system on that disk. The error message "Non-system disk or disk error" is the clue to this problem. Remove the floppy disk and press any key to resume the boot process.

How do I know when the boot process is finished? The boot process is complete when the computer is ready to accept your commands. Usually, the computer displays an operating system prompt or a main screen. The Windows operating system, for example, displays the Windows desktop when the boot process is complete.

If Windows cannot complete the boot process, you are likely to see a menu with an option for Safe Mode. **Safe Mode** is a limited version of Windows that allows you to use your mouse, monitor, and keyboard, but no other peripheral devices (Figure 1-41). This mode is designed for troubleshooting, not real computing tasks. If your computer enters Safe Mode at the end of the boot process, use the Shut Down command on the Start menu to properly shut down and turn off your computer. You can then turn on your computer again. It should complete the boot process in regular Windows mode. If your computer enters Safe Mode again, consult a technician.

FIGURE 1-41

Windows enters Safe Mode as a response to a problem—usually caused by the device driver software that controls a piece of peripheral equipment. You can also force a computer into Safe Mode by pressing the F8 key during the boot sequence.

When a computer is behaving erratically, does rebooting help? Under some circumstances—such as when a computer has been left on for a few weeks straight—the operating system seems to forget how to handle part of its job. Such problems can be caused by transient "soft errors" in the memory circuits that are supposed to hold the operating system instructions. In other cases, areas of memory that are supposed to be reserved for the operating system somehow get overwritten by snippets of application programs. The end effect is the same—parts of the operating system are missing and can't control a particular input, output, or storage function. As a result, a computer might begin to behave erratically. The remedy for this problem is to restore the operating system back to full functionality. Usually, rebooting does the trick. If not, consider the possibility that your computer might have contracted a virus. (More information on viruses can be found in Chapter 4.)

INFOWEBLINKS

Safe Mode can help technically savvy computer owners identify and fix a number of problems caused by installing new hardware devices. To learn more, check out the **Safe Mode InfoWeb**.

www.course.com/np/concepts8/ch01

QUICKCHECK........TECHTALK

1. The boot process loads the ☐ system from the hard disk into memory.

2. During the boot process, the ☐ checks your computer's main circuitry, screen display, memory, and keyboard.

3. Windows ☐ Mode provides a limited version of Windows that allows you to troubleshoot, but not use most peripheral devices.

4. If a computer is behaving erratically, rebooting might restore functionality. True or false? ☐

CHECK ANSWERS

ISSUE

E-MAIL PRIVACY

When you drop an envelope into the corner mailbox, you probably expect it to arrive at its destination unopened, with its contents kept safe from prying eyes. When you make a phone call, you might assume that your conversation will proceed unmonitored by wiretaps or other listening devices. Can you also expect an e-mail message to be read only by the person to whom it is addressed?

In the United States, the Electronic Communications Privacy Act of 2000 prohibits the use of intercepted e-mail as evidence unless a judge approved a search warrant. That doesn't mean the government isn't reading your mail. Heightened security concerns after the September 11, 2001 terrorist attacks resulted in the rapid passage of the Patriot Act, which became law on October 26, 2001. In an effort to assist law enforcement officials, the "Patriot Act" relaxes the rules for obtaining and implementing search warrants and lowers the Fourth Amendment standard for obtaining a court order to compel an ISP to produce e-mail logs and addresses.

To eavesdrop on e-mail from suspected terrorists and other criminals, the FBI developed a technology called Carnivore, which scans through messages entering and leaving an ISP's e-mail system to find e-mail associated with a person who is under investigation. Privacy advocates are concerned because Carnivore scans all messages that pass through an ISP, not just those messages sent to or received by a particular individual.

Although law enforcement agencies are required to obtain a court order before intercepting e-mail, no such restriction exists for employers who want to monitor employee e-mail. According to the American Management Association, 27% of U.S. businesses monitor employee e-mail. But this intentional eavesdropping is only one way in which the contents of your e-mail messages might become public. The recipient of your e-mail can forward it to one or more people—people you never intended for it to reach. Your e-mail messages could pop up on a technician's screen in the course of system maintenance, updates, or repairs. Also, keep in mind that e-mail messages—including those you delete from your own computer—can be stored on backups of your ISP's e-mail server. You might wonder if such open access to your e-mail is legal. The answer in most cases is yes.

The United States Omnibus Crime Control and Safe Streets Act of 1968 and the Electronic Communications Privacy Act of 1986 prohibit public and private employers from engaging in surreptitious surveillance of employee activity through the use of electronic devices. However, two exceptions to these privacy statutes exist. The first exception permits an employer to monitor e-mail if one party to the communication consents to the monitoring. An employer must inform employees of this policy before undertaking any monitoring. The second exception permits employers to monitor employees' e-mail if a legitimate business need exists, and the monitoring takes place within the business-owned e-mail system.

Employees generally have not been successful in defending their rights to e-mail privacy because courts have ruled that an employee's right to privacy does not outweigh a company's rights and interests. Courts seem to agree that because a company owns and maintains its e-mail system, it has the right to monitor the messages it carries.

Like employees of a business, students who use a school's e-mail system cannot be assured of e-mail privacy. When a CalTech student was accused of

sexually harassing a female student by sending lewd e-mail to her and her boyfriend, investigators retrieved all the student's e-mail from the archives of the e-mail server. The student was expelled from the university even though he claimed that the e-mail had been "spoofed" to make it look as though he had sent it, when it had actually been sent by someone else.

Why would an employer want to know the contents of employee e-mail? Why would a school be concerned with the correspondence of its students? It is probably true that some organizations simply snoop on the off chance that important information might be discovered. Other organizations have more legitimate reasons for monitoring e-mail. An organization that owns an e-mail system can be held responsible for the consequences of actions related to the contents of e-mail messages on that system. For example, a school has a responsibility to protect students from harassment. If it fails to do so, it can be sued along with the author of the offending e-mail message. Organizations also recognize a need to protect themselves from false rumors and industrial espionage. For example, a business wants to know if an employee is supplying its competitor with information on product research and development.

Many schools and businesses have established e-mail privacy policies, which explain the conditions under which you can and cannot expect your e-mail to remain private. These policies are sometimes displayed when the computer boots or a new user logs in. Court decisions, however, seem to support the notion that because an organization owns and operates an e-mail system, the e-mail messages on that system are also the property of the organization. The individual who authors an e-mail message does not own all rights related to it. The company, school, or organization that supplies your e-mail account can, therefore, legally monitor your messages. You should use your e-mail account with the expectation that some of your mail will be read from time to time. Think of your e-mail as a postcard, rather than a letter, and save your controversial comments for face-to-face conversations.

INFOWEBLINKS

You'll find lots more information about e-mail privacy (and lack of it) at the **E-mail Privacy InfoWeb**.

www.course.com/np/concepts8/ch01

WHAT DO YOU THINK?

1. Do you think most people believe that their e-mail is private?   ○ Yes   ○ No   ○ Not sure

2. Do you agree with CalTech's decision to expel the student who was accused of sending harassing e-mail to another student?   ○ Yes   ○ No   ○ Not sure

3. Should the laws be changed to make it illegal for employers to monitor e-mail without court approval?   ○ Yes   ○ No   ○ Not sure

4. Would you have different privacy expectations regarding an e-mail account at your place of work as opposed to an account you purchase from an e-mail service provider?   ○ Yes   ○ No   ○ Not sure

SAVE RESPONSES

COMPUTERS IN CONTEXT

HOMELAND SECURITY

Once a localized problem affecting the Middle East and South Asia, terrorism is now spreading around the globe. Governments in many countries are devoting significant resources to combat this growing threat. In the United States, the Department of Homeland Security (DHS) is responsible for reducing America's vulnerability to terrorism and leading a unified national effort to prevent terrorist attacks on American citizens and assets.

Highly publicized efforts of the DHS include rigorous passenger and baggage screening, stepped up border patrols, smallpox vaccinations for military personnel, and a color-coded Homeland Security Advisory System that specifies the current threat level.

Technology is a key component of the DHS strategy. Electronic sniffing devices in airports detect explosives. The PROTECT system, designed to be deployed in subways, uses chemical detectors to sense toxic fumes, video surveillance cameras to monitor subway-train and passenger status, a computer program to predict the dispersion of toxic materials, and a wireless communications system to coordinate emergency responders.

Computer systems assist efforts to identify terrorists among the millions of people who travel into and within U.S. borders. US-VISIT is a system designed to verify the identities of foreign visitors. An inkless fingerprinting system and digital camera collect fingerprints and photographs of visitors, which are compared to travel documents and databases containing terrorist watchlists. US-VISIT integrates data from more than 20 systems, including the Student Exchange Visitor Information System, the National Crime Information Center, and Interpol.

A complex system of watchlists and security triggers (such as buying a one-way ticket or paying with cash) is used to monitor passengers on domestic flights. According to one source, of the more than 600 million passengers who fly during a year, approximately 15% are flagged for closer scrutiny. The DHS hopes a computer system called CAPPS II can reduce flagged passengers to only 5%.

The Multistate Anti-terrorism Information Exchange System (MATRIX) provides the capability to collect, store, analyze, and exchange sensitive terrorist and other criminal intelligence data among state and federal agencies. MATRIX accesses databases containing information about criminal history, driver's licenses, vehicle registrations, and digitized photographs.

Terrorists might use cell phones or e-mail to communicate and plan attacks. The National Security Agency (NSA) uses electronic intercepts to monitor worldwide "chatter." Computerized language translation programs help English-speaking agents sift through communications in other languages. Arabic, for example, presents a fairly complex computer translation problem. The written language uses a script that reads from right to left in which punctuation and vowels are often omitted. The meaning of a particular word can only be interpreted in context. To grasp the problem, imagine that English has no vowels. Does "plc" mean "police" or "place"? The difference could be important in a communication such as "th plns r n plc."

According to the NSA's Web site, "The old adage that 'knowledge is power' has perhaps never been truer than when applied to today's threats against our nation..." The intelligence community's prevailing strategy is to collect as much data as possible—leaving no stone unturned for fear that it might contain a key clue to the next big attack. Electronic surveillance generates mountains of data. NSA is constructing a data center in Colorado designed to collect and store 10 terabytes of data every day—that's about as much data as is stored in the entire Library of Congress with its 29 million books and 530 miles of bookshelves!

But data is not necessarily knowledge. According to one expert, "The billions of dollars spent on homeland defense will inundate intelligence analysts with information: photos from satellites, intercepted e-mails, banking records. Someone—or something—has to separate the information from the noise."

Efforts are underway to analyze and cross-check data to uncover patterns that can signal terrorist activity, but these activities have generated controversy. Privacy advocates worry that data might be used to spy on law-abiding citizens. Civil liberties advocates wonder if honest citizens might be mistakenly flagged as terrorists and have no way to correct their status. Computer experts worry about the security of government databases and their vulnerability to hackers.

On the positive side, homeland security agencies are taking steps to secure the national computer and communications infrastructure with programs that target individual computer owners, corporate computer networks, Internet service providers, and communications carriers.

A DHS division called US-CERT is responsible for analyzing and reducing computer system vulnerabilities, disseminating cyber-threat warning information, and coordinating incident response activities. A terrorist attack on the computer and communications infrastructure is likely to take the form of a virus or worm, so US-CERT monitors malicious code spread by garden-variety hackers, and has been effective in reducing the damage from the Blaster worm, the SoBig virus, and vulnerabilities in the Microsoft Windows operating system.

Individuals can subscribe to US-CERT's Cyber Security Alerts to receive e-mail when threats and

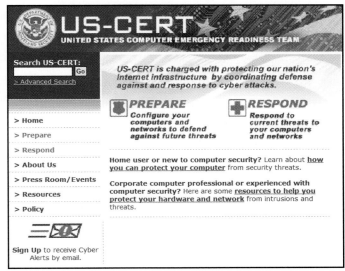

vulnerabilities are discovered. US-CERT also offers a biweekly Cyber Security Tips newsletter with information on how to keep your computer and home network secure. US-CERT's National Cyber Alert System also provides bulletins for technicians about network threats and risk management at the corporate level.

Homeland security efforts are producing job opportunities in government agencies and the private sector. Degree programs at George Washington University, San Diego State University, and several community colleges are preparing graduates for challenging security careers. The Naval Postgraduate School course catalog includes basics, such as Introduction to Homeland Security, and advanced courses in asymmetric conflict and vulnerability analysis.

INFOWEBLINKS

You'll find additional information about this Computers in Context topic by visiting the **Computers and Homeland Security InfoWeb**. ✛

www.course.com/np/concepts8/ch01

INTERACTIVE SUMMARY

To review important concepts from this chapter, fill in the blanks to best complete each sentence. When using the NP8 BookOnCD, click the Check Answers buttons to automatically score your answers. Place your Tracking Disk in the floppy disk drive if you want to save your scores.

A computer is a device that accepts input, [_____] data, stores data, and produces output according to a series of stored instructions. Before a computer processes data, it is temporarily held in [_____]. This data is then processed in the [_____] (CPU). The idea of a [_____] program means that a series of instructions for a computing task can be loaded into a computer's memory.

Computers are grouped into categories, such as personal computers, handhelds, mainframes, super-computers, servers, workstations, and videogame consoles. A [_____] computer is a type of microcomputer designed to meet the needs of an individual. Computers process, store, and transmit data in [_____] format as a series of 1s and 0s. Each 1 or 0 is called a [_____]. Eight bits, called a [_____], represent one character—a letter, number, or punctuation mark. Data becomes [_____] when it is presented in a format that people can understand and use.

An [_____] system, such as Windows, UNIX, or Mac OS, is essentially the master controller for all activities that take place within a computer. [_____] software is any set of computer programs that helps a person carry out a task. Although "Windows" is the name of an operating system, the term "Windows software" refers to application software designed for computers that run the Windows operating system.

✴ CHECK ANSWERS

The Internet is a collection of local, regional, national, and international computer [_____] that are linked together to exchange data and distribute processing tasks. The main routes of the Internet are referred to as the Internet [_____]. Communication between all the devices on the Internet is made possible by a standard set of rules called [_____]. The Internet hosts a wide variety of activities, such as Web browsing, e-commerce, e-mail, bulletin boards, chat groups, instant messaging, Internet telephony, digital broadcasts, remote access, downloads, uploads, and peer-to-peer file sharing.

Many people access the Internet using a dial-up connection that simply requires a telephone line and a [_____]. Faster access methods include cable modem service, ISDN, DSL, and satellite service. Regardless of the access method, individuals cannot typically connect directly to the Internet backbone and, therefore, need to use an [_____] as an intermediary. Both national ISPs and local ISPs have advantages that cater to different computing lifestyles.

Access to the Internet is not restricted, but access to some areas requires a [_____] and password. Passwords are most secure when they consist of two non-related words or a word and a number. Managing multiple passwords can be simplified by selecting a low-security password and a high-security password, and then applying them as necessary.

✴ CHECK ANSWERS

Composed of millions of files stored on Web [_____] all over the world, the Web is one of the most popular aspects of the Internet. Many of these Web-based files are documents that a browser displays as Web [_____]. Other files contain photos, videos, animations, and sound clips that can be incorporated into specific Web pages. Web pages also contain [_____] to related documents and media files. Every Web page has a unique address called a [_____]. Most of them begin with "http", which stands for Hypertext [_____] Protocol, the communications standard that's instrumental in ferrying Web documents to all corners of the Internet. A group of Web pages is usually referred to as a Web [_____].

A [_____] is a software program that runs on your computer and helps you access Web pages. It fetches Web pages and interprets HTML [_____] to properly display the page on your computer screen. Current browsers simply fetch information from a given URL, but they do not have the capability to search for information based on your search specifications. A search [_____] provides the tools you need to search for specific information on the Web. These tools include keyword search input areas, advanced search forms, topic directories, and "agents" that understand queries entered as simple questions.

✤ CHECK ANSWERS

E-mail, short for "electronic mail," can refer to a single electronic message or to the entire system of computers and software that transmits, receives, and stores digital e-mail messages. Any person with an e-mail [_____] can send and receive electronic mail. Basic e-mail activities include composing, reading, replying to, sending, forwarding, and deleting messages. More advanced activities include adding attachments, using HTML format, and maintaining an address book. Most e-mail messages are created in a plain and simple format called [_____] text. It is also possible to create messages in [_____] format, which includes underlining, fancy fonts, colored text, and embedded graphics.

E-mail has similarities with and differences from other forms of communications, but it is the differences that spawned a collection of online communications guidelines called [_____].

An e-mail system consists of e-mail servers, which are accessible to e-mail account holders. Today, consumers can choose between three types of e-mail. [_____] mail holds your incoming mail on an e-mail server until you download it to your computer using e-mail [_____] software. [_____] mail gives you the option of downloading your mail or storing it on the e-mail server. [_____]-based mail allows you to use a browser as e-mail client software.

✤ CHECK ANSWERS

INTERACTIVE KEY TERMS

Make sure you understand all the boldfaced key terms presented in this chapter. If you're using the NP8 BookOnCD, you can use this list of terms as an interactive study activity. First, try to define a term in your own words, and then click the term to compare your definition with the definition presented in the chapter.

Always-on connection, 19
Application software, 12
Beep code, 45
Bit, 11
Blog, 17
Boot process, 44
Browser, 28
Byte, 11
Cable modem, 19
Case sensitive, 22
CD drive, 10
Central processing unit (CPU), 4
Chat group, 17
Client, 9
Computer, 4
Computer network, 8
Computer program, 4
Data, 4
Data file, 11
Desktop computer, 6
Dial-up connection, 18
Digital, 11
Downloading, 16
DSL, 20
DSS, 20
DVD drive, 10
E-commerce, 17
E-mail, 17
E-mail account, 36
E-mail attachment, 37
E-mail client software, 41
E-mail message, 36
E-mail servers, 40
E-mail system, 40
Executable file, 11
File, 11
File extension, 11
File name, 11
Floppy disk drive, 10
Handheld computer, 7
Hard disk drive, 10
Home page, 29
HTML, 27
HTML tags, 30
HTTP, 26
IMAP, 40
Information, 11
Input, 4

Instant messaging, 17
Internet, 15
Internet backbone, 15
Internet telephony, 17
ISDN, 20
ISP, 20
Keyword, 32
LAN, 8
LCD screen, 10
Links, 26
Macs, 13
Mailing list server, 17
Mainframe computer, 8
Memory, 5
Message header, 36
Microcomputer, 6
Microprocessor, 6
MIME, 37
Modem, 10
Monitor, 10
Mouse, 10
Netiquette, 39
Network card, 10
Newsgroups, 17
Notebook computer, 6
Operating system, 12
Output, 5
Password, 22
PCs, 13
PDA, 7
Peer-to-peer, 16
Peripheral device, 11
Personal computer, 6
Platform, 13
POP, 40
POP server, 41
Power-on self-test (POST), 44
Processing, 4
Query, 32
Safe Mode, 46
Search engine, 31
Search operator, 32
Server, 9
Smileys, 39
SMTP server, 42
Software, 4
Sound card, 10
Spam, 40

Spam filter, 40
Storage, 5
Store-and-forward technology, 40
Stored program, 5
Supercomputer, 8
System software, 12
System unit, 10
Tablet computer, 7
TCP/IP, 15
Topic directory, 33
Uploading, 16
URL, 27
Usenet, 17
User ID, 22
Videogame console, 8
Voiceband modem, 18
Web, 26
Web pages, 26
Web servers, 27
Web site, 27
Web-based e-mail, 40
Workstation, 8

INTERACTIVE SITUATION QUESTIONS

Apply what you've learned to some typical computing situations. When using the NP8 BookOnCD, you can type your answers, and then use the Check Answers button to automatically score your responses. Place your Tracking Disk in the floppy disk drive if you want to save your scores.

1. Suppose that you walk into an office and see the devices pictured to the right. You would probably assume that they are the screen and keyboard for a _____ personal computer, _____, or server.

2. You receive a CD from a friend. It contains a file called EverQuest.exe. Because of the file extension, you assume that the disk contains a(n) _____ file that is some type of computer program, rather than a data file.

3. You are a musician and you use your Gateway PC to compose music. Your friend, who has an iMac computer, wants you to try the software she uses. If she loans you her composition software, can you use it on your PC? Yes or no? _____

4. You are a computer technician hired by Ben and Jerry's Ice Cream to set up a Web site. You know that your site requires a unique _____ that pinpoints its location on the Internet, and your server will have to use _____, the standard Internet protocol that transports data between all sorts of computer platforms over the Internet.

5. You want the cheapest Internet connection. You don't mind if the connection is limited to speeds under 56 Kbps and doesn't provide very good video performance. You would probably select an ISP that provides a(n) _____ connection.

6. You need to select a password for your online bank account. Which of the following passwords would be the LEAST secure: jeff683, hddtmrutc, gargantuan, brickcloset, fanhotshot, or high348? _____

7. You want to look at the latest Nike athletic shoes. The URL that will probably get you to Nike's home page is _____.

8. You want to find some Web pages that contain information about snowboarding competitions. You know that your _____ can only fetch and display Web pages, so you'll need to connect to a(n) _____ and enter a query, such as "snowboard competition."

9. If your ISP does not supply you with an e-mail account, you can get a free _____ e-mail account from a site such as Hotmail or Yahoo!.

10. You receive an e-mail message that contains colored text and underlining. You assume that the person who sent the message had his mail software set for _____ format.

✤ CHECK ANSWERS

INTERACTIVE PRACTICE TESTS

Practice tests that consist of 10 multiple-choice, true/false, and fill-in-the-blank questions are available on both the NP8 BookOnCD and the NP8 Web site. The questions are selected at random from a large test bank, so each time you take a test, you'll receive a different set of questions. Your tests are scored immediately, and you can print study guides that help you find the correct answers for any questions that you missed.

www.course.com/np/concepts8/ch01 ✤

CLICK ✤ TO START

REVIEW

ON THE WEB

PROJECTS

An NP8 Project is an open-ended activity that helps you apply the concepts you have learned. Many projects require resources in addition to your textbook, such as current magazines, library materials, or Web access. When you tackle a project, be prepared to use your critical thinking skills, logical analysis, and creativity. Projects for this chapter include:

- **Issue Research: E-mail Privacy**
- **Who Wants to be a Millionaire**
- **Computers in Homeland Security**
- **Micros, Minis, Mainframes, and Supercomputers**

- **Anonymous E-mail?**
- **Get Creative**
- **Describe Your Personal Computer Using Key Terms**

To work with the Projects for this chapter, connect to the **New Perspectives NP8 Web Site**.

www.course.com/np/concepts8/ch01

TECHTV VIDEO PROJECT

The TechTV segment *Predicting Big Surf* highlights one of many unique ways to use the Web. After you watch this video, write a short description of it. Then, browse around the Web to look for other unique applications. Write a short description of at least three applications you found and then explain whether in your opinion they offer good, solid services or are simply gimmicks.

To work with the Video Projects for this chapter, connect to the **New Perspectives NP8 Web Site**.

www.course.com/np/concepts8/ch01

STUDY TIPS

Study Tips help you to organize and consolidate the information in a chapter by making lists, outlines, charts, and sketches. You can use paper and pencil or word processing software to complete most of the Study Tips.

To work with the Study Tips for this chapter, connect to the **New Perspectives NP8 Web Site**.

www.course.com/np/concepts8/ch01

ONLINE GAMES

Test your comprehension of the concepts introduced in Chapter 1 by playing the NP8 Online Games. At the end of each game, you have three options:

- Print a comprehensive study guide complete with page references
- Print your results to be submitted to your instructor
- Save your results to be submitted to your instructor via e-mail

To work with the Online Games for this chapter, connect to the **New Perspectives NP8 Web Site**.

www.course.com/np/concepts8/ch01

STUDENT EDITION LABS

Extend your knowledge of computer basics with the Chapter 1 Student Edition Lab.

The following Student Edition Lab is offered with Chapter 1:

• **E-mail**

To work with the Chapter 1 Student Edition Lab and its corresponding lab assignment, connect to the **New Perspectives NP8 Web Site**.

www.course.com/np/concepts8/ch01

Go to the NP8 New Perspectives Web site for specific lab topics.

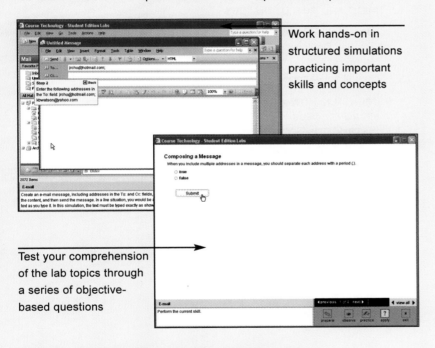

Work hands-on in structured simulations practicing important skills and concepts

Test your comprehension of the lab topics through a series of objective-based questions

Track Your Progress with the Student Edition Labs

• Student Edition Labs test your comprehension of the lab topics through a series of trackable objective-based questions. Your instructor will direct you to either print your results or submit them via e-mail.

• Student Edition Lab Assignments, available on the New Perspectives NP8 Web site, require you to apply the skills learned through the lab in a live environment. Go to the New Perspectives NP8 Web site for detailed instruction on individual Student Edition Lab Assignments.

If you have a SAM user profile, you have access to even more interactive content. Log in to your SAM account and go to your assignments page to see what your instructor has assigned for this chapter.

COMPUTER HARDWARE

CONTENTS

TIP

When using the BookOnCD, the ❋ icons are "clickable" to access resources on the CD. The ✛ icons are clickable to access resources on the Web. You can also access Web resources by using your browser to connect directly to the NP8 New Perspectives Web site at:

www.course.com/np/concepts8/ch02

CHAPTER PREVIEW

Before you begin Chapter 2, you can use the Web-based preview activities to hear an overview of the chapter, check your current level of expertise about key concepts, and look through a list of learning objectives. You can access the preview activities by clicking the icon when using the BookOnCD or going to the New Perspectives NP8 Web site.

CHAPTER OVERVIEW

Whether you are shopping for a new computer, using your trusty laptop, or troubleshooting a problem, it is useful to have some background in hardware terminology. Get your book and highlighter ready, then connect to the New Perspectives NP8 Web site where you can listen to an overview that points out the most important concepts for this chapter.

www.course.com/np/concepts8/ch02 ⊹

CHAPTER PRE-ASSESSMENT

How much do you know about bits and bytes, RAM and ROM, processors and storage, printers and monitors? To gauge your level of knowledge before beginning the chapter, take the pre-assessment quiz at the New Perspectives NP8 Web site. Armed with your results from this quiz, you can focus your study time on concepts that will round out your knowledge of computer hardware and improve your test scores.

www.course.com/np/concepts8/ch02 ⊹

LEARNING OBJECTIVES

When you complete this chapter you should be able to:

- Explain why most computers are digital and how that relates to representing numbers by using 0 and 1 bits
- Describe the role of a microprocessor's ALU, control unit, registers, and instruction set
- List the factors that affect microprocessor performance
- Explain how RAM works and how it differs from disk storage
- List facts about RAM that are important to computer buyers and owners
- Describe the difference between magnetic, optical, and solid state storage
- Use criteria such as versatility, durability, capacity, access time, and data transfer rate to compare storage technologies: floppy disks, hard disks, tapes, CDs, DVDs, and USB Flash drives

- Explain the factors that might help a shopper decide whether to purchase a CRT, LCD, or plasma monitor
- Compare and contrast the technologies and applications for ink jet, solid ink, thermal, dye sublimation, laser, and dot matrix printers
- Describe the components of a computer's expansion bus, including various types of expansion slots and cables
- Explain the hardware compatibility considerations, device drivers, and procedures involved in installing a peripheral device

A detailed list of learning objectives is provided at the New Perspectives NP8 Web site

www.course.com/np/concepts8/ch02 ⊹

DATA REPRESENTATION AND DIGITAL ELECTRONICS

Understanding what makes a computer "tick" can come in handy in today's information age. It helps you decipher computer ads, troubleshoot equipment problems, and make software work. Although scientists are tinkering with exotic technologies such as quantum computers and molecular computers, just about every computer today is an electronic, digital device based on a concept that's as simple as a basic light switch.

DATA REPRESENTATION

What is data representation? People use computers to work with many kinds of data, including numbers, text, music, photos, and videos. **Data representation** is the process of transforming this diverse data into a form that computers can use for processing. Today, computers typically represent data digitally.

How do computers represent data digitally? Most computers are digital devices. A **digital device** works with discrete—distinct and separate—data, such as the digits 1 and 0. In contrast, an **analog device** works with continuous data. As an analogy, a traditional light switch has two discrete states—on and off—so it is a digital device. A dimmer switch, on the other hand, has a rotating dial that controls a continuous range of brightness. It is, therefore, an analog device (Figure 2-1).

Most computers use the simplest type of digital technology—their circuits have only two possible states. For convenience, let's say that one of those states is "on" and the other state is "off." When discussing these states, we usually indicate the "on" state with 1 and the "off" state with 0. So the sequence "on" "on" "off" "off" would be written 1100. These 1s and 0s are referred to as **binary digits**. It is from this term that we get the word "bit"—*bi*nary dig*it*. Computers use sequences of bits to digitally represent numbers, letters, punctuation marks, music, pictures, and videos.

How does a computer represent numbers? **Numeric data** consists of numbers that might be used in arithmetic operations. For example, your annual income is numeric data, as is your age. The price of a bicycle is numeric data. So is the average gas mileage for a vehicle, such as a car or SUV. Computers represent numeric data using the binary number system, also called "base 2."

The **binary number system** has only two digits: 0 and 1. No numeral like "2" exists in this system, so the number "two" is represented in binary as "10" (pronounced "one zero"). You'll recognize the similarity to what happens when you're counting from 1 to 10 in the familiar decimal system. After you reach 9, you run out of digits. For "ten," you have to use "10"—zero is a placeholder and the "1" indicates "one group of tens."

In binary, you just run out of digits sooner—right after you count to 1. To get to the next number, you have to use the zero as a placeholder and the "1" indicates "one group of 2s." In binary then, you count 0 ("zero"), 1 ("one"), 10 ("one zero"), instead of counting 0, 1, 2 in decimal. If you need to brush up on binary numbers, refer to Figure 2-2 on the next page and to the lab at the end of Section A.

FIGURE 2-1

A computer is a digital device, more like a standard light switch than a dimmer switch.

Decimal (Base 10)	Binary (Base 2)
0	0
1	1
2	10
3	11
4	100
5	101
6	110
7	111
8	1000
9	1001
10	1010
11	1011
1000	1111101000

FIGURE 2-2

The decimal system uses ten symbols to represent numbers: 0, 1, 2, 3, 4, 5, 6, 7, 8, and 9. The binary number system uses only two symbols: 0 and 1.

The important point to understand is that the binary number system allows computers to represent virtually any number simply by using 0s and 1s, which conveniently translate into electrical "on" and "off" signals. The average gas mileage for an SUV (11) is 1011 in binary, and can be represented by "on" "off" "on" "on."

How can a computer represent words and letters using bits? **Character data** is composed of letters, symbols, and numerals that are not used in arithmetic operations. Examples of character data include your name, address, and hair color. Just as Morse code uses dashes and dots to represent the letters of the alphabet, a digital computer uses a series of bits to represent letters, characters, and numerals. Figure 2-3 illustrates how a computer can use 0s and 1s to represent the letters and symbols in the text "HI!"

Computers employ several types of codes to represent character data, including ASCII, EBCDIC, and Unicode. **ASCII** (American Standard Code for Information Interchange, pronounced "ASK ee") requires only seven bits for each character. For example, the ASCII code for an uppercase "A" is 1000001. ASCII provides codes for 128 characters, including uppercase letters, lowercase letters, punctuation symbols, and numerals.

A superset of ASCII, called **Extended ASCII**, uses eight bits to represent each character. For example, Extended ASCII represents the letter "A" as 01000001. Using eight bits instead of seven bits allows Extended ASCII to provide codes for 128 more characters than plain ASCII. The additional Extended ASCII characters include boxes, circles, and other graphical symbols. An alternative to the 8-bit Extended ASCII code, called **EBCDIC** (Extended Binary-Coded Decimal Interchange Code, pronounced "EB seh dick"), is usually used only by older, IBM mainframe computers.

Unicode (pronounced "YOU ni code") uses sixteen bits and provides codes for 65,000 characters—a real bonus for representing the alphabets of multiple languages. For example, Unicode represents an uppercase "A" in the Russian Cyrillic alphabet as 0000010000010000.

FIGURE 2-3

A computer treats the letters and symbols in the word "HI!" as character data, which can be represented by a string of 0s and 1s.

01001000   01001001 00100001

Why do ASCII and Extended ASCII provide codes for 0, 1, 2, 3, 4, 5, 6, 7, 8, and 9? The table in Figure 2-4 illustrates the variety of letters and symbols represented by Extended ASCII. You might wonder why the table contains codes for 0, 1, 2, 3, and so on. Aren't these numbers represented by the binary number system? A computer uses Extended ASCII character codes for 0, 1, 2, 3 to represent numerals that are not used for calculations. For example, you don't typically use your social security "number" in calculations, so it is considered character data and represented using Extended ASCII. Likewise, the "numbers" in your street address can be represented by character codes rather than binary numbers.

FIGURE 2-4

The Extended ASCII code uses a series of eight 1s and 0s to represent 256 characters, including lowercase letters, uppercase letters, symbols, and numerals. The first 32 ASCII characters are not shown in this table because they represent special control sequences that cannot be printed. The two "blank" entries are space characters.

Char	Code	Char	Code	Char	Code	Char	Code	Char	Code	Char	Code	Char	Code	Char	Code
	00100000	>	00111110	\	01011100	z	01111010	ÿ	10011000	‖	10110110	⊢	11010100	≥	11110010
!	00100001	?	00111111	]	01011101	{	01111011	Ö	10011001	┐	10110111	╒	11010101	≤	11110011
"	00100010	@	01000000	^	01011110	|	01111100	Ü	10011010	╖	10111000	π	11010110	┌	11110100
#	00100011	A	01000001	_	01011111	}	01111101	¢	10011011	╕	10111001	╫	11010111	⌡	11110101
$	00100100	B	01000010	`	01100000	~	01111110	£	10011100	╣	10111010	╪	11011000	÷	11110110
%	00100101	C	01000011	a	01100001		01111111	¥	10011101	║	10111011	┘	11011001	≈	11110111
&	00100110	D	01000100	b	01100010	Ç	10000000	₧	10011110	╗	10111100	┌	11011010	°	11111000
'	00100111	E	01000101	c	01100011	ü	10000001	ƒ	10011111	╝	10111101	■	11011011	∙	11111001
(	00101000	F	01000110	d	01100100	é	10000010	á	10100000	╜	10111110	▄	11011100	·	11111010
)	00101001	G	01000111	e	01100101	â	10000011	í	10100001	╛	10111111	▌	11011101	√	11111011
*	00101010	H	01001000	f	01100110	ä	10000100	ó	10100010	└	11000000	▐	11011110	ⁿ	11111100
+	00101011	I	01001001	g	01100111	à	10000101	ú	10100011	┴	11000001	▀	11011111	²	11111101
,	00101100	J	01001010	h	01101000	å	10000110	ñ	10100100	┬	11000010	α	11100000	■	11111110
-	00101101	K	01001011	i	01101001	ç	10000111	Ñ	10100101	├	11000011	β	11100001		11111111
.	00101110	L	01001100	j	01101010	ê	10001000	ª	10100110	─	11000100	Γ	11100010		
/	00101111	M	01001101	k	01101011	ë	10001001	º	10100111	┼	11000101	π	11100011		
0	00110000	N	01001110	l	01101100	è	10001010	¿	10101000	╞	11000110	Σ	11100100		
1	00110001	O	01001111	m	01101101	ï	10001011	⌐	10101001	╟	11000111	σ	11100101		
2	00110010	P	01010000	n	01101110	î	10001100	¬	10101010	╚	11001000	µ	11100110		
3	00110011	Q	01010001	o	01101111	ì	10001101	½	10101011	╔	11001001	τ	11100111		
4	00110100	R	01010010	p	01110000	Ä	10001110	¼	10101100	╩	11001010	Φ	11101000		
5	00110101	S	01010011	q	01110001	Å	10001111	¡	10101101	╦	11001011	Θ	11101001		
6	00110110	T	01010100	r	01110010	É	10010000	«	10101110	╠	11001100	Ω	11101010		
7	00110111	U	01010101	s	01110011	æ	10010001	»	10101111	═	11001101	δ	11101011		
8	00111000	V	01010110	t	01110100	Æ	10010010	▒	10110000	╬	11001110	∞	11101100		
9	00111001	W	01010111	u	01110101	ô	10010011	▓	10110001	╧	11001111	φ	11101101		
:	00111010	X	01011000	v	01110110	ö	10010100	�filled	10110010	╨	11010000	ε	11101110		
;	00111011	Y	01011001	w	01110111	ò	10010101	|	10110011	╤	11010001	∩	11101111		
<	00111100	Z	01011010	x	01111000	û	10010110	┤	10110100	╥	11010010	≡	11110000		
=	00111101	[	01011011	y	01111001	ù	10010111	╡	10110101	╙	11010011	±	11110001		

How does a computer convert music and pictures into codes? Music and pictures are not small, discrete objects like numbers or the letters of the alphabet. To work with music and pictures, they must be digitized. The term **digitize** means to convert raw, analog data into digital format represented by 0s and 1s.

A photograph or drawing can be digitized by treating it as a series of colored dots. Each dot is assigned a binary number according to its color. For example, a green dot might be represented by 0010 and a red dot by 1100, as shown in Figure 2-5. A digital image is simply a list of color numbers for all the dots it contains. In a similar way, music can be digitized by assigning binary codes to notes.

FIGURE 2-5

An image can be digitized by assigning a binary number to each dot.

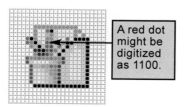

A red dot might be digitized as 1100.

When a computer works with a series of 1s and 0s, how does it know which code to use? All the "stuff" that your computer works with is stored in files as a long—make that really long—series of 1s and 0s. Your computer needs to know whether to interpret those 1s and 0s as ASCII code, binary numbers, or the code for a picture or sound. Imagine the mess if your computer thought that your term paper, stored as ASCII, was an accounting file that contained a series of numbers stored in binary format. It would never be able to reconstruct the words and sentences of your term paper.

To avoid confusion, most computer files contain a **file header** with information on the code used to represent the file data. A file header is stored along with the file and can be read by the computer, but never appears on the screen. By reading the header information, a computer can tell how a file's contents were coded.

QUANTIFYING BITS AND BYTES

How can I tell the difference between bits and bytes? Computer ads include lots of abbreviations relating to bits and bytes. A few key concepts can help you understand what these abbreviations mean. Even though the word "bit" is an abbreviation for "binary digit," it can be further abbreviated, usually as a lowercase "b." A byte, on the other hand, is composed of eight bits and usually abbreviated as an uppercase "B."

Transmission speeds are typically expressed in bits, whereas storage space is typically expressed in bytes. In Chapter 1, for example, you learned that the speed of most voice band modems is 56 Kbps—56 kilobits per second. In a computer ad, you might see the capacity of a hard disk drive described as 40 GB—40 gigabytes.

What do the prefixes kilo-, mega-, and giga- mean? When working with computers, you'll frequently encounter references such as "50 kilobits per second," "1.44 megabytes," and "2.8 gigahertz." Kilo, mega, giga, and similar terms are used to quantify computer data.

In common usage, "kilo," abbreviated as "K," means 1,000. For example, $50 K means $50,000. In the decimal number system we use on a daily basis, the number 1,000 is 10 to the 3rd power, or 10^3. In the world of computers where base 2 is the norm, a "kilo" is precisely 1,024, or 2^{10}. A **kilobit** (abbreviated Kb or Kbit) is 1,024 bits. A **kilobyte** (abbreviated KB or Kbyte) is 1,024 bytes. Kilobytes are often used when referring to the size of small computer files.

The prefix "mega" means a million, or in the context of bits and bytes, precisely 1,048,576 (the equivalent of 2^{20}). A **megabit** (Mb or Mbit) is 1,048,576 bits. A **megabyte** (MB or MByte) is 1,048,576 bytes. Megabytes are often used when referring to the size of medium to large computer files or to floppy disk capacity.

In computer lingo, the prefix "giga" refers to a billion, or precisely 1,073,741,824. As you might expect, a **gigabit** (Gb or Gbit) is approximately one billion bits. A **gigabyte** (GB or GByte) is one billion bytes. Gigabytes are typically used to refer to RAM and hard disk capacity.

Computers—especially mainframes and supercomputers—sometimes work with huge amounts of data, and so terms such as tera- (trillion), peta- (thousand trillion), and exa- (quintillion) are also handy. Figure 2-6 summarizes the terms commonly used to quantify computer data.

FIGURE 2-6
Quantifying Digital Data

Bit	One binary digit
Byte	8 bits
Kilobit	1,024 or 2^{10} bits
Kilobyte	1,024 or 2^{10} bytes
Megabit	1,048,576 or 2^{20} bits
Megabyte	1,048,576 or 2^{20} bytes
Gigabit	2^{30} bits
Gigabyte	2^{30} bytes
Terabyte	2^{40} bytes
Petabyte	2^{50} bytes
Exabyte	2^{60} bytes

DIGITAL ELECTRONICS

How does a computer store and transport all those bits? Because most computers are electronic devices, bits take the form of electrical pulses that can travel over circuits, in much the same way that electricity flows over a wire when you turn on a light switch. All the circuits, chips, and mechanical components that form a computer are designed to work with bits. Most of these essential components are housed within the computer's system unit.

What's inside the system unit? If it weren't for the miniaturization made possible by digital electronic technology, computers would be huge, and the inside of a computer's system unit would contain a complex jumble of wires and other electronic gizmos. Instead, today's computers contain relatively few parts. Desktop computers with large system units are designed so that owners can easily upgrade audio, visual, and storage components. Small desktop and notebook computers, on the other hand, usually provide access for expansion and replacement from outside of the case. In Figure 2-7, you can see what's inside a typical desktop computer.

FIGURE 2-7

A computer's system unit typically contains circuit boards, storage devices, and a power supply that converts current from an AC wall outlet into the DC current used by computer circuitry.

Power supply and fan

Microprocessor located under cooling fan

Expansion cards

CD drive

Floppy disk drive

Hard disk drive

Cables that transfer data from storage devices to system board

Main circuit board (system board)

FIGURE 2-8

A computer chip is classified by the number of miniaturized components it contains—from small-scale integration (SSI) of less than 100 components per chip to ultra large-scale integration (ULSI) of more than 1 million components per chip.

What's a computer chip? The terms "computer chip," "microchip," and "chip" originated as technical jargon for "integrated circuit." An **integrated circuit** (IC), such as the one pictured in Figure 2-8, is a super-thin slice of semiconducting material packed with microscopic circuit elements, such as wires, transistors, capacitors, logic gates, and resistors.

Semiconducting materials (or "semiconductors"), such as silicon and germanium, are substances with properties between those of a conductor (like copper) and an insulator (like wood). To fabricate a chip, the conductive properties of selective parts of the semiconducting material can be enhanced to essentially create miniature electronic pathways and components, such as transistors.

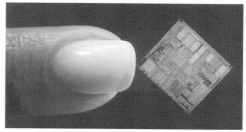

The assortment of chips inside a computer includes the microprocessor, memory modules, and support circuitry. These chips are packaged in a protective carrier that also provides connectors to other computer components. Chip carriers vary in shape and size—including small rectangular **DIPs** (dual in-line package) with caterpillar-like legs protruding from a black, rectangular "body"; long, slim **DIMMs** (dual in-line memory modules); pincushion-like **PGAs** (pin-grid arrays); and cassette-like **SEC cartridges** (single edge contact cartridges). Terms like DIMM and PGA frequently appear in computer ads. Figure 2-9 helps you visualize these components.

INFOWEBLINKS

Find out how thousands of miles of wires and millions of components can be miniaturized to the size of a baby's fingernail by connecting to the **Integrated Circuits InfoWeb.**

www.course.com/np/concepts8/ch02

FIGURE 2-9

Integrated circuits can be used for microprocessors, memory, and support circuitry. They are housed within a ceramic carrier. These carriers exist in several configurations, or "chip packages," such as DIPs, DIMMs, PGAs, and SECs.

A DIP has two rows of pins that connect the IC circuitry to a circuit board.

A DIMM is a small circuit board containing several chips, typically used for memory.

A PGA is a square chip package with pins arranged in concentric squares, typically used for microprocessors.

An SEC cartridge was pioneered by Intel to house Pentium III microprocessors.

How do chips fit together to make a computer? The computer's main circuit board, called a **system board**, "motherboard," or "main board," houses all essential chips and provides connecting circuitry between them. If you look carefully at a system board, you'll see that some chips are permanently soldered in place. Other chips are plugged into special sockets and connectors, which allow chips to be removed for repairs or upgrades. When multiple chips are required for a single function, such as generating stereo-quality sound, the chips might be gathered together on a separate small circuit board, which can then be plugged into a special slot-like connector. Figure 2-10 on the next page provides a handy guide that can help you identify the components on your computer's system board.

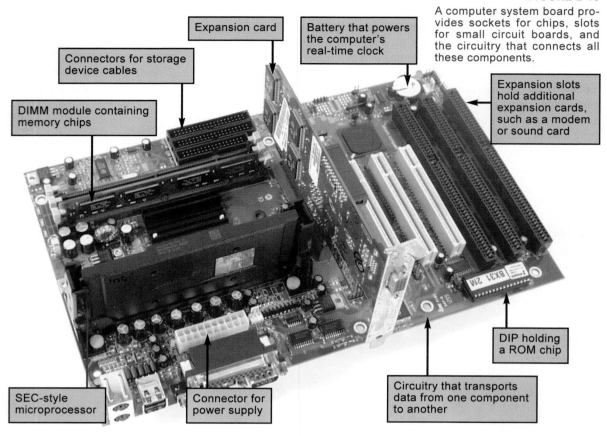

FIGURE 2-10
A computer system board provides sockets for chips, slots for small circuit boards, and the circuitry that connects all these components.

Expansion card

Battery that powers the computer's real-time clock

Connectors for storage device cables

DIMM module containing memory chips

Expansion slots hold additional expansion cards, such as a modem or sound card

DIP holding a ROM chip

SEC-style microprocessor

Connector for power supply

Circuitry that transports data from one component to another

QUICKCHECK......SECTION A

1. Most computers are ⬚ devices that work with discrete numbers, such as 1s and 0s.

2. The ⬚ number system represents numeric data as a series of 0s and 1s.

3. Extended ⬚ uses eight bits to represent each letter of the alphabet.

4. A computer uses ⬚ codes to represent the numerals in your social security number and street address, whereas it uses ⬚ numbers to code numeric data such as your age.

5. A(n) ⬚ is approximately one billion bytes.

6. A(n) ⬚ circuit contains microscopic elements, such as wires, transistors, and capacitors, that are packed onto a very small square of semiconducting material.

7. A computer's ⬚ board is also called a "motherboard" or "main board."

CHECK ANSWERS

LAB

LAB 2-A

WORKING WITH BINARY NUMBERS

In this lab, you'll learn:

- The difference between the binary number system and the decimal number system
- How to count in binary
- How to convert decimal numbers into binary numbers
- How to convert binary numbers into decimal numbers
- How to use the Windows Calculator to convert numbers
- How to work with "powers of two"

INTERACTIVE LAB

CLICK TO START THE LAB

LAB ASSIGNMENTS

1. Start the interactive part of the lab. Insert your Tracking Disk if you want to save your QuickCheck results. Perform each lab step as directed, and answer all the lab QuickCheck questions. When you exit the lab, your answers are automatically graded and your results are displayed.

2. Using paper and pencil, manually convert the following decimal numbers into binary numbers. Your instructor might ask you to show the process that you used for each conversion.

   a. 100   b. 1,000   c. 256   d. 27

   e. 48   f. 112   g. 96   h. 1,024

3. Using paper and pencil, manually convert the following binary numbers into decimal numbers. Your instructor might ask you to show the process that you used for each conversion.

   a. 100   b. 101   c. 1100   d. 10101

   e. 1111   f. 10000   g. 1111000   h. 110110

4. Describe what is wrong with the following sequence:

   10   100   110   1000   1001   1100   1110   10000

5. What is the decimal equivalent of 2^0? 2^1? 2^8?

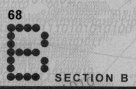

SECTION B

MICROPROCESSORS AND MEMORY

A typical computer ad contains a long list of specifications that describe a computer's components and capabilities. Savvy shoppers understand how these specifications affect computer performance and price. Most computer specifications begin with the microprocessor type and speed. Computer manufacturers want consumers to think that faster is better, but is there a point at which you can pay for speed you won't need? Computer ads also contain information about a computer's memory capacity. Lots of memory can add hundreds of dollars to the cost of a computer. Consumers are right to ask "How much RAM is enough?"

Section B explains how the microprocessor and memory work, and how they affect computer performance and price.

MICROPROCESSOR BASICS

What exactly is a microprocessor? A **microprocessor** (sometimes simply referred to as a "processor") is an integrated circuit designed to process instructions. It is the most important, and usually the most expensive, component of a computer. Although a microprocessor is sometimes mistakenly referred to as "a computer on a chip," it can be more accurately described as "a CPU on a chip" because it contains—on a single chip—circuitry that performs essentially the same tasks as the central processing unit (CPU) of a classic mainframe computer.

What does it look like? Looking inside a computer, you can usually identify the microprocessor because it is the largest chip on the system board, although it might be hidden under a cooling fan. Most of today's microprocessors are housed in a PGA (pin grid array) chip package, as shown in Figure 2-11.

FIGURE 2-11

Today's microprocessors are typically housed in a PGA chip package.

How does a microprocessor work? Inside the chip carrier, a microprocessor is a very complex integrated circuit, containing as many as 300 million miniaturized electronic components. The miniaturized circuitry in a microprocessor is grouped into important functional areas, such as the ALU and the control unit.

The **ALU** (arithmetic logic unit) performs arithmetic operations, such as addition and subtraction. It also performs logical operations, such as comparing two numbers to see if they are the same. The ALU uses **registers** to hold data that is being processed, just as you use a mixing bowl to hold the ingredients for a batch of brownies. The microprocessor's **control unit** fetches each instruction, just as you get each ingredient out of a cupboard or the refrigerator. The computer loads data into the ALU's registers, just as you add all the ingredients to the mixing bowl. Finally, the control unit gives the ALU the green light to begin processing, just as you flip the switch to your electric mixer to begin

blending the brownie ingredients. Figure 2-12 illustrates a microprocessor control unit and ALU preparing to add 2 + 3.

Where does the microprocessor get its instructions? The simple answer is that a microprocessor executes instructions provided by a computer program. However, a microprocessor can't follow just any instructions. A program that contains an instruction to "self destruct" won't have much effect because a microprocessor can perform only a limited list of instructions—"self destruct" isn't one of them.

The list of instructions that a microprocessor can perform is called its **instruction set**. These instructions are hard-wired into the processor's circuitry and include basic arithmetic and logical operations, fetching data, and clearing registers. A computer can perform very complex tasks, but it does so by performing a combination of simple tasks from its instruction set.

MICROPROCESSOR PERFORMANCE FACTORS

What makes one microprocessor perform better than another? Computer ads like the one in Figure 2-13 include microprocessor specifications related to its performance. A microprocessor's performance is affected by several factors, including clock speed, word size, cache size, instruction set, and processing techniques.

What do MHz and GHz have to do with computer performance? The speed specifications that you see in a computer ad indicate the speed of the **microprocessor clock**—a timing device that sets the pace for executing instructions. Most computer ads specify the speed of a microprocessor in megahertz or gigahertz. **Megahertz** (MHz) means a million cycles per second. **Gigahertz** (GHz) means a billion cycles per second.

A cycle is the smallest unit of time in a microprocessor's universe. Every action a processor performs is measured by these cycles. It is important, however, to understand that the clock speed is not equal to the number of instructions a processor can execute in one second. In many computers, some instructions occur within one cycle, but other instructions might require multiple cycles. Some processors can even execute several instructions in a single clock cycle.

A specification such as 3.6 GHz means that the microprocessor's clock operates at a speed of 3.6 billion cycles per second. All other things being equal, a computer with a 2.8 GHz processor is faster than a computer with a 1.5 GHz processor or a 933 MHz processor.

In 2004, a major chip maker began to phase in the use of "processor numbers" (PN) as a replacement for clock speeds. The Pentium 4 3.6 GHz processor became the Pentium 4 560, for example. Processor numbers do not indicate clock speed. They can indicate speed relative to other processors within the same family, but not between different families. For example, the Pentium 4 560 is faster than the Pentium 4 540. However, an Intel M processor 755 is not faster than the Pentium 4 560. Even though 755 is a larger number than 560, the M processor and Pentium 4 are in different processor families. Their processor numbers cannot be compared to each other.

FIGURE 2-12

The control unit fetches the ADD instruction, then loads data into the ALU's registers where it is processed.

FIGURE 2-13

A typical computer ad provides specifications, like those highlighted in yellow, for processor performance.

■ **Intel Pentium 4 560 32-bit processor 3.6 GHz with Hyper-Threading**
■ **1 MB L2 cache**
■ **2 GB 533 MHz SDRAM (max. 4 GB)**
■ **160 GB SATA HD (7200 rpm)**
■ **48X CD-RW + 12X DVD+RW/+R with double-layer write capable**
■ **3.5" 1.44 MB floppy disk drive**
■ **17" LCD TV**
■ **256 MB AGP graphics card**
■ **Sound Blaster PCI sound card**
■ **Altec Lansing speakers**
■ **U.S. Robotics 56 Kbps modem**
■ **Mouse & keyboard**
■ **External drive bays: 2 5.25" bays for disk, tape, or CD drives; 1 3.5" bay for a floppy drive**
■ **Internal drive bays: 1 HDD bay**
■ **8 USB ports: 2 front, 6 back**
■ **2 serial, 1 parallel, and 1 video port**
■ **1 network port (RJ45 connector)**
■ **4 PCI slots and 1 AGP slot**
■ **Windows XP Home Edition**
■ **Home/small business software bundle**
■ **3-year limited warranty**

Which is faster, a 32-bit processor or a 64-bit processor? **Word size** refers to the number of bits that a microprocessor can manipulate at one time. Word size is based on the size of registers in the ALU and the capacity of circuits that lead to those registers. A processor with a 32-bit word size, for example, has 32-bit registers, processes thirty-two bits at a time, and is referred to as a "32-bit processor." Processors with a larger word size can process more data during each processor cycle—a factor that leads to increased computer performance. Today's personal computers typically contain 32-bit or 64-bit processors.

How does the cache size affect performance? **Cache** (pronounced "cash") is sometimes called "RAM cache" or "cache memory." It is special high-speed memory that allows a microprocessor to access data more rapidly than from memory located elsewhere on the system board. Some computer ads specify cache type and capacity. A **Level 1 cache** (L1) is built into the processor chip, whereas a **Level 2 cache** (L2) is located on a separate chip and takes a little more time to get data to the processor. Cache capacity is usually measured in kilobytes.

In theory, a large cache increases processing speed. In today's computers, however, cache size is usually tied to a particular processor brand and model. Cache size is not of particular significance to consumers because it is not configurable. For example, you can't add more L1 cache to your computer without replacing the microprocessor.

How does the instruction set affect performance? As chip designers developed various instruction sets for microprocessors, they tended to add increasingly more complex instructions, each requiring several clock cycles for execution. A microprocessor with such an instruction set uses **CISC** (complex instruction set computer) technology. A microprocessor with a limited set of simple instructions uses **RISC** (reduced instruction set computer) technology. A RISC processor performs most instructions faster than a CISC processor. It might, however, require more of these simple instructions to complete a task than a CISC processor requires for the same task. Most processors in today's Macs use RISC technology; most PCs use CISC technology.

A processor's ability to handle graphics can be enhanced by adding specialized graphics and multimedia instructions to a processor's instruction set. 3DNow!, MMX, and SSE-2 are examples of instruction set enhancements sometimes mentioned in computer ads. Although instruction set enhancements have the potential to speed up games, graphics software, and video editing, they work only with software designed to utilize these specialized instructions.

Can a microprocessor execute more than one instruction at a time? Some processors execute instructions "serially"—that is, one instruction at a time. With **serial processing**, the processor must complete all steps in the instruction cycle before it begins to execute the next instruction. However, using a technology called **pipelining**, a processor can begin executing an instruction before it completes the previous instruction. Many of today's microprocessors also perform **parallel processing**, in which multiple instructions are executed at the same time. Pipelining and parallel processing enhance processor performance.

To get a clearer picture of serial, pipelining, and parallel processing techniques (Figure 2-14), consider an analogy in which computer instructions are pizzas. Serial processing executes only one instruction at a time, just like a pizzeria with one oven that holds only one pizza. Pipelining is similar

FIGURE 2-14

Microprocessor designers have developed techniques for serial, pipelining, and parallel processing.

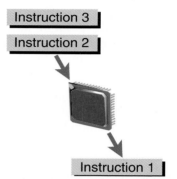

In serial processing, one instruction is processed at a time.

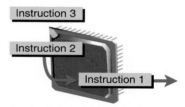

In pipelining, an instruction can begin to be processed before the previous instruction's processing is complete.

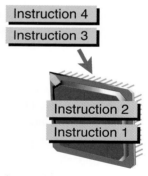

In parallel processing, multiple instructions can be processed at the same time.

TERMINOLOGY NOTE

The term Hyper-Threading, which appears in many computer ads, refers to a technology that enables processors to execute multiple instructions in parallel.

to a pizza conveyor belt. A pizza (instruction) starts moving along the conveyor belt into the oven, but before it reaches the end, another pizza starts moving along the belt. Parallel processing is similar to a pizzeria with many ovens. Just as these ovens can bake more than one pizza at a time, a parallel processor can execute more than one instruction at a time.

With so many factors to consider, how can I compare microprocessor performance? Various testing laboratories run a series of tests to gauge the overall speed of a microprocessor. The results of these tests—called **benchmarks**—can then be compared to the results for other microprocessors. The results of benchmark tests are usually available on the Web and published in computer magazine articles.

TODAY'S MICROPROCESSORS

Which companies produce most of today's popular microprocessors? Intel is the world's largest chipmaker and supplies a sizeable percentage of the microprocessors that power PCs. In 1971, Intel introduced the world's first microprocessor—the 4004. The company has produced a steady stream of new processor models, including the 8088 processor that powered the original IBM PC.

AMD (Advanced Micro Devices) is Intel's chief rival in the PC chip market. Motorola is the main chip supplier for Apple computers. Transmeta Corporation specializes in chips for mobile computing devices, such as tablet computers.

Which microprocessor is best for my PC? Microprocessor models and enhancements seem to appear more frequently than new car models. Intel is continually upgrading its line of Pentium processors. After introducing the original Pentium in 1993, the Pentium II was unveiled in 1997, the Pentium III in 1999, the Pentium 4 in 2000, the Itanium in 2001, and the Itanium2 in 2002. Intel's "budget" Celeron processors are not quite as powerful as the Pentiums, but they do a fine job of running software, and might mean a savings of $100 to $300 on the price of a computer.

AMD's Athlon and Opteron processors are direct competitors to Intel's Pentium and Itanium lines. AMD processors are less expensive than comparable Intel models and have a slight performance advantage according to some benchmarks.

The microprocessor that's "best" for you depends on your budget and the type of work and play you plan to do. The microprocessors marketed with the current crop of computers can handle most business, educational, and entertainment applications (Figure 2-15). You'll want to consider the fastest processor offerings from Intel or AMD if you typically engage in processing-hungry activities, such as 3-D animated computer games, desktop publishing, or video editing.

Can I replace my computer's microprocessor with a faster one? It is technically possible to upgrade your computer's microprocessor, but computer owners rarely do so. The price of the latest, greatest microprocessor can often get you more than halfway to buying an entirely new computer system. Technical factors also discourage microprocessor upgrades. A microprocessor can operate at full efficiency only if all components in the computer can also handle the faster speeds. In many cases, installing a new processor in an old computer can be like attaching a huge outboard engine to a canoe. Safety issues aside, a canoe is not designed to handle all that power, so you can't expect it to go as fast as a high-performance speedboat.

FIGURE 2-15

Today's popular personal computer, server, and workstation microprocessors.

Intel Pentium 4
32-bit processor
PN: 5xx 2.8–3.6 GHz
CISC instruction set Hyper-Threading technology
Popular for desktop computers and servers

Intel Itanium 2
64-bit processor
1.0–1.6 GHz
Popular for workstations and servers

Intel Pentium M
32-bit processor
PN 7xx 1.7–2.6 GHz
Popular for mobile computing devices, such as notebook and tablet computers

Intel Celeron
32-bit processor
PN 3xx 950MHz–2.8 GHz
Popular for low-cost computers

AMD Athlon
32-bit processor
2.0–2.4 GHz
Popular alternative to Intel Pentium processors

Transmeta Crusoe
32-bit processor
500 MHz–1.6 GHz
Used in mobile computing devices, such as tablet computers

Motorola PowerPC
32-bit RISC processor
1.8–2.5 GHz
Used in Apple Power Mac, iMac, and PowerBook computers

INFOWEBLINKS

For updates on popular microprocessors, you can connect to the **Microprocessor Update InfoWeb**.

www.course.com/np/concepts8/ch02

RANDOM ACCESS MEMORY

What is RAM? **RAM** (random access memory) is a temporary holding area for data, application program instructions, and the operating system. In a personal computer, RAM is usually several chips or small circuit boards that plug into the system board within the computer's system unit.

A computer's RAM capacity is invariably included in the list of specifications in a computer ad (Figure 2-16). The amount of RAM in a computer can affect the overall price of a computer system. To understand how much RAM your computer needs and to understand computer ad terminology, it is handy to have a little background on how RAM works and what it does.

FIGURE 2-16

A computer ad typically specifies the amount and type of RAM.

■ **Intel Pentium 4 560 32-bit processor 3.6 GHz with Hyper-Threading**
■ **1 MB L2 cache**
■ **1 GB 533 MHz SDRAM (max. 4 GB)**
■ **160 GB SATA HD (7600 rpm)**
■ **48 X CD-RW + 12 X DVD+RW/+R with double-layer write capable**
■ **3.5" 1.44 MB floppy disk drive**

Why is RAM so important? RAM is the "waiting room" for the computer's processor. It holds raw data waiting to be processed as well as the program instructions for processing that data. In addition, RAM holds the results of processing until they can be stored more permanently on disk or tape. Let's look at an example. When you use personal finance software to balance your checkbook, you enter raw data for check amounts, which is held in RAM. The personal finance software sends the instructions for processing this data to RAM. The processor uses these instructions to calculate your checkbook balance and sends the results back to RAM. From RAM, your checkbook balance can be stored on disk, displayed, or printed (Figure 2-17).

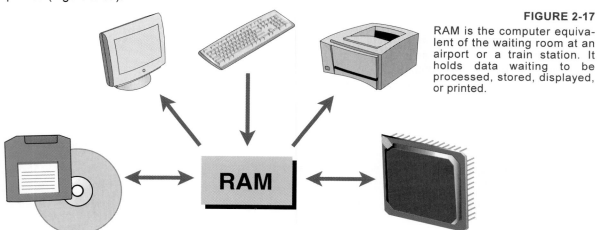

FIGURE 2-17

RAM is the computer equivalent of the waiting room at an airport or a train station. It holds data waiting to be processed, stored, displayed, or printed.

RAM

In addition to data and application software instructions, RAM also holds operating system instructions that control the basic functions of a computer system. These instructions are loaded into RAM every time you start your computer, and they remain there until you turn off your computer.

How does RAM differ from hard-disk storage? People who are new to computers sometimes tend to confuse RAM and hard-disk storage, maybe because both components hold data, because they typically are "hidden" inside the system unit, or because they can both be measured in gigabytes. To differentiate between RAM and hard-disk storage, remember that RAM holds data in circuitry that's directly connected to the system board, whereas hard-disk storage places data on magnetic media. RAM is temporary storage; hard-disk storage is more permanent. In addition, RAM usually has less storage capacity than that of hard-disk storage.

How does RAM work? In RAM, microscopic electronic parts called **capacitors** hold the bits that represent data. You can visualize the capacitors as microscopic lights that can be turned on or off. A charged capacitor is "turned on" and represents a "1" bit. A discharged capacitor is "turned off" and represents a "0" bit. Each bank of capacitors holds eight bits—one byte of data. A RAM address on each bank helps the computer locate data, as needed, for processing (Figure 2-18).

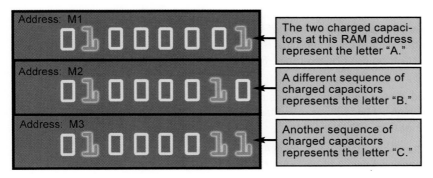

FIGURE 2-18
Each RAM location has an address and uses eight capacitors to hold the eight bits that represent a byte.

In some respects, RAM is similar to a chalkboard. You can use a chalkboard to write mathematical formulas, erase them, and then write an outline for a report. In a similar way, RAM can hold numbers and formulas when you balance your checkbook, and then hold the outline of your English essay when you use word processing software. RAM contents can be changed just by changing the charge of the capacitors.

Unlike disk storage, most RAM is **volatile**, which means it requires electrical power to hold data. If the computer is turned off or the power goes out, all data stored in RAM instantly and permanently disappears. When someone exclaims, "Rats! I just lost my document," it often means the person was entering the text of a document (which was being held in RAM), and the power went out before the data was saved on disk.

How much RAM does my computer need? RAM capacity is expressed in megabytes or gigabytes. Today's personal computers typically feature between 128 MB and 2 GB of RAM. The amount of RAM your computer needs depends on the software you use. RAM requirements are routinely specified on the outside of a software package (Figure 2-19). If you need more RAM, you can purchase and install additional memory up to the limit the computer manufacturer sets. For good basic performance, a computer running Windows software should have at least 256 MB of RAM. Games, desktop publishing, graphics, and video applications tend to run more smoothly with at least 512 MB of RAM.

Can my computer run out of memory? Suppose that you want to work with several programs and large graphics at the same time. Will your computer eventually run out of memory? The answer is "probably not." Today's personal computer operating systems are quite adept at allocating RAM space to multiple programs. If a program exceeds its allocated space, the operating system uses an area of the hard disk, called **virtual memory**, to store parts of programs or data files until they are needed. By selectively exchanging the data in RAM with the data in virtual memory, your computer effectively gains almost unlimited memory capacity.

Too much dependence on virtual memory can have a negative affect on your computer's performance, however, because getting data from a mechanical device, such as a hard disk drive, is much slower than getting data from an electronic device, such as RAM. To minimize virtual memory use, load up your computer with as much RAM as possible.

FIGURE 2-19
Minimum RAM requirements are typically displayed on the package of a software product.

System Requirements:

- Windows XP/2000/NT4 Pentium III with 64 MB of RAM
- Windows ME/98(SE)/98, Pentium III with 32 MB of RAM
- 40 MB hard drive space
- CD-ROM drive
- Mouse
- Internet connection (optional)
- Printer (optional)
- Scanner or digital camera with 32-bit twain interface (optional)

Do all computers use the same type of RAM? No. RAM components vary in speed, technology, and configuration. Many computer ads provide information on all three aspects of RAM, but consumers who want lots of fast RAM for 3-D gaming and desktop publishing have to wade through a thicket of acronyms and technical jargon. To unlock the meaning of RAM specifications, such as "1 GB 533 MHz SDRAM," you need an understanding of a few more acronyms and abbreviations.

RAM speed is often expressed in nanoseconds or megahertz. One **nanosecond** (ns) is 1 billionth of a second. In the context of RAM speed, lower nanosecond ratings are better because it means the RAM circuitry can react faster to update the data it holds. For example, 8 ns RAM is faster than 10 ns RAM.

RAM speed can also be expressed in MHz (millions of cycles per second). Just the opposite of nanoseconds, higher MHz ratings mean faster speeds. For example, 533 MHz RAM is faster than 400 MHz RAM.

Most of today's personal computers use SDRAM or RDRAM. **SDRAM** (synchronous dynamic RAM) is fast and relatively inexpensive. Recent innovations, such as dual channel technology and double data rate (DDR) have increased SDRAM speed. **RDRAM** (rambus dynamic RAM) was first developed for the popular Nintendo 64 game system and then adapted for use in personal computers. RDRAM is more expensive than SDRAM and is usually found in high-performance workstations. RAM is configured as a series of DIPs soldered onto a small circuit board, as shown in Figure 2-20.

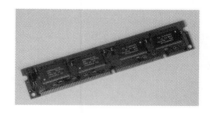

FIGURE 2-20

SDRAM is the most popular type of RAM in today's computers. It is typically available on a small circuit board called a DIMM (dual inline memory module). When adding memory to a computer, check with the computer manufacturer to make sure you purchase the correct RAM type and speed.

READ-ONLY MEMORY

How is ROM different from RAM? **ROM** (read-only memory) is a type of memory circuitry that holds the computer's startup routine. ROM is housed in a single integrated circuit—usually a fairly large, caterpillar-like DIP package—which is plugged into the system board.

Whereas RAM is temporary and volatile, ROM is permanent and non-volatile. ROM circuitry holds "hard-wired" instructions that are a permanent part of the circuitry and remain in place even when the computer power is turned off. This is a familiar concept to anyone who has used a hand calculator that includes various "hard-wired" routines for calculating square roots, cosines, and other functions. The instructions in ROM are permanent, and the only way to change them is to replace the ROM chip.

If a computer has RAM, why does it need ROM too? When you turn on your computer, the microprocessor receives electrical power and is ready to begin executing instructions. As a result of the power being off, however, RAM is empty and doesn't contain any instructions for the microprocessor to execute. Now ROM plays its part. ROM contains a small set of instructions called the **ROM BIOS** (basic input/output system). These instructions tell the computer how to access the hard disk, find the operating system, and load it into RAM. After the operating system is loaded, the computer can understand your input, display output, run software, and access your data.

CMOS MEMORY

Where does a computer store its basic hardware settings? To operate correctly, a computer must have some basic information about storage, memory, and display configurations. For example, your computer needs to know how much memory is available so that it can allocate space for all the programs you want to run. RAM goes blank when the computer power is turned off, so configuration information cannot be stored there. ROM would not be a good place for this information, either, because it holds data on a permanent basis. If, for example, your computer stored the memory size in ROM, you could never add more memory—well, you might be able to add it, but you couldn't change the size specification in ROM. To store some basic system information, your computer needs a type of memory that's more permanent than RAM, but less permanent than ROM. CMOS is just the ticket.

CMOS memory (complementary metal oxide semiconductor memory), pronounced "SEE moss," is a type of chip that requires very little power to hold data. It can be powered by a small battery that's integrated into the system board and automatically recharges while your computer power is on. The battery trickles power to the CMOS chip so that it can retain vital data about your computer system configuration even when your computer is turned off.

When you change the configuration of your computer system—by adding RAM, for example—the data in CMOS must be updated. Some operating systems recognize such changes and automatically perform the update. You can manually change CMOS settings by running the CMOS setup program, as described in Figure 2-21.

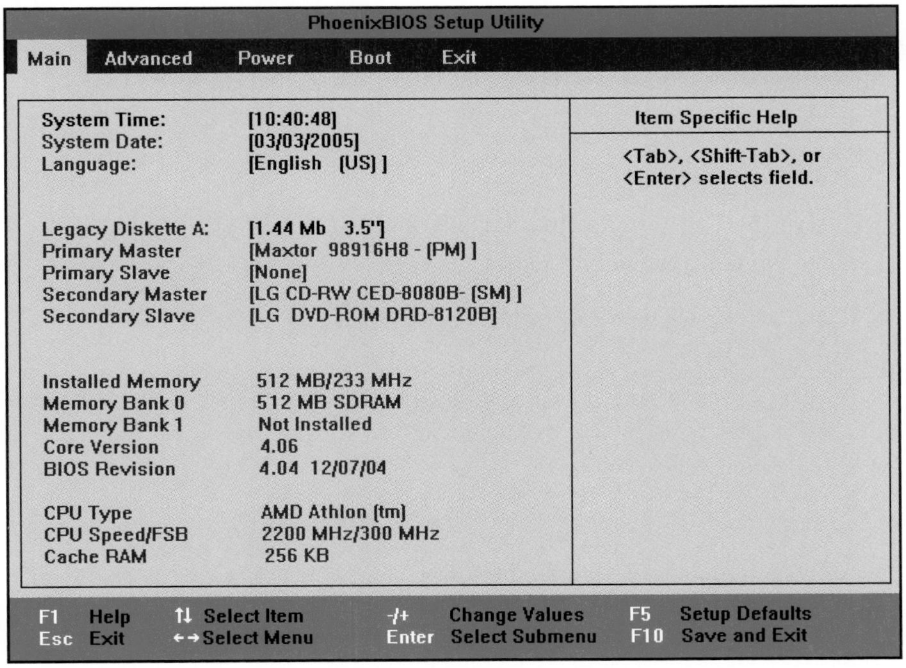

FIGURE 2-21

CMOS holds computer configuration settings, such as the date and time, hard disk capacity, number of floppy disk drives, and RAM capacity. To access the CMOS setup program, hold down the F1 key as your computer boots. But be careful! If you make a mistake with these settings, your computer might not be able to start.

```
                    PhoenixBIOS Setup Utility
 Main    Advanced    Power    Boot    Exit

   System Time:        [10:40:48]                Item Specific Help
   System Date:        [03/03/2005]
   Language:           [English  [US] ]         <Tab>, <Shift-Tab>, or
                                                <Enter> selects field.

   Legacy Diskette A:  [1.44 Mb   3.5"]
   Primary Master      [Maxtor  98916H8 - [PM] ]
   Primary Slave       [None]
   Secondary Master    [LG CD-RW CED-8080B- [SM] ]
   Secondary Slave     [LG  DVD-ROM DRD-8120B]

   Installed Memory    512 MB/233 MHz
   Memory Bank 0       512 MB SDRAM
   Memory Bank 1       Not Installed
   Core Version        4.06
   BIOS Revision       4.04  12/07/04

   CPU Type            AMD Athlon [tm]
   CPU Speed/FSB       2200 MHz/300 MHz
   Cache RAM           256 KB

 F1   Help     ↑↓ Select Item     -/+   Change Values    F5   Setup Defaults
 Esc  Exit     ←→Select Menu    Enter   Select Submenu   F10  Save and Exit
```

If you mistakenly enter the Setup program, follow the on-screen instructions to exit and proceed with the boot process. In Figure 2-21, the Esc (Escape) key allows you to exit the Setup program without making any changes to the CMOS settings.

What information about memory in computer ads is most important? Even though ROM and CMOS have important roles in the operation of a computer, RAM capacity really makes a difference you can notice. The more data and programs that can fit into RAM, the less time your computer will spend moving data to and from virtual memory. With lots of RAM, you'll find that documents scroll faster, games respond more quickly, and many graphics operations take less time than with a computer that has a skimpy RAM capacity.

Most ads specify RAM capacity, speed, and type. Now when you see the specification "512 MB 400 MHz SDRAM (max. 2 GB)" in a computer ad, you'll know that the computer's RAM capacity is 512 megabytes (plenty to run most of today's software), that it operates at 400 megahertz (fairly fast), and that it uses SDRAM (a little slower and less expensive than RDRAM). You'll also have important information about the maximum amount of RAM that can be installed in the computer—2 GB, which is more than enough for the typical computer owner who does a bit of word processing, surfs the Web, and plays computer games.

BUYING A COMPUTER

How do I get the best computer for my money? Different buyers have different needs, so your first step in buying a computer is to assess your budget and think about how you plan to use your computer. Armed with an understanding of the terminology you learned in Sections A and B, you can begin to look at ads and visit online computer stores. The Computer Buyer's Guide InfoWeb is designed to help you get started. Sections C and D provide information about storage and add-on devices that you'll also find useful when shopping for a new computer.

INFOWEBLINKS

The **Computer Buyer's Guide InfoWeb** contains all kinds of tips about how to be a savvy computer shopper. Plus, you'll find worksheets to help assess your needs, compare different computers, and shop for fun accessories. ✝

www.course.com/np/concepts8/ch02

QUICKCHECK......SECTION B

1. The ALU uses ⬚ to hold data as the microprocessor performs arithmetic and logical operations.

2. The ⬚ unit in the CPU fetches instructions and coordinates the operation of the entire computer system.

3. Microprocessor ⬚ sets can be classified as CISC or RISC.

4. A microprocessor's ⬚ speed is provided in a specification such as 3.6 GHz.

5. Some chip makers use a ⬚ number, such as 560, to differentiate microprocessors.

6. RAM is ⬚, which means that it cannot hold data when the computer power is off.

7. A computer does not usually run out of RAM because it can use an area of the hard disk called ⬚ memory.

8. The instructions for loading the operating system into RAM when a computer is first turned on are stored in ⬚ memory.

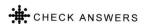 CHECK ANSWERS

LAB 2-B

BENCHMARKING

In this lab, you'll learn:

- Which computer performance factors can be measured by benchmark tests
- How to run a test that identifies a computer's processor type, RAM capacity, and graphics card type
- How to run benchmarking software that analyzes a computer's processor speed and graphics processing speed
- How to interpret the results of a benchmark test
- How to compare the results from benchmark tests that were performed on different system configurations
- When benchmark tests might not provide accurate information on computer performance

_____

INTERACTIVE LAB

CLICK TO START THE LAB ✤

_____

LAB ASSIGNMENTS

1. Start the interactive part of the lab. Insert your Tracking Disk if you want to save your QuickCheck results. Perform each lab step as directed, and answer all the lab QuickCheck questions. When you exit the lab, your answers are automatically graded and your results are displayed.

2. If Microsoft Word is available, use the System Info button to analyze the computer you typically use. Provide the results of the analysis along with a brief description of the computer you tested and its location (at home, at work, in a computer lab, and so on).

PROCESSOR BENCHMARKS

Processor	Quake 3 Arena	Sysmark2000
Athlon 1.466 MHz	204.7	267
Pentium 4 1.5 GHz	219.5	210

3. From the Processor Benchmarks table above, which processor appears to be faster at graphics processing? Which processor appears to be better at overall processing tasks?

4. Explain why you might perform a benchmark test on your own computer, but get different results from those stated in a computer magazine, which tested the same computer with the same benchmark test.

5. Use a search engine on the Web to find benchmark ratings for Intel's Pentium 4 processors. What do these ratings show about the relative performance for 1.5 GHz, 2.4 GHz, and 3.0 GHz Pentium 4s?

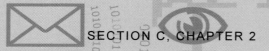

STORAGE DEVICES

Computer manufacturers typically try to entice consumers by configuring computers with a variety of storage devices, such as a floppy disk drive, hard disk drive, and some sort of CD or DVD drive. What's the point of having so many storage devices? As it turns out, none of today's storage technologies is perfect. One technology might provide fast access to data, but it might also be susceptible to problems that could potentially wipe out all your data. A different technology might be more dependable, but it might have the disadvantage of relatively slow access to data.

Smart shoppers make sure their new computers are equipped with a variety of storage devices. Informed computer owners understand the strengths and weaknesses of each storage technology so that they can use these devices with maximum effectiveness. In this section, you'll learn many secrets that can make you a smart storage technology buyer and owner. The storage technologies you'll learn about are now used in a variety of devices—from digital cameras to player pianos—so an understanding of storage technology can be useful outside the boundaries of personal computing.

STORAGE BASICS

What are the basic components of a data storage system? A data storage system has two main components: a storage medium and a storage device. A **storage medium** (storage media is the plural) is the disk, tape, CD, DVD, paper, or other substance that contains data. A **storage device** is the mechanical apparatus that records and retrieves data from a storage medium. Storage devices include floppy disk drives, Zip drives, hard disk drives, tape drives, CD drives, and DVD drives. The term "storage technology" refers to a storage device and the media it uses.

How does a storage system interact with other computer components? You can think of your computer's storage devices as having a direct pipeline to RAM. Data gets copied from a storage device into RAM, where it waits to be processed. After data is processed, it is held temporarily in RAM, but it is usually copied to a storage medium for more permanent safekeeping.

As you know, a computer works with data that has been coded into bits that can be represented by 1s and 0s. When data is stored, these 1s and 0s must be converted into some kind of signal or mark that's fairly permanent, but can be changed when necessary.

Obviously, the data is not literally written as "1" or "0." Instead, the 1s and 0s must be transformed into changes in the surface of a storage medium. Exactly how this transformation happens depends on the storage technology. For example, floppy disks store data in a different way than CD-ROMs. Three types of storage technologies are commonly used for personal computers: magnetic, optical, and solid state.

INFOWEBLINKS

For a table that compares the speeds, costs, and capacities of popular storage devices, and to get an update on the latest computer storage technologies, connect to the **Storage Frontiers InfoWeb**.

www.course.com/np/concepts8/ch02

TERMINOLOGY NOTE

The process of storing data is often referred to as "writing data" or "saving a file" because the storage device writes the data on the storage medium to save it for later use.

The process of retrieving data is often referred to as "reading data," "loading data," or "opening a file."

How does magnetic storage work? Hard disk, floppy disk, and tape storage technologies can be classified as **magnetic storage**, which stores data by magnetizing microscopic particles on the disk or tape surface. The particles retain their magnetic orientation until that orientation is changed, thereby making disks and tapes fairly permanent but modifiable storage media. A **read-write head** mechanism in the disk drive reads and writes the magnetized particles that represent data. Figure 2-22 shows how a computer stores data on magnetic media.

FIGURE 2-22

Before data is stored, particles on the surface of the disk are scattered in random patterns. The disk drive's read-write head magnetizes the particles, and orients them in a positive (north) or negative (south) direction. These patterns of magnetized particles represent 0 and 1 bits.

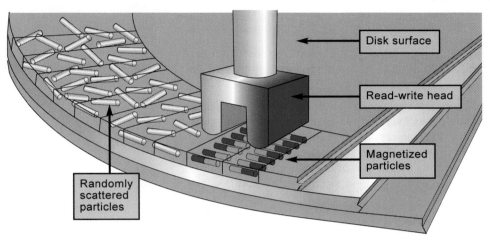

Disk surface

Read-write head

Magnetized particles

Randomly scattered particles

Data stored magnetically can be easily changed or deleted simply by changing the magnetic orientation of the appropriate particles on the disk surface. This feature of magnetic storage provides lots of flexibility for editing data and reusing areas of a storage medium containing unneeded data.

Data stored on magnetic media such as floppy disks can be altered by magnetic fields, dust, mold, smoke particles, heat, and mechanical problems with a storage device. Placing a magnet on a floppy disk, for example, is a sure way of losing data.

Magnetic media gradually lose their magnetic charge, resulting in lost data. Some experts estimate that the reliable life span of data stored on magnetic media is about three years. They recommend that you refresh your data every two years by recopying it.

How does optical storage work? CD and DVD storage technologies can be classified as **optical storage**, which stores data as microscopic light and dark spots on the disk surface. The dark spots, shown in Figure 2-23, are called **pits**. The lighter, non-pitted surface areas of the disk are called **lands**.

Optical storage gets its name because data is read using a laser light, and it is possible to see the data using a high-powered microscope. The transition between pits and lands is interpreted as the 1s and 0s that represent data. An optical storage device uses a low-power laser light to read the data stored on an optical disk.

The surface of an optical disk is coated with clear plastic, making the disk quite durable and less susceptible to environmental damage than data recorded on magnetic media. An optical disk, such as a CD, is not susceptible to humidity, fingerprints, dust, magnets, or spilled soft drinks, and its useful life is estimated at more than 200 years.

FIGURE 2-23

As seen through an electron microscope, the pits on an optical storage disk look like small craters. Each pit is less than 1 micron (one millionth of a meter) in diameter—1,500 pits lined up side by side are about as wide as the head of a pin.

How does solid state storage work? A variety of compact storage cards can be classified as **solid state storage**, which stores data in a non-volatile, erasable, low-power chip. The chip's circuitry is arranged as a grid (Figure 2-24), and each cell in the grid contains two transistors that act as gates. When the gates are open, current can flow and the cell has a value that represents a "1" bit. When the gates are closed by a process called Fowler-Nordheim tunneling, the cell has a value that represents a "0" bit. Very little power is required to open or close the gates, which makes solid state storage ideal for battery-operated devices, such as digital cameras. Once the data is stored, it is non-volatile—the chip retains the data without the need for an external power source.

Some solid state storage requires a device called a **card reader** to transfer data to or from a computer. Other solid state storage plugs directly into a USB port on a computer's system unit.

Solid state storage provides faster access to data than magnetic or optical storage technology because it includes no moving parts. Solid state storage is very durable—it is virtually impervious to vibration, magnetic fields, or extreme temperature fluctuations. On the downside, the capacity of solid state storage does not currently match that of hard disks, or DVDs. The cost per megabyte of storage—about 25¢—is significantly higher than for magnetic or optical storage.

Can I add storage devices to my computer? Many storage devices—especially those for solid state storage media—simply plug into connectors built into your computer's system unit. You'll learn more about these connectors, including USB, in Section D.

As an alternative, you can install storage devices inside your computer's system unit case in "parking spaces" called **drive bays**. An external drive bay provides access from outside the system unit—a necessity for a storage device with removable media, such as floppy disks, CDs, tapes, and DVDs. Internal drive bays are located deep inside the system unit and are designed for hard disk drives, which don't use removable storage media (Figure 2-25).

FIGURE 2-24

A solid state storage medium stores data in a microscopic grid of cells. A card reader transfers data between the card and a computer.

FIGURE 2-25

Most notebook computers provide bays for one floppy disk drive, one hard disk drive, and one CD or DVD drive.

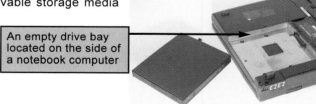

An empty drive bay located on the side of a notebook computer

An empty 5.25" drive bay can hold CD, DVD, tape, or multifunction solid state drives

An empty 3.5" drive bay can hold a floppy disk drive

Most desktop computers have several drive bays, some accessible from outside the case, and others—designed for hard disk drives—without any external access.

Empty drive bays are typically hidden from view with a face plate.

CLICK TO START

Which storage technology is best? Each storage technology has its advantages and disadvantages. If one storage system was perfect, we wouldn't need so many disk and tape drives connected to our computers! To compare storage devices, it is useful to apply the criteria of versatility, durability, speed, and capacity:

- **Versatility.** Some storage devices can access data from only one type of medium. More versatile devices can access data from several different media. A floppy disk drive, for example, can access only floppy disks, whereas a DVD drive can access computer DVDs, DVD movies, audio CDs, computer CDs, and CD-Rs.

- **Durability.** Most storage technologies are susceptible to damage from mishandling or other environmental factors, such as heat and moisture. Some technologies are more susceptible than others to damage that could cause data loss. Optical and solid state technologies tend to be less susceptible than magnetic technologies.

- **Speed.** Quick access to data is important, so fast storage devices are preferred over slower devices. **Access time** is the average time it takes a computer to locate data on the storage medium and read it. Access time for a personal computer storage device, such as a disk drive, is measured in milliseconds (thousandths of a second). One millisecond (ms) is one-thousandth of a second. Lower numbers indicate faster access times. For example, a drive with a 6 ms access time is faster than a drive with an access time of 11 ms.

  Access time is best for random-access devices. **Random access** (also called "direct access") is the ability of a device to "jump" directly to the requested data. Floppy disk, hard disk, CD, and DVD drives are random-access devices, as is solid state storage. A tape drive, on the other hand, must use slower **sequential access** by reading through the data from the beginning of the tape. The advantage of random access becomes clear when you consider how much faster and easier it is to locate a song on a CD (random access) than on a cassette tape (sequential access).

  Data transfer rate is the amount of data a storage device can move per second from the storage medium to the computer. Higher numbers indicate faster transfer rates. For example, a CD-ROM drive with a 600 KBps (kilobytes per second) data transfer rate is faster than one with a 300 KBps transfer rate.

- **Capacity.** In today's computing environment, higher capacity is almost always preferred. Storage capacity is the maximum amount of data that can be stored on a storage medium, and it is measured in kilobytes, megabytes, gigabytes, or terabytes.

FLOPPY DISK TECHNOLOGY

What is floppy disk technology? One of the oldest storage technologies, floppy disks are classified as magnetic storage because data is stored by magnetizing microscopic particles on the disk surface. A **floppy disk** is a round piece of flexible mylar plastic covered with a thin layer of magnetic oxide and sealed inside a protective casing. If you break open the disk casing (something you should never do unless you want to ruin the disk), you would see that the mylar disk inside is thin and literally floppy. Floppy disk technology is used for standard HD DS disks as well as Zip disks.

What is a standard HD DS disk? At one time, just about every personal computer included a floppy disk drive designed for high-density (HD) double-sided (DS) disks. These "standard" floppy disks (Figure 2-26) are still in use. They have a capacity of 1.44 MB—enough space for a 300-page

FIGURE 2-26

A standard floppy disk drive, reads and writes data on a 3.5" HD DS floppy disk.

document or one medium-resolution photograph. Floppy disks are also referred to as "floppies" or "diskettes." It is not correct to call them "hard disks" even though they seem to have a "hard" or rigid plastic casing. The term "hard disk" refers to an entirely different storage technology.

What are the advantages and disadvantages of HD DS floppy disks? When just about every computer had a floppy disk drive, files could be easily transferred from one computer to another using a floppy disk. Floppies are still used in some school computer labs so that students can transport their data to different lab machines or their personal computers. Today, however, many computers do not have a standard floppy disk drive. File transfers tend to take place using other technologies. Solid state storage media is smaller and more durable for mobile applications. Local computer networks and the Internet have made it easy to share data files without physically transporting them from one place to another.

A standard floppy disk's 1.44 MB capacity is not really sufficient for today's media-intensive applications. Many MP3 music files and photos are too large to fit on a floppy. In the past, floppy disks were extensively used to distribute software. CDs and DVDs offer more capacity for distributing the huge files for today's software applications. Web downloads offer more convenience for smaller files.

Can I protect the data on a HD DS floppy disk? An HD DS floppy disk features a **write-protect window** (Figure 2-27). When you open the window, the disk is "write-protected," which means that a computer cannot write data on the disk. Although it sounds like a useful feature, the write-protect window doesn't do much to protect your data from accidental erasures or changes. Typically when you use a disk, you want to save a new file or modify the data in an existing file. To do so, you must close the write-protect window and the disk is no longer protected. Therefore, when you use a disk and the chance of mistakenly deleting data is highest, you're not likely to have the write-protect feature on.

What is a Zip disk? A Zip disk is a special high-capacity floppy disk, available in 100 MB, 250 MB, and 750 MB versions. Zip disks and their drives, shown in Figure 2-28, are manufactured by Iomega. A Zip drive does not read standard HD DS floppy disks and Zip disks cannot be read by a standard floppy disk drive.

What are the advantages and disadvantages of Zip disks? Zip disks offer portability, simplicity, speed, and security. The storage capacity of Zip disks makes them more useful than standard HD DS floppy disks for storing large music and photo files. The process of reading and writing data is relatively fast and easy. Files on a Zip disk can even be password protected to ensure the security of important data.

Even the highest capacity Zip disks have far less capacity than DVDs or hard disks, however. They cannot substitute for a hard disk as primary storage, nor can they substitute for DVDs for video applications.

How can Zip disks store more data than a standard floppy disk? The amount of data that a disk stores depends on its density. **Disk density** refers to the closeness and size of the magnetic particles on the disk surface. The higher the disk density, the smaller the magnetic particles on the disk surface, and the more data it can store. Think of it this way: Just as you can put more lemons than grapefruit in a basket, you can store more data on a disk coated with smaller particles than one with larger particles. Zip disks store data at a higher density than a standard 3.5" floppy disk.

FIGURE 2-27
When the write-protect window is open, the disk drive cannot add, modify, or delete data from a disk.

FIGURE 2-28
A Zip disk requires a special disk drive, but is transportable and provides more storage capacity than a standard floppy disk.

HARD DISK TECHNOLOGY

Why are hard disk drives so popular? Hard disk technology is the preferred type of main storage for most computer systems for three reasons. First, it provides lots of storage capacity. Second, it provides fast access to files. Third, a hard disk is economical. Incredibly, a hard disk typically stores millions of times more data than a floppy disk, but a hard disk drive might cost only three times as much as a floppy disk drive.

How does a hard disk work? A hard disk is one or more platters and their associated read-write heads. A **hard disk platter** is a flat, rigid disk made of aluminum or glass and coated with magnetic iron oxide particles. Each platter has a read-write head that hovers over the surface to read data, as shown in Figure 2-29.

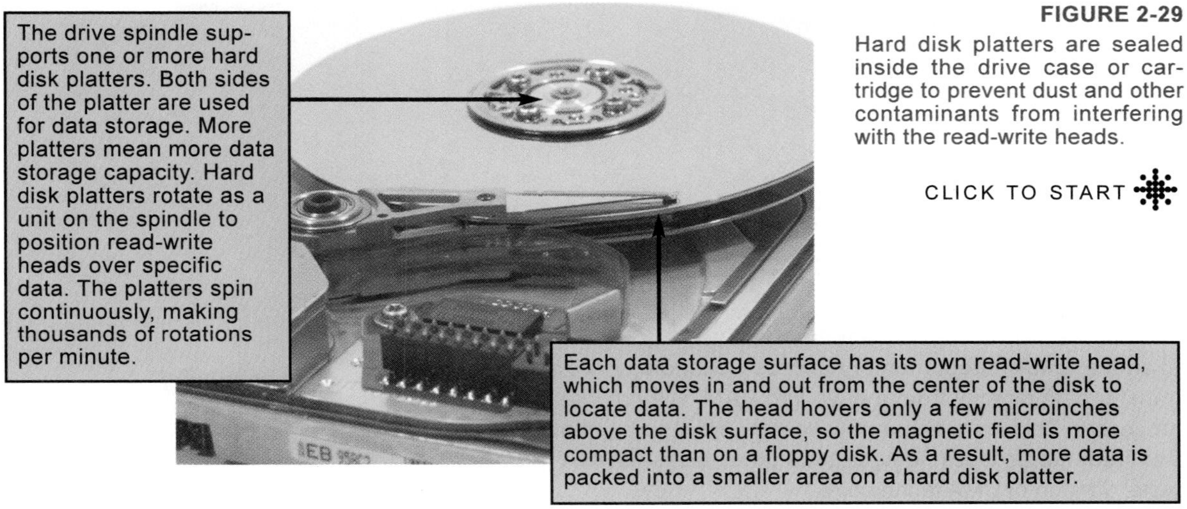

The drive spindle supports one or more hard disk platters. Both sides of the platter are used for data storage. More platters mean more data storage capacity. Hard disk platters rotate as a unit on the spindle to position read-write heads over specific data. The platters spin continuously, making thousands of rotations per minute.

Each data storage surface has its own read-write head, which moves in and out from the center of the disk to locate data. The head hovers only a few microinches above the disk surface, so the magnetic field is more compact than on a floppy disk. As a result, more data is packed into a smaller area on a hard disk platter.

FIGURE 2-29

Hard disk platters are sealed inside the drive case or cartridge to prevent dust and other contaminants from interfering with the read-write heads.

CLICK TO START

Personal computer hard disk platters are typically 3.5" in diameter with storage capacities ranging from 40 to160 GB. Miniature hard drives, such as the 1.8" drive featured on Apple's iPod digital music player, store 20 to 40 GB. The density of particles on the disk surface provide hard disks with capacities far greater than floppy disks. Also, the access time for a hard disk is significantly faster than for a floppy disk. Hard disk access times of 6 to 11 ms are not uncommon, whereas a floppy takes about half a second to spin up to speed and find data. Hard disk drive speed is sometimes measured in revolutions per minute (rpm). The faster a drive spins, the more rapidly it can position the read-write head over specific data. For example, a 7,200 rpm drive is able to access data faster than a 5,400 rpm drive.

Computer ads typically specify the capacity, access time, and speed of a hard disk drive. So "160 GB 8 ms 7200 RPM HD" means a hard disk drive with 160 gigabyte capacity, access time of 8 milliseconds, and speed of 7,200 revolutions per minute.

You might guess that a hard disk drive would fill one platter before storing data on a second platter. However, it is more efficient to store data at the same locations on all platters before moving the read-write heads to the next location. A vertical stack of storage locations is called a "cylinder"—the basic storage bin for a hard disk drive.

What's all this business about Ultra ATA, EIDE, SCSI, and DMA? Computer ads use these acronyms to describe hard disk drive technology. A hard drive mechanism includes a circuit board called a **controller** that

TERMINOLOGY NOTE

You often see the terms "hard disk" and "hard disk drive" used interchangeably. You might also hear the term "fixed disk" used to refer to hard disks.

positions the disk and read-write heads to locate data. Disk drives are classified according to their controllers. Popular drive controllers include SATA,
Ultra ATA, EIDE, and SCSI. Although computer ads often specify the hard
drive controller type, consumers don't really have much choice. If you want
a 160 GB drive, for example, your hardware vendor is likely to offer only
one brand of drive with one type of controller. Figure 2-30 shows a typical
controller mounted on a hard disk drive.

FIGURE 2-30
A hard disk controller circuit
board is typically mounted in
the hard disk drive case.

The storage technology used on many PCs transfers data from a disk,
through the controller, to the processor, and finally to RAM before it is actually processed. Computer ads sometimes specify this technology. For
example, DMA (direct memory access) technology allows a computer to
transfer data directly from a drive into RAM, without intervention from the
processor. This architecture relieves the processor of data-transfer duties
and frees up processing cycles for other tasks. UDMA (ultra DMA) is a
faster version of DMA technology.

What's the downside of hard disk storage? Hard disks are not as
durable as many other storage technologies. The read-write heads in a
hard disk hover a microscopic distance above the disk surface. If a read-
write head runs into a dust particle or some other contaminant on the disk,
it might cause a **head crash**, which damages some of the data on the disk.
To help prevent contaminants from contacting the platters and causing
head crashes, a hard disk is sealed in its case. A head crash can also be
triggered by jarring the hard disk while it is in use. Although hard disks have
become considerably more rugged in recent years, you should still handle
and transport them with care. You should also make sure that you make a
backup copy of the data stored on your hard disk in case of a head crash.

Can I use a second hard disk drive to increase storage space? You
can increase the storage capacity of your computer by adding a second
hard disk drive. A second hard disk drive can also provide backup for your
primary drive. Hard disk drives are available as internal or external units.
Internal drives are inexpensive and can be easily installed in a desktop
computer's system unit. External drives are slightly more expensive and
connect to a desktop or notebook computer using a cable.

Removable hard disks or hard disk cartridges offer even more options.
They contain platters and read-write heads that can be inserted and
removed from the drive much like a floppy disk. Removable hard disks,
such as Iomega's REV drive, provide security for data by allowing you to
remove the hard disk cartridge and store it separately from the computer.

TAPE STORAGE

What's the purpose of a tape drive? As you have learned, a head crash can easily destroy hard disk data. Protecting data on the hard disk is of particular concern because it contains so much data that would be difficult and time-consuming to reconstruct. A **tape backup** is a copy of the data on a hard disk, which is stored on magnetic tape and used to restore lost data. Tape drive manufacturers produce several types of drives and each requires a specific type of tape. Figure 2-31 shows some of the most popular tape formats for personal computer tape drives.

FIGURE 2-31
A tape cartridge is a removable magnetic tape module similar to a cassette tape. Popular tape drives for personal computers use tape cartridges, but there are several specifications and cartridge sizes, including (from top to bottom) ADR (advanced digital recording), Ditto, Travan, and DDS (digital data storage). Check the tape drive manual to make sure you purchase the correct type of tape for your tape drive.

A tape backup device is relatively inexpensive and can simplify the task of reconstructing lost data. A backup tape can hold the entire contents of a hard disk. If the hard drive fails, that data can be copied from the tape to any functional hard disk.

Tape drives are primarily used on business computers. Unlike CDs and DVDs, a tape backup device is not suitable for everyday storage tasks. To find out why, you need to understand how a tape drive works.

How does a tape drive work? A tape is a sequential, rather than a random-access, storage medium. Essentially, data is arranged as a long sequence of bits that begins at one end of the tape and stretches to the other end. The beginning and end of each file are marked with special "header labels." To locate a file, the tape drive must start at one end of the tape and read through all the data until it finds the right header label. A tape can contain hundreds or—in the case of a mainframe—thousands of feet of tape. Access time is measured in seconds, not in milliseconds as for a hard disk drive.

Tape is simply too slow to be practical as your computer's main storage device. Its pokey nature doesn't, however, diminish its effectiveness as a backup device. When you make a backup, you're simply streaming lots of data onto the tape. You don't need to locate specific data or jump back and forth between different files. A sequential device is just fine for this sort of work.

When backing up data, access time is less important than the time it takes to copy data from your hard disk to tape. Manufacturers do not always supply such performance specifications, but most users can expect a tape drive to back up 1 GB in 15-20 minutes. Chapter 4 provides more details on the process and equipment for making backups.

CD AND DVD TECHNOLOGY

Is there a difference between CD and DVD technology? Today, most computers come equipped with some type of optical drive—a CD drive or a DVD drive. The underlying technology for CD and DVD drives is similar, but storage capacities differ.

A computer CD drive is based on the same technology as an audio CD player. A **CD** (compact disc) was originally designed to hold 74 minutes of recorded music. This capacity provides 650 MB of storage space for computer data. Later improvements in CD standards increased the capacity to 80 minutes of music or 700 MB of data.

DVD ("digital video disc" or "digital versatile disk") is a variation of CD technology that was originally designed as an alternative to VCRs, but was quickly adopted by the computer industry to store data. A computer's DVD drive can read disks that contain computer data as well as disks that contain DVD movies.

Originally designed to provide enough storage capacity for a full-length movie, a DVD holds much more data than a CD. The capacity of a DVD is about 4.7 GB (4,700 MB), compared with 650-700 MB on a CD. A **double layer DVD** has two recordable layers on the same side and can store 8.5 GB of data.

How do CD and DVD drives work? CD and DVD drives contain a spindle that rotates the disk over a laser lens. The laser directs a beam of light toward the underside of the disk. Dark "pits" and light "lands" on the disk surface reflect the light differently. As the drive reads the disk, these differences are translated into the 0s and 1s that represent data (Figure 2-32).

FIGURE 2-32
CD and DVD drives use a laser to read data from the underside of a disk.

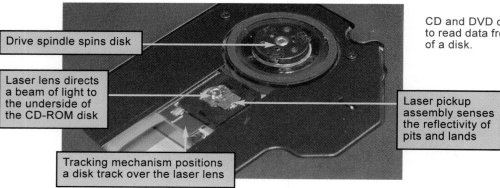

Drive spindle spins disk

Laser lens directs a beam of light to the underside of the CD-ROM disk

Laser pickup assembly senses the reflectivity of pits and lands

Tracking mechanism positions a disk track over the laser lens

Optical drives use several technologies to write data on CD and DVD disks. **Recordable technology** (R) uses a laser to change the color in a dye layer sandwiched beneath the clear plastic disk surface. The laser creates dark spots in the dye that are read as pits. The change in the dye is permanent, so data cannot be changed once it has been recorded.

Rewritable technology (RW) uses "phase change" technology to alter a crystal structure on the disk surface. Altering the crystal structure creates patterns of light and dark spots similar to the pits and lands on a CD. The crystal structure can be changed from light to dark and back again many times, making it possible to record and modify data much like on a hard disk.

The suffixes "R" and "RW" denote specific CD and DVD technologies. For example, CD-R specifies "CD recordable" technology. CD-RW specifies "CD rewritable" technology.

TERMINOLOGY NOTE

DVDs have two types of recordable and two types of rewritable formats. The recordable formats are designated as DVD-R and DVD+R. The rewritable formats are designated as DVD-RW and DVD+RW.

What are my choices for CD and DVD media? Several CD and DVD formats are currently popular for use in personal computers:

- **CD-DA** (compact disc digital audio), more commonly known as "audio CD," is the format for commercial music CDs. Music is typically recorded on audio CDs by the manufacturer, but can't be changed by the consumer.

- **DVD-Video** (digital versatile disc video) is the format for commercial DVDs that contain feature-length films.

- **CD-ROM** (compact disc read-only memory, pronounced "cee dee rom") was the original format for storing computer data. Data is stamped on the disk at the time it is manufactured. Data cannot be added, changed, or deleted from these disks.

- **DVD-ROM** (digital versatile disk read-only memory) contains data stamped onto the disk surface at the time of manufacture. Like CD-ROMs, the data on these disks is permanent, so you cannot add or change data.

- **CD-R** (compact disc recordable) disks store data using recordable technology. The data on a CD-R cannot be erased or modified once you record it. However, most CD-R drives allow you to record your data in multiple sessions. For example, you can store two files on a CD-R disk today, and add data for a few more files to the disk tomorrow.

- **DVD+R** (digital versatile disk recordable) disks store data using recordable technology similar to a CD-R, but with DVD storage capacity.

- **CD-RW** (compact disc rewritable) disks store data using rewritable technology. Stored data can be recorded and erased multiple times, making it a very flexible storage option.

- **DVD+RW** (digital versatile disk rewritable) disks store data using rewritable technology similar to CD-RW, but with DVD storage capacity.

Can I use a single drive to work with any CD or DVD media? Most CD drives can read CD-ROM, CD-R, and CD-RW disks. Most DVD drives can read CD and DVD formats. Storing computer data and creating music CDs requires a recordable or rewritable device. As you can see from the table in Figure 2-33, the most versatile optical storage device is a DVD+R/+RW/CD-RW combo.

INFOWEBLINKS

For more information about current CD and DVD technology, plus tips on how to handle and clean your CDs, connect to the **CD & DVD InfoWeb**.

www.course.com/np/concepts8/ch02

TERMINOLOGY NOTE

Even though CD-ROM and ROM-BIOS both contain the word "ROM," they refer to quite different technologies. ROM BIOS refers to a chip on the system board that contains permanent instructions for the computer's boot sequence. A CD-ROM drive is an optical storage device that's usually installed in one of the system unit's drive bays.

FIGURE 2-33
CD and DVD Capabilities

	Play Audio CDs	Play DVD Movies	Read CD Data	Read DVD Data	Create Music CDs	Store Data on CDs	Store Data on DVDs
CD-ROM Drive	✔		✔				
CD-R Drive	✔		✔		✔	✔	
CD-RW Drive	✔		✔		✔	✔	
DVD/CD-RW Drive	✔	✔	✔	✔	✔	✔	
DVD+R/+RW/CD-RW Drive	✔	✔	✔	✔	✔	✔	✔

Are rewritable CD or DVD drives an acceptable replacement for a hard disk? A rewritable CD or DVD drive is a fine addition to a computer system, but is not a good replacement for a hard disk drive. Unfortunately, the process of accessing, saving, and modifying data on a rewritable disk is relatively slow compared to the speed of hard disk access.

The original CD drives could access 150 KB of data per second. The next generation of drives doubled the data transfer rate and were consequently dubbed "2X" drives. Transfer rates seem to be continually increasing. A 46X CD drive, for example, transfers data at 55.40 Mbps, which is still relatively slow compared to a hard disk drive's transfer rate of 2,560 Mbps.

The speed of a DVD drive is measured on a different scale than a CD drive. A 1X DVD drive is about the same speed as a 9X CD drive. Today's DVD drives typically have 16X speeds for a data transfer rate of 177.28 Mbps.

Is my computer DVD drive the same as the one connected to my TV? Not exactly. Even with the large storage capacity of a DVD, movie files are much too large to fit on a disk unless they are compressed, or shrunk, using a special type of data coding called MPEG-2. The DVD player you connect to your television includes MPEG decoding circuitry, which is not included on your computer's DVD drive. When you play DVD movies on your computer, it uses the CPU as an MPEG decoder. The necessary decoder software is included with Windows or can be located on the DVD itself.

SOLID STATE STORAGE

When would I use solid state storage? Solid state storage is portable, provides fast access to data, and uses very little power, so it is an ideal solution for storing data on mobile devices and transporting data from one device to another. It is widely used in consumer devices, such as digital cameras, MP3 music players, notebook computers, PDAs, and cell phones.

A solid state memory card in a digital camera can hold data for hundreds of snapshots. The card can be removed from the camera and inserted into a card reader that's connected to a computer. Once the data is downloaded, the photos can be edited using the computer's graphics software and trans-mitted via the computer's Internet connection.

Moving data in the other direction, a computer can download MP3 music files and store them on a solid state memory card. That card can be removed from the computer and inserted into a portable MP3 player, so you can hear your favorite tunes while you're on the go.

You can even use solid state storage as you would a floppy disk to trans-port data from one computer to another—say from your home computer to a computer in your school lab or your workplace.

What are my options for solid state storage? Several types of solid state storage are available to today's consumers (Figure 2-34). A **USB flash drive**, such as Sony's MicroVault, is a portable storage device featur-ing a built-in connector that plugs directly into a computer's USB port. A USB flash drive requires no card reader, making it easily transportable from one computer to another. Nicknamed "pen drives" or "keychain drives," USB flash drives are about the size of a highlighter pen and so durable that you can literally carry them on your key ring. You can open, edit, delete, and run files stored on a USB flash drive just as though those files were stored on your computer's hard disk.

FIGURE 2-34
Popular Solid State
Storage Options

USB flash drive: 32 MB–4 GB capacities

CompactFlash card: 8 MB–2 GB capacities

CompactFlash (CF) cards are about the size of a matchbook and provide high storage capacities and access speeds. CompactFlash cards include a built-in controller that reads and writes data within the solid state grid. The built-in controller removes the need for control electronics on the card reader, so the device that connects to your computer to read the card's data is simply an adapter that collects data from the card and shuttles it to the computer's system unit. With their high storage capacities and access speeds, CompactFlash cards are idea for use on high-end digital cameras that require megabytes of storage for each photo.

MultiMedia cards (MMC) offer solid state storage in a package about the size of a postage stamp. Initially used in mobile phones and pages, use of MultiMedia cards has spread to digital cameras and MP3 players. Like CompactFlash cards, MultiMedia cards include a built-in controller, so MMC readers are electronically simple and very inexpensive.

SecureDigital (SD) cards are based on MultiMedia card technology, but feature significantly faster data transfer rates and include cryptographic security protection for copyrighted data and music. SecureDigital cards are popular for storage on digital music players and digital cameras.

SmartMedia cards were originally called "solid state floppy disk cards" because they look much like a miniature floppy disk. Unlike other popular solid state storage, SmartMedia cards do not include a built-in controller, which means that the SmartMedia reader manages the read/write process. These cards are the least durable of the solid state storage media and should be handled with care.

MultiMedia card: 32–512 MB capacities

SecureDigital card: 32 MB–1 GB capacities

SmartMedia card: 32–128 MB capacities

QUICKCHECK......SECTION C

1. A magnetic storage device uses a read-write [_____] to magnetize particles that represent data.

2. Data on an optical storage medium, such as a DVD, is stored as pits and [_____].

3. [_____] time is the average time it takes a computer to locate data on a storage medium and read it.

4. A disk drive is a(n) [_____] access device, whereas a tape drive is a(n) [_____] access device.

5. Higher disk [_____] provides increased storage capacity.

6. Hard disks are susceptible to head [_____], so it is important to make backup copies.

7. CD-RW technology allows you to write data on a disk, and then change that data. True or false? [_____]

8. A(n) [_____] DVD has a capacity of 8.5 GB.

CHECK ANSWERS

INPUT AND OUTPUT DEVICES

This section provides an overview of the most popular input and output devices for personal computers. It begins with input devices, including keyboards, mice, trackpads, and joysticks. Next, a survey of computer display devices helps you sort out the differences among CRT, LCD, and plasma displays. A guide to printers describes today's most popular printer technologies and provides a handy comparison chart. You'll learn about other peripheral devices in later chapters.

You'll also take a look at the computer's expansion bus—the components that carry data to peripheral devices. With an understanding of how the expansion bus works, you'll be able to select, install, and use all kinds of peripherals.

BASIC INPUT DEVICES

What devices can I use to get data into a computer? Most computer systems include a keyboard and pointing device for basic data input. Additional input devices, such as scanners, digital cameras, and graphics tablets, are handy for working with graphical input. Microphones and electronic instruments provide input capabilities for sound and music.

What's special about a computer keyboard's design? The design of most computer keyboards is based on the typewriter's QWERTY layout, which was engineered to keep the typewriter's mechanical keys from jamming. In addition to the basic typing keypad, desktop and notebook computer keyboards include an editing keypad to efficiently move the screen-based insertion point and a collection of function keys designed for computer-specific tasks. Most desktop computer keyboards also include a calculator-style numeric keypad. You can even find tiny keyboards on handheld devices—entering text and numbers is an important part of most computing tasks. Figure 2-35 illustrates a variety of keyboards you might encounter on various computing devices.

FIGURE 2-35
Computer keyboards come in a variety of sizes and styles.

What does a pointing device do? A **pointing device** allows you to manipulate an on-screen pointer and other screen-based graphical controls. The most popular pointing devices for personal computers include mice, trackballs, pointing sticks, trackpads, and joysticks.

How does a mouse work? A standard desktop computer includes a mouse as its primary pointing device. Many computer owners also add a mouse to their notebook computers. A mouse includes one or more buttons that can be "clicked" to input command selections, such as "Start" and "Shut down." To track its position, a computer mouse uses one of two technologies: mechanical or optical (Figure 2-36). Most computer owners prefer the performance of an optical mouse because it provides more precise tracking, greater durability, less maintenance, and more flexibility to use the mouse on a wide variety of surfaces without a mouse pad.

FIGURE 2-36

A mechanical mouse (left) reads its position based on the movement of a ball that rolls over a mouse pad placed on a desk.

An optical mouse uses an onboard chip to track a light beam as it bounces off a surface, such as a desk, clipboard, or mouse pad.

When would I use other pointing devices? A **pointing stick**, or "TrackPoint," looks like the tip of an eraser embedded in the keyboard of a notebook computer. It is a space-saving device that you can push up, down, or sideways to move the on-screen pointer. A **trackpad** is a touch-sensitive surface on which you can slide your fingers to move the on-screen pointer. A **trackball** looks like a mechanical mouse turned upside down. You use your fingers or palm to roll the ball and move the pointer. Pointing sticks, trackpads, and trackballs (Figure 2-37) are typically used with notebook computers as an alternative to a mouse.

A **joystick** looks like a small version of a car's stick shift. Moving the stick provides input to on-screen objects, such as a pointer or an action figure in a computer game. Joysticks, like the one pictured in Figure 2-37, can include several sticks and buttons for arcade-like control when playing computer games.

FIGURE 2-37
Alternative Pointing Devices

Pointing stick   Trackpad   Trackball   Joystick

DISPLAY DEVICES

What are my options for display devices? A computer display screen is usually classified as an output device because it typically shows the results of a processing task. Some screens, however, can be classified as both input and output devices because they include touch-sensitive technology that accepts input. Display devices used for output offer three technology options: CRT, LCD, and plasma (Figure 2-38).

A **CRT** (cathode ray tube) display device uses the same sort of bulky glass tube as a standard television. Gun-like mechanisms in the tube spray beams of electrons toward the screen and activate individual dots of color that form an image. CRT display devices, often simply called "monitors," offer an inexpensive and dependable computer display. They are bulky, however, and consume a fair amount of power.

An **LCD** (liquid crystal display) produces an image by manipulating light within a layer of liquid crystal cells. Modern LCD technology is compact in size and lightweight, and provides an easy-to-read display. LCDs are standard equipment on notebook computers. Standalone LCDs, referred to as "LCD monitors" or "flat panel displays," have also become available for desktop computers as a replacement for CRT monitors. The advantages of LCD monitors include display clarity, low radiation emission, portability, and compactness. They are, however, more expensive than CRT monitors.

Plasma screen technology creates an on-screen image by illuminating miniature colored fluorescent lights arrayed in a panel-like screen. The name "plasma" comes from the type of gas that fills fluorescent lights and gives them their luminescence. Like LCD screens, plasma screens are compact, lightweight, and more expensive than CRT monitors.

CRT, LCD, and plasma screens can be equipped with NTSC (standard American television) or HDTV (high-definition television) circuitry so they accept television signals from an antenna or cable. This technology lets you view computer data and television on the same display device using split-screen or picture-in-picture format.

Which display technology produces the best image? Image quality is a factor of screen size, dot pitch, width of viewing angle, refresh rate, resolution, and color depth. Screen size is the measurement in inches from one corner of the screen diagonally across to the opposite corner. Typical monitor screen sizes range from 13" to 21". On most monitors, the viewable image does not stretch to the edge of the screen. Instead, a black border makes the image smaller than the size specified. Many computer ads now include a measurement of the **viewable image size** (vis).

Dot pitch (dp) is a measure of image clarity. A smaller dot pitch means a crisper image. Technically, dot pitch is the distance in millimeters between like-colored **pixels**—the small dots of light that form an image. A dot pitch between .26 and .23 is typical for today's monitors.

A monitor's **viewing angle width** indicates how far to the side you can still clearly see the screen image. A wide viewing angle indicates that you can view the screen from various positions without compromising image quality. CRT and plasma screens offer the widest viewing angles. Graphics artists tend to prefer CRT screens, which display uniform color from any angle.

In the context of computer displays, **refresh rate** (also referred to as "vertical scan rate") is the speed at which the screen is repainted. Typically, CRT monitors are refreshed 60 times per second (60 Hz) or 75 times per second (75 Hz). The faster the refresh rate, the less the monitor flickers.

FIGURE 2-38
Display Device Technology

CRT

LCD

Gas plasma

INFOWEBLINKS

For up-to-the-minute information on the latest and greatest graphics cards, monitors, and LCD displays, check out the **Display Devices InfoWeb.**

www.course.com/np/concepts8/ch02

The number of colors a monitor can display is referred to as **color depth** or "bit depth." Most PC display devices have the capability to display millions of colors. When set at 24-bit color depth (sometimes called "True Color"), your PC can display more than 16 million colors—and produce what are considered photographic-quality images. Windows allows you to select resolution and color depth. Most desktop owners choose 24-bit color at 1024 x 768 resolution.

The number of horizontal and vertical pixels that a device displays on a screen is referred to as its **resolution**. The resolution for many early PC displays was referred to VGA (Video Graphics Array). Higher resolutions were later provided by **SVGA** (Super VGA), **XGA** (eXtended Graphics Array), **SXGA** (Super XGA), and **UXGA** (Ultra XGA) (Figure 2-39).

At higher resolutions, text and other objects appear smaller, but the computer can display a larger work area, such as an entire page of a document. The two screen shots in Figure 2-40 help you compare a display set at 640 x 480 resolution with a display set at 1024 x 768 resolution.

FIGURE 2-39
Common PC Resolutions

Standard	Resolution
VGA	640 x 480
SVGA	800 x 600
XGA	1024 x 768
SXGA	1280 x 1024
UXGA	1600 x 1200

FIGURE 2-40

The screen on the left shows 1024 x 768 resolution. Notice the size of text and other screen-based objects. The screen on the right shows 640 x 480 resolution. Text and other objects appear larger on the low-resolution screen, but you see a smaller portion of the screen desktop.

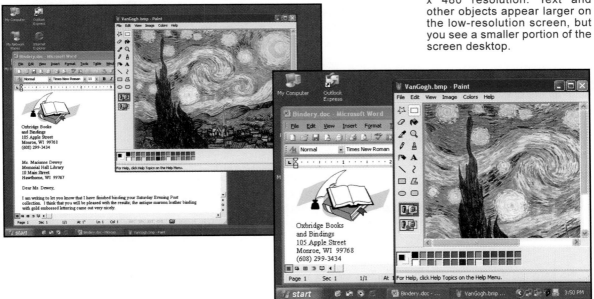

What are the components of a typical computer display system? In addition to a display device, such as a monitor, a computer display system also requires graphics circuitry that generates the signals for displaying an image on the screen. Graphics circuitry, referred to as "integrated graphics", is built into a computer's system board. Graphics circuitry can also be supplied by a small circuit board called a **graphics card** ("graphics board" or "video card"), like the one in Figure 2-41. Today's fastest graphics cards fit into an AGP expansion slot, which you'll learn about later in this section.

A graphics card typically contains a graphics processing unit (GPU) and special video memory, which stores screen images as they are processed, but before they are displayed. Lots of video memory is the key to lightning-fast screen updating for fast action games, 3-D modeling, and graphics-intensive desktop publishing. In addition to video memory, most graphics cards contain special graphics accelerator technology to further boost performance.

FIGURE 2-41

A graphics card is a small circuit board that plugs into the system board.

PRINTERS

What printer technologies are available for personal computers?
Printers are one of the most popular output devices available for personal
computers. Today's best-selling printers typically use ink jet or laser technology. Printer technologies for specialized applications include dot matrix,
solid ink, thermal transfer, and dye sublimation.

How does an ink jet printer work? An **ink jet printer** has a nozzle-like
print head that sprays ink onto paper to form characters and graphics. The
print head in a color ink jet printer consists of a series of nozzles, each with
its own ink cartridge. Most ink jet printers use CMYK color, which requires
only cyan (blue), magenta (pink), yellow, and black inks to create a printout
that appears to have thousands of colors. Alternatively, some printers use
six ink colors to print midtone shades that create slightly more realistic photographic images.

Ink jet printers, such as the one in Figure 2-42, outsell all other types of
printers because they are inexpensive and produce both color and black-
and-white printouts. They work well for most home and small business
applications. Small, portable ink jet printers meet the needs of many mobile
computer owners. Ink jet technology also powers many photo printers,
which are optimized to print high-quality images produced by digital cameras and scanners.

How do laser printers compare to ink jet printers? A **laser printer**,
such as the one in Figure 2-43, uses the same technology as a photocopi-
er to paint dots of light on a light-sensitive drum. Electrostatically charged
ink is applied to the drum and then transferred to paper. Laser technology
is more complex than ink jet technology, which accounts for the higher
price of laser printers.

A basic laser printer produces only black-and-white printouts. Color laser
printers are available, but are somewhat more costly than basic black-and-
white models. Laser printers are often the choice for business printers,
particularly for applications that produce a high volume of printed material.

FIGURE 2-42
Most ink jet printers are small,
lightweight, and inexpensive,
yet produce very good-quality
color output.

FIGURE 2-43
Laser printers are a popular
technology when high-volume
output or good-quality printouts are required.

CLICK TO START ✤

What is a dot matrix printer? When PCs first appeared in the late 1970s,
dot matrix printers were the technology of choice, and they are still
available today. A **dot matrix printer** produces characters and graphics by
using a grid of fine wires. As the print head noisily clatters across the paper,
the wires strike a ribbon and paper in a pattern prescribed by your PC. Dot

matrix printers can print text and graphics—some even print in color using a multicolored ribbon.

Today, dot matrix printers, like the one in Figure 2-44, are used primarily for "back-office" applications that demand low operating cost and dependability, but not high print quality.

Print head contains a matrix of thin wires

FIGURE 2-44

Unlike laser and ink jet technologies, a dot matrix printer actually strikes the paper and, therefore, can print multipart carbon forms.

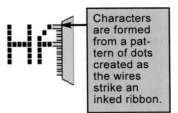

Characters are formed from a pattern of dots created as the wires strike an inked ribbon.

What other printer technologies are available? A **solid ink printer** melts sticks of crayon-like ink and then sprays the liquefied ink through the print head's tiny nozzles. A solid ink printer produces vibrant colors and is sometimes used for professional graphics applications.

A **thermal transfer printer** uses thousands of tiny heating elements to melt the wax from a page-sized ribbon onto specially coated paper or transparency film (the kind used for overhead projectors). This type of printer excels at printing colorful transparencies for presentations, but the fairly expensive per-page costs and the requirement for special paper make it a niche market printer used mainly by businesses.

A **dye sublimation printer** uses technology similar to thermal transfer, but the page-sized ribbon contains dye instead of colored wax. Dye sublimation printers produce excellent color quality—perhaps the best of any printer technology. At $3 to $4 per page, however, these printers are a bit pricey for most personal computer owners.

What features should I look for in a printer? Printers differ in resolution, speed, duty cycle, operating costs, duplex capability, and memory.

■ **Resolution.** The quality or sharpness of printed images and text depends on the printer's resolution—the density of the gridwork of dots that create an image. Printer resolution is measured by the number of dots printed per linear inch, abbreviated as dpi. At normal reading distance, a resolution of about 900 dpi appears solid to the human eye, but a close examination reveals a dot pattern. If you want magazine-quality printouts, 900 dpi is sufficient resolution. If you are aiming for resolution similar to expensive coffee-table books, look for printer resolution of 2,400 dpi or higher.

■ **Print speed.** Printer speeds are measured either by pages per minute (ppm) or characters per second (cps). Color printouts typically take longer than black-and-white printouts. Pages that contain mostly text tend to print more rapidly than pages that contain graphics. Six to ten pages per minute is a typical speed for a personal computer printer.

■ **Duty cycle.** In addition to printer speed, a printer's **duty cycle** determines how many pages a printer is able to churn out. Printer duty cycle is usually measured in pages per month. For example, a personal laser printer has a duty cycle of about 3,000 pages per month (ppm)—that means roughly 100 pages per day. You wouldn't want to use it to produce 5,000 campaign brochures for next Monday, but you would find it quite suitable for printing 10 copies of a five-page outline for a meeting tomorrow.

■ **Operating costs.** The initial cost of a printer is only one of the expenses associated with printed output. Ink jet printers require frequent replacements of relatively expensive print heads. Laser printers require toner cartridge refills. Dot matrix printers require replacement ribbons. When shopping for a printer, you can check online resources to determine how often you'll need to replace printer supplies and how much they are likely to cost.

■ **Duplex capability.** A printer with duplex capability can print on both sides of the paper. This environment-friendly option saves paper but can slow down the print process, especially on ink-jet printers that pause to let the ink dry before printing the second side.

■ **Memory.** A computer sends data for a printout to the printer along with a set of instructions on how to print that data. **Printer Control Language (PCL)** is the most widely used language for communication between computers and printers, but **PostScript** is an alternative printer language that many publishing professionals prefer. The data that arrives at a printer along with its printer language instructions require memory. A large memory capacity is required to print color images and graphics-intensive documents. Some printers accept additional memory, if you find that your printer requires more memory for the types of document you typically print.

Figure 2-45 provides comparative information for ink jet, laser, and dot matrix printers. For specific information on a particular brand and model of printer, check the manufacturer's Web site.

INFOWEBLINKS

Before you shop for a printer, take a look at the buying tips in the **Printer Buyer's Guide InfoWeb**.

www.course.com/np/concepts8/ch02

FIGURE 2-45
Printer Comparison

PRINTER TYPE	MAX. RESOLUTION	SPEED	DUTY CYCLE	OPERATING COST	MEMORY
Ink Jet (B&W) (color)	2400 x 1200	6–12 ppm 1–2 ppm	3,000 ppm	2–4¢ /page 8–20¢/page	256 KB–2 MB
Laser (B&W) (color)	2400 dpi	17 ppm 2–4 ppm	150,000 ppm	1–2¢/page	8–32 MB
Dot Matrix (B&W)	72–360 dpi	5–6 ppm	6,000-60,000 ppm	1.5–.2¢/page	2–128 KB

INSTALLING PERIPHERAL DEVICES

Is it difficult to install a new peripheral device? At one time, installing computer peripherals required a screw driver and extensive knowledge of ports, slots, boards, and device drivers. Today, many peripheral devices connect to an external USB (universal serial bus) port and Windows automatically loads their device drivers, making installation as simple as plugging in a table lamp. USB is currently the most popular technology for connecting peripherals.

On most new computer models, USB ports are conveniently located on the front of the system unit for easy access. Many kinds of peripheral devices—including mice, scanners, and joysticks—are available with USB connections. Several types of storage devices, such as USB Flash drives, also use USB connections.

There are still occasions, however, when a simple USB connection is not available. Installing high-end graphics and sound cards for a multimedia or serious gaming computer typically requires you to open the system unit.

Whether you are working with a simple USB connection or more complex equipment, a little information about the computer's data bus will arm you with the information you need to negotiate the steps for installing most peripheral devices.

How does a computer move data to and from peripheral devices? When you install a peripheral device, you are basically creating a connection for data to flow between the device and the computer. Within a computer, data travels from one component to another over circuits called a **data bus**. One part of the data bus runs between RAM and the microprocessor. Other parts of the data bus connect RAM to various storage and peripheral devices. The segment of the data bus that extends between RAM and peripheral devices is called the **expansion bus**. As data moves along the expansion bus, it can travel through expansion slots, cards, ports, and cables.

What's an expansion slot? An **expansion slot** is a long, narrow socket on the system board into which you can plug an expansion card. An **expansion card** is a small circuit board that gives a computer the capability to control a storage device, an input device, or an output device. Expansion cards are also called "expansion boards," "controller cards," or "adapters." Figure 2-46 shows how to plug an expansion card into an expansion slot.

FIGURE 2-46
An expansion card simply slides into an expansion slot and is secured with a small screw. Before you open the case, make sure you unplug the computer and ground yourself—that's technical jargon for releasing static electricity by using a special grounding wristband or by touching both hands to a metal object.

CLICK TO START ✥

FIGURE 2-47
Factory-Installed Expansion Cards

Graphics card provides a path for data traveling to the monitor.

Modem provides a way to transmit data over phone lines or cable television lines.

Sound card carries data out to speakers and headphones or back from a microphone.

Network card allows you to connect your computer to a local area network.

Expansion cards are built for only one type of slot. If you plan to add or upgrade a card in your computer, you must make sure the right type of slot is available on the system board. Most desktop computers provide four to eight expansion slots, some containing factory-installed expansion cards, such as those listed in Figure 2-47.

Expansion slots are classified as these types:

- **ISA** (Industry Standard Architecture) slots are an old technology, used today only for some modems and other relatively slow devices. Many new computers have few or no ISA slots.

- **PCI** (Peripheral Component Interconnect) slots offer fast transfer speeds and a 32-bit or 64-bit data bus. These slots typically house a graphics card, sound card, video capture card, modem, or network interface card.

- **AGP** (Accelerated Graphics Port) slots provide a high-speed data pathway primarily used for graphics cards.

Do notebook computers contain expansion slots? Most notebook computers are equipped with a special type of external slot called a **PCM-CIA slot** (Personal Computer Memory Card International Association).

Typically, a notebook computer has only one of these slots, but the slot can hold more than one **PC card** (also called "PCMCIA expansion cards" or "Card Bus cards").

What is an expansion port? An **expansion port** is any connector that passes data in and out of a computer or peripheral device. Ports are sometimes called "jacks" or "connectors"—the terminology is inconsistent.

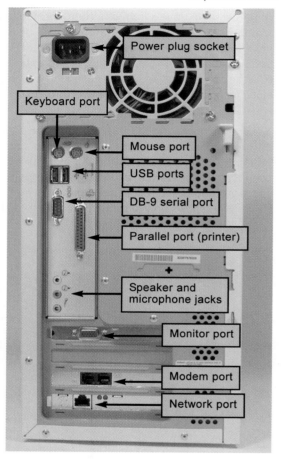

FIGURE 2-48
Expansion Ports

An expansion port is often housed on an expansion card so that it is accessible through an opening in the back of the computer's system unit. A port might also be built into the system unit case of a desktop or notebook computer. The built-in ports supplied with a computer usually include a mouse port, keyboard port, serial port, and USB port. Ports that have been added with expansion cards usually protrude through rectangular cutouts in the back of the case. Figure 2-48 illustrates the major types of expansion ports on a typical desktop computer.

How do I know which cable to use? With so many types of ports, you can expect a corresponding variety of cables. If a cable is supplied with a peripheral device, you can usually figure out where to plug it in by matching the shape of the cable connector to the port. Some manufacturers also color code ports and plugs to make them easy to match. Figure 2-49 on the next page provides information about the computer cables you're most likely to encounter.

Why do some peripheral devices include a disk or CD? Some devices require software, called a **device driver**, to set up communication between your computer and the device. The directions supplied with your peripheral device include instructions on how to install the device driver. Typically, you use the device driver disk or CD one time to get everything set up, and then you can put the disk away in a safe place.

Long-time computer techies probably remember the days when installing a peripheral device meant messing around with little electronic components called dip switches and a host of complex software settings called IRQs. Fortunately, today's PCs include a feature called **Plug and Play** (PnP) that automatically takes care of these technical details. Although it took several years to refine Plug and Play technology, it works quite well for just about every popular peripheral device. If PnP doesn't work, your computer simply won't recognize the device and won't be able to transmit data to it or receive data from it. If you've got a stubborn peripheral device, check the manufacturer's Web site for a device driver update, or call the manufacturer's technical support department.

What's the most important thing to remember about installing peripherals? Installing a peripheral device is not difficult when you remember that it's all about using the expansion bus to make a connection between the system board and a peripheral device. The cable you use must match the peripheral device and a port on the computer. If the right type of port is not available, you might have to add an expansion card. Once the connection is made, PnP should recognize the new device. If not, you'll probably have to install driver software.

FIGURE 2-49
Personal Computer Cables and
Connectors

CONNECTOR	DESCRIPTION	DEVICES
Serial DB-9	Connects to serial port, which sends data over a single data line one bit at a time at speeds of 56 Kbps.	Mouse or modem
Parallel DB-25M	Connects to parallel port, which sends data simultaneously over eight data lines at speeds of 12,000 Kbps.	Printer, external CD drive, Zip drive, external hard disk drive, or tape backup device
USB	Connects to USB port, which sends data over a single data line and can support up to 127 devices. USB-1 carries data at speeds up to 12,000 Kbps; USB-2, at 480,000 Kbps.	Modem, keyboard, joystick, scanner, mouse, external hard disk drive, MP3 player, digital camera
SCSI C-50F	Connects to SCSI port, which sends data simultaneously over 8 or 16 data lines at speeds between 40,000 Kbps and 640,000 Kbps; supports up to 16 devices.	Internal or external hard disk drive, scanner, CD drive, tape backup device
IEEE 1394	Connects to the FireWire port, which sends data at 400,000 Kbps.	Video camera, DVD player
VGA HDB-15	Connects to the video port.	Monitor

QUICKCHECK......SECTION D

1. Computer [_____] devices include mice, trackpads, trackballs, and joysticks.

2. In the context of computer displays, [_____] rate refers to the speed at which the screen image is repainted.

3. The number of dots that form an image on a monitor or printer is referred to as [_____].

4. A printer with [_____] capability can print on both sides of the paper.

5. AGP, PCI, and ISA are types of expansion [_____].

6. A(n) [_____] port provides one of the fastest, simplest ways to connect peripherals.

7. Many peripheral devices come packaged with [_____] driver software.

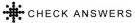 CHECK ANSWERS

TECHTALK

HOW A MICROPROCESSOR EXECUTES INSTRUCTIONS

Remarkable advances in microprocessor technology have produced exponential increases in computer speed and power. In 1965, Gordon Moore, co-founder of chipmaker giant Intel Corporation, predicted that the number of transistors on a chip would double every year. Much to the surprise of engineers and Moore himself, "Moore's law" accurately predicted 30 years of chip development. In 1958, the first integrated circuit contained two transistors. Today's processors feature millions of transistors.

What's really fascinating, though, is how these chips perform complex tasks simply by manipulating those ubiquitous bits. How can pushing around 1s and 0s result in professional-quality documents, exciting action games, animated graphics, cool music, e-commerce Web sites, and street maps? To satisfy your curiosity about what happens deep in the heart of a microprocessor, you'll need to venture into the realm of instruction sets, fetch cycles, accumulators, and pointers.

What kind of instructions does a computer execute? A computer accomplishes a complex task by performing a series of very simple steps, referred to as instructions. An instruction tells the computer to perform a specific arithmetic, logical, or control operation.

To be executed by a computer, an instruction must be in the form of electrical signals—those now familiar 1s and 0s that represent "ons" and "offs." In this form, instructions are referred to as **machine code**. They are, of course, very difficult for people to read, so typically when discussing them, we use more understandable mnemonics, such as JMP, M1, and REG1.

An instruction has two parts: the op code and the operands. An **op code**, which is short for "operation code," is a command word for an operation such as add, compare, or jump. The **operands** for an instruction specify the data, or the address of the data, for the operation. Let's look at an example of an instruction from a hypothetical instruction set:

In the instruction JMP M1, the op code is JMP and the operand is M1. The op code JMP means jump or go to a different instruction. The operand M1 stands for the RAM address of the instruction to which the computer is supposed to go. The instruction JMP M1 has only one operand, but some instructions have more than one operand. For example, the instruction ADD REG1 REG2 has two operands: REG1 and REG2.

The list of instructions that a microprocessor is able to execute is known as its instruction set. This instruction set is built into the microprocessor when it is manufactured. Every task that a computer performs is determined by the list of instructions in its instruction set. As you look at the instruction set in Figure 2-50 on the next page, consider that the computer must use instructions such as these for all the tasks it helps you perform—from database management to word processing.

FIGURE 2-50
A Simple Microprocessor
Instruction Set

Op Code	Operation	Example
INP	Input the given value into the specified memory address	INP 7 M1
CLA	Clear the accumulator to 0	CLA
MAM	Move the value from the accumulator to the specified memory location	MAM M1
MMR	Move the value from the specified memory location to the specified register	MMR M1 REG1
MRA	Move the value from the specified register to the accumulator	MRA REG1
MAR	Move the value from the accumulator to the specified register	MAR REG1
ADD	Add the values in two registers; place the result in the accumulator	ADD REG1 REG2
SUB	Subtract the value in the second register from the value in the first register; place the result in the accumulator	SUB REG1 REG2
MUL	Multiply values in two registers; place the result in the accumulator	MUL REG1 REG2
DIV	Divide the value in the first register by the value in the second register; place the result in the accumulator	DIV REG 1 REG2
INC	Increment (increase) the value in the register by 1	INC REG1
DEC	Decrement (decrease) the value in the register by 1	DEC REG1
CMP	Compare the values in two registers. If values are equal, put 1 in the accumulator; otherwise, put 0 in the accumulator	CMP REG1 REG2
JMP	Jump to the instruction at the specified memory address	JMP P2
JPZ	Jump to the specified address if the accumulator holds 0	JPZ P3
JPN	Jump to the specified address if the accumulator does not hold 0	JPN P2
HLT	Halt program execution	HLT

What happens when a computer executes an instruction? The term **instruction cycle** refers to the process in which a computer executes a single instruction. Some parts of the instruction cycle are performed by the microprocessor's control unit; other parts of the cycle are performed by the ALU. The steps in this cycle are summarized in Figure 2-51.

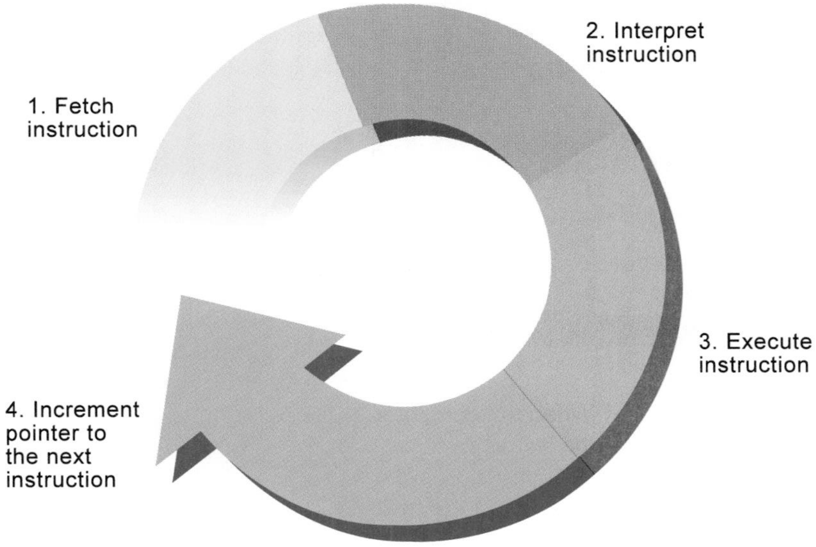

1. Fetch instruction
2. Interpret instruction
3. Execute instruction
4. Increment pointer to the next instruction

FIGURE 2-51
The instruction cycle includes four activities.

What role does the control unit play? The instructions that a computer is supposed to process for a particular program are held in RAM. When the program begins, the RAM address of the first instruction is placed in a part of the microprocessor's control unit called an instruction pointer. The control unit can then fetch the instruction by copying data from that address into its instruction register. From there, the control unit can interpret the instruction, gather the specified data, or tell the ALU to begin processing. Figure 2-52 helps you visualize the control unit's role in processing an instruction.

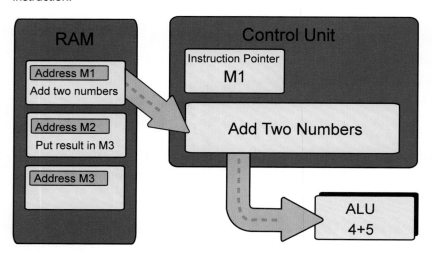

FIGURE 2-52
The control unit fetches instructions, interprets them, fetches data, and tells the ALU which processing operations to perform.

When does the ALU swing into action? The ALU is responsible for performing arithmetic and logical operations. It uses registers to hold data ready to be processed. When it gets the go-ahead signal from the control unit, the ALU processes the data and places the result in an accumulator. From the accumulator, the data can be sent to RAM or used for further processing. Figure 2-53 helps you visualize what happens in the ALU as the computer processes data.

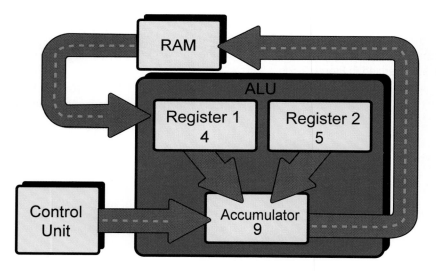

FIGURE 2-53
The ALU uses data from its registers to perform arithmetic and logical operations. The results are placed in another register, called the accumulator.

What happens after an instruction is executed? When the computer completes an instruction, the control unit "increments" the instruction pointer to the RAM address of the next instruction and the instruction cycle begins again. So how does this all fit together? Figure 2-54 on the next page explains how the ALU, control unit, and RAM work together to process instructions.

FIGURE 2-54
The ALU, control unit, and RAM all have a part to play in processing instructions.

1. The instruction pointer indicates the memory location that holds the first instruction (M1).

Control Unit	ALU
Instruction Pointer	**Accumulator**

M1 MMR M6 R1
M2 MMR M7 R2
M3 ADD
M4
M5
M6 100
M7 200

Instruction Pointer: M1
Accumulator:
R1:
Instruction Register:
R2:

2. The computer fetches the instruction and puts it into the instruction register.

M1 MMR M6 R1
M2 MMR M7 R2
M3 ADD
M4
M5
M6 100
M7 200

Instruction Pointer: M1
Accumulator:
R1:
Instruction Register: MMR M6 R1
R2:

3. The computer executes the instruction that is in the instruction register; it moves the contents of M6 into register 1 of the ALU.

M1 MMR M6 R1
M2 MMR M7 R2
M3 ADD
M4
M5
M6 100
M7 200

Instruction Pointer: M1
Accumulator:
R1: 100
Instruction Register: MMR M6 R1
R2:

4. The instruction pointer changes to point to the memory location that holds the next instruction.

M1 MMR M6 R1
M2 MMR M7 R2
M3 ADD
M4
M5
M6 100
M7 200

Instruction Pointer: M2
Accumulator:
R1: 100
Instruction Register:
R2:

5. The computer fetches the instruction and puts it in the instruction register.

M1 MMR M6 R1
M2 MMR M7 R2
M3 ADD
M4
M5
M6 100
M7 200

Instruction Pointer: M2
Accumulator:
R1: 100
Instruction Register: MMR M7 R2
R2:

6. The computer executes the instruction; it moves the contents of M7 into register 2 of the ALU.

M1 MMR M6 R1
M2 MMR M7 R2
M3 ADD
M4
M5
M6 100
M7 200

Instruction Pointer: M2
Accumulator:
R1: 100
Instruction Register: MMR M7 R2
R2: 200

7. The computer fetches the instruction and puts it in the instruction register.

M1 MMR M6 R1
M2 MMR M7 R2
M3 ADD
M4
M5
M6 100
M7 200

Instruction Pointer: M3
Accumulator:
R1: 100
Instruction Register: ADD
R2: 200

8. The computer executes the instruction. The result is put in the accumulator.

M1 MMR M6 R1
M2 MMR M7 R2
M3 ADD
M4
M5
M6 100
M7 200

Instruction Pointer: M3
Accumulator: 300
R1: 100
Instruction Register: ADD
R2: 200

QUICKCHECK........TECHTALK

1. [   ] code instructions are in the form of 0s and 1s.

2. JMP is an example of a(n) [   ] code.

3. An instruction [   ] indicates the instruction to be executed.

4. The results of processing are held in a(n) [   ].

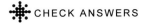 CHECK ANSWERS

ISSUE

COMPUTERS AND THE ENVIRONMENT

Manufacturing an average desktop computer with a CRT monitor requires 48 pounds of chemicals and 529 pounds of fossil fuels, according to a United Nations study. That makes producing a computer more materials-intensive than manufacturing an automobile. Extending the lifespan of your computer might be environmentally friendly, but keeping up with technology probably means replacing your computer every few years.

When it is time to replace your computer, is there a way to do it in an environmentally safe way? According to the National Safety Council, an estimated 300 million computers will be discarded by the year 2007. A recycling company called Back Thru the Future Micro Computer, Inc. (BTTF) estimates that 63 million computers will be retired in 2005 alone, compared with just 20 million that became obsolete in 1998. BTTF also estimates that printer ink cartridges are discarded at the rate of almost eight cartridges every second in the United States alone. A recycling company called GreenDisk estimates that about 1 billion floppy disks, CDs, and DVDs end up in landfills every year.

U.S. landfills already hold more than 2 million tons of computer and electronic parts, which contain toxic substances such as lead, cadmium, and mercury. A computer monitor, for example, can contain up to eight pounds of lead. An Environmental Protection Agency (EPA) report sums up the situation: "In this world of rapidly changing technology, disposal of computers and other electronic equipment has created a new and growing waste stream."

Many computers end up in landfills because their owners are unaware of potential environmental hazards and simply toss them in the garbage. In addition, PC owners typically are not given information on options for disposing of their old machines. Instead of throwing away your old computer, you might be able to sell it; donate it to a local school, church, or community program; have it hauled away by a professional recycling firm; or send it back to the manufacturer. Some artists even accept old computers and use parts in jewelery and craft projects.

Recycled Computer Creations by Gregory Steele, Marquette, MI

With the growing popularity of Internet auctions and dedicated computer reclamation sites, you might be able to get some cash for your old computer. At Web sites such as the Computer Recycle Center at *www.recycles.com*, you can post an ad for your "old stuff." Off the Web, you can find several businesses, such as Computer Renaissance, that refurbish old computers and sell them in retail stores.

Donating your old computer to a local organization doesn't actually eliminate the disposal problem, but it does delay it. Unfortunately, finding a new home for an old computer is not always easy. Most schools and community organizations have few resources for repairing broken equipment, so if your old computer is not in good working order, it could be more of a burden than a gift. In addition, your computer might be too old to be compatible with the other computers in an organization. It helps if you can donate software along with your old computer. To ensure a legal transfer, include the software distribution disks, manuals, and license agreement. And remember, once you donate the software, you cannot legally use it on your new computer unless it is freeware or shareware.

If you cannot find an organization to accept your computer donation, look in your local Yellow Pages or on the Internet for an electronics recycling firm, which will haul away your computer and recycle any usable materials.

Despite private sector options for selling, donating, or recycling old computers, many governments are worried that these voluntary efforts will not be enough to prevent massive dumping of an ever-growing population of obsolete computers.

During the past two years, about half the states have taken some legislative action to curtail the rampant disposal of obsolete computer equipment.

For example, Massachusetts implemented a statewide ban in 2000 on disposing computers in landfills, which helped spur recycling efforts. New Jersey's tough regulations on electronics disposal apply to more than 220 pounds or 100 kilograms, which is about eight monitors. Under those regulations, disposal must be at an approved New Jersey facility and disposal records must be kept for three years. Failure to comply can result in a $2,000 fine.

Many lawmakers in the United States, Japan, and the European Union believe that more legislation is necessary, but they can't agree on an implementation plan. Basic to the issue is the question of "Who pays?" Should it be the taxpayer, the individual consumer, or the computer manufacturer?

Taxpayers typically pick up the tab for electronic waste disposal through municipal trash pick-up fees or local taxes. For example, the Silicon Valley Toxics Coalition estimates that California taxpayers will spend more than $1 billion to manage electronic waste between 2002 and 2006. But is this approach fair to individual taxpayers who generate very little electronic waste?

To make consumers responsible for the cost of recycling the products they buy, some lawmakers suggest adding a special recycling tax to computers and other electronic devices. A proposal in South Carolina, for example, would impose a $5 fee on the sale of each piece of electronic equipment containing

a CRT and require the state treasurer to deposit the fees into a recycling fund for electronic equipment. Of three bills introduced in 2003 in Oregon to address the issue of managing the electronics waste stream, two would impose similar point-of-sale fees on electronic components.

Other lawmakers propose to make manufacturers responsible for recycling costs and logistics. "Extended producer responsibility" refers to the idea of holding manufacturers responsible for the environmental effects of their products through the entire product life cycle, which includes taking them back, recycling them, or disposing of them. Proposed legislation in Europe would require manufacturers to accept returns of their old equipment free of charge and take appropriate steps to recycle it. The economics of a mandatory take-back program are likely to increase product costs because manufacturers would typically pass on recycling costs to consumers.

Some companies currently participate in voluntary producer responsibility programs. Sony's take-back program in Minnesota allows residents to recycle any Sony products at no cost. Using IBM's PC Recycling Service, you can ship any make of computer, including system units, monitors, printers, and optional attachments, to a recycling center for $29.99. Such programs are important steps in the effort to keep our planet green.

INFOWEBLINKS

You'll find much more information about how you can recycle an old computer by connecting to the **Computer Recycling InfoWeb.**

www.course.com/np/concepts8/ch02

 DO YOU THINK?

1. Have you ever thrown away an old computer or other electronic device? ○ Yes ○ No ○ Not sure

2. Are you aware of any options for recycling electronic equipment in your local area? ○ Yes ○ No ○ Not sure

3. Would it be fair for consumers to pay a recycling tax on any electronic equipment that they purchase? ○ Yes ○ No ○ Not sure

SAVE RESPONSES

COMPUTERS IN CONTEXT

MILITARY

In *Engines of the Mind*, Joel Shurkin writes, "If necessity is the mother of invention, then war can be said to be its grandmother." The military, an early pioneer in computer and communication technologies, continues to be the driving force behind technologies that have revolutionized everyday life. During World War II, the U.S. military initiated a classified research program, called Project PX, to develop an electronic device to calculate artillery firing tables; by hand, each table required weeks of grueling calculations. Project PX produced ENIAC (Electrical Numerical Integrator And Calculator), one of the first general-purpose electronic computers. When ENIAC was completed in 1946, the war was over, but ENIAC's versatile architecture could be used for other calculations, such as designing hydrogen bombs, predicting weather, and engineering wind tunnels. ENIAC's technology evolved into the computers used today.

After Project PX, the military continued to support computer research. Like most large corporations, the military used mainframe computers to maintain personnel, inventory, supply, and facilities records. This data was distributed to terminals at other locations via rudimentary networks. Because all data communication flowed through the mainframe, a single point of failure for the entire system was a possible risk. A malfunction or an enemy "hit" could disrupt command and control, sending the military into chaos. Therefore, the armed forces created the Advanced Research Projects Agency (ARPA) to design a distributed communications system that could continue operating without a centralized computer. The result was ARPANET, which paved the way for the data communications system we know today as the Internet.

The U.S. Department of Defense (DoD) currently maintains two data communications networks: SIPRNet, a classified (secret-level) network, and NIPRNet, which provides unclassified services. The DoD's public Web site, called DefenseLINK, provides official information about defense policies, organizations, budgets, and operations.

Computers and communications technology have also become an integral part of high-tech military operations. U.S. Apache helicopters, for example, are equipped with computer-based Target Acquisition Designation Sights, laser range finder/designators, and Pilot Night Vision Sensors. These arcade-style controls are also used by tank drivers in the U.S. Army's 4th Infantry Division. Each vehicle in this "Digitized Division" is equipped with a Force 21 Battle Command Brigade and Below system, which works like a battlefield Internet to transmit data on the location of friendly and enemy forces from one vehicle to another using wireless communication.

Much like a video game, the Force 21 touch screen shows friendly troops in blue, and a global positioning satellite (GPS) system updates their positions automatically. Enemy troops spotted by helicopters are shown as red icons. To get information on any friendly or enemy vehicle, a soldier can simply touch one of these blue or red icons. To send text messages—much like cell phone and computer instant messaging—a soldier touches the Message button.

The built-in GPS system provides location and route information, much like sophisticated mapping programs in luxury cars.

Force 21 computers are installed in shock-resistant cases and equipped with a cooling system that eliminates the need for a fan, which might pull in dust, dirt, or water. The computers run Sun Microsystem's Solaris operating system because it is less vulnerable to viruses and intrusion attacks than Microsoft Windows. To prevent enemy capture and use, Force 21 computers have a self-destruct mechanism that can be triggered remotely.

In addition to pilots and tank drivers, battlefield soldiers will soon be equipped with "wearable" computer and communications equipment. The $2 billion Land Warrior program will provide high-tech weaponry, such as the Integrated Helmet Assembly Subsystem, for soldiers. IHAS is a helmet-mounted device that displays graphical data, digital maps, thermal images, intelligence information, and troop locations. It also includes a weapon-mounted video camera, so that soldiers can view and fire around corners and acquire targets in darkness.

The military has also conducted research in computer simulations that are similar to civilian computer games. "Live" military training is dangerous—weapons are deadly and equipment costs millions of dollars. With computer simulations, however, troops can train in a true-to-life environment without physical harm or equipment damage. Flying an F-16 fighter, for example, costs about $5,000 an hour, but flying an F-16 simulator costs only $500 per hour. The military uses simulators to teach Air Force pilots to fly fighter jets, Navy submarine officers to navigate in harbors, and Marine infantry squads to handle urban combat. Military trainers agree that widespread use of computer games helps prepare troops to adapt quickly to simulations.

A 24-year-old preflight student at Pensacola Naval Air Station modified the Microsoft Flight Simulator game to re-create a T-34C Turbo Mentor plane's controls. After logging 50 hours on the simulator, the student performed so well on a real plane that the Navy used his simulation to train other pilots. Today, a growing cadre of computer and communications specialists are needed to create and maintain increasingly complex military systems.

An army once depended on its infantry, but today's high-tech army depends equally on its database designers, computer programmers, and network specialists. Even previously low-tech military jobs, such as mechanics and dietitians, require some computer expertise. Happily, new recruits are finding military computer systems easy to learn, based on their knowledge of civilian technologies, such as the Internet and computer games.

Although most citizens agree that an adequate national defense is necessary, the cost of defense-related equipment, personnel, and research remains controversial. In 1961, President Dwight Eisenhower warned "We must guard against the acquisition of unwarranted influence, whether sought or unsought, by the military-industrial complex." Many socially motivated citizens and pacifists protested diverting tax dollars from social and economic programs to the military-industrial complex Eisenhower cautioned against. In retrospect, however, military funding contributed to many technologies we depend on today. For example, detractors tried to convince the government that Project PX was doomed to failure, but without ENIAC research, computers might not exist today. Skeptics saw no future for the fruits of ARPANET research, but it led to the Internet, which has changed our lives significantly.

INFOWEBLINKS

You'll find lots more information related to this Computers in Context topic at the **Computers and the Military InfoWeb**.

www.course.com/np/concepts8/ch02

INTERACTIVE SUMMARY

To review important concepts from this chapter, fill in the blanks to best complete each sentence. When using the NP8 BookOnCD, click the Check Answers buttons to automatically score your answers. Place your Tracking Disk in the floppy disk drive if you want to save your scores.

Most of today's computers are electronic, digital devices that work with data coded as binary digits, also known as [   ]. To represent numeric data, a computer can use the [   ] number system. To represent character data, a computer uses Extended [   ], EBCDIC, or Unicode. These codes also provide digital representations for the numerals 0 through 9 that are distinguished from numbers by the fact that they are not typically used in mathematical operations. Computers also [   ] sounds, pictures, and videos into 1s and 0s.

An [   ] is a single 1 or 0, whereas a [   ] is a sequence of eight 1s and 0s. Transmission speeds are usually measured in [   ], but storage space is usually measured in [   ] or gigabytes. In the context of computing, the prefix "kilo" means exactly 1,024. Kb stands for [   ], while the abbreviation KB stands for [   ]. The prefix [   ] means precisely 1,048,576, or about 1 million. The prefix "giga" means about 1 billion; "tera" means about 1 trillion; and "exa" means about 1 quintillion.

The terms "computer chip," "microchip," and "chip" originated as techie jargon for [   ] circuits. These chips are made from a super-thin slice of semiconducting material and are packed with millions of microscopic circuit elements. In a computer, these chips include the [   ], memory modules, and other support circuitry. They are housed inside the computer's system unit on a large circuit board called the [   ].

CHECK ANSWERS

The microprocessor and memory are two of the most important components in a computer. The microprocessor is an [   ] circuit, which is designed to process data based on a set of instructions. Its miniaturized circuitry is grouped into important functional areas. The microprocessor's ALU performs arithmetic and [   ] operations. The [   ] unit fetches each instruction, interprets it, loads data into the ALU's registers, and directs all the processing activities within the microprocessor. In most of today's personal computers, microprocessor performance is measured in [   ]—the number of cycles per second, or clock rate. Other factors affecting overall processing speed include word size, cache size, instruction set complexity, parallel processing, and pipelining.

RAM is a special holding area for data, program instructions, and the [   ] system. It stores data on a temporary basis while it waits to be processed. In most computers, RAM is composed of integrated circuits called [   ] or RDRAM. The speed of RAM circuitry is measured in [   ] or in megahertz (MHz). RAM is different from disk storage because it is [   ], which means that it can hold data only when the computer power is turned on. Computers also contain [   ], which is a type of memory that provides a set of "hard-wired" instructions that a computer uses to boot up. A third type of memory, called [   ], is battery powered and contains configuration settings.

CHECK ANSWERS

Today's personal computers use a variety of storage technologies, including floppy disks, hard disks, CDs, DVDs, tapes, and flash drives. Each storage device essentially has a direct pipeline to a computer's _____ so that data and instructions can move from a more permanent storage area to a temporary holding area and vice versa.

Magnetic storage technology stores data by magnetizing microscopic particles on the surface of a disk or tape. Optical storage technologies store data as a series of _____ and lands on the surface of a CD or DVD. _____ storage technology stores data by activating electrons in a microscopic grid of circuitry.

A standard 3.5" floppy disk formatted for a PC stores _____ MB of data. Zip disks have a higher disk _____, which provides significantly more storage capacity than a standard floppy disk.

A hard disk provides multiple platters for data storage, and these platters are sealed inside the drive case or cartridge to prevent airborne contaminants from interfering with the read-write heads. These disks are less durable than floppy disks, so it is important to make a _____ copy of the data they contain. Computer ads usually contain information about a hard disk's capacity and its _____ card type: SATA, EIDE, Ultra ATA, or SCSI.

Optical storage technologies, such as CD- and DVD-_____, provide good data storage capacity, but do not allow you to alter the disks' contents. _____ technology allows you to write data on a CD or DVD, but you cannot delete or change that data. _____ technology allows you to write and rewrite data on a CD or DVD.

USB _____ drives provide portable, solid state storage.

CHECK ANSWERS

Most computer systems include a keyboard and some type of _____ device for basic data input. A mouse is standard equipment with most desktop computer systems, but alternatives include pointing _____, trackpads, and trackballs.

For output, most computers include a display device. A _____ produces an image by spraying electrons toward the screen. _____ technology produces an image by manipulating light within a layer of liquid crystal cells. _____ screen technology creates an on-screen image by illuminating miniature fluorescent lights arrayed in a panel-like screen. Image quality for a display device is a factor of screen size, dot _____, _____ of viewing angle, resolution, refresh rate, and color _____. A typical computer display system consists of the display device and a _____ card.

For printed output, most PC owners turn to _____ jet printers, although _____ printers are a popular option when low operating costs and high _____ cycle are important. A dot _____ printer is sometimes used for back-office applications and printing multipart forms.

Installing a peripheral device is not difficult when you remember that it is all about using the _____ bus to make a connection between the computer's _____ and a peripheral device. The cable you use must match the peripheral device and a _____ on the computer. If the right type of port is not available, you might have to add an _____ card. Once the connection is made, _____ should recognize the new device. If not, you'll probably have to install device _____ software.

CHECK ANSWERS

INTERACTIVE KEY TERMS

Make sure you understand all the boldfaced key terms presented in this chapter. If you're using the NP8 BookOnCD, you can use this list of terms as an interactive study activity. First, try to define a term in your own words, and then click the term to compare your definition with the definition presented in the chapter.

Access time, 81
AGP, 97
ALU, 68
Analog device, 60
ASCII, 61
Benchmarks, 71
Binary digits, 60
Binary number system, 60
Cache, 70
Capacitors, 73
Card reader, 80
CD, 86
CD-DA, 87
CD-R, 87
CD-ROM, 87
CD-RW, 87
Character data, 61
CISC, 70
CMOS memory, 75
Color depth, 93
CompactFlash, 89
Control unit, 68
Controller, 83
CRT, 92
Data bus, 97
Data representation, 60
Data transfer rate, 81
Device driver, 98
Digital device, 60
Digitize, 62
DIMMs, 65
DIPs, 65
Disk density, 82
Dot matrix printer, 94
Dot pitch, 92
Double layer DVD, 86
Drive bays, 80
Duty cycle, 95
DVD, 86
DVD+R, 87
DVD-ROM, 87
DVD+RW, 87
DVD-Video, 87
Dye sublimation printer, 95
EBCDIC, 61
Expansion bus, 97
Expansion card, 97
Expansion port, 98

Expansion slot, 97
Extended ASCII, 61
File header, 63
Floppy disk, 81
Gigabit, 63
Gigabyte, 63
Gigahertz (GHz), 69
Graphics card, 93
Hard disk platter, 83
Head crash, 84
Ink jet printer, 94
Instruction cycle, 101
Instruction set, 69
Integrated circuit, 64
ISA, 97
Joystick, 91
Kilobit, 63
Kilobyte, 63
Lands, 79
Laser printer, 94
LCD, 92
Level 1 cache, 70
Level 2 cache, 70
Machine code, 100
Magnetic storage, 79
Megabit, 63
Megabyte, 63
Megahertz (MHz), 69
Microprocessor, 68
Microprocessor clock, 69
MultiMedia cards, 89
Nanosecond, 74
Numeric data, 60
Op code, 100
Operands, 100
Optical storage, 79
Parallel processing, 70
PC card, 98
PCI, 97
PCMCIA slot, 97
PGAs, 65
Pipelining, 70
Pits, 79
Pixels, 92
Plasma screen, 92
Plug and Play, 98
Pointing device, 91
Pointing stick, 91

PostScript, 96
Printer Control Language (PCL), 96
RAM, 72
Random access, 81
RDRAM, 74
Read-write head, 79
Recordable technology, 86
Refresh rate, 92
Registers, 68
Resolution, 93
Rewritable technology, 86
RISC, 70
ROM, 74
ROM BIOS, 74
SDRAM, 74
SEC cartridges, 65
SecureDigital, 89
Semiconducting materials, 64
Sequential access, 81
Serial processing, 70
SmartMedia, 89
Solid ink printer, 95
Solid state storage, 80
Storage device, 78
Storage medium, 78
SVGA, 93
SXGA, 93
System board, 65
Tape backup, 85
Thermal transfer printer, 95
Trackball, 91
Trackpad, 91
Unicode, 61
USB flash drive, 88
UXGA, 93
VGA, 93
Viewable image size, 92
Viewing angle width, 92
Virtual memory, 73
Volatile, 73
Word size, 70
Write-protect window, 82
XGA, 93

INTERACTIVE SITUATION QUESTIONS

Apply what you've learned to some typical computing situations. When using the NP8 BookOnCD, you can type your answers, and then use the Check Answers button to automatically score your responses. Place your Tracking Disk in the floppy disk drive if you want to save your scores.

1. Suppose you're reading a computer magazine and you come across the ad pictured to the right. By looking at the specs, you can tell that the microprocessor was manufactured by which company? [ ]

2. The capacity of the hard disk drive in the ad is [ ] and the memory capacity is [ ].

3. The computer in the ad appears to have a(n) [ ] controller card for the hard disk drive.

4. You are thinking about upgrading the microprocessor in your three-year-old computer, which has a 2.6 MHz Pentium microprocessor and 32 MB of RAM. Would it be worthwhile to spend $500 to install a 3.0 GHz Pentium processor? Yes or no? [ ]

5. You're in the process of booting up your computer and suddenly the screen contains an assortment of settings for date and time, hard disk drive, and memory capacity. From what you've learned in this chapter, you can surmise that these are settings stored in the [ ] memory, and that they are best left unmodified.

6. You're looking for a portable storage device that you can use to transport a few files between your home computer and your school computer lab. The school lab computers have no floppy disk drives, but do have USB ports. You should be able to transport your files using a USB [ ] drive.

HOME/SMALL BUSINESS DESKTOP MODEL XP2002

- Pentium 4 560 3.6 GHz
- 1 GB 533 MHz SDRAM
- 80 GB UltraATA HD (7200 rpm)
- 32 X Max CD-RW
- 3.5" 1.44 MB FDD
- 21" 24 dp monitor
- 256 MB AGP graphics card
- Sound Blaster 64v PCI sound card
- Altec Lansing speakers
- U.S. Robotics 56 Kbps modem
- 3-year limited warranty*

$ 1299

7. You want to add a storage device to your computer that reads CD-ROMs, DVD-ROMs, DVD-Videos, and CD-Rs. A DVD/CD-RW will do the job. True or false? [ ]

8. You are a professional graphics designer. A(n) [ ] is likely to give you the best colors from all viewing angles, whereas a(n) [ ] may not show true colors when viewed from some angles.

9. Suppose that you volunteer to produce a large quantity of black-and-white leaflets for a charity organization. It is fortunate that you have access to a(n) [ ] printer with a high duty cycle and low operating costs.

 CHECK ANSWERS

INTERACTIVE PRACTICE TESTS

Practice tests that consist of 10 multiple-choice, true/false, and fill-in-the-blank questions are available on both the NP8 BookOnCD and the NP8 Web site. The questions are selected at random from a large test bank, so each time you take a test, you'll receive a different set of questions. Your tests are scored immediately, and you can print study guides that help you find the correct answers for any questions that you missed.

www.course.com/np/concepts8/ch02

CLICK TO START

REVIEW

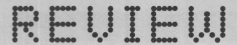

ON THE WEB

PROJECTS

An NP8 Project is an open-ended activity that helps you apply the concepts you have learned. Many projects require resources in addition to your textbook, such as current magazines, library materials, or Web access. When you tackle a project, be prepared to use your critical thinking skills, logical analysis, and creativity. Projects for this chapter include:

To work with the Projects for this chapter, connect to the **New Perspectives NP8 Web Site**.

www.course.com/np/concepts8/ch02

- **Issue Research: Computers and the Environment**
- **Buying a New Computer**
- **Computers in the Military**
- **Calculating Storage Requirements**

- **Sizing Up Future Storage Technologies**
- **Can a Computer Make Errors?**
- **The Jargon of Computer Ads**

TECHTV VIDEO PROJECT

The TechTV segment *Getting Started* demonstrates the basic parts needed to construct a personal computer. While watching the video, make a list of the parts. Use the Web to find an example of each part. Add the manufacturer, model number, and price in your list. Calculate the price of assembling a computer from these parts.

To work with the Video Projects for this chapter, connect to the **New Perspectives NP8 Web Site**.

www.course.com/np/concepts8/ch02

STUDY TIPS

Study Tips help you to organize and consolidate the information in a chapter by making lists, outlines, charts, and sketches. You can use paper and pencil or word processing software to complete most of the Study Tips.

To work with the Study Tips for this chapter, connect to the **New Perspectives NP8 Web Site**.

www.course.com/np/concepts8/ch02

ONLINE GAMES

Test your comprehension of the concepts introduced in Chapter 2 by playing the NP8 Online Games. At the end of each game, you have three options:

- Print a comprehensive study guide complete with page references
- Print your results to be submitted to your instructor
- Save your results to be submitted to your instructor via e-mail

To work with the Online Games for this chapter, connect to the **New Perspectives NP8 Web Site**.

www.course.com/np/concepts8/ch02

STUDENT EDITION LABS

Extend your knowledge of binary numbers and computer hardware with the Chapter 2 Student Edition Labs.

The following Student Edition Labs are offered with Chapter 2:

- **Using Input Devices**
- **Peripheral Devices**
- **Binary Numbers**
- **Understanding the Motherboard**

Go to the NP8 New Perspectives Web site for specific lab topics.

To work with the Chapter 2 Student Edition Labs and their corresponding lab assignments, connect to the **New Perspectives NP8 Web Site**.

www.course.com/np/concepts8/ch02

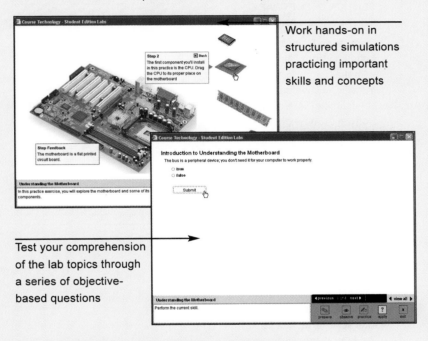

Work hands-on in structured simulations practicing important skills and concepts

Test your comprehension of the lab topics through a series of objective-based questions

Track Your Progress with the Student Edition Labs

- Student Edition Labs test your comprehension of the lab topics through a series of trackable objective-based questions. Your instructor will direct you to either print your results or submit them via e-mail.

- Student Edition Lab Assignments, available on the New Perspectives NP8 Web site, require you to apply the skills learned through the lab in a live environment. Go to the New Perspectives NP8 Web site for detailed instruction on individual Student Edition Lab Assignments.

If you have a SAM user profile, you have access to even more interactive content. Log in to your SAM account and go to your assignments page to see what your instructor has assigned for this chapter.

COMPUTER SOFTWARE

CONTENTS

TIP

When using the BookOnCD, the ❋ icons are "clickable" to access resources on the CD. The ✛ icons are clickable to access resources on the Web. You can also access Web resources by using your browser to connect directly to the NP8 New Perspectives Web site at:

www.course.com/np/concepts8/ch03

CHAPTER PREVIEW

Before you begin Chapter 3, you can use the Web-based preview activities to hear an overview of the chapter, check your current level of expertise about key concepts, and look through a list of learning objectives. You can access the preview activities by clicking the icon when using the BookOnCD or going to the New Perspectives NP8 Web site.

CHAPTER OVERVIEW

Software essentially transforms a computer from one kind of machine to another—from a drafting station to a typesetting machine, from a flight simulator to a calculator, from a filing system to a music remixing turntable. Get your book and highlighter ready, then connect to the New Perspectives NP8 Web site where you can listen to an overview that points out the most important concepts for this chapter.

www.course.com/np/concepts8/ch03

CHAPTER PRE-ASSESSMENT

How much do you know about installing and using software? To gauge your level of knowledge before beginning the chapter, try the pre-assessment quiz at the New Perspectives NP8 Web site. Armed with your results from this quiz, you can focus your study time on concepts that will round out your knowledge of software and improve your test scores.

www.course.com/np/concepts8/ch03

LEARNING OBJECTIVES

When you complete this chapter you should be able to:

- Describe the components of a typical software package, including executable files, support modules, and data modules
- Trace the development of a computer program from its inception as a set of high-level language instructions through its translation into machine language
- Describe the differences between system software and application software
- Describe the way an operating system manages each computer resource
- Identify operating systems for personal computers, PDAs, and servers
- Explain the key features and uses for word processing, desktop publishing, and Web authoring software
- Describe the major features of spreadsheet software

- Describe the key features of database software
- List the types of software available for graphics, video, music, education and reference, entertainment, and business
- Explain how to install and uninstall software, whether it is supplied on CDs or as a Web download
- Describe the differences among new software versions, software patches, and service packs
- Describe the rights granted by copyright law, commercial software licenses, shareware licenses, freeware licenses, open source licenses, and public domain software

A detailed list of learning objectives is provided at the New Perspectives NP8 Web site

www.course.com/np/concepts8/ch03

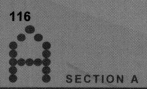

SECTION A

SOFTWARE BASICS

Computer software determines the types of tasks a computer can help you accomplish. Some software helps you create documents, while other software helps you edit home videos, prepare your tax return, or design the floor plan for a new house. But how does software transform your computer into a machine that can help with so many tasks? Section A delves into the characteristics of computer software and explains how it works.

SOFTWARE: THE INSIDE STORY

What is software? As you learned in Chapter 1, the instructions that tell a computer how to carry out a task are referred to as a computer program. These programs form the software that prepares a computer to do a specific task, such as document production, video editing, graphic design, or Web browsing. Software is usually distributed on CDs or DVDs, as shown in Figure 3-1. It also can be made available as a Web download.

What kinds of files are included in a typical software product? Whether it's on a CD or downloaded from the Web, today's software is typically composed of many files. You might be surprised by the number of files that are necessary to make software work. For example, the eVideo-In Pro software includes numerous files with extensions such as .exe, .dll, and .hlp, as shown in Figure 3-2.

FIGURE 3-1

In popular usage, the term "software" usually refers to one or more computer programs and any additional files that are provided to carry out a specific type of task.

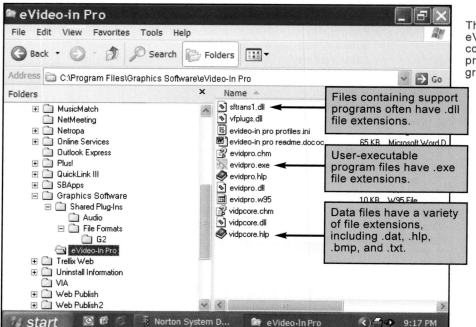

FIGURE 3-2

The files required by the eVideo-In Pro software contain user-executable programs, support programs, and data.

Files containing support programs often have .dll file extensions.

User-executable program files have .exe file extensions.

Data files have a variety of file extensions, including .dat, .hlp, .bmp, and .txt.

At least one of the files included in a software package contains an executable program designed to be launched, or started, by users. On PCs, these programs are stored in files that typically have .exe file extensions and are sometimes referred to as "executable files" or "user-executable files." When using a Windows PC, you can start an executable file by clicking its icon, selecting it from the Start menu, or entering its name in the Run dialog box.

Other files supplied with a software package contain programs that are not designed to be run by users. These "support programs" contain instructions for the computer to use with the main user-executable file. A support program can be "called," or activated, by the main program as needed. In the context of Windows software, support programs often have file extensions such as .dll and .ocx.

In addition to program files, many software packages also include data files. As you might expect, these files contain any data that is necessary for a task, but not supplied by the user, such as Help documentation, a word list for an online spell checker, synonyms for a thesaurus, or graphics for the software's toolbar icons. The data files supplied with a software package sport file extensions such as .txt, .bmp, and .hlp. Figure 3-3 illustrates the relationship between the various files distributed with a typical software package.

TERMINOLOGY NOTE

The term "software" was once used for all non-hardware components of a computer. In this context, software referred to computer programs and to the data the programs used. It could also refer to any data that existed in digital format, such as documents or photos. Using today's terminology, however, the documents and photos you create are usually classified as "data" rather than as "software."

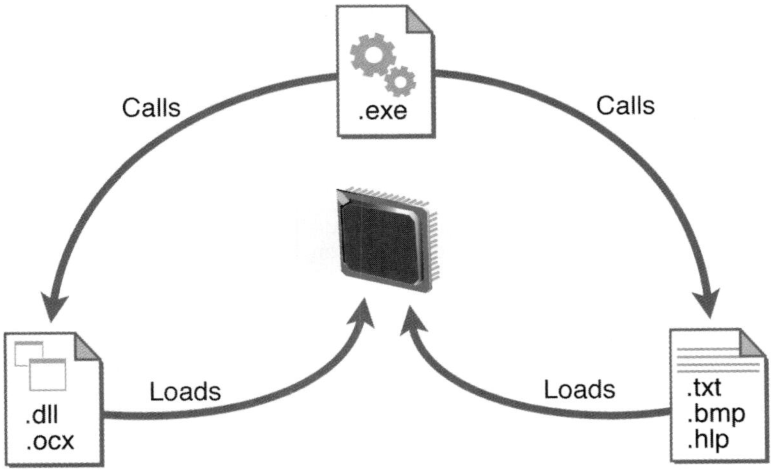

FIGURE 3-3
The main executable file provides the primary set of instructions for the computer to execute and calls various support programs and data files as needed.

Why does software require so many files? The use of a main user-executable file plus several support programs and data files offers a great deal of flexibility and efficiency for software developers. Support programs and data files can usually be modified without changing the main executable file. This modular approach can significantly reduce the time required to create and test the main executable file, which usually contains a long and fairly complex program. The modular approach also allows software developers to reuse their support programs and adapt preprogrammed support modules for use in their own software.

Modular programming techniques are of interest mainly to people who create computer programs; however, these techniques affect the process of installing and uninstalling software, discussed later in this chapter. It is important, therefore, to remember that computer software typically consists of many files that contain user-executable programs, support programs, and data.

PROGRAMMERS AND PROGRAMMING LANGUAGES

Who creates computer software? **Computer programmers** write instructions for the computer programs that become the components of a computer software product. The finished software product is then distributed by the programmers or by **software publishers**—companies that specialize in marketing and selling commercial software.

At one time, businesses, organizations, and individuals had to write most of the software they used. Today, however, most businesses and organizations purchase commercial software (also referred to as "off-the-shelf software") to avoid the time and expense of writing their own. Individuals rarely write software for their personal computers, preferring to select from thousands of software titles available in stores, from catalogs, and on the Internet. Although most computer owners do not write their own software, working as a computer programmer for a government agency, business, or software publisher can be a challenging career.

How does a programmer "write" software? Most software is designed to provide a task-related environment, which includes a screen display, a means of collecting commands and data from the user, the specifications for processing data, and a method for displaying or outputting data. Figure 3-4 illustrates a very simple software environment that converts a Fahrenheit temperature to Celsius and displays the result.

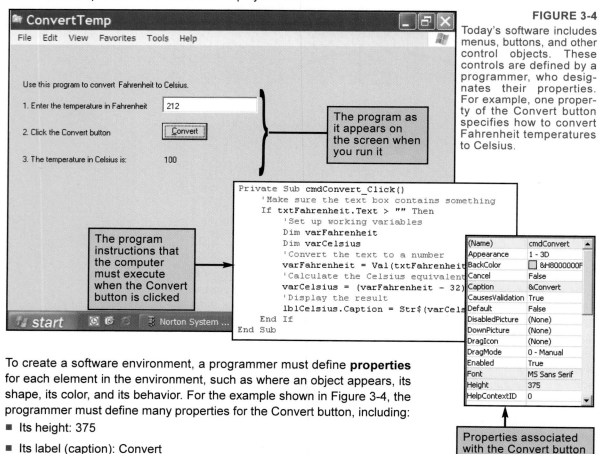

FIGURE 3-4
Today's software includes menus, buttons, and other control objects. These controls are defined by a programmer, who designates their properties. For example, one property of the Convert button specifies how to convert Fahrenheit temperatures to Celsius.

To create a software environment, a programmer must define **properties** for each element in the environment, such as where an object appears, its shape, its color, and its behavior. For the example shown in Figure 3-4, the programmer must define many properties for the Convert button, including:

- Its height: 375

- Its label (caption): Convert

- What happens when you click it: Subtract 32 from Fahrenheit, divide by 1.8, and then display the answer

A **programming language** (sometimes referred to as a "computer language") provides the tools a programmer uses to create software and produce a lengthy list of instructions, called **source code**, which defines the software environment in every detail—what it looks like, how the user enters commands, and how it manipulates data. Most programmers today prefer to use a **high-level language**, such as C++, Java, COBOL, and Visual Basic. These languages have some similarities to human languages and produce programs that are fairly easy to test and modify.

HOW SOFTWARE WORKS

How does a computer process a program? A computer's microprocessor understands only **machine language**—the instruction set that is "hard wired" within the microprocessor's circuits. Therefore, instructions written in a high-level language must be translated into machine language before a computer can use them. Figure 3-5 gives you an idea of what happens to a high-level instruction when it is converted into machine language instructions.

FIGURE 3-5

A simple instruction to add two numbers becomes a long series of 0s and 1s in machine language.

High-level Language Instruction	Machine Language Equivalent	Description of Machine Language Instructions
Answer=FirstNumber+SecondNumber	10001000 00011000 010000000	Load FirstNumber into Register 1
	10001000 00010000 00100000	Load SecondNumber into Register 2
	00000000 00011000 00010000	Perform ADD operation
	10100010 00111000	Move the number from the accumulator to the RAM location called Answer

How are instructions converted to machine language? The process of translating instructions from a high-level language into machine language can be accomplished by two special types of programs: compilers and interpreters. A **compiler** translates all the instructions in a program as a single batch, and the resulting machine language instructions, called **object code**, are placed in a new file (Figure 3-6). Most of the program files on a distribution CD for commercial software are compiled so that they contain machine language instructions that are ready for the processor to execute.

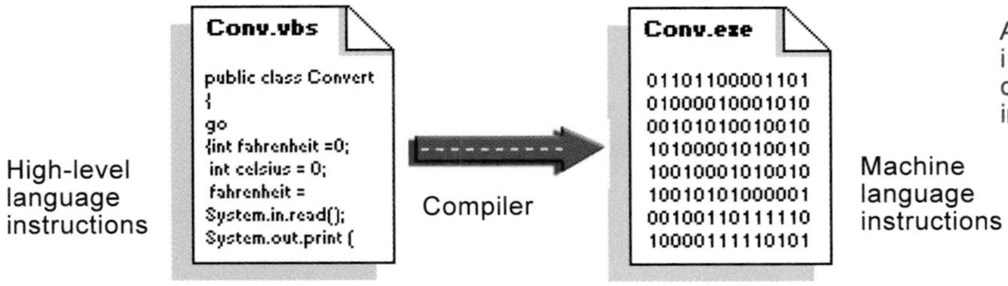

FIGURE 3-6

A compiler converts high-level instructions into a new file containing machine language instructions.

High-level language instructions

```
Conv.vbs

public class Convert
{
go
{int fahrenheit =0;
int celsius = 0;
fahrenheit =
System.in.read();
System.out.print (
```

Compiler

```
Conv.exe

01101100001101
01000010001010
00101010010010
10100001010010
10010001010010
10010101000001
00100110111110
10000111110101
```

Machine language instructions

As an alternative to a compiler, an **interpreter** converts one instruction at a time while the program is running. An interpreter reads the first instruction, converts it into machine language, and then sends it to the microprocessor. After the instruction is executed, the interpreter converts the next instruction, and so on (Figure 3-7 on the next page).

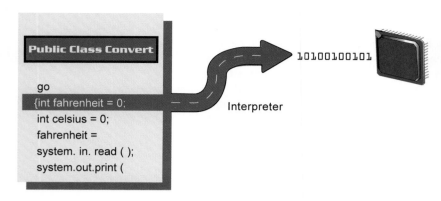

```
Public Class Convert

  go
  {int fahrenheit = 0;
   int celsius = 0;
   fahrenheit =
   system. in. read ( );
   system.out.print (
```

Interpreter

10100100101

FIGURE 3-7

An interpreter converts high-level instructions into machine language instructions while the program is running.

An interpreted program runs more slowly than a compiled program because the translation process happens while the program is running.

CLICK TO START ✦

So how does software work? Assume that a video editing program, such as eVideo-In Pro, is installed on your computer, which is running Windows. Figure 3-8 illustrates how the files included in this software package interact when you edit videos.

FIGURE 3-8

The main executable file loads into RAM when the program runs, and can call various other files as needed.

1. When you start the eVideo-In Pro software, the instructions in the file eVidpro.exe are loaded from disk into RAM and then sent to the microprocessor.

2. eVidpro.exe is a compiled program, so its instructions are immediately executed by the processor.

3. As processing begins, the eVideo-In Pro window opens and the graphical controls for video editing tasks appear. The program waits for you to select a control by clicking it with the mouse.

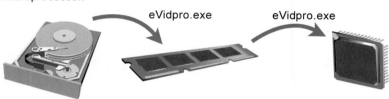

eVidpro.exe   eVidpro.exe

- camera
- VCR
- DVD

4. Based on your selection, eVidpro.exe follows its instructions and performs the actions you specify. Many of the instructions for these actions are included in the main executable file. If not, eVidpro.exe calls a support program, such as Sftrans.dll.

5. If you access eVideo-In Pro Help, eVidpro.exe loads the data file eVidpro.hlp.

6. eVidpro.exe continues to respond to the controls you select until you click the Close button, which halts execution of the program instructions, closes the program window, and releases the space the program occupied in RAM for use by other programs or data.

Sftrans.dll

eVidpro.hlp

APPLICATION SOFTWARE AND SYSTEM SOFTWARE

How is software categorized? Software is categorized as application software or system software. When you hear the word "application," your first reaction might be to envision a financial aid application or a form you fill out to apply for a job, a club membership, or a driver's license. The word "application" has other meanings, however. One of them is a synonym for the word "use." A computer certainly has many uses, such as creating documents, crunching numbers, drawing designs, and editing photographs.

Each use is considered an "application," and the software that provides the computer with instructions for each use is called **application software**, or simply an "application." The primary purpose of application software is to help people carry out tasks using a computer.

In contrast, the primary purpose of **system software**—your computer's operating system, device drivers, and utilities—is to help the computer carry out its basic operating functions. Figure 3-9 illustrates the division between system software and application software. You'll learn more about these software categories in Sections B and C.

FIGURE 3-9
Software can be classified into categories.

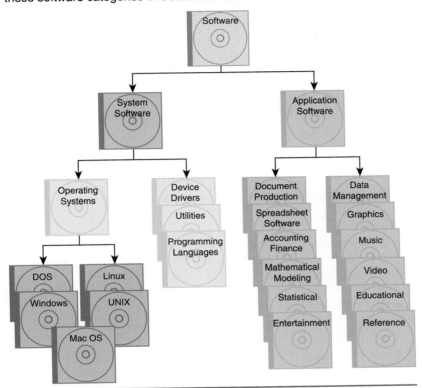

QUICKCHECK......SECTION A

1. When using a Windows PC, you can start a(n) [_____] file by clicking its icon, selecting it from the Start menu, or entering its name in the Run dialog box.

2. A programming language provides tools for creating a lengthy list of instructions called [_____] code.

3. Instructions that are written in a(n) [_____]-level language must be translated into machine language before a computer can use them.

4. As a program is running, a(n) [_____] converts one instruction at a time into machine language.

5. Computer software can be divided into two major categories: [_____] software and system software.

 CHECK ANSWERS

SECTION B

COMPUTER OPERATING SYSTEMS

Chapter 1 explained that an operating system is one factor that determines a computer's platform and compatibility. The term operating system (abbreviated OS) is defined as system software, which acts as the master controller for all activities that take place within a computer system.

An operating system is an integral part of virtually every computer system. It fundamentally affects how you can use your computer. Can you run two programs at the same time? Can you connect your computer to a network? Does your computer run dependably? Does all your software have a similar "look and feel," or do you have to learn a different set of controls and commands for each new program you acquire?

To answer questions like these, it is helpful to have a clear idea about what an operating system is and what it does. Section B provides an overview of operating systems and compares some of the most popular operating systems for personal computers.

OPERATING SYSTEM OVERVIEW

What does an operating system do? A computer's software is similar to the chain of command in an army. You issue a command using application software. Application software tells the operating system what to do. The operating system tells the device drivers, device drivers tell the hardware, and the hardware actually does the work. Figure 3-10 illustrates this chain of command for printing a document or photo.

FIGURE 3-10

A command to print a document is relayed through various levels of software, including the operating system, until it reaches the printer.

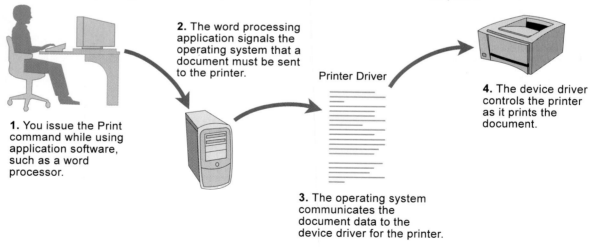

1. You issue the Print command while using application software, such as a word processor.

2. The word processing application signals the operating system that a document must be sent to the printer.

Printer Driver

3. The operating system communicates the document data to the device driver for the printer.

4. The device driver controls the printer as it prints the document.

The operating system interacts with application software, device drivers, and hardware to manage a computer's resources. In the context of a computer system, the term **resource** refers to any component that is required to perform work. For example, the processor is a resource. RAM, storage space, and peripherals are also resources. While you interact with application software, your computer's operating system is busy behind the scenes with tasks such as those listed in Figure 3-11.

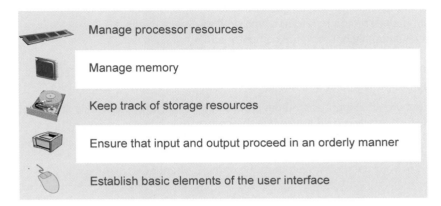

Manage processor resources

Manage memory

Keep track of storage resources

Ensure that input and output proceed in an orderly manner

Establish basic elements of the user interface

FIGURE 3-11
Operating System Tasks

How does the operating system manage processor resources?
Chapter 2 explained how the control unit directs activities within the microprocessor. The operating system also controls the microprocessor—just at a slightly higher level. Every cycle of a computer's microprocessor is a resource for accomplishing tasks.

Many activities—called "processes"—compete for the attention of your computer's microprocessor. Commands are arriving from programs you're using, while input is arriving from the keyboard and mouse. At the same time, data must be sent to the display device or printer, and Web pages are arriving from your Internet connection. To manage all these competing processes, your computer's operating system must ensure that each one receives its share of microprocessor cycles.

Ideally, the operating system should be able to help the microprocessor switch tasks so that, from the user's vantage point, everything seems to be happening at the same time. The operating system also must ensure that the microprocessor doesn't "spin its wheels" waiting for input while it could be working on some other processing task.

Why does an operating system manage memory? A microprocessor works with data and executes instructions stored in RAM—one of your computer's most important resources. When you want to run more than one program at a time, the operating system has to allocate specific areas of memory for each program, as shown in Figure 3-12.

When multiple programs are running, the OS must ensure that instructions and data from one area of memory don't "leak" into an area allocated to another program. If an OS falls down on the job and fails to protect each program's memory area, data can get corrupted, programs can "crash," and your computer displays error messages, such as "General Protection Fault." Your PC can sometimes recover from memory leak problems if you use the Ctrl+Alt+Del key sequence to close the corrupted program.

FIGURE 3-12

The operating system allocates a specific area of RAM for each program that is open and running. The operating system is itself a program, so it requires RAM space, too.

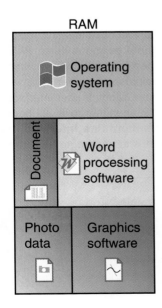

How does the OS keep track of storage resources? Behind the scenes, an operating system acts as a filing clerk that stores and retrieves files from your disks and CDs. It remembers the names and locations of all your files and keeps track of empty spaces where new files can be stored. Chapter 4 explores file storage in more depth and explains how the operating system affects the way you create, name, save, and retrieve files.

Why does the operating system get involved with peripheral devices? Every device connected to a computer is regarded as a resource. Your computer's operating system communicates with device driver software so that data can travel smoothly between the computer and these peripheral resources. If a peripheral device or driver is not performing correctly, the operating system makes a decision about what to do—usually it displays an on-screen message to warn you of the problem.

Your computer's operating system ensures that input and output proceed in an orderly manner, using "buffers" to collect and hold data while the computer is busy with other tasks. By using a keyboard buffer, for example, your computer never misses one of your keystrokes, regardless of how fast you type or what else is happening in your computer system at the same time.

How does the operating system affect the user interface? A **user interface** can be defined as the combination of hardware and software that helps people and computers communicate with each other. Your computer's user interface includes a display device, mouse, and keyboard that allow you to view and manipulate your computing environment. It also includes software elements, such as menus and toolbar buttons. The operating system's user interface defines the "look and feel" for all its compatible software. For example, application software that runs under Windows uses a standard set of menus, buttons, and toolbars based on the operating system's user interface.

Most computers today feature a graphical user interface. Abbreviated "GUI" (sometimes pronounced as "gooey"), a **graphical user interface** provides a way to point and click a mouse to select menu options and manipulate graphical objects displayed on the screen. GUIs were originally conceived at the prestigious Xerox PARC research facility. In 1984, Apple Computer turned the idea into a commercial success with the launch of its popular Macintosh computer, which featured a GUI operating system and applications. Graphical user interfaces didn't really catch on in the PC market until 1992 when Windows 3.1 became standard issue on most PCs, replacing a **command-line interface** that required users to type memorized commands to run programs and accomplish tasks (Figure 3-13).

TERMINOLOGY NOTE

The term "buffer" is technical jargon for a region of memory that holds data waiting to be transferred from one device to another.

FIGURE 3-13

A graphical user interface (below left) features menus and icons that you can manipulate with the click of a mouse.

A command-line interface (below right) requires you to memorize and type commands.

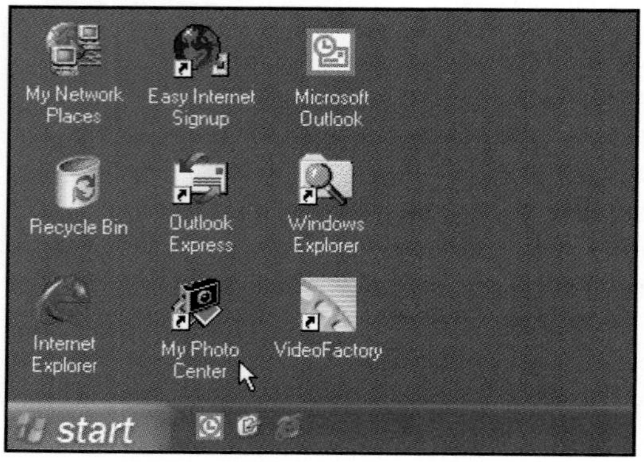

Where is the operating system stored? In some computers—typically handhelds and videogame consoles—the entire operating system is small enough to be stored in ROM. For nearly all personal computers, servers, workstations, mainframes, and supercomputers, the operating system program is quite large, so most of it is stored on a hard disk. The operating system's small **bootstrap program** is stored in ROM and supplies the instructions needed to load the operating system's core into memory when the system boots. This core part of the operating system, called the **kernel**, provides the most essential operating system services, such as memory management and file access. The kernel stays in memory all the time your computer is on. Other parts of the operating system, such as customization utilities, are loaded into memory as they are needed.

Do I ever interact directly with the OS? Although its main purpose is to control what happens "behind the scenes" of a computer system, many operating systems provide helpful tools, called **utilities**, that you can use to control and customize your computer equipment and work environment. Utilities, like those listed below, are typically accessed by using a GUI, such as the familiar Windows desktop.

- **Launch programs.** When you start your computer, Windows displays graphical objects, such as icons, the Start button, and the Programs menu, which you can use to start programs.

- **Manage files.** Another useful utility, called Windows Explorer, allows you to view a list of files, move them to different storage devices, copy them, rename them, and delete them.

- **Get help.** Windows offers a Help system you can use to find out how various commands work.

- **Customize the user interface.** The Control Panel, accessible from the Start menu, provides utilities that help you customize your screen display and work environment.

- **Configure equipment.** The Control Panel also provides access to utilities that help you set up and configure your computer's hardware and peripheral devices (Figure 3-14).

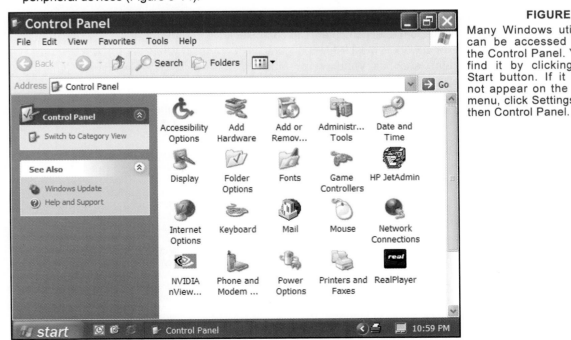

FIGURE 3-14

Many Windows utilities can be accessed from the Control Panel. You'll find it by clicking the Start button. If it does not appear on the Start menu, click Settings and then Control Panel.

Are different operating systems needed for different computing tasks? One operating system might be better suited to some computing tasks than others. To provide clues to their strengths and weaknesses, operating systems are informally categorized and characterized using one or more of the following terms:

A **single-user operating system** expects to deal with one set of input devices—those that can be controlled by one user at a time. Operating systems for handheld computers and many personal computers fit into the single-user category. DOS is an example of a single-user operating system.

A **multiuser operating system** allows a single computer—often a mainframe—to deal with simultaneous input, output, and processing requests from many users. One of its most difficult responsibilities is to schedule all the processing requests that a centralized computer must perform. IBM's OS/390 is one of the most popular mainframe multiuser operating systems.

A **network operating system** (also referred to as a "server operating system") provides communications and routing services that allow computers to share data, programs, and peripheral devices. Novell NetWare, for example, is almost always referred to as a network operating system. The difference between network services and multiuser services can seem a little hazy—especially because operating systems such as UNIX, Linux, and Sun Microsystem's Solaris offer both. The main difference, however, is that multiuser operating systems schedule requests for processing on a centralized computer, whereas a network operating system simply routes data and programs to each user's local computer, where the actual processing takes place.

A **multitasking operating system** provides process and memory management services that allow two or more programs to run simultaneously. Most of today's operating systems, including the OS on your personal computer, offer multitasking services.

A **desktop operating system** is one that's designed for a personal computer—a desktop, notebook, or tablet computer. The computer you use at home, at school, or at work is most likely configured with a desktop operating system, such as Windows or Mac OS. Typically, these operating systems are designed to accommodate a single user, but might also provide networking capability. Today's desktop operating systems invariably provide multitasking capabilities.

Some operating system vendors characterize their products as "home" or "professional" versions. The home version usually has fewer network management tools than the professional version.

WINDOWS, MAC OS, UNIX, LINUX, AND DOS

What's the best-selling operating system? **Microsoft Windows** is installed on more than 80% of the world's personal computers. The number and variety of programs that run on Windows are unmatched by any other operating system, a fact that contributes to its dominant position as the most widely used desktop operating system. Since its introduction in 1985, Windows has evolved through several versions, listed in Figure 3-15.

FIGURE 3-15
Windows Timeline

2001 Windows XP
Featured an updated user interface, used the Windows 2000 32-bit kernel, and supported FAT32 and NTFS file systems.

2000 Windows Me
Featured enhanced multimedia utilities.

2000 Windows 2000
Billed as a "multipurpose network OS for businesses of all sizes" and featured enhanced Web services.

1998 Windows 98
The last Windows version to use the original Windows kernel that accesses DOS.

1995 Windows 95
Featured a revised user interface. Supported 32-bit processors, TCP/IP, dial-up networking, and long file names.

1993 Windows NT
Provided management and security tools for network servers and the NTFS file system.

1992 Windows for Workgroups
Provided peer-to-peer networking, e-mail, group scheduling, and file and printer sharing.

1992 Windows 3.1
Introduced program icons and the file folder metaphor.

1990 Windows 3.0
Introduced graphical controls.

1987 Windows 2.0
Introduced overlapping windows and expanded memory access.

1985 Windows 1.0
Divided the screen into "windows" that allowed users to work with several programs at the same time.

The first versions of Windows, including Windows 3.1, were sometimes referred to as "operating environments" rather than operating systems because they required DOS to supply the operating system kernel. Windows operating environments primarily supplied a point-and-click user interface, complete with graphical screen displays and mouse input. Windows operating environments evolved into today's comprehensive operating systems, that do not require the DOS kernel.

The Windows operating system gets its name from the rectangular work areas that appear on the screen-based desktop. Each work area (or "window") can display a different document or program, providing a visual model of the operating system's multitasking capabilities (Figure 3-16).

INFOWEBLINKS

You'll find lots of current information about Windows at the **Microsoft Windows InfoWeb**.

www.course.com/np/concepts8/ch03

FIGURE 3-16

If you find a Start button sporting the Windows logo in the lower-left corner of the screen, it is a good bet that the computer is running some version of Windows.

The graphical user interface for Windows NT, 98, 2000, and Me (shown at left) features many similarities and some cosmetic differences when compared to the interface for Windows XP (shown below).

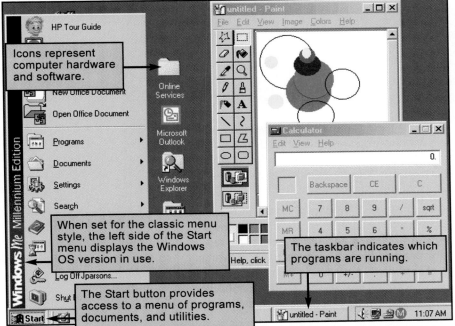

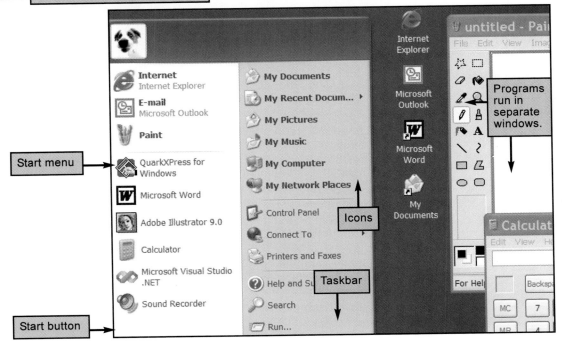

Microsoft currently offers several types of operating systems. Home, Professional, and Workstation editions are designed for personal computers. Server editions are designed for LAN, Internet, and Web servers. Embedded editions are designed for handheld devices, such as PDAs and mobile phones. Figure 3-17 categorizes Windows offerings.

FIGURE 3-17
Microsoft offers several versions of Windows, designed for different computing tasks and equipment.

Personal Computers	LAN, Internet, and Web Servers	PDAs, Mobile Phones, and Non-personal Computer Devices
Windows XP Home Edition Windows XP Professional Windows XP Tablet PC Edition Windows 2000 Professional Windows NT Workstation Windows Me Windows 98 Windows 95 Windows 3.1	Windows Server 2005 Windows Server 2003 Windows 2000 Server Windows NT Server	Windows Mobile OS Pocket PC OS 2002 Pocket PC OS 2000 Windows CE Windows XP Embedded

Is Mac OS similar to Windows? Although **Mac OS** was developed several years before Windows, both operating systems base their user interfaces on the graphical model pioneered at Xerox PARC. Like Windows, Mac OS has been through a number of revisions, including OS X "Tiger" (X meaning version 10), released in 2004.

A quick comparison of Figures 3-16 and 3-18 shows that both Mac and Windows interfaces use a mouse to point and click various icons and menus. Both interfaces feature rectangular work areas to reflect multitasking capabilities. Both operating systems provide basic networking services. A decent collection of software is available for computers that run Mac OS, although the selection is not as vast as the Windows collection. Many of the most prolific software publishers produce one version of their software for Windows and another, similar version for Mac OS.

INFOWEBLINKS

The **Apple InfoWeb** links you to the official site for Apple Computer, Inc.

www.course.com/np/concepts8/ch03

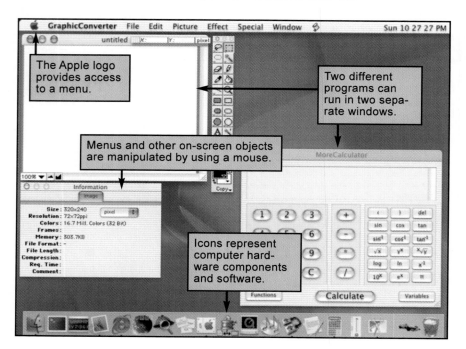

FIGURE 3-18
The Apple logo at the top of the screen is your clue that a computer is running Mac OS.

Are UNIX and Linux the same? The **UNIX** operating system was developed in 1969 at AT&T's Bell Labs. It gained a good reputation for its dependability in multiuser environments, and many versions of it became available for mainframes and microcomputers. In 1991, a young Finnish student named Linus Torvalds developed the **Linux** (pronounced LIH nucks) operating system. Linux was inspired by and loosely based on a UNIX deriviative called MINIX, created by Andrew Tanenbaum.

Linux is rather unique because it is distributed along with its source code under the terms of a General Public License (GPL), which allows everyone to make copies for their own use, to give to others, or to sell. This licensing policy has encouraged programmers to develop Linux utilities, software, and enhancements. Linux is primarily distributed over the Web.

Although Linux is designed for microcomputers, it shares several technical features with UNIX, such as multitasking, virtual memory, TCP/IP drivers, and multiuser capabilities. These features make Linux a popular operating system for e-mail and Web servers as well as for local area networks. Linux has been gaining popularity as a desktop operating system, and some new personal computers now come configured with Linux instead of Windows or Mac OS. Linux typically requires a bit more tinkering than the Windows and Mac desktop operating systems. The comparatively limited number of programs that run under Linux also discourages many nontechnical users from selecting it as the OS for their desktop and notebook computers.

Several Web sites offer a Linux "distribution," which is a package that contains the Linux kernel, system utilities, applications, and an installation routine. Beginner-friendly Linux distributions include Mandrakelinux, Linspire, College Linux, and Xandros Desktop. Most of these distributions include a GUI module that provides a user interface similar to the one pictured in Figure 3-19.

INFOWEBLINKS

If you're interested in exploring the world of "open source" operating systems, start your journey at the **Linux InfoWeb**.

www.course.com/np/concepts8/ch03

FIGURE 3-19

Linux users can choose from several graphical interfaces. Pictured here is the popular KDE graphical desktop.

Why do I keep hearing about DOS? Old-timers in the computer industry sometimes reminisce about DOS. It was the first operating system that many of them used, and its cryptic command-line user interface left an indelible impression. **DOS** (which rhymes with "toss") stands for Disk Operating System. It was developed by Microsoft—the same company that later produced Windows—and introduced on the original IBM PC in 1982. Although IBM called this operating system PC-DOS, Microsoft marketed it to other companies under the name MS-DOS.

After more than 20 years, remnants of DOS still linger in the world of personal computers because it provides part of the operating system kernel for Windows versions 3.1, 95, 98, and Me. Users rarely interact with DOS, however, because it is well hidden by the Windows graphical user interface.

During the peak of its popularity, thousands of software programs were produced for computers running DOS. You can occasionally find some of these programs on the Internet, and run them using the MS-DOS Prompt option (Windows 98, Me, NT, and 2000) or the Command Prompt option (Windows XP) on the Windows Start menu. DOS programs look rather unsophisticated by today's standards, so for most of us, DOS and DOS software are nothing more than footnotes in the history of the computer industry.

HANDHELD AND TABLET OPERATING SYSTEMS

What are the options for handheld operating systems? Two operating systems dominate the realm of handheld computers: Palm OS and Windows Mobile OS, shown in Figure 3-20.

Palm OS is produced by PalmSource, a spinoff of the company that produced some of the first commercially successful PDAs. Palm OS is currently used for popular PDAs such as palmOne Zire and Sony CLIE. It also powers Fossil's wristwatch PDA and smartphones from manufacturers such as palmOne, Samsung, and Kyocera.

Windows Mobile OS is an operating system built on the Microsoft Windows CE technology. As a cousin to Windows XP, Windows Mobile OS sports some features similar to those found on the Windows desktop. Windows Mobile OS is the operating system for a variety of PDAs, phone-enabled PDAs, and smartphones.

INFOWEBLINKS

If you want to find out more about this venerable operating system, connect to the **DOS InfoWeb**.

www.course.com/np/concepts8/ch03

FIGURE 3-20
Palm OS (left) and Windows Mobile OS (right) are two popular PDA operating systems.

Are operating systems for handheld devices similar to desktop operating systems? Operating systems for handheld and desktop devices provide many similar services, such as scheduling processor resources, managing memory, loading programs, managing input and output, and establishing the user interface. But because handheld devices tend to be used for less sophisticated tasks, their operating systems are somewhat simpler and significantly smaller.

By keeping the operating system small, it can be stored in ROM. Without the need to load the OS from disk into RAM, a handheld device's operating system is ready almost instantly when the unit is turned on. Operating systems for handheld devices provide built-in support for touch screens, handwriting input, wireless networking, and cellular communications.

What about operating systems for tablet computers? Windows XP Tablet Edition is the operating system supplied with just about every tablet computer. Its main feature is handwriting recognition, which accepts printed input from the touch-sensitive screen and then converts it into ASCII text, as shown in Figure 3-21.

FIGURE 3-21

Handwriting recognition is one of the main services a tablet computer OS provides.

QUICKCHECK......SECTION B

1. An operating system manages a computer's [_____], such as RAM, storage space, and peripherals.

2. To run more than one program at a time, the operating system must allocate specific areas of [_____] for each program.

3. A graphical [_____] interface provides a way to point and click a mouse to select menu options and manipulate objects that appear on the screen.

4. ROM contains a(n) [_____] program that supplies instructions for loading key parts of the operating system when the computer starts.

5. The core part of an operating system is called its [_____].

6. A desktop operating system, such as Windows, is designed for personal computers. True or false? [_____]

7. Handheld devices, such as PDAs and smartphones typically feature multiuser operating systems. True or false? [_____]

CHECK ANSWERS

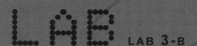
LAB 3-B

USING THE WINDOWS INTERFACE

In this lab, you'll learn:

- Why the standard Windows controls make it easy to learn new Windows software

- What happens when you use the mouse pointer to click, double-click, and right-click an object

- How ToolTips or ScreenTips help you identify icons and toolbar buttons

- How to use the Maximize, Minimize, Restore, and Close buttons

- How to use scroll bars

- How to navigate through a series of menus

- Which menus are common to most Windows applications

- The meaning of menu conventions, such as the ellipsis and triangle

- How to use standard dialog box controls, such as option buttons, spin boxes, tabs, check boxes, and lists

- How to use toolbar buttons

- How to adjust toolbars

- How to take a screenshot and print it

INTERACTIVE LAB

CLICK TO START THE LAB ✦

LAB ASSIGNMENTS

1. Start the interactive part of the lab. Insert your Tracking Disk if you want to save your QuickCheck results. Perform each lab step as directed, and answer all the lab QuickCheck questions. When you exit the lab, your answers are automatically graded and your results are displayed.

2. Draw a sketch or print a screenshot of the Windows desktop on any computer you use. Use ToolTips (or ScreenTips) to identify all the icons on the desktop and the taskbar.

3. Use the Start button and Accessories menu to start an application program called Paint. (If Paint is not installed on your computer, you can use any application software, such as a word processing program.) Draw a sketch or print a screenshot of the Paint (or other application) window and label the following components: window title, title bar, Maximize/Restore button, Minimize button, Close button, menu bar, toolbar, and scroll bar.

4. Look at each of the menu options the Paint software (or other application) provides. Make a list of those that seem to be standard Windows menu options.

5. Draw a sketch of Paint's Print dialog box (or other application's Print dialog box). Label the following parts: buttons, spin bar, pull-down list, option button, and check boxes.

SECTION C

APPLICATION SOFTWARE

Most computers include some basic word processing, e-mail, and Internet access software, but computer owners invariably want additional software to increase their computers' repertory of productivity, business, learning, or entertainment activities. Section C provides an overview of the vast array of application software that's available for personal computers.

DOCUMENT PRODUCTION SOFTWARE

How can my computer help me with my writing? Whether you are writing a 10-page paper, writing software documentation, designing a brochure for your new startup company, or laying out the school newspaper, you will probably use some form of **document production software**. This software assists you with composing, editing, designing, printing, and electronically publishing documents. The three most popular types of document production software are word processing, desktop publishing, and Web authoring (Figure 3-22).

Word processing software, such as Microsoft Word, has replaced typewriters for producing documents such as reports, letters, memos, papers, and manuscripts. Word processing software gives you the ability to create, spell-check, edit, and format a document on the screen before you commit it to paper.

Desktop publishing software (abbreviated DTP) takes word processing software one step further by helping you use graphic design techniques to enhance the format and appearance of a document. Although today's word processing software offers many page layout and design features, DTP software products, such as QuarkXPress and Adobe PageMaker, have sophisticated features to help you produce professional-quality output for newspapers, newsletters, brochures, magazines, and books.

Web authoring software helps you design and develop customized Web pages that you can publish electronically on the Internet. Only a few years ago, creating Web pages was a fairly technical task that required authors to insert special formatting HTML tags, such as <a href="contents.htm">. Now Web authoring software products, such as Microsoft FrontPage and Macromedia Dreamweaver, help nontechnical Web authors by providing easy-to-use tools for composing the text for a Web page, assembling graphical elements, and automatically generating HTML tags.

How does document production software help me turn my ideas into sentences and paragraphs? Document production software makes it easy to let your ideas flow because it automatically handles many tasks that might otherwise distract you. For example, you don't need to worry about fitting words within the margins. A feature called "word wrap" determines how your text will flow from line to line by automatically moving words down to the next line as you reach the right margin. Imagine that the sentences in your document are ribbons of text; word wrap bends the ribbons. Changing the margin size just means bending the ribbon in different

FIGURE 3-22

Popular document production software includes Microsoft Word, QuarkXPress, and Macromedia Dreamweaver.

INFOWEBLINKS

This InfoWeb is your guide to today's best-selling **Document Production Software**.

www.course.com/np/concepts8/ch03

places. Even after you type an entire document, adjusting the size of your right, left, top, and bottom margins is simple (Figure 3-23).

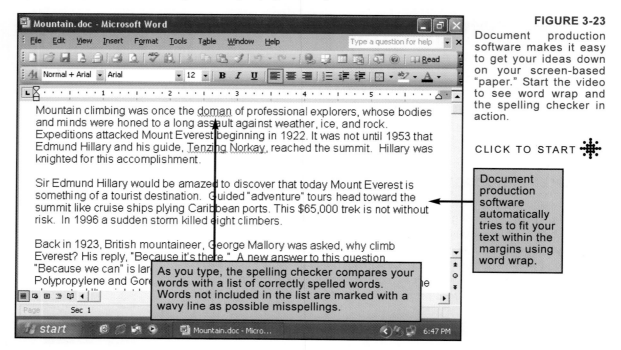

FIGURE 3-23
Document production software makes it easy to get your ideas down on your screen-based "paper." Start the video to see word wrap and the spelling checker in action.

CLICK TO START

What if I'm a bad speller? Most document production software includes a **spelling checker** that marks misspelled words in a document. You can easily correct a misspelled word as you type, or you can run the spelling checker when you finish entering all the text. Some software even has an autocorrecting capability that automatically changes a typo, such as "teh," to the correct spelling ("the").

Although your software's spelling checker helps you correct misspellings, it cannot guarantee an error-free document. A spelling checker works by comparing each word from your document to a list of correctly spelled words that is stored in a data file called a **spelling dictionary**. If the word from your document is in the dictionary, the spelling checker considers the word correctly spelled. If the word is not in the dictionary, the word is counted as misspelled. Sounds okay, right? But suppose your document contains a reference to the city of "Negaunee." This word is not in the dictionary, so the spelling checker considers it misspelled, even though it is spelled correctly. Proper nouns and scientific, medical, and technical words are likely to be flagged as misspelled, even if you spell them correctly, because they do not appear in the spelling checker's dictionary.

Now suppose that your document contains the phrase "a pear of shoes." Although you meant to use "pair" rather than "pear," the spelling checker will not catch your mistake because "pear" is a valid word in the dictionary. Your spelling checker won't help if you have trouble deciding whether to use "there" or "their," "its" or "it's," or "too" or "to." Remember, then, that a spelling checker cannot substitute for a thorough proofread.

Can document production software improve my writing? Because word processing software tends to focus on the writing process, it offers several features that can improve the quality of your writing. These features may not be available in desktop publishing software or Web authoring software, which focus on the format of a document.

Your word processing software is likely to include a **thesaurus**, which can help you find a synonym for a word so that you can make your writing more varied and interesting. A **grammar checker** "reads" through your document and points out potential grammatical trouble spots, such as incomplete sentences, run-on sentences, and verbs that don't agree with nouns.

Your word processing software might also be able to analyze the reading level of your document using a standard **readability formula**, such as the Flesch-Kincaid reading level. You can use this analysis to find out if your writing matches your target audience, based on sentence length and vocabulary.

Can document production software help me break bad writing habits? Most word processing, DTP, and Web authoring software includes a **Search and Replace** feature. You can use this feature to hunt down mistakes that you typically make in your writing. For example, you might know from experience that you tend to overuse the word "typically." You can use Search and Replace to find each occurrence of "typically," and then you can decide whether you should substitute a different word, such as "usually" or "ordinarily."

How do I get my documents to look good? The **format** for a document refers to the way that all the elements of a document—text, pictures, titles, and page numbers—are arranged on the page. The final format of your document depends on how and where you intend to use it. A school paper, for example, simply needs to be printed in standard paragraph format—perhaps double spaced and with numbered pages. Your word processing software has all the features you need for this formatting task. A brochure, newsletter, or corporate report, on the other hand, might require more ambitious formatting, such as columns that continue on noncontiguous pages and text labels that overlay graphics. You might consider transferring your document from your word processing software to your desktop publishing software for access to more sophisticated formatting tools. For documents that you plan to publish on the Web, Web authoring software usually provides the most useful set of formatting tools.

The "look" of your final document depends on several formatting factors, such as font style, paragraph style, and page layout. A **font** is a set of letters that share a unified design. Font size is measured as **point size**, abbreviated pt. (One point is about 1/72 of an inch.) Figure 3-24 illustrates several popular fonts included with document production software.

INFOWEBLINKS

You can add to your font collection by downloading font files from the **Font InfoWeb**.

www.course.com/np/concepts8/ch03

Times New Roman Font	8 pt.
Times New Roman Font	10 pt.
Times New Roman Font	12 pt.
Times New Roman Font	16 pt.
Times New Roman Font	**16 pt. Bold**
Times New Roman Font	16 pt. Green
Arial Font	16 pt.
Comic Sans MS	16 pt.
Georgia Font	**16 pt. Bold Gold**
Dotto	24 pt. Orange

FIGURE 3-24

You can vary the font style by selecting character formatting attributes, such as bold, italics, underline, superscript, and subscript. You can also select a color and size for a font. The font size for the text in a typical paragraph is set at 8, 10, or 12 pt. Titles can be as large as 72 pt.

Paragraph style includes the alignment of text within the margins and the space between each line of text. **Paragraph alignment** refers to the horizontal position of text—whether it is aligned at the left margin, aligned at the right margin, or **fully justified** so that the text is aligned evenly on both the right and left margins. Your document will look more formal if it is fully justified, like the text in this paragraph, than if it has an uneven or "ragged" right margin. **Line spacing** (also called **leading**, pronounced "LED ing") refers to the vertical spacing between lines. Documents are typically single spaced or double spaced, but word processing and DTP software allow you to adjust line spacing in 1 pt. increments.

Instead of individually selecting font and paragraph style elements, document production software typically allows you to define a **style** that lets you apply several font and paragraph elements with a single click (Figure 3-25). For example, instead of applying bold to a title, changing its font to Times New Roman, and then adjusting the font size to 24 pt., you can simply define a Title style as 24 pt., Times New Roman, bold. You can then apply all three style elements at once simply by selecting the Title style.

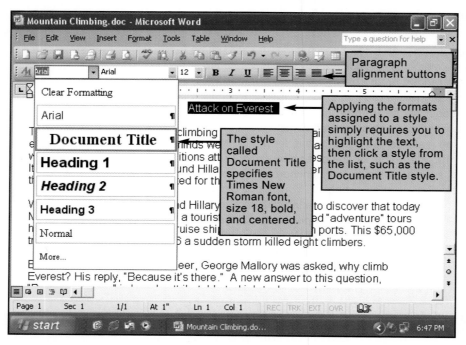

FIGURE 3-25

By defining a style, you can apply multiple font attributes with a single click.

CLICK TO START ✣

Page layout refers to the physical position of each element on a page. In addition to paragraphs of text, these elements might include:

■ **Headers and footers.** A **header** is text that you specify to automatically appear in the top margin of every page. A **footer** is text that you specify to automatically appear in the bottom margin of every page. You might put your name and the document title in the header or footer of a document so that its printed pages won't get mixed up with those of another printed document.

■ **Page numbers.** Word processing and DTP software automatically number the pages of a document according to your specifications, usually placing the page number within a header or footer. A Web page, no matter what its length, is all a single page, so Web authoring software typically doesn't provide page numbering.

- **Graphical elements.** Photos, diagrams, graphs, and charts can be incorporated in your documents. **Clip art**—a collection of drawings and photos designed to be inserted in documents—is a popular source of graphical elements.

- **Tables.** A **table** is a grid-like structure that can hold text or pictures. For printed documents, tables are a popular way to produce easy-to-read columns of data and to position graphics. It may sound surprising, but for Web pages, tables provide one of the few ways to precisely position text and pictures. As a result, Web page designers make extensive and very creative use of tables.

Most word processing is page-oriented because it treats each page as a rectangle that can be filled with text and graphics. Text automatically flows from one page to the next. In contrast, most DTP software is frame-oriented because it allows you to divide each page into several rectangular-shaped **frames** that you can fill with text or graphics. Text flows from one frame to the next, rather than from page to page (Figure 3-26).

Attack on Everest
by Janell Chalmers

Mountain climbing was once the domain of professional explorers, whose bodies and minds were honed to a long assault against weather, ice, and rock. Eventually, even Mount Everest [was conquered in 19]53 [and its first to clim]de, Tenzing Norkay, reached the summit. Hillary was knighted for this accomplishment.

Sir Edmund Hillary would be amazed to discover that today Mount Everest has become something of a tourist destination. Guided "adventure" tours head toward the summit like cruise ships plying

> *"Because it's there."*
> George Mallory

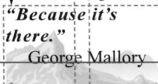

Caribbean ports. This $65,000 trek is not without risk. In 1996 a sudden storm killed eight climbers.

Back in 1923, British mountaineer George Mallory was asked, why climb Everest? His reply, "Because it's there." A new answer to this question, "Because we can" may be largely attributable to new high-tech mountain gear. Nylon, polypropylene and Gore-Tex clothing provide light, yet warm protection from the elements. New, high-tech ultraviolet lenses protect eyes from dangerous "snowblindness."

An other gear makes the mountain seem less

> Wrapping text around a frame adds interest to the layout.

One frame holds the centered title and author's byline. This text is linked to the text in subsequent frames.

"Guide lines" that do not appear on printouts help align text and graphical elements.

Text can link to frames on the next page or on any page of the document.

Does document production software increase productivity? Word processing software, in particular, provides several features that automate tasks and allow you to work more productively. For example, suppose that you want to send prospective employers a letter and your resume. Instead of composing and addressing each letter individually, your software can perform a **mail merge** that automatically creates personalized letters by combining the information in a mailing list with a form letter. Some additional capabilities of word processing software include:

- Automatically generating a table of contents and an index for a document

- Automatically numbering footnotes and positioning each footnote on the page where it is referenced

- Providing document templates and document wizards that show you the correct content and format for a variety of documents, such as business letters, fax cover sheets, and memos

- Exporting a document into HTML format

SPREADSHEET SOFTWARE

What is a spreadsheet? A **spreadsheet** uses rows and columns of numbers to create a model or representation of a real situation. For example, your checkbook register is a type of spreadsheet because it is a numerical representation of the cash flowing in and out of your bank account. Today, **spreadsheet software**, such as Microsoft Excel, provides tools to create electronic spreadsheets. It is similar to a "smart" piece of paper that automatically adds up the columns of numbers you write on it. You can use it to make other calculations, too, based on simple equations that you write or more complex, built-in formulas. As an added bonus, spreadsheet software helps you turn your data into a variety of colorful graphs. It also includes special data-handling features that allow you to sort data, search for data that meets specific criteria, and print reports.

Spreadsheet software was initially popular with accountants and financial managers who dealt with paper-based spreadsheets, but found the electronic version far easier to use and less prone to errors than manual calculations. Other people soon discovered the benefits of spreadsheets for projects that require repetitive calculations—budgeting, maintaining a grade book, balancing a checkbook, tracking investments, calculating loan payments, and estimating project costs.

Because it is so easy to experiment with different numbers, spreadsheet software is particularly useful for **what-if analysis**. You can use what-if analyses to answer questions such as "What if I get an A on my next two economics exams? But what if I get only Bs?" "What if I invest $100 a month in my retirement plan? But what if I invest $200 a month?"

What does a computerized spreadsheet look like? You use spreadsheet software to create an on-screen **worksheet**. A worksheet is based on a grid of columns and rows. Each **cell** in the grid can contain a value, label, or formula. A **value** is a number that you want to use in a calculation. A **label** is any text used to describe data. For example, suppose that your worksheet contains the value $486,000. You could use a label to identify this number as "Income" (Figure 3-27).

INFOWEBLINKS

For links to today's best-selling spreadsheet software, connect to the **Spreadsheet InfoWeb**.

www.course.com/np/concepts8/ch03

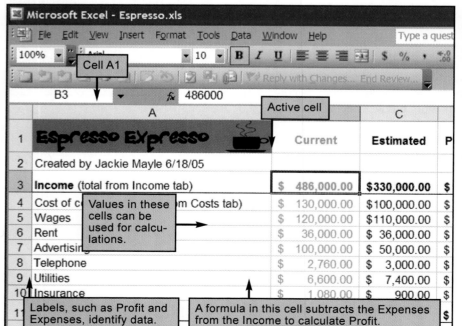

FIGURE 3-27

In a worksheet, each column is lettered and each row is numbered. The intersection of a column and row is called a cell. Each cell has a unique cell reference, or "address," derived from its column and row location. For example, A1 is the cell reference for the upper-left cell in a worksheet because it is in column A and row 1. You can select any cell and make it the active cell by clicking it. Once a cell is active, you can enter data into it.

You can format the labels and values on a worksheet in much the same way as you would format text in a word processing document. You can change fonts and font size, select a font color, and select font styles, such as bold, italic, and underline.

How does spreadsheet software work? The values contained in a cell can be manipulated by formulas placed in other cells. A **formula** works behind the scenes to tell the computer how to use the contents of cells in calculations. You can enter a simple formula in a cell to add, subtract, multiply, or divide numbers. More complex formulas can be designed to perform just about any calculation you can imagine. Figure 3-28 illustrates how a formula might be used in a simple spreadsheet to calculate savings.

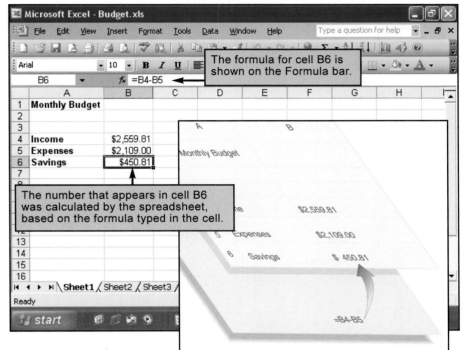

FIGURE 3-28

When a cell contains a formula, it displays the result of the formula rather than the formula itself. To view and edit the formula, you use the Formula bar.

You can think of the formula as working "behind the scenes" to perform calculations and then display the result.

CLICK TO START

FIGURE 3-29

Functions are special formulas provided by spreadsheet software.

A formula, such as =D4-D5+((D8/B2)*110), can contain **cell references** (like D4 and D5), numbers (like 110), and **mathematical operators**, such as the multiplication symbol (*), the division symbol (/), the addition symbol, and the subtraction symbol. Parts of a formula can be enclosed in parentheses to indicate the order in which the mathematical operations should be performed. The operation in the innermost set of parentheses—in this case, (D8/B2)— should be performed first.

You can enter a formula "from scratch" by typing it into a cell, or you can use a built-in **function** provided by the spreadsheet software. To use a function, you simply select one from a list, as shown in Figure 3-29, and then indicate the cell references of any values you want to include in the calculation.

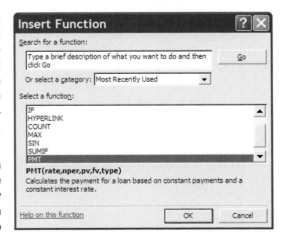

What happens when I modify a worksheet? When you change the contents of any cell in a worksheet, all the formulas are recalculated. This **automatic recalculation** feature ensures that the results in every cell are accurate for the information currently entered in the worksheet.

Your worksheet is also automatically updated to reflect any rows or columns that you add, delete, or copy within the worksheet. Unless you specify otherwise, a cell reference is a **relative reference**—that is, a reference that can change from B4 to B3, for example, if row 3 is deleted and all the data moves up one row.

If you don't want a cell reference to change, you can use an absolute reference. An **absolute reference** never changes when you insert rows or copy or move formulas. Understanding when to use absolute references is one of the key aspects of developing spreadsheet design expertise. Figure 3-30 and its associated tour provide additional information about relative and absolute references.

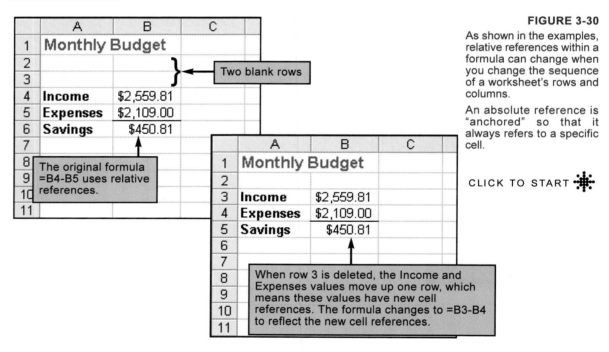

FIGURE 3-30

As shown in the examples, relative references within a formula can change when you change the sequence of a worksheet's rows and columns.

An absolute reference is "anchored" so that it always refers to a specific cell.

CLICK TO START

How will I know which formulas and functions to use when I create a worksheet? To create an effective and accurate worksheet, you typically must understand the calculations and formulas that are involved. If, for example, you want to create a worksheet that helps you calculate your final grade in a course, you need to know the grading scale and understand how your instructor plans to weight each assignment and test.

Most spreadsheet software includes a few templates or wizards for pre-designed worksheets, such as invoices, income-expense reports, balance sheets, and loan payment schedules. Additional templates are available on the Web. These templates are typically designed by professionals and contain all the necessary labels and formulas. To use a template, you simply plug in the values for your calculation.

"NUMBER CRUNCHING" SOFTWARE

Aside from spreadsheets, what other "number crunching" software is available? Spreadsheet software provides a sort of "blank canvas" on which you can create numeric models by simply "painting" values, labels, and formulas. The advantage of spreadsheet software is the flexibility it provides—flexibility to create customized calculations according to your exact specifications. The disadvantage of spreadsheet software is that—aside from a few predesigned templates—you are responsible for entering formulas and selecting functions for calculations. If you don't know the formulas or don't understand the functions, you're out of luck.

In contrast to the "blank canvas" approach provided by spreadsheet software, other "number crunching" software works more like "paint by numbers." It provides a structured environment dedicated to a particular number crunching task, such as statistical analysis, mathematical modeling, or money management.

Statistical software helps you analyze large sets of data to discover relationships and patterns. Products such as SPSS and Statsoft STATISTICA are helpful tools for summarizing survey results, test scores, experiment results, or population data. Most statistical software includes graphing capability so that you can display and explore your data visually.

Mathematical modeling software provides tools for solving a wide range of math, science, and engineering problems. Students, teachers, mathematicians, and engineers, in particular, appreciate how products such as Mathcad and Mathematica help them recognize patterns that can be difficult to identify in columns of numbers (Figure 3-31).

INFOWEBLINKS

For more information about popular "number crunching" software, take a look at the **Numeric Software InfoWeb**.

www.course.com/np/concepts8/ch03

FIGURE 3-31

Mathematical modeling software helps you visualize the product of complex formulas. Here the points from a sphere are graphed onto a plane, to demonstrate the principles behind the Astronomical Clock of Prague.

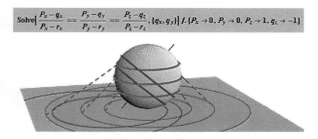

Money management software offers a variety of tools for tracking monetary transactions and investments. In this software category, **personal finance software**, such as Microsoft Money and Intuit Quicken, is designed to keep records of income, expenses, assets, and liabilities using a simple checkbook-like user interface. This software also automates routine financial tasks, such as budgeting, investing, check writing, and bill paying. Many personal financial software products provide direct links to online banking services, so you can use them to check account balances, transfer funds, and pay bills.

Personal financial software produces reports and graphs that show you where your money goes. For example, you can analyze various aspects of your cash flow, such as how much you spent on entertainment last month and how that compares to the previous month.

Tax preparation software is a specialized type of personal finance software designed to help you gather your annual income and expense data, identify deductions, and calculate tax payments. Popular products, such as Intuit TurboTax, even accept data directly from personal finance software to eliminate hours of tedious data entry.

DATABASE SOFTWARE

What is a database? The term "database" has evolved from a specialized technical term into a part of our everyday vocabulary. In the context of modern usage, a **database** is simply a collection of data that is stored on one or more computers. A database can contain any sort of data, such as a university's student records, a library's card catalog, a store's inventory, an individual's address book, or a utility company's customers. Databases can be stored on personal computers, LAN servers, Web servers, mainframes, and even handheld computers.

What is database software? **Database software** helps you enter, find, organize, update, and report information stored in a database. Microsoft Access, FileMaker Pro, and askSam are three of the most popular examples of database software for personal computers. Oracle and MySQL are popular server database software packages. For PDAs, popular choices include HanDBase, Mobile DB, dBNow, and JFile.

How does a database store data? Database software stores data as a series of records, which are composed of fields that hold data. A **record** holds data for a single entity—a person, place, thing, or event. A **field** holds one item of data relevant to a record. You can envision a record as a Rolodex or index card and a series of records as a table (Figure 3-32).

INFOWEBLINKS

For more information about popular database software, connect to the **Database Software InfoWeb**.

www.course.com/np/concepts8/ch03

TERMINOLOGY NOTE

Database software is also referred to as database management software (DBMS).

FIGURE 3-32
A single database record is similar to a Rolodex or an index card. A series of records is usually depicted in table format.

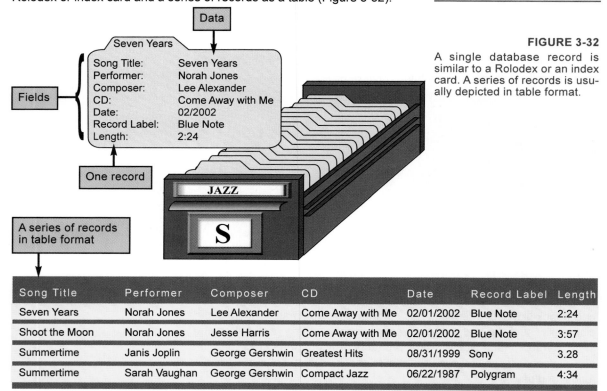

Song Title	Performer	Composer	CD	Date	Record Label	Length
Seven Years	Norah Jones	Lee Alexander	Come Away with Me	02/01/2002	Blue Note	2:24
Shoot the Moon	Norah Jones	Jesse Harris	Come Away with Me	02/01/2002	Blue Note	3:57
Summertime	Janis Joplin	George Gershwin	Greatest Hits	08/31/1999	Sony	3.28
Summertime	Sarah Vaughan	George Gershwin	Compact Jazz	06/22/1987	Polygram	4:34

Database software provides tools to work with more than one collection of records, as long as the records are somehow related to each other. For example, MTV might maintain a database pertaining to jazz music. One series of database records might contain data about jazz songs. It could contain fields such as those shown in Figure 3-32. Another series of records might contain biographical data about jazz performers, including name, birth date, and home town. It might even include a field for the performer's photo.

These two sets of records can be related by the name of the performing artist, as shown in Figure 3-33.

JAZZ PERFORMERS		
Performer	Birth Date	Home Town
Ella Fitzgerald	04/25/1918	Newport News, VA
Norah Jones	03/30/1979	New York,NY
Billie Holiday	04/07/1915	Baltimore, MD
Lena Horne	06/17/1917	Brooklyn, NY

JAZZ SONGS						
Song Title	Performer	Composer	CD	Date	Record Label	Length
Seven Years	Norah Jones	Lee Alexander	Come Away with Me	02/01/2002	Blue Note	2:24
Shoot the Moon	Norah Jones	Jesse Harris	Come Away with Me	02/01/2002	Blue Note	3:57
Summertime	Janis Joplin	George Gershwin	Greatest Hits	08/31/1999	Sony	3.28
Summertime	Sarah Vaughan	George Gershwin	Compact Jazz	06/22/1987	Polygram	4:34

FIGURE 3-33

The two sets of records are related by the Performer field. The relationship allows you to select Norah Jones from the Jazz Performers records and jump to any records in the Jazz Songs records that Norah Jones performed.

How do I create records? Database software provides the tools you need to define fields for a series of records. Figure 3-34 shows a simple form you might use to specify the fields for a database.

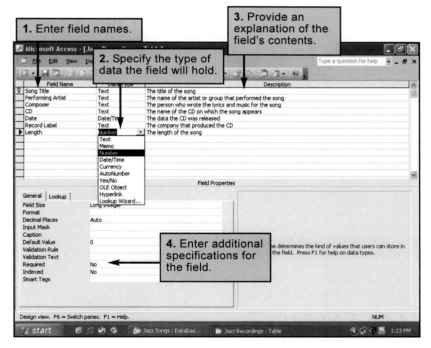

FIGURE 3-34

Database software provides tools for specifying fields for a series of records.

CLICK TO START

When can I enter data? After you've defined fields for a series of records, you can enter the data for each record. Your database software provides a simple-to-use data entry form that allows you to easily fill in the data for each field. Instead of typing data into a database, you can also import data from a commercial database, such as a customer mailing list—you can even download databases from the Web, and then import the data into fields you have defined with your database software.

How do I locate specific data? Many databases contain hundreds or thousands of records. If you want to find a particular record or a group of records, scrolling through every record is much too cumbersome. Instead, you can enter a query, and the computer will quickly locate the records you seek.

Most database software provides one or more methods for making queries. A **query language**, such as SQL (Structured Query Language), provides a set of commands for locating and manipulating data. To locate all performances of *Summertime* before 1990 from a Jazz Songs database, you might enter a query such as:

Select * from JazzSongs where SongTitle = 'Summertime' and Date < '1990'

In addition to a formal query language, some database software provides **natural language query** capabilities. To make such queries, you don't have to learn an esoteric query language. Instead, you can simply enter questions, such as:

Who performed Summertime before 1990?

As an alternative to a query language or a natural language query, your database software might allow you to **query by example** (QBE), simply by filling out a form with the type of data you want to locate. Figure 3-35 illustrates a query by example for *Summertime* performances before 1990.

TERMINOLOGY NOTE

You encountered the term "query" in Chapter 1 in the context of search engines, which allow you to search through a database of information pertaining to the content of Web pages.

A query is a set of keywords and operators that describe information you want to find.

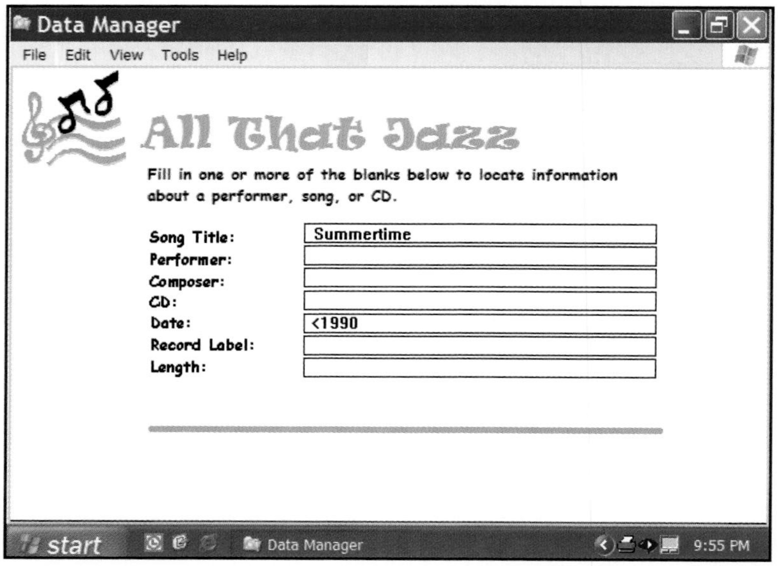

FIGURE 3-35
When you query by example, your database software displays a blank form on the screen, and you enter examples of the data that you want to find.

How can I use search results? Your database software can typically help you print reports, export data to other programs (such as to a spreadsheet where you can graph the data), convert the data to other formats (such as HTML so that you can post the data on the Web), and transmit data to other computers.

Whether you print, import, copy, save, or transmit the data you find in databases, it is your responsibility to use it appropriately. Never introduce inaccurate information into a database. Respect copyrights, giving credit to the person or organization that compiled the data. You should also respect the privacy of the people who are the subject of the data. Unless you have permission to do so, do not divulge names, social security numbers, or other identifying information that might compromise someone's privacy.

GRAPHICS SOFTWARE

What kind of software do I need to work with drawings, photos, and other pictures? In computer lingo, the term **graphics** refers to any picture, drawing, sketch, photograph, image, or icon that appears on your computer screen. **Graphics software** is designed to help you create, manipulate, and print graphics. Some graphics software products specialize in a particular type of graphic, while others allow you to work with multiple graphics formats. If you are really interested in working with graphics, you will undoubtedly end up using more than one graphics software product.

Paint software (sometimes called "image editing software") provides a set of electronic pens, brushes, and paints for painting images on the screen. A simple program called Microsoft Paint is included with Windows. More sophisticated paint software products include JASC Paint Shop Pro and Procreate Painter. Many graphic artists, Web page designers, and illustrators use paint software as their primary computer-based graphics tool.

Photo editing software, such as Adobe Photoshop, includes features specially designed to fix poor-quality photos by modifying contrast and brightness, cropping out unwanted objects, and removing "red eye." Photos can also be edited using paint software, but photo editing software typically offers tools and wizards that simplify common photo editing tasks.

Drawing software provides a set of lines, shapes, and colors that can be assembled into diagrams, corporate logos, and schematics. The drawings created with tools such as Adobe Illustrator and Macromedia Freehand tend to have a "flat" cartoon-like quality, but they are very easy to modify, and look good at just about any size. Figure 3-36 illustrates a typical set of tools provided by drawing software.

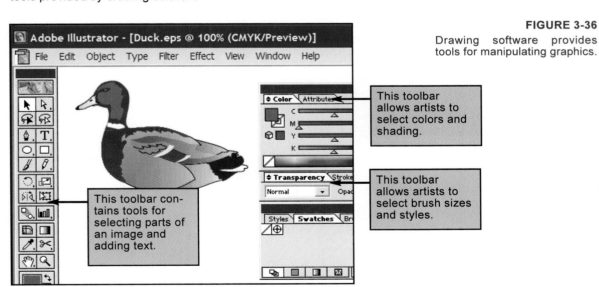

FIGURE 3-36

Drawing software provides tools for manipulating graphics.

3-D graphics software provides a set of tools for creating "wireframes" that represent three-dimensional objects. A wireframe acts much like the framework for a pop-up tent. Just as you would construct the framework for the tent and then cover it with a nylon tent cover, 3-D graphics software can cover a wireframe object with surface texture and color to create a graphic of a 3-D object (Figure 3-37 on the next page).

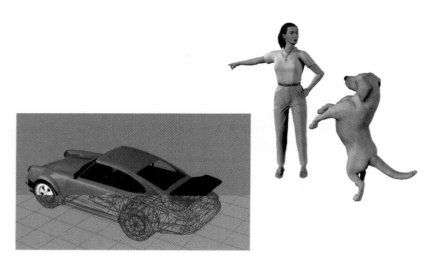

FIGURE 3-37

3-D graphics software provides tools for creating a wireframe that represents a 3-D object.

Some 3-D software specializes in engineering-style graphics, while other 3-D software specializes in figures.

CAD software (computer-aided design software) is a special type of 3-D graphics software designed for architects and engineers who use computers to create blueprints and product specifications. AutoCAD is one of the best-selling professional CAD products. TurboCAD is a low-cost favorite. Scaled-down versions of professional CAD software provide simplified tools for homeowners who want to redesign their kitchens, examine new landscaping options, or experiment with floor plans.

Presentation software supplies the tools you need for combining text, photos, clip art, graphs, animations, and sound into a series of electronic slides, like those in Figure 3-38. You can display electronic slides on a color monitor for a one-on-one presentation or use a computer projection device for group presentations. You can also output the presentation as overhead transparencies, paper copies, or 35 mm slides. Popular presentation software products include Microsoft PowerPoint and Harvard Graphics.

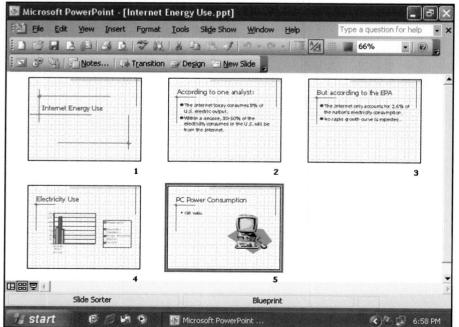

FIGURE 3-38

A computer-based presentation consists of a series of slides, created with presentation software.

CLICK TO START

MUSIC SOFTWARE

Why would I need music software? You don't have to be a musician or composer to have a use for music software. Many types of music software are available. You might be surprised to find how many of them come in handy.

It is possible—and easy—to make your own digital voice and music recordings, which you store on your computer's hard disk. Windows and Mac OS operating system utilities usually supply the necessary **audio editing software**—Sound Recorder on PCs (Figure 3-39) and iTunes on Macs.

FIGURE 3-39

Audio editing software, such as Sound Recorder, provides controls much like those on a tape recorder. Menus offer additional digital editing features, such as speed control, volume adjustments, clipping, and mixing.

Audio editing software typically includes playback as well as recording capabilities. A specialized version of this software called karaoke software integrates music files and on-screen lyrics—everything you need to sing along with your favorite tunes.

Music can be stored in a variety of digital formats on a computer or on a portable audio player, such as Apple's iPod. Digital music formats, such as MP3 and AAC, are not the same formats used to store music on commercial audio CDs. These file formats take up much less storage space than on the original CD.

A variety of software allows you to convert music from commercial CDs for use on computers and portable audio players. **CD ripper software** pulls a track off an audio CD and stores it in "raw" digital format on your computer's hard disk. **Audio encoding software** (sometimes called an "audio format converter") converts the raw audio file into a format such as MP3 or AAC. After the file is converted, you can listen to it on your computer, or you can transfer it to a portable MP3 player.

Ear training software targets musicians and music students who want to learn to play by ear, develop tuning skills, recognize notes and keys, and develop other musical skills. **Notation software** is the musician's equivalent of a word processor. It helps musicians compose, edit, and print the notes for their compositions. For non-musicians, **computer-aided music software** is designed to generate unique musical compositions simply by selecting the musical style, instruments, key, and tempo. **MIDI sequencing software** and software synthesizers are an important part of the studio musician's toolbox. They're great for sound effects and for controlling keyboards and other digital instruments.

TERMINOLOGY NOTE

Some CD ripper software also includes audio encoding software so that ripping and encoding seem to happen within a single operation.

INFOWEBLINKS

At the **Music Software InfoWeb**, you'll find detailed information on popular software in this category.

www.course.com/np/concepts8/ch03

VIDEO EDITING AND DVD AUTHORING SOFTWARE

Is video editing software difficult to use? The popularity of computer-based video editing can be attributed to video editing software, such as Windows Movie Maker and Apple iMovie, now included with Windows computers and Macs. **Video editing software** provides a set of tools for transferring video footage from a camcorder to a computer, clipping out unwanted footage, assembling video segments in any sequence, adding special visual effects, and adding a sound track. Despite an impressive array of features, video editing software is relatively easy to use, as explained in Figure 3-40.

INFOWEBLINKS

Learn more about Apple iMovie and Adobe Premiere at the **Video Editing Software InfoWeb**.

www.course.com/np/concepts8/ch03

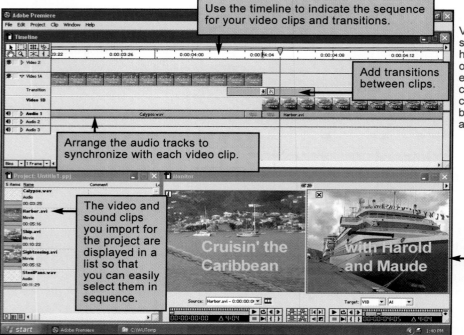

Use the timeline to indicate the sequence for your video clips and transitions.

Add transitions between clips.

Arrange the audio tracks to synchronize with each video clip.

The video and sound clips you import for the project are displayed in a list so that you can easily select them in sequence.

Cruisin' the Caribbean

with Harold and Maude

Preview your video to see how the clips, transitions, and soundtrack all work together.

FIGURE 3-40
Video editing software, such as Adobe Premiere, helps you import a series of video clips from a camera or VCR, arrange the clips in the order of your choice, add transitions between clips, and add an audio track.

With the growing popularity of writable DVD drives, desktop video authors now want to transfer their productions to DVDs and watch them on standard DVD players connected to television sets or projectors. **DVD authoring software** offers tools for creating DVDs with Hollywood-style menus. Just like commercial movies, desktop videos can now include menu selections such as Play Movie, Scene Selection, and Special Features. You can use the remote control for your DVD player to scroll through and select menu options. Examples of DVD authoring software include Sonic DVDit!, ULead DVD MovieFactory, Apple iDVD, and Adobe EncoreDVD.

SOFTWARE SUITES

What is a software suite? A **software suite** is a collection of application software sold as a single package. Office suites, such as Microsoft Office, Star Office, Open Office, and WordPerfect Office, include applications to boost basic productivity: word processing, spreadsheet, and e-mail software. Graphics suites, such as Adobe Creative Suite, Macromedia Studio MX, and CorelDRAW Graphics Suite, typically include paint, draw, and Web graphics tools. Figure 3-41 on the next page lists the components of several popular software suites.

Microsoft Office XP Professional	**Norton SystemWorks**	**Adobe Creative Suite**
Word	Norton AntiVirus	Adobe Illustrator
Excel	Norton Utilities	Adobe Photoshop
Outlook	Norton CleanSweep	Adobe InDesign
PowerPoint	Norton Goback PE	Adobe Acrobat
Publisher	Norton Password	Professional
Access	Manager	Adobe GoLive

FIGURE 3-41

Software suites are available in many applications categories, such as productivity, antivirus, and graphics.

What are the advantages and disadvantages of software suites? Purchasing a software suite is usually much less expensive than purchasing the applications separately. Another advantage is usability. Because all the applications in a suite are produced by the same software publisher, they tend to use similar user interfaces and provide an easy way to transport data from one application to another.

The disadvantage of a software suite is that it might include applications you don't need. If that is the case, you should calculate the price of the applications you *do* need and compare that to the cost of the suite.

EDUCATIONAL AND REFERENCE SOFTWARE

How can I use my computer to learn new things? **Educational software** helps you learn and practice new skills. For the youngest students, educational software, such as MindTwister Math and 3-D Froggy Phonics, teaches basic arithmetic and reading skills. Instruction is presented in game format, and the levels of play are adapted to the player's age and ability.

For older students and adults, software is available for such diverse educational endeavors as learning languages, training yourself to use new software, learning how to play the piano or guitar, improving keyboarding skills, and even learning managerial skills for a diverse workplace. Exam preparation software is available for standardized tests such as the SAT, GMAT, and LSAT. Web-based distance education software tools, such as WebCT and BlackBoard, help instructors keep track of student progress and provide students with interactive study and testing activities.

What's reference software? **Reference software** provides a collection of information and a way to access that information. This type of software includes massive amounts of data—unlike database software, which is shipped without any data. The reference software category spans a wide range of applications—from encyclopedias to medical references, from map software to trip planners, and from cookbooks to telephone books. The options are as broad as the full range of human interests.

Because of the quantity of data it includes, reference software is generally shipped on a CD or DVD, or can be accessed on the Web. Encyclopedias are the most popular software packages in this category. Bestsellers include Microsoft Encarta and Britannica's CD. An encyclopedia on CD-ROM or the Web has several advantages over its printed counterpart. Finding information is easier, for example. Also, electronic formats take up less space on your bookshelf and include interesting video and audio clips. A single CD is cheaper to produce than a shelf full of hard-bound printed books. These lower production costs translate to more affordable products and allow an average person to own a comprehensive encyclopedia.

INFOWEBLINKS

What can you learn on your computer? Check out the **Educational and Reference Software InfoWeb**.

www.course.com/np/concepts8/ch03

ENTERTAINMENT SOFTWARE

What's the best-selling entertainment software? Although some people might get a kick out of watching an animated screen saver, computer games are the most popular type of entertainment software. Over $6 billion of computer and video games are sold each year in the United States alone. Contrary to popular belief, teenage boys are not the only computer game enthusiasts. According to the Interactive Digital Software Association, 90% of all computer games are purchased by people 18 and older. Thirteen percent of gamers are over 50, and about 43% are women.

Computer games are generally classified into subcategories, such as role-playing, action, adventure, puzzles, simulations, and strategy/war games, as described in Figure 3-42.

INFOWEBLINKS

The **Entertainment Software InfoWeb** is your link to the best game sites on the Internet.

www.course.com/np/concepts8/ch03

FIGURE 3-42

Game Categories

Type of Game	Description	Examples
Role-playing	Based on a detailed story line—often one that takes place in a medieval world populated with dastardly villains and evil monsters—the goal is to build a character into a powerful entity that can conquer the bad guys and accumulate treasure.	Diablo, EverQuest, Icewind Dale, Planescape
Action	Like arcade games, action games require fast reflexes as you maneuver a character through a maze or dungeon.	Quake, Doom, Unreal Tournament, Enter the Matrix, Tomb Raider
Adventure	Similar to role-playing games except that the focus is on solving problems rather than building a character into a powerful wizard or fighter.	Myst, The Longest Journey, Return to Monkey Island
Puzzle	Include computerized versions of traditional board games, card games, and Rubik's cube-like challenges.	Tetris, Lemmings
Simulation	Provide a realistic setting, such as the cockpit of an airplane. Players must learn to manipulate controls using the keyboard, joystick, or special-purpose input device. A great way to get your adrenaline pumping without expenses or risks.	Flight Simulator, NASCAR Racing, Mech Warrior
Sports	Place participants in the midst of action-packed sports events, such as a football game, baseball game, hockey final, soccer match, or golf tournament. Most sports games offer arcade-like action and require quick reflexes.	NBA Live, MVP Baseball, SimGolf
Strategy	Players (one player might be the computer) take turns moving characters, armies, and other resources in a quest to capture territory.	Age of Empires, Sim City, Warcraft

How do multiplayer games work? Multiplayer games provide an environment in which two or more players can participate in the same game. Even some of the earliest computer games, like Pong, supplied joysticks for two players. Today's multiplayer games are a far cry from those simplistic games. Now numerous players can use Internet technology to band together or battle one another in sophisticated visual environments.

Massively multiplayer games, such as Battlefield 1942 and EverQuest, operate on multiple Internet servers, each one with the capacity to handle thousands of players at peak times. A new twist in online multiplayer games is "persistent metaworlds," in which objects remain even when play ends. If one player drops an object, for example, it will be there when other players pass by.

Are computer games rated like movies and music? Since it was established in 1994, the Entertainment Software Rating Board (ESRB) has rated more than 10,000 video and computer games. Rating symbols can usually be found in the lower-right corner of the game box. In past years, about 57% of the rated games received an "Everyone" rating. About 32% received a "Teen" rating, and about 10% received a "Mature" rating.

INFOWEBLINKS

Who rates software and how do they do it? Find out at the **Software Ratings InfoWeb**.

www.course.com/np/concepts8/ch03

BUSINESS SOFTWARE

Do businesses use specialized software? The term "business software" is a broad umbrella for vertical and horizontal market software, which are designed to help businesses and organizations accomplish routine or specialized tasks.

What is vertical market software? **Vertical market software** is designed to automate specialized tasks in a specific market or business. Examples include patient management and billing software that is specially designed for hospitals, job estimating software for construction businesses, and student record management software for schools. Today, almost every business has access to some type of specialized vertical market software designed to automate, streamline, or computerize key business activities.

What is horizontal market software? **Horizontal market software** is generic software that just about any kind of business can use. **Payroll software** is a good example of horizontal market software. Almost every business has employees and must maintain payroll records. No matter what type of business uses it, payroll software must collect similar data and make similar calculations to produce payroll checks and W-2 forms. Accounting software and project management software are additional examples of horizontal market software. **Accounting software** helps a business keep track of the money flowing in and out of various accounts. **Project management software** is an important tool for planning large projects, scheduling project tasks, and tracking project costs.

What is groupware? **Groupware** is a type of horizontal market software, designed to help several people collaborate on a single project using LAN or Internet connections. It usually provides the capability to maintain schedules for group members, automatically select meeting times for the group, facilitate communication by e-mail or other channels, distribute documents according to a prearranged schedule or sequence, and allow multiple people to contribute to a single document.

QUICKCHECK......SECTION C

1. Various kinds of _____ production software provide tools for creating and formatting printed and Web-based materials.

2. A spelling checker will find an error in "The sailor tied a complex not." True or false? _____

3. _____ software provides a sort of "blank canvas" on which you can create numeric models by simply "painting" values, labels, and formulas.

4. _____ software stores data as a series of records and allows you to establish relationships between different types of records.

5. CD _____ software transfers files from an audio CD to your computer's hard disk.

6. _____ authoring software allows you to add Hollywood-style menus to digital videos.

 CHECK ANSWERS

SECTION D

SOFTWARE INSTALLATION AND COPYRIGHTS

Software is sold in some surprising places. You might find graphics software at your local art supply store. Your favorite beauty salon might carry *Cosmopolitan*'s makeup and hairstyle makeover software. You might even find homeopathic medicine software on sale at a health food store. Of course, software is also available from traditional sources, including office stores, computer superstores, electronics superstores, and discount stores as well as local computer stores. You can buy software from mail-order catalogs, the software publisher's Web site, and software download sites.

Regardless of how you obtain a new software package, you must install it on your computer before you can use it. That is the first topic in Section D. From time to time, you might want to eliminate some of the software on your computer. The procedure for uninstalling software is the second topic in this section. The section ends with a discussion of software copyrights—important information that will help you understand the difference between legal and illegal software copying.

INSTALLATION BASICS

What's included in a typical software package? The key "ingredients" necessary to install new software are the files that contain the programs and data. These files might be supplied on **distribution media**—one or more CDs or DVDs that are packaged in a box, along with an instruction manual. The files might also be supplied as an Internet download that contains program modules and the text of the instruction manual.

How do I know if a software program will work on my computer? Tucked away at the software publisher's Web site or printed on the software package (Figure 3-43), you'll find **system requirements**, which specify the operating system and minimum hardware capacities necessary for a software product to work correctly.

FIGURE 3-43

System requirements typically can be found on the software box or posted on the download site.

System Requirements

Operating Systems: Windows 95/98/2000/Me/XP
Processor: Pentium class computer
Memory: 16 MB or more
Hard Disk Space: 10 MB free
Network Protocol: TCP/IP
Network Connection: 10/100 Ethernet LAN/WAN, cable modem, DSL router, ISDN router, or dial-up modem

eCourse Internet Works
2005 eCourseWare Corp. All rights reserved. eCourse is a registered trademark of eCourseWare Corp.

Why is it necessary to install most software? When you **install** software, the new software files are placed in the appropriate folders on your computer's hard disk, and then your computer performs any software or hardware configurations necessary to make sure the program is ready to run. During the installation process, your computer usually performs the following activities:

- Copies files from distribution media or downloads files to specified folders on the hard disk

- Uncompresses files that have been distributed in compressed format

- Analyzes the computer's resources, such as processor speed, RAM capacity, and hard disk capacity, to verify that they meet or exceed the minimum system requirements

- Analyzes hardware components and peripheral devices to select appropriate device drivers

- Looks for any system files and players, such as Internet Explorer or Windows Media Player, that are required to run the program but not supplied on the distribution media or download

- Updates necessary system files, such as the Windows Registry and the Windows Start menu, with information about the new software

Are all files for the software provided on the distribution media? With Windows and other operating systems, application software programs share some common files. These files are often supplied by the operating system and perform routine tasks, such as displaying the Print dialog box, which allows you to select a printer and specify how many copies of a file you want to print. These "shared" files are not typically provided on the new software's distribution media or download because the files should already exist on your computer. The installation routine attempts to locate these files. It then notifies you if any files are missing, and provides instructions for installing them.

Are all the files for the new software installed in the same folder? Most executable files and data files for new software are placed in the folder you specify. Some support programs for the software, however, might be stored in other folders, such as Windows/System. The location for these files is determined by the software installation routine. Figure 3-44 maps out the location of files for a typical Windows software installation.

FIGURE 3-44

When you install software, its files might end up in different folders. Files for the eVideo-In Pro software are installed in two folders.

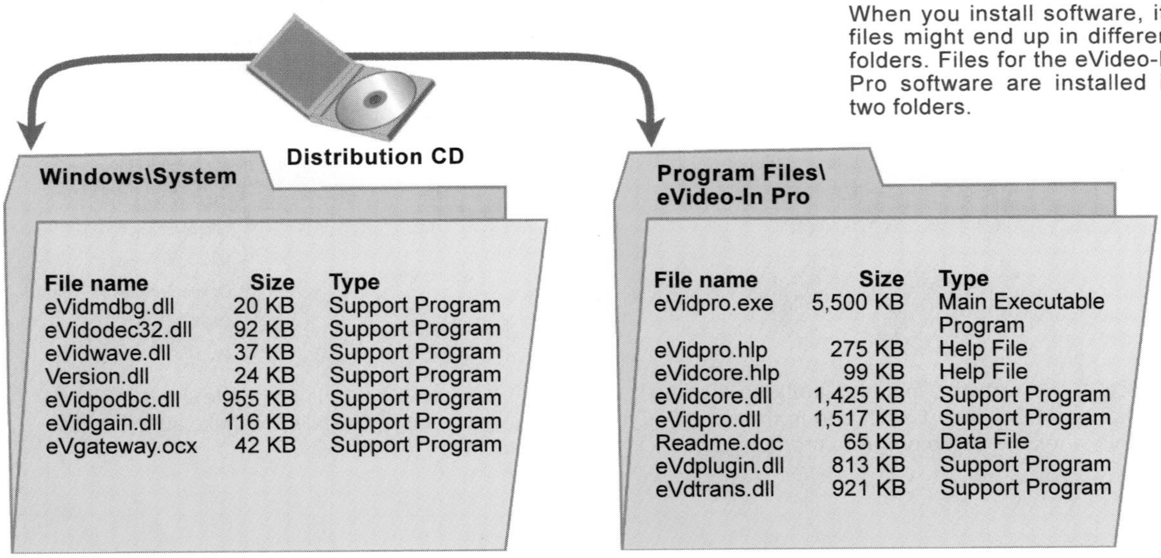

Distribution CD

Windows\System

File name	Size	Type
eVidmdbg.dll	20 KB	Support Program
eVidodec32.dll	92 KB	Support Program
eVidwave.dll	37 KB	Support Program
Version.dll	24 KB	Support Program
eVidpodbc.dll	955 KB	Support Program
eVidgain.dll	116 KB	Support Program
eVgateway.ocx	42 KB	Support Program

Program Files\ eVideo-In Pro

File name	Size	Type
eVidpro.exe	5,500 KB	Main Executable Program
eVidpro.hlp	275 KB	Help File
eVidcore.hlp	99 KB	Help File
eVidcore.dll	1,425 KB	Support Program
eVidpro.dll	1,517 KB	Support Program
Readme.doc	65 KB	Data File
eVdplugin.dll	813 KB	Support Program
eVdtrans.dll	921 KB	Support Program

INSTALLING FROM DISTRIBUTION MEDIA

How do I install software from distribution media? Installation procedures vary, depending on a computer's operating system. Take a look at the installation process on a computer running Windows.

Windows software typically contains a **setup program** that guides you through the installation process. Figure 3-45 shows you what to expect when you use a setup program.

FIGURE 3-45
Installing from
Distribution Media

1 Insert the first distribution CD, or DVD. The setup program should start automatically. If it does not, look for a file called Setup.exe and then run it.

○ **Full Installation**
○ **Custom Installation**

3 Select the installation option that best meets your needs. If you select a full installation, the setup program copies all files and data from the distribution medium to the hard disk of your computer system. A full installation gives you access to all features of the software.

If you select a custom installation, the setup program displays a list of software features for your selection. After you select the features you want, the setup program copies only the selected program and data files to your hard disk. A custom installation can save space on your hard disk.

5 If the software includes multiple distribution CDs, insert each one in the specified drive when the setup program prompts you.

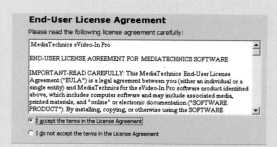

2 Read the license agreement, if one is presented on the screen. By agreeing to the terms of the license, you can proceed with the installation.

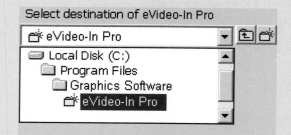

4 Follow the prompts provided by the setup program to specify a folder to hold the new software program. You can use the default folder specified by the setup program or a folder of your own choosing, You can also create a new folder during the setup process.

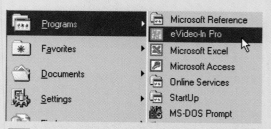

6 When the setup is complete, start the program you just installed to make sure it works.

INSTALLING DOWNLOADED SOFTWARE

Is the installation process different for downloaded software? The installation process is slightly different for Windows software that you download. Usually all the files needed for the new software are **zipped** to consolidate them into one large file, which is compressed to decrease its size and reduce the download time. As part of the installation process, this downloaded file must be reconstituted, or **unzipped**, into the original collection of files (Figure 3-46).

FIGURE 3-46
Installing Downloaded
Software

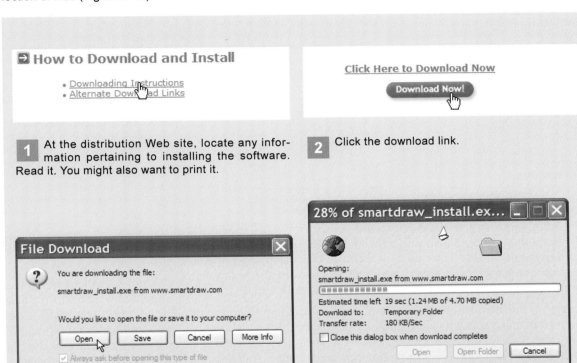

1 At the distribution Web site, locate any information pertaining to installing the software. Read it. You might also want to print it.

2 Click the download link.

3 If you are downloading from a trusted site and have antivirus software running, click the Open button in the File Download dialog box.

4 Wait for the download to finish. Typically, the setup program included in the download starts automatically.

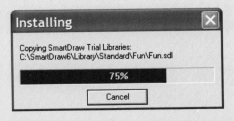

5 Use the setup program to specify a folder to hold the new software program. You can use the default folder specified by the setup program or a folder of your own choosing. You can also create a new folder during the setup process.

6 Wait for the setup program to uncompress the downloaded file and install the software in the selected directory. During this process, respond to license agreement and other prompts. When the installation is complete, test the software to make sure it works.

Downloadable software can be provided in several different formats. Some automatically install themselves, but others require manual procedures. A downloadable file typically is set up as a **self-installing executable file**, **self-executing zip file**, or **non-executing zip file** (Figure 3-47).

FIGURE 3-47
Downloadable File Formats

Self-installing Executable Files

Under the most automated installation system, the process of downloading new software automatically initiates the entire installation process.

The software download is packaged as one large file with an .exe extension. This file automatically unzips itself and starts the setup program. You simply follow the setup program prompts to acknowledge the license agreement, indicate the folder for the software files, and complete the installation.

Self-executing Zip Files

Downloaded files with .exe extensions do not always install themselves. Some are simply self-executing zip files, which automatically unzip the software's files, but do not automatically start the setup program.

To install software from a self-executing zip file, you start the executable file to unzip the files for the new software. One of these files will be the Setup.exe program. Next, you manually start the setup program and follow its prompts to complete the installation.

Non-executing Zip Files

If you download software and it arrives as one huge file with a .zip extension, you must locate this file on your hard disk and then use Windows XP or a program such as WinZip to unzip it.

After unzipping the file, you must run the setup program to acknowledge the license agreement, indicate the folder for the software files, and complete the installation.

Is installing a software update different from installing the original version? After you purchase and install software, you might have the opportunity to update it. A software update can be distributed as a new version, patch, or service pack. A new version of software entirely replaces an old version, and is installed in much the same way as the original.

In contrast, a **software patch** is a small section of program code that replaces part of the software you currently have installed. The term **service pack**, which usually applies to operating system updates, is a set of patches that correct problems and address security vulnerabilities. Patches and service packs are usually distributed via the Internet and automatically install themselves when you download them. It is always a good idea to install patches and service packs when they become available.

TERMINOLOGY NOTE

Some software provides an Automatic Update option that periodically checks the software publisher's Web site for updates, downloads updates automatically, and installs them without user intervention.

The advantage of Automatic Update is convenience. The disadvantage is that changes are made to your computer without your knowledge.

UNINSTALLING SOFTWARE

How do I get rid of software? With some operating systems, such as DOS, you can remove software simply by deleting its files. Other operating systems, such as Windows and Mac OS, include an **uninstall routine**, which deletes the software's files from various folders on your computer's hard disk. The uninstall routine also removes references to the program from the desktop and from operating system files, such as the file system and, in the case of Windows, the Windows Registry (Figure 3-48).

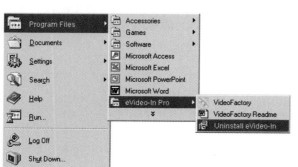

FIGURE 3-48

To uninstall any Windows application software, first look for an Uninstall option listed on the same menu you use to start the program. If that option is not available, use Add/Remove Programs from the Control Panel.

SOFTWARE COPYRIGHTS

Is it legal to copy software? After you purchase a software package, you might assume that you can install it and use it in any way you like. In fact, your "purchase" entitles you to use the software only in certain prescribed ways. In most countries, computer software, like a book or movie, is protected by a copyright. A **copyright** is a form of legal protection that grants the author of an original "work" an exclusive right to copy, distribute, sell, and modify that work, except under special circumstances described by copyright laws. These exceptions include:

1. The purchaser has the right to copy software from distribution media or a Web site to a computer's hard disk in order to install it.

2. The purchaser can make an extra, or backup, copy of the software in case the original copy becomes erased or damaged.

3. The purchaser is allowed to copy and distribute sections of a software program for use in critical reviews and teaching.

Most software displays a **copyright notice**, such as "© 2005 eCourse," on one of its screens. This notice is not required by law, however, so programs without a copyright notice are still protected by copyright law. People who circumvent copyright law and illegally copy, distribute, or modify software are sometimes called software pirates, and their illegal copies are referred to as pirated software.

SOFTWARE LICENSES

What is a software license? In addition to copyright protection, computer software is often protected by the terms of a software license. A **software license**, or "license agreement," is a legal contract that defines the ways in which you may use a computer program. For personal computer software, you will find the license on the outside of the package, on a separate card inside the package, on the CD packaging, or in one of the program files.

Typically, computer owners purchase the right to use software that is distributed under a **single-user license** that limits use of the software to only one person at a time. Schools, organizations, and businesses sometimes purchase a **site license**, **multiple-user license**, or **concurrent-use license**, which allows more than one person to use the software.

Most legal contracts require signatures before the terms of the contract take effect. This requirement becomes unwieldy with software—imagine having to sign a license agreement and return it before you can use a new software package. To circumvent the signature requirement, software publishers typically use two techniques to validate a software license: shrink-wrap licenses and installation agreements.

When you purchase computer software, the distribution media are usually sealed in an envelope, plastic box, or shrink wrapping. A **shrink-wrap license** goes into effect as soon as you open the packaging. Figure 3-49 explains more about the mechanics of a shrink-wrap license.

An **installation agreement** is displayed on-screen when you first install software. After reading the software license on the screen, you can indicate that you accept the terms of the license by clicking a designated button—usually labeled "OK," "I agree," or "I accept." If you do not accept the terms, the software does not load and you will not be able to use it.

INFOWEBLINKS

To read the actual text of software copyright laws, connect to the **Software Copyright InfoWeb**.

www.course.com/np/concepts8/ch03

TERMINOLOGY NOTE

A site license is generally priced at a flat rate and allows software to be used on all computers at a specific location.

A multiple-user license is priced per user and allows the allocated number of people to use the software at any time.

A concurrent-use license is priced per copy and allows a specific number of copies to be used at the same time.

FIGURE 3-49

When software has a shrink-wrap license, you agree to the terms of the software license by opening the package. If you do not agree with the terms, you should return the software in its unopened package.

Software licenses are often lengthy and written in "legalese," but your legal right to use the software continues only as long as you abide by the terms of the software license. Therefore, you should understand the software license for any software you use. To become familiar with a typical license agreement, you can read through the one in Figure 3-50.

FIGURE 3-50

When you read a software license agreement, look for answers to the following questions:

Am I buying the software or licensing it?

When does the license go into effect?

Under what circumstances can I make copies?

Can I rent the software?

Can I sell the software?

What if the software includes a distribution CD and a set of distribution floppy disks?

Does the software publisher provide a warranty?

Can I loan the software to a friend?

Software License Agreement

Important - READ CAREFULLY: This License Agreement ("Agreement") is a legal agreement between you and eCourse Corporation for the software product, eCourse GraphWare ("The SOFTWARE"). By installing, copying, or otherwise using the SOFTWARE, you agree to be bound by the terms of this Agreement. The SOFTWARE is protected by copyright laws and international copyright treaties. The SOFTWARE is licensed, not sold.

GRANT OF LICENSE. This Agreement gives you the right to install and use one copy of the SOFTWARE on a single computer. The primary user of the computer on which the SOFTWARE is installed may make a second copy for his or her exclusive use on a portable computer.

OTHER RIGHTS AND LIMITATIONS. You may not reverse engineer, decompile, or disassemble the SOFTWARE except and only to the extent that such activity is expressly permitted by applicable law.

The SOFTWARE is licensed as a single product; its components may not be separated for use on more than one computer. You may not rent, lease, or lend the SOFTWARE.

You may permanently transfer all of your rights under this Agreement, provided you retain no copies, you transfer all of the SOFTWARE, and the recipient agrees to the terms of this Agreement. If the software product is an upgrade, any transfer must include all prior versions of the SOFTWARE.

You may receive the SOFTWARE in more than one medium. Regardless of the type of medium you receive, you may use only one medium that is appropriate for your single computer. You may not use or install the other medium on another computer.

WARRANTY. eCourse warrants that the SOFTWARE will perform substantially in accordance with the accompanying written documentation for a period of ninety (90) days from the date of receipt. TO THE MAXIMUM EXTENT PERMITTED BY APPLICABLE LAW, eCourse AND ITS SUPPLIERS DISCLAIM ALL OTHER WARRANTIES AND CONDITIONS EITHER EXPRESS OR IMPLIED, INCLUDING, BUT NOT LIMITED TO, IMPLIED WARRANTIES OF MERCHANTABILITY, FITNESS FOR A PARTICULAR PURPOSE, TITLE, AND NON-INFRINGEMENT, WITH REGARD TO THE SOFTWARE PRODUCT.

Are all software licenses similar? Copyright laws have fairly severe restrictions on copying, distributing, and reselling software; however, a license agreement might offer additional rights to consumers. The licenses for commercial software, shareware, freeware, open source, and public domain software specify different levels of permission for software use, copying, and distribution.

Commercial software is typically sold in computer stores or at Web sites. Although you "buy" this software, you actually purchase only the right to use it under the terms of the software license. A license for commercial software typically adheres closely to the limitations provided by copyright law, although it might give you permission to install the software on a computer at work and on a computer at home, provided that you use only one of them at a time.

Shareware is copyrighted software marketed under a "try before you buy" policy. It typically includes a license that permits you to use the software for a trial period. To use it beyond the trial period, you must pay a registration fee. A shareware license usually allows you to make copies of the software and distribute them to others. If they choose to use the software, they must pay a registration fee as well. These shared copies provide a low-cost marketing and distribution channel. Registration fee payment relies on the honor system, so unfortunately many shareware authors collect only a fraction of the money they deserve for their programming efforts. Thousands of shareware programs are available, encompassing just about as many applications as commercial software.

Freeware is copyrighted software that—as you might expect—is available for free. Because the software is protected by copyright, you cannot do anything with it that is not expressly allowed by copyright law or by the author. Typically, the license for freeware permits you to use the software, copy it, and give it away, but does not permit you to alter it or sell it. Many utility programs, device drivers, and some games are available as freeware.

Open source software makes the uncompiled program instructions—the source code—available to programmers who want to modify and improve the software. Open source software may be sold or distributed free of charge in complied form, but it must, in every case, also include the source code. Linux is an example of open source software, as is FreeBSD—a version of UNIX designed for personal computers.

Public domain software is not protected by copyright because the copyright has expired, or the author has placed the program in the public domain, making it available without restriction. Public domain software may be freely copied, distributed, and even resold. The primary restriction on public domain software is that you are not allowed to apply for a copyright on it.

QUICKCHECK......SECTION D

1. System [_____] specify the operating system and minimum hardware capacities required for software to work correctly.

2. During the [_____] process, your computer performs many tasks, including updating the Windows Registry and Start menu.

3. The [_____] program typically asks for your consent to the license agreement and confirms the folder into which you want files copied.

4. The files for downloaded software are usually [_____] into one large compressed file.

5. You can [_____] software using the Control Panel's Add/Remove Programs option.

6. Linux is an example of [_____] source software.

7. [_____] domain software is not copyrighted, making it available for use without restriction, except that you cannot apply for a copyright on it.

 CHECK ANSWERS

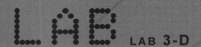 LAB 3-D

INSTALLING AND UNINSTALLING SOFTWARE

In this lab, you'll learn:

- How to use a setup program to install Windows application software from a distribution CD
- What to do if the setup program doesn't automatically start
- The difference between typical, compact, and custom installation options
- How to specify a folder for a new software installation
- How to install downloaded software
- How to install an upgrade
- How to uninstall a Windows application
- What happens, in addition to deleting files, when you uninstall a software application
- How to locate the program that will uninstall a software application
- Why you might not want to delete all of the files associated with an application

INTERACTIVE LAB

CLICK TO START THE LAB

LAB ASSIGNMENTS

1. Start the interactive part of the lab. Insert your Tracking Disk if you want to save your QuickCheck results. Perform each lab step as directed, and answer all the lab QuickCheck questions. When you exit the lab, your answers are automatically graded and your results are displayed.

2. Browse the Web and locate a software application that you might like to download. Use information supplied by the Web site to answer the following questions:

   a. What is the name of the program and the URL of the download site?

   b. What is the size of the download file?

   c. According to the instructions, does the download file appear to require manual installation, is it a self-executing zip file, or is it a self-installing executable file?

3. On the computer you typically use, look through the list of programs (click Start, then select Programs to see a list of them). List the names of any programs that include their own uninstall routines.

4. On the computer you typically use, open the Control Panel and then open the Add/Remove Programs dialog box. List the first 10 programs that are currently installed on the computer.

TECHTALK
THE WINDOWS REGISTRY

To many computer owners, the Windows Registry is simply a mysterious "black box" that is mentioned occasionally in articles about computer troubleshooting. Certainly, it is possible to use a computer without intimate knowledge of the Registry; however, the Registry is the "glue" that binds together many of the most important components of a PC—the computer hardware, peripheral devices, application software, and system software. After reading this TechTalk section, you should have a basic understanding of the Registry and its role in the operation of a computer system.

Why does a PC need the Registry? Reflect back for moment on what you know so far about how a computer works. You know that you use menus, dialog boxes, and other controls provided by application software to direct the operations a computer carries out. For some operations—particularly those involving hardware—the application software communicates with the operating system. The operating system might communicate with device drivers or, in some cases, it can directly communicate with a peripheral device.

To act as an intermediary between software and peripheral devices, your operating system needs information about these components—where they are located, what's been installed, how they are configured, and how you want to use them. CMOS memory holds the most essential data about your computer's processing and storage hardware, but the **Windows Registry** keeps track of your computer's peripheral devices and software so that the operating system can access the information it needs to coordinate the activities in a computer system. Figure 3-51 lists some of the items the Registry tracks.

Where can I find the Registry? The contents of the Registry are stored in multiple files in the Windows folder of your computer's hard disk and combined into a single database when Windows starts. Although each version of Windows uses a slightly different storage scheme, the basic organization and function of the Registry are similar in all versions.

Windows 95, 98, and Me store the entire contents of the Registry in two files: System.dat and User.dat. System.dat includes configuration data for all the hardware and software installed on a computer. User.dat contains user-specific information, sometimes called a "user profile," which includes software settings and desktop settings. Windows 2000 and XP divide Registry data among about two dozen files.

What does the Registry look like? The Registry has a logical structure that appears as a hierarchy of folders, similar to the directory structure of your hard disk, as shown in Figure 3-52.

FIGURE 3-51
Items Tracked by the Windows Registry

User preferences for desktop colors, icons, pointers, shortcuts, and display resolution

Sounds that are assigned to various system events, such as clicking and shutting down

The capability of your CD-ROM drive for playing audio CDs and autorunning computer CDs

The options that appear on a shortcut menu when you right-click an object

The computer's network card settings and protocols

The location of the uninstall routines for all installed software

FIGURE 3-52
The Windows Registry is organized as a hierarchy of folders and files.

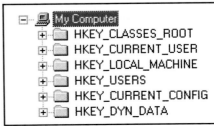

There are six main folders in the Registry, and their names begin with HKEY. Each folder contains data that pertains to a particular part of a computer system, as described in Figure 3-53.

FIGURE 3-53
Registry Folder Contents

Folder	Contents
HKEY_CLASSES_ROOT	This folder contains data that associates file extensions with a particular application and a list of desktop shortcuts to programs.
HKEY_CURRENT_USER	Information for the current user is transferred here from the HKEY_USERS folder.
HKEY_LOCAL_MACHINE	This folder contains computer-specific information about hardware configuration and software preferences. This information is used for all users who log on to this computer.
HKEY_USERS	This folder contains individual preferences for each person who uses the computer.
HKEY_CURRENT_CONFIG	This folder links to the section of HKEY_LOCAL_MACHINE appropriate for the current hardware configuration.
HKEY_DYN_DATA	This folder points to the part of HKEY_LOCAL_MACHINE that maintains data for Plug and Play devices. This data is dynamic and can change as devices are added and removed from the system.

What does the Registry data look like? The Registry contains thousands of esoteric-looking data entries, such as those shown in Figure 3-54.

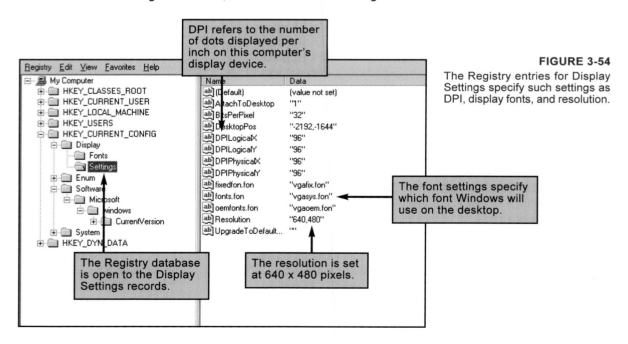

FIGURE 3-54
The Registry entries for Display Settings specify such settings as DPI, display fonts, and resolution.

Can I make changes to the Registry? You change the Registry indirectly whenever you install or remove software or hardware. The setup program for your software automatically updates the Registry with essential information about the program's location and configuration. Device drivers and the Windows Plug and Play feature provide similar update services for hardware.

You can also make changes to the Windows Registry by using the dialog boxes for various configuration routines provided by the operating system and application software. For example, if you want to change the desktop colors for your user profile, you can do so by selecting the Settings option from the Start menu, clicking Control Panel, and then selecting the Display option. Any changes you make to settings in the Display Properties dialog box (Figure 3-55) will be recorded in the Windows Registry.

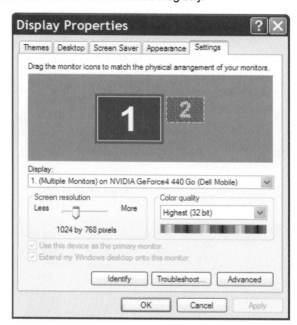

FIGURE 3-55

Changes that you make when using the Display Properties dialog box automatically update the corresponding entries in the HKEY_CURRENT_CONFIG folder of the Registry.

QUICKCHECK........TECHTALK

1. The Windows Registry contains settings and preferences for the peripheral devices and software that are installed on a computer. True or false?

2. The Registry is stored in the [   ] folder.

3. In the hierarchy of Registry folders, each folder name begins with [   ].

4. The [   ] program automatically updates the Registry when you install software.

 CHECK ANSWERS

ISSUE

SOFTWARE PIRACY

Software is easy to steal. You don't have to walk out of a Best Buy store with a $495 DVD Workshop software box under your shirt. You can simply borrow your friend's DVD Workshop distribution CDs and install a copy of the program on your computer's hard disk. It seems so simple that it couldn't be illegal. But it is.

Piracy takes many forms. End-user piracy includes friends loaning distribution disks to each other and installing software on more computers than the license allows.

Counterfeiting is the large-scale illegal duplication of software distribution media and sometimes even its packaging. According to Microsoft, many software counterfeiting groups are linked to organized crime and money-laundering schemes that fund a diverse collection of illegal activities, such as smuggling, gambling, extortion, and prostitution. Counterfeit software is sold in retail stores and through online auctions—often the packaging looks so authentic that buyers have no idea they have purchased illegal goods.

Internet piracy uses the Web as a way to illegally distribute unauthorized software. In "Net" jargon, the terms "appz" and "warez" (pronounced as "wares" or "war EZ") refer to pirated software. Some warez has even been modified to eliminate serial numbers, registration requirements, expiration dates, or other forms of copy protection. The Business Software Alliance (BSA) estimates that more than 800,000 Web sites illegally sell or distribute software.

In many countries, including the United States, software pirates are subject to civil lawsuits for monetary damages and criminal prosecution, which can result in jail time and stiff fines. Nonetheless, software piracy continues to have enormous impact. According to the Software and Information Industry Association (SIIA), a leading anti-piracy watchdog, revenue losses from business software piracy typically exceed $2 billion per year. This figure reveals only part of the piracy problem—it does not include losses from rampant game and educational software piracy, which are estimated to exceed $12 billion a year.

A small, but vocal, minority of software users, such as members of GNU (which stands for "Gnu's Not UNIX"), believes that data and software should be freely distributed. Richard Stallman writes in the GNU Manifesto, "I consider that the golden rule requires that if I like a program I must share it with other people who like it. Software sellers want to divide users and conquer them, making each user agree not to share with others. I refuse to break solidarity with other users in this way. I cannot in good conscience sign a nondisclosure agreement or a software license agreement."

Is software piracy really damaging? Who cares if you use a program without paying for it? Software piracy is damaging because it has a negative effect on the economy. Software production makes a major contribution to the United States economy, employing more than 2 million people and accounting for billions of dollars in corporate revenue. A BSA economic impact study concluded that lowering global piracy from an average of 36% to only 26% would add more that 1 million jobs and $400 billion in worldwide economic growth.

Decreases in software revenues can have a direct effect on consumers, too. When software publishers are forced to cut corners, they tend to reduce customer service and technical support. As a result, you, the consumer, get put on hold when you call for technical support, find fewer free technical support sites, and encounter customer support personnel who are only moderately knowledgeable about their products. The bottom line—software piracy negatively affects customer service.

As an alternative to cutting support costs, some software publishers might build the cost of software piracy into the price of the software. The unfortunate result is that those who legitimately license and purchase software pay an inflated price.

According to a 2003 BSA/IDC report on global software piracy, about 36% of the software currently in use is pirated. China has the world's highest piracy rate—92% of the software used in China is believed to be pirated. In Russia the piracy rate is 87%. In the United States, an estimated 22% of software is pirated. In Japan, the rate is 29%.

Piracy Rates by Region (as percent of total in use)

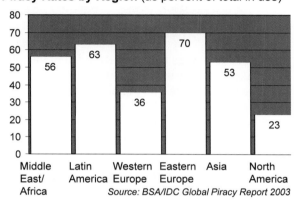

Source: BSA/IDC Global Piracy Report 2003

Although the rate of business software piracy might be declining, total piracy appears to be growing by one or two percentage points each year. Analysts fear that the Internet is a major factor in piracy increases. As Internet access becomes available to subscribers in countries such as China, piracy could skyrocket. To make matters worse, increased access to high-speed Internet connections makes it much easier to quickly download large software files.

As a justification of high piracy rates, some observers point out that people in many countries simply might not be able to afford software priced for the U.S. market. This argument could apply to China, where the average annual income is equivalent to about U.S.$3,500, and in North Korea, where the average income is only U.S.$900. A Korean who legitimately purchases Microsoft Office for U.S.$250 would be spending more than one-quarter of his or her annual income.

Many countries with a high incidence of software piracy, however, have strong economies and respectable per capita incomes. To further discredit the theory that piracy stems from poverty, India—which has a fairly large computer-user community, but a per capita income of only U.S.$1,600—is not among the top 10 countries with high rates of software piracy.

If economic factors do not account for the pervasiveness of software piracy, what does? The incidence of piracy seems to be higher among small business and consumer personal computer users than corporations and government agencies. Some analysts suggest that people need more education about software copyrights and the economic implications of piracy. Other analysts believe that copyright enforcement must be increased by implementing more vigorous efforts to identify and prosecute pirates.

INFOWEBLINKS

You can read the GNU Manifesto and other thought-provoking articles about software piracy by going to the **Copyright and Piracy InfoWeb**.

www.course.com/np/concepts8/ch03

WHAT DO YOU THINK?

1. Do you believe that software piracy is a serious issue?   ○ Yes   ○ No   ○ Not sure

2. Do you know of any instances of software piracy?   ○ Yes   ○ No   ○ Not sure

3. Do you think that most software pirates understand that they are doing something illegal?   ○ Yes   ○ No   ○ Not sure

4. Should software publishers try to adjust software pricing for local markets?   ○ Yes   ○ No   ○ Not sure

SAVE RESPONSES

COMPUTERS IN CONTEXT

JOURNALISM

In the ancient world, news spread by word of mouth, relayed by bards and merchants who traveled from town to town—in essence, the first reporters to "broadcast" the news. The news business is all about gathering and disseminating information as quickly as possible. Technology has played a major role in news reporting's evolution from its bardic roots to modern 24-hour "live" news networks.

Johann Gutenberg's printing press (ca. 1450), the first technological breakthrough in the news business, made it feasible to publish news as printed notices tacked to walls in the town square. As paper became more economical, resourceful entrepreneurs sold broadsheets to people eager for news, and the concept of a newspaper was born. The first regularly published newspapers appeared in Germany and Holland in 1609, and the first English newspaper, the *Weekly News*, was published in 1622.

But the news spread slowly. In the early 1800s, it took four weeks for newspapers in New York to receive reports from London. With the advent of the telegraph in 1844, however, reporters from far-flung regions could "wire" stories to their newspapers for publication the next day. The first radio reporters in the 1920s offered live broadcasts of sports events, church services, and variety shows. Before the 1950s, black-and-white newsreels shown in movie theaters provided the only visual imagery of news events, but television gave viewers news images on a nightly basis.

Technology has benefited print journalism, too. For decades, typesetters transferred reporters' handwritten stories into neatly set columns of type. Today, reporters use computers and word processing software to tap out their stories and run a preliminary check of spelling and grammar.

Stories are submitted via computer network to editors, who use the same software to edit stories to fit time and space constraints. The typesetting process has been replaced by desktop publishing software and computer to plate (CTP) technology. Digital pages produced with desktop publishing software are sent to a raster image processor (RIP), which converts the pages into dots that form words and images. After a page has been RIPed, a platesetter uses lasers to etch the dots onto a physical plate, which is then mounted on the printing press to produce printed pages. CTP is much faster and more flexible than typesetting, so publishers can make last-minute changes to accommodate late-breaking stories.

Personal computers have also added a new dimension to the news-gathering process. Reporters were once limited to personal interviews, observation, and fact gathering at libraries, but can now make extensive use of Internet resources and e-mail. Web sites and online databases provide background information on all sorts of topics. Other resources include newsgroups and chat rooms, where reporters can monitor public opinion on current events and identify potential sources.

Most major networks maintain interactive Web sites that offer online polls and bulletin boards designed to collect viewers' opinions. Although online poll respondents are not a representative sample of the population, they can help news organizations gauge viewer opinions and determine whether news coverage is comprehensive and effective.

E-mail has changed the way reporters communicate with colleagues and sources. It's often the only practical method for contacting people in remote locations or distant time zones, and it's useful with reluctant sources, who feel more comfortable providing information under the cloak of anonymous Hotmail or Yahoo! accounts. "Vetting" e-mail sources—verifying credentials such as name, location, and occupation—can be difficult, however, so reporters tend not to rely on these sources without substantial corroboration.

For broadcast journalism, digital communications play a major role in today's "live on the scene" television reporting. Most news organizations maintain remote production vans, sometimes called "satellite news gathering (SNG) trucks," that travel to the site of breaking news, raise their antennas, and begin to broadcast. These complete mobile production facilities include camera control units, audio and video recording equipment, and satellite or microwave transmitters.

On-the-scene reporting no longer requires a truck full of equipment, however. Audiovisual editing units and video cameras have gone digital, making them easier to use and sized to fit in a suitcase. A new breed of "backpack journalists" carry mini-DV cameras, notebook computers, and satellite phones. Jane Ellen Stevens, a pioneer backpack journalist specializing in science and technology, has reported since 1997 from remote locations, such as a space camp in Russia.

Backpack journalists can connect their minicams to notebook computers with a FireWire cable, transfer their video footage to the hard disk, and then edit the footage using consumer-level video editing software. The resulting video files, compressed for transmission over a satellite phone, are sent to newsroom technicians, who decompress and then broadcast them—all in a matter of seconds.

One drawback of backpack journalists' use of minicams and compression is that the video quality usually isn't as crisp as images filmed with studio cameras. News organizations with high standards were hesitant to use this lower quality video, but have found that viewers would rather see a low-quality image now than a high-quality image later. To many viewers, a few rough edges just make the footage seem more compelling, more "you are there."

A recent tour de force in SNG was the brainchild of David Bloom, an NBC reporter embedded with the U.S. Army 3rd Infantry Division during Operation Iraqi Freedom. He helped modify an M-88 tank recovery vehicle into a high-tech, armored SNG vehicle. The $500,000 "Bloommobile" featured a gyrostabilized camera that could produce jiggle-free video as the tank blasted over sand dunes at 50 mph. Tragically, Bloom died while covering the conflict, but many viewers vividly remember his exhilarating reports as the Bloommobile raced down desert roads, trundled along with army supply convoys, and narrowly escaped enemy fire.

Computers, the Internet, and communications technology make it possible to instantly broadcast live reports across the globe, but live reporting is not without controversy. A reporter who arrives at the scene of a disaster with microphone in hand has little time for reflection, vetting, and cross-checking, so grievous errors, libelous images, or distasteful video footage sometimes find their way into news reports. Jeff Gralnick, former executive producer for ABC News, remarks, "In the old days, we had time to think before we spoke. We had time to write, time to research and time to say, 'Hey, wait a minute.' Now we don't even have the time to say, 'Hey, wait a nanosecond.' Just because we can say it or do it, should we?" Technology has given journalists a powerful arsenal of tools for gathering and reporting the news, but has also increased their accountability for accurate, socially responsible reporting.

INFOWEBLINKS

You'll find lots more information related to this topic at the **Computers and Journalism InfoWeb.**

www.course.com/np/concepts8/ch03

INTERACTIVE SUMMARY

To review important concepts from this chapter, fill in the blanks to best complete each sentence. When using the NP8 BookOnCD, click the Check Answers buttons to automatically score your answers. Place your Tracking Disk in the floppy disk drive if you want to save your scores.

[_____] consists of computer programs and data files that work together to provide a computer with the instructions and data necessary for carrying out a specific type of task, such as document production, video editing, graphic design, or Web browsing. Computer [_____] write instructions for the programs that become the components of a computer software product. To understand how software is installed and uninstalled, it is important for computer owners to recognize that today's software typically consists of many files.

To create a software environment, a programmer must define the [_____] for each element in the environment, such as where an object appears, its shape, its color, and its behavior. A computer programming [_____] provides the tools a programmer uses to create software. Most programmers today prefer to use [_____] languages, such as C, C++, Java, Ada, COBOL, and Visual Basic. A computer's microprocessor understands only [_____] language, however, so a program that is written in a high-level language must be compiled or interpreted before it can be processed. A [_____] translates all the instructions in a program as a single batch, and the resulting machine language instructions, called [_____] code, are placed in a new file. An alternative method of translation uses an [_____] to translate instructions one at a time while the program runs.

CHECK ANSWERS

A computer's software is like the chain of command in an army. [_____] software tells the operating system what to do. The operating system tells the device drivers, device drivers tell the hardware, and the hardware actually does the work. The operating system interacts with application software, device drivers, and hardware to manage a computer's [_____]. In addition, many operating systems also influence the "look and feel" of your software, or what's known as the user [_____].

The core part of an operating system is called the [_____]. In addition to this core, many operating systems provide helpful tools, called [_____], that you can use to control and customize your computer equipment and work environment. Operating systems are informally categorized and characterized using one or more of the following terms: A [_____] operating system expects to deal with one set of input devices—those that can be controlled by one person at a time. A [_____] operating system is designed to deal with input, output, and processing requests from many users. A [_____] operating system provides process and memory management services that allow two or more programs to run simultaneously. A [_____] operating system is one that's designed for a personal computer—either a desktop or notebook computer. Popular desktop operating systems include Windows 95/98/Me/XP and Mac OS. Popular [_____] operating systems include Windows NT/2000, Linux, and UNIX. Operating systems for PDAs are typically smaller than PC operating systems and can fit in [_____].

CHECK ANSWERS

Document [_____] software assists you with composing, editing, designing, printing, and electronically publishing documents. The three most popular types of document production software include word processing, desktop publishing, and Web authoring. [_____] software is similar to a "smart" piece of paper that automatically adds up the columns of numbers you write on it. You can use it to make other calculations, too, based on simple equations that you write or more complex, built-in formulas. Because it is so easy to experiment with different numbers, this type of software is particularly useful for [_____] analyses. [_____] software helps you store, find, organize, update, and report information stored in one or more tables. When two sets of records are [_____], database software allows you to access data from both tables at the same time. [_____] software, including paint, photo editing, drawing, CAD, 3-D, and presentation software, is designed to help you create, manipulate, and print images.

Music and video editing software, educational and reference software, and entertainment software round out the most popular categories of personal computer software. A software [_____] is a "bundled" collection of application software sold as a single package.

For businesses, [_____] market software is designed to automate specialized tasks in a specific market or business. [_____] market software is generic software that can be used by just about any kind of business. [_____] is a type of horizontal market software designed to help several people collaborate on a single project using LAN or Internet connections.

✦ CHECK ANSWERS

When you [_____] software, the new software files are placed in the appropriate folders on your computer's hard disk, and then your computer performs any software or hardware configurations that are necessary to make sure the program is ready to run. The [_____] files and data files for the software are placed in the folder you specify. Some [_____] programs for the software, however, might be stored in different folders, such as Windows\System. Windows software typically contains a [_____] program that guides you through the installation process.

To install application software from a [_____] CD, simply place the CD in the drive and wait for the setup program to begin. The installation process is slightly different for application software that you download. Usually all the files needed for the new software are consolidated into one large file, which is [_____] to decrease its size and reduce the download time. This large, downloaded file must be reconstituted, or [_____], into the original collection of files as a first step in the installation process. A self-installing [_____] file automatically unzips the downloaded file and starts the setup program. A self-executing [_____] file automatically unzips the software's files, but does not automatically start the setup program.

A [_____] is a form of legal protection that grants the author of an original "work" an exclusive right to copy, distribute, sell, and modify that work, except under special circumstances described by copyright laws. A software [_____] is a legal contract that defines the ways in which you may use a computer program. Licenses for commercial, shareware, freeware, open source, and public domain software provide consumers with different sets of rights pertaining to copying and distribution.

✦ CHECK ANSWERS

INTERACTIVE KEY TERMS

Make sure that you understand all of the boldfaced key terms presented in this chapter. If you're using the NP8 BookOnCD, you can use this list of terms as an interactive study activity. First, try to define a term in your own words, then click the term to compare your definition with the definition that is presented in the chapter.

Absolute reference, 140
Application software, 121
Automatic recalculation, 140
Bootstrap program, 125
Cell, 138
Cell references, 139
Clip art, 137
Command-line interface, 124
Commercial software, 158
Compiler, 119
Computer programmers, 118
Concurrent-use license, 157
Copyright, 157
Copyright notice, 157
Database, 142
Desktop operating system, 126
Distribution media, 152
DOS, 130
Field, 142
Font, 135
Footer, 136
Format, 135
Formula, 139
Frames, 137
Freeware, 159
Fully justified, 136
Function, 139
Grammar checker, 135
Graphical user interface, 124
Graphics, 145
Groupware, 151
Header, 136
High-level language, 119
Install, 153
Installation agreement, 157

Interpreter, 119
Kernel, 125
Label, 138
Leading, 136
Line spacing, 136
Linux, 129
Mac OS, 128
Machine language, 119
Mail merge, 137
Mathematical operators, 139
Microsoft Windows, 126
Multiple-user license, 157
Multitasking operating system, 126
Multiuser operating system, 126
Natural language query, 144
Network operating system, 126
Non-executing zip file, 156
Object code, 119
Open source software, 159
Page layout, 136
Palm OS, 130
Paragraph alignment, 136
Paragraph style, 136
Point size, 135
Programming language, 119
Properties, 118
Public domain software, 159
Query by example, 144
Query language, 144
Readability formula, 135
Record, 142
Relative reference, 140
Resource, 123
Search and Replace, 135
Self-executing zip file, 156

Self-installing executable file, 156
Service pack, 156
Setup program, 154
Shareware, 158
Shrink-wrap license, 157
Single-user license, 157
Single-user operating system, 126
Site license, 157
Software license, 157
Software patch, 156
Software publishers, 118
Software suite, 148
Source code, 119
Spelling checker, 134
Spelling dictionary, 134
Spreadsheet, 138
Style, 136
System requirements, 152
System software, 121
Table, 137
Thesaurus, 135
Uninstall routine, 156
UNIX, 129
Unzipped, 155
User interface, 124
Utilities, 125
Value, 138
What-if analysis, 138
Windows Mobile OS, 130
Windows Registry, 161
Worksheet, 138
Zipped, 155

SOFTWARE KEY TERMS

INTERACTIVE SITUATION QUESTIONS

Apply what you've learned to some typical computing situations. When using the NP8 BookOnCD, you can type your answers, then use the Check Answers button to automatically score your responses. Place your Tracking Disk in the floppy disk drive if you want to save your scores.

1. While using several programs at the same time, your computer displays an error message that refers to a general protection fault. You recognize this problem as a potential [_____] leak and decide to close the corrupted program using Ctrl+Alt+Del.

2. If your goal is to produce a printed brochure that contains numerous graphics and looks professionally typeset, you should use DTP software that provides [_____]-oriented layout, instead of a word processor that provides page-oriented layout.

3. You've volunteered to create some graphics for a nonprofit organization, but you'll need a variety of graphics software tools for the organization's computer. Your first choice is to consider a graphics [_____] that bundles together paint, draw, and Web graphics software.

4. Suppose that you've been hired to organize a professional skateboard competition. When you consider how you'll need to use computers, you realize that you must collect information on each competitor and keep track of every competitive event. With at least two types of related records, you'll probably need to use [_____] software.

5. Imagine that you just purchased a new software package. You insert the distribution CD, but nothing happens. No problem—you can manually run the [_____] program, which will start the install routine.

6. You are preparing to download a new software program from the Web. The download consists of one huge file with an .exe extension. You recognize this as a self-[_____] executable file that will automatically unzip itself and start the installation routine.

7. You download an open source software program from the Web. You assume that the download includes the uncompiled [_____] code for the program as well as the [_____] version.

CHECK ANSWERS

INTERACTIVE PRACTICE TESTS

Practice tests that consist of 10 multiple-choice, true/false, and fill-in-the-blank questions are available on both the NP8 BookOnCD and the NP8 Web site. The questions are selected at random from a large test bank, so each time you take a test, you'll receive a different set of questions. Your tests are scored immediately, and you can print study guides that help you find the correct answers for any questions that you missed.

www.course.com/np/concepts8/ch03

CLICK TO START

REVIEW

ON THE WEB

PROJECTS

An NP8 Project is an open-ended activity that helps you apply the concepts you have learned. Many projects require resources in addition to your textbook, such as current magazines, library materials, or Web access. When you tackle a project, be prepared to use your critical thinking skills, logical analysis, and creativity. Projects for this chapter include:

- **Issue Research: Software Piracy**
- **Application Software**
- **Computers in Journalism**
- **Software Applications: What's Available**

- **Productivity Suites and Groupware**
- **Where's the Shareware?**
- **Legal Beagle**

To work with the Projects for this chapter, connect to the **New Perspectives NP8 Web Site**.

www.course.com/np/concepts8/ch03

TECHTV VIDEO PROJECT

The TechTV segment *Software Vending Machines* highlights an innovative way to get software into the hands of consumers. After watching the video, write a short description of how this technology works. Next, suppose you are asked to invest in this company. What do you see as the advantages and disadvantages of this technology? Do alternative technologies exist that might be more effective? Discuss your thoughts on these questions.

To work with the Video Projects for this chapter, connect to the **New Perspectives NP8 Web Site**.

www.course.com/np/concepts8/ch03

STUDY TIPS

Study Tips help you to organize and consolidate the information in a chapter by making lists, outlines, charts, and sketches. You can use paper and pencil or word processing software to complete most of the Study Tips.

To work with the Study Tips for this chapter, connect to the **New Perspectives NP8 Web Site**.

www.course.com/np/concepts8/ch03

ONLINE GAMES

Test your comprehension of the concepts introduced in Chapter 3 by playing the NP8 Online Games. At the end of each game, you have three options:

- Print a comprehensive study guide complete with page references
- Print your results to be submitted to your instructor
- Save your results to be submitted to your instructor via e-mail

To work with the Online Games for this chapter, connect to the **New Perspectives NP8 Web Site**.

www.course.com/np/concepts8/ch03

STUDENT EDITION LABS

Extend your knowledge of software with the Chapter 3 Student Edition Labs.

The following Student Edition Labs are offered with Chapter 3:

- **Working with Windows**
- **Word Processing**
- **Spreadsheets**
- **Databases**
- **Presentation Software**
- **Installing and Uninstalling Software**
- **Advanced Spreadsheets**

Go to the NP8 New Perspectives Web site for specific lab topics.

To work with the Chapter 3 Student Edition Labs and their corresponding lab assignments, connect to the **New Perspectives NP8 Web Site**.

www.course.com/np/concepts8/ch03

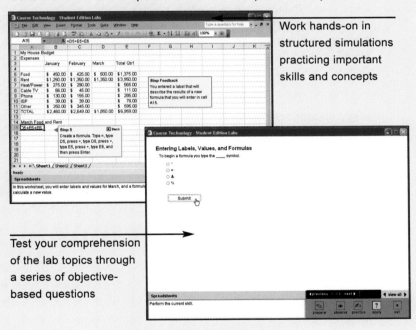

Work hands-on in structured simulations practicing important skills and concepts

Test your comprehension of the lab topics through a series of objective-based questions

Track Your Progress with the Student Edition Labs

- Student Edition Labs test your comprehension of the lab topics through a series of trackable objective-based questions. Your instructor will direct you to either print your results or submit them via e-mail.

- Student Edition Lab Assignments, available on the New Perspectives NP8 Web site, require you to apply the skills learned through the lab in a live environment. Go to the New Perspectives NP8 Web site for detailed instruction on individual Student Edition Lab Assignments.

If you have a SAM user profile, you have access to even more interactive content. Log in to your SAM account and go to your assignments page to see what your instructor has assigned for this chapter.

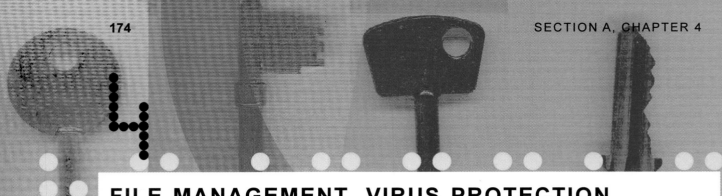

FILE MANAGEMENT, VIRUS PROTECTION, AND BACKUP

CONTENTS

LABS

✳ Working with Windows Explorer
✳ Backing Up Your Computer

TIP

When using the BookOnCD,
the ✳ icons are "clickable" to
access resources on the CD.
The ✚ icons are clickable to
access resources on the Web.
You can also access Web
resources by using your browser to connect directly to the
NP8 New Perspectives Web
site at:

www.course.com/np/concepts8/ch04

CHAPTER PREVIEW

Before you begin Chapter 4, you can use the Web-based preview activities to hear an overview of the chapter, check your current level of expertise about key concepts, and look through a list of learning objectives. You can access the preview activities by clicking the ✚ icon when using the BookOnCD or going to the New Perspectives NP8 Web site.

CHAPTER OVERVIEW

Your important documents, music collection, and digital photos are stored in files on your computer. This chapter tells you how to organize your files for easy access and how to protect them from viruses and equipment failures. Get your book and highlighter ready, then connect to the New Perspectives NP8 Web site where you can listen to an overview that points out the most important concepts for this chapter.

www.course.com/np/concepts8/ch04 ✚

CHAPTER PRE-ASSESSMENT

How much do you know about computer file management and viruses? To gauge your level of knowledge before beginning the chapter, take the pre-assessment quiz at the New Perspectives NP8 Web site. Armed with your results from this quiz, you can focus your study time on concepts that will round out your knowledge of computer files and improve your test scores.

www.course.com/np/concepts8/ch04 ✚

LEARNING OBJECTIVES

When you complete this chapter you should be able to:

- Create valid names for files and folders, plus demonstrate that you can construct and trace file paths

- Demonstrate how to use file management features of application software and operating system utilities

- Describe how a computer physically stores data on disks, but represents this storage system with a logical model

- Explain how file viruses, boot sector viruses, macro viruses, Trojan horses, worms, and Denial of Service attacks affect files and disrupt computer operations

- Describe how a computer owner can use antivirus software to avoid, find, and remove viruses

- Demonstrate that you can implement a viable backup and restore plan

- Compare the advantages and disadvantages of using tapes, floppy disks, a second hard disk, CDs, Zip disks, networks, and Web sites for backups

A detailed list of learning objectives is provided at the New Perspectives NP8 Web site

www.course.com/np/concepts8/ch04 ✚

A

SECTION A

FILE BASICS

The term "file" was used for filing cabinets and collections of papers long before it became part of the personal computer lexicon. Today, a computer file—or simply a "file"— is defined as a named collection of data that exists on a storage medium, such as a disk, CD, DVD, or tape. A file can contain a group of records, a document, a photo, music, a video, an e-mail message, or a computer program.

Computer files have several characteristics, such as a name, format, location, size, and date. To make effective use of computer files, you'll need a good understanding of these file basics, and that is the focus of Section A.

FILE NAMES, EXTENSIONS, AND FORMATS

What are the rules for naming files? Every file has a name and might also have a file extension. When you save a file, you must provide a valid file name that adheres to specific rules, referred to as **file-naming conventions**. Each operating system has a unique set of file-naming conventions. You can use Figure 4-1 to determine whether file names, such as *Nul, My File.doc, Report:2002,* and *Bud01/02.txt,* are valid under the operating system you use.

FIGURE 4-1
File-Naming Conventions

	DOS and Windows 3.1	Windows 95/98/Me/XP/NT/2000	Mac OS (Classic)	UNIX/Linux
Maximum length of file name	8-character file name plus an extension of 3 characters or less	File name and extension cannot exceed 255 characters	1–31 characters	14–256 characters (depending on UNIX/Linux version), including an extension of any length
Spaces allowed	No	Yes	Yes	No
Numbers allowed	Yes	Yes	Yes	Yes
Characters not allowed	* / [ ] ; " = \ : , | ?	* \ : < > | " / ?	:	* ! @ # $ % ^ & ( ) { } [ ] " \ ? ; < > /
File names not allowed	Aux, Com1, Com2, Com3, Com4, Con, Lpt1, Lpt2, Lpt3, Prn, Nul	Aux, Com1, Com2, Com3, Com4, Con, Lpt1, Lpt2, Lpt3, Prn, Nul	Any file name is allowed	Any filename is allowed
Case sensitive	No	No	No	Yes (use lowercase)

Why are certain characters and words not allowed in a file name? If an operating system attaches special significance to a symbol, you might not be able to use it in a file name. For example, DOS and Windows use the colon (:) character to separate the device letter from a file name or folder, as in *C:Music*. A file name such as *Report:2002* is not valid because the operating system would become confused about how to interpret the colon.

Some operating systems also contain a list of **reserved words** that are used as commands or special identifiers. You cannot use these words alone as a file name. You can, however, use these words as part of a longer file name. For example, under Windows XP, the file name *Nul* would not be valid, but you could name a file something like *Nul Committee Notes.doc* or *Null Set.exe*.

Are file extensions important? As explained in Chapter 1, a file extension is an optional file identifier that is separated from the main file name by a period, as in *Paint.exe*. With some operating systems, such as Windows and DOS, file extensions work like tickets that admit people to different plays, movies, or concerts. If you have the right ticket, you get in. If a file has the right extension for a particular application program, you'll see it in the list of files you can open with that software. For example, files with a .doc extension appear in the Open and Save As lists when you're working with Microsoft Word software.

A file extension is usually related to the **file format**, which is defined as the arrangement of data in a file and the coding scheme used to represent the data. Files containing graphics are usually stored using a different file format than files containing text. Hundreds of file formats exist, and you'll encounter many of them as you use a variety of software. Most software programs have what's called a **native file format** for storing files. For example, Microsoft Word stores files in DOC format, whereas Adobe Illustrator stores graphics files in AI format. When using a software application such as Microsoft Word to open a file, the program displays any files that have the file extension for its native file format, as shown in Figure 4-2.

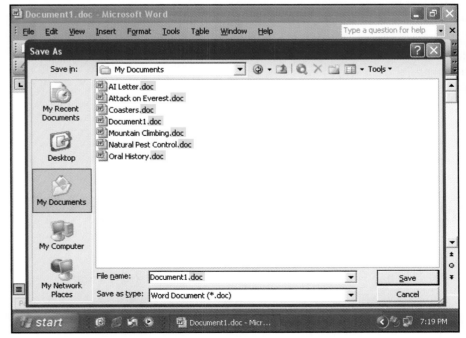

FIGURE 4-2

The next time you use software, take note of the file extensions that appear when you look at the list of files in the Open dialog box. If you don't see any file extensions, you've discovered the results of a Windows setting that can hide (but not erase) file extensions.

If Windows is set to hide file extensions, you can view them by opening Windows Explorer, selecting the Tools menu, selecting Folder Options, then changing the "Hide file extensions" option.

CLICK TO START

FILE LOCATIONS, FOLDERS, AND PATHS

How do I designate a file's location? To designate a file's location, you must first specify where the file is stored. As shown in Figure 4-3, each of a PC's storage devices is identified by a device letter—a convention that is specific to DOS and Windows. The floppy disk drive is usually assigned device letter A and is referred to as "drive A." A device letter is usually followed by a colon, so drive A could be designated as A: or as 3.5" Floppy (A:). The main hard disk drive is usually referred to as "drive C." Additional storage devices can be assigned letters D through Z. Although most PCs stick to the standard of drive A for the floppy disk drive and drive C for the hard disk drive, the device letters for CD, Zip, and DVD drives are not standardized. For example, the CD-writer on your computer might be assigned device letter E, whereas the CD-writer on another computer might be assigned device letter R.

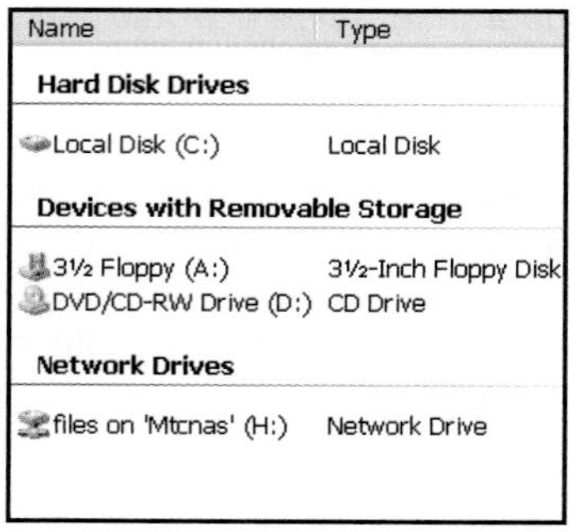

What's the purpose of folders? An operating system maintains a list of files called a **directory** for each storage disk, tape, CD, or DVD. The main directory of a disk is referred to as the **root directory**. On a PC, the root directory is identified by the device letter followed by a backslash. For example, the root directory of the hard disk drive would be C:\. You should try to avoid storing your data files in the root directory of your hard disk; instead, store them in a subdirectory.

A root directory can be subdivided into smaller lists. Each list is called a **subdirectory**. When you use Windows, Mac OS, or a Linux graphical file manager, these subdirectories are depicted as **folders** because they work like folders in a filing cabinet to store an assortment of related items. Each folder has a name, so you can easily create a folder called *Documents* to hold reports, letters, and so on. You can create another folder called *My Music* to hold your MP3 files. Folders can be created within other folders. You might, for example, create a folder within the *My Music* folder to hold your jazz collection and another folder to hold your reggae collection.

A folder name is separated from a drive letter and other folder names by a special symbol. In DOS and Microsoft Windows, this symbol is the backslash (\ ). For example, the folder for your reggae music (within the *My Music* folder on drive C) would be written as *C:\ My Music\Reggae*.

Imagine how hard it would be to find a specific piece of paper in a filing cabinet that was stuffed with a random assortment of reports, letters, and newspaper clippings. By storing a file in a folder, you assign it a place in an organized hierarchy of folders and files.

A computer file's location is defined by a **file specification** (sometimes called a **path**), which includes the drive letter, folder(s), file name, and extension. Suppose that you have stored an MP3 file called *Marley One Love* in the *Reggae* folder on your hard disk drive. Its file specification would be as follows:

FIGURE 4-3

The Windows operating system labels storage devices with letters, such as A: and C:.

Name	Type
Hard Disk Drives	
Local Disk (C:)	Local Disk
Devices with Removable Storage	
3½ Floppy (A:)	3½-Inch Floppy Disk
DVD/CD-RW Drive (D:)	CD Drive
Network Drives	
files on 'Mtcnas' (H:)	Network Drive

C:\My Music\Reggae\Marley One Love.mp3

| Drive letter | Primary folder | Secondary folder | File name | File extension |

FILE SIZES AND DATES

What's the significance of a file's size? A file contains data, stored as a group of bits. The more bits, the larger the file. **File size** is usually measured in bytes, kilobytes, or megabytes. Knowing the size of a file can be important. Compared to small files, large files fill up storage space more quickly, require longer transmission times, and are more likely to be stripped off e-mail attachments by a mail server. Your computer's operating system keeps track of file sizes and supplies that information when you request a listing of files.

Is the file date important? Your computer keeps track of the date that a file was created or last modified (Figure 4-4). The **file date** is useful if you have created several versions of a file and want to make sure you know which version is the most recent. It can also come in handy if you have downloaded several updates of a software package, such as an MP3 player, and you want to make sure you install the latest version.

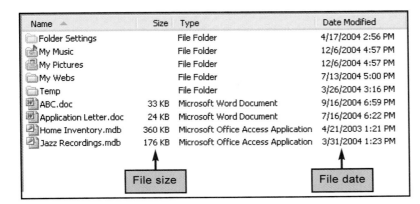

FIGURE 4-4

File sizes and dates can provide information that is useful when working with files.

QUICKCHECK......SECTION A

1. Windows file-naming [_____] are different than for Linux.

2. When using Windows, you cannot use a reserved word, such as Aux, as a file name. True or false? [_____]

3. Microsoft Word uses DOC as its [_____] file format.

4. On a computer running Windows, the hard disk letter is usually designated as [_____].

5. The root directory of a disk can be divided into smaller lists called [_____], that are depicted as folders.

6. A file's location is defined by a file path, which includes the drive letter, one or more [_____], file name, and extension.

7. A file's [_____] can be important information when you are planning to transmit it to another computer over a network.

 CHECK ANSWERS

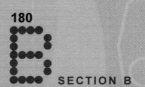

SECTION B

FILE MANAGEMENT

File management encompasses any procedure that helps you organize your computer-based files so that you can find and use them more efficiently. Depending on your computer's operating system, you can organize and manipulate your files from within an application program or by using a special file management utility the operating system provides. Section B offers an overview of application-based and operating system-based file management.

APPLICATION-BASED FILE MANAGEMENT

How does a software application help me manage files? Applications, such as word processing software or graphics software, typically provide a way to open files and save them in a specific folder on a designated storage device. An application might also have additional file management capabilities, such as deleting, copying, and renaming files. Take a look at an example of the file management capabilities in a typical Windows application—Microsoft Word.

Suppose you want to write a letter to the editor of your local newspaper about the rising tide of graffiti in your neighborhood. You would open your word processing software and type the document. As you type, the document is held in RAM. At some point, you'll want to save the document. To do so, you click File on the menu bar, and then select the Save As option. The Save As dialog box, shown in Figure 4-5, opens and allows you to specify a name for the file and its location on one of your computer's storage devices.

FIGURE 4-5

The Save As dialog box is used to name a file and specify its storage location.

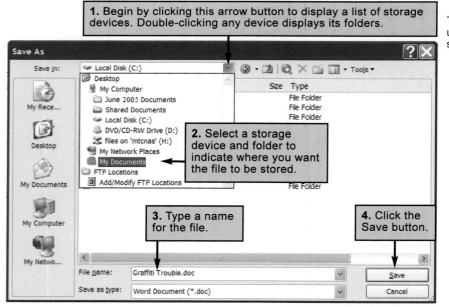

1. Begin by clicking this arrow button to display a list of storage devices. Double-clicking any device displays its folders.

2. Select a storage device and folder to indicate where you want the file to be stored.

3. Type a name for the file.

4. Click the Save button.

What's the difference between the Save option and the Save As option? Most Windows applications provide a curious set of options on the File menu. In addition to the Save As option, the menu contains a Save option. The difference between the two options is subtle, but useful. The Save As option allows you to select a name and storage device for a file, whereas the Save option simply saves the latest version of a file under its current name and at its current location.

A potentially confusing aspect of these options occurs when you try to use the Save option for a file that doesn't yet have a name. Because you can't save a file without a name, your application displays the Save As dialog box, even though you selected the Save option. The flowchart in Figure 4-6 will help you decide whether to use the Save or Save As command.

What other options are available in the Save As dialog box? The Save As dialog box displayed by Windows applications allows you to do more than just save a file. You can use it to rename a file, delete a file, or create a folder, as shown in Figure 4-7.

FIGURE 4-6

Should I use the Save or Save As command?

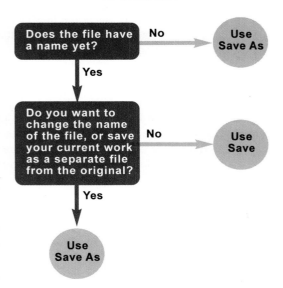

FIGURE 4-7

The Save As dialog box not only helps you select a name and destination drive for a file, but also allows you to rename files, delete files, create folders, and rename folders.

CLICK TO START

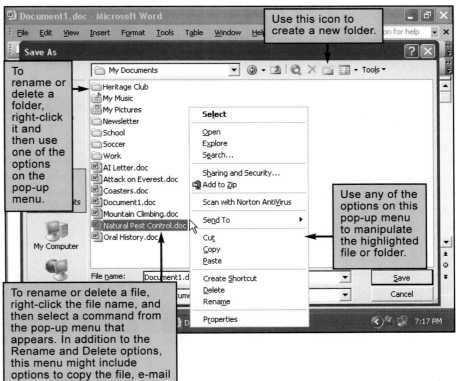

FILE MANAGEMENT UTILITIES

How does the operating system help me manage files? Although most application software gives you access to commands you can use to save, open, rename, and delete individual files, you might want to work with groups of files or perform other file operations that are inconvenient within the Open or Save dialog boxes.

Most operating systems provide **file management utilities** that give you the "big picture" of the files you have stored on your disks and help you work with them. For example, Windows provides a file management utility that can be accessed from the My Computer icon or from the Windows Explorer option on the Start menu. On computers with Mac OS, the file management utility is called the "Finder." These utilities, shown in Figure 4-8, help you view a list of files, find files, move files from one place to another, make copies of files, delete files, discover file properties, and rename files.

FIGURE 4-8

The Windows file management utility can be tailored to show files as icons (top) or as a list (middle).

Mac OS provides a file management utility called the Finder (bottom).

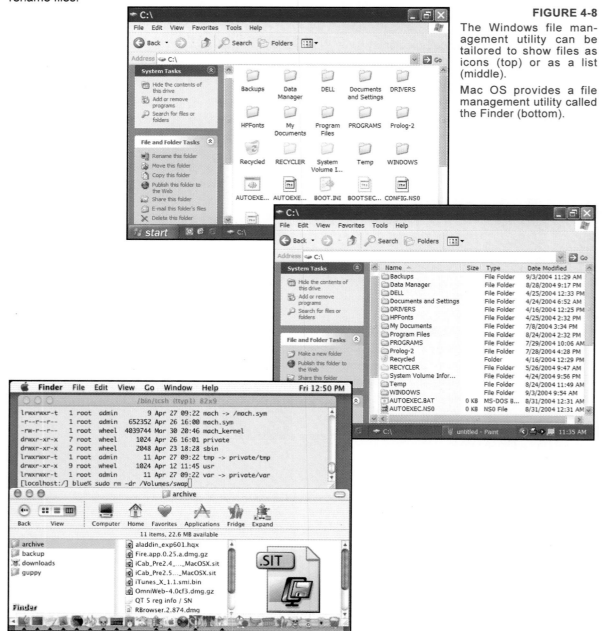

FILE MANAGEMENT METAPHORS

How can a file management utility help me visualize my computer's file storage? File management utilities often use some sort of **storage metaphor** to help you visualize and mentally organize the files on your disks and other storage devices. These metaphors are also called **logical storage models** because they are supposed to help you form a mental (logical) picture of the way in which your files are stored.

What storage metaphors are typically used for personal computers? After hearing so much about files and folders, you might have guessed that the filing cabinet is a popular metaphor for computer storage. In this metaphor, each storage device of a computer corresponds to one of the drawers in a filing cabinet. The drawers hold folders and the folders hold files.

Another storage metaphor is based on a hierarchical diagram that is sometimes referred to as a "tree structure." In this metaphor, a tree represents a storage device. The trunk of the tree corresponds to the root directory. The branches of the tree represent folders. These branches can split into small branches representing folders within folders. The leaves at the end of a branch represent the files in a particular folder. Figure 4-9 illustrates the tree lying on its side so that you can see the relationship to the metaphor shown in the next figure, Figure 4-10.

The tree structure metaphor offers a useful mental image of the way in which files and folders are organized. It is not, however, particularly practical as a user interface. Imagine the complexity of the tree diagram from Figure 4-9 if it were expanded to depict branches for hundreds of folders and leaves for thousands of files.

For practicality, storage metaphors are translated into more mundane screen displays. Figure 4-10 shows how Microsoft programmers combined the filing cabinet metaphor with the tree structure metaphor in the Windows Explorer file management utility.

FIGURE 4-9

You can visualize the directory of a disk as a tree on its side. The trunk corresponds to the root directory, the branches to folders, and the leaves to files.

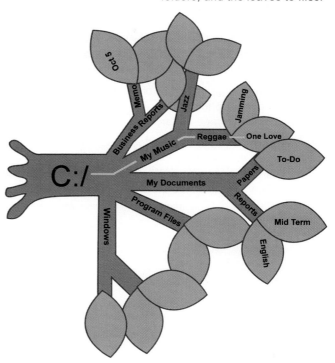

FIGURE 4-10

Windows Explorer borrows folders from the filing cabinet metaphor and places them in a hierarchical structure similar to a tree on its side.

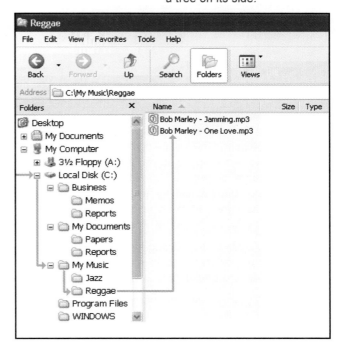

WINDOWS EXPLORER

How do I use a file management utility? As an example of a file management utility, take a closer look at **Windows Explorer**, a utility program bundled with the Windows operating system and designed to help you organize and manipulate the files stored on your computer.

The Windows Explorer window is divided into two "window panes." The pane on the left side of the window lists each of the storage devices connected to your computer, plus several important system objects, such as My Computer, My Network Places, and the Desktop.

An icon for a storage device or other system object can be "expanded" by clicking its corresponding plus-sign icon. Expanding an icon displays the next level of the storage hierarchy—usually a collection of folders.

A device icon or folder can be "opened" by clicking directly on the icon rather than on the plus sign. Once an icon is opened, its contents appear in the pane on the right side of the Windows Explorer window. Figure 4-11 illustrates how to manipulate the directory display.

FIGURE 4-11

Windows Explorer makes it easy to drill down through the levels of the directory hierarchy to locate a folder or file.

CLICK TO START ✤

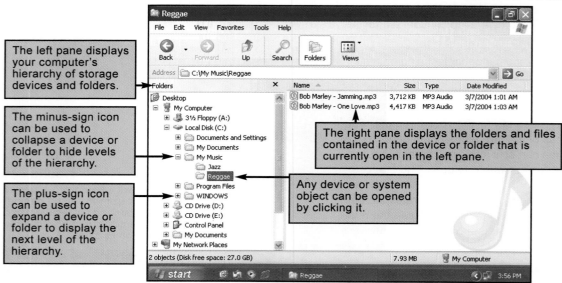

The left pane displays your computer's hierarchy of storage devices and folders.

The minus-sign icon can be used to collapse a device or folder to hide levels of the hierarchy.

The plus-sign icon can be used to expand a device or folder to display the next level of the hierarchy.

The right pane displays the folders and files contained in the device or folder that is currently open in the left pane.

Any device or system object can be opened by clicking it.

Can I work with more than one file or folder at a time? To work with a group of files or folders, you must first select them. You can accomplish this task in several ways. You can hold down the Ctrl key as you click each item. This method works well if you are selecting files or folders that are not listed consecutively. As an alternative, you can hold down the Shift key while you click the first item and the last item you want to select. By using this method, you select the two items that you clicked and all the items in between. Windows Explorer displays all the items you selected by highlighting them. After a group of items is highlighted, you can use the same copy, move, or delete procedure that you would use for a single item.

What can I do with the folders and files that are listed in Windows Explorer? In addition to locating files and folders, Windows Explorer provides a set of procedures (shown in Figure 4-12 on the next page) that help you manipulate files and folders in the following ways:

■ **Rename.** You might want to change the name of a file or folder to better describe its contents.

■ **Copy.** You can copy a file from one device to another—for example, from a floppy disk in drive A to the hard disk in drive C. You can also make a copy of a document so that you can revise the copy and leave the original intact.

■ **Move.** You can move a file from one folder to another or from one storage device to another. When you move a file, it is erased from its original location, so make sure you remember the new location of the file. You can also move folders from one storage device to another or move them to a different folder.

■ **Delete.** You can delete a file when you no longer need it. You can also delete a folder. Be careful when you delete a folder because most file management utilities also delete all the files within a folder.

FIGURE 4-12
Windows Explorer helps you delete, copy, move, and rename files.

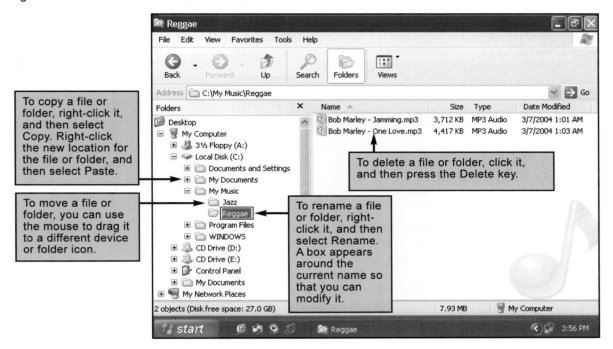

To copy a file or folder, right-click it, and then select Copy. Right-click the new location for the file or folder, and then select Paste.

To move a file or folder, you can use the mouse to drag it to a different device or folder icon.

To delete a file or folder, click it, and then press the Delete key.

To rename a file or folder, right-click it, and then select Rename. A box appears around the current name so that you can modify it.

FILE MANAGEMENT TIPS

A file management utility provides tools and procedures to help you keep track of your program and data files, but these tools are most useful when you have a logical plan for organizing your files and when you follow some basic file management guidelines. The following tips pertain to managing files on your own computer. When working with files on lab computers, follow the guidelines from your instructor or lab manager.

■ **Use descriptive names.** Give your files and folders descriptive names, and avoid using cryptic abbreviations.

■ **Maintain file extensions.** When renaming a file, keep the original file extension so that you can easily open it with the correct application software.

■ **Group similar files.** Separate files into folders based on subject matter For example, store your creative writing assignments in one folder and your MP3 music files in another folder.

■ **Organize your folders from the top down.** When devising a hierarchy of folders, consider how you want to access files and back them up. For example, it is easy to specify one folder and its subfolders for a backup. If your important data is scattered in a variety of folders, however, making backups is more time consuming.

- **Consider using the My Document default directory.** Windows software typically defaults to the *My Documents* folder for storing data files. You might want to use *My Documents* (Figure 4-13) as your main data folder, and add subfolders as necessary to organize your files.

- **Do not mix data files and program files.** Do not store data files in the folders that hold your software—on Windows systems, most software is stored in subfolders of the *Program Files* folder.

- **No files in the root directory.** Although it is acceptable to create folders in the root directory, it is not a good practice to store programs or data files in the root directory of your computer's hard disk.

- **Access files from the hard disk.** For best performance, copy files from floppy disks or CDs to your computer's hard disk before accessing them.

- **Follow copyright rules.** When copying files, make sure you adhere to copyright and license restrictions.

- **Delete files you no longer need.** Deleting unneeded files and folders helps keep your list of files from growing to an unmanageable size.

- **Be aware of storage locations.** When you save files, make sure the drive letter and folder name specify the correct storage location.

- **Back up!** Back up your folders regularly.

PHYSICAL FILE STORAGE

Is data stored in specific places on a disk? So far, you've seen how an operating system such as Windows can help you visualize computer storage as files and folders. This logical storage model, however, has little to do with what actually happens on your disk. The structure of files and folders you see in Windows Explorer is called a "logical" model because it is supposed to help you create a mental picture. The **physical storage model** describes what actually happens on the disks and in the circuits. As you will see, the physical model is quite different from the logical model.

Before a computer can store a file on a disk, CD, or DVD, the storage medium must be formatted. The **formatting** process creates the equivalent of electronic storage bins by dividing a disk into **tracks** and then further dividing each track into **sectors**. Tracks and sectors are numbered to provide addresses for each data storage bin. The numbering scheme depends on the storage device and the operating system. On floppy, Zip, and hard disks, tracks are arranged as concentric circles; on CDs and DVDs, one or more tracks spiral out from the center of the disk (Figure 4-14).

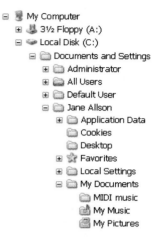

FIGURE 4-13

Windows XP supplies a series of default folders, including *My Documents*, that many users find convenient for storing their data.

- My Computer
  - 3½ Floppy (A:)
  - Local Disk (C:)
    - Documents and Settings
      - Administrator
      - All Users
      - Default User
      - Jane Allson
        - Application Data
        - Cookies
        - Desktop
        - Favorites
        - Local Settings
        - My Documents
          - MIDI music
          - My Music
          - My Pictures

FIGURE 4-14

A process called formatting prepares the surface of a disk to hold data.

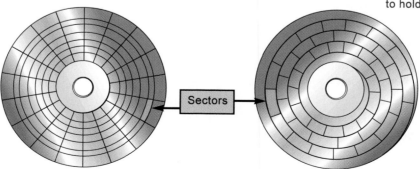

Disks are divided into tracks and wedge-shaped sectors—each side of a floppy disk typically has 80 tracks divided into 18 sectors. Each sector holds 512 bytes of data.

On a typical CD, a single track is about three miles long and is divided into 336,000 sectors. Each sector holds 2,048 bytes of data.

How does a disk get formatted? Today, most floppy, Zip, and hard disks are preformatted at the factory; however, computer operating systems provide **formatting utilities** you can use to reformat some storage devices—typically floppy and hard disks. Formatting utilities are also supplied by the companies that manufacture hard disk drives, writable CD drives, and writable DVD drives.

When you use a formatting utility, it erases any data that happens to be on the disk, and then prepares the tracks and sectors necessary to hold data. You might consider reformatting some of your old floppy disks (instead of just deleting the files they contain) if you really want to make them blank before you reuse them. The screen tour associated with Figure 4-15 demonstrates how to use Windows to format a floppy disk.

FIGURE 4-15

Windows includes a floppy disk formatting utility, which can be accessed from the A: (Floppy disk) icon in the My Computer window or Windows Explorer.

CLICK TO START

How does the operating system keep track of a file's location? The operating system uses a **file system** to keep track of the names and locations of files that reside on a storage medium, such as a hard disk. Different operating systems use different file systems. Most versions of Mac OS use the Macintosh Hierarchical File System (HFS). Ext2fs (extended 2 file system) is the native file system for Linux. Windows NT, Windows 2000, and Windows XP use a file system called **NTFS** (New Technology File System). The file system for Windows 3.1 was called FAT16. Windows 95, 98, and Me use a file system called **FAT32**.

To speed up the process of storing and retrieving data, a disk drive usually works with a group of sectors called a **cluster** or a "block." The number of sectors that form a cluster varies, depending on the capacity of the disk and the way the operating system works with files. A file system's primary task is to maintain a list of clusters and keep track of which are empty and which hold data. This information is stored in a special index file. If your computer uses the FAT32 file system, for example, this index file is called the **File Allocation Table** (FAT). If your computer uses NTFS, it is called the **Master File Table** (MFT).

Each of your disks contains its own index file so that information about its contents is always available when the disk is in use. Unfortunately, storing this crucial file on disk also presents a risk because if the index file is damaged by a hard disk head crash or scratch, you'll generally lose access to all the data stored on the disk. Index files become damaged all too frequently, so it is important to back up your data.

When you save a file, your PC's operating system looks at the index file to see which clusters are empty. It selects one of these clusters, records the file data there, and then revises the index file to include the file name and its location.

A file that does not fit into a single cluster spills over into the next contiguous (meaning adjacent) cluster unless that cluster already contains data. When contiguous clusters are not available, the operating system stores parts of a file in noncontiguous (nonadjacent) clusters. Figure 4-16 helps you visualize how an index file, such as the MFT, keeps track of file names and locations.

FIGURE 4-16

Each colored cluster on the disk contains part of a file. Bio.txt is stored in contiguous clusters. Jordan.wks is stored in noncontiguous clusters.

A computer locates and displays the Jordan.wks file by looking for its name in the Master File Table.

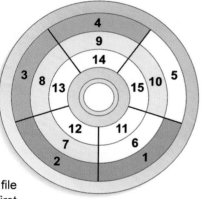

Master File Table

File	Cluster	Comment
MFT	1	Reserved for MFT files
DISK USE	2	Part of MFT that contains list of empty sectors
Bio.txt	3, 4	Bio.txt file stored in clusters 3 and 4
Jordan.wks	7, 8, 10	Jordan.wks file stored noncontiguously in clusters 7, 8, and 10
Pick.wps	9	Pick.wps file stored in cluster 9

When you want to retrieve a file, the OS looks through the index for the file name and its location. It moves the disk drive's read-write head to the first cluster that contains the file data. Using additional data from the index file, the operating system can move the read-write heads to each of the clusters containing the remaining parts of the file.

What happens when a file is deleted? When you click a file's icon and then select the Delete option, you might have visions of the read-write head somehow scrubbing out the clusters that contain data. That doesn't happen. Instead, the operating system simply changes the status of the file's clusters to "empty" and removes the file name from the index file. The file name no longer appears in a directory listing, but the file's data remains in the clusters until a new file is stored there. You might think that this data is as good as erased, but it is possible to purchase utilities that recover a lot of this "deleted" data—law enforcement agents, for example, use these utilities to gather evidence from deleted files on the computer disks of suspected criminals.

To delete data from a disk in such a way that no one can ever read it, you can use special **file shredder software** that overwrites "empty" sectors with random 1s and 0s. You might find this software handy if you plan to donate your computer to a charitable organization, and you want to make sure your personal data no longer remains on the hard disk.

Can deleted files be undeleted? The Windows Recycle Bin and similar utilities in other operating systems are designed to protect you from accidentally deleting hard disk files you actually need. Instead of marking a file's clusters as available, the operating system moves the file to the Recycle Bin folder. The "deleted" file still takes up space on the disk, but does not appear in the usual directory listing.

Files that appear in the directory listing for the Recycle Bin folder can be undeleted so that they again appear in the regular directory. The Recycle Bin can be emptied to permanently delete any files it contains.

How does a disk become fragmented? As a computer writes files on a disk, parts of files tend to become scattered all over the disk. These **fragmented files** are stored in noncontiguous clusters. Drive performance generally declines as the read-write heads move back and forth to locate the clusters containing the parts of a file. To regain peak performance, you can use a **defragmentation utility** to rearrange the files on a disk so that they are stored in contiguous clusters (Figure 4-17).

FIGURE 4-17

Defragmenting a disk helps your computer operate more efficiently. Consider using a defragmentation utility at least once a month to keep your computer running in top form.

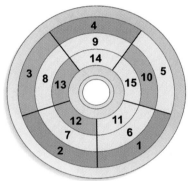

Fragmented disk

On the fragmented disk (left), the purple, yellow, and blue files are stored in noncontiguous clusters.

When the disk is defragmented (right), the sectors of data for each file are moved to contiguous clusters.

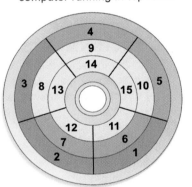

Defragmented disk

QUICKCHECK......SECTION B

1. The _____ option on an application's File menu allows you to save the latest version of a file under its current name and at its current location.

2. A storage _____, such as a filing cabinet or tree, helps you visualize and mentally organize your computer files.

3. Windows _____ is software provided by the operating system and designed to help you organize and manipulate files.

4. A hard disk stores data in concentric _____, which are divided into wedge-shaped _____.

5. File _____ software overwrites deleted files with random 1s and 0s.

CHECK ANSWERS

LAB 4-B

WORKING WITH WINDOWS EXPLORER

In this lab, you'll learn:

- How to access Windows Explorer
- How to expand and collapse the directory structure to locate folders and files
- How to rename or delete a file or folder
- The basic principles for creating an efficient directory structure for your files
- How to create a folder
- How to select a single file or a group of files
- How to move files from one folder to another

LAB ASSIGNMENTS

1. Start the interactive part of the lab. Insert your Tracking Disk if you want to save your QuickCheck results. Perform each lab step as directed, and answer all the lab QuickCheck questions. When you exit the lab, your answers are automatically graded and your results are displayed.

2. Use Windows Explorer to look at the directory of the hard disk or floppy disk that currently contains most of your files. Draw a diagram showing the hierarchy of folders. Write a paragraph explaining how you could improve this hierarchy, and draw a diagram to illustrate your plan.

3. Use a new floppy disk or format an old disk that doesn't contain important data. Create three folders on the disk: Music, Web Graphics, and Articles. Within the Music folder, create four additional folders: Jazz, Reggae, Rock, and Classical. Within the Classical folder, create two more folders: Classical MIDI and Classical MP3. If you have Internet access, go on to #4.

4. Use your browser software to connect to the Internet, and then go to a Web site, such as *www.zdnet.com* or *www.cnet.com*. Look for a small graphic (remember, you have only 1.44 MB of space on your floppy disk!) and download it to your Web Graphics folder. Next, use a search engine such as *www.google.com* or *www.yahoo.com* to search for "classical MIDI music." Download one of the compositions to the Music\Classical\Classical MIDI folder. Open Windows Explorer and expand all the directories for drive A. Open the Music\Classical\Classical MIDI folder and make sure your music download appears. Capture a screenshot. Follow your instructor's directions to submit this screenshot as a printout or an e-mail attachment.

INTERACTIVE LAB

CLICK TO START THE LAB ✦

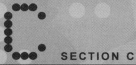

COMPUTER VIRUSES

Viruses are one of the biggest threats to the security of your computer files. In 1981, there was one known computer virus. Today, the count exceeds 70,000. Between 600 and 900 new viruses appear every month. Viruses are spreading more rapidly than ever. The Michelangelo virus infected 75,000 computers in seven months; the Melissa virus reached 3.5 million computers in 10 hours; and a virus called I-love-you took only three hours to reach 72 million. Today, MyDoom, Sasser, and Netsky infections affect hundreds of millions of computers despite vigorous eradication efforts.

Computer viruses invade all types of computers, including mainframes, servers, personal computers, and even handheld computers. To defend your computer against viruses, you should understand what they are, how they work, and how to use antivirus software.

VIRUSES, TROJAN HORSES, AND WORMS

What kind of code can attack my computer? The term **malicious code** (sometimes called "malware") refers to any program or set of program instructions designed to surreptitiously enter a computer and disrupt its normal operations. Malicious code, including viruses, worms, and Trojan horses, is created and unleashed by individuals referred to as "hackers" or "crackers."

The term "hacker" originally referred to a highly skilled computer programmer. Today, however, the terms "hacker" and "cracker" usually refer to anyone who uses a computer to gain unauthorized access to data, steal information, distribute viruses, or crash a computer system. Spreading a computer virus is a crime in many countries, including the United States.

What is a computer virus? A **computer virus** is a set of program instructions that attaches itself to a file, reproduces itself, and spreads to other files. It can corrupt files, destroy data, display an irritating message, or otherwise disrupt computer operations. A common misconception is that viruses spread themselves from one computer to another, but they can replicate themselves only on the host computer. Viruses spread because people distribute infected files by exchanging disks and CDs, sending e-mail attachments, exchanging music on file-sharing networks, and downloading software from the Web. Be cautious of floppy disks, homemade CDs, and Web sites that contain games and other supposedly fun stuff. Check these files with antivirus software before you copy or use them.

Many computer viruses infect files executed by your computer—files with extensions such as .exe, .com, or .vbs. When your computer executes an infected program, it also executes the attached virus instructions. These instructions then remain in RAM, waiting to infect the next program your computer runs or the next disk it accesses.

In addition to replicating itself, a virus might deliver a **payload**, which could be as harmless as displaying an annoying message or as devastating as corrupting the data on your computer's hard disk. A **trigger event**, such as a specific date, can unleash some viruses. For example, the Michelangelo virus triggers on March 6, the birthday of artist Michelangelo.

TERMINOLOGY NOTE

Viruses that deliver their payloads on a specific date are sometimes referred to as "time bombs."

Viruses that deliver their payloads in response to some other system event are referred to as "logic bombs."

A key characteristic of viruses is their ability to "lurk" in a computer for days or months, quietly replicating themselves. While this replication takes place, you might not even know that your computer has contracted a virus; therefore, it is easy to inadvertently spread infected files to other people's computers.

A virus can be classified as a file virus, boot sector virus, or macro virus. A **file virus** infects application programs, such as games. A **boot sector virus** Infects the system files your computer uses every time you turn it on. These viruses can cause widespread damage and recurring problems. A **macro virus** infects a set of instructions called a "macro"—a miniature program that usually contains legitimate instructions to automate document and worksheet production. When you view a document containing an infected macro, the macro virus duplicates itself into the general macro pool, where it is picked up by other documents (Figure 4-18).

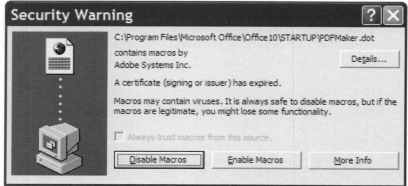

FIGURE 4-18

Today, programs with macro capabilities warn you if a document contains a macro and allow you to disable macros. Macro security warnings do not necessarily mean that a document contains a macro infected with a virus. Scanning the macro with antivirus software, however, can detect the presence of a virus.

How is a Trojan horse different from a virus? A **Trojan horse** is a computer program that seems to perform one function while actually doing something else. Technically, it is not the same as a virus because, unlike a virus, a Trojan horse is not designed to make copies of itself. Trojan horses are notorious for stealing passwords. For example, one Trojan horse arrives as an e-mail attachment named Picture.exe, which leads you to believe you've received some type of graphics software. If you open this file, however, it searches for America Online (AOL) user information and tries to steal your login and e-mail passwords. Trojan horses can also generate official-looking forms that are actually fake (Figure 4-19).

Security Measures

As part of our continuing commitment to protect your account and to reduce the instance of fraud on our website, we are undertaking a period review of our member accounts.

Before signing in, please confirm that you are the owner of this account.

Please fill in the correct information to verify your identity.

	Full Name
	Card & expiration date
	Your card number
3-digit validation code on back of card (cw2)
	ATM PIN-Code

Click Once To Continue

Image Copyright @ F-Secure Corporation

FIGURE 4-19

A Trojan horse called Padodor watches your browser window for text strings such as "Sign in" and "Log in." It then displays a fake login screen like the one shown here to collect your credit card numbers and ATM PIN code.

Messages that demand your PayPal account number, your AOL password, or your ATM PIN are additional examples of Trojan horses currently making the rounds.

Many Trojan horses have **backdoor** capability, which allows unauthorized access to victims' computers. A backdoor allows remote hackers to download and execute files on your computer, upload a list of other infected computers, and use your computer as a relay station for breaking into other computers.

Some Trojan horses delete files and cause other trouble. Although a Trojan horse is not defined as a program that replicates itself, some Trojan horses do contain a virus, which can replicate and spread. Other Trojan horses are carried by worms. Virus experts use the term **blended threat** to describe threats that combine more than one type of malicious program. Common blended threats include Trojan-horse/virus combinations and worm/virus combinations.

What's a worm? With the proliferation of network traffic and e-mail, worms have become a major concern in the computing community. Unlike a virus, which is designed to spread from file to file, a **worm** is designed to spread from computer to computer. Most worms take advantage of communications networks—especially the Internet—to travel within e-mail and TCP/IP packets, jumping from one computer to another. Some worms simply spread throughout a network. Others also deliver payloads that vary from harmless messages to malicious file deletions.

How do worms spread? Mass-mailing worms have become especially troublesome. A **mass-mailing worm** spreads by sending itself to every address in the address book of an infected computer. Mass-mailing worms such as Klez, Netsky, MyDoom, and Bagle have made headlines and caused havoc on personal computers, LANs, and Internet servers. To make these worms difficult to track, the "From" line of the infected message sometimes contains a **spoofed address** of a randomly selected person from the address book rather than the address of the computer that actually sent the mail.

Mass-mailing worms often include an attachment that contains the worm. Opening the attachment unleashes the worm. Some mass-mailing worms contain a Web link that installs a worm, Trojan horse, or virus (Figure 4-20). Sasser and other mass-mailing worms, however, require no user interaction to infect a computer.

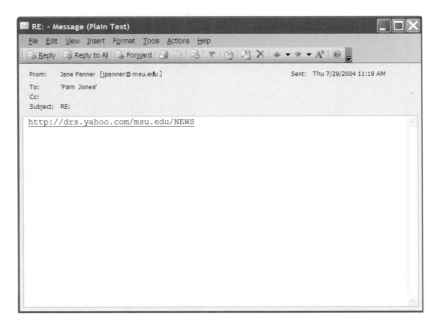

FIGURE 4-20

A mass-mailing worm called Wallon contains a link to a Web site. Clicking the link downloads several files, including the worm, which replicates by sending itself to addresses listed on the infected computer.

The conventional wisdom for avoiding e-mail-borne infections is not to open suspicious attachments—especially those with executable file extensions, such as .exe. Most computer owners recognize that an attachment called Amazing Photo.exe that arrives from an unknown sender probably contains a virus. Hackers, however, have become proficient at using "social engineering" techniques to make e-mail messages and their attachments seem legitimate. For example, a virus called Netsup looks like a message from your e-mail postmaster that says, "A message sent could not be delivered to one or more of its recipients correctly. This is a permanent error. Attached is a copy of the original message." Opening the attachment to view the undelivered mail triggers the worm.

Another prevalent example of social engineering is a message that appears to have been sent by Microsoft imploring you to install software updates (Figure 4-21). The so-called update contains a worm. If you're uncertain about the legitimacy of an e-mail that arrives from a reputable organization, check its Web site before responding.

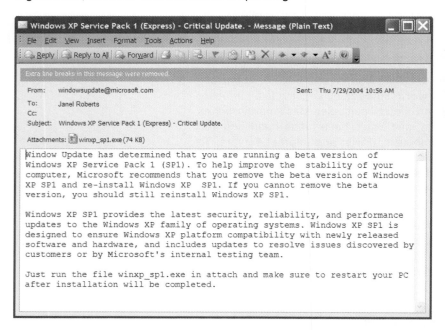

FIGURE 4-21
You might be tempted to install the operating system service pack in this e-mail that seems to have been sent by Microsoft. Don't do it! This worm is an example of social engineering techniques used to make infected e-mail messages look legitimate.

Worms can also spread via HTML scripts. Chapter 1 explained that you can set your e-mail software to use HTML format, which provides a variety of font colors, types, and sizes for your messages. Unfortunately, e-mail that's in HTML format can harbor worms hidden in program-like "scripts" that hackers embed in the HTML tags. These worms are difficult to detect—even for antivirus software. As a result, many people stick with plain-text, non-HTML e-mail.

Although e-mail is currently the primary vehicle used to spread worms, hackers have also devised ways to spread worms over file-sharing networks, such as Kazaa. Some worms are designed to spread over instant messaging links. Worms such as Cabir can even infect mobile phones.

What are the most common threats? Before widespread use of the Internet, viruses were the biggest threat to computer security. Today, however, worms have become the biggest threat. Looking toward the future,

INFOWEBLINKS

The old saying "know thy enemy" applies to viruses and worms. To learn more details about current threats, visit the **Virus Descriptions InfoWeb**.

www.course.com/np/concepts8/ch04

experts predict an increase of blended threats that combine worm-like distribution with virus payloads. Worms that spread through channels other than e-mail are likely to become more prevalent, too. Figure 4-22 highlights some landmarks and trends in the development of malicious code.

Date	Threats	Trends
1981	Cloner	The first known virus begins to spread. Cloner infects files on disks formatted for Apple II computers. The prevalence of disk-borne viruses continues well into the1990s with Jerusalem (1987), Michelangelo (1992), and others.
1988	Internet Worm	The first major worm attack via the Internet sets the stage for today's prolific crop of mass-mailing worms.
1998	Back Orifice	First Trojan horse designed to allow a remote hacker to gain unauthorized access to a computer.
1999	Melissa	Macro viruses, such as Melissa and Laroux, are prevalent for several years and cause trouble by infecting Microsoft Word and Excel files.
2000	Love Letter	One of the fastest spreading mass-mailing worms of all time. Followed by Sobig, Blaster, and MyDoom (2004).
2001	Code Red	Worms designed for Denial of Service attacks gather steam. Code Red, which targeted the White House, is followed by Blaster (2001) and Slammer (2003).
2002	Klez	Klez is a mass-mailing worm that is particularly difficult to eradicate. Because the "From" address is spoofed, it is is almost impossible to locate infected computers.
2003	Mimail	Social engineering takes center stage and users are confused by fake e-mails from seemingly legitimate companies, such as PayPal, Microsoft, and Wells Fargo.
2004	Sasser Netsky Xombe MyDoom, Zafi Bagle	Worms, such as Sasser, begin to emerge that infect computers without user interaction, such as opening an infected e-mail attachment. Mass-mailing worms are still most prevalent. Worms that spread via instant messaging and handheld devices begin to emerge.

What are the symptoms of a malicious code attack? Some viruses have noticeable—and usually annoying—symptoms. Remember, however, that many infections have no recognizable symptoms. Your computer can contract a worm, for example, that never displays an irritating message or attempts to delete your files, but merrily replicates itself through your e-mail until it eventually arrives at a server where it can do some real damage to a network communication system.

What kind of damage is caused by malicious code? The current crop of viruses, Trojan horses, and worms cause various problems, ranging from displaying harmless messages to bringing down Web sites. The list of malware activities below illustrates why everyday computer users and security specialists are concerned.

Network traffic jam. When worms are active, they generate traffic on LANs and the Internet. Service deteriorates as download time increases for files, Web pages, and e-mail messages.

Denial of Service. A **Denial of Service attack** is designed to generate a lot of activity on a network by flooding its servers with useless traffic—enough traffic to overwhelm the server's processing capability and essentially bring all communications to a halt. Successful DoS attacks have been launched against Microsoft, the White House, and the controversial Internet ad agency DoubleClick.

Browser reconfiguration. Some worms block users from accessing certain Web sites and can change your home page setting. They can also set up a redirection routine that downloads malicious code from an infected Web site, even when you enter a legitimate Web address.

Delete and modify files. Many viruses are designed to delete files on a personal computer's hard disk. Some malicious code modifies the Windows Registry and can cause system instability.

Access confidential information. Trojan horses are notorious for using backdoors to steal passwords and credit card numbers. Worms can also scan files and Web sites for e-mail addresses.

Performance degradation. Malicious code requires system resources to send mail and scan files. While a virus or worm is active, your computer might seem to perform slower than normal.

Disable antivirus and firewall software. Some viruses—called **retro viruses**—are designed to attack antivirus software by deleting the files that contain virus descriptions or corrupting the main executable virus-scanning program. One antivirus vendor calls them "anti-antivirus viruses."

ANTIVIRUS SOFTWARE

How can I avoid viruses and worms? Keeping viruses, Trojan horses, and worms out of your computer is preferable to trying to eliminate these pesky programs after they have taken up residence. After malicious code infiltrates your computer, it can be difficult to eradicate. Certain viruses are particularly tenacious—just the process of booting up your computer can trigger their replication sequence or send them into hiding.

These are the top three steps you can take to prevent your computer from becoming infected:

☑ Use antivirus software on every computing device you own.

☑ Keep software patches and operating system service packs up to date.

☑ Do not open suspicious e-mail attachments.

What is antivirus software? **Antivirus software** is a set of utility programs that can look for and eradicate viruses, Trojan horses, and worms. This essential software is available for handheld computers, personal computers, and servers. Popular antivirus software for personal computers includes McAfee VirusScan, Norton AntiVirus, and F-Secure Anti-Virus.

How does antivirus software work? Antivirus software uses several techniques to find viruses. As you know, some viruses attach themselves to an existing program. The presence of such a virus often increases the length of the original program. The earliest antivirus software simply examined the programs on a computer and recorded their length. A change in the length of a program from one computing session to the next indicated the possible presence of a virus.

To counter early antivirus software, hackers became more cunning. They created viruses that insert themselves into unused portions of a program file without changing its length. Antivirus software developers fought back. They designed software that examines the bytes in an uninfected application program and calculates a checksum. A **checksum** is a number calculated by combining the binary values of all bytes in a file. Each time you run an application program, antivirus software calculates the checksum and compares it with the previous checksum. If any byte in the application program has changed, the checksum will be different, and the antivirus software assumes that a virus is present.

Today's viruses, Trojan horses, and worms are not limited to infecting program files, so modern antivirus software attempts to locate viruses by

---

INFOWEBLINKS

If you don't have antivirus software for your computer, you should get it. Use the **Antivirus Software InfoWeb** to link to Web sites where you can purchase and download antivirus software.

www.course.com/np/concepts8/ch04

searching your computer's files and memory for virus signatures. A **virus signature** is a section of the virus program, such as a unique series of instructions, that can be used to identify a known virus, much as a fingerprint is used to identify an individual.

When should I use antivirus software? The short answer is "all the time." Most antivirus software allows you to specify what to check and when to check it. You can, for example, fire it up only when you receive a suspicious e-mail attachment, or you can set it to look through all the files on your computer once a week. The best practice, however, is to keep your antivirus software running full-time in the background so that it scans all files the moment they are accessed and checks every e-mail message as it arrives. The scanning process requires a short amount of time, which creates a slight delay in downloading e-mail and opening files. The wait is worth it, however, when you can feel confident that the files you open have been scanned for viruses.

How often should I get an update? The information antivirus software uses to identify and eradicate viruses, Trojan horses, and worms is stored in one or more files usually referred to as "virus definitions." New viruses and variations of old viruses are unleashed just about every day. To keep up with these newly identified pests, antivirus software vendors provide virus definition updates, which are usually available as Web downloads (Figure 4-23). You should check your antivirus vendor's Web site for the latest updates of antivirus software every few weeks or when you hear of a new virus making headlines.

How reliable is antivirus software? Considering the number of existing viruses and the number of viruses debuting every month, antivirus software is surprisingly reliable. Viruses try to escape detection in many ways. **Multi-partite viruses** (pronounced multi-PAR-tite) are able to infect multiple types of targets. For example, a multi-partite virus might combine the characteristics of a file virus (which hides in .exe files) and a boot sector virus (which hides in the boot sector). If your antivirus software looks for that particular virus only in .exe files, the virus could escape detection by hiding in the boot sector as well.

Polymorphic viruses mutate to escape detection by changing their signatures. **Stealth viruses** remove their signatures from a disk-based file and temporarily conceal themselves in memory. Antivirus software can find stealth viruses only by scanning memory.

Unfortunately, antivirus software is not 100% reliable. On rare occasions, it might not identify a virus, or it might conclude that your computer has a virus when one does not actually exist. Despite these rare mistakes, the protection you get is worth the required investment of time and money. Remember that without antivirus software, your computer is susceptible to all the nasty little programs that can cause damage to your files and irritate the friends whose computers you infect.

VIRUS HOAXES

What's a virus hoax? Some virus threats are very real, but you're also likely to get e-mail messages about "viruses" that don't really exist. A **virus hoax** usually arrives as an e-mail message containing dire warnings about a supposedly new virus on the loose (Figure 4-24 on the next page).

TERMINOLOGY NOTE

Because today's antivirus software scans for virus signatures, it is sometimes referred to as "virus scanning software."

FIGURE 4-23

It is important to get regular updates for your antivirus software. Some antivirus vendors feature an electronic update service that you can set to automatically download and install updated virus definitions.

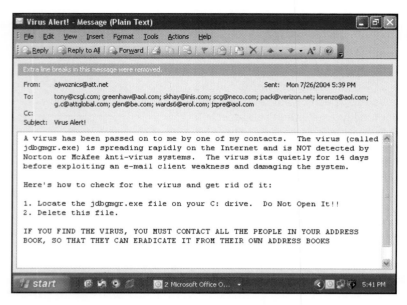

FIGURE 4-24

A virus hoax tends to contain telltale characteristics, such as:

- Warns of a "new" or "dangerous" virus spreading on the Internet.
- Contains a long list of people in the To: or Cc: boxes.
- Cites some "authority" to make you think the alert is official.
- Includes some technical jargon that supposedly explains the virus attack.
- Provides instructions, such as reformatting your computer's hard disk drive or deleting a file, for eradicating the virus. The instructions can cause more damage than the virus itself!
- Urges you to send the e-mail message to everyone in your address book.

What should I do about virus hoaxes? When you receive an e-mail message about a virus, don't panic. Many of them are hoaxes. If you are uncertain, check one of the many antivirus Web sites. There you can look up the alleged virus by name to see if it is a real threat or a hoax.

If the virus is a real threat, the antivirus Web site can provide information to determine whether your computer has been infected. You can also find instructions for eradicating the virus and updating the list of virus definitions your computer's antivirus software uses. If the virus threat is a hoax, you can ignore it. Under no circumstances should you forward virus hoax messages to other people.

INFOWEBLINKS

Some Web sites specialize in tracking hoaxes. For links to these sites, visit the **Hoax InfoWeb**.

www.course.com/np/concepts8/ch04

QUICKCHECK......SECTION C

1. The key characteristic of a virus is that it can replicate itself. True or false? [ ]

2. Many Trojan horses have [ ] capability, which allows unauthorized access to victims' computers.

3. Many mass-mailing worms are difficult to trace because they contain [ ] addresses.

4. Social [ ] is a technique used by hackers to make e-mail messages and their attachments seem legitimate.

5. A virus [ ] is a section of the virus program, such as a unique series of instructions, that can be used to identify a known virus.

6. [ ] viruses mutate to escape detection by changing their signatures.

 CHECK ANSWERS

SECTION D

DATA BACKUP

Computer experts universally recommend that you make backups of your data. It sounds pretty basic, right? Unfortunately, this advice tells you what to do, not how to do it. It fails to address some key questions, such as: Do I need special backup equipment and software? How often should I make a backup? How many of my files should I back up? What should I do with the backups?

In this last section of Chapter 4, you'll find the answers to your questions about backing up data that's stored on a personal computer. You'll begin by looking at how to devise a backup plan that's right for you, and then review your equipment and software options. Along the way, you should pick up lots of practical tips to help you keep your data safe.

BACKUP AND RESTORE PROCEDURES

Why do I need to make backups? Have you ever mistakenly copied an old version of a document over a new version? Has your computer's hard disk drive gone on the fritz? Did a virus wipe out your files? Has lightning "fried" your computer system? These kinds of data disasters are not rare; they happen to everyone. You can't always prevent them, so you need a backup plan that helps you recover data that's been wiped out by operator error, viruses, or hardware failures.

How do I make a backup? A **backup** is a copy of one or more files that has been made in case the original files become damaged. A backup is usually stored on a different storage medium from the original files. For example, you can back up files from your hard disk to a different hard disk, a writable CD or DVD, tape, floppy disk, or Web site. The exact steps you follow to make a backup depend on your backup equipment, the software you use to make backups, and your personal backup plan. That said, the list in Figure 4-25 gives you a general idea of the steps in a typical backup session.

FIGURE 4-25

These are the steps in a typical backup session.

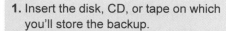
CLICK TO START

1. Insert the disk, CD, or tape on which you'll store the backup.

2. Start the software you're using for the backup.

3. Select the folders and files you want to back up.

4. Give the "go ahead" to start copying data.

5. Feed in additional disks, CDs, or tapes if prompted to do so.

6. Clearly label each disk, CD, or tape.

7. Test your backup.

How do I restore data? In technical jargon, you **restore** data by copying files from a backup to the original storage medium or its replacement. As with the procedures for backing up data, the process you use to restore data to your hard disk varies, depending on your backup equipment and software. It also depends on exactly what you need to restore.

After a hard disk crash, for example, you'll probably need to restore all your backup data to a new hard disk. On the other hand, if you inadvertently delete a file or mistakenly copy one file over another, you might need to restore only a single file from the backup. Most software designed to back up and restore data allows you to select which files you want to restore. A typical session to restore data follows the steps in Figure 4-26.

What's the best backup plan? A good backup plan allows you to restore your computing environment to its pre-disaster state with a minimum of fuss. Unfortunately, no single backup plan fits everyone's computing style or budget. You must devise your own backup plan that's tailored to your particular computing needs.

The checklist in Figure 4-27 outlines factors you should consider as you formulate your own backup plan.

FIGURE 4-26
These are the steps in a typical restore session.

1. Start the software you used to make the backup.
2. Select the file or files you want to restore.
3. Insert the appropriate backup tape or disk.
4. Wait for the files to be copied from the backup to the hard disk.

FIGURE 4-27
Backup Tips

☑ Decide how much of your data you want, need, and can afford to back up.

☑ Create a realistic schedule for making backups.

☑ Make sure you have a way to avoid backing up files that contain viruses.

☑ Find out what kind of boot disks you might need to get your computer up and running after a hard disk failure or boot sector virus attack.

☑ Make sure you can test your restore procedure so that you can successfully retrieve the data you've backed up.

☑ Find a safe place to store your backups.

☑ Decide what kind of storage device you'll use to make backups.

☑ Select software to handle backup needs.

Do I have to back up every file? A **full-system backup** contains a copy of every program, data, and system file on a computer. The advantage of a full-system backup is that you can easily restore your computer to its pre-disaster state simply by copying the backup files to a new hard disk. A full-system backup takes a lot of time, however, and automating the process requires a large-capacity tape backup device or a second hard disk drive.

A workable alternative to a full system backup is a "selective" backup that contains only your most important data files. A backup of these files ensures that your computer-based documents and projects are protected from many data disasters. You can back up these files on floppy disks, Zip disks, removable hard disks, an external hard disk, CDs, or DVDs. The disadvantage of this backup strategy is that because you backed up only data files, you must manually reinstall all your software in addition to restoring your data files.

If your strategy is to back up your important data files, the procedure can be simplified if you've stored all these files in one folder or its subfolders. For example, Windows users might store their data files in folders contained in the *My Documents* folder. A folder called *My Documents\Music* might hold MP3 files, a *My Documents\Reports* folder can hold reports, a *My Documents\Art* folder can hold various graphics files, and so on. With your data files organized under the umbrella of a single folder, you are less likely to omit an important file when you make backups.

Some applications, such as financial software, create files and update them without your direct intervention. If you have the option during setup, make sure these files are stored under the My Documents umbrella. Otherwise, you must discover the location of the files and make sure they are backed up with the rest of your data.

In addition to data files you create, a few other types of data files might be important to you. Consider making backups of the files listed in Figure 4-28.

FIGURE 4-28

Back up these files in addition to your documents, graphics, and music files.

Internet connection information. Your ISP's phone number and IP address, your user ID, and your password are often stored in an encrypted file somewhere in the *Windows\System* folder. Your ISP can usually help you find this file.

E-mail folders. If you're using POP e-mail software, your e-mail folder contains all the e-mail messages you've sent and received, but not deleted. Check the Help menu on your e-mail program to discover the location of these files.

E-mail address book. Your e-mail address book might be stored separately from your e-mail messages. To find the file on a Windows computer, use the Search or Find option on the Start menu to search for "Address Book."

Favorite URLs. If you're attached to the URLs you've collected in your Favorites or Bookmarks list, you might want to back up the file that contains this list. To find the file, search your hard disk for "Favorites" or "Bookmarks."

Downloads. If you paid to download any files, you might want to back them up so that you don't have to pay for them again. These files include software, which usually arrives in the form of a compressed .exe file that expands into several separate files as you install it. For backup purposes, the compressed .exe file should be all you need.

What about backing up the Windows Registry? Windows users often hear a variety of rumors about backing up the Windows Registry. The Registry, as it is usually called, is an important group of files the Windows operating system uses to store configuration information about all the devices and software installed on a computer system. If the Registry becomes damaged, your computer might not be able to boot up, launch programs, or communicate with peripheral devices. It is a good idea to have an extra copy of the Registry in case the original file is damaged.

As simple as it sounds, backing up the Registry can present a bit of a problem because the Registry is always open while your computer is on. Some software that you might use for backups cannot copy open files. If you use such software, the Registry will never make its way onto a backup. Windows users whose backup plans encompass all files on the hard disk must make sure their backup software provides an option for including the Windows Registry. Even if a full-system backup is not planned, many experts recommend that you at least copy the Registry to a separate folder on the hard disk or to a floppy disk. If you do so, you should update this copy whenever you install new software or hardware.

INFOWEBLINKS

For more detailed information on backup techniques, such as backing up the Registry, take a look at the **Backup Techniques InfoWeb**.

www.course.com/np/concepts8/ch04

How do I avoid backing up files that contain viruses? Viruses can damage files to the point that your computer can't access any data on its hard disk. In this case, it is really frustrating when you restore data from a backup only to discover that the restored files contain the same virus that wiped out your data. If your antivirus software is not set to constantly scan for viruses on your computer system, you should run an up-to-date virus check as the first step in your backup routine.

How often should I back up my data? Your backup schedule depends on how much data you can afford to lose. If you're working on an important project, you might want to back up the project files several times a day. Under normal use, however, most people schedule a once-a-week backup. If you work with a To Do list, use it to remind yourself when it is time to make a backup.

Where should I store my backups? Store your backups in a safe place. Don't keep them at your computer desk because a fire or flood that damages your computer could also wipe out your backups. In addition, a thief who steals your computer might also scoop up nearby equipment and media. Storing your backups at a different location is the best idea, but at least store them in a room apart from your computer.

How do I choose a backup device? The backup device you select depends on the value of your data, your current equipment, and your budget. If you can afford a tape drive, buy one, install it, and use it. Otherwise, use what you have—your writable CD drive, Zip drive, or floppy disk drive. If you have several backup options available, use the table in Figure 4-29 to evaluate the strengths and weaknesses of each one.

FIGURE 4-29
Storage Capacities
of Backup Media

	Device Cost	Media Cost	Capacity	Comments
Floppy disk	$20–$50	25¢	1.44 MB	Low capacity means that you have to wait around to feed in disks
Zip disk	$200 (average)	$9	750 MB	Holds much more than a floppy but a backup still requires multiple disks
External hard disk	$200 (average)	N/A	80 GB (average)	Fast and convenient, but might hold only one backup
Removable hard disk	$149 (average)	$100	2 GB (average)	Fast, limited capacity, but disks can be removed and locked in a secure location
CD-R	$50 (average)	50¢	680 MB	Limited capacity, can't be reused, long shelf life
CD-RW	$50 (average)	75¢	680 MB	Limited capacity, reusable, very slow
Writable DVD	$100 (average)	50¢	4.7 GB	Good capacity, reasonable media cost
Tape	$300 (average)	$50	40 GB (average)	Great capacity, reasonable media cost, convenient—you can let backups run overnight
USB Flash drive	$15–$500	N/A	32 MB–4 GB	Convenient and durable, but high-capacity models are expensive
Web site	N/A	$5.95 per month	N/A	Transfer rate depends on your Internet connection; security and privacy of your data might be a concern

DISK, CD, AND DVD BACKUP

What's the easiest way to back up my important data? Today, most computers are equipped with a writable CD or DVD drive with adequate storage capacity for a typical computer owner's data files. An easy way to back up your important data is simply copying selected files to a writable CD or DVD. No special software is necessary for this task. The software supplied with your CD or DVD writer includes a formatting routine that prepares a disk to hold data and allows you to select the files you want to copy, or "burn," as a backup.(Figure 4-30).

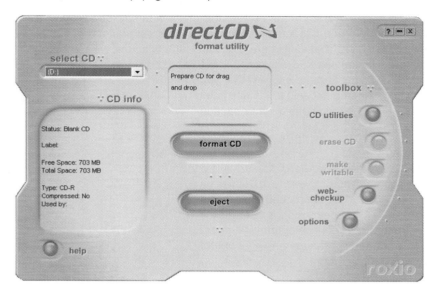

What are the limitations of CDs and DVDs? The major disadvantage of backing up your data on CDs and DVDs is that the writing process is slow—slower than writing data to tape or a removable hard disk. Further, although it is feasible to back up your entire system on a series of CDs or DVDs, you would have to use special backup software, monitor the backup process, and switch disks occasionally. CDs and DVDs are more practical for backing up a select group of important data files.

Unfortunately, if you simply back up data files, the process of restoring a crashed computer is cumbersome. You must load the operating system, device drivers, and application software from original distribution disks before copying your data from CDs or DVDs to your computer's hard disk.

Can I use floppy disks and Zip disks to back up my data? Floppy disks are inexpensive and just about every computer has a floppy disk drive. The 1.44 MB capacity of a floppy disk is suitable for storing several documents, but does not provide enough capacity for digital photos or most MP3 music files. If you have no other means to back up your data, at least copy your e-mail address book and important document files to floppy disks.

Zip disks with 100 MB or 250 MB capacity are sufficient for backups of documents and most digital graphics files. Several 750 MB Zip disks might be enough for backing up all your data files and could be feasible for a full-system backup if you have not installed lots of application software.

NETWORK AND INTERNET BACKUP

Can I store backup files on a network server? If your computer is connected to a local area network, you might be able to use the network server as a backup device. Before entrusting your data to a server, check with the network administrator to make sure you are allowed to store a large amount of data on the server. Because you might not want strangers to access your data, you should store it in a password-protected, non-shared folder. You also should make sure the server is backed up on a regular basis so that your backup data won't be wiped out by a server crash.

Can I store my backups on the Internet? Several Web sites offer fee-based backup storage space. When needed, you can simply download backup files from the Web site to your hard disk. These sites are practical for backups of your data files, but space limitations and download times make them impractical for a full-system backup. Experts suggest that you should not rely on a Web site as your only method of backup. If a site goes out of business or is the target of a Denial of Service attack, your backup data might not be accessible.

HARD DISK AND TAPE BACKUP

Can I back up to a second hard disk? A second hard disk drive is a good backup option—especially if it has equivalent capacity to your main hard disk. This capacity allows the backup process to proceed unattended because you won't have to swap disks or CDs. Speed-wise, a hard disk is faster than many tape drives. Unfortunately, like your computer's main hard disk, a backup hard disk is susceptible to head crashes, making it one of the least reliable storage options.

Internal hard disk drives are inexpensive, but they are not desirable backup devices because they are susceptible to electrical damage and any other catastrophe that besets your computer. External hard disk drives, like the one shown in Figure 4-31, are preferred for backups because they can be disconnected from your computer and stored in a safe place. An internal hard disk drive with removable disks is also an acceptable option because the disks can be removed for safe storage.

What about using a tape drive for backups? Tape drives are typically used in business computing situations, when a full-system backup is desirable. Some computer owners with a large amount of important data also install tape drives for their home systems. Tape drives are fairly inexpensive and fast enough to back up an entire hard disk in less than two hours. A tape drive with the capacity to hold the entire contents of a computer's hard disk can be left unattended as the backup proceeds. To make a tape backup, you typically use **backup software**—a set of utility programs designed to back up and restore files.

What does backup software do? Backup software usually includes options that make it easy to schedule periodic backups, define a set of files that you want to regularly back up, and automate the restoration process.

Backup software differs from most copy routines because it typically compresses all the files for a backup and places them in one large file. Under the direction of backup software, this file can spread across multiple tapes if necessary. The file is indexed so that individual files can be located, uncompressed, and restored.

Where can I get backup software? Backup software is supplied with most tape drives. Some versions of Windows include Microsoft Backup software, which you can usually find by clicking the Start button, and then

FIGURE 4-31

An external hard disk drive typically connects to your computer's USB port. The drive can easily be disconnected when not in use and stored in a safe place.

selecting Accessories and System Tools. You can also purchase and download backup software from companies that specialize in data protection software.

Whatever backup software you use, remember that it needs to be accessible when it comes time to restore your data. If the only copy of your backup software exists on your backup tapes, you will be in a Catch-22 situation. You won't be able to access your backup software until you restore the files from your backup, but you won't be able to restore your files until your backup software is running! Make sure you keep the original distribution CD for your backup software or a disk-based copy of any backup software you downloaded from the Web.

How do I use backup software? Backup software provides tools for scheduling backup dates and selecting the files you want to back up. The scheduling feature allows you to automate the backup process and reduces the chance that you'll forget to make regular backups. Backup software can also save time and storage space by offering options for full, differential, or incremental backups.

What is a full backup? A **full backup** makes a fresh copy of every file in the folders you've specified for the backup. In contrast to a full-system backup, a full backup does not necessarily contain every file on your computer. A full backup might contain only your data files, for example, if those are the files you want to regularly back up.

What is a differential backup? A **differential backup** makes a backup of only those files that were added or changed since your last full backup session. After making a full backup of your important files, you can make differential backups at regular intervals. If you need to restore all your files after a hard disk crash, first restore the files from your full backup, and then restore the files from your latest differential backup.

What is an incremental backup? An **incremental backup** makes a backup of the files that were added or changed since the last backup—not necessarily the files that changed from the last full backup, but the files that changed since any full or incremental backup. After making a full backup of your important files, you can make your first incremental backup containing the files that changed since the full backup. When you make your second incremental backup, it will contain only the files that changed since the first incremental backup. To restore files from an incremental backup, files from a full backup are restored first, followed by files from each incremental backup, starting with the oldest and ending with the most recent. The video associated with Figure 4-32 describes the difference between full, differential, and incremental backups.

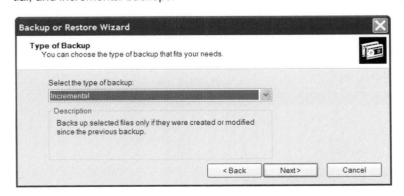

FIGURE 4-32

Full, incremental, and differential backups each take a slightly different approach to backing up files.

CLICK TO START

How many backup tapes do I need? Computer systems with tape back-up usually contain essential business data, and it is critical that data from the backups can be restored in case of a hard disk crash. In this situation, one backup tape is not sufficient. Data security experts recommend maintaining a rotating set of backups—typically using three backup tapes.

To maintain a rotating backup, use one tape for the first backup, and then use a different tape for the next backup. Use another tape for the third backup. For the fourth backup, you can overwrite the data on the first backup tape; for the fifth backup, overwrite the data on the second tape, and so on. So that you know which backup is the most recent, write the date of the backup on the tape label.

How can I be sure that my tape backup works? If your computer's hard disk crashes, you do not want to discover that your backup tapes are blank! To prevent such a disastrous situation, it is important to enable the "read after write" or "compare" option backup software provides. These options force the software to check the data in each sector as it is written to make sure it is copied without error. You should also test your backup by trying to restore one file. Try it with one of your least important data files, just in case your backup is faulty.

BOOT AND RECOVERY DISKS

What is a boot disk? If your computer's hard disk is out of commission, you might wonder how it can access the operating system files needed to carry out the boot process. If your hard disk failed or a virus wiped out the boot sector files on your hard disk, you will not be able to use your normal boot procedure.

A **boot disk** is a floppy disk or CD containing the operating system files needed to boot your computer without accessing the hard disk. A bare-bones boot disk simply loads the operating system kernel. You can make a boot disk using My Computer or Windows Explorer, as shown in Figure 4-33. The boot disk you create, however, boots DOS, not Windows.

FIGURE 4-33

To create an MS-DOS boot disk, insert a blank floppy disk in drive A. Open My Computer or Windows Explorer, and then right-click the Drive A icon. Select Format and check the box labeled Create an MS-DOS startup disk.

A more sophisticated boot disk—sometimes referred to as a **recovery CD**—loads hardware drivers and user settings as well as the operating system. Recovery CDs are sometimes included with new computer systems. Some computer manufacturer Web sites offer a download that creates a recovery CD. The operating system might also supply a method for creating recovery CDs. For example, the Windows XP Backup utility creates a set of **Automated System Recovery** disks (Figure 4-34).

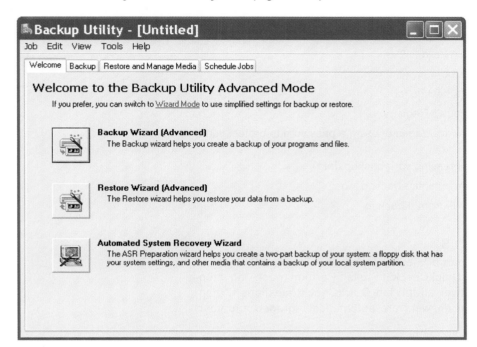

FIGURE 4-34

Windows XP includes an Automated System Recovery Wizard that helps you create a boot disk containing your system settings.

The contents and capabilities of recovery CDs vary. Some are designed to restore your computer to its "like new" state and wipe out all your data. Others attempt to restore user settings, programs, and data. Before you depend on a recovery CD, make sure you know what it contains and how to use it in case of a system failure.

QUICKCHECK......SECTION D

1. When backing up selected files, rather than making a full backup, you should make a copy of the Windows [ ] and keep it updated every time you install new hardware or software.

2. The backup process is simplified if you store all your important data files in a single [ ].

3. One of the best devices for home backup is a(n) [ ] hard disk drive.

4. A(n) [ ] backup copies only those files that have changed since your last backup session.

5. A(n) [ ] CD helps restore a computer system by loading hardware drivers and user settings as well as the operating system.

 CHECK ANSWERS

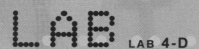

LAB 4-D

BACKING UP YOUR COMPUTER

In this lab, you'll learn:

- How to start the Windows Backup utility
- How to use the Backup Wizard
- How to create a backup job
- Which files to select for a backup job
- How to back up the Windows Registry
- The advantages and disadvantages of using a password to protect your backup data
- The implications of compressing your backup data
- How to restore data from an entire backup job
- How to restore a single file from a backup

INTERACTIVE LAB

CLICK TO START THE LAB

LAB ASSIGNMENTS

1. Start the interactive part of the lab. Insert your Tracking Disk if you want to save your QuickCheck results. Perform each lab step as directed, and answer all the lab QuickCheck questions. When you exit the lab, your answers are automatically graded and your results are displayed.

2. Describe where most of your data files are stored, and estimate how many megabytes of data (not programs) you have in all these files. Next, take a close look at these files and estimate how much data (in megabytes) you cannot afford to lose. Finally, explain what you think would be the best hardware device for backing up this amount of data.

3. Draw a sketch or capture a screenshot of the Microsoft Backup window's toolbar. Use ToolTips, ScreenTips, or the window's status bar to find the name of each toolbar button. Use this information to label the buttons on your sketch or screenshot.

4. Assume that you will use Microsoft Backup to make a backup of your data files. Describe the backup job you would create—specify the folders you must include. It is not necessary to list individual files unless they are not within one of the folders you would back up. Make sure you indicate whether you would use password protection, the type of compression you would select, and how you would handle the Windows Registry.

TECHTALK

FILE FORMATS

As you learned earlier in the chapter, the way data is stored in a file is referred to as its file format (or file type) and is indicated by its file extension. Most computer users quickly catch on to the basic idea that a file extension provides a clue as to which application software is needed to open the file. For example, files with .doc extensions typically can be opened using Microsoft Word.

Although a basic understanding of file formats might be sufficient for computer "newbies," a more in-depth understanding can come in handy. This TechTalk is designed to take your current knowledge of file formats in the Windows environment and kick it up a notch so that you'll become more adept at using and manipulating the files stored on your computer.

Why should I know about file formats? Some operating systems do a fairly good job of shielding users from the intricacies of file formats. For example, Windows uses a file association list to link a file extension to its corresponding application software. This handy feature allows you to open a data file without first opening an application, simply by double-clicking the file from within Windows Explorer or selecting it from the Documents list that's accessible from the Start menu.

Of course, your application software also shields you from the messy task of searching through directories to find the files it will open. When you use the Open dialog box, most applications automatically comb through the files on a specified device and in a specified folder to display only those that have the "right" file extensions.

With all this help from the operating system and your application software, it might seem that knowing about file formats is unimportant. You might, however, find it useful to understand file formats so that you can easily accomplish tasks such as those listed in Figure 4-35.

What determines a file's format? Although a file extension is a good indicator of a file's format, it does not really define the format. You could use the Rename command to change a QuickTime movie called Balloons.mov to Balloons.doc. Despite the .doc extension, the file is still in QuickTime format because the data elements in the file are arranged in a specific configuration unique to QuickTime.

The format of a file might include a header, data, and possibly an end-of-file marker. You might recall that file headers were defined in Chapter 2. A file header is a section of data at the beginning of a file that contains information about a file—typically the date it was created, the date it was last updated, its size, and its file type.

A file header should not be confused with the headers appearing at the top of each page in a document created with a word processor. Instead, envision a file header as a hidden Post-It note that's attached to the beginning of a file. Although it is hidden to users, computers can read the information in a file header to determine the file's format.

FIGURE 4-35

Understanding file formats helps you perform the following tasks:

- Figure out the correct format for e-mail attachments that you send to friends or colleagues.

- Find the right player software for music and media files that you download from the Web.

- Discover how to work with a file that doesn't seem to open.

- Convert files from one format to another.

The remaining contents of a file depend on whether it contains text, graphics, audio, or multimedia data. A text file, for example, might contain sentences and paragraphs interspersed with codes for centering, boldfacing, and margin settings. A graphics file might contain color data for each pixel, followed by a description of the color palette. The file format dictates the arrangement of this data. Figure 4-36 illustrates the layout for a Windows bitmap file and contrasts it with the layout of a GIF file.

Bitmap File Format	GIF File Format
File header	File header
Bitmap header	Logical screen descriptor
Color palette	Global color table
Bitmap data	Local image descriptor
	Local color table
	Image data
	End-of-file character

FIGURE 4-36
Although bitmap and GIF file formats contain graphics, the file layouts differ.

Which file formats am I most likely to encounter? A software program typically consists of at least one executable file with an .exe file extension. It might also include a number of support programs with extensions such as .dll, .vbx, and .ocx. Configuration and startup files usually have .bat, .sys, .ini, and .bin extensions. In addition, you'll find files with .hlp and .tmp extensions. Files with .hlp extensions hold the information for a program's Help utility. Files with .tmp extensions are temporary files. When you open a data file with software applications, such as word processors, spreadsheets, and graphics tools, your operating system makes a copy of the original file and stores this copy on disk as a temporary file. It is this temporary file that you work with as you view and revise a file.

To the uninitiated, the file extensions associated with programs and the operating system might seem odd. Nevertheless, executable and support files—even so-called temporary files—are crucial for the correct operation of your computer system. You should not manually delete them unless they become corrupted. The table in Figure 4-37 lists the file extensions typically associated with the operating system and executable files.

INFOWEBLINKS

The **File Formats InfoWeb** provides a list of file extensions and their corresponding software.

www.course.com/np/concepts8/ch04

FIGURE 4-37
OS and Executable Extensions

Type of File	Description	Extension
Batch file	A sequence of operating system commands executed automatically when the computer boots	.bat
Configuration file	Information about programs the computer uses to allocate the resources necessary to run them	.cfg .sys .mif .bin .ini
Help	The information displayed by online Help	.hlp
Temporary file	A sort of "scratch pad" that contains data while a file is open, but is discarded when you close the file	.tmp
Support program	Program instructions executed along with the main .exe file for a program	.ocx .vbx .vbs .dll
Program	The main executable files for a computer program	.exe .com

The list of data file formats is long, but becoming familiar with the most popular formats and the type of data they contain is useful. Figure 4-38 provides this information in a convenient table. Where noted, a file format is associated with a particular software program.

FIGURE 4-38
Data File Extensions

Type of File	Extension
Text	.txt .dat .rtf .doc (Microsoft Word and WordPad) .wpd (WordPerfect)
Sound	.wav .mid .mp3 .au .ra (RealAudio)
Graphics	.bmp .pcx .tif .wmf .gif .jpg .png .eps .ai (Adobe Illustrator)
Animation/video	.flc .fli .avi .mpg .mov (QuickTime) .rm (RealMedia)
Web pages	.htm .html .asp .vrml
Spreadsheets	.xls (Microsoft Excel) .wks (Lotus 1-2-3) .dif
Database	.mdb (Microsoft Access)
Miscellaneous	.pdf (Adobe Acrobat) .ppt (Microsoft PowerPoint) .zip (WinZip) .pub (Microsoft Publisher) .qxd (QuarkExpress)

How do I know which files a program will open? A software application can open files that exist in its native file format, plus several additional file formats. For example, Microsoft Word opens files in its native DOC format, plus files in formats such as HTML (.htm or .html), Text (.txt), and Rich Text Format (.rtf). Within the Windows environment, you can discover which formats a particular software program can open by looking at the *Files of type* list in the Open dialog box, as shown in Figure 4-39.

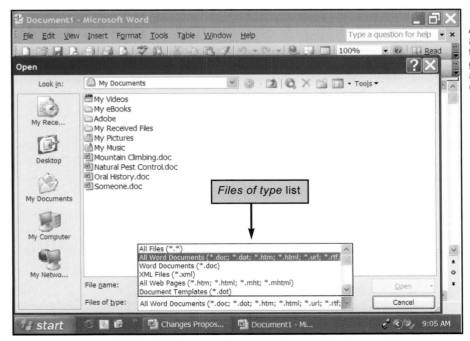

Why can't I open some files? Suppose you receive an e-mail attachment called Cool.tif. "Aha!" you say to yourself, "My Photoshop software ought to open that file." You try—several times—but all you get is an error message. When a file doesn't open, one of three things probably went wrong:

- The file might have been damaged—a techie would call it "corrupted"—by a transmission or disk error. Although you might be able to use special file recovery software to repair the damage, it is usually easier to obtain an undamaged copy of the file from its original source.

- Someone might have inadvertently changed the file extension. While renaming the Cool file, perhaps the original .bmp extension was changed to .tif. If you have a little time, you can change the file extension and try to open the file. If a file contains a graphic, chances are that it should have the extension for one of the popular graphics formats, such as .bmp, .gif, .jpg, .tif, or .pcx. Otherwise, you should contact the source of the file to get accurate information about its real format.

- Some file formats exist in several variations, and your software might not have the capability to open a particular variation of the format. You might be able to open the file if you use different application software. For example, Photoshop might not be able to open a particular file with a .tif file extension, but CorelDraw might open it.

What if all my software fails to open a particular file format? Although a computer might be able to discover a file's format, it might not necessarily know how to work with it. Just as you might be able to identify a helicopter, you can't necessarily fly it without some instructions. Your computer also requires a set of instructions to use most file formats. These instructions are provided by software. To use a particular file format, you must make sure your computer has the corresponding software.

Suppose you download a file with a .rm extension and none of your current software works with this file format. Several Web sites provide lists of file extensions and their corresponding software. By looking up a file extension in one of these lists, you can find out what application software you'll need to find, buy, download, and install.

Many files downloaded from the Web require special "player" or "reader" software. For example, PDF text files require software called Acrobat Reader, MP3 music files require software called an MP3 player, and RM video files require the RealMedia Player software. Typically, you can follow a link from the Web page that supplied your file download to find a site from which you can download the necessary player or reader software.

How do I know what kinds of file formats I can send to my friends, colleagues, and instructor? Unless you know what application software is installed on your friends' computers, you won't know for certain whether they can open a particular file you've sent. There's a good chance, however, that your friends can open files saved in common file formats represented by the extensions listed in Figure 4-40. You should check with the recipient before sending files in less common, proprietary formats, such as Adobe Illustrator's AI format and QuarkExpress's QXD format.

Is it possible to convert a file from one format to another? Perhaps you created a Word document on your PC, but you need to convert it into a format that's usable by your colleague who owns a Mac. Or suppose you want to convert a Word document into HTML format so that you can post it on the Web. You might also want to convert a Windows bitmap (.bmp)

FIGURE 4-40
Extensions for Common
File Formats

.bmp	.tif
.gif	.doc
.txt	.wav
.jpg	.mid
.htm	.html
.xls	.rtf
.mp3	.aac
.wmv	.wma

graphic into GIF format so that you can include it on a Web page. The easiest way to convert a file from one format to another is to find an application program that works with both file formats. Open the file using that software, and then use the Export option, or the Save As dialog box, to select a new file format, assign the file a new name, and save it (Figure 4-41).

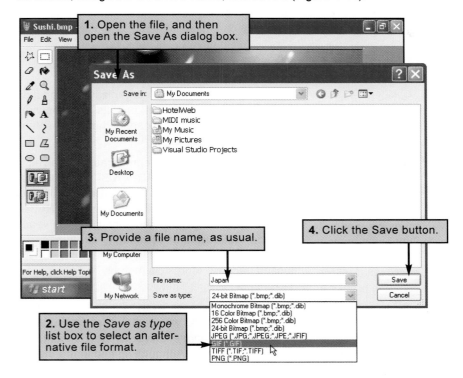

1. Open the file, and then open the Save As dialog box.

3. Provide a file name, as usual.

4. Click the Save button.

2. Use the *Save as type* list box to select an alternative file format.

FIGURE 4-41

An easy way to convert a file from one format to another is to open it with an application that supports both file formats, and then use the Save As dialog box to select an alternative file format.

CLICK TO START

Many file formats convert easily to another format, and the resulting file is virtually indistinguishable from the original. Some conversions, however, do not retain all the characteristics of the original file. When you convert a DOC file into HTML format, for example, the HTML page does not contain any of the headers, footers, superscripts, page numbers, special characters, or page breaks that existed in the original DOC file.

When you need a conversion routine for an obscure file format, or if you need to convert between many different file formats, consider specialized conversion software, available through commercial or shareware outlets.

INFOWEBLINKS

Conversion software runs the gamut from simple shareware to "industrial-strength" commercial packages. The **Conversion Software InfoWeb** will help you compare what's available.

www.course.com/np/concepts8/ch04

QUICKCHECK........TECHTALK

1. A file [_____] is a section of data at the beginning of a file that contains information about the file type.

2. File extensions, such as .ocx, .vbx, .vbs, and .dll, typically indicate [_____] programs.

3. The [_____] file format for Microsoft Word is DOC.

4. [_____] software can help you transform one file type into a different file type.

 CHECK ANSWERS

ISSUE

COMPUTER CRIME

It doesn't take any special digital expertise to master-mind some computer crimes. Setting fire to a computer doesn't require the same finesse as writing a stealthy virus, but both can have the same disastrous effect on data. "Old-fashioned" crimes, such as arson, that take a high-tech twist because they involve a computer can be prosecuted under traditional laws.

Traditional laws do not, however, cover the range of possibilities for computer crimes. Suppose a person unlawfully enters a computer facility and steals backup tapes. That person might be prosecuted for breaking and entering. But would common breaking and entering laws apply to a person who uses an off-site terminal to "enter" a computer system without authorization? And what if a person copies a data file without authorization? Has that file really been "stolen" if the original remains on the computer?

Many countries have computer crime laws that specifically define computer data and software as personal property. These laws also define as crimes the unauthorized access, use, modification, or disabling of a computer system or data. But laws don't necessarily stop criminals. If they did, we wouldn't have to deal with malicious code and intrusions.

Computer Crime Gambits

Data diddling: Unauthorized alterations to data stored on a computer system, such as a student changing grades stored in a school's computer.

Identity theft: Unauthorized copying of personal information, such as credit card numbers, passwords, social security numbers, and bank account PINs.

Salami shaving: Redirecting small, unnoticeable amounts of money from large amounts.

Denial of Service: An attempt to disrupt the operations of a network or computer system, usually by flooding it with data traffic.

Information theft: Unauthorized access to a computer system, such as military or government computers, to gain restricted information.

Virus distribution: Launching viruses, worms, and Trojan horses.

Vandalism: Intentional defacement of Web sites.

Computer crimes—costly to organizations and individuals—include a variety of gambits, such as virus distribution, data diddling, identity theft, and salami shaving.

One of the first computer crime cases involved a worm unleashed on the ARPANET in 1990 that quickly spread through government and university computer systems. The worm's author, Robert Morris, was convicted and sentenced to three years' probation, 400 hours of community service, and a $10,000 fine. This relatively lenient sentence was imposed because Morris claimed he had not intended to cripple the entire network.

A 1995 high-profile case involved a computer hacker named Kevin Mitnick, who was accused of breaking into dozens of corporate, university, government, and personal computers. Although vilified in the media, Mitnick had the support of many hackers and other people who believed that the prosecution grossly exaggerated the extent of his crimes. Nonetheless, Mitnick was sentenced to 46 months in prison and ordered to pay restitution in the amount of $4,125 during his three-year period of supervised release. The prosecution was horrified by such a paltry sum—an amount that was much less than its request for $1.5 million in restitution.

Forbes reporter Adam L. Penenberg took issue with the 46-month sentence imposed by Judge Marianne Pfaelzer and wrote, "This in a country where the average prison term for manslaughter is three years. Mitnick's crimes were curiously innocuous. He broke into corporate computers, but no evidence indicates that he destroyed data. Or sold anything he copied. Yes, he pilfered software—but in doing so left it behind. This world of bits is a strange one, in which you can take something and still leave it for its rightful owner. The theft laws designed for payroll sacks and motor vehicles just don't apply to a hacker."

In 1999, Melissa virus author David L. Smith pleaded guilty in federal court to purposely spreading a computer virus with the intent to cause damage. The charge carried a maximum prison sentence of five years and a $250,000 fine. Smith received a more lenient sentence: 20 months in prison, 3 additional years of supervised release, 100 hours of community service, and a $5,000 fine. Analyst Lorna Koetzle remarked: "It is a stiff sentence akin to a zero tolerance approach, but the people who commit these attacks believe that only the stupid get caught and that they are not stupid."

More recently, officials made two arrests in connection with the Blaster worm. A 24-year-old Romanian and an American teenager apparently downloaded copies of the worm source code, altered it slightly, and sent their versions back out again. The Romanian was allegedly angered by his treatment by one of his professors. The American teenager was just trying to see what he could get away with.

Under Romanian law, distributing a virus can mean a 15 year prison sentence. The U.S. Patriot Act and the Cyber-Security Enhancement Act carry even stiffer penalties—anywhere from 10 years to life in prison.

A CNET reporter questions the fairness of such penalties: "What bothers me most is that here in the United States, rapists serve, on average, 10 years in prison. Yet if, instead of assaulting another human being, that same person had released a virus on the Net, the criminal would get the same or an even harsher sentence."

Law makers hope that stiff penalties will deter cyber criminals. U.S. Attorney John McKay is quoted as saying, "Let there be no mistake about it, cyber-hacking is a crime. It harms persons, it harms individuals, it harms businesses. We will investigate, track down and prosecute cyber-hackers."

These cases illustrate our culture's ambivalent attitude toward computer hackers. On the one hand, they are viewed as evil cyberterrorists who are set on destroying the glue that binds together the Information Age. From this perspective, hackers are criminals who must be hunted down, forced to make restitution for damages, and prevented from creating further havoc.

From another perspective, hackers are viewed more as Casper the Friendly Ghost in our complex cyber-machines—as moderately bothersome entities whose pranks are tolerated by the computer community, along with software bugs and hardware glitches. Seen from this perspective, a hacker's pranks are part of the normal course of study that leads to the highest echelons of computer expertise. "Everyone has done it," claim devotees, "even Bill Gates (founder of Microsoft) and Steve Jobs (founder of Apple Computer)."

Which perspective is right? Are hackers dangerous cyberterrorists or harmless pranksters? Before you make up your mind about computer hacking and cracking, you might want to further investigate several landmark cases by following links at the Computer Crime InfoWeb.

INFOWEBLINKS

Who's in the cybercrime news? How are cybercriminals caught? The **Computer Crime InfoWeb** provides answers to these questions and more.

www.course.com/np/concepts8/ch04

WHAT DO YOU THINK?

1. Should a computer virus distribution sentence carry the same penalty as manslaughter? ⭘Yes ⭘No ⭘Not sure

2. Should it be a crime to steal a copy of computer data while leaving the original data in place and unaltered? ⭘Yes ⭘No ⭘Not sure

3. Should hackers be sent to jail if they cannot pay restitution to companies and individuals who lost money as the result of a prank? ⭘Yes ⭘No ⭘Not sure

4. Do you think that a hacker would make a good consultant on computer security? ⭘Yes ⭘No ⭘Not sure

⬧ SAVE RESPONSES

COMPUTERS IN CONTEXT

LAW ENFORCEMENT

Sirens wail. Blue lights strobe the night. A speeding car slows and pulls off to the side of the road. It looks like a routine traffic stop, but the patrol car is outfitted with a mobile data computer. The police officers on this high-tech force have already checked the speeding car's license plate number and description against a database of stolen cars and cars allegedly used in kidnapping and other crimes.

Mounted in the dashboard of marked and unmarked police cars, a mobile data computer resembles a notebook computer with its flat-panel screen and compact keyboard. Unlike a consumer-grade notebook, however, the computers in police cruisers use hardened technology designed to withstand extreme conditions, such as high temperatures in parked vehicles. The dashboard-mounted computer communicates with an office-based server using a wireless link, such as short-range radio, CDPD (cellular digital packet data) technology, or Wi-Fi. With this wireless link, police officers can access data from local, state, and national databases.

One national database, the National Crime Information Center (NCIC), is maintained by the FBI and can be accessed by authorized personnel in local, state, and federal law enforcement agencies. The system can process more than 2.4 million queries per day related to stolen vehicles, wanted criminals, missing persons, violent gang members, stolen guns, and members of terrorist organizations.

The officers who pulled over the speeding car received information from the NCIC that the car was stolen, so they arrested the car's occupant and took him to the police station for booking.

At the police station, digital cameras flash and the suspect's mug shot is automatically entered into an automated warrants and booking system. The system stores the suspect's complete biographical and arrest information, such as name, aliases, addresses, social security number, charges, and arrest date. The system also checks for outstanding warrants against the suspect, such as warrants for other thefts. Booking agents can enter those charges into the system, assign the new inmate to a cell, log his personal items, and print a photo ID or wrist band.

Automated warrants and booking systems have been proved to increase police productivity. New York City's system handles more than 300,000 bookings per year, with gains in productivity that have put nearly 300 officers back into action investigating crimes and patrolling neighborhoods.

As part of the booking process, the suspect is fingerprinted. A standard fingerprint card, sometimes called a "ten-print card," contains inked prints of the fingers on each hand, plus name, date of birth, and other arrest information. Now, however, instead of using ink, a biometric scanning device can electronically capture fingerprints. Text information is entered via keyboard and stored with digital fingerprint images.

The fingerprint information can be transmitted in digital format from local law enforcement agencies to the FBI's Automated Fingerprint Identification System

(AFIS). This biometric identification methodology uses digital imaging technology to analyze fingerprint data. Using sophisticated algorithms, AFIS can classify arriving prints for storage or search the collection of 600 million fingerprint cards for matching prints.

Conventional crimes, such as car theft, are often solved by using standard investigative techniques with information from computer databases. To solve cybercrimes, however, often the special skills of computer forensic investigators are required.

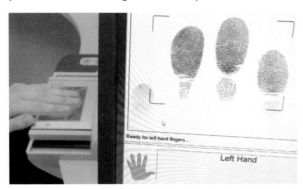

Ready for left hand fingers...

Left Hand

Computer forensics is the scientific examination and analysis of data located on computer storage media, conducted to offer evidence of computer crimes in court. Computer crimes can be separated into two categories. The first includes crimes that use computers, such as transmitting trade secrets to competitors, reproducing copyrighted material, and distributing child pornography. The second includes crimes targeted at computers, such as Denial of Service attacks on servers, Web site vandalism, data theft, and destructive viruses. Computer forensics can be applied to both categories.

Whether a computer is suspected as the origin of a cyber attack or is suspected of holding evidence, the first step in the forensic process is to use disk imaging software to make an exact replica of the information stored on the hard disk. The disk image is then collected on a write-once medium that cannot be altered with "planted" evidence, and the forensic scientist begins analyzing the disk image data with simple search software that looks through files for keywords related to the crime. In the case of the "Gap-Toothed Bandit" who was convicted for robbing nine banks, analysis of the disk image revealed word processing files containing notes he handed to tellers demanding money.

Criminals typically attempt to delete files with incriminating evidence, but a good forensic scientist can retrieve data from deleted files with undelete software or data recovery software. Temporary Internet or cache files can also yield evidence, pointing law enforcement officers to Web sites the suspect visited that might be fronts for illegal activity.

When a computer is a target of a cyber attack, forensic investigators use three techniques to track the source. The first option is to make an immediate image of the server's hard disk and look through its log files for evidence of activity coming from unauthorized IP addresses. A second technique is to monitor the intruder by watching login attempts, changes to log files, and file access requests. Sophisticated intruders might be able to detect such monitoring, however, and cover their tracks. A third technique is to create a "honeypot"—an irresistible computer system or Web site containing fake information that allows investigators to monitor hackers until identification is possible.

Despite the many techniques and tools available to forensic investigators, they have three main constraints. First, they must adhere to privacy regulations and obtain warrants to set up wiretaps or gather information from ISPs about their customers. Second, they must scrupulously document their procedures so that the evidence they produce cannot be discredited in court as "planted" or fabricated. Third, forensic investigators must examine a wide range of alternatives pertaining to the crime, such as the chance that an IP or e-mail address used to commit a cybercrime doesn't belong to an innocent bystander being spoofed by the real hacker.

Privacy, documentation, and evidentiary constraints cost forensic investigators time, and failure to adhere to strict standards can sometimes allow criminals to avoid conviction and penalties. But even within these constraints, careful forensic investigation is an important aspect of catching and convicting high-tech criminals.

INFOWEBLINKS

For more information about police and FBI technology, connect to the **Computers in Law Enforcement InfoWeb**.

www.course.com/np/concepts8/ch04

INTERACTIVE SUMMARY

To review important concepts from this chapter, fill in the blanks to best complete each sentence. When using the NP8 BookOnCD, click the Check Answers buttons to automatically score your answers. Place your Tracking Disk in the floppy disk drive if you want to save your scores.

A computer [_____] is a named collection of data that exists on a storage medium, such as a hard disk, floppy disk, CD, DVD, or tape. Every file has a name and might also have a file extension. The rules for naming a file are called file-naming [_____]. These rules typically do not allow you to use certain characters or [_____] words in a file name. A file [_____] is usually related to a file format, which is defined as the arrangement of data in a file and the coding scheme used to represent the data. A software program's [_____] file format is the default format for storing files created with that program.

A file's location is defined by a file [_____] (sometimes called a "path"), which includes the storage device, folder(s), file name, and extension. In Windows, storage devices are identified by a drive letter, followed by a [_____]. An operating system maintains a list of files called a directory for each storage disk, tape, CD, or DVD. The main directory of a disk is sometimes referred to as the [_____] directory, which can be subdivided into several smaller lists called subdirectories that are depicted as [_____].

CHECK ANSWERS

File [_____] encompasses any procedure that helps you organize your computer-based files so that you can find and use them more effectively. [_____]-based file management uses tools provided with a software program to open and save files. Additional tools might also allow you to create new folders, rename files, and delete files. The Save and Save As dialog boxes are examples of these file management tools.

Most operating systems provide file management [_____] that give you the "big picture" of the files you have stored on your disks. The structure of folders that you envision on your disk is a logical model, which is often represented by a storage [_____], such as a tree structure or filing cabinet. Windows Explorer is an example of a file management utility provided by an operating system. Windows Explorer allows you to find, rename, copy, move, and delete files and folders. In addition, it allows you to perform these file management activities with more than one file at a time.

The way that data is actually stored is referred to as the [_____] storage model. Before a computer stores data on a disk, CD, or DVD, it creates the equivalent of electronic storage bins by dividing the disk into [_____], and then further dividing the disk into [_____]. This dividing process is referred to as [_____]. Each sector of a disk is numbered, providing a storage address that the operating system can track. Many computers work with a group of sectors, called a [_____], to increase the efficiency of file storage operations. An operating system uses a file system to track the physical location of files. The file system for Windows 95, 98, and Me is called FAT32; for Windows NT, 2000, and XP, it is called [_____].

CHECK ANSWERS

A computer virus is a set of program instructions that attaches itself to a file, reproduces itself, and spreads to other files. You might encounter several types of viruses. A virus that attaches itself to an application program, such as a game utility, is known as a [_____] virus. A boot [_____] virus infects the system files your computer uses every time you turn it on. A [_____] virus infects a set of instructions that automates document and worksheet production.

A Trojan horse is a computer program that seems to perform one function while actually doing something else. Such programs are notorious for stealing [_____], although some delete files and cause other problems.

A [_____] is a program designed to spread from computer to computer. Most take advantage of communications networks—especially the Internet—to travel within e-mail and TCP/IP packets, jumping from one computer to another. Today, mass [_____] worms, such as MyDoom, are one of the most common threats to computer networks. Many worms are designed to trigger Denial of [_____] attacks that flood networks and block access to servers.

[_____] threats that combine a worm or Trojan horse with a virus are becoming more prevalent.

Viruses can slip into your computer from a variety of sources, such as floppy disks, homemade CDs, and Web sites that contain games and other supposedly fun stuff. E-mail [_____] are another common source of viruses. HTML-formatted e-mail is susceptible to viruses and worms hidden in program-like "scripts" that are embedded in HTML tags.

[_____] software can help prevent viruses from invading your computer system and can root out viruses that take up residence. This software typically scans for a virus [_____] and is sometimes referred to as virus scanning software.

CHECK ANSWERS

A backup is a copy of one or more files that has been made in case the original files become damaged. For safety, a backup is usually stored on a different storage medium from the original files. A good backup plan allows you to [_____] your computing environment to its pre-disaster state with a minimum of fuss.

No single backup plan fits everyone's computing style or budget. Your personal backup plan depends on the files you need to back up, the hardware you have available to make backups, and your backup software. In any case, it is a good idea to back up the Windows [_____] and make sure your files are free of [_____]. Backups should be stored in a safe place, away from the computer.

Backups can be recorded on floppy disks, writable CDs and DVDs, networks, Web sites, a second hard disk, or tapes. Many computer owners depend on writable CDs for backups, and use My Computer or Windows [_____] to simply select files and copy files to the backup. [_____] drives and backup software are typically used in business situations when a full-system backup is desirable. Backup software differs from most copy routines because it [_____] all the files for a backup into one large file.

In addition to file backups, you should have a [_____] disk containing the operating system files and settings needed to start your computer without accessing the hard disk.

CHECK ANSWERS

INTERACTIVE KEY TERMS

Make sure you understand all the boldfaced key terms presented in this chapter. If you're using the NP8 BookOnCD, you can use this list of terms as an interactive study activity. First, try to define a term in your own words, and then click the term to compare your definition with the definition presented in the chapter.

Antivirus software, 196
Automated System Recovery, 207
Backdoor, 193
Backup, 199
Backup software, 204
Blended threat, 193
Boot disk, 206
Boot sector virus, 192
Checksum, 196
Cluster, 187
Computer virus, 191
Defragmentation utility, 189
Denial of Service attack, 195
Differential backup, 205
Directory, 178
FAT32, 187
File Allocation Table, 187
File date, 179
File format, 177
File management utilities, 182
File-naming conventions, 176
File shredder software, 188
File size, 179
File specification, 178
File system, 187
File virus, 192
Folders, 178

Formatting, 186
Formatting utilities, 187
Fragmented files, 189
Full backup, 205
Full-system backup, 200
Incremental backup, 205
Logical storage models, 183
Macro virus, 192
Malicious code, 191
Mass-mailing worm, 193
Master File Table, 187
Multi-partite viruses, 197
Native file format, 177
NTFS, 187
Path, 178
Payload, 191
Physical storage model, 186
Polymorphic viruses, 197
Recovery CD, 207
Reserved words, 177
Restore, 200
Retro viruses, 196
Root directory, 178
Sectors, 186
Spoofed address, 193
Stealth viruses, 197
Storage metaphor, 183

Subdirectory, 178
Tracks, 186
Trigger event, 191
Trojan horse, 192
Virus hoax, 197
Virus signature, 197
Windows Explorer, 184
Worm, 193

INTERACTIVE SITUATION QUESTIONS

Apply what you've learned to some typical computing situations. When using the NP8 BookOnCD, you can type your answers, and then use the Check Answers button to automatically score your responses. Place your Tracking Disk in the floppy disk drive if you want to save your scores.

1. Suppose you are using Microsoft Word and you want to open a file. When your software lists the documents you can open, you can expect them to be in Word's [_____] file format, which is DOC.

2. Can you use a Windows application, create a document, and store it using the file name I L*ve NY ? Yes or no? [_____]

3. When you want to work with several files—to move them to different folders, for example—it would be most efficient to use a file management utility, such as Windows [_____].

4. When specifying a location for a data file on your hard disk, you should avoid saving it in the [_____] directory.

5. Suppose you have a floppy disk containing data you no longer need. You can use a(n) [_____] utility to erase the data on the disk and re-create all the tracks and sectors on the disk.

6. You have an old computer that you will donate to a school, but you want to make sure its hard disk contains no trace of your data. To do so, you should use file [_____] software that overwrites "empty" sectors with random 1s and 0s.

7. You receive e-mail from PayPal asking you to renew your account by entering your current user ID and password. You assume that a hacker is using [_____] engineering to make a Trojan horse appear to be a legitimate message.

8. You receive an e-mail message that says, "Your computer has contracted a virus. You can remove it by using the program attached to this message." Would you assume that this message is a hoax? Yes or no? [_____]

9. You just bought a tape drive and you make a full-system backup. Before you depend on this backup, you should [_____] it to make sure you can successfully restore the data in the event of a hard disk crash.

10. Your hard disk crashed for some unknown reason. Now when you switch on the computer power, all you get is an "Error reading drive C:" message. Your first reaction should be to reach for a(n) [_____] CD that contains the operating system files and device drivers needed to start your computer without accessing the hard disk.

 CHECK ANSWERS

INTERACTIVE PRACTICE TESTS

Practice tests that consist of 10 multiple-choice, true/false, and fill-in-the-blank questions are available on both the NP8 BookOnCD and the NP8 Web site. The questions are selected at random from a large test bank, so each time you take a test, you'll receive a different set of questions. Your tests are scored immediately, and you can print study guides that help you find the correct answers for any questions that you missed.

www.course.com/np/concepts8/ch04

CLICK ✦ TO START

REVIEW
ON THE WEB

PROJECTS

An NP8 Project is an open-ended activity that helps you apply the concepts you have learned. Many projects require resources in addition to your textbook, such as current magazines, library materials, or Web access. When you tackle a project, be prepared to use your critical thinking skills, logical analysis, and creativity. Projects for this chapter include:

- **Issue Research: Computer Crime**
- **Hoax!**
- **Computer Forensics**
- **Antivirus Software**
- **Cyber Crime**
- **Biometrics**
- **Web Backup Sites**

To work with the Projects for this chapter, connect to the **New Perspectives NP8 Web Site.**

www.course.com/np/concepts8/ch04

TECHTV VIDEO PROJECT

The TechTV segment *MS Windows Security Hole* highlights one of many security problems that plague computer owners. After watching the video, write a short description of the security hole, and discuss how it relates to hackers, viruses, and worms. Explore the Microsoft Web site *www.microsoft.com* and list any security updates needed by your computer. If you are using your own personal computer, you can install these updates. If you are working on a lab computer, obtain permission from the lab manager before installing Windows updates.

To work with the Video Projects for this chapter, connect to the **New Perspectives NP8 Web Site.**

www.course.com/np/concepts8/ch04

STUDY TIPS

Study Tips help you to organize and consolidate the information in a chapter by making lists, outlines, charts, and sketches. You can use paper and pencil or word processing software to complete most of the Study Tips.

To work with the Study Tips for this chapter, connect to the **New Perspectives NP8 Web Site.**

www.course.com/np/concepts8/ch04

ONLINE GAMES

Test your comprehension of the concepts introduced in Chapter 4 by playing the NP8 Online Games. At the end of each game, you have three options:

- Print a comprehensive study guide complete with page references
- Print your results to be submitted to your instructor
- Save your results to be submitted to your instructor via e-mail

To work with the Online Games for this chapter, connect to the **New Perspectives NP8 Web Site.**

www.course.com/np/concepts8/ch04

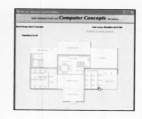

STUDENT EDITION LABS

Extend your knowledge of file management and backup procedures with the Chapter 4 Student Edition Labs.

The following Student Edition Labs are offered with Chapter 4:

- **Maintaining a Hard Drive**
- **Managing Files and Folders**
- **Keeping Your Computer Virus Free**
- **Backing Up Your Computer**

Go to the NP8 New Perspectives Web site for specific lab topics.

To work with the Chapter 4 Student Edition Labs and their corresponding lab assignments, connect to the **New Perspectives NP8 Web Site**.

www.course.com/np/concepts8/ch04

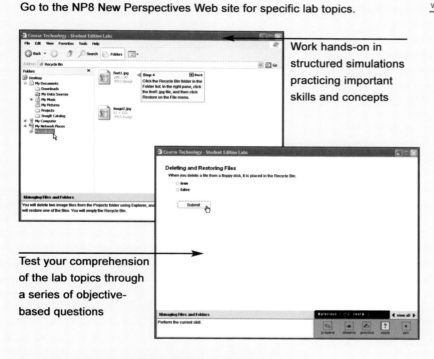

Work hands-on in structured simulations practicing important skills and concepts

Test your comprehension of the lab topics through a series of objective-based questions

Track Your Progress with the Student Edition Labs

- Student Edition Labs test your comprehension of the lab topics through a series of trackable objective-based questions. Your instructor will direct you to either print your results or submit them via e-mail.

- Student Edition Lab Assignments, available on the New Perspectives NP8 Web site, require you to apply the skills learned through the lab in a live environment. Go to the New Perspectives NP8 Web site for detailed instruction on individual Student Edition Lab Assignments.

If you have a SAM user profile, you have access to even more interactive content. Log in to your SAM account and go to your assignments page to see what your instructor has assigned for this chapter.

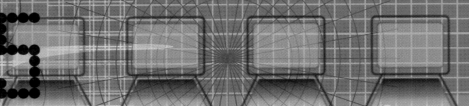

INTERNET AND LAN TECHNOLOGY

CONTENTS

TIP

When using the BookOnCD,
the ✳ icons are "clickable"
to access resources on the
CD. The ✚ icons are clickable to access resources on
the Web. You can also access
Web resources by using your
browser to connect directly to
the NP8 New Perspectives
Web site at:

www.course.com/np/concepts8/ch05

CHAPTER PREVIEW

Before you begin Chapter 5, you can use the Web-based preview activities to hear an overview of the chapter, check your current level of expertise about key concepts, and look through a list of learning objectives. You can access the preview activities by clicking the ✦ icon when using the BookOnCD or going to the New Perspectives NP8 Web site.

CHAPTER OVERVIEW

Today, computing is all about getting connected—accessing the Internet from home or your local Starbucks, hooking into your school network from your dorm room or the campus commons, and checking your e-mail from your notebook computer, PDA, or cell phone. Get your book and highlighter ready, then connect to the New Perspectives NP8 Web site where you can listen to an overview that points out the most important concepts for this chapter.

www.course.com/np/concepts8/ch05 ✦

CHAPTER PRE-ASSESSMENT

How much do you know about computer networks, TCP/IP, and Wi-Fi? To gauge your level of knowledge before beginning the chapter, take the pre-assessment quiz at the New Perspectives NP8 Web site. Armed with your results from this quiz, you can focus your study time on concepts that will round out your knowledge of networks and improve your test scores.

www.course.com/np/concepts8/ch05 ✦

LEARNING OBJECTIVES

When you complete this chapter you should be able to:

- Describe the characteristics of various networks, such as HomePLC, HomePNA, Ethernet, Wi-Fi, Token Ring, FDDI, MANs, WANs, LANs, NANs, PANs, client/server, and peer-to-peer

- Diagram Shannon's model of a communications network

- List the types of cables and other links typically used for data communications networks

- Make a list of network devices, explain the role of each one, and indicate whether they are typically used on the Internet or with LANs

- Describe the role of communications protocols and list some protocols associated with the Internet and LANs

- Explain the difference between packet switching and circuit switching technology

- Briefly recount the history of the Internet

- Draw a conceptual diagram illustrating the Internet backbone, NAPs, NSPs, routers, and ISPs

- Explain when and why you might use Ping and Traceroute utilities

- Explain the differences between permanent IP addresses, dynamic IP addresses, private IP addresses, and domain names

- Describe the advantages and disadvantages of dial-up, cable modem, DSL, ISDN, T1, T3, and wireless Internet access

- Explain when and why it is important to implement security measures, such as antivirus software, firewalls, and Network Address Translation

A detailed list of learning objectives is provided at the New Perspectives NP8 Web site

www.course.com/np/concepts8/ch05 ✦

SECTION A

NETWORK BUILDING BLOCKS

Today, networks are everywhere and network technology is evolving rapidly. Just when you think you have dial-up under control, along comes cable access and Wi-Fi. Just as you get comfortable with your school's campuswide network, everyone is issued notebook computers that use some sort of wireless connections. Although network technology continues to evolve, it is based on a set of fairly stable concepts. If you understand these network building blocks, working with new network technologies will be a piece of cake.

NETWORK ADVANTAGES AND CHALLENGES

Why is networking computers advantageous? In the early years of the personal computer's popularity, networks were scarce. Most personal computers functioned as standalone units, and computing was essentially a solitary activity in which one person interacted with a limited set of software tools, such as a word processor, spreadsheet, database, and games.

Some computer engineers, however, had the foresight to anticipate that personal computers could be networked to provide advantages not available with standalone computers. One of the most significant network ideas was conceived by Bob Metcalfe in 1976. His plan for transporting data between computers, shown in Figure 5-1, has become a key element in just about every computer network, including the Internet.

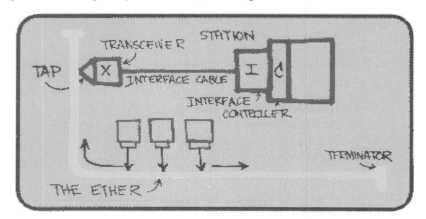

FIGURE 5-1

In 1976, Bob Metcalfe drew this diagram of a network technology, which he called "Ethernet."

Today, the pervasiveness of networks has dramatically changed the face of computing by offering **shared resources**—hardware, software, and data made available for authorized network users to access. Networks offer the following advantages:

■ **Sharing networked hardware can reduce costs.** In an office environment, for example, a single expensive color printer can be purchased and attached to a network, instead of the expensive alternative of purchasing color printers for each employee who wants to generate color printouts.

■ **Sharing networked hardware can provide access to a wide range of services and specialized peripheral devices.** A network can allow multiple users to access Internet services through a single Internet connection. Networked peripheral devices, such as scanners, photo printers, plotters, high-capacity storage devices, and computer-aided manufacturing (CAM) equipment, can be accessed by any authorized network users.

■ **Sharing networked software can reduce costs.** Although purchasing and installing a single software copy for an entire network might be technically possible, it is typically not allowed under the terms of a single-user license agreement. However, software site licenses for network use are usually less expensive than purchasing single-user versions of a product for each network user.

■ **Sharing data on a network is easy.** To transfer data between stand-alone computers, a file is usually copied to some type of removable storage media, and then carried or mailed to the other computer where it is copied onto the hard disk. Networks can provide authorized users with access to data stored on network servers or workstations.

■ **Networks enable people to work together regardless of time and place.** Using groupware and other specialized network application software, several people can work together on a single document, communicate via e-mail and instant messaging, and participate in on-line conferences and Webcasts (Figure 5-2).

FIGURE 5-2
An Internet teleconference links participants from multiple geographical locations.

Do networks have disadvantages? The primary disadvantage of networks is their vulnerability to unauthorized access. Whereas a standalone computer is vulnerable to on-premises theft or access, network computers are vulnerable to unauthorized access from many sources and locations.

Through unauthorized use of a network workstation, intruders can access data stored on the network server or other workstations. Networks connected to the Internet are vulnerable to intrusions from remote computers in distant states, provinces, or countries. Wireless networks can be tapped from a specially equipped "snooping" computer in a car that's being driven by a hacker. You'll learn more about network security threats and countermeasures later in this chapter.

Networks are also more vulnerable than standalone computers to malicious code. Whereas the most prevalent threat to standalone computers is disk-borne viruses, networks are susceptible to an ever increasing number of worms, Trojan horses, and blended threats.

Most computer owners are enthusiastic about the benefits provided by networks and believe that those benefits outweigh the risks of intrusions and viruses—especially if their computers can be protected by security aids, such as antivirus software.

NETWORK CLASSIFICATIONS

Are there different kinds of networks? In the past, a great diversity of network technologies existed as engineers pioneered new ideas to make data transport faster, more efficient, and more secure. Today, networks are becoming more standardized, but some diversity remains necessary to accommodate networking environments that range from simple household networks to complex global banking networks.

How are networks classified? It would be nice if networks could be classified simply and we could define a "personal computer network," for example, as consisting of technologies X, Y, and Z. Networks, however, exist in many variations because each one is constructed from a collection of technologies. The network you use in a school lab might be referred to as an "Ethernet," but at the same time it might also be called a "fiber-optic network," and it could further be described as a "local area network." The network you use at home might also be referred to as a "local area network," but it might use HomePLC technology instead of fiber optics and might not be classified as Ethernet.

To understand network classifications and make sense of the network options available for your computer, think of a network as composed of several layers of technology. The technology from a single layer is often used in casual conversation to classify a network, even though it does not provide a complete description of the technologies used in all layers.

Network layers important for classification are described in Figure 5-3. The remainder of Section A explains the components of these network layers in more detail.

FIGURE 5-3
Network Technology Layers

Geographical scope	The area in which network devices are located	WAN, MAN, LAN, NAN, PAN
Organizational structure	The hierarchy of devices connected to a network	Client/server, peer-to-peer
Physical topology	The physical layout and relationship between network devices	Star, bus, ring, mesh, tree
Network links	The technologies for cables and signals that carry data	Twisted-pair cable, coaxial cable, fiber-optic cable, RF signals, microwaves, infrared light, power line, phone line
Bandwidth	The capacity of a network for carrying data	Broadband, narrowband
Communications protocols	The transportation standards that provide an orderly way to package data and make sure data is not corrupted in transit	TCP/IP, SPX/IPX (Novell networks), NetBEUI/NetBIOS (Microsoft networking), AppleTalk

GEOGRAPHIC SCOPE: PANS, NANS, LANS, WANS, AND MANS

Why is geographic scope important? Localized networks typically include a small number of computers, which can be connected using basic equipment. As the area of network coverage expands, the number of workstations grows, specialized devices are sometimes required to boost signals, and the diversity of devices requires sophisticated management tools and strategies. From a geographic perspective, networks can be classified as PANs, NANs, LANs, MANs, and WANs.

What are the options? **PAN** (personal area network) is a term sometimes used to refer to the interconnection of personal digital devices within a range of about 30 feet (10 meters) and without the use of wires or cables. For example, a PAN could be used to wirelessly transmit data from a notebook computer to a PDA or portable printer.

A **NAN** (neighborhood area network) provides connectivity within a limited geographical area, usually spread over several buildings. These networks are becoming popular as local coffee shops and computer hobbyists offer wireless Internet connections.

A **LAN** (local area network) is a data communications network that typically connects personal computers within a very limited geographical area—usually a single building. LANs use a variety of wired and wireless technologies, standards, and protocols. School computer labs and home networks are examples of LANs.

A **MAN** (metropolitan area network) is a public high-speed network capable of voice and data transmission within a range of about 50 miles (80km). Examples of MANs that provide data transport services include local ISPs, cable television companies, and local telephone companies.

A **WAN** (wide area network) covers a large geographical area and usually consists of several smaller networks, which might use different computer platforms and network technologies. The Internet is the world's largest WAN. Networks for nationwide banks and multi-location "superstores" can be classified as WANs.

ORGANIZATIONAL STRUCTURE: CLIENT/SERVER AND PEER-TO-PEER

How are networks structured? A typical organizational chart diagrams the hierarchy of personnel in a business. In a hierarchical business, the president at the top of the chart is the main decision maker. In a "flattened," decentralized chart, decisions are shared among peers. Like a business, networks also have an organizational structure that provides a conceptual model of the way data is stored and transported. The two most prevalent network organizational structures are client/server and peer-to-peer.

What is the difference between a client/server network and a peer-to-peer network? A **client/server network** contains one or more computers configured with server software and other computers, configured with client software, that access the servers. The server provides a centralized repository for data and a transfer point through which data traffic flows. Web sites, retail point-of-sale networks, school registration systems, online databases, and Internet-based multiplayer games typically use a client/server organizational structure.

A **peer-to-peer network** (sometimes called P2P) treats every computer as an "equal" so that workstations can store network data, which can be transported directly to other workstations without passing through a central server. P2P technology forms the basis for file-sharing networks, such as Kazaa and Microsoft Networking provided with Windows. Figure 5-4 contrasts the client/server structure with the peer-to-peer structure.

FIGURE 5-4

In a client/server network, a server is the most important resource. In a peer-to-peer network, every computer is treated as an equal resource.

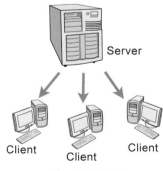

Client/server

Peer-to-peer

PHYSICAL TOPOLOGY

How are the devices on a network physically arranged? Each connection point on a network is referred to as a **node**. A network node typically contains one of the following devices:

- **Server:** A computer responsible for storing data and programs

- **Workstation:** A personal computer connected to a network

- **Networked peripheral:** A device, such as a printer or scanner, directly connected to a network rather than to a workstation

- **Network device:** An electronic device that broadcasts network data, boosts signals, or routes data to its destination

The arrangement of devices in a network is referred to as its **physical topology**. Figure 5-5 illustrates star, ring, bus, mesh, and tree topologies; the pathways shown between nodes can be linked by physical cables or wireless signals.

What are the advantages of each topology? A network arranged as a **star topology** features a central connection point for all workstations and peripherals. The central connection point is not necessarily a server—more typically it is a network device called a **hub**, which is designed to broadcast data to workstations and peripherals. Some hubs are also repeaters. A **repeater** can boost the strength of the signal that carries data over any network topology when the distance between two nodes exceeds the carrying capacity of their connecting links.

Many home networks are arranged in a star topology. The advantage of this topology is that any link can fail without affecting the rest of the network. Its primary disadvantage is that it requires quite a bit of cable to link all the devices—a disadvantage that disappears with wireless networks. Although the failure of a link does not affect the rest of the network, you can see from Figure 5-5 that a device with a failed link would be cut off from the network and unable to receive data.

A **ring topology** connects all devices in a circle, with each device having exactly two neighbors. Data is transmitted from one device to another around the ring. This topology minimizes cabling, but failure of any one device can take down the entire network. Ring topologies, once championed by IBM, are infrequently used in today's networks.

A **bus topology** uses a common backbone to connect all network devices. The backbone functions as a shared communication link, which carries network data. The backbone stops at each end of the network with a special device called a "terminator." Bob Metcalfe's 1976 network plan was based on a bus topology. However, bus networks work best with a limited number of devices. Bus networks with more than a few dozen computers are likely to perform poorly, and if the backbone cable fails, the entire network becomes unusable.

A **mesh topology** connects each network device to many other network devices. Data traveling on a mesh network can take any of several possible paths from its source to its destination. These redundant data pathways make a mesh network very robust. Even if several links fail, data can follow alternative functioning links to reach its destination—an advantage over networks arranged in a star topology. The original plan for the Internet was based on mesh topology.

FIGURE 5-5
Network Topologies

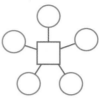

Star topology

Ring topology

Bus topology

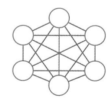

Mesh topology

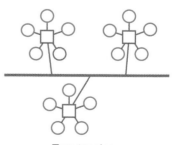

Tree topology

A **tree topology** is essentially a blend of star and bus networks. Multiple star networks are connected into a bus configuration by a backbone. Tree topologies offer excellent flexibility for expansion—a single link to the backbone can add an entire group of star-configured devices. This link can be accomplished using the same type of hub used as the central connection point in a star network. Most of today's school and business networks are based on tree topologies.

Can various networks be interconnected? Yes. Two similar networks can be connected by a device called a **bridge**, which simply transfers data without regard to its format. Networks that use different topologies and technologies can be interconnected by using gateways. **Gateway** is a generic term for any device or software code used to join two dissimilar networks by converting data sent from one network into a format compatible to the receiving network. A gateway can be implemented completely in software, completely in hardware, or as a combination of the two.

The most commonly used gateway is a **router**, an electronic device that joins two or more networks. For example, a home network can use a router and a DSL or cable modem to join the home's LAN to the Internet's WAN. A router acts as a LAN's point of presence to a larger network and can include bridging or conversion capabilities to interact with dissimilar networks. A router accepts incoming data transmissions and distributes them to devices attached to its local network. It also shuttles data from a local network to other networks, as shown in Figure 5-6.

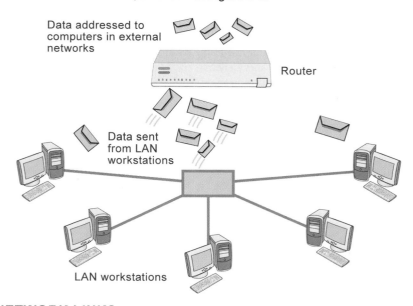

Data addressed to computers in external networks

Router

Data sent from LAN workstations

LAN workstations

FIGURE 5-6

A router typically connects a LAN to a WAN and filters transmissions between them.

The router forwards messages destined for other networks (orange), but keeps local messages (green) within the network.

NETWORK LINKS

What connects the nodes of a network? Data can travel from one network device to another over a cable or through the air. A **communications channel**, or "link," is a physical path or a frequency for a signal transmission. For example, Channel 12 on your TV tuner is a specific frequency used to broadcast audiovisual data for a television station. This data might also be carried over another channel, such as coaxial cable, as part of a cable TV system.

Data in a **wired network** travels from one device to another over cables. Data in a **wireless network** travels through the air, eliminating the need for cables.

What are popular network cabling options? If you install your own home network, it is likely to require twisted-pair cables to connect network devices, such as workstations and hubs. A **twisted-pair cable** is a popular, inexpensive cable designed for telephone and network installations. It typically contains four pairs of copper wires. Each pair of wires is independently insulated and then twisted together, which gives this cable its name. Twisted-pair cables are frequently used in school labs and small business LANs as well as home networks.

When purchasing twisted-pair cable, you have shielding and category options. Shielded twisted-pair cable (STP) contains shielding, which reduces signal noise that might interfere with data transmitted over unshielded cable (UTP). Cable categories (abbreviated as CAT) indicate carrying capacity. CAT 1 is sufficient for telephone cabling, whereas CAT 5 provides more capacity for networking. Twisted-pair cables typically terminate with plastic RJ-11 plugs for telephones or RJ-45 plugs for computer networks (Figure 5-7).

INFOWEBLINKS

Make your own fiber-optic cable with duct tape and flashlights? You'll find some fun facts as well as solid technical information at the **Fiber Optics InfoWeb**.

www.course.com/np/concepts8/ch05

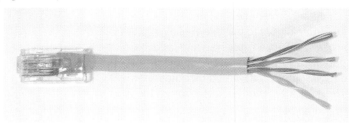

FIGURE 5-7
Twisted-pair cable is popular for LANs.

Coaxial cable, often called "coax cable" (pronounced CO ax), consists of a copper wire encased in a nonconducting insulator, a foil shield, a woven metal outer shield, and a plastic outer coating. It is the cable of choice for cable television because its high capacity simultaneously carries signals for hundreds of television channels, with additional capacity for carrying cable modem signals. If you use a cable modem, you'll probably use a coaxial cable to connect it to the cable wall outlet. A coaxial cable is typically terminated with metal BNC or F-type connectors, as shown in Figure 5-8.

FIGURE 5-8
Coaxial cable is a common component of cable television systems.

Fiber-optic cable is a bundle of extremely thin strands of glass. Each strand, called an optical fiber, is much thinner than a human hair. A fiber-optic cable usually consists of a strong inner support wire, multiple strands of optical fiber (each covered by a plastic insulator), and a tough outer covering (Figure 5-9). Unlike twisted-pair and coaxial cables, fiber-optic cables do not conduct or transmit electrical signals. Instead, miniature lasers convert data into pulses of light that flash through the cables. Fiber-optic cables are an essential part of the Internet backbone and are increasingly found on business and campus networks.

FIGURE 5-9
Fiber-optic cables have good carrying capacity, but are costly and require special installation tools and techniques.

USB, serial, parallel, SCSI, and FireWire cables can also be pressed into service as communications channels. They are typically used to transport data between a computer and a network or communications device. For example, you might use a USB cable to connect your computer to a cable modem or a serial cable to connect your computer to a voiceband modem. Some home networks allow you to make use of existing electrical wiring, using special adapters that connect computers to electrical wall outlets.

What are the options for wireless networks? Most wireless LANs transport data as **RF signals** (radio frequency signals). RF signals—commonly called "radio waves"—are sent and received by a **transceiver** (a combination of a transmitter and a receiver) that is equipped with an antenna. Every network workstation, peripheral device, and hub is equipped with a transceiver, which sends and receives data (Figure 5-10).

Microwaves (the waves themselves, not your oven!) provide another option for transporting data. Like radio waves, microwaves are electromagnetic signals, but they behave differently. Microwaves can be aimed in a single direction and have more carrying capacity than radio waves. However, microwaves cannot penetrate metal objects and work best for "line-of-sight" transmission when a clear path exists between the transmitter and receiver. Microwave installations typically provide data transport for large corporate networks.

Radio and microwave transmissions cannot bend around the surface of the earth to reach far-flung towers, so earth-orbiting **communications satellites** play an important role in long-distance communications. A signal can be relayed from a ground station to a communications satellite. On board the satellite, a **transponder** receives a signal, amplifies it, and then retransmits the signal back to a ground station on earth. Satellites provide a way for people in remote areas to connect personal computers to the Internet.

Today most people are familiar with remote controls that use **infrared light** beams to change television channels. Infrared can also carry data signals, but only for short distances and with a clear line of sight. Its most practical use seems to be for transmitting data between devices connected to a PAN.

ANALOG AND DIGITAL SIGNALS

What's the difference between analog and digital signals? When data is transmitted it usually takes the form of an electromagnetic signal. You can think of these signals as waves that ripple through cables or through the air. Digital signals are transmitted as bits using a limited set of frequencies. Analog signals can assume any value within a specified range of frequencies. Figure 5-11 helps you visualize the difference between digital and analog waves.

Are digital signals better than analog signals? At its most primitive level, digital equipment must be sensitive to only two frequencies—one that represents 1s and one that represents 0s. In contrast, analog equipment such as a telephone or a microphone, must be sensitive to a wide range of audible frequencies, or else it will not be able to pick up and transport very high or very low sounds. The beauty of digital signals is that they require simple circuitry and are easy to "clean up" after being affected by noise.

To understand how digital waves might get cleaned up, suppose that a computer network uses different voltages to transmit 0s and 1s. A "perfect" 0 is sent as -5 volts and a perfect 1 is sent as +5 volts. What if, during transmission, some interference changes the voltage of a "perfect" 1 to +3

Wireless hub

Wireless network card for workstation

FIGURE 5-11
Digital and Analog Wave Forms

The signals carried on a digital channel are depicted as a stepped wave.

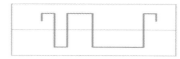

An analog signal is depicted as a smooth wave.

volts? When the signal is received, the receiving device realizes that +3 volts is not one of the two valid voltages. It "guesses" that a 1 bit (+5 volts) was actually transmitted, and "cleans" the signal by reestablishing its voltage to +5.

In contrast, suppose that interference changes a 1,200 Hz wave in an analog transmission to a 1,233 Hz wave. The receiving device cannot determine whether the 1,233 Hz signal is an error or just one of the many analog values that were originally sent. The 1,233 Hz signal, therefore, remains part of the transmission, even if it is the result of static. Most modern networks carry digital signals rather than analog signals.

BANDWIDTH

What's bandwidth? Networks must move data and move it quickly. **Bandwidth** is the transmission capacity of a communications channel. Just as a four-lane freeway can carry more traffic than a two-lane street, a high-bandwidth communications channel can carry more data than a low-bandwidth channel. For example, the coaxial cable that brings you more than 100 channels of cable TV has a higher bandwidth than your home telephone line. The bandwidth of a digital channel is usually measured in bits per second (bps). The bandwidth of an analog channel is typically measured in hertz (Hz).

To better grasp the significance of bandwidth in a communications network, imagine a dial-up connection's 56 Kbps bandwidth as a narrow bike path that allows a limited amount of slow traffic. A 1.5 Mbps connection through your cable TV company is equivalent to a two-lane highway. A typical LAN, such as a college computer lab, might provide 100 Mbps bandwidth—similar to a 260-lane expressway.

High-bandwidth communications systems, such as cable TV and DSL, are sometimes referred to as **broadband**, whereas systems with less capacity, such as the telephone system, are referred to as **narrowband**.

COMMUNICATIONS PROTOCOLS

How does data travel over a network? In 1948, Claude Shannon, an engineer at the prestigious Bell Labs, published an article describing a communications system model applicable to today's voice and data networks.

In Shannon's model, data from a source, such as a network workstation, is encoded and sent over a communications channel to a destination, such as a network printer, storage device, server, or workstation. When data arrives at its destination, it is decoded. Transmission can be disrupted by interference called "noise," which has the potential to corrupt data, making it erroneous or unintelligible (Figure 5-12). Networks use protocols to set standards for encoding and decoding data, guiding data to its destination, and mitigating the effects of noise.

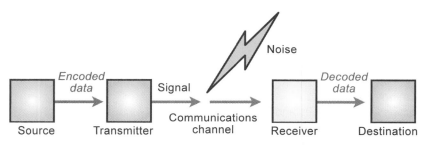

FIGURE 5-12
A communications system basically sends information from a source to a destination. Although the path between the source and destination might appear to be straight in the diagram, the data can pass through several devices, which convert it to electrical, sound, light, or radio signals; beam it up to satellites; route it along the least congested links; or clean up parts of the signal that have been distorted by noise.

What is a protocol? In general, a "protocol" is a set of rules for interacting and negotiating. In some respects, it is like signals between the pitcher and catcher in a baseball game. Before the ball is thrown, the catcher and pitcher use hand signals to negotiate the speed and style of the pitch.

In the context of networks, the term "protocol," or **communications protocol**, refers to a set of rules for efficiently transmitting data from one network node to another. The best-known protocol is probably TCP/IP—popular because it is the protocol that regulates Internet data transport. Figure 5-13 lists some popular communications protocols.

What can protocols do? Protocols perform several important network functions, including:

- Dividing messages into packets
- Affixing addresses to packets
- Initiating transmission
- Regulating the flow of data
- Checking for transmission errors
- Acknowledging receipt of transmitted data

What's a packet? When you send a file or an e-mail message, you might suppose that it is transmitted as an entire unit to its destination. This is not the case. Your file is actually chopped up into small pieces called packets. A **packet** is a "parcel" of data that is sent across a computer network. Each packet contains the address of its sender, the destination address, a sequence number, and some data. When packets reach their destination, they are reassembled back into the original message according to the sequence number (Figure 5-14).

FIGURE 5-13

Network Protocols

Protocol	Main Use
TCP/IP	Internet
NetBIOS/NetBEUI	Microsoft networks
AppleTalk	Macintosh networks
IPX/SPX	Novell networks

FIGURE 5-14

Before transmission, messages are divided into packets. Upon arriving at their destination, packets are reassembled into the original message.

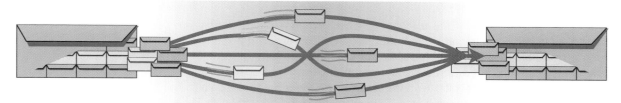

Why not just send an entire message? Some communications networks, such as the telephone system, use a technology called **circuit switching**, which essentially establishes a dedicated, private link between one telephone and another for the duration of a call. This type of switching provides callers with a direct pipeline over which streams of voice data can flow. Unfortunately, circuit switching is rather inefficient. For example, when someone is "on hold," no communication is taking place—yet the circuit is reserved and cannot be used for other communications.

A more efficient alternative to circuit switching, **packet switching** technology divides a message into several packets that can be routed independently to their destination. By dividing messages into equal-size packets, they are easier to handle than an assortment of small, medium, large, and huge files.

Packets from many different messages can share a single communications channel, or "circuit." Packets are shipped over the circuit on a "first come, first served" basis. If some packets from a message are not available, the system does not need to wait for them. Instead, the system moves on to send packets from other messages. The end result is a steady stream of data (Figure 5-15).

FIGURE 5-15

Packet switching networks (left) provide a more efficient communications system than circuit switching networks (right).

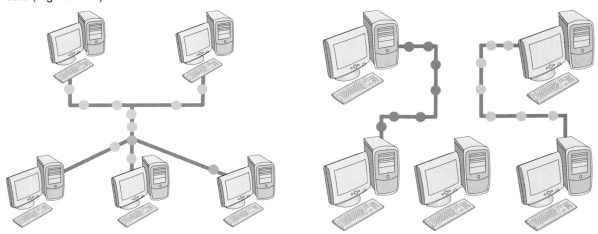

How are packets routed to their destinations? Every device on a network has an address. Every packet that travels over a network includes the address of its destination device, similar to the way a letter contains the address of a house or mailbox. Communications protocols specify the proper format for addresses within a particular type of network. When a packet reaches a network node, a router examines the address and sends the packet along to its destination or to another router that's closer to the packet's destination.

How does a protocol initiate a transmission? When a message has been divided into packets and each packet has been addressed, it is ready for transmission. A major challenge of network communications is coordinating the transmission and reception of each packet. The transmitting computer sends a series of bits, but if the receiving device is not ready, data can get lost and messages can become hopelessly garbled. Several categories of protocols handle this aspect of data transmission.

A **synchronous protocol** coordinates sending and receiving devices by using a clock signal. The transmitting computer sends data at a fixed clock rate, and the receiving computer expects the incoming data at the same fixed rate. Much of the communication between components on a computer's motherboard is synchronous. Most data communications systems, however, send and receive data using asynchronous protocol.

The rules for an **asynchronous protocol** require the transmitting computer to send a start bit that indicates the beginning of a packet. Data is then transmitted as a series of bytes—the number of bytes is specified by the protocol. A stop bit marks the end of the data.

Before sending a start bit, two devices might have to negotiate their communications protocols through a process called **handshaking**. The transmitting device sends a signal that means "I want to communicate." It then waits for an acknowledgement signal from the receiving device. The two devices then "negotiate" a transmission speed and protocol that both can handle. The sounds you hear as two modems or fax machines connect are examples of handshaking.

How do protocols regulate the flow of data? Communications channels, protocols, and devices provide different capabilities for sending and receiving data. For example, you use a walkie-talkie differently from the way you use a telephone. A walkie-talkie requires you to press a button when you are ready to send and release the button when you are ready to receive. In contrast, a telephone does not require any special action to switch between talking and listening. The signals that represent data can flow over a network in three ways:

Simplex: Signals travel in only one direction. A radio transmitter uses simplex communication—it can transmit, but not receive, signals.

Half duplex: Signals can be sent and received, but not at the same time. A walkie-talkie (Figure 5-16) is an example of half-duplex communication because only one party can talk at a time.

Full duplex: Signals can be sent and received at the same time, over the same channel—for example, a telephone conversation.

Most data communications networks operate in half-duplex or full-duplex mode. But you don't have to worry about holding down the "Talk" button, even if your network operates in half-duplex mode. Communications protocols take care of the flow of data behind the scenes.

How does a protocol make sure that data arrives without errors? Computers use error-checking protocols to ensure accurate delivery of data. Internet protocols use a simple **checksum**—a number that represents the total number of bits being sent. That number is affixed to each packet. As data arrives, a second checksum is calculated and compared to the original. If the checksums are not the same, the receiving device assumes that data has been corrupted and requests retransmission. Some LANs use an alternative error-checking calculation called a **cyclic redundancy check**.

What part of a network specifies protocols? Some protocols are handled by hardware, whereas other protocols are handled by software. For example, physically changing a signal, say from the +5 volt pulse that emanates from a computer's motherboard to a 1,233 Hz "tone" that can travel over a telephone line, takes place in the circuitry of a modem. On the other hand, software usually provides the specification for creating packets.

FIGURE 5-16

On some networks data can be transmitted and received, but not at the same time—similar to the way a walkie-talkie works.

QUICKCHECK......SECTION A

1. Networks offer shared [_____], such as printers, software applications, and storage space.

2. Most school computer labs are examples of [_____] (Hint: Use the abbreviation), whereas the Internet is a WAN.

3. The central point of connection in a network is often a [_____].

4. A(n) [_____] switching network divides messages into small parcels and handles them on a "first come, first served" basis, whereas a(n) [_____] switching network establishes a dedicated connection between two devices.

CHECK ANSWERS

SECTION B

LOCAL AREA NETWORKS

LANs used to be a fairly esoteric and quirky technology that required certified technicians to "magically" keep all the connections up and running. As the technology stabilized, LANs became a must-have tool for small business. Today, everyone has jumped onto the LAN bandwagon. Small networks are popping up in homes, apartments, and dorm rooms. The key attraction: A LAN allows several computers to share a high-speed (and expensive) Internet connection.

Section B provides some general background on LANs and specific details on how to set one up. For information about connecting a LAN to the Internet, refer to Section D.

LAN STANDARDS

What are LAN standards? LAN technologies are standardized by the Institute of Electrical and Electronics Engineers (IEEE) *Project 802 - Local Network Standards*. IEEE standards are available for most types of commercial networks. An IEEE designation number, such as IEEE 802.3, is sometimes used to refer to a network standard in articles and advertisements. For network technicians, IEEE designation numbers help identify compatible network technologies. Historically, several LAN standards have experienced popularity, including ARCnet, Token Ring, and FDDI.

What is ARCnet? Introduced in 1977, **ARCnet** (Attached Resource Computer network) is one of the oldest, simplest, and least expensive LAN technologies. The original ARCnet standard supported transmission rates of 2.5 Mbps. Later versions of ARCnet offered 20 and 100 Mbps transmission rates. A special advantage of ARCnet permits twisted-pair, coax, and fiber-optic cables to be mixed on the same network to connect up to 255 workstations. Although no longer popular for LANs, ARCnet technology is now deployed for applications such as industrial control, building automation, transportation, robotics, and casino gaming.

What is Token Ring technology? A **Token Ring network**, defined by the IEEE 802.5 standard, passes data around a ring topology using a signal called a "token" to control the flow of data. When the token is available, a network device attaches a packet to the token to be carried to its destination. After delivering the packet, the token returns to the sending device, announces a successful delivery, and becomes available to circulate and pick up additional packets (Figure 5-17). The original Token Ring standard carried data at 4 Mbps. In 1989, the speed was increased to 16 Mbps.

Token Ring technology was intensively marketed by IBM and found a home on many networks that are still operational. However, new network technologies offered faster and less expensive solutions, and by 1999 it was clear that Token Ring was headed for gradual extinction.

FIGURE 5-17

To send data on a Token Ring network, a workstation must wait for the token to become available. A packet is then attached to the token and circles around the network until it reaches its destination.

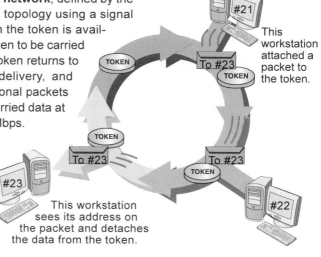

This workstation attached a packet to the token.

This workstation sees its address on the packet and detaches the data from the token.

What is the FDDI standard? **FDDI** (Fiber Distributed Data Interconnect) offers 100 Mbps speeds over fiber-optic cables. As defined by the IEEE 802.8 standards, an FDDI network supports up to 500 devices, cabled as a dual ring—the second ring provides redundancy in case the first ring fails. Like Token Ring networks, FDDI uses a token to control data transmission. Typically, the FDDI ring links network devices, such as servers and routers. Workstations do not connect directly to the ring, but instead connect by twisted-pair cable to a router, as shown in Figure 5-18.

FDDI networks became a popular campus network technology and made some inroads into small businesses. By 1999, however, FDDI was losing ground to less expensive technologies that offered faster data transfer rates.

So what are the current LAN standards? Today, most LANs are configured with Ethernet technology and use compatible Wi-Fi standards in applications that require wireless access. These technologies are worth a more detailed look.

ETHERNET

How does Ethernet work? In 1980, Bob Metcalfe's 1976 concept for Ethernet became commercially available. **Ethernet**, defined by IEEE 802.3, simultaneously broadcasts data packets to all network devices. A packet is accepted only by the device to which it is addressed (Figure 5-19).

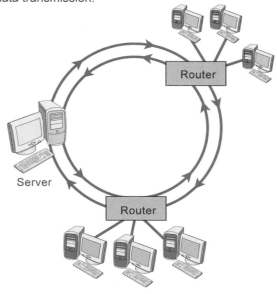

FIGURE 5-18

FDDI networks connect routers and servers using a double ring topology. Workstations connect to a router rather than to the ring.

FIGURE 5-19

On an Ethernet, a packet is broadcast to every device, but is accepted only by the device to which it is addressed.

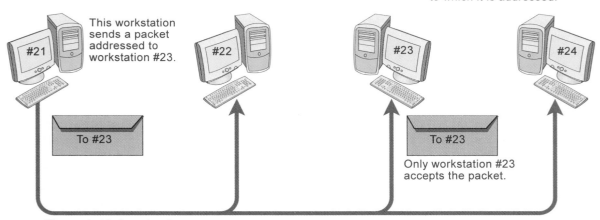

This workstation sends a packet addressed to workstation #23.

#21   #22   #23   #24

To #23   To #23

Only workstation #23 accepts the packet.

The packet is broadcast to every device.

An integral part of Ethernet technology relies on **CSMA/CD** protocol (Carrier Sense Multiple Access with Collision Detection). CSMA/CD takes care of situations in which two network devices attempt to transmit packets at the same time. A "collision" occurs as two signals travel over the network. CSMA/CD protocol detects the collision, deletes the colliding signals, and resets the network. The two devices wait for random time periods before the next transmission to prevent a collision from reoccurring (Figure 5-20).

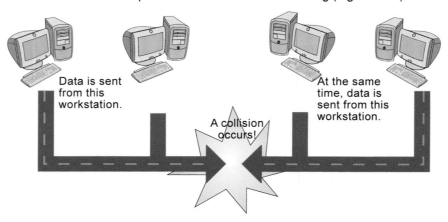

Data is sent from this workstation.

At the same time, data is sent from this workstation.

A collision occurs!

How fast is an Ethernet network? The original Ethernet standard carried data over a coaxial cable bus topology at 10 Mbps. Today, the term "Ethernet" refers to a family of LAN technologies that offer various data transmission rates over fiber-optic and twisted-pair cables arranged in a bus or star topology. Of the Ethernet variations shown in Figure 5-21, Fast Ethernet is currently the most popular for small to medium LANs, such as you might find in homes and small businesses.

FIGURE 5-21
Ethernet Standards

Ethernet Standard	IEEE Designation	Speed	Cable
10BaseT Ethernet	IEEE 802.3	10 Mbps	CAT 3 or CAT 5
Fast Ethernet	IEEE 802.3u	100 Mbps	CAT 5 or fiber-optic
Gigabit Ethernet	IEEE 802.3z	1000 Mbps	CAT 5 or fiber-optic
10 Gig Ethernet	IEEE 802.3ae	10 Gbps	Fiber-optic

What equipment is required for a home Ethernet? A basic Ethernet network requires an Ethernet card in each workstation and any peripheral device attached directly to the network. An **Ethernet card** is a type of network interface card (NIC), or network adapter, designed to support Ethernet protocols. Many desktop, notebook, and tablet computers include a preinstalled Ethernet card. Ethernet circuitry is also included in some printers and other peripheral devices.

Add-on Ethernet cards for desktop computers fit into a slot inside the system unit. Add-on Ethernet cards for notebook and tablet computers are designed to fit in a PCMCIA slot. The cost of add-on Ethernet cards, such as those shown in Figure 5-22, can be as low as $15.

In addition to Ethernet cards, a home Ethernet network requires some type of link between network nodes—typically CAT 5 twisted-pair cable. These cables link workstations and peripherals to a central connection point called

FIGURE 5-22
Ethernet Cards

an Ethernet hub. Today, most Ethernet hubs also serve as routers. Ethernet hubs are available in many configurations offering various numbers of ports. Your hub should have enough ports to accommodate the number of devices you plan to connect to the network. A five-port or an eight-port hub is typical for home networks. A 16-port hub, such as the one in Figure 5-23, might be used in a small business.

FIGURE 5-23

An Ethernet hub or combination hub/router features a collection of ports for connecting servers, workstations, and peripheral devices.

What additional equipment is needed for large Ethernet installations? Large Ethernets typically stretch over a sizable geographic area and connect many workstations. A simple step up from a basic single-hub network is to connect several hubs using an **uplink port**. A repeater can boost signals between distant workstations. A bridge can be used to connect two smaller Ethernet segments. Enterprise devices called concentrators allow network builders to add modules containing Ethernet ports to a rack-like case. Equipment for large networks can become quite specialized and beyond the scope of this textbook.

Why is Ethernet so popular? Despite challenges from other technologies, Ethernet has emerged as the leading LAN technology. It is currently used in approximately 85% of LANs worldwide. Ethernet's success is attributable to several factors:

- Ethernet networks are easy to understand, implement, manage, and maintain.
- As a nonproprietary technology, Ethernet equipment is available from a variety of vendors, and market competition keeps prices low.
- Current Ethernet standards allow extensive flexibility in network topology to meet the needs of small and large installations.

Ethernet 802.3 standards pertain to wired networks. Ethernet's cousin, Wi-Fi, provides standards for popular wireless networking options.

WI-FI

What is Wi-Fi? **Wi-Fi** (Wireless Fidelity) refers to a set of wireless networking technologies defined by IEEE 802.11 standards that are compatible with Ethernet. A Wi-Fi network transmits data as radio waves over predefined frequencies, much like cordless telephones. Wi-Fi networks operate at 2.4 or 5 GHz, as shown in Figure 5-24.

INFOWEBLINKS

Ethernet is definitely cool. See what the "Ether" is all about at the **Ethernet InfoWeb**.

www.course.com/np/concepts8/ch05

FIGURE 5-24
Wi-Fi Standards

IEEE Designation	Frequency	Speed	Range	Pros/Cons
IEEE 802.11b	2.4 GHz	11 Mbps	100–150 feet	Original standard
IEEE 802.11a	5 GHz	54 Mbps	25–75 feet	Not compatible with 802.11b
IEEE 802.11g	2.4 GHz	54 Mbps	100–150 feet	Faster than, but compatible with, 802.11b

What are the pros and cons of Wi-Fi? The big attraction of Wi-Fi is the absence of wires and cables running through walls and between floors. Wireless networks are especially desirable for notebook and tablet computers that don't otherwise need to be tethered to electrical outlets for true portability.

Wi-Fi is similar to cordless telephones in that it uses unlicensed frequencies, such as 2.4 GHZ and 5 GHz. Whereas the frequencies used for broadcast TV, radio, and cable TV require a license from the FCC (Federal Communications Commission), setting up a Wi-Fi NAN requires no license.

When compared to wired networks, Wi-Fi has three disadvantages: slow transmission rates, susceptibility to interference, and lack of security. The fastest Wi-Fi standards operate at a maximum speed of 54 Mbps, but actual throughput is about half the maximum speed.

In a typical office environment, Wi-Fi's range varies from 25 to 150 feet, although considerably more range is possible with additional equipment. Thick cement walls, steel beams, and other environmental obstacles can, however, drastically reduce this range to the point that signals cannot be reliably transmitted. Wi-Fi signals can also be disrupted by interference from electronic devices operating at the same frequency, such as 2.4 GHz cordless telephones.

Wi-Fi signals that travel through the air are easy to intercept by any suitably equipped receiving device within the network's range of service. A practice called **war driving** or "LAN-jacking" occurs when hackers cruise around with a Wi-Fi-equipped notebook computer set up in "promiscuous mode" to search for Wi-Fi signals coming from home and corporate Wi-Fi networks. War drivers can access and use unsecured Wi-Fi networks to hack into files and gain unauthorized access to larger, wired networks.

Preventing Wi-Fi signal interception is difficult, but encrypting transmitted data using **WEP** (Wired Equivalent Privacy) is an essential step in making your data useless to intruders. The WEP algorithm has been broken, however, so although it is adequate for a typical home network, corporations must establish additional security measures. Despite security concerns and other potential drawbacks, Wi-Fi is becoming increasingly popular in corporate, school, and home networks.

What equipment is required for a Wi-Fi network? As with a wired Ethernet network, every workstation and network peripheral requires a network interface card. A **Wi-Fi card** includes a transmitter, receiver, and antenna to transmit signals. Wi-Fi cards for notebook or tablet computers can plug into a PCMCIA slot or USB port. Wi-Fi capability can be added to a desktop computer as a Wi-Fi card that fits into a system unit slot with the antenna protruding out of the back or as a small box that connects to a USB port. Yet another option is to use a wireless adapter to convert a standard Ethernet port into a wireless port. Figure 5-25 illustrates various Wi-Fi cards.

A **wireless access point** performs the same function as a hub or router in a wired Ethernet network by broadcasting signals to any devices with compatible Wi-Fi cards. Many wireless access points also include ports for connecting wired devices and a cable modem (Figure 5-26).

INFOWEBLINKS

For the latest information on Wi-Fi equipment and pricing, check out the **Wireless LAN InfoWeb**.

www.course.com/np/concepts8/ch05

FIGURE 5-25
Wi-Fi Cards

FIGURE 5-26
A wireless access point provides a central point for data transmitted over a Wi-Fi network.

Are any alternative wireless networking technologies available? **Bluetooth** is a short-range wireless network technology that's designed to make its own connections between electronic devices, without wires, cables or any direct action from a user. Unlike Wi-Fi, Bluetooth is not typically used to connect a collection of workstations. Instead, Bluetooth connectivity replaces the short cables that would otherwise tether a mouse, keyboard, or printer to a computer. Bluetooth can also be used to link devices in a PAN, connect home entertainment system components, and to synchronize PDAs with desktop base stations.

Bluetooth is built into some peripheral devices and can be added to personal computers using a variety of add-on cards. The cool feature of Bluetooth-enabled devices is that they automatically find each other and strike up a conversation without any user input at all. Bluetooth operates at the same 2.4 GHz frequency as Wi-Fi, but offers peak transmission rates of only 1 Mbps over a range of about 30 feet (Figure 5-27).

HOMEPNA AND HOMEPLC NETWORKS

What's HomePNA? A **HomePNA network** utilizes existing telephone wiring to connect network devices. The HomePNA network standard uses a special NIC and cable to connect each computer to a standard telephone wall jack. The NICs contain circuitry that eliminates the need for hubs. When your computer is connected to a HomePNA network, you can typically use the phone to make a call and send information over the network at the same time because the network frequency is different from the voice frequency. You cannot, however, make a voice call while a dial-up Internet connection is active.

What's HomePLC? A **HomePLC network**, or "power line network," uses a special NIC to connect a computer to a standard electrical outlet. Data, transmitted as low-frequency radio waves, travels along the electrical wiring until it reaches another network device. Unfortunately, power line fluctuations caused by fluorescent lights, baby monitors, dimmer switches, amateur band radios, air-conditioning units, or other major appliances can disrupt the signal and cause momentary loss of network connections.

How do LAN technologies compare? LANs operate at different speeds, over various distances, and provide unique advantages and disadvantages. Figure 5-28 compares the LAN standards presented in this section.

FIGURE 5-27
Microsoft produces a wireless keyboard, mouse, and Bluetooth transceiver, which provide a wire-free, uncluttered work area and flexibility to type and point from anywhere within 30 feet of the transceiver.

INFOWEBLINKS

For the latest information on HomePNA and HomePLC networks, connect to the **Home Network InfoWeb**.

www.course.com/np/concepts8/ch05

FIGURE 5-28
LAN Technology Comparison

Network Type	Advantages	Disadvantages	Speed
Ethernet	Inexpensive; reliable; standard technology; fast	Unsightly cables; might require running cables through walls, ceilings, and floors	10 Mbps, 100 Mbps, 1 Gbps, 10 Gbps
Wi-Fi	No cables required	Each device requires a transceiver, which adds costs; signals can be intercepted; susceptible to interference from large metal objects and other wireless devices	11 Mbps (802.11b) 54 Mbps (802.11a and 802.11g)
Bluetooth	Inexpensive; reliable; built into many popular devices	Slow; limited range; little security	1 Mbps
HomePLC	No cables required; uses any standard electrical outlet	Susceptible to electrical Interference; very slow	2 Mbps
HomePNA	No cables required; uses existing telephone wiring	Requires telephone jacks near computers; slow transmission speed	10 Mbps

INSTALLING A LAN

How do I set up a simple LAN? Setting up a small LAN is easy. Equipment for HomePLC and HomePNA LANs is typically sold in kit form, with detailed instructions on setup procedures. To set up an Ethernet or Wi-Fi LAN, most consumers purchase parts from a computer, electronics, or office store, and follow the setup instructions provided with the hub or router. Figure 5-29 provides an overview of Ethernet and Wi-Fi setup.

FIGURE 5-29

Installing a LAN

1. To begin, make sure every computer and peripheral you'll connect to the network contains a NIC. If a card is not built in, you must install one.

Devices you intend to connect using cables require Ethernet cards. Devices slated for wireless connections require Wi-Fi cards.

CLICK TO START

2. Place the hub or router in a central location and plug it into a surge-protected outlet.

If you are planning to link your LAN to the Internet, connect the hub or router to your Internet connection. (More details on the options for Internet connections are presented in Section D.)

3. For an Ethernet, run cables from the hub or router to the NIC in each device.

Turn on network devices one at a time. Windows should automatically detect the NICs and establish a connection to the network.

INFOWEBLINKS

Your basic shopping list for a simple Ethernet LAN is at the **Building a LAN InfoWeb**.

www.course.com/np/concepts8/ch05

USING A LAN

How do I access network resources? If you use Windows, it automatically detects the network any time you turn on a workstation. Depending on your network setup, you might be asked to log in by entering a user ID and password. Once access is established, you can use any shared resources for which you have been given authorization.

You can access shared folders and drives on other workstations in a variety of ways. For example, you can use My Computer to access shared resources listed under the My Network Places icon, or you can use **drive mapping** to assign a drive letter to a storage device located on a different workstation (Figure 5-30).

FIGURE 5-30

In this drive mapping example, a server's drive C is mapped as drive F by a workstation.

After the mapping is complete, the server's hard disk appears in the workstation's directory as drive F and can be used just as though it were a drive connected directly to the workstation.

CLICK TO START

How do I specify which resources can be shared by other workstations? Workstation owners can specify whether files and locally attached printers can be accessed from other workstations on the network. Windows allows you to designate a special folder for files you want to share with others. You can allow others to view and edit these files, or you can limit access only to viewing. You can also allow other network users to access your computer's entire hard disk or locally connected printer.

QUICKCHECK......SECTION B

1. A(n) [_____] LAN simultaneously broadcasts data packets over all network links and uses CSMA/CD protocol to handle collisions.

2. Today's most popular wireless LAN technology is compatible with Ethernet and called [_____].

3. [_____] is a short-range technology used for PANs.

4. A Home [_____] network uses existing telephone wiring, whereas a Home [_____] uses power lines.

CHECK ANSWERS

SECTION C

INTERNET TECHNOLOGY

To most people, the Internet seems like old hat. Even people who haven't used the Internet know a lot about it from watching the news, reading magazines, and watching movies. Using the Internet is actually pretty easy. Browsing Web sites, shopping at the Net mall, sending e-mail, and chatting online? No problem.

But what makes the Internet "tick"? How can one network offer so much information to so many people? Section C pulls back the curtain and gives you a glimpse of what happens behind the scenes of the Net.

BACKGROUND

How did the Internet get started? The history of the Internet begins in 1957 when the Soviet Union launched Sputnik, the first man-made satellite. In response to this display of Soviet superiority, the U.S. government resolved to improve its scientific and technical infrastructure. One of the resulting initiatives was the Advanced Research Projects Agency (ARPA).

ARPA swung into action with a project designed to help scientists communicate and share valuable computer resources. The ARPANET, created in 1969, connected computers at UCLA, Stanford Research Institute, University of Utah, and University of California at Santa Barbara (Figure 5-31). In 1985, the National Science Foundation (NSF) used ARPANET technology to create a similar, but larger, network, linking not just a few mainframe computers, but entire LANs at each site. Connecting two or more networks creates an "internetwork" or "internet." The NSF network was an internet (with a lowercase "i"). As this network grew throughout the world, it became known as the Internet (with an uppercase "I").

FIGURE 5-31

An original diagram of the ARPANET included four nodes, depicted as circles.

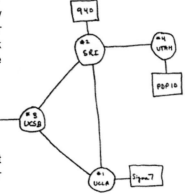

Early Internet pioneers—mostly educators and scientists—used primitive command-line user interfaces to send e-mail, transfer files, and run scientific calculations on Internet supercomputers. Finding information was not easy. Without search engines, Internet users relied on word of mouth and e-mail to keep informed about new data and its location. "The data you need is on the Stanford computer in a file called Chrome.txt." was typical of messages between colleagues.

How did the Internet become so popular? In the early 1990s, software developers created new user-friendly Internet access tools, and Internet accounts became available to anyone willing to pay a monthly subscription fee. Today, the Internet connects computers all over the globe and supplies information to people of all ages and interests.

How big is the Internet today? With an estimated 200 million nodes and 500 million users, the Internet is huge. Although exact figures cannot be determined, it is estimated that Internet traffic exceeds 100 terabytes each week—about 100 trillion bytes. That's approximately 10 times the amount of data stored in the entire printed collection of the U.S. Library of Congress.

INTERNET STRUCTURE

How is the Internet structured? Surprisingly, the Internet is not "owned" or operated by any single corporation or government. It is a data communications network that grew over time in a somewhat haphazard configuration as networks connected to other networks.

In Chapter 1 you learned that the Internet backbone provides the main high-speed routes for data traffic. At one time, the topology of the Internet backbone and interconnected networks might have resembled a spine with ribs connected along its length. Today, however, it more resembles a map of interstate highways with many junctures and redundant routes.

How does the backbone tie the Internet together? The Internet backbone consists of high-speed fiber-optic links connecting high-capacity routers that direct network traffic. Backbone links and routers are maintained by **network service providers** (NSPs), such as AT&T, MCI, Qwest, Sprint, and UUNET. NSP equipment and links are tied together by **network access points** (NAPs), so that, for example, data that begins its journey on an AT&T link can cross over to a Sprint link, if necessary, to reach its destination.

Large ISPs connect directly to backbone routers. Smaller ISPs typically connect to a larger ISP to gain Internet access and supply it to their customers. Figure 5-32 shows a simplified, conceptual diagram of the Internet backbone and its components.

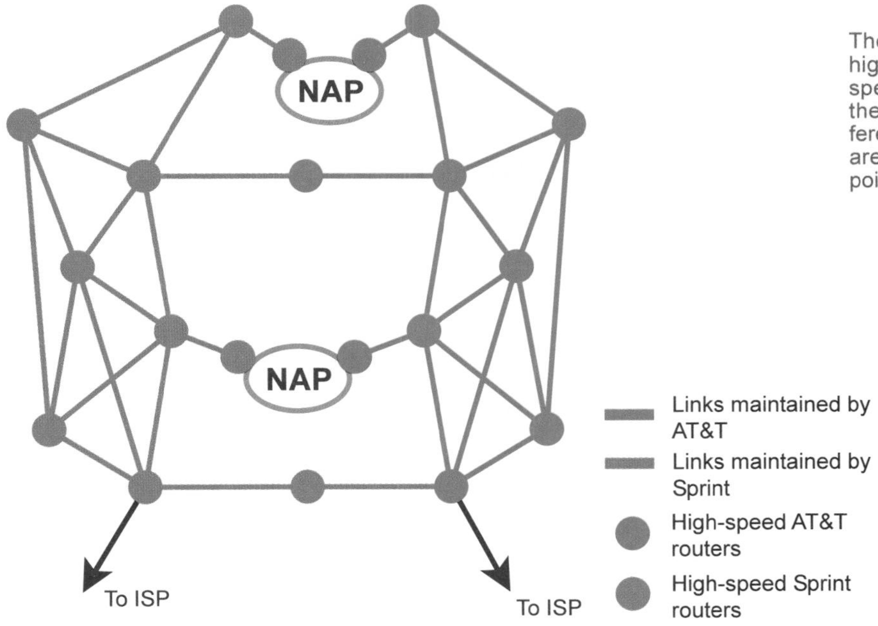

FIGURE 5-32

The Internet backbone includes high-speed routers and high-speed fiber-optic links. Parts of the backbone maintained by different communications companies are connected at network access points (NAPs).

Is it possible to track data as it travels over the Internet? You can track the route of data you send using Internet utilities, such as Ping and Traceroute. An Internet utility called **Ping** (Packet Internet Groper) sends a signal to a specific Internet address and waits for a reply. If a reply arrives, Ping reports that the computer is online and displays the elapsed time, or **latency**, for the round-trip message. Ping is useful for finding out whether a site is up and running. Ping is also useful for determining whether a connection is adequate for online computer games or videoconferencing.

A utility called **Traceroute** records a packet's path—including intermediate routers—from your computer to its destination. Figure 5-33 contains a Traceroute report.

INFOWEBLINKS

Would you like a color map showing your data's path through cyberspace? Check out the **Traceroute Utilities InfoWeb**.

www.course.com/np/concepts8/ch05

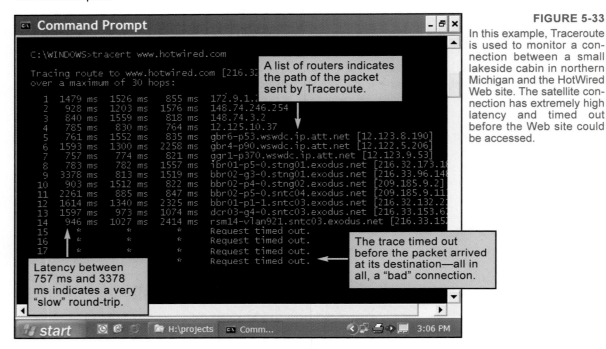

FIGURE 5-33

In this example, Traceroute is used to monitor a connection between a small lakeside cabin in northern Michigan and the HotWired Web site. The satellite connection has extremely high latency and timed out before the Web site could be accessed.

How fast does data travel over the Internet? Using Ping or Traceroute, you can discover how long data is in transit from point A to point B. On average, data within North America usually arrives at its destination 110–120 ms (milliseconds) after it is sent. Overseas transmission usually requires a little more time.

ISP INFRASTRUCTURE

What kinds of network devices are part of an ISP? An ISP operates network devices that handle the physical aspects of transmitting and receiving data from your computer. For example, an ISP that offers telephone modem connections must maintain a bank of modems that answer when your computer dials the ISP's access number.

Many ISPs operate e-mail servers to handle incoming and outgoing mail for their subscribers and Web servers for subscriber Web sites. An ISP might also operate a server that translates an address, such as *www.google.com*, into a valid, numeric Internet address, such as 208.50.141.12. You'll learn more about this topic later in the chapter. ISPs can also maintain servers for chat groups, instant messaging, music file sharing, FTP, and other file transfer services. Figure 5-34 on the next page illustrates the equipment at a typical ISP.

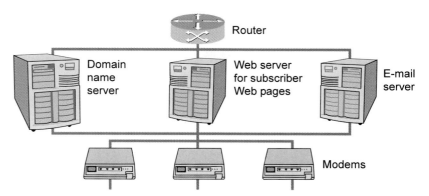

FIGURE 5-34
ISP Equipment

How does my computer fit into the structure of the Internet? Your computer connects to the Internet in one of two ways (Figure 5-35). It can link directly to an ISP connection, such as voiceband modem, cable modem, direct satellite service, or DSL. Or, if your computer is part of a LAN, an Internet connection can be provided by a LAN link. Section D provides detailed information on linking computers and networks to the Internet.

INTERNET PROTOCOLS

Why does the Internet use TCP/IP? When the Internet was still the ARPANET, its communications protocols were slow and prone to crashes. Improvements were definitely in order, and by 1977, new protocols, including TCP/IP, were implemented. From a practical perspective, TCP/IP provides a standard that is easy to implement, public, free, and extensible.

Is TCP/IP limited to the Internet? No. TCP/IP is also used on LANs and WANs. A local area network that uses TCP/IP is called an **intranet**. Intranets are popular with businesses that want to store information as Web pages but not provide them for public access. An intranet that provides private, external access is called an **extranet**.

How does TCP/IP work? TCP/IP is a combination of protocols. **TCP** (Transmission Control Protocol) breaks a message or file into packets. **IP** (Internet Protocol) is responsible for addressing packets so that they can be routed to their destination.

Is TCP/IP the only Internet protocol? No. Several other protocols are used with TCP/IP on the Internet. Figure 5-36 briefly describes some of them.

FIGURE 5-35
Your computer can connect to the Internet as a standalone device or part of a LAN.

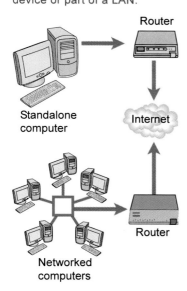

FIGURE 5-36
Protocols Used on the Internet

Protocol	Name	Function
HTTP	Hypertext Transfer Protocol	Exchanges information over the Web
FTP	File Transfer Protocol	Transfers files between local and remote host computers
POP	Post Office Protocol	Transfers mail from an e-mail server to a client Inbox
SMTP	Simple Mail Transfer Protocol	Transfers e-mail messages from client computers to an e-mail server
IMAP	Internet Mail Access Protocol	An alternative to POP
TELNET	Telecommunication Network	Allows users who are logged on to one host to access another host
SSL	Secure Sockets Layer	Provides secure data transfer over the Internet

IP ADDRESSES

Does the Internet use a special addressing scheme? The "IP" part of TCP/IP defines the format for the addresses that identify computers on the Internet. As a result, these addresses are referred to as **IP addresses**; however, you might also see them referred to as "TCP/IP addresses" or "Internet addresses."

An IP address is a series of numbers, such as 204.127.129.1. When written, an IP address is separated into four sections by periods for the convenience of human readers. Each section is called an **octet** (Figure 5-37). The number in a section cannot exceed 255. In binary representation, each section of an IP address requires 8 bits, so the entire address requires 32 bits.

204.127.129.1

Octet   Octet   Octet   Octet

FIGURE 5-37
Each section of an IP address, called an octet, can contain a number from 0–255.

Does each octet correspond to part of a URL? Although an IP address, such as 216.247.67.77, might correspond to a URL, such as *http://www.mediatechnics.net*, the octets do not map to the parts of a URL. That means the first octet, 216, does not correspond to *http://*. Nor does the second octet, 247, map to *www.* Instead, IP address octets designate specific networks and subnetworks. Octets 216.247, for example, designate a network called Interland that hosts the MediaTechnics Web site.

Do I need a permanent IP address? A computer can have a permanently assigned **static IP address** or a temporarily assigned **dynamic IP address**. As a rule of thumb, computers on the Internet that act as servers use static IP addresses. Typically, ISPs, Web sites, Web hosting services, and e-mail servers are constantly connected to the Internet and require static addresses.

Theoretically, the IP addressing scheme provides approximately 4.3 billion unique addresses—a meager number considering the growing demands of today's information-hungry consumers. Happily, you don't need a static IP address to engage in client (as opposed to server) activities, such as surfing the Web, sending and receiving e-mail, listening to Internet radio, or participating in chat groups. A "temporary" dynamic IP address suffices for these activities.

When do I get a dynamic IP address? Every ISP controls a unique pool of IP addresses, which can be assigned as needed to subscribers. ISPs assign Dynamic IP addresses for most dial-up connections and some DSL, ISDN, or cable modem connections.

When you use a dial-up connection, for example, your ISP assigns a temporary IP address to your computer for use as long as it remains connected. When you end a session, that IP address goes back into a pool of addresses that can be distributed to other subscribers when they log in.

INFOWEBLINKS

Want to know how to find your current IP address? It's easy. You can find out how at the **IP Address InfoWeb**.

www.course.com/np/concepts8/ch05

Your computer is rarely assigned the same IP address it had during a previous dial-up session. As a dial-up "nomad" with no permanent address, you can't feasibly run a Web site or other server-related activities from your computer because your previous IP address—the one that your customers recorded in their Favorites lists and the one that appears in search engines—does not remain assigned to your computer after you log off.

The address situation for DSL, ISDN, and cable modem subscribers varies, depending on the ISP. You might be assigned a static IP address; you might be given a dynamic address each time you connect; or you might be allocated a semi-permanent address that lasts for several months. If you want to operate a server over a DSL, ISDN, or cable modem connection, ask your ISP about its method of address allocation and its policies on allowing server activities.

DOMAIN NAMES

What's a domain name? Although IP addresses work for communication between computers, people find it difficult to remember long strings of numbers. Therefore, many Internet servers also have an easy-to-remember name, such as *nike.com*. The official term for this name is "fully qualified domain name" (FQDN), but most people just refer to it as a **domain name**. By convention, you should type domain names using all lowercase letters.

A domain name is a key component of URLs and e-mail addresses. It is the Web server name in a URL and the e-mail server name in an e-mail address. For example, in the URL *www.msu.edu/infotech*, the domain name is *msu.edu*. In the e-mail address *jbillings@msu.edu*, the domain name is also *msu.edu*.

A domain name ends with an extension that indicates its **top-level domain**. For example, in the domain name *msu.edu*, *edu* indicates that the computer is maintained by an educational institution. Some of the most commonly used top-level domains are listed in Figure 5-38.

Domain	Description
biz	Unrestricted use; usually for commercial businesses
com	Unrestricted use; usually for commercial businesses
edu	Restricted to North American educational institutions
gov	Restricted to U.S. government agencies
info	Unrestricted use
int	Restricted to organizations established by international treaties
mil	Restricted to U.S. military agencies
net	Unrestricted use; traditionally for Internet administrative organizations
org	Unrestricted use; traditionally for professional and nonprofit organizations

FIGURE 5-38
Top-level Domains

Country codes also serve as top-level domains. Canada's top-level domain is ca; the United Kingdom's is uk; Australia's is au. A domain with growing popularity is tv. Originally assigned to the small Polynesian island of Tuvalu, the tv domain has been obtained by a professional management team and is available for a fee to media-related Web sites.

How are domain names related to IP addresses? Every domain name corresponds to a unique IP address that has been entered into a huge database called the **Domain Name System** (DNS). Computers that host this database are referred to as **domain name servers**. A domain name, such as *travelocity.com*, must be converted into an IP address before any packets can be routed to it. For example, when you type the URL *www.travelocity.com* into your browser, the browser's first step is to contact a domain name server to get the IP address for the Travelocity Web server, as shown in Figure 5-39.

FIGURE 5-39

A domain name request is routed through your ISP to your designated domain name server, which searches through its database to find a corresponding IP address. The IP address can then be attached to packets, such as requests for Web pages.

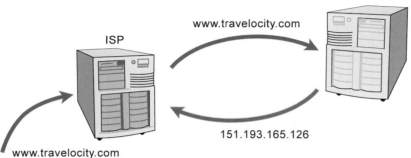

The Domain Name System is based on a distributed database. Amazingly, this database is not stored as a whole in any single location; instead, it exists in parts all over the Internet. Your Internet connection is set up to access one of the many domain name servers that reside on the Internet. When you enter a domain name or URL, it is sent to your designated domain server, which can do one of three things:

- It can send back the IP address that corresponds to the domain name.

- If your domain name server does not have a record of the domain name, it can contact another domain name server and request the IP address.

- It can send back the address for a domain name server that is more likely to have the IP address of the domain name you requested.

The servers in the Domain Name System are quite efficient and typically manage to supply IP addresses in a matter of milliseconds.

Do I need my own domain name? For client-style Internet activities, such as Web browsing, e-mail, and chat, you do not need your own domain name. You might, however, want a domain name if you plan to operate your own Web server or if you establish a Web site using servers provided by a Web site hosting service.

Suppose you decide to set up a Web site called Rocky Mountain Photos. If you would like people to access your site by typing *www.rockymtnphotos.com*, you must obtain the *rockymtnphotos.com* domain name. In contrast, if your Web site is set up on a Web server supplied by your ISP, your own domain name might not be necessary because you use the domain of the ISP's Web server. For example, if you set up your Rocky Mountain Photos on AOL's Hometown Web server, your URL might be *hometown.aol.com/rockymtnphotos*.

How do I get a domain name? An organization called **ICANN** (Internet Corporation for Assigned Names and Numbers) is recognized by the United States and other governments as the global organization that coordinates technical management of the Internet's Domain Name System. It supervises several for-profit Accredited Domain Registrars, which handle domain name requests.

INFOWEBLINKS

Where can you register a domain name? What are the current fees? These questions are answered at the **Domain Name InfoWeb**.

www.course.com/np/concepts8/ch05

The first step in registering a domain name is to find out whether the name is available. By connecting to an Accredited Domain Registrar Web site, you can enter a domain name, as shown in Figure 5-40.

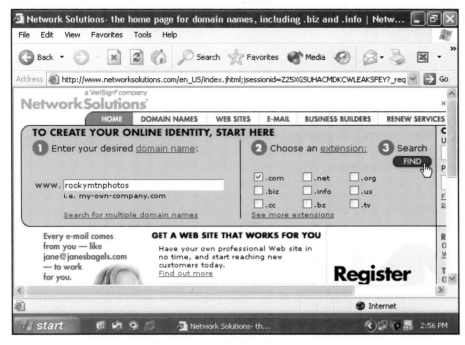

FIGURE 5-40

The first step in registering a domain name is to find out whether the name is currently in use or reserved for future use.

If a domain name is not available, consider using a different top-level domain, such as biz instead of com.

After you've found an available domain name you like, you can continue the registration process by filling out a simple online form.

CLICK TO START ✦

Is a fee required to obtain a domain name? You can register a domain name for a minimal annual fee—currently between $10 and $50, depending on the registration service.

Some domain names are not currently in use, yet they are not available because they are reserved. Internet entrepreneurs have made a business of registering high-profile domain names with the intention of reselling them. For example, the domain name *team.com* is "for sale" for the tidy sum of $250,000; *science.tv* has a price tag of $100,000. To obtain one of these domain names, you must purchase it from the seller. After you pay for the name, you can register it for the standard annual fee.

QUICKCHECK......SECTION C

1. Network [＿＿＿＿＿＿] providers, such as AT&T and UUNET, maintain links and routers on the Internet backbone.

2. A utility called [＿＿＿＿＿＿] checks whether a network computer is online and displays the elapsed time for a round-trip message.

3. The [＿＿＿＿＿＿] protocol breaks a message or file into packets; [＿＿＿＿＿＿] is responsible for addressing packets so that they can be routed to their destination. Hint: Use acronyms.

4. Internet servers typically have a(n) [＿＿＿＿＿＿] IP address.

5. An Internet address, such as *msu.edu*, is called a fully qualified [＿＿＿＿＿＿] name.

✦ CHECK ANSWERS

LAB

LAB 5-C

TRACKING PACKETS

In this lab, you'll learn:

- How Ping and Traceroute work
- How to use the Ping and Tracert utilities supplied by Windows
- How to interpret Ping and Tracert reports to determine the speed and reliability of your Internet connection
- How to access and use a graphical Traceroute utility
- What's on the Boardwatch Web site
- How to find and use Web-based Ping and Traceroute utilities
- The advantages and disadvantages of Web-based Ping and Traceroute utilities
- How to access the Internet Traffic Report Web site
- The meaning of a "traffic index"
- How to interpret data and graphs at the Internet Traffic Report Web site
- How to use Internet traffic data with Ping and Traceroute reports to pinpoint problems with your Internet connection

LAB ASSIGNMENTS

1. Start the interactive part of the lab. Insert your Tracking Disk if you want to save your QuickCheck results. Perform each lab step as directed, and answer all the lab QuickCheck questions. When you exit the lab, your answers are automatically graded and your results are displayed.

2. Use the Ping utility that's supplied by Windows to ping *www.abc-news.com*. Record the IP address for the ABC News site, plus the minimum, maximum, and average times. For each time, indicate whether it would be considered poor, average, or good.

3. Use the Tracert utility that's supplied by Windows to trace a packet between your computer and *www.excite.com*. Print the Traceroute report listing transmission times. Circle any pings on the report that indicate high latency.

4. Locate a Web-based Ping utility and use it to ping *www.gobledegok.com*. Indicate the URL for the Web site where you found the Ping utility. Explain the results of the ping.

5. Connect to the Internet Traffic Report Web site, make a note of the date and time, and then answer the following questions:

   a. What is the traffic index for Asia?

   b. How does the index for Asia compare with the traffic index for North America?

   c. During the previous 24 hours in Europe, what was the period with the worst response time?

INTERACTIVE LAB

CLICK TO START THE LAB

SECTION D

INTERNET ACCESS

One of the most challenging aspects of the Internet is selecting a connection. Although most people begin with a dial-up connection, many soon explore high-speed Internet access options. Interest is also growing in using home-based LAN and wireless Internet access.

In this section of the chapter, you'll discover why online interactive game players shun direct satellite connections. You'll learn why cable and DSL modems leave your computer open to hackers who cruise the Internet searching for user IDs, passwords, and launching points for bothersome viruses. And you won't be left in suspense—you'll learn how to close up those security holes to prevent unwanted intrusions.

DIAL-UP CONNECTIONS

How does a dial-up connection work? A dial-up connection uses **POTS** (plain old telephone service) to transport data between your computer and your ISP. To understand how it works, you'll need a little background on telephone communications.

The telephone communications system uses a tiered network to transport calls locally, cross-country, and internationally. At each level of the network, a switch creates a connection so that a call eventually has a continuous circuit to its destination. The first tier of this network uses a star topology to physically connect each telephone in a city to a switch in what's called a "switching station," "local switch," or "central office."

The second tier of the telephone network links several local switching stations. Connections then fan out to switches maintained by many different local and long-distance telephone companies, as shown in Figure 5-41.

FIGURE 5-41

The telephone system connects your telephone to a local switch. Local switches are connected to other nearby local switches and to long-haul communications links.

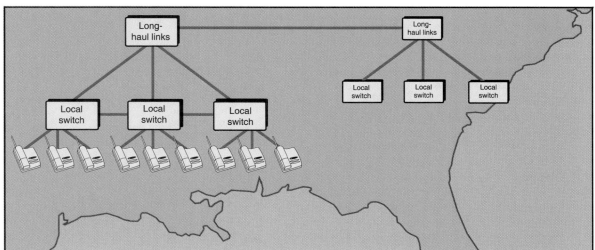

When you use a dial-up connection, your computer's modem essentially places a regular telephone call to your ISP. Your call is routed through the telephone company's local switch and out to the ISP. When the ISP's computer "answers" your call, a dedicated circuit is established between you and your ISP—just as though you had made a voice call and someone at the ISP had "picked up" the phone. The circuit remains connected for the duration of your call and provides a communications link that carries data between your computer and the ISP. As your data arrives at the ISP, a router sends it out over the Internet. Figure 5-42 illustrates the path of your data when you use a dial-up connection.

FIGURE 5-42

When you use an ISP to access the Internet, your data travels through the local telephone switch to your ISP, which sends it onto the Internet.

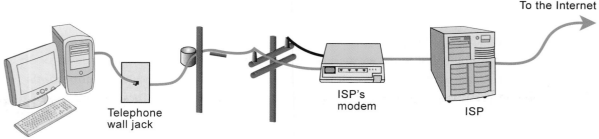

How does a modem work? The signals that represent data bits exist in your computer as digital signals. The telephone system, however, expects to work with human voices, so the "stuff" that it carries must be in the format of analog audio tones. It's as though you are trying to move a bunch of ice cubes through a tube. If the cubes won't fit through the tube, you can melt them into water, which can flow through the tube. A voiceband modem—usually referred to simply as a "modem"—converts the signals from your computer into signals that can travel over telephone lines. A modem transmits a 1,070 Hz tone for a 0 and a 1,270 Hz tone for a 1.

The word "modem" is derived from the words "modulate" and "demodulate." In communications terminology, **modulation** means changing the characteristics of a signal, as when a modem changes a digital pulse into an analog audio signal. **Demodulation** means changing a signal back to its original state, as when a modem changes an audio signal back to a digital pulse (Figure 5-43).

INFOWEBLINKS

If you're curious about the latest modem technology, speed, and prices, check out the **Modem InfoWeb**.

www.course.com/np/concepts8/ch05

FIGURE 5-43

When you transmit data, your modem modulates the signal that carries your data. A modem at the other end of the transmission demodulates the signal.

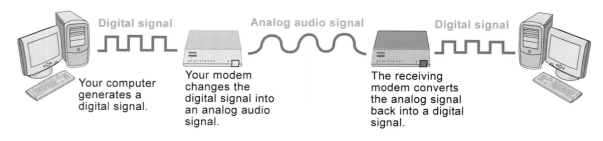

When your computer's modem initiates a connection, it sends a signal that is equivalent to picking up the receiver of a telephone to get a dial tone. It then dials the ISP by emitting a series of tones—the same tones you'd produce if you punched in the ISP's number using a phone keypad. The modem then waits for the ISP's modem to answer the call. After the ISP's modem answers, the two modems begin to negotiate communications protocols, such as transmission rate. The series of beeps, tones, and whooshing sounds you hear when you connect to your ISP is the sound of your modem "talking" to the ISP's modem. When the negotiation, or "handshaking," is complete, data transmission can begin.

Why doesn't new digital telephone technology eliminate the need for a modem? Although telephone companies went digital long ago, their digital switches kick into action only after your call arrives at the local switching station. The technology between your telephone and your local switch would be recognizable to Alexander Graham Bell. The "local loop," as it is sometimes called, is designed to carry analog voice signals.

To transport data over this local loop, the digital signals from your computer must be converted into analog tones that can travel over the telephone lines to your local switch. When these signals arrive at the local switch, they are converted into digital signals—but not in the same digital format as they originated from your computer—so that they can be sent over the digital section of the telephone network. With all this conversion, it seems amazing that data actually reaches its destination!

Can I talk and send data at the same time? When your computer is connected to your ISP via dial-up, data is transmitted over the same frequencies normally used for voice conversations. If you have only one telephone line, you cannot pick up your telephone receiver, dial your friend, and carry on a voice conversation while you are sending data. Some modems use technology similar to call waiting that allows you to remain connected to your ISP and temporarily suspend data transfers while answering a voice call. It is also possible to use the Internet to carry voice signals from your computer's microphone to the sound card of another computer. This technology, called **Voice over IP** (VoIP), allows you to play games, for example, and chat about your moves—all while you are online.

How fast is a modem? When modems were a new technology, their speed was measured as **baud rate**—the number of times per second that a signal in a communications channel varies or makes a transition between states. An example of such a transition is the change from a signal representing a 1 bit to a signal representing a 0 bit. A 300-baud modem's signal changes state 300 times each second, but—and this is the tricky part—each baud doesn't necessarily carry one bit. So a 300-baud modem might be able to transmit more than 300 bits per second.

To help consumers make sense of modem speeds, they are now measured in bits per second. (If you're a stickler for details, you'll realize that bps is actually a measure of capacity, but everyone calls it "speed.") Since 1998, most modems use a standard called **V.90** to provide a theoretical maximum speed of 56 Kbps. Actual data transfer speeds are affected by factors such as the quality of your local loop connection to the telephone switch. Even with a "perfect" connection, a 56 Kbps modem tops out at about 44 Kbps. Slightly faster speeds might be possible with **V.92** and **V.44** modems (Figure 5-44), as they gain widespread support from dial-up ISPs.

INFOWEBLINKS

At the **Voice over IP InfoWeb**, you'll find links to software downloads and more information about using the Internet as a voice channel.

www.course.com/np/concepts8/ch05

FIGURE 5-44
Modems with V.92/V.44 technology are gradually replacing the V.90 standard.

Many Internet connection methods provide faster **downstream** (the data you receive) transmission rates than **upstream** (the data you send) rates. Dial-up connections are no exception; 44 Kbps is a typical downstream speed for a 56 Kbps modem. Upstream, the data rate drops to about 33 Kbps or less.

CABLE MODEM CONNECTIONS

How does a cable modem work? The cable television system was originally designed for remote areas where TV broadcast signals could not be received in an acceptable manner with an antenna. These systems were called "community antenna television," or CATV. The CATV concept was to install one or more large, expensive satellite dishes in a community, catch TV signals with these dishes, and then send the signals over a system of cables to individual homes.

The satellite dish "farm" at which television broadcasts are received and retransmitted is referred to as the **head-end**. From the head-end, a cabling system branches out and eventually reaches consumers' homes.

The topology of a CATV system looks a lot like the physical topology for a computer network. And that is just what is formed when your cable TV company becomes your Internet provider. A router and high-speed connection from the head-end to the Internet provide the potential for Internet connectivity over every cable in the system. Your computer becomes part of a neighborhood LAN like the one depicted in Figure 5-45.

FIGURE 5-45

Cables from the CATV head-end extend out as a series of "trunks." The trunks are then connected to "feeders" that serve neighborhoods. The connection from a feeder to a consumer's home is referred to as a "drop."

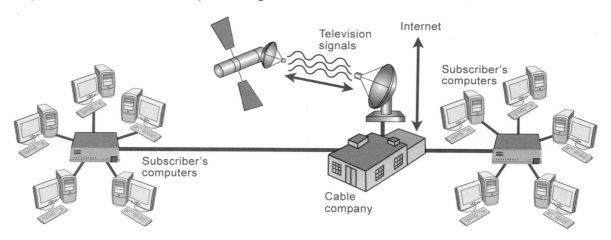

Are television and data signals carried over the same cable? The lowest-capacity coaxial cable the CATV system uses has a far greater carrying capacity than POTS lines. To offer both television and Internet access, the cable's bandwidth is divided among three activities. As shown in Figure 5-46, a CATV cable must provide bandwidth for television signals, incoming data signals, and outgoing data signals.

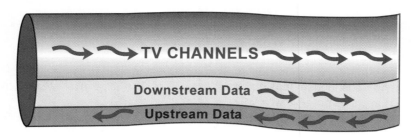

FIGURE 5-46

A CATV cable has enough bandwidth to support TV channels and data flowing downstream as well as data flowing upstream.

How do I set up a cable modem connection? When you configure your computer to access the Internet with a cable modem, you are essentially connecting to an Ethernet-style LAN that connects a neighborhood of cable subscribers. The two requirements for this type of connection are circuitry to handle Ethernet protocols and a **cable modem**, which converts your computer's signal into one that can travel over the CATV network.

Some cable modems include Ethernet circuitry, so they can be connected to your computer using a USB cable. Otherwise, your computer must be equipped with an Ethernet card. Figure 5-47 shows how to connect a cable modem to a desktop computer's Ethernet card.

INFOWEBLINKS

For an in-depth look at cable modem technology, connections, bandwidth, and security, follow the links at the **Cable Modem InfoWeb**.

www.course.com/np/concepts8/ch05

FIGURE 5-47
If your home has only one CATV cable outlet, you need to use a splitter to link your cable modem and television. If you have multiple cable outlets, you can connect your cable modem directly to any one of them.

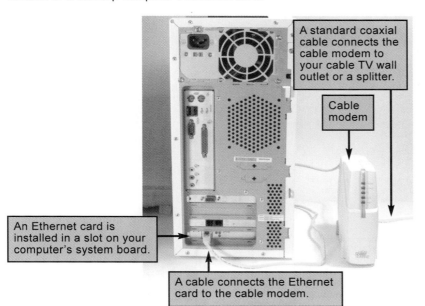

A standard coaxial cable connects the cable modem to your cable TV wall outlet or a splitter.

Cable modem

An Ethernet card is installed in a slot on your computer's system board.

A cable connects the Ethernet card to the cable modem.

Unlike a dial-up connection that's connected only for the duration of your call, a cable modem provides an **always-on connection** that is "on" whenever your computer is powered up—whether or not you are online using a browser, an e-mail client, FTP, or other Internet utility. With an always-on connection, you might have the same IP address for days or even months, depending on your ISP. Because your computer is connected to the Internet for long periods of time, an always-on connection is particularly vulnerable to hackers. Gaining access to unprotected computers allows hackers to steal data, launch virus attacks, and send e-mail from your account.

What's the significance of becoming part of a "neighborhood network"? When your cable connection is up and running, your computer becomes part of a neighborhood data network that includes any of your neighbors who subscribe to cable modem access. Two issues become significant: bandwidth and security.

The cable you share with your neighbors has a certain amount of bandwidth. As more and more neighbors use the service, it might seem to get slower and slower. As an analogy, consider the luggage conveyor belt in an airport, which moves at a constant speed. If you have three pieces of luggage and you are the only passenger on the plane, your bags arrive one right after another. However, if you just arrived on a full 747, your bags are intermixed with those of hundreds of other passengers, and it takes longer to collect them.

Your cable company's network carries packets at a constant speed. However, if many of your neighbors are sending and receiving packets at the same time, those packets seem to arrive more slowly.

As for the security issue, in the early days of cable modem service, some cable modem users were unpleasantly surprised when they happened to open Windows Network Neighborhood, only to be greeted with a list of their neighbors' computers! When you have an Ethernet card in your PC, Windows automatically takes inventory of the LAN during bootup. It looks for any computers on the network that have file and printer sharing activated, and then lists them in the My Network Places window, as shown in Figure 5-48.

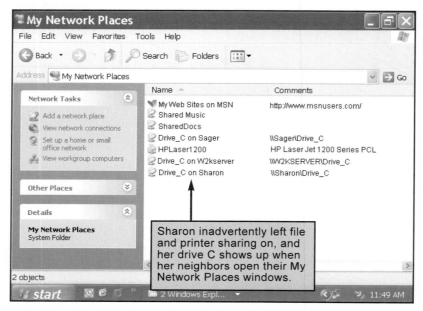

FIGURE 5-48
If your PC is part of a network and has file and printer sharing activated, other network users might be able to access your files by opening the My Network Places window.

Today, most cable companies use DOCSIS-compliant cable modems that block "crossover" traffic between subscribers. **DOCSIS** (Data Over Cable Service Interface Specification) is a security technology that filters packets to certain ports, including the port Windows uses for networking. DOCSIS secures your computer from your neighbors, but it does not close up all the security holes that are opened when you use an always-on connection.

DSL, ISDN, T1, AND T3

What other options are available for high-speed Internet access? Although the standard equipment provided by telephone companies limits the amount of data you can transmit and receive over a voiceband modem, the copper wire that runs from your wall jacks to the switching station actually has a fair amount of capacity. Several services, such as DSL, ISDN, T1, and T3, take advantage of this capacity to offer high-speed digital communications links for voice and data.

What is DSL? **DSL** (digital subscriber line) is a high-speed, digital, always-on, Internet access technology that runs over standard phone lines. It is one of the fastest Internet connections that's affordable to individual consumers. Several variations of this technology exist, including ADSL (asymmetric DSL, with downstream speed faster than upstream speed), SDSL (symmetric DSL, with the same upstream and downstream speed), HDSL (high-rate DSL), and DSL lite.

TERMINOLOGY NOTE

The acronym xDSL refers to the entire group of DSL technologies (including symmetric DSL, HDSL, and so on), but xDSL is not a separate variation of DSL.

DSL is digital, so data doesn't need to be changed into analog form and then back to digital as it does when you use a dial-up connection. Data is transmitted over your local loop in pure digital form, bypassing the bottleneck of analog-to-digital-to-analog conversion and escaping the requirement to use the narrow bandwidth allocated to voice transmissions. The result is fast data transmission over standard copper telephone cable.

A DSL connection can simultaneously carry voice and data, if permitted by your DSL provider. You can then use your DSL line for voice calls instead of your POTS line. The digital data and analog voice signals travel over the DSL line to the local switching station. There the voice signals are transferred to the telephone company's regular lines. The data signals are interpreted by special equipment called a **DSLAM** (DSL Access Multiplexor) and routed over high-speed lines to a DSL provider or directly to the Internet.

In many areas, DSL is a joint venture between the telephone company and the DSL provider. The telephone company is responsible for the physical cabling and voice transmission. The DSL provider is responsible for data traffic. Figure 5-49 illustrates how DSL handles voice and data.

INFOWEBLINKS

Nationwide, DSL vendors are grouping and regrouping. How might this affect your Internet access? You'll find up-to-date consumer information at the **DSL InfoWeb**.

www.course.com/np/concepts8/ch05

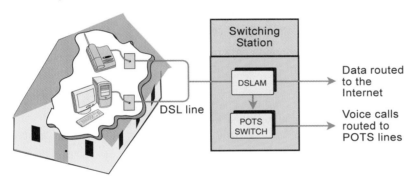

FIGURE 5-49

Voice and data signals travel over DSL to a special device at the local telephone switching station, where they are divided and routed to an ISP or to the regular telephone network.

The speed of a DSL connection varies according to the characteristics of your telephone line, the equipment at your local switch, and your distance from the switching station. Most DSL modems are rated for 1.5 Mbps downstream. A DSL signal deteriorates over distance, however, which limits dependable DSL service to customers who live within three "cable" miles of a switching station. When shopping for a DSL connection, you should inquire about actual speed, find out if the upstream rate differs from the downstream rate, and check your distance from the switching station.

How do I install DSL? Most DSL installations require trained service technicians. Your DSL provider requests your local telephone company to designate a telephone line for the DSL connection. This line might utilize unused twisted pairs in your current telephone line, or it might require a new line from the nearest telephone pole to the telephone box outside your house. This line is connected to a DSL switch at the phone company's local switching office.

Next, a technician from the DSL provider makes a service call to run cables and install a DSL wall jack, if necessary. The technician usually installs a **DSL modem**, which manages the interface between your computer and a DSL line. If the modem includes Ethernet circuitry, a USB cable connects the modem to your PC. Other types of DSL modems connect to your computer's Ethernet card (Figure 5-50).

FIGURE 5-50

In a typical DSL installation, a twisted-pair cable connects your computer's Ethernet card to a DSL modem, which is plugged into a wall jack.

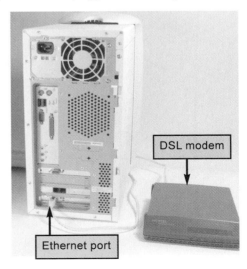

Is ISDN faster than DSL? **ISDN** (Integrated Services Digital Network) connections move data at speeds of 64 Kbps or 128 Kbps—not as fast as DSL or cable modems but faster than a dial-up connection. As with DSL, ISDN is an all-digital service with the potential to simultaneously carry voice and data. A device called an **ISDN terminal adapter** connects a computer to a telephone wall jack and translates the computer's digital signals into a different kind of digital signal that can travel over the ISDN connection.

ISDN service is typically regarded as a high-speed Internet connection option for businesses that maintain small LANs. The service is usually obtained from a local telephone company or a dedicated ISDN service provider. ISDN availability and pricing vary from place to place.

Who uses T1 or T3 service? **T1** (or T-1) is a high-speed (1.544 Mbps) digital network developed by AT&T in the early 1960s to support long-haul voice transmission in North America. Similar service is available in Europe under CEPT (Conference of European Postal and Telecommunications) standards.

A T1 line consists of 24 individual channels. Each channel has a capacity of 64 Kbps and can be configured to carry voice or data. T1 lines provide a dedicated link between two points, so they are popular for businesses and ISPs that want a high-speed connection to the Internet, regardless of cost.

A **T3** (or T-3) connection consists of 672 channels and supports data rates of about 43 Mbps. Sometimes referred to as DS3 (Digital Service-3) lines, T3 lines provide many of the links on the Internet backbone.

Both T1 and T3 services are considered dedicated, leased lines, which means they are essentially rented from the telephone company and are not usually shared by other customers. T1 and T3 services are usually too expensive for individuals.

DIRECT SATELLITE ACCESS

How does satellite access work? Most people are familiar with services that provide access to "pay TV" over a personal satellite dish. Many companies that provide satellite TV also offer satellite Internet access.

Direct satellite service (DSS) uses a geosynchronous or low-earth satellite to transmit television, voice, or computer data directly to and from a satellite dish, or "base station," owned by an individual. A satellite Internet modem connects the satellite dish to a computer, as shown in Figure 5-51.

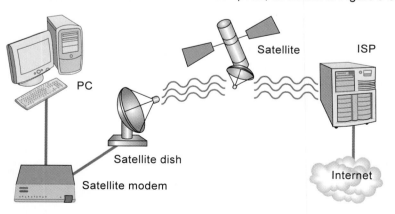

FIGURE 5-51
DSS Internet Connection

What are the pros and cons of direct satellite service? In many rural areas, DSS is the only alternative to a dial-up connection. Satellite service typically offers 500 Kbps downstream speed but only 40–60 Kbps upstream.

On the downside, satellite data transport is subject to latency delays of one second or more, which occur as your data is routed between your computer and a satellite that orbits 22,200 miles above the earth. Latency might not pose much of a problem for general Web surfing and downloading MP3 files, but it can become a showstopper for interactive gaming that requires quick reactions. Satellite transmission and reception can be blocked by adverse weather conditions, such as rain and snow, which makes this type of data transport less reliable than most wired options.

As with cable modem service, satellite data transport speeds might seem to decline when other users subscribe to the service because the satellite's bandwidth is shared among all users. Equipment and installation costs for DSS are often higher than dial-up, ISDN, DSL, or cable modem service.

LAN INTERNET ACCESS

How can I connect to the Internet through a LAN? A LAN provides a cost-effective way to share one Internet connection among several computers. School computer labs and businesses usually provide Internet access via LANs.

LAN Internet access is also feasible for home networks. A single cable TV, DSL, ISDN, or satellite connection can be cabled into your home LAN and accessed by all its workstations. Before connecting multiple computers to a single Internet connection, check with your service provider. Some have restrictions on sharing connections.

To establish LAN Internet access, you need:

- An operational wired or wireless LAN
- A router or a hub with router capabilities
- A high-speed Internet connection, such as DSL, ISDN, or cable TV
- A modem that corresponds to your Internet connection type

A LAN, such as your home Ethernet or Wi-Fi network, can easily be connected to the Internet in several ways, illustrated in Figure 5-52.

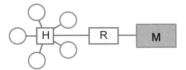

Connect a hub (H) to a router (R) and the router to a cable, DSL, ISDN, or satellite modem (M).

Connect a hub/router (H/R) to a cable, DSL, ISDN, or satellite modem (M).

Typically, routers are configured to automatically distribute IP addresses to LAN workstations via DHCP (Dynamic Host Configuration Protocol). Most Windows computers are configured to request an IP address via DHCP, so the computer and router can work together to establish a connection for each computer.

Networks typically use always-on connections, so it is important to implement security measures to protect data on network servers and workstations. Refer to the TechTalk at the end of this chapter for information on Internet access security.

INFOWEBLINKS

The **Satellite InfoWeb** dishes out lots of goodies about satellite Internet access—the technology, service providers, prices, and even reviews from disgruntled computer game players.

www.course.com/np/concepts8/ch05

FIGURE 5-52
Connecting a LAN to the Internet

Connect a device (D) containing modem and routing circuitry directly to the outlet for DSL, ISDN, or satellite service.

MOBILE INTERNET ACCESS

Can I access Internet services using mobile devices? When you are not using a computer with access to your home Internet connection, you can use a mobile Internet connection to surf the Web and check your e-mail. Devices such as cell phones, PDAs, notebook computers, and tablet computers can be easily configured for mobile Internet access. Currently, the two most popular options for mobile Internet access are Wi-Fi hotspots and cellular phone service.

What is a Wi-Fi hotspot? A **Wi-Fi hotspot** is wireless broadband Internet service offered in public locations such as Starbucks, Borders Books & Music, FedEx Kinko's, libraries, schools, and airports (Figure 5-53). Any Wi-Fi equipped device that enters a hotspot can gain access to the network's services. Some Wi-Fi hotspots offer free service; others require a service plan or one-time use fee. A company that maintains Wi-Fi hotspots is sometimes referred to as a **WISP** (wireless ISP). U.S.-based WISPs include T-Mobile, Verizon, Sprint, and AT&T Wireless.

What are the advantages and disadvantages of Wi-Fi hotspots? In a typical scenario, you might take your notebook computer—equipped with a Wi-Fi card—to your local Starbucks cafe. You buy a cup of cappuccino, sit down in a comfortable chair, and switch on your computer. Windows networking utilities automatically sense a Wi-Fi network and establish a connection using your T-Mobile account. You can then surf the Web, just as though you were at home using a connection supplied by your desktop ISP.

Wi-Fi hotspot technology offers the convenience of broadband Internet access outside your home. Theoretically, Wi-Fi networks can pump data through at 56 Mbps. However, hotspot providers such as Verizon advertise peak speeds of only 1.5 Mbps. Actual speed can vary depending on your distance from the access point, the number of people logged in, and interference from other networks. The biggest advantage of Wi-Fi hotspots is that you're using your notebook computer with its large screen, full keyboard, sophisticated software, and all your data. With some other wireless options, such as PDAs, you're limited to a small screen, cell phone keypad, and small amount of storage space.

Wi-Fi hotspot availability is currently limited. Many small towns have no hotspots, and in big cities coverage is localized. On the bright side, hotspot coverage is expanding. Web sites such as *www.wi-fihotspotlist.com* help you find Wi-fi hotspots in a specific city. Another drawback is that Wi-Fi service plans are not interchangeable. You cannot, for example, access a T-Mobile hotspot if you have a Verizon Wi-FiAccess service plan. Access plans can be expensive, too. Daily plans for 24 hours of access run $5-$6. Monthly unlimited access is about the same as basic cell phone service.

How can I use my cell phone service to access the Internet? You can subscribe to a WAP plan offered by your cellular phone provider, as explained in the following paragraphs, or you can use a cellular-ready modem with your notebook computer (described later in this section).

What is WAP? **WAP** (Wireless Access Protocol) is a communications protocol that provides Internet access from handheld devices, such as cell phones and PDAs. WAP-enabled devices contain a microbrowser that simplifies Web and e-mail access on a small, low-resolution screen (Figure 5-54). You can obtain WAP-enabled devices and services from many mobile telecommunications providers, such as T-Mobile, Verizon, Cingular, and CellularOne.

FIGURE 5-53

Starbucks Wi-Fi hotspots offer wireless Internet access to customers with T-Mobile accounts.

FIGURE 5-54

The advantage of WAP-enabled devices is their portability. The disadvantage is their small, low-res screens. Although various schemes for scrolling over a full-sized Web page have been tried, most WAP users stick to Web sites specially designed for small screen devices.

What kind of services are available from handheld devices? Cell phones and PDAs might not have huge screens, full-size keyboards, and full-featured application software, but they offer an expanding array of useful services.

■ **Short message service (SMS).** Also known as text messaging, SMS allows cell phone and PDA users to enter short messages and send them to other cell phones where they are displayed on screen. Text messaging uses less airtime than a voice message. Innovative uses include using SMS to pay for merchandise purchased from vending machines. The cost of the purchase is added to the user's phone bill.

■ **Multimedia messaging (MMS).** Camera phones can take still photos and/or videos that can be sent to other mobile phones or to e-mail addresses. Camera phones make it easy to snap a picture while shopping to get your friend's opinion. Cell phone photos have even been used to solve crimes. Despite a ban on photography, "cellcerting" has become popular as concert-goers snap shots of live action so their friends can participate. Camera phones have been banned from many gyms, however, because of privacy concerns. Picture messaging and video messaging usually require activation and incur additional service charges.

■ **Music fingerprinting.** With music fingerprinting technology, songs can be identified from an audio snippet captured on your cell phone. Suppose you're listening to a song on the radio. You missed the introduction and don't know the song title. Just dial GraceNote or Music Kube, hold your cell phone to the music source, and in a few seconds you'll know the name of the song and have an opportunity to buy the album.

■ **Games.** You can download wireless versions of popular Activision, NBA, Lord of the Rings, and Xbox games. Multiplayer games are even in the works—but make sure you have unlimited air time before you get into lengthy battles!

■ **City guides.** Use your cell phone to access information about restaurants and find the nearest ATM, gas station, or mall.

■ **E-mail.** Exchange e-mail messages with personal computer users as well as other cell phone users. Your cellular service provider usually supplies an e-mail account. Some services do not, however, allow you to use your desktop POP account or a Web-based e-mail service, such as HotMail or Yahoo! Mail.

■ **News, sports, stocks, and weather.** You can subscribe to personalized content through your cellular provider or third party. You'll get sports scores as the game progresses, and you can watch the stock ticker from your online trading account.

What are my options for handheld devices? When shopping for a handheld device to access the Internet, you should consider screen size, keypad functionality, and network connection options. Color screens—the bigger the better—are essential for a look similar to your desktop browser. A 26-letter keypad sure beats double- and triple-thumbing to enter text. And why have one device for Wi-Fi hotspots and another device for cellular access? PDAs such as Hewlett-Packard's iPAQ 6315 (Figure 5-55) offer cellular, Wi-Fi, and Bluetooth connectivity.

Cellular service providers offer dual-band, tri-band, and quad-band phones. The "band" refers to the radio frequency used to transmit calls. Cellular service in major U.S. cities tends to use the 1,900 MHz band. Many rural areas are covered by 850 MHz service. You benefit from a dual-band phone if you use your phone outside big cities. If you plan to use your phone in Europe, you might consider a tri-band phone that also works in the 900 MHz band or a quad-band phone that adds 1,800 MHz capability.

TERMINOLOGY NOTE

The term "smartphone" refers to a cell phone that includes computer capabilities, such as e-mail, Web browsing, and gaming. The term is occasionally used to refer to PDAs with cellular access, but more often they are referred to as "smartphone/PDAs."

FIGURE 5-55

HP's iPAQ PDA offers a large color screen and clip-on keyboard. It can connect to Wi-Fi hotspots and GSM/GPRS cellular networks using quad-band frequencies in the U.S. and Europe. This PDA also offers Bluetooth connectivity to printers and other PAN devices.

What are my options for cellular service? Cellular technology is evolving rapidly and generates a real alphabet soup of acronyms, such as G1, AMPS, CDMA, GSM, and GPRS. First-generation (G1) cell phones are analog, operate in the 800 MHz band, and offer few features beyond voice communications. Second-generation (G2) cell phones offer digital voice service, e-mail, and limited Internet access, but have slow data transmission speeds. An in-between generation, sometimes called G2.5, combines second-generation technology with GPRS (general packet radio service) to provide always-on network connections and broadband data transmission speeds. G3 cell phones offer always-on broadband connections with speeds up to 2 Mbps.

Within each generation are technology subcategories. With the exception of GPRS, which is often combined with GSM, a cellular service provider's network typically offers only one technology. Figure 5-56 can help you understand technologies that might be mentioned in cell phone advertising.

FIGURE 5-56
Cellular Network Technologies

Generation	Service		Features
G1	AMPS	(advanced mobile phone service)	Analog voice service No data service
G2	CDMA	(code division multiple access)	Digital voice service 9.6 Kbps–14.4 Kbps speed Enhanced calling features, such as caller ID No always-on data connection
	TDMA	(time division multiple access)	
	PDC	(personal digital cellular)	
	GSM	(global system for mobile communications)	
G2.5	GPRS	(general packet radio service)	Adds always-on data transfers at 171.2 Kbps to CDMA, TDMA, and GSM networks
G3	W-CDMA	(wide-band code division multiple access)	Superior digital voice service Always-on data service at 2 Mbps speed Broadband multimedia data services
	UTMS	(universal mobile telecommunications system)	
	CDMA-2000	(time division synchronous code-division multiple access)	

Can I connect my notebook computer to my cell phone service? Some cell phones connect to your computer and act as a wireless modem to transmit data over the Internet. Another option is to purchase a cellular-ready modem packaged as a PC card that slips easily into the PCMCIA port of a notebook or tablet computer.

With either method, data transfer speeds using basic cell phone service, top out at 14.4 Kbps or less—only a fraction of the speed of a dial-up connection. Some cellular carriers, however, offer special data transfer services that match or exceed 56 Kbps dial-up speeds. These services are fairly expensive. For example, one company charges $80 per month for its nationwide talk plan and high-speed data service.

Cell phone and notebook combinations are practical only for mobile computer users who want to use their notebook computers in areas not serviced by Wi-Fi hotspots.

INTERNET CONNECTION ROUNDUP

What's the best Internet connection? The best Internet connection depends on your budget and what's available in your area. Most people begin with a dial-up connection and eventually look around for a connection that offers higher access speeds. Cable modem service is usually the first choice, when available. If cable modem service is not available, or proves slower or less dependable than expected, the next choice would be DSL or satellite service, if available.

If several Internet connection services are available to you, the table in Figure 5-57 can help you evaluate their requirements, costs, advantages, and disadvantages.

FIGURE 5-57
Internet Access Options

	Dial-up	ISDN	DSL	Cable	Satellite	Wi-Fi Hotspot	Cellular Service
Downstream speed (max)	56 Kbps	128 Kbps	384 Kbps–1.5 Mbps	1.5 Mbps	500 Kbps	11 or 56 Mbps	14.4 Kbps to 2 Mbps
Upstream speed (max)	33 Kbps	128 Kbps	128 Kbps–1.5 Mbps	56–256 Kbps	40–60 Kbps	11 or 56 Mbps	14.4, Kbps to 2 Mbps
Downstream speed (avg)	44 Kbps	128 Kbps	384 Kbps	800 Kbps	400 Kbps	1.5 Mbps	171 Kbps
Latency	100–200 ms	10–30 ms	10–20 ms	10–20 ms	1–3 seconds	3-4 ms	200–500 ms
Image file (2 MB) download time	6 minutes	2 minutes	43 seconds	20 seconds	40 seconds	10 seconds	1.5 minutes
Short video (72 MB) download time	4 hours	78 minutes	26 minutes	12 minutes	25 minutes	5 minutes	1 hour
Requirements	Telephone line, ISP, voiceband modem	Computer must be located within 3 miles of local telephone switch	Computer must be located within 3 miles of local telephone switch	CATV service that provides Internet access	Clear view of southern sky	Wi-Fi equipped computer or PDA, access to Wi-Fi hotspot	Cellular service, cable to connect modem to cell phone
Monthly fee	$10–$30	$50–$100	$30–$200	$30–$50	$35–$80	$0–$20	$10–$50
Installation cost	$0	$0–$300	$0–$200	$0–$50	$200–$300	$0–$50	$0–$50

QUICKCHECK......SECTION D

1. Many types of Internet connections offer faster [＿＿＿＿＿＿＿] transmission rates than [＿＿＿＿＿＿＿] transmission rates.

2. [＿＿＿＿＿＿＿] connections, such as DSL or ISDN, are particularly vulnerable to security breaches.

3. [＿＿＿＿＿＿＿] provides high-speed Internet access over standard phone lines and comes in symmetric and asymmetric versions.

4. DSS is the best Internet service for gamers because of its high latency. True or false? [＿＿＿＿]

5. Many Starbucks offer Wi-Fi [＿＿＿＿＿＿＿].

 CHECK ANSWERS

LAB

LAB 5-D

SECURING YOUR CONNECTION

In this lab, you'll learn:

- How to use Windows utilities, online utilities, and firewall software to check the security of your Internet connection
- Why an unauthorized intruder might want to gain access to your computer
- The significance of communications ports as an intrusion risk factor
- How a Trojan horse can open up ports on your computer to provide intruders with full access to your computer system
- How to use the Windows Netstat utility to check your computer's open ports
- How to use an online utility to get a hacker's view of your computer
- Why Windows file and printer sharing can make your computer files vulnerable
- How to disable file and printer sharing for a computer that is not connected to a LAN
- How the NetBEUI protocol differs from TCP
- How to unbind a service, such as file and printer sharing, from a protocol by using Control Panel's Network Connections icon
- What features to look for in personal firewall software
- How to use firewall software, add packet filtering rules, and interpret firewall reports

INTERACTIVE LAB

CLICK TO START THE LAB

LAB ASSIGNMENTS

1. Start the interactive part of the lab. Insert your Tracking Disk if you want to save your QuickCheck results. Perform each lab step as directed, and answer all the lab QuickCheck questions. When you exit the lab, your answers are automatically graded and your results are displayed.

2. Use the Netstat utility to scan any computer that you typically use. Write out the Netstat report or print it. To print the report, copy it to Paint or Word, and then print. Explain what the Netstat report tells you about that computer's security.

3. Connect to the *grc.com* site and access the Shields Up! tests. Test the shields and probe the ports for the same computer you used for Assignment 2. Explain the similarities and differences between the Shields Up! report and the Netstat report for this computer. Which report indicates more security risks? Why?

4. In the lab, you learned which dialog boxes to use for disabling Windows file and printer sharing, plus a technique for unbinding TCP from file and printer sharing. Without actually changing the settings, use the dialog boxes to determine whether file and printer sharing is active or disabled on your computer. Also, discover whether file and printer sharing is bound to TCP on your computer. Report your findings and indicate whether these settings are appropriate for network access and security.

TECHTALK
INTERNET ACCESS SECURITY

Whether you work with a standalone computer or a LAN, Internet connections pose two kinds of risks: malicious code and intrusions. As you learned in Chapter 4, to deal with malicious code, such as viruses and worms, it is important to run antivirus software on standalone computers and all network workstations. To prevent intrusions, you need to take additional precautions. This TechTalk explains the most important steps you can take to secure your Windows-based computer from intrusions.

Should I worry about intrusions when using a standalone computer? A standalone computer with an always-on DSL, ISDN, or cable modem connection is particularly susceptible to intrusions. Without any visible sign or warning, hackers can infiltrate your computer to obtain personal information or use your computer as a launching pad for attacks on other machines. If you have an always-on connection, you should take steps to secure your computer from intrusions (Figure 5-58).

How do I secure a standalone computer? One of the easiest steps to enhance your computer's security is to turn it off when you aren't using it. When your computer is turned off, it is not vulnerable to intrusions. Putting your computer into sleep mode or activating a screen saver is not sufficient protection. Your computer must be shut down and turned off.

You should also keep your computer up-to-date with the latest Windows security patches and service packs. Hackers look for holes or vulnerabilities in Windows and Internet Explorer and work out ways to exploit them to gain unauthorized access to computers. As Microsoft develops security patches, they are posted at *www.windowsupdate.microsoft.com.* Check the site frequently to download the most recent patches.

You can also use Windows Automatic Updates to periodically check for patches. To configure Automatic Updates, go to Control Panel, select System, and select a setting from the Automatic Updates tab (Figure 5-59). When updates are available, you'll see the New Updates icon on the taskbar:

Your computer should be configured to run **firewall software**, which is designed to analyze and control incoming and outgoing packets. This software helps keep your computer secure in several ways. It makes sure that incoming information was actually requested and is not an unauthorized intrusion. It blocks activity from suspicious IP addresses and—best of all—it reports intrusion attempts so that you can discover whether any hackers are trying to break into your computer.

FIGURE 5-58

Standalone Computer Security Checklist

✔ Turn your computer off when not in use.

✔ Make sure operating system security patches and service packs are up to date.

✔ Disable file and printer sharing.

✔ Check security settings in Internet Explorer.

✔ Enable the Internet Connection Firewall.

FIGURE 5-59

To configure your computer for Automatic Updates, use Control Panel's System icon.

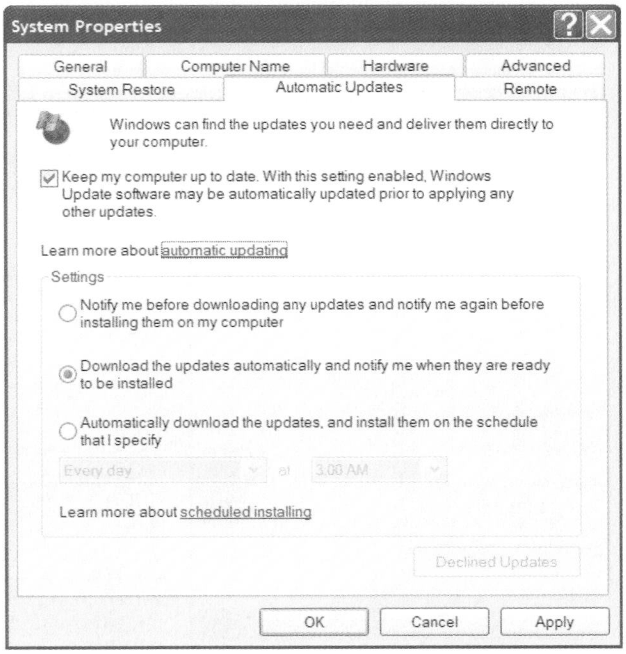

How can I get firewall protection? Windows XP includes firewall software called Internet Connection Firewall (ICF) or Windows Firewall. To activate and configure it, use Control Panel's Network Connections option (Figure 5-60 left). For earlier Windows versions or non-Windows operating systems, Tiny Personal Firewall and BlackICE are popular personal firewall products.

FIGURE 5-60
Activating Windows Internet Connection Firewall (left) and setting Internet Explorer security options (right) is easy.

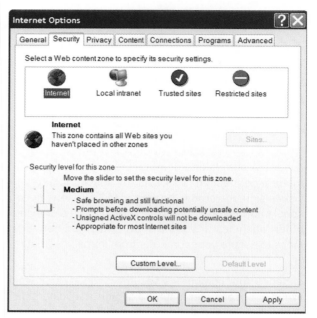

What other Windows security options should I use? You should also check Internet Explorer's security options. Most experts agree that the Medium setting allows maximum flexibility for browsing while providing a good level of protection from intrusions. To check this setting, open Internet Explorer and select Internet Options from the Tools menu (Figure 5-60 right).

If your computer is not connected to a LAN or used for access to a public Wi-Fi network, you should deactivate file and printer sharing. Figure 5-61 demonstrates this procedure for Windows XP.

FIGURE 5-61
When you turn off file and printer sharing, your files and printer cannot be accessed by other network users.

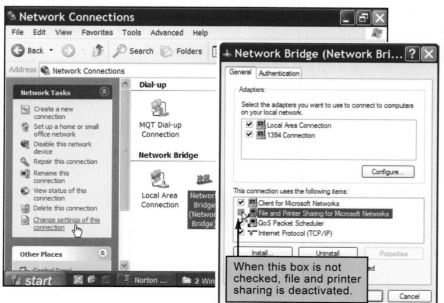

What about LAN security? Many security measures for LANs are the same as for standalone computers. You should not, however, deactivate file and printer sharing, which would defeat the purpose of having a network. You should not activate ICF. Instead, use firewall software designed for networks. LAN managers should establish user IDs and passwords for all users and close all "backdoors," such as default passwords. LAN managers also should consider using Network Address Translation to add another layer of security. See Figure 5-62.

What is Network Address Translation? A LAN requires a device with routing capabilities, and that device can become part of a network's security defenses. **Network Address Translation** (NAT) uses private IP addresses to hide LAN workstations from Internet intruders. Here's how it works. Your ISP typically assigns an IP address to your high-speed connection. This address is visible to the rest of the Internet. Within your LAN, however, workstations can use "hidden" private Internet addresses.

When the IP addressing scheme was devised, three ranges of addresses were reserved for internal or "private" use: 10.0.0.0—10.255.255.255, 172.16.0.0—172.31.255.255, and 192.168.0.0—192.168.255.255. These **private IP addresses** cannot be routed over the Internet. If you assign private IP addresses to your workstations, they are essentially hidden from hackers, who see only the IP address for your router.

You might wonder how you can transmit and receive data from a workstation with a nonroutable address. Your router maintains a NAT table that keeps track of the private IP addresses assigned to each workstation. For outgoing packets, the router substitutes its own address for the address of the workstation. When a response to a packet arrives, the router forwards it to the appropriate workstation. In that way, only the router's address is publicly visible. The router should, of course, be protected by antivirus software and firewall software.

Is it possible to secure connections for remote users? Sales representatives and telecommuters often have to access corporate networks by using a remote connection from home or a customer's office. It is possible to secure these remote connections by setting up **virtual private network** (VPN) access to a remote access server that uses Point-to-Point Tunneling Protocol or Layer Two Tunneling Protocol.

To initiate a VPN connection, dial your ISP as usual. After the connection is established, a second connection to the remote access server creates an encrypted channel for data transmission. Windows XP and several standalone products provide VPN software. Figure 5-63 illustrates how a VPN operates.

QUICKCHECK........TECHTALK

1. An important security measure for a standalone computer is putting it into sleep mode when not in use. True or false? [＿＿＿＿＿]

2. Windows Internet Connection [＿＿＿＿＿＿＿] blocks activity from suspicious IP addresses.

3. A(n) [＿＿＿＿＿＿＿] private network provides secure remote access to corporate networks.

FIGURE 5-62

Network Workstation Security Checklist

✔ Make sure operating system security patches and service packs are up to date.

✔ Install a router and NAT.

✔ Check security settings in Internet Explorer.

✔ Install firewall software.

✔ Control access by using passwords.

✔ Close all "backdoors."

FIGURE 5-63
Virtual Private Network

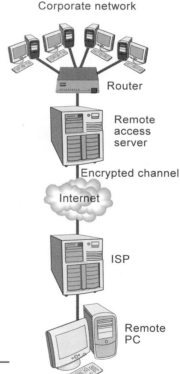

Corporate network

Router

Remote access server

Encrypted channel

Internet

ISP

Remote PC

ISSUE

FREE WI-FI

How would you like high-speed Internet access that requires no cables, no modem, and best of all—no subscription fees? Free community wireless access in cities as diverse as San Francisco, Miami, New York, Prague, and Amsterdam is made possible by free WLANs (wireless LANs). Dubbed "renegade WLANs" by some members of the press, these free networks are operated by public-spirited individuals who like to tinker with technology and want to provide a useful community service. Free WLAN operators typically subscribe to a DSL or cable provider for high-speed Internet access. They pay their monthly fees, but instead of limiting access to their own personal use, they distribute their connections to friends, neighbors, and just about anyone who passes by with the right computer equipment.

Free WLANs are based on Wi-Fi technology, which uses the 802.11b networking standard to create wireless Ethernet-compatible LANs. The technology itself is not inherently renegade. It is used for many mainstream applications. Wi-Fi networks are popular in corporations and universities where users are mobile and the flow of information typically requires broadband capacity.

The 802.11b standard uses an unlicensed telecommunications spectrum, so it is perfectly legal to set up an antenna to transmit and receive Wi-Fi signals without obtaining a broadcast license or paying any fees to the Federal Communications Commission.

Not only is it legal, setting up a Wi-Fi antenna is simple and inexpensive. A basic Wi-Fi antenna can be created with a few wires and an empty Pringles container. Fancier antennas require a ravioli can—really!

Using a Wi-Fi network is even cheaper and easier than setting one up. Many notebook computers have built-in Wi-Fi transceivers and software. If a transceiver is not built into your computer, you can add one for less than $100. With a Wi-Fi-ready computer, you can literally walk down the street, and your computer will look for and connect to any available Wi-Fi network.

Some free WLAN advocates envision a nationwide web of interconnected Wi-Fi networks that will form "a seamless broadband network built by the people, for the people." In this vision of a world connected by free WLANs, libraries can offer Internet access to people in low income neighborhoods. Local schools could get wired without exorbitant cabling expenses. Parents, kids, and grandparents, as well as corporate executives, could exchange e-mail and instant messages from locations that include the kitchen table, the corner coffee shop, and the Little League field.

But some broadband providers, such as AT&T and Time Warner Cable, fear that every user of a free wireless network is one less paying customer. According to one industry analyst, "The telecom industries are addicted to the one-wire, one-customer philosophy." Sharing an Internet connection that is intended for single-user access does not coexist with this philosophy. Most subscriber agreements contain wording that limits use of a broadband connection to one user and perhaps immediate family members. Although wording varies from one provider to another, most agreements expressly prohibit subscribers from using their connections for commercial purposes. Some free WLAN operators don't believe that sharing is commercial use. "I'm sharing it with people," says one free WLAN provider, "I'm not selling it. I'm not making a profit off it."

Whether or not free WLANs are legal, their benefits are tempered by several potentially negative repercussions. For example, tightening up subscriber agreements to eliminate the sharing loophole could affect many broadband subscribers who currently operate private wired or wireless networks that link several computers to a single Internet connection. Broadband providers could force private network operators to purchase more expensive multiuser licenses—an option that might be too expensive for many home networks.

Most free WLANs are operated as a hobby. Some operators are very conscientious, but others have a laid-back attitude toward quality of service: If no one gets charged, no one can complain when the network doesn't work. Consequently, free WLAN access can be unreliable. If broadband providers threaten to pull out of areas where free WLANs are popular, community members might have to choose between unreliable free WLAN service offered by hobbyists and more reliable, but more costly, services supplied by for-profit providers.

The wisdom of unregulated network availability is called into question by the proliferation of free WLANs. A publicly accessible LAN that requires no passwords or accounts can be used anonymously for a variety of illegal and dangerous activities. Like drug dealers who use public telephones to avoid taps and traces, terrorists and other criminals can simply walk into a free WLAN zone, tap into the Internet, and walk away without leaving a trace.

Widespread distribution of free WLANs can reduce the bandwidth available to paying customers. If your neighbor sets up a free WLAN that becomes popular with customers in a nearby coffee house, your previously sedate network neighborhood might suddenly become an overcrowded metropolis with major Internet access traffic jams.

Despite possible repercussions, the free WLAN movement appears to be growing and becoming more controversial. Some industry analysts expect a battle similar to the one that ensued when Napster's peer-to-peer music-sharing network was attacked by the music industry. The free WLAN controversy could pit a group of telecommunications giants against a rag-tag alliance of free WLAN advocates. The outcome has the potential to affect broadband subscribers everywhere.

INFOWEBLINKS

The **Free WLAN InfoWeb** provides more details about Wi-Fi technology and renegade LANs. ⊹

www.course.com/np/concepts8/ch05

WHAT DO YOU THINK?

1. Have you ever accessed a free WLAN?

○ Yes   ○ No   ○ Not sure

2. Do you believe that pirate WLANs can survive alongside for-profit broadband ISPs?

○ Yes   ○ No   ○ Not sure

3. Are broadband providers justified in limiting the terms of their service agreements to "one subscription, one customer"?

○ Yes   ○ No   ○ Not sure

⁘ SAVE RESPONSES

COMPUTERS IN CONTEXT

EDUCATION

The first educational application of computers emerged in the 1960s, when huge mainframes with clunky interfaces introduced students to computer-aided instruction (CAI). Based on B. F. Skinner's research—remember dogs salivating when a bell rings?—CAI uses basic drill and practice: The computer presents a problem, the student responds, and the computer evaluates the response. Studies in the 1970s indicated that CAI systems, such as PLATO (Programmed Logic for Automated Teaching Operations), improved student test scores, but students found the mainframe's monochrome display and the CAI's regimented drill format boring. Recent incarnations of CAI, such as an "alien invader" style elementary math program, use snazzy graphics and arcade formats to grab learners' attention.

Educators looking for ways to harness computers' interactive and programmable nature arrived at the idea of computer-based training (CBT). CBT is formatted as a series of tutorials, beginning with a pretest to see whether students have the prerequisite skills and ending with a CAI-style drill and practice test to determine whether students can move on to the next tutorial segment. Today, CBT is a popular approach to learning how to use computer software.

Another educational approach, called computer-aided learning (CAL), uses the computer more as a source of information than an assessment mechanism. Students using CAL make decisions about their level of expertise, what material is relevant, and how to pace their own learning. Exploratory CAL environments include Seymour Papert's Logo programming language; students can investigate geometry concepts by using Logo to program a graphical turtle on-screen.

In addition to CAI, CBT, and CAL, simulations have become a popular educational tool. The computer mimics a real-world situation through a narrative description or with graphics. Students are given options and respond with a decision or an action. The computer evaluates each response and determines its consequences. Oregon Trail, a simulation popular with elementary school students, describes events that beset a group of pioneers traveling in a wagon train. Students respond to each event, while learning bits of history, money-handling skills, conservation, and decision making.

Most educators believe that computers can help create an individualized and interactive learning environment, which can make learning more effective and efficient. Although 99% of American public schools have computers and 93% of students use them in some way, these statistics can be deceiving. The reality falls far short of the ideal situation—every student having access to a computer throughout the school day.

The challenge is to figure out how to realize computers' potential in an educational setting when supplying computers for every student is often cost prohibitive. Compromise solutions have been tried with varying degrees of success. Some schools have installed learning labs where students go for scheduled lab time. In elementary schools, often a few computers are placed in special work areas of classrooms and used for small group projects or individual drill and practice. Some schools have relegated most computers to the library, where they are connected to the Internet and used for research. In some classrooms, a single computer can be used as an effective presentation device.

A few schools without the budget for enough desktop computers have opted for inexpensive PDAs instead. "Students need to use technology just as you and I do, not just one hour a day," says one teacher in support of PDAs. Students use standard PDA software for educational tasks: tracking nutritional intake for health class, collecting data from experiments in biology class, graphing functions in math class, translating phrases for French class, and maintaining to-do lists. The biggest drawback to more widespread educational use of PDAs, however, is a lack of software specifically designed for education.

As another option, some schools—primarily colleges—have confronted the problem of computer access by requiring all incoming first-year students to purchase notebook computers. Many colleges, for example, provide Internet connections in dorm rooms and library study carrels or offer campuswide Wi-Fi service. Students can tote their notebook computers to class and take notes. They can contact instructors via e-mail, use the Internet as a research resource, and run educational software.

Another educational use of computers can be seen in distance education (DE) courses (also called "distance learning"). Historically, distance education meant correspondence study or courses delivered by radio or television, but the meaning has been broadened to encompass any educational situation in which students and instructors aren't in the same place. Therefore, most DE courses today require students to have access to a computer and an Internet connection. DE courses are offered to K-12 students, college students, military personnel, business people, and the general public. Most students who choose DE courses do so because they want to learn at their own pace, at a convenient time, and in a location close to home. Single parents who must deal with the realities of child care, working professionals who cannot relocate to a college town, and physically disabled students find distance education handy.

Distance education has the potential of increasing the pool of students for a course by making it financially feasible; for example, an advanced Kanji course could be offered at a midwestern university with only 10 on-campus Japanese majors if enough distance education students can boost enrollment.

The Internet hosts a wide variety of DE courses, both credit-earning and noncredit courses. Several course management systems (CMSs), such as Blackboard and WebCT, help teachers prepare and manage DE courses. These systems are popular with degree-granting institutions that offer credit-earning DE courses in their course catalogs (subject to the usual course fees and requirements). Course management software typically runs from a server maintained by a school system, college, or university. Using Web browsers, teachers access the CMS to post an online syllabus, develop Web pages with course content, create a database of questions for online assessment, manage e-mail, set up online discussion groups, and maintain a gradebook. Students using Internet-connected computers and standard Web browsers can access course materials, submit assignments, interact with other students, and take tests.

Computers and the Internet have opened opportunities for life-long learning. Prospective students can use a search engine to easily find non-credit courses and tutorials for a wide range of topics, including pottery, dog grooming, radio astronomy, desktop publishing, and drumming. Some tutorials are free, and others charge a small fee. Several Web sites, such as Barnes & Noble University and OnlineLearning.com, offer a good choice of fee-based or free courses. In a society that promotes learning as a lifelong endeavor, the Internet has certainly made it possible for students of all ages to pursue knowledge and skills simply by using a computer and an Internet connection.

INFOWEBLINKS

You'll find lots more information related to this Computers in Context topic at the **Computers and Education InfoWeb**.

www.course.com/np/concepts8/ch05

INTERACTIVE SUMMARY

To review important concepts from this chapter, fill in the blanks to best complete each sentence. When using the NP8 BookOnCD, click the Check Answers buttons to automatically score your answers. Place your Tracking Disk in the floppy disk drive if you want to save your scores.

Computer networks offer several advantages, including shared [   ], such as hardware, software, and data. Networks can be classified by geographical scope as PANs, [   ], MANs, NANs and WANs. Organizationally, they can be classified as client/[   ] or peer-to-peer. Physical network topologies include star, bus, [   ], mesh, and tree.

The central connection device in a star network is called a [   ]. A device called a [   ] amplifies and regenerates signals so that they can retain the necessary strength to reach their destination. Two similar networks can be connected by a device called [   ]. Two dissimilar networks can be connected using a hardware or software [   ], such as a router.

Data is transmitted over a variety of communications channels, including twisted-pair cables, coaxial cable, fiber-optic cable, RF signals, microwaves, infrared light, and laser light. The transmission capacity of a channel is called [   ]. High-capacity communications systems, such as cable TV, are sometimes referred to as [   ], whereas systems with less capacity, such as the telephone system, are referred to as [   ]. The transmission capacity of a digital channel is usually measured in [   ] per second (bps).

The rules for orderly communications are established by communications [   ], such as TCP/IP. A [   ] is a parcel of data that is sent across a computer network. Most computer networks use [   ] switching technology that allows data from several different sources to share a single communications channel.

✦ CHECK ANSWERS

A LAN (local [   ] network) connects computers, called workstations, within a limited geographical area. Today, most LANs are based on the Ethernet standard, which uses CSMA/CD to detect [   ]. A basic Ethernet network requires an Ethernet card in each workstation. Network devices are typically connected by CAT 5 cables, which converge at a centrally located Ethernet [   ].

Ethernet's wireless cousin, called [   ], is specified under IEEE 802.11 standards. A wireless [   ] point performs the same functions as a hub or router in a wired Ethernet. Because airborne signals from a wireless network are easy to intercept, it is essential to provide a basic level of security using [   ] encryption.

An alternative wireless technology, which is called [   ], transmits data over a short distance and is typically used for PANs. For home networks, HomePNA uses existing telephone wiring and Home [   ] uses existing electrical wiring.

Setting up a small LAN is easy. After the hardware and connections are in place, Windows detects the network any time you turn on a workstation. Workstation users can use drive [   ] to assign drive letters to storage devices located on other workstations and to designate files and folders to be shared with other network users.

✦ CHECK ANSWERS

The Internet has its roots in a network called [   ], which was developed in 1969. Gradually this network grew until it spanned the globe. In the early 1990s, user-friendly Internet access tools, such as graphical browsers, attracted millions of people to the Internet.

Network [   ] providers, such as MCI, UUNET, and AT&T, supply high-speed links for the Internet backbone. The acronym [   ] refers to points where equipment and links from these companies intersect. Internet [   ] direct data to the proper path according to its address.

An Internet utility called [   ] helps you discover whether a host, such as a Web server, is "alive." This utility also reports the elapsed time, called [   ], for a packet to travel from your computer to the host and back. Another utility, called [   ], records the path of a packet as it travels from your computer to its destination.

Most people access the Internet through an [   ], which provides modems, e-mail servers, domain name servers, and routers. The Internet protocol suite is [   ], which breaks a message into packets and then attaches an IP address. A computer can have a permanently assigned [   ] IP address or a temporary [   ] IP address. In addition to an IP address, many Internet servers also have a corresponding [   ] name, which is tracked by a large database called the [   ] Name System.

CHECK ANSWERS

Dial-up connections use POTS to transport data between your computer and your ISP over a "local loop" that carries [   ], not digital, signals. A modem [   ] your computer's digital signal so that it can travel over telephone lines. To restore a signal to its original state, it must be [   ]. Like many other Internet access technologies, a dial-up connection's [   ] transmission rate is usually faster than the [   ] rate.

A cable modem provides Internet access over the same [   ] cables that carry television signals from the cable company's head-end to your home. Some cable modems connect to a port provided by an [   ] card, whereas other cable modems connect to a USB port.

DSL connections are similar to cable connections in several ways, except that a DSL connection uses specially conditioned telephone lines that carry [   ] signals over the local loop. A similar, but slower, service is called [   ].

[   ] connections, such as DSL and cable, are active any time your computer is turned on. With such a connection, security becomes an issue.

Direct [   ] service provides another high-speed Internet access method that might be the only option in rural areas.

LANs can also provide Internet connections. Typically, a [   ] connects the LAN to a single DSL, cable, or T1 Internet connection that can be shared by all the LAN workstations.

Mobile Internet access is available from Wi-Fi [   ] and cellular services. Notebook computers equipped with Wi-Fi capability and a compatible service plan can gain access to network services, such as an Internet connection. Cellular devices use [   ] protocol to handle e-mail and Web browsing on devices with small, low-res screens.

CHECK ANSWERS

INTERACTIVE KEY TERMS

Make sure you understand all the boldfaced key terms presented in this chapter. If you're using the NP8 BookOnCD, you can use this list of terms as an interactive study activity. First, try to define a term in your own words, and then click the term to compare your definition with the definition presented in the chapter.

Always-on connection, 259
ARCnet, 238
Asynchronous protocol, 236
Bandwidth, 234
Baud rate, 257
Bluetooth, 243
Bridge, 231
Broadband, 234
Bus topology, 230
Cable modem, 259
Checksum, 237
Circuit switching, 235
Client/server network, 229
Coaxial cable, 232
Communications channel, 231
Communications protocol, 235
Communications satellites, 233
CSMA/CD, 240
Cyclic redundancy check, 237
Demodulation, 256
Direct satellite service, 262
DOCSIS, 260
Domain name, 251
Domain name servers, 252
Domain Name System, 252
Downstream, 258
Drive mapping, 245
DSL, 260
DSL modem, 261
DSLAM, 261
Dynamic IP address, 250
Ethernet, 239
Ethernet card, 240
Extranet, 249
FDDI, 239
Fiber-optic cable, 232
Firewall software, 269
Full duplex, 237

Gateway, 231
Half duplex, 237
Handshaking, 236
Head-end, 258
HomePLC network, 243
HomePNA network, 243
Hub, 230
ICANN, 252
Infrared light, 233
Intranet, 249
IP, 249
IP addresses, 250
ISDN, 262
ISDN terminal adapter, 262
LAN, 229
Latency, 248
MAN, 229
Mesh topology, 230
Microwaves, 233
Modulation, 256
NAN, 229
Narrowband, 234
Network access points, 247
Network Address Translation, 271
Network service providers, 247
Node, 230
Octet, 250
Packet, 235
Packet switching, 235
PAN, 229
Peer-to-peer network, 229
Physical topology, 230
Ping, 248
POTS, 255
Private IP addresses, 271
Repeater, 230
RF signals, 233
Ring topology, 230

Router, 231
Shared resources, 226
Simplex, 237
Star topology, 230
Static IP address, 250
Synchronous protocol, 236
T1, 262
T3, 262
TCP, 249
Token Ring network, 238
Top-level domain, 251
Traceroute, 248
Transceiver, 233
Transponder, 233
Tree topology, 231
Twisted-pair cable, 232
Uplink port, 241
Upstream, 258
V.44, 257
V.90. 257
V.92, 257
Virtual private network, 271
Voice over IP, 257
WAN, 229
WAP, 264
War driving, 242
WEP, 242
Wi-Fi, 241
Wi-Fi card, 242
Wi-Fi hotspot, 264
Wired network, 231
Wireless access point, 242
Wireless network, 231
WISP, 264

INTERACTIVE SITUATION QUESTIONS

Apply what you've learned to some typical computing situations. When using the NP8 BookOnCD, you can type your answers, and then use the Check Answers button to automatically score your responses. Place your Tracking Disk in the floppy disk drive if you want to save your scores.

1. You're installing a LAN and you decide to go with Ethernet. You'll typically use Category [____] cables to connect each workstation to a(n) [_____].

2. You're finally ready to get a high-speed Internet connection. Because the cable modem provided by your CATV company contains Ethernet circuitry, you can simply connect the modem to your computer's [_____] port (shown in the photo at right).

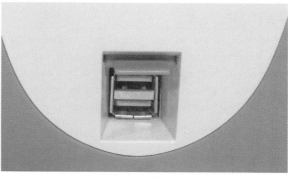

3. Your Internet access seems very slow one day. You might be able to discover the source of the slowdown using a networking utility called [_____].

4. Suppose that you decide to open a little Web store to sell handcrafted pottery. Your Web site will need a(n) [_____] IP address, and you'll want to register a(n) [_____] name.

5. Imagine that your computer contains a 56 Kbps modem that uses the V.90 standard. You can expect about 44 Kbps [_____] speed and about 33 Kbps as the maximum [_____] speed.

6. Suppose you have installed a cable modem on a standalone PC. To secure your computer, you should first use Control Panel's Network Connections icon to turn off file and printer [_____]. You should also activate Internet Connection [_____] software.

7. Suppose you live in a rural area that is not serviced by a cable TV company. Your best bet for high-speed Internet access is probably direct [_____] service.

8. You install an 802.11b network, but it seems to stop working at various times. To begin troubleshooting, you look for any devices, such as cordless phones, that use the [_____] GHz frequency.

9. Your PC is connected to a LAN, and you want to regularly access a file that's stored on one of the LAN workstations. You'd like to access that computer's hard disk as though it were connected to your own computer, so you decide to [_____] the workstation's hard disk drive as drive F.

10. You arrive at work and one of your co-workers tells you that the "router is down." You can surmise that your workstation will not be able to access the [_____] until the router is fixed.

CHECK ANSWERS

INTERACTIVE PRACTICE TESTS

Practice tests that consist of 10 multiple-choice, true/false, and fill-in-the-blank questions are available on both the NP8 BookOnCD and the NP8 Web site. The questions are selected at random from a large test bank, so each time you take a test, you'll receive a different set of questions. Your tests are scored immediately, and you can print study guides that help you find the correct answers for any questions that you missed.

www.course.com/np/concepts8/ch05

CLICK TO START

REVIEW

ON THE WEB

PROJECTS

An NP8 Project is an open-ended activity that helps you apply the concepts you have learned. Many projects require resources in addition to your textbook, such as current magazines, library materials, or Web access. When you tackle a project, be prepared to use your critical thinking skills, logical analysis, and creativity. Projects for this chapter include:

- **Issue Research: Free WLANs**
- **Build a LAN**
- **Computers in Education**
- **Communications Across the Globe**
- **Building a Home Network**
- **Claude Shannon**
- **Phone, Cable, or Satellite**
- **The Internet: Fact and Fantasy**
- **Wireless Ways**

To work with the Projects for this chapter, connect to the **New Perspectives NP8 Web Site**.

www.course.com/np/concepts8/ch05

TECHTV VIDEO PROJECT

The TechTV video clip *Free Wi-Fi Blankets San Francisco* highlights a growing trend in many cities. After watching the video clip, write a short summary and explain why San Francisco is ideally suited for this technology. Next, use a Wi-Fi hotspot locator on the Web to get lists of hotspots in three of your favorite cities. Can you tell how many of these hotspots are free and how many require a service plan? Write a summary of your findings.

To work with the Video Projects for this chapter, connect to the **New Perspectives NP8 Web Site**.

www.course.com/np/concepts8/ch05

STUDY TIPS

Study Tips help you to organize and consolidate the information in a chapter by making lists, outlines, charts, and sketches. You can use paper and pencil or word processing software to complete most of the Study Tips.

To work with the Study Tips for this chapter, connect to the **New Perspectives NP8 Web Site**.

www.course.com/np/concepts8/ch05

ONLINE GAMES

Test your comprehension of the concepts introduced in Chapter 5 by playing the NP8 Online Games. At the end of each game, you have three options:

- Print a comprehensive study guide complete with page references
- Print your results to be submitted to your instructor
- Save your results to be submitted to your instructor via e-mail

To work with the Online Games for this chapter, connect to the **New Perspectives NP8 Web Site**.

www.course.com/np/concepts8/ch05

STUDENT EDITION LABS

Extend your knowledge of wired and wireless networking with the Chapter 5 Student Edition Labs.

The following Student Edition Labs are offered with Chapter 5:

• **Networking Basics**   • **Wireless Networking**

Go to the NP8 New Perspectives Web site for specific lab topics.

To work with the Chapter 5 Student Edition Labs and their corresponding lab assignments, connect to the **New Perspectives NP8 Web Site**.

www.course.com/np/concepts8/ch05

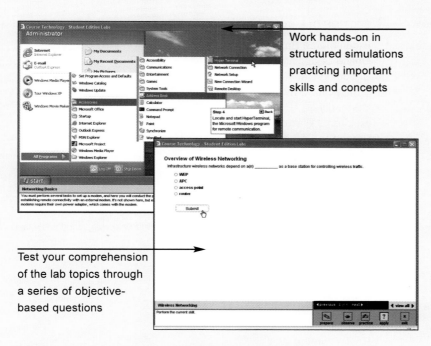

Work hands-on in structured simulations practicing important skills and concepts

Test your comprehension of the lab topics through a series of objective-based questions

Track Your Progress with the Student Edition Labs

• Student Edition Labs test your comprehension of the lab topics through a series of trackable objective-based questions. Your instructor will direct you to either print your results or submit them via e-mail.

• Student Edition Lab Assignments, available on the New Perspectives NP8 Web site, require you to apply the skills learned through the lab in a live environment. Go to the New Perspectives NP8 Web site for detailed instruction on individual Student Edition Lab Assignments.

If you have a SAM user profile, you have access to even more interactive content. Log in to your SAM account and go to your assignments page to see what your instructor has assigned for this chapter.

WEB PAGES, WEB SITES, AND E-COMMERCE

CONTENTS

TIP

When using the BookOnCD, the ✳ icons are "clickable" to access resources on the CD. The ✚ icons are clickable to access resources on the Web. You can also access Web resources by using your browser to connect directly to the NP8 New Perspectives Web site at:

www.course.com/np/concepts8/ch06

CHAPTER PREVIEW

Before you begin Chapter 6, you can use the Web-based preview activities to hear an overview of the chapter, check your current level of expertise about key concepts, and look through a list of learning objectives. You can access the preview activities by clicking the ✛ icon when using the BookOnCD or going to the New Perspectives NP8 Web site.

CHAPTER OVERVIEW

When the Internet was first developed, only a handful of scientists and science fiction writers envisioned it as an interlinked network of information attracting billions of visitors to a virtual global village. Today, the Web is one of the most popular services the Internet offers. Get your book and highlighter ready, then connect to the New Perspectives NP8 Web site where you can listen to an overview that points out the most important concepts for this chapter.

www.course.com/np/concepts8/ch06 ✛

CHAPTER PRE-ASSESSMENT

How much do you know about Web technology and e-commerce? To gauge your level of knowledge before beginning the chapter, take the pre-assessment quiz at the New Perspectives NP8 Web site. Armed with your results from this quiz, you can focus your study time on concepts that will round out your knowledge of the Web and improve your test scores.

www.course.com/np/concepts8/ch06 ✛

LEARNING OBJECTIVES

When you complete this chapter you should be able to:

- Describe the roles that HTML, XHTML, HTTP, URLs, browsers, and Web servers play in bringing Web pages to your desktop
- Explain why cookies are useful in an environment that is based on a stateless protocol, and provide some concrete examples of their use
- Identify some Web page design tools and discuss their advantages and disadvantages
- Describe how HTML tags, cascading style sheets, links, buttons, hot spots, frames, forms, and tables are used in the design and creation of Web pages
- Identify the elements that typically form a Web page
- Explain how to test and post Web pages
- Describe how DHTML, XML, and XSL technologies work to enhance Web pages

- List some advantages and disadvantages of using JavaScript, VBScript, Java applets, and ActiveX controls
- Discuss why e-commerce has become so popular with consumers and merchants
- List some threats to the security of credit card numbers and other sensitive data during e-commerce transactions
- Describe how the following e-commerce technologies work: shopping carts, SSL, one-time-use credit cards, electronic wallets, and person-to-person payment systems

A detailed list of learning objectives is provided at the New Perspectives NP8 Web site

www.course.com/np/concepts8/ch06 ✛

SECTION A

WEB TECHNOLOGY

In 1990, a British scientist named Tim Berners-Lee developed specifications for HTML, HTTP, and URLs. He hoped that these technologies would help researchers share information by creating access to a sort of "web" of electronic documents.

Berners-Lee's free Web software appeared on the Internet in 1991, but the Web didn't take off until 1993 when Marc Andreessen and his colleagues at the University of Illinois created Mosaic, a graphical browser. Andreessen later formed his own company and produced a browser called Netscape, which put the Web into the hands of millions of Web "surfers." In this section of the chapter, you'll peel back the layers of Web technologies to take a look at what happens "behind" your browser window.

THE WEB, THE NET, AND HYPERTEXT

What's the difference between the Web and the Internet? The Internet is basically a collection of computers and cables that form a communications network, similar in many ways to the telephones and cables that form the telephone system. The Internet is designed to carry computer data, just as the telephone network is designed to carry conversations. The Internet carries a variety of data, including e-mail, videoconferences, and instant messages. The Internet also carries text, graphical, and audio data that form Web pages.

In the words of Tim Berners-Lee, "The Web is an abstract (imaginary) space of information. On the Net, you find computers—on the Web, you find documents, sounds, videos, and information. On the Net, the connections are cables between computers; on the Web, connections are hypertext links." In other words, the Internet is a communications system, and the Web is an interlinked collection of information that flows over that communications system.

What is hypertext and what does it have to do with the Web? Two of the most important elements of the Web—Hypertext Transfer Protocol (HTTP) and Hypertext Markup Language (HTML)—contain "hypertext" in their names. A **hypertext** is a group of interlinked files. Hypertext is a key concept for understanding the Web, but the idea of hypertext originated much earlier than the Web, or even the Internet. In 1945, an engineer named Vannevar Bush wrote the article "As We May Think," which described a microfilm-based machine called the Memex that linked associated information or ideas through "trails." The idea resurfaced in the mid-1960s when Harvard graduate Ted Nelson coined the term "hypertext" to describe a computer system that could store literary documents, link them according to logical relationships, and allow readers to comment and annotate what they read. Nelson sketched the diagram in Figure 6-1 to explain his idea of a computer-based "web" of "links."

FIGURE 6-1

Ted Nelson's early sketch of project Xanadu—a distant relative of the Web—used the terms "links" and "web."

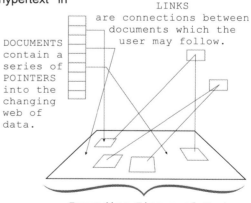

LINKS
are connections between documents which the user may follow.

DOCUMENTS contain a series of POINTERS into the changing web of data.

Expanding Tissue of Text, Data, and Graphics

On today's Web, many aspects of hypertext have become a reality. Every Web page is based on a document that is stored in a file and identified by a unique address called a URL. To access any one of these documents, you can type its URL. You can also click an underlined word or phrase called a **hypertext link** (or simply a "link") to access related documents.

HTTP and HTML are two of the major ingredients that define the Web. If you add URLs, browsers, and Web servers to this recipe, you'll have a pretty complete menu of the basic technologies that make the Web work.

How does the Web work? A Web server stores data for Web pages that form a Web site. One way to store data for a Web page is as a file called an **HTML document**—a plain text, or ASCII, document with embedded HTML tags. Some of these tags specify how the document is to be displayed when viewed in a browser. Other tags contain links to related document, graphics, sound, and video files that are also stored on Web servers.

As an alternative to HTML documents, Web servers can store Web page data in other types of files, such as databases. This data can be assembled into HTML format "on the fly" in response to Web page requests.

To "surf" the Web, you use Web client software called a browser. When you type a URL into the browser's Address box, you are requesting HTML data for the Web page you want to view. Your browser creates a request for the specified data by using a command the HTTP communications protocol provides.

In the meantime, the Web server has been "listening" for incoming HTTP requests. When your request arrives, the Web server examines it, locates the Web page data you requested, and sends it to your computer. When your request is fulfilled, the server moves on to service other requests. If additional elements are needed for the Web page your browser is displaying—a graphic, for example—your browser must issue a new request to the server for that element. Figure 6-2 illustrates how a Web server and browser interact to display a Web page stored as an HTML document.

TERMINOLOGY NOTE

The terms URL (Uniform Resource Locator), HTTP (Hypertext Transfer Protocol), and HTML (Hypertext Markup Language) were introduced in Chapter 1.

FIGURE 6-2

Web browsers and Web servers exchange HTTP messages.

CLICK TO START ✣

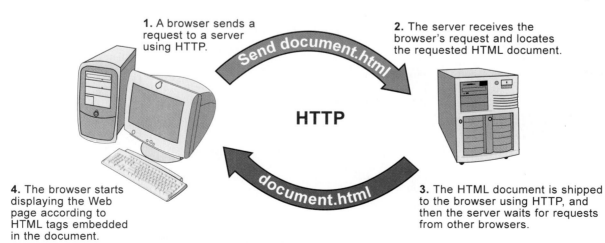

1. A browser sends a request to a server using HTTP.

Send document.html

2. The server receives the browser's request and locates the requested HTML document.

HTTP

4. The browser starts displaying the Web page according to HTML tags embedded in the document.

document.html

3. The HTML document is shipped to the browser using HTTP, and then the server waits for requests from other browsers.

HTML AND XHTML

What is HTML? HTML is a set of specifications for creating HTML documents that a browser can display as a Web page. HTML is called a **markup language** because authors mark up their documents by inserting special instructions, called HTML tags, that specify how the document should appear when displayed on a computer screen or printed.

Tim Berners-Lee developed the original HTML specifications in 1990. These specifications were revised several times by the **World Wide Web Consortium** (W3C), but many of the early revisions did not gain widespread acceptance. HTML 3.2, introduced in 1997, was the first widely adopted revision of the original HTML specifications. HTML version 4.0 was introduced in late 1997, and HTML 4.01 in 1999.

XHTML is the follow-up version to HTML 4. Rather than calling it HTML 5, the W3C preferred to name it XHTML 1.0 to reflect its extensibility. XHTML includes all HTML 4 tags, but it can be extended by adding customized tags. Today's Web operates according to XHTML standards, even though people commonly refer to the technology simply as HTML.

How do HTML tags work? In an HTML document, HTML tags, such as <hr /> and <b>, are enclosed in angle brackets. These tags are treated as instructions to the browser. When your browser displays a Web page on your computer screen, it does not show the tags or angle brackets. Instead, it attempts to follow the tags' instructions. Figure 6-3 illustrates how the <hr /> tag produces a horizontal rule on a Web page.

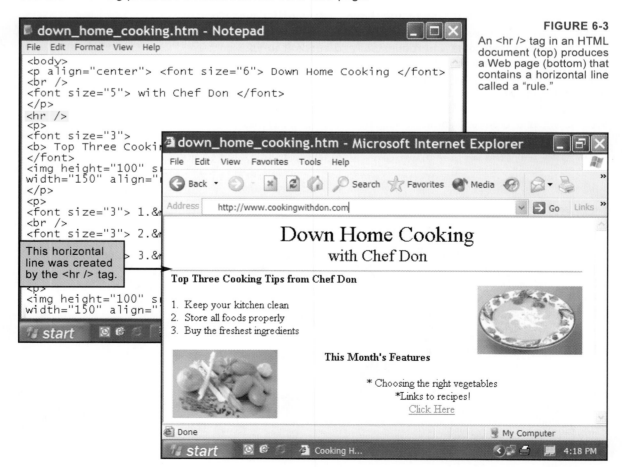

FIGURE 6-3
An <hr /> tag in an HTML document (top) produces a Web page (bottom) that contains a horizontal line called a "rule."

The <hr /> tag is called a **self-closing tag**, which is a single tag that includes a closing "/" symbol. A space between the "hr" and "/" is included for maximum compatibility with various browsers.

Unlike the self-closing <hr /> tag, most HTML tags work in pairs. An opening tag begins an instruction, which stays in effect until a closing tag appears. Closing tags always contain a slash. For example, the following sentence contains opening and closing bold tags:

<b>Caterpillars</b> love sugar.

When displayed by a browser, the word "Caterpillars" will be bold, but the other words in the sentence will not be bold.

HTML is not a case-sensitive language, but XHTML style requires tags to be lowercase so that they work on case-sensitive servers. Notice, too, that in self-closing tags such as <hr />, the slash comes at the end of the tag, whereas in a closing tag such as </b>, the slash comes at the beginning.

In addition to formatting, HTML tags can be used to specify how to incorporate graphics on a page. Some people are surprised to learn that HTML documents contain no graphics. Of course, graphics do appear on many of the Web pages displayed in your browser window, so how do they get there? The <img src> tag specifies the name and location of the graphics file to be displayed as part of a Web page. Figure 6-4 illustrates how graphics are incorporated into a Web page.

FIGURE 6-4

An <img src> tag in an HTML document (top) produces a graphic when your browser displays the Web page (bottom).

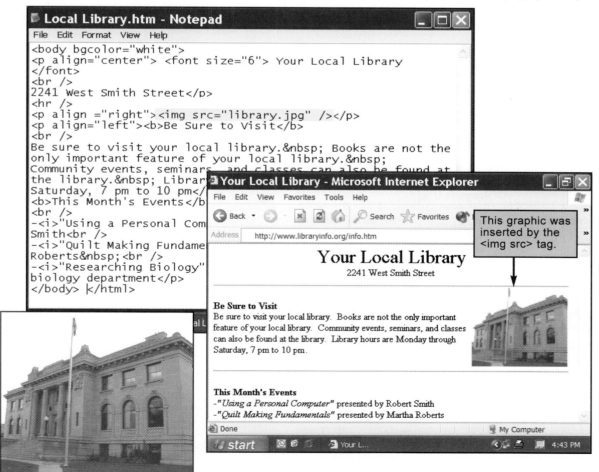

HTML tags do more than make a Web page look pretty. They also produce links that connect you to other Web documents. The <a href> tag specifies the information your browser needs to display links that allow you to jump to related Web pages. Figure 6-5 illustrates <a href> tags that produce links to two Web pages.

FIGURE 6-5

<a href> tags in an HTML document produce underlined links when your browser displays the Web page.

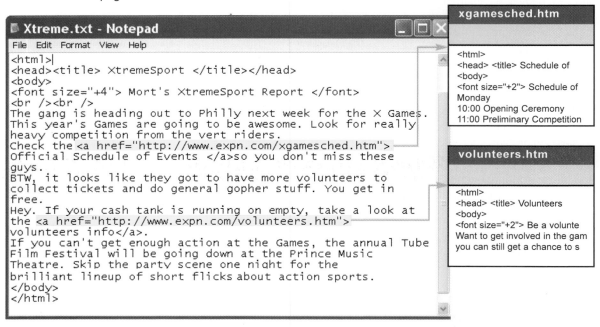

The <a href> HTML tag contains the URL for the linked page. Text between the <a href> and </a> tags (such as "volunteers info" in Figure 6-6) appears as an underlined link when the Web page is displayed in a browser.

<a href = "http://www.expn.com/volunteers.htm">volunteers info</a>
URL for linked page   Text for underlined link

FIGURE 6-6

The components of the <a href> tag (left) specify the location of the linked page and the underlined text to display as the link (below).

So HTML documents look a lot different from Web pages, right? Exactly. An HTML document is like a screenplay, and your browser is like a director who makes a screenplay come to life by assembling cast members and making sure they deliver their lines correctly. As the HTML screenplay unfolds, your browser must follow the instructions in an HTML document to display the lines of text on your computer screen in the right color, size, and position. If the screenplay calls for a graphic, your browser must collect it from the Web server and display it. Although the HTML screenplay exists as a permanent file, the Web page you see on your computer screen exists only for the duration of the "performance."

Technically speaking, you can distinguish HTML documents—the "screenplay"—from Web pages—the performance. However, in everyday conversation, the term "Web page" is often used for the HTML document as well as the Web page displayed on screen.

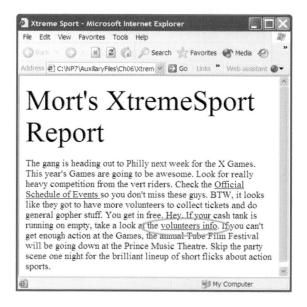

Can I see the HTML tags used to create a Web page? Your browser is designed to display nicely formatted Web pages, not a messy source document filled with HTML tags. However, if you are curious about how a page is constructed or you would like to duplicate the features of a Web page, you can view the source document and its HTML tags by using a menu option on your browser. Figure 6-7 explains.

FIGURE 6-7

Most browsers include a menu option for viewing an HTML source document and the HTML tags it contains. This example illustrates how to view source HTML while using Internet Explorer.

CLICK TO START

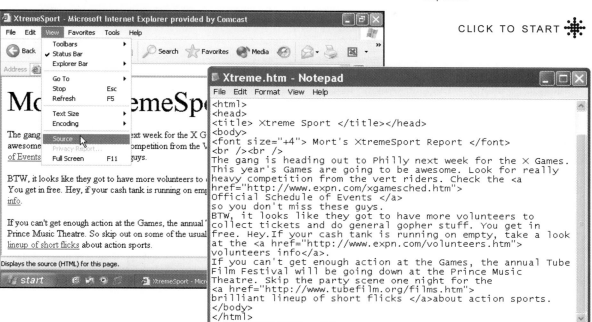

What are the most commonly used HTML tags? HTML includes hundreds of tags. For convenience, these tags can be classified into four groups. **Formatting tags** change the appearance of text and work in much the same way as the formatting options in a word processor that create bold and italic text, adjust text size, change text color, arrange text in table format, or center text on a page. **Link tags** specify where and how to display links to other Web pages and e-mail addresses. **Media tags** specify how to display media elements, such as graphics, sound clips, or videos. **Operational tags** specify the basic setup for a Web page, provide ways for users to interact with a page, and offer ways for Web pages to incorporate information derived from databases.

WEB BROWSERS

Why do I need a browser to access the Web? In Chapter 1, you learned that a Web browser—usually referred to simply as a "browser"—is a software program that runs on your computer and helps you access Web pages. Technically, a browser is the client half of the client/server software that facilitates communication between a personal computer and a Web server. The browser is installed on your computer, and the Web server software is installed on a server somewhere on the Internet.

Your browser plays two key roles. First, it uses HTTP to send messages to a Web server—usually a request for a specific HTML document. Second, when it receives an HTML document from a Web server, your browser interprets the HTML tags to display the requested Web page.

What are some of today's most popular browsers?
Netscape Navigator version 1.0 was published in December 1994. "Netscape," as it is generally called, quickly became the most popular browser on both Macintosh and PC platforms. Numerous revisions added pioneering features, such as frames, plug-ins, and JavaScript support. Netscape is currently published by Netscape Communications, a subsidiary of AOL.

In 1998, Netscape source code became open source software, managed by an organization known as Mozilla. The organization's main product, a browser called Mozilla, was all but ignored by most computer owners. In 2004, however, a new version of Mozilla, dubbed Firefox, rapidly gained popularity because it offered effective security features.

Internet Explorer (IE) version 1.0 was published by Microsoft in August 1995. The program code for the original IE 1.0 browser was licensed from a Netscape spin-off called Spyglass, which provided IE with many of the same features as Netscape. Until IE 4.0 appeared in 1997, however, Microsoft's browser was unable to match Netscape's popularity. Today, IE has supplanted Netscape as the dominant browser across Mac and PC platforms. It is also available for Linux and several versions of UNIX. AOL's browser is a slightly modified version of IE.

Before Firefox, Opera was one of the few alternatives to IE and Netscape. First published in December 1996, Opera began as a Norwegian phone company project to develop a small and fast browser for computers with meager memory and processing resources. Unlike IE and Netscape, which descended from Mosaic, Opera was written from scratch; as a result, it has some unique features, such as page zoom and a multidocument display. Versions of Opera are available for Windows, Linux, UNIX, and Mac OS.

Should I upgrade my browser when new versions become available? It is a good idea to upgrade when a new version of your browser appears. Both IE and Netscape updates are free. Therefore, you can get up-to-date browser functionality simply by spending a few minutes downloading and installing an update.

The problem with using an old version of a browser is that some Web pages depend on new HTML features supported only by the latest browser versions. Without the latest upgrade, you might encounter errors when your browser tries to display a page, but cannot interpret some of the HTML. In other cases, your browser might display the Web page without errors, but you will not see all the intended effects.

Another important reason to upgrade is for increased security. As hackers discover and take advantage of security holes, browser publishers try to patch the holes. Upgrades usually contain patches for known security holes, although new features might sometimes open new holes.

FIGURE 6-8

Today's popular browsers from top to bottom: Netscape Navigator, Internet Explorer, Opera, and Firefox.

HELPER APPLICATIONS, PLUG-INS, AND PLAYERS

Why do I have to download software to view some Web pages?
Native file formats for early browsers were typically limited to documents in
HTML format and graphics files in GIF and JPEG formats. Today, browsers
work with additional file formats, but they do not have built-in support for
several proprietary file formats commonly used on the Web, such as PDF,
QuickTime, and Flash.

If you click a link that leads to a file stored in a format your browser cannot handle, you can usually download software necessary to read the file
format. For example, you might be directed to the Adobe Web site to
download the Acrobat Reader software that handles PDF files. To display an animation, you might need Macromedia's Flash software. For
movies, you might need the QuickTime player. The software your browser calls upon to read non-native file formats can take the form of a helper
application, plug-in, or player.

What is a helper application? A **helper application** is a program that
extends a browser's ability to work with file formats. The process of
installing a helper application creates an association between the browser
and a file format, such as PDF, SWF, or MOV. Whenever your browser
encounters one of these file formats, it automatically runs the corresponding helper application, which in turn opens the file.

Is a plug-in the same as a helper application? A **plug-in** is a type of
helper application, pioneered by Netscape developers, that can be activated from an <embed> tag inserted in an HTML document. For example,
<embed src = "sample.swf"> instructs a browser to activate the plug-in that
works with the SWF file format, which can in turn open the sample.swf file.
Recent versions of Internet Explorer, however, do not respond to the
<embed> tag and, therefore, are not able to use Netscape-style plug-ins.
Instead, IE uses ActiveX components, which are activated by the <object>
tag. Aside from this technical distinction, today's helper applications and
plug-ins are very similar from the user's perspective. The current trend is to
use the term **player** to refer to any helper application or plug-in that helps
a browser display a particular file format. Figure 6-9 shows a list of players
downloaded for use with Internet Explorer.

INFOWEBLINKS

For information about the most
popular players, connect to the
Browser Players InfoWeb.

www.course.com/np/concepts8/ch06

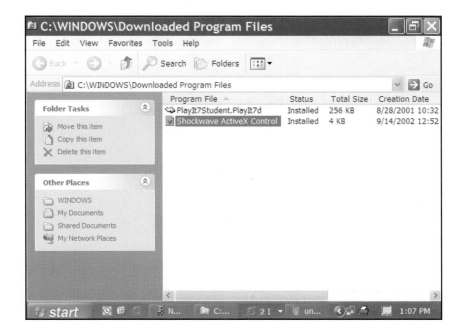

FIGURE 6-9
Windows XP lists some
installed players in the
Downloaded Program Files
folder. Other players might
be installed in different
folders.

HTTP

How does HTTP work? HTTP is a protocol that works with TCP/IP to get Web resources to your desktop. A Web resource can be defined as any chunk of data that has a URL, such as an HTML document, a graphic, or a sound file.

HTTP includes commands called "methods" that help your browser communicate with Web servers. GET is the most frequently used HTTP method. The GET method is typically used to retrieve the text and graphics files necessary for displaying a Web page. This method can also be used to pass a search query to a file server.

HTTP transports your browser's request for a Web resource to a Web server. Next, it transports the Web server's response back to your browser.

An HTTP exchange takes place over a pair of sockets. A **socket** is an abstract concept that represents one end of a connection. Although a packet switching network doesn't actually make point-to-point connections between network nodes, many people find it handy to visualize network connections as a communication line with a doorway-like "socket" at each end.

In an HTTP exchange, your browser opens a socket, connects to a similar open socket at the Web server, and issues a command, such as "send me an HTML document." The server receives the command, executes it, and sends a response back through the socket. The sockets are then closed until the browser is ready to issue another command. Figure 6-10 demonstrates the messages that flow between your browser and a Web server to retrieve an HTML document.

FIGURE 6-10

HTTP messages flow between a browser and a Web server.

CLICK TO START

1. The URL in the browser's Address box contains the domain name of the Web server that your browser contacts.

2. Your browser opens a socket and connects to a similar open socket at the Web server.

3. Next, your browser generates and sends an HTTP message through the socket.

4. The server sends back the requested HTML document through the open sockets.

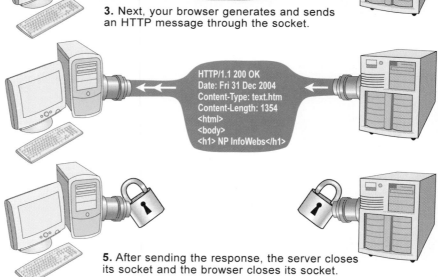

5. After sending the response, the server closes its socket and the browser closes its socket.

Does a browser have to request each Web page element separately?
Yes. HTTP is classified as a **stateless protocol**, which maintains no record
of previous interactions and handles each request based entirely on information that comes with it. HTTP generally allows only one request and
response per session. As a result, your browser can request an HTML document during a session, but as soon as the document is sent, the session
is closed, and the Web server "forgets" that your browser ever made a
request. To make additional requests—for example, to request a graphic
that's supposed to be displayed on a Web page—your browser must open
another session. You can understand, then, that to assemble a complex
Web page with several graphics, buttons, and sounds, your browser makes
many HTTP requests to the Web server.

What if a Web server cannot find the file a browser requested? A
Web server's response to a browser's request includes an **HTTP status
code** that indicates whether the browser's request could be fulfilled. The
status code 200 means that the request was fulfilled—the requested HTML
document, graphic, or other resource was sent. Anyone who surfs the Web
has encountered the "404 Not Found" message. Your browser displays this
message when a Web server sends a 404 status code to indicate that the
requested resource does not exist. HTTP status codes are summarized in
Figure 6-11.

FIGURE 6-11
HTTP Status Codes

Code	Message	Description
200	OK	The request succeeded, and the resulting resource, such as a file or script output, has been sent.
301	Moved Permanently	The resource has been moved.
302	Moved Temporarily	The resource is temporarily not available.
303	See Other	The resource has moved to another URL and should be automatically retrieved by the client.
404	Not Found	The requested resource doesn't exist.
500	Server Error	An unexpected server error, such as encountering a scripting error, has occurred.

WEB SERVERS

How does a Web server understand HTTP requests? A Web server
is configured to include HTTP software. This software is always running
when the server is "up" and ready to fulfill requests. One of the server's
ports is dedicated to listening for HTTP requests. When a request
arrives, the server software analyzes the request and takes whatever
action is necessary to fulfill it.

Why does a Web server need a special port for HTTP requests? The
computer that runs Web server software might have other software running
on it as well. For example, a computer might operate as a Web server, as
an e-mail server, and as an FTP (File Transfer Protocol) server all at the
same time! To efficiently handle these diverse duties, a computer devotes
one port to HTTP requests, one port to handling e-mail, and another port to
FTP requests. Traditionally, port 80 is devoted to HTTP traffic, port 25 deals
with SMTP e-mail traffic, and port 21 handles FTP.

The way that a computer allocates one port to each service helps explain how it is possible for a Web server to be "down" when the computer is still up and running. A computer runs separate software for each service it offers. As long as the right software is running, the service is available. Suppose, however, that a server encounters a bug in the HTTP software and stops working. That server is no longer able to fulfill HTTP requests, even though it can continue to deal with e-mail and FTP.

Can a Web server handle more than one request at a time? Just as a multiple-outlet strip can accept many electrical plugs, a single port on a Web server can connect to many sockets that carry requests from browsers. The number of socket connections that a port can handle depends on the server's memory and operating system, but at minimum, hundreds of requests can be handled at the same time.

Some large-volume sites, such as *yahoo.com* and *amazon.com*, have more traffic than any single Web server can handle. These sites tend to use a group of multiple servers, also known as a **server farm**, to handle the thousands of requests that come in each second (Figure 6-12).

FIGURE 6-12
Large-volume Web sites often use a server farm to handle thousands of Web page requests.

Is a Web server the same as a Web site? Not necessarily. Most Web server software can be configured so that the server responds to requests addressed to more than one IP address or domain name. In such a case, one computer running one Web server program can act like multiple Web sites. This type of shared hosting is typically supplied to small Web sites that don't have enough traffic to justify the cost of operating their own Web servers.

Similarly, very large Web sites with lots of traffic often configure multiple Web servers to respond to requests for the same IP address or domain name. When you connect to *www.hotmail.com*, for example, you are usually redirected to one of several identically configured file servers.

What happens when traffic exceeds the capacity of Web servers? In a classic example of demand exceeding capacity, the first online Victoria's Secret lingerie show frustrated thousands of shoppers as images appeared at a snail's pace and eventually the servers crashed. During the Iraq conflict, the Army home page, which typically takes 4 seconds to load on a high-speed connection, averaged more than 80 seconds at peak times because the site was inundated with traffic from family members of Army personnel and others interested in information about the unfolding war.

Excessive demand can occur when special circumstances attract people to a Web site or when a worm launches a denial-of-service attack. When traffic exceeds capacity, a Web server can take a long time to fulfill Web page requests—some requests might even time out and produce a "page not found" error. If you experience excessive delays from a Web site, try again at another time, when traffic might be lighter.

COOKIES

What is a "cookie"? A **cookie** is a small chunk of data generated by a Web server and stored in a text file on your computer's hard disk. Figure 6-13 contains an example.

Cookie: jqstudent@sarasota.fl.us/

SITESERVER ID=9022591d2390f3b8639aa3c7cf1ca8f5 sarasota.fl.us/
0 642859008 31887777 2868194304 29411026 *

FIGURE 6-13
A cookie is created by a Web server and stored on your computer's hard disk.

Cookies allow a Web site to store information on a client computer for later retrieval. Web sites use cookies to:

- Monitor your path through a site to keep track of the pages you viewed or the items you purchased.

- Gather information that allows a Web server to present ad banners targeted to products you previously purchased at that Web site.

- Collect personal information you type into a Web page form and retain it for the next time you visit the Web site.

Why do Web sites use cookies? In many respects, cookies are a "fix" for the problems caused by HTTP's stateless protocol. Cookies are frequently used to remind a Web server who you are each time your browser makes a request.

Suppose that you use your browser to visit a popular online music store. You search for your favorite bands, listen to some sample tracks, and select a few CDs you want to purchase. After browsing through 20 or 30 pages, you eventually go to the checkout counter where you see a list of the CDs you selected. You fill out a form that requests your name, shipping address, and payment information.

Although you might have been browsing at the music site for 30 minutes or more, from the perspective of the site's server, that activity could just as well have been carried out by several people, each one spending only a few seconds at the site. Because HTTP is a stateless protocol, each time you connect to a different page, the server regards it as a new visit.

Cookies allow the music site's server to identify you so that your requests won't get mixed up with those of other people visiting the site. Cookies also enable the server to keep track of your activity and compile a list of your purchases.

How do cookies work? When your browser connects to a site that uses cookies, it receives an HTTP "Set-cookie" message from the Web server. This cookie message contains some information that your browser stores on your computer's hard disk. The cookie information can include a customer number, a shopping cart number, a part number, or any other data. In addition, the cookie usually contains the date the cookie expires and the domain name of the host that created the cookie. A server that creates a cookie can request it the next time you connect to one of its Web pages.

Are cookies safe and private? Cookies are a relatively safe technology. A cookie is data, not a computer program or script. Although a cookie is sent to your computer and stored there, it cannot be executed to activate a virus or worm.

INFOWEBLINKS

At the **Cookies InfoWeb**, you'll find links to a collection of articles that focus on cookie technology, including how they affect security and privacy.

www.course.com/np/concepts8/ch06

Cookies have several important privacy features. First, cookies don't use your name for identification purposes. Instead, a Web server sends your browser a randomly generated number, which is saved in the cookie and used to identify you and keep track of your activity on the site. Your name is not associated with your cookies unless you entered it into a form, which is then transferred to the cookie.

The second privacy feature of cookies is that they can contain only as much information as you disclose while using the Web site that sets the cookie. A cookie cannot rummage through your hard disk to find the password for your e-mail account, the number for your checking account, or the PIN for your credit card. However, if you enter your credit card number in the process of making an online purchase, it is possible for the cookie to store that number. Most reputable Web sites do not store such sensitive information in cookies—a site's privacy policy often supplies information on this important privacy and security topic.

The third privacy characteristic is that a cookie can be accessed only by the site that created it. For example, if the *www.cduniverse.com* server creates a cookie that contains your preference for rap music, no other Web site should be able to access this cookie and send you junk mail about discount rap CDs. Unfortunately, this aspect of cookie privacy can be defeated—you'll learn more about this topic in the e-commerce section.

Does my computer have to accept cookies? Most browsers include security settings that block cookies (Figure 6-14). Unfortunately, on many Web sites, cookies are the only mechanism available for tracking your activity or remembering your purchases. If you turn off cookies, you probably won't be able to make online purchases, you'll have to manually enter your user IDs and passwords, and you won't be able to take advantage of targeted marketing (such as when a music Web site keeps track of your favorite bands and shows you their new CDs).

A more sophisticated approach to cookie security is provided by **P3P** (Platform for Privacy Preferences Project), which defines a standard set of security tags that become part of the HTTP header for every cookie. This header, called a **Compact Privacy Policy**, describes how a Web site uses cookie data. Based on your security preferences, your browser can use this header data to decide whether to accept the cookie. Compact Privacy Policy headers are supported by recent versions of most browsers.

P3P standards do not ensure your privacy. Although your browser might supply some personal data to a company because the Compact Privacy Policy promised not to distribute or sell that data to other businesses, several months later, the policy might change.

How long do cookies stay on my computer? A Web developer can program a cookie to "time out" after a designated period of time. When a cookie reaches the end of its predefined lifetime, your Web browser simply erases it.

FIGURE 6-14

Most browsers allow you to block cookies, but doing so might make it impossible to shop at some Web sites.

You can also delete cookies, but first you must discover where they are stored. Netscape stores cookies in one large file called *Cookies.txt* on a PC or in *Magiccookie* on a Macintosh. IE stores each cookie in a separate file. Refer to your browser documentation to discover which folder holds your cookies. Most browsers allow you to delete unwanted cookies, as shown in Figure 6-15.

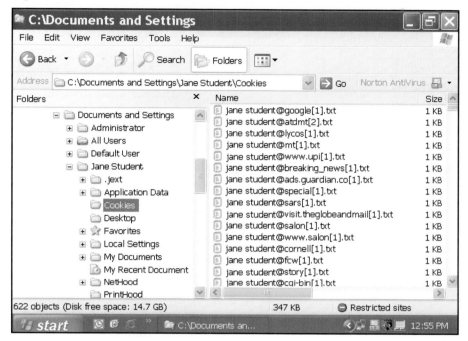

FIGURE 6-15

IE typically stores cookies as individual files on your computer's hard disk. You can view a list of cookies stored on your computer and delete those you no longer want.

QUICKCHECK......SECTION A

1. A hypertext [_____] can be specified by a Web page author using the <a href> tag.

2. Web servers listen for incoming [_____] requests.

3. The followup version to HTML 4 is called [_____] to reflect its extensibility.

4. A Web [_____] is the client half of the client/server software that provides access to information on the Web.

5. You might need to install a(n) [_____] to display some types of data, such as Quicktime movies or Flash animations.

6. HTTP is a(n) [_____] protocol, so each time you connect to a different page, the Web server regards it as a new connection.

7. A(n) [_____] is a small chunk of data generated by a Web server and stored as a text file on your computer's hard disk.

CHECK ANSWERS

LAB 6-A

WORKING WITH COOKIES

In this lab, you'll learn:

- How Web servers use cookies
- Why cookies might pose a threat to your privacy
- How to locate cookies stored on your computer
- How to view the contents of a cookie
- How to delete a single cookie created by Internet Explorer
- How to delete all the cookies stored on your computer
- How to limit the space allocated to cookies created by Internet Explorer
- How to block cookies
- What a session cookie is
- How to set cookie prompts and use the cookie prompt dialog box
- How to take advantage of P3P and Compact Privacy Policies
- The differences between first-party and third-party cookies
- How to "opt out" of receiving third-party cookies

INTERACTIVE LAB

CLICK TO START THE LAB

LAB ASSIGNMENTS

1. Start the interactive part of the lab. Insert your Tracking Disk if you want to save your QuickCheck results. Perform each lab step as directed, and answer all the lab QuickCheck questions. When you exit the lab, your answers are automatically graded and your results are displayed.

2. Use Windows Explorer to look at the cookies stored on your computer. Indicate how many cookies are currently stored. Examine the contents of one cookie, and indicate whether you think it poses a threat to your privacy.

3. Indicate the name and version of the browser you typically use. To find this information, open your browser, and then select the About option from the Help menu. Next, look at the cookie settings your browser provides. Describe how you would adjust these settings to produce a level of privacy protection that is right for your needs.

4. Adjust your browser settings so that you are prompted whenever a Web server attempts to send a cookie to your computer. Go to several of your favorite Web sites and watch for third-party cookies. When you receive a message from a third-party Web site, record the name of the third-party site and the contents of the cookie it is attempting to send. Finally, indicate whether you would accept such a cookie.

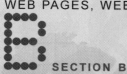

SECTION B

BASIC WEB PAGE AUTHORING

So you want to make your own Web pages? No problem. With today's Web-related software tools, creating a basic Web page has never been easier. In this section of the chapter, you'll learn about the components of a Web page and discover some tips for incorporating graphics, creating menus, adding navigation buttons, and posting your finished pages to a Web server.

WEB PAGE AUTHORING TOOLS

What tools can I use to create Web pages? You have several choices when it comes to Web page authoring tools. You can use a text editor, HTML conversion tools, online Web authoring tools, or Web authoring software.

How do I use a text editor? The most difficult—and some would say old-fashioned—way to create Web pages is to use a text editor, such as Notepad. A **text editor** is similar to word processing software. Unlike word processing software, however, a text editor creates an ASCII document with no hidden formatting codes. When you use a text editor to create an HTML document, you simply type the HTML tags along with the text that you want the browser to display on a Web page.

When saving the document you create with a text editor, make sure you specify an .html or .htm file extension so that browsers recognize it as an HTML document. If you want to create Web pages using a text editor, like the one shown in Figure 6-16, you need a good HTML reference book.

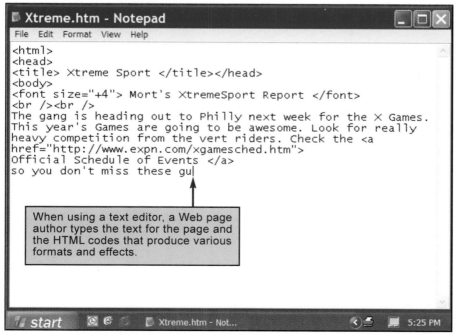

FIGURE 6-16

The most "primitive" Web page authoring tool is a simple text editor, such as Notepad.

What is an HTML conversion tool? An HTML conversion tool is a feature included in many of the software applications you use every day. Microsoft Word, for example, allows you to create a standard DOC file and then use the File menu's Save As Web Page option to convert the document into HTML format. You might also find HTML conversion capabilities in your spreadsheet, presentation, or desktop publishing software. To discover if an application has an HTML option, check the File, Save As, or Export menus. Converting a document into HTML format sometimes produces an unusual result, however, because some of the features and formatting in your original document might not be possible within the world of HTML.

What kind of Web authoring tools can I find online? A third option for budding Web page authors is to use a set of online Web page authoring tools. These tools are provided by some ISPs and other companies that host Web pages for individuals and businesses. Working with these tools is quite simple—you type, select, drag, and drop elements onto a Web page. These simple tools are great for beginners, but they sometimes omit features included with more sophisticated authoring tools.

What's Web authoring software? A fourth option for creating Web pages is a special category of software called **Web authoring software**, which provides tools specifically designed to enter and format Web page text, graphics, and links (Figure 6-17). Popular Web authoring products include Microsoft FrontPage and Macromedia Dreamweaver.

Some Web authoring software has features that help you manage an entire Web site, as opposed to simply creating Web pages. Web site management tools include the capability to automatically link pages within a site and easily change those links. They are also capable of checking all the external links at a site to make sure they still link to valid Web pages—that's a valuable feature for today's constantly changing Web!

INFOWEBLINKS

For help in selecting software to design your own Web pages, connect to the **Web Authoring Tools InfoWeb**.

www.course.com/np/concepts8/ch06

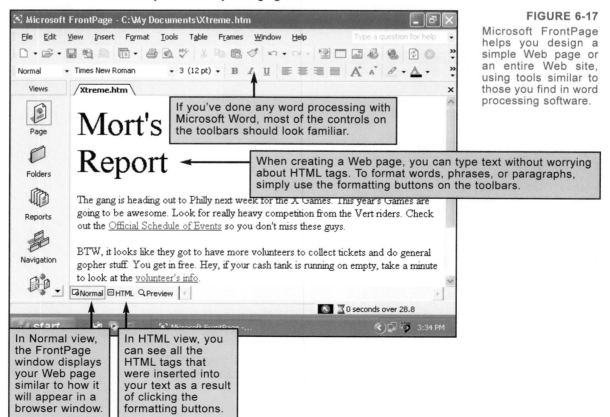

FIGURE 6-17
Microsoft FrontPage helps you design a simple Web page or an entire Web site, using tools similar to those you find in word processing software.

BASIC WEB PAGE COMPONENTS

What are the components of a Web page? A Web page consists of text, links, and media elements, such as graphics, sound, and video. These components can be displayed and combined in various ways to create unique, eye-catching pages.

The HTML document for a Web page is divided into two sections: the head and the body. If you create an HTML document using a text editor, you must manually enter the tags that begin and end these two sections. If you use Web authoring software, these tags are automatically entered for you. Figure 6-18 outlines the sections of an HTML document.

The **head section** begins with the <head> HTML tag and contains information that defines some global properties for the document. Information in the head section of an HTML document can include the following:

- The Web page title that appears in the title bar of the browser window
- Global formatting information
- Information about the page that can be used by search engines
- Scripts that add interactivity to the Web page

The **body section** of an HTML document begins with the <body> HTML tag. It contains the text you want the browser to display, the HTML tags that format the text, plus a variety of links—including links to graphics, sounds, and videos. Most Web pages use headers to break up the text into organized sections. A **Web page header** (casually referred to as a "heading") is simply a subtitle displayed in a font that is a different size or color from the normal text in the paragraphs that appear on the page. HTML supports six predefined levels of headings, with H1 using the largest font and H6 using the smallest font. Figure 6-19 illustrates the basic components of a typical Web page.

FIGURE 6-18

The framework for an HTML document consists of two sections: the head and the body.

```
<html>
<head>
<title>
This text appears on the
title bar of the browser
window
</title>
</head>

<body>
This text is displayed in
the browser window as
the Web page
</body>

</html>
```

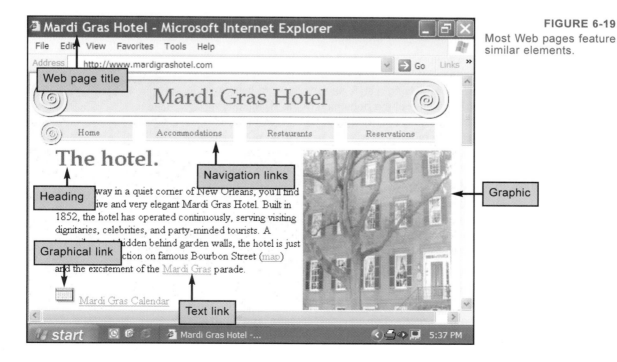

FIGURE 6-19

Most Web pages feature similar elements.

FORMATS, STYLES, AND STYLE SHEETS

How do I format the text on a Web page? When working with Web authoring software, you can simply highlight the text you want to format, and then select the formatting attributes from a list.

When you create Web pages with a text editor, you can format text by inserting HTML tags, such as <font size="4" face="Arial" color="#121212">. Figure 6-20 lists some formatting tags typically used in an HTML document.

FIGURE 6-20
HTML Formatting Tags

Tag	Use
<font size="xxx">	Specify a font size by inserting a number between the quotes
<font color="color">	Specify a color name or number between the quotes
<b>	Bold text
<i>	Italicize text
<u>	Underline text
<align="direction">	Specify paragraph alignment by inserting right, center, or left between the quotes
<bgcolor="color">	Specify a background color for the entire page

What is a style? In the world of Web pages, a style is essentially the same as in the world of word processing. It is a combination of attributes—such as bold, italic, green, and Arial—that specifies the way text is displayed. You can use styles for emphasis and decoration. Just don't get carried away with all the possibilities for colors, sizes, and fonts. Choose a base font that is easy to read for paragraphs of text. Also, use a consistent set of styles for headers.

What is a style sheet? A style sheet—officially referred to as a **cascading style sheet** (CSS)—acts as a "template" that can control the layout and design of a Web page. Style sheets, like the one in Figure 6-21, work with HTML tags to make it easy to globally change one or more formats on a Web page without modifying individual HTML tags.

Suppose you are creating a Web page and you plan to include 20 key terms in a bold green 12-point font. You could specify this font style 20 times—one time for each key term. Using a style sheet, however, you can simply define the style as h2 one time at the beginning of the HTML document, and then apply it by using a single HTML tag (if you are using a text editor) or by selecting the style from a list (if you are using Web authoring software). If you later decide to make all these key terms a different color, you can change only the initial definition for the style, and then the change will "cascade" through the entire page.

Rather than define styles in each HTML document for a Web site, you can set up an **external style sheet** that contains formatting specifications for a group of Web pages. All these Web pages can use this external style sheet by means of a link placed in their head sections.

Are style sheets universally supported by all browsers? The main disadvantage of style sheets is that some of their features are not uniformly supported by all browsers. For example, an HTML document that uses style sheets might be displayed differently in Netscape and IE. If you decide to use style sheets for the Web pages you create, it is important to preview your pages using the browsers that visitors to your Web site might use.

FIGURE 6-21
Styles can be defined in the head section or as a separate document. Here, the head section defines the font used throughout the document for the text in normal paragraphs (p) and in heading 2 (h2).

```
<head>

p { font-size: 12pt;
font-family: Garamond, serif; }

h2 { color: green;
font-weight: bold;
font-size: 12pt;}

</head>
```

WEB PAGE GRAPHICS, SOUND, AND ANIMATION

How are graphics incorporated into Web pages? As you learned in Section A, the HTML document that your browser receives does not actually contain any graphics. Instead, it contains an <img src> HTML tag that references a graphic. When displaying a Web page, your browser retrieves the specified graphic and displays it with the rest of the page.

If you use a text editor to create a Web page, you must manually enter the complete tag, such as <img src="truck.gif">, which includes the file name for the graphic. When using Web page authoring software, you can use a menu option to select the graphic from a list of files stored on your computer. Figure 6-22 illustrates how you select a graphic when creating a Web page with FrontPage software.

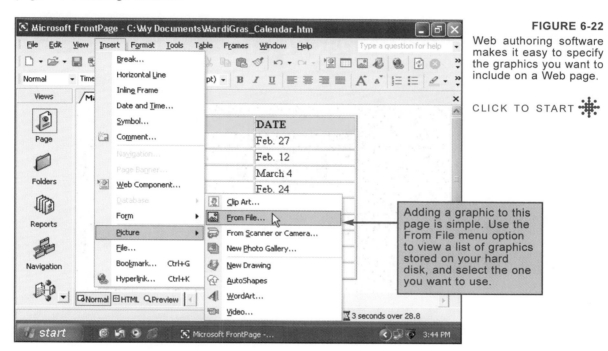

FIGURE 6-22

Web authoring software makes it easy to specify the graphics you want to include on a Web page.

CLICK TO START

Can I use any graphic format on a Web page? Most of the graphics used for Web pages are stored in GIF, JPEG, or PNG format. All three graphics formats use compression techniques to store graphical images in a relatively small number of bytes. Keeping graphics files small helps Web pages download swiftly and appear quickly in the browser window. You'll learn more about graphics formats and their use on the Web in Chapter 7.

How do I include sound? You can include sound files in the foreground or background of a Web page. The <a href> tag creates a foreground link that visitors can click to hear the sound. The HTML looks like this:

<a href="FileName.wav"> Click here for music </a>

A second method, commonly referred to as "background sound," uses the <embed> tag to attach a sound file that starts to play as soon as a browser displays the Web page. The Web page can show a popup window containing sound controls, or the music can play completely in the background. The HTML looks like this:

<embed src="FileName.wav">

What about video and animation? Videos and animations can add a dynamic element to Web pages. They can be added to Web pages using the simple <embed> tag, the <a href> tag, or the more complex <object> tag.

An **animated GIF** is a graphics file that consists of a sequence of frames or related images. Animated GIFs, such as the one shown in Figure 6-23, are supported by most browsers and offer one of the easiest ways to add simple animation to a Web page.

FIGURE 6-23

When an animated GIF is displayed, your browser cycles through the frames, resulting in a simple repeating animation. In this example, the spacecraft spins to illustrate its operation in space.

CLICK TO START

Flash animation is a proprietary technology developed by Macromedia that requires client software for viewing. Many computer owners have downloaded the Flash client, making it one of the most popular animation formats. Flash provides more flexibility than animated GIFs and can be used for more complex animations.

Popular video formats, such as QuickTime, MPEG, and AVI, are used for Web-based and disk-based video playback. Variations of these formats are specially designed to handle the communications details for Web playback. To play video, your computer needs corresponding player software, usually specified at the Web site.

LINKS, BUTTONS, AND HOT SPOTS

How do links work? Typically, a link appears on a Web page as underlined blue text, but a link can be any color, might not be underlined, and could look like a graphic or a button. Remember from Chapter 1 that the arrow-shaped pointer changes to a pointing hand when it moves over any text or graphics link in the browser window.

The HTML that indicates a link (Figure 6-24) specifies two elements: a destination and a label.

FIGURE 6-24

The destination specifies a URL—usually the Web page that appears as a result of clicking the link. The label is the wording for the underlined text that appears on the Web page as the clickable link.

<a href = "http://www.e-course.com/instructions.html" > Click for instructions. </a>

Link destination

Link label that appears on the Web page

The <a href> link tag also allows a Web page author to specify whether the linked page will appear in the current browser window or a new browser window. You've probably encountered Web page links that create a new window. When used effectively, new windows help you easily return to previous pages. Too many new windows, however, can clutter your screen.

How can I turn a graphic into a link? Instead of a text label, you can use an image as a clickable link. These graphical links can connect to other Web pages or graphics. You might have encountered graphical links called "thumbnails" that expand in size when clicked. Graphical links can even look like buttons, complete with labels and icons.

Suppose you want to create a Web page that displays a photograph of a sports car. You want your Web page visitors to be able to click the sports car to see a list of its features. The HTML tag might look like the one in Figure 6-25.

FIGURE 6-25

This link shows an image of a sports car from the file *sports car.jpg*. When clicked, this graphical link displays the information contained in the file named *features.html*.

<a href = "http://www.cars.com/features.html">	<img src = "sports car.jpg"> </a>	
Link destination	HTML graphics tag	File name for graphic

What kinds of links can I add to a page? Text and graphics links can specify a variety of destinations.

- An **internal link** (also called a "local link" or "page link") links to other pages at the same Web site. Web page authors typically use these links for navigation within a Web site.

- An **external link** (also called a "remote link") links to pages outside the Web site. You can create links to any Web site in the world, but it is a good idea to check the site's policies on external links. A site might ask that you create links only to its main page rather than to a specific page within the site.

- An **intrapage link** (also called an "anchor link") is a type of link used to jump to a different location within the current Web page. These links are handy for a long page that's divided into sections. User group FAQs are often structured as a long page of questions and answers. The page begins with a list of questions. Each question is linked to its answer, which appears farther down the page.

- A **mailto link** automatically opens a preaddressed e-mail form that can be filled in and sent. These links are often used as a method for contacting the Webmaster who maintains the site or a customer service representative.

How do "hot spots" work? While browsing the Web, you've probably encountered graphics divided into several clickable areas. These images might be maps that allow you to click a region to view a list of local attractions, businesses, or dealers. You might even come across a Web site with a photo on the main page that is divided into areas representing different parts of the Web site.

A clickable map, photo, or diagram (Figure 6-26) is referred to as an **image map**, and each link within the image map is sometimes referred to as a **hot spot**. Hot spots are defined by a set of HTML tags that specify the coordinates and destination page for each clickable area. A Web authoring tool makes it easy to drag over an area of an image, and then use menus and dialog boxes to specify the destination page for each hot spot.

FIGURE 6-26

Using Web page authoring software, hot spots can be defined by dragging over areas of the graphic. Here hot spots define areas of the moon. When the image map is complete, clicking one of these hot spots produces information about that area of the moon.

What is a broken link? A nonfunctioning link is called a **broken link**. A Web page link works only as long as a file with the corresponding URL exists on the server. If the requested file has been deleted or its name changed, the link will not function properly (Figure 6-27).

It is the responsibility of Web page authors to periodically check links on their Web pages to make sure they work. To test links, an author can manually click through them or use the link checking feature of Web authoring software. Broken links must be removed or edited to reflect the correct URL for a destination page.

HTML FORMS

What is an HTML form? An **HTML form** (usually referred to simply as a "form") is a series of fill-in blanks created using the HTML <form> and <input> tags. Forms are used to collect user input for e-commerce orders, site registrations, opinion polls, and so on.

What happens to the data that's entered into a form? The information you enter into an HTML form is held in the memory of your computer, where your browser creates temporary storage bins that correspond to the input field names designated by the form's HTML tags. Your address, in the form shown in Figure 6-28, might be temporarily held in a memory location that's called "Customer Address." When you click a Submit button, your browser gathers the data from memory and sends it to a specially designated program on an HTTP server, where it can be processed and stored.

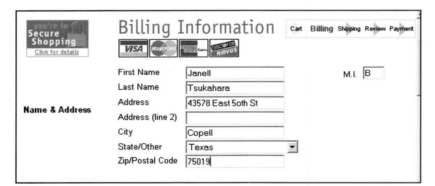

What happens to form data after it arrives at a server? The HTTP message containing your data also contains the name of a small CGI or ASP program called a "script" that accepts the form data after it arrives at the server. **CGI** (Common Gateway Interface) is a set of specifications or standards for how servers can handle a variety of HTTP requests. Using these specifications, programmers and Web page authors can write CGI scripts that run on a server to handle data submitted as HTTP messages. These scripts can be written using a variety of programming and scripting languages, such as Perl, C, C++, C#, and Java.

ASP (Active Server Pages) is a server-side technology developed by Microsoft as an alternative to CGI. ASP scripts, like CGI scripts, run on a server and deal with data submitted as HTTP messages. ASP scripts can be written in VBScript, Perl, REXX, or JScript—Microsoft's version of JavaScript.

The CGI or ASP script that accepts data from a form specifies how the server should deal with the data. In an e-commerce environment, the data is typically part of a purchase transaction, so it is processed to calculate the total price of the order and then stored in the company's database.

FIGURE 6-27

When a broken link points to a nonexistent HTML document, your browser typically produces a 404 Not Found error. When a broken link points to a nonexistent graphic or other non-HTML file, your browser usually displays a broken link icon, shown below.

FIGURE 6-28

HTML forms are typically used to collect payment and shipping information at the "checkout counter" of e-commerce Web sites.

TABLES AND FRAMES

Why are tables such an integral part of many Web pages? A **Web page table** (usually referred to simply as a "table") is a grid of cells that can be used as a layout tool for specifying the placement of text and graphics on a Web page. Tables are an important part of Web page design because HTML does not include a formatting feature for multiple columns. Without tables, authors would have very little control over the position of text and graphics displayed in the browser window. The effectiveness of tables is clear in Figure 6-29, where one Web page uses tables and the other page does not.

FIGURE 6-29

The Web page displayed at left uses a table to position graphics and text. Without a table, the Web page at right simply displays text and graphics in a single column.

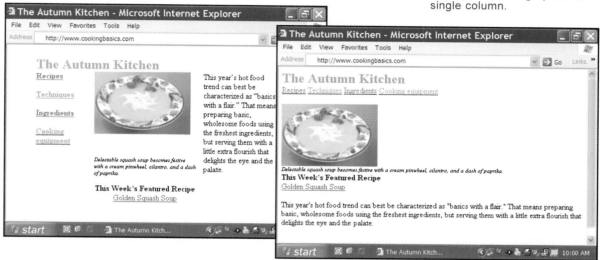

How flexible are tables? The cells of a table can contain text or graphics, but all the columns and rows in a table do not have to be the same size—they can be sized according to the material they contain. This feature of tables makes them a flexible layout tool. Many Web page designers put the entire contents of a Web page into a single table.

Tables are easy to create—especially when using Web authoring software or word processing software that converts documents into HTML format. You simply define the number of columns and rows for a table, and then specify the size for each row and column. You can merge two or more cells to create a larger cell, or you can subdivide a cell to make it smaller.

What's a frame? An **HTML frame** (or simply "frame") is part of a Web page that scrolls independently of other parts of the page so that titles and menus remain visible while you scroll through text and graphics. Frames also allow your browser to display multiple documents at the same time. Frames have fallen out of favor—in part because some Web designers littered Web pages with frames that remained visible after visitors linked to other sites.

A typical use of frames, shown in Figure 6-30, is to display a stationary banner at the top of a page and a set of links on the left side of the screen that do not move as you scroll through the main text on the Web page.

FIGURE 6-30

Expert Web designers suggest using frames sparingly and making sure that frames close when linking to other sites.

CLICK TO START

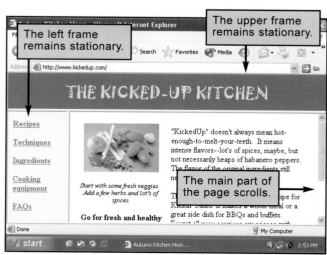

TESTING AND POSTING WEB PAGES

How do I get my Web pages on the Internet? Creating a Web page is not the end of the publishing process. You also must test your pages, transfer them to a Web server, and test all your links, as explained by the steps in the following list:

1. Test each page locally. When you complete the first draft of a Web page, you must test it to verify that every element is displayed correctly by any browsers that visitors to your Web page might use. You can accomplish this task without connecting to the Web. Simply open a browser, and then enter the local file name for the HTML document you created for your Web page. Repeat this process for any other browsers you expect visitors to use. One caution: Your hard disk drive is much faster than a dial-up connection, so the text and graphics for your Web page are displayed faster during your local test than for someone viewing your page over the Internet. Figure 6-31 shows you how to test Web pages offline.

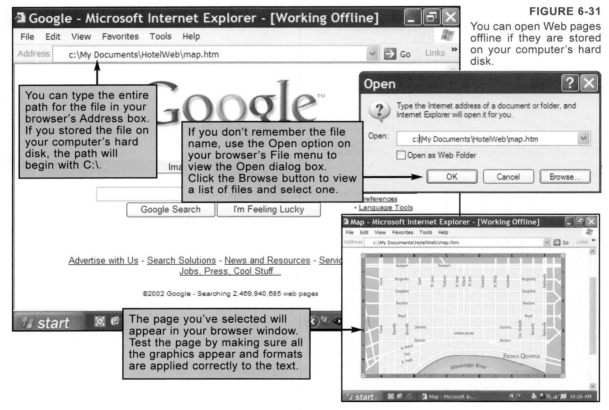

FIGURE 6-31
You can open Web pages offline if they are stored on your computer's hard disk.

You can type the entire path for the file in your browser's Address box. If you stored the file on your computer's hard disk, the path will begin with C:\.

If you don't remember the file name, use the Open option on your browser's File menu to view the Open dialog box. Click the Browse button to view a list of files and select one.

The page you've selected will appear in your browser window. Test the page by making sure all the graphics appear and formats are applied correctly to the text.

2. Transfer pages to a Web server. Whether you're publishing a single page, a series of pages, or an entire Web site, you must put your pages on a Web server—a process called "posting." Although Web server software is available for your home computer, you probably will not want to leave your computer on continuously with a live dial-up, DSL, or cable link to the Internet. Instead, you should look for a site that will "host" your pages by providing space for your HTML files on a Web server.

Some universities allocate space for student Web pages and resumes. ISPs, such as America Online and AT&T WorldNet, also offer space for subscriber Web pages. If you are setting up a site for your business, consider a Web hosting service that, for a monthly fee, provides space on a reliable Web server in a secure data center.

The process of posting a Web page consists of transferring from your computer to the hard disk of a Web server the file containing your HTML document and all associated media files, such as graphics, sound, and video files. To accomplish the transfer for pages you've created using a text editor or word processor, you can use a file transfer utility, such as WSFTP. Web authoring software usually provides a menu option that automates the process of posting HTML documents and associated media files.

Regardless of the posting tool you use, it is necessary to follow the posting procedure required by your hosting service. You need to obtain a password that allows you to save files on the server, and you need to know the URL for the server and folder that will hold your files.

3. Test all pages and links. After you post your pages on a Web server, make sure you can access each page, and then test the links between your pages as well as the links to pages on other sites.

4. Update your site to keep it current. Periodically, you should review the information on your Web pages and verify that the links still connect to existing Web pages. You can easily change your pages and then test them offline before reposting them. You might encounter "Under Construction" signs at some Web sites, but they aren't usually necessary. You should handle your construction and revision work offline.

INFOWEBLINKS

Before you post Web pages, take a good look at them. For hints about creating effective Web pages and avoiding design disasters, check the links at the **Web Page Design Tips InfoWeb**.

www.course.com/np/concepts8/ch06

QUICKCHECK......SECTION B

1. A text editor, such as Notepad, creates a(n) [＿＿＿＿＿＿＿] document to which you can manually add HTML tags.

2. Some Web [＿＿＿＿＿＿＿] software not only offers tools for creating Web pages, but also includes Web site management tools for checking external links.

3. The [＿＿＿＿＿＿＿] section of an HTML document can contain information that defines global formatting and scripts.

4. A(n) [＿＿＿＿＿＿＿] sheet acts as a template that controls the formats for Web page headers, fonts, and colors.

5. The three graphics formats most commonly used for Web pages are GIF, [＿＿＿＿＿＿＿], and PNG.

6. For Web-based animation, the most popular technology is [＿＿＿＿＿＿＿].

7. Clicking a(n) [＿＿＿＿＿＿＿] link automatically opens a pre-addressed e-mail form.

8. An image map contains clickable [＿＿＿＿＿＿＿].

9. Many Web page authors and designers use tables as a layout tool for positioning the elements of a Web page. True or false? [＿＿＿＿＿]

10. After creating one or more Web pages, you have to [＿＿＿＿＿] them before they can be accessed by others.

 CHECK ANSWERS

WEB PAGE EXTENSIONS, SCRIPTS, AND PROGRAMS

Originally, Web pages were static, unchanging, and maybe a little boring. After a page was downloaded and displayed in your browser window, that was it. The only way to change it was to download an update to the entire page. Suppose, for example, that a Web designer wants a star to appear next to any item you select from a list displayed on a Web page. With basic HTML, the only way to accomplish that feat is to make the list item a hot spot, and link it to a copy of the same page in which a star appears next to the selected item.

Basic HTML does not provide much flexibility in two key areas. First, it does not allow Web pages to change in appearance after they are downloaded and displayed, and it does not provide a convenient way for users to interact with Web pages. To address these deficiencies, technologies such as Web page extensions, scripts, and programming tools are now available. With these tools, Web page design goes far beyond basic HTML. Students who plan careers as Web page designers need to learn how to use them. For people who simply browse the Web, a basic grasp of these tools is also valuable for understanding usability, security, and privacy issues.

DHTML

What is DHTML? **DHTML** (Dynamic HTML) is typically used to describe the combination of HTML tags, cascading style sheets, and scripts that enables Web page authors to animate the pages they create. DHTML allows the appearance of a Web page to change after it's loaded into the browser, without any additional communication with the Web server for an update. DHTML is sometimes described as "animating HTML." For example, after a Web page appears in the browser window, a chunk of text can change color, or a graphic can move from one location to another, in response to some user action, such as a mouse movement or mouse click (Figure 6-32).

FIGURE 6-32

DHTML effects usually activate as a result of a "mouseover." In this example, moving the mouse over the map zooms the map to a larger size.

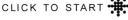

CLICK TO START

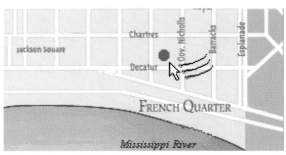

Is DHTML a replacement for HTML? DHTML is not a replacement for HTML. In fact, DHTML is not a scripting language at all. It is simply a term used to describe a method for using HTML in combination with a few other technologies to make Web pages more, well, dynamic.

Do all browsers support DHTML? All of today's popular personal computer browsers support DHTML. However, each browser supports DHTML somewhat differently. As a result, the tags and scripts that a Web page author uses for dynamic effects to be displayed by the Netscape browser could differ from the tags required to achieve the same effects with Internet Explorer.

If you ever noticed a message such as "This site is best when viewed with Netscape," you might have encountered a Web page that includes DHTML effects that work only when the page appears in the Netscape browser window. When you encounter these Web pages, it might be possible to obtain information from the site regardless of the browser you use. You just might not be able to see all the dynamic effects if you are not using the recommended browser.

XML AND XSL

What is XML? **XML** (Extensible Markup Language) is a method for putting structured data, such as spreadsheet cells or database records, into a text file. As with HTML, XML uses tags and attributes to mark up the contents of a file. Whereas HTML tags, such as <b>, focus on the format or appearance of a document, XML tags essentially define fields of data. For example, XML tags, such as <part number>, <price>, and <weight>, explicitly identify a particular kind of information—much like a field heading in a database.

As the name suggests, XML is extensible, which means that individual users and groups of users can create their own tags and even their own markup languages. A series of specialized tags pertaining to sports, for example, can be formalized as a markup language and used to record data, store it, and then exchange it in a variety of formats, such as Web pages and printed documents. Figure 6-33 lists some markup languages created with XML.

How does XML work? Suppose an automobile manufacturing group wants a standard way to store and exchange information about car features and prices. The group can specify new tags, such as <dealer_price> and <suggested_retail_price>, which can be inserted into XML documents along with corresponding data.

Of course, these new tags must be defined somewhere, so the XML specifications provide for **DTD files** (Document Type Definition files), which contain the tags used in an XML file. DTD files can exist in the same location as the XML file or on a server elsewhere on the Web. This flexibility makes it possible for an entire industry to define and use the same tags by referencing a DTD file on a known server. The tool for reading XML documents is referred to as an **XML parser** and is included in all of today's popular browsers.

What is XSL? **XSL** (Extensible Stylesheet Language) is a technology that's similar to XML, but can be used to create customized tags that control the display of data in an XML document. The files containing the definitions for new XSL tags can be stored in the same location as the XML file, or they can be referenced from a server anywhere on the Internet. XSL and XML work well together to produce customized, flexible, and platform-independent Web pages.

INFOWEBLINKS

To learn more about DHTML, XML, and XSL, you can access the **Beyond HTML InfoWeb.**

www.course.com/np/concepts8/ch06

FIGURE 6-33
XML Applications

Real Estate Transaction Standard (RETS)
Designed to allow realtors and county clerks to access real estate transaction information.

Green Building XML
Helps architects, engineers, and builders obtain and calculate energy efficiency data for construction projects.

Robotic Markup Language (RoboML)
Allows researchers, designers, and manufacturers to communicate and archive data used by human-robot interface agents.

OpenGIS Geography Markup Language
Designed for geographers and mapmakers to record and exchange topographic details and coordinate reference points.

SportsML
Helps recruiters, sportswriters, and coaches record and exchange sports scores, schedules, standings, and statistics for a wide variety of competitions.

DocBook
Enables authors and technical writers to create and store the contents of books and papers about computer hardware and software.

Chemical Markup Language
Helps researchers record, exchange, and display chemical information, particularly at the molecular level.

JAVASCRIPT AND VBSCRIPT

Is it possible to add programs to a Web page? Standard HTML provides a way to display text and graphics on a Web page and link to other Web pages, but because it isn't a programming language, HTML does not provide a way to perform complicated tasks or respond to user actions. Scripting languages, such as JavaScript and VBScript, allow a Web designer to embed simple program instructions, called "scripting statements," directly into the text of an HTML document. A series of these scripting statements is called a **script**. Scripting statements are not displayed by the browser; instead, they instruct the browser to perform specific actions or respond to specific user actions.

How would a Web page author use a scripting language? Scripting languages allow Web pages to become more interactive and incorporate activities that would otherwise require a computer program. Scripts enable e-commerce sites to verify credit card information. They also make it possible to create interactive Web pages, such as loan payment calculators. Scripts work with cookies to deliver custom Web pages, such as those Amazon.com generates each time you return to the site. Scripts don't replace normal HTML—they extend and enhance it.

What are the most popular scripting languages? **JavaScript** and **VBScript** are the most popular scripting languages, but alternatives do exist, including PerlScript, Python, REXX, and Awk.

How do scripts work? Scripts can run on the client or the server. A **client-side script** consists of scripting statements embedded in an HTML document. The statements are executed by the browser, which must have the capability to deal with that scripting language. Most of today's browsers can handle JavaScript, but only IE has the built-in capability to execute VBScript.

A **server-side script** consists of statements that run on the server. Server-side scripts accept data submitted by a form, process that data, and then generate a custom HTML document that is sent to the browser for display. Because the server-side script is interpreted on the server, the browser receives only straight HTML code. The browser does not receive scripts that it must process, which eliminates many of the compatibility problems with client-side scripting.

What's a scripting error? If you've used the Web a lot, you have almost certainly encountered your share of JavaScript error messages, similar to the one in Figure 6-34.

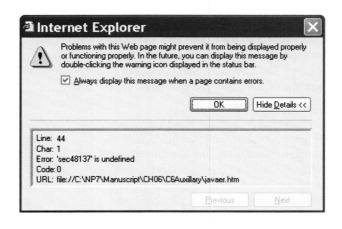

FIGURE 6-34

A JavaScript error means that your browser cannot execute the instructions in a JavaScript.

The Windows XP error message might contain a prompt asking if you want to debug the problem. A JavaScript error can be corrected only by the programmer, so your response to this prompt is "no."

A **scripting error** occurs when a browser or server cannot execute one or more statements in a script. In some cases, scripting errors occur when one of the statements does not adhere to the rules of the scripting language. Usually, these "syntax errors" are caused by a careless Web page author who neglects to test pages before posting them. In other cases, scripting errors occur because the browser that's trying to run the script does not support one of the commands.

Some browsers do not include support for a particular scripting language. For example, Opera and Netscape version 6 do not support VBScript. If support for a scripting language is missing, you can download a player, provided one is available for your browser. For example, IE6 users might find it necessary to download and install the Java Virtual Machine to correctly display Web pages that include JavaScript.

Whatever the cause, if you encounter a scripting error message, you can sometimes close the error message dialog box and continue to access information from the Web site. In some instances, the script is tied to a key aspect of the Web site, and you might have to use a different browser to view its pages.

JAVA APPLETS

What's a Java applet? Java, a high-level programming language developed by Sun Microsystems, has become a popular programming tool for Web-based projects. Small Java applications are called **Java applets**.

How do applets work? A programmer or Web page author can use the Java programming language to write Java applet source code, which is stored in a file with a .java file extension. This source code is compiled into a format called **bytecode** with a .class file extension. A reference to this bytecode file is included in an HTML document using the <applet> HTML tag. When an HTML document contains an <applet> tag, your browser downloads the specified bytecode file and then executes the applet using a **Java Virtual Machine** (JVM). Figure 6-35 helps you visualize this process.

FIGURE 6-35

Programmers can create Java applet source code, compile it, and then include it in an HTML document, where it is executed by a browser.

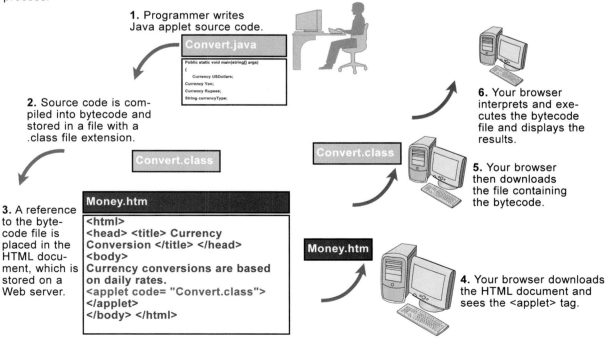

1. Programmer writes Java applet source code.

```
Convert.java
Public static void main(string[] args)
{
    Currency USDollars;
    Currency Yen;
    Currency Rupees;
    String currencyType;
```

2. Source code is compiled into bytecode and stored in a file with a .class file extension.

`Convert.class`

3. A reference to the bytecode file is placed in the HTML document, which is stored on a Web server.

```
Money.htm
<html>
<head> <title> Currency
Conversion </title> </head>
<body>
Currency conversions are based
on daily rates.
<applet code= "Convert.class">
</applet>
</body> </html>
```

`Convert.class`

`Money.htm`

6. Your browser interprets and executes the bytecode file and displays the results.

5. Your browser then downloads the file containing the bytecode.

4. Your browser downloads the HTML document and sees the <applet> tag.

What's the difference between Java applets and JavaScript?
Although their names would lead you to believe that they are similar, Java
applets and JavaScript are two very different technologies. The table in
Figure 6-36 summarizes their differences.

FIGURE 6-36
Java Applet and
JavaScript Comparison

Java Applets	JavaScript
Must be compiled into bytecode	Not compiled
Stored as a separate file or embedded in HTML document	Entire script stored with the HTML document
Referenced using the <applet> or <object> HTML tags	Referenced using the <script> HTML tag
Requires the browser to use a Java Virtual Machine	Requires a JavaScript interpreter
Programmers and Web page authors must use Java programming tools	No special programming tools required

How safe are Java applets? A Java applet is a program that your
browser downloads and runs on your computer. You might wonder if a
Java applet could contain a virus that would take up residence in your
computer system or a worm that would spread over your network. The
technology for Java applets was designed with security in mind. The
applets you download from the Web have the following restrictions:

- They are not allowed to open, modify, delete, or create files on your
  computer.

- They are not allowed to make any network connections except to the
  originating site.

- They are not allowed to start other programs.

You can see from this list that applets are prohibited from the activities that
characterize viruses and worms. Because they cannot attach themselves
to files (thereby modifying them), delete files on your hard disk, mail themselves to people in your address book, and so on, applets are considered
a fairly safe technology.

A more troublesome aspect of Java applets is that they are sometimes
blocked by network firewalls. When an applet is blocked, your browser
might display a Security Exception error message, or you might see the
broken graphics link icon. If you encounter such problems on your network,
you should refer to your personal firewall documentation or consult your
network manager.

INFOWEBLINKS

Maybe you're interested in
adding Java applets to your
Web pages. You'll find links to
online tutorials at the **Java
Applets InfoWeb**.

www.course.com/np/concepts8/ch06

ACTIVEX CONTROLS

What is an ActiveX control? Sometimes when you connect to a Web site, you might see a dialog box containing a security warning, such as the one in Figure 6-37. To better understand what this warning means, you need some background information about ActiveX controls.

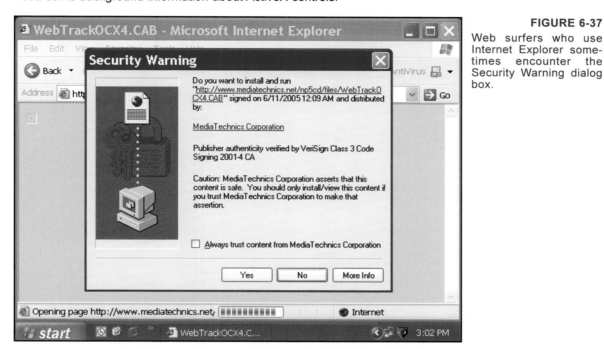

FIGURE 6-37
Web surfers who use Internet Explorer some-times encounter the Security Warning dialog box.

An **ActiveX control** is a compiled computer program that can be refer-enced from within an HTML document, downloaded, installed on your computer, and executed within the browser window. ActiveX controls can be used on the server side, too. Programmers and Web page authors use programming languages, such as C++ and Visual Basic, to create these controls, which can be applied in a wide variety of ways to make Web pages interactive and provide the functionality many consumers expect after using full-featured applications, such as word processing, graphics, and entertainment software.

How do ActiveX controls differ from Java applets? ActiveX controls are installed on your computer's hard disk, whereas Java applets are simply downloaded into memory and run. The advantage of installing an ActiveX control is that it is available locally the next time you want to use it. Java applets cannot be installed on your computer—they are downloaded every time they are used.

Another key difference between the two technologies is that Java applets work on many computer platforms, but ActiveX controls are designed only for the Windows platform—in fact, ActiveX components work only on Windows PCs using the IE browser. ActiveX, which is a Microsoft technol-ogy, is currently not supported by Netscape or non-Windows operating sys-tems, such as Linux or Mac OS.

INFOWEBLINKS

ActiveX controls are used in all sorts of Windows soft-ware—not just Web-based applications. You can get the scoop on ActiveX controls, including how they affect security, by linking to the **ActiveX InfoWeb**.

www.course.com/np/concepts8/ch06

Are ActiveX controls safe? Most ActiveX controls are safe. However, an ActiveX control is a full-fledged program, which gives it the potential to include routines that alter or delete data on your computer's hard disk. If you use IE as your browser, you can adjust its security settings so that it never downloads any ActiveX controls; it downloads and installs only those controls with signed digital certificates; or it downloads and installs any ActiveX controls. Figure 6-38 shows IE options for ActiveX security settings.

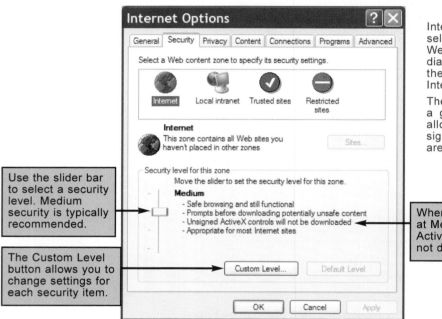

Use the slider bar to select a security level. Medium security is typically recommended.

The Custom Level button allows you to change settings for each security item.

When security is set at Medium, unsigned ActiveX controls are not downloaded.

FIGURE 6-38
Internet Explorer allows you to select a level of security for Web browsing. To access the dialog box, select Tools from the menu bar, then select Internet Options.

The Medium setting gives you a good level of security, and allows your browser to use signed ActiveX controls, which are usually safe.

What is a digital certificate? ActiveX controls include digital certificates to increase their security. A **digital certificate** is an electronic attachment to a file, such as an ActiveX control, that verifies the identity of its source. It is similar to a check cashing card or the stamp you get on your hand when a bouncer checks your ID at the entry to a club. In the world of ActiveX controls, a digital certificate means that the control was created by an identifiable person or company, which can be held accountable for its contents.

An individual programmer, a Web author, or a company can apply for a digital certificate through a **certificate authority** such as VeriSign. Applicants must provide information to verify their identities. The certificate authority then confirms this information before issuing a certificate. Most certificates must be renewed annually for fees ranging from $20 for an individual certificate to $3,000 for a corporate certificate.

A digital certificate can be electronically attached to any ActiveX control the applicant creates. That control is then referred to as "signed"—it is as though the programmer signed his or her name to it. The certificate authority never reviews the ActiveX control itself, so a digital certificate does not ensure that the control is virus-free. Instead, a certificate provides consumers with the name of the person who created the control—the theory being that malicious programmers would not put their names on certificates that travel with an ActiveX control infected with a virus or worm.

INFOWEBLINKS

The **Digital Certificates InfoWeb** explains their use in monitoring ActiveX controls and in verifying consumer and merchant identities in an e-commerce transaction.

www.course.com/np/concepts8/ch06

How does a digital certificate work? Suppose you connect to a Web page that includes an ActiveX control, and your browser's security setting is Medium—the recommended setting for the average Web surfer. When your browser encounters the HTML tag that references a signed ActiveX control, it displays a warning message to alert you that an ActiveX component is trying to install itself. Your browser reads the digital certificate, displays the name of the person or company that signed it, and verifies that the component was not altered since it was signed.

After examining this information, you can decide whether you want your browser to download and install the ActiveX control. To avoid viruses, you should not accept ActiveX controls that are unsigned, signed with "weird" names, or have been changed since they were created. Figure 6-39 shows an example of a valid digital certificate.

FIGURE 6-39

A valid digital certificate contains the certificate holder's name. To ensure that the certificate is legitimate, you can click the underlined links to connect to the certificate holder's Web site and the Web site of the certificate authority.

QUICKCHECK......SECTION C

1. If you want to put structured data, such as spreadsheet cells, into an HTML document, you can use _____ tags to identify the contents of each field.

2. To create interactive Web pages, such as loan payment calculators and online tests, developers can insert _____ into HTML documents.

3. A(n) _____ applet is stored as a bytecode and activated by an <applet> HTML tag.

4. A(n) _____ control is a compiled program that can be referenced from within an HTML document, downloaded, installed on your computer, and executed.

5. A digital _____ carries an electronic signature to verify the source of a program, file, script, or control.

 CHECK ANSWERS

LAB

LAB 6-C

BROWSER SECURITY SETTINGS

In this lab, you'll learn:

- How to adjust the security settings for Internet Explorer
- The significance of Internet, Local Intranet, Trusted, and Restricted security zones
- How to view settings for each security zone
- How to add sites to a security zone
- How to adjust zone security settings
- Why ActiveX controls pose a potential security threat
- The difference between signed and unsigned ActiveX controls
- The recommended security settings for ActiveX controls
- How to adjust ActiveX control security settings
- Why downloads pose a potential security threat to your computer
- How to activate the recommended download security settings
- Why Java applets pose a potential security threat to your computer
- The significance of Java permission levels
- How to activate the recommended Java security settings

LAB ASSIGNMENTS

1. Start the interactive part of the lab. Insert your Tracking Disk if you want to save your QuickCheck results. Perform each lab step as directed, and answer all the lab QuickCheck questions. When you exit the lab, your answers are automatically graded and your results are displayed.

2. Check the Internet zone security setting on the computer you typically use. Indicate whether the setting is High, Medium, Medium-low, Low, or Custom. Describe how this setting handles ActiveX controls, downloads, and Java applets.

3. On the computer you typically use, find out whether any Web sites are listed in the Trusted or Restricted zones. Would you make changes to the list of sites for these zones? Explain why or why not.

4. Activate the Prompt setting for the Download ActiveX controls security setting. After you have done so, use your browser to connect to *http://www.infoweblinks.com/np6/samples/activex.htm*, where you should encounter an ActiveX control security alert. Use your computer's PrtSc key to capture a screenshot of the warning. Paste the screenshot into Paint and then print it. Would you accept this ActiveX control? Why or why not?

SECTION D

E-COMMERCE

One of the most popular activities on the Web is shopping. It has the same allure as catalogs—you can shop at your leisure, anonymously, and in your pajamas. But the economics of the Web provide opportunities that go beyond retail catalogs. Even small businesses and individual artists can post Web pages that display their wares.

The Internet was opened to commercial use in 1991. Since then, thousands of businesses have taken up residence at Web sites. This section of the chapter focuses on e-commerce and the technologies a typical shopper might encounter on the Web.

E-COMMERCE BASICS

What is e-commerce? Chapter 1 introduced e-commerce as Internet activities that include online shopping, electronic auctions, online banking, and online stock trading. Although the experts don't always agree on its definition, **e-commerce** is typically used to describe financial transactions that are conducted electronically over a computer network. It encompasses all aspects of business and marketing processes enabled by Internet and Web technologies.

E-commerce "wares" include many kinds of physical products, digital products, and services. Physical products offered at e-commerce sites include such goods as clothing, shoes, skateboards, and cars. Most of these products can be shipped to buyers through the postal service or a parcel delivery service.

Increasingly, e-commerce goods include digital products, such as news, music, video, databases, software, and all types of knowledge-based items. The unique feature of these products is that they can be transformed into bits and delivered over the Web. Consumers can get them immediately upon completing their orders, and no one pays shipping costs.

E-commerce merchants also peddle services, such as arranging trips, online medical consultation, and remote education. Some of these services can be carried out by computers. Others require human agents. Services can be delivered electronically, as in the case of a distance education course, or they might produce some physical product, such as a cruise ship ticket.

Who is the typical e-commerce customer? The demographics of e-commerce have not yet stabilized. Whereas the typical e-commerce consumer in 1995 was a 30-something white male, in recent years, females and teens have entered the online shopping fray in droves.

Most of the e-commerce activities Web surfers enjoy are classified as **B2C** (business-to-consumer) e-commerce. In the B2C model, businesses supply goods and services to individual consumers. In the **C2C** (consumer-to-consumer) model, consumers sell to each other (Figure 6-40). This model includes wildly popular online auctions and rummage sales. **B2B** (business-to-business) e-commerce involves one enterprise buying goods or services from another enterprise. **B2G** (business-to-government) e-commerce aims to help businesses sell to governments.

FIGURE 6-40

B2C and C2C e-commerce offer consumers many types of goods and services.

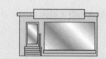

Online storefronts sell a variety of goods, such as clothing, books, toys, music, food, sports gear, and electronics.

Online auctions provide consumers with a worldwide market for antiques, collectibles, and other new and used items.

Online schools offer credit and noncredit courses, tutorials, and even college degrees.

Online ticket and reservation systems provide concert and event tickets plus air, hotel, and car reservations.

Online information services sell subscriptions to news archives, databases, and online magazines.

How profitable is e-commerce? E-commerce enhances traditional business models by offering efficiency and opportunities for automation, computerization, and digitization. As with a traditional "brick and mortar" business, profit in an e-commerce business is the difference between income and expenses.

One of the advantages of e-commerce is its ability to increase profit margins by cutting costs. For example, a typical catalog order placed over the phone costs the merchant $2.50, whereas an online transaction costs about 35 cents. A hotel reservation made online costs the innkeeper 80% less than a booking by phone. A withdrawal or deposit costs the bank about a dollar when handled by a teller, about 25 cents on an ATM, and only a penny on the Web.

E-commerce merchants also gain income by hosting advertising space for banner and popup ads. A **banner ad** is an advertisement, typically embedded at the top of a Web page. A **popup ad**, such as the one in Figure 6-41, is an advertisement that appears in a separate window when you enter a Web site or connect to Web pages. When you click a banner or popup ad, your browser connects directly to the advertiser's Web site, where you can find product information and make a purchase.

Banner and popup ads earn revenue for hosting merchants based on **click-through rate**—the number of times that site visitors click the ad to connect to the advertiser's site. The hosting merchant is paid a small fee for each click through. Click-through rates have declined in recent years because most consumers simply ignore the ads or install **ad-blocking software** to prevent ads from appearing on their screens. The most recent version of Internet Explorer includes a configurable feature to block popup ads.

E-commerce has matured from its early days, when investors were happy to throw money at any e-commerce scheme, through a "dot.com bust," when sites with flawed business models closed down. Today, e-commerce is rebuilding its image, based on more realistic business plans and responsible management.

Is e-commerce popular worldwide? North America accounts for about half of all e-commerce activity, and Western Europe and Asian Pacific regions account for most of the rest. The low volume of e-commerce activity in Africa, Eastern Europe, and Russia can be attributed to several factors, including lack of Internet access, language barriers, depressed economies, shipping limitations, and merchant policies.

Today's e-commerce model is aimed at English speakers with Internet access and a credit card. Although a handful of Web sites offer language alternatives, non-English speakers have difficulty using search engines and reading product descriptions. In regions where electricity and telephone service are not available, Internet access is simply not possible (Figure 6-42). Many e-commerce merchants do not accept checks or cash and might not accept credit cards issued by non-U.S. banks. Even if cash payment is accepted, the price of goods remains beyond the budget of many people in developing countries.

FIGURE 6-41

Popup ads appear as separate windows.

FIGURE 6-42

In some regions of the world, e-commerce obstacles include language barriers, economic factors, and even lack of electrical service.

ONLINE SHOPPING

What makes online shopping so special? E-commerce offers some unique advantages over brick-and-mortar stores and mail-order catalogs. Customers can easily search through large catalogs. They can configure products online, see actual prices, and build an order over several days. Customers can easily compare prices between multiple vendors.

Merchants are always looking for ways to attract customers. The Web and its search engines give merchants a way to be found by customers without expensive, national advertising. Even small merchants can reach a global market. Web technology also allows merchants to track customer preferences and produce individually tailored marketing.

How does an e-commerce store work? E-commerce seems simple from the perspective of a shopper who connects to an online store, browses the electronic catalog, selects merchandise, and then pays for it. The screentour in Figure 6-43 walks you through a typical shopping session.

FIGURE 6-43

In a typical shopping session, you connect to an online storefront and use navigation controls to browse through the merchant's catalog. As you browse, you can drop items into your electronic shopping cart. At the checkout counter, you enter the information necessary to pay for the items you selected.

CLICK TO START

Behind the scenes, an e-commerce site uses several technologies to display merchandise, keep track of shoppers' selections, collect payment data, attempt to protect customers' privacy, and prevent credit card numbers from falling into the wrong hands.

An e-commerce site's domain name, such as *www.amazon.com*, acts as the entry to the online store. A Web page at this location—sometimes referred to as an "electronic storefront"—welcomes customers and provides links to various parts of the site. The goods and services for sale appear in a customer's browser window.

An e-commerce site usually includes some mechanism for customers to select merchandise and then pay for it. Customer orders might be processed manually in a small business. Most high-volume e-commerce businesses, however, use as much automation as possible; their order-processing systems automatically update inventories, and then print packing slips and mailing labels.

SHOPPING CARTS

What's an online shopping cart? If you've done any shopping online, you've probably used an **online shopping cart**—a cyberspace version of the metal cart you wheel around a store and fill up with merchandise.

How do shopping carts work? As mentioned earlier, HTTP is a stateless protocol, which fulfills a single request for a Web resource and then immediately forgets about it. Under these circumstances, you might wonder how it is possible for an online retail store to remember the items you put in your shopping cart.

Most shopping carts work because they use cookies to store information about your activities on a Web site. Cookies work with shopping carts in one of two ways, depending on the e-commerce site. An e-commerce site might use cookies as a storage bin for all the items you load into your shopping cart, as shown in Figure 6-44.

FIGURE 6-44

Shopping cart items can be stored in a cookie.

ADD TO CART

1. When you click the Add to Cart button, the merchant's server sends a message to your browser to add that item number to the cookie, which is stored on your computer.

ITEM #B7655

Cookies

VIEW CART

2. When you check out, the server asks your browser for all the cookie data that pertains to your shopping cart items.

Cookies

3. Your browser sends those cookies along with a request for an order summary.

Your order:

1 Blender $29.95

1 Wok $38.49

4. The Web server uses the cookies to produce a Web page listing the items you want to purchase.

Some e-commerce sites use cookies simply as a way to uniquely identify each shopper. These sites use your unique number to store your item selections in a server-side database (Figure 6-45).

FIGURE 6-45

Shopping cart items can be stored in a database.

Order for CART #2098-2

| 1 Blender | B7655 | $29.95 |
| 1 Wok | GJK4-31 | $38.49 |

4. When you check out, your browser sends your shopping cart number to the server, which retrieves all your selections from the database.

1. When you connect to a merchant's site, the server sends your browser a cookie that contains your unique shopping cart number.

WEB SERVER

DATABASE

CART # 2098-2

ITEM # B7655

3. The Web server sends this number and your merchandise selection to the database, where it is stored in a record that corresponds to your shopping cart number.

CART # 2098-2

Cookies

WEB SERVER
CART # 2098-2

BUY IT

2. When you select an item to purchase, your browser reads your shopping cart ID number from the cookie, and then sends this number to the merchant's Web server.

TRANSACTION PRIVACY AND SECURITY

Is it safe to shop online? Online shoppers are justifiably worried that personal information and credit card numbers supplied in the course of an e-commerce transaction might be hijacked and used inappropriately. Web sites can surreptitiously collect data about your browsing and purchasing habits. Credit card numbers can be stolen and used without authorization.

How does e-commerce affect my privacy? Merchants who market goods and services are eager to get the attention of prospective customers, but they sometimes use spyware that has the potential to compromise your privacy. **Spyware** is any technology that surreptitiously gathers information. In the context of the Web and e-commerce, spyware secretly gathers information and relays it to advertisers or other interested parties. Web-based marketers use several spyware techniques, including ad-serving cookies and clear GIFs.

What is an ad-serving cookie? When you connect to a Web site, you expect it to store an innocuous cookie on your computer's hard disk. Some Web sites, however, feature banner ads supplied by third-party marketing firms. If you click the ad, this third party can create an **ad-serving cookie** (Figure 6-46) and use it to track your activities at any site containing banner ads from that third party. The marketing firms that distribute ad-serving cookies claim that this data is simply used to select and display ads that might interest you, but privacy advocates are worried that shopper profiles can be compiled, sold, and used for unauthorized purposes.

FIGURE 6-46

Ad-serving cookies can be created and stored on your computer's hard disk without your knowledge.

What is a clear GIF? A **clear GIF** or "Web bug" is typically a 1x1 pixel graphic on a Web page. Clear GIFs can be used to set cookies to third-party Web sites. Unlike ad-serving cookies, you don't have to click a banner ad to receive a GIF-activated cookie. Simply viewing the page that contains a clear GIF sets the cookie. Cookies created with clear GIFs have the same uses and potential for misuse as ad-serving cookies.

Can I do anything about spyware? Ad-blocker software and antispyware are designed to block ad-serving cookies, clear GIFs, and other spyware—some even block banner and popup ads altogether. These products are becoming quite popular, despite their tendency to slightly slow your browser's response time.

INFOWEBLINKS

For more information about software you can install to block ads, ad-serving cookies, and clear GIFs, check out the **Ad Blocker InfoWeb**.

www.course.com/np/concepts8/ch06

Can credit card numbers get intercepted? Many shoppers worry that their credit card numbers might get intercepted while traveling over the Internet. A **packet sniffer** (officially called a "protocol analyzer") is a computer program that monitors data as it travels over networks. Most network devices read only the packets addressed to them and ignore the packets addressed to other devices. However, a packet sniffer can observe and open any packet traveling on the network. Packet sniffers have legitimate uses in system maintenance, but hackers can also use them to pilfer data as it travels from customers' computers to e-commerce sites.

To protect your data from packet-sniffing hackers, you should engage in electronic transactions only over a secure connection. A **secure connection** encrypts the data transmitted between your computer and a Web site. Even if a hacker can capture the packets containing your payment data, this data must be decrypted before it can be used for illicit purposes. Technologies that create secure connections include SSL and S-HTTP.

What is SSL? **SSL** (Secure Sockets Layer) is a protocol that encrypts data traveling between a client computer and an HTTP server. This encryption protocol creates what's called an "SSL connection" using a specially designated port—typically Port 443 rather than Port 80, which is used for unsecured HTTP communication. Web pages that provide an SSL connection start with *https:* instead of *http:*.

What is S-HTTP? **S-HTTP** (secure HTTP) is an extension of HTTP that simply encrypts the text of an HTTP message before it is sent. Although SSL and S-HTTP both use encryption techniques to securely transmit data, they are technically different. Whereas SSL creates a secure connection between a client and a server, over which any amount of data can be sent securely, S-HTTP is simply designed to encrypt and then transmit an individual message.

How do I know if a connection is secure? Your browser helps you identify when you are using a secure connection. Figure 6-47 explains.

TERMINOLOGY NOTE

Secure connections differ from secure Web sites. A secure connection encrypts the data transmitted between your computer and a Web site. A secure Web site, such as an online banking site, uses password security to prevent unauthorized access to pages on the site.

FIGURE 6-47

Secure connections are indicated by a dialog box, URL, and taskbar icon.

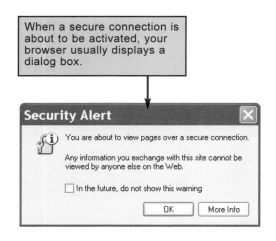

When a secure connection is about to be activated, your browser usually displays a dialog box.

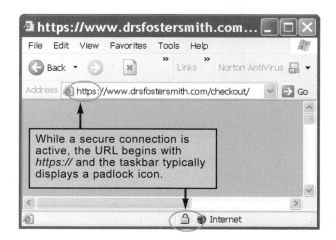

While a secure connection is active, the URL begins with *https://* and the taskbar typically displays a padlock icon.

What is the danger of a database break-in? An increasing number of businesses report that their customer databases have been accessed without authorization. In some cases, thousands of credit card numbers are stolen. Security-conscious e-commerce merchants protect their databases by limiting access and encrypting data. Unfortunately, not all businesses follow these practices. Even when databases seem secure, hackers might find security holes and retrieve sensitive data.

As a consumer, you cannot prevent database break-ins, but you can take steps to ensure that the credit card number stored in a merchant's database is of little use to a hacker. Several credit card companies offer **one-time-use credit card** numbers, which allow consumers to make purchases while keeping their actual card numbers hidden.

A one-time-use credit card number works for a single online purchase. Your credit card company tracks the purchases you incur with one-time-use numbers and adds the charges to your monthly credit card statement. One-time-use numbers cannot be used twice, so even if a hacker steals the number, it will not be accepted for any online or offline purchases.

Should I worry about dishonest employees? An online break-in into the database of a merchant or credit card processing service is a fairly high-tech crime, but your credit card number can be compromised by low-tech methods as well. If a merchant collects your credit card number instead of routing it directly to a credit card processing service, a dishonest employee who works for the merchant might be able to obtain your card number while processing your order. Individual consumers can't do much to prevent this type of theft, but the likelihood of it occurring is low—you take a similar risk every time you pay for a meal by allowing a waiter to take your credit card back to a cashier station or give your credit card number over the phone.

What is a fake storefront? A fake storefront appears to be an online store, but is in fact a fraudulent Web site, designed exclusively for the purpose of collecting credit card numbers from unwary shoppers. These sites might have all the trappings of a real e-commerce site—they might even offer a secure connection for transmitting your credit card number. When your data is received, however, it is stored in a database that belongs to a hacker, who can use the data for illegitimate transactions. Figure 6-48 explains how you can avoid fake storefronts.

FIGURE 6-48
The URLs for fake storefronts often differ from the real thing by a single character. For example, hackers might create a fake storefront using the URL *www.ediebauer.com*—similar to the legitimate store at *www.eddiebauer.com*.

To protect yourself from fake storefronts, make sure to type the URL correctly. Better yet, type the store name—Eddie Bauer, for example—in a search engine such as Google, and use the link provided to reach the site's home page.

Can hackers steal credit card numbers from my hard disk? One additional security problem is worth noting. If your computer is connected with an always-on network connection, such as a DSL or a cable modem, unwanted intruders could find their way into the files stored on your computer's hard disk. If your credit card number exists in any file—for example, in an order confirmation sent to you in an e-mail message—a hacker could find it. As explained in Chapter 5, to block intruders from accessing your computer's hard disk, you should install firewall software.

ELECTRONIC WALLETS

What is an electronic wallet? An **electronic wallet** (also called a "digital wallet") is software that stores billing and shipping information that a customer submits when finalizing an e-commerce purchase. Electronic wallets, such as Microsoft Passport and Yahoo! Wallet, might also hold a digital certificate that verifies your identity.

You can create an electronic wallet by subscribing at the wallet provider's site. After you create your electronic wallet, it pops up on your screen when you make a purchase at a participating merchant's site (Figure 6-49).

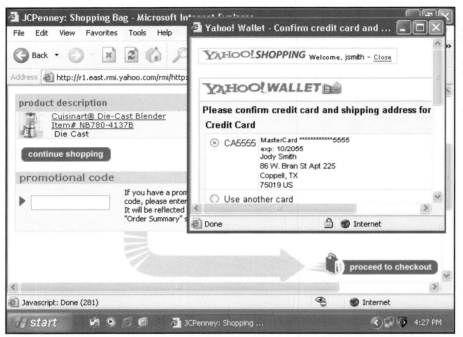

FIGURE 6-49

An electronic wallet can transfer your billing and shipping information to an e-commerce Web server when you check out.

CLICK TO START

How does an electronic wallet work? The data for an electronic wallet can be stored on your computer or on a server maintained by a wallet provider—usually a financial institution, such as a bank or credit card company. Server-side wallets are sometimes referred to as "thin wallets" because they don't require much storage space on your computer.

A wallet requires client-side and server-side software. The client-side software resides on your computer—usually in the form of a browser plug-in. The server-side wallet software resides on an HTTP server that the merchant maintains. Many "brands" of wallets exist, and a server uses data only from a compatible wallet.

When you proceed to an online checkout, software on the merchant's server sends an HTTP message to your PC that looks for and activates compatible wallet software. By clicking a Submit button, your payment data is transferred from your electronic wallet to the server.

How safe is an electronic wallet? Most wallets implement **SET** (Secure Electronic Transaction)—a security method that relies on cryptography and digital certificates to ensure that transactions are legitimate as well as secure. Even if a hacker gains access to your wallet file from your computer or a server, the data it contains will be difficult to decode. Of course, you don't have to decode the contents of your electronic wallet before using it, so you might wonder if a hacker could simply copy your wallet and use the whole encrypted file just as you do. Your wallet is protected by a password, which acts as a PIN to prevent unauthorized use.

Electronic wallets have several vulnerabilities, however. Security analysts were stunned to discover that it is possible to steal credit card numbers from an electronic wallet simply by getting the victim to open an e-mail message. Hackers might also be able to snag data as it flows from an electronic wallet to a merchant's site by using Trojan horse technology to collect your wallet password. Consumers should carefully study current security bulletins before trusting their data to electronic wallets.

PERSON-TO-PERSON PAYMENT SERVICES

What is a person-to-person payment? A **person-to-person payment** (sometimes called an "online payment") offers an alternative to credit cards. It can be used to pay for auction items and to wire money over the Internet. An online service called PayPal pioneered person-to-person payments. PayPal's model has since been copied by several other service providers.

How does a person-to-person payment work? The process begins when you open an account at a person-to-person payment service. Some services require you to deposit some money in your account—just as though you were opening a bank account. Other services allow you to supply your credit card number, which is billed only as you make purchases. You receive a user ID and password that enable you to access your account to make purchases and deposit additional funds. Money can be sent to anyone who has an e-mail account, as shown in Figure 6-50.

Is person-to-person payment safe? The major advantage of person-to-person payments is that the payment service is the only entity that sees your credit card number—merchants, auction dealers, and other payment recipients never receive your credit card number and, therefore, can't misuse it or store it on an unsecured computer. Currently, however, the person-to-person payment industry is in its infancy, and companies are still scrambling to offer reliable, long-term service to customers. Consumer advocates recommend using these services with caution and keeping your account balances low.

FIGURE 6-50

Using a person-to-person payment service.

1. To use a person-to-person payment service, simply log in to your account, enter the recipient's e-mail address, and indicate the payment amount.

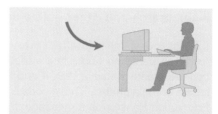

2. The recipient immediately receives an e-mail notification of your payment.

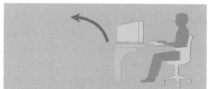

3. The recipient connects to the payment site to "pick up" the money by transferring the funds to a checking account, requesting a check, or sending the funds to someone else.

QUICKCHECK......SECTION D

1. Examples of B2C e-commerce include online auctions and wholesale clearance sites where businesses sell goods to each other. True or false? [   ]

2. A clear [   ] or Web bug can be used to set cookies to a third-party site.

3. A padlock icon at the bottom of your browser window indicates an S-HTTP or [   ] connection. Hint: Use the abbreviation.

4. A packet [   ] is a computer program that monitors data as it travels over networks and is sometimes used by hackers to intercept packets.

5. Most electronic [   ] use SET cryptography and digital certificates.

CHECK ANSWERS

TECHTALK

ENCRYPTION

At one time, encryption was synonymous with spies, secret agents, and an assortment of cloak-and-dagger activities. The average person's exposure to encryption was pretty much limited to Captain Midnight decoder rings and pig Latin. Today, the situation is different. Encryption is one of the most important technologies for maintaining your privacy and the security of important information, such as your credit card number. This TechTalk is designed to provide a basic background in encryption, which you can apply when participating in e-commerce and other online activities.

Is encryption the same as coding? In the context of computers, the word "code" is bantered about in a variety of ways. Programmers write computer code to create software. ASCII and EBCDIC codes are used to represent the letters of the alphabet. These codes, however, are not the same as encryption. Encryption transforms a message in such as way that its contents are hidden from unauthorized readers. Encryption is designed to keep messages secret. Its purpose, therefore, is quite different from simple coding schemes, such as ASCII and EBCDIC, which are designed to transform data into formats that are publicly known and shared.

How does encryption work? An original message—one that has not yet been encrypted—is referred to as **plaintext** or "cleartext." An encrypted message is referred to as **ciphertext**. The process of converting plaintext into ciphertext is called **encryption**. The reverse process—converting ciphertext into plaintext—is called **decryption**. In an e-commerce transaction, for example, your credit card number exists as plaintext, which is encrypted into ciphertext for its journey over a secure connection to the merchant. When the ciphertext arrives at its destination, it is decrypted back into the original plaintext credit card number.

Messages are encrypted by using a cryptographic algorithm and key. A **cryptographic algorithm** is a specific procedure for encrypting or decrypting a message. A **cryptographic key** (usually just called a "key") is a word, number, or phrase that must be known to encrypt or decrypt a message.

For example, Julius Caesar made extensive use of an encryption method called simple substitution, which could have been used to turn the plaintext message "Do not trust Brutus" into GRQRWWUXVWEUXWXV. The cryptographic algorithm was to offset the letters of the alphabet. The key was 3. Anyone who knew this algorithm and key could set up a transformation table like the one in Figure 6-51 to encrypt or decrypt messages for Caesar.

FIGURE 6-51

The algorithm for Caesar's encryption technique was to offset the letters of the alphabet—in this case by three letters. A simple transformation table was used to encrypt or decrypt a message. For example, if a "G" appears in the encrypted message, it would be a "D" in the original unencrypted message.

Ciphertext letters:

D E F G H I J K L M N O P Q R S T U V W X Y Z A B C

Equivalent plaintext letters:

A B C D E F G H I J K L M N O P Q R S T U V W X Y Z

What's the difference between strong and weak encryption? Caesar's simple substitution key is an example of **weak encryption** because it is easy to decrypt even without the algorithm and key. Unauthorized decryption is sometimes referred to as "breaking" or "cracking" a code. You could crack Caesar's code in several ways. For example, you could discover the key by making 25 different transformation tables, each with a different offset (assuming that the encryption method uses the letters of the alphabet in sequence and not at random). You could also analyze the frequency with which letters appear—in English documents, E, T, A, O, and N appear most frequently—and you can piece together the message by guessing the remaining letters.

Strong encryption is loosely defined as "very difficult to break." Of course, with continuous advances in technology, strong encryption is a moving target. For example, several encryption methods that were considered "impossible" to break 10 years ago have recently been cracked by using networks of personal computers. The encryption methods used for most e-commerce transactions are considered "strong" but not unbreakable.

How long does it take to "break" strong encryption? Encryption methods can be broken by the use of expensive, specialized, code-breaking computers. The cost of these machines is substantial, but not beyond the reach of government agencies, major corporations, and organized crime. Encryption methods can also be broken by standard computer hardware—supercomputers, mainframes, workstations, and even personal computers. These computers typically break codes using a **brute-force method**, which consists of trying all possible keys (Figure 6-52).

The length of a computer-readable encryption key is measured in bits. A bit, as you know, can be a 1 or a 0. Unlike the PIN example in which each digit could be one of 10 possible numbers, in a computer-readable encryption key, each digit can be one of two possible numbers: 0 or 1. Figuring out how many numbers you must try to break a computer code requires a calculation using powers of two rather than powers of 10. A 32-bit key, therefore, could be one of about 4.2 billion (2^{32}) numbers. Surprisingly, it would be possible to try all these numbers and discover the key by using an average personal computer.

To discover a 40-bit key, you would have to try about 1 trillion possible combinations—a week's worth of processing time on a personal computer. 56-bit and 64-bit encryption—once thought to be unbreakable by any computer in the private sector—require a lot of computing power, but have been broken by combining the power of many personal computers connected over the Internet. 128-bit encryption and 256-bit encryption are probably secure for several years. Most encryption today uses a 128-bit key.

Another way to understand how the length of a key affects the strength of encryption is to consider this rule of thumb: Beginning with a 40-bit key, each additional bit doubles the time it would take to discover the key. If a personal computer takes one week to crack a 40-bit key, it takes two weeks to crack a 41-bit key, four weeks to crack a 42-bit key, and eight weeks to crack a 43-bit key. A 128-bit key takes $2^{(128-40)}$ times longer to crack than a 40-bit key—that's 309,485,009,821,345,068,724,781,056 times longer!

FIGURE 6-52

Is your PIN secure?

Suppose that a criminal steals an ATM card. The card cannot be used, however, without the correct PIN. A four-digit PIN could be one of 10,000 possible combinations.

If you're mathematically inclined, you'll realize that each digit of the PIN could be one of 10 possibilities: 0, 1, 2, 3, 4, 5, 6, 7, 8, or 9, so 10^4 or 10x10x10x10 possible PINs exist.

To discover a PIN number by brute force, a criminal must try, at most, 10,000 possibilities. Although it would take a person quite a long time to figure out and try all 10,000 possibilities, a computer could polish them off as quickly as the ATM would accept them.

What's public key encryption? Caesar's encryption method is an example of symmetric key encryption, which is also called "secret key" or "conventional" encryption. With **symmetric key encryption**, the key used to encrypt a message is also used to decrypt the message.

Symmetric key encryption is often used to encrypt stationary data, such as corporate financial records. It is not, however, a very desirable encryption method for data that's on the move. The person who encrypts the data must get the key to the person who decrypts the data, without the key falling into the wrong hands. On a computer network, key distribution is a major security problem because of the potential for a packet sniffer to intercept the key.

To eliminate the key-distribution problem, Whitfield Diffie and Martin Helman introduced a concept called **public key encryption** (PKE) in 1975. It uses asymmetric key encryption, in which one key is used to encrypt a message, but another key is used to decrypt the message. Figure 6-53 illustrates how public key encryption works.

FIGURE 6-53

Public key encryption uses two keys. A public key is used to encrypt a message. A private key is used to decrypt the message.

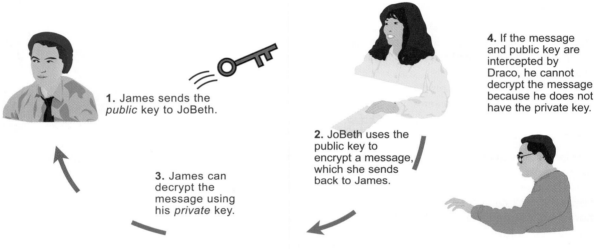

1. James sends the *public* key to JoBeth.

2. JoBeth uses the public key to encrypt a message, which she sends back to James.

3. James can decrypt the message using his *private* key.

4. If the message and public key are intercepted by Draco, he cannot decrypt the message because he does not have the private key.

Public key encryption is a crucial technology on the Web, particularly for e-commerce. When you use an SSL connection to transmit your credit card number, the server sends a public key to your browser. Your browser uses this public key to encrypt the credit card number. After it's encrypted, no one—not even you—can use this public key to decrypt the message. The encrypted message is sent to the Web server, where the private key is used to decrypt it.

Public key encryption is not perfect. The mathematics of PKE make it easier to crack than symmetric key encryption. To get a level of security equal to 80-bit symmetrical encryption requires a 1024-bit public encryption key! As a result of these huge keys, PKE encryption and decryption usually require lots of processing time—about 1000 times more than for symmetric encryption. For this reason, PKE is best used for short messages, such as e-commerce transactions and e-mail.

What are the most commonly used encryption methods? **RSA** (named for its inventors—Ron Rivest, Adi Shamir, and Leonard Adleman) is the most commonly used public key encryption algorithm. In addition to being the technology used for SSL connections, RSA is used to encrypt the data in most digital certificates. **DES** (Data Encryption Standard) is an encryption method based on an algorithm developed by IBM and the U.S. National Security Agency. It uses 56-bit symmetric key encryption. Although it was once the cornerstone of government encryption, DES is being replaced by AES, which offers stronger encryption. **AES** (Advanced Encryption Standard) is an encryption standard that uses three key sizes of 128, 192, or 256 bits. It is based on the Rijndael (pronounced "rain doll") encryption algorithm.

What kind of encryption can I use on my computer? When you engage in an e-commerce transaction, secure connections that encrypt your data are provided by the e-commerce site. In most cases, this is all the encryption necessary for the transaction. Even if you were to further encrypt your data, it is unlikely that the e-commerce server would be equipped to handle the decryption. You might, however, want to encrypt other data, such as your e-mail messages or your data files.

When personal computer users want to encrypt e-mail or other documents, they turn to Phillip Zimmerman's **PGP** (Pretty Good Privacy) software. In addition to encrypting data files, this software lets you digitally sign a message, which verifies to the recipient that you are the sender and that no tampering is involved.

PGP is a type of public key encryption. When you first use PGP, the software generates a private key and a public key. You must keep your private key hidden. You e-mail the public key to the people you have authorized to send encrypted messages to you.

The people who receive your public key can store it in their PGP programs, which they then use to encrypt messages. When they send these messages to you, you can decrypt them using your private key. PGP software is available as a free download from several Web sites. Figure 6-54 contains an example of a public key generated by PGP.

-----BEGIN PGP PUBLIC KEY BLOCK-----

Version: 5.0

mQCNAi44C30AAAEEAL1r6BylvuSAvOKIk9ze9yCK+ZPPbRZrpXIRFBbe
+U8dGPMb9XdJS4L/cy1fXr9R9j4EfFsK/rgHV6i2rE83LjWrmsDPRPSaizz+
EQTIZi4AN99jiBomfLLZyUzmHMoUoE4shrYgOnkc0u101ikhieAFje77j/F3
596pT6nCx/9/AAURtCRBbmRyZSBCYBNhcmQgPGFiYWNhcmRAd2Vsb
C5zZi5jYS51cz6JAFUCBRAuOA6O7zYZz1mqos8BAXr9AgCxCu8CwGZR
dpfSs65r6mb4MccXvvfxO4TmPi1DKQj2FYHYjwYONk8vzA7XnE5aJmk5J
/dChdvflU7NvVifV6AF=GQv9

-----END PGP PUBLIC KEY BLOCK-----

INFOWEBLINKS

For additional resources on using ciphertext to protect data, including PGP software that you can use on your PC, connect to the **Encryption InfoWeb**.

www.course.com/np/concepts8/ch06

FIGURE 6-54
PGP software generates a huge public key. Each person's public key is unique. You can send this key, via e-mail, to anyone who might want to send you an encrypted message.

QUICKCHECK........TECHTALK

1. In an e-commerce transaction, your credit card number exists as
    [_____], which is encrypted into [_____].

2. [_____] key encryption uses the same key to encrypt a message as it does to decrypt the message.

3. [_____] key encryption uses one key to encrypt a message, but another key to decrypt the message.

4. [_____] is public key encryption software that is popular with personal computer owners who want to encrypt e-mail and data files.

 CHECK ANSWERS

ISSUE

INFORMATION QUALITY

The Internet provides access to a virtually bottomless pool of information, but in its vast depths truth mingles with lies, rumors, myths, and urban legends. The Internet is uncensored and unregulated. Anyone with a Web page or an e-mail account can rapidly and widely distribute information, which is often redistributed and forwarded like a chain letter on steroids.

You might have received an e-mail from a Nigerian businessman who is "looking for a reliable person to handle a very confidential transaction which involves the transfer of a huge sum of money." As the story goes, this businessman is smuggling millions of dollars out of his country for the bereaved widow of a martyred freedom fighter or the son of a deposed dictator. He needs a place to temporarily stash the money and is willing to pay a substantial handling fee for the use of your bank account. All you have to do is supply your bank account number!

Called an "advance fee fraud," this many-layered scam is widely circulated and surprisingly successful. Although it seems improbable that anyone would believe such an outlandish proposal, the U.S. Secret Service reports, "Advance fee fraud grosses hundreds of millions of dollars annually and the losses are continuing to escalate. In all likelihood, there are victims who do not report their losses to authorities due to either fear or embarrassment."

Have you heard that Wet Swiffers are poisoning pets? Have any of your friends used Mountain Dew as a contraceptive? Did Oracle database developer and CEO Larry Ellison give a graduation speech at Yale in which he told students they should have dropped out like he did? Did actor Andy Kaufman, quirky star of *Taxi*, fake his death? Are smallpox vac-

cinations part of a government conspiracy to reduce the population of third-world countries?

The prevalence of false information is graphically described in the *Chicago Tribune*: "America is awash in a growing and often disruptive avalanche of false information that takes on a life of its own in the electronic ether of the Internet, talk radio, and voicemail until it becomes impervious to denial and debunking."

The most plausible Internet rumors sometimes contain a grain of truth that becomes distorted. A recent rumor spreading on the Internet warns that two bills before Congress will reinstate a military draft "within the year" and make it mandatory for women as well as men. Although two bills relating to compulsory military service exist, they have never gotten out of committee and the Selective Service Agency claims that it is not getting ready to conduct a draft.

A widely circulated e-mail message claims that voting rights for African Americans will expire in 2007. Inquiries from genuinely worried voters prompted the following clarification on the NAACP Web site: "The right of African Americans and of all citizens to vote free of discrimination based on race or color is guaranteed by the Fifteenth Amendment to the United States Constitution and does not expire." The site goes on to explain that certain special provisions of the Voting Rights Act of 1965, such as pre-clearance of voting regulations and bilingual voting materials, are up for renewal in 2007 and are likely to be passed.

During the 2004 presidential campaign, many Vietnam veterans were enraged by a news clipping of John Kerry giving a speech with "Hanoi Jane" Fonda during an anti-war rally. The article was false and the photo was a digital manipulation of two separate photos from the Corbis photo database. Although this photo was a fake, John Kerry did speak at an anti-war rally in 1970 and a genuine photo exists showing him in the audience a few rows behind Fonda.

Even with so many rumors, myths, and fakes circulating on the Internet, is it fair to say that the Internet has a monopoly on false information? Probably not. Even well-established newspapers, magazines, and television news shows report stories that are later found to be misleading or untrue.

Before the Internet became a ubiquitous part of modern life, certain rules of thumb helped distinguish truth from lies and fact from fiction. In *The Truth About URLs*, Robin Raskin writes, "When printed junk mail floods our overcrowded mailboxes we have some antennae for the bogus causes and the fly-by-night foundations. We've come to expect *The New York Times* to be a credible source of information; we're not as sure about *The National Enquirer...* It takes years to establish these sorts of cultural cues for knowing whether we're getting good information or a bum steer."

Perhaps the Internet has not been around long enough for us to establish the cultural cues we need

to distinguish fact from fiction in Web pages, e-mails, online chats, and discussion groups. You can, however, get some help from the Web itself. Several sites keep track of the myths and so-called urban legends that circulate on the Internet. Before you spread rumors about Wet Swiffers or forward e-mails about an impending military draft, you might want to check one of these sites for the real scoop.

Who should be responsible for the accuracy of information? Holding writers accountable for their "facts" does not seem to work, and governments, already overburdened with other problems, have scant resources available to sift through mountains of information and set the record straight. It seems, then, that the burden of verifying facts is ultimately left to the reader. Many people, however, do not have the time, motivation, expertise, or resources to verify facts before they pass them through the information mill.

We live in an information age. Ironically, much of the information that we hear and read just isn't true. False and misleading information is not unique to our time, but now it propagates more rapidly, fed by new technologies and nurtured by spin doctors. As one commentator suggested, "The danger is that we are reaching a moment when nothing can be said to be objectively true, when consensus about reality disappears. The Information Age could leave us with no information at all, only assertions."

INFOWEBLINKS

You'll find more fascinating Internet myths and substantive articles about disinformation at the **Urban Legends InfoWeb**.

www.course.com/np/concepts8/ch06

WHAT DO YOU THINK?

1. Would you agree that it sometimes seems difficult to determine whether information is true or false?   ○ Yes ○ No ○ Not sure

2. Do older people tend to be more susceptible than younger people to false information that's disseminated over the Internet?   ○ Yes ○ No ○ Not sure

3. Have you ever received an e-mail that contained false information or visited a Web site that provided inaccurate information?   ○ Yes ○ No ○ Not sure

4. Do you have your own set of rules to help you evaluate the truth of information that's disseminated over the Internet?   ○ Yes ○ No ○ Not sure

 SAVE RESPONSES

.se
COMPUTERS IN CONTEXT
FASHION INDUSTRY

Fashion is big business. Worldwide, clothing sales generate more than $200 billion in revenue. Shoes, accessories, and jewelry bump this industry's revenue even higher. Competition is tough as designers, manufacturers, and retailers compete for customer dollars. In the fashion industry, trends change quickly. As the saying goes, "Today's style is tomorrow's markdown." Fashion industry players look for every competitive advantage. It is no surprise that technology plays a major role in this glitzy industry.

Fashion begins with designers, such as Miuccia Prada, John Galliano, and Ralph Lauren. Their runway extravaganzas set off fashion trends that eventually work their way to retail stores. Fashion runways went high-tech in 1999 when lingerie manufacturer Victoria's Secret produced a Webcast watched by over 1 million. Now, with inexpensive digital technology, even haute couture wannabes can stage their own online runway shows. Young designers without the cash to stage elaborate runway shows can turn to companies such as Nouveau Media, a video production company that creates "Fashion Video Shorts." These digital runway videos can be produced on DVDs and displayed on TV monitors in retail stores or broadcast as commercials. In streaming media format, the videos can be accessed from a Web site.

Although runway fashions are typically conceived with a sketch and stitched by hand, designs are adapted for the ready-to-wear market by using computer-assisted design (CAD) tools, such as pattern-making software. Garments are constructed by sewing together sections of fabric that form arms, fronts, backs, collars, and so forth. The set of templates used to cut fabric sections is called a pattern. Pattern-making is a tricky 3D challenge because flat pieces of fabric eventually become garments shaped to conform to curved body contours. Pattern making software helps designers visualize how flat pieces fit together and drape when sewn. Once a master pattern is complete, pattern-making software automatically generates a set of patterns for each garment size.

Fashion requires fabric, and computers play a major role in fabric design and manufacturing. Computer software, such as ArahWeave, lets fabric designers experiment with colors, yarns, and weaves while viewing detailed, realistic on-screen samples. Fabric designs can be stored in a variety of formats for weaving machines. A few older mechanical weaving machines are controlled by punched cards. Digital fabric designs can be transferred to punched cards with a dedicated card punch machine. Most of today's weaving mills use computerized machinery that directly accepts digital input to control threads and patterns. Networks tie looms to CAD stations and to the Internet. Fabric designs can be stored in XML format, transmitted to a fabric manufacturer via the Internet, and used directly by computerized weaving machines.

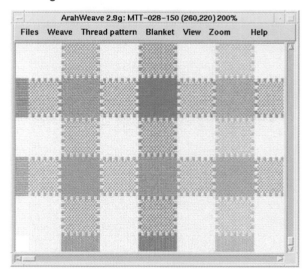

Clothing production, warehousing, and shipping are also highly automated. Benetton's high-tech facility at Castrette, Italy can produce over 110 million garments per year. Its automated distribution center uses a workforce of only 24 people to handle 40,000 boxes of merchandise daily. Radio frequency identification (RFID) tags—sometimes called "smart labels"—can be attached to individual garments or to packing boxes as an important tool for controlling inventory.

RFID technology uses a tiny computer chip with built-in antenna and the capacity to store between 64 and 128 bits of data about a garment—its SKU number, size, model, dye lot, manufacturing date, and so on. An RFID reader that can retrieve data from tags is used to track merchandise from the manufacturing plant through the distribution chain to the retailer. RFID tags are becoming popular for all types of merchandise. Businesses that use them can save time and money. For example, RFID tags can reduce the time it takes to do a physical inventory by a factor of 10. Privacy advocates, however, are worried because these tags remain active even after you bring your merchandise home. Could a thief circle your house with an RFID scanner to find out what's inside? Could a stalker follow your movements by tracking the RFID tag embedded in your sweater? After customers protested a plan to attach RFID tags to every sweater, Benetton currently uses the tags only on shipping cartons.

In response to competition from offshore companies, U.S. clothing manufacturers pioneered Quick Response (QR)—a business model for compressing supply chains to quickly obtain raw materials, such as fabric, yarn, buttons, and zippers. Sophisticated software tools, such as the Sourcing Simulator, simplify QR planning.

Online shopping has become routine, but one drawback of catalog and online ordering is the cost associated with restocking returned merchandise. Can an online customer find out how a garment will fit and look before ordering it? In 1998, Lands' End offered "My Virtual Model" technology that allows shoppers to create a custom model of themselves by choosing from a variety of hair colors, face shapes, and body types. The model can "try on" clothes to show online customers how they would look when wearing the garments.

More recently, Land's End toured the country with a body-scanning device to collect actual measurements from thousands of customers. Body-scanning devices use cameras and lasers to capture approximately 300,000 data points that can be pieced together into a 3D image.

Body scanners are also helping the fashion industry by collecting research data. Sizing standards fell by the wayside as "vanity sizing" added an inch or two to a garment so that consumers can feel good about themselves by fitting into smaller sizes. In the U.S. clothing industry, a comprehensive study of body shapes and sizes can help standardize sizing and eliminate much of the trial and error involved in finding apparel that fits. Collecting data from body scans is part of this ongoing research effort.

No discussion of fashion and computers would be complete without highlighting wearable technology. Clothing that contains digital devices has made its way out of the laboratory and onto store shelves. For example, Burton Snowboards, electronic fabric manufacturer SOFTswitch, and Apple teamed up to create the limited-edition Burton Amp, a jacket with integrated iPod controls designed for snowboarders to control music from the sleeve of their jackets without fumbling with zippers, gloves, and small control buttons.

Another "wearable," originally popular with secret service agents, is the SCOTTeVEST, a jacket with pockets for cell phone, PDA, MP3 player, and built-in wiring to connect these devices into a personal area network (PAN). Available as a jacket or vest and in men's and women's sizes, the jacket can now be purchased by civilians.

With a growing emphasis on the use of technology in fashion design and manufacturing, fashion degree programs at colleges and technical schools have added courses such as computer-aided fashion design, computer-based pattern drafting, pattern grading and computer-aided drafting, and wearable computers.

INFOWEBLINKS

You'll find information related to this Computers in Context topic at the **Computers and Fashion InfoWeb**.

INTERACTIVE SUMMARY

To review important concepts from this chapter, fill in the blanks to best complete each sentence. When using the NP8 BookOnCD, click the Check Answers buttons to automatically score your answers. Place your Tracking Disk in the floppy disk drive if you want to save your scores.

The basic building blocks for today's Web were developed in 1990 by a British scientist named Tim Berners-Lee. The Web did not "take off," however, until 1993 when Marc Andreessen and his colleagues developed a Web [   ] called Mosaic. The Web is an abstract or imaginary space of information, whereas the [   ] is the communications network that carries Web data.

The Web is based on Ted Nelson's concept of a [   ]—a series of documents that are stored electronically and linked together according to logical relationships. On today's Web, these documents are stored in [   ] format and then displayed as Web [   ] by a browser. HTML is a set of specifications for creating documents that contain special instructions called HTML [   ], which specify how the document should appear when displayed on a computer screen.

In an HTML document, these tags are set apart from normal text by [   ] brackets. In addition to HTML documents, Web browsers are designed to deal with [   ] file formats, such as GIF, JPEG, and PNG. A browser can also work with other file formats if the necessary helper application, plug-in, or [   ] has been installed.

HTML documents are transmitted from a Web server to a browser by means of the [   ] protocol. This protocol is [   ], which means that as soon as a request is fulfilled, the Web server "forgets" that your browser ever made a request. To keep track of an individual who clicks through several pages on a Web site, a Web server resorts to a [   ]—a small chunk of data that is generated by a Web server, sent to a browser, and then stored on the client computer's hard disk.

✦ CHECK ANSWERS

Many software tools are available today that make it easy to create Web pages. A Web page author can use a [   ] editor, such as Notepad, to create Web pages "from scratch" by manually embedding HTML tags within the text of a document. It is also possible to use the HTML conversion routines included with many standard software applications. Another route is to use specialized Web [   ] software, such as Microsoft FrontPage.

An HTML document is divided into two sections. The [   ] section contains information used to define global properties for the document. The [   ] section contains the text you want the browser to display, the HTML tags that format the text, and a variety of links. In addition to embedding HTML tags within the text, a Web page can be format-

ted with a [   ] style sheet, which allows Web page designers to change formats throughout an HTML document without modifying individual HTML tags. In addition to formatting specifications, HTML tags can be used to add graphics and links to Web pages. The <img src> tag can be used to specify a [   ]. The <a href> tag is used to specify a [   ]. Graphics and links can be combined to create an [   ] map that contains clickable hot spots. To control the position of text and graphics on a Web page, many authors place these elements in the cells of a [   ]. In the context of Web pages, a [   ] is part of a Web page that scrolls independently of other parts of the Web page.

✦ CHECK ANSWERS

HTML was designed to create static Web pages. With basic HTML, once a Web page appeared in a browser window, the only way to change the appearance of the page was to download an update to the entire page. [_____] is a method for updating Web pages "on the fly"—typically as the result of a mouseover or a mouse click. A technology called [_____] can be used to incorporate structured data, such as spreadsheet data or database records, into a text file by adding special-purpose tags. These tags explicitly identify a particular kind of information, much like a field heading in a [_____]. A technology called [_____] is similar to XML, but can be used to create customized HTML tags that control the appearance of an XML document.

Another way to add animation and interactivity to Web pages is to use [_____] languages, such as JavaScript and VBScript. Unfortunately, browsers offer slightly different support for these languages, which sometimes results in a [_____] error if the browser can't execute a particular instruction. In addition to JavaScript and VBScript, Java has become a popular programming tool for Web-based projects. Small Java programs are referred to as Java [_____]. ActiveX provides another Web development tool. An ActiveX [_____] is a compiled computer program that can be referenced from within an HTML document, downloaded, installed on your computer, and executed within the browser window. This technology has potential security loopholes, which can be avoided by the use of digital [_____].

CHECK ANSWERS

The Internet was opened up to commercial use in 1991, and since then, e-commerce has become one of the fastest growing activities on the Web. E-commerce "wares" include physical products, [_____] products, and services. Most of the e-commerce activities that a typical Web surfer enjoys are classified as business-to-[_____], but with online auctions, consumer-to-[_____] e-commerce is also popular.

E-commerce merchants take advantage of automation and digitization to increase profit margins by cutting [_____]. Many online merchants attempt to gain income by providing space for banner ads and [_____] ads. Some Web pages—and not just those displayed by e-commerce sites—can contain [_____], such as ad-serving cookies and Web bugs, that surreptitiously gathers information and sends it to advertisers or other interested parties.

E-commerce customers typically collect the items they want to purchase in an online [_____] cart. These carts store a customer's selections in a [_____] on the client computer or in a server-side database.

When it is time to check out, a customer can use an electronic [_____] to automatically enter billing and shipping information. Many online customers are worried about their credit card numbers falling into the wrong hands. Most e-commerce sites establish a [_____] connection by using SSL or S-HTTP to avoid [_____] sniffer software that could intercept it. Savvy shoppers are also wary of [_____] storefronts that are designed to look like a legitimate store, but are operated by credit card thieves.

CHECK ANSWERS

INTERACTIVE KEY TERMS

Make sure you understand all the boldfaced key terms presented in this chapter. If you're using the NP8 BookOnCD, you can use this list of terms as an interactive study activity. First, try to define a term in your own words, and then click the term to compare your definition with the definition presented in the chapter.

Ad-blocking software, 320
Ad-serving cookie, 323
ActiveX control, 315
AES, 331
Animated GIF, 304
ASP, 307
B2B, 319
B2C, 319
B2G, 319
Banner ad, 320
Body section, 301
Broken link, 306
Brute-force method, 329
Bytecode, 313
C2C, 319
Cascading style sheet, 302
Certificate authority, 316
CGI, 307
Ciphertext, 328
Clear GIF, 323
Click-through rate, 320
Client-side script, 312
Compact Privacy Policy, 296
Cookie, 295
Cryptographic algorithm, 328
Cryptographic key, 328
Decryption, 328
DES, 330
DHTML, 310
Digital certificate, 316
DTD files, 311
E-commerce, 319

Electronic wallet, 326
Encryption, 328
External link, 305
External style sheet, 302
Flash animation, 304
Formatting tags, 289
Head section, 301
Helper application, 291
Hot spot, 305
HTML document, 285
HTML form, 306
HTML frame, 307
HTTP status code, 293
Hypertext, 284
Hypertext link, 285
Image map, 305
Internal link, 305
Intrapage link, 305
Java applets, 313
JavaScript, 312
Java Virtual Machine, 313
Link tags, 289
Mailto link, 305
Markup language, 286
Media tags, 289
One-time-use credit card, 325
Online shopping cart, 322
Operational tags, 289
P3P, 296
Packet sniffer, 324
Person-to-person payment, 327
PGP, 331

Plaintext, 328
Player, 291
Plug-in, 291
Popup ad, 320
Public key encryption, 330
RSA, 330
Script, 312
Scripting error, 313
Secure connection, 324
Self-closing tag, 287
Server farm, 294
Server-side script, 312
SET, 326
S-HTTP, 324
Socket, 292
Spyware, 323
SSL, 324
Stateless protocol, 293
Strong encryption, 329
Symmetric key encryption, 330
Text editor, 299
VBScript, 312
Weak encryption, 329
Web authoring software, 300
Web page header, 301
Web page table, 306
World Wide Web Consortium, 286
XHTML, 286
XML, 311
XML parser, 311
XSL, 311

INTERACTIVE SITUATION QUESTIONS

Apply what you've learned to some typical computing situations. When using the NP8 BookOnCD, you can type your answers, and then use the Check Answers button to automatically score your responses. Place your Tracking Disk in the floppy disk drive if you want to save your scores.

1. Suppose that you are about to check out at an online store, but you don't see any indication that your transaction data will be protected by a secure connection. It would be best, under these circumstances, to use PGP software to encrypt your shipping and billing data. True or false?

2. Your friend, who is a little "computer phobic," is going to be creating his first Web page and asks you to recommend some software for the task. Which one requires the least knowledge of HTML tags: Notepad or Microsoft Word?

3. Suppose you visit a Web site that has eye-catching pages. You want to know how these pages were formatted, so you use one of the options on your browser's menu to view the [   ] HTML document.

4. Suppose you click a link at a Web site and get a message that the file cannot be displayed because it is in PDF format. To view the file, you need an updated version of your browser. True or false?

5. Suppose you're performing a local test of a Web page you created. All the page elements appear to be correctly positioned and formatted. You're also happy to discover that your large graphics files are displayed quite quickly by your browser. Can you expect similar performance after you post the page on a Web site? Yes or no?

6. You're poking around in an HTML document and you notice a tag that references a file with a .class file extension. You assume that this file contains the bytecode for a Java [   ].

7. Suppose your browser's security setting is Medium. You can expect your browser to display a security warning message any time that a(n) [   ] control tries to install itself on your computer.

8. One of your relatives wants to try online shopping, but is suspicious that her credit card number might get stolen from a merchant's server by a hacker using a packet sniffer. Is it correct to tell her that she can best avoid these potential rip-offs by a secure connection, such as SSL? Yes or no?

9. Suppose you're the high bidder in an online auction for a handmade quilt. The person who is selling the quilt does not accept credit cards and suggests that you use a(n) [   ] payment service to, in effect, wire your payment electronically.

10. You're looking through a list of cookies stored on your computer, but don't remember visiting sites such as bannerbank, hotlog, and ad.bb. You can assume that these cookies were created by [   ], such as ad-serving cookies.

CHECK ANSWERS

INTERACTIVE PRACTICE TESTS

Practice tests that consist of 10 multiple-choice, true/false, and fill-in-the-blank questions are available on both the NP8 BookOnCD and the NP8 Web site. The questions are selected at random from a large test bank, so each time you take a test, you'll receive a different set of questions. Your tests are scored immediately, and you can print study guides that help you find the correct answers for any questions that you missed.

www.course.com/np/concepts8/ch06

CLICK TO START

REVIEW

ON THE WEB

PROJECTS

An NP8 Project is an open-ended activity that helps you apply the concepts you have learned. Many projects require resources in addition to your textbook, such as current magazines, library materials, or Web access. When you tackle a project, be prepared to use your critical thinking skills, logical analysis, and creativity. Projects for this chapter include:

- **Issue Research: Information Quality**
- **No One Knows**
- **Computers in Fashion**

- **Web Site Makeover**
- **Internet Censorship**
- **Virtual Reality**

To work with the Projects for this chapter, connect to the **New Perspectives NP8 Web Site**.

www.course.com/np/concepts8/ch06

"On the Internet, nobody knows you're a dog."

TECHTV VIDEO PROJECT

The TechTV segment *Find the Best Deals Online* offers tips for using the e-pinions Web site. While watching the video, make a note of the features that make e-pinions such a helpful site. Go online and check out these features for yourself. Suppose you're looking for a digital music player and a hotel in Savannah, Georgia. Print a few sample pages showing choices, opinions, and detailed information. Indicate your personal selections using a highlighter. Did the e-pinions site live up to your expectations?

To work with the Video Projects for this chapter, connect to the **New Perspectives NP8 Web Site**.

www.course.com/np/concepts8/ch06

STUDY TIPS

Study Tips help you organize and consolidate the information in a chapter by making lists, outlines, charts, and sketches. You can use paper and pencil or word processing software to complete most of the Study Tips.

To work with the Study Tips for this chapter, connect to the **New Perspectives NP8 Web Site**.

www.course.com/np/concepts8/ch06

ONLINE GAMES

Test your comprehension of the concepts introduced in Chapter 6 by playing the NP8 Online Games. At the end of each game, you have three options:

- Print a comprehensive study guide complete with page references
- Print your results to be submitted to your instructor
- Save your results to be submitted to your instructor via e-mail

To work with the Online Games for this chapter, connect to the **New Perspectives NP8 Web Site**.

www.course.com/np/concepts8/ch06

STUDENT EDITION LABS

Extend your knowledge of the Web with the Chapter 6 Student Edition Labs.

The following Student Edition Labs are offered with Chapter 6:

- **Protecting Your Privacy Online**
- **Creating Web Pages**
- **Getting the Most Out of the Internet**
- **Electronic Commerce**
- **Web Design Principles**

Go to the NP8 New Perspectives Web site for specific lab topics.

To work with the Chapter 6 Student Edition Labs and their corresponding lab assignments, connect to the **New Perspectives NP8 Web Site**.

www.course.com/np/concepts8/ch06

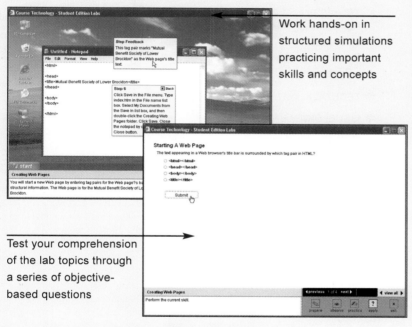

Work hands-on in structured simulations practicing important skills and concepts

Test your comprehension of the lab topics through a series of objective-based questions

Track Your Progress with the Student Edition Labs

- Student Edition Labs test your comprehension of the lab topics through a series of trackable objective-based questions. Your instructor will direct you to either print your results or submit them via e-mail.

- Student Edition Lab Assignments, available on the New Perspectives NP8 Web site, require you to apply the skills learned through the lab in a live environment. Go to the New Perspectives NP8 Web site for detailed instruction on individual Student Edition Lab Assignments.

If you have a SAM user profile, you have access to even more interactive content. Log in to your SAM account and go to your assignments page to see what your instructor has assigned for this chapter.

7

MP3

DIGITAL MEDIA

CONTENTS

TIP

When using the BookOnCD, the ❋ icons are "clickable" to access resources on the CD. The ✛ icons are clickable to access resources on the Web. You can also access Web resources by using your browser to connect directly to the NP8 New Perspectives Web site at:

www.course.com/np/concepts8/ch07

CHAPTER PREVIEW

Before you begin Chapter 7, you can use the Web-based preview activities to hear an overview of the chapter, check your current level of expertise about key concepts, and look through a list of learning objectives. You can access the preview activities by clicking the ⌗ icon when using the BookOnCD or going to the New Perspectives NP8 Web site.

CHAPTER OVERVIEW

Digital media, such as photos, movies, 3-D games, and music, are all part of today's computer environment. Get your book and highlighter ready, then connect to the New Perspectives NP8 Web site where you can listen to an overview that points out the most important concepts for this chapter.

www.course.com/np/concepts8/ch07 ⌗

CHAPTER PRE-ASSESSMENT

How much do you know about bitmap graphics, vectors, 3-D animation, digital sound, and video? To gauge your level of knowledge before beginning the chapter, take the pre-assessment quiz at the New Perspectives NP8 Web site. Armed with your results from this quiz, you can focus your study time on concepts that will round out your knowledge of digital media and improve your test scores.

www.course.com/np/concepts8/ch07 ⌗

LEARNING OBJECTIVES

When you complete this chapter you should be able to:

- Describe the advantages, disadvantages, and uses for digital media, such as bitmap graphics, vector graphics, 3-D graphics, 3-D animations, desktop video, waveform audio, MIDI music, speech synthesis, and speech recognition

- List the equipment and software that can be used to work with various types of digital media

- Identify digital media files by their file extensions

- Understand the advantages and disadvantages of using each type of digital media on the Web

- Explain how resolution, image size, color depth, and color palettes can be manipulated to adjust the file size of a bitmap graphic

- Describe procedures required to convert bitmap graphics into vectors and vector graphics into bitmaps

- Explain how wireframes, rendering, and ray tracing apply to 3-D graphics

- Define the differences between digital video and 3-D animation

- Describe how to shoot, capture, edit, and process digital video

- Explain how window size, frame rate, and compression affect file size for a desktop video

- Describe the formats used for digital music

- Explain how to download music files and transfer them to portable audio players

A detailed list of learning objectives is provided at the New Perspectives NP8 Web site

www.course.com/np/concepts8/ch07 ⌗

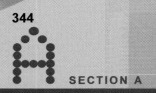

SECTION A

BITMAP GRAPHICS

A digital camera seems easy to use. Point it, shoot the photo, and....what next? How do you transfer digital photos from camera to computer? How can you print them? How do you get them ready to become e-mail attachments? How do you prepare them for Web pages? To understand the wide range of possibilities for digital photos, you'll need some background information about bitmap graphics—the topic for this section of the chapter.

BITMAP BASICS

What is a bitmap graphic? A **bitmap graphic**, also called a "raster graphic" or simply a "bitmap," is composed of a grid of dots, and the color of each dot is stored as a binary number. Think of a grid superimposed on a picture. The grid divides the picture into cells, called pixels. Each pixel is assigned a color, which is stored as a binary number. Figure 7-1 illustrates these basic characteristics of a bitmap graphic.

TERMINOLOGY NOTE

The term "pixel" is derived from "picture element." It is the smallest element that can be manipulated by a computer display device or printer.

FIGURE 7-1

A bitmap graphic is divided into a grid of individually colored pixels. The color number for each pixel is stored in binary format.

Where would I encounter bitmap graphics? Bitmap graphics are typically used to create realistic images, such as photographs. You might also encounter bitmaps in the form of cartoons, images that appear in computer games, and rendered images produced by 3-D graphics software. When you use a digital camera or camera-enabled cell phone, your photos are stored as bitmaps. A scanner produces bitmaps. The photos you send or receive as e-mail attachments are bitmaps, as are most Web page graphics.

How do I create bitmap images? You can create a bitmap graphic from scratch using the tools provided by graphics software—specifically a category of graphics software referred to as **paint software**. You might be familiar with paint software such as Adobe Photoshop, Jasc Paint Shop Pro, and Microsoft Paint (included with Windows). These programs have tools for freehand sketching, filling in shapes, adding realistic shading, and creating effects that look like oil paints, charcoal, or watercolors. If your freehand sketching talent maxes out with stick figures, you can also create bitmap graphics by using a scanner or digital camera.

SCANNERS AND CAMERAS

How do I convert a printed image into a bitmap? When you have a printed image, such as a photograph, a page from a magazine, or a picture from a book, you can use a **scanner** to convert the printed image into a bitmap graphic. A scanner essentially divides an image into a fine grid of cells and assigns a digital value for the color of each cell. As the scan progresses, these values are transferred to your computer's hard disk and stored as a bitmap graphics file. Scanners, such as the one pictured in Figure 7-2, are inexpensive and easy to use.

INFOWEBLINKS

For more information about scanning equipment, connect to the **Scanner Buyers Guide InfoWeb**.

www.course.com/np/concepts8/ch07

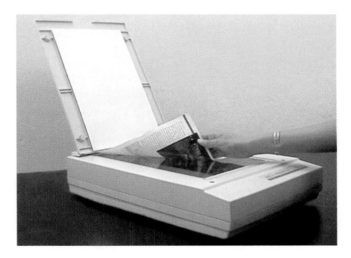

FIGURE 7-2

To scan an image, turn on the scanner and start your scanner software. Place the image face down on the scanner glass, and then use the scanner software to initiate the scan. The scanned image is saved in RAM and can then be saved on your computer's hard disk.

CLICK TO START

When should I use a digital camera rather than a scanner? Whereas a scanner digitizes printed images, a **digital camera** digitizes real objects. Instead of taking a photo with a conventional camera, developing the film, and then digitizing it with a scanner, a digital camera, such as the one in Figure 7-3, takes a photo in digital format, which you can then transfer directly to your computer.

INFOWEBLINKS

You'll learn more about digital cameras and accessories at the **Digital Camera Buyers Guide InfoWeb**.

www.course.com/np/concepts8/ch07

FIGURE 7-3

The controls for a digital camera are very similar to those for an analog, or film, camera. To take a photo, you simply point and shoot.

CLICK TO START

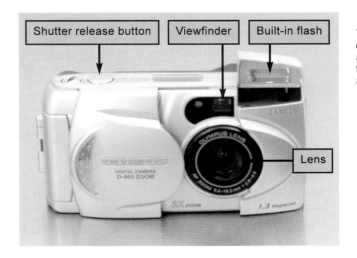

Shutter release button | Viewfinder | Built-in flash

Lens

How does a digital camera store images? Some digital cameras store images on floppy disks, CDs, mini-CDs, or miniature hard disk drives. Other digital cameras store images in removable solid-state storage modules, sometimes called "memory cards." Solid state storage is a popular technology for digital cameras. Like RAM, it can be erased and reused. Unlike RAM, solid state storage holds data without consuming power, so it doesn't lose data when the camera is turned off. Figure 7-4 illustrates several digital camera storage options.

FIGURE 7-4

Storage options for digital cameras vary in capacity from 8 MB to 1 GB. The number of photos that can be stored depends on their resolution. High-resolution photos require more storage space than low-resolution photos. As few as two high-res photos might fit on an 32 MB card, whereas the same card might hold hundreds of low-res images.

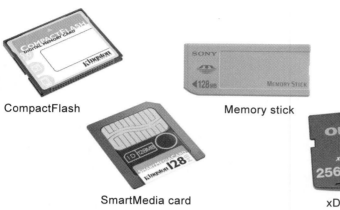

CompactFlash

Memory stick

SmartMedia card

xD-Picture card

Microdrive

How can I get images out of the camera? Digital cameras allow you to preview images while they are still in the camera and delete those you don't want. The photos you want to keep can be transferred directly to some printers, but typically you transfer the photo data to your computer's hard disk. Depending on your camera, this transfer can be achieved in several ways:

■ **Media transfer.** If your camera stores data on floppy disks or CDs, you can simply remove the media from your camera and insert it into the appropriate drive of your computer.

■ **Direct cable transfer.** If your computer and your camera have FireWire ports (also called IEEE-1394 ports), you can connect a cable between these two ports to transfer the photo data. You can use a similar transfer method if your computer and camera have USB ports or serial ports. A USB-2 or FireWire port provides good transfer speed. USB-1 ports are somewhat slower, and serial ports are quite slow.

■ **Infrared port.** Some cameras can "beam" the data from your camera to your computer's infrared port. This method eliminates the need for a cable but is much slower than using a FireWire, USB, or serial port.

■ **Card readers.** A card reader is a small device connected to your computer's USB or serial port and designed to read data contained in a solid state memory card. A card reader acts in the same way as an external disk drive by treating your memory cards like floppy disks. To transfer the photo data from a memory card, you remove it from the camera and insert it into the card reader, as shown in Figure 7-5.

■ **Floppy disk adapters.** A **floppy disk adapter** is a floppy disk-shaped device that contains a slot for a memory card. You simply insert the memory card into the floppy disk adapter, and then insert the adapter into your computer's floppy disk drive.

FIGURE 7-5

A card reader transfers photo data from a memory card to your computer's hard disk.

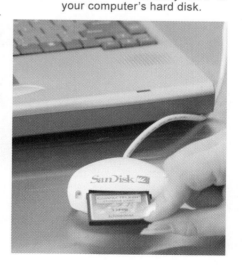

■ **E-mail.** Cell phone photos can be transferred to a computer by e-mailing the photo to your e-mail account. The photo arrives as an attachment, which can be saved as a separate file.

Regardless of the technology you use, transferring photo data from your camera to your computer requires software, which might be supplied along with your camera, with your card reader, or by a standalone graphics software package, such as Adobe Photoshop. This software allows you to select a file format, specify a file name, and determine the location for each image file. You'll learn about your choices for file formats later in this section, but most cameras store photos in JPEG or TIFF formats.

After you store your digital photos on your computer's hard disk, you can modify them, send them as e-mail attachments, print them, post them on Web pages, or archive them onto a CD.

MODIFYING BITMAP GRAPHICS

What characteristics of a bitmap can I modify? Because bitmap graphics are coded as a series of bits that represent pixels, you can use graphics software to modify or edit this type of graphic by changing individual pixels. You can retouch old photographs to eliminate creases, spots, and discoloration (Figure 7-6). You can modify photos to wipe out red eye or erase the "rabbit ears" that ruined an otherwise good family portrait. You can even design eye-catching new pictures with images you cut and paste from several photos or scanned images.

Whether you acquire an image from a digital camera or a scanner, bitmap graphics tend to require quite a bit of storage space. Although a large graphics file might provide the necessary data for a high-quality printout, these files take up space on your hard disk and can require lengthy transmission times that clog up mailboxes and make Web pages seem sluggish. The size of the file that holds a bitmap depends on its resolution and color depth. Read on to see how these factors affect file size and how you can alter them to create smaller graphics files, suitable for e-mail attachments and Web pages.

IMAGE RESOLUTION

How does resolution pertain to bitmap graphics? The dimensions of the grid that forms a bitmap graphic are referred to as its resolution. The resolution of a graphic is usually expressed as the number of horizontal and vertical pixels it contains. For example, a small graphic for a Web page might have a resolution of 150 x 100 pixels—150 pixels across and 100 pixels high.

How does resolution relate to image quality? High-resolution graphics contain more data than low-resolution graphics. With more data, it is possible to display and print high-quality images that are smoother and cleaner than images produced using less data. For example, a photograph of a cat taken with an inexpensive digital camera might produce a graphic with a resolution of 1600 x 1200. Camera manufacturers sometimes express the resolution of digital cameras as **megapixels** (millions of pixels)—the total number of pixels in a graphic. A resolution of 1600 x 1200 would be expressed as 1.9 megapixels (1600 multiplied by 1200). A photo of the same cat using a more expensive 3.5 megapixel digital camera with 2160 x 1440 resolution contains more pixels and produces a higher-quality image than the low-resolution photo.

FIGURE 7-6

Bitmap graphics can be easily modified. Many graphics software products include wizards that help you retouch photographs.

Before

After

How does resolution relate to the file size of a graphic? Each pixel in a bitmap graphic is stored as one or more bits. The more pixels in a bitmap, the more bits needed to store the file.

How does resolution relate to the physical size of an image? A bitmap graphic is simply a collection of data. Unlike a printed photograph, a bitmap has no fixed physical size. The size at which a bitmap is displayed or printed depends on the density as well as the resolution (dimensions) of the image grid.

Imagine that each bitmap image and its grid come on a surface that you can stretch or shrink. As you stretch the surface, the grid maintains the same number of horizontal and vertical cells, but each cell becomes larger and the grid becomes less dense. As you shrink the surface, the grid becomes smaller and more dense. The graphic retains the same resolution no matter how much you stretch or shrink the graphic's physical size, as shown in Figure 7-7.

FIGURE 7-7
When this bitmap graphic is enlarged, it still retains its original resolution—24 x 24.

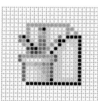

Original graphic at 24 x 24 resolution

Enlarged graphic still has 24 x 24 resolution

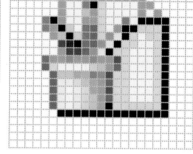

This concept of stretching and shrinking without changing resolution is important for understanding what happens when bitmaps are displayed and printed. The denser the grid, the smaller the image will appear. The density of an image grid can be expressed as dots per inch (dpi) for a printer or scanner or as pixels per inch (ppi) on a monitor.

How do I specify the size of a printed image? Most graphics software allows you to specify the size at which an image is printed without changing the resolution of the bitmap graphic. You'll get the highest print quality if the resolution of the graphic meets or exceeds the printer's dpi. An ink jet printer with a resolution of 1440 x 720 dpi produces a very dense image grid. If each pixel of a 1600 x 1200 graphic was printed as a single dot on this printer, the resulting image would be very high quality but just a bit wider than 1 inch. You can specify a larger size for the printout, in which case the printer must create additional data to fill the print grid. This process can produce a fuzzy and blocky image if the printed image gets very large.

As a rule of thumb, when you incorporate an image in a desktop-published document, or when you print photographs, you should work with high-resolution bitmaps so that you can produce high-quality output. To capture high-resolution bitmaps, use the highest resolution provided by your digital camera. When scanning an image, choose a dpi setting on your scanner that is at least as high as the dpi for the printout.

How does a bitmap's resolution relate to what I see on the screen? In Chapter 2, you learned that you can set your computer monitor to a particular resolution, such as 1024 x 768. When you display a bitmap graphic on the screen, each pixel of the graphic typically corresponds to one pixel on the screen. If the resolution of your graphic is 1024 x 768 and your monitor is set at 1024 x 768 resolution, the image appears to fill the screen. If you view a 3.1 megapixel image on the same monitor, the image is larger than the screen, and you have to scroll or set the zoom level to view it (Figure 7-8).

Can I change a graphic's file size? The resolution and corresponding file size of a graphic might not be right for your needs. For example, if you take a photo with a 3.1 megapixel camera, it is unsuitable for a Web page. Not only would it take a long time to download, but it would be larger than most screens. A 3.1 megapixel graphic is also not suitable for an e-mail attachment. Uploading and downloading such a large file—especially over a dial-up connection—would take much too long. Reducing the resolution of a bitmap can reduce its file size and on-screen display size. Most experts recommend that Web graphics not exceed 100 KB and that e-mail attachments not exceed 500 KB.

You can reduce the size of a bitmap by cropping it. **Cropping** refers to the process of selecting part of an image—just like cutting out a section of a photograph. Cropping decreases resolution and file size by reducing the number of pixels in a graphic. You can also reduce file size by removing pixels from the entire graphic; however, this process changes the image quality.

Bitmap graphics are **resolution dependent**, which means that the quality of the image depends on its resolution. If you reduce the resolution, the computer eliminates pixels from the image, reducing the size of the image grid. For example, if you reduce the resolution from 2160 x 1440 (3.1 megapixels) to 1080 x 720 (.8 megapixels), the image grid becomes a quarter of its original size. The file size is reduced by a similar amount. However, the computer threw away data with the pixels, which can reduce image quality.

If you attempt to enlarge a bitmap by increasing its resolution, your computer must somehow add pixels because no additional picture data exists. But what colors should these additional pixels become? Most graphics software uses a process called **pixel interpolation** to create new pixels by averaging the colors of nearby pixels. For some graphics, pixel interpolation results in an image that appears very similar to the original. Other images—particularly those with strong curved or diagonal lines—develop an undesirable **pixelated**, or "bitmappy," jagged appearance (Figure 7-9).

FIGURE 7-8
When viewing an image larger than the screen, you must scroll to see all parts of the image or set the zoom level of your graphics software to less than 100%. You should understand, however, that changing the zoom level stretches or shrinks only the size of the image grid. It has no effect on the printed size of a graphic or the graphic's file size.

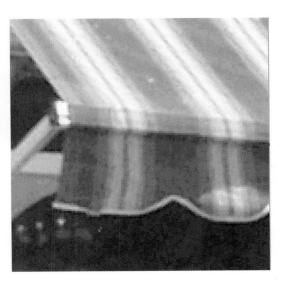

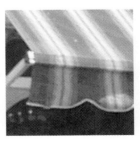

The figure above has a resolution of 130 x 130. The figure at right was enlarged to a resolution of 260 x 260, but it has a rough, pixelated appearance.

FIGURE 7-9
When you increase the resolution of an existing graphic, the file size increases, but the quality might deteriorate.

7

COLOR DEPTH AND PALETTES

What is color depth? **Color depth** is the number of colors available for use in an image. As the number of colors increases, image quality improves, but file size also increases. You can limit color depth to decrease the file size required for a graphic. To find out how this works, take a look at the storage requirements for various color depths. Then you can turn to the procedures for reducing color depth.

How does color depth relate to file size? To answer this question, go back to the old days of computing when monitors were simple monochrome devices. Each screen pixel could be either "on" or "off." A **monochrome bitmap** is displayed by manipulating the pattern of "off" and "on" pixels displayed on-screen. To store the data for a monochrome bitmap, an "on" pixel is represented by a 1 bit. An "off" pixel is represented by a 0 bit. Each row of the bitmap grid is stored as a series of 0s and 1s, as shown in Figure 7-10.

FIGURE 7-10

Each pixel in a monochrome bitmap graphic is stored as a bit.

1. The image can originate as a black-and-white silhouette, as a black-and-white photograph, or even as a color photo.

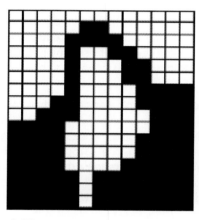

2. The computer divides the picture into a matrix.

3. If a cell is white, it is coded as a 1. If the cell is black, it is coded as a 0.

Monochrome bitmaps require very little storage space. Suppose you create a full-screen monochrome bitmap with your monitor's resolution set to 640 x 480. Your screen displays 307,200 pixels (that's 640 multiplied by 480). Each pixel is set to display a black dot or a white dot. When you store the graphic, each dot requires only one bit. Therefore, the number of bits required to represent a full-screen picture is the same as the number of pixels on the screen. At a resolution of 640 x 480, a full-screen graphic requires 307,200 bits of storage space. The number of bytes required to store the image is 307,200 divided by 8 (remember that there are eight bits in a byte). Your full-screen monochrome bitmap would, therefore, require only 38,400 bytes of storage space.

But what about color? Today's color monitors require a more complex storage scheme. Each screen pixel displays a color based on the intensity of red, green, and blue signals it receives. A pixel appears white if the red, green, and blue signals are set to maximum intensity. If red, green, and blue signals are equal but at a lower intensity, the pixel displays a shade of gray. If the red signal is set to maximum intensity, but the blue and green signals are off, the pixel appears in brilliant red. A pixel appears purple if it receives red and blue signals. You get the idea.

Each red, green, and blue signal is assigned a value ranging from zero to 255. Zero represents the absence of color, and 255 represents the highest intensity level for that color. These values produce a maximum of 16.7 million colors. A graphic that uses this full range of colors is referred to as a **True Color bitmap** or a **24-bit bitmap**. You might be able to guess where the "24-bit" term comes from. The data for each pixel requires three bytes of storage space—eight bits for blue, eight bits for green, and eight bits for red—for a total of 24 bits. Although True Color bitmaps produce photographic-quality images, they also produce very large files. Because each pixel requires three bytes, a 3.1 megapixel True Color bitmap would require a 9.3 MB file!

You might occasionally encounter a **32-bit bitmap**. Just like a 24-bit bitmap, it displays 16.7 million colors. The extra bits are used to define special effects, such as the amount of transparency, for a pixel. These files are even larger than those containing 24-bit bitmaps. A 3.1 megapixel 32-bit bitmap would be about 10 MB.

Files containing full-screen 24-bit and 32-bit bitmaps are typically too large for e-mail attachments and Web pages because they require excessively long upload and download times. Earlier in the chapter, you learned that you can reduce a bitmap's file size by removing pixels. Another way to shrink a bitmap file is to reduce its color depth.

How can I reduce color depth? To reduce the color depth of a bitmap, you can use your graphics software to work with color palettes. A **color palette** (also called a "color lookup table" or "color map") is the digital version of a kidney-shaped artist's palette that holds the selection of colors an artist uses for a particular painting. A digital color palette allows you to select a group of colors to use for a bitmap graphic.

The advantage of a palette is that if it contains only 256 colors, you can store the data for each pixel in 8 bits instead of 24 bits, which reduces the file to a third of the size required for a True Color bitmap.

How does a color palette work? A color palette is stored as a table within the header of a graphics file. Each palette contains a list of 256 color numbers. Each of these numbers is mapped to a 24-bit number that corresponds to the actual levels of red, green, and blue required to display the color. Figure 7-11 explains how this table works.

Pixels in the upper-left corner of an image		
0	2	2
1	1	3
2	4	4
3	3	253

Color Palette	
Index #	RGB Value
0	000 000 000
1	060 000 255
2	020 167 167
3	120 060 060
4	180 060 060
5	255 000 000
.	
.	
.	
253	255 060 060
254	255 000 255
255	255 255 255

FIGURE 7-11

A color palette is a subset of all possible colors. Each color in the palette is numbered, and its number points to the full 24-bit RGB (red, green, blue) value stored in the graphics file header.

How do I select a color palette? Most graphics software offers a selection of ready-made palettes that you can choose by using the color palette or color picker tool. Ready-made palettes usually include a grayscale palette, a system palette, and a Web palette.

A **grayscale palette** uses shades of gray, or "gray scales," to display images that look similar to black-and-white photographs. Most grayscale palettes consist of 256 shades of gray. Figure 7-12 illustrates a grayscale palette and a grayscale bitmap graphic.

FIGURE 7-12

Grayscale bitmaps look like black-and-white photographs.

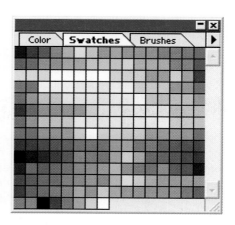

A **system palette** is the collection of colors the operating system uses for graphics that represent desktop icons and controls. Windows, for example, uses a system palette containing 20 permanent colors and 236 colors that can be changed, depending on the application.

A **Web palette** (also called a "Web-safe palette" or a "browser palette") contains a standard set of colors used by Internet Web browsers. Because most browsers support this palette, it is typically regarded as a safe choice when preparing graphics for Internet distribution. Figure 7-13 shows the collection of colors used by system and Web palettes.

FIGURE 7-13

The Windows system palette and Web palette are usually provided by graphics software.

Your graphics software might offer additional palettes. They are likely to include a "woodsy" palette that works well for outdoor photographs, a pastel palette that works well with images filled with predominantly light colors, and a flesh-tone palette that's designed to work nicely for portraits.

What if a palette doesn't contain the colors needed for an image? A particular 256-color palette sometimes does not contain the "right" selection of colors for an image. For example, the Windows system palette does not have a wide selection of orange tones for a Halloween or sunset photo. To make up for the lack of colors, your graphics software can dither the image. **Dithering** uses patterns composed of two or more colors to produce the illusion of additional colors and shading, relying on the human eye to blend colors and shapes.

Most graphics software provides options that let you control dithering. You can experiment with these options to find the best one for a particular image. Figure 7-14 illustrates different types of dithering.

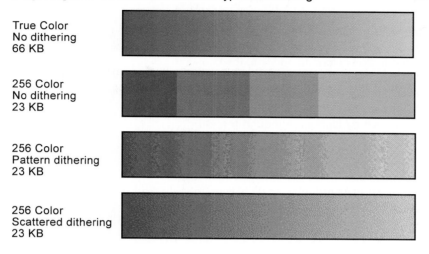

True Color
No dithering
66 KB

256 Color
No dithering
23 KB

256 Color
Pattern dithering
23 KB

256 Color
Scattered dithering
23 KB

When should I reduce color depth? As a rule of thumb, bitmap graphics that you want to print should remain in True Color format. Any graphics that will be sent as e-mail attachments, posted on a Web site, or viewed only on-screen should be reduced to a 256-color palette or compressed into a small file using JPEG format.

BITMAP GRAPHICS FORMATS

Are there different kinds of bitmap graphics? Many graphics file formats exist, and most graphics software offers a choice of popular formats, such as BMP, PCX, TIFF, JPEG, GIF, and PNG.

BMP, pronounced "bee-em-pee" or "bump," is the native bitmap graphics file format of the Microsoft Windows environment. Microsoft Paint, included as part of Microsoft Windows, creates BMP graphics files. The BMP format supports True Color and can be used for a wide variety of graphics applications, such as photographs, illustrations, and graphs. BMP files are not compressed in any way, so this format typically creates the largest graphics files of any file format. BMP graphics are not supported by most browsers, so they are not used on the Web.

PCX is one of the original personal computer bitmap graphics file formats. PCX graphics are usually 8-bit (256 colors) and are automatically compressed to reduce file size without any loss of image quality. Because it's not supported by browsers, PCX is not used on the Web.

TIFF (Tag Image File Format), or TIF, is a flexible and platform-independent graphics file format supported by most photo-editing software packages. Scanners and digital cameras commonly store bitmaps in TIFF format because it supports True Color and can be easily converted into other graphics file formats. TIFF is an excellent choice for DTP projects, but it is not supported by most browsers.

JPEG (pronounced JAY peg), which stands for Joint Photographic Experts Group, is a graphics format with built-in compression that stores True Color bitmap data very efficiently in a small file. The JPEG format is popular for Web graphics. When creating or converting an image in JPEG format, you can control the level of compression and the resulting file size.

The compression process eliminates some image data, however, so highly compressed files suffer some quality deterioration. The TechTalk section of this chapter covers compression in more detail.

GIF (pronounced GIF or JIFF), or Graphics Interchange Format, was specifically designed to create images that can be displayed on multiple platforms, such as PCs and Macs. GIF graphics are a very popular format for Web graphics, but they are limited to 256 colors. In addition, the compression algorithm that's built into the GIF format is patented by UniSys Corporation. Currently, UniSys allows individuals to freely use GIF graphics on Web sites, as long as those graphics are created by using graphics software that contains GIF routines licensed by UniSys. Although the GIF format is popular, some Web developers express concern about further restrictions or fees that UniSys might require in the future.

PNG (Portable Network Graphic), pronounced "ping," is a graphics format designed to improve on the GIF format. A PNG graphic can display up to 48-bit True Color (trillions of colors). Unlike JPEG, PNG compresses bitmap data without losing any data, so compressed images retain the same high quality as the originals. Unlike GIF, PNG is a public domain format without any restrictions on its use.

How do I know which graphics format to use? Selecting the best graphics file format to use depends on what you intend to do with the image. Figure 7-15 summarizes popular uses for each format.

BMP	Graphical elements, such as buttons and other controls used in computer programs
PCX	Not used with much frequency today
TIFF	High-resolution scanned images and digital photos used in desktop publishing; high-quality digital photos reproduced on special photo printers
JPEG	Photographic or scanned images that might be used in a variety of applications, such as DTP or Web pages, where flexibility in file size is important
GIF	Popular format for Web graphics
PNG	An alternative to GIF for Web graphics

FIGURE 7-15

Choosing a bitmap graphics format depends on how the image is used.

QUICKCHECK......SECTION A

1. Images from a digital camera can be transferred to a computer by using a(n) [_____], serial, or FireWire cable.

2. A 3.5 megapixel digital camera captures images with a 2160 x 1440 [_____].

3. Bitmap graphics are resolution [_____], so that reducing the resolution also reduces the image quality.

4. A(n) [_____] palette produces images that resemble black and white photographs.

5. The [_____] format is a good choice for desktop publishing, but not for Web graphics.

6. The most popular 256-color formats for Web graphics include [_____] and PNG.

 CHECK ANSWERS

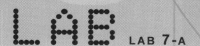 LAB 7-A

WORKING WITH BITMAP GRAPHICS

In this lab, you'll learn:

- How to identify common bitmap graphics file extensions
- How to capture an image from the Web
- How to find the properties of a graphic
- How to eliminate red eye from a photo
- How to manipulate brightness, contrast, and sharpness
- How to make a photo look "old"
- The differences between cropping and resizing
- How to change the size of an image
- How to reduce file size
- How to select a palette
- How to apply a dithering technique
- How to prepare graphics for the Web
- How to prepare a graphic to use as an e-mail attachment
- The effects of lossy compression

INTERACTIVE LAB

CLICK TO START THE LAB

LAB ASSIGNMENTS

1. Start the interactive part of the lab. Insert your Tracking Disk if you want to save your QuickCheck results. Perform each lab step as directed, and answer all the lab QuickCheck questions. When you exit the lab, your answers are automatically graded and your results are displayed.

2. Use the Start button to access the Programs menu for the computer you typically use. Make a list of the available bitmap graphics software.

3. Capture a photographic image from a digital camera, scanner, or Web page. Save it as "MyGraphic." Open the image using any available graphics software. Use this software to discover the properties of the graphic. Indicate the source of the graphic, and then describe its file format, file size, resolution, and color depth.

4. Prepare this graphics file to send to a friend as an e-mail attachment that is smaller than 200 KB. Describe the steps that were required.

5. Suppose you want to post this image on a Web page. Make the necessary adjustments to file size and color depth. Describe the resulting graphic in terms of its resolution, color depth, palette, and dithering.

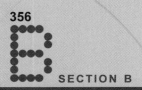
VECTOR AND 3-D GRAPHICS

If you've played any computer games recently or watched a hit movie such as *ROBOTS* or *Cars*, you've seen the product of computer-generated 3-D animated graphics. To the uninformed, these photorealistic action characters might seem little more than fancy cartoons. After you understand the way they are created, however, you'll appreciate the incredible amount of computing power that's required.

This section of the chapter begins with two-dimensional vector graphics, one of the basic building blocks for 3-D animated graphics. You'll find out how they differ from bitmaps and why you might want to use them. After covering the basics for two-dimensional graphics, the section progresses to static 3-D graphics and then to animated 3-D graphics.

VECTOR GRAPHICS BASICS

What is a vector graphic? Unlike a bitmap graphic created by dividing an image into a grid of pixels, a **vector graphic** consists of a set of instructions for re-creating a picture. Instead of storing the color value for each pixel, a vector graphic file contains the instructions the computer needs to create the shape, size, position, and color for each object in an image. These instructions are similar to those a drafting teacher might give students: "Draw a 2" (or 112-pixel) circle. Locate this circle 1" down and 2" in from the right edge of the work area. Fill the circle with yellow." The Stonehenge image shown in Figure 7-16 was created as a vector graphic.

FIGURE 7-16
A vector graphic is formed from lines and shapes, which can be colored or shaded.

The parts of a vector graphic are created as separate objects. For example, the Stonehenge image was created with a series of roughly rectangular objects for the stones and a circular object for the sun. These objects are layered according to the artist's specifications. In the Stonehenge image, the sun object is layered behind the stones and clouds. This characteristic of vector graphics gives artists a great deal of flexibility in arranging and editing image elements.

How can I identify vector graphics? It can be difficult to accurately identify a vector graphic just by looking at an on-screen image. One clue that an image might be a vector graphic is a flat, cartoon-like quality. Think of clip art images—they are typically stored as vector graphics. For a more definitive identification, however, you should check the file extension. Vector graphics files have file extensions such as .wmf, .dxt, .mgx, .eps, .pict, and .cgm.

How do vector graphics compare with bitmap graphics? Vector graphics are suitable for most line art, logos, simple illustrations, and diagrams that might be displayed and printed at various sizes. When compared to bitmaps, vector graphics have several advantages and disadvantages. You should take the following distinctions into account when deciding which type of graphic to use for a specific project.

■ **Vector graphics resize better than bitmaps.** When you change the size of a vector graphic, the objects change proportionally and maintain their smooth edges. Whereas a circle in a bitmap graphic might appear to have jagged edges after it is enlarged, a circle in a vector graphic appears as a smooth curve at any size, as shown in Figure 7-17.

FIGURE 7-17

Unlike bitmaps, vector graphics can be resized without becoming pixelated.

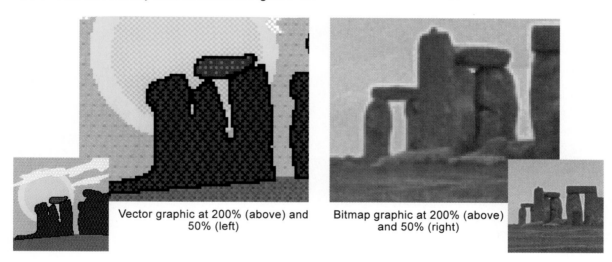

Vector graphic at 200% (above) and 50% (left)

Bitmap graphic at 200% (above) and 50% (right)

■ **Vector graphics usually require less storage space than bitmaps.** The storage space required for a vector graphic reflects the complexity of the image. Each instruction requires storage space, so the more lines, shapes, and fill patterns in the graphic, the more storage space it requires. The Stonehenge vector graphic used as an example in this chapter requires less than 4 KB of storage space. A True Color photograph of the same image requires 1,109 KB.

■ **It is easier to edit an object in a vector graphic than an object in a bitmap graphic.** In some ways, a vector graphic is like a collage of objects. Each object can be layered over other objects, but moved and edited independently. You can individually stretch, shrink, distort, color, move, or delete any object in a vector graphic. For example, if you delete some of the stones from the Stonehenge vector image, the background layers remain. In contrast, most bitmap graphics are constructed as a single layer of pixels. If you erase the pixels for some of the stones in the Stonehenge photograph, you'll create a "hole" of white pixels (Figure 7-18).

FIGURE 7-18

Vector graphic objects are layered, so it is easy to move and delete objects without disrupting the rest of the image. In contrast, deleting a shape from a bitmap image leaves a "hole" because the image is only one layer of pixels.

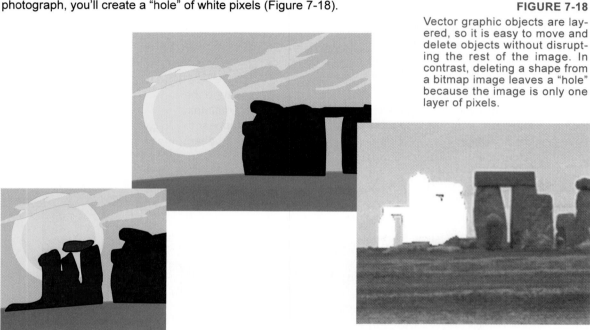

■ **Vector graphics are not usually as realistic as bitmap images.** Most vector images tend to have a cartoon-like appearance instead of the realistic appearance you expect from a photograph. This cartoon-like characteristic of vector images results from the use of objects filled with blocks of color. Your options for shading and texturing objects are limited, which tends to give vector graphics a "flat" appearance.

FIGURE 7-19

A digitizing tablet allows you to trace line drawings for a vector graphic.

What tools do I need to create vector graphics? Neither scanners nor cameras produce vector graphics. Architects and engineers sometimes use a digitizing tablet, such as the one in Figure 7-19, to turn a paper-based line drawing into a vector graphic. A **digitizing tablet** (sometimes called a "2-D digitizer") is a device that provides a flat surface for a paper-based drawing and a pen or "puck" that you can use to click the endpoints of each line on the drawing. The endpoints are converted into vectors and stored.

Usually, vector graphics are created "from scratch" with vector graphics software, referred to as **drawing software**. Popular drawing software includes Adobe Illustrator, Macromedia Freehand, and Corel Designer. Drawing software is sometimes packaged separately from the paint software used to produce bitmap graphics. In other cases, it is included with bitmap software as a graphics software suite.

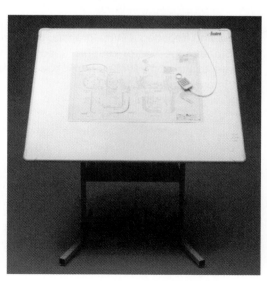

Vector graphics software provides an array of drawing tools that you can use to create objects, position them, and fill them with colors or patterns. For example, you can use the filled circle tool to draw a circle filled with a solid color. You can create an irregular shape by connecting points to outline the shape. Figure 7-20 illustrates how to use drawing tools to create a vector graphic.

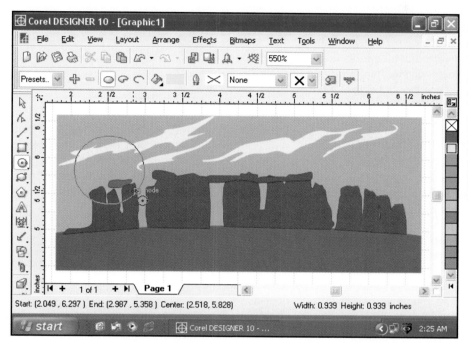

The sun is a circle filled with a gradient.

The clouds are created as a series of short line segments and filled with color.

The stones are created as a series of short line segments and filled with black.

The background is a filled rectangle.

FIGURE 7-20

To draw a circle, select the filled circle tool, and then drag the mouse pointer to indicate the circle's location and size. A color palette allows you to select the circle color. After you create the circle object, you can move it and change its size or color. You can also create irregular shapes for objects, such as clouds, by connecting short line segments.

CLICK TO START

Vector graphics software helps you easily edit individual objects within a graphic by changing their sizes, shapes, positions, or colors. For example, the data for creating the circle is recorded as an instruction, such as CIRCLE 40 Y 200 150, which means create a circle with a 40-pixel radius, color it yellow, and place the center of the circle 200 pixels from the left of the screen and 150 pixels from the top of the screen. If you move the circle to the right side of the image, the instruction that the computer stores for the circle changes to something like CIRCLE 40 Y 500 150—500 pixels from the left instead of 200.

INFOWEBLINKS

To learn more about popular vector graphics software, you can connect to the **Vector Graphics Software InfoWeb**.

www.course.com/np/concepts8/ch07

When filling in a shape with color, your graphics software might provide tools for creating gradients. A **gradient** is a smooth blending of shades from one color to another or from light to dark. Gradients, as shown in Figure 7-21, can be used to create shading and three-dimensional effects.

FIGURE 7-21
Gradients can create the illusion of three dimensions, such as making this shape appear to be a tube.

Some vector graphics software provides tools that apply bitmapped textures to vector graphic objects, giving them a more realistic appearance. For example, you can create a vector drawing of a house, and then apply a bricklike texture derived from a bitmap photograph of real bricks. Graphics that contain both bitmap and vector data are called **metafiles**.

VECTOR-TO-BITMAP CONVERSION

Is it possible to convert a vector graphic into a bitmap? A vector graphic can be converted quite easily into a bitmap graphic through a process called rasterizing. **Rasterization** works by superimposing a grid over a vector image and determining the color for each pixel. This process is typically carried out by graphics software, which allows you to specify the output size for the final bitmap image. On a PC, you can also rasterize a vector graphic by using the Print Screen key to take a screenshot of a vector image. It is important to output your rasterized images at the size you ultimately need. If you rasterize a vector image at a small size and then try to enlarge the resulting bitmap image, you will likely get a poor-quality pixelated image, such as the one in Figure 7-22.

After a vector graphic is converted to a bitmap, the resulting graphic no longer has the qualities of a vector graphic. For example, if you convert the Stonehenge vector graphic into a bitmap, the sun is no longer an object that you can easily move or assign a different color.

How about converting a bitmap graphic into a vector graphic? Converting a bitmap graphic into a vector graphic is more difficult than converting from a vector to a bitmap. To change a bitmap graphic into a vector graphic, you must use special tracing software. **Tracing software** locates the edges of objects in a bitmap image and converts the resulting shapes into vector graphic objects.

Tracing software products, such as Adobe Streamline and ImpressionX, work best on simple images and line drawings. They do not usually produce acceptable results when used on complex, detailed photos. Tracing capabilities are included in some general-purpose graphics software, but standalone tracing software offers more flexibility and usually produces better results.

INFOWEBLINKS

Looking for software to convert between vector images and bitmaps? You'll find helpful links at the **Vector-Bitmap Conversion InfoWeb**.

www.course.com/np/concepts8/ch07

FIGURE 7-22
When vector images are rasterized, they become bitmaps and can't be enlarged without becoming pixelated.

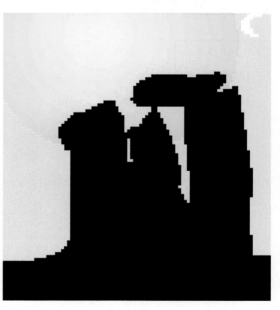

VECTOR GRAPHICS ON THE WEB

Do vector graphics work on the Web? Web browsers were originally designed to support a limited number of graphics formats—GIF and JPEG—and these formats were exclusively bitmaps. Built-in browser support for vector graphics has been slow, but plug-ins and players are currently available for several of the most popular Web-based vector graphics formats.

Which vector graphics formats can be used on the Web? A graphics format called **SVG** (Scalable Vector Graphics) is designed specifically for the Web (Figure 7-23). Graphics in SVG format are automatically resized when displayed on different screens or when printed. SVG supports gradients, drop shadows, multiple levels of transparency, and other effects, along with portability to other platforms, such as handheld computers and cellular phones. SVG graphic objects can include regular and irregular shapes, images, and text, and they can be animated. You can add SVG files to HTML and XML documents by using the <embed> tag.

Despite the simplicity of the SVG format, today **Flash** is the most popular vector graphics format for the Web. As Chapter 6 explained, Macromedia's Flash software creates a popular vector graphics format that is stored in files with .swf extensions. Flash graphics can be static or animated. Flash players are shipped with most browsers, and player updates can be downloaded from the Macromedia site.

Flash animations have advantages over other formats, such as animated GIFs. You should recall that an animated GIF is essentially a series of slightly different bitmap images displayed in sequence to achieve animation effects. As a bitmap-based format, GIF files are fairly large. Most Flash animations fit in compact files and, therefore, can be transferred from a Web server to a browser more rapidly than animated GIFs.

What are the advantages of using vector graphics on the Web? Vector graphics have several advantages:

■ **Consistent quality.** On Web pages, vector graphics appear with the same consistent quality on all computer screens. This capability makes it possible for browsers to adjust the size of an image "on the fly" to fit correctly on a screen, regardless of its size or resolution. These adjustments don't carry any penalty in terms of image quality—a "large" version of a vector graphic displayed on a monitor set at 1024 x 768 resolution has the same sharp detail and smooth curves as the original image sized to fit a smaller screen set at 640 x 480 resolution. This flexibility is important for Web pages that might be viewed at different resolutions on PCs, Macs, or other platforms.

■ **Searchable.** Another advantage is that any text contained in a vector image is stored as actual text, not just a series of colored dots. This text can be indexed by search engines so that it can be included in keyword searches. For example, suppose a vector drawing was used to produce a diagram describing the service box where your telephone line enters your house. One of the components in this diagram is labeled "telephone test jack." If you enter "telephone test jack" into a search engine, the service box diagram will likely turn up in the list of search results.

■ **Compact file size.** A third advantage of vector graphics on the Web is their compact file sizes. A fairly complex graphic can be stored in a file that is under 30 KB—that's kilobytes, not megabytes. These files require little storage space and can be transmitted swiftly from a Web server to your browser.

FIGURE 7-23

SVG graphics are typically used on the Web for maps, ads, organizational charts, and flowcharts.

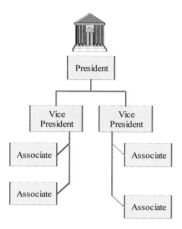

INFOWEBLINKS

Connect to the **Web-based Vector Graphics InfoWeb** for an update on the latest vector graphics formats for the Web.

www.course.com/np/concepts8/ch07

3-D GRAPHICS

How do vector graphics relate to 3-D graphics? Like vector graphics, **3-D graphics** are stored as a set of instructions. For a 3-D graphic, however, the instructions contain the locations and lengths of lines that form a wireframe for a three-dimensional object. The **wireframe** acts in much the same way as the framework of a pop-up tent. Just as you would construct the framework for the tent, and then cover it with a nylon tent cover, a 3-D wireframe can be covered with surface texture and color to create a graphic of a 3-D object. The process of covering a wireframe with surface color and texture is called **rendering**. The rendering process, shown in Figure 7-24, outputs a bitmap image.

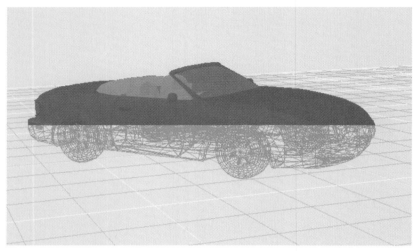

FIGURE 7-24

3-D graphics are based on a wireframe, which can be rendered into a bitmap image that looks three-dimensional.

For added realism, the rendering process can take into account the way that light shines on surfaces and creates shadows. The technique for adding light and shadows to a 3-D image is called **ray tracing**. Before an image is rendered, the artist selects a location for one or more light sources. The computer applies a complex mathematical algorithm to determine how the light source affects the color of each pixel in the final rendered image. This process can take time—hours for a complex image, even using today's most powerful personal computers. Figure 7-25 shows the image from the previous figure rendered with an additional light source and ray tracing.

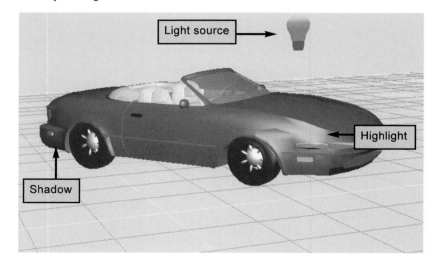

FIGURE 7-25

Ray tracing adds realism to 3-D graphics by adding highlights and shadows that are produced by a light source.

What tools do I need to create 3-D graphics? To create 3-D graphics, you need 3-D graphics software, such as AutoCad or Caligari trueSpace. This software has tools for drawing a wireframe and viewing it from any angle. It provides rendering and ray tracing tools, along with an assortment of surface textures that you can apply to individual objects. Figure 7-26 takes you on a tour of a popular 3-D graphics software package.

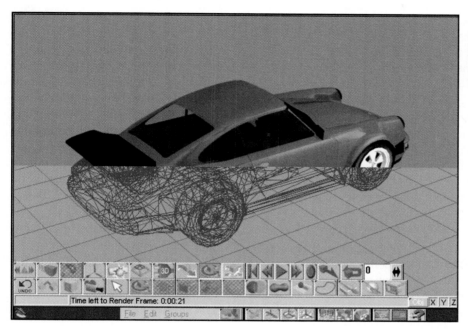

FIGURE 7-26
3-D graphics software provides tools for drawing a wireframe and then specifying colors and textures for rendering.

CLICK TO START

3-D graphics software runs on most personal computers, although some architects and engineers prefer to use high-end workstations. A fast processor, lots of RAM, and a fast graphics card with its own video RAM all speed up the rendering process. Experts recommend using at least a 1 GHz Pentium PC or a Macintosh G3 equipped with a high-resolution, 17" or larger monitor. A graphics card designed for 3-D work and loaded with at least 128 MB of memory is also useful.

Is it possible to animate 3-D graphics? 3-D graphics can be animated to produce special effects for movies or to create interactive, animated characters and environments for 3-D computer games. Animated special effects, such as the massive battle scenes in *Lord of the Rings: Return of the King*, are created by rendering a sequence of bitmaps, in which one or more objects are moved or otherwise changed between each rendering. In traditional hand-drawn animation, a chief artist draws the keyframes, and then a team of assistants creates each of the in-between images—24 of these images for each second of animation. For 3-D computer animation, the computer creates the in-between images by moving the object and rendering each necessary image. All the images are then combined into a single file, creating essentially a digital movie.

Graphics design companies such as Pixar Animation Studios and DreamWorks use 3-D animation techniques to produce animated feature films as well as special effects. The first full-length animated 3-D movie was *Toy Story*, released in 1995 by Walt Disney Studios and Pixar. Digitally animated films, such as *ROBOTS*, *The Polar Express*, and *The Incredibles*, illustrate the growing sophistication of 3-D animation.

INFOWEBLINKS

For additional resources about 3-D software (and shareware), rendering, ray tracing, and 3-D animated graphics, check out the **3-D Graphics InfoWeb**.

www.course.com/np/concepts8/ch07

Do game and movie animation require similar tools and techniques? An important characteristic of special effects and animated films is that rendering can be accomplished during the production phase of the movie and incorporated into the final footage. In contrast, 3-D computer game animation happens in "real time." Each frame that makes the image seem to move must be rendered while you are playing the game—a process that requires an incredible amount of computer power. To give you a handle on the immensity of the task, consider a game like Doom displayed on a computer monitor that's set at 1024 x 768 resolution (Figure 7-27). At this resolution, the screen contains 786,432 pixels (1024 multiplied by 768). If the game is presented in 32-bit color, each frame of the animation requires 25,165,824 bits (multiply 786,432 times 32).

Computer game designers believe that on-screen animation looks smoothest at 60 frames per second, which means your computer must handle 1,509,949,440—that's more than 1 billion—bits of information every second just to put the 3-D image onto the screen. In addition, the computer must process even more data to keep track of the movements of each player. To handle all this data, your computer's main processor gets help from a graphics processor located on your computer's graphics card. These graphics processors vary in their capabilities. For the fastest graphics capability, look for graphics cards billed as 3-D accelerators.

Can I create my own animated 3-D graphics? You can create 3-D animations on a standard PC or Mac with commercially available software, but professional 3-D software, such as Maya and Discrete 3ds max, is expensive and has a steep learning curve. If you want to dabble with 3-D animations before making an expensive software investment, you might try Curious Labs Poser, Corel Bryce, or one of the shareware programs listed in the 3-D Graphics InfoWeb (page 363). Whether you use a commercial or shareware package, be prepared to spend lots of time with the manual before you are able to produce any original animations.

FIGURE 7-27

Classic computer games, such as Doom, established building blocks for animation technologies used to create today's fast-action, visually detailed computer games.

QUICKCHECK......SECTION B

1. Unlike bitmaps, vector graphics can be enlarged without becoming pixelated. True or false? [＿＿＿＿＿]

2. Whereas the software used to work with bitmap graphics is often referred to as paint software, vector graphics software is usually referred to as [＿＿＿＿＿＿] software.

3. 3D graphics are based on a(n) [＿＿＿＿＿＿＿] that can be covered with surface texture and color.

4. The technique of adding light and shadows to a 3-D image is called ray [＿＿＿＿＿＿].

5. A vector graphic can be easily converted into a bitmap through a process called [＿＿＿＿＿＿].

6. Today, [＿＿＿＿＿＿] is the most popular vector graphics format for the Web.

CHECK ANSWERS

SECTION C

DIGITAL VIDEO

In the previous sections, you learned about GIF and Flash animations—popular options for adding motion to Web pages. You also learned about using animated 3-D graphics for movie special effects and computer games. Digital animation is typically created from scratch by an artist with the help of a computer. In contrast, digital video is based on footage of real objects filmed and then stored as bits. Digital video encompasses several technologies, including those that produce theater-quality DVD movies, desktop videos, Web-based videos, and PDA videos. In this section, you'll take a look at what you can do with affordable, easy-to-use desktop video tools. You'll also explore how to transfer digital videos onto DVD and then add interactive menus to access selected scenes and special features.

DIGITAL VIDEO BASICS

What is digital video? A video is a series of still frames, like those in Figure 7-28, projected at a rate fast enough to fool the human eye into perceiving continuous motion. **Digital video** uses bits to store color and brightness data for each video frame. The process is similar to storing the data for a series of bitmap images in which the color for each pixel is represented by a binary number.

FIGURE 7-28

A video is composed of a series of frames.

Unlike analog video, digital video retains image quality no matter how many times it is copied. Videos in digital format can be easily manipulated on a personal computer, putting the world of movie-making at your fingertips.

Footage for digital videos can be supplied by a video camera, videotape, television, DVD, or even a digital video recording device such as TiVo. You can use a consumer-quality camcorder and your personal computer to edit this footage into videos suitable for a variety of personal and professional uses, such as video wedding albums, product sales videos, training videos, video holiday greeting cards, documentaries for nonprofit organizations, and video scrapbooks. These videos can be stored on a hard disk or distributed on CDs, DVDs, videotapes, memory cards, or the Web.

Are there different kinds of digital videos? Digital video is sometimes classified by its platform. The term **desktop video** refers to videos that are constructed and displayed using a personal computer. **Web-based video** is incorporated in Web pages and accessed with a browser. **DVD video** refers to commercial DVDs that contain feature-length films. **PDA video** refers to small-format video designed to be viewed on a PDA or cell phone screen.

How do I create digital video? To understand how you can create your own digital videos, you'll need information about four procedures summarized in Figure 7-29 and explained in the rest of this section.

1. Produce video footage. Select equipment for filming videos and use effective filming techniques.

2. Transfer video footage to a computer. Transfer video footage from cameras, video tape, TVs, and DVRs.

3. Edit video footage. Use software to select video segments, arrange them into a video, and add a soundtrack.

4. Store and play video. Select digital video file formats for playback on desktop, Web, PDA, and DVD platforms.

FIGURE 7-29
Desktop video requires a few fairly simple steps.

PRODUCING VIDEO FOOTAGE

Is it necessary to use a digital video camera for filming digital video? You can use a digital or an analog video camera to shoot video footage. As you might expect, a **digital video camera** stores footage as a series of bits. The video data can be stored on a tape in much the same way that computer data is stored on a backup tape. Video data can also be stored on 3'' miniDVDs. Digital video tape formats include miniDV, DVCPro, and DVCam. MiniDV is the most popular and generally the format used by consumer digital video cameras.

You can also use an analog video camera to shoot footage that eventually becomes digital video. As with digital video cameras, the footage is stored on tape, but instead of storing bits, an **analog video camera** stores video signals as a continuous track of magnetic patterns. The three most popular analog video formats are Hi8, S-VHS, and VHS.

Another option for shooting video footage is a small, inexpensive **videoconferencing camera** (often called a "Web cam" or "Web camera") that attaches directly to a computer (see Figure 7-30). These cameras capture a series of still photos, which are stored in digital format directly on your computer's hard disk. Web cameras typically produce rather low-quality video. These cameras are not usually battery powered and must remain tethered to your computer, which tends to limit your videos to "talking heads."

FIGURE 7-30
A Web camera, such as this popular D-Link model, sits on top of a computer monitor. It is designed mainly for "talking head" applications, such as online video chats and video conferences.

What are the advantages of a digital video camera? A digital video camera captures video data in digital format, which can then be transferred directly to a computer for editing. In addition, digital cameras generally produce higher quality video than analog or videoconferencing cameras. Images tend to be sharper and more colorful. A common misconception is that because desktop, Web-based, and PDA videos are shown on a small computer screen at a fairly low resolution, a cheap camera won't make a difference. Just the opposite is true. The higher the quality of the original video, the better the final video will look.

Does desktop video require special filming techniques? When videos are processed and stored on a personal computer, some of the image data is eliminated to reduce the video file to a manageable size. Simpler videos tend to maintain better quality as they are edited, processed, and stored. Camera movements, fast actions, patterned clothing, and moving backgrounds all contribute to the complexity of a video and should be minimized. The techniques listed in Figure 7-31 can help you produce video footage that maintains good quality as it is edited and processed.

- Use a tripod to maintain a steady image.
- Move the camera slowly if it is necessary to pan from side to side.
- Zoom in and out slowly.
- Direct your subjects to move slowly, when possible.
- Position your shot to eliminate as much background detail and movement as possible.
- Ask the subjects of your video to wear solid-colored clothing, if possible.

FIGURE 7-31
Video Filming Tips

VIDEO TRANSFER

How do I transfer video footage to my computer? Video footage can originate from a variety of sources, including video cameras, video tape, DVRs (digital video recorders), and even your TV. To digitally edit and process digital video, you must transfer the video footage from its source to your computer. After the footage is transferred and stored on a random-access device, such as your computer's hard disk, you can easily cut out unwanted footage, rearrange clips, and add a soundtrack.

The basic method for transferring video footage to your computer is to send the data over a cable that connects your video source to your computer (Figure 7-32). Analog video footage from TV, video tape, and analog video cameras must be converted into digital format before it is stored on your computer's hard disk. Video that originates as a digital signal might transfer directly to your computer, or it might require conversion to a computer-compatible format.

How do I convert video from analog devices? The process of converting analog video signals into digital format is referred to as **video capture** and requires a video capture device that connects your computer to the video source via cable. Your computer's graphics card might include video capture capabilities. If not, you can purchase a separate video capture

FIGURE 7-32
You can transfer video footage to a hard disk by connecting a cable between a video camera and a computer. When the transfer is complete, the cable can be disconnected.

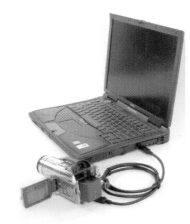

device that connects to your computer's USB port or a video capture card that plugs into one of your computer's PCI slots.

Most video capture devices support a variety of analog video sources, such as cameras and VCRs. The trick is to find a cable with a connector at one end that plugs into the video output port of your analog video source and a plug at the other end that's compatible with your video capture device. Figure 7-33 illustrates the equipment necessary for capturing video from an analog camera.

FIGURE 7-33

After it has been installed in your computer, a video capture card can be connected to an analog camera's video-out and audio-out ports.

How do I transfer data from a digital camera to my computer? The data from a digital camera requires no conversion, so it can be transferred directly to your computer's hard disk. Most digital cameras provide a USB or FireWire port for this purpose. Your computer needs a corresponding port to accept the cable from the camera. Figure 7-34 explains where to find your computer's FireWire and USB ports.

FIGURE 7-34

FireWire ports (top) and USB ports (bottom) can be located on the front or back of the computer's system unit.

Can I capture video from a digital video recorder? A digital video recorder (DVR), like those used with TiVo service, is a device that records television signals received by an antenna, through a cable, or via satellite. Signals that originate from antenna or cable are converted from analog into digital format and stored on a built-in hard disk. Satellite signals, already in digital format, are converted or unscrambled as necessary before being stored. DVRs are controlled by customized operating systems, usually based on Linux.

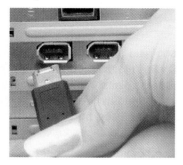

It seems like it would be easy to transfer video files from this computer-like device to your personal computer for editing. Some DVRs store data in proprietary formats designed to discourage copying and distribution, however. These proprietary formats can make it difficult to convert DVR videos into formats that can be manipulated on a computer. Consumers, however, are demanding more compatibility between DVRs and computers. Until DVR manufacturers provide standard video formats, it is easier to capture analog video direct from the TV using a video capture device.

How do I control the transfer process? Whether you transfer footage from an analog camera or a digital camera, you must use **video capture software** to control the transfer process. Video capture software allows you to start and stop the transfer, select a file format for storing your video footage, and specify the file for each video clip. Video capture software is supplied with video editing software and with video capture devices.

Videos are easier to edit if you divide them into several files, each containing a one- or two-minute video clip. Some video capture software automatically creates clips by detecting frame changes, such as when you turn your camera off, pause, or switch to a new scene (Figure 7-35).

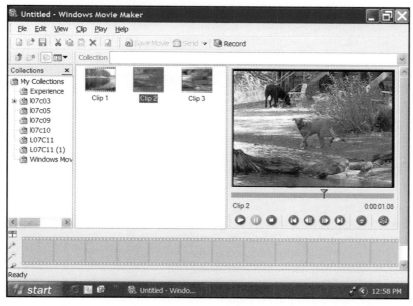

FIGURE 7-35
Videos should be transferred as a series of short clips.

Most digital video cameras store data in DV format. Despite the use of real-time compression to filter out unnecessary data as you record with your camera, DV format contains lots of data. When transferred to your computer, a DV clip requires roughly 1 GB of storage per 5 minutes of video. If you have the disk capacity, you'll get the best quality video if you transfer all this data. If disk space is tight, however, you can whittle digital video down to a more manageable size by using your video capture software to decrease the video display size, reduce the frame rate, and compress file data.

■ **Decrease video display size.** A smaller video window contains fewer pixels than a full-screen window and requires fewer bits to represent the data. Whereas a 720 x 480 video window contains 345,600 pixels, a 320 x 240 window contains only 76,800 pixels and fits in a file one-fourth the size. That's a big advantage. If you're creating Web-based videos designed to be displayed in a small window, or if you're designing video for handheld devices, consider decreasing the resolution at this stage of the process.

■ **Reduce the frame rate. Frame rate** refers to the number of frames shown per second. Digital video cameras record 30 frames per second (fps). Feature films are typically projected at a rate of 24 frames per second. If you intend to output your digital videos to DVDs, you should maintain a high frame rate. Most desktop video, however, has a frame rate of only 15 fps. Reducing the frame rate tends to increase the blurriness of a video, especially for fast-action sequences. If your videos are destined for desktop, Web, or PDA playback, you can reduce the frame rate at this stage of the process because the finished video will be displayed at a lower frame rate.

■ **Compress data.** Most video capture software stores video footage in AVI, MOV, or MPEG files. MPEG offers the most compression and produces the smallest files. MPEG compression works by eliminating data, however, and that can decrease image quality. MPEG format is a good option if storage space is a concern or if your videos are destined for the Web or a PDA.

VIDEO EDITING

Do I need special equipment for video editing? Before camcorders went digital, editing a video consisted of recording segments from one videotape onto another tape. This process, called **linear editing**, required two VCRs at minimum. Professional video editors used expensive editing equipment, beyond the budget of most consumers.

Today's **nonlinear editing** simply requires a computer hard disk and video editing software. The advantage of nonlinear editing is that you can use a random-access device to easily edit and arrange video clips. Video editing requires lots of hard disk space, however, so before you begin an editing session, make sure your computer's hard disk has several gigabytes of available storage space.

How do I edit a video? After your video footage is transferred to your computer and stored on the hard disk, you can begin to arrange your video clips by using video editing software, such as Adobe Premiere, Roxio VideoWave, Windows Movie Maker, or Ulead VideoStudio. Your completed video consists of video tracks containing video segments and transitions, plus audio tracks containing voices and music. Most video editing software allows you to overlay a video track with several audio tracks. Figure 7-36 illustrates how to lay out video and audio tracks.

INFOWEBLINKS

The **Video Editing InfoWeb** contains tips about editing digital videos, updates on the latest consumer-level software, and links to the most popular digital video sites.

www.course.com/np/concepts8/ch07

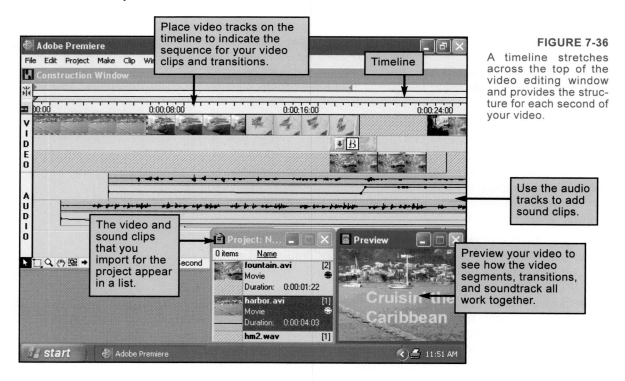

FIGURE 7-36

A timeline stretches across the top of the video editing window and provides the structure for each second of your video.

VIDEO OUTPUT

How does video footage become a digital video? After you edit your video clips, arrange them on a timeline, and specify a soundtrack, your video editing software combines the data from all the video and audio files you selected into a single file, which is stored on your computer's hard disk as a digital video.

You can save your digital video in a variety of file formats and select compression techniques to achieve a file size that's best for desktop, Web-based, PDA, or DVD video. Figure 7-37 describes some popular video file formats—**AVI**, **QuickTime**, **MPEG**, **RealMedia**, **WMV**, and **VOB**.

FIGURE 7-37
Popular Digital Video Formats

Format	Extension	Platform	Description and Use
AVI (Audio Video Interleave)	.avi	PC	Often the format for storing digital clips from video cameras; used for desktop video on the PC platform
QuickTime Movie	.mov	PC, Mac, UNIX, Linux	One of the most popular formats for desktop and streaming Web videos
MPEG (Moving Pictures Experts Group)	.mpg or .mpeg	PC, Mac, UNIX, Linux	Versions include MPEG1, MPEG2, and MPEG4; used for desktop video, PDA video, and streaming Web video
RealMedia	.rm	PC, Mac, UNIX, Linux	Produced by RealNetworks, a popular format for streaming Web videos
WMV (Windows Media Video)	.wmv	PC	Offers sophisticated compression options for high-quality images; used for desktop video, PDA video, and streaming video over the Web
VOB (Video Object)	.vob	Standalone DVD players, PCs, Macs, Linux	Industry-standard format for standalone DVD players

Which compression techniques should I use? Suppose you decide to store your video as an AVI file for desktop viewing. You can compress that AVI file using various compression ratios and by reducing the frame rate or frame size. The videos in Figure 7-38 illustrate the differences in image quality and file size that result from using different compression ratios and frame rates.

FIGURE 7-38
Different compression ratios and frame rates can have a remarkable effect on video quality and file size.

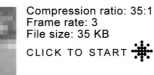
Compression ratio: 35:1
Frame rate: 3
File size: 35 KB

CLICK TO START

Compression ratio: 14:1
Frame rate: 10
File size: 76 KB

CLICK TO START

Compression ratio: 3:1
Frame rate: 15
File size: 353 KB

CLICK TO START

A **codec** (compressor/ decompressor) is the software that compresses a file when a video is created and decompresses the file when the video is played. Popular codecs include MPEG, Indeo, Cinepak, DivX, and Video 1. Each codec uses a unique compression algorithm and allows you to specify a level of compression. The TechTalk section of this chapter provides details about how video compression works.

It is important to understand that the codec used to compress a video also must be used to decompress the video when it is played. Videos intended for a widespread audience should use one of the codecs included in popular video players, such as QuickTime or Windows Media Player.

DESKTOP, PDA, AND WEB VIDEO

How are desktop videos used? Desktop videos are usually displayed on a computer screen with popular video player software, such as the RealMedia player, Windows Media Player, or Apple's QuickTime player. Desktop videos are typically stored on hard disk or CD, and they are sometimes sent as e-mail attachments.

Can I view movies on my PDA? Some PDAs and smartphones can be configured to play digital videos (Figure 7-39), including movie trailers, TV shows, and even feature-length movies. The device requires video or multimedia player software, such as Pocket TV or Windows Media Player, and storage capacity for the video file—usually on a solid-state memory card. Videos specially optimized for handheld devices can be downloaded from Web sites to your computer, then transferred to handheld storage and played. Popular formats for handheld video include MPEG and WMV.

How do Web-based videos work? A video for a Web page is stored on a Web server in a file. Usually, a link for the video file appears on the Web page. When you click the link, the Web server transmits a copy of the video file to your computer. If you have the correct video player installed on your computer, the video appears on your computer screen.

The transfer of a digital video file from the Web to your computer can happen in one of two ways, depending on the video format. In one case, your computer waits until it receives the entire video file before starting to play it. For large video files, you might wait several minutes or more before the video starts. An alternative method, called **streaming video**, sends a small segment of the video to your computer and begins to play it. While this first segment plays, the Web server sends the next part of the file to your computer, and so on, until the video ends. With streaming video technology, your computer essentially plays the video while it continues to receive it.

How do I add a video to a Web page? You can add two styles of video to your Web pages. The first style, called external video, simply displays a link to a video file. An HTML tag, such as <a href="ducks.avi"> 1.5 MB AVI Video </a>, indicates the file that contains the video (ducks.avi) and the text for the link (1.5 MB AVI Video). When the link is clicked, the video file is downloaded, and the video player is opened and displayed as a separate window in which the video appears.

A second style of Web video uses the <embed> tag to create an internal video, also referred to as an "in-place video." Instead of opening a separate window for the video player, an internal video plays within the Web page. Figure 7-40 on the next page illustrates external and internal Web page videos.

TERMINOLOGY NOTE

MPEG is potentially confusing because it is a file format and a codec. Files in MPEG format use the MPEG codec. Files in other formats, such as AVI and MOV, can also use the MPEG codec to compress file contents.

FIGURE 7-39
You can watch digital videos on some PDAs and cell phones.

INFOWEBLINKS

The **Video Players InfoWeb** provides lots of handy information about Microsoft Media Player, QuickTime, and other video player software. ✚

www.course.com/np/concepts8/ch07

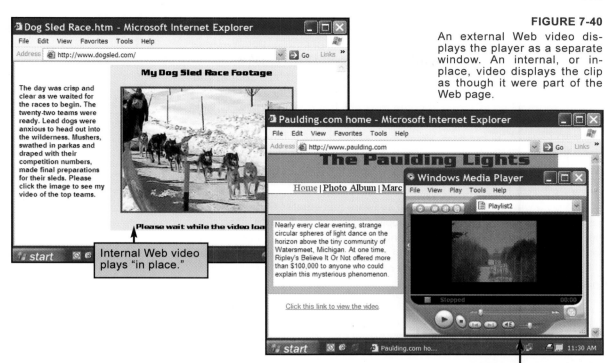

FIGURE 7-40
An external Web video displays the player as a separate window. An internal, or in-place, video displays the clip as though it were part of the Web page.

External Web video displays video in a separate window.

How does Internet connection speed affect Web videos? Although it is possible to play streaming videos over a dial-up connection, it is truly an unsatisfying experience. New compression techniques are able to jam more video data into a smaller package, but images tend to be fuzzy and motion is often jerky.

High-speed Internet connections provide much more bandwidth for streaming video. Videos designed to be transmitted over high-speed connections can play in a larger video window, use less compression, and display better image quality. Until everyone has a high-speed connection, however, many Web sites provide one video file that's optimized for dial-up connections and a better quality video file that's optimized for DSL, cable, and ISDN connections (Figure 7-41).

What are the best formats for Web videos? Today's most popular Web video formats include MPEG4, MOV, WMV, and RM. All these formats offer streaming video and allow developers to adjust compression levels to produce file sizes optimized for dial-up or broadband connections.

DVD VIDEO

Can standalone DVD players work with desktop and Web video formats? Although DVD players work with MPEG files, many DVD players are not able to read desktop video or Web file formats, such as AVI, MOV, and WMV. Further, these players can read DVDs formatted for video, but not DVDs formatted for computer data storage. If you create a digital video, store it in MPEG format on your computer's hard disk, and then copy the MPEG to a DVD, you will be able to view the video on most computers, but not on most TV or home theater DVD players. So don't be surprised if your home theater DVD player can't read a DVD containing the Robots.mov movie trailer you downloaded from the Web, or your HappyNewYear.wmv video greeting card. If you want to view DVDs on your TV or home theater DVD player, you should store them in DVD-video format.

FIGURE 7-41
Many Web sites offer separate versions of video files for dial-up and broadband connections.

VIDEO LIBRARY

Gotta Have Gadgets:
Whether you're a millionaire or managing on a tight budget, these gadgets you've gotta have.

 Watch video:
dial-up |broadband

Superstar Wannabe
Recognize these actors? One of them is destined for superstardom.

 Watch video:
dial-up |broadband

Gutter Derby
Candidates in Ohio bring negative campaigning to new depths.

 Watch video:
dial-up |broadband

What format is used for DVD video? Commercial DVD movies are stored using the industry-standard DVD-video disk format. Video data is stored on these DVDs as VOB (video object) files using MPEG2 compression. Many computers include software that reads VOB files so that you can view DVD movies on your computer screen. Standalone DVD players, like those attached to TVs and home theaters, are designed to work with VOB files. Some standalone DVD players support additional formats, such as VCD (video CD), but if you want to distribute digital videos for playback on standalone DVD players, you can expect the best results by using DVD-video format.

How do I store my digital videos so they can be viewed by standalone DVD players? You simply use software that creates DVD video. For example, DVD authoring software supplies tools for assembling video clips as a series of scenes, creating a menu structure to access these scenes, and transferring this production onto a DVD in standard DVD-video format. The software supplied with your DVD drive might also include an option for burning DVD videos.

Can I use any type of DVD media? Commercial DVD movies are stamped onto DVD-ROM disks, a format that can be universally read by any DVD player. Your computer can burn data on DVD-R, DVD+R, or DVD-RW disks. Because the DVD industry has not achieved a single media standard, some standalone DVD players are not able to read one or more of these disk types. DVD+R seems to be compatible with the widest variety of DVD players, whereas DVD-RWs seem to be the least compatible. Before you distribute your videos on DVDs, test them on the target DVD player if possible.

QUICKCHECK......SECTION C

1. [_____] video refers to digital videos constructed and displayed using a personal computer.

2. The process of converting analog video signals into digital format is referred to as video [_____].

3. The size of a video file can be reduced by three techniques: shrinking the size of the video window, reducing the [_____] rate, and compressing the video data.

4. When transferring video to your computer's hard disk, you get the best quality if you use MPEG compression. True or false? [_____]

5. PDA videos are stored in MP3 files, similar to those used on portable audio players. True or false? [_____]

6. Some Web pages feature [_____] video, which sends a small segment of the video to your computer and begins to play it. While this first segment plays, the Web server sends the next part of the file to your computer, and so on, until the video ends.

7. DVD video requires files stored in [_____] format.

 CHECK ANSWERS

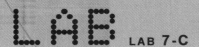

LAB 7-C

VIDEO EDITING

In this lab, you'll learn:

- How to identify and use the basic tools provided by video editing software
- How to select clips for a video and arrange them on the timeline
- How to add transitions
- What sound formats are acceptable for video sound clips
- How to select sound clips for a video and arrange them on the timeline
- How to preview a video
- How to identify popular video formats and codecs
- How characteristics such as frame rate, frame size, sound sampling, and codecs affect file size
- How to specify a codec and other video attributes
- How to find out which video players are installed on a computer
- How to find the properties of a Web-based video
- The differences between streaming and nonstreaming video formats

INTERACTIVE LAB

CLICK TO START THE LAB

LAB ASSIGNMENTS

1. Start the interactive part of the lab. Insert your Tracking Disk if you want to save your QuickCheck results. Perform each lab step as directed, and answer all the lab QuickCheck questions. When you exit the lab, your answers are automatically graded and your results are displayed.

2. Use Control Panel's Add or Remove Programs icon to make a list of the video players available on your computer.

3. Locate a video clip on the Web and indicate the URL of the Web page on which it can be found. Describe the video's properties, including file size and format.

4. Play the video you located for Lab Assignment #3. Describe the video's visual and sound qualities, and discuss how they relate to your Internet connection speed. Also, describe the length and content of the video, the use of transitions or special effects (if any), and the use of sound tracks. If you could edit this video yourself, what changes would you make to produce a more effective video?

SECTION D

DIGITAL SOUND

Computers can record, store, and play back sounds, such as narrations, sound effects, and music. Swapping music files over the Internet is currently the most popular use of digital sound, but digital sound plays a key role in other very interesting applications.

How would you like to quit messing with your computer keyboard and enter commands and documents simply by speaking into a microphone? Would you like to add music and sound effects to your Web pages? Maybe you'd like to pull tracks from your audio CDs and remaster them into your own collection of favorite songs. This section of the chapter covers a wide-ranging selection of digital sound concepts and technologies that you're likely to find handy for personal and professional use.

WAVEFORM AUDIO

What is waveform audio? **Waveform audio** is a digital representation of sound. Music, voice, and sound effects can all be recorded as waveforms. To digitally record sound, samples of the sound are collected at periodic intervals and stored as numeric data. Figure 7-42 shows how a computer digitally samples a sound wave.

FIGURE 7-42
Sampling a Sound Wave

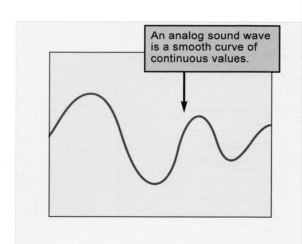

An analog sound wave is a smooth curve of continuous values.

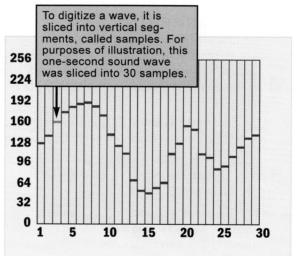

To digitize a wave, it is sliced into vertical segments, called samples. For purposes of illustration, this one-second sound wave was sliced into 30 samples.

Sample	Sample Height (Decimal)	Sample Height (Binary)
1	130	10000010
2	140	1000110
3	160	10100000
4	175	10101111
5	185	10111001

The height of each sample is converted into a binary number and stored. The height of sample 3 is 160 (decimal), so it is stored as its binary equivalent—10100000.

Does sampling rate affect sound quality? **Sampling rate** refers to the number of times per second that a sound is measured during the recording process. It is expressed in hertz (Hz). One thousand samples per second is expressed as 1,000 Hz or 1 KHz (kilohertz). Higher sampling rates increase the quality of the sound recording but require more storage space than lower sampling rates.

The height of each sample can be saved as an 8-bit number for radio-quality recordings or a 16-bit number for high-fidelity recordings. The audio CDs you buy at your favorite music store are recorded at a sampling rate of 44.1 KHz, which means a sample of the sound is taken 44,100 times per second. Sixteen bits are used for each sample. To achieve stereo effects, you must take two of these 16-bit samples. Therefore, each sample requires 32 bits of storage space. When you sample stereo CD-quality music at 44.1 KHz, you can store only eight seconds of music on a 1.44 MB floppy disk. Forty-five minutes of music—the length of a typical album—require about 475 MB.

To conserve space, applications that do not require such high-quality sound use much lower sampling rates. Voice is often recorded with a sampling rate of 11 KHz (11,000 samples per second). This rate results in lower quality sound, but the file is about one fourth the size of a file for the same sound recorded at 44.1 KHz. Figure 7-43 illustrates how sampling rate affects sound quality.

FIGURE 7-43

A higher sampling rate produces more true-to-life sound quality. Use your BookOnCD to compare the quality of these audio clips, which were digitized at different sampling rates.

CLICK TO START

CLICK TO START

CLICK TO START

How does a computer produce waveform audio? Your computer's sound card is responsible for transforming the bits stored in an audio file into music, sound effects, and narrations. A **sound card** is a device that contains a variety of input and output jacks, plus audio-processing circuitry. A desktop computer's sound card (Figure 7-44) is usually plugged into a PCI expansion slot inside the system unit. Alternatively, sound card circuitry might be built into the system board. Notebook computers rarely feature a separate sound card because manufacturers save space by incorporating sound circuitry into the system board.

FIGURE 7-44

A sound card that plugs into a slot in a desktop computer's system unit is standard equipment on many PCs.

A sound card is typically equipped to accept input from a microphone and send output to speakers or headphones. For processing waveform files, a sound card contains a special type of circuitry called a **digital signal processor**, which performs three important tasks. It transforms digital bits into analog waves when you play back a waveform audio file. It transforms analog waves into digital bits when you make a sound recording. It also handles compression and decompression, if necessary.

To play a digitally recorded sound, the bits from an audio file are transferred from disk to the microprocessor, which routes them to your computer's sound card. The digital signal processor handles any necessary decompression, and then transforms the data into analog wave signals. These signals are routed to the speakers and voilà! You have sound (Figure 7-45).

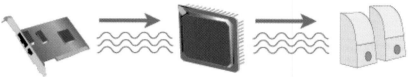

The sound card receives data from the microprocessor.

The sound card's digital signal processor decompresses data and converts it to analog signals.

The sound card sends analog signals to speakers.

FIGURE 7-45
Most sound cards use a digital signal processor to convert bits into an analog signal.

How can I recognize a waveform audio file? You can recognize a waveform audio file by looking at its file extension. Waveform audio can be stored in a variety of file formats. The table in Figure 7-46 provides an overview of the most popular waveform audio formats, including **AAC**, **AIFF**, **MP3**, **RealAudio**, **Wave**, and **WMA**.

FIGURE 7-46
Popular Waveform Audio File Formats

Audio Format	File Extension	Advantages	Disadvantages
AAC (Advanced Audio Compression)	.aac	Very good sound quality; compressed format, used on iTunes music download site	Files are copy protected and use is limited to approved devices
AIFF (Audio Interchange Format)	.aif	Excellent sound quality; supported in browsers without a plug-in	Audio data is stored in raw, uncompressed format, so files are very large
MP3 (also called MPEG-1 Layer 3)	.mp3	Good sound quality even though the file is compressed; can be streamed over the Web	Requires a standalone player or browser plug-in
RealAudio	.ra, rx	High degree of compression produces small files; data can be streamed over the Web	Sound quality is not up to the standards of other formats; requires a player or plug-in
Wave	.wav	Good sound quality; supported in browsers without a plug-in	Audio data is stored in raw, uncompressed format, so files are very large
WMA (Windows Media Audio)	.wma	Compressed format, very good sound quality; used on music download sites	Files can be copy protected; requires Windows Media Player 9 or above

What type of software is required to record and play waveform audio files? To play an audio file on your computer, you must use audio or media player software. Player software tends to support several audio file formats. In the Windows environment, for example, you can use Windows Media Player to play Wave, AIF, and MP3 formats. Some players, however, do not allow you to record audio data. For example, you cannot use Windows Media Player to record sound. For recording, you must use Microsoft Sound Recorder.

Software that plays and records various audio file formats might be included with your computer's operating system, packaged with your sound card, or available on the Web.

Can I add waveform audio files to my Web pages? Yes. Waveform files can be embedded into a Web page using an HTML tag, such as <embed src="daisy.wav"> or <bgsound src="imagine.wav">. Wave format files are supported by most Web browsers, so it is a popular audio file format. RealAudio, AIFF, and MP3 can also be delivered over the Web.

Web-based waveform audio is often delivered in streaming format to avoid lengthy delays while the entire audio file is downloaded. As with videos, waveform audio files can be streamed over the Internet so that they play as they are downloaded. Streaming audio provides the technology for real-time Internet radio broadcasts and voice chat sessions.

PORTABLE AUDIO PLAYERS

How can I listen to my digital music collection when I'm away from my computer? A **portable audio player** like the one in Figure 7-47 is a pocket-sized, battery-powered device that stores digital music. You can transfer a series of digital music tracks, called a "playlist," from your computer's hard disk to your portable audio player and you'll have a great collection of music wherever you go.

Where can I get digital music? Digital music is available from a wide variety of sources. At online music stores, such as iTunes Music Store, MusicMatch, Napster 2.0, MSN Music, and Walmart Music Downloads, individual songs can be downloaded for less than $1 each. The download price of an entire album is typically less than $10.

You can find free digital music, too. Famous performing artists and rock star wannabes post sample tracks from their CDs on Web sites. If fans like the music in these samples, they can purchase and download the entire song or CD.

You can also digitize music from your CD collection by using CD ripper software that converts CD-audio music into computer-friendly waveform audio format.

What are the most popular file formats for portable audio players? The first generation of online music was distributed in MP3 format. MP3 is a compressed waveform audio format that stores digitized music, vocals, and narrations in such a way that the sound quality is very good, but the file size remains relatively small—small enough to download from the Web. A CD track that requires 32 MB of storage space shrinks to approximately 3 MB in MP3 format.

Although MP3 remains a popular audio file format, newer standards offer better sound quality and compression. Apple is promoting the AAC format at its iTunes Music Store. Microsoft is promoting its WMA format at the Walmart Music Downloads site and at MSN Music.

TERMINOLOGY NOTE

Portable audio players are also called MP3 players and digital music players.

FIGURE 7-47
A Portable Audio Player

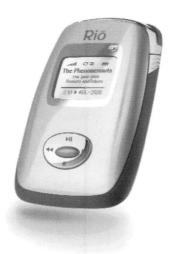

Can I play any digital music format on my portable audio player?
Some portable audio players support a variety of digital music formats,
whereas others support only one format. For example, Sony's first digital
audio Walkman supports only a proprietary ATRAC3plus format and
requires conversion for music downloaded in AAC or MP3 format. In contrast, Apple's iPod supports several digital music formats, including AAC.
MP3, WAV, and AIFF. When purchasing a portable audio player, you
should consider which music formats you are likely to use.

What's all the buzz about the iPod? Consumers demand convenience
and prefer not to purchase two devices when a single device meets their
needs. Market demand and technological innovation produce convergence, such as when PDAs gain Wi-Fi compatibility or when cell phones
feature digital cameras.

As an example of convergence, take a portable audio player, outfit it with a
screen, add a high capacity mini-hard disk, include personal organizer software, throw in a few games, and provide connections for an external
microphone and memory card reader. What you get is the Apple iPod
(Figure 7-48). Not only can you use it to store a huge collection of digital
music, you can use the hard disk drive as a portable mass storage device
for document, photo, and video files. You can use it as a voice recorder and
as a personal organizer for storing contacts and appointments. The iPod's
versatility has led at least one college to experiment with issuing them to all
incoming students.

MIDI MUSIC

What is MIDI music? Waveform audio is a digital version of a real analog
sound signal. In contrast, **synthesized sound** is an artificially created, or
synthetic, sound. Synthesized sound can be classified as MIDI music or
synthesized speech.

MIDI (Musical Instrument Digital Interface) specifies a standard way to
store music data for synthesizers, electronic MIDI instruments, and computers. Unlike waveform sound files, which contain digitized recordings of
real sound passages, MIDI files contain instructions for creating the pitch,
volume, and duration of notes that sound like various musical instruments.

MIDI is a music notation system that allows computers to communicate
with music synthesizers. The computer encodes the music as a **MIDI
sequence** and stores it as a file with a .mid, .cmf, or .rol file extension. A
MIDI sequence is analogous to a player-piano roll that contains punched
information indicating which musical notes to play. A MIDI sequence contains instructions specifying the pitch of a note, the point at which the note
begins, the instrument that plays the note, the volume of the note, and the
point at which the note ends.

Most computer sound cards are equipped to generate music from MIDI
files, and many can capture music data from a MIDI instrument as well. A
MIDI-capable sound card contains a **wavetable** (sometimes called a
"patch set"), which is a set of prerecorded musical instrument sounds. The
sound card accesses these sounds and plays them as instructed by the
MIDI file. For example, if a sound card receives a MIDI instruction for a
trumpet to play middle C, it accesses the trumpet's middle C patch and
routes it to the speaker until it receives a MIDI instruction to stop the note.

What are the advantages and disadvantages of MIDI? MIDI files are
much more compact than waveform audio files. Depending on the exact

INFOWEBLINKS

The **Portable Music InfoWeb**
is chock full of information on
where to download digital
music, how to rip tracks from
your CDs, and what you can
expect form the newest
portable audio players.

www.course.com/np/concepts8/ch07

FIGURE 7-48
Apple's iPod portable audio
player is also a handy mass
storage device.

piece of music, three minutes of MIDI music might require only 10 KB of storage space, whereas the same piece of music stored in a high-quality, uncompressed waveform file might require 15 MB of storage space.

One of the big disadvantages of MIDI is that it does not produce high-quality vocals. Another disadvantage is that it does not have the full resonance of "real" sound. Most musicians can easily identify MIDI recordings because they simply lack the tonal qualities of symphony-quality sound. You can compare the differences by using the Click to Start buttons in Figure 7-49.

FIGURE 7-49

MIDI music tends not to have the full resonance of waveform audio. Use your BookOnCD to listen to these two sound clips and see if you can tell the difference.

CLICK TO START

CLICK TO START

When would I use MIDI music? MIDI is a good choice for adding background music to multimedia projects and Web pages. Using a procedure similar to that for waveform audio files, you can add a link to a MIDI file by inserting a tag such as <embed src="sousa.mid"> within an HTML document. Most browsers include built-in support for MIDI music.

You can use music composition software to create your own snappy tunes or get permission to use MIDI files you find on the Web. For composing your own MIDI music, you can input notes from a MIDI instrument, such as an electronic keyboard, directly to your computer. The input is typically handled by music composition software (Figure 7-50), which you can also use to edit notes and combine the parts for several instruments.

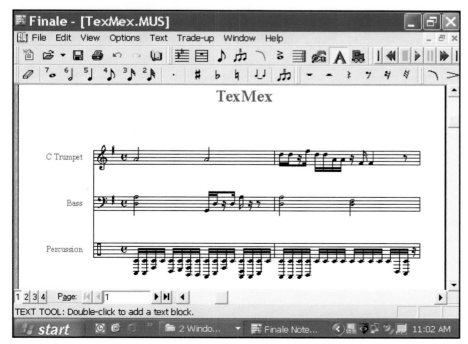

FIGURE 7-50

Music composition software provides tools for entering notes, specifying instruments, printing sheet music, and saving compositions in formats such as MIDI.

CLICK TO START

SPEECH RECOGNITION AND SYNTHESIS

What's the difference between speech synthesis and speech recognition? **Speech synthesis** is the process by which machines, such as computers, produce sound that resembles spoken words. **Speech recognition** (or "voice recognition") refers to the ability of a machine to "understand" spoken words.

If you've dialed information lately to obtain a telephone number, you've probably encountered speech recognition and speech synthesis. An automated operator asks you to speak the name of the person whose telephone number you seek. The name you speak is collected by a speech recognition unit, which attempts to spell out the name and then look for it in a database. If it locates the name and telephone number, a synthesized voice "speaks" the telephone number.

How does speech synthesis work? Most speech synthesizers string together basic sound units called **phonemes**. For example, the phonemes "reh" and "gay" produce the word "reggae." A basic speech synthesizer consists of **text-to-speech software**, which generates sounds that are played through your computer's standard sound card. As an alternative, some speech synthesizers are special-purpose hardware devices.

Speech synthesis is a key technology in wireless communication, such as accessing your e-mail via cell phone—a speech synthesizer "reads" your e-mail messages to you. A speech synthesizer can also read a computer screen aloud, which unlocks access to computers and the Internet for individuals with visual disabilities.

How does speech recognition work? On a personal computer, a speech recognition system typically collects words spoken into a microphone that's attached to the sound card. The sound card's digital signal processor transforms the analog sound of your voice into digital data. This data is then processed by speech recognition software.

Speech recognition software analyzes the sounds of your voice and converts them to phonemes. Next, the software analyzes the content of your speech. It compares the groups of phonemes to the words in a digital dictionary that lists phoneme combinations along with their corresponding English (or French, Spanish, and so on) words. When a match is found, the software displays the correctly spelled word on the screen.

Speech recognition software can be integrated with word processing software so that you can enter text simply by speaking into a microphone. Going beyond word processing, speech recognition can be used to activate Windows controls instead of using a mouse. Most speech recognition software also works with your browser, allowing you to "voice surf" the Web.

Microsoft Office includes speech recognition software you can activate by using the Speech icon in Control Panel. The first step in using Microsoft speech recognition is training the computer to recognize your speaking style—your accent, pronunciation, and idiomatic expressions. Training consists of reading a series of short text passages into a microphone attached to your computer. Figure 7-51 lists tips for successful voice recognition training.

FIGURE 7-51
Tips for Voice Recognition Training

■ Speak at a consistent volume.

■ Speak at a steady pace, without speeding up and slowing down.

■ Speak naturally, without exaggerated pauses between words or syllables.

■ Work in a quiet environment so that the computer hears your voice instead of the sounds around you.

■ Use a good quality microphone and keep it in the same position.

You can train your computer by using the Voice Training Wizard, which displays paragraphs of text, waits for you to read them, and creates your personal speech profile (Figure 7-52).

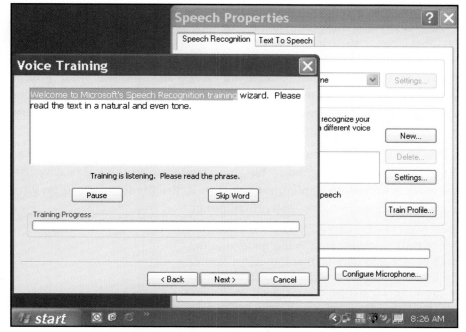

When training is complete, you can use Microsoft speech recognition to verbally issue commands in Windows and dictate text in Microsoft Word and Excel, plus any other Windows applications designed to support this feature.

QUICKCHECK......SECTION D

1. [   ] music is primarily designed for instrumental sounds, whereas [   ] audio can deal with vocals, music, and narrations.

2. The number of times per second that a sound wave is measured is referred to as the [   ] rate.

3. The most popular waveform audio formats for music downloads are MP3, WMA, and [   ]. (Hint: Use the abbreviation.)

4. You can transfer a series of digital music tracks, called a [   ], from your computer's hard disk to your portable audio player, and you'll have a great collection of music wherever you go.

5. Speech [   ] software translates spoken words into text that appears on a computer screen or is stored in a file.

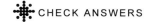 CHECK ANSWERS

TECHTALK
DATA COMPRESSION

As you learned throughout this chapter, digital media files can be quite large. For example, one second of video requires 56 MB of storage space; a 1024 x 768 True Color bitmap graphic requires 2.3 MB; and a 45-minute waveform audio file might be as large as 475 MB. Large files need lots of storage space, require lengthy transmission times, and easily become fragmented, thereby reducing the efficiency of your computer's hard disk drive.

If you could reduce the size of a file without losing any of its data, you would be able to minimize these problems. This TechTalk is designed to help you understand the basic way that compression algorithms work and how to apply compression to the files you store on your computer, post on Web sites, and transmit as e-mail attachments.

What is data compression? **Data compression** is the general term used to describe the process of recoding data so that it requires fewer bytes of storage space. The process is similar in concept to condensing and reconstituting orange juice. To condense orange juice, water is removed. To compress a file, bytes are removed, which reduces the file size. Data compression is reversible. Just as water can be added to reconstitute orange juice, bytes previously removed from a file can be restored so that the data is returned to its original form (Figure 7-53). The process of reversing data compression is sometimes referred to as uncompressing, decompressing, extracting, or expanding a file.

FIGURE 7-53
Compression reduces the number of bytes in a file.

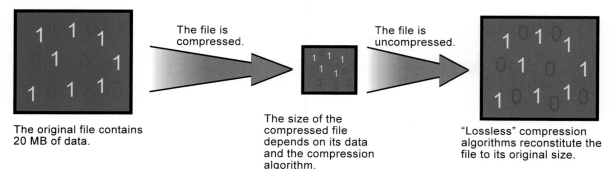

The original file contains 20 MB of data.

The file is compressed.

The size of the compressed file depends on its data and the compression algorithm.

The file is uncompressed.

"Lossless" compression algorithms reconstitute the file to its original size.

When data is compressed, the size of the file that holds the data shrinks. The amount of shrinkage is referred to as the **compression ratio**. A compression ratio of 20:1, for example, means that a compressed file is 20 times smaller than the original file. The advantages of compressed files are that they can often fit on a single removable disk, and they take less time to upload or e-mail. The disadvantage of compressed files is that you might be required to manually uncompress them before using them.

Data compression is based on a **compression algorithm**—the steps that are required to shrink the data in a file and reconstitute the file to its original state. Many compression algorithms, such as Huffman, Lempel-Ziv Welch, and Shannon-Fano, are named after their inventors. As you learned earlier in this chapter, a compression algorithm is incorporated into a codec, which a computer uses to compress and decompress file data.

How do compression algorithms work? Some compression algorithms are designed to shrink text files; other algorithms are for graphics, sound, or video data. Some compression algorithms are generalized and work for any type of data. Although most of today's codecs contain sophisticated compression algorithms beyond the scope of this book, you can look at some examples of simple compression algorithms to get a general idea of how they work.

Dictionary-based compression replaces common sequences of characters with a single codeword, or symbol, which points to a dictionary of the original characters or to the original occurrence of the word. Figure 7-54 illustrates how this type of compression might work on a short text sample.

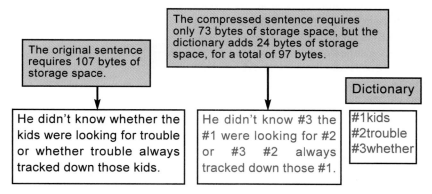

The compressed sentence requires only 73 bytes of storage space, but the dictionary adds 24 bytes of storage space, for a total of 97 bytes.

The original sentence requires 107 bytes of storage space.

| He didn't know whether the kids were looking for trouble or whether trouble always tracked down those kids. | He didn't know #3 the #1 were looking for #2 or #3 #2 always tracked down those #1. | **Dictionary** #1kids #2trouble #3whether |

FIGURE 7-54
Dictionary-based Text Compression

Statistical compression, such as the well-known Huffman algorithm, takes advantage of the frequency of characters to reduce the file size. Characters that appear frequently are recoded as short bit patterns, and those that appear infrequently are assigned longer bit patterns.

For example, in the word "passages," the letter "s" appears with the most frequency. It is used for three of the eight characters—a probability of .375 (3 divided by 8). The letter "a" appears twice—a probability of .25. The letters "p," "g," and "e" each appear once, so each has a probability of .125. To compress this word, you can replace the ASCII codes for each letter with new shorter codes. The letters that appear most frequently have the shortest codes. After compression, the original word, which required 64 bits, requires only 18 bits. Figure 7-55 illustrates.

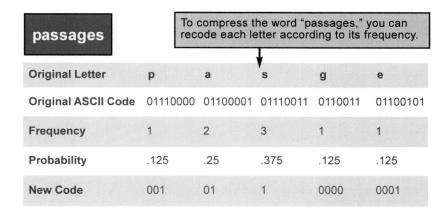

passages

To compress the word "passages," you can recode each letter according to its frequency.

Original Letter	p	a	s	g	e
Original ASCII Code	01110000	01100001	01110011	0110011	01100101
Frequency	1	2	3	1	1
Probability	.125	.25	.375	.125	.125
New Code	001	01	1	0000	0001

FIGURE 7-55
Statistical Text Compression

0111000001100001011100110111001101100001011001110110010101110011

The original ASCII code for "passages" was 64 bits.

001011101000000011

The compressed code is only 18 bits.

In the two examples of text compression described on the previous page, file size is reduced without any data loss. This **lossless compression** provides the means to compress a file and then reconstitute all the data into its original state. TIFF, PCX, and GIF graphics formats also use lossless compression. In contrast, **lossy compression** "throws away" some of the original data during the compression process. Lossy compression can be applied to graphics, videos, and sounds because, in theory, the human eye or ear won't miss the lost information. JPEG, MP3, and MPEG file formats use lossy compression. Most lossy compression techniques have adjustable compression levels so that you can decide how much data you can afford to lose.

Spatial compression takes advantage of redundant data in a file by looking for patterns of bytes and replacing them with a message that describes the pattern. **Run-length encoding** (RLE) is an example of a lossless spatial compression technique that replaces a series of similarly colored pixels with a code that indicates the number of pixels and their colors. As a simple example, suppose that a section of a picture has 167 consecutive white pixels, and each pixel is described by one byte of data, as in a 256-color bitmap image. An RLE codec compresses this series of 167 bytes into as few as two bytes, as shown in Figure 7-56.

FIGURE 7-56

In an uncompressed file, each pixel of a 256-color bitmap requires one byte to indicate its color. For example, a white pixel might be coded 11111111. Run-length encoding compresses graphical data by recoding like-colored pixels when they appear in a series.

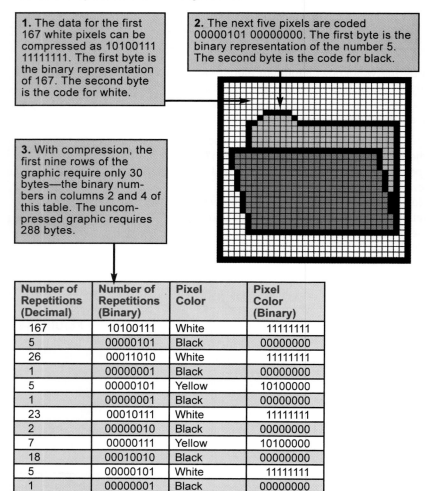

1. The data for the first 167 white pixels can be compressed as 10100111 11111111. The first byte is the binary representation of 167. The second byte is the code for white.

2. The next five pixels are coded 00000101 00000000. The first byte is the binary representation of the number 5. The second byte is the code for black.

3. With compression, the first nine rows of the graphic require only 30 bytes—the binary numbers in columns 2 and 4 of this table. The uncompressed graphic requires 288 bytes.

Number of Repetitions (Decimal)	Number of Repetitions (Binary)	Pixel Color	Pixel Color (Binary)
167	10100111	White	11111111
5	00000101	Black	00000000
26	00011010	White	11111111
1	00000001	Black	00000000
5	00000101	Yellow	10100000
1	00000001	Black	00000000
23	00010111	White	11111111
2	00000010	Black	00000000
7	00000111	Yellow	10100000
18	00010010	Black	00000000
5	00000101	White	11111111
1	00000001	Black	00000000
25	00011001	Yellow	10100000
1	00000001	White	11111111
1	00000001	Black	00000000

JPEG is a lossy version of run-length encoding that can be applied to images, such as photographs, that don't have large areas of solid color. A True Color photograph might not have any adjoining pixels of the same color. Applying RLE to such a photo would not result in any compression whatsoever. JPEG "preprocesses" an image by tweaking the colors in adjoining pixels so that they are the same color whenever possible. After this preprocessing is complete, run-length encoding techniques can be applied with more success. Figure 7-57 illustrates a section of a noncompressed image and a section of that same image after JPEG compression has been applied.

FIGURE 7-57

JPEG compression can slightly adjust the colors of adjacent pixels to make them the same. These like-colored pixels can then be compressed with RLE.

What about compressing sound and video files? **Temporal compression** is a technique that can be applied to video footage or sound clips to eliminate redundant or unnecessary data between video frames or audio samples. For example, if you are working with a video of a "talking head," the background image is likely to contain lots of redundant information that doesn't change from one frame to the next.

Non-compressed JPEG image

JPEG image with 35% compression

As the temporal compression algorithm begins to analyze frames, the first frame becomes a **key frame** that contains all the data. Key frames are stored at preset intervals or whenever a cut, wipe, or transition changes the scene. As the compression algorithm analyzes subsequent frames in the video, it stores only the data that is different from data in the key frame. If the image data from all frames is maintained, the compression is lossless. If slight changes between frames are eliminated, the compression is lossy. MPEG uses temporal and spatial compression algorithms, both of which are lossy. As a result, videos compressed with MPEG codecs have some image quality degradation.

Can I compress any kind of file? Some file formats automatically compress file data. Other formats allow you to select whether you want to compress the file and specify a level of compression. PCX, GIF, and MP3 files are always compressed. The software you use to save and open these files contains the codecs necessary to compress and decompress them. Codecs for JPEG, MPEG, AVI, DivX, and QuickTime files typically allow you to select compression levels before saving a graphics or video file. Some TIFF files are compressed, but others are not—it depends on the software used to store the file.

Most files that contain documents and databases are not stored in compressed format. BMP and Wave files are also stored as "raw," noncompressed bits. If you want to compress these files before sending them as e-mail attachments, for example, you can do so manually. BMP and DOC file sizes might shrink by as much as 70%. Other noncompressed file formats, such as Wave, might compress by about 20%. File formats such as GIF, MP3, MPEG, and JPEG hardly shrink at all when you zip them because they are already stored in a compressed format.

How do I manually compress files? To manually compress a file, such as a Word document or a Windows bitmap image, you can work with a **file compression utility**, which uses lossless compression to shrink one or more files into a single new file. PKZIP and WinZip are popular shareware programs that compress and decompress files. You can zip any kind of file, including program or data files. You cannot use a compressed file until it has been decompressed.

Compressing a file is sometimes called "zipping," and decompressing a file is sometimes called "unzipping." Technically, however, zipping not only compresses files, but can also combine several files into a single compressed file that can be unzipped into the original separate files.

For example, suppose you want to send three files to your boss. The original files are called Technology.xls, Award.doc, and Insurance.mdb. You can zip all three files into a single compressed file called Report.zip (Figure 7-58). Simply attach this one file to an e-mail and send it to your boss. When Report.zip is unzipped, it produces the three original files.

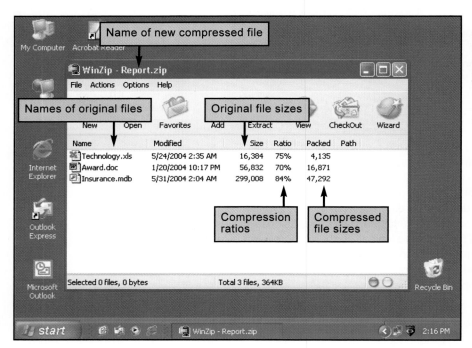

FIGURE 7-58

Popular file compression utilities, such as WinZip, zip one or more files into a new compressed file with a .zip extension.

CLICK TO START

Zipping can come in handy when you want to send several files as an e-mail attachment. It works particularly well for bitmap graphics and documents because they contain raw, uncompressed data. Remember, however, that JPEG graphics are already compressed and do not shrink significantly if you zip them.

Windows XP includes a built-in compression feature that allows you to create compressed folders. Any files that you drag into a compressed folder are automatically compressed. Compressed folders are fairly easy to use. You don't have to do anything special to open a file from a compressed folder. Simply double-click the file as usual, and Windows automatically decompresses the file before displaying its contents.

When you create a compressed folder, Windows automatically adds a .zip extension to the folder name. In this way, the folder is treated like a zipped file by other compression utilities, such as PKZIP and WinZip. So if you want to e-mail several bitmap graphics, for example, you can save them as usual in BMP format. Next, create a compressed folder called Photos (Figure 7-59). Windows automatically adds a .zip extension to the folder name. Drag the three bitmaps into the Photos folder. Attach the Photos folder to your e-mail message. The attachment will be named Photos.zip. The recipient of your e-mail can open the attachment by using Windows or a file compression utility.

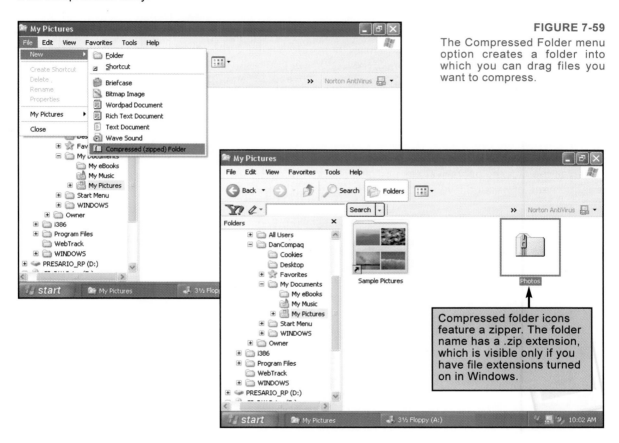

FIGURE 7-59

The Compressed Folder menu option creates a folder into which you can drag files you want to compress.

Compressed folder icons feature a zipper. The folder name has a .zip extension, which is visible only if you have file extensions turned on in Windows.

QUICKCHECK........TECHTALK

1. A compression [ ] is a measurement of the amount of shrinkage—the original file size compared to the compressed file size.

2. A compression [ ] is the steps required to shrink the data in a file and reconstitute the file back to its original state.

3. Dictionary-based and statistical text compression are examples of [ ] compression, which loses no data during the compression process.

4. JPEG is an example of [ ] compression, in which data is eliminated during the compression process.

 CHECK ANSWERS

ISSUE

DIGITAL RIGHTS MANAGEMENT

Suppose you purchase a music CD of your favorite recording group. Now you want to transfer the file to your computer, rip the best tracks, and transfer them to your portable audio player. But wait! That CD is copy protected and your computer CD drive won't read it. You purchased the disk. Can't you listen to the music on any device you choose? The answer is "yes" and "no." Yes, copyright law gives you the right to make copies for your personal use and transfer works into a format that works on your equipment. However, the growing pervasiveness of digital rights management may curtail your ability to exercise these rights.

It is easy to copy digital material. Before the dawn of the digital age, copies produced by analog equipment, such as photocopiers and audio tape dubbing machines, were of considerably poorer quality than the originals. Copies of digital materials, however, are indistinguishable from the originals, and that factor has encouraged an alarming increase in software, music, and movie piracy.

Piracy made world headlines in a dispute about sharing music on Napster. In 1999, an 18-year-old student named Shawn Fanning developed a Web-based technology for sharing MP3 music files. This technology, dubbed "Napster" after Shawn's nickname, quickly became one of the hottest applications on the Internet. In less than a year, its user base exceeded 25 million. Many of these music lovers downloaded hundreds of songs without paying for any of them.

Almost immediately, Napster ran afoul of the Recording Industry Association of America (RIAA), a watchdog organization that represents record companies, such as Columbia Records, Motown Records, and Epic Nashville. The RIAA compiled a list of 12,000 copyrighted songs that Napster technology made available as free downloads.

The RIAA filed suit, accusing Napster of contributing to copyright infringement, which considerably reduced the revenues of record companies and artists. The ensuing court battle stirred up a caldron of issues that relate to the use and abuse of digital media, including music, photos, and videos. After shutting down Napster's free download network, music piracy continued unabated. The RIAA then initiated a series of lawsuits targeting individuals who allegedly maintained large collections of pirated music.

The Napster experience hardened the resolve of digital stakeholders to stop illegal copying. The battle against piracy took shape as a concept called digital rights management (DRM), vigorously supported by Microsoft and backed by a host of industry leaders.

Today, digital rights management encompasses a variety of technologies implemented by copyright holders, such as record companies and software publishers, which restrict the usage of digital material. DRM systems address piracy by using a variety of technologies for manipulating data, media, devices, and transactions.

Software copy protection techniques include reading data written to places on a disk or CD-ROM that the drive cannot normally access, using hardware that must be plugged into the computer when the software is run, requiring a serial number during the installation process, and using Internet product activation that checks the validity of an installation. Most software copy protection schemes have proved to be costly for publishers or inconvenient for consumers.

Cable television has a long history of signal scrambling and encryption to prevent piracy. Consumers seem to tolerate this form of DRM because once the signal arrives, it is descrambled and can be archived to TiVo or video tape just as any broadcast television program.

Many consumers are not aware that they pay a surcharge for every blank audio tape or CD they purchase. Collected revenues from this surcharge go to music publishers to compensate recording artists for the fact that many people duplicate works without authorization.

Most of today's music download sites encrypt music files and embed codes that limit the number of times they can be copied and the devices on which they can be played. Apple's FairPlay DRM system is used on the iTunes Music Store, Microsoft's DRM-enabled Windows Media Player 9 is used on Walmart's Music Download site, and RealNetworks secure RealAudio (.rax) format protects files downloaded from the RealPlayer Music Store. These formats are not compatible with each other and require different players. Music from several different download sites cannot be compiled into a single playlist.

It is becoming more common for music CDs to use play-protection technology designed to make the CD unusable in devices, such as computer CD-R drives, that can also be conveniently used for duplicating CDs. Consumers who purchase these protected CDs find that they cannot be copied to a computer hard disk, then ripped to produce an MP3 file for a portable audio player.

Commercial movie DVDs use CSS (Content-Scrambling System) encryption to make DVDs playable only on authorized DVD players equipped with decryption key circuitry. Movies purchased in the United States and Canada cannot be played on devices manufactured for the European or Asian markets, so continent-jumping travelers and expatriates have to take along their DVD players or abandon their DVD collections.

Despite DRM technologies and the inconveniences imposed on consumers, digital piracy remains rampant. According to an article about digital rights management posted on Wikipedia, "To date, all DRM systems have failed to meet the challenge of protecting the rights of the rights holder while also allowing the use of the rights of the purchaser. None have succeeded in preventing criminal copyright infringement by organized, unlicensed, commercial pirates."

Current DRM technologies do not seem able to distinguish between pirates and legitimate consumers. As a result, DRM technologies essentially pose restrictions on consumers that go beyond the intended limitations of copyright law.

Circumventing DRM is possible and it would seem OK to do so for legitimate reasons, such as making a backup copy. However, the Digital Millennium Copyright Act, makes it illegal to circumvent any technological measure that controls access to a work.

The current status of DRM seems to conflict with the original intent of copyright law to allow consumers to manipulate and copy works for their own use. Can technology eventually offer a solution that prevents piracy, but allows individuals to exercise their rights to fair use of copyrighted materials?

INFOWEBLINKS

You'll find information related to this controversy at the **Digital Rights Management InfoWeb**.

www.course.com/np/concepts8/ch07

WHAT DO YOU THINK?

1. Have you had trouble using software, music CDs, or movie DVDs because of copy protection?   ◯ Yes   ◯ No   ◯ Not sure

2. In your opinion, do sites like the iTunes Music Store provide consumers with enough flexibility for copying files and creating playlists?   ◯ Yes   ◯ No   ◯ Not sure

3. Do you think digital rights management technologies are justified because of the high rate of piracy?   ◯ Yes   ◯ No   ◯ Not sure

 SAVE RESPONSES

COMPUTERS IN CONTEXT

FILM

In 1895, eager Parisians crowded into a busy café to watch the first public presentation of an exciting new invention—the Cinematograph. The 10-minute film, mostly scenes of everyday life, was a smashing success and ushered in the motion picture era. Early films were short, grainy, grayscale, and silent, but technology quickly improved. In the New York debut of *The Jazz Singer* (1927), Al Jolson spoke the first words in a feature film, "Wait a minute, wait a minute. You ain't heard nothin' yet!" The audience rose to its feet, applauding wildly. In 1935, RKO studios released *Becky Sharp*, the first feature-length movie filmed from beginning to end in Technicolor—a real milestone for the film industry.

Even before "talkies" and Technicolor, filmmakers sought ways to escape the bounds of reality through special effects. As early as 1925, directors such as Willis O'Brien used stop-motion photography to animate dinosaurs, giant gorillas, and sword-wielding skeletons. Special-effects technologies—miniatures, blue screens, puppets, claymation, and composite shots—were used with varying degrees of skill over the next 50 years. Films such as Stanley Kubrick's masterpiece, *2001: A Space Odyssey* (1968), and George Lucas's original *Star Wars* (1977) stretched these technologies to their limits, but audiences demanded even more spectacular, yet "realistic," effects.

In 1982, Disney released *TRON*, a movie about a computer programmer who becomes trapped in the depths of a computer where programs are human-like creatures at the whim of an evil Master Control Program. The movie included the first primitive attempts at computer-generated footage—30 minutes of computer-generated imagery (CGI) created by two Cray XMP supercomputers.

CGI uses rendering techniques to create a 3-D scene from a 2-D image, a camera angle, and a light source. Sophisticated algorithms determine how textures, colors, and shadows appear in the rendered scene. Camera angles can be changed at will, and fantastic effects can be created by bending or stretching the image, manipulating light, creating textures, and adding movement to the scene.

Rendered scenes can be set in motion with computer animation techniques. Manual animation requires a painstaking process called "in-betweening," in which an artist draws a series of incrementally different images to produce the illusion of movement. Computers can easily generate in-between images and free up human animators for more challenging work.

A captivating animation special effect called morphing was first seen on the big screen in James Cameron's *Abyss* (1989) and later used in *Terminator 2* (1991) and other movies. Like in-betweening, morphing starts out with animators defining the morph's start and end points—for example, in *Terminator 2*, the liquid metal face of the T-1000 robot and actor Robert Patrick's face. The start and end points are rendered into digital images, and then the computer generates all the in-between images. Human animators tweak the images by inserting small discrepancies for a touch of less-than-perfect realism in the final image.

Although the process might sound simple, morphing complex objects realistically and believably takes a tremendous amount of time and computer power. The five-minute morphing sequence in *Terminator 2* took special-effects company Industrial Light and Magic a year to create.

Memorable computer-generated scenes from 2002 blockbusters include the breathtaking aerial scenes in *Spiderman*, a furry blue monster called Sully careening downhill in *Monsters, Inc.*, and the endless army of Uruk-hai marching down the valley toward Helm's Deep in *The Two Towers*. Spiderman's acrobatic swing through Manhattan was generated with three professional rendering products: Maya, Houdini, and RenderMan. The Uruk-hai were created with MASSIVE, a custom program that gave each computer-generated warrior a unique sequence of actions. To individually animate each of Sully's 2,320,413 blue hairs, animators developed software called Fizt, a dynamic simulator.

Rendering, morphing, and other special-effects processing require sophisticated computer systems. Pixar Inc., the company that provided the technology behind *Toy Story*, *Shrek 2*, *Monsters, Inc.*, and many other feature-length animated films, uses a cluster of computers dubbed the "RenderFarm." Consisting of more than 100 Sun SPARCstation computers, the network can process 16 billion instructions per second. A movie such as *Toy Story* took more than 800,000 computer hours to produce using the RenderFarm. That might seem like a long time, but if Pixar animators had attempted to use a single-processor computer, it would have taken 43 years to finish the job!

Other CGI variations are being used for increasingly sophisticated effects. Special-effects guru John Gaeta developed bullet time and image-based rendering for *The Matrix* (1999). It has been used for stunning visual effects in movies such as *The Matrix: Reloaded* (2003), *The Matrix: Revolutions* (2003),

and *Hero* (2002/2004). Bullet time produces reality-defying action sequences that slow time to a tantalizing crawl and then crank it back up to normal speed as the camera pivots rapidly around the scene. The effect requires a computer to meticulously trigger a circular array of more than 100 still cameras in sequence. Image-based rendering generates a digital image based on photos of objects, scenes, or people. The 2-D photos can be digitally manipulated to create 3-D objects, eliminating the need for conventional CGI's computationally intensive 3-D wireframes and ray tracing. Neo battles hundreds of Agent Smiths in a world created by image-based rendering.

Sophisticated animation and rendering techniques now come close to producing realistic human figures. Animations were once clearly two-dimensional and far from lifelike, but CGI renderings are becoming more difficult to distinguish from real actors. What might happen in the future is the subject of *Simone* (2002), starring Al Pacino as a washed-up director who is given a hard disk containing code for a computer-generated movie star. Pacino uses her as the leading lady in a string of hits, all the while keeping her identity secret. According to reviewer Leigh Johnson, it becomes clear that Simone, a computer-generated image, is more authentic than the people watching her. It is one of the film's main themes, expressed by Pacino's character: "Our ability to manufacture fraud now exceeds our ability to detect it."

The implications of computer-generated actors are just emerging. Not only do they blur the line between reality and fiction, but they also raise puzzling questions for actors and their agents, directors, and programmers. Is it possible to create CGI doubles for long-dead actors, such as Marilyn Monroe and James Dean? If so, who controls their use and profits from their work? Can aging actors sign contracts for use of their "young" CGI counterparts? Would it be legal and ethical for programmers to create and market virtual characters based on real actors or a compilation of the best traits of popular stars? As is often the case, new technologies present issues along with their benefits—issues you might want to consider the next time you watch a movie.

INFOWEBLINKS

To find more information on this topic, visit the **Computers and Film InfoWeb**.

www.course.com/np/concepts8/ch07

INTERACTIVE SUMMARY

To review important concepts from this chapter, fill in the blanks to best complete each sentence. When using the NP8 BookOnCD, click the Check Answers buttons to automatically score your answers. Place your Tracking Disk in the floppy disk drive if you want to save your scores.

A [_____] graphic is composed of a grid of dots, and the color of each dot is stored as a binary number. Both scanners and cameras produce images in bitmap format. The [_____] of the grid that forms a bitmap graphic is referred to as its resolution. High-resolution graphics typically produce better image quality than low-resolution graphics, but require more storage space. It is possible to change the resolution and/or the file size of a bitmap graphic, but because bitmaps are resolution [_____], these changes can reduce image quality. For example, enlarging a bitmap requires your computer to fill in missing pixels, which often results in a jagged or [_____] image. As a rule of thumb, images that you intend to print should remain at full size and resolution. When sending bitmap files as e-mail attachments, they can be [_____]

in size or resolution to produce a file that is less than 500 KB.

Color [_____] refers to the number of colors available for use in an image. For example, a bitmap graphic composed of 256 colors requires only [_____] bits to store the data for each pixel, whereas 24 bits are required for each pixel in a [_____] Color graphic. Grayscale, system, and Web palettes use eight bits to represent each pixel. If a palette does not contain the right selection of colors, an image can be [_____] using scattered or patterned techniques. Popular bitmap graphics formats include BMP, PCX, TIFF, GIF, JPEG, and PNG. Of these formats, GIF, JPEG, and PNG are supported by most Web browsers.

❖ CHECK ANSWERS

Unlike a bitmap graphic, created by superimposing a grid of pixels over an image, a [_____] graphic consists of a set of instructions for creating a picture. These graphics are created by using a type of graphics software called [_____] software. They are stored as a collection of [_____] and their corresponding sizes, colors, and positions. You can identify these graphics by their flat cartoon-like appearance and their file extensions: .wmf, .dxt, .mgx, .eps, .pict, and .cgm.

A vector graphic can be converted into a bitmap by a process called [_____]. Once converted, however, the resulting graphic loses the object-editing qualities it had in its vector state. In contrast, changing a bitmap image to a vector graphic is not easy. It requires the help of [_____] software, which works best on simple line drawings. Vector

graphics have not been popular on the Web because they have not been supported by browsers. Two vector graphics formats, [_____] and Flash, are gaining popularity, despite the fact that they require browser plug-ins or players.

3-D graphics are stored as a set of instructions that contain the locations and lengths of lines that form a [_____] for a 3-D object. These lines form a framework that can be covered by colored, patterned, and textured surfaces. This process, called [_____], produces a bitmap image of the 3-D object. [_____] tracing adds highlights and shadows to the image. 3-D graphics can be animated to produce special effects for movies and animated characters for 3-D computer games.

❖ CHECK ANSWERS

Whereas animated 3-D graphics are created from scratch by an artist, digital video is usually based on footage of real objects, filmed and then stored as bits. Videos that are constructed and played on a personal computer are called [_____] videos. Video footage is typically stored on a computer's [_____] disk for editing, and then it can be transferred to CDs, DVDs, or videotape.

A video is composed of a series of bitmap graphics. Each one is called a [_____]. Popular desktop video file [_____] include AVI, QuickTime, MPEG, RealMedia, WMV, and VOB. When video footage is filmed using an analog camera, it can be converted into digital format by a video [_____] device. Footage from a digital video camera requires no conversion and can be streamed directly from camera to computer through a [_____] or USB port. After video footage has been stored on a [_____]-access device, such as a hard disk, it can be easily edited.

Raw video footage contains a huge amount of data. The size of a video file can be reduced by three techniques: shrinking the size of the video window, reducing the [_____] rate, and [_____] the video data. A [_____] is the software or hardware that compresses and decompresses files, such as graphics and videos. Videos can be added to Web pages by using techniques such as [_____] video, which transmits the first segment of a video, begins to play it, and then continues to transfer additional segments. Digital videos can be transferred to DVDs, which use files in the [_____] format.

CHECK ANSWERS

Music, voice, and sound effects can all be recorded and digitally stored as [_____] audio. To digitally record sound, [_____] of the sound are collected at periodic intervals and stored as numeric data. High-quality sound is usually sampled at 44.1 [_____], and each stereo sample requires 32 bits of storage space. To conserve space, radio-quality recordings of speaking voices are often recorded at lower sampling rates.

A computer's [_____] card is responsible for transforming the bits stored in an audio file into music, sound effects, and narrations. It contains digital [_____] processing circuitry that transforms bits into analog sound, records analog sounds as digital bits, and handles audio compression. Waveform audio file formats include Wave, Audio Interchange Format, RealAudio, AAC, WMA, and MP3. Most portable audio players work with waveform formats, such as [_____], used by the iTunes Music Store.

MIDI music is [_____] sound that is artificially created. Unlike waveform sound files, which contain digitized recordings of real sound passages, MIDI files contain [_____] for creating the pitch, volume, and duration of notes made by musical instruments. MIDI files are typically much smaller than waveform audio files for similar musical passages, so they are ideal for Web pages. However, MIDI music tends to lack the full resonance of symphony-quality sound that can be achieved with waveform audio.

Speech [_____] is the process by which machines, such as computers, produce sound that resembles spoken words. Speech [_____] refers to the ability of machines to "understand" spoken words.

CHECK ANSWERS

INTERACTIVE KEY TERMS

Make sure you understand all the boldfaced key terms presented in this chapter. If you're using the NP8 BookOnCD, you can use this list of terms as an interactive study activity. First, try to define a term in your own words, and then click the term to compare your definition with the definition presented in the chapter.

24-bit bitmap, 351
32-bit bitmap, 351
3-D graphics, 362
AAC, 378
AIFF, 378
Analog video camera, 366
AVI, 371
Bitmap graphic, 344
BMP, 353
Codec, 372
Color depth, 350
Color palette, 351
Compression algorithm, 384
Compression ratio, 384
Cropping, 349
Data compression, 384
Desktop video, 365
Dictionary-based compression, 385
Digital camera, 345
Digital signal processor, 378
Digital video, 365
Digital video camera, 366
Digitizing tablet, 358
Dithering, 352
Drawing software, 358
DVD video , 365
File compression utility, 388
Flash, 361
Floppy disk adapter, 346
Frame rate, 369
GIF, 354
Gradient, 360

Grayscale palette, 352
JPEG, 353
Key frame, 387
Linear editing, 370
Lossless compression, 386
Lossy compression, 386
Megapixels, 347
Metafiles, 360
MIDI, 380
MIDI sequence, 380
Monochrome bitmap, 350
MP3, 378
MPEG, 371
Nonlinear editing, 370
Paint software, 344
PCX, 353
PDA video, 365
Phonemes, 382
Pixel interpolation, 349
Pixelated, 349
PNG, 354
Portable audio player, 379
QuickTime, 371
Rasterization, 360
Ray tracing, 362
RealAudio, 378
RealMedia, 371
Rendering, 362
Resolution dependent, 349
Run-length encoding, 386
Sampling rate, 377
Scanner, 345

Sound card, 377
Spatial compression, 386
Speech recognition, 382
Speech recognition software, 382
Speech synthesis, 382
Statistical compression, 385
Streaming video, 372
SVG, 361
Synthesized sound, 380
System palette, 352
Temporal compression, 387
Text-to-speech software, 382
TIFF, 353
Tracing software, 360
True Color bitmap, 351
Vector graphic, 356
Video capture, 367
Video capture software, 368
Videoconferencing camera, 366
VOB, 371
Wave, 378
Waveform audio, 376
Wavetable, 380
Web-based video, 365
Web palette, 352
Wireframe, 362
WMA, 378
WMV, 371

INTERACTIVE SITUATION QUESTIONS

Apply what you've learned to some typical computing situations. When using the NP8 BookOnCD, you can type your answers, and then use the Check Answers button to automatically score your responses. Place your Tracking Disk in the floppy disk drive if you want to save your scores.

1. You have an old photograph that you want to incorporate in a brochure for your antiques business. To convert the photo into digital format, you use a(n) _____.

2. Suppose you receive a bitmap image from one of your friends, but it seems curiously "blocky" or pixelated. Either this image was captured using a very low-resolution camera, or the size of the image was _____.

3. Imagine that you are preparing a series of bitmap graphics for a Web site. To decrease the download time for each graphic, you can remove pixels or reduce the color _____.

4. Suppose you are designing a logo for a client. You know the design will undergo several revisions, and you understand that the logo will be used at various sizes. You decide it would be best to use drawing software to create the logo as a(n) _____ graphic.

5. What if you created a diagram as a vector graphic, but you want to post it on the Web as a bitmap so that it can be viewed without a plug-in or player. You can convert the vector into a bitmap using a process called _____.

6. After you finish arranging video clips and adding a soundtrack, you can select a video file format and a compression technique. For example, you might store the video in AVI format and use the Cinepak _____ to compress the file.

7. Suppose you click a Web page link to a video, but it is barely watchable because it is so jerky, and the sound doesn't coordinate with the images. You would expect this type of problem if you are using a slow, _____ Internet connection.

8. Suppose you are creating an English-as-a-Second-Language Web page and you want to add links to sound files that pronounce English phrases. If you want the sound files to play without the aid of a plug-in or player, you should use the Audio Interchange Format or _____ file format.

9. Imagine that you're a musician and you are asked to synthesize some music for the opening screen of a Web site. For this project, you would most likely work with _____ music.

10. Suppose you visit a Web site that allows you to enter sentences, and then it reads the sentences back to you. The site even gives you a choice of a female or male voice. You assume that this site uses speech _____ technology.

✦ CHECK ANSWERS

INTERACTIVE PRACTICE TESTS

Practice tests that consist of 10 multiple-choice, true/false, and fill-in-the-blank questions are available on both the NP8 BookOnCD and the NP8 Web site. The questions are selected at random from a large test bank, so each time you take a test, you'll receive a different set of questions. Your tests are scored immediately, and you can print study guides that help you find the correct answers for any questions that you missed.

www.course.com/np/concepts8/ch07 ✦

CLICK ✦ TO START

REVIEW
ON THE WEB

PROJECTS

An NP8 Project is an open-ended activity that helps you apply the concepts you have learned. Many projects require resources in addition to your textbook, such as current magazines, library materials, or Web access. When you tackle a project, be prepared to use your critical thinking skills, logical analysis, and creativity. Projects for this chapter include:

- **Issue Research: Digital Rights management**
- **Group Project: Graphics Equipment Tradeshow**
- **Computers in Film**
- **Graphics Software**
- **MP3 Compression**
- **Digital Cameras**
- **Explore the GIF Controversy**

To work with the Projects for this chapter, connect to the **New Perspectives NP8 Web Site**.

www.course.com/np/concepts8/ch07

TECHTV VIDEO PROJECT

The TechTV segment *Online Music Stores and Services* highlights some of the post popular sites for downloading music. The host for this segment evaluates music sites based on five criteria. Watch the video and make a list of these criteria. Then go online and create your own comparison of two music download sites using these criteria.

To work with the Video Projects for this chapter, connect to the **New Perspectives NP8 Web Site**.

www.course.com/np/concepts8/ch07

STUDY TIPS

Study Tips help you to organize and consolidate the information in a chapter by making lists, outlines, charts, and sketches. You can use paper and pencil or word processing software to complete most of the Study Tips.

To work with the Study Tips for this chapter, connect to the **New Perspectives NP8 Web Site**.

www.course.com/np/concepts8/ch07

ONLINE GAMES

Test your comprehension of the concepts introduced in Chapter 7 by playing the NP8 Online Games. At the end of each game, you have three options:

- Print a comprehensive study guide complete with page references
- Print your results to be submitted to your instructor
- Save your results to be submitted to your instructor via e-mail

To work with the Online Games for this chapter, connect to the **New Perspectives NP8 Web Site**.

www.course.com/np/concepts8/ch07

STUDENT EDITION LABS

Extend your knowledge of digital media with the Chapter 7 Student Edition Labs.

The following Student Edition Labs are offered with Chapter 7:

- **Working with Graphics**
- **Working with Video**
- **Working with Audio**

Go to the NP8 New Perspectives Web site for specific lab topics.

To work with the Chapter 7 Student Edition Labs and their corresponding assignments, you can connect to the **New Perspectives NP8 Web Site**.

www.course.com/np/concepts8/ch07

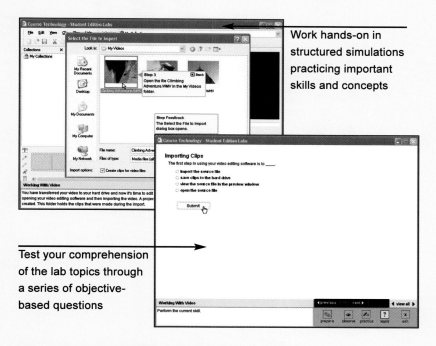

Work hands-on in structured simulations practicing important skills and concepts

Test your comprehension of the lab topics through a series of objective-based questions

Track Your Progress with the Student Edition Labs

- Student Edition Labs test your comprehension of the lab topics through a series of trackable objective-based questions. Your instructor will direct you to either print your results or submit them via e-mail.

- Student Edition Lab Assignments, available on the New Perspectives NP8 Web site, require you to apply the skills learned through the lab in a live environment. Go to the New Perspectives NP8 Web site for detailed instruction on individual Student Edition Lab Assignments.

If you have a SAM user profile, you have access to even more interactive content. Log in to your SAM account and go to your assignments page to see what your instructor has assigned for this chapter.

8

THE COMPUTER INDUSTRY: HISTORY, PRODUCTS, AND CAREERS

CONTENTS

TIP

When using the BookOnCD, the 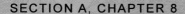 icons are "clickable" to access resources on the CD. The ✝ icons are clickable to access resources on the Web. You can also access Web resources by using your browser to connect directly to the NP8 New Perspectives Web site at:

www.course.com/np/concepts8/ch08

CHAPTER PREVIEW

Before you begin Chapter 8, you can use the Web-based preview activities to hear an overview of the chapter, check your current level of expertise about key concepts, and look through a list of learning objectives. You can access the preview activities by clicking the ✦ icon when using the BookOnCD or going to the New Perspectives NP8 Web site.

CHAPTER OVERVIEW

On a cold winter day in 1937, John Atanasoff sat in a roadside tavern, deep in thought about a device to solve algebraic equations. Suddenly he smiled, grabbed a cocktail napkin, and scribbled some quick notes. They were the design for the first electronic digital computer. Since then, the computer industry has become one of the most prolific sources of innovation in history. Get your book and highlighter ready, and then connect to the New Perspectives NP8 Web site where you can listen to an overview that points out the most important concepts for this chapter.

www.course.com/np/concepts8/ch08 ✦

CHAPTER PRE-ASSESSMENT

How much do you know about the origins of computers, product life cycles, and computer careers? To gauge your level of knowledge before beginning the chapter, take the pre-assessment quiz at the New Perspectives NP8 Web site. Armed with your results from this quiz, you can focus your study time on concepts that will round out your knowledge of the computer industry and improve your test scores.

www.course.com/np/concepts8/ch08 ✦

LEARNING OBJECTIVES

When you complete this chapter you should be able to:

- Outline the development of calculating and computer devices, beginning with simple counting aids and continuing through developments that led to today's computer technology
- Describe the hardware, software, and operating system characteristics for computer prototypes and the four generations of computers
- List the factors that changed personal computers from hobbyists' kits to widely used productivity and communications tools
- Describe the role of the computer and IT industries in today's global economy
- Explain the life cycle of typical hardware and software products

- Discuss the advantages and disadvantages of various marketing channels for consumers who want to purchase computers and related products
- Describe the job outlook, working conditions, and salaries for computer professionals
- Differentiate between computer engineering, computer science, and information systems degree programs
- Demonstrate how to create a resume that works in today's technology-driven job market

A detailed list of learning objectives is provided at the New Perspectives NP8 Web site

www.course.com/np/concepts8/ch08 ✦

SECTION A
COMPUTER HISTORY

Like so many inventions throughout history, the computer evolved as inventors tinkered with various devices. As a result, it is difficult for historians to point to one development and say that it represents the first calculator or the first computer. Keeping that uncertainty in mind, it is, nonetheless, interesting to trace the development of computers. Knowing the history of computers helps you understand the design and capabilities of today's digital computers. It also helps you understand how the computer industry of today came into being.

MANUAL CALCULATORS

What came before computers? Even before recorded history, humans used counting aids, such as pebbles and notched sticks, to keep track of quantities—the number of sheep in a flock, for example, or the number of oil jars purchased from a merchant. Many transactions, however, required calculations.

A calculation is based on an algorithm—the step-by-step process by which numbers are manipulated. Even simple paper-and-pencil addition requires an algorithm. The steps include adding the rightmost digits first, carrying a 1 if necessary, and then moving left to any remaining digits, where the process is repeated. A **manual calculator** is a device that assists in the process of numeric calculations, but requires the human operator to keep track of the algorithm.

A manual calculator called an **abacus** first appeared around 1200 in China, and then in Japan around 1600. An abacus, like the one in Figure 8-1, consists of beads mounted on sticks within a rectangular frame. Each bead represents a quantity—1, 5, 10, 50, and so on. To use an abacus, you must learn the algorithm for manipulating the beads.

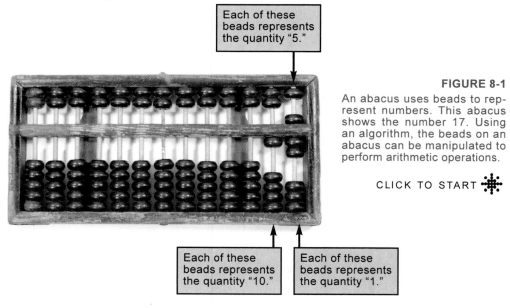

Each of these beads represents the quantity "5."

Each of these beads represents the quantity "10."

Each of these beads represents the quantity "1."

FIGURE 8-1

An abacus uses beads to represent numbers. This abacus shows the number 17. Using an algorithm, the beads on an abacus can be manipulated to perform arithmetic operations.

CLICK TO START

Other manual calculators include the oddly named Napier's Bones and the slide rule. John Napier, the Scottish Laird of Merchiston, made two contributions to the field of mathematics. He invented logarithms and a device for multiplication and division. The device consisted of several rods, divided into 10 squares, each labeled with 2 numbers. The rods were positioned according to the numbers in a calculation, and the result was determined by adding values shown in a specific location on the rods. These rods were often constructed out of bones, so they came to be called **Napier's Bones** (Figure 8-2).

In 1621, an English mathematician named William Oughtred used Napier's logarithms to construct the first **slide rule**. Slide rules, like the one pictured in Figure 8-2, remained in use as an essential tool for students, engineers, and scientists through the 1960s.

INFOWEBLINKS

Want to learn more about manual and mechanical computing devices? Connect to the **Calculating Devices InfoWeb**.

www.course.com/np/concepts8/ch08

FIGURE 8-2
Napier's Bones (left) evolved into the slide rule (right).

CLICK TO START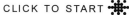

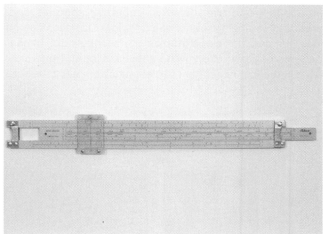

MECHANICAL CALCULATORS

When did machines begin to perform calculations? Manual calculators, such as the abacus and slide rule, require the operator to apply algorithms to perform calculations. In contrast, a **mechanical calculator** implements algorithms autonomously. To work a mechanical calculator, the operator simply enters the numbers for a calculation, and then pulls a lever or turns a wheel to carry out the calculation. No thinking—or at least very little—is required.

Mechanical calculators were developed as early as 1623, when a German professor named Wilhelm Schickard created a mechanical calculator (called **Schickard's Calculator**) with a series of interlocking gears. Each of the 10 spokes on a gear represented a digit. Every time a gear completed a full circle, it activated the gear to the left, moving it one notch to "carry the 1." A similar mechanism is used to advance the mileage on a car's odometer.

In 1642, a Frenchman named Blaise Pascal developed the **Pascaline**, a mechanical device that could be used to perform addition, subtraction, multiplication, and division. Yet another mechanical calculator—now called the **Leibniz Calculator**—was created by a German baron named Gottfried Wilhelm von Leibniz in 1673. It was not until 1820, however, that Thomas **deColmar's Arithmometer** became the first mass-produced calculator. These devices, unlike today's battery-powered calculators, operated under manual power by turning a crank or pulling a lever.

When did calculating devices begin to operate without human power? In 1822, an English mathematician named Charles Babbage proposed a device called the **Difference Engine** that would operate using steam power—cutting-edge technology during Babbage's lifetime. The Difference Engine was intended to quickly and accurately calculate large tables of numbers used for astronomical and engineering applications. The blueprints for the Difference Engine called for more than 4,000 precision-engineered levers, gears, and wheels. Babbage worked on the Difference Engine until 1833, but he was unable to fabricate gears with the necessary precision to create a working version of this complex mechanical device.

In 1834, Babbage began designing a new general-purpose calculating device, called the **Analytical Engine**. Computer historians believe that the Analytical Engine design embodies many of the concepts that define the modern computer, including memory, a programmable processor, an output device, and user-definable input of programs and data. Babbage proposed storing programs and data for calculations on punched cards, an idea that probably came from using punched cards to control the color and patterns of yarns used in the Jacquard loom. Punched cards were later used in the first generation of electronic computing devices (Figure 8-3).

INFOWEBLINKS

At the **Charles Babbage InfoWeb**, you'll find sketches, photos, and original documents describing the Analytical and Difference Engines, including programming notes by mathematician Ada Byron.

www.course.com/np/concepts8/ch08

FIGURE 8-3
Charles Babbage conceived of a device called the Analytical Engine, which embodied many of the characteristics that define modern computers. For example, he proposed storing programs and data for calculations on punched cards, much like those used in 1970s mainframes.

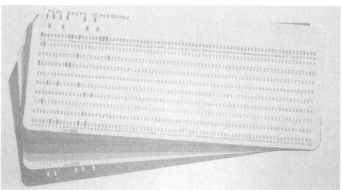

The U.S. Census provided incentive for the next generation of calculating machines. Compiling data from the 1880 census dragged on until 1887—just three years before the next census was to begin. With a surge in population, Census Bureau administrators feared that the 1890 census could not be completed before the 1900 census would begin. Clearly a faster way of tabulating census results was required.

The U.S. Census Bureau held a competition to find a way to tabulate the 1890 census. Herman Hollerith won the competition with a design for an electronic punched card tabulating device. Each card contained areas to represent fields, such as "nationality." Once punched, the cards were fed into a card reader that used an array of metal rods to electronically read data from the cards and tabulate the results. The **Hollerith Tabulating Machine** was effective. The 1890 census was tallied in six months, and only two additional years were required to complete all statistical calculations.

Hollerith incorporated The Tabulating Machine Company in 1896. In 1924, the name of the company was changed to International Business Machines, better known today as IBM. Since it was founded, IBM has become a major player in the computer industry.

The first half of the 20th century ushered in an era of growth in the business machine industry, which at that time produced typewriters and mechanical calculating devices. IBM faced tough competition from companies such as Burroughs, National Cash Register, Olivetti, and Remington. Some of these companies would later venture into the computer industry.

COMPUTER PROTOTYPES

Who invented the computer? The question "Who invented the computer?" doesn't have a simple answer because the modern digital computer evolved from a series of prototypes developed by various groups of people. A **prototype** is an experimental device that typically must be further developed and perfected before going into production and becoming widely available.

Between 1937 and 1942, an Iowa State University professor, John V. Atanasoff, and a graduate student, Clifford E. Berry, worked on a prototype for an electronic computer. The **Atanasoff-Berry Computer** (ABC) was the first to use vacuum tubes instead of mechanical switches. Its design also incorporated the idea of basing calculations on the binary number system. The ABC, shown in Figure 8-4, is often considered the first electronic digital computer. According to one historian, "The ABC first demonstrated in 1939 may not have been much of a computer, just as the Wrights' model was not much of an airplane, but it opened the way."

FIGURE 8-4

The Atanasoff-Berry Computer (ABC) gained national attention when it was pulled from obscurity in a 1972 patent dispute. Sperry Rand claimed to have a patent on digital computer architecture. The court declared the patent claim invalid because it was based on the work of Atanasoff and Berry.

While Atanasoff worked on the ABC, a German engineer named Konrad Zuse developed a computer called the **Z3,** which, like the ABC, was designed to work with binary numbers. Built in Nazi Germany during World War II, the Z3 was cloaked in secrecy, even though Hitler believed that computers had no strategic use in the war effort. Information on Zuse's invention did not surface until long after the war ended. So although Zuse was on the trail of modern computer architecture, his work had little effect on the development of computers.

Even with the work of Atanasoff and Zuse, it was not clear that computers were destined to be binary electronic devices. IBM had an entirely different computer architecture in mind. In 1939, IBM sponsored an engineer named Howard Aiken, who embarked on an audacious plan to integrate 73 IBM Automatic Accounting Machines into a single unified computing unit. What emerged was a mechanical computer officially named the IBM Automatic Sequence Controlled Calculator (ASCC), but now usually referred to as the **Harvard Mark I** (Figure 8-5) because it was moved to Harvard University shortly after completion.

FIGURE 8-5
Constructed of relay switches, rotating shafts, and clutches, the Harvard Mark 1 was described as sounding like a "roomful of ladies knitting." The device was 51 feet long and 8 feet tall and weighed about 5 tons.

Although the Harvard Mark I was one of the first working computers, as a prototype, it strayed considerably from the path of development leading to modern computers. The Harvard Mark I was digital but used decimal rather than binary representation, which is used by today's computers. In contrast, the ABC, with its electronic vacuum tubes and binary representation, was a much closer prototype of the generations of computers to come.

Aiken was a fine engineer but did not quite grasp the far-reaching potential of computers. In 1947, he predicted that only six electronic digital computers would be required to satisfy the computing needs of the entire United States—a sentiment that echoed an earlier statement made by Thomas J. Watson, then chairman of IBM.

Were prototypes able to perform any "real" computing? Some computer prototypes were pressed into service barely before they were completed. In 1943, a team of British developers created **COLOSSUS**, an electronic device designed to decode messages encrypted by the German Enigma machine. COLOSSUS contained 1,800 vacuum tubes, used binary arithmetic, and was capable of reading input at the rate of 5,000 characters per second. COLOSSUS successfully broke the Enigma codes and gave the Allies a major advantage during World War II.

In 1943, a team headed by John W. Mauchly and J. Presper Eckert started work on ENIAC, a gigantic, general-purpose electronic computer. **ENIAC** (Electronic Numerical Integrator and Computer) was designed to calculate trajectory tables for the U.S. Army, but wasn't finished until November 1945, three months after the end of World War II. ENIAC was over 100 feet long and 10 feet high and weighed 30 tons. This gigantic machine contained over 18,000 vacuum tubes and consumed 174,000 watts of power. It could perform 5,000 additions per second and was programmed by manually connecting cables and setting 6,000 switches—a process that generally took two days to complete.

ENIAC was formally dedicated at the Moore School of Electrical Engineering of the University of Pennsylvania on February 15, 1946, and immediately pressed into service making atomic energy calculations and computing trajectories for new missile technologies. ENIAC received several upgrades and remained in service until 1955.

INFOWEBLINKS

Read more about the ABC, Z3, COLOSSUS, ENIAC, and other early computers at the **Computer Prototype InfoWeb**.

GENERATIONS OF COMPUTERS

What was the first commercially successful computer? A computer called the **UNIVAC** is considered by most historians to be the first commercially successful digital computer. The first UNIVAC computer was constructed under the auspices of the Eckert-Mauchly Computer Corp. By the time the first UNIVAC was completed in 1951, the Eckert-Mauchly Computer Corp. had fallen into financial distress and been acquired by Remington Rand, one of IBM's chief rivals in the business machine arena. Forty-six UNIVAC computers were delivered to Remington Rand's customers between 1951 and 1958.

At 14.5 feet long, 7.5 feet high, and 9 feet wide, UNIVAC was physically smaller than ENIAC, but more powerful. UNIVAC could read data at the rate of 7,200 characters per second, and complete 2.25 million instruction cycles per second. It had RAM capacity of 12,000 characters (12 KB), and used magnetic tape for data storage and retrieval. The cost of a UNIVAC averaged about $930,000.

How did computers progress from room-sized behemoths to modern personal computers? Early computers, such as the Harvard Mark I, ENIAC, and UNIVAC, used technology that required lots of space and electrical power. As technology evolved, relay switches and vacuum tubes were replaced with smaller, less power-hungry components. Computer historians generally agree that computers have evolved through four distinct generations, and in each generation, computers became smaller, faster, more dependable, and less expensive to operate.

What characterized the first generation of computers? **First-generation computers** can be characterized by their use of vacuum tubes, such as those in Figure 8-6, to store individual bits of data. A **vacuum tube** is an electronic device that controls the flow of electrons in a vacuum. Each tube can be set to one of two states. One state is assigned a value of 0 and the other a value of 1. Vacuum tubes respond more quickly than mechanical relays, resulting in faster computations but they also have several disadvantages. They consume a lot of power, much of which is wasted as heat. They also tend to burn out quickly. ENIAC, the prototype for first-generation computers, contained about 18,000 tubes, and every tube was replaced at least once in the first year of operation.

INFOWEBLINKS

Historians are not in total agreement about the number of computer generations. You can find more information about historians' views regarding this topic by connecting to the **Computer Generations InfoWeb**.

www.course.com/np/concepts8/ch08

FIGURE 8-6

Vacuum tubes resemble light bulbs and were used as the main processing and memory technology for first-generation computers. Although no longer used in computers, vacuum tubes can still be found in televisions, computer monitors, high-end stereo systems, and guitar amplifiers.

In addition to vacuum tube technology, first-generation computers were characterized by custom application programs, made to order for the specific task the computer was to perform. Programming first-generation computers was difficult. As the computer era dawned, programmers were forced to think in 1s and 0s to write instructions in machine language. Before the first generation ended, programmers had devised rudimentary compilers that allowed them to write instructions using assembly language op codes, such as LDA and JNZ. Assembly language was a small step forward, but like machine language, it was machine specific and required programmers to learn a different set of instructions for each computer.

Although many companies recognized the potential of machines to perform fast calculations, first-generation computers did not seem ready for "prime time." That said, many business machine companies, such as IBM, Burroughs, and National Cash Register (NCR), began research and development efforts into fledgling computer technologies. Companies in the electronics industry, such as General Electric, RCA, Control Data, and Honeywell, also showed interest in the new field of computing.

How did second-generation computers differ from first-generation computers? **Second-generation computers** used transistors instead of vacuum tubes. First demonstrated in 1947 by AT&T's Bell Laboratories, **transistors** regulate current or voltage flow and act as a switch for electronic signals. Transistors performed functions similar to vacuum tubes, but they were much smaller, cheaper, less power hungry, and more reliable. By the late 1950s, transistors, such as those in Figure 8-7, had replaced vacuum tubes as the processing and memory technology for most computers.

FIGURE 8-7

Transistors first sparked a revolution in the entertainment industry by providing a small, power-efficient technology for portable radios. Later, transistors were incorporated in computers to replace large, hot, power-hungry vacuum tubes.

Several successful transistorized computers were manufactured by companies such as IBM, Burroughs, Control Data, Honeywell, and Sperry Rand (which was the new name given to Remington Rand after its merger with Sperry Corp). In addition to the important hardware breakthrough provided by transistors, an equally important development in software differentiated second-generation computers from their first-generation ancestors.

First-generation computers didn't have operating systems, as we know them today. Instead, each software application included the instructions necessary for every aspect of the computing job, including input, output, and processing activities. Programmers were quick to realize that this style of programming was terribly inefficient. For example, although virtually every program sent results to a printer, every program was required to have its own print routine. As programmers found themselves writing print routines over and over again for every program, they began to look for a more efficient method to standardize such routines and consolidate them into programs that any application software could access. These routines were gathered together into operating systems, which became a characteristic of second-generation computers.

Computer manufacturers such as IBM developed operating systems that provided standardized routines for input, output, memory management, storage, and other resource management activities. Application programmers were no longer required to write resource management routines. These operating systems allowed programmers to write application software that "called" the operating system's standard routines.

Early proprietary operating systems developed by IBM and other computer manufacturers were designed to work only on a particular computer model. Each of these operating systems had a unique set of commands to call its routines. Early operating systems were a step in the right direction, but unfortunately, learning to use each one was like learning a new and unique programming language. It was not until the third generation of computers that portable operating systems, such as CP/M and UNIX, provided programmers with similar operating system commands across hardware platforms.

In addition to operating systems, second-generation computers also ran programming language compilers that allowed programmers to write instructions using English-like commands rather than the binary numbers of machine language. High-level languages, such as COBOL (Common Business-Oriented Language) and FORTRAN (Formula Translator), were available for use on second-generation computers and remain in use today. The availability of high-level computer programming languages made it possible for third parties to develop software, and that capability was instrumental in the birth of the software industry.

What are the characteristics of third-generation computers? **Third-generation computers** became possible in 1958, when Jack Kilby at Texas Instruments and Robert Noyce at Fairchild Semiconductor independently developed integrated circuits (Figure 8-8). Integrated circuit technology made it possible to pack the equivalent of thousands of vacuum tubes or transistors onto a single miniature chip, greatly reducing the physical size, weight, and power requirements for devices such as computers.

FIGURE 8-8

Jack Kilby's original integrated circuit was a key development for creating today's small, fast, and efficient computers.

Two of the first computers to incorporate integrated circuits were the **RCA Spectra 70** and the wildly successful **IBM 360**. The first orders for IBM 360s computers were filled in 1965—a date regarded by many historians as the advent of third-generation computers.

In 1965, Digital Equipment Corp. (DEC) introduced the **DEC PDP-8**, the first commercially successful minicomputer. As explained in Chapter 1, minicomputers were designed to be smaller and less powerful than mainframe computers, while maintaining the capability to simultaneously run multiple programs for multiple users. Thousands of manufacturing plants, small businesses, and scientific laboratories were attracted to the speed, small size, and reasonable cost of the PDP-8.

DEC introduced a succession of minicomputers that stole a share of the mainframe market. Eventually, IBM and other mainframe makers introduced their own minicomputers, but the "star" for minicomputers faded as microcomputers gained processing power and networking became easier. DEC was purchased by Compaq in 1998. By 2000, the **IBM AS/400** (renamed the iSeries 400) was one of the few remaining devices that could be classified as a minicomputer. Today, demand for minicomputers is satisfied by high-end personal computers and servers, and the term "minicomputer" has generally fallen into disuse.

How did microprocessor technology affect the computer industry?
The technology for **fourth-generation computers** appeared in 1971, when Ted Hoff developed the first general-purpose microprocessor. Called the Intel 4004, this microprocessor dramatically changed the computer industry, resulting in fourth-generation microprocessor-based computer systems that were faster, smaller, and even less expensive than third-generation computers.

Microprocessor manufacturers soon flourished. Early industry leaders included Intel, Zilog, Motorola, and Texas Instruments. Intel's 4004 microprocessor (Figure 8-9) was smaller than a corn flake but matched the computing power of ENIAC. The 4004 packed the equivalent of 2300 transistors or vacuum tubes on a single chip and was able to perform 60,000 instructions per second. The 4004 was followed by the 8008, the first commercial 8-bit microprocessor, and then the 8080.

In 1974, Motorola released the 6800 8-bit microprocessor. A few months later, ex-Motorola engineers working at MOS Technologies created the 6502, an 8-bit microprocessor that was used in the Apple II and Commodore personal computer systems.

In 1976, Zilog introduced the Z80 microprocessor, an enhanced 8080 microprocessor that was used in many early computer systems. In the same year, Intel released the 8085, a further enhancement of the 8080.

Both Intel and Motorola continued development of advanced microprocessors. The Intel line, used in most Windows-compatible computers, included the 8086, 8088, 80286, 80386, 80486, Pentium, and Itanium microprocessors. The Motorola line of microprocessors grew to include the 68000 series processors used in Apple Macintosh computers, plus the PowerPC processors developed in the early 1990s and used in current Macintosh computer systems.

Today, microprocessors are key components of computers—ranging from PDAs to supercomputers. Intel reigns as the world's leading microprocessor manufacturer, although microprocessors are also produced by companies such as Hitachi, Texas Instruments, Sun Microsystems, AMD, Toshiba, and Motorola.

PERSONAL COMPUTERS

Who invented the personal computer? In the early 1970s, many hobbyists built their own computer systems based on integrated circuit and microprocessor technologies. One such system was the **Mark-8** developed by Jonathan A. Titus, who was featured in the July 1974 issue of *Radio-Electronics*. These early personal computers were not commercially produced or widely available, but they are often considered forerunners of today's personal computer.

In 1975, Ed Roberts and the MITS (Micro Instrument and Telemetry Systems) company announced the **MITS Altair**, which many historians believe to be the first commercial microcomputer (Figure 8-10). The Altair was based on the Intel 8080 processor and sold as a kit for $395 or fully assembled for $650—about one-fourth the price of a 1975 Volkswagen Beetle. The Altair was a computer for the hobbyist. The kit came unassembled in a box containing a processor and 256 bytes of memory—not 256 KB, just 256 bytes. It had no keyboard, no monitor, and no permanent storage device.

FIGURE 8-9

The Intel 4004 microprocessor was small—only 1/8" by 1/16" compared to today's Pentium microprocessors. The 4004's 2,300 transistors provided much less processing power than the Pentium III, with its 9.5 million transistors, or the Pentium 4, with 42 million transistors.

FIGURE 8-10

The Altair computer made the cover of *Popular Electronics* in January 1975.

Programming the Altair computer meant flipping individual switches on the front of the system unit. Output consisted of flashing lights, and the only programming language available was 8080 machine language. Although it was typically sold as a kit, required assembly, and was too limited to perform significant computational tasks, the Altair was snapped up by hobbyists.

In 1977, Steve Jobs and Steve Wozniak founded Apple Computer Corporation and released the **Apple I**, a kit containing a system board with 4 KB of RAM that sold for $666.66. Other companies, such as Commodore, Atari, and Radio Shack, pursued the hobbyist market, but with preassembled computers.

FIGURE 8-11
The Apple II was the most popular computer of its time.

How did personal computers become so successful?
In 1978, Apple introduced a preassembled computer called the **Apple II**, which featured color graphics, expansion slots, a disk drive, a 1.07 MHz 6502 processor, and 16 KB of RAM for $1,195. The Apple II, shown in Figure 8-11, was a very successful product. One of the main reasons behind its success was a commercial software program called **VisiCalc**—the first electronic spreadsheet. This program landed computers on the radar screen of business users and clearly marked a turning point where personal computers appealed to an audience beyond hobbyists.

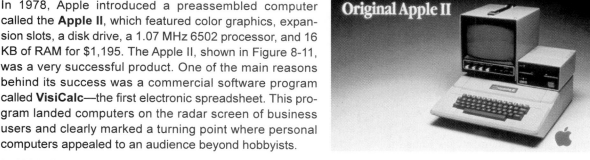

In 1981, IBM began marketing what it called a "personal computer" or "PC," based on the 8088 processor. When the PC version of VisiCalc became available, the IBM PC quickly became the top-selling personal computer, far surpassing IBM's expectations.

The $3,000 **IBM PC**, shown in Figure 8-12, shipped with a 4.77 MHz Intel 8088 processor, 16 KB of RAM, and single-sided 160 KB floppy disk drives. The IBM PC was soon followed by the **IBM PC XT**, which featured RAM upgradable to 640 KB, and a 10 MB hard disk drive.

FIGURE 8-12
The IBM PC, launched in 1981, evolved into today's popular Windows-based PCs.

IBM PCs were constructed with off-the-shelf parts that could be easily obtained from many electronics wholesalers. Within months, dozens of companies used these parts to produce "clones" of IBM-compatible computers that could run the same software and use the same expansion cards as the IBM PC and XT. These companies were also able to obtain essentially the same operating system used by IBM.

The IBM PC used an operating system called PC-DOS that was marketed by a young entrepreneur named Bill Gates, founder of a fledgling software company called Microsoft. Microsoft marketed a similar operating system, called MS-DOS, to PC clone makers. Many of the companies that produced IBM clones failed, but some, such as Dell and Hewlett-Packard, became major forces in the personal computer industry.

Although hobbyists and the business community had embraced computers, these machines were still considered difficult for the average person to use. That perception began to change in 1983, when Apple introduced a product called the **Apple Lisa**. A key feature of the Lisa was its graphical user interface—an idea borrowed from the **Xerox Alto** computer. At $10,000, the Lisa proved too expensive for most consumers. Apple stuck to its commitment to graphical user interfaces, however, and in 1984, released the first **Apple Macintosh** (Figure 8-13). The $2,495 Macintosh featured a graphical user interface that made programs easier to use than those on the command-line-based IBM PC. The Macintosh became the computer of choice for graphical applications such as desktop publishing.

FIGURE 8-13

The Apple Macintosh computer popularized graphical user interfaces.

By the late 1980s, the computer industry had begun to consolidate around two primary platforms—the MS-DOS-based IBM-compatible platform and the Apple Macintosh. Although dozens of companies produced IBM-compatible systems that ran the same software and used the same hardware as the IBM PC, Apple attempted to keep its system proprietary. As more IBM-compatible computers were sold, the market for IBM-compatible hardware and software continued to grow. By the mid-1990s, IBM-compatible computer systems accounted for more than 90% of all personal computer sales. The Apple Macintosh accounted for most of the remainder, with other proprietary platforms accounting for a very small percentage of new computer sales.

Even as computer sales soared, and graphical user interfaces, such as Windows 3.1, made computers easier to use, many people simply could not think of any reason to own one. They preferred to write short notes on paper rather than learn how to use a word processor. It seemed easier to punch numbers into a handheld calculator than tackle the complexities of electronic spreadsheets. Why buy a computer if it didn't offer some really enticing perks? That attitude began to change in the late 1980s when the Internet opened to public use. In a flurry of activity, graphical browsers appeared, ISPs provided inexpensive connections, e-mail began to fly, and e-commerce sites opened their doors. Personal computers had finally achieved mass popularity.

INFOWEBLINKS

At the **Computer Museum InfoWeb** you'll find links to detailed timelines of computer history, photos of old computers, plus additional accounts of the computer industry's early days.

www.course.com/np/concepts8/ch08

QUICKCHECK......SECTION A

1. The abacus and slide rule are examples of [＿＿＿＿＿＿＿＿] calculators, which require the operator to apply an algorithm to perform calculations.

2. Charles [＿＿＿＿＿＿＿＿] designed a general-purpose calculating device, called the Analytical Engine, that embodied many of the concepts that define the modern computer.

3. Computers designed by Atanasoff, Zuse, and Aiken are usually considered to be computer [＿＿＿＿＿＿＿＿] because they were experimental models.

4. The first generation of computers can be characterized by its use of [＿＿＿＿＿＿＿＿] tubes to store individual bits of data, whereas second-generation computers used [＿＿＿＿＿＿＿＿].

5. Third-generation computers were based on [＿＿＿＿＿＿＿＿] circuit technology, and fourth-generation computers are characterized by [＿＿＿＿＿＿＿＿] technology.

CHECK ANSWERS

SECTION B

THE COMPUTER AND IT INDUSTRIES

The industries that supply computer goods and services are in a continual state of change as new products appear and old products are discontinued; as corporations form, merge, and die; as corporate leadership shifts; as consumers' buying habits evolve; and as prices steadily decrease.

Before you venture out to buy computers, peripheral devices, or software; before you commit yourself to a computer career; or before you buy stock in computer companies, you should arm yourself with some basic knowledge about the computer and information technology industries. In this section of the chapter, you'll learn about the scope and economics of these dynamic industries.

INDUSTRY OVERVIEW

Is there a difference between the computer industry and the information technology industry? The term "computer industry" is used in a variety of ways. Narrowly defined, the **computer industry** encompasses those companies that manufacture computers (Figure 8-14) and computer components, such as microprocessors. It is also used more broadly to include software publishers and peripheral device manufacturers.

FIGURE 8-14

Manufacturers such as Apple, Dell, Hewlett-Packard, IBM, and Intel are representative of companies in the computer industry.

A broader term, **information technology industry** (or IT industry), is typically used to refer to the companies that develop, produce, sell, or support computers, software, and computer-related products. It includes companies in the computer industry; software publishers; communications service vendors, such as AT&T; information services, such as the Nexus online law library; and service companies, such as EDS.

The terms "computer industry" and "IT industry" are sometimes used interchangeably in news reports and publications, leaving the reader to discern whether the subject is limited to computer manufacturers and distributors. In this textbook, the term "computer industry" is used in its more limited sense, and "IT industry" refers to the broader group of companies that provide computer, software, and telecommunications equipment and services.

Is every company that uses computers part of the IT industry? No. A bank uses computers to track money flowing in and out of accounts, but it is classified as part of the banking industry. A clothing store might use computers to monitor inventory, but it is classified as part of the apparel industry. Such businesses make use of information technology, but they are definitely not part of the computer industry and are not considered part of the IT industry either.

What kinds of companies are included in the IT industry? Companies in the IT industry can be separated into several broad categories, sometimes referred to as "sectors" or "segments," including equipment manufacturers, chipmakers, software publishers, service companies, and retailers.

Equipment manufacturers design and manufacture computer hardware and communications products, such as personal computers, mainframe computers, PDAs, mice, monitors, storage devices, routers, scanners, and printers. Examples of these companies include computer manufacturers IBM and Hewlett-Packard. Network hardware companies, such as Cisco and Linksys, are also examples of equipment manufacturers.

Chipmakers design and manufacture computer chips and circuit boards including microprocessors, RAM, system boards, sound cards, and graphics cards. Intel, AMD, Transmeta, and Texas Instruments are examples of chipmakers.

Software publishers create computer software, including applications, operating systems, and programming languages. Examples of software companies are Microsoft, Adobe Systems, and Computer Associates.

Service companies provide computer-related services, including business consulting, Web site design, Web hosting, Internet connections, computer equipment repair, network security, and product support. Classic examples of service companies include AOL and the computer consulting giant, EDS (Electronic Data Systems).

Retailers (sometimes called "resellers") include companies that sell computer products through retail stores, direct sales representatives, mail-order catalogs, and Web sites. Well-known resellers include CompUSA, which operates retail stores, and mail-order retailers PC Connection and MicroWarehouse.

Although some companies fit neatly into one of the above categories, other companies operate in two or more areas. For example, Dell manufactures hardware but also resells that hardware directly to individuals and businesses. Sun Microsystems is known for its Sun servers and workstations but also develops and sells software, such as operating systems and the Java programming language. IBM designs and manufactures computer chips and circuit boards as well as producing personal computers, servers, and mainframes.

The IT industry also encompasses large conglomerates with one or more divisions devoted to computer hardware, software, or services. As an example, Japanese-owned Hitachi produces a wide variety of electronic devices, but it is also one of the world's largest chipmakers.

INFOWEBLINKS

The computer industry makes a tremendous contribution to global financial resources. For links to information on company stock values, venture over to the **NASDAQ InfoWeb**.

www.course.com/np/concepts8/ch08

What about "dot coms"? The 1990s spawned a group of Internet-based companies that came to be called "dot coms." The dot com moniker came from the companies' domain names, which inevitably ended with ".com"; many of the companies even incorporated ".com" into their official company names.

Amazon.com was one of the first Internet-based companies. Founded in 1995, the company's mission is to "use the Internet to transform book buying into the fastest, easiest, and most enjoyable shopping experience possible." To "transform book buying," Amazon.com set up a Web site where customers can buy books online, without walking into a "brick and mortar" store.

Unless a dot com sells computers, peripherals, or software online, it is probably not considered part of the computer industry, but experts disagree on whether dot coms rightfully belong to the IT industry. Some experts group dot coms under the IT umbrella because they make extensive use of computer equipment and have developed key e-commerce technologies. Other analysts classify dot coms by their core businesses. For example, dot coms that sell clothing would be in the apparel industry, music vendors would be in the entertainment industry, and an online stock broker would be in the financial industry.

FIGURE 8-15

Silicon Valley is home to many companies in the IT industry.

What is the significance of Silicon Valley? The area of California called Silicon Valley that stretches south and east from San Francisco's Golden Gate bridge was the birthplace of integrated circuits, microprocessors, and personal computers. Early IT industry pioneers attracted the attention of many other technology companies who wanted to be in the middle of the action. Today, well-known companies, such as Cisco, Sun Microsystems, Oracle, Hewlett-Packard, AMD, 3Com, and Silicon Graphics, all have headquarters in California's Silicon Valley (Figure 8-15).

Although Silicon Valley has a reputation as the home of the IT industry, many top IT players are located elsewhere. Microsoft is located near Seattle. EDS is headquartered in Plano, Texas and Dell is just outside Austin. North Carolina's Research Triangle (Raleigh-Durham-Chapel Hill) is home base for IBM's largest hardware lab and several small research startups. Colorado's Front Range (the Boulder-Denver-Longmont area) hosts tape drive manufacturer Exabyte and desktop publishing software vendor Quark, Inc. Software publisher Computer Associates is based in New York. Unisys, a high-end server manufacturer, has its headquarters near Philadelphia. Outsourcing and offshoring spread the computer industry to additional locations both in the United States and abroad.

What are outsourcing and offshoring? Like companies in many industries, computer companies make significant use of outsourcing to reduce the price of materials and labor. **Outsourcing** is defined as the use of components or labor from outside suppliers. Most computer companies do not manufacture all the components used to assemble their computers. Instead they depend on components from other companies, such as microprocessors from Intel, hard drives from Seagate, and LCD panels from

Samsung. Software publishers also make use of outsourcing by hiring outside firms to develop products and manufacture packaging. Outsourcing offers economies of scale and expertise to companies in the highly competitive computer industry.

Computer companies also make use of offshoring to help keep product prices competitive. **Offshoring** is defined as relocating business processes, such as development and production, to lower-cost locations in other countries.

U.S. computer companies have established manufacturing and development facilities in countries such as India, Malaysia, Thailand, and Mexico, where labor is inexpensive but reliable. Computer manufacturer Dell Inc. maintains a cadre of offshore technicians to staff customer call centers. The next time you dial technical support, you might be connected to a technician in India. Companies such as Microsoft and Oracle make extensive use of programmers based in India, who telecommute, when necessary, via the Internet (Figure 8-16). The use of offshore resources has become increasingly controversial. You can read about the pros and cons in the Offshoring Issue at the end of this chapter.

FIGURE 8-16
The IT industry reaches globally for programmers and manufacturing facilities.

Where can I find information about the IT industry? Whether you are planning to purchase a computer, embark on a computing career, or invest in a computer company, you can dig up lots of information on IT and computer companies from a wide variety of computer and business publications. The IT Sources InfoWeb provides an up-to-date guide to publications and other IT industry resources.

ECONOMIC FACTORS

How has the IT industry affected the economy? The IT industry has been described as the most dynamic, most prosperous, most economically beneficial industry the world has ever known. That statement might be a bit of an exaggeration, but the IT industry unquestionably has fueled the economies of many countries. Worldwide consumption of IT industry products is estimated to be more than U.S.$800 billion annually.

By dollar value, the biggest computer hardware producing countries are the United States, Japan, Taiwan, Singapore, and China. Despite the increasing globalization of the IT industry, however, it remains dominated by the United States. The majority of IT workers are in the United States, even though about two-thirds of industry revenues are from non-U.S. companies.

What about the dot com bubble? A stock market "bubble" refers to a sharp rise in stock values of a particular industry, which is later followed by a sudden decline. During the later part of the 1990s, the information technology sector experienced a stock market bubble, which burst in 2001 (Figure 8-17). The bubble was fueled by a dot com frenzy. Entrepreneurs seemed to believe that any Internet-based business was destined for success. Investors believed that dot coms were the key to quick profits. Stock sold like hotcakes on the technology-specialized NASDAQ stock exchange.

Dot com stock values soared as investors poured money into online businesses. These businesses needed equipment and employees, which had a positive effect on other sectors of the IT industry by boosting computer sales, networking equipment sales, and IT employment. Unfortunately, many dot coms lacked experienced management teams and realistic business plans, burned through startup capital without making a profit, and then went bankrupt.

A high rate of dot com business failures during 2001 and 2002 meant a decline in equipment orders, Web site hosting contracts, and IT sector job openings. Nonetheless, strength in worldwide markets for IT equipment and services continues to buoy up the industry, and most analysts believe a steady recovery now is in progress. Although another dot com boom is doubtful, analysts believe that well-conceived and professionally managed online businesses can be a profitable part of the IT industry.

What accounts for the success of the IT industry? As with many situations involving the economy, the factors that account for the success of the IT industry cannot be pinpointed with certainty. It is likely, however, that population growth and business globalization are two important factors that contribute to huge investments in information technology.

The worldwide population more than doubled over the past 50 years, and a recent study predicts that the population will peak at 9 billion by 2070. Keeping track of the information relating to all these people—births, deaths, marriages, property ownership, taxes, purchases, banking records, and licenses—certainly seems impossible without the use of computers. Governments and private businesses have discovered that they can become much more efficient with a liberal application of computers and other information technologies.

As a business globalizes, it encounters new competitors with technological advantages. Intense global competitive pressure keeps companies looking for ways to cut costs and raise productivity. Keeping up with the Joneses—or Muramotos, Cordobas, Faisals, and Orlovs—becomes a priority for survival. If your business competitor offers automated online order tracking, for example, you might lose customers unless you can offer the same service. Bottom line: If your business competitors turn to technology, so must you. In our highly populated global economy, information technology products are an effective alternative to manual record-keeping systems (Figure 8-18).

FIGURE 8-17
Dot Com Bubble Timeline

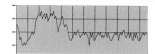

May 1997 Amazon.com stock initial public offering (IPO) kicks off the dot com frenzy.

November 1998 theglobe.com earns $100 million during its IPO, making it the most successful stock offering in history.

March 2000 NASDAQ reaches its all-time high of 5048; stocks are trading for an average of $55.92 per share.

December 2000 By year's end, venture capitalists have invested an estimated $20 billion in 12,450 dot com startups.

January 2001 17 dot coms each spend over $2 million for a 30-second ad during the Super Bowl.

June 2001 By mid-year, 345 dot coms have closed their doors or filed for bankruptcy protection.

August 2001 theglobe.com goes out of business.

September 2002 NASDAQ bottoms out at 1,184, much lower than its 5,048 peak. Average price per share is $14.07.

August 2004 Google has a successful IPO—a sign that consumers are regaining confidence in dot com stocks.

FIGURE 8-18
Manual record-keeping systems of the past have gradually been replaced by computerized archives.

PRODUCT DEVELOPMENT

Why do so many new computer products appear each year?
Automobile manufacturers introduce new models every year, which incorporate new features and give customers an incentive to buy. IT manufacturers and publishers introduce new products for the same reasons as their counterparts in the automotive industry. New products, such as a computer with a faster microprocessor, a DVD player, or a Windows upgrade, are designed to attract customers and generate sales.

In contrast to the automotive industry, however, the IT industry is not on an annual cycle. As a result, the computer marketplace seems rather chaotic because new product announcements, availability dates, and ship dates all occur at irregular intervals.

The equipment manufacturing segment of the IT industry is relatively young, and technology, rather than marketing, is the major force that drives product development. New technologies spur a flurry of development activity and generate new products designed to increase sales. For example, the debut of W-Fi technology stimulated development of Wi-Fi hubs and cards, Wi-Fi enabled notebook computers, Internet access points in coffee shops and airports, and Wi-Fi access plans from companies such as T-Mobile.

Technological breakthroughs do not necessarily adhere to a schedule, however. Companies cannot always predict when a new technology will appear or how it might be incorporated into new products. As a result, the life cycle of computer hardware and some computer products is short, whereas other products have a long life cycle.

What are the stages in the life cycle of a typical hardware product?
In the computer industry, the life cycle of a new computer model usually includes five stages: product development, product announcement, introduction, maintenance, and retirement, as shown in Figure 8-19.

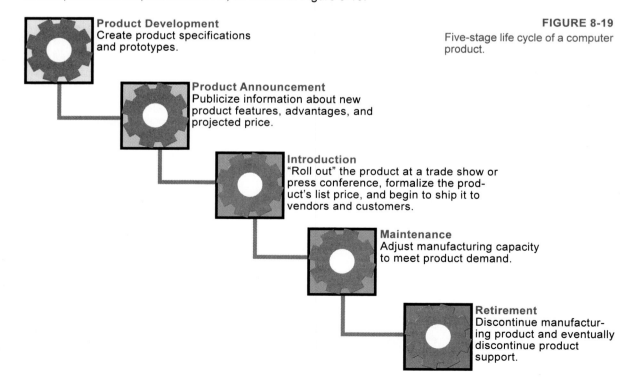

FIGURE 8-19

Five-stage life cycle of a computer product.

Product Development
Create product specifications and prototypes.

Product Announcement
Publicize information about new product features, advantages, and projected price.

Introduction
"Roll out" the product at a trade show or press conference, formalize the product's list price, and begin to ship it to vendors and customers.

Maintenance
Adjust manufacturing capacity to meet product demand.

Retirement
Discontinue manufacturing product and eventually discontinue product support.

- **Product development.** Product development often takes place "under wraps." Developers use fanciful code names, such as Sawtooth and Longhorn, to refer to their products. Inevitably, news of these products leaks out and causes much speculation among industry analysts.

- **Product announcement.** Sometime during the development process, a company makes a product announcement to declare its intention to introduce a new product. Products are often announced at trade shows and press conferences. As a consumer, you should be wary of making purchase or investment decisions based on product announcements. A product announcement can precede the actual launch by several years. Some products, referred to as **vaporware**, are announced but never produced.

- **Introduction.** When a new product becomes available, it is usually added to the vendor's product line and featured prominently in advertisements. Initial supplies of the product generally remain low while manufacturing capacity increases to meet demand. Consumers who want a scarce product must pay a relatively high list price—sometimes called **MSRP** (manufacturer's suggested retail price)—set by the manufacturer.

- **Maintenance.** As supply and demand for a product reach an equilibrium, the price of the product decreases slightly. Usually the price decrease is caused by retail discounting rather than a change to the MSRP. This discounted price is usually referred to as the **street price**. Over time, the manufacturer might also reduce the MSRPs of products with older technology to keep them attractive to buyers.

- **Retirement.** Gradually, a company's oldest products are discontinued as demand for them declines. As you can see from the ad in Figure 8-20, the least expensive products tend to have slower processors, less RAM, and lower-capacity hard disk drives. If your budget is not severely limited, a computer in the middle of a vendor's product line usually gives you the most computing power per dollar.

FIGURE 8-20

A typical manufacturer's product line.

Edge 2500 Notebook

- Pentium M 705 1.5 GHz
- 14.1" XGA TFT
- 256 MB DDR SDRAM
- 40 GB Ultra ATA HD
- 24X CD-RW Drive
- 32 MB Video RAM
- 56K Fax Modem

$749

Edge 4200 Notebook

- Intel Pentium M 725 1.6 GHz
- 15" XGA TFT Display
- 512 MB DDR SDRAM
- 80 GB Ultra ATA HD
- 24X CD-RW/8X DVD Drive
- 64 MB Video RAM
- Ethernet port

$1,499

Edge 8200 Notebook

- Intel Pentium M 755 2 GHz
- 15" UXGA TFT Display
- 2 GB DDR RAM
- 100 GB Ultra ATA HD
- 12X CD/DVD +RW +R Drive
- 128 MB Video RAM
- Ethernet/Wi-Fi port

$2,499

Is the life cycle of a software product similar to that of a hardware product? Software, like hardware, begins with an idea that is shaped by a design team and marketing experts. A team of programmers then works to produce executable programs and support modules for the new software product.

Most software products undergo extensive testing before they are released. The first phase of testing, called an **alpha test**, is carried out by the software publisher's in-house testing team. Errors, or "bugs," found during the alpha test phase are fixed, and then the software enters a second testing phase called a **beta test**. Typically, a beta test is conducted by a team of off-site testers, such as a professional testing company. Sometimes a software publisher releases a "beta version" of the software to select individuals and companies in the general public to expose the software to the widest possible variety of computers and operating environments. Although it can be exciting to test a yet-to-be-released software package, beta versions are typically "buggy" and can cause unexpected glitches in your computer. Beta testing requires a high tolerance for frustration.

A newly published software package can be an entirely new product, a new version (also called a "release") with significant enhancements, or a revision designed to add minor enhancements and eliminate bugs found in the current version.

When a new software product first becomes available, the publisher often offers a special introductory price that's designed to entice customers. For example, several software products that now carry a list price of $495 were introduced at a special price of $99. Even after the introductory price expires, most vendors offer sizable discounts. Expect software with a list price of $495 to be offered for a street price of about $299.

Unlike computer hardware products, older versions of software typically do not remain in the vendor's product line. Soon after a new version of a software product is released, the software publisher usually stops selling earlier versions. When a publisher offers a new version of the software that you are using, it is a good idea to upgrade, but you can wait for several months until the initial rush for technical support on the new product subsides. If you don't upgrade, you might find that the software publisher offers minimal technical support for older versions of the program. Also, if you let several versions go by without upgrading, you might lose your eligibility for special upgrade pricing.

MARKET SHARE

How do computer companies stack up against each other? Industry analysts often use market share as a gauge of a company's success. **Market share** refers to a company's share, or percentage, of the total market "pie." For example, Microsoft's share of the total personal computer operating system market is about 80%. The remaining 20% share is distributed among Apple and several Linux vendors.

In worldwide hardware sales, Dell leads the pack with more than 16% market share, followed closely by Hewlett-Packard (Figure 8-21).

FIGURE 8-21
Worldwide market share for personal computer vendors in the second quarter of 2004.

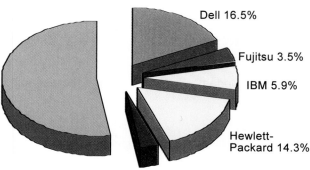

Source: Gartner, Inc.

Market share graphs for personal computer manufacturers, software publishers, operating system developers, Internet service providers, and handheld computer manufacturers provide a roadmap to the changing fortunes of companies in the computer industry. Competition is fierce in all segments of the industry, and market share is one indicator of a company's ability to "steal" sales from its rivals. The top companies are constantly challenged, not only by their peers, but by startup companies in lower tiers of the industry.

What's the relevance of market tiers? Since 1981, hundreds of companies have produced personal computers. Industry analysts have classified these companies into **market tiers**, or categories. Although analysts do not agree on which companies belong in each tier, the concept of tiers helps explain price differences and changing market shares.

The top (first) tier in any segment of the computer industry consists of large companies that have been in the computer business for many years, and have an identifiable share—usually more than 2%—of total computer sales. IBM and Hewlett-Packard are two venerable members of the top tier of the computer industry. The second tier includes newer companies with sales volume just below the cutoff level for identifiable market share and somewhat fewer financial resources than companies in the first tier. Most analysts place companies such as Gateway in this tier. The third tier consists of smaller startup companies that sell primarily through mail order (Figure 8-22).

FIGURE 8-22
Market Tiers

First Tier

Prices Computer prices from first-tier vendors are generally higher than computers offered by second-tier or third-tier vendors. Pricing reflects overhead costs that include facilities, professional management teams, a large workforce, and cutting-edge research.

Quality Many consumers believe that computers sold by first-tier companies offer better quality and are a safer purchasing decision than computers from other tiers.

Resources Substantial financial resources help these companies contribute many of the innovations that make computers faster, more powerful, and more convenient.

Service A stable first-tier company is likely to provide continuing support, honor warranties, and maintain an inventory of replacement parts.

Second Tier

Prices Computers from second-tier companies are typically less expensive than those from first-tier firms.

Quality Most PCs are constructed from off-the-shelf circuit boards, cases, and chips. Components in the computers sold by second-tier companies are often the same as those in computers sold by first-tier firms.

Resources Second-tier companies typically maintain low prices by minimizing operating costs. These companies have limited research and development budgets.

Service Some second-tier companies maintain a relatively small workforce by contracting with other companies to provide repair and warranty work.

Third Tier

Prices Computers from third-tier companies often appear to be much less expensive than those in other tiers.

Quality A consumer who is knowledgeable about the market and has technical expertise can often get a bargain on a good-quality computer from a third-tier company. Low pricing might reflect low overhead costs of a small company, but it could reflect poor-quality components.

Resources Third-tier companies usually do not have substantial financial resources and are more likely to go out of business than companies in the other tiers.

Service If a company goes out of business, its customers may be left without technical support.

MARKETING CHANNELS

Why are computer equipment and software sold through so many outlets? Hardware manufacturers and software publishers try to reach consumers by making their products available through a variety of sources. Computer hardware and software are sold through marketing outlets called **marketing channels**. These channels, shown in Figure 8-23, include computer retail stores, mail-order/Internet outlets, value-added resellers, and manufacturer direct.

FIGURE 8-23

Computer hardware and software are sold through several marketing channels.

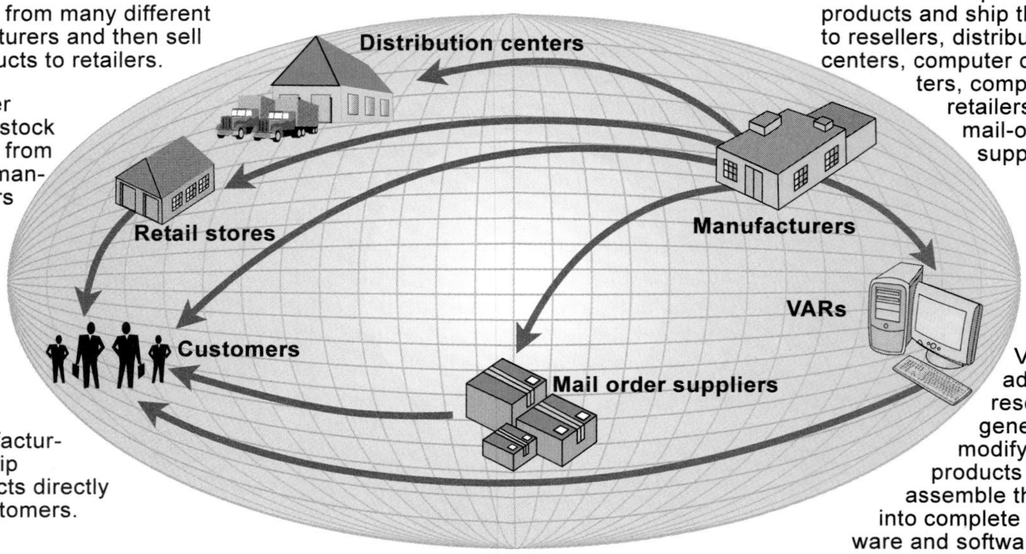

Distribution centers stock products from many different manufacturers and then sell the products to retailers.

Computer retailers stock products from several manufacturers and sell these products to customers.

Some manufacturers ship products directly to customers.

Manufacturers produce products and ship them to resellers, distribution centers, computer centers, computer retailers, and mail-order suppliers.

Value-added resellers generally modify products or assemble them into complete hardware and software solutions targeted at specific businesses.

Mail-order suppliers specialize in taking phone orders and shipping products to customers using U.S. mail or courier services.

Isn't a computer retail store the best channel for hardware and software products? A **computer retail store** purchases computer products from a variety of manufacturers, and then sells those products to consumers. Computer retail stores are either small local shops or nationwide chains, such as CompUSA, that specialize in the sale of microcomputer software and hardware. Computer retail store employees are often knowledgeable about a variety of computer products and can help you select a hardware or software product to fit your needs. Many computer retail stores also offer classes and training sessions, answer questions, provide technical support, and repair hardware products.

A computer retail store is often the best shopping option for buyers who are likely to need assistance after their purchases, such as beginning computer users or those with plans for complex computer networks. Retail stores can be a fairly expensive channel for hardware and software, however. Their prices reflect the cost of purchasing merchandise from a distributor, maintaining a retail storefront, and hiring a technically qualified staff.

What about office and electronics stores? Today, computers, peripherals, and software are sold from a variety of retail outlets, including electronics stores, such as Best Buy, Circuit City, and Radio Shack. Office superstores, such as Staples, Office Depot, and Office Max, also sell computer wares.

Prices at these outlets vary. Service tends to be less professional than from a dedicated computer retail store, so it is important for consumers to ask about service facilities and policies.

How does the mail-order channel compare to retail? **Mail order** is a special instance of retailing in which a vendor takes orders by telephone or from an Internet site, and then ships the product directly to consumers. Mail-order suppliers, such as MicroWarehouse and CDW.com, generally offer low prices but might provide only limited service and support. A mail-order supplier is often the best source of products for buyers who are unlikely to need support or who can troubleshoot problems by calling a help desk.

Experienced computer users who can install components, set up software, and do their own troubleshooting are often happy with mail-order suppliers. Inexperienced computer users might not be satisfied with the assistance they receive.

Do some manufacturers and publishers sell direct? **Manufacturer direct** refers to hardware manufacturers that sell their products directly to consumers without a "middleman," such as a retail store. IBM has a long tradition of direct sales, and that model has been emulated by several hardware manufacturers and some software publishers. A company's sales force usually targets large corporate or educational customers, where large-volume sales can cover the sales representative's costs and commissions.

For personal computer hardware, Dell Computers pioneered Web-based direct sales to individual customers. Its innovative Web site allows customers to select from a variety of standard models or configure their own custom builds (Figure 8-24). A "just-in-time" inventory model allows Dell to build each customer's computer as it is ordered, which eliminates costly inventories of computers that quickly become outdated. The obvious advantage of direct sales is that by cutting out the retailer, a manufacturer can make more profit on each unit sold. The disadvantage is that the manufacturer must provide customers with technical support—a potentially costly service that requires large teams of technical support personnel.

FIGURE 8-24

At Dell's Web site, customers can order a custom-built computer by simply clicking to add various hardware options.

CLICK TO START

What's a VAR? **VAR** stands for value-added reseller. A value-added reseller combines commercially available products with specialty hardware or software to create a computer system designed to meet the needs of a specific industry. Although VARs charge for their expertise, they are often the only source for specialized computer systems. For example, if you own a video rental store and want to automate the rental process, the best type of vendor might be a VAR that offers a complete hardware and software package tailored to the video rental business. Otherwise, you must piece together the computer, scanner, printer, and software components yourself. VARs are often the most expensive channel for hardware and software, but their expertise can be crucial to ensure that the hardware and software work correctly in a specific environment.

Do so many channels confuse consumers? Consumers can benefit from a variety of channels. Because the price of computer equipment and software tends to vary by channel, consumers can shop for the best price and the most appropriate level of support.

Although consumers benefit from a variety of channels, vendors within the channels often find that other channel vendors pirate their sales—a process referred to as **channel conflict**. In the early days of the IT industry, hardware manufacturers and software publishers awarded exclusive territories to their retail vendors. An Apple computer dealer in Spokane, for example, was assured of sales to any customers in the local area who wanted a Macintosh. Mail-order vendors, however, were also able to attract the business of Spokane customers, creating a channel conflict. To avoid such conflicts, Apple did not allow its computers to be sold through mail-order channels.

INDUSTRY REGULATION

Is the IT industry regulated in any way? Some aspects of the IT industry are regulated by government agencies, but many aspects are self-regulated. Unlike the airline industry, which is regulated by agencies such as the Federal Aviation Authority (FAA), most countries do not have a single government agency dedicated to regulating the IT industry. The IT industry encompasses many activities, however, and consequently, it is subject to regulation from a variety of broad-based government agencies, such as the FCC and FTC (Figure 8-25).

Many governments are enacting laws that restrict access to particular Internet activities and content. For example, several Caribbean countries recently enacted laws that regulate online casino operators. In 1996, the U.S. Congress enacted the Communications Decency Act, which made it illegal to put indecent material online where children might see it. Parts of this legislation were contested and ultimately nullified by the U.S. Supreme Court, but the desire for decency without censorship has not died among lawmakers. In an effort to avoid further government regulations, many Internet service companies are establishing their own policies for policing and monitoring their customers' online activity.

In many countries, export restrictions affect the type of technology that can be sold to foreign governments and individuals. For example, before being exported from the United States, software and hardware products that contain certain encryption algorithms must be registered with the U.S. government. Additional government regulations that pertain to law enforcement, national security, e-commerce, and taxation can also affect the way the IT industry conducts its business and engineers products.

FIGURE 8-25
IT Industry Regulation

Internet activity is affected by policies of the U.S. Federal Communications Commission (FCC), which regulates interstate and international communications by television, wire, radio, satellite, and cable.

The U.S. Federal Trade Commission (FTC) and Department of Justice police the business practices of the IT industry, just as they police other industries.

How does the IT industry perceive government regulation? Most IT industry leaders oppose further regulation of their industry. They remain skeptical of government regulations that might limit their ability to explore new technologies and offer them to the public. To avoid further government intervention, the IT industry has taken steps toward self-regulation.

Several organizations provide a forum for the IT industry to examine issues, express views, work out self-governing policies, and set standards. The Information Technology Industry Council has become one of the major trade associations for computer manufacturers, telecommunications suppliers, business equipment dealers, software publishers, and IT service providers. As part of its mission, this organization provides a powerful lobbying group, which works with lawmakers to minimize legislation that might curtail technology innovation and use.

The Software and Information Industry Association, formerly known as the Software Publishers Association, has 600 members. This organization focuses on protecting the intellectual property of members and lobbying for a legal and regulatory environment that benefits the entire IT industry. Its anti-piracy program is instrumental in identifying and prosecuting software and Internet piracy cases.

Organizations such as the IEEE Standards Association help the IT industry standardize technology, such as microprocessor architecture and network protocols, as well as programming languages and multimedia components.

QUICKCHECK......SECTION B

1. The computer industry can be divided into several broad categories called [_____] or segments.

2. [_____] Valley is regarded as the birthplace of integrated circuits, microprocessors, and personal computers.

3. To stay competitive, many companies turn to [_____], which locates development and production to lower-cost locations in other countries.

4. Internet-based companies called [_____] coms fueled a stock market boom that turned into a bust.

5. The life cycle of a new computer model typically includes five stages: product development, product announcement, introduction, maintenance, and [_____].

6. Some products, referred to as [_____], are announced but never produced.

7. Computer companies use a variety of marketing [_____], such as retail stores and VARs, to reach consumers.

 CHECK ANSWERS

SECTION C

CAREERS FOR COMPUTER PROFESSIONALS

Today, it seems that just about everyone uses computers at work. Secretaries use computers for word processing, auto mechanics use computers for engine diagnostics, bartenders use computers for tracking drink orders, architects use computers to draw blueprints, teachers use computers to automate grade books, and the list goes on. In fact, it is difficult to find a job nowadays that does not make use of computers in some capacity.

But who writes the software that's used by all these workers? Who designs their hardware, configures their networks, and troubleshoots their technical glitches? In this part of the chapter, you'll learn about a special cadre of workers within the IT industry called "computer professionals." You'll find out who they are, what they do, who employs them, and how much they're paid. Maybe you'll even get a glimpse of your own future, if you're considering a career in IT.

JOBS AND SALARIES

What is a "computer professional?" Despite the widespread deployment of computers, not everyone who uses a computer is considered a computer professional. In 1999, the U.S. Congress crafted an amendment to the Fair Labor Standards Act that essentially defines a **computer professional** as any person whose primary occupation involves the design, configuration, analysis, development, modification, testing, or security of computer hardware or software. The actual wording of the definition is provided in Figure 8-26.

FIGURE 8-26

The term "computer professional" is defined in a 1999 amendment to the U.S. Fair Labor Standards Act.

Any employee who is a computer systems, network, or database analyst, designer, developer, programmer, software engineer, or other similarly skilled worker whose primary duty is:

(i) The application of systems or network or database analysis techniques and procedures, including consulting with users, to determine hardware, software, systems, network, or database specifications (including functional specifications);

(ii) The design, configuration, development, integration, documentation, analysis, creation, testing, securing, or modification of, or problem resolution for, computer systems, networks, databases, or programs, including prototypes, based on and related to user, system, network, or database specifications, including design specifications and machine operating systems;

(iii) The management or training of employees performing certain duties described in clause (i) or (ii);

(iv) A combination of duties described in clauses (i), (ii), or (iii), the performance of which requires the same level of skills.

What kinds of jobs are typically available to computer professionals? Many computer professionals work in an **Information Systems department**—the wing of a business or organization responsible for computer, data, software, and support services. An IS department is also responsible for prioritizing an organization's information needs, modifying old systems as necessary, and creating new systems.

Historically, IS departments were part of an organization's Finance department because computers were initially deployed for accounting and inventory management functions. As computers began to assist with a wider variety of business tasks, some organizations changed their organizational charts to make the IS department a separate entity reporting directly to the chief executive officer or president. This reorganization provided IS departments with more autonomy to make budget decisions and prioritize projects. In addition, it provided more interaction with employees and managers from other departments.

Most IS departments are headed by a **chief information officer** (CIO), or "director." The CIO heads a hierarchy of computer professionals, who might be organized as in Figure 8-27. The following descriptions highlight typical responsibilities and skills for various IS department jobs:

A **systems analyst** investigates the requirements of a business or organization, its employees, and its customers in order to plan and implement new or improved computer services. This job requires the ability to identify problems and research technical solutions. Good communications skills are essential for interacting with managers and other employees.

A **computer programmer** (sometimes described as a programmer/analyst) designs, codes, and tests computer programs. In addition, programmers modify existing programs to meet new requirements or eliminate bugs. Computer programming requires concentration and a good memory for the countless details that pertain to a programming project. Programming projects range from entertainment and games to business and productivity applications. Programmers get satisfaction from devising efficient ways to make a computer perform specific jobs, tasks, and routines.

A **security specialist** analyzes a computer system's vulnerability to threats from viruses, worms, unauthorized access, and physical damage. Security specialists install and configure firewalls and antivirus software. They also work with management and employees to develop policies and procedures to protect computer equipment and data. Computer security is punctuated by "crises" when a virus hits, or a security breach is discovered. A security specialist must have wide-ranging knowledge of computers as well as communications protocols that can be applied for a quick resolution to any crisis that occurs.

A **database administrator** analyzes a company's data to determine the most effective way to collect and store it. Database administrators create databases, data entry forms, and reports. They also define backup procedures, provide access to authorized users, and supervise the day-to-day use of databases.

FIGURE 8-27

The organizational structure of information systems departments vary. This organizational structure might typically be found in a mid-size business.

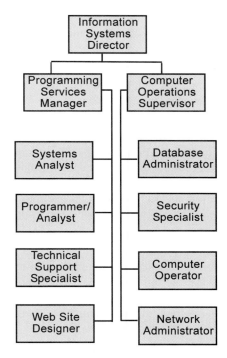

A **network specialist/administrator** plans, installs, and maintains one or more local area networks. They also provide network accounts and access rights to approved users. They troubleshoot connectivity problems and respond to requests from the network's users for new software. Network specialists/administrators might be responsible for maintaining the security of a network, plus they often pick up Webmaster duties to maintain an organization's Web site.

A **computer operator** typically works with minicomputers, mainframes, and supercomputers. Computer operators monitor computer performance, install software patches and upgrades, perform backups, and restore data as necessary.

A **technical support specialist** troubleshoots hardware and software problems. Good interpersonal skills and patience are required for this job.

A **Web site designer** creates, tests, posts, and modifies Web pages. A good sense of design and artistic talent are required for this job, along with an understanding of how people use graphical user interfaces. Familiarity with Web tools, such as HTML, XML, JavaScript, and ActiveX, is becoming more important for this job, as is a knowledge of computer programming and database management.

Do computer professionals work outside of IS departments? In addition to jobs in IS departments, computer professionals also find work in companies that produce computer hardware and software. Some of these jobs include the following:

A **technical writer** creates documentation for large programming projects and writes the online or printed user manuals that accompany computers, peripheral devices, and software. Some technical writers work for computer magazines, writing columns about the latest hardware products, software, and automated business solutions. Good writing and communications skills are valuable for this job, as is an ability to quickly learn how to use new computers and software.

A **computer salesperson**, or "sales rep," sells computers. Sales reps might pay personal visits to potential corporate customers or staff the order desk of a mail-order computer company. Sales reps' starting salaries tend to be low but are usually supplemented by commissions and bonuses. Effective sales reps tend to have good interpersonal skills, an ability to remember technical specifications, and an understanding of business problems and solutions.

A **quality assurance specialist** participates in alpha and beta test cycles of software, looking for bugs or other usability problems. This job title sometimes refers to assembly-line workers who examine and test chips, circuit boards, computers, and peripheral devices. An effective QA specialist has a good eye for detail and a passion for perfection.

A **computer engineer** designs and tests new hardware products, such as computer chips, circuit boards, computers, and peripheral devices.

A **manufacturing technician** participates in the fabrication of computer chips, circuit boards, system units, or peripheral devices. Some of these jobs require basic screwdriver skills, whereas others require special training in microlithography.

These job descriptions are but a sample of those in IS departments and the IT industry. Additional job titles are listed in Figure 8-28. You'll find even more at the IT Careers InfoWeb.

FIGURE 8-28
Jobs for Computer Professionals

Account Representative
Applications Systems Analyst
Applications Programmer
Art Director - Web
Associate Editor - Web
Associate Producer -Web
Assoc. Product Manager - Web
Business Development Director
Business Development Manager
Business Systems Analyst
Client/Server Programmer
Computer Operations Manager
Computer Operations Supervisor
Computer Operator
Content Engineer - Web
Creative Director - Web
Data Architect
Data Control Clerk
Data Entry Clerk
Data Entry Supervisor
Data Security Analyst
Data Security Manager
Data Security Supervisor
Data Warehouse Specialist
Database Administrator
Database Analyst
Database Librarian
Documentation Specialist
E-commerce Manager
Electronic Data Interchange Specialist
Graphical User Interface Programmer
Hardware Engineer
Help Desk Support Technician
Information Systems Auditor
Information Technology Director
Interface Designer
Intranet Applications Manager
LAN Support Technician
Mail Server Administrator
Mainframe Programmer
Network Administrator
Network Analyst
Operating Systems Programmer
PC Maintenance Technician
Software Engineer
Software Quality Assurance Specialist
Technical Librarian
Trainer
Telecommunications Specialist
Webmaster
Web Site Designer

What's the outlook for computer careers? According to an Information Technology Association of America study, in 2000, the IT workforce totaled about 10.4 million, but lost 500,000 jobs in 2001 as the dot com bubble burst. A small but steady upswing from 2002 through 2004 brought the IT workforce close to its year 2000 peak. In coming years, the highest demand may be for technical support personnel, enterprise systems specialists, database developers/administrators, and security specialists.

As in the past, economic trends could cause significant changes in the job market. In preparing for an IT career, flexibility is the key. You should be willing to train and then retrain as new skills are needed to work with emerging technologies.

What can I expect as a salary for an IT industry job? Web sites such as *www.bls.gov* provide salary data for various IT industry jobs. In addition to data from the Bureau of Labor Statistics, you can find comparative IT industry salary averages using a standard Web search engine.

As with almost every industry, the compensation rates for jobs in the IT industry vary. Jobs that require college degrees and certification typically pay more than jobs that require a high school diploma and some on-the-job training. IT industry salaries also vary by geographic location. In the United States, the highest salaries tend to be offered in the Northeast and on the West Coast. Figure 8-29 shows the range of salaries for selected IT jobs in the United States.

INFOWEBLINKS

Before making a career decision, it is important for you to research current industry trends and the general economic outlook. The **Career Outlook InfoWeb** will help you access Web resources on this topic.

www.course.com/np/concepts8/ch08

FIGURE 8-29
IT Industry Average
Base Salaries

Job Title	Northeast	Southeast	N. Central	S. Central	Western
Software Developer	$72,000	$70,000	$71,000	$68,000	$77,000
Database Administrator	$85,500	$76,000	$77,500	$80,000	$88,000
Web Applications Programmer	$72,500	$68,000	$66,500	$65,000	$76,000
Network Administrator	$66,000	$57,000	$62,000	$62,500	$67,500
Applications Development Analyst	$69,000	$61,500	$63,500	$68,500	$73,000
Telecommunications Engineer	$68,500	$65,500	$67,000	$66,000	$74,000
Customer Support Analyst	$52,000	$43,500	$47,500	$49,000	$51,000
Quality Assurance Analyst	$60,000	$50,000	$53,000	$55,000	$63,000
Security Analyst	$67,500	$59,500	$63,000	$63,000	$71,500

Average base salary paid to an individual with a Bachelor's Degree in a relevant field of work and 3-5 years of relevant work experience.
Source: 2004 IT Market Compensation Study, people3, Inc., A Gartner Company. Data effective as of 3/1/2004.
Copy Right: people3, Inc., A Gartner Company. All Rights Reserved.

WORKING CONDITIONS

What are the advantages of working in the computer industry? Many technology companies offer employee-friendly working conditions that include child care, flexible hours, and the opportunity to work from home. As in any industry, the exact nature of a job depends on the company and the particular projects that are in the works. Some jobs and projects are more interesting than others.

Are IT workers typically satisfied with their jobs? Job satisfaction depends on many factors, such as working conditions, salary, benefits, and job security. When the economy is slow, job satisfaction declines as companies downsize their workforces and the burden of work increases for the employees who remain. Companies might also turn to outsourcing and off-shoring to reduce costs, making in-house jobs less secure. When the economy is good, job satisfaction increases because wages tend to rise, job security is more certain, and it is easier to leave a job you don't like to seek a better one.

Data gathered for the *Best Places to Work in IT* survey indicate that IT employees want basics, such as good salaries, paid vacations, and health care coverage. They are most satisfied, however, when their jobs offer access to cutting-edge technology, training opportunities that help advance careers, and flexibility to establish balance between work and personal life.

What about part-time or contract work? The average IT industry employee works a 40-hour week, and often longer hours are required. Part-time workers are defined as those who are required to be on the job for fewer than 40 hours a week. The number of part-time workers in the computer industry is similar to other industries.

The IT industry has an unusually large number of contract and temporary workers. A **contract worker** is typically hired as a consultant (Figure 8-30). Contract workers are not official employees of a company. They might be paid by the job, rather than by the hour; they are not eligible for a company's health insurance benefits or retirement plan, and they must pay self-employment taxes.

IT businesses benefit from the ability to hire contract workers. The pool of IT contract workers offers a selection of people with specialized skills. Contract workers can be added to a company's staff when needed, instead of hiring full-time workers who might later be laid off if the company is forced to downsize. A few businesses, however, have been accused of misusing contract workers by hiring them for years at a time without paying benefits. Potential contract workers are advised to carefully read their contracts and understand the terms of employment.

Can I work at an IT job from home? Workers in many industries are interested in **telecommuting**—using available technology to work from home or an off-site location. In recent years, businesses have begun to allow telecommuting because it makes financial sense. Telecommuters tend to be more productive and work longer hours because they have no commute time, and they are not interrupted by routine office chatter.

Telecommuting also has disadvantages. Some workers need supervision or they procrastinate. The home environment can be distracting, which reduces productivity. Security is also a concern—especially the security of data transmitted from home workers to corporate networks.

The Internet and telecommunications technologies have made an impact on the availability of telecommuting opportunities for workers. It has become common for employees to collaborate through e-mail, fax, groupware, and videoconferencing. Although the majority of IT workers still commute to work, industry observers expect the number of telecommuting IT workers to increase. Programming and customer support are likely to be the first jobs with a significant number of telecommuting workers.

How safe are computers, monitors, and other electronic equipment? Most people in the IT industry work at desk jobs, and spend many hours of the workday gazing at a computer monitor and typing on a keyboard. According to the BLS, "Data entry keyers and others who work at video terminals for extended periods of time may experience musculoskeletal strain, eye problems, stress, or repetitive motion illnesses, such

FIGURE 8-30
Contract Workers

Many IT workers prefer contract work. It provides variety and new challenges, plus the opportunity to learn new skills while working with different businesses. IT contract workers often earn more than permanent full-time workers doing the same work. Contract workers command anywhere from $25 to $350 an hour, although health insurance and other benefits are not included.

as carpal tunnel syndrome." To avoid these health hazards, workers should be aware of the ergonomics of their work areas.

Ergonomics is the study of work and work environments. The U.S. Occupational Safety and Health Administration (OSHA) further explains ergonomics as "the science of designing the job to fit the worker, rather than physically forcing the worker's body to fit the job." Ergonomics provides guidelines for making work environments safer and healthier. For example, Figure 8-31 illustrates how to use ergonomic guidelines to set up your computer, desk, and chair to avoid potentially disabling musculoskeletal injuries.

FIGURE 8-31

OSHA guidelines help you set up your computer work area according to ergonomic guidelines.

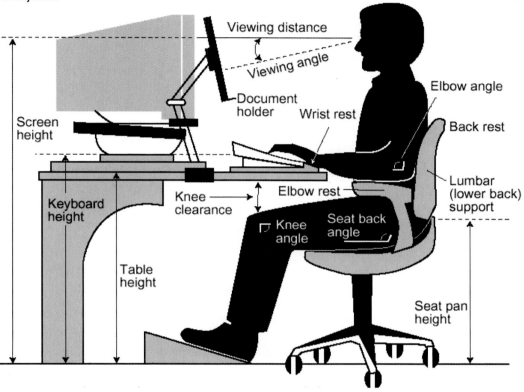

Who is a typical computer professional? As you might expect, IT industry workers are younger than their counterparts in most other industries. About 32% of IT industry workers are 25–34 years old, whereas only 22% of all workers are in that age group.

As with many technical occupations, men outnumber women in the IT industry. In the United States only 26% of programmers are women, although in India, that figure is 38%. Fewer than 25% of the members of the World Wide Web Consortium staff, which sets the standard for HTML and other Web protocols, are women. Only a handful of women head major IT corporations, even though IT is considered one of the industries with the fewest barriers to women.

Minorities are increasingly taking advantage of opportunities in the IT industry. The typical IT workplace in the United States is populated by a large percentage of people of Asian, European, and Indian descent. The number of African Americans in the IT industry is growing slowly. Although the Latino population is the fastest-growing segment of United States society, it remains the most underrepresented in the IT workforce.

The general attitude among IT industry human resource managers is "If you're good, we'll hire you." But being "good" means having the right set of qualifications and experience for the job. The disturbing news is that despite various scholarship incentives, women and minorities continue to shy away from the engineering, computer science, and information system degrees necessary to gain entry to IT industry careers.

EDUCATION

What are the basic qualifications for IT industry jobs? Qualifications for most IT industry jobs include some type of higher education, certification, or computer experience. A bachelor's degree in a computer-related discipline is the most prevalent job requirement, but some employers accept a two-year associate's degree. High demand for IT workers in the past prompted employers to hire high school graduates and college students who seemed able to "learn fast." A maturing IT industry, however, has made employers more selective. The table in Figure 8-32 shows the educational level of the current IT workforce.

Level Completed	Percent of IT Workers
High school graduate, high school equivalency, or less	8
Some college, no degree	16
Associate's degree	10
Bachelor's degree	48
Graduate degree	18

FIGURE 8-32
Educational Level of IT Workers

Do I need a computer science degree to work in the computer industry? Computer science is only one of the many computer-related degrees that colleges and universities offer. Each of these degrees emphasizes a particular aspect of information technology:

■ **Computer engineering** focuses on the design of computer hardware and peripheral devices, often at the chip level. The curriculum includes basic studies in calculus, chemistry, engineering, physics, computer organization, logic design, computer architecture, microprocessor design, and signal processing. Students learn how to design new computer circuits, microchips, and other electronic components, plus they learn how to design new computer instruction sets and combine electronic or optical components to provide powerful, cost-effective computing. A degree in computer engineering provides excellent qualifications for working at a chip manufacturer, such as Intel, Motorola, IBM, or Texas Instruments.

■ **Computer science** focuses on computer architecture and how to program computers to make them work effectively and efficiently. The curriculum includes courses in programming, algorithms, software development, computer architecture, data representation, logic design, calculus, discrete math, and physics. Students investigate the fundamental theories of how computers solve problems, and they learn how to write application programs, system software, computer languages, and device drivers. Computer science graduates generally find jobs as programmers, with good possibilities for advancement to software engineers, object-oriented/GUI developers, and project managers in technical applications development. Computer scientists work as theorists, inventors, and researchers in fields as diverse as artificial intelligence, virtual reality, and computer games.

■ **Information systems**, or information technology, degree programs, typically offered by a university's College of Business, focus on applying computers to business problems. The curriculum includes course work in business, accounting, computer programming, communications, systems analysis, and human psychology. For students who want to become computer professionals but lack strong math aptitude, most academic advisors recommend the information systems degree. An information systems degree usually leads to a programming or technical support job, with good possibilities for advancement to systems analyst, project manager, database administrator, network manager, or other management positions.

What kinds of computer jobs require only an associate's degree? Colleges, community colleges, and technical schools offer several computer-related associate's degrees, ranging from computer programming to graphic design, networking, and telecommunications. The curriculum for these programs varies from one degree program to another, but all tend to require intensive course work. Graduates of two-year programs typically find employment as entry-level technicians, programmers, and support personnel. Advancement opportunities might be limited, however, without additional education or certification.

Do I need a graduate degree? Master's degrees in software engineering have been difficult to find, except at large research universities with well-established computer science programs. A master's degree in computer science is available at most four-year colleges and universities that offer graduate degrees. Another option at the graduate level is to pursue a master's degree in information systems or a master's degree in business administration (MBA). Any of these graduate degrees would help you get a management position in the computer industry.

Doctoral degrees are available in software engineering, applications software engineering, systems software development, and management information systems. A doctoral degree in any of these areas would qualify you for advanced technical research or for a position as a college professor (Figure 8-33).

FIGURE 8-33

Master's and doctoral degrees provide qualifications for management-level industry jobs, private sector and government research, and college teaching.

Where can I find information on computer-related degree programs? Peterson's is a comprehensive resource for educational services. Its Web site at *www.petersons.com* has become a primary resource for locating educational programs as well as providing testing services for admissions and certification. Peterson's maintains a searchable database of two-year and four-year programs that prepare you for a variety of IT jobs. You can find additional information at the Web sites of various technical schools, community colleges, and universities.

CERTIFICATION

How important is certification? Certification alone is rarely sufficient to qualify you for a job in the IT industry. Paired with a college degree or extensive experience, however, several studies suggest that certification can improve your chances for employment, increase your credibility in the workplace, and lead to higher salaries. Many employers view certification with some degree of skepticism, so the value of a certificate depends on where, when, and how it is obtained. Critics of certification exams, for example, maintain that a multiple-choice test cannot accurately measure a person's ability to deal with real-world equipment and software. Bottom line: Certification is only part of your total package of qualifications.

What type of certification is available? Certification falls into two broad categories: certificates of completion and certification exams. **Certificates of completion** are offered to students who successfully complete one or more courses on a specific topic. Community colleges and technical schools often offer certificates of completion in a variety of computer-related areas, such as Information Technology Specialist, LAN Administrator, User Support Specialist, PC/Hardware Support Specialist, and IT Operations Specialist.

FIGURE 8-34

Your local bookstore and the Internet provide sources for independent study materials that can help you prepare for an IT certification exam.

A **certification exam** is an objective test that verifies your level of knowledge about a particular technology or subject. Approximately 300 computer-related certification exams are offered in areas of specialty that range from desktop publishing to network installation. Most of these exams use multiple-choice format, last several hours, and require substantial testing fees. You can prepare for a certification exam with independent study materials (Figure 8-34), online tutorials, or an exam preparation class. Certification exams can be divided into several categories:

▪ **General computer knowledge.** IC3 certification, offered by Certipoint, covers basic computing knowledge and skills. General certification is also offered by the International Computer Driving License (ICDL).

The Institute for Certification of Computing Professionals (ICCP) offers several generalized certification exams, including the CCP (Certified Computing Professional) exam. According to the ICCP Web site, "Professionals certified with ICCP serve as consultants, working with local, state, and federal government; in accounting and banking; in high schools, technical schools, and universities; in the manufacturing industry; in insurance and numerous other fields."

▪ **Software applications.** Many certification exams allow you to demonstrate your prowess with a specific software application. The Microsoft Office Specialist certification is perhaps the most popular, but of limited value to most computer professionals who are expected to be able to quickly learn such applications on their own. Certification in productivity applications is most valuable for entry-level secretarial and clerical positions as well as help desk personnel.

Autodesk offers the AutoCAD Certified Professional exam on the use of its 3-D design software. Certification is also available for popular Adobe software applications, such as Illustrator, PageMaker, and Premiere. Macromedia offers certification for its Dreamweaver, Flash, and ColdFusion software products.

■ **Database administration.** Databases require a high level of expertise, not only in the use of database software, but in the conception and design of database structures. Many computer professionals have sought certification in database systems, such as Oracle, Access, Sybase, and DB2. The most popular database certification exams include the Microsoft Certified Database Administrator (MCDBA) and Oracle Certified Database Administrator.

■ **Networking.** Among computer professionals, network certification might be the most useful. One of the earliest network certification exams was offered by Novell, publisher of the NetWare network operating system. Microsoft offers a corresponding MCSE certification (Microsoft Certified Systems Engineer). Network hardware certification includes the Cisco Certified Network Professional (CCNP), offered by network equipment supplier Cisco Systems.

■ **Computer hardware.** One of the most popular computer hardware certification exams is the A+ Certification, sponsored by the Computing Technology Industry Association (CompTIA). This exam is designed to certify the competency of entry-level computer service technicians for installing, configuring, upgrading, troubleshooting, and repairing personal computer systems. A+ Certification provides good credentials for employment in a computer store or computer repair shop.

■ **Computer security.** With the proliferation of computer viruses and worms, analysts predict that computer security will become a hot niche for IT workers. CompTIA offers the Security+ certification exam, which covers topics such as cryptography, access control, authentication, external attack, and operational security. The International Information Systems Security Consortium offers a Certified Information System Security Professional (CISSP) exam.

INFOWEBLINKS

For a comprehensive list of certification exams and tips on how to prepare for them, connect to the **Certification InfoWeb**.

www.course.com/np/concepts8/ch08

QUICKCHECK......SECTION C

1. The term "computer professional" is loosely defined as programmers and systems analysts who work in the IT industry. True or false?

    [   ]

2. A [   ] specialist analyzes a computer system's vulnerability to threats from viruses, worms, unauthorized access, and physical damage.

3. The advantage of [   ] is reduced commute time, but disadvantages include distractions and security risks.

4. Most IT jobs are safe when [   ] guidelines are followed to set up your computer, desk, and lighting to avoid potentially disabling musculoskeletal injuries.

5. [   ] systems degree programs focus on applying computers to business problems.

6. IC3 and ICDL are examples of computer [   ] exams.

 CHECK ANSWERS

SECTION D

JOB HUNTING RESOURCES

In earlier sections of this chapter, you learned about the events that created today's computer and IT industries. You then learned about becoming a computer professional and working in these industries. In this section of the chapter, you'll find out how to hunt for a job using up-to-date tools and techniques. Although the focus is hunting for jobs in the IT industry, you'll find that many of the tips and techniques apply to job hunting in any field.

JOB HUNTING BASICS

How do I find a job in the IT industry? In many ways, finding a job in the IT industry is just like finding a job in any other industry. Effective job seekers begin by taking stock of their qualifications, identifying job titles relevant to their skills, identifying potential employers, and considering the geographic area in which they want to work. They then create a carefully worded resume, look for job openings, contact potential employers, and work with employment agencies and recruiting firms. Figure 8-35 summarizes the steps in a job hunt.

Conventional wisdom about job hunting applies to a broad spectrum of industries, such as financial, automotive, hospitality, and even entertainment. But one job-hunting strategy is not necessarily effective for every job in every industry. Take a closer look at the job hunting process, and examine how hunting for an IT job might differ from a job search in other industries.

How can I use the Internet to find a job? The Internet has become an important tool for job hunters. In 1994, about 10,000 resumes were posted on the Web. By 1998, that number exceeded 1 million. Today, the Web plays host to an estimated 2.5 million resumes.

The Internet can figure into your job hunt in several ways, including researching potential jobs and employers, posting your resume, locating job leads, and corresponding with potential employers. Career counselors warn of placing too much emphasis on the online aspects of your job search. "Don't put all your eggs in the online basket" is often-repeated advice. Job-hunting experts advise IT job seekers to spend no more than 50% of their total job-hunting efforts online; the other 50% should be spent making contacts with recruiters, placement agencies, career counselors, and mentors. Rather than accept that advice outright, consider it with regard to your employment needs, geographical location, and current employment situation.

Where do I start? You should begin by defining the jobs for which you are qualified. In the IT industry, job titles are not standardized. For example, the job title for a person who provides employee or customer support over the phone might be "Help Desk Operator," "Customer Support Technician," "Support Specialist," "Personal Computer Specialist," "Technology Support Specialist," or "Inbound Telephone Service Consultant."

FIGURE 8-35
Job Hunting Steps

Define the job you want

Create your resume

Look for job openings

Supply potential employers with resume

Prepare for interviews

Evaluate job offers

Accept a new job

INFOWEBLINKS

At the **Online Job Hunting InfoWeb**, you'll find lots of tips for using technology to find a job.

www.course.com/np/concepts8/ch08

Nonstandardized job titles can pose a problem for job hunters, especially those who use search engines to locate job openings. Failure to enter one of the many titles for a job might mean that a job hunter misses a good opportunity. Although many job search sites maintain their own lists of equivalent job titles, job hunters in the IT industry should take some time to compile their own lists of equivalent job titles and relevant search terms. You can compile such a list by entering the key phrases "job titles" and "computer industry" into a general search engine such as Google. Connect to the sites the search produces, and take note of any job titles that seem applicable.

RESUMES FOR TODAY'S JOB MARKET

Do I need an online resume? As a computer professional, you are expected to use technology effectively for everyday tasks. You can demonstrate this ability to prospective employers by the way you treat your resume. You can prepare your resume in formats suitable for different computer platforms and delivery methods, as shown in Figure 8-36.

■ **Print.** You should save one version of your resume as a beautifully formatted word processing file. You might consider using desktop publishing software to put the finishing touches on your resume before you print it on high-quality paper. Make sure the file that holds your resume converts easily into formats that can be read by Mac, PC, and Linux computers, in case a prospective employer asks you to attach your resume file to an e-mail message.

Before sending your resume as an attachment, try to discover the format that is easiest for your prospective employer to use. Microsoft's Rich Text Format produces files with .rtf extensions, which can be read by a variety of word processing software. Microsoft's document format, which uses the .doc extension, is also widely used.

■ **E-mail.** Some career counselors advise against the use of e-mail attachments, suggesting that many employers never open attachments for fear of e-mail viruses. Instead of attaching your resume, you can simply paste it into the body of an e-mail message. To make sure it is formatted for maximum readability, you might want to create a plain ASCII version of your resume, without fancy fonts, bullets, or symbols. This ASCII version might also be useful for online job posting sites that store your resume information in a searchable database. Making an attractive ASCII version of your resume can be a real challenge, but it is one of the topics covered in the lab at the end of this section.

■ **HTML.** You might also want to create an HTML version of your resume. You can paste this version into an HTML-formatted e-mail message or post it on a Web site provided by your school or ISP.

You might be able to provide just your resume's URL to prospective employers—not a bad strategy if you send out e-mail with a general "Do you have any job openings?" inquiry.

FIGURE 8-36
Job seekers can format their resumes for printed output, e-mail delivery, or Web posting.

Should an IT industry resume contain any special elements?
Regardless of the industry in which you seek employment, an effective
resume is clear, correct, and easy to read. When developing your resume,
you can ask friends, coworkers, and career counselors to review your
drafts and provide suggestions for improvement. Figure 8-37 shows a short
checklist of resume writing guidelines.

In the past, tips on how to create the "perfect"
resume applied to a conventional process in which
a recruiter sifted through a pile of resumes that
arrived by surface mail. Job seekers spent hours
agonizing over the weight, texture, and color of the
paper on which they printed their resumes.
Selecting a font that showed just the right degree of
individuality became almost as important as selecting the most dynamic adjectives and verbs.

Conventional tips about paper color, fonts, and
wording remain valid for hard-copy resumes.
However, today's job seekers often place resumes
in online databases, which are initially scanned not
by human eyes, but by a computer.

**How can my resume get maximum exposure in
an online job database?** For resumes that
become part of a computer-searchable database,
experts recommend that you focus on nouns, not
verbs. At one time, the trend was to pepper your
resume with action phrases and power verbs, such
as "implemented successful solutions" and "created
innovative algorithms." When employers use a job
site's search engine to locate potential employees,
however, they typically search for particular skills by
entering nouns associated with programming language names, software, computer equipment,
analysis methodologies, and business sectors.
They might also enter buzzwords and acronyms,
such as XML, B2B, client/server, API, and P2P,
which relate to specific IT tools and methods. Job
seekers should try to envision the search terms that
employers might enter, and then include applicable
terms in their resumes.

Tips for an Effective Resume

Be clear and concise

- Eliminate unnecessary words, phrases, and sentences.
- Be economical with words when describing tasks, duties, titles, and accomplishments.
- Be brief and to the point without selling yourself short.

Place the most important point first

- List your qualifications by importance and relevance to the job you seek.
- Summarize skills at the top of the resume.
- Use a bold font to emphasize skills and accomplishments that are required for the position you seek.
- Include pertinent information about training, certification, and professional affiliations, but avoid personal information, such as church affiliation and hobbies, that is not directly related to the job.

Use language effectively

- Target terms and wording to prospective employers.
- Use industry jargon wherever appropriate.
- Use action verbs to maintain the reader's interest.
- Use past and present tenses consistently. Double-check grammar and spelling.
- When posting information in a database, use nouns that describe your skills.

In addition to computer-related search terms, employers sometimes
search for terms that indicate a job applicant's personality, communication
skills, and work ethic. When appropriate, adjectives such as "enthusiastic,"
"team player," "industrious," "honest," "capable," and "experienced" can be
effective in helping an online recruiter pull your resume from those submitted by thousands of other applicants.

What other factors are important for online resumes? Today's trend to search resumes online has implications for all job seekers, not just those in the IT industry. For example, if you use word processing software to create a resume that's organized in columns, the information might become scrambled. Most online search engines "read" down each column, instead of scanning across columns from left to right. For example, suppose that you use two columns to list your previous employment, like this:

Project Manager	MultiNat Inc., Hanover, CO
Database Administrator	Shorelance Equipment, Denver, CO

When posted online, the formatting codes that produce multiple columns might be ignored, producing a single column of jumbled information, like this:

Project Manager

Database Administrator

MultiNat Inc., Hanover, CO

Shorelance Equipment, Denver, CO

To avoid problems with column formats, use a single column, like this:

Project Manager, MultiNat Inc., Hanover, CO

Database Administrator, Shorelance Equipment, Denver, CO

Experience is important, but the old style of "dating" your tenure at a job supplies little information for online searches. Information such as "Intern IBM from 2003-2005" does not produce a "hit" for a recruiter searching online for "IBM >2 years." By modifying your online resume to "Intern IBM, 2 years: 2003-2005," you provide better information for electronic searches.

WEB PORTFOLIOS

Can my personal home pages play a role in my job search? Your personal home pages can be an effective supplement to your job hunt. In addition to posting your resume, you can use your Web site to showcase talents in a Web portfolio. A **Web portfolio** is a hypertext version of your resume, which might contain links to relevant Web sites, such as past employers, your alma mater, and samples of your work. For example, a programmer might include a link to one of her particularly well-documented and elegant programs, or a Web designer might provide links to sites that he designed.

Current technology gives you the ability to personalize your Web pages with photos or even "video portraits" that demonstrate your speaking and communications abilities. However, some human resource directors are nervous about any information that indicates an applicant's age, gender, ethnicity, or physical characteristics. Decisions based on such factors could be viewed as discriminatory. You might want to keep such multimedia presentations on hand but supply them only when requested.

Just remember that your personal home pages are an open book to prospective employers. If you don't want them to know the details about last summer's vacation, you should remove such extraneous material from your Web site. Even if you don't supply the URL for your personal home pages to prospective employers, remember that your Web site can be easily found simply by entering your name in a search engine, such as Yahoo!

INFOWEBLINKS

Because of their extensive knowledge about computers, job seekers in the IT industry may be able to understand the implications of online resume searches better than their counterparts in other industries. It doesn't hurt to get some tips from the experts at the **Resume Guide InfoWeb**.

www.course.com/np/concepts8/ch08

JOB LISTINGS

What's the best way to find job openings? Successful job hunting usually requires several strategies. One strategy is to look for job openings and initiate contact with an employer by submitting an application. A second strategy is to post an online resume that can be found by recruiters who then initiate contact. A third strategy is to develop a liaison with a recruiting firm, which acts as an intermediary between job seekers and potential employers.

Where can I find a list of job openings? To find job openings, you can begin with the usual sources of job listings: the newspaper's Help Wanted section, your school's career placement office, and your local state employment agency. Typically, you'll move quickly to online resources, especially if you seek employment beyond your local city. For example, several Web sites enable you to search the current Help Wanted ads from major metropolitan newspapers. Many other local papers place the Help Wanted section online at their own sites. If you search for employment in a particular city, these Help Wanted resources can prove quite useful.

Many employers—and a large percentage of IT industry employers—maintain Web sites that include links to information about their job openings. If you have a short list of companies that you'd like to work for, check out their Web sites (Figure 8-38).

FIGURE 8-38
Many companies include "jobs" links at their Web sites.

JOB BANKS

An **online job bank** maintains a database that contains thousands of job openings posted by employers. The largest job banks span just about every industry. Others are devoted to specific industries. Several online job banks, like the one in Figure 8-39, specialize in the IT industry.

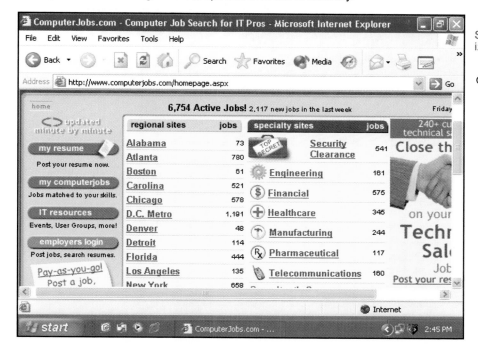

FIGURE 8-39
Some job banks special-ize in the IT industry.

CLICK TO START

You can search most online job databases by job title, geographic location, or company. These searches are typically free, although you might be required to register before searching. When registering, follow common sense to protect your privacy. Do not, for example, provide your social security number. Although it is required for jobs in the United States, your social security number should be given only to your employer after you receive a job offer.

If your search turns up a job that looks promising, you might be provided with the information necessary to contact the employer directly with a letter of application and resume. If the information for direct contact is not sup-plied, most job banks provide a way to apply online by sending your resume information to the employer through the job bank's Web site. To use the "apply online" feature, you're typically required to register with the job bank.

Do I have to manually search every online job bank? At last count, the Internet offered more than 2,500 job banks, each with unique job announcements. Searching all these sites manually would be a full-time job in itself! Search agents and metasearch tools allow you to automate the search process across many sites.

INFOWEBLINKS

Connect to the **Online Job Banks InfoWeb** for links to the most popular Web-based job databases.

www.course.com/np/concepts8/ch08

A **job search agent** is an automated program that searches one or more databases and notifies you when it finds any leads that match your specified criteria. To use a job search agent, you configure it with keywords that describe the type of job you want, your geographical limitations, and salary requirements. You then launch the agent and it searches for matching job announcements. When a match is found, the search agent generates an e-mail message with the information you need to access the job posting and respond. Most job banks provide access to free job search agents.

Some search agents work within one specific site—typically an online job bank. Other search agents visit multiple Web sites. The key advantage of a job search agent, such as the one shown in Figure 8-40, is that you don't have to be online while it works.

FIGURE 8-40

An online search agent autonomously searches for jobs that match your requirements.

CLICK TO START

A **metasearch tool** is a software program that performs broad-based Web searches, such as searching more than one job database at a time. In some respects, a metasearch tool is similar to a multi-site job search agent, except that when you use a metasearch tool, you must remain online. Instead of notifying you by e-mail, a metasearch tool supplies a list of links to applicable job postings, similar to the links provided by a standard search engine, such as Google.

How well do job banks protect my privacy? Job seekers who post their resumes at online job banks should be aware of potential threats to their privacy. Even if you specify an expiration date for your resume, a job bank might store it for many years. Such information can be used to compile a profile of you, which can be misused by advertisers or individuals interested in "stealing" identities. Some job banks might distribute your resume or personal information without your authorization. Sometimes job banks sell resumes to employers and pass personal information to advertisers. Before posting your resume, always check the job bank's privacy policy.

To protect your privacy, you might consider removing most of the contact information, such as your address and phone number, from your online resume. You should provide an e-mail address, but not the address of the business e-mail account supplied by your employer. Also, make sure your e-mail address is not linked to a personal profile, as it is on America Online and some other Internet provider sites. You can open a Web-based e-mail account specifically devoted to job hunting. By the way, consider your e-mail user ID carefully. Employers might respond better to an e-mail address such as excellentprogrammer@hotmail.com than an address such as bigbertha@hotmail.com.

Many job seekers are hesitant to post their resumes for fear that their current employers will learn they are preparing to "jump ship." Some job banks allow you to block access to your resume by specific employers. If that is not possible, you can disguise the name of your employer by substituting a generic description of it. For example, Epson America might become "a multinational company specializing in digital printer technology."

HEAD HUNTERS AND EMPLOYMENT AGENCIES

What's a "head hunter"? The term "head hunter" refers to a recruitment firm. These firms are contacted by companies seeking new employees. A head hunter looks through its database of job seekers and attempts to find suitable candidates. Head hunters are continually searching for workers to add to their databases. They use a variety of techniques to find workers with high-demand skills—even workers who might not be actively seeking a new job.

FIGURE 8-41

Head hunters and employment agencies can help you find a job, but make sure you understand the fee structure and privacy policies before you agree to participate.

Head hunter recruitment fees are usually paid by the companies that hire them. They are paid only if they make a placement. Fees are typically based on a percentage of the employee's salary—not because the employee pays the fees, but because head hunters command higher fees for finding scarce high-level executives.

Companies usually ask head hunters to help fill managerial and executive positions. However, during boom times in the IT industry, qualified applicants at all levels of the corporate ladder sometimes become scarce, and head hunters are asked to recruit even entry-level workers, such as junior programmers.

What about employment agencies? An employment agency (or placement service) works on behalf of employees rather than employers. The focus of an employment agency is to find employers for people who seek work (Figure 8-41). State-run employment agencies and those operated by schools typically offer placement services for free. Most colleges and universities offer some type of placement service and encourage students to tap into resources offered by career counselors, alumni, and on-campus recruiters. Private employment agencies, however, usually charge a fee for their services. At some agencies the fee is due up front, whereas other agencies charge only when a job offer is accepted.

EVALUATING JOB OPENINGS

What factors should I consider before responding to a job opening?
A job application takes time—your time and a recruiter's time. Before you apply for a job, most career counselors suggest that you gather some background information about the company and its location. This information can help you decide whether the job is worth pursuing.

If you decide to go ahead with an application, the information you gather can also help you formulate some intelligent questions to ask if you're invited for an interview. You might also be able to use the Web to find out about your prospective employer's financial status and corporate culture and gather information about the town that could become your new home.

How do I find information about a company's finances and corporate culture? To find information about a company, start at its Web site. Most companies provide a set of "About us" pages that describe the company's mission. You can also check reports such as *Computerworld*'s "100 Best Places to Work in IT" and *Fortune* magazine's "100 Best Places to Work."

How do I find information about the quality of life in a particular city? Web sites such as *www.homefair.com* provide online tools that help you calculate the cost of moving, the cost of living, and the quality of life in a selected location. Such sites offer comparative information about crime rates, demographics, school systems, the local economy, air quality, and water quality as well as cultural, sports, and leisure activities. You can also connect to the city's Chamber of Commerce Web site, which might have additional information about lifestyles in the area.

INFOWEBLINKS

If you need to explore a company's finances, corporate culture, or geographical location, use the links provided by the **Companies and Places InfoWeb**.

www.course.com/np/concepts8/ch08

QUICKCHECK......SECTION D

1. You can demonstrate your ability to use technology for everyday tasks by preparing your resume in a variety of [   ], such as HTML, DOC, and ASCII.

2. For resumes that you intend to post on a computer-searchable [   ], experts recommend that you focus on nouns rather than verbs.

3. A Web [   ] is a hypertext version of your resume, which might include links to relevant Web sites and samples of your work.

4. A job search [   ] is an automated program that searches one or more databases and notifies you when it finds any leads that match your specified criteria.

5. A(n) [   ] tool performs broad-based Web searches similar to the way a search engine works.

6. The best way to protect your privacy is to make sure that your job bank encrypts the data you post. True or false? [   ]

 CHECK ANSWERS

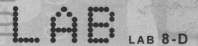

LAB 8-D

ONLINE JOB HUNTING

In this lab, you'll learn:

- How to register with an online job bank
- How to submit your resume online
- Why the file that you use for your printed resume might not be appropriate for posting online
- The characteristics of an ASCII document
- How to convert a formatted resume to an ASCII resume
- How to "fix" an ASCII resume so that it presents information in an easy-to-read format
- How to post an ASCII resume at a job bank
- How to enter a job search by keyword or category
- Creative ways to use keywords in a search specification
- How to configure a search agent
- How to find information on salaries, employers, and places to live

---

INTERACTIVE LAB

CLICK TO START THE LAB

LAB ASSIGNMENTS

1. Start the interactive part of the lab. Insert your Tracking Disk if you want to save your QuickCheck results. Perform each lab step as directed, and answer all the lab QuickCheck questions. When you exit the lab, your answers are automatically graded and your results are displayed.

2. Write a paragraph that describes your ideal job. Next, create a list of search specifications that you could enter at an online job bank to find job openings for your ideal job. Connect to an online job bank and enter your search specifications. Describe the results. If your results were not satisfactory, try modifying your search specifications. Record what seems to be the most effective search, and, if possible, print the job listings that resulted from your search.

3. Using word processing or desktop publishing software, create a one-page resume that highlights your current skills and experience. Print this resume. Convert the resume into an ASCII document, tidy up the format, and then print it.

4. Use the Web to find information about the corporate culture at Microsoft. Summarize your findings, and list each Web site you visited to find information.

5. Use the Web to compare Macon, GA to San Diego, CA. Write a one-page summary of the strengths and weaknesses of each city, and then explain which city you would prefer to live in. List the URLs for any Web sites you used for this assignment.

TECHTALK
THE FUTURE OF COMPUTING

The computer industry has been running on Moore's law since 1965, when Gordon Moore, co-founder of Intel, predicted that the number of transistors per integrated circuit would double about every year. He originally forecasted that this trend would continue through 1975, but Moore's law is expected to hold true until at least 2012. By that year, Intel estimates that it can integrate 1 billion transistors onto a production chip that will operate at 10 GHz. After that, however, Moore's law is expected to encounter some major technological obstacles.

What is the problem with today's technology? Current computer technology is silicon based. Chipmakers can now pack about 400 million transistors on a chip by shrinking components down to 130 nanometers (billionths of a meter). Making these features even smaller, however, requires new and expensive fabrication facilities. Many semiconductor experts believe that commercial fabrication methods cannot economically make silicon transistors much smaller than 100 nanometers. Even if chipmakers could figure out a cost-effective way to etch them onto a chip, ultrasmall silicon components might not work reliably. At transistor dimensions of around 50 nanometers, the electrons begin to obey quantum laws, which cause erratic behavior.

What are the alternatives to silicon-based computers? Researchers are experimenting with three technologies that might supplant silicon: molecular computing, biological computing, and quantum computing.

What's molecular computing? **Molecular computing** can be described as the use of individual molecules to build components that perform functions identical or analogous to those of transistors and other key components of today's microchips. Molecules are small—much smaller than even the microscopic components that populate today's highly miniaturized chips. To put the size differential in perspective, imagine a semiconductor-based transistor enlarged to the size of the printed page you're currently reading. A molecular device would be the size of the period at the end of this sentence. Put another way, molecular electronic devices are about 500 times smaller than today's silicon transistors.

Some of the most promising research into molecular technologies involves carbon nanotubes, first discovered by Japanese scientist Sumio Iijima in 1991. A carbon nanotube is a single, cylinder-shaped molecule that's about 50,000 times thinner than a human hair (Figure 8-42). The electrical properties of carbon nanotubes are similar to those of the semiconductors used in today's microprocessors. Because carbon nanotubes are so small, they could be used for microprocessors and memory, providing up to 30,000 times more memory capacity and 10,000 times more speed than today's DRAM chips.

FIGURE 8-42

In 2002, IBM researchers were able to construct a prototype carbon-nanotube transistor that outperformed today's silicon transistors. Some analysts believe that carbon nanotube technology is currently the computer industry's best chance for replacing silicon-based computer circuitry. Researchers warn, however, that nanotube computers are not expected to be feasible for at least 10 years.

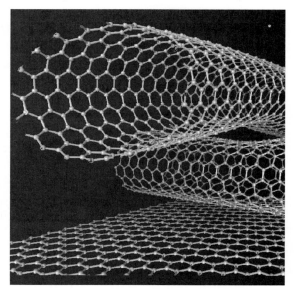

What is biological computing? **Biological computing** is a multidisciplinary field that integrates the work of computer scientists, molecular biologists, geneticists, mathematicians, physicists, and others. One much-talked-about application of biological computing focuses on using DNA strands. DNA (deoxyribonucleic acid) molecules are the basic building blocks of genes.

Just as a string of binary data is encoded using 1s and 0s, a strand of DNA is encoded with four nucleotides represented by the letters A, T, C, and G. In the cell, DNA is modified biochemically by a variety of enzymes. For example, one enzyme cuts DNA and another enzyme pastes it back together. Other enzymes function as copiers. Even others function as repair units. Scientists have developed techniques for performing many of these cellular operations in a test tube.

How do these enzymatic operations relate to computing? Just as a microprocessor's ALU contains circuitry for addition, subtraction, and logical operations, DNA has cutting, copying, pasting, and repairing operations that can be harnessed to solve computational problems. In 1994, Leonard Adleman performed the first DNA computation to solve the classic Hamiltonian Path problem, which is popularly called the "traveling salesman" problem. As Figure 8-43 shows, the problem is to help the salesman find the most efficient way to visit each city, starting in LA and ending in NY.

FIGURE 8-43

The "traveling salesman" problem is solved by finding the best route for a visit to each city. Note that routes between cities are limited to those shown by arrows. The problem becomes more and more difficult to solve as the number of cities and routes increases.

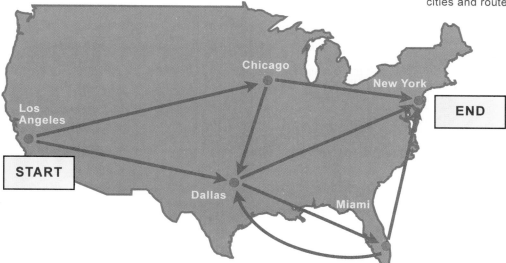

To solve the problem with DNA, you must first decide on city codes that can be represented by the A, T, C, and G nucleotides. For example, you could code each city as shown in Figure 8-44.

FIGURE 8-44

Patterns of nucleotides can be used to code information, such as city names.

CITY NAME	NUCLEOTIDE CODE
Los Angeles	GCTACG
Chicago	CTAGTA
Dallas	TCGTAC
Miami	CTACGG
New York	ATGCCG

Your next step is to generate DNA molecules for every possible route. For example, the route LA -> Chicago -> Dallas -> Miami -> NY would be represented by the DNA strand **GCTACG**CTAGTA**TCGTACCTACGGATGCCG**.

This step results in a test tube full of DNA strands for all routes between the cities, but not all these strands represent routes that begin in LA and end in NY, as required by the salesman. You can use a technique called Polymerase Chain Reaction to selectively amplify the DNA strands that begin in LA and end in NY.

After using this technique, the test tube is filled with DNA strands of various lengths that represent itineraries between LA and NY, but you want the shortest route. To discover the shortest route, a process called Gel Electrophoresis forces the DNA through an electric field, which sorts the DNA by size. After the sorting is complete, you can cut out the shortest strands for further analysis.

Unfortunately, some of these strands do not include all five cities—some might have the salesman travel back and forth between LA, Dallas, Miami, and NY, but never reach Chicago. The final step is to pull out the strands that include all five cities, as shown in Figure 8-45.

FIGURE 8-45

To complete the process and find the solution, a process called Affinity Purification performs a series of steps that collect only DNA strands that include all five cities.

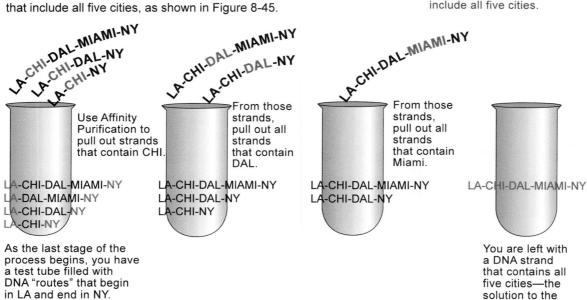

As the last stage of the process begins, you have a test tube filled with DNA "routes" that begin in LA and end in NY.

You are left with a DNA strand that contains all five cities—the solution to the problem.

Is DNA computing practical? Applying DNA to solve the traveling salesman problem involved a complex algorithm and a variety of molecular biology techniques. Adleman's initial attempt to solve the problem took seven days of DNA computing time. Your standard desktop computer could solve the same problem in less than a second. Nevertheless, the potential of DNA computing is staggering. Nucleotides that can be used to represent data are spaced a mere 0.35 nanometers apart along the DNA molecule, giving DNA a remarkable storage density of nearly 18 MB per linear inch. In two dimensions, the data density is over 1 million gigabits per square inch. In comparison, your computer's hard disk drive stores only 7 gigabits per square inch.

Significantly, the storage capacity of DNA matches its processing capacity because enzymes can work on many DNA molecules simultaneously. This parallel operating capacity could allow a DNA-based computer to solve a complex mathematical problem in hours, in contrast to the years of computing time required by today's silicon-based sequential processors.

What's quantum computing? **Quantum computing** is the application of quantum mechanics to computer systems. It has been described as "a bizarre, subatomic world in which two electrons can be two places at the same time." The description is fairly accurate. The principles of quantum computing certainly seem to stretch the limits of credibility.

Today's digital computers work with bits, and each bit can represent a 0 or 1. Bits are easy to understand because they correspond to known characteristics of our physical world: electrical current that is on or off, particles magnetized with positive or negative polarity, and so on. Quantum computers, on the other hand, have their roots in quantum theory, which deals with atomic particles, such as electrons, protons, and neutrons. According to scientists, an isolated individual particle—an electron, for example—might exist in multiple states and locations until it is observed and measured. It further seems that a particle might be able to exist in more than one state at a time.

Suppose that a computer can be constructed to work with these atomic particles instead of conventional bits. A quantum bit, called a **qubit**, can theoretically exist in multiple states. A qubit would have the potential not just to represent a 1 or a 0, but to represent both 1 and 0 at the same time. A computer containing 500 qubits could represent as many as 2,500 states. Unlike a classic digital computer, which would use 500 bits to represent *one* of these 2,500 states at a time, a quantum computer could represent all 2,500 states simultaneously. Then with one tick of the quantum computer's system clock, a calculation could be performed on all 2,500 machine states. Eventually, observing the system causes it to coalesce into a single state corresponding to a single answer.

Will quantum computers replace desktops? Quantum computers are at least 20 years down the road, according to most researchers, and they are probably not destined to tackle desktop tasks, such as word processing and e-mail. Large-scale cryptography, on the other hand, is ideal for quantum computing and could provide security experts with tools for cracking encrypted data. Another potential use for quantum computers is modeling and indexing very large databases, an application that could become crucial if the Web continues to grow at its current rate.

QUICKCHECK........TECHTALK

1. [_____] law predicted that the number of transistors per integrated circuit would double about every year.

2. Carbon nanotubes are one of the most promising technologies for [_____] computing.

3. The storage density of [_____] is over 1 million gigabits per square inch. Hint: Use the acronym.

4. In a quantum computer, data is represented by [_____], instead of the 0 and 1 bits familiar to users of today's silicon-based electronic digital computers.

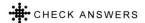 CHECK ANSWERS

ISSUE

OFFSHORING

Have you ever called a customer service number and encountered a friendly voice with a foreign accent on the other end of the line? Has it ever occurred to you that this support technician might be sitting at a desk on the other side of the world—in India, Singapore, or the Philippines, for example?

Computer and telecommunications technologies have made it possible for companies such as American Express, America Online, and Dell to move their call centers to India, the Philippines, and other countries. You might not, however, be able to determine a call center's location because according to an article in the *New York Times*, offshore customer service representatives are not allowed to disclose their locations to customers.

Outsourcing and offshoring have come under increasing criticism. Some analysts believe these business practices are causing unemployment in many sectors of the U.S. economy—including the IT industry. Other experts disagree, and view outsourcing and offshoring as part of economic globalization.

Outsourcing is an established business practice that can reduce product costs, cut consumer prices, and help businesses remain competitive. The range of outsourced jobs includes manufacturing; electrical engineering; back-office functions like accounting, human resources, call centers, and data analysis; and IT-related work, such as software development, maintenance, support, and quality assurance.

Electronic Data Systems (EDS), founded in 1962 by former presidential candidate Ross Perot, gets credit for turning IT outsourcing into a major business. In 1969, when Blue Shield of Pennsylvania could no longer handle the state's Medicare processing workload, EDS took over responsibility for managing the system and hiring employees.

Outsourcing seemed a good business practice and did not generate much controversy when jobs remained within national boundaries. As jobs were outsourced to other countries with significantly cheaper labor, the term "offshoring" was born and analysts became increasingly concerned about its effect on unemployment at home.

India, the first country to host offshore contact centers for U.S. businesses, is currently on the leading edge of IT offshoring. China, the Philippines, Mexico, Canada, and Russia are also considered strong contenders.

The major lure of offshoring is reduced cost of labor in developing nations. Whereas the salary for a U.S.-based programmer with three to four year's experience would be $45,000 to $55,000 a year, programmers in India can easily charge a fraction of the cost—around $15,000 to $19,000 a year. News reports cite several high-tech workers who claim they were laid off after training their offshore replacements.

The downside of offshoring is rooted in language barriers and cultural differences. For example, in several Asian countries, it is customary to answer indirectly instead of giving an outright "yes" or "no" as would normally be the case in the U.S. An Asian technician who says "Very difficult" might actually mean "no." A Mexican software engineer's enthusiastic "Yes!" might really mean, "I'll have to think about it."

Miscommunication can be costly. Dell Computers was forced to discontinue its offshore business-customers call center because of mounting complaints about "bad service." New York financial services firm Lehman Brothers stopped offshoring its computer help desk to Wipro in India because of unsatisfactory service.

On both the national and state levels, politicians are faced with a dilemma: Should they focus on protecting their constituents' jobs or saving taxpayer money? Voters are clearly voicing their anxiety over job security. Because it became a major election issue last year, the State of Indiana prematurely ended a $15.2 million offshoring contract to upgrade the state's unemployment claims computer system, even though the contract saved taxpayers $8.1 million.

Consumers, however, vote with their wallets, and few are willing to pay more for U.S.-produced goods and services. Businesses that maintain a high-cost onshore workforce could find themselves unable to compete in a global marketplace. If the business goes bankrupt, all its employees join the unemployment ranks.

It is difficult to precisely assess the pros and cons of offshoring. A survey conducted by *CFO* magazine reported that some companies had no cost savings whatsoever, or only nominal savings of less than 15%. Less than half of the companies in the study reported savings of more than 20%. In contrast to this data, Forrester Research, an independent technology research company, claims that its offshoring clients typically reap benefits ranging from 25% to 45%. How many domestic jobs have moved offshore? Estimates vary between 300,000 and 1 million—less than 2 tenths of a percent of all U.S. workers. Forrester Research projects a loss of 3.4 million jobs by 2015.

As the offshoring debate continues, IEEE-USA, an organizational unit of the world's largest technical professional society, recommends the following:

- The Federal Government must collect and publish reliable statistics on the kinds and numbers of manufacturing and service jobs that are being moved offshore.
- Government procurement rules should favor work done in the United States and should restrict the offshoring of work in any instance where there is not a clear long-term economic benefit to the nation or where the work supports technologies that are critical to our national economic or military security.
- New U.S. workforce assistance programs should be created to help displaced high-tech workers regain productive employment and ensure that employed workers can acquire the knowledge and skills they need to remain competitive.
- A coordinated national strategy must be developed to sustain U.S. technological leadership and promote jobs creation in response to the concerted strategies other countries are using to capture U.S. industries, jobs, and markets.

Not since the industrial revolution has technology provided tools for such a significant change as economic globalization. Our response as individuals and as a nation is likely to have a far-reaching effect on future lifestyles, so keeping tabs on this issue is important.

INFOWEBLINKS

You'll find additional information about this issue at the **Offshoring InfoWeb**.

www.course.com/np/concepts8/ch08

WHAT DO YOU THINK?

1. Have you ever contacted a call center that you suspected was located outside the United States? ⭘Yes ⭘ No ⭘ Not sure

2. Are you surprised that high-tech jobs, such as software engineering, requiring advanced skills can be handled by offshore firms? ⭘Yes ⭘ No ⭘ Not sure

3. Are you against offshoring? ⭘Yes ⭘ No ⭘ Not sure

 SAVE RESPONSES

COMPUTERS IN CONTEXT

TRAVEL

Ramon Stoppelenburg left his home in the Netherlands with a backpack, a digital camera, a laptop computer, and a cell phone. He left behind the one thing most travelers would never be caught without—money! Instead, he set up a Web site called *Let Me Stay For a Day.* Every few days, Ramon updated his Web site with a journal entry, a picture or two, and his travel itinerary. After viewing the Web site, more than 3,600 people from 72 different countries have offered money, meals, and lodging. Using the Web as his travel agent, Ramon has traveled through 17 countries, written more than 500 journal entries, taken more than 7,000 photographs, and spent U.S. $0 of his own money.

Ramon Stoppelenburg's adventure might be unconventional, but it demonstrates the growing role that computers play in the travel industry. Since the 1960s, computer-based GDSs (global distribution systems) have managed and distributed travel related information, such as flight schedules, ticket prices, and passenger itineraries. GDSs were originally proprietary systems installed in airport terminals and used only by authorized airline employees. Today, GDSs are used by travel agents, hotel employees, and airline ticketing clerks. They also provide the power behind some travel-related Web sites.

The SABRE system, one of the oldest and largest GDSs, caters primarily to travel industry professionals. In 1953, American Airlines President C. R. Smith happened to be seated next to IBM Sales Representative R. Blair Smith on a flight from Los Angeles to New York. Their chance meeting led to the development of the Semi-Automatic Business Research Environment—commonly known as SABRE. When SABRE went online in 1964, it became the first e-commerce system in the world, allowing American Airlines agents in airport terminals to automate up to 26,000 passenger reservation transactions per day. Other airlines quickly followed suit, and competing GDSs were launched by United Airlines, TWA, and Amadeus, a partnership of European Airlines.

Before SABRE, flight reservations required cumbersome manual transactions. Travel agents used teletypes to communicate with airlines to reserve seats and generate tickets. Processing a round-trip reservation could take up to 3 hours and involved as many as 12 people. Today, SABRE and other GDSs manage information from hundreds of airlines, thousands of hotels, and a multitude of other travel-related organizations, such as car rental companies, cruise lines, and tour operators. Travel agents can compare fare information, generate itineraries, and print tickets instantly. Schedule and rate changes are available immediately—no waiting for new rates to be printed and distributed.

Although GDSs are still in demand, some experts believe that their early popularity is now contributing to their demise. Most GDSs were built before the Internet and the Web were invented, and the hardware and software they rely on is now considered outdated. Compared to modern information systems, GDSs are difficult and expensive to maintain, and their use often requires special training. The information stored on a GDS was historically available only to professional travel agents.

The use of GDSs has been affected by a fundamental change in the travel industry characterized by a shift away from marketing through tour guides and travel agents. Many travel-related companies now prefer to market directly to consumers through Web sites and telephone sales. Some GDSs have been modified for consumer-level Web accessibility. These GDSs now provide the power behind popular travel Web sites such as Expedia.com and Travelocity.com.

GDS-powered Web sites offer consumers the same information that was previously available only to travel professionals who subscribed to a GDS service. Consumers can search for flights, compare fares, research travel destinations, and find hotel and car rental fees from one easy-to-use Web site. The GDS components of these systems continue to use old hardware and software, however, and the ongoing cost of maintenance is high.

In 2001, five airlines—American, Continental, Delta, Northwest, and United—launched a new travel-related Web site called Orbitz.com. Unlike other travel Web sites, this new site was not powered by a traditional GDS. Instead, Orbitz.com was built from the ground up, using modern hardware and software. Like GDS-based sites, Orbitz.com maintains information about flights, fares, hotels, rental cars, and cruises. Consumers can search for travel deals and discounts or research specific destinations.

Even before Orbitz.com went live, it was the subject of criticism and lawsuits. For example, the American Association of Travel Agents (AATA) claimed that Orbitz.com could publish special pricing not available through the standard fare schedules. If travel agents were unable to access the special online pricing, the AATA predicted that consumers would eventually stop using the services of travel agencies to book flights, rental cars, and other travel services. In July 2003, the Department of Transportation Inspector General closed the federal review after finding no evidence of any anti-competitive behavior by Orbitz, and in fact determined that Orbitz provides a valuable service to consumers and promotes competition in the travel marketplace. Despite a federal probe, Orbitz.com opened to much fanfare in June 2001 and quickly became one of the most popular travel-related Web sites.

Web-based travel services represent one of the few bright spots on the e-commerce landscape after the dot com bubble burst. Despite traveler's trepidation about terror threats, online travel sites appear to be profitable.

Hotel and transportation reservations represent only one segment of the travel-related services found on the Internet. The Web provides an abundance of trip planning information. MapQuest.com provides road maps and driving destinations between cities all over the globe. Web sites maintained by popular travel guides, such as Frommers.com and Fodors.com, provide information that helps travelers plan where to eat, where to stay, and what to see. The Web also offers travelogues, reviews, blogs, and message boards with postings from individual travelers. Web sites and Blogs, such as TravelAdvisor.com and Epinions.com, encourage tourists and business travelers to post reviews about favorite restaurants, hotels, and tourist attractions.

Computers aren't used only for planning travel. Many travelers opt to take PDAs or laptops on the road, or stop at local Internet cafes and spend some time browsing the Web or sending e-mail messages. Web-based e-mail services such as Hotmail or Yahoo! Mail make it simple and inexpensive to keep in touch with friends, family, clients, and colleagues while on the road. Travelers with digital cameras can even send vacation photos to friends and relatives via e-mail or post the photos on a personal Web site. Travelers can download street maps and tourist information to their PDAs, calculate exchange rates, and even translate simple phrases from one language to another.

INFOWEBLINKS

You'll find lots more information and links related to this Computers in Context topic at the **Computers and Travel InfoWeb.**

www.course.com/np/concepts8/ch08

▌▌▌ ▌ INTERACTIVE SUMMARY

To review important concepts from this chapter, fill in the blanks to best complete each sentence. When using the NP8 BookOnCD, click the Check Answers buttons to automatically score your answers. Place your Tracking Disk in the floppy disk drive if you want to save your scores.

Even before recorded history, humans used various [_____] aids, such as pebbles and notched sticks, to keep track of quantities. By 1200, a [_____] calculator, called the abacus, had appeared in China. In Europe, a popular calculating device called Napier's Bones was transformed into the slide rule in 1621, and became the calculating tool of choice in Europe and later the Americas. Manual calculators require the operator to apply an [_____] to perform calculations. In contrast, [_____] calculators, such as the Pascaline and deColmar's Arithmometer, are designed to carry out calculations autonomously. In 1822, an English mathematician named Charles [_____] proposed to build a device, called the Difference Engine, that would operate using steam power. He also designed a second device,

called the [_____] Engine, which embodied many of the concepts that define the modern computer. In the 1930s and 1940s, several [_____] computers were developed, including the Atanasoff-Berry Computer, Z3, Harvard Mark I, COLOSSUS, and ENIAC. Most of these early computers used [_____] tubes, which paved the way for the architecture of first-generation computers, such as UNIVAC. Second-generation computers were smaller and less power hungry because they were designed to use [_____]. Third-generation computers were even smaller due to the use of [_____] circuits. The key technology for fourth-generation computers, including personal computers, is the [_____].

✽ CHECK ANSWERS

The [_____] industry encompasses those companies that manufacture computers. A broader term, IT industry, is typically used to refer to the companies that develop, produce, sell, or support computers, software, and computer-related products. The IT industry has fueled the economies of many countries, but despite a trend toward [_____], the IT industry remains dominated by the United States. It is likely that population growth and business globalization are two important factors in the success of this industry. The life cycle of a typical hardware product includes product development, product announcement, introduction, [_____], and retirement. The life cycle of a software product is similar, except that old versions of a software product do not typically remain in the publisher's product line. Soon after a new version of a software product is released, the publisher discontinues sales of the old version. Hardware and

software products are sold through marketing [_____], such as retail stores, mail-order/Internet outlets, value-added resellers, and manufacturer direct. The price you pay for computer-related merchandise, and the support you receive after the sale, can depend on the type of channel from which the computer was purchased. Retail stores and VARs tend to have the highest prices. In most countries, including the United States, the IT industry is not regulated by a dedicated government agency. Instead, the IT industry is subject to broad-based [_____] that pertains to anti-monopoly laws, communications rules, and gambling restrictions. To avoid government regulations that target technology companies, the IT industry has attempted to regulate itself by creating organizations to set standards and disseminate information to technology companies, government, and the general public.

✽ CHECK ANSWERS

A computer [　　　　　] is defined as any person whose primary occupation involves the design, configuration, analysis, development, modification, testing, or security of computer hardware or software. The IT industry encompasses a wide variety of jobs for computer professionals, and the career outlook appears to be relatively positive. Salaries and working conditions are quite favorable, and IT jobs are typically regarded as safe if [　　　　　] guidelines are followed for setting up your work area.

Demographics in the IT industry indicate that computer professionals tend to be slightly younger than their counterparts in other occupations. Men outnumber women. Although many IT workers are of European, Asian, and Indian descent, other ethnic groups are underrepresented. The typical IT worker puts in a 40+ hour week, although part-time work is also available. Many computer professionals are [　　　　　] workers, who arrange to work for a company on a temporary basis, usually as consultants for particular projects.

Although these workers are usually highly paid, they are not official employees of a company and are not eligible for company health care or retirement benefits.

Education is an important key to most IT industry jobs. Over 50% of IT workers have at least a bachelor's degree, many from computer-oriented curricula. Computer [　　　　　] degree programs focus on the design of computer hardware and peripheral devices. Computer [　　　　　] degree programs focus on digital computer architecture and how to program computers to make them work effectively and efficiently. Information [　　　　　] degree programs focus on applying computers to business problems. In addition to a college degree, certification provides job applicants with marketable credentials, through certificates of completion or certification exams. Certification exams are offered in areas such as general computer knowledge, software applications, database administration, networking, security, and computer hardware.

✦ CHECK ANSWERS

Finding a job in the IT industry is similar in many ways to finding a job in any other industry. Effective job seekers begin by devising a search strategy that identifies potential employers, defines a geographic area for the search, and zeroes in on specific job titles. They then create a carefully worded [　　　　　], which can be posted online, e-mailed, or printed.

Job openings can be found in local newspapers, at employers' Web sites, or in the databases provided by online job [　　　　　]. Instead of manually searching through several job databases, you can use a job search [　　　　　], which is an automat-

ed program that searches one or more databases even while you are offline, and then notifies you when it finds any job listings that match your specified criteria. Another valuable online search tool, called a [　　　　　] tool, is a software program that searches more than one job database while you are online. Job seekers are sometimes contacted by recruiting firms, called [　　　　　] hunters, that are hired by companies to find candidates with specific qualifications. Many job seekers also tap into the free services offered by state-run employment agencies and school-based placement services.

✦ CHECK ANSWERS

INTERACTIVE KEY TERMS

Make sure you understand all the boldfaced key terms presented in this chapter. If you're using the NP8 BookOnCD, you can use this list of terms as an interactive study activity. First, try to define a term in your own words, and then click the term to compare your definition with the definition presented in the chapter.

Abacus, 402
Alpha test, 420
Analytical Engine, 404
Apple I, 411
Apple II, 411
Apple Lisa, 411
Apple Macintosh, 412
Atanasoff-Berry Computer, 405
Beta test, 420
Biological computing, 447
Certificates of completion, 434
Certification exam, 434
Channel conflict, 424
Chief information officer, 427
Chipmakers, 414
COLOSSUS, 406
Computer engineer, 428
Computer engineering, 432
Computer industry, 413
Computer operator, 428
Computer professional, 426
Computer programmer, 427
Computer retail store, 422
Computer salesperson, 428
Computer science, 432
Contract worker, 430
Database administrator, 427
DEC PDP-8, 409
deColmar's Arithmometer, 403
Difference Engine, 404
ENIAC, 406
Equipment manufacturers, 414

Ergonomics, 431
First-generation computers, 407
Fourth-generation computers, 410
Harvard Mark I, 406
Hollerith Tabulating Machine, 404
IBM 360, 409
IBM AS/400, 409
IBM PC, 411
IBM PC XT, 411
Information systems, 433
Information Systems department, 427
Information technology industry, 413
Job search agent, 442
Leibniz Calculator, 403
Mail order, 423
Manual calculator, 402
Manufacturer direct, 423
Manufacturing technician, 428
Mark-8, 410
Market share, 420
Market tiers, 421
Marketing channels, 422
Mechanical calculator, 403
Metasearch tool, 442
MITS Altair, 410
Molecular computing, 446
MSRP, 419
Napier's Bones, 403
Network specialist/administrator, 428
Offshoring, 416
Online job bank, 441
Outsourcing, 415

Pascaline, 403
Prototype, 405
Quality assurance specialist, 428
Quantum computing, 449
Qubit, 449
RCA Spectra 70, 409
Retailers, 414
Schickard's Calculator, 403
Second-generation computers, 408
Security specialist, 427
Service companies, 414
Slide rule, 403
Software publishers, 414
Street price, 419
Systems analyst, 427
Technical support specialist, 428
Technical writer, 428
Telecommuting, 430
Third-generation computers, 409
Transistors, 408
UNIVAC, 407
Vacuum tube, 407
Vaporware, 419
VAR, 424
VisiCalc, 411
Web portfolio, 439
Web site designer, 428
Xerox Alto, 411
Z3, 405

INTERACTIVE SITUATION QUESTIONS

Apply what you've learned to some typical computing situations. When using the NP8 BookOnCD, you can type your answers, and then use the Check Answers button to automatically score your responses. Place your Tracking Disk in the floppy disk drive if you want to save your scores.

1. Suppose that you were an accountant in 1979, and you wanted to use a state-of-the-art personal computer and software for your work. You would probably have selected an Apple II computer and _____ software.

2. You work as a manufacturing technician in a chip fabrication plant. Your aunt asks if you're in the IT industry. Your response: _____

3. Suppose that you visit a software publisher's Web site and gather information about a software package that has an MSRP of $495. Instead of purchasing the software directly from the software publisher, you check a few other sites because you expect the _____ price to be less.

4. You receive an e-mail from a software publisher that offers to supply you with a free copy of a new operating system if you become part of a beta test program. You are hesitant about participating because beta software versions often contain _____ that can cause unexpected glitches in your computer.

5. After studying and gaining practical experience on how to analyze a computer system's vulnerability to threats from viruses, worms, unauthorized access, and physical damage, you are ready for a job as a(n) _____ specialist.

6. In looking for an IT industry job in the United States, you think it is important to take into consideration the fact that the highest salaries tend to be offered on the West Coast and in _____ states.

7. You signed on with an IT company as a(n) _____ worker, fully realizing that you will not be considered an official employee of the company, nor will you be eligible for the company's health care or retirement benefits.

8. You want to make sure your computer is set up so that you can avoid disabling musculoskeletal injuries, like carpal tunnel syndrome. You can look for _____ guidelines on the Web, which offer advice on how to position your computer monitor and where to place lighting.

9. Your friend is not strong in math, but really wants to work with computers. You suggest that your friend consider a(n) _____ systems degree.

10. To supplement your computer science degree, you decide to take a(n) _____ exam to become a Microsoft Certified Systems Engineer.

11. As part of your job hunting activities, you are planning to create your resume in several different _____, for use in the body of an e-mail message, as a Web page, and as a printed document.

12. Because your online resume might be subject to machine searches, you know that it is important to focus on _____, rather than verbs, and include industry-specific tools, programming languages, methods, and buzzwords.

✦ CHECK ANSWERS

INTERACTIVE PRACTICE TESTS

Practice tests that consist of 10 multiple-choice, true/false, and fill-in-the-blank questions are available on both the NP8 BookOnCD and the NP8 Web site. The questions are selected at random from a large test bank, so each time you take a test, you'll receive a different set of questions. Your tests are scored immediately, and you can print study guides that help you find the correct answers for any questions that you missed.

www.course.com/np/concepts8/ch08 ✦

CLICK ✦ TO START

ON THE WEB

PROJECTS

An NP8 Project is an open-ended activity that helps you apply the concepts you have learned. Many projects require resources in addition to your textbook, such as current magazines, library materials, or Web access. When you tackle a project, be prepared to use your critical thinking skills, logical analysis, and creativity. Projects for this chapter include:

- **Issue Research: Offshoring**
- **Web Resumes**
- **Computers and Travel**
- **Certification**
- **The Computer Industry**
- **Careers**

To work with the Projects for this chapter, connect to the **New Perspectives NP8 Web Site.**

www.course.com/np/concepts8/ch08

TECHTV VIDEO PROJECT

Your TechTalk host on the *PC Pioneer Trail* takes you on a virtual tour of memorable Silicon Valley locations. As you watch the video, create a list of the places and people who contributed to the booming PC industry. Choose any one of the computer pioneers or innovations on your list and use the Web to find more in-depth information. Use your findings to write a one-minute script that could be used by a Silicon Valley tour guide for a bus full of tourists.

To work with the Video Projects for this chapter, connect to the **New Perspectives NP8 Web Site.**

www.course.com/np/concepts8/ch08

STUDY TIPS

Study Tips help you to organize and consolidate the information in a chapter by making lists, outlines, charts, and sketches. You can use paper and pencil or word processing software to complete most of the Study Tips.

To work with the Study Tips for this chapter, connect to the **New Perspectives NP8 Web Site.**

www.course.com/np/concepts8/ch08

ONLINE GAMES

Test your comprehension of the concepts introduced in Chapter 8 by playing the NP8 Online Games. At the end of each game, you have three options:

- Print a comprehensive study guide complete with page references
- Print your results to be submitted to your instructor
- Save your results to be submitted to your instructor via e-mail

To work with the Online Games for this chapter, connect to the **New Perspectives NP8 Web Site.**

www.course.com/np/concepts8/ch08

STUDENT EDITION LABS

Extend your knowledge of computer concepts with the Student Edition Labs.

There are currently no Student Edition Labs directly related to the topics covered in Chapter 8, however, you can go to the NP8 New Perspectives Web site to access Student Edition Labs for review and additional exploration.

Go to the NP8 New Perspectives Web site for specific lab topics.

To work with the Student Edition Labs and their corresponding lab assignments, you can connect to the **New Perspectives NP8 Web Site**.

www.course.com/np/concepts8/ch08

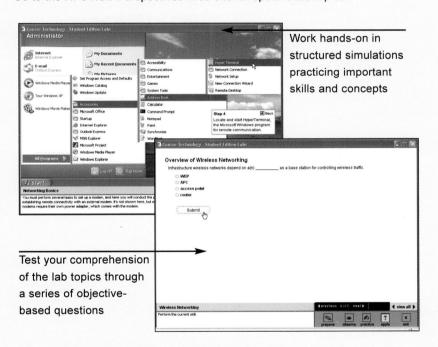

Work hands-on in structured simulations practicing important skills and concepts

Test your comprehension of the lab topics through a series of objective-based questions

Track Your Progress with the Student Edition Labs

- Student Edition Labs test your comprehension of the lab topics through a series of trackable objective-based questions. Your instructor will direct you to either print your results or submit them via e-mail.

- Student Edition Lab Assignments, available on the New Perspectives NP8 Web site, require you to apply the skills learned through the lab in a live environment. Go to the New Perspectives NP8 Web site for detailed instruction on individual Student Edition Lab Assignments.

If you have a SAM user profile, you have access to even more interactive content. Log in to your SAM account and go to your assignments page to see what your instructor has assigned for this chapter.

INFORMATION SYSTEMS ANALYSIS AND DESIGN

CONTENTS

TIP

When using the BookOnCD,
the ✱ icons are "clickable" to
access resources on the CD.
The ✚ icons are clickable to
access resources on the Web.
You can also access Web
resources by using your browser to connect directly to the
NP8 New Perspectives Web
site at:

www.course.com/np/concepts8/ch09

CHAPTER PREVIEW

Before you begin Chapter 9, you can use the Web-based preview activities to hear an overview of the chapter, check your current level of expertise about key concepts, and look through a list of learning objectives. You can access the preview activities by clicking the ⌖ icon when using the BookOnCD or going to the New Perspectives NP8 Web site.

CHAPTER OVERVIEW

On a day-to-day basis, you interact with information systems as you shop, register for classes, and pay your bills. How does an information system differ from the computer on your desktop? Get your book and highlighter ready, then connect to the New Perspectives NP8 Web site where you can listen to an overview that points out the most important concepts for this chapter.

www.course.com/np/concepts8/ch09 ⌖

CHAPTER PRE-ASSESSMENT

How much do you know about the way computer systems fit into organizations? To gauge your level of knowledge before beginning the chapter, take the pre-assessment quiz at the New Perspectives NP8 Web site. Armed with your results from this quiz, you can focus your study time on concepts that will round out your knowledge of information systems and improve your test scores.

www.course.com/np/concepts8/ch09 ⌖

LEARNING OBJECTIVES

When you complete this chapter you should be able to:

- Describe how information systems help organizations fulfill their missions, deal with threats, and take advantage of opportunities

- Contrast and compare the characteristics of transaction processing systems, management information systems, decision support systems, and expert systems

- Apply the PIECES framework to classify problems that reduce the effectiveness of an information system

- Describe various models for the system development life cycle (SDLC), and explain the focus of the structured, information engineering, object-oriented, and rapid application development approaches to system development

- List the activities that take place in each phase of the system development life cycle

- Describe alternative hardware and software solutions that a project team might consider

- Explain the differences between unit testing, integration testing, system testing, and acceptance testing

- Describe the advantages and disadvantages of direct, parallel, phased, and pilot conversion techniques

- Explain how user feedback helps system operators identify and fix "bugs"

A detailed list of learning objectives is provided at the New Perspectives NP8 Web site

www.course.com/np/concepts8/ch09 ⌖

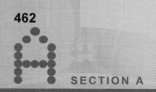

SECTION A

INFORMATION SYSTEMS

You are probably a member of an organization, such as a student club, fraternity or sorority, sports team, or political party. You also deal with all kinds of organizations every day: your school, stores, banks, and government agencies. Most organizations use information systems to operate more effectively, gather information, and accomplish tasks. In this section, you'll review some basic concepts about organizations and find out how information systems enhance organizational activities.

INFORMATION SYSTEMS IN ORGANIZATIONS

What is an information system? An **information system** collects, stores, and processes data to provide useful, accurate, and timely information, typically within the context of an organization. Although an information system does not necessarily have to be computerized, today most information systems rely on computers and communications networks to store, process, and transmit information with far more efficiency than would be possible with a manual system. In this textbook, the term "information system" always refers to a system that uses computers and usually includes communications networks.

What's the official definition of "organization"? An **organization** is a group of people working together to accomplish a goal. According to Peter Drucker, one of today's most influential writers about business and management, "the purpose of an organization is to enable ordinary people to do extraordinary things." Organizations have accomplished amazing feats, such as sending astronauts into space, providing live television coverage of global events, and inventing freeze-dried ice cream. They also accomplish all kinds of day-to-day, routine tasks, such as offering banking services, selling merchandise, and policing your neighborhood.

Any organization that seeks profit by providing goods and services is called a **business**. Some organizations are formed to accomplish political, social, or charitable goals that do not include amassing profit. Such an organization is known as a **nonprofit organization**.

Every organization has a goal or plan that's often referred to as its **mission**. All activities that take place in an organization, including those that involve computers, should contribute to this mission. The written expression of an organization's mission is called a mission statement. A **mission statement** describes not only an organization's goals, but also the way in which those goals will be accomplished. Companies publish their mission statements in corporate reports and on the Web (Figure 9-1).

FIGURE 9-1
A Web-based mission statement for the Pacific Whale Foundation.

HOME

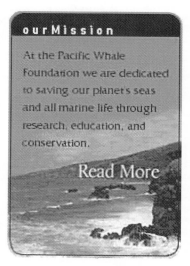

ourMission

At the Pacific Whale Foundation we are dedicated to saving our planet's seas and all marine life through research, education, and conservation.

Read More

Who uses information systems? An information system is used by the people in an organization and its customers. You've undoubtedly used many information systems—for example, when registering for classes, getting cash from an ATM, and purchasing merchandise on the Web. You might even work for a business or nonprofit organization where you have access to an information system.

Not everyone in an organization uses an information system in the same way. An information system must support the needs of people who engage in many different organizational activities.

To coordinate the activities of their employees, most organizations use a hierarchical structure. An **organizational chart**, such as the one in Figure 9-2, depicts the hierarchy of employees in an organization.

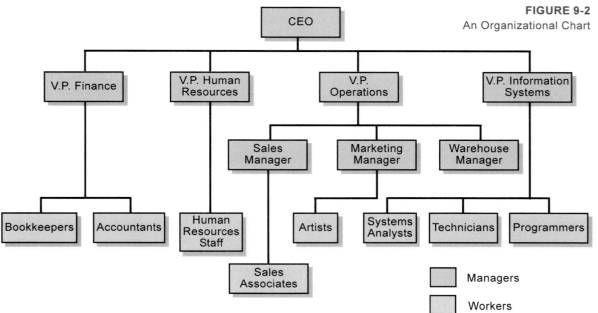

FIGURE 9-2
An Organizational Chart

In many organizations, and most businesses, employees can be classified as workers or managers. **Workers** are the people who directly carry out the organization's mission. For example, they assemble cars, write newspaper articles, sell merchandise, answer telephones, lay bricks, cut trees, or fix engines. Workers typically collect data for information systems. For example, as a checkout clerk rings up sales, her cash register records each item in a database.

Managers determine organizational goals and plan how to achieve those goals. They approve new products, authorize new construction, and supervise workers. Executive managers plan an organization's long-range goals for profitability, market share, membership levels, and so on. This emphasis on long-range and future goals is referred to as **strategic planning**.

Mid-level managers are responsible for figuring out how to achieve those long-range goals through sales, marketing, or new product development. They set incremental goals that can be achieved in a year or less—a process referred to as **tactical planning**. Low-level managers are responsible for scheduling employees, ordering supplies, and other activities that make day-to-day operations run smoothly—a process referred to as **operational planning**. Information systems can provide some or all of the data needed for strategic, tactical, and operational planning.

How do information systems help the people in an organization? An information system can help the people in an organization perform their jobs more quickly and effectively by automating routine tasks, such as reordering inventory, taking customer orders, or sending out renewal notices. Information systems can also help people solve problems.

One of the major functions of an information system is to help people make decisions in response to problems. According to Herbert Simon, who is well known for his insights into organizational behavior, the decision-making process has three phases, shown in Figure 9-3.

Phase 1: Recognize a problem or a need to make a decision.

Phase 2: Devise and analyze possible solutions or actions to solve the problem.

Phase 3: Select an action or a solution.

FIGURE 9-3
The three decision-making phases are usually clear cut, leading to decisions that are objective, standardized, and based on factual data.

All problems are not alike, but they can be classified into three types: structured, semi-structured, and unstructured. An everyday, run-of-the-mill, routine problem is called a **structured problem**. When you make decisions in response to structured problems, the procedure for obtaining the best solution is known, the objective is clearly defined, and the information necessary to make the decision is easy to identify. An example of a structured problem is figuring out which customers should receive overdue notices. The information for this decision is usually stored in a file cabinet or computer system. The method for reaching a solution is to look for customers with outstanding balances, and then check whether the due dates for their payments fall before today's date.

A **semi-structured problem** is less routine than a structured problem. When solving a semi-structured problem, the procedure for arriving at a solution is usually known; however, it might involve some degree of subjective judgment. Also, some of the information regarding the problem might not be available, might lack precision, or might be uncertain. An example of a semi-structured problem for a retail business is deciding how much inventory to stock for the holidays. The decision can be based on the previous year's sales, with some adjustment for the current year's consumer confidence index. The consumer confidence index, however, might or might not accurately predict consumer spending over the holidays. Because of this uncertainty, determining the appropriate amount of holiday inventory would be classified as a semi-structured problem.

An **unstructured problem** requires human intuition as the basis for finding a solution. Information relevant to the problem might be missing, and few, if any, parts of the solution can be tackled using concrete models. If experts are presented with the same problem data, but they disagree on a solution, it is likely an unstructured problem. An example of an unstructured problem might be whether Saks Fifth Avenue should stock Japanese-inspired evening gowns. The purchasing agent for women's clothing makes this decision based on her intuition of customer taste and fashion trends.

Can an information system solve all three types of problems? Traditionally, information systems have contributed most to solving structured problems, but tools have emerged to help people tackle

INFOWEBLINKS

Case studies provide detailed accounts of successful and unsuccessful information systems. To read some of these case studies, connect to the **IS Case Study InfoWeb**.

www.course.com/np/concepts8/ch09

semi-structured and unstructured problems as well. Despite these tools and the data they provide, many semi-structured and unstructured problems continue to be solved based on "guesstimates."

An information system's ability to assist with problem solving and decision making depends on the data it collects and makes available. Some information systems collect and store **internal information** generated by the organization itself. Other information systems store or provide access to **external information** generated by sources outside the organization. Later in this section, you'll learn how different types of information systems deal with internal and external information.

Do organizations require different kinds of information systems? Because organizations have different missions and face different problems, they require different kinds of information systems. An information system might have one or more of the following components: a transaction processing system, a management information system, a decision support system, or an expert system. Let's take a closer look at each of these systems.

TRANSACTION PROCESSING SYSTEMS

What's a transaction? In an information system context, a **transaction** is an exchange between two parties that is recorded and stored in a computer system. When you order a product at a Web site, buy merchandise in a store, or withdraw cash from an ATM, you are involved in a transaction.

What is a transaction processing system? Many organizational activities involve transactions. A **transaction processing system** (TPS) provides a way to collect, process, store, display, modify, or cancel transactions. Most transaction processing systems allow many transactions to be entered simultaneously. The data collected by a TPS is typically stored in databases, and can be used to produce a regularly scheduled set of reports, such as monthly bills, weekly paychecks, annual inventory summaries, daily manufacturing schedules, or periodic check registers. Figure 9-4 lists some examples of business transaction processing systems.

FIGURE 9-4
Business Transaction
Processing Systems

Point-of-sale (POS) systems record items purchased at each cash register and calculate the total amount due for each sale. Some POS systems automatically verify credit cards, calculate change, and identify customers who previously wrote bad checks.

Order-entry/invoice systems provide a way to input, view, modify, and delete customer orders. These systems help track the status of each order and create invoices. **E-commerce** systems are specialized order-entry/invoice systems designed to collect online orders and process credit card payments.

General accounting systems record the financial status of a business by keeping track of income, expenses, and assets.

Payroll systems track employee hours, calculate deductions and taxes, generate paychecks, and produce data for year-end reports, such as W-2 and K1.

Early transaction processing systems, such as banking and payroll applications of the 1970s, used **batch processing** to collect and hold a group of transactions for processing until the end of a day or pay period. An entire batch was then processed without human intervention, until all transactions were completed or until an error occurred.

In contrast to batch processing, most modern transaction processing systems use **online processing**—an interactive method in which each transaction is processed as it is entered. Such a system is often referred to as an **OLTP system** (online transaction processing system). OLTP uses a "commit or rollback" strategy to ensure that each transaction is processed correctly. This strategy is crucial because most transactions require a sequence of steps, and every step must succeed for the transaction to be completed.

How does commit or rollback work? If you withdraw cash from an ATM, the bank's computer must make sure your account contains sufficient funds before it allows the ATM to deliver cash and deducts the withdrawal from your account. If the ATM is out of cash, however, the transaction fails, and the withdrawal should not be deducted from your account. A TPS can **commit** to a transaction and permanently update database records only if every step of the transaction can be successfully processed. If even one step fails, however, the entire transaction fails and a **rollback** returns the records to their original state. Figure 9-5 diagrams the processes that take place in a typical TPS, and the video that accompanies the figure provides additional information about commit and rollback.

FIGURE 9-5

A transaction processing system is characterized by its ability to:

- Collect, display, and modify transactions
- Store transactions
- List transactions

CLICK TO START ✳

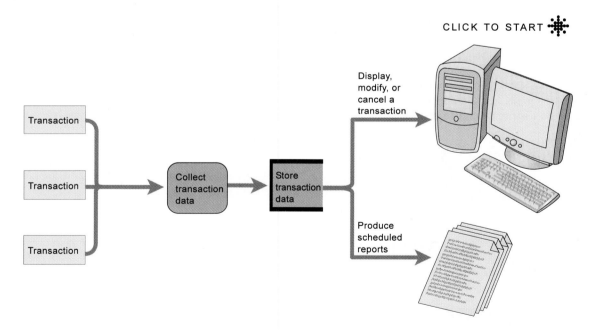

What are the limitations of transaction processing systems? Although a TPS excels at maintaining transaction data entered by clerical personnel and online customers, its reporting capabilities are limited. A typical TPS generates **detail reports**, which provide a basic record of completed transactions. However, managers need more sophisticated reports to help them understand and analyze data. These reports are usually created by a management information system.

MANAGEMENT INFORMATION SYSTEMS

What is a management information system? The term "management information system" is used in two contexts. It can be a synonym for the term "information system," or it can refer to a specific category or type of information system. We'll use the term **management information system** (MIS, pronounced em-eye-ess) in this second context, to refer to a type of information system that uses the data collected by a transaction processing system, and manipulates the data to create reports that managers can use to make routine business decisions in response to structured problems. As Figure 9-6 shows, an MIS is characterized by the production of periodic reports that managers use for structured and routine tasks.

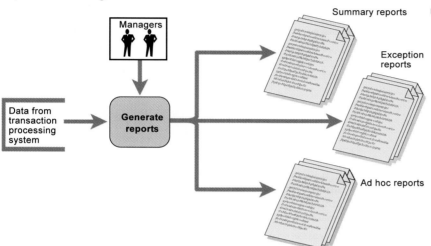

One of the major goals of an MIS is to increase the efficiency of managerial activity. Different levels of management have different information needs. In response to these different needs, an MIS can produce scheduled reports or ad hoc reports. **Scheduled reports**, such as monthly summaries, follow a fixed format and are produced according to a preset timetable. An **ad hoc report** (sometimes called a "demand report") is a customized report, generated to supply specific information not available in scheduled reports.

The scheduled reports produced by an MIS include summary and exception reports. A **summary report** combines, groups, or totals data. For example, a summary report might show total annual sales for the past five years. Summary reports are useful in tactical and strategic planning. An **exception report**, such as the one shown in Figure 9-7, contains information that is outside normal or acceptable ranges.

```
              Low Inventory-May 30
  Item#  Description   Minimum    Current   Vendor
                       Quantity   Quantity
  J506   Qualo-bag        12         10     REI
  05D-8  Sm. Backpack     48         22     REI
  B99A   Med. Backpack    48         40     REI
  L2020  Canteen          24          3     ZB Ind.
  D2990  Flashlight       36          8     ZB Ind.
  6-334  Tent stakes     112         24     Granot
```

FIGURE 9-6

A management information system is characterized by its ability to:

■ Produce routine and on-demand reports

■ Provide useful information for managerial activities

■ Increase managerial efficiency

■ Provide information used for structured, routine decisions

CLICK TO START ✣

FIGURE 9-7

Exception reports help managers take action, such as reordering inventory. Managers also use exception reports to analyze potential problems, such as continued inventory shortages or an excessive number of customers making late payments.

How does an MIS differ from a TPS? Whereas a TPS simply records data, an MIS can consolidate data by grouping and summarizing it. For example, modern library systems typically contain both a TPS and an MIS, which serve different functions, as Figure 9-8 explains.

FIGURE 9-8
A library's TPS performs different functions than its MIS.

TPS

Purpose: Track books by maintaining a database of titles, checkout dates, and so forth

Users: Library patrons locating books and librarians checking books in and out

Key characteristic: Managing transactions as books are checked in and out

MIS

Purpose: Provide librarians with summary and exception reports needed to manage the collection

Users: Librarians requesting and analyzing reports

Key characteristics: Summary reports indicate how many books are checked out each day, each week, each month, or each year; Exception reports list long-overdue books

What are the limitations of a management information system? A traditional MIS is based on the data collected by a transaction processing system. The MIS software used to generate reports might not be flexible enough to provide managers with the exact information needed. Further, an MIS usually cannot create models or projections—two important strategic planning tools. Today's competitive business environment calls for more sophisticated data manipulation tools, such as those that decision support systems provide.

DECISION SUPPORT SYSTEMS

What's a decision support system? A **decision support system** (DSS) helps people make decisions by directly manipulating data, analyzing data from external sources, generating statistical projections, and creating data models of various scenarios. A DSS provides tools for routine decisions, non-routine decisions, structured problems, and even semi-structured problems in which a decision might be based on imprecise data or require "guesstimates."

A special type of decision support system, called an **executive information system** (EIS), is designed to provide senior managers with information relevant to strategic management activities—such as setting policies, planning, and preparing budgets—based on information from the organization's database, where all current operational and financial data can be found.

A decision support system derives its name from the fact that it "supports" the decision maker; that is, it provides the tools a decision maker needs to analyze data. A DSS does not make decisions, however. That task remains the responsibility of the human decision maker.

Decision makers use DSSs to design decision models and make queries. A **decision model** is a numerical representation of a realistic situation, such as a cash-flow model of a business that shows how income adds to cash accounts and expenses deplete those accounts. A **decision query** is a question or set of instructions describing data that must be gathered to make a decision.

A DSS typically includes modeling tools, such as spreadsheets, so that managers can create a numerical representation of a situation and explore "what-if" alternatives. DSS statistical tools help managers study trends before making decisions. In addition, a DSS usually includes data from an organization's transaction processing system, and it might include or access external data, such as stock market reports, as shown in Figure 9-9.

FIGURE 9-9

A decision support system is characterized by its ability to:

- Support, rather than replace, managerial judgment

- Create decision models

- Improve quality of decisions

- Solve semi-structured problems

- Incorporate external data

CLICK TO START

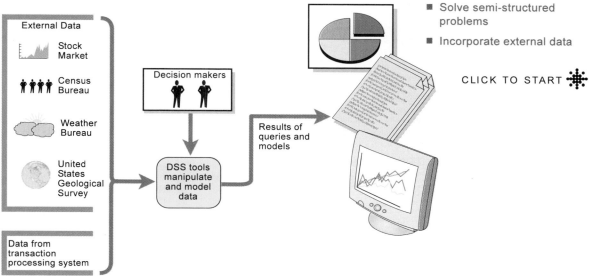

What kinds of decisions can a DSS handle? A DSS can be used to tackle diverse problems because it contains a good selection of decision support tools. A manager of a camping supply business might use a DSS to project demand for camping equipment before deciding how much new inventory to order. The DSS can access data on past sales from the company's transaction processing system. It can also access external data from government reports and commercial information services. This data can be manipulated to examine what-if scenarios, such as "What if higher national park fees decrease the number of campers, and demand for camping equipment declines by 2%?"

What are the limitations of a DSS? A DSS helps people manipulate the data needed to make a decision but does not actually make a decision. Instead, a person must analyze the data and reach a decision. A DSS is not a substitute for human judgment. Therefore, a DSS is appropriate in situations where it is used by trained professionals.

Many organizations, however, would like an alternative in which not every decision needs to be made by a highly paid expert. The major limitation of most decision support systems is that their use requires in-depth knowledge of the business problem that underlies the decision, plus a good background on what-if models and statistics. When organizations want an information system to make decisions without direct guidance from an experienced decision maker, they turn to expert systems.

INFOWEBLINKS

The Web contains lots of information about DSSs. At the **DSS InfoWeb**, you can explore their history and learn about state-of-the-art DSS software.

www.course.com/np/concepts8/ch09

EXPERT SYSTEMS AND NEURAL NETWORKS

What is an expert system? An **expert system**, sometimes referred to as a "knowledge-based system," is a computer system designed to analyze data and produce a recommendation, diagnosis, or decision based on a set of facts and rules, as shown in Figure 9-10.

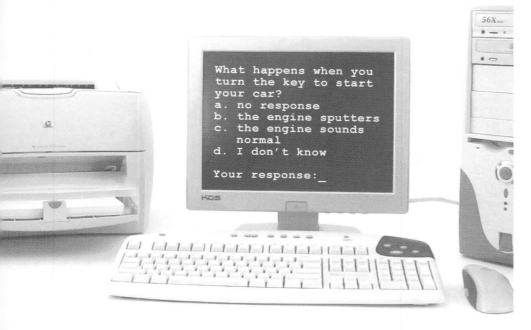

FIGURE 9-10
A simple expert system, such as this auto-mechanic expert, collects information about car trouble by asking questions. Answers are analyzed according to a set of facts and rules to produce a repair recommendation.

RULE 1:
IF the result of trying the starter is the engine sputters and the headlights dim,
THEN the recommended action is recharge the battery.

RULE 2:
IF the result of switching on the headlights is they don't light up or the result of turning the key to start the car is no response,
THEN the recommended action is recharge or replace the battery.

RULE 3:
IF the gas tank is empty,
THEN the recommended action is refuel the car.

RULE 4:
IF the tail pipe emits black smoke ...

The facts and rules for an expert system are usually derived by interviewing one or more experts, and then incorporated into a **knowledge base**. The knowledge base is stored in a computer file and can be manipulated by software called an **inference engine**. The process of designing, entering, and testing the rules in an expert system is referred to as **knowledge engineering**.

What kinds of decisions can an expert system make? An expert system is not a general-purpose problem solver or decision maker. Each expert system is designed to make decisions in a particular area or "domain." For example, an expert system created for use at the Campbell Soup Company captured the knowledge of an expert cooking-vat operator to help less experienced employees troubleshoot problems that might arise during the cooking and canning process. Other expert systems have been developed to locate mineral deposits, diagnose blood diseases, evaluate corporate financial statements, underwrite complex insurance policies, order a customized personal computer, and recommend stock purchases.

How does an expert system work? When it is time to make a decision, the inference engine begins analyzing the available data by following the rules in the knowledge base. If the expert system needs additional data, it checks external databases, looks for the data in a transaction processing system, or asks the user to answer questions. Figure 9-11 outlines the flow of information in an expert system and summarizes its capabilities.

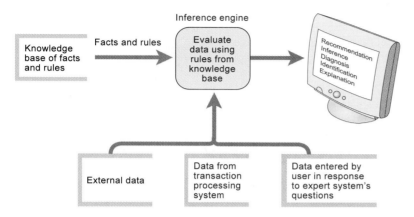

FIGURE 9-11
An expert system is characterized by its ability to:

- Replicate the reasoning of a human expert

- Produce a recommendation or decision

- Work with internal or external data

CLICK TO START

How are expert systems built? Expert systems can be created with a computer programming language, but an expert system shell offers a set of tools designed to simplify the development process. An **expert system shell** is a software tool containing an inference engine and a user interface that developers use to enter facts and rules for a knowledge base. An expert system shell also has tools for testing a knowledge base to make certain it produces accurate decisions. One of these tools is a trace feature that displays the inference engine's progress as it analyzes each fact and rule in the knowledge base.

Can an expert system deal with uncertainty? Expert systems are often designed to deal with data that is imprecise, or with problems that have more than one solution. Using a technique called **fuzzy logic**, an expert system can deal with imprecise data by asking for a level of confidence. For example, suppose an expert system is helping you identify a whale you spotted off the California coast. The expert system asks, "Did you see a dorsal fin?" You're not sure. You think you saw one, but it could have been a shadow. If the expert system is using fuzzy logic, it will let you respond with something like "I'm 85% certain I saw a dorsal fin." Based on the confidence level of your answers to this and other questions, the expert system might be able to tell you that it is "pretty sure," maybe 98% confident, that you saw a gray whale.

Is it possible to build an expert system without an expert? An expert system begins with a set of facts and rules. But if the rules are not known, a computer can "learn" how to make decisions based on hundreds or thousands of lightning-fast trial and error attempts. A **neural network** uses computer circuitry to simulate the way a brain might process information, learn, and remember. For example, a neural network could be connected

INFOWEBLINKS

At the **Expert System and Neural Network InfoWeb**, you'll find information about the history and current availability of these fascinating technologies.

www.course.com/np/concepts8/ch09

to a digital projector that displays photos of people's faces. Which faces are males and which are females? The neural network begins with a list of criteria with no values attached. "Hair length" might be one criteria, but the neural network is not programmed to expect that females usually have longer hair than men. Based on the evidence, a neural network begins to establish its own criteria—its own rules—about the data.

Neural networks have been successfully implemented in many business and financial applications where identification and trend analysis are important. A useful application of neural networks takes place in video surveillance systems, such as one that analyzes video footage of busy central London streets, watching for faces that match those of known terrorists (Figure 9-12).

FIGURE 9-12
Neural networks have been developed for a variety of applications, including surveillance.

QUICKCHECK......SECTION A

1. Effective information systems are designed to support the goals that help an organization accomplish its [   ].

2. Mid-level managers are responsible for [   ] planning, whereas executive managers engage in [   ] planning.

3. Information systems are effective for solving everyday, run-of-the-mill [   ] problems.

4. [   ] processing holds a group of transactions for later processing, whereas [   ] handles each transaction as it is entered.

5. A(n) [   ] makes it possible to produce scheduled, ad hoc, and exception reports. Hint: Use the acronym.

6. A(n) [   ] model is a numerical representation of a realistic situation that can be incorporated in a DSS.

7. A(n) [   ] system is designed to make decisions based on a series of rules derived from the knowledge of a specialist.

CHECK ANSWERS

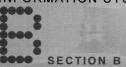
SYSTEMS ANALYSIS

The computer industry abounds with tales of information systems developed at great expense, but that failed to meet expectations because they didn't work correctly, were too complex to use, or weren't flexible enough to meet changing business needs. As Frederick Brooks observes in his book *The Mythical Man-Month*, "One can expect the human race to continue attempting systems just within or just beyond our reach, and software systems are perhaps the most intricate and complex of all man's handiwork."

Whether you are part of a team that is developing a complex corporate information system, or you are developing a small information system for your own use, you will be more likely to succeed if you analyze the purpose of the information system, carefully design the system, test it thoroughly, and document its features. In this section of the chapter, you'll learn about the planning and analysis that's required for an information system.

PLANNING PHASE

How does an information system project begin? Creating an information system can be compared to building a house. You don't just grab a hammer and start nailing pieces of wood together. It is important to have a plan. The process of planning and building an information system is referred to as **systems analysis and design**. This process begins with a planning phase.

FIGURE 9-13

What does the planning phase entail? The **planning phase** for an information system project includes the activities listed in Figure 9-13. The goal of these activities is to create a **Project Development Plan**. Before the project proceeds beyond the planning phase, the Project Development Plan must typically be reviewed and approved by management. This planning document includes:

- A short description of the project, including its scope

- A justification for the project, which includes an estimate of the project costs and potential financial benefits

- A list of project team participants

- A schedule for the project, including an outline of its phases

Do computers offer tools for planning activities? Project planning begins in the planning phase, but stretches throughout the entire project. As the project takes shape, project managers break down the work into tasks and milestones, which can be scheduled and assigned. As tasks are completed, the schedule can be updated and adjusted.

Project management software is an effective tool for planning and scheduling. It helps managers track and visualize the complex interactions between tasks. Popular examples include open source software, such as Open WorkBench, and commercial software, such as Microsoft Project.

Planning Phase Activities:

✓ Assemble the project team

✓ Justify project

✓ Choose development methodology

✓ Develop a project schedule

✓ Produce a Project Development Plan

ASSEMBLE PROJECT TEAM

Who supervises the development project? Information system problems are usually relayed to an organization's Information Systems department. Depending on the scope of the problem and the expertise of the IS department, an information systems project can be managed in house or outsourced.

Who participates in the process of building an information system? Whether the project is handled in house or outsourced, a system development project team, or "project team" for short, is a group of people who are assigned to analyze and develop an information system.

The composition of a project team depends on the scope of the project. Large and complex projects tend to have sizable project teams, with a majority of the people on the team being systems analysts or other computer professionals. Smaller projects tend to have fewer members on the project team, and a higher percentage of team members are likely to be users rather than computer professionals. Whether the project is large or small, the project team is usually headed by a member of the IS department staff.

In addition to the project team, other members of the organization might be asked to participate in various phases of the project. A widely accepted technique called **joint application design** (JAD) is based on the idea that the best information systems are designed when end users and systems analysts work together on a project as equal partners. JAD provides a structured methodology for planning and holding a series of meetings, called JAD sessions, in which users and analysts jointly identify problems and look for solutions (Figure 9-14).

TERMINOLOGY NOTE

As described in Chapter 8, systems analysts are responsible for analyzing information requirements, designing new information systems, and supervising their implementation. Systems analysts also create specifications for application software, and then give those specifications to computer programmers, who, in turn, create software to meet those specifications.

FIGURE 9-14
JAD helps users and analysts identify problems with an information system and look for effective solutions.

JUSTIFY PROJECT

Why are new information systems developed? The justification for a new information system usually emerges from a serious problem with the current system, a threat to the organization's success, or an opportunity to improve an organization's products or services through technology. If the current information system is manual, for example, it might not be cost effective, efficient, or competitive. Computerized information systems can become obsolete when the hardware is out of date, or when the software no longer meets the needs of the business mission.

What kinds of threats and opportunities can affect an organization? Most organizations exist in a rapidly changing and competitive environment, where many opportunities and threats can be effectively handled only by using computers. A well-known business analyst, Michael Porter, created the Five Forces model, shown in Figure 9-15, to illustrate how opportunities and threats can affect an organization.

FIGURE 9-15

Michael Porter's Five Forces model illustrates the factors that affect competition among business rivals.

CLICK TO START

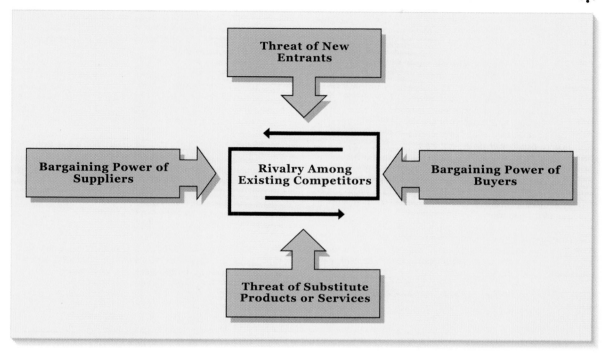

How can an information system help an organization respond to threats and opportunities? To be successful in its mission, an organization must respond effectively to opportunities and threats. An organization has a choice of three fundamental responses:

- **Make improvements.** An organization can become better at what it does by cutting costs, lowering prices, improving its products, offering better customer service, and so on. Computers often provide ways to make businesses run more efficiently, and they can supply timely information that helps improve customer service. For example, to keep up with other automakers, DaimlerChrysler developed a new information system that uses the Internet to track vehicle design, manufacturing, and supply.

- **Change the industry.** An organization can change the nature of an industry. Computers and related technologies, such as the Internet, often make such changes possible. For example, Amazon.com pioneered the idea of selling books on the Web, which was a major change to an industry in which success depended on the number of store franchises that could be placed in shopping malls.

- **Create new products.** An organization can create a new product, such as flavored potato chips, or a new service, such as overnight package delivery. Although creativity and invention usually spring from the minds of people, computers can contribute to research and development efforts by collecting and analyzing data, helping inventors create models and explore simulations, and so on.

A new information system might be only one aspect of a larger plan to evolve an organization into a stronger, more competitive entity. The business community has embraced several business practices, summarized in Figure 9-16, that use information systems as a key component for transforming organizations.

FIGURE 9-16
Business Practices Glossary

BPR (Business Process Reengineering): An ongoing iterative process that helps businesses rethink and radically redesign practices to improve performance, as measured by cost, quality, service, and speed.

CRM (Customer Relationship Management): A technique for increasing profitability by improving the relationship between a company and its customers. It helps a business increase sales by identifying, acquiring, and retaining customers. It can also cut costs by automating sales, marketing, and customer service. Information systems make it possible to collect and process the large volumes of customer data required for CRM and to efficiently transform this data into useful information.

EAI (Enterprise Application Integration): The use of networked, compatible software modules and databases to provide unrestricted sharing of data and business processes throughout an organization.

EDI (Electronic Data Interchange): The ability to transfer data between different companies using networks, such as the Internet, which enables companies to buy, sell, and trade information.

ERP (Enterprise Resource Planning): A system of business management that integrates all facets, or "resources," of a business, including planning, manufacturing, sales, and marketing. An information system running special ERP software is a key technology that allows a business to track the information necessary to monitor its resource use.

JIT (Just In Time): A manufacturing system in which the parts needed to construct a finished product are produced or arrive at the assembly site just when they are needed. JIT typically reduces costs by eliminating substantial warehousing costs and obsolete parts.

MRP (Manufacturing Resource Planning): Calculates and maintains an optimum manufacturing plan based on master production schedules, sales forecasts, inventory status, open orders, and bills of material. If properly implemented, it improves cash flow and increases profitability. MRP provides businesses with the ability to be proactive rather than reactive in the management of their inventory levels and material flow.

TQM (Total Quality Management): A technique initiated by top management that involves all employees and all departments and focuses on quality assurance in every product and service offered to customers.

INFOWEBLINKS

You'll find more information about terms such as BPR, TQM, JIT, and CRM at the **Business Practices InfoWeb**.

www.course.com/np/concepts8/ch09

How does the project team identify problems and opportunities? The members of the project team can use a variety of techniques, such as interviews and data analysis, to identify problems and opportunities. For example, James Wetherbe's **PIECES framework** helps classify problems in an information system. Each letter of PIECES stands for a potential problem, as shown in Figure 9-17.

FIGURE 9-17
Wetherbe's PIECES

Performance
A performance problem means that an information system does not respond quickly enough to users or takes too long to complete processing tasks.

Information
An information problem means that users don't receive the right information at the right time in a usable format.

Economics
An economics problem means that the system costs too much to operate or use.

Control
A control problem means that information is available to unauthorized users or that authorized users are not given the authority to make decisions based on the information they receive.

Efficiency
An efficiency problem means that too many resources are used to collect, process, store, and distribute information.

Service
A service problem means that the system is too difficult or inconvenient to use.

SYSTEM DEVELOPMENT LIFE CYCLE

What is a system development life cycle? The project team typically proceeds according to a system development methodology chosen by the IS department. Several development methodologies exist, based on various views of the system development life cycle.

A **system development life cycle**—usually referred to as **SDLC**—is an outline of a process that helps develop successful information systems. An SDLC is divided into phases, such as those in Figure 9-18.

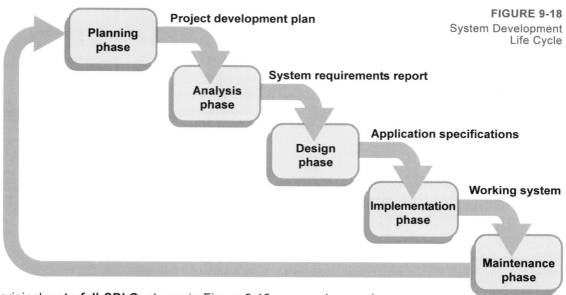

FIGURE 9-18
System Development
Life Cycle

The original **waterfall SDLC**, shown in Figure 9-18, approaches each phase as a discrete step in the development process. One phase is supposed to be completed before the next phase can begin. In reality, this model is impractical because it is not possible to neatly compartmentalize the development process. For example, it is difficult to complete the design phase until analysts and programmers have a chance to work with software tools to be purchased later in the implementation phase. A **modified waterfall SDLC** allows overlap between SDLC phases. An **iterative SDLC** allows phases to repeat, if necessary, as the project progresses. Figure 9-19 illustrates modified waterfall and iterative SDLC models.

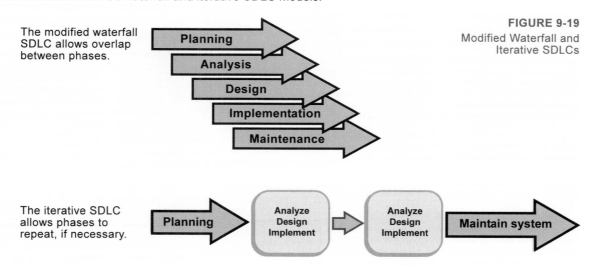

FIGURE 9-19
Modified Waterfall and
Iterative SDLCs

How do different SDLCs affect project development? An organization typically develops an information system according to a specific methodology and a set of related development tools. The **structured methodology** focuses on the processes that take place within an information system. The **information engineering methodology** focuses on the data an information system collects before working out ways to process that data. The **object-oriented methodology** treats an information system as a collection of objects that interact with each other to accomplish tasks. A methodology called **rapid application development** (RAD) proceeds with the project team creating a series of prototypes that users can evaluate. User comments are incorporated into the next prototype, and the process continues until the system is acceptable. In many cases, RAD shortens the development schedule, which is why it is called "rapid" application development.

What marks the end of the planning phase? After the development methodology has been selected, the project team can draw up a project schedule, complete the Project Development Plan, and request permission to begin the next phase of the project.

ANALYSIS PHASE

What happens in the analysis phase? The goal of the **analysis phase** is to produce a list of requirements for a new or revised information system. Tasks for the analysis phase are listed in Figure 9-20.

STUDY THE CURRENT SYSTEM

Why study the current system? Typically, a new information system is designed to replace a system or process that is already in place. It is important to study the current system to understand its strengths and weaknesses before planning a new system.

How does the project team discover what happens in the current system? Some members of the project team might have first-hand experience with the current system. They can often provide an overview of the system and identify key features, strengths, and weaknesses. To obtain additional information about the current system, project team members can interview people who use the system or observe the system in action. The project team usually documents the current system using data flow diagrams, such as the one in Figure 9-21.

FIGURE 9-20

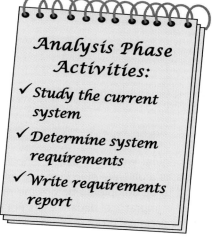

Analysis Phase Activities:

✓ Study the current system

✓ Determine system requirements

✓ Write requirements report

FIGURE 9-21

This diagram can graphically illustrate the way a school's current information system schedules workshops, enrolls students, and creates class rosters.

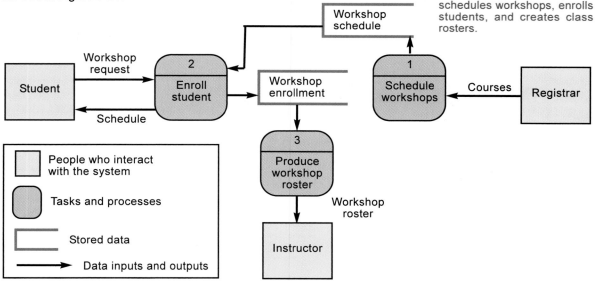

DETERMINE SYSTEM REQUIREMENTS

How does the project team determine what the new system should do? **System requirements** are the criteria for successfully solving the problem or problems identified in an information system. These requirements guide the design and implementation for a new or updated information system. They also serve as an evaluation checklist at the end of the development project, so they are sometimes called **success factors**. A new or updated information system should meet the requirements the project team defines.

The project team determines requirements by interviewing users and studying successful information systems that solve problems similar to those in the current system. Another way to determine requirements is to construct a prototype as an experimental or trial version of an information system. Often the prototype is not a fully functioning system because it is designed to demonstrate only selected features that might be incorporated into a new information system. A systems analyst shows the prototype to users, who evaluate which features of the prototype are important for the new information system.

How does the project team document system requirements? The project team can use a variety of tools to diagram the current system and specify what it does. These tools help the team produce documentation that is also useful in later phases of the SDLC. It can be difficult, however, to maintain this documentation as the project progresses. A **CASE tool** (computer-aided software engineering tool) is a software application designed for documenting system requirements, diagramming current and proposed information systems, scheduling development tasks, and developing computer programs. CASE tools automate many of the routine housekeeping tasks required by systems analysis and design, such as changing the labels used to describe elements in a database. Figure 9-22 shows a screen from a CASE tool called Visible Analyst.

INFOWEBLINKS

You'll find more information about CASE software, including links to downloads, at the **CASE Tools InfoWeb**.

www.course.com/np/concepts8/ch09

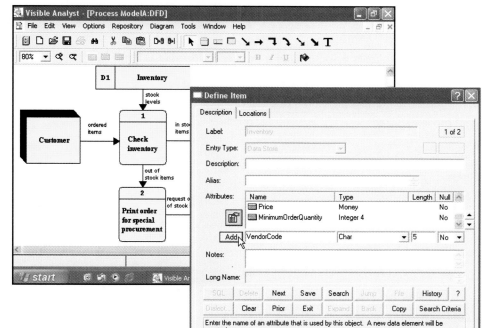

FIGURE 9-22

CASE tools help project team members manage all the details of system documentation. In this example, the project team is defining fields for the Inventory object depicted on the DFD.

CLICK TO START

What marks the end of the analysis phase of the SDLC? After the project team studies the current system and determines system requirements, the analysis phase concludes when the project team produces a written report that documents its findings. The **System Requirements Report**, outlined in Figure 9-23, typically contains diagrams that illustrate what the new information system should do. The report also includes narrative descriptions and diagrams showing the new system's users, data, processes, objects, and reports. If management or the project sponsor approves the report, the project can move on to the design phase.

FIGURE 9-23

A System Requirements Report describes the objectives for a new information system.

Title Page	**3 Recommendations** The rationale for developing or not developing the proposed system
Table of Contents	
Executive Summary	**4 Time and Cost Estimates** An estimate of the time and cost required to implement additional phases of the project
1 Introduction Project background Problems and opportunities that prompted the project Brief description of the current system	**5 Expected Benefits** A description of the benefits that can be expected if the project team's recommendations are followed
2 Findings Description of the scope of the proposed project List of general requirements for the proposed information system	**Appendices** Diagrams, interviews, and other documentation gathered by the project team

QUICKCHECK......SECTION B

1. Project [＿＿＿＿＿＿＿＿] software helps project leaders schedule and track a project's milestones and tasks.

2. In the planning phase, one of the main goals is to produce a Project [＿＿＿＿＿＿＿＿] Plan.

3. Users and analysts work together to identify problems and look for solutions in a development process called [＿＿＿＿＿＿＿＿] application design.

4. When justifying a new information system, the project team should consider threats and [＿＿＿＿＿＿＿＿] that affect the organization.

5. In the [＿＿＿＿＿＿＿＿] SDLC, one phase of the process must be completed before the next phase can begin.

6. To fulfill the main goal of the analysis phase, the project team produces [＿＿＿＿＿＿＿＿] for a new or revised information system.

7. A(n) [＿＿＿＿＿＿＿＿] tool helps the project team document the current system by automating many of the housekeeping tasks involved in diagramming and documenting an information system.

CHECK ANSWERS

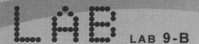 **LAB 9-B**
WORKING WITH DFDs

In this lab, you'll learn:

- The purpose of data flow diagrams (DFDs) in the system development life cycle
- How to read a leveled set of DFDs
- The meaning of each DFD symbol
- The differences between Gane/Sarson DFD notation and Yourdon/Coad DFD notation
- How to label data flows, entities, data stores, and processes
- How to create a context DFD
- How to "explode" a DFD to show additional levels of detail
- Why "black holes" and "miracles" indicate DFD errors

INTERACTIVE LAB

CLICK TO START THE LAB

LAB ASSIGNMENTS

1. Start the interactive part of the lab. Insert your Tracking Disk if you want to save your QuickCheck results. Perform each lab step as directed, and answer all the lab QuickCheck questions. When you exit the lab, your answers are automatically graded and your results are displayed.

2. Use paper and pencil, graphics software, or a CASE tool to create a context DFD for a video rental store. Use Gane/Sarson notation. Remember that the store purchases as well as rents videos and DVDs.

3. Explode the DFD you created in Assignment 2 so that it represents the main processes and data stores for the video rental store. Make sure you label data flows, processes, entities, and data stores. Before you finalize your DFD, make sure it contains no black holes or miracles.

4. Convert the DFD you drew in Assignment 3 to Yourdon/Coad notation.

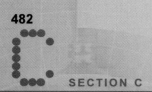

SECTION C

SYSTEM DESIGN

Many aspects of designing an information system resemble an architectural construction project. Suppose that during the analysis phase, an architect determines the elements a new building will contain. A single-family home, for example, might require bedrooms, bathrooms, closets, a kitchen, living room, dining room, and laundry room. In the design phase, the architect must figure how to arrange these elements. Should all the rooms be on the same floor? How many bedrooms? Where will the closets be located? Where will the doors be placed to create the best traffic pattern? As the architect answers these questions, the design for the house begins to emerge. In Section C, you'll learn how a project team designs a new information system.

DESIGN PHASE

What happens in the design phase? In the analysis phase, the project team determines *what* the new information system must do. In the **design phase** of the SDLC, the project team must figure out *how* the new system will fulfill the requirements specified in the System Requirements Report. The activities that typically take place during the design phase for an information system are listed in Figure 9-24.

IDENTIFY POTENTIAL SOLUTIONS

How does the project team come up with solutions? There might be more than one way to solve the problems and meet the requirements identified in the analysis phase of the SDLC. Some potential solutions might be better than others—more effective, less costly, or less complex. Therefore, it is not a good idea to proceed with the first solution that comes to mind. The project team should instead identify several potential hardware and software solutions by brainstorming and researching case studies on Web sites and in computer magazines.

What hardware alternatives are available? A myriad of hardware options are available for information systems. Mainframes, servers, and personal computers are the most commonly used components, but in some information systems, handhelds or even supercomputers play a role. When evaluating hardware solutions for a new information system, the project team considers the overall architecture of the information system based on level of automation, processing methodology, and network technology.

■ **Level of automation and computerization.** Some information systems provide a higher level of automation than others. For instance, a point-of-sale system with a low level of automation might require the checkout clerk to enter credit card numbers from a keypad. At a higher level of automation, a magnetic strip reader automates the process of

FIGURE 9-24

Design Phase Activities:

✓ Identify potential solutions

✓ Evaluate solutions and select the best

✓ Select hardware and software

✓ Develop application specifications

✓ Obtain approval to implement the new system

entering a credit card number. A further level of automation is achieved by using a pressure-sensitive digitizing pad and stylus to collect customer signatures (Figure 9-25). With signatures in digital format, the entire transaction record becomes electronic, and the business does not need to deal with paper credit card receipts.

FIGURE 9-25
Automation options, such as this device that digitizes signatures, might be considered by the project team as it brainstorms solutions.

Automation alternatives can affect many aspects of an information system. In the point-of-sale example, a credit card number can be stored using a few bytes. Storing a digitized signature, however, might require far more disk space and a special type of database software. The project team should consider the pros and cons of different levels of computerization and automation because they affect all aspects of the planned information system.

■ **Processing methodology.** An information system can be designed for **centralized processing**, in which data is processed on a centrally located computer. An alternative design option is **distributed processing**, in which processing tasks are distributed to servers and workstations. Typically, centralized processing requires a more powerful computer—usually a mainframe—to achieve the same response speed as distributed processing. Distributed processing in a client/server or peer-to-peer environment is very popular because it provides high levels of processing power at a low cost. However, these distributed architectures present more security problems than a single, centralized computer—a factor that the project team must consider within the context of selecting a solution.

■ **Network technology.** An information system, by its very nature, is designed to serve an entire organization. That organization includes many people who work in different rooms, different buildings, and perhaps even different countries. Virtually every information system requires a network, so the project team must examine network alternatives, such as LANs, extranets, intranets, and the Internet. Many information systems require a complex mixture of networks, such as a LAN in each branch office connected to a company intranet, with customers accessing selected data via the Internet.

What software alternatives are available? The project team might consider software alternatives, such as whether to construct the system "from scratch," use an application development tool, purchase commercial software, or select a turnkey system (Figure 9-26).

Creating an information system "from scratch" using a programming language can take many months or years. It is usually costly, but offers the most flexibility for meeting the system requirements. As an analogy, baking a cake from scratch allows you some flexibility in the ingredients you choose—margarine instead of shortening, for example. However, baking from scratch requires a lot of time and work to sift the flour with the salt; mix the sugar, eggs, shortening, and milk; combine the dry and wet ingredients; and so forth.

During the design phase, the project team can analyze the costs and benefits of developing an information system from scratch. If it appears to be a feasible solution, the team can also select the programming language to use.

An **application development tool** is essentially a type of software construction kit containing building blocks that can be assembled into a software product. Application development tools include expert system shells and database management systems.

An application development tool is the programmer's "cake mix," which contains many of the ingredients necessary for quickly and easily developing the modules for an information system. Although application development tools usually speed up the development process, they might not offer the same level of flexibility as a programming language.

Commercial software for an information system is usually a series of pre-programmed software modules, supplied by a software developer or value added reseller (VAR). Commercial software eliminates much of the design work required with programming languages or application development tools. However, commercial software requires extensive evaluation to determine how well it meets the system requirements. Following through with the cake analogy, commercial software is equivalent to buying a pre-made cake that you simply slice and serve.

Commercial software is available for standard business functions, such as human resource management, accounting, and payroll. It is also available for many vertical market businesses and organizations, such as law offices, video stores, medical offices, libraries, churches, e-commerce, and charities. Although most commercial software has some customization options, in many cases, it cannot be modified to exactly meet every system requirement, which necessitates adjustments in an organization's procedures. The project team must decide if the benefits of commercial software can offset the cost and inconvenience of procedural changes.

A **turnkey system** is essentially an "information system in a box," which consists of hardware and commercial software designed to offer a complete information system solution. In terms of the cake analogy, a turnkey system is like going out to dinner and simply ordering your choice of cake for dessert. A turnkey system might seem like a quick and easy solution, and it looks attractive to many project teams. Like commercial software, however, a turnkey system must be extensively evaluated to determine whether it can satisfy system requirements.

FIGURE 9-26
Software Alternatives

Programming Language

Pros: Can be exactly tailored to system requirements

Cons: Requires development time and expertise

Application Development Tool

Pros: Requires less time than programming languages

Cons: Might limit developers on the way they implement some system features

Commercial Software

Pros: Little or no programming required, so requires minimal development time

Cons: Software features might not exactly match business needs; might require extensive customization

Turnkey System

Pros: Minimal effort required to select and set up equipment and software

Cons: Requires time and expertise to evaluate

EVALUATE SOLUTIONS AND SELECT THE BEST

How does the team choose the best solution? To determine the best solution, the project team devises a list of criteria for comparing each potential solution. This list includes general criteria related to costs, benefits, and development time. The list also includes technical criteria, such as the flexibility of the solution and its adaptability for future modifications and growth. Finally, the list includes functional criteria that indicate how well the solution satisfies the specified requirements.

Each criterion is assigned a weight to indicate its importance. The project team then evaluates the criteria for each solution and assigns raw scores. The raw score for each criterion is multiplied by the weight, and these weights are added to produce a total score for each solution. Sound complicated? It isn't, especially if the project team uses a **decision support worksheet**. Take a few moments to study Figure 9-27, and you'll quickly see how it works.

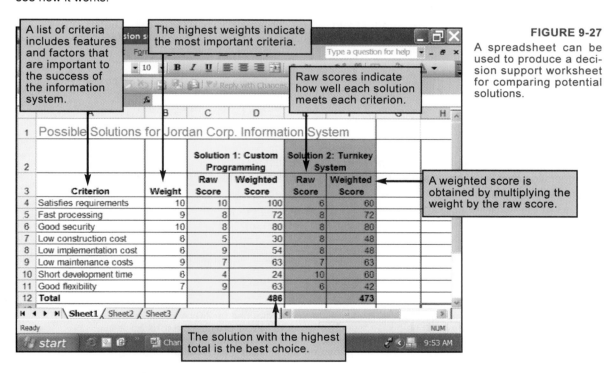

FIGURE 9-27

A spreadsheet can be used to produce a decision support worksheet for comparing potential solutions.

A list of criteria includes features and factors that are important to the success of the information system.

The highest weights indicate the most important criteria.

Raw scores indicate how well each solution meets each criterion.

A weighted score is obtained by multiplying the weight by the raw score.

The solution with the highest total is the best choice.

Possible Solutions for Jordan Corp. Information System

Criterion	Weight	Solution 1: Custom Programming		Solution 2: Turnkey System	
		Raw Score	Weighted Score	Raw Score	Weighted Score
Satisfies requirements	10	10	100	6	60
Fast processing	9	8	72	8	72
Good security	10	8	80	8	80
Low construction cost	6	5	30	8	48
Low implementation cost	6	9	54	8	48
Low maintenance costs	9	7	63	7	63
Short development time	6	4	24	10	60
Good flexibility	7	9	63	6	42
Total			**486**		**473**

SELECT HARDWARE AND SOFTWARE

How does the project team find the right hardware and software for the new information system? After the project team selects a solution, the next task is to select the hardware and software needed to implement the solution. Sometimes more than one vendor sells the hardware and software necessary for the new system, so an organization might have a choice of vendors.

The method for selecting the hardware, software, and vendor depends on the project team's understanding of what is required for the solution. Sometimes the team knows exactly what brand, model, or version of hardware and software are required. At other times, the team has a general understanding, but needs vendor help selecting specific products. RFPs and RFQs (described on the next page) help the team collect information for these important decisions.

What's an RFP? A **request for proposal** (RFP) is a document that describes the information system problem and the requirements for the solution. An RFP essentially asks a vendor to recommend hardware and software for the solution and to describe the vendor's qualifications for implementing the solution. A project team usually issues an RFP to vendors when its members believe that a vendor has more knowledge and experience in the solution area. Look at the sample RFP in Figure 9-28.

FIGURE 9-28
RFP Excerpt

RFP for The University Library Information System

The purpose of this request for proposal (RFP) and subsequent vendor presentations is to identify a vendor with whom The University will negotiate a contract to supply, install, and support an integrated library system. This system must be capable of supporting an online public access catalog, cataloging and authority control, acquisitions and serials control, circulation, and reserve. It should be capable of supporting media booking, interlibrary loan and document delivery, and preservation control. Proposals are due 10 August 3:00pm, Purchasing Dept.

A letter of intent to propose should be received by the University by 5:00pm CDT, July 13, 2005. Letters should be sent to the following address:

What's an RFQ? A **request for quotation** (RFQ) is a request for a formal price quotation on a list of hardware and software. A project team issues an RFQ to vendors when it knows the make and model of the equipment and the titles of the software packages needed but wants to compare prices from different vendors. Compare the RFQ in Figure 9-29 with the RFP in the previous figure.

FIGURE 9-29
RFQ Excerpt

City Hall Information System RFQ

The Information Technology Office is seeking qualified vendors for the quotation of network equipment required for the expansion of the city hall facility. A list of hardware and software is provided below. Prospective vendors MUST provide the total price including shipping charges and the applicable sales tax. Any deviation from the specifications MUST be noted on the quotation and a written explanation is strongly encouraged to support the substitutions. Bids submitted with equipment other than those stated in the specifications may be rejected.

Part Description	Part Number	Quantity	Price
1. Cisco Catalyst 3750 24 10/100/1000T + 4 SFP Enhanced Multilayer Switch	WS-C3750G-24TS-E	1	
2. Cisco Catalyst 3750 24 10/100/1000T + 4 SFP Standard Multilayer Switch	WS-C3750G-24TS-S	2	

How does the project team evaluate an RFP or RFQ? The project team can evaluate RFPs or RFQs by constructing a decision table similar to the one used for evaluating solutions. The basis for choosing hardware and software typically includes general criteria, such as cost and delivery time. In addition, it is important for the project team to consider the vendor's reliability, expertise, and financial stability. Technical criteria for hardware might include processing speed, reliability, upgradability, maintenance costs, and warranty. Technical criteria for software might include reliability, compatibility, and the availability of patches to fix program errors.

DEVELOP APPLICATION SPECIFICATIONS

What happens after the project team selects a solution? Exactly what happens next in the system design phase depends on the type of solution selected. If a turnkey solution is selected, the next step might be to get approval to move into the implementation phase of the SDLC. In contrast, if the project team selected a solution that requires custom programming, the team's systems analysts will create a set of **application specifications** that describe the way the information system's software should interact with users, store data, process data, and format reports (Figure 9-30).

```
BEGIN

FIND item in INVENTORY with matching inventory-ID

IF record cannot be found

        DISPLAY "No inventory item matches the Inventory ID."

ELSE

        READ item record

        SET discontinued-item to YES

        WRITE item record

        DISPLAY "Item [inventory-ID] is now marked as
        discontinued."

ENDIF

END
```

FIGURE 9-30
This excerpt from a project team's application specifications describes in detail the process for discontinuing an inventory item.

This part of the SDLC is sometimes referred to as the "detailed design phase" because its goal is to create very detailed specifications for the completed information system. Detailed application specifications can be developed only after selecting the hardware and software for an information system. For example, the specifications for a program that runs on a Windows-based LAN might require quite a different user interface and processing model than a program that runs on a centralized mainframe computer and is accessed via the Internet.

What is the importance of application specifications? Application specifications are a key element in developing an effective information system. Not only do these specifications serve as a blueprint for the new system, but they play a critical role in ensuring that the development process proceeds efficiently.

Many projects fail because of constant, unmanaged demand for changes, even before the system is implemented. This failure to constrain change is often referred to as **feature creep** because new features tend to creep into the development process with a snowballing effect on other features, costs, and schedules. It might be important to change some specifications during the development process because of changes in business needs, laws, or regulations. Proposed changes should be managed within a formal process that includes written **change requests**, which detail the scope of a proposed change and can be evaluated by project team members.

What happens to the completed specifications? Application specifications are similar to the pages of an architectural blueprint that show the detailed plan for electrical wiring or plumbing. In a large information systems project, the specifications are given to a programming team or application developer who creates the software. In a small information systems project, you as the user might develop your own specifications. Then you might give the specifications to a programmer or, if you have the expertise, you might create the software yourself.

OBTAIN APPROVAL TO IMPLEMENT THE NEW SYSTEM

When can the project team actually begin to build the new information system? In the design phase of the SDLC, the project team chooses a solution, selects hardware and software, and designs detailed application specifications. Before the solution is implemented, the project team typically must seek approval from management. The approval process might be fairly informal, simply involving a discussion with the CIO. In contrast, some organizations require a much more formal process for obtaining approval, in which the project team submits a written proposal that's supplemented by presentations to management and user groups. After the project team's proposal is approved, the project can move to the next phase of development.

QUICKCHECK......SECTION C

1. In the design phase of the SDLC, a project team identifies several potential [＿＿＿＿＿＿＿] and then selects the one that offers the most benefits at the lowest cost.

2. The project team should consider [＿＿＿＿＿＿＿] processing methodologies, such as a client/server and peer-to-peer.

3. A(n) [＿＿＿＿＿＿＿] development tool is essentially a software construction kit containing building blocks that can be assembled into the software for an information system.

4. The project team can send out a(n) [＿＿＿＿＿＿＿] to ask vendors to recommend solutions. HInt: use the acronym.

5. Application [＿＿＿＿＿＿＿] describe the way an application should interact with users, store data, process data, and format reports.

CHECK ANSWERS

SECTION D
IMPLEMENTATION AND MAINTENANCE

After the plan for an information system is approved, it's time to start building it. During the implementation phase of the SDLC, an organization puts together the components for the new information system. After an information system is installed and tested, it enters the final phase of the SDLC—the maintenance phase. Most people have experience with information systems in the maintenance phase because that is when a system provides its services. At the end of this section, you'll learn what happens during the maintenance phase and the important role played by people who use the system.

IMPLEMENTATION PHASE

What happens during the implementation phase? During the **implementation phase** of the SDLC, the project team supervises the tasks necessary to construct the new information system. The tasks that take place during the implementation phase can include any of those listed in Figure 9-31.

PURCHASE AND INSTALL HARDWARE AND SOFTWARE

Does a new information system typically require new hardware? Most new information systems require new hardware, which can either replace old equipment or be connected to existing equipment. During the implementation phase, new hardware is purchased, installed, and tested to ensure that it operates correctly.

How about new software? Many information systems require new software, such as a commercial application, a programming language, an application development tool, or an expert system shell. During the implementation phase, this software must be installed and tested to ensure that it works correctly. Software testing can reveal problems that result from incompatibilities with the existing hardware or an incorrect installation of the software. These problems must be corrected before continuing with system development. Some problems might result from bugs (errors) in the software, which must be corrected by the software publisher.

FIGURE 9-31

Implementation Phase Activities:

✓ *Purchase and install hardware and/or software*

✓ *Create applications*

✓ *Test applications*

✓ *Finalize documentation*

✓ *Train users*

✓ *Convert data*

✓ *Convert to new system*

CREATE APPLICATIONS

What's the next step in the implementation phase? The next step in the implementation phase depends on the software tools selected for the project.

When the software for an information system is created by using a programming language or application development tool, programmers must create and test all the new software modules. Chapter 11 provides more information about the programming process.

When an information system is constructed using commercial software, that software has been written and tested by the software publisher.

Nevertheless, the software sometimes must be customized. **Software customization** is the process of modifying a commercial application to reflect an organization's needs. Customization might include modifying the user interface, enabling or disabling the mouse, selecting the menus that appear on-screen, and designing forms or reports. The extent to which commercial software can be customized depends on the options available in the application. For example, some commercial software offers options for customizing report formats, while other software does not.

TEST APPLICATIONS

How can the team ensure that a new information system works? A rigorous testing process is the only way to make sure a new information system works. Different types of testing during the implementation phase help identify and fix problems before the information system is incorporated into day-to-day business activities.

What is application testing? **Application testing** is the process of trying out various sequences of input values and checking the results to verify that the application works correctly. Application testing is performed in three ways: unit testing, integration testing, and system testing.

As each application module is completed, it undergoes **unit testing** to ensure that it operates reliably and correctly. When all modules have been completed and tested, **integration testing** is performed to ensure that the modules operate together correctly. Unit testing and integration testing are usually performed in a test area. A **test area** is a place where software testing can occur without disrupting the organization's regular information system. A test area might be located in an isolated section of storage on the computer system that runs the organization's regular information system, or it might be located on an entirely separate computer system.

When a problem is discovered during unit testing or integration testing, the team must track down the source of the problem and correct it. Unit testing and integration testing are then repeated to make sure the problem is corrected, and no new problems were introduced when the original problem was fixed.

After unit and integration testing are completed, **system testing** ensures that all hardware and software components work together correctly. If an existing information system is modified, system testing is performed when the new or modified units are combined with the rest of the existing system. In a completely new information system, system testing is performed to simulate daily work loads and make sure processing speed and accuracy meet the specifications. Figure 9-32 summarizes the three stages of application testing.

FIGURE 9-32

Unit, integration, and system testing ensure that applications work.

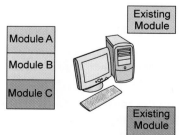

Module A
Module B
Module C

Unit testing ensures that each module of the application software works correctly.

Module A
Module B
Module C

Integration testing ensures that all the modules work together correctly.

Module A
Module B
Module C
Existing Module
Existing Module

System testing ensures that new modules work with the rest of the system hardware and software.

FINALIZE DOCUMENTATION

One of the most important tasks during the implementation phase is to make sure the information system is completely documented so that it can be used effectively and modified easily. The documentation for an information system can be broadly categorized as system or user documentation.

System documentation describes a system's features, hardware architecture, and programming. The target audience for system documentation is programmers, designers, and analysts who might maintain the system on a day-to-day basis and implement modifications. Much of the information required for system documentation is generated in the analysis and design phases of the SDLC. These documents should be reviewed for accuracy, however, because features sometimes change as a result of problems or opportunities encountered during implementation. Many project teams turn to automated applications that produce documentation from completed source code. These tools help the team retrofit the documentation to the actual system, which might differ somewhat from the original system and application specifications.

User documentation describes how to interact with the system to accomplish specific tasks. It typically includes a list of features and instructions on how to use them. It might also list common errors and describe how to correct them.

Both system and user documentation can be supplied in printed format, but the current trend is to supply documentation in digital format as electronic documents, online help, or hyperlinked HTML documents. Electronic documents are often stored in a standard format, such as PDF, which can be accessed by Adobe Acrobat. Online help systems, such as the familiar Windows Help files, can be customized to provide help for information system modules. HTML documents can be posted for Web access via the Internet or a corporate intranet.

TRAIN USERS

How do employees learn how to use the new information system? In preparation for using a new information system, users need extensive training, which might include software orientation, hardware operation, data entry, and backup procedures (Figure 9-33).

During these training sessions, users learn how to interact with the interface, use the new system to perform day-to-day tasks, and find additional information in user manuals or procedure handbooks. A **procedure handbook** is a type of user documentation that contains step-by-step instructions for performing specific tasks. It often takes the place of a lengthy user manual because in a large organization, an employee in a particular department usually performs specific tasks and does not need to know how all features of the system work.

CONVERT DATA

What happens to data from the old system? The data for a new information system might exist in card files, file folders, or an old information system. This data must be loaded into the new system—a process called "data conversion." For example, suppose that a local building inspector's office has a manual system for issuing and renewing construction permits. It has more than 8,000 permits on record. If this office computerizes its operations, it must convert these 8,000 records into an electronic format that the new computerized system can access.

FIGURE 9-33

Training sessions for a new information system can be conducted by members of the project team or outsourced to professional trainers.

When converting data from a manual system to a computer system, the data can be typed or scanned electronically into the appropriate storage media (Figure 9-34).

When converting data from an existing computer system to a new system, a programmer typically writes conversion software to read the old data and convert it into a format that is usable by the new system. Without such software, users would be forced to manually reenter data from the old system into the new system.

CONVERT TO NEW SYSTEM

How does a business switch from the old information system to the new system? **System conversion** refers to the process of deactivating an old information system and activating the new one. It is also referred to as "cutover" or "go live." There are several strategies for converting to a new system.

A **direct conversion** means that the old system is completely deactivated and the new system is immediately activated. Direct conversion usually takes place during non-peak hours to minimize disruption to normal business routines. Direct conversion is risky, however, because if the new system does not work correctly, it might need to be deactivated and undergo further testing. In the meantime, the old system must be reactivated, and transactions that were entered into the new system must be reentered into the old system so that business can continue.

A **parallel conversion** avoids some of the risk of direct conversion because the old system remains in service while some or all of the new system is activated. Both the old and new systems operate in parallel until the project team can determine whether the new system is performing correctly. Parallel conversion often requires that all entries be made in both the new and old systems, which is costly in terms of time, computer resources, and personnel. Parallel conversion is fairly safe but often not practical because of the cost and duplication of effort.

Phased conversion works well with larger information systems that are modularized. In a phased conversion, the new system is activated one module at a time. After the project team determines that one module is working correctly, the next module is activated, and so on, until the entire new system is operational. In a phased conversion, each module of the new system must work with both the old and new systems, which greatly increases the complexity and cost of application development.

A **pilot conversion** works well in organizations with several branches that have independent information processing systems. The new information system is activated at one branch. If the system works correctly at one branch, it is activated at the next branch. During a pilot conversion, some method must be developed to integrate information from branches using the new system with information from branches still using the old system.

When is the new information system formally "live"? A new or upgraded information system undergoes a final test called acceptance testing. **Acceptance testing** is designed to verify that the new information system works as required. The procedures for acceptance testing are usually designed by users and systems analysts, and often include the use of real data to demonstrate that the system operates correctly under normal and peak data loads. Acceptance testing usually marks the completion of the implementation phase.

FIGURE 9-34
Some organizations have a lot of data that must be converted from paper-based documents into digital format. Even using scanners, this process can take a long time, require extra personnel, and be quite costly.

MAINTENANCE PHASE

What happens during the maintenance phase? The **maintenance phase** of the SDLC involves day-to-day operation of the system, making modifications to improve performance, and correcting problems. After an information system is implemented, it remains in operation for a period of time. During this time, maintenance activities ensure that the system functions as well as possible. Figure 9-35 lists the major maintenance activities for a typical information system.

The term "maintenance phase" is a bit misleading because it seems to imply that the information system is maintained in a static state. On the contrary, during the maintenance phase, an information system is likely to undergo many changes to meet an organization's needs. Changes during the maintenance phase can include the following:

- Upgrades to operating system and commercial software

- User interface revisions to make the system easier to use

- Application software revisions to fix bugs and add features

- Hardware replacements to enhance performance

- Security upgrades

FIGURE 9-35

Maintenance Phase Activities:
✓ *Operate equipment*
✓ *Make backups*
✓ *Provide help to users*
✓ *Fix bugs*
✓ *Optimize for speed and security*
✓ *Revise software as necessary to meet business needs*

How important is system security during this phase? To combat an escalating number of viruses, worms, Denial of Service attacks, and intrusions, security has become a top priority for the maintenance phase of an information system's life cycle. Maintaining security is an ongoing activity. Some of the maintenance phase duties of a security specialist include:

- Keeping user accounts up to date by creating new accounts as required and promptly deleting accounts for employees who cease to be employed

- Staying up-to-date on new virus threats and taking appropriate action to guard against them

- Keeping informed about potential security problems with operating systems, e-mail systems, and application software used in the information system, and applying updates and security patches as needed

- Watching for unusual system activity or network traffic that might indicate a security breach

Who is responsible for system maintenance? In an information system that revolves around a mainframe computer or minicomputer, the task of operating the computer on a day-to-day basis is usually the responsibility of the **system operator**. The system operator performs system backups and data recovery, monitors system traffic, and troubleshoots operational problems. Additional responsibilities might include installing new versions of the operating system and software applications, but in some organizations, these responsibilities are delegated to a systems programmer. A **systems programmer** is the operating system "guru," whose responsibilities include installing new versions of the operating system and modifying operating system settings to maximize performance.

In an information system that revolves around a microcomputer network, a network manager or network specialist is typically responsible for day-to-day operations and system maintenance. Some maintenance activities might also fall on the shoulders of individual users, who are often charged with the responsibility of backing up their workstations and performing workstation installations of new software.

Why do maintenance activities include user support? Even after in-depth training, employees sometimes forget procedures or have difficulty when they encounter a new set of circumstances. These employees turn to the IS department for help. Many organizations establish a help desk to handle end-user problems. The **help desk** is staffed by technical support specialists who are familiar with the information system's software. Support specialists keep records of problems and solutions.

When you use an information system, you are likely to have questions. Your first source of information is your procedure handbook or user manual, similar to the one in Figure 9-36.

FIGURE 9-36

When you have questions about how to use an information system, first check the documentation. If you can't find an answer there, call the help desk.

Help desk personnel have little tolerance for people who ask questions that are clearly answered in the documentation. You should not hesitate, however, to ask about procedures or problems that are not covered in the documentation. Your questions can often promote much-needed modifications in the information system. For example, suppose you encounter a problem with an update procedure and call the help desk. The help desk technician begins to troubleshoot the problem and soon realizes that it is caused by a programming error not caught during system testing. This bug is recorded in a "bug report" that is routed to the programming group, which can determine its severity and take steps to fix it.

How long does the maintenance phase last? The maintenance phase is the longest SDLC phase and lasts until the system is retired. Although the analysis, design, and implementation phases of the SDLC are costly, for many organizations, the maintenance phase is the most expensive because it is the longest.

The maintenance phase often accounts for 70% of the total cost of an information system. As shown in Figure 9-37 on the next page, maintenance costs follow a U-shaped curve—an information system requires the most maintenance at the beginning and end of its life cycle.

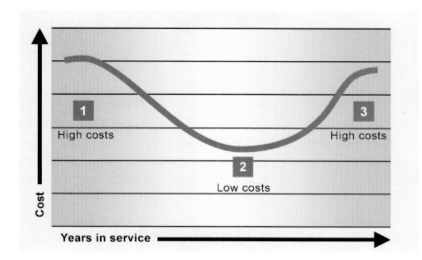

FIGURE 9-37
Maintenance Phase Costs

1. When a new information system first goes "live," maintenance costs are high while programmers work out the bugs and users clamor for support.

2. After most of the bugs are fixed and users become familiar with the information system, maintenance costs decrease.

3. As an information system nears the end of its useful life span, repair costs rise, and changing business practices begin to require modifications that are time consuming and expensive to implement.

When does the maintenance phase end? The maintenance phase continues until an information system is no longer cost effective or until changes in the organization make the information system obsolete. It is not unusual for an information system to remain in operation for 20 years or more. Eventually an information system's useful or cost-effective life nears a close. It is then time to begin the system development life cycle again.

QUICKCHECK......SECTION D

1. The [   ] phase follows the design phase.

2. When the project team selects commercial software, it usually has to be [   ] to reflect the organization's needs.

3. [   ] testing ensures that a software module operates reliably and correctly, whereas [   ] testing checks to make sure all the modules work with each other.

4. The target audience for [   ] documentation is programmers, designers, and analysts.

5. A(n) [   ] handbook can take the place of a lengthy user manual.

6. A(n) [   ] conversion is more risky than other types of conversion because all parts of the new system go live at once.

7. The final phase of testing, in which users verify that the entire system works as specified, is called [   ] testing.

8. During the [   ] phase, security is a top priority, but operating system upgrades, software revisions, hardware replacements, and user interface revisions also take place.

CHECK ANSWERS

TECHTALK

DOCUMENTATION TOOLS

Throughout the analysis and design phases of the SDLC, the project team documents its work, describing the current system and requirements for the new system. As you might expect, lengthy narrative descriptions are not the most convenient method for documentation. In the world of systems analysis and design, one picture—or diagram—is really worth a thousand words.

This TechTalk provides an overview of the diagrams that a project team might use to document an enrollment system for workshops offered by a university's Continuing Education Department. You'll first look at diagrams the project team would use when following a structured system development methodology. You'll then learn about diagrams the project team would use when following an object-oriented methodology.

STRUCTURED DOCUMENTATION TOOLS

Where does the project team begin with structured documentation?
The core of structured documentation is the **data flow diagram** (DFD), which graphically illustrates how data moves through an information system. You can think of a DFD as a map that traces the possible paths for data traveling from entities (such as customers) to processes (such as printing) or storage areas. In DFD terminology, an **external entity** is a person, organization, or device outside the information system that originates or receives data. A **data store** is a filing cabinet, disk, or tape that holds data. A **process** is a manual or computerized routine that changes data by performing a calculation, updating information, sorting a list, and so on. An arrow symbolizes a **data flow** and indicates how data travels from entities to processes and data stores. Each of these elements is represented on a DFD by a symbol, as shown in Figure 9-38.

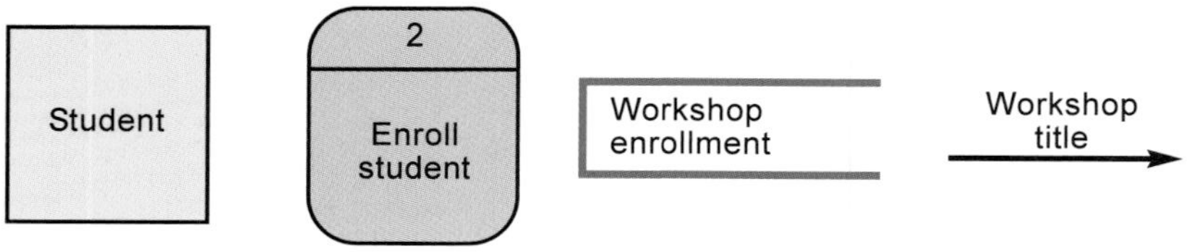

FIGURE 9-38
Data Flow Diagram Symbols

| Student | Enroll student (2) | Workshop enrollment | Workshop title → |

An external entity is represented by a square labeled with a noun.

A process is represented by a rounded rectangle, which is numbered and labeled with a verb phrase (except for the process numbered 0, which gives the system's name).

A data store is represented by an open rectangle labeled with the name of a data file.

A data flow is represented by an arrow labeled with a description of the data.

What does a DFD look like? In a completed DFD, data flow arrows show the path of data to and from external entities, data stores, and processes. Figure 9-39 explains how to read a DFD.

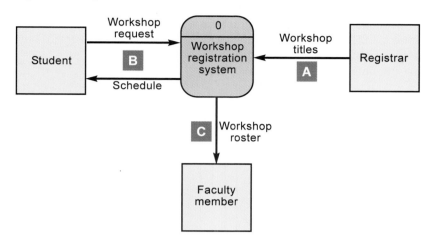

FIGURE 9-39
DFD for Workshop Registration System

A The registrar produces the list of workshops offered and submits it to the registration system.

B A student submits a request to enroll in a workshop. The workshop registration system processes the request and produces a schedule of workshops in which the student is enrolled.

C A faculty member receives a list of the students enrolled in a workshop.

Why doesn't the DFD show the detail of the system? The DFD in the previous figure is called a **context diagram**, and it simply provides an overview of the information system. This context DFD can be "exploded" to show more details. Figure 9-40 illustrates how the rectangle labeled 0 in the previous diagram is exploded to show the more detailed processes that take place within the system. It also shows the two data stores that can be accessed by processes.

FIGURE 9-40

In this exploded DFD for workshop registration, the orange area corresponds to the single process depicted in the context diagram.

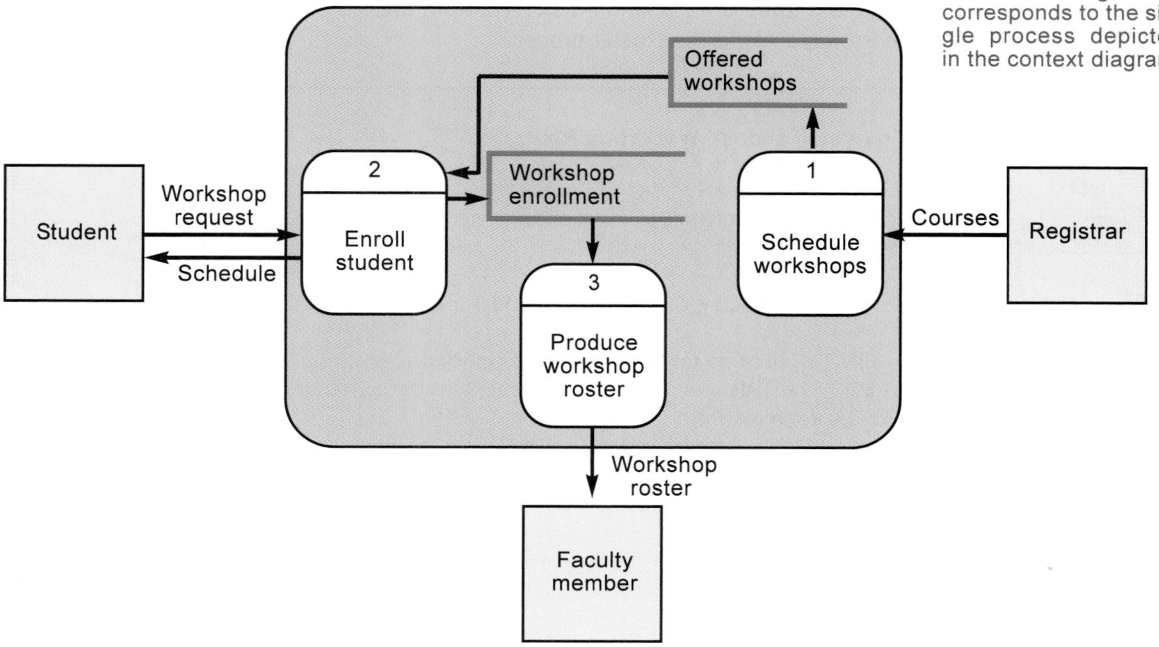

How do I find out what data is included in each data store? A DFD
does not provide a direct mechanism for listing the data in a data store. For
that purpose, a project team typically uses a **data dictionary**, which contains a detailed description of the records stored in a database. A complete
data dictionary can supply the specifications necessary to construct the
database for a new information system. CASE tools usually provide a way
to attach the data dictionary to its corresponding data store on a DFD.
Figure 9-41 shows an excerpt from the data dictionary for the Offered
Workshops data store.

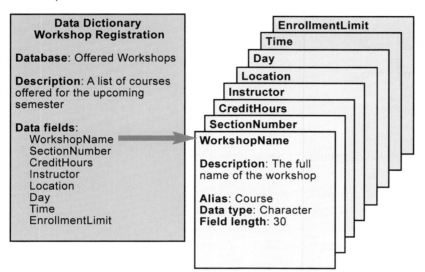

FIGURE 9-41
A data dictionary lists each field
in a file or database, and then
provides a detailed description
of each field.

Can a DFD provide the specifications programmers need to write
applications for an information system? Although DFDs can be
exploded to show more and more detailed levels of processing activity,
they do not typically include enough detail for programmers. Instead, the
project team provides programmers with **process specifications**, which
explain exactly what happens in each process of a DFD. Many CASE tools
provide a way to attach a process specification to its corresponding
process on a DFD. For example, Figure 9-42 shows an excerpt from the
process specification for the Produce Workshop Roster process.

FIGURE 9-42
A Process Specification

```
           3

        Produce
        workshop
         roster
```

Process: Produce Workshop Roster

FOR each SectionNumber
    PRINT SectionNumber, WorkshopName, CreditHours, and
    EnrollmentLimit

    PRINT Instructor, Location, Day, and Time

    FIND all records for SectionNumber in Workshop Enrollment database
    SORT records in ascending alphabetical order by StudentLastName
    FOR each record
        Print StudentLastName, FirstName, MiddleInitial,
        SocialSecurityNumber

OBJECT-ORIENTED DOCUMENTATION TOOLS

How do documentation tools differ for object-oriented analysis and design? In structured design, the goal is to create documentation that indicates how to design databases and write the applications that allow people to interact with those databases. In contrast, object-oriented design tools provide blueprints for creating data objects and the routines that allow people to interact with those objects. The current standard for object-oriented documentation is called **UML** (Unified Modeling Language). Three of the most frequently used UML tools include use case diagrams, sequence diagrams, and class diagrams.

What is a use case diagram? A **use case diagram** documents the users of an information system and the functions they perform. In object-oriented jargon, the people who use the system are called **actors**. Any task an actor performs is called a **use case**. Figure 9-43 shows a simple use case diagram for a workshop registration system.

Does a use case diagram explode like a DFD? No. To fill in the detail for a use case, the project team uses a **sequence diagram**, which depicts the detailed sequence of interactions that take place. Figure 9-44 shows the sequence diagram for the Enroll in a Workshop use case and explains how to interpret it.

FIGURE 9-43

A use case diagram for a workshop registration system depicts two use cases—one in which a student enrolls in a workshop and one in which the student drops the workshop.

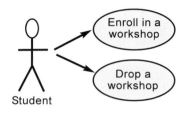

FIGURE 9-44

Sequence Diagram for the Enroll in a Workshop Use Case

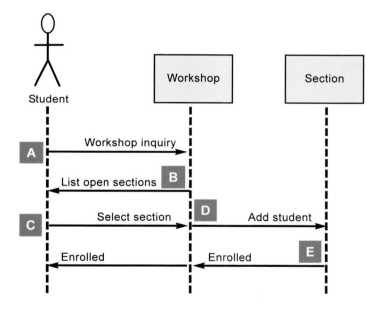

A A student enters the title or number of a workshop that he or she wants to take.

B The Workshop object displays a list of sections that are open.

C The student selects a section.

D The student is added to the workshop roster for the section.

E The student receives confirmation of the enrollment.

What is the composition of an object? A key element of object-oriented development is defining objects. In the previous diagram, the student interacted with two objects: the Workshop object and the Section object. A **class diagram** provides the name of each object, a list of each object's attributes, a list of methods, and an indication of the cardinality between objects. An attribute is simply any data element that is stored as part of an object. A method is any behavior that an object is capable of performing. Cardinality refers to the number of associations that can exist between objects. You'll find detailed definitions of object-oriented terms, such as classes, attributes and methods, in Chapter 11. Figure 9-45 illustrates a class diagram for the workshop registration system.

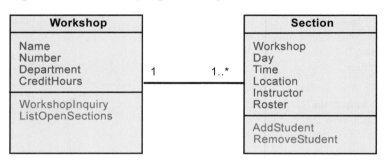

FIGURE 9-45

This class diagram shows each object's attributes (in blue) and methods (in green). The cardinality between objects (indicated by 1 and 1..*) means that each workshop may have one or more sections.

Class diagrams can be further refined to show inheritance—how objects inherit attributes and methods from a class. In objected-oriented terminology, a class is a group of objects with similar characteristics. For example, consider a school that offers sections of the same workshop on campus, at extension centers, and over the Web. All these sections have common attributes, such as a name, scheduled day and time, instructor, and roster. However, extension center workshops might require additional fees, and self-paced, Web-based workshops might not meet on a particular date and time. Figure 9-46 shows a modified class diagram in which On-Campus Section, Extension Section, and Web Section are subclasses of the Section object.

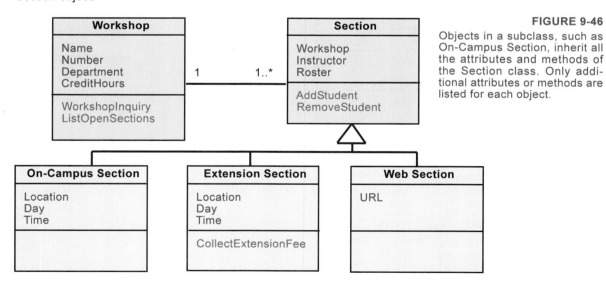

FIGURE 9-46

Objects in a subclass, such as On-Campus Section, inherit all the attributes and methods of the Section class. Only additional attributes or methods are listed for each object.

How do the various object-oriented diagrams fit together? A use case diagram provides an overview of the actors and use cases in an information system. A sequence diagram provides detailed steps showing how the actor interacts with objects. The objects are defined in detail in a class diagram. Figure 9-47 illustrates how these diagrams are linked conceptually, although a project team would not actually create such a linked diagram in practice.

FIGURE 9-47
Conceptual Links Among
Object-Oriented Diagrams

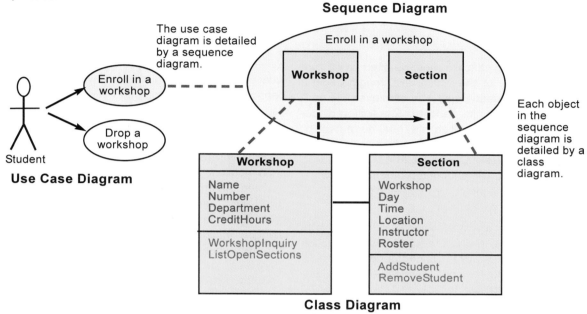

Sequence Diagram

The use case diagram is detailed by a sequence diagram.

Each object in the sequence diagram is detailed by a class diagram.

Use Case Diagram

Class Diagram

Is it necessary to document the methods associated with an object? Yes, the methods associated with an object can be documented using a technique similar to the process specifications produced as part of structured analysis and design, providing a complete set of system documentation for a project.

QUICKCHECK........TECHTALK

1. A(n) [_____] is a diagramming tool used in the process of structured analysis and design that depicts the possible paths for data traveling from entities (such as customers) to processes (such as printing) or storage areas.

2. A(n) [_____] dictionary can be used to describe the contents of a data store.

3. The current standard for object-oriented analysis and design diagramming is abbreviated as [_____].

4. A(n) [_____] case diagram documents the users of an information system and the functions that they perform.

5. A(n) [_____] diagram provides the name of each object, a list of each object's attributes, a list of methods, and an indication of the cardinality between objects.

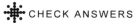 CHECK ANSWERS

ISSUE

PROFESSIONAL ETHICS

When discussing ethical issues, we often do so from the perspective of the victim. We imagine how it might feel if someone else—an employer, the government, cyberpunks, and so on—pilfered our original artwork from a Web site, read our e-mail, or stole our credit card number from an e-commerce site. It is quite possible, however, that at some time in your career, you will encounter situations in which you could become the perpetrator—the copyright violator, the snoop, or the thief.

Every day, computer professionals must cope with ethical dilemmas, in which the right course of action is not entirely clear, or in which the right course of action is clear, but the consequences—such as getting fired—are not easy to face.

Suppose, for example, that you are hired to manage a local area network in a prestigious New York advertising agency. On your first day of work, your employer hands you a box containing the latest upgrade for Microsoft Office and asks you to install it on all computers in the organization. When you ask if the agency owns a site license, your boss responds, "No, do you have a problem with that?" What would you reply? Would you risk your job by insisting that the agency order enough copies for all the computers before you install it? Or would you go ahead and install the software, assuming that your boss would take responsibility for this violation of the software license agreement?

Now imagine that you're hired as a programmer for a local public school system. One day, the superintendent of schools calls you into her office and asks if you can write software that will monitor online access and provide reports to management. From your understanding of the school's network and Web access, you realize that it would be easy to write such monitoring software. You also realize, however, that the superintendent could use the software to track individual teachers and students as they visit Web sites. You ask the superintendent if faculty and students would be aware of the monitoring software, and she replies, "What they don't know won't hurt them." Should you write the program? Should you write the program, but start a rumor that monitoring software is being used to track faculty and student Web access? Should you pretend that it would be technically impossible to write such software? Should you tell the superintendent that federal criminal law does not permit interception of electronic communications without consent?

A code of ethics is designed to help computer professionals thread their way through a sometimes tangled web of ethical decisions. Published by many professional organizations—such as the Association for Computing Machinery, the British Computer Society, the Australian Computer Society, and the Computer Ethics Institute—each code varies in detail but supplies a similar set of overall guiding principles for professional conduct.

One of the shortest codes is published by the Computer Ethics Institute (see sidebar on next page). These 10 guidelines are short and to the point but have drawn fire from critics, such as Dr. N. Ben Fairweather, the Centre for Computing and Social Responsibility's resident philosopher and research fellow, who states, "It is easy to find exceptions to the short dos and don'ts of the 'ten commandments'... indeed, every time such a short code of ethics falls into unwarranted disrepute, the whole idea of acting morally is brought into disrepute too." Dr. Fairweather seems to suggest that hard and fast rules might not apply to all situations.

Computer Ethics Institute Professional Code

1. Thou shalt not use a computer to harm other people.

2. Thou shalt not interfere with other people's computer work.

3. Thou shalt not snoop around in other people's files.

4. Thou shalt not use a computer to steal.

5. Thou shalt not use a computer to bear false witness.

6. Thou shalt not use or copy software for which you have not paid.

7. Thou shalt not use other people's computer resources without authorization.

8. Thou shalt not appropriate other people's intellectual output.

9. Thou shalt think about the social consequences of the program you write.

10. Thou shalt use a computer in ways that show consideration and respect.

and Professional Conduct contains 21 guidelines, including "ACM members must obey existing local, state, province, national, and international laws unless there is a compelling ethical basis not to do so." It goes on to say, "...sometimes existing laws and rules may be immoral or inappropriate and, therefore, must be challenged. Violation of a law or regulation may be ethical when that law or rule has inadequate moral basis or when it conflicts with another law judged to be more important. If one decides to violate a law or rule because it is viewed as unethical, or for any other reason, one must fully accept responsibility for one's actions and for the consequences."

A code of ethics can provide guidelines, but it might not offer ready answers to every dilemma that arises in the course of your career. When confronted with a difficult ethical decision, you should consider ethical guidelines, but also consider the policies of your workplace and relevant laws. You might also seek legal advice, consult the human resources advocate at your job, or ask advice from your union representative. Sometimes even talking to a trusted friend helps you recognize the correct course of action.

Ultimately, the decision abut the right course of action is yours, and you must be willing to take responsibility for the consequences of your decision.

In some cases the code's intent is not accurately reflected in the wording. For example, the guideline "Thou shalt not use or copy software for which you have not paid" obviously does not include public domain and open source software. Similarly, the idea that you should "think about the social consequences of the program you write" is valid, but *what* should you think about? This guideline does not offer helpful criteria for distinguishing between socially useful programs and those that might be damaging.

Not all codes of ethics are this short and snappy, however. Some codes attempt to offer more detailed guidance. For example, the ACM's Code of Ethics

---

INFOWEBLINKS

You'll find additional information about professional ethics at the **Ethics in Computing InfoWeb**.

www.course.com/np/concepts8/ch09

WHAT DO YOU THINK?

1. Would you follow your boss's orders to install unlicensed software?   ○ Yes ○ No ○ Not sure

2. If you went ahead and installed the software, but it was later discovered by the software publisher, do you think you should be held responsible?   ○ Yes ○ No ○ Not sure

3. Is Dr. Fairweather correct in suggesting that hard and fast ethical rules might not apply to all situations?   ○ Yes ○ No ○ Not sure

 SAVE RESPONSES

COMPUTERS IN CONTEXT

ARCHITECTURE AND CONSTRUCTION

A cluster of hardhats study a dog-eared blueprint. Sun-bronzed laborers perch on a makeshift bench, munching sandwiches and waving to a group of carpenters hauling 2x4s onto a foundation. The sounds of hammers, shovels, and power tools fill the air from early morning through late afternoon. It is a typical construction site: an ant hill of activity where a structure of some sort is eventually assembled—a house, a shopping mall, or a skyscraper.

Behind the scenes of this ant hill, computer technology has added a high-tech flavor to construction projects with real-time interactive computer graphics, broadband wireless communications, distributed database management systems, wearable and vehicle-mounted computers, global positioning satellites, and laser-guided surveying systems. Architects use computers to create blueprints. Contractors use computers for cost estimates and scheduling. Computers are even starting to appear on the job site, carried as handheld devices and embedded in construction equipment.

In the past, architects typically drew construction plans by hand on semitransparent film called vellum. To create a blueprint, they overlaid the vellum on special blue paper and then ran it through a machine that exposed it to intensified light and ammonia. Minor changes to a design were possible, but for major changes, architects often needed to create a new set of vellum drawings.

With the advent of computers and computer-aided design (CAD) software, architects realized they could be more productive—and make design changes more easily—by replacing their drafting tables with computers running CAD software, much as writers replaced their typewriters with computers running word processing software. Using plotters with wide print beds, architects were able to produce computer-generated blueprints similar to those they created at a drafting table.

Initially, architects used CAD software to create 2-D floor plans and elevations. Today architects use 3-D CAD software that offers a greatly expanded toolset. Architects can begin with a simple 2-D floor plan, and then use CAD tools to draw interior and exterior walls, ceilings, and roofs. Standard building materi-

als, such as doors and windows, can be selected from a list of clip-art objects and dragged into position with a mouse. Electrical, plumbing, and framing schematics can also be added. Any elements of the drawing can be displayed or hidden—for example, when discussing the design with an electrical contractor, an architect can hide the plumbing details. These 3-D wireframe drawings with building, electrical, and plumbing elements added can be rotated and viewed from any angle.

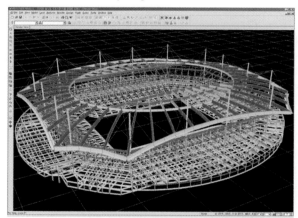

Inexpensive inkjet printers have replaced expensive first-generation plotters and give architects the option of printing in realistic color. Using 3-D CAD software, they can also apply textures and colors to convert wireframes into 3-D models that can be viewed from the inside or outside. Architects sometimes use an animated version of a 3-D model for "virtual reality" walkthroughs.

After an architect has completed the building plans, a contractor estimates the project's price tag by calculating the cost of materials and labor. Computerized spreadsheets, such as Excel, are a popular tool for cost estimates. Large contracting firms often use commercial software specifically designed for construction estimates.

Contractors are also responsible for scheduling the tasks in a construction project, such as excavating the building site, erecting the foundation and frame, assembling the roof, adding wiring and plumbing, and doing interior finish work. Large construction projects, such as malls and government buildings, can involve thousands of tasks and many subcontractors. Computerized scheduling tools, such as Gantt charts, PERT (program evaluation and review technique) diagrams, and CPM (Critical Path Management) software, make it possible to plan and track each construction phase and break a project down into a series of tasks. For each task, planners enter its estimated duration and how it relates to other tasks. For example, drywall work that requires eight days depends on interior framing, electrical work, and plumbing being finished first. Given information about all the tasks in a project, planning software can create a master schedule showing both best- and worst-case completion dates, and contractors can easily update the schedule based on actual construction progress.

At a high-tech construction site, computers can play several roles. A site supervisor can use a wireless handheld computer to view and update the construction schedule stored on a desktop computer at the contractor's main office. Rather than refer to a set of printed—and possibly outdated—plans, the supervisor can refer to up-to-date plans transmitted from the home office. A supervisor might even wear a hardhat-mounted computer that collects multimedia data, such as video and sound, to document site inspections. A voice-activated microphone records the supervisor's comments and adds them to the digital video, which can be uploaded to a database in the contractor's main office.

Computers also play a role in guiding bulldozers during site preparation by using construction software developed at Ohio State University that works with

the global positioning system (GPS). A GPS receiver is mounted on a vehicle that traverses the site. GPS signals are collected and entered in the software program, which creates a map and a plan for site preparation. A wireless computer monitor mounted in each bulldozer's cab receives data from the software and displays it to the operator. The system allows construction crews to stake and grade a site with to-the-centimeter accuracy.

Computers embedded in robots are used extensively on large construction projects in Japan. These "single task robots" perform specific jobs. For example, a concrete-task robot might lay forms, bend rebar, pour concrete, and screed the surface to a smooth finish. Other robots weld steel components, apply paint, or install tile. Single-task robots have been successful because they shield human workers from dangerous and difficult jobs and typically work faster and more consistently than humans. However, trained technicians are required to set up and monitor robot work.

Although construction robots are widely used in Japan, they aren't popular with contractors in many other parts of the world. Industry observers speculate that Japan's shortage of unskilled laborers differentiates it from countries where labor is readily available and relatively inexpensive. In the United States, for example, college students working in construction is a long-standing summer tradition—but one that might be changing. In a recent survey, students viewed construction work as "dirty and undesirable" and, out of 252 career choices, ranked it as 251.

Construction robots might help fill the labor gap in countries like the United States, but potential barriers, such as union regulations, could discourage their use. Some observers question how building trade union agreements might affect construction site robots. According to one supervisor's worst-case scenario, "Millwrights will want to set up the device, electricians will want to fix the electronic controls, equipment operators will want to run it, cement finishers will want to adjust it, and laborers will be expected to clean it." The future of computer-powered robots at construction sites is still unclear and illustrates the controversies that sometimes surround technology as it filters into society and the workplace.

INFOWEBLINKS

You'll find lots more information related to this topic by connecting to the **Computers and Construction InfoWeb.**

www.course.com/np/concepts8/ch09

INTERACTIVE SUMMARY

To review important concepts from this chapter, fill in the blanks to best complete each sentence. When using the NP8 BookOnCD, click the Check Answers buttons to automatically score your answers. Place your Tracking Disk in the floppy disk drive if you want to save your scores.

[_____] systems play a key role in helping organizations achieve goals, which are set forth in a [_____] statement. Computers can be used by people at all levels of an organization. Workers use information systems to produce and manipulate information. Managers depend on information systems to supply data that is essential for long-term [_____] planning and short-term tactical planning.

Transaction [_____] systems provide an organization with a way to collect, display, modify, or cancel transactions. These systems encompass activities such as general accounting, inventory tracking, and e-commerce. [_____] information systems typically build on the data collected by a TPS to produce reports that managers use to make the business decisions needed to solve routine, structured problems.

A decision [_____] system helps workers and managers make non-routine decisions by constructing decision models that include data collected from internal and external sources.

An [_____] system is designed to analyze data and produce a recommendation or decision based on a set of facts and rules called a [_____] base. These facts and rules can be written using an expert system shell or a programming language. An [_____] engine evaluates the facts and rules to produce answers to questions posed to the system. Using a technique called [_____] logic, these systems can deal with imprecise data and problems that have more than one solution. If the rules for an expert system are not known, a neural [_____] might be used to enable a computer to "learn" how to make a decision.

CHECK ANSWERS

The process of planning and building an information system is referred to as systems [_____] and design. The development process is supervised by an organization's Information Systems (IS) department, but the [_____] team usually includes members from other departments as well. System development follows some type of system development [_____] cycle (SDLC), which consists of several "phases." In the [_____] SDLC, one phase of the SDLC must be completed before the next phase can begin. In practice, however, most project teams use a modification of this model in which phases can overlap or repeat.

A project team can use one of several approaches to the system development process. For example, the

[_____] methodology focuses on the processes that take place in an information system. The information [_____] methodology focuses on the data that an information system collects. The object-[_____] methodology treats an information system as a collection of interacting objects.

A project begins with a [_____] phase in which a member of the IS department creates a Project Development Plan. The project team then proceeds to the [_____] phase, with the goal of producing a list of requirements for a new or revised information system.

CHECK ANSWERS

In the [＿＿＿＿＿＿＿＿] phase of the SDLC, the project team identifies potential solutions, evaluates those solutions, and then selects the best one. The team members might consider various levels of [＿＿＿＿＿＿], such as scanning magnetic credit card strips instead of entering credit card numbers from a keyboard. The project team might also consider whether a [＿＿＿＿＿＿] processing model would be better than a distributed processing model. Several alternative [＿＿＿＿＿＿] technologies might provide connectivity solutions. Alternative software solutions include the use of programming languages, application development tools, or commercial software. It is also possible that a [＿＿＿＿＿＿] system might offer a complete hardware and software solution. The project team can use a [＿＿＿＿＿＿] support worksheet to eval-

uate solutions based on general, technical, and functional criteria.

After the project team selects a solution, it can then select the specific hardware and software products to build the new information system. The project team might send out a request for [＿＿＿＿＿＿], asking vendors to recommend a solution and specify hardware and software requirements. As an alternative, when team members know exactly what hardware and software they need for the solution, they can send out a request for [＿＿＿＿＿＿], which simply asks for vendor prices. After selecting hardware and software, the team can develop [＿＿＿＿＿＿] specifications that describe the way the new information system should interact with the user, store data, process data, and format reports.

⟐ CHECK ANSWERS

During the [＿＿＿＿＿＿] phase of the SDLC, the project team supervises the technicians who set up new hardware, install programming languages and other application [＿＿＿＿＿＿] tools, create and test applications, and customize software. The team also finalizes the system documentation and trains users. In this phase, three types of testing ensure that new software works correctly. [＿＿＿＿＿＿] testing is performed on each module, and then [＿＿＿＿＿＿] testing is performed to make sure that all of the modules work together correctly. [＿＿＿＿＿＿] testing ensures that the software components work correctly on the hardware and with other, perhaps older, elements of the information system.

When application testing is complete, data is converted from the old system to the new one, users are trained, and the new system goes live. Four types of information system "go live" conversions are possible. During a [＿＿＿＿＿＿] conversion, the old system is completely deactivated and the new system is immediately activated. For a [＿＿＿＿＿＿]

conversion, both the old and new systems operate until it can be determined that the new system is performing correctly. In a [＿＿＿＿＿＿] conversion, the new system is activated one module at a time. In a [＿＿＿＿＿＿] conversion, the new information system is activated at one branch or office of an organization before being activated in other locations. At the end of the conversion process, the information system undergoes a final test called [＿＿＿＿＿＿] testing, designed to assure the system's owner that the new system works as specified.

After installation, an information system enters the [＿＿＿＿＿＿] phase of its life cycle. During this phase, a [＿＿＿＿＿＿] operator typically performs backups, monitors system utilization, and troubleshoots operational problems. As users discover bugs, programmers must fix them. Ongoing user support from a help [＿＿＿＿＿＿] might also be required.

⟐ CHECK ANSWERS

INTERACTIVE KEY TERMS

Make sure you understand all the boldfaced key terms presented in this chapter. If you're using the NP8 BookOnCD, you can use this list of terms as an interactive study activity. First, try to define a term in your own words, and then click the term to compare your definition with the definition presented in the chapter.

INTERACTIVE SITUATION QUESTIONS

Apply what you've learned to some typical computing situations. When using the NP8 BookOnCD, you can type your answers, and then use the Check Answers button to automatically score your responses. Place your Tracking Disk in the floppy disk drive if you want to save your scores.

1. Suppose that you own a small bookstore located in a mall. Business seems to be declining, and you suspect that many of your former customers are now shopping at online bookstores. What can you do about declining sales? You realize that this problem falls into the category of a(n) [_____] problem, and you might not be able to solve it using the data supplied by your MIS.

2. Your friend just graduated and started work in a local pharmacy. She tells you about the pharmacy's computer system that warns of dangerous drug interactions by examining the patient's prescription record and sometimes asking the pharmacist to enter age and allergy information. The system that she describes sounds like a(n) [_____] system.

3. An article in your local newspaper describes a new airport security system as "a sophisticated facial-recognition system powered by advanced computer technology that learns on its own." This technology sounds like a(n) [_____] network.

4. As a member of the IS staff at a large corporation, you often hear about problems with the current information system. One recently discovered problem is that when an employee quits (or gets fired), sometimes the network manager is not notified, and the former employee continues to have access to company data over the Internet. Using the PIECES framework, you would classify this as a(n) [_____] problem.

5. Your county provides online access to property records. You simply enter the address of the property or the owner's name. However, each search seems to take longer than one minute. According to the PIECES framework, this delay would be classified as a(n) [_____] problem.

6. Your roommate works in the Data Entry department for a large corporation and has been asked to participate in a JAD session. When asked about it, you explain to your roommate that JAD stands for [_____] application design, and this probably means the corporation is working on a new information system.

7. You just started working in the IS department for a very small company that's developing a new information system. Your coworkers are trying to track down a discrepancy that resulted from a change in the name of a data field. Although you don't say it, you realize that such a problem would not have occurred if the project team used [_____] tools.

8. On your last job, you worked as an admitting clerk in a hospital. One day you were told to begin using the hospital's new information system. The next day, you were told to go back to using the old system until further notice. You suspect that these events occurred as a result of a failed attempt at a(n) [_____] conversion.

✦ CHECK ANSWERS

INTERACTIVE PRACTICE TESTS

Practice tests that consist of 10 multiple-choice, true/false, and fill-in-the-blank questions are available on both the NP8 BookOnCD and the NP8 Web site. The questions are selected at random from a large test bank, so each time you take a test, you'll receive a different set of questions. Your tests are scored immediately, and you can print study guides that help you find the correct answers for any questions that you missed.

www.course.com/np/concepts8/ch09 ✦

CLICK ✦ TO START

REVIEW

ON THE WEB

PROJECTS

An NP8 Project is an open-ended activity that helps you apply the concepts you have learned. Many projects require resources in addition to your textbook, such as current magazines, library materials, or Web access. When you tackle a project, be prepared to use your critical thinking skills, logical analysis, and creativity. Projects for this chapter include:

- **Issue Research: Professional Ethics**
- **Project Development Team**
- **Exploring an Information System**

- **Request for Proposal**
- **Information Systems Department Careers**
- **Mission Statement**
- **Decision Support Software**

To work with the Projects for this chapter, connect to the **New Perspectives NP8 Web Site**.

www.course.com/np/concepts8/ch09

TECHTV VIDEO PROJECT

The TechTV segment *Making Flowcharts Using Office XP* demonstrates how to make organizational charts, flow charts, and other types of hierarchical diagrams. After watching the video, use Microsoft Word to duplicate the organizational chart on page 463. Then use one of Word's other diagram types to create a diagram of your own.

To work with the Video Projects for this chapter, connect to the **New Perspectives NP8 Web Site**.

www.course.com/np/concepts8/ch09

STUDY TIPS

Study Tips help you to organize and consolidate the information in a chapter by making lists, outlines, charts, and sketches. You can use paper and pencil or word processing software to complete most of the Study Tips.

To work with the Study Tips for this chapter, connect to the **New Perspectives NP8 Web Site**.

www.course.com/np/concepts8/ch09

ONLINE GAMES

Test your comprehension of the concepts introduced in Chapter 9 by playing the NP8 Online Games. At the end of each game, you have three options:

- Print a comprehensive study guide complete with page references
- Print your results to be submitted to your instructor
- Save your results to be submitted to your instructor via e-mail

To work with the Online Games for this chapter, connect to the **New Perspectives NP8 Web Site**.

www.course.com/np/concepts8/ch09

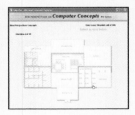

STUDENT EDITION LABS

Extend your knowledge of project management with the Chapter 9 Student Edition Lab.

The following Student Edition Lab is offered with Chapter 9:

• **Project Management**

To work with the Chapter 9 Student Edition Lab and its corresponding lab assignment, connect to the **New Perspectives NP8 Web Site**.

www.course.com/np/concepts8/ch09

Go to the NP8 New Perspectives Web site for specific lab topics.

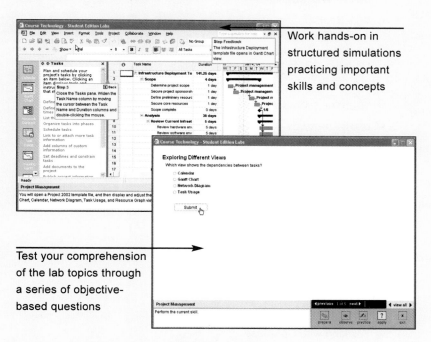

Work hands-on in structured simulations practicing important skills and concepts

Test your comprehension of the lab topics through a series of objective-based questions

Track Your Progress with the Student Edition Labs

• Student Edition Labs test your comprehension of the lab topics through a series of trackable objective-based questions. Your instructor will direct you to either print your results or submit them via e-mail.

• Student Edition Lab Assignments, available on the New Perspectives NP8 Web site, require you to apply the skills learned through the lab in a live environment. Go to the New Perspectives NP8 Web site for detailed instruction on individual Student Edition Lab Assignments.

If you have a SAM user profile, you have access to even more interactive content. Log in to your SAM account and go to your assignments page to see what your instructor has assigned for this chapter.

10

DATABASES

CONTENTS

TIP

When using the BookOnCD, the ❋ icons are "clickable" to access resources on the CD. The ✛ icons are clickable to access resources on the Web. You can also access Web resources by using your browser to connect directly to the NP8 New Perspectives Web site at:

www.course.com/np/concepts8/ch10

CHAPTER PREVIEW

Before you begin Chapter 10, you can use the Web-based preview activities to hear an overview of the chapter, check your current level of expertise about key concepts, and look through a list of learning objectives. You can access the preview activities by clicking the ⊹ icon when using the BookOnCD or going to the New Perspectives NP8 Web site.

CHAPTER OVERVIEW

Databases are a key component of information systems that you encounter when shopping online, registering for classes, and paying bills. To really understand how databases work, you need a little background on database theory, including data models, data management tools, database design, and query languages. Get your book and highlighter ready, then connect to the New Perspectives NP8 Web site where you can listen to an overview that points out the most important concepts for this chapter.

www.course.com/np/concepts8/ch10 ⊹

CHAPTER PRE-ASSESSMENT

How much do you know about databases? To gauge your level of knowledge before beginning the chapter, take the pre-assessment quiz at the New Perspectives NP8 Web site. Armed with your results from this quiz, you can focus your study time on concepts that will round out your knowledge of databases and improve your test scores.

www.course.com/np/concepts8/ch10 ⊹

LEARNING OBJECTIVES

When you complete this chapter you should be able to:

- Define basic database terminology, such as fields, records, record types, and cardinality
- Describe the characteristics of hierarchical, network, relational, and object-oriented databases
- Explain the capabilities of various data management tools, such as commercial applications, word processing software, spreadsheet software, file management software, and database management software

- Describe various ways to provide access to databases via the Web
- Explain how to design an effective relational database
- Use your knowledge of SQL queries to describe how to add records, delete records, search for information, update fields, and simultaneously access data from multiple tables

A detailed list of learning objectives is provided at the New Perspectives NP8 Web site

www.course.com/np/concepts8/ch10 ⊹

FILE AND DATABASE CONCEPTS

In today's wired world, you probably interact directly with several databases, such as when you modify your e-mail address book, order a pay-per-view movie, register online for classes, or select merchandise from an e-commerce Web site. Section A begins with a short review of basic database terminology pertaining to files, fields, and records before tackling the key concept of record types. After you understand record types, it is easy to grasp the last topic in this section, which describes hierarchical, network, relational, and object-oriented database models.

Throughout the chapter, most of the examples focus on WebMusic, a fictitious Web-based music store. WebMusic's information system stores data about CD prices, monitors inventory levels, maintains customer records, and reports which CDs are the top sellers. It also keeps track of customer orders, prints shipping labels, and produces quarterly sales reports. The characteristics of WebMusic's database are typical of many databases you encounter on and off the Web.

DATABASES AND STRUCTURED FILES

What is a database? In the broadest definition, a **database** is a collection of information. Today, databases are typically stored as computer files. The tasks associated with creating, maintaining, and accessing the information in these files are referred to as data management, file management, or database management.

Computer databases evolved from manual filing systems, such as library card catalogs and Rolodexes. Manual filing systems and most computer databases contain data organized as structured files. A **structured file** uses a uniform format to store data for each person or thing in the file (Figure 10-1).

FIELDS

What is the basic element of a structured file? A **field** contains the smallest unit of meaningful information, so you might call it the basic building block for a structured file or database. Each field has a unique **field name** that describes its contents. For example, in the WebMusic database, the field name ArtistName might describe a field containing the name of the artist or band that recorded the CD.

A field can be variable length or fixed length. A **variable-length field** is like an accordion—it expands to fit the data you enter, up to some maximum number of characters. A **fixed-length field** contains a predetermined number of characters (bytes). The data you enter in a fixed-length field cannot exceed the allocated field

FIGURE 10-1

A Rolodex is often used to store names and addresses. Each card is preprinted with places to enter a person's name, address, city, state, ZIP code, and telephone number. Because all cards have a uniform organization, the Rolodex is a structured file, which could easily be converted into a computer database.

length. Moreover, if the data you enter is shorter than the allocated length, blank spaces are automatically added to fill the field. The fields in Figure 10-2 are fixed length. The underscores indicate the number of characters allocated for each field.

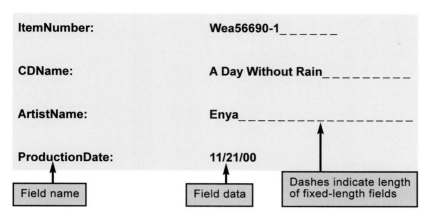

FIGURE 10-2

WebMusic uses fixed-length fields to store most of its data.

RECORDS

What is a record? Unlike the music world where a "record" refers to an old-fashioned recording medium that preceded cassette tapes and CDs, in the world of computing a **record** refers to a collection of data fields. Each record stores data about one entity—a person, place, thing, or event. For example, if you have a group of index cards and each index card lists information about a particular CD, then each index card is a record. You can visualize a record as a Rolodex card, but computer databases typically display records as rows in a table or as forms (Figure 10-3).

FIGURE 10-3

Records can be displayed as rows in a table or as forms.

CLICK TO START

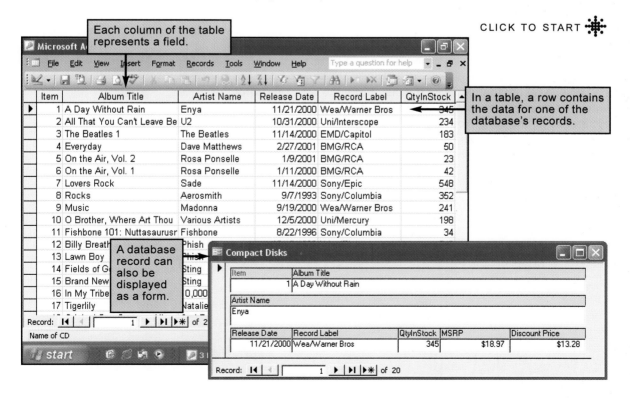

What's involved in defining the structure for records in a file? A database designer defines the fields for a database. This task is similar to designing a blank form for a manual record-keeping system or card file. Each kind of record is referred to as a **record type**. Different record types are necessary for storing data about different types of entities. For example, WebMusic uses one record type for storing information about customers and another record type for storing information about music CDs. WebMusic uses four other record types for storing additional data. All six record types are illustrated in Figure 10-4.

CUSTOMERS	COMPACT DISKS	CD DESCRIPTION
CustomerNumber	ItemNumber	ItemNumber
FirstName	CDName	Description
LastName	ArtistName	
Street	ProductionDate	
City	Publisher	
State	QtyInStock	
ZipCode	MSRP	
EmailAddress	DiscountPrice	
PhoneNumber	CDCover	

ORDER DETAILS	ORDERS	TRACKS
OrderNumber	OrderNumber	ItemNumber
ItemNumber	CustomerNumber	TrackTitle
Qty	TotalPrice	TrackLength
DiscountPrice	OrderDate	TrackSample

FIGURE 10-4

WebMusic stores data in six record types.

A record type, similar to a blank form, is usually shown without any data in the fields. A record that contains data is referred to as a **record occurrence**, or simply "a record." WebMusic's database includes a record occurrence for the song "You Raise Me Up" on Josh Groban's *Closer* CD (Figure 10-5). The field names are defined by the record type called Tracks.

TRACKS		TRACKS	
ItemNumber		ItemNumber:	B0000CFW87
TrackTitle		TrackTitle:	You Raise Me Up
TrackLength		TrackLength:	258
TrackSample		TrackSample	URaiseMeUp.mp3

FIGURE 10-5

A record type (left) is simply a list of fields, whereas a record occurrence (right) contains data for a particular entity. In this case, the entity is a track called "You Raise Me Up" on Josh Groban's *Closer* CD. This record type contains a field called TrackSample that stores the name of an MP3 file customers can listen to before deciding to purchase the entire CD.

RELATIONSHIPS AND CARDINALITY

How do record types pertain to files and databases? A structured file that contains only one record type is often referred to as a **flat file**. Flat files can be used to store simple data, such as names and addresses. In contrast, a database can contain a variety of different record types. WebMusic needs six record types (refer back to Figure 10-4 for a list), so a database rather than a flat file is required.

A key characteristic of a database is its ability to maintain relationships so that data from several record types can be consolidated or aggregated into essentially one unit for data retrieval and reporting purposes.

What are relationships? In database jargon, a **relationship** is an association between data that's stored in different record types. For example, WebMusic's Customers record type is related to the Orders record type because customers place orders. Figure 10-6 helps you visualize the relationship between these two record types.

FIGURE 10-6

For optimum efficiency, WebMusic stores general information about customers in one set of records, but stores information about individual orders in a different set of records. For example, data in the CustomerNumber field can be used to find all the orders placed by a customer, such as Jorge Rodriguez.

CUSTOMERS

CustomerNumber:	171109
FirstName:	Jorge
LastName:	Rodriguez
Street:	101 Las Vegas Court
CustomerNumber:	171109
City:	Taos
State:	NM
ZipCode:	87571
EmailAddress:	jrod@hotmail.com
PhoneNumber:	505-555-3412

ORDERS

OrderNumber:	02-3422901
CustomerNumber:	171109
TotalPrice:	$52.28

OrderNumber:	03-4873392
CustomerNumber:	171109
TotalPrice:	$23.89

OrderNumber:	03-9872655
CustomerNumber:	171109
TotalPrice:	$46.58
OrderDate:	9/30/05

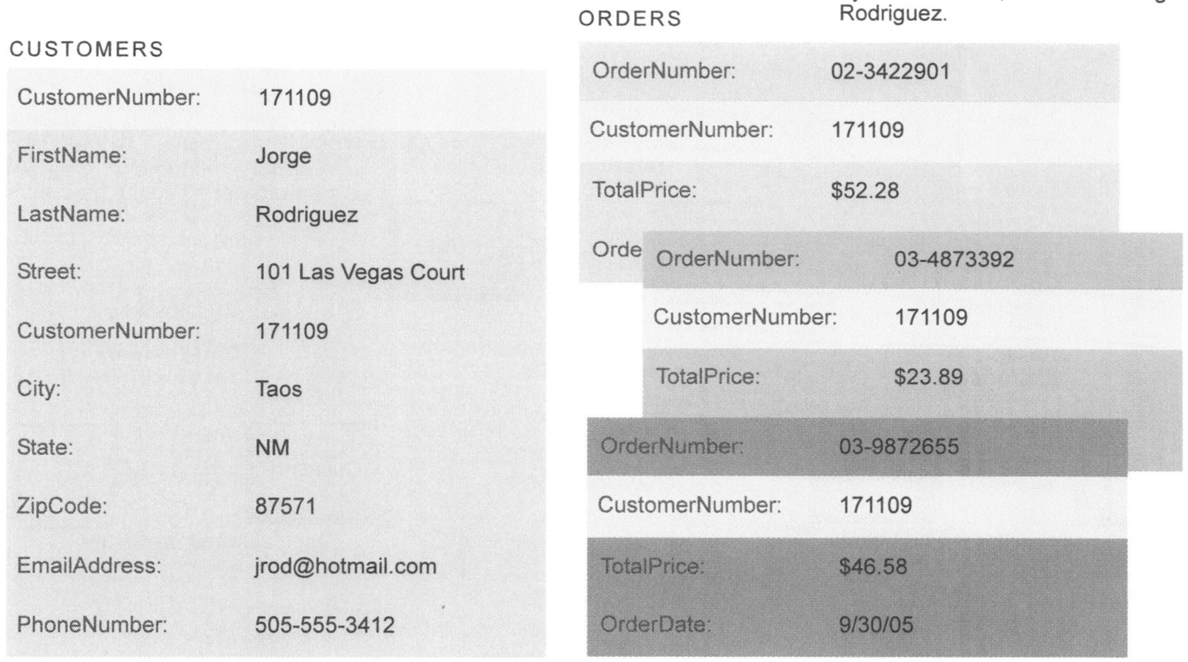

The WebMusic database stores basic information about a customer, such as Jorge Rodriguez, in the Customers record type.

Jorge's orders are stored in the Orders record type and can be located using the relationship provided by the CustomerNumber field.

One important aspect of the relationship between record types is cardinality. **Cardinality** refers to the number of associations that can exist between two record types. For example, a WebMusic customer can place more than one order. The reverse is not true, however. A particular order cannot be placed jointly by two customers. When one record is related to many records, the relationship is referred to as a **one-to-many relationship**.

In contrast, a **many-to-many relationship** means that one record in a particular record type can be related to many records in another record type, and vice versa. For example, a CD contains many songs. At the same time, a song could be included on several different CDs. For example, George Harrison's song "Something" was included in the Beatles *Abbey Road* album and the "best hits" release, *The Beatles 1*.

18

A **one-to-one relationship** means that a record in one record type is related to only one record in another record type. This kind of relationship is rare in the world of databases. It is sometimes used to conserve disk space when an item of information will not be stored for every record in the database.

For example, the marketing director at WebMusic sometimes wants to include a description of a CD in the database, but only for top-selling CDs. If a Description field is included in the Compact Disks record type, it will be empty for most records. Empty fields take up space on the disk, so it's not desirable to have fields that will most likely be blank. Creating another record type, called CD Description, allows this data to be stored efficiently. Only top-selling CDs would have a corresponding CD Description record. The CD record and its corresponding description would have a one-to-one relationship.

The relationship between record types can be depicted graphically with an **entity-relationship diagram** (sometimes called an "ER diagram" or "ERD"). Figure 10-7 shows ERDs for one-to-many, many-to-many, and one-to-one relationships.

INFOWEBLINKS

You can connect to the **Data Relationships InfoWeb** for more information on relationships and various ways to depict them in diagrams.

www.course.com/np/concepts8/ch10

Many-to-many relationship

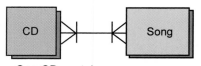

One CD contains many songs, and a song can be included on several different CDs.

FIGURE 10-7

An entity-relationship diagram depicts each record type as a rectangle. Relationships and cardinality are shown by connecting lines.

One-to-one relationship

A CD has only one description.

One-to-many relationship

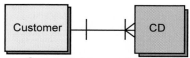

One customer can order many CDs.

KEY TO ERD SYMBOLS

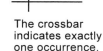

The crossbar indicates exactly one occurrence.

The crossbar and crow's foot indicate one or more occurrences.

HIERARCHICAL, NETWORK, RELATIONAL, AND OBJECT-ORIENTED DATABASES

Am I limited to one type of database? Several database models exist. Some models work with all the relationships described earlier in this section, whereas other models work with only a subset of the relationships. The four main types of database models in use today are hierarchical, network, relational, and object oriented.

What's the simplest database model? The simplest database model arranges record types as a hierarchy. In a **hierarchical database**, a record type is referred to as a **node** or "segment." The top node of the hierarchy is referred to as the **root node**. Nodes are arranged in a hierarchical structure as a sort of upside-down tree. A **parent node** can have more than one **child node**. A child node, however, can have only one parent node. The relationship between a parent node and a child node in a hierarchical database is always one-to-many, as shown in Figure 10-8.

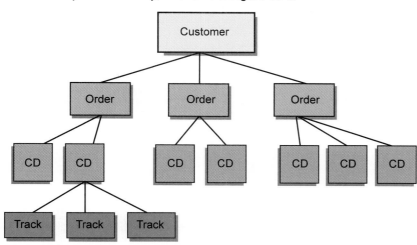

FIGURE 10-8

In this hierarchical database, CDs, Tracks, and Orders are nodes. All of the relationships are one-to-many.

Although the hierarchical database model is the earliest and simplest type of database, it remains in use today for storing data characterized by fairly simple relationships and routine, predictable search requirements. For example, Windows uses a hierarchical database to store Registry data that keeps track of the software and hardware configuration of your PC. In addition, databases created with XML (Extensible Markup Language) tags support a hierarchical database model.

Which database model allows many-to-many relationships? The **network database** model allows many-to-many relationships in addition to one-to-many relationships. Related record types are referred to as a **network set**, or simply a "set." A set contains an owner and members. An **owner** is similar to a parent record in a hierarchical database. A **member** is roughly equivalent to child records (Figure 10-9).

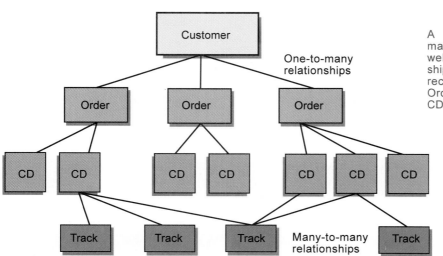

FIGURE 10-9

A network database allows many-to-many relationships as well as one-to-many relationships. The Customer and Order records form a set, as do the Order and CD records, and the CD and Track records.

What's a relational database? Although the network database model seems like a good idea, such databases are difficult to create, manipulate, and maintain. The relational database model quickly replaced it and is the most popular database model today. A **relational database** stores data in a collection of related tables. Each **table** (also called a "relation") is a sequence, or list, of records. All the records in a table are of the same record type. Each row of a table is equivalent to a record and is sometimes called a **tuple**. Each column of the table is equivalent to a field, sometimes called an **attribute**. Figure 10-10 illustrates relational database terminology.

FIGURE 10-10
WebMusic uses a relational database to store records in a series of tables, such as Customers, Orders, CDs, and Tracks.

Tables

CUSTOMERS	ORDERS	CDs	TRACKS
Customer 2	Order 1	CD1	Track 1
Customer 2	Order 2	CD2	Track 2
Customer 3	Order 3	CD3	Track 3

WebMusic's database contains several tables, including one called Tracks.

TRACKS

ItemNumber	TrackTitle	TrackLength	TrackSample
Wea56690-1	Only Time	198	OnlyTime.mp3
Wea56690-1	Tempus Vernum	154	Tempv.mp3
Wea56690-1	Fallen Embers	209	FallenEm.mp3

The Tracks table contains rows (also called tuples). Each row stores one record containing data about the content of a CD track.

Each column of the table contains data for a field, or attribute, of the table.

In a relational database, relationships are specified through the use of common data stored in the fields of records in different tables. This method of establishing relationships allows the tables to be essentially independent, but the tables can be consolidated for a particular task as required. Relationships can be added, changed, or deleted on demand. Figure 10-11 illustrates how a relationship can be established using the ItemNumber field in two tables.

FIGURE 10-11
In a relational database, two tables are related by similar fields—in this example, by ItemNumber.

COMPACT DISKS

ItemNumber	CDName	ArtistName	Production Date	Qty in Stock	MSRP
Wea56690-1	A Day Without Rain	Enya	11/21/00	345	14.95
B0002GMSC0	Autobiography	Ashlee Simpson	7/20/04	234	16.95
B0000CFW87	Closer	Josh Groban	11/11/03	183	19.95
RCA-00-134	Everyday				

TRACKS

ItemNumber	TrackTitle	Track Length	TrackSample
Wea56690-1	Only Time	198	OnlyTime.mp3
Wea56690-1	Tempus Vernum	154	Tempv.mp3
Wea56690-1	Fallen Embers	209	FallenEm.mp3
0002GMSC0	Pieces of Me	141	PiecesOfMe.mp3

The ItemNumber Wea56690-1 links records in both tables that refer to the Enya CD *A Day Without Rain*.

What's an object-oriented database? An **object-oriented database** stores data as objects, which can be grouped into classes and defined by attributes and methods. Chapter 11 covers object-oriented terminology in detail, but in the context of object-oriented databases, a class defines a group of objects by specifying the attributes and methods these objects share.

The attributes for an object are equivalent to fields in a relational database. A method is any behavior that an object is capable of performing. There is no equivalent to a method in a non-object-oriented database. Specifications for the object-oriented database model are provided by standards organizations, such as the Object Data Management Group (ODMG). Figure 10-12 explains how data is stored in an object-oriented database.

FIGURE 10-12

An object-oriented database can easily store data about different types of orders. A class called Orders holds data and methods common to all types of orders. An object called Phone Orders inherits all the characteristics of Orders, but it has attributes and methods unique to orders placed by telephone. The Web Orders object has attributes and methods unique to orders placed via the Web.

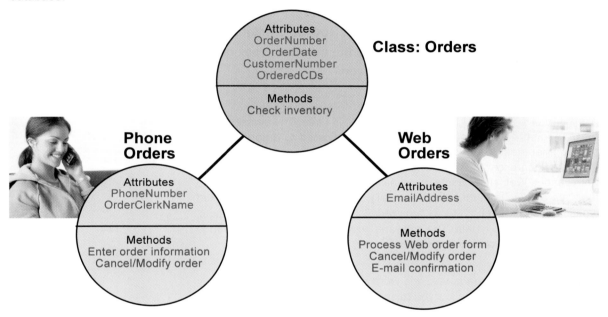

Class: Orders

Attributes
OrderNumber
OrderDate
CustomerNumber
OrderedCDs

Methods
Check inventory

Phone Orders

Attributes
PhoneNumber
OrderClerkName

Methods
Enter order information
Cancel/Modify order

Web Orders

Attributes
EmailAddress

Methods
Process Web order form
Cancel/Modify order
E-mail confirmation

QUICKCHECK......SECTION A

1. A structured file uses a uniform [＿＿＿＿＿＿＿] to store data.

2. A(n) [＿＿＿＿＿＿＿] is a collection of data fields that pertain to an entity, such as a person, place, or thing.

3. A database consists of one or more record [＿＿＿＿＿＿＿] that contain data.

4. A(n) [＿＿＿＿＿＿＿] file is a structured file containing only one record type.

5. The simplest database is based on the [＿＿＿＿＿＿＿] database model.

6. A(n) [＿＿＿＿＿＿＿] database is one that can link record types through shared fields on demand.

 CHECK ANSWERS

18

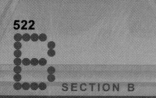

SECTION B

DATA MANAGEMENT TOOLS

One of the first decisions to make when creating a database is what type of data management tools to use. Different tools are designed for different uses. Simple tools that easily store address book information might not be suited for managing a worldwide airline reservation system. On the other hand, database software designed for huge corporations might be overkill for keeping track of your social calendar or storing customer data for a small business. Some tools provide ways to display information from a database on the Web, and some are designed only to print basic reports. How do you know which data management tools to use for a project? Section B describes the different types of tools available and explains how to decide which one best suits your needs.

DATA MANAGEMENT SOFTWARE

Are simple data management tools available? Yes. The simplest tools for managing data are software packages dedicated to a specific data management task, such as keeping track of appointments or managing your checking account. You can purchase these tools or download them from various Web sites. Some are available as shareware. Although these tools are easy to use, they don't generally allow you to create new record types because the record types are predefined. To use one of these tools, you simply enter your data. The software includes menus that allow you to manipulate your data after entering it.

How about a simple, generic tool that allows me to define a file structure? Most spreadsheet and word processing software packages feature simple tools that allow you to specify fields, enter data, and manipulate it. For example, your word processing software probably allows you to maintain data as a set of records, as shown in Figure 10-13.

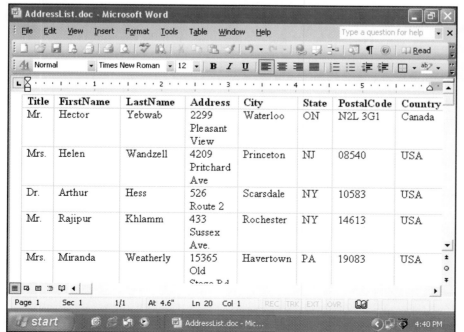

FIGURE 10-13

Microsoft Word allows you to create a table of information, such as a mailing list, which you can edit, sort, search, and print. In addition, you can merge data from the table with a template letter to create form letters, mailing labels, and envelopes.

CLICK TO START ⊹

Some spreadsheet software also includes basic data management features. It's quite easy to create simple flat files using a spreadsheet. Depending on the spreadsheet software, it may be possible to sort records, validate data, search for records, perform simple statistical functions, and generate graphs based on the data. Figure 10-14 illustrates Microsoft Excel data functions.

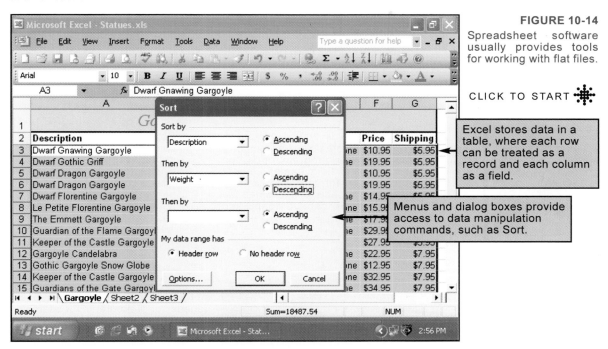

FIGURE 10-14

Spreadsheet software usually provides tools for working with flat files.

CLICK TO START

Excel stores data in a table, where each row can be treated as a record and each column as a field.

Menus and dialog boxes provide access to data manipulation commands, such as Sort.

The simple file management tools provided by word processing and spreadsheet software are popular for individuals who want to maintain flat files that contain hundreds, not thousands, of records. These tools work well for a simple address book, an inventory of household goods, a record of health insurance costs, and a variety of other simple lists. They do not, however, offer database capabilities for establishing relationships between different record types, and they are not powerful enough to maintain the large volume of records required for business information systems.

Can I create my own data management software? It is possible to simply enter data as an ASCII text file, and then use a programming language to write routines to access that data. Custom software can be created to accommodate hierarchical, network, relational, and object-oriented databases as well as flat files.

Custom data management software has the advantage of being tailored to the exact needs of a business or an individual. This advantage is offset, however, by several disadvantages. Custom software requires skilled programmers. The development time for each module can be lengthy and costly. In addition, programmer efforts are sometimes redundant because similar modules are often required for different data files. For example, programmers who write a report routine for one data file might have to repeat their efforts a few weeks later for a different data file.

Poorly designed custom software can result in **data dependence**—a term that refers to data and program modules being so tightly interrelated that they become difficult to modify. Imagine a database in which programs and data all exist in one large file! It would be impossible to access the data while editing any of the programs. Furthermore, changing the file structure in any way might make the programs unusable.

Modern database software supports **data independence**, which means separating data from the programs that manipulate data. As a result, a single data management tool can be used to maintain many different files and databases. In addition, standard search, sort, and print routines continue to function, regardless of changes to field names or record structure. Figure 10-15 further explains data dependence and independence.

FIGURE 10-15

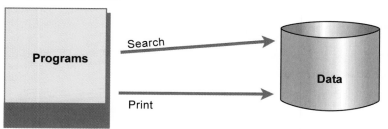

Data dependence is typically found in poorly written custom software when programmers tie the program code too tightly to specific field names, record structures, report formats, and calculations. If these aspects of the database change, programs cannot adapt and must be rewritten.

Data independence is a design concept based on the idea that databases are most flexible when programs that manipulate a database are not too tightly tied to the structure of fields, records, calculations, and reports.

Commercial database software promotes data independence because a generic set of programs for searching and printing can be used on any set of data.

What's the best data management tool? The best tool depends on several factors. When selecting a data management tool, consider its cost, versatility, and ease of use (Figure 10-16).

FIGURE 10-16
Data Management Tools

Tool	Cost	Versatility	Ease of Use
Dedicated software, such as an address book	Inexpensive shareware available for simple applications; dedicated software for business applications can be costly	Typically dedicated to a single type of database	Easy; minimal setup required because fields are predefined
Word processing software	Most computers include word processing software	Best for simple flat files, such as mailing lists	Easy; uses an interface familiar to most users
Spreadsheet software	Most computers include spreadsheet software	Best for simple flat files that involve calculations	Easy; uses an interface familiar to most users
Custom software	Expensive development and programming time	Very versatile because programs can be tailored to any data	The programming can be difficult, but the final result may be easy to use
Database software	Basic shareware database software is inexpensive; high-end database software can be expensive	High-end packages provide excellent versatility	High-end database software often has a steep learning curve

DATABASE MANAGEMENT SYSTEMS

What kinds of tools are specifically designed for creating and manipulating databases? The term **DBMS** (database management system) refers to software that is designed to manage data stored in a database. Each DBMS typically specializes in one of the four database models, but some DBMS software offers versatility by dealing with a variety of models and data.

An **XML DBMS**, for example, is optimized for handling data that exists in XML format. An **OODBMS** (object-oriented database management system) is optimized for the object-oriented database model, allowing you to store and manipulate data classes, attributes, and methods. An **RDBMS** (relational database management system) allows you to create, update, and administer a relational database. Today's popular RDBMS software also provides the capability to handle object classes and XML data, making it unnecessary to purchase a separate OODBMS or XML DBMS.

Which DBMS should I use for my projects? Today most database projects are implemented with a relational database management system. The particular RDBMS package you choose, however, depends on the scope of your project, the number of people who will simultaneously access the database, and the expected volume of records, queries, and updates.

Entry-level RDBMS software, such as Microsoft Access, is designed for personal and small business uses, such as managing a diet-and-exercise log or maintaining customer information. An entry-level DBMS typically includes all the tools you need to manipulate data in a database, create data entry forms, query the database, and generate reports, as shown in Figure 10-17.

INFOWEBLINKS

Get the latest scoop on relational, object-oriented, and XML database software at the **DBMS InfoWeb.**

www.course.com/np/concepts8/ch10

FIGURE 10-17

An entry-level DBMS usually includes all the tools you need to manipulate data in a database.

CLICK TO START

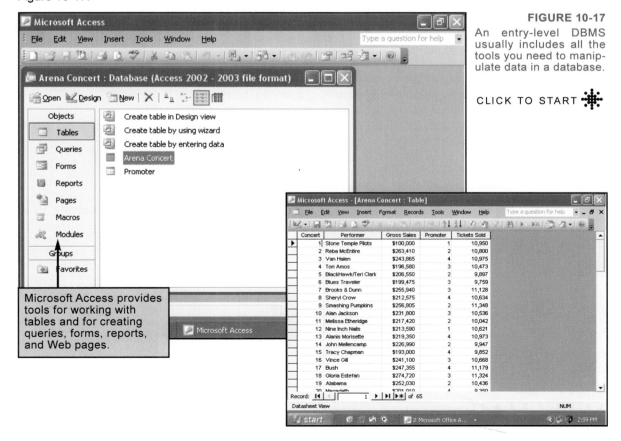

Microsoft Access provides tools for working with tables and for creating queries, forms, reports, and Web pages.

If an entry-level DBMS is located on a network, it is possible for multiple users to access the database at the same time. As shown in Figure 10-18, each workstation typically uses database client software to communicate with the DBMS. **Database client software** allows any remote computer or network workstation to access data in a database.

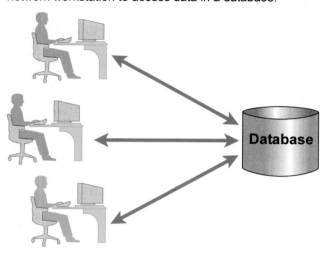

FIGURE 10-18
Multiple users can access a database using client software.

An entry-level DBMS that resides on a network server might be able to handle many simultaneous searches. However, these DBMSs have limited capabilities to deal with problems that arise when multiple users attempt to update the same record at the same time. This limited multiuser capability might be able to handle, for example, a civic center ticketing system operated by a box office clerk. It would not be sufficient, however, to handle the volume of simultaneous transactions for Ticketmaster's 3,800 retail ticket center outlets, 20 telephone call centers worldwide, and online Web site.

In situations with many users who make simultaneous updates, it is usually necessary to move to database server software, such as Oracle Database, IBM DB2 Universal Database, or Microsoft SQL Server. **Database server software** is designed to manage billions of records and several hundred transactions every second. It provides optimum performance in client/server environments, such as LANs and the Internet. It can also handle a **distributed database**, in which a database is stored on different computers, on different networks, or in different locations. As shown in Figure 10-19, database server software replaces an entry-level DBMS, and users continue to communicate with the server by means of client software.

FIGURE 10-19
Database server software is optimized to provide fast access to multiple simultaneous users.

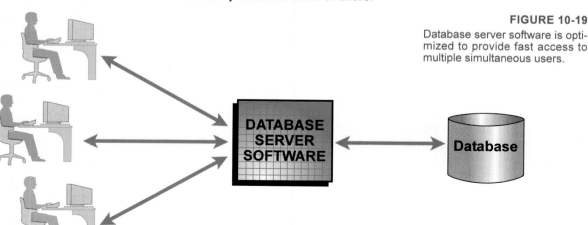

DATABASES AND THE WEB

Is it possible to access a database over the Web? The Web provides both opportunities and challenges for accessing the information in a database. Obviously, with its global reach, the Web provides an opportunity for many people to gain access to data from many locations. Web access is constrained, however, by the stateless nature of HTTP and the necessity to provide access by using a browser as client software. Providing access to databases via the Web requires some "tricks." It does not, however, require special databases or special DBMSs. Web access to hierarchical, network, relational, and object-oriented databases is possible—although access to relational databases is most common, simply because so many databases are stored in relational format.

What's the simplest way to provide Web access to a database? A technique called **static Web publishing** is a simple way to display the data in a database by converting a database report into an HTML document, which can be displayed as a Web page by a browser. Static publishing provides extremely limited access to a database because it creates a Web page that essentially displays a "snapshot" of your data at the time the report was generated. Data on the Web page cannot be manipulated, except to be searched in a rudimentary way by the Find feature of your Web browser.

The advantages of static publishing include security and simplicity. Your data remains secure because you have not provided direct access to your database, so unauthorized users cannot change your data. Static publishing is simple because most entry-level DBMS software includes a menu option that allows you to easily produce an HTML page from a database report, as shown in Figure 10-20.

INFOWEBLINKS

The **Web Databases InfoWeb** offers links to lots of useful tips about database access via the Web.

www.course.com/np/concepts8/ch10

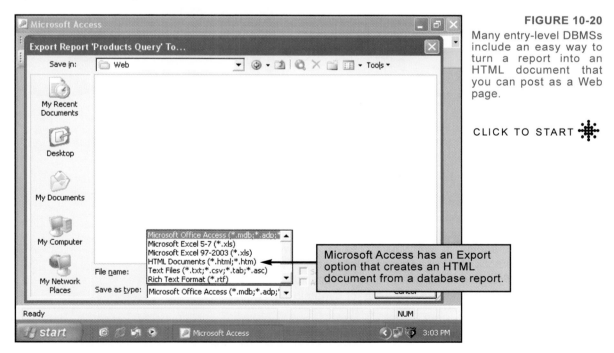

FIGURE 10-20

Many entry-level DBMSs include an easy way to turn a report into an HTML document that you can post as a Web page.

CLICK TO START

Microsoft Access has an Export option that creates an HTML document from a database report.

What if I want to provide access to current data? Each time regular customers at WebMusic connect to the site, they see Web pages tailored to their music preferences. Country music fans, for example, see descriptions of the latest hits out of Nashville and a list of discount CDs by their favorite artists. Obviously, these pages cannot be the result of static publishing. They are created by a **dynamic Web publishing** process that generates customized Web pages as needed, or "on the fly."

Dynamic Web publishing relies on a program or script, referred to as a **server-side program**, that resides on a Web server and acts as an intermediary between your browser and a DBMS. In the WebMusic example, a server-side program reads a cookie from the customer's computer to find the unique number assigned to the customer. The server-side program then uses the customer number to generate a query, which is sent to the database server software. This software accesses the database to locate the customer's music preferences and favorite artists. The server-side program then asks the database server software to locate all the specials that apply to this customer's preferences. A list of applicable CDs, descriptions, and prices is sent back to the Web server, where it is formulated as an HTML document and sent to the browser. The architecture for dynamic publishing requires a Web server in addition to database server software, a database, and a browser, as shown in Figure 10-21.

FIGURE 10-21

Dynamic Web publishing requires several components, including a Web server, database server software, database, and browser.

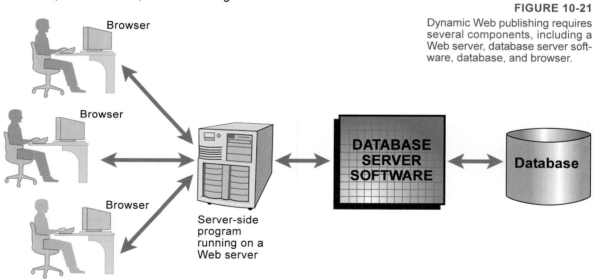

Browser

Browser

Browser

Server-side program running on a Web server

DATABASE SERVER SOFTWARE

Database

Is it possible to add and update database records via the Web? In several situations, such as e-commerce, it is important for people to use a browser to add or update records in a database. For example, the process of ordering merchandise at WebMusic creates a new order record, changes the QtyInStock field in the CompactDisks table, and creates a customer record for first-time customers. These dynamic database updates require an architecture similar to that used for dynamic Web publishing, plus the use of forms.

A form can collect data, such as customer name and address, or it can collect the specifications for a query, such as a search for Garth Brooks CDs. A completed form is sent from your browser to the Web server, which strips the data or query out of the document and sends it to the DBMS. Results are sent to the Web server, formatted into an HTML document, and sent back to your browser.

A form usually exists on a Web server, which sends the form to your browser. Most forms are created using the HTML <form> tag and <input> tag. Figure 10-22 illustrates an HTML document with <input> tags and shows the Web page form it produces.

FIGURE 10-22

An HTML document (top) produces a form (lower-right) when displayed by a browser.

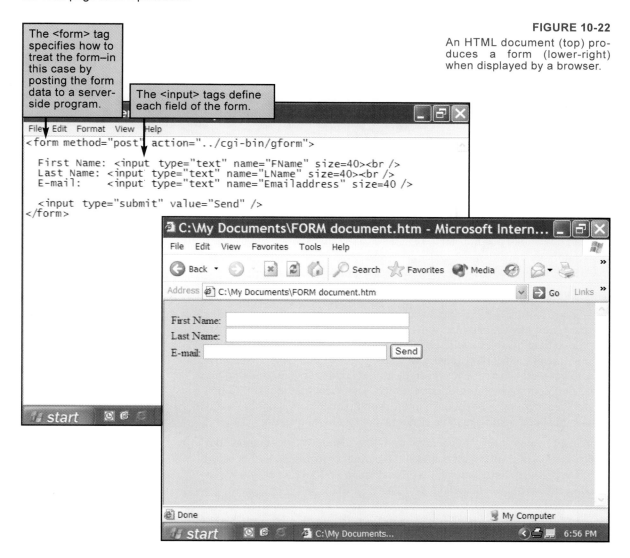

The <form> tag specifies how to treat the form—in this case by posting the form data to a server-side program.

The <input> tags define each field of the form.

```
File  Edit  Format  View  Help
<form method="post" action="../cgi-bin/gform">

  First Name:  <input type="text" name="FName" size=40><br />
  Last Name:  <input type="text" name="LName" size=40><br />
  E-mail:     <input type="text" name="Emailaddress" size=40 />

  <input type="submit" value="Send" />
</form>
```

C:\My Documents\FORM document.htm - Microsoft Intern...

File Edit View Favorites Tools Help

Back · Search Favorites Media

Address C:\My Documents\FORM document.htm Go Links

First Name: _____
Last Name: _____
E-mail: _____ Send

Done My Computer

start C:\My Documents... 6:56 PM

An emerging technology called **XForms** provides an alternative to HTML forms. XForms offer more flexibility than HTML forms, and they interface with XML documents. XForms are designed as the successor to HTML forms for interactive exchange of data over the Web, such as e-commerce. Use of XForms requires an XForms-enabled browser or a plug-in that adds XForms capability.

How do I create server-side programs? Several tools, including ASP, CGI, and PHP, help you create server-side programs. As you learned in Chapter 6, ASP (Active Server Pages) technology can be used to generate an HTML document that contains scripts, which are run before the document is displayed as a Web page. These scripts are small embedded programs that can be designed to get user input, run queries, and display query results.

INFOWEBLINKS

What's going on with XForms technology? Which browsers support it? You can find out at the **XForms InfoWeb**.

www.course.com/np/concepts8/ch10

ASP technology, developed by Microsoft, originally worked only on Windows-based Web servers. A plug-in is now available for UNIX servers. Figure 10-23 illustrates how an ASP script displays database information that has been requested by a remote user.

FIGURE 10-23

An ASP script can collect user input, run queries, and display query results.

Display query results

HTML

ASP script

Run queries

Database

CGI (Common Gateway Interface) offers a non-proprietary way to create HTML pages based on data in a database. A CGI script can be written in a variety of programming languages, such as C, C++, Java, and Perl.

PHP (PHP: Hypertext Preprocessor) is a cross-platform scripting language that can be used to accomplish the same tasks as CGI scripts. Specialized Web database development tools, such as ColdFusion, provide a way to link HTML pages to a database without programming or scripting.

XML DOCUMENTS

How does XML relate to the Web and databases? XML is a markup language that allows field tags, data, and tables to be incorporated into a Web document. It was developed in response to several deficiencies that become apparent as HTML gained widespread use. For example, suppose you are interested in speeches given by Martin Luther King, Jr. Entering his name in a search engine produces thousands of entries, including MLK biographies, streets and schools named after the famous civil rights leader, historic locations relating to the civil rights movement, and so on.

Wouldn't it be nice if King's speeches were stored in HTML documents that identified their content as speeches and their author as Martin Luther King, Jr.? XML provides tags that can be embedded in an XML document to put data in context, as shown in Figure 10-24.

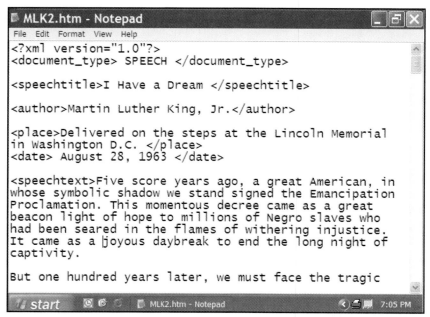

FIGURE 10-24

A document with XML tags allows you to make a targeted search for author = Martin Luther King, Jr. and document_type = SPEECH.

How is XML typically used today? One of XML's most positive contributions to data management is the potential to add context to the information contained in a widely diverse pool of documents on the Web. Although it is easy to see how XML tags might make the free-form documents currently on the Web much easier to manage, today XML is more often used for structured data.

As explained in Chapter 6, XML is often used to specify a standard structure of fields and records, such as SportsML, DocBook, and Chemical Markup Language, for storing data that can be accessed from a browser. Using this standard structure, data entered into an XML document can be identified by field names. Figure 10-25 provides an example of an XML document that contains data similar to that in WebMusic's CompactDisks table.

How do I query an XML database? The way you query an XML database depends on how it was created, where it is stored, and whether you have authorization for access. Direct access to XML databases is provided by XML query engines, such as XPath and XQuery. Direct access to an XML database, however, requires knowledge of its location, access rights, and a list of field names. Therefore, like many relational databases, access to an XML database is provided by some type of client software designed specifically to accept queries, access the database, and return results. XML database clients can be offered as browser plug-ins.

What are the pros and cons of XML databases? Storing data in an XML document offers several advantages. It is "portable" so that it can be easily accessed from virtually any computer platform—PCs, Macs, Linux computers, mainframes, and even handhelds. All that's required on the platform is an XML-enabled browser, such as Internet Explorer or Netscape Navigator.

XML documents are not, however, optimized for many operations you would customarily associate with databases, such as fast sorts, searches, and updates.

To get the best out of XML and relational databases, some experts recommend storing data in a relational database, managing it with RDBMS software, and using server-side software to generate XML documents for exchanging data via the Web. Some RDBMSs include features that allow a database server to receive queries in the form of XML commands. After receiving a query, the database compiles the results and uses XML to format the data into a Web page, as shown in Figure 10-26.

FIGURE 10-26
Manipulating XML data with an RDBMS.

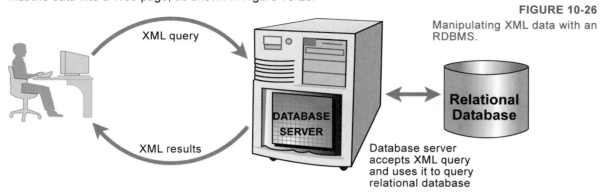

Database server accepts XML query and uses it to query relational database

As you can see, many techniques exist for storing, accessing, and displaying the data from databases. Individuals can use simple tools to create personal databases, such as address books. Corporate database managers, however, need to be familiar with more complex tools used to distribute data over networks and the Web. Sometimes more than one tool has the potential to work for a specific application. Now that you've had an introduction to the options, you should be able to evaluate when and how to use them.

QUICKCHECK......SECTION B

1. A custom database can be stored as a simple [_____] file and accessed by routines written in a standard programming language.

2. Spreadsheet software typically includes some data management features suitable for working with relational databases. True or false? [_____]

3. Modern database software supports data [_____], which means keeping data separated from the program modules that manipulate the data.

4. [_____] Web publishing uses the data in a database to generate customized Web pages as needed.

5. ASP, CGI, and PHP are used to create XML documents that are processed on a server before being sent to your browser. True or false? [_____]

✦ CHECK ANSWERS

SECTION C

DATABASE DESIGN

The key to an effective database is its initial design. In a well-designed database, data can be flexibly manipulated to produce timely, meaningful, and accurate information for decision making. Bad database design can lead to messy databases, lost records, and inaccurate data.

The goal of good database design is to store information so that it is easy to access and maintain, but concise enough to take up as little disk space as possible. Section C looks at databases from the perspective of the database designer and describes how to create an efficient structure for a relational database. You can even apply many of these design principles when you create your own databases.

DEFINING FIELDS

How does a database designer know what data to store? The term **database structure** refers to the arrangement of fields, tables, and relationships in a database. The first step in structuring a relational database is to determine what data must be collected and stored. To do so, a database designer might begin by consulting users and studying the current filing system to compile a list of available data as well as any additional data necessary to produce on-screen output or printed reports.

If you are designing the database structure for WebMusic, for example, you would probably recognize that data such as CD Name, Artist Name, Production Date, Item Number, Publisher, Qty In Stock, MSRP (manufacturer's suggested retail price), Discount Price, and CD Cover Photo should be collected and stored.

After the database designer determines what data to store, the next step is to organize that data into fields. It is usually easy to break data into fields just by using common sense and considering how people might want to access the data. Any data that people would want to search for, sort on, or use in a calculation should be in its own field.

Why are last names stored in a different field than first names? The treatment of first and last names illustrates the concept of breaking data into fields. A database designer could define a field called Name to hold an entire customer's name, such as Gilbert B. Grape. With the entire name in one field, however, the database would not be able to access individual parts of the name, making it difficult to alphabetize customers by last name or to produce a report in which names appear in a format such as Grape, Gilbert B. (Figure 10-27).

First Name * | Gilbert   MI * | B.

Last Name * | Grape

Gilbert B. Grape   Grape, Gilbert B.

FIGURE 10-27

When a field contains an entire name, it is difficult to individually manipulate the first name, last name, and middle initial. A more flexible design provides separate fields for each part of the name.

What makes each record unique? Although two people might have the same name or two paychecks might contain the same amount, a computer must have some way to differentiate between records. A **primary key** is a field that contains data unique to a record. Designers commonly designate fields such as SocialSecurityNumber and PartNumber as primary keys.

How does a database designer know what data types to use? The data that can be entered into a field depends on the field's data type. From a technical perspective, a **data type** specifies the way data is represented on the disk and in RAM. From a user perspective, the data type determines the way data can be manipulated. When designing a database, each field is assigned a data type.

Data can be broadly classified as numeric or character. As you learned in Chapter 2, character data contains letters, numerals, and symbols not used for calculations. Numeric data contains numbers that can be manipulated mathematically by adding, averaging, multiplying, and so forth. As an example, the DiscountPrice field in Figure 10-28 contains numeric data, which can be added to the prices for other CDs to calculate a total price when a customer buys more than one CD.

FIGURE 10-28

Numeric data can be used for calculations.

DiscountPrice | $12.97

INVOICE

Qty	CD Title	Discount Price
1	Tigerlily	$12.97
1	Autobiography	$14.97
1	Everyday	$14.97
	Total	$42.91

There are several numeric data types, including real, integer, and date. Database designers assign the **real data type** to fields that contain numbers with decimal places—prices, percentages, and so on. The **integer data type** is used for fields that contain whole numbers—quantities, repetitions, rankings, and so on. Database designers typically use the integer data type unless the data requires decimal places because real numbers require more storage space. As you might expect, the **date data type** is used to store dates in a format that allows them to be manipulated, such as when you want to calculate the number of days between two dates.

The **text data type** is typically assigned to fixed-length fields that hold character data—people's names, CD titles, and so on. Text fields sometime hold data that looks like numbers, but doesn't need to be mathematically manipulated. Telephone "numbers" and ZIP codes are examples of data that looks numeric, but is stored in text fields because database users would never want to add two telephone numbers together or find the average of a group of ZIP codes. As a rule of thumb, information such as telephone numbers, ZIP codes, Social Security numbers, and item numbers should be stored in text fields.

A **memo data type** usually provides a variable-length field into which users can enter comments. For example, the WebMusic database might contain a memo field for storing comments about a particular CD, such as "Winner of the 2003 Best CD of the Year award!"

The **logical data type** (sometimes called a Boolean or yes/no data type) is used for true/false or yes/no data using minimal storage space. For example, a database designer might define a logical field called OnSale, which would contain a Y if a CD is on a special sale or N if the CD is not on sale.

Some file and database management systems also include additional data types, such as BLOBs and hyperlinks. A **BLOB** (binary large object) is a collection of binary data stored in a single field of a database. BLOBs can be just about any kind of data you would typically store as a file, such as an MP3 music track. For example, the WebMusic database could store a short sample of each song on a CD in a BLOB field called TrackSample.

The **hyperlink data type** stores URLs used to link directly from a database to a Web page. For example, data stored in a hyperlink field of the WebMusic database might provide a link to a musician's Web site. Figure 10-29 summarizes the most commonly used data types in today's databases.

FIGURE 10-29
Commonly Used Data Types

Data Type	Description	Sample Field	Sample Data
Real	Numbers that include decimal places	DiscountPrice	9.99
Integer	Whole numbers	QTY	5
Date	Month, day, and year	OrderDate	9/30/2005
Text	Letters or numerals not used for calculations	Name ZipCode	Gilbert 49866
Logical	Data that can have one of two values	InStock	Y
Memo	Variable length comment field	Awards	Golden Globe 2004
BLOB	Binary data	SampleTrack	[An MP3 file]
Hyperlink	URLs	MusicianWebSite	www.nataliemerchant.com

How does a database handle computations? When a customer looks for a CD at WebMusic's Web site, three pieces of pricing information are provided. The first is the manufacturer's suggested retail price, or MSRP. The second is the discounted price that WebMusic offers. The third is the amount of money a customer will save by purchasing the CD through WebMusic. The CompactDisks record type, however, contains only two pieces of pricing information—MSRP and DiscountPrice. The third piece of information—the amount of money a customer saves by purchasing through WebMusic—is a computed field.

A **computed field** is a calculation that a DBMS performs during processing, and then temporarily stores in a memory location. An efficiently designed database uses computed fields whenever possible because they do not require disk storage space. Figure 10-30 illustrates how a computed field produces the amount saved with purchases at WebMusic's discount price.

TERMINOLOGY NOTE

A computed field works somewhat like a function in a spreadsheet; you set up a formula for the calculation, which is applied to compute the data.

FIGURE 10-30
Creating a Computed Field

MSRP	$18.97
DiscountPrice	$13.28

The database includes a field containing the MSRP and another field containing the discount price.

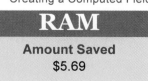

RAM
Amount Saved
$5.69

The amount in one field can be subtracted from the amount in the other field. The result is temporarily stored in a "field" in RAM and can appear on a screen or report.

Can a database designer prevent people from entering inaccurate data? There's an old saying in the computer industry: "garbage in, garbage out." This adage is especially true when dealing with databases. The information produced by reports and processing routines is only as accurate as the information in the database. Unfortunately, data entry errors can compromise the accuracy and validity of a database. When designing a database, it is important to think ahead and envision potential data entry errors. Most DBMSs provide tools that database designers can use to prevent some, but not all, data entry errors.

People who enter data into a database sometimes have difficulty deciding whether to use uppercase or lowercase characters. In a **case sensitive database**, uppercase letters are not equivalent to their lowercase counterparts. For example, in a case sensitive database, the artist name "Jewel" is not equivalent to "jewel." Inconsistent use of case can lead to several problems. A search for "jewel" will not produce records for "Jewel" or "JEWEL." Furthermore, in a sorted or indexed list, "jewel" and "JEWEL" might not be grouped together.

Most, but not all, DBMSs give database designers an option to turn case sensitivity on or off. They might also have the option to force data to all uppercase or all lowercase as it is entered. Neither technique is an infallible solution to case sensitivity, but as you gain experience designing databases, you'll become more familiar with the advantages and disadvantages of each technique.

People who enter data might not be consistent about the way they enter numbers. For example, a data entry operator might enter a telephone number as 555-555-7777, (555) 555-7777, or 1-555-555-7777. If multiple data entry operators enter telephone numbers in different formats, it becomes difficult to produce nicely formatted reports or locate a particular telephone number. To prevent this sort of inconsistent formatting, a database designer can specify a field format. A **field format** is a "picture" of what the data is supposed to look like when it's entered. If someone attempts to enter data in the wrong format, the database rejects that entry. A telephone number field might use a field format such as the one shown in Figure 10-31.

FIGURE 10-31

A field format helps maintain consistent data by providing a structure for entering data into a field.

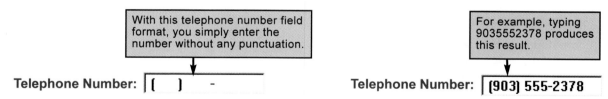

With this telephone number field format, you simply enter the number without any punctuation.

Telephone Number: [   ]   -

For example, typing 9035552378 produces this result.

Telephone Number: (903) 555-2378

Sometimes people who enter data simply make a mistake and press the wrong keys. Preventing every typographical error is not possible. However, it is possible to catch some of these errors by using field validation rules, list boxes, or lookups.

A **field validation rule** is a specification that the database designer sets up to filter data entered into a particular field. For example, the price of CDs in the WebMusic database ranges from $0 (for promotions) to $75. No CDs have an MSRP greater than $100. When intending to enter $19.98 in the MSRP field, however, the omission of a decimal point could set the price of a CD to $1998.00! When designing the WebMusic database, a database designer can use a field validation rule to limit entries in the MSRP field to less than $100. If the DBMS receives a number such as 1998 in the MSRP field, it displays a message requesting the correct price.

Another technique that prevents typographical and case-sensitivity errors is to limit data entry to the items on a specified list. For example, the state abbreviation for Michigan might be entered as MI, Mi, Mich, or NI if your fingers slipped. However, most databases allow the database designer to specify a list of acceptable entries for each field. Most people are familiar with clickable lists of state abbreviations, such as the one in Figure 10-32.

Database designers can also prevent entry errors by using lookup routines. A **lookup routine** validates an entry by searching for the same data in a file or database table. For example, suppose that a WebMusic employee is entering new CDs. It is important that each CD has a unique item number. When data is entered in the ItemNumber field, the database can use a lookup routine to search every existing record to make sure the new item number does not duplicate an already existing item number.

NORMALIZATION

How does a database designer group fields into tables? A process called **normalization** helps database designers create a database structure that can save storage space and increase processing efficiency. The goal of normalization is to minimize **data redundancy**—the amount of data that is repeated or duplicated in a database. To normalize a database, one of the designer's main tasks is to decide how best to group data into tables.

The first step to grouping fields is to get an idea of the "big picture" of the data. Often, groupings correspond to the physical items, or entities, that are tracked in the database. For example, WebMusic data is grouped into several tables: CompactDisks, Tracks, Customers, Orders, and OrderDetails. Some of these groupings seem obvious, but other groupings might seem a bit puzzling. You might wonder why it is necessary to use two tables—Orders and Order Details—to store data about an order. Why won't one table suffice? To answer this question, first take a look at the data relevant to each order in Figure 10-33.

FIGURE 10-32

Clickable lists are an easy way for users to enter data in a standard format.

INFOWEBLINKS

Explore normalization and work with several examples at the **Database Normalization InfoWeb**.

www.course.com/np/concepts8/ch10

FIGURE 10-33

A typical WebMusic order contains customer data and data about the merchandise being ordered.

WebMusic Order

OrderNumber	8097656		LastName	Rodriguez
OrderDate	12/15/05		FirstName	Jorge
CustomerNumber	3422211		Street	101 Las Vegas Court
			City	Taos
			State	NM	ZipCode	87571

Quantity	Item#	Item	Price
1	EMD789600	The Beatles 1	$18.97
1	RCA5644-09	Everyday	$20.98
		TotalPrice	$39.95

18

If the customer information and order information are grouped in the same table, each time Jorge Rodriguez places an order, his name, shipping address, billing address, telephone number, and e-mail address must be entered and stored. This data redundancy not only requires extra storage space, but also could lead to storing inconsistent or inaccurate data. The solution is to create separate tables for Orders and Customers, which can be related by including a CustomerNumber field in both tables, as shown in Figure 10-34.

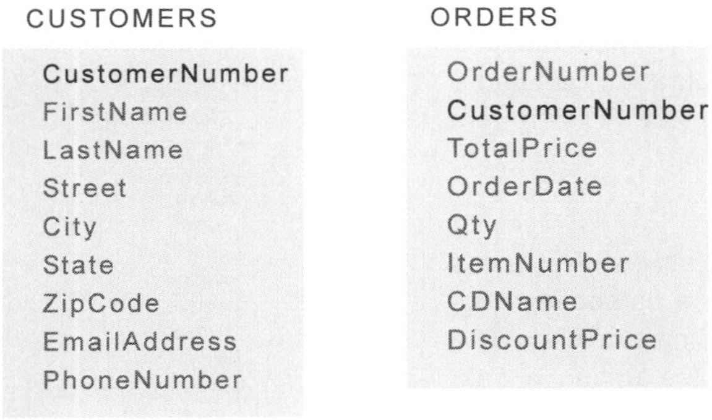

CUSTOMERS

CustomerNumber
FirstName
LastName
Street
City
State
ZipCode
EmailAddress
PhoneNumber

ORDERS

OrderNumber
CustomerNumber
TotalPrice
OrderDate
Qty
ItemNumber
CDName
DiscountPrice

FIGURE 10-34
Fields for each order are separated into two tables—one for customer information and one for order information.

Even after separating customer data from order data, the structure of the WebMusic database can be further improved. The Orders table in the previous figure allows customers to order only one CD because the fields for ItemNumber and DiscountPrice occur only once. Obviously, the WebMusic database is required to handle orders for more than one CD.

It might seem reasonable to provide several fields for the CDs on an order. Perhaps they could be named ItemNumber1, ItemNumber2, ItemNumber3, and so on. But how many fields should the database designer provide? If the designer provides fields for ordering 10 items, the database still cannot handle large orders for more than 10 CDs. Furthermore, if a customer orders fewer than 10 CDs, space is wasted by having empty fields in each record.

You might recognize that a one-to-many relationship exists between an order and the ordered items. That clue indicates that the database designer should separate the data into two tables, such as Orders and OrderDetails. These two tables are related by the OrderNumber field. Figure 10-35 illustrates how the Orders table is further normalized into two tables to store data more efficiently.

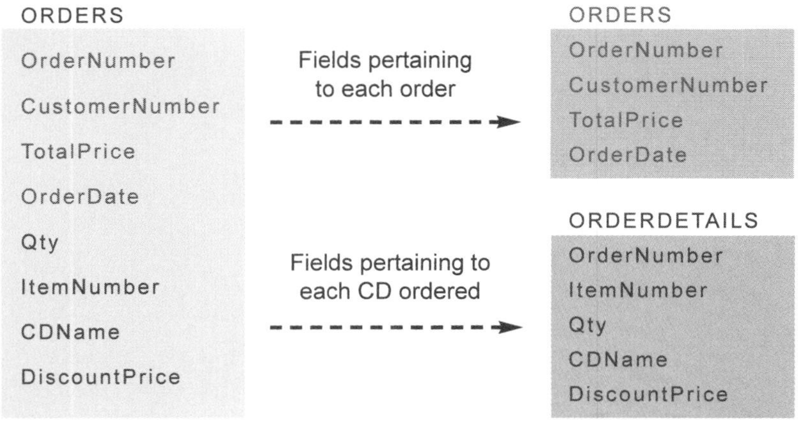

ORDERS

OrderNumber
CustomerNumber
TotalPrice
OrderDate
Qty
ItemNumber
CDName
DiscountPrice

Fields pertaining to each order - - - - - - - - - ->

Fields pertaining to each CD ordered - - - - - - - - - ->

ORDERS

OrderNumber
CustomerNumber
TotalPrice
OrderDate

ORDERDETAILS

OrderNumber
ItemNumber
Qty
CDName
DiscountPrice

FIGURE 10-35
The fields pertaining to the ordered merchandise are further divided into two record types and related by the OrderNumber field.

ORGANIZING RECORDS

How are database records organized? Records can be organized in different ways depending on how people want to use them. For example, a customer visiting WebMusic's Web site will most often view the information in the CompactDisks table by CDName or ArtistName. The inventory manager usually wants the data sorted by QtyInStock so that it is easy to see which CDs must be reordered. In contrast, the marketing manager is more interested in the ProductionDate, so that new CDs can be aggressively priced. No single way of organizing the data accommodates everyone's needs, but tables can be sorted or indexed in multiple ways.

What happens when the data in a table is sorted? A table's **sort order** is the order in which records are stored on disk. Sorted tables typically produce faster queries and updates because they take advantage of clever algorithms that quickly pinpoint records. In a sorted table, new records are inserted to maintain the order. If no sort order is specified, new records are appended to the end of the file, resulting in a file that is not in any particular order. Queries and updates within an unsorted database are slow because the only algorithm for searching an unsorted table requires a sequential look at each record.

Most DBMSs use a sort key to determine the order in which records are stored. A table's **sort key** is one or more fields used to specify where new records are inserted in a table. A table can have only one sort key at a time, but the sort key can be changed. Changing a sort key can take a long time, however, because the process physically rearranges records on the disk. The database designer usually specifies the sort key for a database table at the time the database structure is created.

How is indexing different from sorting? A database index is very similar to an index in a book that contains a list of keywords and pointers to the pages where they can be found. A **database index** contains a list of keys, and each key provides a pointer to the record that contains the rest of the fields related to that key. Figure 10-36 illustrates how an index works.

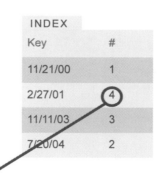

FIGURE 10-36

When indexed by date, the index file contains a list of keys and the record number that contains more information about the CD released on that date.

CLICK TO START

INDEX	
Key	#
11/21/00	1
2/27/01	4
11/11/03	3
7/20/04	2

COMPACTDISKS

#	ItemNumber	CDName	ArtistName	Production Date	QtyInStock	MSRP
1	Wea56690-1	A Day Without Rain	Enya	11/21/00	345	14.95
2	B0002GMSC0	Autobiography	Ashlee Simpson	7/20/04	234	16.95
3	B0000CFW87	Closer	Josh Groban	11/11/03	183	19.95
4	RCA-00-134	Everyday	Dave Matthews	2/27/01	50	14.95

10

Unlike a sort order, an index has no bearing on the physical sequence of records on disk. An index simply points to the record where the data can be found. The advantage of an index over a sort is that a table can have multiple indexes, but only one sort order. For example, the CompactDisks table could be indexed by CDName to facilitate searches for CD titles. The same table could also be indexed by ArtistName to facilitate searches using artist names.

Database tables should be indexed by any field or fields that are commonly used as search fields. The database designer typically creates indexes at the time the database structure is designed. Indexes can also be created at a later date, as needed.

DESIGNING THE INTERFACE

Does a database designer have control over the user interface? The way that database records, queries, and reports appear on the screen depends on the user interface. An operating system typically provides some conventions for the user interface, such as dialog and button styles, but additional design decisions must be made for the database user interface.

Designing the database user interface can be a challenging task. If a company's database includes multiple tables used by many different people, a professional user interface designer usually creates and maintains the user interface. Large databases might even require a group of user interface designers.

The interface for smaller databases, such as those used by small businesses or individuals, is most likely created by the database designer. Some DBMSs include tools to create database interfaces. Others require separate tools for this task.

What makes a good database interface? A well-defined user interface for a database should be clear, intuitive, and efficient. Take a moment to look at the data entry screen in Figure 10-37, and imagine that you are using the screen to finalize the purchase of several CDs from WebMusic.

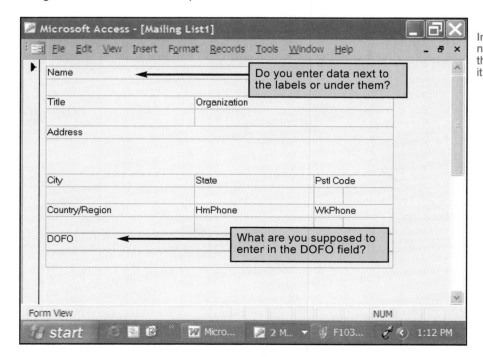

FIGURE 10-37

Imagine entering your own name and address using this on-screen form. Does it seem easy to use?

Using the data entry screen pictured on the previous page might be awkward because it does not follow good user interface design principles. The data entry fields seem out of order, and users might have difficulty discerning which entry box corresponds to each label. In addition, several fields have cryptic labels that don't provide good clues about the data you're supposed to enter.

To improve this database interface, a designer might consider the following principles:

■ Arrange fields in a logical order beginning at the top-left of the screen. The first fields should be those used most often or those that come first in the data entry sequence.

■ Provide visual clues to the entry areas. An edit box, line, or shaded area can delineate data entry areas.

■ Entry areas should appear in a consistent position relative to their labels. By convention, labels are placed left of the entry areas or above them.

■ Provide a quick way to move through the fields in order. By convention, the tab key performs this function.

■ If all fields do not fit on a single screen, use scrolling or create a second screen.

■ Provide buttons or other easy-to-use controls for moving from one record to another.

■ Supply on-screen instructions to help ensure that data is entered correctly. Web databases can benefit from links to help pages.

Figure 10-38 contains an improved interface for the database in the previous figure.

INFOWEBLINKS

Compare the good, the bad, and the ugly at the **Database Interface InfoWeb**.

www.course.com/np/concepts8/ch10

FIGURE 10-38

A well-designed data input screen should be easy to use.

[Figure showing a data entry form with callouts:]

- Fields are arranged in logical order.
- Data entry areas are clearly delineated as white spaces.

Last Name	First Name	
Title	Organization Name	
Address		
City	State	Postal Code
Country/Region	Home Phone	Work Phone

Enter the date of your first order or enter your password in the space below:

- On-screen instructions help users enter data correctly.

Help   Dial   Page 1 2

Record: 1 of 22

Form View   NUM

- Navigation controls make it easy to view additional records.
- Buttons make it easy to get to the second page of this record.

DESIGNING REPORT TEMPLATES

How can I display or print data as a formatted report? A **report generator** is a software tool that provides the ability to create report templates for a database. End users might use report generators, but more typically they are used by database designers.

A **report template** contains the outline or general specifications for a report, including such elements as the report title, fields to include, fields to subtotal or total, and report format specifications. The template does not, however, contain data from the database. Data is merged into the template when you actually run a report.

As an example, you might create a report template called CDPriceGroup, which specifies the following:

- The title of the report is WebMusic CDs by Price.

- The report contains data from the CompactDisks table, arranged in four columns, with data from the DiscountPrice, CDName, ArtistName, and QtyInStock fields.

- The headings for the columns are Discount Price, CD Name, Artist Name, and Qty In Stock.

- The report is grouped by price.

These specifications would be used to produce a report similar to the one shown in Figure 10-39.

FIGURE 10-39

A report template contains the specifications to produce this report.

WebMusic CDs by Price   Report Date: 08/05

Discount Price	CD Name	Artist Name	Qty In Stock
$11.97			
	Original Sun Greatest Hits	Carl Perkins	10
	In My Tribe	10,000 Maniacs	231
	Rocks	Aerosmith	352
	Scarecrow	John Mellencamp	521
$13.28			
	O Brother Where Art Thou?	Various Artists	198
	Cuttin' Heads	John Mellencamp	632
	Everyday	Dave Matthews Band	50
	A Day Without Rain	Enya	345
$13.99			
	Scarecrow	Garth Brooks	327

When a report is actually produced, it is based on the data currently contained in the database table. For example, the report on the previous page was produced on August 4th and includes CDs that were stored in the database as of that date. Now suppose that on October 4th, WebMusic changes the price of several CDs. The CDPriceGroup report template is used again to print a report on October 4th. This report, shown in Figure 10-40, follows the same format as the previous report, but includes the price changes and current quantity in stock.

FIGURE 10-40

Using the same report specifications as the 08/05 report, but different data.

WebMusic CDs by Price

Report Date: 10/05

Discount Price	CD Name	Artist Name	Qty In Stock
$11.97			
	Original Sun Greatest Hits	Carl Perkins	50
	In My Tribe	10,000 Maniacs	198
$13.28			
	Rocks	Aerosmith	345
	Scarecrow	John Mellencamp	421
	O Brother Where Art Thou?	Various Artists	198

How does the database designer create effective report templates?
The reports created by a report generator can be displayed, printed, saved as files, or output as Web pages. Some data management software also provides tools to output data as graphs, sounds, or graphics. The database designer can create templates for reports that effectively present information by observing the following guidelines:

- Supply only the information required. Too much information can make it difficult to identify what is essential.

- Present information in a usable format. For example, if subtotals are necessary for making a decision, include them. The people who use reports should not have to make additional manual calculations.

- Information should be timely. Reports must arrive in time to be used for effective decision making. Some decisions require periodic information—for example, monthly sales reports. Other decisions require ongoing information, such as current stock prices, that will be best satisfied by a continuous display.

- Information should be presented in a clear, unambiguous format and include necessary titles, page numbers, dates, labels, and column headings.

- Present information in the format most appropriate for the audience. In many cases, a traditional report organized in rows and columns is most appropriate. In other cases, graphs might be more effective.

LOADING DATA

How is data loaded into database tables? After the design for the database structure is complete, it is time to load the database with an initial set of data. For example, before the WebMusic database went online, it was populated with data for all the CDs in the inventory.

Data can be loaded into a database manually by using generic data entry tools supplied with the DBMS or by using a customized data entry module created by the database designer. Entering data manually can take a long time, however, and mistakes such as misspellings are common.

If the data exists electronically in another type of database or in flat files, it is usually possible to transfer the data using a custom-written conversion routine or import and export routines. A **conversion routine** converts the data from its current format into a format that can be automatically incorporated into the new database. It takes some time and requires knowledge about database formats to write conversion routines, but for large databases, it's much quicker to convert data than to re-enter it manually. Converting data also results in fewer errors.

Some DBMSs provide built-in import and export routines that automatically convert data from one file format to another. An import routine brings data into a database. For example, if data was previously stored as a spreadsheet file, an import routine in Microsoft Access can be used to transfer data from the spreadsheet to an Access database. In contrast, an export routine copies data out of a software package, such as spreadsheet software, and into the database. Typically, you would use either an import routine or an export routine, but not both.

QUICKCHECK......SECTION C

1. A(n) primary _____ contains data unique to a record, such as a Social Security number or ISBN.

2. Real, integer, text, logical, BLOB, and date are examples of data _____ .

3. A computed field is calculated during processing and stored temporarily in memory. True or false? _____

4. In a case _____ database, a data entry such as MI is not the same as Mi.

5. To filter the data entered into a particular field, the database designer can set up a field _____ rule.

6. One of the goals of the normalization process is to minimize data _____ .

7. A report _____ contains the outline or general specifications for a report, but does not contain data from the database.

 CHECK ANSWERS

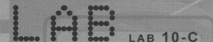 LAB 10-C

WORKING WITH DATABASE SOFTWARE

In this lab, you'll learn:

- How relational database software depicts data as tables, records, and fields
- How to use tables and forms to view data
- How to create a table
- How to use primary keys
- How to enter and edit data
- Why relationships between tables are so important
- How to sort data and create an index
- How to search for data
- How to set filters
- How to create queries
- How to view the SQL code for a query
- How to create a report
- How to modify a report in Design view

INTERACTIVE LAB

CLICK TO START THE LAB

LAB ASSIGNMENTS

1. Start the interactive part of the lab. Insert your Tracking Disk if you want to save your QuickCheck results. Perform each lab step as directed, and answer all the lab QuickCheck questions. When you exit the lab, your answers are automatically graded and your results are displayed.

2. A friend wants to create a table to store information about a collection of old books. List the fields you might include in the table to store information about the books. For each field, specify the field name, data type (text, numeric, date, etc.), and field length. Indicate the primary key(s), and describe how you would sort and/or index the data.

3. Use Microsoft Access or any available file or database management software to create the structure for the table you specified in Assignment 2. Enter at least 10 records. Print a list of all your data.

4. Make a list of five queries that might be useful if your database had hundreds of records. Try these queries on your table. For each query, list the records that were selected.

5. Sketch a report on paper that uses some of the fields in your table. Make sure your report contains a title and headings for each field. Specify whether you would like to align your data at the right, center, or left of each column. Use your software to generate and print the report.

SQL

Adding records, finding information, and making updates are all important aspects of database use. Most people who access a database on a "casual" basis—to shop online or withdraw cash from an ATM, for example—interact with very simple user interfaces. These user interfaces shield users from the intricacies of sophisticated query languages. Nevertheless, a little background in query languages can help you understand the power and capabilities of databases. In Section D, you'll explore the SQL database query language by working with examples that illustrate major database functions, such as deleting records, adding records, searching for information, updating records, and joining tables.

SQL BASICS

How does a query language like SQL work? Query languages like **SQL** (Structured Query Language) typically work behind the scenes as an intermediary between the database client software provided to users, and the database itself. Database client software provides an easy-to-use interface for entering search specifications, new records, data updates, and so on. The client software collects your input, and then converts it into an **SQL query**, which can operate directly on the database to carry out your instructions, as shown in Figure 10-41.

TERMINOLOGY NOTE

The American National Standards Institute's official pronunciation of SQL is "ESS que el," but you also hear it called "SEE quell."

FIGURE 10-41
Database client software provides database users with simple forms that can be used to enter search specifications or update data.

Client software converts these entries into SQL commands, which interact directly with the database to locate data, update records, and perform other functions the user requests.

Database

Query language

SELECT CDName FROM CompactDisks WHERE ArtistName = 'Garth Brooks'

Search

Artist: Garth Brooks

Title:

Label:

Format: ⦿ CD ◯ Cassette ◯ DVD Audio

Search Now   Clear the Form

Form-based user interface

What does a simple SQL query look like? An SQL query is a sequence of words, much like a sentence. For example, an SQL query that searches for a song called "Fly Away" in WebMusic's database might look like this:

SELECT TrackTitle FROM Tracks WHERE TrackTitle = 'Fly Away'

The SQL query language provides a collection of special command words called **SQL keywords**, such as SELECT, FROM, INSERT, and WHERE, which issue instructions to the database. Although the SQL examples in this section of the chapter use uppercase letters for keywords, most implementations of SQL accept either uppercase or lowercase keywords.

Most SQL queries can be divided into three simple elements that specify an action, the name of a database table, and a set of parameters. Let's look at each of these elements.

How does SQL specify the action that I want carried out in the database? An SQL query typically begins with an action keyword, or command, which specifies the operation you want carried out. For example, the command word **DELETE** removes a record from a table. Figure 10-42 lists some of the most commonly used SQL command words.

FIGURE 10-42
SQL Command Words

Command	Description	Example
CREATE	Create a database or table	CREATE TABLE CompactDisks
DELETE	Remove a record from a table	DELETE FROM Tracks WHERE TrackTitle = 'Yesterday'
INSERT	Add a record	INSERT INTO CD Description (ItemNumber, Description) VALUES ('RCA8766098', 'In the Top 10 list for 28 weeks!')
JOIN	Use the data from two tables	SELECT FROM CompactDisks JOIN Tracks ON CompactDisks.ItemNumber = Tracks.ItemNumber
SELECT	Search for records	SELECT FROM CompactDisks WHERE ArtistName = 'Garth Brooks'
UPDATE	Change data in a field	UPDATE CompactDisks SET DiscountPrice = 15.95 WHERE ItemNumber = 'RCA6578988'

How does SQL specify which table to use? SQL keywords such as USE, FROM, or INTO can be used to construct a clause specifying the table you want to access. The clause consists of the keyword followed by the name of the table. For example, the clause **FROM Tracks** indicates that you want to use WebMusic's Tracks table.

An SQL query that begins with **DELETE FROM Tracks** means that you want to delete something from the Tracks table. To complete the query, you provide the parameters that specify which record you want to delete.

18

How does SQL specify parameters? The term **parameter** refers to detailed specifications for a command. Keywords such as WHERE usually begin an SQL clause containing the parameters for a command. Suppose that WebMusic's inventory manager wants to delete all the CDs in the WebMusic database recorded by Phish. The SQL looks like this:

DELETE FROM CompactDisks WHERE ArtistName = 'Phish'

SQL com- mand word	FROM clause specifies the table to use	WHERE clause specifies the field name and its contents

Now that you've learned the basic structure of an SQL query, take a closer look at the SQL for specific database tasks, such as adding records, searching for information, updating fields, organizing records, and joining tables.

ADDING RECORDS

How are records added to a database? Suppose you want to purchase a new CD from the WebMusic site. As a first-time customer, you fill out a form with your name, address, and so on. The client software that you use collects the data you enter in the form and generates an SQL statement using the **INSERT** command, which adds your data to the Customers table of the WebMusic database. Figure 10-43 shows the Customer form, the SQL statement that adds the customer data to the database, and the data that is added to the Customers table.

FIGURE 10-43

Data from the Customer form is added to the database.

Customer form

| First Name: | Jorge | Last Name: | Rodriguez |

Address Line 1
(or company name): 101 Las Vegas Court

Address Line 2
(optional):

City: Taos

State/Province/Region: NM

ZIP/Postal Code: 87571

Phone Number: 5055553412

SQL statement

INSERT INTO Customers (LastName, FirstName, Street, City, State, ZipCode, PhoneNumber) VALUES ('Rodriguez', 'Jorge', '101 Las Vegas Court', 'Taos', 'NM', '87571', '5055553412')

Customers table

LastName	FirstName	Street	City	State	ZipCode	PhoneNumber
Rodriguez	Jorge	101 Las Vegas Court	Taos	NM	87571	505-555-3412
Bleuman	Jonathan	5022 Lake St.	Negaunee	MI	49866	906-555-2131
Wincheta	Daisy	499 Table Mesa	Boulder	CO	80301	303-555-6902
Venkata	Patel	872 Old York Way	Durango	CO	81301	970-555-4438
Wong	Joy	822 Park Place	New York	NY	10023	212-555-9903
Helwig	Nathaniel	5 Winsome Drive	Cheyenne	WY	82003	303-555-3223
Chen	Lu-Chi	2235 Overview Trail	San Francisco	CA	94118	415--555-9001
Walton	William	500 Vista Mesa Pl...	...	NM	87504	505-555-1111
Bolduc	Luc	41 Rue S...	...	M...	...	...555-...487
	Kallie					

SEARCHING FOR INFORMATION

How do SQL queries carry out searches? One of the most common database operations is to query for a particular record or group of records by using the **SELECT** command. Suppose you're looking for Beyonce CDs. You fill in the Search box at the WebMusic site, as shown in Figure 10-44.

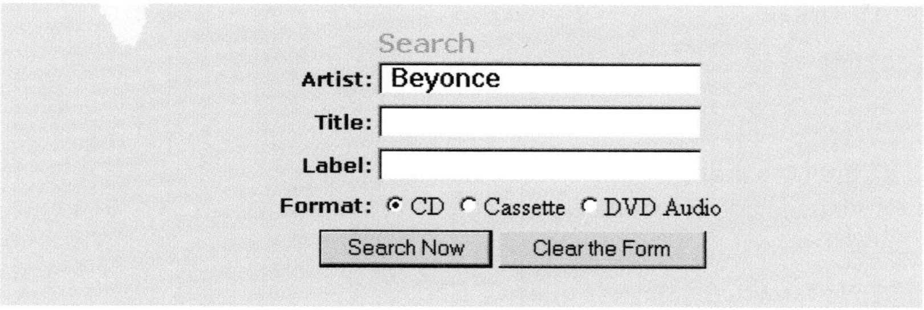

Search

Artist: | Beyonce |

Title: | |

Label: | |

Format: ⊙ CD ○ Cassette ○ DVD Audio

[Search Now] [Clear the Form]

FIGURE 10-44
Search form used by customers to query the database. Here the search is for Beyonce CDs.

The database client software uses your search specification to create the SQL query:

SELECT CDName, CDCover FROM CompactDisks

WHERE ArtistName = 'Beyonce'

As a result of this query, the WebMusic Web page displays a list beginning with *Dangerously in Love*—one of Beyonce's CDs—and a photo of the CD cover. Take a closer look at this query.

The phrase **SELECT CDName, CDCover** specifies that the database should show you only the title and CD cover. Until you confirm that this is the CD you're interested in, it will not show you additional information, such as the price or list of tracks. **FROM CompactDisks** tells the DBMS to search for the CD in the CompactDisks table. **WHERE ArtistName = 'Beyonce'** specifies that the record you want contains the data "Beyonce" in the ArtistName field.

Can SQL perform complex searches? Yes, SQL uses search operators to form complex queries. Chapter 1 introduced the concept of search operators, such as AND, OR, and NOT. Because search operators were originally the idea of mathematician George Boole, they are also referred to as **Boolean operators**. Let's see how they work in the context of SQL queries.

How does AND work in an SQL query? AND (sometimes indicated by a + sign) is used when you want to retrieve records that meet more than one criteria. For example, say a customer wants to find all the CDs by Beyonce, but wants to display only CDs that are on sale for less than $10.00. You might enter something like **Beyonce <$10.00** in the WebMusic search box. The database client creates an SQL query:

SELECT CDName FROM CompactDisks
WHERE ArtistName = 'Beyonce' AND
DiscountPrice < 10.00

WHERE ArtistName = 'Beyonce' AND DiscountPrice < 10.00 is the search criteria. In this example, a record is selected only if the ArtistName field contains Beyonce, and the value in the DiscountPrice field is less than $10.00. If the artist's name is Beyonce, but the discount price is $10.00 or more, the record is not selected. The AND operator specifies that both of the search criteria must be true for the record to be selected.

INFOWEBLINKS

At the **Boolean InfoWeb**, you can learn how a guy born in 1815 had such an immense effect on a modern technology like the Web.

www.course.com/np/concepts8/ch10

18

How does OR differ from AND? Two variations of the OR operator exist. One variation, the "inclusive OR," designates records that meet one of the criteria or both. The other variation, called the "exclusive OR," designates records that meet one criterion or the other, but not both.

SQL uses the inclusive OR. A query such as:

```
SELECT CDName FROM CompactDisks
WHERE ArtistName = 'Beyonce' OR
DiscountPrice < 10.00
```

produces all the Beyonce CDs and all the CDs that are less than $10.00, regardless of the artist. These results also include Beyonce CDs that are less than $10.00, if any exist in the database.

You can combine AND and OR clauses to formulate complex queries. For example, Beyonce was in the band Destiny's Child before she started releasing CDs as a solo artist. If you'd like a list of Beyonce or Destiny's Child CDs for less than $10.00, you can use a query like the following:

```
SELECT CDName FROM CompactDisks
WHERE (ArtistName = 'Beyonce' OR ArtistName =
'Destiny's Child') AND DiscountPrice < 10.00
```

Note the use of parentheses around the OR clause. Parentheses tell the DBMS to process this part of the query first. The placement of parentheses can change the results of a query, sometimes drastically. Compare the previous query to the following query:

```
SELECT CDName FROM CompactDisks
WHERE ArtistName = 'Beyonce' OR (ArtistName =
'Destiny's Child' AND DiscountPrice < 10.00)
```

The first query (in blue) returns CDs by Beyonce or Destiny's Child that are less than $10.00. The second query (in green) returns all CDs by Beyonce, regardless of price, and any CDs by Destiny's Child that cost less than $10.00.

How does NOT work in an SQL query? The NOT operator can be used to omit records from a search by specifying a not-equal relationship. For example, the following query returns all records in the CompactDisks table where the ArtistName is not equal to Beyonce:

```
Select CDName from CompactDisks
WHERE NOT(ArtistName = 'Beyonce')
```

Sometimes NOT relationships are specified with a not-equal operator, such as <> or !=, depending on the specifications of the query language. For example, the following query returns the same records as one that uses the NOT operator:

```
Select CDName from CompactDisks
WHERE ArtistName <> 'Beyonce'
```

UPDATING FIELDS

Can I change the contents of a record? You can change records in a database only if you have authorization to do so. At WebMusic's site, for example, customers do not have authorization to change CD prices or alter the name of the songs on a CD. The process of purchasing a CD, however, does cause an update in the WebMusic database. Suppose you purchase Beyonce's *Dangerously in Love* CD. Your purchase reduces the number of *Dangerously in Love* CDs in WebMusic's inventory. To accomplish this update, one of the software modules in WebMusic's inventory system issues an SQL **UPDATE** command to reduce the number in the QtyInStock field of the *Dangerously in Love* record:

UPDATE CompactDisks

SET QtyInStock = QtyInStock - 1

WHERE CDName = 'Dangerously in Love'

Is it possible to update a group of records? In addition to changing the data in a single record, SQL can perform a **global update** that changes the data in more than one record at a time. Suppose you're WebMusic's marketing manager, and you want to put all The Rolling Stones CDs on sale by reducing the DiscountPrice to $9.95. You could do it the hard way by searching for an ArtistName field that contains "The Rolling Stones," adjusting the DiscountPrice field for that record, and then looking for the next Rolling Stones CD. However, it would be easier to change all the records with a single command. The following SQL statement accomplishes this global update:

UPDATE CompactDisks

SET DiscountPrice = 9.95

WHERE ArtistName = 'The Rolling Stones'

Let's see how this command performs a global update. The UPDATE command means you want to change the data in some or all of the records. CompactDisks is the name of the record type containing the data you want to change. **SET DiscountPrice = 9.95** tells the DBMS to change the data in the DiscountPrice field to $9.95. **WHERE ArtistName = 'The Rolling Stones'** tells the DBMS to change only those records where the artist name is The Rolling Stones.

What are the limitations of the global UPDATE command? Although the global update function is powerful, it works only for records that have similar characteristics—for example, all CDs by The Rolling Stones or all CDs produced in 2005. Custom programming is required to perform global operations on information that does not have any similar characteristics. Figure 10-45 provides an example.

INFOWEBLINKS

From all these examples, you can tell that SQL is a key factor in database manipulation. At the **SQL InfoWeb**, you'll find additional examples and links to tutorials.

www.course.com/np/concepts8/ch10

FIGURE 10-45

Database designers can write modules that provide custom update capabilities.

WebMusic's marketing manager picks 10 CDs each week to place on a special promotional sale. These CDs have no common data that can be used to formulate a global UPDATE command.

Custom programming would allow the marketing manager to simply submit a list of 10 CDs as a document. The module would "read" the document and issue an UPDATE command for each of the chosen CDs.

JOINING TABLES

How is data retrieved from more than one table at a time? Recall that the process of normalization creates tables that can be related by fields that exist in both tables. In SQL terminology, creating a relationship between tables is referred to as **joining tables**.

Suppose you want some information on Enya CDs. It would be nice to see not only the CD name and cover, but also a list of the songs included on the CD. The songs, however, are not stored in the same table as the rest of the CD data. The CompactDisks table holds the CD name, the artist's name, the production date, and other data about the CD. The Tracks table holds the name of each song track, the track length, and an MP3 sample of the track. Both tables also contain an ItemNumber field.

Earlier in the chapter you learned that a relationship can exist between WebMusic's CompactDisks table and Tracks table, based on the data in the ItemNumber field, as shown in Figure 10-46.

FIGURE 10-46

Records in the CompactDisks table and Tracks table both include an ItemNumber field. When the data in these fields is the same, the records refer to the same entity—in this case, an Enya CD called *A Day Without Rain*.

COMPACTDISKS

ItemNumber	CDName	ArtistName	Production Date	Qty in Stock	MSRP
Wea56690-1	A Day Without Rain	Enya	11/21/00	345	14.95
B0002GMSC0	Autobiography	Ashlee Simpson	7/20/04	234	16.95
B0000CFW87	Closer	Josh Groban	11/11/03	183	19.95
RCA-00-134	Everyday				

TRACKS

ItemNumber	TrackTitle	Track Length	TrackSample
Wea56690-1	Only Time	198	OnlyTime.mp3
Wea56690-1	Tempus Vernum	154	Tempv.mp3
Wea56690-1	Fallen Embers	209	FallenEm.mp3
Wea56690-1	Wild Child	258	WildChild.mp3

To take advantage of the relationship between these two tables, you first have to join the tables. Why? Remember that in a relational database, the tables are essentially independent unless you join them together. The SQL **JOIN** command allows you to temporarily join and simultaneously access the data in more than one table.

How does the JOIN command work? A single SQL query can retrieve data from the CompactDisks table and the Tracks table for Enya CDs. To do so, however requires some way to distinguish the data contained in each table. In the example, both tables contain a field called ItemNumber. How can you differentiate the ItemNumber field that belongs to the CompactDisks table from the ItemNumber field in the Tracks table?

SQL uses dot notation to make this distinction. CompactDisks.ItemNumber is the full specification for the ItemNumber field in the CompactDisks table. Tracks.ItemNumber specifies its counterpart in the Tracks table.

When joining two tables, the convention is to use the full specification for table and field name. Figure 10-47 dissects an SQL query that joins two WebMusic tables.

FIGURE 10-47
The JOIN command links the CompactDisks and Tracks tables to produce the CD name, cover, price, and tracks for item number Wea56690-1.

SELECT CompactDisks.CDName,

CompactDisks.CDCover,

CompactDisks.DiscountPrice,

Tracks.TrackTitle

FROM CompactDisks JOIN Tracks on

CompactDisks.ItemNumber =

Tracks.ItemNumber

WHERE CompactDisks.ItemNumber = 'Wea56690-1'

The SELECT clause specifies the fields that should appear. CompactDisks.CDName refers to the CDName field of the CompactDisks table.

The JOIN command links the CompactDisks and Tracks tables.

The tables are joined when the same data appears in the ItemNumber fields of records from the two tables.

The WHERE clause specifies that you want to see the Enya CD with item number Wea56690-1.

How extensive is SQL? In this section, you were introduced to some of the most commonly used SQL commands, and you explored how they might be used in the context of an e-commerce music business. SQL is a very extensive and powerful language that can be used not only to manipulate data, but also to create databases, tables, and reports. Because SQL is one of the most popular database tools, many computer professionals consider SQL fluency an essential career skill.

QUICKCHECK......SECTION D

1. SQL [_____] include SELECT, FROM, and INSERT.

2. The term "parameter" refers to detailed specifications for a command. True or false? [_____]

3. AND, OR, and NOT are examples of [_____] operators and are used to specify relationships between search criteria.

4. In SQL, the DATA command adds fields to a database. True or false? [_____]

5. To search for data in a specific field, you can use the SQL command [_____].

6. The SQL [_____] command can change the data in a specified field in one or more records.

7. In SQL, the JOIN command allows you to add fields to a database. True or false? [_____]

 CHECK ANSWERS

10

TECHTALK

DATA ANALYSIS

Databases contain a wealth of information. What many people don't realize is that a database often contains more information than it holds in its fields and records. Consider an order-entry database. Hidden in the order details is a complete history of sales trends over the life span of the database. Customer records contain marketing data that can be broken down by region, state, or city. This "hidden" information can be revealed by a technique called data analysis. This TechTalk is designed to give you a basic understanding of data analysis concepts and methods.

What kinds of information can I find by using data analysis? Data analysis refers to the process of interpreting existing information to discover trends and patterns. It provides many kinds of information. Because it uses statistical tools to aggregate or sift through data, the process of data analysis can produce information that is not readily apparent from simply looking at "raw" data. Data analysis can produce useful information from summaries, predictions, and classifications.

■ **Summaries.** The simplest information found by data analysis is a summary of existing information. This includes reports such as all sports equipment sales by region over the past five years, the most popular destinations for Christmas travel versus Fourth of July travel broken down by state, or the 10 best-selling books in the $10.00 to $20.00 price range.

■ **Predictions.** More complex data analysis can reveal sequences of events that predict future trends and patterns (Figure 10-48). A furniture store might find that customers who purchase a sofa often buy a coffee table within three to six months. The store could use that information to target those customers who buy sofas, and market directly to them. For example, the store could send every sofa purchaser a coupon good for 25% off the price of a coffee table.

■ **Classifications.** Data analysis can also be used to classify information. A pizza delivery franchise can use data analysis to classify the areas where its pizza shops are located by gathering information on population densities, home prices, and number of working parents who are likely to order pizza for dinner. Knowing which classifications are most likely to produce high sales figures allows the chain to pinpoint the most desirable locations for new pizza shops.

The information produced by data analysis is highly valuable to decision makers. The success or failure of an organization can lie in its ability to accurately predict future events and patterns and make decisions based on those predictions. No one can see the future, but data analysis can help people make informed decisions about the future based on information about the past.

FIGURE 10-48

Data analysis can reveal trends hidden among the detailed data in a database.

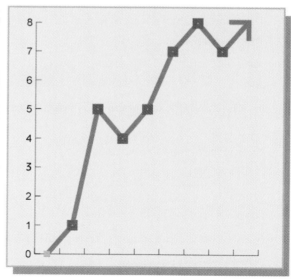

Does data analysis require a special type of information system?
Most data analysis methods fall under the broader scope of decision support systems. As described in Chapter 9, a decision support system, or DSS, provides decision makers with tools to analyze information. Today's decision support systems vary in their sophistication. Some offer only rudimentary tools for summarizing and extracting data, whereas others provide tools for complex data analysis.

Today's most advanced data analysis method is referred to as **OLAP** (online analytical processing). An OLAP system consists of computer hardware, database software, and analytical tools optimized for summarizing, consolidating, viewing, and synthesizing data.

The architecture of an OLAP system is usually not the same as transaction processing architecture. Broadly speaking, a transaction processing system (TPS) is optimized to provide maximum performance for inserting, updating, and deleting information from a database. In contrast, an OLAP system is used to analyze existing data, generate summaries, and expose patterns and trends in the data. Because the data in an OLAP system rarely changes, it makes more sense for an OLAP system to be optimized to quickly perform complex searches, calculate summaries, and produce aggregated data.

What methods are used to analyze information in an OLAP system?
Many OLAP systems support a data analysis technique called data mining. **Data mining** refers to the use of statistical tools for automated extraction of predictive information from large databases. For example, a store that sells kitchen equipment and cookbooks might notice that 50% of the people who buy *The New Sushi Cookbook* also buy rice cookers. Data mining is the method used to clarify some of these "hidden" relationships so that organizations can benefit from information that is not obvious. Data mining typically looks at the relationships between data along a single dimension. Decision makers who "mine data" seek an answer to the question, "How does X affect Y?" (or, in this example, "How does a cookbook purchase affect the purchase of cooking equipment?")

OLAP also allows decision makers to look for relationships between multiple data dimensions. For example, imagine a sales history database for a national bookstore. A typical OLAP query might retrieve the total sales of all nonfiction books for bookstores in Indiana in the month of January 2005. This query consists of three dimensions—the category of the book (nonfiction), the store location (Indiana), and the time period (January 2005).

The information used for OLAP queries is often represented as a data cube. A **data cube** is a three-dimensional model of the data in a database. Each dimension of a data cube corresponds to a dimension of the OLAP query, as shown in Figure 10-49.

INFOWEBLINKS

The **Data Analysis InfoWeb** provides links to OLAP, data mining, data warehouses, and multidimensional databases.

www.course.com/np/concepts8/ch10

FIGURE 10-49

A data cube represents data in multiple dimensions. This data cube has three dimensions—months, states, and book categories.

The black cube represents data for nonfiction books sold in Indiana in January 2005.

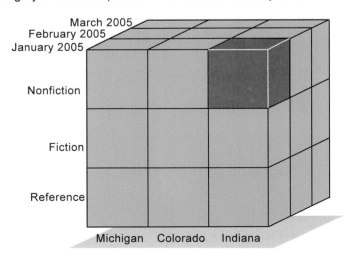

18

Does an OLAP system require a special type of database? The database used for an OLAP system is often referred to as a data warehouse. A **data warehouse**, or "information warehouse," is a collection of information organized for analysis. A data warehouse can contain data from only one database, but more often it contains information from a variety of sources. These sources include flat files, databases, spreadsheets, text files, and any other source of historical information an organization maintains. Data from these sources can be exported to a data warehouse, which is typically stored with the help of a relational database management system, or RDBMS.

The process of populating a data warehouse with data typically requires custom conversion routines. During the conversion, incomplete or inaccurate data is corrected or eliminated. For example, suppose customer information from a transaction processing system is being added to a data warehouse. If some customer records don't include a ZIP code, the conversion routine could attempt to find the correct ZIP code or simply discard records without ZIP codes. This process ensures that the data warehouse receives only customer information that is complete and accurate.

Depending on how the data warehouse is used, sometimes the conversion routines summarize information rather than convert all the raw data. For example, suppose a data warehouse is used to analyze sales by region. It might be necessary to store only the number of customers per ZIP code, in which case any "extra" customer information, such as name, address, and e-mail address, can be eliminated. Data can also be summarized by date. For example, a bookstore might include only the number of books sold per month by title, rather than the number of books on each particular invoice. These kinds of "shortcuts" in the conversion process make data analysis faster and more precise than if the analysis was performed on the raw data. Figure 10-50 summarizes the process of populating a data warehouse.

FIGURE 10-50

When data is moved into a data warehouse, conversion routines can summarize or change data before storing it.

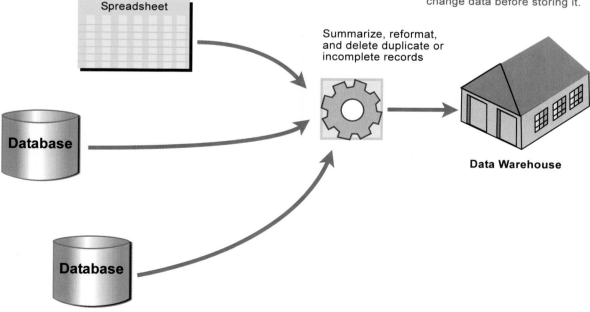

To facilitate the use of data cubes and multidimensional analysis, some OLAP systems are based on a **multidimensional database**, which provides built-in methods to display and store data in a multidimensional structure. Organizing data in a multidimensional database requires that all the data be converted into a multidimensional format. Because this process is often time consuming, many large OLAP systems retain information in an RDBMS. To support multidimensional analysis with an RDBMS, however, it is usually necessary to create additional tables to store aggregated and summarized data as well as dimension-specific data. With these additional tables, an RDBMS can essentially "mimic" an MDBMS (multidimensional database management system) for purposes of data analysis.

Can I use any DBMS for data analysis? Data analysis usually involves large amounts of data and complex queries. As a result, entry-level DBMSs usually don't include sophisticated data analysis tools, nor do they supply the speed to adequately support a data warehouse. However, most professional DBMSs include tools for data analysis. These tools offer sophisticated ways to convert and summarize information from a variety of sources, and query languages optimized for working with OLAP systems.

How is data analysis used today? The *MIT Technology Review* recently labeled data mining as one of the 10 emerging technologies that will "change the world." Data mining and other sophisticated data analysis techniques are useful tools in many fields. Scientists use data analysis to understand global warming trends. Economists use data mining to examine the relationships between consumer spending patterns and various factors such as military action and technology innovations. It is also used to develop risk tables for insurance companies and develop profiles of loan defaulters (for example, they tend to write loan applications in pencil) for banks.

Data analysis also has controversial uses, such as profiling terrorists according to their nationality, religion, background, and activities. Controversy also exists over Google's Gmail plan to offer free e-mail service to subscribers who are willing to let Google computers scan their e-mail content to help with more targeted advertising. Privacy advocates are concerned with the potential misuse of data analysis to assemble and market profiles on individuals.

QUICKCHECK........TECHTALK

1. A(n) [_____] system is optimized to quickly perform complex searches, summarize data, and calculate aggregates.

2. Data [_____] refers to the use of statistical tools for automated extraction of predictive information from large databases.

3. A data [_____] is a three-dimensional model of OLAP data.

4. A data [_____] is a database that consists of information from a variety of sources organized and optimized for data analysis.

5. An entry-level DBMS does not typically include analysis tools, nor does it supply the speed to adequately support a data warehouse. True or false?
[_____]

18

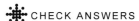 CHECK ANSWERS

ISSUE

PRIVACY

You might be astonished by the amount of information stored about you in computer databases. Your bank has information on your financial status, credit history, and the people, organizations, and businesses to which you write checks. School records indicate something about your ability to learn and the subjects that interest you. Medical records indicate the state of your health. Credit card companies track the places you shop and what you purchase in person, by mail, or on the Web. Your phone company stores your phone number, your address, and a list of the phone numbers you dial. The driver's license bureau has your physical description. Your Internet cookies track many of the Web sites you frequent. By compiling this data—a process sometimes referred to as "profiling"—an interested person or company could guess some very private things about you, such as your political views or even your sexual orientation.

When records were stored on index cards and in file folders, locating and distributing data constituted a laborious process that required hand transcriptions or photocopies of piles of papers. Today, this data exists in electronic format and is easy to access, copy, sell, ship, consolidate, and alter.

Privacy advocates point out the potential for misusing data that has been collected and stored in computer databases. A University of Miami law professor, A. Michael Froomkin, writes that it is becoming increasingly possible to "assemble an individual data profile of extraordinary detail by cross referencing multiple, extensive databases. These profiles have uses in commerce, in law-enforcement; some applications are benign, some less so."

In response to terrorist threats, the Pentagon is working on a controversial project called Terrorist Information Awareness (TIA) designed to mine data from databases that store information about passports, visas, work permits, car rentals, airline reservations, arrests, bank accounts, school grades, medical history, and fingerprints. Government data miners cite patterns in the activities of the September 11 hijackers and believe that data mining could uncover terrorists. Privacy advocates note, however, that every data set contains patterns. The big question is whether any set of seemingly innocent activities, such as credit card purchases, can be correlated with impending terrorist acts.

The potential for error and privacy violation in the Terrorist Information Awareness project is sobering. According to an editorial in *Scientific American*, "Suppose that there are 1,000 terrorists in the U.S. and that the data-mining process has an amazing 99 percent success rate. Then 10 of the terrorists will probably still slip through—and 2.8 million innocent people will also be fingered." The editorial goes on to suggest that broad dragnets, such as data mining, are less likely to work than more targeted solutions, such as inspecting trucks that enter sensitive areas and beefing up airplane cockpit doors.

Privacy advocates are encouraging lawmakers to closely monitor government snooping and restrict private-sector sale and distribution of information about individuals. Some legislation is in place for certain private-sector institutions. For example, the 1999 Financial Services Modernization Act requires financial institutions to supply clients with an annual notice explaining how personal information is collected and shared. This legislation also requires financial institutions to provide a way for clients to opt out of such information exchanges.

Legislation passed by the U.S. Congress in 2001 established regulations to protect the confidentiality of medical records by requiring a patient's consent before medical information can be disclosed. Health insurance companies, doctors, pharmacists, and other health care providers must provide patients with notification that explains how personal medical information may be used and what patient rights are under the new privacy regulation. Generally, patients are asked to sign a document stating that they received this notification.

The issue of privacy is not simple. Information about you is not necessarily "yours." Although you might "reveal" information about yourself on an application form, other information about you is collected without your direct input. For example, suppose you default on your credit card payments. The credit card company has accumulated information on your delinquent status. Shouldn't it have the freedom to distribute this information, for example, to another credit card company?

People are not always unwilling victims of privacy violations. Many individuals knowingly let companies gather profiling information to get free products. For example, thousands of people signed up for Google's Gmail service even though they knew their e-mail messages could be scanned to develop marketing profiles.

Unfortunately, private information can be garnered from your computer without your permission. Spyware is a type of software containing code that tracks personal information from your computer and passes it on to third parties, without your authorization or knowledge. Spyware might be embedded in an application that you download, or it can download itself from unscrupulous Web sites—a process called a "driveby download."

Databases containing personal information do offer positive benefits. For example, many Web surfers appreciate the shortcuts offered by software agents that assemble a customer profile in order to recommend books, CDs, videos, news articles, and other targeted goods and services. These users might willingly give up some measure of privacy for the convenience afforded by these agents. For another example, the LEXIS-NEXIS database has been used for several socially beneficial activities, such as locating heirs to estates, reuniting family members, finding pension beneficiaries, and tracing the influence of personal donations in politics.

The electronic privacy issue appears to be heading toward some type of compromise between strict privacy and wholesale collection/distribution of personal data. Check out the Privacy InfoWeb for more information on the issue as well as tips and computer programs you can use to protect your privacy online.

INFOWEBLINKS

You'll find lots more information about privacy issues at the **Privacy InfoWeb**.

www.course.com/np/concepts8/ch10

⊔⊔⊞⩑⊤ DO YOU THINK?

1. Do you think data about you should be distributed only after your permission is obtained? ⭕Yes ⭕ No ⭕ Not sure

2. Can you identify an actual incident when you discovered that data about you was distributed without your approval? ⭕Yes ⭕ No ⭕ Not sure

3. Do you think the information you provide on paper forms is more private than information you enter into Web-based forms? ⭕Yes ⭕ No ⭕ Not sure

4. Have you thought about ways to protect your privacy? ⭕Yes ⭕ No ⭕ Not sure

 SAVE RESPONSES

18

COMPUTERS IN CONTEXT

MEDICINE

The heath care industry was an early adopter of computer technology for traditional data processing applications, such as client billing and employee payroll. A computer's ability to process and store thousands of records helps reduce hospital administrative costs. Linking hospital billing to health insurance companies streamlines cumbersome manual procedures for submitting insurance claims. These "behind-the-scenes" applications do not, however, directly affect the quality of health care, where computer technology has recently made a significant contribution.

Until recent years, paper charts dangled from the foot of every hospital bed and additional information was stored in thick file folders in nursing stations or the hospital's medical records department. Patient records include doctors' diagnoses, laboratory test results, medication schedules, and charts depicting a patient's vital signs. The process of maintaining these paper-based records is time consuming and quite open to errors. Effective treatments might be dangerously delayed while a slip of paper that holds laboratory results wends its way through the hospital corridors. In a hospital where a patient's condition can change suddenly and unexpectedly, health care providers need instant and ubiquitous access to the information contained in the patient's record.

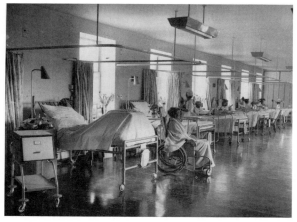

Today, technology allows hospitals to store patient records in computer databases that are instantly accessible to doctors, nurses, and other health care workers. A nurse can access a patient's record from a computer in the nursing station to check care instructions and enter vital statistics. Doctors can access a patient's record from an office or home computer to check progress, order tests, and make decisions when minutes count. Lab technicians can enter test results immediately into a patient's record. Patient records tie into a comprehensive hospital information system (HIS) that integrates just about every aspect of hospital management. Even the hospital dietitian can access relevant parts of a patient's record to work out menus that fit a patient's dietary needs, while avoiding allergies.

According to Ray Kurzweil, "medicine is among the most knowledge-intensive professions." Most doctors agree that medicine has grown too complex to have all the answers "in their heads." Today, in just about every aspect of their practices, doctors use computer applications and Internet technologies.

At one time, doctors dictated the results of an examination or surgical procedure. The dictated notes were later transcribed into computer records by staff members. Today's technology allows doctors to enter this information directly into computerized patient records by typing or by dictating into a speech recognition system that digitally converts the spoken word into computer text.

The Internet supplies physicians with many informational and diagnostic resources. Health libraries provide online access to reference databases, such a MEDLINE, and medical reference books, such as *Stat Ref*. Doctors use drug databases to choose appropriate medications, avoid dangerous drug interactions, determine correct dosages, and print out prescriptions. One pediatrician says, "I use the computer to make sure the medicine will work with any other medicines the patient takes, the patient won't be allergic, and to check for warnings about certain foods or alcohol."

The Internet's ability to rapidly disseminate information worldwide makes it a crucial tool for tracking global health threats. During the SARS outbreak in 2003, Web sites maintained by the World Health Organization (WHO) and Centers for Disease Control (CDC) provided statistics on the spread of infection. They also kept doctors, researchers, and reporters up to date on efforts to identify the virus, develop a vaccine, and devise treatment options.

Many doctors use Internet technology to communicate with their colleagues via e-mail and send imaging data, such as X-rays, to specialists. Telemedicine uses communications links to supply medical services at a distance. It can be used to provide specialty medical services to rural patients, and allow medical personnel from several locations to collaborate on patient diagnosis and treatment.

Once limited to telephone consultations and fax transmission of paper-based patient records, today telemedicine takes full advantage of the Internet to transfer electronic patient records, still images, and even full motion video sequences. Images from diverse sources, such as x-rays, MRIs, and CT scans, stored in the standard DICOM (Digital Imaging and Communications in Medicine) format, can be easily transferred over the Internet and displayed using a single software package.

Computers have become an integral part of modern medical equipment. The use of x-rays was a huge medical breakthrough in the early 1900s, but x-rays capture only a two-dimensional image. A technology called CT (computerized tomography) essentially assembles a series of x-ray images taken from slightly different angles. A computer works with the data to generate a three-dimensional image that can be rotated and viewed from any angle.

Computers, data, and telecommunications technology team up in a number of mobile medical devices that have revolutionized emergency medical services. An EMS worker describes a device used to monitor suspected heart attack patients: "We can do a comprehensive 12-lead EKG at the scene and the computer inside the LifePak 12 tells us what kind of arrhythmia we may be dealing with and even gives us suggestions for treatments."

Today, most patients want to be informed participants in their health care team. Patients use the Web to find information on diseases, drugs, and treatment options. Doctors frequently recommend health-related Web sites and support groups to patients. Patients can gather information from these sites at their own pace and refer back to it as necessary. The availability of information on the Web reduces the need for doctors to make lengthy explanations that patients often cannot absorb or remember during an office visit.

The computer's use in medicine is not without potential pitfalls. Online patient records raise issues of confidentiality. Many patients are concerned about unauthorized access to their records by employers, Human Resources staff, and hackers.

The Health Insurance Portability and Accountability Act (HIPAA) requires insurance companies to protect the privacy of its policy holders from inappropriate use or disclosure. Insurance company employees are allowed to look at clients' personal health information only in the course of administering claims. Insurance companies are not allowed to disclose personal health information to any other company or to a client's employer without permission. Insurance companies are, however, allowed to divulge information to government agencies if a serious threat to public health and safely exists. HIPAA also gives patients the right to amend incorrect or missing information in their records, and it allows clients to request a list of the disclosures.

The next time you're in a hospital or doctor's office, look around for computers. You're sure to find these essential tools used to improve the effectiveness of health care.

INFOWEBLINKS

You can find more information for this Computers in Context topic at the **Computers and Medicine InfoWeb**.

www.course.com/np/concepts8/ch10

INTERACTIVE SUMMARY

To review important concepts from this chapter, fill in the blanks to best complete each sentence. When using the NP8 BookOnCD, click the Check Answers buttons to automatically score your answers. Place your Tracking Disk in the floppy disk drive if you want to save your scores.

A database is a collection of information, typically stored as computer files. Computer databases evolved from manual file processing technology in which data is stored in a single _____ file that uses a uniform format for every item the file contains. A _____ holds the smallest unit of meaningful information. A series of data fields forms a _____, which stores data about one entity—a person, place, thing, or event.

Each kind of record is referred to as a record type. A record that contains data is sometimes referred to as a record _____. A _____ file contains only one record type. In contrast, a _____ can contain a variety of different record types.

In a database, records can be related by one-to-_____ relationships, one-to-many relationships, or many-to-many relationships. The number of associations that can exist between two record types is referred to as _____. Relationships can be depicted graphically by using _____-relationship diagrams.

_____ databases allow only one-to-many relationships. _____ databases allow one-to-many and many-to-many relationships. _____ databases exist as a series of tables that can be related by common fields. The relationships between these tables can be added, changed, or deleted on demand. An object-oriented database stores data in objects that can be grouped into _____ and defined by attributes and methods.

✦ CHECK ANSWERS

Flat files can be created and manipulated by using a variety of tools, including word processing and spreadsheet software. For databases composed of more than one record type, however, it is best to use a database management system, which is abbreviated as _____.

An entry-level database management system typically handles many simultaneous searches, but has limited capability to deal with multiple simultaneous updates. Handling billions of records and performing hundreds of transactions every second require database _____ software.

The data in a database can be accessed via the Web. A simple process called _____ Web publishing converts a database report into an HTML document, which can be displayed by a browser. More sophisticated _____ Web publishing produces data from a database on demand. HTML forms and XForms not only provide search capabilities, but can also be used to add or modify data in a database with a Web browser. _____ documents provide a Web-based data management tool that uses special tags as field names within a document.

✦ CHECK ANSWERS

The first step in designing a relational database is to define its fields by specifying a field name and data type. Integer, date, and _____ data types are used for fields containing data that might be mathematically manipulated. The _____ data type is used for fixed-length fields containing text that is not intended to be mathematically manipulated. The _____ data type is a variable-length field for entering text. The _____ data type is used to store true/false or yes/no data. The _____ data type can be used to store URLs. The _____ data type is used to store binary data, such as MP3 files or graphics. When designing fields, a database designer can also include field formats, field _____ rules, and lookup routines to reduce data entry errors.

The number of tables in a database can be determined by a process called _____, which helps a database designer group fields into record types and avoid data redundancy. A database designer must also consider how to sort or index records. The _____ key for a table specifies the order in which records are stored and indicates where new records are inserted in a table. A database _____ provides an alternative way to organize records, using a series of keys and pointers to temporarily arrange data without affecting the physical sequence of records specified by the sort order. A database designer might also be responsible for designing the database user interface and report templates as well as the conversion routines for loading the initial set of data into the database.

CHECK ANSWERS

SQL is a database query language that typically works behind the scenes as an intermediary between the database _____ software provided to users and the database itself. Although the specifications for searches and other database tasks are collected by easy-to-use graphical user interfaces, those specifications are converted into SQL _____, which can communicate directly with the database.

An SQL query contains SQL _____, such as SELECT, FROM, INSERT, JOIN, and WHERE, plus _____ that specify the details of the command. Records can be removed from a database using the SQL _____ command. Records can be added to a table using the SQL _____ command. To search for data, you can use the SQL _____ command. To change or replace the data in a field requires the SQL _____ command. SQL also provides a _____ command that can be used to temporarily consolidate two tables so that data can be accessed simultaneously from both of them.

CHECK ANSWERS

18

INTERACTIVE KEY TERMS

Make sure you understand all the boldfaced key terms presented in this chapter. If you're using the NP8 BookOnCD, you can use this list of terms as an interactive study activity. First, try to define a term in your own words, and then click the term to compare your definition with the definition presented in the chapter.

Attribute, 520
BLOB, 535
Boolean operators, 549
Cardinality, 517
Case sensitive database, 536
Child node, 519
Computed field, 535
Conversion routine, 544
Data analysis, 554
Data cube, 555
Data dependence, 524
Data independence, 524
Data mining, 555
Data redundancy, 537
Data type, 534
Data warehouse, 556
Database, 514
Database client software, 526
Database index, 539
Database server software, 526
Database structure, 533
Date data type, 534
DBMS, 525
DELETE, 547
Distributed database, 526
Dynamic Web publishing, 528
Entity-relationship diagram, 518
Field, 514
Field format, 536

Field name, 514
Field validation rule, 536
Fixed-length field, 514
Flat file, 517
Global update, 551
Hierarchical database, 519
Hyperlink data type, 535
INSERT, 548
Integer data type, 534
JOIN, 552
Joining tables, 552
Logical data type, 534
Lookup routine, 537
Many-to-many relationship, 517
Member, 519
Memo data type, 534
Multidimensional database, 557
Network database, 519
Network set, 519
Node, 519
Normalization, 537
Object-oriented database, 521
OLAP, 555
One-to-many relationship, 517
One-to-one relationship, 518
OODBMS, 525
Owner, 519
Parameter, 548
Parent node, 519

Primary key, 534
RDBMS, 525
Real data type, 534
Record, 515
Record occurrence, 516
Record type, 516
Relational database, 520
Relationship, 517
Report generator, 542
Report template, 542
Root node, 519
SELECT, 549
Server-side program, 528
Sort key, 539
Sort order, 539
SQL, 546
SQL keywords, 547
SQL query, 546
Static Web publishing, 527
Structured file, 514
Table, 520
Text data type, 534
Tuple, 520
UPDATE, 551
Variable-length field, 514
XForms, 529
XML DBMS, 525

INTERACTIVE SITUATION QUESTIONS

Apply what you've learned to some typical computing situations. When using the NP8 BookOnCD, you can type your answers, and then use the Check Answers button to automatically score your responses. Place your Tracking Disk in the floppy disk drive if you want to save your scores.

1. You're working for a company that's just getting started with a database project. The boss wants "the most standard kind of database," so you recommend using ⬚ database management software.

2. You are analyzing a company's customer and order information. Because each customer can place multiple orders, you know this is a(n) ⬚ -to-many relationship.

3. You are designing a record type that holds customer information. You should use a(n) ⬚ data type for the fields that hold information such as telephone numbers and Social Security numbers because although this data looks like numbers, you'll never need to use it to perform mathematical calculations.

4. You are creating a movie review database, and one field stores the "star rating" that a popular reviewer gave each movie. Movies are rated from one to four stars, so the "Stars" field is valid only if the number is between 1 and 4. To ensure that nobody enters a value below 1 or above 4, you can use a field ⬚ rule to filter the data as it's entered into the table.

5. You want to print a professionally designed list of all the records in your database. To organize and format the list, you use a report generator to create a reusable report ⬚.

6. You own a fly-fishing shop and maintain an inventory database that, along with inventory data, stores the names of the wholesalers from which

you buy each item. Hot Rod Wholesalers just changed its name to Northern Rod and Reel, so you need to update your database. The best way to accomplish this task would be to perform a(n) ⬚ update that changes every instance of "Hot Rod Wholesalers" to "Northern Rod and Reel."

7. You are designing the structure for a mail-order catalog company. You recognize that a many-to-many relationship exists between an order and the items listed on the order. That clue indicates that you should separate the data into two ⬚, one called Orders and the other called OrderDetails.

8. Your friend is working on some Web pages, and you notice that they contain tags such as <editor>Ella Ellison</editor>

<born>1960/05/26</born>

You surmise that your friend is using ⬚ instead of HTML.

 CHECK ANSWERS

INTERACTIVE PRACTICE TESTS

Practice tests that consist of 10 multiple-choice, true/false, and fill-in-the-blank questions are available on both the NP8 BookOnCD and the NP8 Web site. The questions are selected at random from a large test bank, so each time you take a test, you'll receive a different set of questions. Your tests are scored immediately, and you can print study guides that help you find the correct answers for any questions that you missed.

 CLICK TO START

REVIEW

ON THE WEB

PROJECTS

An NP8 Project is an open-ended activity that helps you apply the concepts you have learned. Many projects require resources in addition to your textbook, such as current magazines, library materials, or Web access. When you tackle a project, be prepared to use your critical thinking skills, logical analysis, and creativity. Projects for this chapter include:

- **Issue Research: Protecting Your Privacy**
- **DMV**
- **Computers in Medicine**

- **Normalization**
- **Toy Store**

To work with the Projects for this chapter, connect to the **New Perspectives NP8 Web Site.**

www.course.com/np/concepts8/ch10

TECHTV VIDEO PROJECT

The TechTV segment, *Controversial Digital Bouncers Track Bar Patrons in Canadian City*, explains a controversial use of databases. After watching this video clip, write a short summary of what it had to say about this database's pros and cons. Then provide your own reaction to this use of database technology.

To work with the Video Projects for this chapter, connect to the **New Perspectives NP8 Web Site.**

www.course.com/np/concepts8/ch10

STUDY TIPS

Study Tips help you to organize and consolidate the information in a chapter by making lists, outlines, charts, and sketches. You can use paper and pencil or word processing software to complete most of the Study Tips.

To work with the Study Tips for this chapter, connect to the **New Perspectives NP8 Web Site.**

www.course.com/np/concepts8/ch10

ONLINE GAMES

Test your comprehension of the concepts introduced in Chapter 10 by playing the NP8 Online Games. At the end of each game, you have three options:

- Print a comprehensive study guide complete with page references
- Print your results to be submitted to your instructor
- Save your results to be submitted to your instructor via e-mail

To work with the Online Games for this chapter, connect to the **New Perspectives NP8 Web Site.**

www.course.com/np/concepts8/ch10

STUDENT EDITION LABS

Extend your knowledge of databases with the Chapter 10 Student Edition Lab.

The following Student Edition Lab is offered with Chapter 10:

• **Advanced Databases**

Go to the NP8 New Perspectives Web site for specific lab topics.

To work with the Chapter 10 Student Edition Lab and its corresponding lab assignment, connect to the **New Perspectives NP8 Web Site**.

www.course.com/np/concepts8/ch10

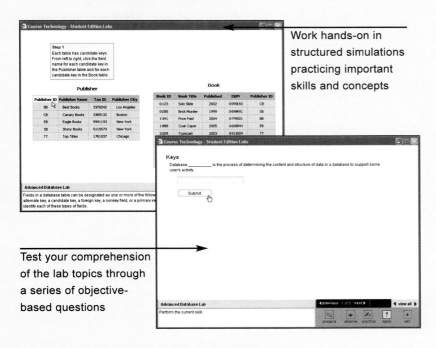

Work hands-on in structured simulations practicing important skills and concepts

Test your comprehension of the lab topics through a series of objective-based questions

Track Your Progress with the Student Edition Labs

• Student Edition Labs test your comprehension of the lab topics through a series of trackable objective-based questions. Your instructor will direct you to either print your results or submit them via e-mail.

• Student Edition Lab Assignments, available on the New Perspectives NP8 Web site, require you to apply the skills learned through the lab in a live environment. Go to the New Perspectives NP8 Web site for detailed instruction on individual Student Edition Lab Assignments.

If you have a SAM user profile, you have access to even more interactive content. Log in to your SAM account and go to your assignments page to see what your instructor has assigned for this chapter.

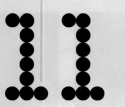

11

COMPUTER PROGRAMMING

CONTENTS

TIP

When using the BookOnCD, the ❋ icons are "clickable" to access resources on the CD. The ✚ icons are clickable to access resources on the Web. You can also access Web resources by using your browser to connect directly to the NP8 New Perspectives Web site at:

www.course.com/np/concepts8/ch11

CHAPTER PREVIEW

Before you begin Chapter 11, you can use the Web-based preview activities to hear an overview of the chapter, check your current level of expertise about key concepts, and look through a list of learning objectives. You can access the preview activities by clicking the icon when using the BookOnCD or going to the New Perspectives NP8 Web site.

CHAPTER OVERVIEW

A computer without software is like a VCR without tapes, a car without gas, or a swimming pool without water. It is pretty much useless, unless you use it as a doorstop. So where does software come from and how is it created? Get your book and highlighter ready, then connect to the New Perspectives NP8 Web site where you can listen to an overview that points out the most important concepts for this chapter about computer programming.

www.course.com/np/concepts8/ch11

CHAPTER PRE-ASSESSMENT

How much do you know about computer programmers and programming languages? To gauge your level of knowledge before beginning the chapter, take the pre-assessment quiz at the New Perspectives NP8 Web site. Armed with your results from this quiz, you can focus your study time on concepts that will round out your knowledge of computer programming and improve your test scores.

www.course.com/np/concepts8/ch11

LEARNING OBJECTIVES

When you complete this chapter you should be able to:

- Describe the role of computer programmers and software engineers

- Categorize today's popular computer programming languages by generation and paradigm

- Explain the process of planning, coding, and testing a computer program

- Describe the advantages and disadvantages of generic text editors, program editors, and VDEs for coding computer programs

- Define the term algorithm and describe how it relates to procedural programming

- Identify various tools that programmers use to plan programs, such as flowcharts, structured English, pseudocode, UML diagrams, and decision tables

- Follow the control structures for a procedural program

- Describe the major concepts of object-oriented programming, such as objects, classes, inheritance, messages, methods, polymorphism, and encapsulation

- Create some basic facts and rules using Prolog syntax

- Describe how a declarative language, such as Prolog, satisfies goals by instantiation

A detailed list of learning objectives is provided at the New Perspectives NP8 Web site

www.course.com/np/concepts8/ch11

11

SECTION A

PROGRAMMING BASICS

Even if you are not planning to become a computer programmer or software engineer, you are likely to use many computer programs during your career. When you realize that your word processing software contains in excess of 750,000 lines of code, you can understand how a few bugs might exist. You can also understand why you would not want to undertake the task of writing word processing software on your own—that project is best left to professional programming teams. Although you would not typically write the productivity software you use, you might have the opportunity to participate in the development of software applications that are specific to your needs. Understanding the basics of computer programming will help you constructively plan and productively participate in the development process.

COMPUTER PROGRAMMING AND SOFTWARE ENGINEERING

What is program code? As you learned in earlier chapters, a computer program is a set of step-by-step instructions that tell a computer how to solve a problem or carry out a task. The instructions that make up a computer program are sometimes referred to as **code**, probably because program instructions for first-generation computers were entered as binary codes. Coding refers to entering the list of commands that become a computer program. Today, program code contains familiar English-like words. Figure 11-1 illustrates the code for a short program that converts feet and inches into centimeters.

FIGURE 11-1

A typical computer program consists of lines of code that tell a computer how to solve a problem or carry out a task. This program is written in a computer programming language called Pascal.

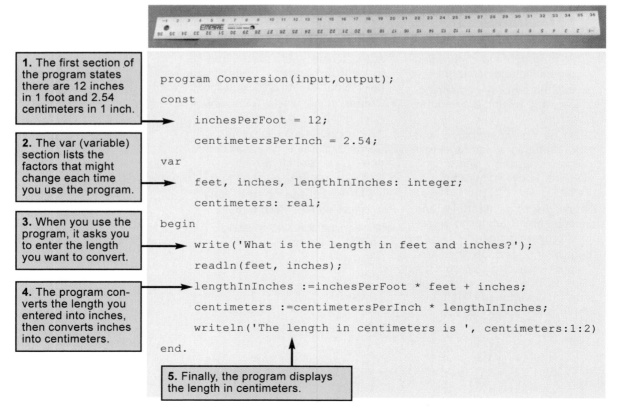

1. The first section of the program states there are 12 inches in 1 foot and 2.54 centimeters in 1 inch.

2. The var (variable) section lists the factors that might change each time you use the program.

3. When you use the program, it asks you to enter the length you want to convert.

4. The program converts the length you entered into inches, then converts inches into centimeters.

```pascal
program Conversion(input,output);
const
     inchesPerFoot = 12;
     centimetersPerInch = 2.54;
var
     feet, inches, lengthInInches: integer;
     centimeters: real;
begin
   write('What is the length in feet and inches?');
   readln(feet, inches);
   lengthInInches :=inchesPerFoot * feet + inches;
   centimeters :=centimetersPerInch * lengthInInches;
   writeln('The length in centimeters is ', centimeters:1:2)
end.
```

5. Finally, the program displays the length in centimeters.

A computer program is typically stored as a file and transferred into RAM when needed, but a computer program can also be embedded in computer hardware—in a ROM chip, for example. As explained in Chapter 3, a computer program can exist as a single module that provides all the instructions necessary for a software application, device driver, or operating system. Alternatively, a computer program might consist of several modules that form a software application or operating system.

How big is a typical computer program? Compared to commercial application software, the programs that you'll work with in this chapter are relatively tiny. By Department of Defense standards, a "small" program is one with fewer than 100,000 lines of code. A "medium-sized" program is one with 100,000 to 1 million lines. A "large" program is one with more than 1 million lines. Research has shown that, on average, one person can write, test, and document only 20 lines of code per day. It is not surprising, then, that most commercial programs are written by programming teams and take many months or years to complete.

Who creates computer programs? The people who develop computer programs are referred to as computer programmers ("programmers" for short) or software engineers. A computer programmer typically focuses on coding computer programs, whereas software engineers tend to focus on designing and testing activities (Figure 11-2).

What's the difference between computer programming and software engineering? The term **computer programming** encompasses a broad set of activities that include planning, coding, testing, and documenting. Most computer programmers participate to some extent in all of these phases of program development, but focus on the coding process.

Software engineering is a development process that uses mathematical, engineering, and management techniques to reduce the cost and complexity of a computer program while increasing its reliability and modifiability. It can be characterized as more formalized and rigorous than computer programming. It is used on large software projects where cost overruns and software errors might have disastrous consequences.

Some software engineering activities overlap with the systems analysis and design activities presented in Chapter 9. To distinguish between the two, remember that systems analysis and design encompass all aspects of an information system, including hardware, software, people, and procedures. In contrast, software engineering tends to focus on software development.

FIGURE 11-2

Like a computer programmer, a software engineer designs, codes, tests, and documents software, but tends to focus on designing and testing activities.

Software engineers approach these activities using formalized techniques based on mathematical proofs, computer science research, and engineering theory. For example, a computer programmer might code a search routine by simply instructing the computer to step through a list looking for a match.

In contrast, a software engineer might consider several sophisticated methods for implementing the search, and select the one that provides the greatest efficiency based on the computer architecture and the data being processed.

11

PROGRAMMING LANGUAGES AND PARADIGMS

What is a programming language? A **programming language**, or "computer language," is a set of keywords and grammar rules designed for creating instructions that a computer can ultimately process or carry out. Most people are familiar with some names of programming languages, such as BASIC, C, Pascal, FORTRAN, Java, and COBOL. But many other programming languages, such as 8088 assembly, FORTH, LISP, and APL, remain relatively unknown to the general public.

Just as an English sentence is constructed from various words and punctuation that follow a set of grammar rules, each instruction for a computer program consists of keywords and parameters that are held together by a set of rules. A **keyword**, or "command," is a word with a predefined meaning for the compiler or interpreter that translates each line of program code into machine language. Keywords for the Pascal computer language include WRITE, READ, IF...THEN, and GOSUB.

Keywords can be combined with specific **parameters**, which provide more detailed instructions for the computer to carry out. Keywords and parameters are combined with punctuation according to a series of rules called **syntax**, as shown in Figure 11-3.

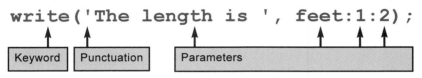

FIGURE 11-3

An instruction for a computer program consists of keywords and parameters, formed into sentence-like statements according to a set of syntax rules.

How are programming languages categorized? Programming languages are categorized in several ways. They can be divided into two major categories: low-level languages and high-level languages. They are also categorized by generation and by paradigm.

What is a low-level language? A **low-level language** typically includes commands specific to a particular CPU or microprocessor family. Low-level languages require a programmer to write instructions for the lowest level of the computer's hardware—that is, for specific hardware elements, such as the processor, registers, and RAM locations. Low-level languages include machine languages and assembly languages.

What is a high-level language? A **high-level language** uses command words and grammar based on human languages to provide what computer scientists call a "level of abstraction" that hides the underlying low-level assembly or machine language. High-level languages, such as COBOL, BASIC, Java, and C, make the programming process easier by replacing unintelligible strings of 1s and 0s or cryptic assembly commands with understandable commands, such as PRINT and WRITE. High-level language commands eliminate many lines of code by substituting a single high-level command for multiple low-level commands (Figure 11-4).

High-level Pascal command	Low-level assembly commands

`Total:=5+4`	`LDA 5`
	`STA Num1`
	`LDA 4`
	`ADD Num1`
	`STA Total`
	`END`

FIGURE 11-4

A single high-level command does the work of multiple low-level commands.

How did programming evolve from low-level to high-level languages? The first computers were programmed without programming languages. Technicians rewired a computer's circuitry to prepare it for various processing tasks (Figure 11-5). The idea of storing programs in computer memory paved the way for computer programming languages, which allowed a programmer to write a series of commands and load them into the computer for execution. Programming languages were very primitive at first, but they evolved through many generations into the computer languages of today.

What was the first generation of programming languages? Machine languages were the first languages available for programming computers and, therefore, they are sometimes referred to as **first-generation languages**. A **machine language** consists of a set of commands, represented as a series of 1s and 0s, corresponding to the instruction set that is hardwired into the circuitry of a microprocessor.

A machine language is specific to a particular CPU or microprocessor family. For example, the machine language that is hardwired into a Pentium 4 processor includes many unique commands that are not wired into older PC 8088 microprocessors or Macintosh-based PowerPC microprocessors. Although machine languages still work on today's computers, programmers rarely use machine languages to write programs.

What is a second-generation language? An **assembly language** allows programmers to use abbreviated command words, called op codes, such as LDA for "load," rather than the 1s and 0s used in machine languages. At the time assembly languages were first introduced, they were hailed as a significant improvement over machine languages, and came to be known as **second-generation languages**.

Like a machine language, an assembly language is classified as a low-level language because it is machine specific—each assembly language command corresponds on a one-to-one basis to a machine language instruction. As you might expect, the assembly language instructions for a Pentium 4 microprocessor differ from those for an 8088 or a PowerPC microprocessor. An assembly language is useful when a programmer wants to directly manipulate what happens at the hardware level. Today, programmers typically use assembly languages to write system software, such as compilers, operating systems, and device drivers.

What is a third-generation language? When high-level languages were originally conceived in the 1950s, they were dubbed **third-generation languages** because they seemed a major improvement over machine and assembly languages. Third-generation languages used easy-to-remember command words, such as PRINT and INPUT, to take the place of several lines of assembly language op codes or endless strings of machine language 0s and 1s. Third-generation languages, such as COBOL and FORTRAN, were used extensively for business and scientific applications. Pascal and BASIC were popular teaching languages. C remains popular today for system and application software development, for example to develop Microsoft Windows and Linux.

Many computer scientists believed that third-generation languages would eliminate programming errors. Errors certainly became less frequent, and program development time decreased significantly. Programmers using third-generation languages still made a variety of errors, however, so computer language development continued to progress.

FIGURE 11-5

Technicians programmed the first computers by changing the circuitry.

11

What is a fourth-generation language? In 1969, computer scientists began to develop high-level languages, called **fourth-generation languages**, which more closely resemble human languages, or "natural languages," than do third-generation languages. Fourth-generation languages, such as SQL and RPG-I, eliminate many of the strict punctuation and grammar rules that complicate third-generation languages. Today, fourth-generation languages are typically used for database applications. A single SQL command, such as SORT TABLE Kids on Lastname, can replace many lines of third-generation code, as shown in Figure 11-6.

FIGURE 11-6

A single command written in a fourth-generation language can replace many lines of third-generation code.

```
SORT TABLE Kids on Lastname
```

```
PUBLIC SUB Sort(Kids As Variant, inLow As Long, inHi As Long)
    DIM pivot   As Variant
    DIM tmpSwap As Variant
    DIM tmpLow  As Long
    DIM tmpHi   As Long
    tmpLow = inLow
    tmpHi = inHi
     pivot = Kids((inLow + inHi) \ 2)
    WHILE (tmpLow <= tmpHi)
       WHILE (Kids(tmpLow) < pivot And tmpLow < inHi)
          tmpLow = tmpLow + 1
       WEND
       WHILE (pivot < Kids(tmpHi) And tmpHi > inLow)
          tmpHi = tmpHi - 1
       WEND
     IF (tmpLow <= tmpHi) THEN
          tmpSwap = Kids(tmpLow)
          Kids(tmpLow) = Kids(tmpHi)
          Kids(tmpHi) = tmpSwap
          tmpLow = tmpLow + 1
          tmpHi = tmpHi - 1
       END IF
    WEND
    IF (inLow < tmpHi) THEN Sort Kids, inLow, tmpHi
    IF (tmpLow < inHi) THEN Sort Kids, tmpLow, inHi
END SUB
```

What about fifth-generation languages? In 1982, a group of Japanese researchers began work on a fifth-generation computer project that used Prolog—a computer programming language based on a declarative programming paradigm, which is described in detail later in the chapter. Prolog and other declarative languages became closely identified with the fifth-generation project and were classified by some experts as **fifth-generation languages**. Other experts disagree with this classification and instead define fifth-generation languages as those that allow programmers to use graphical or visual tools to construct programs, instead of typing lines of code. You'll learn more about visual programming later in the chapter.

What is the best programming language? Hundreds of programming languages exist, and each has unique strengths and weaknesses. Although it might be possible to select the best language for a particular project, most computer scientists would find it difficult to agree on one all-time "best" language. The table in Figure 11-7 on the next page briefly describes some of the programming languages discussed in this chapter.

INFOWEBLINKS

Programmers can choose from a wide array of programming languages. You can learn more about the most popular languages by visiting the **Programming Languages InfoWeb**.

www.course.com/np/concepts8/ch11

FIGURE 11-7 Selected Programming Languages

Ada: A high-level programming language developed under the direction of the Department of Defense and originally intended for military applications.

APL (A Programming Language): Scientific language used to manipulate tables of numbers.

BASIC (Beginner's All-purpose Symbolic Instruction Code): Developed by John Kemeny and Thomas Kurtz in the mid-1960s; simple, interactive programming language.

C: Developed in the early 1970s by Dennis Ritchie at Bell Laboratories; used today for a wide range of commercial software.

C++ and **C#**: Languages derived from C that provide object-oriented (OO) capabilities.

COBOL (COmmon Business Oriented Language): Procedural language developed in the early 1960s and used extensively for mainframe business applications.

CPL (Combined Programming Language): A language developed in the 1960s for scientific and commercial programming.

Eiffel: An advanced OO language developed in 1988 with syntax similar to C.

FORTRAN (FORmula TRANslator): One of the original third-generation languages, FORTRAN was developed in the 1950s and is still used today for scientific applications.

Haskell: A functional programming language named for the mathematician Haskell Brooks Curry.

Java: A high-level C++ derivative developed by Sun Microsystems and used extensively for Web-based programming.

LISP (LISt Processing): Developed in 1959 by famed AI researcher John McCarthy, LISP is used for artificial intelligence applications.

Pascal: Named in honor of Blaise Pascal, who invented one of the first mechanical adding machines, Pascal is a third-generation language developed to teach students programming concepts.

PL/1 (Programming Language 1): A complex business and scientific language developed in 1964 by IBM that combines FORTRAN, COBOL, and ALGOL.

Prolog (PROgramming in LOGic): Declarative language developed in 1972 and used for artificial intelligence applications.

RPG (Report Program Generator) and **RPG-II**: An IBM programming platform introduced in 1964 for easily generating business reports.

Scheme: A dialect of LISP, used for computer research and teaching.

SIMULA (SIMUlation LAnguage): Believed to be the first object-oriented programming language.

Smalltalk: Classic object-oriented programming language developed by Xerox researchers in 1980.

Visual Basic: Windows-based software development kit created by Microsoft in the early 1990s that assists programmers in developing Windows-based applications.

What is a programming paradigm? In addition to being classified by level and by generation, programming languages can also be classified by paradigm. Programmers approach problems in different ways. Whereas one programmer might focus on the steps required to complete a specific computation, another programmer might focus on the data that forms the basis for the computation. The phrase **programming paradigm** refers to a way of conceptualizing and structuring the tasks a computer performs. Quite a number of programming paradigms exist, and they are not mutually exclusive. A programmer might use techniques from multiple paradigms while planning and coding a program.

Some programming languages support a single paradigm. Other programming languages—referred to as **multiparadigm languages**—support more than one paradigm. Figure 11-8 provides a brief description of today's most popular programming paradigms. Sections B, C, and D of this chapter give you a detailed look at three classic paradigms—procedural, object-oriented, and declarative.

FIGURE 11-8
Programming Paradigms

Paradigm	Languages	Description
Procedural	BASIC, Pascal, COBOL, FORTRAN, Ada	Emphasizes linear, step-by-step algorithms that provide the computer with instructions on how to solve a problem or carry out a task
Object-oriented	Smalltalk, C++, Java	Formulates programs as a series of objects and methods that interact to perform a specific task
Declarative	Prolog	Focuses on the use of facts and rules to describe a problem
Functional	LISP, Scheme, Haskell	Emphasizes the evaluation of expressions, called "functions"
Event-driven	Visual Basic, C#	Focuses on selecting user interface elements and defining event-handling routines that are triggered by various mouse or keyboard activities

11

PROGRAM PLANNING

How does a programmer plan a computer program? Suppose a group of market analysts—or even a group of hungry students—wants to determine which pizza shop offers customers the best deal. Problems you might try to solve using a computer often begin as questions—for example, "Which pizza place has the best deal?" But such questions might not be stated in a way that helps you devise a method for a computer to arrive at an answer.

A question like "Which pizza place has the best deal?" is vague. It does not specify what information is available or how to determine the best deal. Do you know the price of several pizzas at different pizza places? Do you know the sizes of the pizzas? Do you know how many toppings are included in each price? What does "best deal" mean? Is it merely the cheapest pizza? Is it the pizza that gives you the most toppings for the dollar? Is it the biggest pizza you can get for the $24.63 that you and your friends managed to scrape together? The programming process begins with a problem statement that helps you clearly define the purpose of a computer program.

What is a problem statement? In the context of programming, a **problem statement** defines certain elements that must be manipulated to achieve a result or goal. A good problem statement for a computer program has three characteristics:

■ It specifies any assumptions that define the scope of the problem.

■ It clearly specifies the known information.

■ It specifies when the problem has been solved.

Study Figure 11-9 and see if you can formulate a problem statement that is better than the initial vague question, "Which pizza place has the best deal?"

FIGURE 11-9

Which pizzeria offers the best deal?

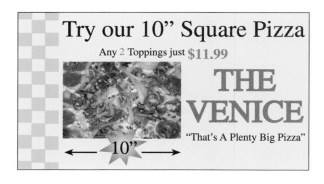

What is an assumption? In a problem statement, an **assumption** is something you accept as true in order to proceed with program planning. For example, with the pizza problem, you can make the assumption that you want to compare two pizzas. Furthermore, you can assume that some pizzas are round and others are square. To simplify the problem, you might also assume that none of the pizzas are rectangular—that is, none will have one side longer than the other. This assumption simplifies the problem because you need to deal only with the "size" of a pizza, rather than the "length" and "width" of a pizza. A fourth assumption for the pizza problem is that the pizzas you compare have the same toppings. Finally, you can assume that the pizza with the lowest cost per square inch is the best buy.

How does "known information" apply to a problem statement? The **known information** in a problem statement is the information that you supply to the computer to help it solve a problem. For the pizza problem, the known information includes the prices, shapes, and sizes of pizzas from two pizzerias. The known information is often included in the problem statement as "givens." For example, a problem statement might include the phrase, "given the prices, shapes, and sizes of two pizzas... ."

How can a problem statement specify when a problem is solved? After identifying the known information, a programmer must specify how to determine when the problem has been solved. Usually this step means specifying the output you expect. Of course, you cannot specify the answer in the problem statement. You won't know, for example, whether VanGo's Pizzeria or The Venice has the best deal before you run the program, but you can specify that the computer should output which pizza is the best deal.

Suppose that the best deal means getting the biggest pizza at the lowest price; in other words, the best deal is the pizza that has the lowest price per square inch. In this case, a pizza that costs 5¢ per square inch is a better deal than a pizza that costs 7¢ per square inch. The problem is solved, therefore, when the computer has calculated the price per square inch for both pizzas, compared the prices, and printed a message indicating which one has the lower price per square inch. You could write this part of the problem statement as, "The computer will calculate the price per square inch of each pizza, compare the prices, then print a message indicating which pizza has the lower price per square inch."

FIGURE 11-10
Pizza Problem Statement

What's the problem statement for the pizza program? You can incorporate your assumptions, known information, and expected output into a problem statement, such as the one in Figure 11-10.

Assuming that there are two pizzas to compare, that both pizzas contain the same toppings, and that the pizzas could be round or square, and given the prices, shapes, and sizes of the two pizzas, the computer will print a message indicating which pizza has the lower price per square inch.

Does the problem statement provide sufficient planning to begin coding? Formulating a problem statement provides a minimal amount of planning, which is sufficient for only the simplest programs. A typical commercial application requires far more extensive planning, which includes detailed program outlines, job assignments, and schedules. To some extent, program planning depends on the language and paradigm used to code a computer program. Program planning tools, such as flowcharts, structured English, pseudocode, UML diagrams, and decision tables, are discussed in Sections B, C, and D of this chapter.

Regardless of the tools used, when planning is complete, programmers can begin coding, testing, and documenting.

PROGRAM CODING

How do I code a computer program? The process of coding a computer program depends on the programming language you use, the programming tools you select, and the programming paradigm that best fits the problem you're trying to solve. Programmers typically use a generic text editor, a program editor, or a VDE to code computer programs.

What is a generic text editor? A **generic text editor** (or simply a "text editor") is any word processor that can be used for basic text editing tasks, such as writing e-mail, creating documents, or coding computer programs. Notepad, an accessory program supplied with Microsoft Windows, is one of

11

the most popular generic editors used for programming PCs. When using a generic editor to code a computer program, you simply type in each instruction. The lines of code are stored in a file, which can be opened and modified using the usual editing keys. Figure 11-11 shows the use of a generic text editor to enter program code.

CLICK TO START

FIGURE 11-11
A text editor such as Notepad allows programmers to enter lines of code using a familiar word processing interface.

What is a program editor? A **program editor** is a type of text editor specially designed for entering code for computer programs. These editors are available from several commercial, shareware, and freeware sources. Features vary, but can include helpful programming aids, such as keyword colorizing, word completion, keyboard macros, and search/replace, as shown in Figure 11-12.

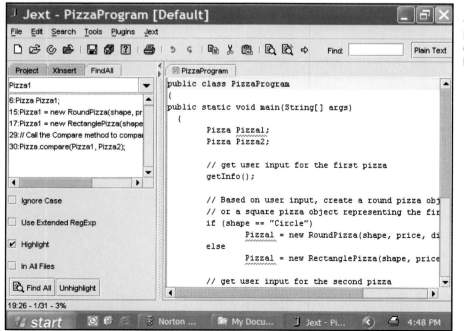

FIGURE 11-12
The Jext program editor is specially designed for entering code for computer programs.

What is a VDE? A **VDE** (visual development environment) provides programmers with tools to build substantial sections of a program by pointing and clicking rather than typing lines of code. A typical VDE is based on a **form design grid** that a programmer manipulates to design the user interface for a program.

By using various tools provided by the VDE, a programmer can add objects, such as controls and graphics, to the form design grid. In the context of a VDE, a **control** is a screen-based object whose behavior can be defined by a programmer. Frequently used controls include menus, toolbars, list boxes, text boxes, option buttons, check boxes, and graphical boxes. Figure 11-13 shows a form design grid and illustrates a variety of controls that can be added.

FIGURE 11-13
A form design grid is an important part of a VDE. This form was designed for the pizza program using Visual Basic.

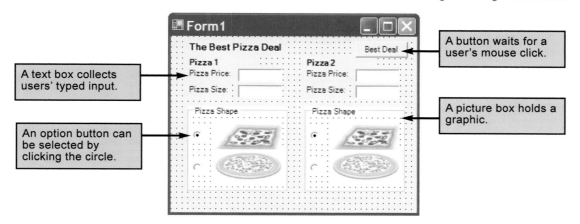

A text box collects users' typed input.

An option button can be selected by clicking the circle.

A button waits for a user's mouse click.

A picture box holds a graphic.

A control can be customized by specifying values for a set of built-in **properties**. For example, a button control can be customized for the pizza program by selecting values for properties such as shape, color, font, and label (Figure 11-14).

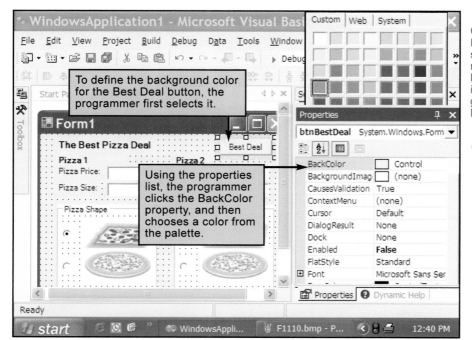

To define the background color for the Best Deal button, the programmer first selects it.

Using the properties list, the programmer clicks the BackColor property, and then chooses a color from the palette.

FIGURE 11-14
Controls, such as the Best Deal button, can be selected by a programmer from a properties list. Here a programmer is selecting the background color for the Best Deal button.

CLICK TO START

In a visual development environment, each control comes with a predefined set of events. Within the context of programming, an **event** is defined as an action, such as a click, drag, or key press, associated with a form or control. A programmer can select the events that apply to each control. For example, a programmer might decide that pizza program users will be allowed to left-click either the Round Pizza or Square Pizza button in each Pizza Shape box. Users will not be allowed to right-click, double-click, or drag these buttons, however.

An event usually requires the computer to make some response. Programmers write **event-handling code** for the procedures that specify how the computer responds to each event. For example, if a user clicks an icon depicting a round pizza, an event-handling procedure might set a variable called pizzashape equal to "round." When a user clicks the Best Deal button, another event-handling procedure must perform the calculations to determine which pizza is the best deal. Event-handling code is usually entered using a program editor supplied by the visual development environment. Figure 11-15 illustrates how event-handling code works.

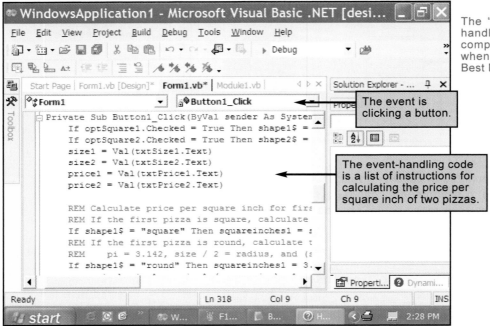

FIGURE 11-15
The "Best Deal" event-handling code tells the computer what to do when users click the Best Deal button.

Is a visual development environment better than an editor? A programmer's choice of development tools depends on what is available for a particular programming language and the nature of the programming project. Although visual development environments are available for several of today's most popular languages, VDEs are not available for every programming language. Microsoft Visual Basic was one of the first programming languages to feature a visual development environment. Today, VDEs are also available for programming languages such as C++, C#, Java, and Prolog.

Generic text editors and program editors provide a fine tool set for programs with minimal user interfaces. Many so-called "back-end applications," such as device drivers, middleware, and scripts embedded in HTML documents, require little or no user interaction and, therefore, can be created just as easily with an editor as with a visual development environment.

A visual development environment is a powerful tool for programming software applications for GUI environments, such as Windows. Most GUI applications are "event-driven," which means that when launched, the program's interface appears on the screen and waits for the user to initiate an event by clicking a menu, dragging an object, double-clicking an icon, typing text, or clicking a button. The fact that the sequence of user actions cannot be predicted introduces a level of complexity that doesn't fit well with traditional programming languages, which tend to approach programs as a fixed sequence of procedures.

Visual development environments have spawned an approach to programming that is sometimes referred to as the **event-driven paradigm**, in which a programmer develops a program by selecting user interface elements and specifying event-handling routines. The programmer is never required to deal with the overall program sequence because the VDE automatically combines user interface elements and event-handling routines into a file that becomes the final computer program. This event-driven paradigm can significantly reduce development time and simplify the entire programming process.

PROGRAM TESTING AND DOCUMENTATION

How does a programmer know if a program works? A computer program must be tested to ensure that it works correctly. Testing often consists of running the program and entering test data to see whether the program produces correct results. If testing does not produce the expected results, the program contains an error, sometimes called a "bug." This error must be corrected, and then the program must be tested again and again until it runs error-free.

What can cause program errors? When a program doesn't work correctly, it is usually the result of an error made by the programmer. A **syntax error** occurs when an instruction does not follow the syntax rules, or grammar, of the programming language. For example, the BASIC command `If AGE = 16 Then "You can drive."` produces a syntax error because the command word PRINT is missing. The correct version of the command is `If AGE = 16 Then Print "You can drive."` Syntax errors are easy to make, but they are usually also easy to detect and correct. Figure 11-16 lists some common syntax errors.

Another type of program bug is a **runtime error**, which, as its name indicates, shows up when you run a program. Some runtime errors result from instructions that the computer can't execute. The BASIC instruction `DiscountPrice = RegularPrice/0` produces a runtime error because dividing by 0 is a mathematically impossible operation that the computer cannot perform.

Some runtime errors are classified as logic errors. A **logic error** is an error in the logic or design of a program, such as using the wrong formula to calculate the area of a round pizza. Logic errors can be caused by an inadequate definition of the problem or an incorrect formula for a calculation, and are usually more difficult to identify than syntax errors.

How do programmers find errors? Programmers can locate errors in a program by reading through lines of code, much like a proofreader. They can also use a tool called a **debugger** to step through a program and monitor the status of variables, input, and output. A debugger is sometimes packaged with a programming language or can be obtained as an add-on.

FIGURE 11-16
Common Syntax Errors

■ Omitting a keyword, such as THEN

■ Misspelling a keyword, such as PIRNT

■ Omitting required punctuation, such as a period

■ Using incorrect punctuation, such as a colon where a semicolon is required

■ Forgetting to close parentheses

11

Do computer programs contain any special documentation? Anyone who uses computers is familiar with program documentation in the form of user manuals and help files. Programmers also insert documentation called **remarks** or "comments" into the program code. Remarks are identified by language-specific symbols, such as // in Java, or keywords, such as Rem in BASIC.

Remarks are useful for programmers who want to understand how a program works before modifying it. For example, suppose you are assigned to make some modifications to a 50,000-line program that calculates income tax. Your task would be simplified if the original programmer included remarks that identify the purpose of each section of the program and explain the basis for any formulas used to perform tax calculations.

A well-documented program contains initial remarks that explain its purpose and additional remarks in any sections of a program where the purpose of the code is not immediately clear. For example, in the pizza program, the purpose of the expression `3.142 * (size1 / 2) ^2` might not be immediately obvious. Therefore, it would be helpful to have a remark preceding the expression, as shown in Figure 11-17.

FIGURE 11-17

A series of remarks in a BASIC program can explain to programmers the method used to calculate the square inches in a round pizza.

```
Rem  The program calculates the number of square inches

Rem  in a round pizza using the formula pi r squared

Rem  pi = 3.142, size/2 = radius,

Rem  and (size/2)^2 = radius squared

Rem  SquareInches = 3.142*(size/2)^2
```

QUICKCHECK......SECTION A

1. The instructions that make up a computer program are sometimes referred to as code. True or false? [   ]

2. Software [   ] plan and develop computer software using formalized techniques based on mathematical proofs, computer science research, and engineering theory.

3. A programming language typically supports one or more programming [   ], such as procedural, object-oriented, or declarative.

4. [   ]-generation programming languages, such as COBOL and FORTRAN, use easy-to-remember command words.

5. A(n) [   ] development environment provides programmers with tools to build substantial sections of a program by pointing and clicking.

6. Programmers can use software called a(n) [   ] to step through a program and find errors.

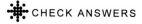 CHECK ANSWERS

LAB 11-A

USING A VISUAL DEVELOPMENT ENVIRONMENT

In this lab, you'll learn:

- To use the basic tools provided by the Visual Basic VDE

- How to work with a form design grid

- How to select controls, such as buttons, menus, and dialog boxes, for the graphical user interface of a computer program

- The way that a visual development environment displays properties for a control

- How to set properties that modify the appearance and operation of a control

- About the variety of events that can affect a control

- How to add code that specifies how a control responds to events

- How to add a component to the Visual Basic toolbox, and then incorporate it into a program

- How to save and test a program

- How to compile a program and run the executable version

LAB ASSIGNMENTS

1. Start the interactive part of the lab. Insert your Tracking Disk if you want to save your QuickCheck results. Perform each lab step as directed, and answer all the lab QuickCheck questions. When you exit the lab, your answers are automatically graded and your results are displayed.

2. Draw a sketch of the main screen of your favorite word processing program. Identify five controls (such as menus, toolbars, lists, buttons, and scroll bars) provided by the programmer. Describe the external events (such as clicks, double-clicks, right-clicks, and mouseovers) to which each control responds.

3. Suppose you are preparing to write a program that calculates the number of calories you burn while exercising. The program requires users to enter their weight, the distance travelled, and the elapsed time in minutes from the beginning of the exercise to the end. Users should also be able to select from the following types of exercises: jogging, walking, swimming, and bicycling. After these calculations are entered, users should click a Calculate button to display the results of the calorie calculation. A Clear button should allow users to enter a new set of weight, distance, and time data. Sketch a form design grid like the one you used in the lab, and indicate where you would place each control necessary for this program's user interface.

INTERACTIVE LAB

CLICK TO START THE LAB

11

PROCEDURAL PROGRAMMING

Early approaches to computer programming were based on writing step-by-step instructions for the computer to follow. This technique is still in widespread use today and provides an easy starting point for learning what programming is all about. In this section, the examples are written in BASIC because it is one of the easiest programming languages to grasp.

ALGORITHMS

What is procedural programming? The traditional approach to programming uses a **procedural paradigm** (sometimes called an "imperative paradigm") to conceptualize the solution to a problem as a sequence of steps. A program written in a procedural language typically consists of self-contained instructions in a sequence that indicates how a task is to be performed or a problem is to be solved.

A programming language that supports the procedural paradigm is called a **procedural language**. Machine languages, assembly languages, COBOL, FORTRAN, C, and many other third-generation languages are classified as procedural languages. Procedural languages are well suited for problems that can be easily solved with a linear, or step-by-step, algorithm. Programs created with procedural languages have a starting point and an ending point. The flow of execution from the beginning to the end of a program is essentially linear—that is, the computer begins at the first instruction and carries out the prescribed series of instructions until it reaches the end of the program.

What is an algorithm? An **algorithm** is a set of steps for carrying out a task that can be written down and implemented. For example, the algorithm for making a batch of macaroni and cheese is a set of steps that includes boiling water, cooking the macaroni in the water, and making a cheese sauce (Figure 11-18). The algorithm is written down, or expressed, as instructions in a recipe. You can implement the algorithm by following the recipe instructions.

An important characteristic of a correctly formulated algorithm is that carefully following the steps guarantees that you can accomplish the task for which the algorithm was designed. If the recipe on a macaroni package is a correctly formulated algorithm, by following the recipe, you should be guaranteed a successful batch of macaroni and cheese.

How do I write an algorithm? An algorithm for a computer program is a set of steps that explains how to begin with known information specified in a problem statement and how to manipulate that information to arrive at a solution. Algorithms are usually written in a format that is not specific to a particular programming language. This approach allows you to focus on formulating a correct algorithm, without becoming distracted by the detailed

FIGURE 11-18

The algorithm for making macaroni and cheese is expressed as a recipe.

syntax of a computer programming language. In a later phase of the software development process, the algorithm is coded into instructions written in a programming language so that a computer can implement it.

How do I figure out an algorithm? To design an algorithm, you might begin by recording the steps you take to solve the problem manually. If you take this route with the pizza problem, you must obtain initial information about the cost, size, and shape of each pizza. The computer also needs this initial information, so part of your algorithm must specify how the computer gets it. When the pizza program runs, it should ask the user to enter the initial information needed to solve the problem. Your algorithm might begin like this:

> **Ask the user for the shape of the first pizza and hold it in RAM as Shape1.**
>
> **Ask the user for the price of the first pizza and hold it in RAM as Price1.**
>
> **Ask the user for the size of the first pizza and hold it in RAM as Size1.**

Next, your algorithm should specify how to manipulate this information. You want the computer to calculate the price per square inch, but a statement like "Calculate the price per square inch" neither specifies how to do the calculation, nor deals with the fact that you must perform different calculations for square and round pizzas. A more appropriate set of statements for the algorithm is shown in Figure 11-19.

INFOWEBLINKS

Donald Knuth's multivolume collection of programming algorithms, called *The Art of Computer Programming*, is considered one of the best scientific monographs of the twentieth century. You'll find information about this book and more at the **Algorithms InfoWeb**.

www.course.com/np/concepts8/ch11

FIGURE 11-19

The algorithm for calculating the price per square inch must work for square pizzas as well as round ones.

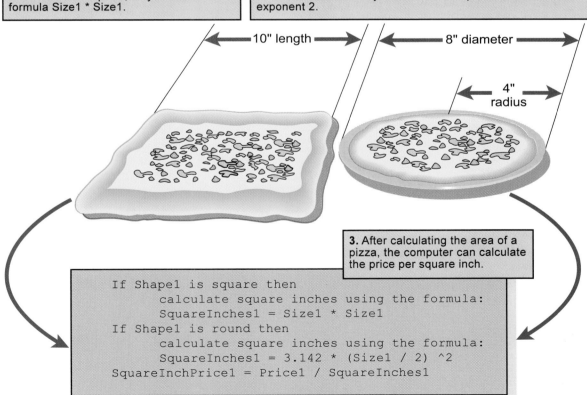

1. To calculate the area of a square pizza, multiply the length of one side by the length of the other side. The sides are the same size in a square, so you can use the formula Size1 * Size1.

2. To calculate the area of a round pizza, use the formula for the area of a circle: πr^2. π is approximately 3.142. r^2 is the square of the radius of the circle. The size of a pizza is its diameter, so you need to divide the diameter by 2 to get the radius, using Size1 / 2. Then you need to square the radius. ^2 is the notation that you use on a computer to indicate the exponent 2.

10" length

8" diameter

4" radius

3. After calculating the area of a pizza, the computer can calculate the price per square inch.

```
If Shape1 is square then
     calculate square inches using the formula:
     SquareInches1 = Size1 * Size1
If Shape1 is round then
     calculate square inches using the formula:
     SquareInches1 = 3.142 * (Size1 / 2) ^2
SquareInchPrice1 = Price1 / SquareInches1
```

11

So far, the algorithm describes how to calculate the price per square inch of one pizza. It should specify a similar process for calculating the price per square inch of the second pizza.

Finally, the algorithm should specify how the computer decides what to display as the solution. You want the computer to display a message indicating which pizza has the lowest square-inch cost, so your algorithm should include steps like the following:

> **If SquareInchPrice1 < SquareInchPrice2 then display the message "Pizza 1 is the best deal."**

> **If SquareInchPrice2 < SquareInchPrice1 then display the message "Pizza 2 is the best deal."**

But don't forget to indicate what you want the computer to do if the price per square inch is the same for both pizzas:

> **If SquareInchPrice1 = SquareInchPrice2 then display the message "Both pizzas are the same deal."**

The complete algorithm for the pizza problem is shown in Figure 11-20.

FIGURE 11-20
The algorithm for the pizza problem, written in structured English, has five main sections.

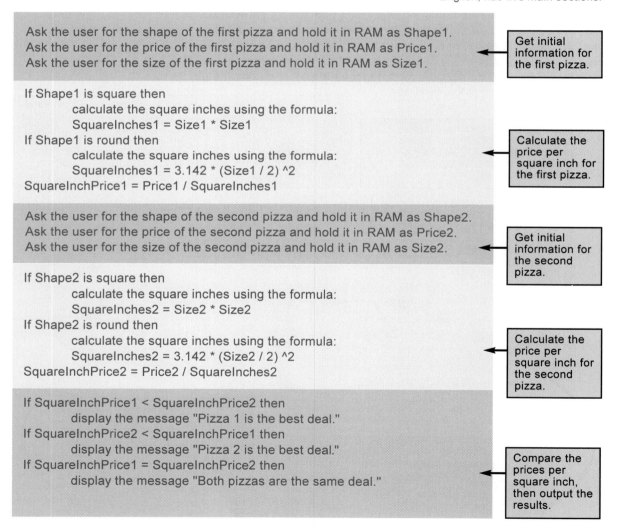

Ask the user for the shape of the first pizza and hold it in RAM as Shape1.
Ask the user for the price of the first pizza and hold it in RAM as Price1.
Ask the user for the size of the first pizza and hold it in RAM as Size1.

> Get initial information for the first pizza.

If Shape1 is square then
      calculate the square inches using the formula:
      SquareInches1 = Size1 * Size1
If Shape1 is round then
      calculate the square inches using the formula:
      SquareInches1 = 3.142 * (Size1 / 2) ^2
SquareInchPrice1 = Price1 / SquareInches1

> Calculate the price per square inch for the first pizza.

Ask the user for the shape of the second pizza and hold it in RAM as Shape2.
Ask the user for the price of the second pizza and hold it in RAM as Price2.
Ask the user for the size of the second pizza and hold it in RAM as Size2.

> Get initial information for the second pizza.

If Shape2 is square then
      calculate the square inches using the formula:
      SquareInches2 = Size2 * Size2
If Shape2 is round then
      calculate the square inches using the formula:
      SquareInches2 = 3.142 * (Size2 / 2) ^2
SquareInchPrice2 = Price2 / SquareInches2

> Calculate the price per square inch for the second pizza.

If SquareInchPrice1 < SquareInchPrice2 then
      display the message "Pizza 1 is the best deal."
If SquareInchPrice2 < SquareInchPrice1 then
      display the message "Pizza 2 is the best deal."
If SquareInchPrice1 = SquareInchPrice2 then
      display the message "Both pizzas are the same deal."

> Compare the prices per square inch, then output the results.

EXPRESSING AN ALGORITHM

What's the best way to express an algorithm? You can express an algorithm in several different ways, including structured English, pseudocode, and flowcharts. These tools are not programming languages, and they cannot be processed by a computer. Their purpose is to give you a way to document your ideas for program design.

Structured English is a subset of the English language with a limited selection of sentence structures that reflect processing activities. Refer to Figure 11-20 on the previous page to see how structured English can be used to express the algorithm for the pizza problem.

Another way to express an algorithm is with pseudocode. **Pseudocode** is a notational system for algorithms that has been described as a mixture of English and your favorite programming language. Pseudocode is less formalized than structured English, so the structure and wording are left up to you. Also, when you write pseudocode, you are allowed to incorporate command words and syntax from the computer language you intend to use for the actual program. Compare Figure 11-20 with Figure 11-21 and see if you can identify some of the differences between structured English and pseudocode.

INFOWEBLINKS

For additional examples of ways to express algorithms, connect to the **Pseudocode & Flowcharts InfoWeb**.

www.course.com/np/concepts8/ch11

FIGURE 11-21

Pseudocode for the pizza program mixes some English-like instructions, such as "display prompts," with programming commands, such as "input."

```
display prompts for entering shape, price, and size
input Shape1, Price1, Size1
if Shape1 = square then
        SquareInches1 ← Size1 * Size1
if Shape1 = round then
        SquareInches1 ← 3.142 * (Size1 / 2) ^2
SquareInchPrice1 ← Price1 / SquareInches1
display prompts for entering shape, price, and size
input Shape2, Price2, Size2
if Shape2 = square then
        SquareInches2 ← Size2 * Size2
if Shape2 = round then
        SquareInches2 ← 3.142 * (Size2 / 2) ^2
SquareInchPrice2 ← Price2 / SquareInches2
if SquareInchPrice1 < SquareInchPrice2 then
        output "Pizza 1 is the best deal."
if SquareInchPrice2 < SquareInchPrice1 then
        output "Pizza 2 is the best deal."
if SquareInchPrice1 = SquareInchPrice2 then
        output "Both pizzas are the same deal."
```

A third way to express an algorithm is to use a **flowchart**. A flowchart is a graphical representation of the way a computer should progress from one instruction to the next when it performs a task. The flowchart for the pizza program is shown in Figure 11-22 on the next page.

FIGURE 11-22
The pizza program flowchart illustrates how the computer should proceed through the instructions in the final program.

CLICK TO START ✣

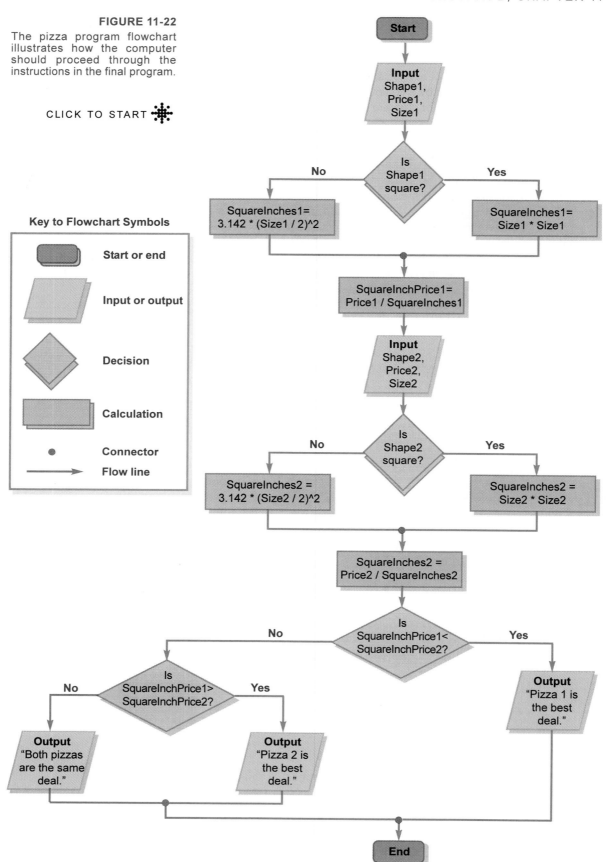

How do I know if my algorithm is correct? Before finalizing the algorithm for a computer program, you should perform a **walkthrough** to verify that your algorithm works. To perform a walkthrough for a simple program, you can use a calculator, paper, and pencil to step through a sample problem using realistic "test" data.

For more complex programs, a walkthrough might consist of a verbal presentation to a group of programmers who can help identify logical errors in the algorithm and suggest ways to make the algorithm more efficient. Figure 11-23 illustrates how to check the pseudocode for the pizza program.

FIGURE 11-23
Pseudocode Walkthrough

Pseudocode	Explanation
display prompts for entering shape, price, and size	User asked to enter the first pizza's shape, price, and size
input Shape1, Price1, Size1	User enters square, $10.00, 12

if Shape1 = square **then**
    SquareInches1 ← Size1 * Size1
if Shape1 = round **then**
    SquareInches1 ← 3.142 * (Size1 / 2) ^2
	The first pizza is square, so the computer calculates:
	12 * 12 = 144 for SquareInches1

SquareInchPrice1 ← Price1 / SquareInches1	The computer also calculates: $10.00/144 = .069 for SquareInchPrice1
display prompts for entering shape, price, and size	User asked to enter the second pizza's shape, price, and size:
input Shape2, Price2, Size2	User enters round, $10.00, 12

if Shape2 = square **then**
    SquareInches2 ← Size2 * Size2
if Shape2 = round **then**
    SquareInches2 ← 3.142 * (Size2 / 2) ^2
	The second pizza is round, so the computer calculates:
	$3.142*(12/2)^2 = 113.112$ for SquareInches2

SquareInchPrice2 ← Price2 / SquareInches2	The computer also calculates $10.00/113.112 = .088 for SquareInchPrice2

if SquareInchPrice1 < SquareInchPrice2 **then**
    output "Pizza 1 is the best deal."
if SquareInchPrice2 < SquareInchPrice1 **then**
    output "Pizza 2 is the best deal."
if SquareInchPrice1 = SquareInchPrice2 **then**
    output "Both pizzas are the same deal."
	.069 < .088 so pizza 1 is the best deal

11

SEQUENCE, SELECTION, AND REPETITION CONTROLS

How do I specify the order in which program instructions are performed by the computer? Unless you specify otherwise, sequential execution is the normal pattern of program execution. During **sequential execution**, the computer performs each instruction in the order it appears—the first instruction in the program is executed first, then the second instruction, and so on, to the last instruction in the program. Here is a simple program written in the BASIC computer language that outputs This is the first line., and then outputs This is the second line.

```
Print "This is the first line."
Print "This is the second line."
```

Is there an alternative to sequential execution? Some algorithms specify that a program must execute instructions in an order different from the sequence in which they are listed, skip some instructions under certain circumstances, or repeat instructions. **Control structures** are instructions that specify the sequence in which a program is executed. Most programming languages have three types of control structures: sequence controls, selection controls, and repetition controls.

A **sequence control structure** changes the order in which instructions are carried out by directing the computer to execute an instruction elsewhere in the program. In the following simple BASIC program, a GOTO command tells the computer to jump directly to the instruction labeled "Widget." By performing the GOTO statement, the program never carries out the command **Print "This is the second line."**

```
Print "This is the first line."
Goto Widget
Print "This is the second line."
Widget: Print "All done!"
End
```

The flowchart in Figure 11-24 shows how the computer follows a series of sequential commands, and then "jumps" past other commands as the result of a GOTO command.

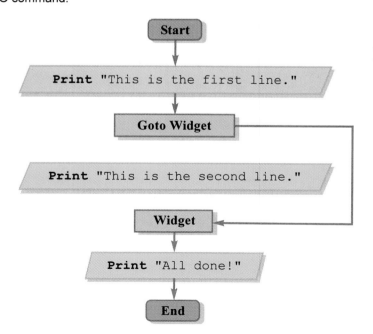

FIGURE 11-24

Executing a GOTO command directs the computer to a different part of the program.

CLICK TO START

Although it is the simplest control structure, the GOTO command is rarely used by skilled programmers because it can lead to programs that are difficult to understand and maintain. In 1968, the journal *Communications of the ACM* published a now-famous letter from Edsger Dijkstra, called "Go To Statement Considered Harmful." In his letter, Dijkstra explained that injudicious use of the GOTO statement in programs makes it difficult for other programmers to understand the underlying algorithm, which in turn means that such programs are difficult to correct, improve, or revise.

Experienced programmers prefer to use sequence controls other than GOTO to transfer program execution to a subroutine, procedure, or function. A **subroutine**, **procedure**, or **function** is a section of code that is part of a program, but is not included in the main sequential execution path. A sequence control structure directs the computer to the statements they contain, but when these statements have been executed, the computer neatly returns to the main program. Figure 11-25 shows the execution path of a program that uses the GOSUB command to transfer execution to a subroutine.

INFOWEBLINKS

Read Dijkstra's letter and find out why the GOTO command is considered bad programming at the **GOTO InfoWeb**.

www.course.com/np/concepts8/ch11

FIGURE 11-25

Executing a GOSUB command directs the computer to a different section of the program.

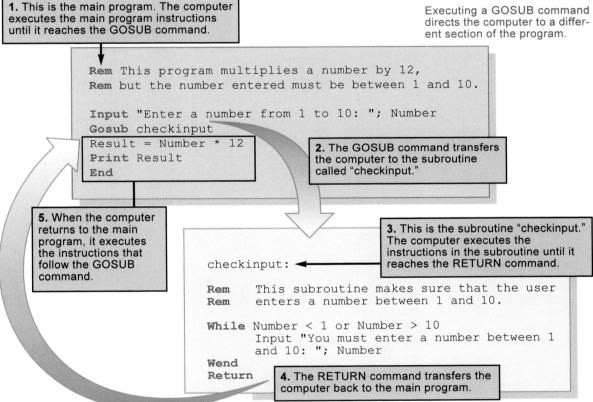

1. This is the main program. The computer executes the main program instructions until it reaches the GOSUB command.

```
Rem This program multiplies a number by 12,
Rem but the number entered must be between 1 and 10.

Input "Enter a number from 1 to 10: "; Number
Gosub checkinput
Result = Number * 12
Print Result
End
```

2. The GOSUB command transfers the computer to the subroutine called "checkinput."

5. When the computer returns to the main program, it executes the instructions that follow the GOSUB command.

3. This is the subroutine "checkinput." The computer executes the instructions in the subroutine until it reaches the RETURN command.

```
checkinput:

Rem    This subroutine makes sure that the user
Rem    enters a number between 1 and 10.

While Number < 1 or Number > 10
       Input "You must enter a number between 1
       and 10: "; Number
Wend
Return
```

4. The RETURN command transfers the computer back to the main program.

11

Can the computer make decisions while it executes a program? A **selection control structure**, also referred to as a "decision structure" or "branch," tells a computer what to do, based on whether a condition is true or false. A simple example of a selection control structure is the IF...THEN...ELSE command.

The following program uses this command to decide whether a number entered is greater than 10. If the number is greater than 10, the computer prints `That number is greater than 10`. If the number is not greater than 10, the program performs the ELSE instruction and prints `That number is 10 or less`.

```
Input "Enter a number from 1 to 10: "; Number
If Number > 10 Then Print "That number is greater than 10."
Else Print "That number is 10 or less."
End
```

Figure 11-26 uses a flowchart to illustrate how a computer follows commands in a decision structure.

FIGURE 11-26

The computer executes a decision indicated on the flowchart by the question in the diamond shape.

CLICK TO START

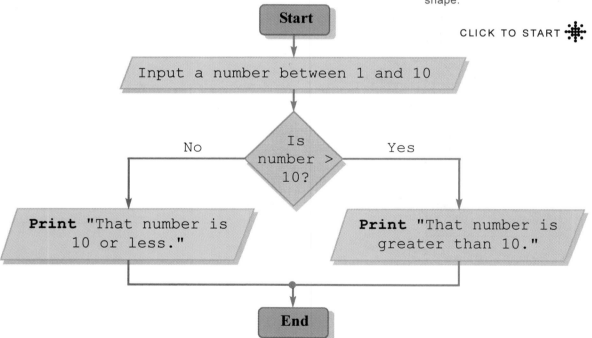

Can a computer automatically repeat a series of instructions? A **repetition control structure** directs the computer to repeat one or more instructions until a certain condition is met. The section of code that repeats is usually referred to as a **loop** or "iteration." Some of the most frequently used repetition commands are FOR...NEXT, DO...WHILE, DO...UNTIL, and WHILE...WEND.

The keyword FOR, DO, or WHILE marks the beginning of a loop. The keyword NEXT, UNTIL, or WEND (which means "while ends") marks the end of a loop. The following simple BASIC program uses a FOR...NEXT command to print a message three times:

```
For N = 1 to 3

   Print "There's no place like home."

Next N

End
```

Follow the path of program execution in Figure 11-27 to see how a computer executes a series of commands in a repetition structure.

FIGURE 11-27

To execute a loop, the computer repeats one or more commands until some condition indicates that the looping should stop.

CLICK TO START

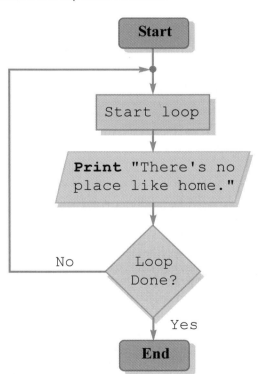

To get a better idea of how a FOR...NEXT loop works, pretend that you're the computer executing the FOR...NEXT instructions below. You can use the box labeled N in the margin as a RAM location. As the computer, you would also have a screen on which to display output—use the Screen Output box. Now, walk through the loop.

```
For N = 1 to 3
   Print "There's no place like home."
Next N
End
```

1. As the computer, the first time you see the instruction `For N = 1 to 3`, you set N equal to 1. To do so, write the number 1 in the N box in the margin.

2. You would then execute the next instruction, `Print "There's no place like home."` To do so, write the phrase "There's no place like home." in the Screen Output box.

N

3. The instruction `Next` sends you back to the command `For N = 1 to 3`. Because this occasion is the second time you have executed this statement, put a 2 in the N box in the margin (you can erase the 1 that was there previously).

4. You must check whether the value in box N is greater than 3. Why? Because the command `For N = 1 to 3` means you can continue to loop only if N is 3 or less. N is only 2, so you can proceed.

5. Go to the next instruction, which is `Print "There's no place like home."` Write this sentence again in the Screen Output box.

Screen Output

6. Moving on, you reach the `Next` statement again, which sends you back to the For statement.

7. Continue by changing the value in the N box to 3. Check the N box to make sure it does not contain a value greater than 3. It doesn't, so continue.

8. The next line instructs you to `Print "There's no place like home."` Write this sentence again in the Screen Output box. The `Next` statement sends you back to the For statement. Increase the value in the N box to 4. This time when you check whether the value in N is greater than 3, it is. That means the loop is complete, and you should jump to the statement past the end of the loop.

9. The next statement is `End`, so you've completed the program.

How do I use control structures to write a program? To write the code for the pizza program, you use the control structures, keywords, and syntax provided by your programming language. The completed pizza program, written in BASIC, is provided in Figure 11-28.

FIGURE 11- 28

Each line of code for the pizza program consists of keywords (shown in blue) and parameters.

```
Rem The Pizza Program
Rem This program tells you which of two pizzas is the best deal
Rem    by calculating the price per square inch of each pizza.
Rem Collect initial information for first pizza.
Input "Enter the shape of pizza 1:"; Shape1$
Input "Enter the price of pizza 1:"; Price1
Input "Enter the size of pizza 1:"; Size1

Rem Calculate price per square inch for first pizza.
Rem If the first pizza is square, calculate square inches by multiplying one side
Rem    by the other.
If Shape1$ = "square" Then SquareInches1 = Size1 * Size1
Rem If the first pizza is round, calculate the number of square inches where
Rem    pi = 3.142, size / 2 = radius, and (size / 2) ^2 = radius squared.
If Shape1$ = "round" Then SquareInches1 = 3.142 * (Size1 / 2)^2
SquareInchPrice1 = Price1 / SquareInches1

Rem Collect initial information for second pizza.
Input "Enter the shape of pizza 2:"; Shape2$
Input "Enter the price of pizza 2:"; Price2
Input "Enter the size of pizza 2:"; Size2

Rem Calculate price per square inch for second pizza.
If Shape2$ = "square" Then SquareInches2 = Size2 * Size2
If Shape2$ = "round" Then SquareInches2 = 3.142 * (Size2 / 2)^2
SquareInchPrice2 = Price2 / SquareInches2

Rem Decide which pizza is the best deal and display results.
If SquareInchPrice1 < SquareInchPrice2 Then Message$ = "Pizza 1 is the best deal."
If SquareInchPrice2 < SquareInchPrice1 Then Message$ = "Pizza 2 is the best deal."
If SquareInchPrice1 = SquareInchPrice2 Then Message$ = "Both pizzas are the same deal."
Print Message$
End
```

Lines that begin with Rem contain "remarks" that explain each section of the program. The computer does not execute the remarks.

Data is stored in variables, or memory locations, in RAM. The variable Shape2$ stores text, such as the word "round." The $ indicates a text variable. Other variables, such as Price1 and Size1, store numbers; they do not include $ as part of the variable name.

PROCEDURAL LANGUAGES AND APPLICATIONS

What are the most popular procedural languages? All the first programming languages were procedural. FORTRAN, developed in the United States in 1954, was the first widely used, standardized computer language. Its implementation of the procedural paradigm set the pattern for other popular procedural languages, such as COBOL, FORTH, APL, ALGOL, PL/1, Pascal, C, Ada, and BASIC.

In 1958, a group of European researchers created a new programming language, dubbed "ALGOL," an acronym for "ALGOrithmic Language." ALGOL was used for research applications and is the ancestor of several languages in widespread use today. CPL, created by Ken Thompson of AT&T Bell Laboratories, descended from ALGOL and evolved into the C language. Pascal, the popular teaching language created by Niklaus Wirth, was an important step in the development of Ada.

11

What kinds of problems are best suited to the procedural approach? The procedural approach is best used for problems that can be solved by following a step-by-step algorithm. One of the original problems tackled by computers was computing missile trajectories. Missiles follow an arcing path called a trajectory. Aim too high or too low, and the missile misses its target.

The factors that affect a missile's trajectory include the angle of the gun, weight of the missile, wind direction, wind speed, temperature, and distance to target. However, after these factors are known for a particular target, the calculation follows a simple mathematical algorithm. Therefore, the steps for calculating trajectories remain the same, regardless of the data. That concept is the key to understanding the kinds of problems that are best suited for the procedural approach.

The procedural approach has been widely used for transaction processing, which is characterized by the use of a single algorithm applied to many different sets of data. For example, in the banking industry, the algorithm for calculating checking account balances is the same, regardless of the amounts deposited and withdrawn. Many problems in math and science also lend themselves to the procedural approach.

What are the advantages and disadvantages of the procedural paradigm? The procedural approach and procedural languages tend to produce programs that run quickly and use system resources efficiently. It is a classic approach understood by many programmers, software engineers, and system analysts.

The downside of the procedural paradigm is that it does not fit gracefully with certain types of problems—those that are unstructured or those with very complex algorithms. The procedural paradigm has also been criticized because it forces programmers to view problems as a series of steps, whereas some problems might better be visualized as interacting objects or as interrelated words, concepts, and ideas.

QUICKCHECK......SECTION B

1. BASIC is an easy to understand programming paradigm because it requires no algorithms. True or false? [   ]

2. COBOL, FORTRAN, and C are examples of [   ] languages.

3. Structured English, pseudocode, and [   ] are used by programmers to express algorithms.

4. A(n) [   ] control tells a computer what to do, based on whether a condition is true or false, whereas a(n) [   ] control can change the order in which program instructions are executed.

5. A subroutine is a section of code that is part of a program, but is not included in the main execution path. True or false? [   ]

6. The section of a program that contains a repetition control is sometimes referred to as an "iteration" or a(n) "[   ]."

CHECK ANSWERS

SECTION C

OBJECT-ORIENTED PROGRAMMING

The procedural paradigm forced programmers to view every problem in terms of a step-by-step algorithm. It soon became clear, however, that not every problem fit into the procedural pigeon hole. Alternative programming paradigms and languages were quick to appear, but none achieved the widespread popularity of the procedural paradigm until the emergence of "OO." The abbreviation "OO," which stands for object oriented, is used to describe a programming paradigm as well as a variety of computer programming languages.

In this section, you'll find out what OOP (object-oriented programming) is all about. Java is used for the examples in this section of the chapter because it is today's most popular language for implementing object-oriented programs.

OBJECTS AND CLASSES

What is the basic focus of the object-oriented paradigm? The **object-oriented paradigm** is based on the idea that the solution for a problem can be visualized in terms of objects that interact with each other. In the context of this paradigm, an **object** is a unit of data that represents an abstract or a real-world entity, such as a person, place, or thing. For example, an object can represent a $10.99 small round pepperoni pizza. Another object can represent a pizza delivery guy named Jack Flash. Yet another object can represent a customer who lives at 22 W. Pointe Rd.

What's the difference between an object and a class? The real world contains lots of pizzas, customers, and delivery guys. These objects can be defined in a general way by using classes. Whereas an object is a single instance of an entity, a **class** is a template for a group of objects with similar characteristics. For example, a Pizza class defines a group of gooey Italian snacks that are made in a variety of sizes, crafted into rectangular or round shapes, and sold for various prices. A class can produce any number of unique objects, as shown in Figure 11-29.

CLASS: Pizza

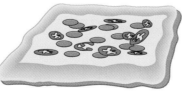

Pizza objects

FIGURE 11-29

A class, such as the Pizza class, is a general template for a group of objects with similar characteristics.

11

How do I define the classes I need to solve a problem? When taking the object-oriented approach to a problem, one of the first steps is to identify the objects that pertain to a solution. As you might expect, the solution to the pizza problem requires some pizza objects.

Certain characteristics of pizzas provide information necessary to solve the problem. This information—the price, size, and shape of a pizza—provides the structure for the Pizza class. A class is defined by attributes and methods. A **class attribute** defines the characteristics of a set of objects.

Each class attribute typically has a name, scope, and data type. One class attribute of the Pizza class might be named "pizzaPrice." Its scope can be defined as public or private. A **public attribute** is available for use by any routine in the program. A **private attribute** can be accessed only from the routine in which it is defined. The pizzaPrice attribute's data type can be defined as "double," which means that it can be any decimal number, such as 12.98. Figure 11-30 describes the data types most often used to describe class attributes.

TERMINOLOGY NOTE

The data types used to define class attributes are similar to the data types for defining database fields, but the terminology is slightly different.

FIGURE 11-30
Class Attribute Data Types

Data Type	Description	Example
Int	Integer whole numbers	10
Double	Numbers with decimal places	12.99
String	Multiple characters, symbols, and numerals	Square
Boolean	Limited to two values	T or F

OO programmers often use **UML** (Unified Modeling Language) diagrams to plan the classes for a program. The UML diagram in Figure 11-31 shows one possible way to envision the Pizza class.

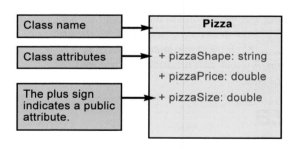

FIGURE 11- 31
The core of a UML diagram is a rectangular shape that contains information about a class.

How do I code a class when writing a program? Although a programmer typically completes the overall program plan before coding, jump ahead to take a quick look at the Java code for the attributes in the Pizza class. The first line of code defines the name of the class. Each subsequent line defines the scope, data type, and name of an attribute. The curly brackets simply define the start and end of the class.

```
class Pizza
{

  public string pizzaShape;

  public double pizzaPrice;

  public double pizzaSize;

}
```

INHERITANCE

How flexible are classes for defining different types of objects? The object-oriented paradigm endows classes with quite a bit of flexibility. For the pizza program, objects and classes make it easy to compare round pizzas to rectangular pizzas rather than just to square pizzas.

Suppose you want to compare a 10-inch round pizza to a rectangular pizza that has a length of 11 inches and a width of 8 inches. The Pizza class in Figure 11-31 on the previous page holds only one measurement for each pizza—pizzaSize. This single attribute won't work for rectangular pizzas, which might have a different length and width. Should you modify the class definition to add attributes for pizzaLength and pizzaWidth? No, because these attributes are necessary only for rectangular pizzas, not for round pizzas. An OO feature called "inheritance" provides flexibility to deal with objects' unique characteristics.

What is inheritance? In object-oriented jargon, **inheritance** refers to passing certain characteristics from one class to other classes. For example, to solve the pizza problem, a programmer might decide to add a RoundPizza class and a RectanglePizza class. These two new classes can inherit attributes from the Pizza class, such as pizzaShape and pizzaPrice. You can then add specialized characteristics to the new classes. The RectanglePizza class can have attributes for length and width, and the RoundPizza class can have an attribute for diameter.

The process of producing new classes with inherited attributes creates a superclass and subclasses. A **superclass**, such as Pizza, is any class from which attributes can be inherited. A **subclass** (or "derived class"), such as RoundPizza or RectanglePizza, is any class that inherits attributes from a superclass. The set of superclasses and subclasses that are related to each other is referred to as a **class hierarchy**. The UML diagram in Figure 11-32 shows the Pizza class and its subclasses.

FIGURE 11-32

The subclass attributes shown in blue (pizzaShape and pizzaPrice) are inherited from the Pizza superclass. The attributes in red are unique to the subclasses. The plus sign indicates that these attributes are public.

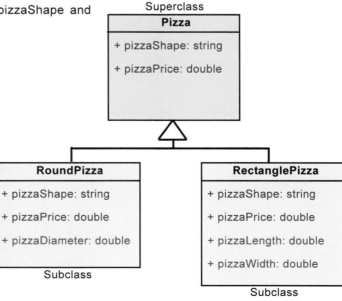

How do I code a subclass? Java uses the "extends" command to link a subclass to a superclass. The statement `class RectanglePizza extends Pizza` means "create a class called RectanglePizza that's derived from the superclass called Pizza." Figure 11-33 contains the Java code that creates attributes for the RectanglePizza class.

```
class RectanglePizza extends Pizza
{
        double pizzaLength;
        double pizzaWidth;
}
```

FIGURE 11-33

Using the extends command, the RectanglePizza class inherits the pizzaShape and pizzaPrice attributes from the Pizza super-class. The pizzaLength and pizzaWidth attributes are unique to the RectanglePizza class.

METHODS AND MESSAGES

How does an OO program use objects? An OO program can use objects in a variety of ways. A basic way to use objects is to manipulate them with methods. A **method** is a segment of code that defines an action. The names of methods usually end in a set of parentheses, such as compare() or getArea().

What can a method do? A method can perform a variety of tasks, such as collecting input, performing calculations, making comparisons, executing decisions, and producing output. For example, the pizza program can use a method named compare() to compare the square-inch prices of two pizzas and display a message indicating which pizza is the best deal.

What does a method look like when it has been coded in Java? A method begins with a line that names the method and can include a description of its scope and data type. The scope—public or private—specifies which parts of the program can access the method. The data type specifies the kind of data, if any, that the method produces. The initial line of code is followed by one or more lines that specify the calculation, comparison, or routine that the method performs. Figure 11-34 illustrates the code for the compare() method.

FIGURE 11-34

Java code for the compare() method.

```
public compare( Pizza Pizza1, Pizza Pizza2 )
{
        if (Pizza1.SquareInchPrice < Pizza2.SquareInchPrice )
            System.out.println("Pizza 1 is the best deal!");

        if (Pizza1.SquareInchPrice > Pizza2.SquareInchPrice )
            System.out.println("Pizza 2 is the best deal!");

        if (Pizza1.SquareInchPrice == Pizza2.SquareInchPrice
            System.out.println("The pizzas are the same deal!");
}
```

The method manipulates pizza objects.

The method title includes its scope and name.

The body of the method contains logic statements that determine which pizza is the best deal and print the result.

What activates a method? A method is activated by a **message**, which is included as a line of program code, sometimes referred to as a "call." For example, in a Java program, a line of code such as `compare(Pizza1, Pizza2)` produces a message used to activate or "call" the compare() method.

In the object-oriented world, objects often interact to solve a problem by sending and receiving messages. For example, a pizza object might receive a message asking for the pizza's area or price per square inch.

How do methods relate to classes? Methods can be defined along with the class they affect. The getSquareInchPrice() method pertains to pizzas of any shape, so it can be defined as part of the Pizza class. To calculate the square-inch price, however, it is necessary to know the area of a pizza. That calculation can be achieved by defining a getArea() method.

The area calculation for round pizzas is different from the calculation for rectangular pizzas, so the getArea() method should become part of the RoundPizza and RectanglePizza subclasses, as indicated by the UML diagram in Figure 11-35.

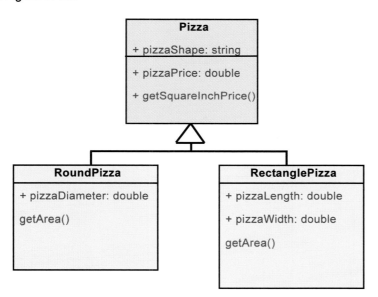

FIGURE 11-35

The getSquareInchPrice() method is defined as part of the Pizza class, whereas the getArea() method is defined within the RoundPizza and RectanglePizza classes.

11

How does the getArea() method work? If you have been thinking ahead a bit, you might wonder how a programmer can define the getArea() method to perform two different calculations—one that calculates the area of a rectangle by multiplying its length times its width, and another that calculates the area of a circle using the formula πr^2. An object-oriented concept called polymorphism makes it possible to assign more than one formula to the getArea() method.

What is polymorphism? **Polymorphism**, sometimes called "overloading," is the ability to redefine a method in a subclass. It allows programmers to create a single, generic name for a procedure that behaves in unique ways for different classes.

In the pizza program, for example, both the RectanglePizza and RoundPizza classes can have a getArea() method. The calculation that getArea() performs is defined one way for the RectanglePizza class and another way for the RoundPizza class. Figure 11-36 illustrates how polymorphism allows subclasses to tailor methods to fit their unique requirements.

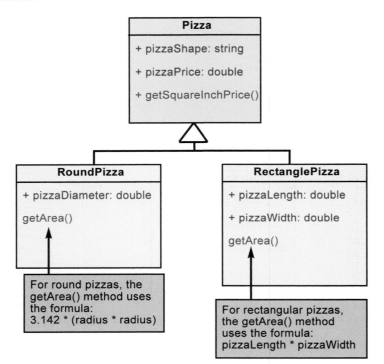

FIGURE 11-36

Polymorphism allows a programmer to define different getArea() methods for each subclass.

How does the code for the round getArea() method differ from the code for the rectangle getArea() method? The code for the getArea() method defined in the RoundPizza class asks users for the pizza's diameter. The method then divides the diameter by 2 to arrive at the radius. The value for the radius is used in the πr^2 calculation—3.142 * (radius * radius)—for the area of a circle.

The getArea() method defined in the RectanglePizza class asks users to enter the length of the pizza and then its width. This data is used in the calculation that multiplies length times width to produce the area of a rectangular pizza. Figure 11-37 illustrates the Java code for the getArea() methods.

FIGURE 11-37

The getArea() methods for round and rectangular pizzas.

```
getArea()

//Method to calculate the area of a round pizza
{
        pizzaDiameter = Keyin.inDouble("Enter the diameter of the pizza: ");

        radius = pizzaDiameter/2;

        pizzaArea = 3.142 * (radius*radius);


}
```

```
getArea()

//Method to calculate the area of a rectangular pizza
{
        pizzaLength = Keyin.inDouble("Enter the length of the pizza: ");

        pizzaWidth  = Keyin.inDouble("Enter the width of the pizza: ");

        pizzaArea = pizzaLength * pizzaWidth;
}
```

What are the advantages of polymorphism? Polymorphism provides OO programs with easy extensibility and can help simplify program code. For example, it would be easy to extend the pizza program to work with triangular pizzas, if one of the pizzerias decides to get creative with pizza shapes. To extend the program, you would simply define a TrianglePizza class that includes attributes for pizzaWidth and pizzaHeight and tailor its getArea() method for calculating the area of a triangle.

The ability to tailor the getArea() method for round and square pizzas allows programmers to avoid complex logic and to simplify program code. As you can imagine, creating separate methods with unique names, such as getAreaRoundPizza(), getAreaRectanglePizza(), and getAreaTrianglePizza(), would add to the program's complexity and make it more difficult to extend the program for other pizza shapes.

11

OBJECT-ORIENTED PROGRAM STRUCTURE

What does the completed pizza program look like in Java? So far in this section of the chapter, you have learned how objects and methods interact to solve the pizza problem. You know that the pizza program uses a Pizza class and two subclasses: RectanglePizza and RoundPizza. You also know that these classes include getSquareInchPrice() and getArea() methods to perform calculations that supply data for solving the problem. You should also remember that the compare() method is used to manipulate pizza objects to determine which is the best deal.

The classes and methods defined for the pizza program must be placed within the structure of a Java program, which contains class definitions, defines methods, initiates the comparison, and outputs results. Figure 11-38 provides an overview of the program structure.

Pizza Class Definition

Define Pizza as a class with attributes for shape and price. Define the getSquareInchPrice() method that collects input for the pizza price, then calculates a pizza's square-inch price.

RectanglePizza Class Definition

Define RectanglePizza as a subclass of Pizza with attributes for length and width. Define the getArea() method that collects input for the pizza length and width to calculate area.

RoundPizza Class Definition

Define RoundPizza as a subclass of Pizza with an attribute for diameter. Define a getArea() method that collects input for the pizza diameter, then calculates area.

Compare() Method

Compare the square-inch price of two pizzas and output results.

Main Module

Set up variables, create objects for Pizza1 and Pizza2, and activate the getArea(), getSquareInchPrice(), and compare() methods.

FIGURE 11-38
Program Structure for the Pizza Program

How does a Java program begin? The computer begins executing a Java program by locating a standard method called main(), which contains code to send messages to objects by calling methods. For the pizza program, the main() method includes code that defines a few variables and then asks the user to enter the shape of the first pizza. If the shape entered is "Round" the program creates an object called Pizza1 that is a member of the RoundPizza class. If the shape entered is "Rectangle" the program creates an object called Pizza1 that is a member of the RectanglePizza class.

After the pizza object is created, the program uses the getArea() method to calculate its area. The program then uses the getSquareInchPrice() method to calculate the pizza's square-inch price. When the calculations are complete for the first pizza, the program performs the same process for the second pizza. Finally, the program uses the compare() method to compare the square-inch prices of the two pizzas and output a statement about which one is the best deal.

Because it is not the goal of this section to teach you the particulars of Java programming, don't worry about the detailed syntax of the Java code. Instead, refer to Figure 11-39 to get an overview of the activity that takes place in the main() method for the pizza program.

FIGURE 11-39

Java code for the main module of the Pizza Program.

```java
public static void main(String[] args)    ← 1. Main() method title
  {

    Pizza Pizza1;    ← 2. Define variables used in
    Pizza Pizza2;        the main() method.
    String pizzaShape;

    pizzaShape = Keyin.inString("Enter the shape of the first pizza: ");
    if (pizzaShape.equals("Round"))    ← 3. Collect input for the shape of the
      {                                    first pizza, then create an object
      Pizza1 = new RoundPizza();           called Pizza1 that belongs to the
      }                                    RoundPizza or RectanglePizza class.
    else
       Pizza1 = new RectanglePizza();

                                       4. Use the getArea() and getSquareInchPrice()
    Pizza1.getArea();    ←             methods to calculate area and square-inch
    Pizza1.getSquareInchPrice();       price for the first pizza.

    pizzaShape = Keyin.inString("Enter the shape of the second pizza: ");
    if (pizzaShape.equals("Round"))    ← 5. Collect input for the shape of the second
       Pizza2 = new RoundPizza();         pizza, then create an object called Pizza2
    else                                  that belongs to the RoundPizza or
       Pizza2 = new RectanglePizza();     RectanglePizza class.

                                       6. Use the getArea() and getSquareInchPrice()
    Pizza2.getArea();    ←             methods to calculate area and square-inch price for
    Pizza2.getSquareInchPrice();       the second pizza.

    compare(Pizza1, Pizza2);    ←      7. Use the compare() method
  }                                    to determine which pizza is the
                                       best deal, then print results.
```

11

What happens when the completed pizza program runs? When you run the pizza program, it looks for the main() method. This method displays an onscreen prompt that asks for the pizza's shape. The getArea() method displays a prompt for the pizza's diameter (for a round pizza) or the pizza's length and width (for a rectangular pizza). A similar series of prompts appears for the second pizza. The program concludes when the compare() method displays a statement about which pizza is the best deal. The software tour for Figure 11-40 lets you see what happens when the OO pizza program runs.

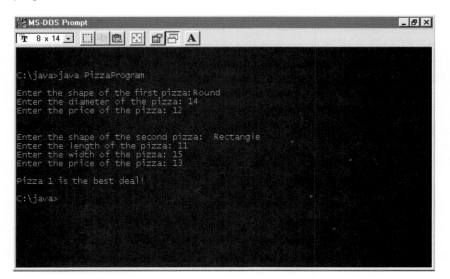

FIGURE 11-40
When the pizza program runs, on-screen prompts ask for the shape, size, and price of each pizza; then the program displays a message that indicates which pizza is the best deal.

CLICK TO START

OBJECT-ORIENTED LANGUAGES AND APPLICATIONS

How did object-oriented languages originate? Computer historians believe that SIMULA (SIMUlation LAnguage) was the first computer language to work with objects, classes, inheritance, and methods. SIMULA was developed in 1962 by two Norwegian computer scientists for the purpose of programming simulations and models. SIMULA laid the foundation for the object-oriented paradigm, which was later incorporated into other computer languages, such as Eiffel, Smalltalk, C++, and Java.

The second major development in object-oriented languages came in 1972 when Alan Kaye began work on the Dynabook project at the Xerox Palo Alto Research Center (PARC). Dynabook was a prototype for a notebook-sized personal computer, intended to handle all the information needs of adults and children. Kaye developed a programming language called Smalltalk for the Dynabook that could be easily used to create programs based on real-world objects. Dynabook never became a commercial product, but Smalltalk survived and is still in use today. Smalltalk is regarded as a classic object-oriented language, which encourages programmers to take a "pure" OO approach to the programming process.

Which object-oriented languages are popular today? As the object-oriented paradigm gained popularity, several existing programming languages were modified to allow programmers to work with objects, classes, inheritance, and polymorphism. The concept for the Ada programming language originated in 1978 at the U.S. Department of Defense. The first versions of Ada were procedural, but in 1995, the language was modified to incorporate object-oriented features. A similar transformation took place with the C language in 1983, except that the object-oriented version earned a new name—C++. Hybrid languages, such as Ada95, C++, Visual Basic, and C#, give programmers the option of using procedural and object-oriented techniques.

Java is one of the newest additions to the collection of object-oriented languages. Originally planned as a programming language for consumer electronics, such as interactive cable television boxes, Java evolved into an object-oriented programming platform for developing Web applications. Java was officially launched by Sun Microsystems in 1995 and has many of the characteristics of C++, from which it derives much of its syntax. Like C++, Java can also be used for procedural programming, so it is sometimes classified as a hybrid language.

What kinds of applications are suitable for object-oriented languages? The object-oriented paradigm can be applied to a wide range of programming problems. Basically, if you can envision a problem as a set of objects that pass messages back and forth, the problem is suitable for the OO approach.

What are the advantages and disadvantages of the OO paradigm? The object-oriented paradigm is cognitively similar to the way human beings perceive the real world. Using the object-oriented approach, programmers might be able to visualize the solutions to problems more easily. Facets of the object-oriented paradigm can also increase a programmer's efficiency because encapsulation allows objects to be adapted and reused in a variety of different programs. **Encapsulation** refers to the process of hiding the internal details of objects and their methods. After an object is coded, it becomes a "black box," which essentially hides its details from other objects and allows the data to be accessed via methods. Encapsulated objects can be easily reused, modified, and repurposed.

A potential disadvantage of object-oriented programs is runtime efficiency. Object-oriented programs tend to require more memory and processing resources than procedural programs. Programmers, software engineers, and system analysts can work together to weigh the tradeoffs between the OO approach and runtime efficiency.

QUICKCHECK......SECTION C

1. The _____ paradigm is based on the idea that computer programs can be visualized in terms of objects that interact with each other.

2. A class is a template for a group of objects with similar characteristics. True or false? _____

3. OO programmers often use _____ diagrams to plan the classes for a program. (Hint: Use the abbreviation.)

4. The process of passing certain characteristics from a superclass to a subclass is referred to as _____.

5. In an OO program, objects send and receive _____ to initiate actions, which the programmer defines by creating a(n) _____.

11

DECLARATIVE PROGRAMMING

As the 1950s drew to a close, computers were primarily used for number-crunching tasks, such as calculating missile trajectories, tabulating census data, and processing payrolls. A few visionary computer scientists saw beyond these limited number-crunching applications and began to explore ways in which computers could make decisions and solve problems by manipulating non-numeric data, including words and concepts. Procedural programming languages, such as FORTRAN and COBOL, did not have the flexibility to deal efficiently with non-numeric data, so non-procedural languages were developed. This section explains a type of non-procedural programming that follows the declarative paradigm and gives you a little taste of the Prolog language.

THE DECLARATIVE PARADIGM

What is the declarative paradigm? Non-procedural languages, such as LISP, Scheme, Haskell, and Prolog, can be grouped into one of two paradigms, functional or declarative. The **functional paradigm** emphasizes the evaluation of expressions, called "functions," rather than the execution of commands. The **declarative paradigm** attempts to describe a problem without specifying exactly how to arrive at a solution.

What is unique about the declarative paradigm? In earlier sections of this chapter, you learned that procedural programming focuses on a step-by-step algorithm that instructs the computer how to arrive at a solution. You also learned that the object-oriented approach emphasizes classes and methods that form objects. In contrast, the declarative paradigm describes aspects of a problem that lead to a solution. Although the declarative paradigm might sound similar to the procedural paradigm, the procedural paradigm focuses on an algorithm that describes the solution, whereas the declarative paradigm focuses on describing the problem. Figure 11-41 summarizes these differences.

What are the building blocks for the declarative paradigm? Many declarative programming languages, such as Prolog, use a collection of facts and rules to describe a problem. In the context of a Prolog program, a **fact** is a statement that provides the computer with basic information for solving a problem. In the pizza problem, for example, these facts might include:

A pizza has a price of $10.99, a size of 12 inches, and a round shape.

Another pizza has a price of $12.00, a size of 11 inches, and a square shape.

In the context of a Prolog program, a **rule** is a general statement about the relationship between facts. For example, the following rule is useful for solving the problem of which pizza is a better deal:

A pizza is a better deal if its square-inch price is less than the square-inch price of another pizza.

FIGURE 11-41
Paradigm Comparison

Procedural paradigm:

■ Programs detail how to solve a problem

■ Very efficient for number-crunching tasks

Object-oriented paradigm:

■ Programs define objects, classes, and methods

■ Efficient for problems that involve real-word objects

Declarative paradigm:

■ Programs describe the problem

■ Efficient for processing words and language

To apply the "betterdeal" rule, additional rules are necessary to calculate the square-inch price of each pizza. You'll look at these rules in more detail later in this section.

How does a programmer plan a declarative program? The core of most declarative programs is a set of facts and rules that describe a problem. The logic for the pizza program is very simple because the solution depends on a single factor: the lowest square-inch price. Declarative programs with such simple logic don't require much planning. In contrast, programs that deal with multiple factors have more complex logic and often require planning tools, such as decision tables.

A **decision table** is a tabular method for visualizing and specifying rules based on multiple factors. As an example, suppose your decision to buy a pizza depends not just on its price, but on whether you can get it delivered and how soon it is ready. These three factors produce eight possible situations. In which of those eight situations would you purchase a pizza? What if the best-priced pizza is ready in less than 30 minutes, but it can't be delivered? What if the best-priced pizza won't be ready for an hour? Figure 11-42 illustrates how a programmer might construct a decision table that describes all the rules pertaining to pizza prices, delivery, and time.

FIGURE 11-42
Decision Table

Lowest price	Y	N	Y	N	Y	N	Y	N
Delivery available	Y	Y	N	N	Y	Y	N	N
Ready in less than 30 minutes	Y	Y	Y	Y	N	N	N	N
Buy it?	Y	Y	N	N	Y	N	N	N

PROLOG FACTS

How does a programmer code facts? Return to the simple problem of deciding which of two round or square pizzas is the best deal based on price per square inch. The first step in coding the program is to enter facts that describe the prices, shapes, and sizes of two pizzas. The fact "The shape of a pizza is round." can be coded in Prolog like this:

```
shapeof(pizza,round).
```

The words in parentheses are called arguments. An **argument** represents one of the main subjects that a fact describes. The word outside the parentheses, called the **predicate**, describes the relationship between the arguments. In other words, the predicate "shapeof" describes the relationship between "pizza" and "round." Figure 11-43 points out some important syntax details pertaining to capitalization and punctuation for Prolog facts.

FIGURE 11-43
A Prolog fact follows specific syntax rules.

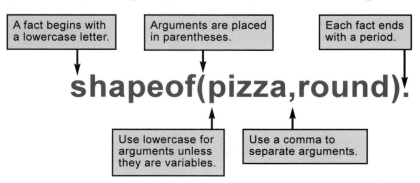

11

Although it might seem obvious that "round" describes the shape of a pizza, the predicate cannot be omitted. In many cases, the predicate can drastically change the meaning of a fact. For example, the facts in Figure 11-44 have the same arguments, (joe,fish), but the predicates give the facts very different meanings.

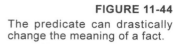
FIGURE 11-44
The predicate can drastically change the meaning of a fact.

```
hates(joe,fish).
```
Joe hates fish.

```
name(joe,fish).
```
Joe is the name of a fish.

```
playscardgame(joe,fish).
```
Joe plays a card game called fish.

For the pizza program, a series of facts can be used to describe a pizza:

```
priceof(pizza1,10).

sizeof(pizza1,12).

shapeof(pizza1,square).
```

Another set of similar facts can be used to describe a second pizza:

```
priceof(pizza2,12).

sizeof(pizza2,14).

shapeof(pizza2,round).
```

Facts can have more than two arguments. For example, a single fact can be used to fully describe a pizza:

```
pricesizeshape(pizza1,10,12,square).
```

Using a series of facts to describe a pizza has some advantages and some disadvantages over using a single fact. A single fact tends to make a program more compact, whereas multiple facts might provide more flexibility. The structure of a fact also affects the syntax for goals that produce information.

What is a goal? The facts in a Prolog program are useful even without any rules. Prolog can manipulate facts in several ways without explicit programming. Each fact in a Prolog program is similar to a record in a database. You can "query" a program's "database" by asking a question, called a **goal** in Prolog jargon. Suppose you have entered the following facts:

```
priceof(pizza1,10).

sizeof(pizza1,12).

shapeof(pizza1,square).

priceof(pizza2,12).

sizeof(pizza2,14).

shapeof(pizza2,round).
```

You can ask questions by entering goals from the ?- prompt. For example, the goal `?- shapeof(pizza1,square)` means "Is the shape of pizza1 square?" Prolog searches through the facts to see if it can satisfy the goal by finding a match. If a match is found, Prolog responds with "yes"; otherwise, it responds with "no." This exercise might seem trivial because you are working with a small set of facts, which are all visible on the screen. Many programs, however, contain hundreds of facts, which cannot be displayed on a single screen or easily remembered by a programmer.

Prolog allows you to ask open-ended questions by replacing constants with variables. A **constant**, such as "pizza1," "square," or "10," represents an unchanging value or attribute. A Prolog **variable** is like a placeholder or an empty box, into which Prolog can put information gleaned from a fact. A Prolog variable begins with an uppercase letter to distinguish it from a constant. The argument Pizza is a variable, whereas pizza1 is a constant. The argument Inches is a variable, whereas 14 is a constant.

Prolog variables are handy tools for formulating open-ended goals. As an example, suppose you want to find the size of pizza2. You can obtain this information by using the variable Inches in the goal:

```
?- sizeof(pizza2,Inches).
```

Prolog looks for any facts that have sizeof as a predicate and pizza2 as the first argument. It responds with the actual value of the second argument:

```
Inches = 14
```

Much of the power and flexibility of the Prolog language stem from its ability to sift through facts trying to match predicates, compare constants, and instantiate variables. The screentour for Figure 11-45 demonstrates various Prolog queries.

TERMINOLOGY NOTE

Although variables and constants are presented in terms of the declarative paradigm, they are also used in other paradigms. For example, the procedural program in Figure 11-28 contains variables such as Shape1$ and Price1.

FIGURE 11-45

The ?- prompt allows you to query a set of Prolog facts and rules.

CLICK TO START ✦

SWI-Prolog (version 3.4.5)

```
Welcome to SWI-Prolog (Version 3.4.5)
Copyright (c) 1990-2000 University of Amsterdam.
Copy policy: GPL-2 (see www.gnu.org)

For help, use ?- help(Topic). or ?- apropos(Word).

?- consult('pizza.txt').

Yes
?- sizeof(pizza2,Inches).     ◄——  The query asks for the
                                    size of pizza2 in inches.
Inches = 14

Yes
?- ■
```

Prolog finds the fact sizeof(pizza2,14) and displays the value of the second argument—14—as the pizza's size in inches.

start   SWI-Prolog (versi...   10:20 AM

What is instantiation? Finding a value for a variable is referred to as **instantiation**. To solve the goal `?- sizeof(pizza2,Inches)`, Prolog "instantiates" the value 14 to the variable Inches. Instantiation means "to make a temporary assignment." When a Prolog program discovers that the size of pizza2 is 14 inches, it instantiates, or assigns, the value 14 to the variable Inches.

Prolog can perform multiple instantiations. You can ask for the sizes of both pizzas by using the query `?- sizeof(Pizza,Inches)`. Capitalizing the words Pizza and Inches signifies that both are variables. Prolog can instantiate Pizza to pizza1 and then instantiate it to pizza2:

```
Pizza = pizza1

Inches = 12

Pizza = pizza2

Inches = 14
```

You can also formulate queries in which you tell Prolog not to instantiate a variable. For example, suppose you want to know the prices of the pizzas, but you don't need to know which price corresponds to a particular pizza. You can enter the query `?- priceof(_,Price)`, which means, "What are the prices?" Prolog would reply with:

```
Price = 10

Price = 12
```

Instantiation can be used to produce information that is not implicitly stored in the database. Suppose you want to know the size of the round pizza. The database does not contain a fact like `sizeofroundpizza(14)`; however, you can use a conjunction of two goals, as shown in Figure 11-46, to obtain the size of the round pizza.

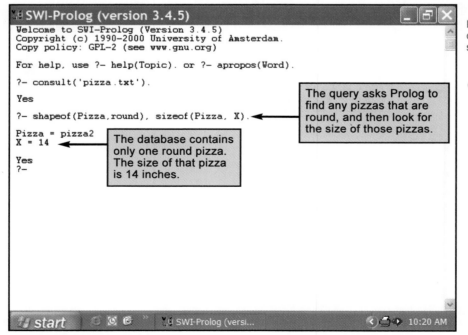

FIGURE 11-46
Prolog uses a process called instantiation to satisfy goals.

CLICK TO START ✦

Instantiation is one of the keys to understanding how Prolog works. Unlike a procedural programming language, which is designed to step through a series of statements in a path prescribed by the programmer, Prolog can autonomously run through every possible instantiation, backtracking if necessary to deal with multiple variables.

Backtracking refers to a process by which every possible solution is tried. For example, backtracking would enable a Prolog program to analyze every possible move in a chess game. If you envision solutions as the branches on a tree, backtracking begins by following one branch seeking a solution. If the solution is not found, it backs up to the trunk and follows another branch (Figure 11-47).

Instantiation and backtracking are powerful tools when used by savvy programmers. They work in the context of Prolog facts and Prolog rules. Take a look at how a programmer codes Prolog rules; then you can see how those rules work.

PROLOG RULES

How does a programmer code Prolog rules?
The pizza program requires a rule that states, "A pizza is a better deal if its price per square inch is less than the price per square inch of the other pizza." Translated into Prolog code, this rule becomes:

```
betterdeal(PizzaX,PizzaY) :-
        squareinchprice(PizzaX,AmountX),
        squareinchprice(PizzaY,AmountY),
        AmountX < AmountY.
```

FIGURE 11-47
Backtracking can follow every "branch" to cover all possible combinations of facts. The program first checks Branch1, Limb1, Facts 1, 2, and 3. Then it backtracks to Branch1, moves to Limb2, and checks Facts X, Y, and Z.

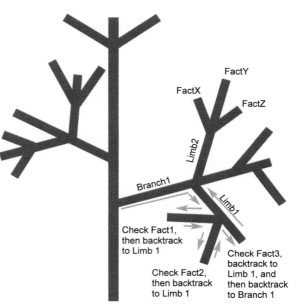

Take a look at the logic behind this rule. A Prolog rule consists of a head, body, and connecting symbol, as described in Figure 11-48.

FIGURE 11-48
A Prolog rule consists of a head and one or more clauses that form the body of the rule.

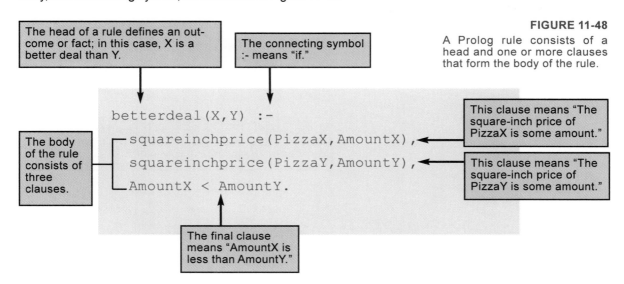

The head of a rule defines an outcome or fact; in this case, X is a better deal than Y.

The connecting symbol :- means "if."

The body of the rule consists of three clauses.

```
betterdeal(X,Y) :-
        squareinchprice(PizzaX,AmountX),
        squareinchprice(PizzaY,AmountY),
        AmountX < AmountY.
```

This clause means "The square-inch price of PizzaX is some amount."

This clause means "The square-inch price of PizzaY is some amount."

The final clause means "AmountX is less than AmountY."

11

How do Prolog rules work? To understand how the betterdeal rule works, you'll need to perform a bit of "magic" to determine the price per square inch of each pizza. In the completed pizza program, the computer can calculate the square-inch price using a rule the programmer provides. Because you don't yet have such a rule, temporarily assume that the square-inch price of the first pizza is .0694 (6.94 cents) and the square-inch price of the second pizza is .0612 (6.12 cents). These facts would be stated as:

`squareinchprice(pizza1,.069).` **and**
`squareinchprice(pizza2,.0612).`

Now, suppose you enter the query `?- betterdeal(pizza1,pizza2).`, which translates to "Is pizza1 a better deal than pizza2?" Figure 11-49 illustrates how Prolog uses the betterdeal rule to answer your query.

FIGURE 11-49
Prolog executes the betterdeal rule.

Facts for the pizza program

```
priceof(pizza1,10).

sizeof(pizza1,12).

shapeof(pizza1,square).

priceof(pizza2,12).

sizeof(pizza2,14).

shapeof(pizza2,round).

squareinchprice(pizza1,.069).

squareinchprice(pizza2,.0612).
```

The betterdeal rule

```
betterdeal(PizzaX,PizzaY) :-

    squareinchprice(PizzaX,AmountX),

    squareinchprice(PizzaY,AmountY),

    AmountX < AmountY.
```

The query

```
?- betterdeal(Pizza1,Pizza2)
```

1. Prolog instantiates pizza1 to PizzaX and pizza2 to PizzaY.

```
betterdeal(pizza1,pizza2) :-

    squareinchprice(pizza1,AmountX),

    squareinchprice(pizza2,AmountY),

    AmountX < AmountY.
```

2. Prolog looks through the facts to find the squareinchprice for pizza1 and pizza2. These prices are instantiated to AmountX and AmountY.

```
betterdeal(pizza1,pizza2) :-

    squareinchprice(pizza1,.0694),

    squareinchprice(pizza2,.0612),

    .0694 < .0612.
```

3. The last line now contains a statement that is not true—.0694<.0612—which invalidates the rule and produces "no" as a response to your query, "Is pizza1 a better deal than pizza2?"

Does the order of rules affect the way a Prolog program runs? When coding programs in a procedural language, such as C, Pascal, or BASIC, the order of program instructions is critically important. For example, if you place input statements for pizza size and price after the code that calculates the price per square inch, the program produces an error.

In contrast, the order or sequence of rules in a Prolog program is, in most cases, not critical. For example, the completed Prolog pizza program might use four rules. One rule describes how to determine the better deal. One rule describes the area of a square pizza. Another rule describes the area of a round pizza. A final rule describes how the square-inch price relates to the area and price of a pizza, as shown in Figure 11-50.

FIGURE 11-50

The four rules for the pizza program can appear in any order and produce the correct output.

```
betterdeal(PizzaX,PizzaY) :-

   squareinchprice(PizzaX,Amount1),

   squareinchprice(PizzaY,Amount2),

   Amount1 < Amount2.
```

The betterdeal rule determines if PizzaX is less expensive than PizzaY.

```
area(Pizza,Squareinches) :-

   sizeof(Pizza,Side),

   shapeof(Pizza,square),

   Squareinches is Side * Side.
```

This area rule calculates the area of a square pizza.

```
area(Pizza,Squareinches) :-

   sizeof(Pizza,Diameter),

   shapeof(Pizza,round),

   Radius is Diameter/2

   Squareinches is 3.142 * (Radius * Radius).
```

This area rule calculates the area of a round pizza.

```
squareinchprice(Pizza,Amount) :-

   area(Pizza,Squareinches),

   priceof(Pizza,Dollars),

   Amount is Dollars / Squareinches.
```

The squareinchprice rule calculates the price for a square inch of pizza.

11

What does the complete pizza program look like in Prolog? The complete pizza program includes the facts that describe two pizzas and rules that describe betterdeal, square-inch price, and area. Figure 11-51 contains the Prolog code for the entire pizza program.

FIGURE 11-51
The complete Prolog program.

```
priceof(pizza1,10).
sizeof(pizza1,12).
shapeof(pizza1,square).
priceof(pizza2,12).
sizeof(pizza2,14).
shapeof(pizza2,round).
betterdeal(PizzaX,PizzaY) :-
    squareinchprice(PizzaX,Amount1),
    squareinchprice(PizzaY,Amount2),
    Amount1 < Amount2.
area(Pizza,Squareinches) :-
    sizeof(Pizza,Side),
    shapeof(Pizza,square),
    Squareinches is Side * Side.
area(Pizza,Squareinches) :-
    sizeof(Pizza,Diameter),
    shapeof(Pizza,round),
    Radius is Diameter/2,
    Squareinches is 3.142 * (Radius * Radius).
squareinchprice(Pizza,Amount) :-
    area(Pizza,Squareinches),
    priceof(Pizza,Dollars),
    Amount is Dollars / Squareinches.
```

INPUT CAPABILITIES

Can I generalize the program for any pizzas? A version of the pizza program that contains facts, such as `priceof(pizza1,10)` and `priceof(pizza2,12)` is limited to specific pizzas that cost $10.00 and $12.00. The program can be generalized by collecting input from the user and storing it in variables or by asserting new facts at runtime.

How do I collect input from the user? If you think back to the procedural programming section of this chapter, you might recall that the BASIC program collected the size, shape, and price of each pizza by using Input statements such as:

```
Input "Enter the size of pizza1: ", Size1
```

That Input statement displayed the prompt "Enter the size of pizza1:" and then stored the number entered in a variable called Size1. Prolog has similar capabilities. Examine the following program code to see how a Prolog program collects user input, then take the screentour in Figure 11-52 to see how the program interacts with users when it is run.

> The pizzainfo rule displays prompts and collects input for pizza prices, sizes, and shapes.

> Prolog uses the write predicate to display a prompt for input.

> The read predicate gathers input entered by the user, then the assertz predicate creates a fact, such as price-of(pizza1,12).

```prolog
pizzainfo(complete) :-
write(user,'enter price of pizza1: '),
read(user,Price1), assertz(priceof(pizza1,Price1)),
write(user,'enter size of pizza1: '),
read(user,Size1), assertz(sizeof(pizza1,Size1)),
write(user,'enter shape of pizza1: '),
read(user,Shape1), assertz(shapeof(pizza1,Shape1)),
write(user,'enter price of pizza2: '),
read(user,Price2), assertz(priceof(pizza2,Price2)),
write(user,'enter size of pizza2: '),
read(user,Size2), assertz(sizeof(pizza2,Size2)),
write(user,'enter shape of pizza2: '),
read(user,Shape2), assertz(shapeof(pizza2,Shape2)).
```

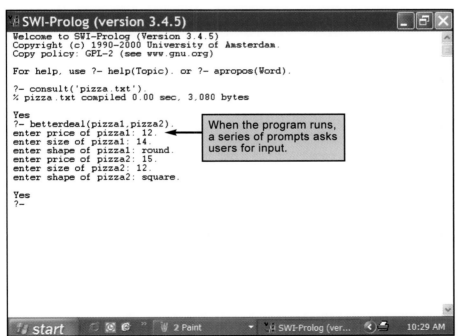

> When the program runs, a series of prompts asks users for input.

FIGURE 11-52

When the pizza program runs, the pizzainfo rule collects input for the prices, the sizes, and the shapes of two pizzas.

CLICK TO START

How can I add facts at runtime? Another way of generalizing the pizza program is to exclude all the facts about the two pizzas. The program then consists only of the four rules. When the program runs, you can use Prolog's built-in asserta predicate to temporarily add facts to the beginning of the program. The command `asserta(priceof(pizza1,10)).` temporarily adds the fact that pizza1 costs $10.

11

DEBUGGING WITH TRACE

How do I test a Prolog program? As with programs written in procedural or object-oriented languages, you should test your Prolog programs by entering test data to make sure the calculations and logic are performed correctly. Most Prolog compilers provide a **trace feature** that allows you to track through each instantiation. The trace feature is especially handy for monitoring the state of each variable as Prolog works through each fact and rule. Figure 11-53 shows a sample trace of a Prolog query that asks for the area of the square pizza.

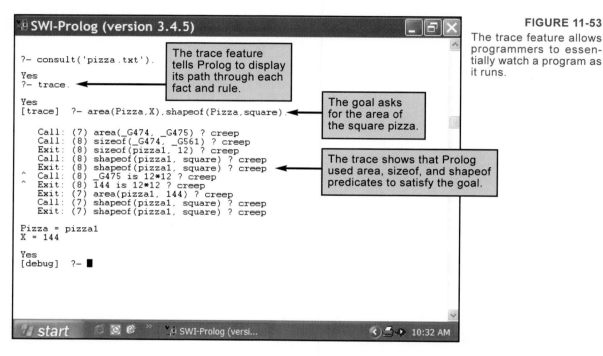

FIGURE 11-53
The trace feature allows programmers to essentially watch a program as it runs.

DECLARATIVE LANGUAGES AND APPLICATIONS

What kinds of problems are suitable for the declarative approach?
As you have seen from the pizza example, it is possible to use a declarative language to solve a problem that involves calculations. However, problems that require intensive computation are not usually best suited for the declarative paradigm. As a rule of thumb, declarative programming languages are most suitable for problems that pertain to words and concepts rather than to numbers. These languages are a good choice for applications such as:

■ Databases that contain complex relationships—for example, a genealogy database used to trace ancestral lineage or a street and highway database used for mapping routes

■ Decision support systems that handle semi-structured problems—for example, a decision support system that helps determine tactics for military campaigns or a system that helps planners efficiently allocate energy resources

■ Expert systems that require analysis of multiple, interrelated factors—for example, an expert system that helps troubleshoot appliance repairs or a program that translates documents from one language to another

What are the advantages and disadvantages of declarative languages? Declarative languages offer a highly effective programming environment for problems that involve words, concepts, and complex logic. As you learned in this chapter, declarative languages offer a great deal of flexibility for querying a set of facts and rules. These languages also allow you to describe problems using words rather than the abstract structures procedural and object-oriented languages require.

Currently, declarative languages are not commonly used for production applications. To some extent, today's emphasis on the object-oriented paradigm has pushed declarative languages out of the mainstream, both in education and in the job market. Many aspiring programmers are never introduced to declarative languages, so they are not included in the languages evaluated for a specific project.

Declarative languages have a reputation for providing minimal input and output capabilities. Although many of today's Prolog compilers provide access to Windows and Mac user interface components, programmers are often unaware of this capability.

A final disadvantage of declarative languages is their relatively poor performance on today's personal computer architecture, which is optimized for sequential processing. Declarative languages run much more efficiently on parallel architectures, which are only now emerging in the personal computer market.

QUICKCHECK......SECTION D

1. The declarative programming paradigm focuses on describing a(n) [_____], whereas the procedural paradigm focuses on an algorithm that describes a(n) [_____].

2. A(n) [_____] table is a tabular method for visualizing and specifying rules based on multiple factors.

3. In the Prolog fact partnumber(desk,12367), "desk" and "12367" are referred to as [_____], whereas "partnumber" is referred to as the [_____].

4 A Prolog attribute can be a(n) [_____], such as "pizza" (with a lowercase "p"), or it can be a(n) [_____], such as "Pizza" (with an uppercase "P").

5. Finding the value for a variable while solving a Prolog goal is called [_____].

6. In a Prolog [_____], the :- connecting symbol means "if."

 CHECK ANSWERS

11

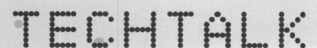

TECHTALK

PROGRAMMING TOOLS

The software tools shipped with today's personal computers typically do not include programming languages. If you want to try your hand at programming, your first step is to obtain some programming tools, such as an editor, a compiler, components, and a debugger. This TechTalk begins with an overview of basic programming tools. It concludes with information about how programming tools, such as SDKs and IDEs, are distributed.

What's the most important programming tool? Although programmers spend most of their time interacting with a program editor or VDE (visual development environment), coding tools are not the most important element of the programmer's toolbox. You can use the coolest program editor or visual development environment, but without a compiler or interpreter, the computer cannot run the programs you code. Because of their key role in translating high-level instructions into executable machine language, compilers and interpreters are the most important programming tools.

A microprocessor is designed to perform a repertoire of very basic activities, discussed in Chapter 2, such as add, load, and stop. These basic activities are defined in a microprocessor's built-in machine language instruction set. The programs that you write in a high-level language must be translated into machine language instructions that coincide with a microprocessor's instruction set. A program can be translated into executable code in one of two ways: It can be compiled or interpreted.

How does a computer compile a program? A **compiler** translates a program written in a high-level language into low-level instructions before the program is executed. The commands that you write in a high-level language are referred to as **source code**. The low-level instructions that result from compiling the source code are referred to as **object code**. Some compilers produce executable files that contain machine language instructions. Other compilers produce files that contain intermediate language instructions.

An **intermediate language** is a set of low-level instructions that can be converted easily and quickly into machine language. For example, when the source code for a Java program is compiled, it produces a file containing intermediate language instructions called **bytecode** (Figure 11-54). This bytecode can be distributed to PC or Mac owners. The bytecode is converted into machine language by software called a **Java Virtual Machine** (JVM) when the program is run. The JVM for a PC converts the bytecode into machine language instructions that work on a Pentium processor. The JVM for a Mac converts the bytecode into machine language for the PowerPC processor.

Microsoft's .NET Framework also features an intermediate language. The **.NET Framework** is a set of tools for building, deploying, and running software applications. Programs constructed within the .NET Framework are compiled into an intermediate language called **MSIL** (Microsoft Intermediate Language). The MSIL version can be distributed for use on any computer platform supported by the .NET Framework.

FIGURE 11-54

An intermediate language provides low-level instructions that can be compiled quickly for a specific computer platform.

High-level language

```
X2 := X * X
```

↓

Intermediate language

```
ldloc fpXTemp
    dup
    mul
    stloc fpX2
```

Machine language

```
0001100000010011
1000001011000100
0100001111100000
0100001100111100
1010000000010000
1010000001000101
1010101110010000
```

MSIL is converted into executable code by using a platform-specific **CLR** (common language runtime) module. For example, when you run the program on a PC, the PC version of the CLR compiles an executable version of the program.

The .NET Framework is very efficient because it compiles programs written in a variety of languages, such as Visual Basic, C#, and Eiffel, into the same MSIL. End users require only one CLR to produce executable code, regardless of the language the programmer uses. End users save space on their computers because they don't need separate CLRs for C#, Visual Basic, and C++ programs.

How does an interpreter differ from a compiler? An **interpreter** reads one high-level or intermediate language instruction at a time and converts it into machine language for immediate processing. After an instruction is executed, the interpreter reads the next instruction, converts it into machine language, and so forth.

Is a compiler better than an interpreter? Compiled programs typically run faster than interpreted programs because the computer does not spend time translating instructions before executing them.

In contrast to compiled programs, interpreted programs run more slowly and require interpreter software on end-user computers. For example, any users who want to run a Java program supplied as bytecode must have the Java Virtual Machine installed on their computers so that the bytecode can be translated into machine code as the program runs.

The major advantage of an interpreter is its ability to simplify the process of testing and debugging a program. As each line of a program is interpreted, it is examined for errors. If a line contains an error, program execution stops, allowing the programmer to view the error and fix it before continuing.

Debugging a compiled program is a bit more complex. The compiler attempts to compile the entire program and accumulates a list of errors. This list is displayed to the programmer, who must then locate the errors in the program and correct them. Figure 11-55 illustrates the different techniques required for debugging compiled and interpreted programs.

FIGURE 11-55

The debugging process is different for interpreters and compilers.

Using a Compiler

1 Compile the entire program.

2 Run the compiled program.

3 Use the error report to fix as many errors as possible.

4 Recompile the revised program and rerun it.

Using an Interpreter

1 Start the program.

2 Execution halts when the program encounters an error.

3 Fix the error, then run the program again.

4 Continue to fix and run until the program runs from start to end without error.

Can a programmer choose whether to use a compiler or an interpreter? The choice between an interpreter and a compiler is tied to the programming language that's used to code a program. Some programming languages—most versions of BASIC, for example—provide only an interpreter. Other programming languages, such as C, C++, Pascal, and FORTRAN, provide only a compiler.

Many programmers prefer to use an interpreter during the development and testing phases, and then use a compiler to convert the program into an intermediate language or an executable file for distribution. Some programming languages, such as Visual Basic and LISP, provide both an interpreter and a compiler. Interpreters are so popular for debugging that an interpreter-based debugging add-on, called an interactive debugger, is available for use with programming languages that once featured only a compiler.

Do I need components for my programming projects? Every feature of a lengthy computer program is not necessarily created from scratch. Components can be incorporated into a program, saving days, weeks, or months of programming time. A **component** is a prewritten module, typically designed to accomplish a specific task. For example, one component might provide spreadsheet capabilities, while another component might provide encryption capabilities. Figure 11-56 elaborates on components.

What's an API? In the context of computer programming, **API** is an abbreviation for "application program interface" or "application programming interface." An API is a set of application program or operating system functions that programmers can access from within the programs they create. For example, the Windows API includes code for an assortment of dialog box controls familiar to anyone who uses a PC. The ability to browse through file folders is one element of the Windows API that might be useful in any application program that allows users to open or save files. Programmers can make use of this built-in Windows feature in their own programs by adding code to invoke the SHBrowseForFolder API, as shown in Figure 11-57.

FIGURE 11-56

Suppose you plan to write an e-mail client that automatically encrypts e-mail messages before sending them. Instead of spending many days creating lines of code to handle the encryption, you can use an encryption component.

> Encryption Component
> Copyright ComponentSoftware, Inc.
>
> This component applies a 128-bit key RSA encryption algorithm to a text string delineated by use of get-string.

■ The encryption component is supplied as a short program.

■ In the main module that you're creating, add a line of code that references the component.

■ Instructions for creating code to reference the component are supplied with the component's documentation.

■ Include the component on your distribution CD with the rest of the modules you create.

■ Components are available for several of today's popular programming languages. Most can be downloaded from the Web where they are offered as commercial products or shareware.

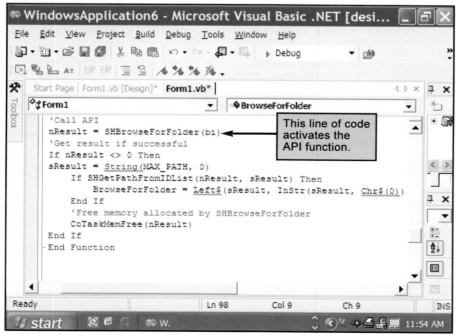

FIGURE 11-57

APIs give programmers control over commonly used program building blocks, such as browsing through file folders.

What's the difference between an API and a component? An API provides programmers with a detailed set of function calls, whereas a component limits programmer control to a good, but not overly extensive, set of predefined combinations. Using API functions, a programmer has a lot of control over details, but typically must learn about and apply many API functions to completely define a task.

In contrast, components provide less control over details, but require less programming. For example, using a component, a programmer might have to add only a single line of code to include a pop-up window in a program. The component might not offer as many options as an API function, however.

Where can I get programming tools? Some programmers like to obtain programming tools "a la carte" by picking up a compiler from one Web site, selecting an interactive debugger from another Web site, and using any handy editor, such as Notepad. More typically, programmers download or purchase an SDK or IDE that contains a collection of programming tools.

An **SDK** (software development kit) is a collection of language-specific programming tools that enables a programmer to develop applications for a specific computer platform, such as Windows PCs. A basic SDK includes a compiler, documentation about the language and syntax, and installation instructions. More sophisticated SDKs might also include an editor, a debugger, a visual user interface design module, and APIs. The components of an SDK are sometimes a hodgepodge of tools without consistent user interfaces for the programmer. For a more polished development environment, programmers turn to IDEs.

An **IDE** (integrated development environment) is a type of SDK that packages a set of development tools into a sleek programming application. The modules in the application—editor, compiler, debugger, and user interface development tool—have a uniform set of menus and controls, which simplifies the programming process.

SDKs and IDEs are available on the Web as shareware or commercial products. Some of these development tools—especially IDEs—are so large that they are not practical to download without a high-speed Internet connection. For programmers limited to dial-up speeds, SDKs and IDEs can be ordered on the Web and shipped on CDs.

INFOWEBLINKS

Programmers can select from a wide variety of components. To find out what's available, connect to the **Components InfoWeb**.

www.course.com/np/concepts8/ch11

QUICKCHECK........TECHTALK

1. A(n) [ ] converts source code into object code stored in executable files that contain [ ] language instructions.

2. Bytecode and MSIL are examples of [ ] languages, which can be converted into machine language by using a Java Virtual Machine or Microsoft's CLR, respectively.

3. Prewritten modules called [ ] are designed to be incorporated into programs and provide building blocks that can save programmers days, weeks, or months of development time.

4. Programmers can use detailed [ ] functions to access application programs or operating system features.

 CHECK ANSWERS

HUMAN FACTORS

A student in Singapore found her 15 minutes of fame when she thumbed 26 words into her cell phone in less than 44 seconds, beating the previous 67-second record. Although some people can use a cell phone keypad to rapidly enter text messages, for most people, a numeric keypad is a frustrating tool for entering text. In addition to the exasperation of dealing with controls for gadgets such as cell phones and remote controls, you probably have pet peeves about the software interfaces for Web sites, productivity software, and computer games.

Today's programming languages provide programmers with sophisticated tools for coding and testing software. Why is it, then, that computers and computer software are so often characterized as being difficult to use? How is it that one of the new words in the computer lexicon is "techno-rage"? What prompts comments such as "My machine sometimes makes me feel like an idiot!"

Programmer and user interface designer Alan Cooper offers an explanation and solution in his book *The Inmates Are Running the Asylum*. The book's title is a metaphor for what Cooper perceives as the current state of computer programming. The "inmates" are computer programmers and the "asylum" is the frustrating, seemingly demented world of computer technology, with its cryptic error messages, puzzling user manuals, and inscrutable "modes" of operation.

According to Cooper, programmers don't intentionally create bad technology products. "Programmers aren't evil. They work hard to make their software easy to use. Unfortunately, their frame of reference is themselves, so they only make it easy to use for other software engineers, not for normal human beings." Cooper suggests that it is possible to create intuitive, easy-to-use technology products by devoting more time to developing detailed product specifications with the assistance of an "interactive designer" who is familiar with the psychology and habits of a typical computer user.

Paul Somerson, writing in *PC Computing* magazine, asserts, "You shouldn't have to plod through manuals, or spend hours waiting on support lines just to get your work done. This stuff is way, way too hard and overcomplicated." Somerson proposes a 10-point User's Bill of Rights that begins "1. All computers should be forced to work the way people do, rather than the other way around."

The first point of Somerson's Bill of Rights echos the last point of another User's Bill of Rights, developed by Clare-Marie Karat, a psychologist and IBM researcher.

The Computer User's Bill of Rights

1. The user is always right. If there is a problem with the use of the system, the system is the problem, not the user.

2. The user has the right to easily install software and hardware systems.

3. The user has the right to a system that performs exactly as promised.

4. The user has the right to easy-to-use instructions for understanding and utilizing a system to achieve desired goals.

5. The user has the right to be in control of the system and to be able to get the system to respond to a request for attention.

6. The user has the right to a system that provides clear, understandable, and accurate information regarding the task it is performing and the progress toward completion.

7. The user has the right to be clearly informed about all system requirements for successfully using software or hardware.

8. The user has the right to know the limits of the system's capabilities.

9. The user has the right to communicate with the technology provider and receive a thoughtful and helpful response when raising concerns.

10. The user should be the master of software and hardware technology, not vice-versa. Products should be natural and intuitive to use.

Source: Clare-Marie Karat, IBM Thomas J. Watson Research Center

Karat agrees with Cooper's comments about programmers being unable to understand the people who use their software. She says, "The profile of the people who use systems has changed, while the system, and the culture in which they have developed, have not adjusted…The engineers and computer scientists who design hardware and software know little about the needs and frustrations of consumers."

BusinessWeek columnist Stephen H. Wildstrom published Karat's Bill of Rights and asked for reader feedback. The response was overwhelming and led Wildstrom to comment in a follow-up article, "The computer industry has a lot of baffled, frustrated, and unhappy customers." Surprisingly, many readers disagreed with the tenets of the Bill of Rights. For example, Jef Raskin, a member of the Macintosh computer design team, pointed out that "the mouse was not intuitive. A person seeing one for the first time had no idea how to use it."

Until we are able to implant some kind of "instant computer genius" chip at birth, it might be that people will just have to invest some time learning how to use a computer. "It shouldn't take a Ph.D. to understand that a few hours invested in learning about the computer and its software will make subsequent products intuitively usable," wrote one concerned *BusinessWeek* reader. Other readers questioned how much simplicity one could really expect from a computer. A computer that is as simple to use as a toaster would seem unlikely. As readers pointed out, a toaster is designed to do only one thing, whereas a computer can perform many different tasks, depending on the software it uses.

Some efforts to simplify operating system software have created another band of disgruntled users who complain that important features are now "hidden" based on feedback from novice testers who considered such features too "advanced" or confusing. Some controls, such as those for setting up networks, are not easy to understand, but could be crucial for a successful installation. Hiding those controls because they might confuse beginners has only caused more advanced users to become frustrated.

Who is right? Can technology be simplified, yet remain powerful enough to accomplish complex tasks? A branch of ergonomics called Human Factors, or Human-Computer Interaction (HCI), focuses on factors that make computers easy or difficult to use. The Human Factors InfoWeb provides more information about HCI and offers some additional food for thought on the usability controversy.

INFOWEBLINKS

You can read more about user-oriented software design at the **Human Factors InfoWeb**.

www.course.com/np/concepts8/ch11

WHAT DO YOU THINK?

1. Can you think of a specific instance when you have become frustrated with a software user interface? ○ Yes ○ No ○ Not sure

2. Is it possible to make computer software significantly easier to use? ○ Yes ○ No ○ Not sure

3. Would you agree that programmers do not understand the viewpoint of a typical computer user and consequently produce bad software? ○ Yes ○ No ○ Not sure

11

SAVE RESPONSES

COMPUTERS IN CONTEXT
AGRICULTURE

Agriculture might seem like a low-tech enterprise, but many farmers are turning to technology for help managing their finances, crops, and livestock. Even home gardeners who need little more than a few seed packets and a hoe are digging into computer and Internet resources for tips on combating garden pests, growing spectacular roses, and producing a bumper crop of veggies. Need to identify the pesky insect that's eating your tomatoes? Worried about the black spots appearing on your apple trees? Trying to figure out if that sprout is a flower or a weed? Many of your gardening questions are answered at sites sponsored by Prince Edward Island Forestry and Agriculture Information Centre, the National Gardening Association, Organic Gardening.com, and many more.

Computers first sprouted up on farms to take care of financial matters. Farming, like any business, is all about the bottom line—the profit that's left after paying for seed, feed, fertilizer, machinery, taxes, utilities, and labor. Tracking income and expenses provides essential information for analyzing ways to improve operations and generate more profit. To keep track of finances, farmers typically use generic small-business accounting software, such as Quicken, or vertical market software designed especially for farming.

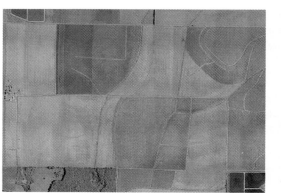

Farmers also use computers to maintain and analyze production records for crops and livestock. The Manitoba Milk Revenue Analyzer is an Excel spreadsheet template designed to help farmers pick the best dairy management scenario by analyzing factors such as feed costs and milk production levels. The colorfully named CowChips decision support software can help farmers improve cow herds and explore production, marketing, and financial alternatives.

How does a farmer decide whether to plant fields with soybeans or wheat? The Internet offers resources such as The Alberta Agriculture, Food, and Rural Development Web site where farmers can use an interactive crop cost calculator to compare profit potential for up to four crops. The calculator uses average market value for each crop and expected yield per acre based on the farm's growing zone. It produces a table that shows costs and estimated profit for each crop.

Suppose that a farmer decides to plant durum wheat. How much seed is needed? Too much seed is wasted money. Not enough seed produces scanty crops. A Web-based seed calculator helps farmers decide how much seed is necessary to produce the desired plant population. It also provides instructions for calibrating the seeder so that it sows the correct amount of seed. And what if chickweeds are choking out the sunflower crop? Alberta's Agriculture Web site offers an expert system to determine the most effective herbicide.

Farmers use the Internet to gather information about weather, market reports, farm equipment, loans, crops, and livestock. Lively discussions take place in "ag" chat groups, such as Farm Business, Crop Scouting, Cattle Talk, Hog Talk, and Insect Chat. Farmers subscribe to e-mail newsletters, such as ePigSense, and tap government resources, such as the USDA (United States Department of Agriculture) Hogs and Pigs Quarterly report.

The cutting edge of agricultural technology revolves around remote sensing, satellite imaging, geographical information systems, and global positioning systems. Remote sensing involves gathering information about an object without being in physical contact with it. For agriculture, two of the most often used remote sensing tools are satellite imaging and aerial photography. Weather satellite images are readily available and help farmers decide the best days to plant and harvest crops. Topographical satellite images can help farmers analyze drainage patterns to prevent crops from being flooded. Other satellite images can be used for crop surveillance—looking for areas of low yield, drought, disease, and infestation.

A graphical information system (GIS) is a computer-based tool for storing data and creating layered maps of the earth's surface. A GIS can store data about many factors important to farmers, such as soil moisture, salinity, nitrogen levels, and acidity. To collect data for a GIS, farmers use a global positioning system (GPS) and a variety of monitoring devices. Throughout the growing season, farmers use GPSs to find specific locations in their fields where they record data from soil sampling and observations of weed growth, unusual plant stress, and growth conditions. They can enter this data into a GIS program, along with data from satellite images, to create maps that help them gauge where to plant, what to plant, and how to care for plants.

The experience of a North Dakota farmer illustrates how data from satellite images and GPS observations can be combined in a GIS to create valuable agricultural maps. The farmer was producing a bountiful harvest of sugar beets, but the crop's sugar content was low. The farmer enlisted the help of agriculture experts at a nearby university who obtained a satellite image of the fields that showed areas of high and low production. The next step was to take soil samples—one every half acre. A handheld GPS was used to make sure samples were taken in an exact half-acre grid pattern. The satellite and soil sample data were then entered into a GIS, which produced a map overlaid with a multicolored grid. Grid colors cor-

responded to the amount of nitrogen that should be applied for best production. But how to apply these varying levels of nitrogen in each small area? The farmer used GPS-equipped machinery to spread the correct amount of nitrogen in each area of the field. This selective fertilization, along with crop rotation to further even out nitrogen levels, increased the beets' sugar content and the farmer's income.

Applying detailed agricultural data collected with a GPS is called "precision farming." Several specialized tools, such as GPS-equipped yield monitors, help farmers collect data on bushels per acre, wet and dry bushels, total pounds, acres per hour, acres worked, and grain moisture content. Yield monitors are usually installed on the combines that harvest crops. The data is recorded on a memory card for later analysis and mapping.

Although a variety of agricultural technologies are available, not all farmers embrace them with equal enthusiasm. Barriers to using technology such as computers, GISs, GPSs, and satellite imaging include cost, training, and concerns about reliability, privacy, and security. The cost of obtaining satellite images, for example, has been the biggest deterrent to regular use of this data; the main barrier to the use of computers is simply a lack of expertise. Busy farmers might not have time to learn how to use even basic computer programs, and a fairly complex GIS database application can seem particularly daunting. University and government agencies are targeting farmers with special extension courses on agriculture-specific software for accounting, livestock decision support, and crop management. The goal is to make these technology tools part of the legacy that's handed down to the next generation of farmers.

INFOWEBLINKS

You'll find lots more information at the **Computers and Agriculture InfoWeb**.

www.course.com/np/concepts8/ch11

11

INTERACTIVE SUMMARY

To review important concepts from this chapter, fill in the blanks to best complete each sentence. When using the NP8 BookOnCD, click the Check Answers buttons to automatically score your answers. Place your Tracking Disk in the floppy disk drive if you want to save your scores.

Each line of instructions for a computer program is referred to as [   ]. Computer programmers focus on [   ] computer programs, but also plan, test, and document computer programs. In contrast, software [   ] tend to focus on designing and [   ] activities.

A computer programming language is a set of [   ] and grammar rules for creating instructions that can ultimately be processed by a computer. The first programming languages were low-level [   ] languages. Second-generation programming languages, called [   ] languages, allowed programmers to write programs consisting of abbreviated op codes instead of 1s and 0s. Third-generation languages provided programmers with easy-to-remember command words, such as PRINT and INPUT. Fourth-generation languages eliminated many of the strict punctuation and [   ] rules that complicated third-generation languages.

Experts believe that [   ] languages, such as Prolog, constitute a fifth generation of computer languages. Other experts define fifth-generation languages as those that allow programmers to use graphical or visual tools to construct programs.

Before program code can be written, a programmer needs a clear problem [   ], which includes a list of assumptions, a description of known information, and a specification for what constitutes a solution. With a clear plan, a programmer can begin coding using a generic text editor, a program editor, or a [   ] development environment. A program is not complete until it has been tested to ensure that it contains no [   ] errors or runtime errors. All computer programs should include internal documentation in the form of [   ], which are explanatory comments inserted into a computer program along with lines of code.

CHECK ANSWERS

Programming [   ] affect the way programmers conceptualize and approach a computer program. Every computer language supports one or more programming approaches. Languages such as COBOL and FORTRAN support a traditional approach to programming called the [   ] paradigm, which is based on a step-by-step [   ]. Various planning tools, such as structured English, [   ], and flowcharts, help programmers plan the steps for a procedural program.

Procedural languages provide a variety of [   ] structures that allow program-

mers to specify the order of program execution. A [   ] control structure directs the computer to execute one or more instructions, not coded as a simple succession of steps. A [   ] control provides a choice of paths, based on whether a condition is true or false. A [   ] control, or "loop," repeats one or more instructions until a certain condition is met. The procedural paradigm provides a solid approach to problems that can be solved by following a set of steps. Procedural languages tend to produce programs that run quickly and use [   ] resources efficiently.

CHECK ANSWERS

The object-oriented paradigm is based on the idea that the solution to a problem can be visualized in terms of objects that [_____] with each other. An object is a single instance of an entity. Programmers can use a [_____] as a template for a group of objects with similar characteristics. Classes can be derived from other classes through a process called [_____]. The set of superclasses and subclasses that are related to each other is referred to as a class [_____]. OO programmers often use [_____] Modeling Language diagrams to plan the classes for a program.

Objects interact to solve problems by exchanging [_____], which initiate an action, process, or procedure. OO programmers can create [_____] to define what happens once an action is initiated. Methods provide good flexibility because a concept called [_____], or "overloading," allows programmers to create a single, generic name for a procedure that behaves in unique ways for different classes. The OO paradigm allows programmers to hide the internal details of objects and their methods. This process, called [_____], allows objects to be easily reused, modified, and repurposed.

Computer historians believe [_____] was the first computer language to work with objects, classes, inheritance, and methods. It is a language called [_____], however, that is regarded as the classic object-oriented programming language. The object-oriented paradigm has become so popular that many procedural languages have been given OO capabilities. [_____], which originated at the Department of Defense, was originally a procedural language, but now includes OO features. The C language was modified into a language called [_____], and again modified into C#, which allows programmers to work with objects. Recent versions of [_____] Basic also offer programmers the option of working within the object-oriented paradigm.

 CHECK ANSWERS

Programming languages such as Prolog support the [_____] programming paradigm because they encourage programmers to describe a [_____] rather than its solution.

Prolog programs are typically built from a collection of facts and rules. A Prolog fact begins with a [_____], such as shapeof, followed by a series of [_____] within parentheses, such as (pizza,round). Each Prolog rule has a [_____], which defines an outcome or fact, followed by the notation :-, which means "if." The body of the rule consists of one or more clauses that define conditions that must be satisfied to validate the head of the rule. Prolog uses a process called [_____] to evaluate facts and rules to determine whether they are true.

A programmer can test a program and follow the sequence of instantiation and the state of each variable by using a handy [_____] feature.

Declarative languages, such as Prolog, can be used for problems that require calculations, but those problems are typically better suited to [_____] languages. As a rule of thumb, declarative languages are best suited for problems that pertain to words and concepts rather than numbers. They are a good choice for applications such as [_____] that contain complex relationships among records, decision support systems that handle semi-structured problems, and expert systems that require analysis of multiple, interrelated factors.

CHECK ANSWERS

11

INTERACTIVE KEY TERMS

Make sure you understand all the boldfaced key terms presented in this chapter. If you're using the NP8 BookOnCD, you can use this list of terms as an interactive study activity. First, try to define a term in your own words, and then click the term to compare your definition with the definition presented in the chapter.

.NET Framework, 620
Ada, 575
Algorithm, 584
API, 622
APL, 575
Argument, 609
Assembly language, 573
Assumption, 576
Backtracking, 613
BASIC, 575
Bytecode, 620
C, 575
C#, 575
C++, 575
Class, 597
Class attribute, 598
Class hierarchy, 599
CLR, 621
COBOL, 575
Code, 570
Compiler, 620
Component, 622
Computer programming, 571
Constant, 611
Control, 579
Control structures, 590
CPL, 575
Debugger, 581
Decision table, 609
Declarative paradigm, 608
Eiffel, 575
Encapsulation, 607
Event, 580
Event-driven paradigm, 581
Event-handling code, 580
Fact, 608
Fifth-generation languages, 574
First-generation languages, 573
Flowchart, 587

Form design grid, 579
FORTRAN, 575
Fourth-generation languages, 574
Function, 591
Functional paradigm, 608
Generic text editor, 577
Goal, 610
Haskell, 575
High-level language, 572
IDE, 623
Inheritance, 599
Instantiation, 612
Intermediate language, 620
Interpreter, 621
Java, 575
Java Virtual Machine, 620
Keyword, 572
Known information, 577
LISP, 575
Logic error, 581
Loop, 593
Low-level language, 572
Machine language, 573
Message, 601
Method, 600
MSIL, 620
Multiparadigm languages, 575
Object, 597
Object code, 620
Object-oriented paradigm, 597
Parameters, 572
Pascal, 575
PL/1, 575
Polymorphism, 602
Predicate, 609
Private attribute, 598
Problem statement, 576
Procedural language, 584
Procedural paradigm, 584

Procedure, 591
Program editor, 578
Programming language, 572
Programming paradigm, 575
Prolog, 575
Properties, 579
Pseudocode, 587
Public attribute, 598
Remarks, 582
Repetition control structure, 593
RPG, 575
Rule, 608
Runtime error, 581
Scheme, 575
SDK, 623
Second-generation languages, 573
Selection control structure, 592
Sequence control structure, 590
Sequential execution, 590
SIMULA, 575
Smalltalk, 575
Software engineering, 571
Source code, 620
Structured English, 587
Subclass, 599
Subroutine, 591
Superclass, 599
Syntax, 572
Syntax error, 581
Third-generation languages, 573
Trace feature, 618
UML, 598
Variable, 611
VDE, 579
Visual Basic, 575
Walkthrough, 589

INTERACTIVE SITUATION QUESTIONS

Apply what you've learned to some typical computing situations. When using the NP8 BookOnCD, you can type your answers, and then use the Check Answers button to automatically score your responses. Place your Tracking Disk in the floppy disk drive if you want to save your scores.

1. A friend asks you for help writing a computer program to calculate the square yards of carpet needed for a dorm room. The statement "the living room floor is rectangular" is an example of a(n) [   ]. The length and width of the room are examples of [   ] information, which you would probably obtain as [   ] from the user.

2. Continuing with the carpet example, you devise a set of steps, or a(n) [   ], to solve the problem. You then use a computer language to write the [   ] shown below, which expresses the algorithm.

```
Input "Enter the width of the room
   in feet: "; width
Input "Enter the length of the room
   in feet: "; length
Print "Carpet needed:"
Print length*width & " square feet"
Print (length*width)/9 & "square
   yards"
```

3. Examine the code shown below. This program prints [   ] lines of text.

```
For n = 1 To 5
    Print "Loop number " & n
Next n
```

4. You've just joined a programming team that is developing a Java program for an earth-moving equipment vendor. The lead programmer shows you a UML with labels such as Cranes, Trucks, and Front-end Loaders. With your background in object-oriented programming, you can tell

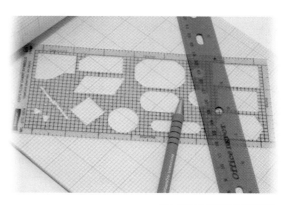

immediately that these are [   ], which will be coded as a series of attributes, such as `private string manufacturer`.

5. While browsing through several programs posted online, you come across the following code and realize it is written using the [   ] programming language.

```
male(frodo).
male(mungo).
male(largo).
male(balbo).
female(berylla).
female(belladonna).
female(primula).
female(sella).
parents(mungo,berylla,balbo).
parents(frodo,primula,drogo).
parents(largo,berylla,balbo).
parents(sella,berylla,balbo).
brother_of(X,Y):-
    male(Y),
    parents(X,Mother,Father),
    parents(Y,Mother,Father).
```

 CHECK ANSWERS

11

INTERACTIVE PRACTICE TESTS

Practice tests that consist of 10 multiple-choice, true/false, and fill-in-the-blank questions are available on both the NP8 BookOnCD and the NP8 Web site. The questions are selected at random from a large test bank, so each time you take a test, you'll receive a different set of questions. Your tests are scored immediately, and you can print study guides that help you find the correct answers for any questions that you missed.

REVIEW
ON THE WEB

PROJECTS

An NP8 Project is an open-ended activity that helps you apply the concepts you have learned. Many projects require resources in addition to your textbook, such as current magazines, library materials, or Web access. When you tackle a project, be prepared to use your critical thinking skills, logical analysis, and creativity. Projects for this chapter include:

- **Issue Research: Human-Computer Interaction**
- **Algorithm Exchange**
- **Computers in Context: Agriculture**
- **Programming Languages**
- **Grading Computer Literacy Exams**
- **The Tourist Problem**
- **Genealogy**

To work with the Projects for this chapter, connect to the **New Perspectives NP8 Web Site**.

www.course.com/np/concepts8/ch11

TECHTV VIDEO PROJECT

In the TechTV segment *Design Your Own Video Game*, the guest is a young programmer who talks about Blitz Basic and demonstrates some simple game programs. As you watch the video, make a list of at least 10 terms presented in the video that are included in the Interactive Key Terms list for Chapter 11. Write a short definition for each of these terms. Also, make a list of at least two terms from the video that were not presented in Chapter 11. Use the Web or other sources to find definitions for these terms.

To work with the Video Projects for this chapter, connect to the **New Perspectives NP8 Web Site**.

www.course.com/np/concepts8/ch11

STUDY TIPS

Study Tips help you to organize and consolidate the information in a chapter by making lists, outlines, charts, and sketches. You can use paper and pencil or word processing software to complete most of the Study Tips.

To work with the Study Tips for this chapter, connect to the **New Perspectives NP8 Web Site**.

www.course.com/np/concepts8/ch11

ONLINE GAMES

Test your comprehension of the concepts introduced in Chapter 11 by playing the NP8 Online Games. At the end of each game, you have three options:

- Print a comprehensive study guide complete with page references
- Print your results to be submitted to your instructor
- Save your results to be submitted to your instructor via e-mail

To work with the Online Games for this chapter, connect to the **New Perspectives NP8 Web Site**.

www.course.com/np/concepts8/ch11

STUDENT EDITION LABS

Extend your knowledge of visual programming with the Chapter 11 Student Edition Labs.

The following Student Edition Lab is offered with Chapter 11:

• **Visual Programming**

Go to the NP8 New Perspectives Web site for specific lab topics.

To work with the Chapter 11 Student Edition Lab and its corresponding lab assignment, connect to the **New Perspectives NP8 Web Site**.

www.course.com/np/concepts8/ch11

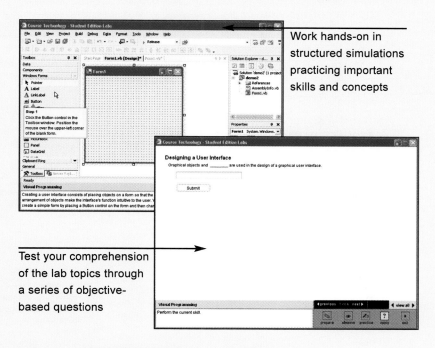

Work hands-on in structured simulations practicing important skills and concepts

Test your comprehension of the lab topics through a series of objective-based questions

Track Your Progress with the Student Edition Labs

• Student Edition Labs test your comprehension of the lab topics through a series of trackable objective-based questions. Your instructor will direct you to either print your results or submit them via e-mail.

• Student Edition Lab Assignments, available on the New Perspectives NP8 Web site, require you to apply the skills learned through the lab in a live environment. Go to the New Perspectives NP8 Web site for detailed instruction on individual Student Edition Lab Assignments.

If you have a SAM user profile, you have access to even more interactive content. Log in to your SAM account and go to your assignments page to see what your instructor has assigned for this chapter.

12.

BEYOND DESKTOP COMPUTING

CONTENTS

TIP

When using the BookOnCD, the ❄ icons are "clickable" to access resources on the CD. The ✚ icons are clickable to access resources on the Web. You can also access Web resources by using your browser to connect directly to the NP8 New Perspectives Web site at:

www.course.com/np/concepts8/ch12

CHAPTER PREVIEW

Before you begin Chapter 12, you can use the Web-based preview activities to hear an overview of the chapter, check your current level of expertise about key concepts, and look through a list of learning objectives. You can access the preview activities by clicking the icon when using the BookOnCD or going to the New Perspectives NP8 Web site.

CHAPTER OVERVIEW

Most of us don't think of modern computers as huge, number-crunching machines tended by a cadre of engineers and scientists. However, large-scale computing systems exist today, and the tasks they handle go far beyond the capabilities of personal computers. Get your book and high-lighter ready, then connect to the New Perspectives NP8 Web site where you can listen to an overview that points out the most important concepts for this chapter.

www.course.com/np/concepts8/ch12

CHAPTER PRE-ASSESSMENT

How much do you know about enterprise and high-performance computing? To gauge your level of knowledge before beginning the chapter, take the pre-assessment quiz at the New Perspectives NP8 Web site. Armed with your results from this quiz, you can focus your study time on concepts that will round out your knowledge of large-scale computing and improve your test scores.

www.course.com/np/concepts8/ch12

LEARNING OBJECTIVES

When you complete this chapter you should be able to:

- Define enterprise computing and describe its key characteristics
- Explain how enterprise systems achieve hardware and application integration
- Define high-performance computing and list some examples of high-performance computing applications
- Explain how the term "compute-intensive" relates to high-performance computing
- Describe the input, processing, output, and storage hardware of a typical enterprise computing system

- Explain how supercomputers, servers, and personal computers contribute to the architecture of high-performance computing systems
- Describe and diagram centralized, distributed, tiered, and grid computing architectures
- Discuss how quality of service relates to large-scale computer systems

A detailed list of learning objectives is provided at the New Perspectives NP8 Web site

www.course.com/np/concepts8/ch12

SECTION A

LARGE-SCALE COMPUTING

You might not think large-scale computer systems affect you, but if you've ever used an ATM, purchased an airline ticket, or filed your taxes online, you've interacted with a large-scale enterprise computing system. On the other side of the large-scale computing spectrum, high-performance computing systems power many research projects and commercial endeavors, such as processing the data collected by the Hubble telescope or creating complex investment risk models for financial institutions. In this section, you learn the definitions of enterprise computing and high-performance computing. You'll also find out how these two types of systems differ from each other and from standard information systems.

ENTERPRISE COMPUTING

What is enterprise computing? **Enterprise computing** is defined as one or more information systems that share data and typically supply information to hundreds or thousands of users who may be located in diverse geographical locations. Enterprise computing systems also offer more than one service, and they process a large number of transactions.

For example, UPS (United Parcel Service) uses an enterprise computing system to track and deliver more than 13 million packages every day. Each package is accompanied by a waybill containing the shipper's name and address, the recipient's name and address, and a tracking number. The information on the waybill is required by several departments within UPS, as shown in Figure 12-1.

Making waybill and tracking information available to customers, drivers, sorting centers, and various UPS departments is not simple because data must be accessed from a variety of computers and communications equipment, which require data in several different formats. An enterprise computing system is able to unite these disparate hardware platforms and software applications by creating what appears to be one large information system, accessible to a variety of customers and company employees. Without its enterprise computing system, UPS would not have the technology to handle the shipping volume required to remain one of the world's leading parcel delivery couriers.

FIGURE 12-1

Information from a waybill can be accessed by customers and employees in many departments, making an enterprise system an important tool for UPS operations.

CLICK TO START

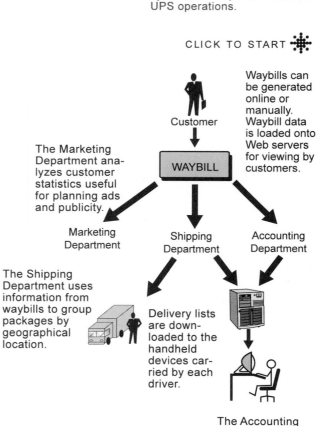

Customer

Waybills can be generated online or manually. Waybill data is loaded onto Web servers for viewing by customers.

The Marketing Department analyzes customer statistics useful for planning ads and publicity.

WAYBILL

Marketing Department

Shipping Department

Accounting Department

The Shipping Department uses information from waybills to group packages by geographical location.

Delivery lists are downloaded to the handheld devices carried by each driver.

The Accounting Department accesses waybill information for billing.

What's the difference between an enterprise system and an information system? The difference between an enterprise system and an information system is one of scope. Whereas an information system is dedicated to one set of related tasks, an enterprise computing system encompasses the tasks associated with multiple information systems, as well as the task of integrating these systems to work together and share data. An enterprise system usually includes several information systems, such as a transaction processing system, management information system, decision support system, and possibly an expert system.

UPS's LANs handle word processing, e-mail, and other office functions. A transaction processing system handles payroll and accounting. A decision support system allows the Marketing Department to analyze data and make marketing decisions. A Web server provides online access to shipping rates, package tracking information, and transit times. An enterprise computing system integrates these diverse information systems so that they can share data and computing resources. For example, UPS's enterprise system allows the Web site to automatically display a package's delivery status, using data collected by a UPS driver, when a package is delivered to its destination.

What is the scale of an enterprise system? Enterprise computing systems are classified as "large-scale" systems because they contain from a few dozen to several thousand computers. The size of a specific system depends on several factors—the size of the organization, the number of transactions processed each day, the number of users accessing data, and the geographical area in which computers and users are located.

To get some idea of the scale of enterprise computing systems, consider that SABRE's ticketing system distributes airline, hotel, tour, and car rental information to more than 56,000 travel agencies worldwide. The computer systems that run online games might be required to handle as many as 118,000 simultaneous players during peak times. Parcel delivery services require systems that handle millions of packages every day (Figure 12-2). These statistics are impressive, especially when you realize these companies are growing, and their computer systems are expanding every year.

FIGURE 12-2

The enterprise computing system used by UPS boasts 14 mainframes, 293 terabytes of storage space, 2,445 mid-range computers, 225,000 personal computers, 5,500 servers, and 70,000 wireless DIADs—the "delivery information acquisition devices" carried by UPS drivers.

Can an enterprise computing system expand to meet the demands of a growing business? A well-designed computer system must change to meet demand. Standard information systems, however, often have limited capacity for expansion. For example, imagine a nationwide health insurance company with a processing center in Denver, Colorado. When the number of claims outstrips the processing center's capacity, the company opens a new office in St. Louis, Missouri. The offices have similar, but separate, information systems. Claims from the eastern U.S. are routed to the St. Louis office, while claims from western states are routed to the Denver office. These separate information systems prove to be less than optimal, however, because they cannot share data for clients who move or receive medical care in more than one region.

An enterprise computing system is a better solution for the health insurance company because it is designed for scalability. **Scalability** refers to the ability of a computer system to shrink or grow as requirements change. "Scaling up" and "scaling out" are two methods for increasing the capacity of computer systems. **Scaling up** means increasing individual machine performance by adding processors, memory, and storage capacity. **Scaling out** means adding more computers to increase the overall size of a system.

Successful enterprise systems provide cost-effective and time-sensitive scalability. Cost-effective scalability means the system can grow without a large financial investment. Time-sensitive scalability means the system can be scaled without disabling it for a long period of time.

Enterprise computing systems can offer several scalability options. For example, enterprise-level claims-processing application software can allow Denver and St. Louis offices to share one database in which all claims are stored. Another enterprise solution would be to set up a distributed database server with one node in Denver and another in St. Louis. A third option would be to set up two database servers and synchronize them at specified intervals. These options are illustrated in Figure 12-3.

FIGURE 12-3

An enterprise computing system's scalability options include sharing a database, distributing the database, or synchronizing databases at specified time intervals.

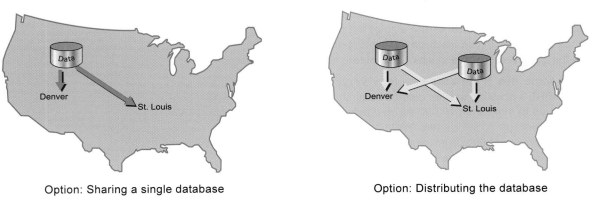

Option: Sharing a single database   Option: Distributing the database

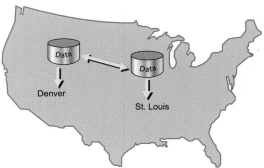

Option: Periodically synchronizing two databases

What is enterprise system integration? The process of connecting two or more information systems in a way that allows scalability and data sharing is referred to as **enterprise system integration**. This process encompasses both enterprise hardware integration and enterprise application integration.

Enterprise hardware integration refers to the process of connecting different types of hardware. Specialized hardware or software allows different types of devices to interoperate. For example, suppose the reporters and editors who work for a newspaper publisher use Windows computers on a LAN for word processing and research. The publisher's graphic design and layout experts use Macintosh computers connected to an AppleTalk network. Each LAN also includes printers, scanners, and other devices such as tape backup units. To allow a reporter using a Windows computer to print documents on a printer connected to the AppleTalk network, at least two links must be established:

■ A physical link allows the reporter's computer to communicate with the printer on the AppleTalk LAN. Typically this link is established by connecting the AppleTalk and the Windows LANs so that computers on either network can access the printer.

■ A link between systems allows the two devices to understand each other's commands and data. This link is accomplished through software or hardware drivers.

After these two links are established, the hardware is integrated and a reporter can print directly to the printer on the Macintosh network. This example takes into account only two separate LANs. In a typical large-scale computing system, hardware integration can involve hundreds or even thousands of diverse devices and LANs. Figure 12-4 shows how an enterprise system integrates many different hardware devices.

FIGURE 12-4

Enterprise-level hardware integration links diverse types of processing, input, output, and storage equipment.

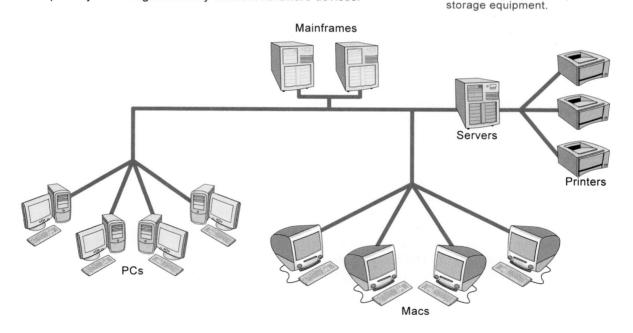

Mainframes

Servers

Printers

PCs

Macs

Enterprise application integration (EAI) is the process of configuring software applications to exchange data. Applications that exchange data can streamline processing by allowing quick and easy access to all information pertaining to a query, procedure, or transaction. For example, your cell phone service provider can integrate its billing, transaction, and subscription software so that you can go to one Web site to pay your bill, view recent telephone call data, or change your calling plan.

How can an enterprise integrate applications? Enterprise application integration can be achieved using four techniques: database linking, application linking, data warehousing, and common virtual systems.

■ **Database linking** is a process that allows databases to share or replicate information as required. For example, the company that issues your credit card uses a computer system to process credit card charges. Data about cardholder transactions is stored in a database. Because hundreds of thousands of transactions are processed every day, one database server is not sufficient; multiple database servers are required. These servers and their databases must be linked to share information, so that, for example, you are not allowed to exceed your credit limit. Database management software usually automates this linking and makes EAI possible.

FIGURE 12-5
Application linking helps customer service representatives seamlessly access data from two applications.

■ **Application linking** is a process that allows computer systems to share information among software applications. Linked applications work together to provide services and display information previously available only by accessing each of the multiple applications individually. For example, credit-card company customer service representatives who answer customer questions about credit balances, late payments, and lost cards use a software application to keep track of customer questions and requests for information. Customer service representatives also require access to transaction records. One way to access this information is to allow customer service representatives to link directly to the transaction processing database. However, this scheme would force customer service representatives to access two separate applications for every customer query, slowing down service and introducing potential errors. A better solution would be to link the two applications, so that the customer service application automatically accesses the transaction database and displays transaction information formatted and filtered for customer service use (Figure 12-5).

■ **Data warehousing** is the process of collecting historic data so that it can be analyzed to uncover trends and predict future behaviors. For example, your credit card company might use data warehousing to predict spending trends, market new services to prospective customers, and detect fraud. Have you ever wondered how your credit card company determines whether your credit card has been stolen? Sophisticated data warehousing techniques can collect, analyze, and predict fraudulent behavior. One common fraud technique—the theft of newly issued cards directly from a mailbox—can be detected by combining and analyzing data from transaction systems and customer information systems. A newly issued card that is suddenly used for an unusual number of transactions would fit the theft profile and be flagged as a possible stolen card.

■ A **common virtual system** links all enterprise components into what appears to be one unified system. Transactions or processes running on a common virtual system have immediate access to any data stored on the enterprise system, regardless of where the data exists. In the case of a credit card company, a common virtual system allows a person with the appropriate security access to locate a particular credit card transaction, and then quickly access information about the cardholder who performed the transaction, information about marketing trends for that marketing segment, sales data from the store where the transaction took place, and any other relevant information stored in the credit card company's enterprise computing system.

INFOWEBLINKS

Learn more about enterprise techniques that protect against fraud by connecting to the **EAI InfoWeb**. ✠

www.course.com/np/concepts8/ch12

HIGH-PERFORMANCE COMPUTING

What is high-performance computing? In 1996, thousands of people watched as chess champion Garry Kasparov nearly met his match playing chess against a computer nicknamed Deep Blue. He barely won the six-game series, but immediately challenged the computer to a rematch. IBM designers went to work upgrading and improving Deep Blue. The following year, Kasparov resigned the match only 19 moves into the sixth game. Deep Blue had won (Figure 12-6).

FIGURE 12-6
Kasparov played Deep Blue on a conventional chess board. Moves were relayed to the computer by a technician stationed at a keyboard.

Deep Blue is probably the best known example of high-performance computing. The term **high-performance computing** (HPC) refers to a branch of computer science that focuses on ways to optimize computer processing capabilities. High-performance computing systems are designed to handle computationally complex tasks, extremely large data sets, and operations that require lightning-fast response. For example, Deep Blue was optimized for playing chess and had the capacity to evaluate 200 million chess moves every second.

High-performance computing systems are not limited to playing chess. They are used for a wide range of tasks, including car design, weather forecasting, earthquake prediction, and genetic research. Many HPC applications involve scientific research, such as simulating the aerodynamics of space vehicles or modeling the folding action of a protein.

HPC is uniquely suited for cutting-edge research, which typically requires massive numbers of computations based on complex numerical models and huge data sets. Conventional computing systems are far too slow to complete such computations in a reasonable period of time. For example, an HPC computer called ASCI Q performs calculations for the U.S. Department of Energy at a rate of 30 teraFLOPS. To put that processing speed into perspective, in one hour a supercomputer running at 30 teraFLOPS can complete calculations that would require months of processing on today's fastest personal computers.

INFOWEBLINKS

The Deep Blue development team is working on an even more sophisticated chess-playing computer. You'll find more information about interesting HPC projects at the **HPC Applications InfoWeb**.

www.course.com/np/concepts8/ch12

12

What's a teraFLOP? Whereas the processing speed of a typical personal computer is measured in megahertz, the speed of HPC systems is typically measured in FLOPS or MIPS.

FLOPS is an acronym for "floating-point operations per second." Floating-point numbers, such as 5.0, .333, and 3.142, can include fractional parts and are typically displayed with decimal places. In contrast, integers are whole numbers. Floating-point operations take much longer to compute than integer operations and occur frequently in HPC applications.

MIPS is the acronym for "millions of instructions per second" and indicates the speed at which a computer executes instructions of any kind. Figure 12-7 highlights the difference in processing speed for personal computers and high-performance computers.

FIGURE 12-7
Processing Speed

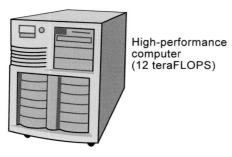

High-performance computer (12 teraFLOPS)

Measurement	Abbreviation	Instructions per Second
MegaFLOPS	MFLOPS	1 million
GigaFLOPS	GFLOPS	1 billion
TeraFLOPS	TFLOPS	1 trillion
PetaFLOPS	PFLOPS	1000 trillion

3.2 GHz Pentium 4 computer (about 6 gigaFLOPS)

What is "compute intensive"? A **compute-intensive** problem is one that requires massive amounts of data to be processed using complex mathematical calculations. Molecular calculations, atmospheric models, and cosmological research are all examples of projects that require massive numbers of data points to be manipulated, processed, and analyzed.

Scientists at the Department of Energy had a compute-intensive problem on their hands when they studied the atomic behaviors of materials used for magnetic storage devices, such as hard disks and magnetic tapes. The study required a series of 30 trillion calculations for every atom in a cube of iron two millionth of a centimeter across. Because a cube this size contains 1,458 atoms, its analysis required an astounding 45 quadrillion calculations! Even more astounding: The analysis was not complete. A complete analysis would require calculations for an iron cube containing 27,000 atoms—about 20 times more atoms than in the original project.

The complexity of the calculations required for much of today's critical research in medicine, engineering, climatology, and space exploration is what drives computer scientists to develop newer and faster HPC systems. Even with the massive computing power now available, some compute-intensive calculations are still not feasible.

INFOWEBLINKS

For additional examples of compute-intensive problems that affect research related to many aspects of your daily life, connect to the **Compute-intensive Problems InfoWeb**.

www.course.com/np/concepts8/ch12

How does high-performance computing differ from enterprise computing? High-performance computing focuses on compute-intensive problems, whereas enterprise computing distributes its processing capabilities over a wide range of processing tasks that might take place within an organization. Historically, high-performance computing was applied to scientific and engineering problems, but enterprise computing was applied to business problems. Within the historical context, high-performance computing was carried out by supercomputers, in contrast to enterprise computing, which was carried out by networks of mainframes, minicomputers, terminals, and personal computers.

Today, high-performance computing and enterprise computing can overlap in some situations. HPC has been applied to business tasks that involve very large data sets or compute-intensive calculations. For example, Google operates a huge network of computer servers dedicated to indexing vast streams of Web data and servicing search queries. Although Google officially admits to operating more than 10,000 servers, experts estimate the number is between 45,000 and 80,000, with at least 126 teraflops of processing speed—well into the realm of high-performance computing.

Similarly, some enterprise technologies have had an effect on high-performance computing. Whereas high-performance computing installations were once centered on a single supercomputer, many of these monolithic supercomputers have been replaced by clusters of distributed computers, accessible using a variety of personal computers, workstations, and terminals. In the next sections of this chapter, you learn more about the hardware and network configurations used for high-performance and enterprise computing.

QUICKCHECK......SECTION A

1. The main difference between an enterprise system and an HPC system is processing power. True or false? [   ]

2. When an enterprise system is scaled [   ], the overall size of the system is increased by adding more computers.

3. Enterprise system [   ] connects two or more information systems in a way that provides scalability and data sharing.

4. A common [   ] system is an enterprise system in which all components are linked and appear to be one unified system.

5. The branch of computer science that focuses on ways to optimize computer processing capabilities is called high-[   ] computing.

6. HPC systems are designed for compute-[   ] problems, which require massive amounts of data to be processed using complex mathematical calculations.

7. The acronyms [   ] and MIPS are used to measure the speed of HPC systems.

 CHECK ANSWERS

 12

SECTION B

COMPONENTS OF LARGE-SCALE COMPUTING SYSTEMS

Enterprise and high-performance computing systems work on a completely different scale than smaller, traditional information systems and personal computers. Enterprise computing systems contain hundreds or thousands of computers, hardware devices, and software packages. High-performance systems might not incorporate as many devices as enterprise systems, but the massive amounts of data they process and the speed at which they operate put them on a different level from standard information systems. In this section, you learn about the hardware and software technologies that form the foundation for enterprise and HPC systems.

ENTERPRISE HARDWARE

What types of hardware can be incorporated into an enterprise system? An enterprise computing system can include a diverse array of processing, storage, input, and output hardware. For example, a single enterprise system might consist of UNIX, Macintosh, and Windows computers; output devices ranging from high-speed printers to video output devices; and input devices including digital cameras, credit card readers, and UPC scanning devices such as the ones used in supermarkets and other retail stores.

Some enterprise systems incorporate proprietary devices designed for a specific organization or application. For example, package sorters who work at UPS distribution centers use wearable Bluetooth scanners to collect data from waybills. Data is wirelessly transmitted to waist-worn Wi-Fi devices, and then relayed to the company network.

UPS drivers carry small portable DIADs (Delivery Information Acquisition Devices) that scan bar codes, record customer signatures, and transmit data to distribution centers via Bluetooth, Wi-Fi, or cellular service (Figure 12-8). The devices also link to GPS satellites so that drivers can find customer locations for package pickup and delivery.

FIGURE 12-8

Specialized input devices, such as this UPS scanner, can be part of an enterprise computing system.

As technology improves and an organization's needs change, a true enterprise-level computing system should be capable of evolving to increase productivity and add new technologies. Expansion often presents a challenge, however, because many enterprise computing systems must incorporate legacy systems.

What is a legacy system? A **legacy system** is a computer system that has become outdated because of technology advances or changing organizational requirements. Many legacy systems are old mainframes or minicomputers that provided the first generation of computerization for a business or organization.

Although you might expect 20- or 30-year-old legacy systems to be long retired, some remain in operation for a variety of reasons. A legacy system might perform adequately even though newer technology exists. In addition, replacing a legacy system might be prohibitively expensive, considering the cost of new hardware, new software, installation time, training people to use the new system, and converting large quantities of data to a new format. Legacy systems can be incorporated into a new enterprise computing system, but they typically carry with them a special set of challenges (Figure 12-9).

Allstate Insurance is an example of a company that successfully integrated its legacy systems into a full-featured, Web-enabled enterprise system. Allstate's split with Sears—the company's previous owner—prompted a massive restructuring on both the corporate and technological levels. Allstate's information system consisted of a legacy software application running on IBM AS/400s, which stored approximately 35 million insurance policies and associated data. Allstate managers soon realized that maintaining the company's competitive edge required a computer system upgrade.

Reformatting and moving the legacy data was too complex and time consuming to be economically feasible, so methods had to be developed to allow more modern computers to access the legacy data. To accomplish the integration, software developers at Allstate created programs that allowed Windows PCs to access data stored on the AS/400s.

Software developers then created Web pages and applications to run on Windows PCs, using modern tools not available for the AS/400. The result was the "Good Hands Network"—a cutting-edge enterprise system that allowed customers, Allstate employees, and independent insurance agents to access data stored on Allstate's legacy computers.

What types of computers form the core of an enterprise computing system? The core of an enterprise computing system typically consists of one or more fast servers. These servers usually contain multiple processors. An enterprise system can include servers with different types of processors and operating systems. UNIX-based servers from Sun Microsystems, mainframe servers from IBM, and Intel-based servers from Dell and other vendors typically provide the core processing power for many of today's enterprise computing systems.

Current enterprise computing systems often include several blade servers. A **blade server**, also referred to as a "high-density server," is a modular electronic circuit board containing one or more processors and, depending on the model, some storage. It is configured to perform a single dedicated task, such as providing access to Web pages.

FIGURE 12-9
Legacy systems force developers to deal with problems not usually encountered with new systems.

- Repairs can be difficult because replacement parts are not available or the manufacturer is no longer in business.

- An older computer system might do its specific job adequately, but it might lack hardware or software drivers necessary to interface with newer, faster printers or other output devices.

- Application software and operating system upgrades might not be available because the product has been discontinued, or the software publisher is out of business.

A blade server generates less heat and uses less electricity than a standard desktop computer. Blade servers are designed to be inserted into a rack containing many other such servers. These rack-mounted devices can be designed to share a power supply and cooling fan. Using blade servers, like the one shown in Figure 12-10, allows an organization to minimize space and power requirements and can often shrink a whole room of computers into one floor-to-ceiling cabinet.

FIGURE 12-10

A blade server is a compact unit dedicated to processing and storage tasks.

A blade server is typically mounted in a rack along with other servers.

Do enterprise systems use specialized storage devices? The larger a computer system becomes, the more data it must store. An enterprise system usually stores many gigabytes or even terabytes of data. For example, Wal-Mart's invoicing and payroll systems have the capacity to store 50 terabytes of data. That's equal to the information stored on over 5 billion Web pages! Figure 12-11 illustrates a high-capacity storage device that might be included in a typical enterprise system.

Enterprise systems use specialized storage systems, designed to store large amounts of data. An organization implements these storage systems for the same reasons it might have a central library or repository for physical resources, such as books or printed reports. Rather than store data in individual departments or computers, it is easier to organize, maintain, and retrieve information stored in a central location. Enterprise storage options include RAID, SANs, and NAS.

What is RAID? RAID (redundant array of independent disks) is a storage system that uses a process called "striping" to break files into smaller blocks, which are stored across multiple hard disks. RAID is faster and more resilient than single hard disks. When retrieving data, all the disks work in parallel, which provides quick access. If any one RAID disk fails, its contents can be automatically reconstructed based on parity data stored on the other disks. Even with a failed disk, data in the RAID can be accessed normally.

FIGURE 12-11

An enterprise computing system might incorporate high-capacity storage devices, such as IBM 2104 Expandable Storage Plus, which provides 1027 gigabytes of storage, with expansion capabilities up to 14 terabytes.

What is a SAN? A **storage area network** (SAN) is a network of storage devices and data servers designed to function as a node on a wider network. A SAN storage device, such as a hard disk or tape, simply stores data. A SAN data server manages a group of storage devices. When network workstations access or store data on a SAN, they interact with the SAN in the same way they might interact with a standard storage device. A request for file access is captured by the SAN data server, and all the SAN storage devices work together as an integrated whole to retrieve data, as shown in Figure 12-12.

FIGURE 12-12

A storage area network consists of storage devices and a SAN data server. The SAN can be accessed from any of the enterprise network's servers, such as the NT, UNIX, and Linux servers shown here.

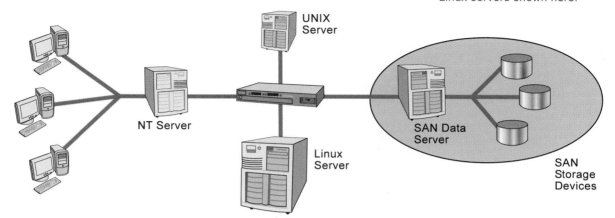

SANs are typically found in the corporate data centers of large supermarket chains, financial institutions, and other nationwide companies. SANs are also used to store the data that populates Web pages. For example, BN.com, the Web-based bookseller owned by Barnes & Noble, uses a SAN to store up to 7 terabytes of order and inventory data. Other advantages of SANs include scalability and storage management. SANs are easily scalable because storage devices or servers can be added at any time. SANs also typically offer **storage management services**, such as the ability to automatically store multiple copies of every file or maintain exact copies of storage media via mirroring.

What is mirroring? **Mirroring** is the process of creating a real-time "mirror image" of a storage medium, such as a hard disk or CD. Mirroring a hard disk, for example, requires two hard disks—a master and a mirror. Whenever a file is created, changed, or deleted on the master disk, that file is also created, changed, or deleted on the mirror disk. Mirroring differs from copying because it happens in real time. If the master disk fails, the mirror disk can immediately take over the duties of the master disk. SANs make mirroring easy because they contain multiple storage devices, but mirroring can be accomplished with any storage system that contains at least two distinct storage mediums.

What is NAS? Network attached storage, or NAS, refers to storage devices designed to be attached directly to a network without requiring a server for management. A NAS device typically contains a built-in network interface card. Each NAS device is assigned an IP address by the network administrator and can be connected directly to any network, as shown in Figure 12-13.

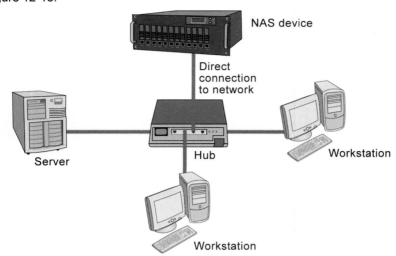

FIGURE 12-13

Network attached storage contains a built-in network card for direct connection to a network.

Do enterprise systems require special input devices? Adding data to an enterprise computing system can be accomplished in a variety of ways. Much of the data stored by enterprise computing systems has been entered from a keyboard. Enterprise systems also collect data using a wide variety of other input devices, such as optical scanners and digital cameras.

As the amount of input to an enterprise system grows, the speed at which it is collected and converted to computer-readable format becomes more and more important. A variety of input devices can provide enterprise systems with high-speed and automated input capabilities required for large amounts of data. High-speed input devices, such as scanners, quickly and accurately handle large volumes of input.

Banks deal with a very high volume of checks that must be read, sorted, and cleared. Two technologies, MICR and OCR, allow banks to automate check processing. **MICR** (magnetic ink character recognition) is a legacy technology developed in the 1950s. MICR automates check sorting by reading a routing code printed on the check in a special font, using magnetic ink. This specially printed routing code allows magnetic readers to sort checks with almost 100% accuracy. MICR is also fast—modern MICR readers can process up to 2,400 checks (like the one in Figure 12-14) per minute.

FIGURE 12-14

Printed checks that contain MICR or OCR printing can be read quickly by a high-volume input device.

OCR (optical character recognition) is more sophisticated than MICR. Dedicated OCR devices read a special font, but require no special inks. Software-based OCR readers can read a variety of fonts, but are not as accurate or as fast as dedicated OCR readers. Similar technology is used for optical mark recognition devices that read filled-in circles on multiple choice tests, ballots, and evaluation forms.

Automated input devices, such as handheld scanners, bypass manual data entry and all its associated errors. For example, employees at Wal-Mart use handheld bar-code scanners to take inventory. These automated input devices record bar codes for each item, and communicate wirelessly with the store's central computer to update the inventory database. Using these input devices not only decreases the number of errors that might occur during a manual inventory count, but also supplies the central Wal-Mart computer with a list of low-stock items that should be reordered immediately. Wal-Mart's sophisticated enterprise computing system is a key factor in the company's status as the world's premiere discount emporium.

FIGURE 12-15
A self-checkout device allows customers to scan their own purchases.

One of the most ambitious enterprise input devices is an automated self-checkout lane, which allows supermarket customers to scan, bag, and pay for their purchases without the assistance of a checkout clerk, as shown in Figure 12-15. In addition to reducing labor costs, these self-checkout devices have the potential to increase throughput after customers become familiar with the technology.

Do enterprise systems require special output devices? An enterprise system can use just about any standard output device, but speed and reliability are top priorities, especially if the quantity of output is high. Enterprise systems use a variety of high-speed printers, such as line printers, when large quantities of data must be printed. A **line printer** prints an entire line of text at a time instead of printing one character at a time. Some line printers produce output at speeds that exceed 1,800 lines a minute. Line printers are often used to print utility bills and credit card statements.

Organizations that frequently run large print jobs might group printers together into clusters. Printer clusters are managed by a **printer server**, which organizes print jobs and manages them using a print queue. Computers on the network send print jobs to the printer server, which then places them in the queue and starts the print job when a printer becomes available. Some organizations set up print labs—rooms containing general-use printers as well as specialized printers configured to print forms, envelopes, or other specialized output. These printers can be accessed through a printer server or directly from any computer on the network.

An increasingly popular form of output is information compiled into Web pages. An online retailer such as Amazon.com must produce Web pages that display the results of queries, order and shipping information, and customer service information. With more than 39 million active customers, Amazon.com must be able to quickly format and display information requested by customers. To do so, Amazon.com has high-speed servers dedicated to the creation of Web-based output.

Web-based output is replacing several legacy devices, such as ticker tapes and airline tickets. Instead of referring to a strand of paper streaming out of a teletype machine, stock market investors now rely on stock quotes posted on Web pages. Companies such as ETrade and Datek not only display stock quotes, but allow investors to buy, sell, and research stocks online.

You might expect enterprise computing systems to include high-speed printers for producing Publisher's Clearinghouse-style mass mailings. Such tasks, however, are typically outsourced to print shops equipped with high-speed, dedicated printing equipment. In addition to the need for high-speed printers, mass mailings and other large print jobs often require services difficult to maintain in-house, such as book binding and envelope stuffing.

HPC HARDWARE

Does high-performance computing require a supercomputer? In Chapter 1, a supercomputer was defined as any computer that is, at the time of its construction, one of the fastest computers in the world. Some HPC applications require supercomputer processing speeds. One of the fastest computers in the world at the time of this writing, Earth Simulator consists of 640 powerful computers linked by 83,000 high-speed cables (Figure 12-16). The computer performs at an amazing speed of 40 teraFLOPS. This state-of-the-art supercomputer covers an area the size of four tennis courts. Earth Simulator is designed to model all aspects of the atmosphere and analyze weather-related problems, such as global warming and abrupt climate change.

FIGURE 12-16
Japan's Earth Simulator Supercomputer

Building and maintaining a supercomputer like Earth Simulator is not an inexpensive or easy proposition. Fortunately, most HPC applications don't require the processing speeds offered by Earth Simulator and other supercomputers. Standard HPC systems are typically required to operate at speeds that approach or exceed 1 gigaFLOPS (1 billion floating-point operations per second). With new technological advances, it is possible to achieve this level of processing without a monolithic supercomputer. IBM, Hewlett-Packard, Cray, NEC, and other companies all offer HPC systems with high-speed processing, but without the complexity and costs associated with supercomputers.

What's the alternative to a supercomputer for HPC systems? Believe it or not, you can construct a high-performance computing system in your garage using off-the-shelf personal computers. Technological advances such as high-speed network interface cards and multiprocessor computers make it possible to build relatively low-cost "garage" HPC systems that operate at speeds exceeding 1 gigaFLOPS. One such network technology, called fibre channel, transports data between computers at a rate of up to 1 Gbps (or 1 billion bits per second) over a maximum distance of 6 miles.

INFOWEBLINKS

What's the latest news about supercomputers? You can visit the **Supercomputer InfoWeb** to learn more about these amazing machines.

www.course.com/np/concepts8/ch12

Low-cost personal computers that utilize multiprocessor architecture also have made homegrown HPC systems more accessible. **Multiprocessor architecture** refers to computers that contain two or more processors. Many of today's off-the-shelf servers and personal computers are available with up to four processors, and some feature even more. Connecting several of these multiprocessor computers using high-speed networking can produce a high-performance system that might not rival Earth Simulator, but is adequate for most academic and many scientific uses. In Section C of this chapter, you learn the details about clustering and grid architectures that turn a collection of off-the-shelf computers into a high-performance computing system.

What role does parallel processing play in high-performance computing? Connecting several processors has little effect on processing speed if only one of the processors executes programs. Multiprocessor architecture can carry out high-performance computing only when the processors are configured for parallel processing.

Parallel processing is the simultaneous use of more than one processor to execute a program. It is achieved by dividing a problem or program into sections and assigning sections to each processor. This technique increases processing speed because the problem is simultaneously being solved by as many processors as are available. Parallel processing is a key to achieving the processing speeds necessary for high-performance computing systems, whether those systems are based on an expensive supercomputer or a low-cost, off-the-shelf alternative.

Parallel processing can be divided into two main categories: symmetric multiprocessing and massively parallel processing. **Symmetric multiprocessing** (SMP) makes use of a single operating system to control multiple processors, which share a common bus and memory (Figure 12-17). SMP, once a technology unique to supercomputers, is now available on many off-the-shelf personal computers and servers, such as the Apple G5 and the Dell Precision. Typically, an SMP personal computer has 2 to 16 processors. An SMP server might have as many as 64 processors.

FIGURE 12-17

For symmetric multiprocessing, a computer's operating system controls multiple processors that share a common bus and memory.

CLICK TO START

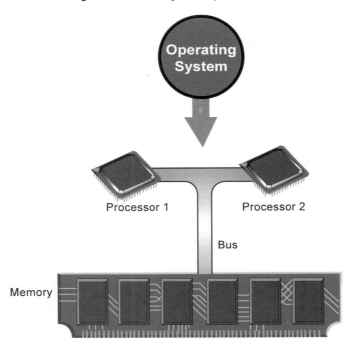

12

Massively parallel processing, or MPP, is the process of linking multiple processors, each with its own bus, memory, and operating system, as shown in Figure 12-18. An MPP system can consist of hundreds or even thousands of processors. On an MPP system, a problem or computation is divided into sections, and each section is distributed to a processor for simultaneous execution.

FIGURE 12-18

Massively parallel processing systems contain multiple processors, each with its own OS, bus, and memory. Application software typically controls the tasks assigned to each processor.

CLICK TO START

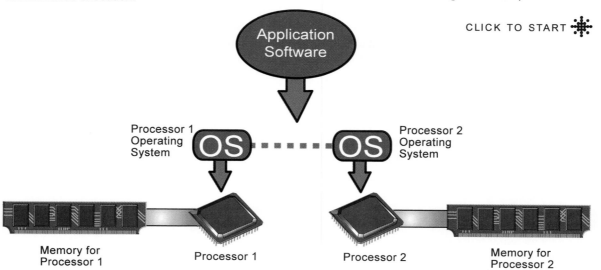

Regardless of the type of parallel processing, applications must be specifically written to take advantage of the parallel processing capabilities of multiple processors. Most MPP systems run custom software, written to take advantage of all the processors available on the system. SMP systems, however, are often used to run off-the-shelf applications such as DBMSs, transaction processing applications, and Web hosting packages. Although any off-the-shelf products can generally run on SMP systems, not all take advantage of multiple processors.

A similar situation holds true even for personal computer owners. For example, Apple's Power Mac G5 computer can be configured with two microprocessors that operate in parallel. Only a limited number of software packages take advantage of the G5's parallel processing capabilities, however. Some music, graphics, and video editing products, such as Adobe Premiere, Bibble, Alias Maya, DVD Studio Pro, and Apple First Cut Pro, include specially written program code to support parallel processing on the G5 computer. Most word processing, productivity, and personal finance applications do not. Owners and managers of multiprocessing computer systems can check software documentation to verify that an application supports true parallel processing.

ENTERPRISE SOFTWARE

What software is used on a typical enterprise system? Enterprise systems run a variety of software applications, which might be custom written or available as off-the-shelf commercial software. These applications range from standard accounting and inventory programs to Web-based catalogs and order-entry systems. Enterprise systems also run a variety of utility software for database access, backup, security, and transaction processing. Figure 12-19 lists some of the utilities commonly used on enterprise computing systems.

FIGURE 12-19
Enterprise Computing Utilities

Utility	Description
Veritas Cluster Server	A utility that allows up to 32 Solaris, HP-UX, or Windows NT computers to be configured in a cluster
Microsoft SQL Server Enterprise Edition	A DBMS that can support large Web sites and high-end OLTP applications as well as offer clustering support and advanced analysis tools
Microsoft Exchange Enterprise Server	An e-mail server that can be distributed across multiple servers and offers the potential to manage millions of mailboxes
IBM Enterprise Information Portal	An information integration tool for querying and browsing information stored in diverse formats across a large network
Computer Associates Unicenter	A utility designed to manage and maintain information about current computer systems and analyze workload to accurately forecast future needs
IBM WebSphere Application Server	An enterprise-level package that provides transaction management, security, and clustering services
Sun Java 2 Platform, Enterprise Edition	A development environment that allows organizations to easily create custom enterprise-level applications
Computer Associates BrightStor Enterprise Backup	A high-performance data protection application, allowing data on multiple, diverse platforms to be backed up to a centralized backup server
Symantec Enterprise Security Manager	A centralized virus protection server utility designed to protect a network from virus attacks

Although it is possible to use most standard software applications on an enterprise system, many organizations use software designed specifically for enterprise systems. These enterprise-level software applications include features not required on standard information systems. The characteristics of enterprise-level applications are still emerging, but these applications usually include at least some of the following features:

■ **Multiplatform availability.** Enterprise-level software applications typically run on more than one platform and allow information to be shared among platforms. For example, enterprise-level backup software not only runs on many different operating systems and hardware types, but also allows these different computers to interact.

- **Scalability.** Enterprise-level software applications are typically scalable. A growing organization might require additional processing and storage capabilities. Enterprise-level applications allow additional computers, hardware devices, and software to be connected to a system. For example, an enterprise-level DBMS allows scalability through its ability to distribute data among several database servers.

- **Redundancy.** Enterprise-level software applications usually do not have one point of failure. For example, suppose Amazon.com customer software resides on a single server. If that server fails, customers cannot search Amazon's Web site for specific products. An enterprise-level software application would divide queries among several redundant servers. If one server fails, the remaining servers can take over the workload.

What role does software play in integrating legacy applications? An enterprise system might encompass applications that are not enterprise-level and cannot communicate directly with other applications running on the enterprise system. Some of these non-enterprise applications originated on legacy systems. Others have been pressed into service because an enterprise-level version of the application is not available. Making these applications and their data accessible to other enterprise applications requires special software routines called middleware. **Middleware** is a type of software that acts as an intermediary between two other software packages, typically by formatting data from one software package so that it can be used by another software package.

You might have seen some of the famous pictures from *TimeLife*'s collection of 22 million photographs—the soldier kissing a nurse on V-J Day or the theater full of people wearing 3-D glasses. These photographs were originally stored on magnetic tape and indexed by using an Informix DBMS running on a Sun computer. Today, access to these photographs is possible because middleware translates the HTTP request from a browser (Figure 12-20) to an SQL-based query the Informix DBMS can understand and process.

INFOWEBLINKS

Middleware is a key technology for today's enterprise systems. Learn more at the **Middleware InfoWeb**.

www.course.com/np/concepts8/ch12

FIGURE 12-20

Middleware makes it possible to access Web-based *TimeLife* photos.

Middleware can be written using standard programming languages such as C++ and Java, or it can be written using languages and protocols specifically designed for communicating among diverse systems. One such protocol, called **SOAP** (Simple Object Access Protocol), allows a program running on one operating system, such as Windows, to communicate with a program running on a different operating system, such as Linux, using Web-based communications protocols such as HTTP and XML (Figure 12-21). Other tools for creating middleware include SNMP and Java 2 Platform Enterprise Edition.

FIGURE 12-21

SOAP defines exactly how to encode an HTTP or XML file in order to call a program from another operating system, send parameters, and receive a response.

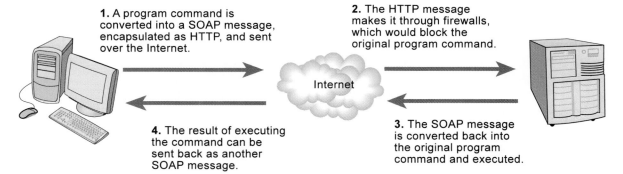

1. A program command is converted into a SOAP message, encapsulated as HTTP, and sent over the Internet.

2. The HTTP message makes it through firewalls, which would block the original program command.

Internet

4. The result of executing the command can be sent back as another SOAP message.

3. The SOAP message is converted back into the original program command and executed.

HPC SOFTWARE

Does high-performance computing require special software?
Unlike enterprise systems, high-performance computing systems rarely run commercial software. Custom software offers two important advantages for high-performance computing: speed and specialized applications.

Organizations use custom software to increase computational speed. Commercial software applications are usually written to run on a variety of computers and hardware devices and, as such, are written primarily with compatibility and interoperability in mind. In contrast, custom software routines are tightly coupled with the hardware that runs them. Custom software is almost always faster than commercial software because it can be optimized to take full advantage of hardware capabilities. For example, high-performance software can be customized to use all available processors and virtually eliminate processor idle time. In the same way, software can be designed to use specialized high-speed input and output devices at their maximum capacities.

Speed is not the only benefit of custom software. Organizations develop custom software for high-performance systems because these systems often perform tasks for which commercial software is not available. Most HPC projects involve very specialized research, and there is no off-the-shelf application with the required sophistication, speed, or specialized content. Also, the complexity of HPC hardware often makes it impossible to run off-the-shelf applications.

IBM's Blue Gene Supercomputer is designed to model protein folding, a biological phenomenon thought to be at least partially responsible for diseases such as Alzheimer's, cystic fibrosis, and mad cow. Blue Gene requires custom software for speed and because the necessary application software is not available commercially.

Modeling proteins is a big job, even for a supercomputer. Scientists estimate three years to model 100 milliseconds of a protein-folding scenario at 1 petaFLOPS speeds. However, they believe the use of sophisticated software techniques, such as streamlined algorithms, threading, and the ability of simulations to migrate from one thread to another, can considerably speed up the modeling process.

Designing, writing, and testing sophisticated HPC software requires time, expertise, and financial resources. An ongoing effort of the National HPCC Software Exchange (NHSE) makes a selection of HPC software available on the Web. The NHSE Web site (Figure 12-22) includes links to download sites, software reviews, and tutorials about HPC algorithms.

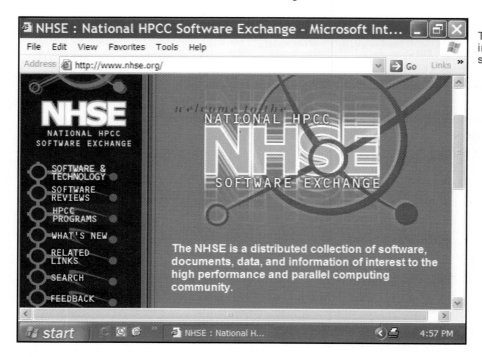

FIGURE 12-22
The NHSE Web site includes links to HPC software.

QUICKCHECK......SECTION B

1. A legacy computer is a modular electronic board designed to be inserted into a rack and used as the core of an enterprise computing system. True or false? ☐

2. The acronym ☐ refers to a storage system that uses a system of striping data, whereas a storage ☐ network is a network of storage devices and data servers.

3. MICR and ☐ are examples of technologies used by banks to automate check processing.

4. Network ☐ storage devices attach directly to a network without requiring a server for management.

5. Computers like Apple's G5 Power Mac increase performance by using ☐ processing.

6. ☐ is a type of software that acts as in intermediary between two software packages so that they can exchange data.

 CHECK ANSWERS

ENTERPRISE AND HIGH-PERFORMANCE ARCHITECTURE

Today's mega roller coasters offer a heart-stopping ride, and yet their architecture makes them much safer than the rickety wooden structures that populated carnivals in the days of poodle skirts and saddle shoes. A structure's architecture specifies its components and the way in which those components are assembled. The architecture of a well-built structure is effective, efficient, and reliable.

The architecture of a computer system specifies its components and how those components are connected. The "right" architecture for a specific enterprise or high-performance computer system depends on a variety of factors, such as geographical coverage, number of users, desired response time, required processing time, and security. In this section, you learn more about the design, organization, and configuration of enterprise and high-performance computer systems.

CENTRALIZED ARCHITECTURE

What is the simplest architecture for enterprise and high-performance systems? The earliest computer systems that provided services for enterprises were based on centralized architecture. A **centralized computing system** consists of one central computer surrounded by terminals, as shown in Figure 12-23.

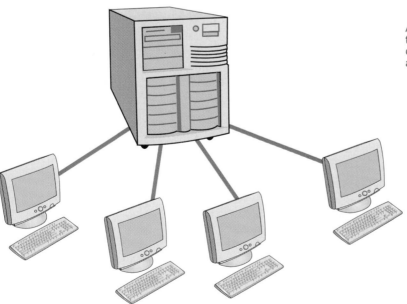

FIGURE 12-23

A centralized computing system typically consists of a mainframe computer that processes data for a collection of terminals.

In a centralized computing system, the primary processing device is typically a mainframe computer, referred to as a **host computer**, which performs most or all of the processing for the entire system. Users communicate processing requests to the host computer using terminals. A **terminal** is an input/output device that features a keyboard and screen, but has no storage capacity and very limited processing capability. Popular terminals for centralized legacy systems include the IBM 3270 and DEC's VT-100.

Personal computers can also be connected to mainframe hosts. These PCs, however, must run **terminal emulation software**, which makes them appear to the host computer as "dumb terminals" unable to store or process any data. Figure 12-24 shows an example of a terminal.

FIGURE 12-24
A terminal resembles a personal computer, but a close look usually reveals that a terminal has no storage device. A typical terminal features a display unit and a keyboard unit, but rarely a separate system unit.

Although centralized architecture is not a popular choice for today's enterprise systems, some centralized systems have been integrated into larger enterprise systems. For example, most libraries installed a computerized card catalog in the 1970s or early 1980s. These centralized systems still perform adequately today, and replacement or upgrading is not necessary. Some libraries, however, want to expand computer services, offering patrons Web access to the card catalog and providing library staff with a variety of management tools. To offer such services, a library might incorporate its centralized legacy system into a larger, less centralized enterprise system.

Centralized architecture is a popular option for high-performance computer systems. High-performance computing rarely requires the flexibility, availability, and compatibility of an enterprise system. Therefore, a centralized system might be an adequate choice. Centralized architecture is sometimes the only choice available for the very fastest high-performance systems because they often rely on one very fast, high-powered supercomputer to perform most, if not all, of the processing required.

What are the advantages and disadvantages of centralized architecture? Centralized computing systems are the simplest of the many architectures in use today. Centralized architecture allows many people to use straightforward tools to access services provided by a host computer. Because the host computer performs all of the processing, no middleware is required. Terminals do not store data or programs required by other components of the system, so terminal malfunctions have little effect on the functionality of the entire system.

Administering a centralized system is also very easy. Because the host computer is the only device on the network that processes data or stores files, administering the system is almost as simple as administering a single computer. No client software exists on the terminals, so upgrading or installing new software involves only the host system. Monitoring user access and processing speed, adding new users, and other administration tasks are similarly easy.

Centralized architecture has disadvantages as well. Because all the processing takes place on a single host computer, if that computer fails, the entire system fails. Centralized systems often have scalability limits based on the storage, memory, processing, and connectivity capacity of the host computer. For example, adding 100 terminals might not be possible without purchasing, installing, and configuring a more powerful host computer.

DISTRIBUTED ARCHITECTURE

What is a distributed computer system? A **distributed computer system** is a collection of connected computers in which processing, data, and application software are dispersed among more than one physical computer. Distributed computer systems are commonly used for both standard information systems and enterprise systems. A simple distributed system might consist of only two computers connected in a client/server configuration—for example, a database server with a client computer connected to it. More complex distributed systems consist of multiple servers, storage devices, and client computers. The largest distributed system is the Internet itself, with millions of servers connected to millions of clients. Figure 12-25 illustrates an example of a distributed computer network designed for a medium-sized business.

FIGURE 12-25
A distributed computer system includes a variety of servers and clients, all with the capability to process and store data.

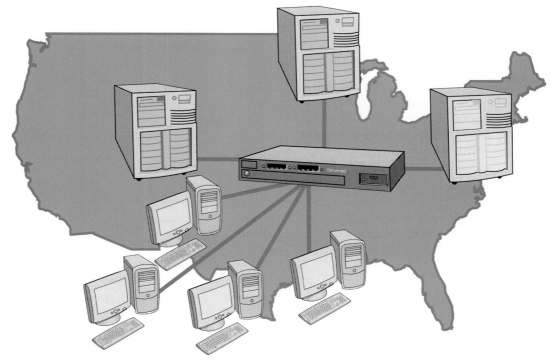

What are the advantages and disadvantages of distributed computer systems? Distributed computer systems are popular because of their scalability, reasonable cost, and performance. In contrast to centralized systems, whose scalability is limited to a single host computer's processing capability, distributed systems can be scaled up or down by adding or removing devices. A small organization might require only one server connected to five or ten workstations. As the organization grows, a distributed system makes it possible to add more workstations, connect additional servers, and group computers into an efficient structure.

Distributed systems can also be scaled to encompass a large geographical area. Even a small organization might need to share data among sites located in different cities or states. A distributed system can span cities and connect users located just about anywhere around the world.

Distributed architecture is cost-effective because specialized hardware or software is typically not required. Most modern operating systems allow computers to be connected simply by installing a standard network card and connecting a few cables. Because standard hardware and software are used, the system can be upgraded as newer components appear on the market. Also, distributed systems allow organizations to put expensive, fast computers to work doing the most difficult and complex functions, while using low-end, slower, less expensive machines for those tasks without such high requirements. For example, a university's distributed system might use an expensive mainframe server to run its student record software and a moderately priced blade server for accounting, but use inexpensive desktop PCs as employee workstations and student registration terminals.

The main disadvantage of distributed systems is the level of complexity involved in management. Problems can be difficult to track down because every computer on a distributed network processes data and interacts with other computers. For example, in a distributed system infected with a virus, finding infected computers and containing the virus is much more difficult than with a centralized system.

Upgrading and installing new software and hardware on a distributed system can also be time consuming. Hardware upgrades, such as installing faster network cards, can involve every computer on the network. Software upgrades must be coordinated to prevent multiple versions of the same software from running on the system.

For most organizations, the advantages of distributed systems outweigh the disadvantages. Consequently, most enterprise systems and an increasing number of high-performance computing systems are based on distributed computing architecture. The table in Figure 12-26 summarizes the advantages and disadvantages of distributed systems.

FIGURE 12-26
Advantages and Disadvantages of Distributed Systems

Advantages	Disadvantages
Easily scalable	System management is more complex than centralized systems.
Expandable over a large geographical area	Viruses and other problems have the potential to affect many users.
Uses standard hardware and software	Repairs and upgrades often take place on equipment located at remote sites.
Simple tasks handled by inexpensive computers	Software upgrades must be coordinated.

TIERED ARCHITECTURE

What is a tier? Computers in a distributed system are often connected in a tiered architecture. The term **tier** refers to a group or layer of computers that perform a particular task. A **tiered computer system** can have two tiers, three tiers, four tiers, or more. Any tiered system, regardless of the number of tiers, is often referred to as an **n-tier system**. An enterprise accounting system could, for example, be based on three-tier architecture, as shown in Figure 12-27.

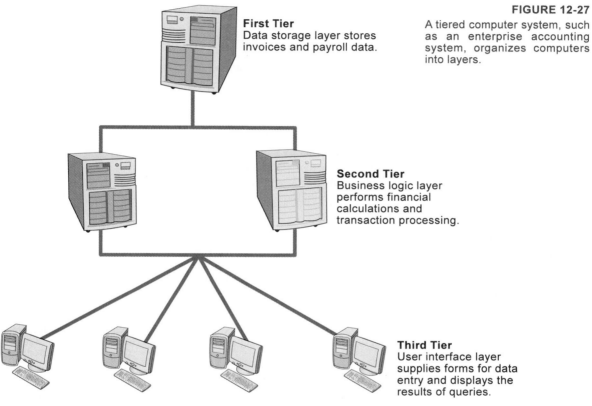

First Tier
Data storage layer stores invoices and payroll data.

Second Tier
Business logic layer performs financial calculations and transaction processing.

Third Tier
User interface layer supplies forms for data entry and displays the results of queries.

FIGURE 12-27

A tiered computer system, such as an enterprise accounting system, organizes computers into layers.

In a tiered computer system, each tier consists of one or more computers. In the accounting system example, the business logic tier consists of one server that processes invoices and another server that processes payroll. In contrast, the data storage tier consists of a single computer that runs database server software. The user interface tier consists of computers for employees who access the system. Each tier in a distributed system can interact with one or more of the other tiers. For example, the user interface tier interacts only with the business logic tier, but the business logic tier interacts with both the user interface and data storage tiers.

What are the advantages of tiered architecture? The major advantage of a tiered system is that each tier is independent and can be changed or upgraded without affecting other tiers. For instance, if the user interface tier in the accounting example is running on Macintosh computers and the organization decides to change to Windows computers, the change could be accomplished without altering the business logic or data storage tiers.

Tiered architecture also allows an enterprise to switch software more easily than with a non-tiered system. Instead of obtaining new software for every computer in an enterprise, it might be possible to switch software only within a single tier.

GRID ARCHITECTURE

What is a grid computing system? In the movie *The Matrix*, a computer programmer named Neo discovers humanity has been trapped inside a cyber world and is being used to generate power for an evil artificial intelligence that has taken over the earth. The cyber world called "the matrix" is generated as a sort of 3-D computer grid. This matrix is science fiction, but the idea of grids applies to computer systems that exist today. Computer grids generate massive processing power by using many relatively simple computers, which work together to achieve processing speeds that rival some of the world's top HPC systems.

A **grid computing system** is a network of diverse computers, such as PCs, Macs, workstations, and servers, in which each computer is treated as a generic and equal processing resource. Grid systems require a connection to one or more computers running **grid management software**, which divides problems into pieces that are farmed out to individual computers on the grid for processing.

Each computer on the grid runs **grid client software** that contains the program necessary to process a piece of the problem. In this manner, complex calculations or tasks can be performed in parallel by using as many computers as are available on the grid. Grid computing systems can be public or private. Some grid systems use computers connected to the Internet as resources; others operate on private networks.

Aside from the computers that run grid management software, none of the computers on the grid is specialized or tiered. In many distributed information systems, computers perform specialized tasks; one computer might be designated as a database server, whereas another computer might be dedicated to processing graphics. In contrast, the computers in a grid system are treated as equal processing resources. Because of this approach, grid systems can be easily scaled simply by adding or removing computers. Figure 12-28 illustrates the basic architecture of a grid computing system.

FIGURE 12-28

A grid computing system uses a diverse variety of computers as generic and equal resources.

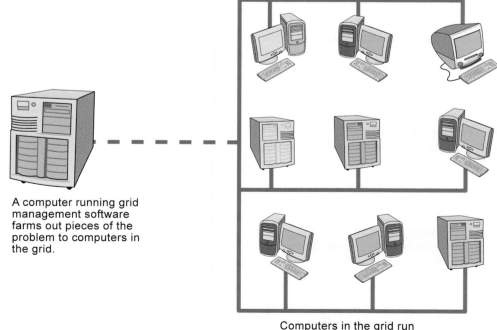

A computer running grid management software farms out pieces of the problem to computers in the grid.

Computers in the grid run grid client software.

Where are grid systems used? Because of their scalability, low cost, and high performance, grid computing systems play a central role in high-performance computing. One of the most famous examples of a grid system is the SETI@home project.

The Search for Extraterrestrial Intelligence, or SETI, was originally conceived by David Gedye, a computer scientist with an interest in astronomy. Scientists and astronomers have been watching the skies and listening to interstellar signals for decades, looking for anomalies that might prove the existence of intelligent life on other planets. Radio telescopes gather a huge amount of raw data from far-off corners of the galaxy. Searching through this data to find signals that might have been sent by another civilization could easily consume the resources of the fastest and most expensive high-performance computer available.

In 1994, Gedye realized that thousands of computers connected to the Internet sit idle for hours while the people who own them are in meetings, talking on the telephone, sleeping, or otherwise occupied. If these idle processing cycles could be harnessed, they would supply all the computing power required to analyze SETI radio telescope data. Gedye gathered support from many organizations and launched the SETI@home project.

SETI@home consists of a grid management system and millions of privately owned personal computers whose owners donate idle processing time to the project. The SETI@home grid management system receives and stores raw data from the Arecibo radio telescope in Puerto Rico, divides this data into small segments for analysis, and farms it out to one of the privately owned computers.

People who wish to donate their computers' idle processing cycles to the SETI@home project can download and install grid client software from the project's Web page (Figure 12-29). This software includes a special screen saver, grid access software, and the software routines for processing radio telescope data. Whenever the PC is idle, the SETI screen saver becomes active and signals the grid that it is ready to process SETI data. When processing is complete, the results are uploaded to the SETI@home system.

INFOWEBLINKS

For more information about this fascinating use of grid computing, take a look at the **SETI@home InfoWeb**.

www.course.com/np/concepts8/ch12

FIGURE 12-29

The SETI@home grid system performs at an average speed of 15 teraFLOPS. This level of performance rivals some of the fastest high-performance systems at a fraction of the cost.

For comparison, a supercomputer called ASCI White operates at 12 teraFLOPS, but its $110 million price tag is significantly higher than the $500,000 cost to set up the SETI@home grid.

12

What kinds of problems are best solved using grid systems? Grid computing systems perform best on problems that can be divided into smaller problems, which can be processed in any sequence and at any time. One example of this type of problem is the process used to "crack" encryption algorithms, which are based on keys formed from very long numbers. The longer the number, the more keys are possible. For example, 56 digits can generate many more keys than 12 digits. Modern computerized encryption algorithms, which use 56-digit keys, were once thought to be unbreakable because the key can be any one of billions of numbers.

In theory, discovering an encryption key borders on the impossible, but is that true in today's computerized world? In 1997, a company called RSA Security Inc. set up a series of contests that awarded monetary prizes to the first person who could crack messages encrypted with a variety of common encryption algorithms. The contest caught the eye of a group of scientists who had an interest in encryption techniques and distributed computing. The group, led by scientist Jeff Lawson, realized it would be possible to win the contest using simple "brute force" computing, which means trying every possible key. All that was needed was enough computer processing power to try all the different key combinations.

Lawson's group, Distributed.net, obtained the processing power by using a grid system. Group members created grid management software to divide keys into blocks and assign each block to one of the computers on the grid for processing. Each computer on the grid does the same thing—it starts with the first key in its block, checks it against the encrypted message to see if it's the correct key and, if unsuccessful, moves on to the next key. As more people donate their idle computer cycles to the project, the processing proceeds faster and faster. Using grid technology, Distributed.net cracked several encryption keys once thought to be unbreakable.

The first victory, RSA's RC5-56 challenge, was cracking a 56-bit code in 250 days. Over the course of the project, Distributed.net received donated cycles from more than 500,000 computers. The grid processed more than 34 quadrillion keys at a peak rate of 7 billion keys a second—the equivalent of 26,000 Pentium computers! In 2002, Distributed.net broke 64-bit encryption in 1,757 days with the help of 331,252 grid participants who tested 15,769,938,165,961,326,592 keys. It is now working on breaking 72-bit encryption.

In addition to analyzing radio telescope signals and breaking codes, grid computing projects currently exist for applications such as studying global climate changes, predicting earthquakes, playing chess, searching for new medicines, and cracking codes (Figure 12-30). Sony is even considering a grid of Internet-connected PlayStation 3 gaming consoles to enhance online game performance.

Some analysts predict Web-based grid computing systems can eventually supply high-performance processing power to organizations, in much the same way electrical power grids supply electricity—customers just plug into the grid to tap its massive processing power.

Not all computing tasks are suited to grid systems, however. Some problems cannot be divided into small processing segments for grid systems; other problems require extensive human interaction or highly specialized equipment.

FIGURE 12-30
Public Grid Computing Projects

First distributed computing network to play online chess.

Study climate change in the 21st century and examine effects on food production, ecosystems, water resources, and energy demand.

Crack encryption algorithms.

Medical research into cancer, anthrax, and smallpox.

Collect data and design models to predict earthquakes.

INFOWEBLINKS

RSA Security Inc. continues to hold contests challenging people to break commonly used encryption algorithms. Think you can solve one? Find out more at the **Cracking Contests InfoWeb**.

www.course.com/np/concepts8/ch12

Is the Internet a grid system? Although some parts of the Internet offer resources for grid computing systems, the Internet is better described as a distributed system that includes both tiered and grid systems. In fact, just about any computer on the Internet could be part of a grid system and part of an enterprise system at the same time. A computer located on a desk in an office could easily be part of an enterprise system, a distributed system, and a grid system. The different types of architectures are not mutually exclusive.

CLUSTERING

What is clustering? In a computing system, a **cluster** is a group of two or more devices connected together to distribute processing, input, output, or storage workloads, and adapt to equipment failure. Processing clusters (Figure 12–31) can be thought of as "super servers." They provide the same functions as a normal server, but because a cluster consists of more than one computer, it is not as susceptible to equipment failure and offers speed benefits. Clusters are often used as servers for business-critical functions, such as e-mail, storage, Web sites, and e-commerce. Clusters also serve as the platform for online massively parallel multiplayer games, such as EverQuest and Battlefield 1942.

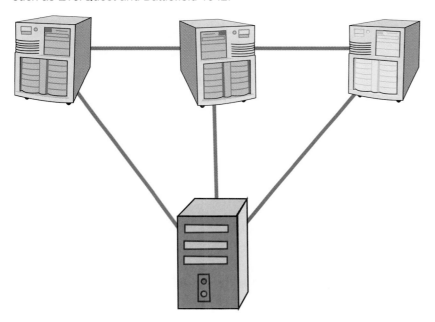

FIGURE 12-31

A cluster is a group of computers that performs the functions of a single server on a network.

CLICK TO START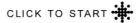

Each computer in a cluster is called a **cluster node**. Every node requires special cluster management software. In addition, application software used by the cluster must be "cluster-aware," meaning that it supports the distribution of work among several servers. Cluster management software is available from third-party software publishers. Some operating systems, such as Windows Server 2003, offer built-in cluster support. Clusters are an important configuration option for computer systems because they can improve reliability, offer parallel processing, and handle variable workloads.

Clusters can be incorporated into both enterprise and high-performance computing systems. Enterprise systems use clusters primarily to support services that must be available continuously, and HPC systems commonly use the parallel processing abilities of a cluster.

What is fault tolerance? **Fault tolerance** refers to a computer system's ability to react gracefully to unexpected software or hardware failures. A cluster implements fault tolerance by detecting node failure and transferring workloads, as required. This process of transferring service from a failed node to a working node is referred to as **cluster failover**. The ability to handle failures without a break in service makes clustering ideal for situations that require 24/7 operation—jargon for "up and running 24 hours a day, 7 days a week." As shown in Figure 12-32, the availability of more than one server in a cluster makes it possible to failover to a secondary server if the main server fails.

FIGURE 12-32

When one computer in a cluster fails, a process called cluster failover transfers service to a working computer.

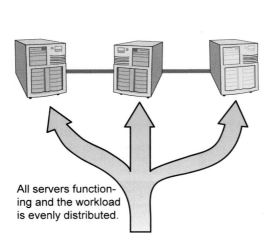

All servers function-ing and the workload is evenly distributed.

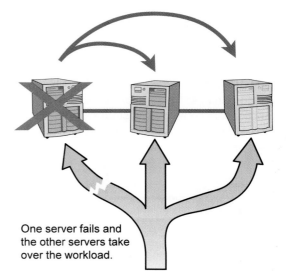

One server fails and the other servers take over the workload.

How do clusters optimize resources? Clusters optimize computing resources by allowing cluster nodes to share workloads and data. **Load balancing** refers to the practice of distributing processing and storage tasks among the nodes of a cluster in a way that optimizes the performance of the entire system. Load balancing is most often performed by the application running on the cluster, as opposed to the cluster management software or operating system.

To understand how load balancing works, consider a cluster of two servers and one storage device configured to handle e-mail for an ISP. All incoming mail is held on the shared storage device until the recipient is ready to receive it. How does this cluster handle many simultaneous requests for e-mail from ISP subscribers? It would be possible to configure the cluster so that one computer—call it Server A—handles as many e-mail requests as it can until it is overwhelmed. When Server A is operating at full capacity, Server B might begin to process e-mail requests, too. This scheme, although logical, does not make effective use of a cluster's load balancing capabilities because as a computer reaches maximum capacity, its efficiency tends to decrease.

A better scheme for load balancing distributes the workload before Server A becomes overwhelmed. When Server A reaches a specified level of performance—say, 60% of capacity—Server B is configured to "kick in" and help with the workload.

Is every node in a cluster active at all times? A cluster can be configured as an **active-active cluster** so that all nodes are active at the same time. The application software for an active-active cluster must perform load balancing activities to allow each node to participate in the application processing functions. Designing a software application to run on an active-active cluster is a difficult and time-consuming process and, as a result, very few applications available today are truly active-active. For true parallel computing, however, active-active clustering is required.

A more common configuration is an **active-passive cluster**, which contains one node active at all times, and additional nodes ready in case of failover. As with an active-active cluster, applications for an active-passive cluster must be cluster-aware and designed to allow failover.

What is a Beowulf cluster? A **Beowulf cluster** is a collection of off-the-shelf computers interconnected and configured as a cluster to handle high-performance computing tasks. The original Beowulf (pronounced BAY oh wolf) system was developed in 1994 at the Goddard Space Flight Center by Thomas Sterling and Donald Becker. They theorized that a high-performance computer system running in the gigaFLOPS range could be created using a cluster of standard, off-the-shelf hardware and software. Their theory turned out to be correct, and they were able to create the first Beowulf system out of 16 Intel DX4 computers connected by 10 Mbps Ethernet.

Although a Beowulf cluster might seem similar to grid computing, there are differences between the two. The computers on a Beowulf cluster are dedicated to the cluster and run cluster applications. In contrast, nodes on a grid system are usually personal desktop systems that run desktop applications in addition to grid applications. Cluster nodes are also under the administrative jurisdiction of the cluster, whereas grid nodes are administered by individual PC owners. Today, Beowulf clusters are popular with organizations such as educational research facilities, which require fast systems, but are unable to pay the high costs associated with high-performance computers. In addition to being cost-effective to build, Beowulf clusters can be upgraded easily and inexpensively as new technology appears on the market.

TERMINOLOGY NOTE

When Beowulf clusters meet pop culture, it produces a "flash mob supercomputer." The basic idea is modeled after flash mobs, where a group of strangers gather at a predetermined time to perform some kind of (usually silly) activity before disbanding. A flash mob supercomputer is formed when computer owners gather together and connect their machines into a cluster that forms a supercomputer. So far, the goal of these events has been to demonstrate the viability of supercomputing outside of established research centers.

QUICKCHECK......SECTION C

1. A centralized computing system uses a simple architecture in which [_____] communicate with a single mainframe computer.

2. Computers in a(n) [_____] computing system are often connected in a(n) [_____] architecture with layers for the user interface, business logic, and data storage.

3. A(n) [_____] computing system is a network of computers in which each computer is treated as a generic and equal resource.

4. Clustered computers offer [_____] tolerance because a process called cluster [_____] transfers service from an inoperable node to a working node.

5. A(n) [_____] mob supercomputer is formed when computer owners bring their machines to a central location and connect them as a cluster.

 CHECK ANSWERS

 12

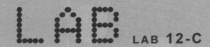

LAB 12-C

GRID COMPUTING

In this lab, you'll learn:

- The basic elements of a grid computing system, such as SETI@home
- The purpose of grid client software
- How to download and install grid client software
- The methods grid client software use to become active during idle CPU cycles
- What happens on a client computer during a typical processing session
- How to view the results produced by the SETI@home screensaver
- The role of server-side computers for managing a grid
- The configuration of SETI@home servers
- How server-side computers integrate the results uploaded by grid clients
- To recognize the security threats to grid clients, and take steps to safeguard your computer
- About the security threats to grid servers and how to determine whether security measures seem like appropriate protection for grid clients
- How to determine whether a grid project is legitimate

INTERACTIVE LAB

CLICK TO START THE LAB

LAB ASSIGNMENTS

1. Start the interactive part of the lab. Insert your Tracking Disk if you want to save your QuickCheck results. Perform each lab step as directed, and answer all the lab QuickCheck questions. When you exit the lab, your answers are automatically graded and your results are displayed.

2. Connect to the SETI@home Web site at *setiathome.ssl.berkeley.edu/* and locate as much information as you can about security. After reading this information, do you feel confident that all necessary steps have been taken to protect grid participants? Why or why not?

3. Enter the search term "donate CPU cycles" in a Web search engine, and then follow one of the links to a site (other than SETI@home) that requests your idle CPU cycles for a charitable cause. Describe the purpose of the project. Determine the approximate size of the grid client software and what sort of data it processes.

4. Browse through the site you found in Assignment 3 to determine whether you think it is legitimate. Write a one-page report that describes the site, includes its URL, and includes specific details about how you evaluated the site's legitimacy.

SECTION D

QUALITY OF SERVICE

In 1999, women's clothing retailer Victoria's Secret planned to broadcast its annual lingerie fashion show live on the Web. It would be one of the first massive Webcasts in Internet history. To attract viewers, the company advertised during the Super Bowl. The publicity campaign generated so much interest that more than 1.5 million people attempted to log on to the fashion show—far more than the anticipated 500,000 viewers. The company's Web servers were overwhelmed and eventually crashed. The Victoria's Secret Web site crash and other similar incidents illustrate just one of the many factors that can have a negative effect on the quality of service offered by large-scale computing systems. This section examines the goals and risks related to enterprise-level quality of service.

RELIABILITY, AVAILABILITY, AND SERVICEABILITY

What is quality of service? The term **quality of service** (QoS) refers to the level of performance a computer system provides. When quality of service is good, data flows swiftly through the system, software is easy and intuitive to use, and work is completed quickly and without error. When quality of service is poor, users experience long waits, software is clumsy to use, and information is difficult to find.

Most Web surfers have encountered unreliable dial-up connections, difficult-to-navigate Web sites, and slow search engines. An enterprise computing system with poor quality of service might exhibit delays during peak usage periods or it might crash. For organizations, poor quality of service can produce unhappy customers, inefficient employees, and revenue losses.

Three key concepts ensure good quality of service: reliability, availability, and serviceability. Computer systems are reliable when they can be count-

FIGURE 12-33
Anarchy Online

ed on to function correctly. Availability refers to the ability of the system to be continuously accessible to all the people who use it. Systems exhibit serviceability when they are easily upgraded or repaired.

Quality of service can affect the success of an entire organization or business—a lesson learned the hard way by an online game company called Funcom. Funcom publishes a Web-based game, called Anarchy Online, set in a futuristic world where players create characters that battle aliens, band together to venture on futuristic missions, or simply chat with in-game friends (Figure 12-33).

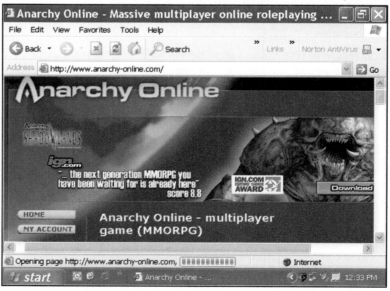

Anarchy Online was eagerly anticipated, and on its release date gamers flooded Funcom's servers attempting to register, pay their fees, and start playing. The results were dismal. Credit card registration was handled on an unsecure server, making people reluctant to give out their credit card numbers. Other parts of the registration process, such as verifying the CD key, didn't work because of a software bug. If players managed to complete the registration process, they encountered an overloaded server unable to handle the number of players trying to log in. All this trouble might have been overlooked if the game itself had proceeded smoothly. However, players found themselves struggling through a game in which their characters could barely move because of bandwidth problems, and using a system that repeatedly crashed because of bugs in the software.

Funcom had a discouraging quality-of-service problem on its hands. The company quickly fixed numerous bugs in the software and reconfigured its hardware to speed up play. Despite these measures, Funcom lost many customers. Approximately three months after the game was released, Funcom reported 50,000 paying subscribers. In contrast, Dark Ages of Camelot, a competing game without quality-of-service problems, boasted 108,000 paying subscribers three months after its release date.

Who monitors quality of service? Quality of service is usually monitored by an organization's Information Services (IS) Department. Some organizations maintain separate quality-of-service teams within the IS Department, and other organizations make QoS a responsibility of the entire IS Department. As systems grow, some organizations outsource QoS duties to companies that specialize in the field. Regardless of who does the job, quality of service involves setting standards, developing metrics to monitor system performance, and optimizing systems that do not meet desired standards.

What are quality-of-service metrics? A **quality-of-service metric** is a technique for measuring a specific QoS characteristic. Data for these metrics can be gathered by monitoring system performance and analyzing responses to user satisfaction surveys. Businesses typically use several metrics to evaluate QoS. **Response time**, one of the most common QoS metrics, is the time period that begins when a user initiates a request for information and ends when the request is fulfilled. For software running locally, response times of longer than two seconds are usually considered unacceptable.

Slow response time causes short delays while employees wait for the system to process information. In an organization with hundreds of employees, a three-second per hour per employee processing delay can easily add up to hundreds of days of lost productivity. Other QoS metrics are described in Figure 12-34.

INFOWEBLINKS

The vast scope and scale of today's online games require several enterprise-level technologies. You can check out the **Online Games InfoWeb** for links to some of today's hottest games and information about online game technology.

www.course.com/np/concepts8/ch12

FIGURE 12-34
QoS Metrics

QoS Metric	Description
Throughput	Amount of data processed in a particular time interval
Accuracy	Number of errors occurring in a particular time interval for a particular function
Downtime	Amount of time a system is not available for processing
Capacity	Available storage space, number of users, number of connections, or number of packets
User levels	Number of users at peak, average, and low times
Response time	Time period between when a user initiates a request for information and when the request is fulfilled

The data collected by various metrics must be interpreted according to QoS standards the business or organization sets. For example, a small organization might require its e-mail server to be up and running during standard business hours. Repairs and upgrades can be performed at night and on weekends. A larger organization, however, could have offices located in different time zones, employees who work late at night or on weekends, and workers who need access to e-mail 24 hours a day, 7 days a week. Although both companies measure the same metric—the amount of e-mail server uptime—the acceptable level for the first organization is very different from the acceptable level for the second organization.

QoS software is available to monitor system performance and report metrics, such as bandwidth use, number of users connected, and peak usage periods. QoS software is also useful for simulating system stress. For example, one popular Web-based QoS package (Figure 12-35) advertises that it can simulate up to 1 million concurrent users and over 10,000 new users every second.

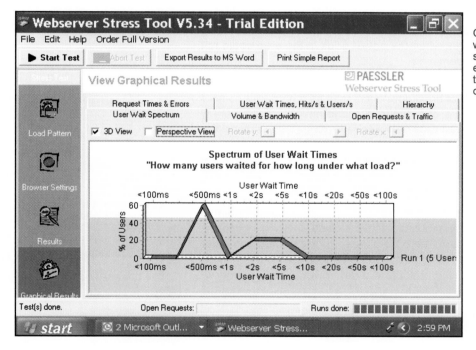

FIGURE 12-35

One type of QoS software helps organizations stress-test their computer systems by simulating thousands of simultaneous logons.

RISK MANAGEMENT

What is risk management? Computer systems are threatened by viruses, natural disasters, power outages, malicious hackers, and a host of other risk factors. In the context of computer systems, **risk management** is the process of identifying potential threats to computer equipment and data, implementing plans to avoid as many threats as possible, and developing steps to recover from unavoidable disasters. Although it might not be cost-effective or even possible to protect a computer system from all threats, a good risk management plan provides a level of protection that is technologically and economically feasible. The goals of risk management are to reduce downtime, maintain good quality of service, and promote business continuity.

What are the most common threats to large-scale computer systems? As with personal computers, common threats to enterprise computing systems include natural disasters, power outages, software failures, hardware breakdowns, human error, security breaches, acts of war, and viruses. When disaster strikes the PC on your desktop, it is a major inconvenience, but just for one person. The threats to an enterprise system can affect thousands of people.

■ **Natural disasters** include fires, floods, hurricanes, and other such unforeseeable events. A natural disaster can completely shut down a computer system, cutting off service to all customers, and potentially destroy the system completely. For example, when a tornado touched down in downtown Fort Worth, Texas, it traveled over a mile through some of the densest parts of the downtown area and caused more than $400 million in damage. Many small businesses lost their entire computer systems in this disaster.

■ **Power outages** can be caused by natural disasters, overloaded power grids, planned brownouts, and rolling blackouts. For example, the IS Departments of many California businesses had to contend with rolling blackouts in the early 2000s when the power grids in the area could not keep up with rising power demands.

■ **Hardware breakdowns** can occur in any hardware component of a computer system. The risk of breakdown increases as a hardware component ages, but breakdowns can occur in brand-new hardware. Many devices are rated with a **mean time between failures** (MTBF) statistic. For example, a MTBF rating of 125,000 hours means that, on average, a device could function for 125,000 hours before failing. MTBF ratings are averages, however, so a blade server with a 125,000 MTBF rating might operate for only 10 hours before it fails, for example.

■ **Human errors** refer to mistakes made by computer operators. Common errors within an enterprise computing system include entering inaccurate data and failing to follow required procedures. Poorly trained computer operators were blamed for the biggest North American blackout in history, which left more than 50 million people without power in the summer of 2003. (Figure 12-36).

FIGURE 12-36

Human error was blamed for a blackout that cascaded from the midwestern United States, across the northeast, and into Canada.

- **Software failures** can be caused by bugs or flawed software design. A tiny memory leak might be undetectable in a small computing system, but it can be disastrous on a system consisting of hundreds or thousands of computers. Other bugs may cause security leaks. Hackers continue to discover bugs in Microsoft software that allow unauthorized access to servers.

- **Security breaches** include stolen data, physical intrusions, and deliberate sabotage. In one of the most publicized security cases, Omega Engineering Corporation, an instrumentation manufacturer for customers such as NASA and the U.S. Navy, fired network administrator Tim Lloyd for performance problems. Little did the company know that before being fired, the disgruntled employee had written a six-line computer program that would ultimately cost his former employer $10 million dollars in financial losses. Lloyd had set up a "time bomb" that erased all the information on his employer's file server and destroyed all the backup tapes. Tim Lloyd was eventually tried and convicted of computer sabotage, but Omega Engineering never regained its foothold in the market.

- **Acts of war** once affected only computer systems located on battle fronts. With a recent increase in terrorist incidents, however, civilian areas have become targets. Acts of war, such as bombing, can cause physical damage to computer systems. Cyberterrorism can also cause damage, using viruses and worms to destroy data and otherwise disrupt computer-based operations, which now include critical national infrastructures such as power grids and telecommunications systems.

- **Viruses** can damage just about any computer system. You might have experienced the nuisance of rooting out a virus from your personal computer. That inconvenience pales when compared to the potential effect of a virus on an enterprise computing system. The MyDoom worm, spread via e-mail, infected Web sites, and caused an estimated $250 million in damage when it infected millions of computers worldwide.

How are large-scale computer systems protected from threats? No computer system can be completely risk-free, but several proactive measures can protect systems from threats. These countermeasures can be grouped into four categories: deterrents, preventive countermeasures, corrective procedures, and detection activities.

- **Deterrents** reduce the likelihood of deliberate attack. Common deterrents include security features such as multilevel authentication and password protection. Monitoring software that tracks users, file updates, and changes to critical systems also act as deterrents. Physical deterrents, such as providing only limited access to critical servers, also fall under this category (Figure 12-37).

- **Preventive countermeasures** shield vulnerabilities to render an attack unsuccessful or reduce its impact. Firewalls that prevent unauthorized access to a system are one example of a preventive countermeasure.

- **Corrective procedures** reduce the effect of an attack. Data backups, disaster recovery plans, and the availability of redundant hardware devices all are examples of corrective procedures.

- **Detection activities** recognize attacks and trigger preventive countermeasures or corrective procedures. For example, antivirus software detects viruses entering a system and can be configured to automatically clean the system or quarantine infected files. Theft or vandalism can be detected by periodic hardware inventories.

FIGURE 12-37
Physical deterrents, such as fingerprint and retinal scans, provide one line of defense against disasters.

DATA CENTERS

Does a data center help minimize risks? The hardware and software for most enterprise and many high-performance computing systems are housed in a data center. A **data center** is a specialized facility designed to house and protect computer systems and data. A data center typically includes special security features, such as fireproof construction, earthquakeproof foundations, sprinkler systems, power generators, secure doors and windows, and antistatic floor coverings.

Data centers are designed to proactively reduce the risk of data loss that might occur as a result of a disaster. The best way to protect against risk is to avoid it altogether, and data centers can reduce or negate the effects of specific types of disasters. For example, NTT/Verio, an ISP that supplies Web hosting services in more than 170 countries, currently operates from more than 20 data centers located in the U.S., Europe, Australia, and Asia. The company stores data for thousands of organizations, and loss of information in even one data center would be a disaster. NTT/Verio managers designed a series of data centers with risk prevention in mind. Each data center incorporates special risk management features for dealing with fires, power outages, security, and environmental concerns.

FIGURE 12-38
Many critical data centers are located in underground bunkers.

Data centers can be located in the basement of a building or even underground (Figure 12-38). One commercial data center, USDCO, is housed 85 feet below ground in an abandoned gypsum mine near Grand Rapids, Michigan. Underground data centers provide some level of protection against natural disasters, such as storms and fires, and are not susceptible to extreme changes in surface temperature. In general, data centers are not located in earthquake, flood, or tornado prone areas.

Data centers typically include equipment to keep computers functioning during power outages. Most areas experience occasional power failures or blackouts, which can be costly to organizations whose goal is to offer 24/7 coverage. To avoid downtime, one of the most basic requirements for a data center is a supply of uninterrupted power from high-capacity, battery-operated UPSs (uninterruptible power supplies) and backup power generators. A data center must also protect and maintain its own power grid. For example, fuel tanks must be protected against explosions or fire, and batteries must be kept at room temperature for proper functioning.

Physical security is critical to data centers. Most data centers limit physical access via fingerprint identification systems, badges, or security guards. Steel doors divide the centers into secure areas. Motion detectors and automated alarm systems prevent unauthorized movement through the building. In addition, many data centers are located close to police and fire departments.

Conditions in a data center must be monitored at all times. Computerized detection systems monitor sensing devices that track temperature, humidity, water, smoke, fire, air flow, power levels, security systems, and many other metrics. Cameras can be placed in air ducts, under raised floors, and in computer chassis to detect intruders, pests such as mice or rats, or chemical leaks. Figure 12-39 shows the features of a typical data center.

DISASTER RECOVERY PLANS

What if disaster strikes? Despite the best risk prevention measures, disasters that destroy data can and do occur. One of the most destructive disasters in history was the World Trade Center collapse on September 11, 2001. Surprisingly, very few companies affected by the disaster experienced critical data loss. Most companies were able to reconstitute their computer systems because the World Trade Center bombing eight years earlier prompted many companies in the towers to design disaster recovery plans. A **disaster recovery plan** is a step-by-step plan that describes the methods used to secure data against disaster and explains how an organization will recover lost data if and when a disaster occurs.

For example, Kemper Insurance, located on the 35th and 36th floors of the north tower of the World Trade Center, designed a disaster recovery plan after the 1993 bombing. Kemper's disaster recovery plan not only detailed what to do in case of disaster, but it also required a mock disaster recovery exercise at least once a year. In these yearly exercises, IT employees went through the process of reconstructing the company's computer system from scratch at an off-site location. They configured new hardware, installed the required software, and restored data from backup tapes. In response to the 9/11 catastrophe, Kemper Insurance IT employees followed the disaster recovery plan and re-created the computer system at another Kemper Insurance site. Kemper Insurance was up and running by 4:00 a.m. on September 12—less than 24 hours after one of the largest disasters in history.

FIGURE 12-39

A data center is designed to protect equipment and data from a variety of disasters.

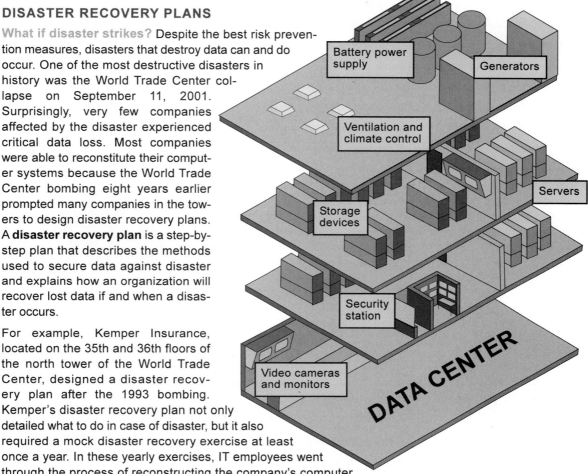

Battery power supply

Generators

Ventilation and climate control

Servers

Storage devices

Security station

Video cameras and monitors

DATA CENTER

12

Disaster recovery plans must deal not only with calamities such as the World Trade Center collapse; they also must take into account day-to-day events that could potentially cause data loss. Backup tapes can become corrupted, an employee might spill coffee onto the most critical storage device in the building, or a virus can slow down the network to the point that it's unusable. A well-formulated disaster recovery plan should account for all kinds of trouble, from the most minor "glitch" to the most destructive disaster. Specifically, an enterprise-wide disaster recovery plan should:

FIGURE 12-40

Publications such as the *Disaster Recovery Journal* help risk management professionals design and update disaster recovery plans.

■ Ensure the safety of people on the premises at the time of a disaster

■ Continue critical business operations

■ Minimize the duration of a serious disruption to operations

■ Minimize immediate damage and prevent additional losses

■ Establish management succession and emergency powers

■ Facilitate effective coordination of recovery tasks

A disaster recovery plan can mean the difference between an organization rebounding after a disaster or simply ceasing to exist. The Kemper Insurance example illustrates how quickly and easily information can be recovered, even from severe disasters. Disaster recovery plans are as critical to data security as data backups, firewalls, and password protection. As a critical component of computer system management, disaster recovery is the focus of numerous publications and conferences (Figure 12-40).

QUICKCHECK......SECTION D

1. The term quality of service refers to the ability of online customer service agents to help Web shoppers. True or false? [＿＿＿]

2. [＿＿＿＿] is a quality-of-service [＿＿＿＿] that measures the amount of data processed in a particular time interval.

3. [＿＿＿＿] is a term that refers to systems that are not operational or not available for processing.

4. The process of identifying potential threats to computer systems, implementing plans to avoid threats, and developing steps to recover from disasters is referred to as [＿＿＿＿] management.

5. Preventive [＿＿＿＿], such as firewalls, shield vulnerabilites.

6. A data center is a RAID-based storage facility specifically designed to withstand attacks from internal auditors. True or false? [＿＿＿]

❖ CHECK ANSWERS

TECHTALK

HIERARCHICAL STORAGE MANAGEMENT

Have you ever wondered how big businesses, governments, and other large organizations store all the information they collect and generate? The IRS alone processes more than 232 million tax returns every year, and that data must be stored for at least seven years. IBM researchers estimate that one exebyte of online information exists today—that's equivalent to a stack of telephone books reaching from the earth to the moon and back. Additional data exists in corporate and government archives. The process of organizing and storing all this information is a challenge, even with fast computers and large storage devices. As a result, most large organizations collect old data and organize it in storage archives. One way that organizations archive data is through the use of hierarchical storage management.

What is hierarchical storage management? **Hierarchical storage management** (HSM) refers to the practice of moving infrequently accessed data to a succession of increasingly inexpensive storage devices. The process of moving data from one storage device to another can be automated by using HSM software. A major advantage of HSM systems is cost savings. As data ages, it can be moved from expensive hard disk storage to less expensive storage media, such as optical disks and digital tapes.

An HSM system uses a variety of tiered storage devices, referred to as a "storage hierarchy," to store managed data. A **storage hierarchy** is a collection of several types of storage devices, usually organized from high-cost, fast media at the top of the hierarchy, to slower, low-cost media at the bottom. An HSM system typically has between one and three tiers, depending on the organization's requirements. As data ages, it is moved from the top tier of the hierarchy toward the lowest tier. For example, a file can be moved from the first storage tier to the second storage tier when it hasn't been accessed in 30 days. The first storage tier is often a hard disk or other fast-access storage medium. The second tier might be an optical disk drive or a tape drive. If the file has not been accessed for another 30 days—making it 60 days since the last access—it is then moved to the third tier. The process of moving data as it ages from one storage tier to another is referred to as **migration** or "relocation" (Figure 12-41).

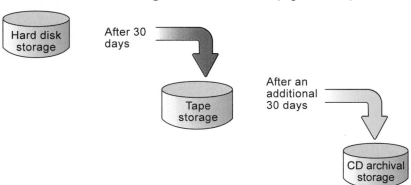

FIGURE 12-41

Data in an HSM system migrates to lower levels of the storage hierarchy.

12

What happens when someone needs to access migrated data? Data is retrieved from long-term storage by recalling it. In the context of HSM, the term **recall** refers to locating and retrieving data from the storage hierarchy. Recall is sometimes referred to as "restoration." When a file is recalled, it is removed from long-term storage and placed in its original location. After a file is recalled, it remains in its original location and is subject to its original migration criteria.

How do HSM systems work? An HSM system allows administrators to set migration criteria to determine when and to which location a file is relocated. The first decision an administrator is required to make is which files will migrate. Certain files, such as executable files and system files, should never migrate. Other files, such as old data files, very large files, and any files such as tax documents required to be stored for a specified time period, should migrate. Migration criteria might include file creation date, date of last access, file size, file name, and file type.

After the system administrator determines which files are to migrate, he or she must decide how the files will progress through the storage hierarchy. A file does not necessarily move through each successive level of the storage hierarchy. It might move from the top level of the hierarchy directly to the bottom level. For example, an administrator might know that certain files, such as outdated inventory reports, will be accessed rarely and can be moved directly to the bottom tier of the storage hierarchy.

When moving a file to a different level of the hierarchy, software that controls an HSM system does not eradicate all traces of the file from its original location. Instead, it truncates the file, leaving behind the file name, size, and attributes. The data contained in the file is moved to long-term storage, and a pointer is left in its place. The pointer, called a **stub** or "placeholder," allows an HSM system to locate the data later, just as the call number on a library book allows you to find a particular book on a library shelf. Figure 12-42 explains how HSM applications truncate files.

FIGURE 12-42

The migration process leaves behind a stub that can be used to access migrated data.

To the end user, a stub is indistinguishable from the original file. Stubs can be opened, copied, or even deleted, just like normal files. The only difference a user might notice is a short pause while the HSM system locates and restores data to the truncated file.

CLICK TO START ✦

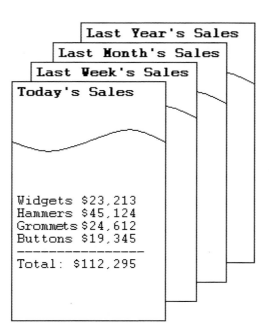

When files migrate, a stub is left behind pointing to the files' new locations.

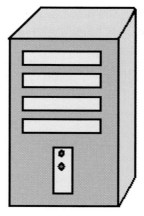

HSM Storage Device

Newer forms of HSM are designed to work with diverse types of digitally formatted information. One modern use for HSM is the migration and recall of e-mail files. Most organizations preserve e-mail for business and legal reasons. HSM products can work directly with e-mail applications to move old e-mail messages to hierarchical storage devices. As with standard HSM files, migrating and recalling e-mail is seamless to the user.

How does hierarchical storage management benefit enterprise computing? Enterprise computing systems maintain massive amounts of data. Much of this data is accessed infrequently. Accounting and tax data for past years, for example, must be retained for a considerable time, but might be accessed only sporadically. Other information, such as marketing documents, white papers, and research results, must be stored indefinitely in case future employees need it. HSM allows this type of information to be stored inexpensively, but located easily and retrieved when necessary.

Storage costs are a major benefit of HSM systems (Figure 12-43). Hard disk drives offer fast access time, but hard drive storage is relatively expensive and not easily expandable. Removable media, such as digital tapes and optical platters, are infinitely expandable simply by adding new tapes or platters to the system, and they are also inexpensive.

Some HSM systems also offer security benefits. Most HSM software can be configured to automatically make copies of data using several methods. Storage media can be mirrored, automatically making two or more copies of every piece of media the HSM system uses. Data itself can be stored multiple times; for example, the system administrator can configure HSM software to copy important data to three different media before truncating the original files. HSM software can also make backups of storage media automatically at periodic intervals.

Most HSM systems also have a reporting and alerting feature. Because so much HSM activity occurs behind the scenes and is undetectable to the average user, HSM applications must have some way of notifying an administrator in case of failure or error. Some HSM software packages have an administrative interface that reports any errors. Other more sophisticated HSM software can be configured to issue an alert to an administrator's e-mailbox or pager. For example, an HSM application could be configured to automatically e-mail a system administrator if all media in the system are full, and new tapes or optical platters must be installed.

FIGURE 12-43
HSM offers cost benefits for storing large files.

A major league sports team can store digital movies of every game the team plays. Coaches and players refer to these games as part of the training process. Each movie might require several gigabytes of storage space, and storing these files on hard disks in an organized and logical manner would require large, costly hard disk drives. Instead, a sports team can use an HSM system to store a stub for each movie, but maintain the large movie files on inexpensive, easily expandable media, such as digital tapes.

QUICKCHECK........TECHTALK

1. _____ storage management (HSM) refers to the practice of moving infrequently accessed data to a succession of increasingly inexpensive storage devices.

2. In an HSM system, the process of moving data from one storage tier to another is referred to as _____.

3. When an HSM system moves data to long-term storage, a pointer, called a(n) _____, is left in its place.

4. The major reason for implementing an HSM system is to decrease the _____ of data storage.

12

CHECK ANSWERS

ISSUE

DONATED CPU CYCLES

"Volunteer your PC. Don't just make a donation. Make a difference." It's an appealing slogan, and the trademarked tag line for a company that uses donated CPU cycles to look for a cure for cancer. Similar projects are tackling AIDS research, searching for extraterrestrial life, looking for a cure for smallpox, studying global climate change, and cracking codes.

Should you and your computer volunteer to participate in these projects? Are they legitimate? Can your computer really make a difference in solving such large and complex problems? Would participation open your computer to viruses and other intrusions? To answer these questions, you'll need to apply what you've learned about grid computing.

As explained in Section C of this chapter, grid computing is a type of distributed computing that works by tapping into the idle computing resources of thousands of personal computers connected to a local area network or the Internet. It breaks down large projects into many small processing tasks, and then distributes those tasks to individual computers connected to the network.

As one analyst explains grid computing, "By combining thousands of ordinary PCs to work on extremely large computational projects, problems can be solved more quickly and less expensively than by conventional methods. Now regular people can help fuel research and projects that previously may have required a bank of supercomputers or a hundred years to complete."

To participate in a grid computing project, you download grid client software that provides your computer with instructions for processing the problem and submitting your results. Grid computing tasks are typically processed during idle CPU cycles—when your computer is not being used for other tasks—so they should not interfere with the speed or reliability of your own computer work.

Many of today's grid computing projects use the Internet to harness computer processing power from the homes and dorm rooms of thousands of individual volunteers.

The idea of distributing processing tasks among many personal computers is not a new one. The first Beowulf clusters were on the drawing board in 1994. Recent flash mob supercomputer experiments have shown that groups of low-powered computers can be connected without too much difficulty into a low-cost surrogate for a supercomputer.

One of the first Internet-based grid computing projects, SETI@home, was designed to search for extraterrestrial intelligence. Since the project started in 1999, more than 5 million people have donated the equivalent of 2 million years of CPU time to analyzing radiotelescope data for any signals that could have come from an alien civilization.

The potential of grid computing is astounding. As one project manager explains, "What we're talking about is the possibility of getting something like 50 teraFLOPS of computer capacity—almost for free." Of course, you've heard the old adage "Nothing in life is free." And so it is with grid computing. Although the processor cycles might be "free," grid computing requires software and a computer to consolidate the results sent in by thousands of volunteers. Projects require advertising and managers—and none of this overhead is free. Some projects are financed by donations, corporations, and organizations. A leukemia research project, for example, is jointly sponsored by Intel, the American Cancer Society, and the National Foundation for Cancer Research. Other projects, however, might rely on financial support from commercial revenues.

One grid computing venture runs several nonprofit and for-profit projects. Although it uses nonprofit projects to recruit volunteers, donated CPU cycles are sometimes used, without their owners' knowledge, to run commercial tasks. As a result, you might volunteer your computer's CPU cycles for a humanitarian nonprofit project, but your computer might also be used to process an inventory management job for a commercial business. The company that runs the grid computing venture gets paid for this service, but you don't. Financial issues aside, some computer owners find it a bit disturbing that their computers are processing data from unknown sources and for unknown purposes.

Grid computing also poses a potential security threat. SETI@home has been attacked by hackers trying to simulate alien signals! A harmless prank? Perhaps. But grid client software—downloaded by thousands or millions of volunteers—is a highly attractive target for hackers. Grid computing also offers opportunities for terrorist and criminal organizations. For example, a terrorist organization might set up a grid for a seemingly innocent humanitarian cause to gain access to enough computing power to crack encrypted government communications.

Installing a grid client on your own computer is your choice, but what about configuring work or school computers to donate CPU cycles? An employee at a Georgia college faced legal action after installing software on school computers to participate in RSA's 64-bit code breaking challenge. The State of Georgia attempted to fine the employee 59 cents per minute for the bandwidth used, a total of $415,000. Although the case never went to court, the employee accepted a plea agreement to probation, a small fine, and community service. The moral of that story: Get clearance before installing grid clients on a computer you don't own.

On the question about the effectiveness of grid computing projects, the jury is still out. Grid computing works best for problems that can be broken down into many small independent calculations. It is less effective when individual calculations affect each other. It fails at weather forecasting, for example, where a disturbance in one part of the atmosphere affects neighboring weather systems. Potential volunteers might have difficulty assessing the likelihood that a particular problem can be solved by using grid computing. Therefore, a certain degree of trust is required, and can be established only after this technology acquires a more substantial track record.

INFOWEBLINKS

You'll find more information about philanthropic uses of your computer's CPU cycles at the **Idle CPUs InfoWeb**. ✦

www.course.com/np/concepts8/ch12

ЫНАТ DO YOU THINK?

1. Have you ever participated in a grid computing project? ○ Yes ○ No ○ Not sure

2. Would you participate in a purely nonprofit grid computing project that appeared to be legitimate? ○ Yes ○ No ○ Not sure

3. Would you participate in a grid computing project without asking for compensation if you knew some of your CPU cycles were being sold to profit-based businesses? ○ Yes ○ No ○ Not sure

✦ SAVE RESPONSES

12

COMPUTERS IN CONTEXT

BANKING

For most of history, banks used low-tech methods to track one of the world's most cherished commodities—wealth. Checking accounts were in widespread use as early as 1550, when wealthy Dutch traders began depositing money with cashiers for safekeeping. The use of printed checks became popular in England in the late 18th century—so popular that banks found it difficult to process a steadily increasing stream of checks, including those drawn on accounts from other banks.

An unverified story that has become part of bank lore describes the origin of a solution to the check processing problem. As the story goes, a London bank messenger stopped for coffee and got to talking with a messenger from another bank. Realizing that they were delivering checks drawn on each other's banks, the two messengers decided to exchange checks there in the coffee house. This event evolved into a system of check clearinghouses where representatives from various banks met periodically to exchange checks and reconcile totals in cash. By 1839, British clearinghouses were annually processing in excess of £954 million of checks—equivalent to U.S.$250 billion in today's money.

Bank clearinghouses were described in an essay, *The Economy of Machinery and Manufactures*, written by Charles Babbage in 1832. He also included a reference to the "possibility of performing arithmetical calculations by machinery" along with a description of the Difference Engine, then under construction in his workshop.

This dream of automated check clearing did not, however, become reality until more than a century later when S. Clark Beise, senior vice president at Bank of America, contracted with Stanford Research Institute (SRI) to develop a computer system to automate check processing. SRI completed a prototype in 1955 that used mechanical sorting equipment to queue up each check and MICR technology to read check numbers. In 1959, the first ERMA (Electronic Recording Machine-Accounting) system went into service. With ERMA handling calculations, 9 employees could handle the job that once required 50 people. By 1966, 32 regional ERMA systems operated by Bank of America were processing more than 750 million checks per year. ERMA and similar check processing technologies quickly integrated with bank transaction processing systems to become the bedrock of today's banking technology.

Output from check sorting machines can be submitted to the Automated Clearing House (ACH) network, which offers a secure, batch-oriented data exchange system that can be accessed by financial institutions. On a daily basis, banks submit check data and receive a report of balances due to other banks. These balances can be reconciled by electronic funds transfer over the Federal Reserve's FedWire telecommunications network.

An upswing in check fraud during the 1960s made it increasingly difficult to cash checks at local merchants. As an alternative to trying to cash checks at banks and local merchants, automatic teller machines (ATMs) were first installed in the 1970s. A typical ATM connects to a bank's front-end processor—a computer that maintains account balances for in-network customers and monitors suspicious activity. The front-end processor is separated from the bank's main computer system for security.

Some ATMs exchange data with the front-end processor by using dedicated dial-up telephone lines. Other ATMs use always-on leased lines. Legacy protocols such as SNA and 3270 bisync, are being replaced by the standard Internet Protocol (IP) that can be routed through more affordable connections, such as cable, ISDN, DSL, or Internet VPN.

ATMs are expensive—about $50,000 to purchase a machine, install it, and operate it for one year. Banks have offset this cost by charging transaction fees and reducing the number of bank tellers. Once a promising entry-level occupation, bank tellers today earn less than $20,000 per year. Although tellers continue to accept deposits, process withdrawals, and cash payroll checks, they are increasingly pressed into customer service roles—opening new accounts, issuing ATM cards, resolving disputed transactions, and assisting customers who have lost bank cards or checkbooks. Despite this shift in job description, the number of bank teller jobs is expected to fall at least 10% by 2010.

ATMs offer access to bank services from convenient locations where customers shop, eat, and hang out with friends. The Internet takes banking convenience one step further and provides round-the-clock account access from customers' homes, schools, or work PCs. Today, most banks and credit unions offer some type of online banking (also called home banking, Internet banking, or electronic banking).

Basic online banking services allow customers to access checking account and bankcard activity, transfer funds between checking and savings accounts, view electronic images of checks and deposit slips, download and print monthly statements, and reorder checks. Customers can also pay bills online by scheduling payment dates and amounts. Many credit card and utility companies offer e-billing services that automatically forward electronic bills to customers' online

banking accounts. For monthly fixed-amount bills, such as car loans, online banking offers automatic payment options that deduct funds from specified checking or savings accounts.

For managing assets more effectively, online banking sites also offer sophisticated tools, including account aggregation, stock quotes, rate alerts, and portfolio management programs. Most online banking sites are also compatible with personal finance software, such as Managing Your Money, QuickBooks, Microsoft Money, and AOL BankNOW, so that transaction data can be shuttled between customer's local computers and their online banking services.

A cadre of customer support personnel staff online help desks for customers with questions about online banking. Webmasters, computer security specialists, and network technicians are also part of banking's new job corps.

Online banking services are typically housed on a secure Web server, and customers are not allowed direct access to the bank's transaction processing system. Customer privacy is maintained by the use of passwords and SSL connections that encrypt data as it is sent to and from customers' browsers.

Successful banks are built on good business decisions. Bank managers are increasingly working with business intelligence tools to look for trends in customer behavior, analyze competing financial institutions, and examine current business practices. Tools for these activities include data warehouses that collect and organize data, data mining software that organizes and analyzes data in a meaningful way, and statistical tools that formulate comparisons and trendlines.

Today, banking rests on multilayered technologies that incorporate check processing equipment, transaction processing systems, business intelligence software, ACH networks, FedWire, ATM networks, the Internet, and Web servers. Many banking practices originated from batch check processing, and only gradually have banks begun to move to more modern online transaction processing (OLTP) systems that store scanned images of checks and instantly update accounts when a purchase is made or a bill is paid.

INFOWEBLINKS

For more information about this Computers in Context topic, check the **Computers and Banking InfoWeb.**

www.course.com/np/concepts8/ch12

12

INTERACTIVE SUMMARY

To review important concepts from this chapter, fill in the blanks to best complete each sentence. When using the NP8 BookOnCD, click the Check Answers buttons to automatically score your answers. Place your Tracking Disk in the floppy disk drive if you want to save your scores.

[_____] computing is defined as one or more information systems that share data. They typically supply information to hundreds or thousands of users. The difference between an enterprise computing system and an information system is one of [_____]. Information systems are usually dedicated to one set of related tasks, whereas enterprise systems encompass the tasks of multiple information systems.

The ability of a computer system to change to meet demand is referred to as [_____]. Increasing individual machine performance by adding processors, memory, and storage capacity is referred to as scaling up. Scaling out means adding more computers to increase the overall size of a system. The process of connecting two or more information systems in a way that allows scalability and data sharing is referred to as enterprise system integration.

Enterprise [_____] integration refers to the process of connecting different types of computing, storage, input, and output devices. Enterprise [_____] integration (EAI) is the process of connecting software applications so that they can exchange data. EAI consists of four techniques: database linking, application linking, data warehousing, and common virtual systems.

High-[_____] computing (HPC) is the branch of computer science that focuses on ways to optimize the processing capabilities of computers. HPC systems usually are designed to process compute-[_____] problems.

✦ CHECK ANSWERS

Enterprise computing systems contain many diverse types of hardware. Enterprise systems may have to integrate a [_____] system, which might use outdated technology, but performs critical processing tasks. A [_____] server is a modular electronic circuit board containing one or more processors.

Enterprise systems can use high-capacity storage systems called storage [_____] networks. Another type of storage system commonly found on enterprise systems is [_____] attached storage. [_____] is the process of creating a real-time copy of a piece of storage media.

The core of an HPC system can be a [_____] like Earth Simulator, or it could be a collection of interconnected, less powerful computers. Many HPC systems consist of computers that use multiprocessor architecture, that is, computers designed and built to use two or more processors. [_____] processing is the simultaneous use of more than one processor to execute a program. [_____] multiprocessing uses a single operating system to control multiple processors. [_____] parallel processing links multiple processors, each with its own bus, memory, and operating system.

Enterprise-level software applications typically include multiplatform support, are scalable, and support redundant equipment resources that avoid a single point of [_____]. Software developers use [_____] to allow applications on an enterprise system to share data. High-performance systems typically use [_____] software designed and written for a specific HPC system.

✦ CHECK ANSWERS

The simplest architecture for enterprise and high-performance systems is a [_____] computing system. Many of these systems consist of a [_____] computer, which performs most or all of the processing, and [_____] for user input and output. It is also possible for these systems to include personal computers, which use terminal [_____] software to make them appear to the host computer as "dumb terminals."

A [_____] computing system is a collection of connected computers in which data and application software are dispersed to more than one physical computer. These systems are often organized in [_____], which group computers into layers that perform specific tasks.

A [_____] computing system is a network of computers in which each computer is treated as a generic and equal resource. These systems perform best on problems that can be divided into smaller problems and processed in any sequence, at any time.

A cluster is a group of two or more servers connected together to distribute workloads and adapt to system failure. Each computer on a cluster is referred to as a cluster [_____]. Clusters are fault [_____]; that is, they react gracefully to unexpected failures. Transferring service from a failed node to a working node is called cluster [_____]. Load [_____] is the practice of distributing processing and storage tasks among the nodes of a cluster. A cluster configured so that all nodes are active at the same time is referred to as an [_____] cluster. A cluster configured so that there is one active node and additional nodes that are ready in case of failover is called an [_____] cluster. A cluster of off-the-shelf computers configured to perform HPC tasks is called a [_____] cluster.

CHECK ANSWERS

The term quality of [_____] (QoS) refers to the level of performance a computer system provides. QoS [_____] are the measurements used to evaluate the quality of computer system performance. One of the most common of these measurements is [_____] time—the time period that begins when a user initiates a request for information and ends when the request is fulfilled.

Risk [_____] is the process of identifying potential threats to computer equipment and data and then determining how to minimize or avoid those threats. Natural disasters are a common risk, as are power outages, software failures, and hardware breakdowns. Common risk [_____] include security features and monitoring software. [_____] countermeasures shield vulner-abilities to render an attack unsuccessful or reduce its impact. [_____] procedures reduce the effect of an attack. [_____] activities discover attacks and trigger preventative or corrective measures.

A data center is a specialized facility designed to house and protect computer systems and data. These centers are typically fireproof and earthquakeproof and include features such as power generators and antistatic floor coverings. A disaster [_____] plan is a step-by-step plan that describes the methods used to secure data against disasters and explains how an organization will recover lost data if and when a disaster occurs.

CHECK ANSWERS

12

INTERACTIVE KEY TERMS

Make sure you understand all the boldfaced key terms presented in this chapter. If you're using the NP8 BookOnCD, you can use this list of terms as an interactive study activity. First, try to define a term in your own words, and then click the term to compare your definition with the definition presented in the chapter.

INTERACTIVE SITUATION QUESTIONS

Apply what you've learned to some typical computing situations. When using the NP8 BookOnCD, you can type your answers, and then use the Check Answers button to automatically score your responses. Place your Tracking Disk in the floppy disk drive if you want to save your scores.

1. You're the chief information officer at a large company that just purchased a smaller company whose computer system must be incorporated with the existing system. You realize that this is best done using a(n) [＿＿＿＿＿] computing system.

2. While browsing the Web, you find a site that describes an ongoing project to find very large prime numbers. You can download a client program that allows your computer to help in the search. You realize that this is an example of a(n) [＿＿＿＿＿] computing system.

3. You work in the IT Department of an organization. One day a small fire destroys the main computer room. You don't panic because you know exactly how to rebuild the system. Your organization's disaster [＿＿＿＿＿] plan has step-by-step instructions on what to do.

4. Your company recently implemented a 24/7 policy for its e-mail system. The CEO is very concerned that equipment failure could cause the e-mail system to go down. By connecting several servers together, you create a(n) [＿＿＿＿＿] that allows the e-mail system to failover to additional servers in case the main e-mail server fails.

5. You're a scientist working in a research lab. You have masses of data that must be analyzed, but your existing computer system is too slow to do it in a timely manner. You realize that you need a high-[＿＿＿＿＿] computing system to do the job.

6. Your company administers a Web site that must be available all the time. You worry that disasters such as earthquakes or fires might cause the system to fail. The area where the system is located also has frequent power outages and brownouts. You decide to move the system to a data [＿＿＿＿＿], which offers disaster protection, backup power supplies, and additional risk management features.

7. You're a computer programmer assigned to make a legacy inventory system share data with a Web-based retail system. You decide to create [＿＿＿＿＿] that allows applications on the two diverse systems to share data.

8. You're shopping for a new personal computer to produce some training videos. The video software offers parallel processing capabilities. The specs on the computer you want to purchase indicate that it has [＿＿＿＿＿] architecture, so it seems likely that it can use the parallel processing features of your software.

✦ CHECK ANSWERS

INTERACTIVE PRACTICE TESTS

Practice tests that consist of 10 multiple-choice, true/false, and fill-in-the-blank questions are available on both the NP8 BookOnCD and the NP8 Web site. The questions are selected at random from a large test bank, so each time you take a test, you'll receive a different set of questions. Your tests are scored immediately, and you can print study guides that help you find the correct answers for any questions that you missed.

www.course.com/np/concepts8/ch12 ✦

CLICK ✦ TO START

12

REVIEW

ON THE WEB

PROJECTS

An NP8 Project is an open-ended activity that helps you apply the concepts you have learned. Many projects require resources in addition to your textbook, such as current magazines, library materials, or Web access. When you tackle a project, be prepared to use your critical thinking skills, logical analysis, and creativity. Projects for this chapter include:

- **Issue research: Donating CPU Cycles**
- **Become a Disaster Expert**
- **Computers in Banking**
- **Internet QoS**
- **Legacy Systems**
- **High-performance Computing**

To work with the Projects for this chapter, connect to the **New Perspectives NP8 Web Site.**

www.course.com/np/concepts8/ch12

TECHTV VIDEO PROJECT

The TechTV clip *Predicting the Future of AI* features an interview with MIT professor Marvin Minsky, a well-known pioneer in artificial intelligence. As you watch the video look for Minsky's ideas about the computer processing power needed for "smart" computers. Can today's personal computers exhibit intelligence, or would a "smart" computer require supercomputer processing power like chess-playing Deep Blue? Research this question on the Web and then write a short paper summarizing your prediction for the future of AI.

To work with the Video Projects for this chapter, connect to the **New Perspectives NP8 Web Site.**

www.course.com/np/concepts8/ch12

STUDY TIPS

Study Tips help you to organize and consolidate the information in a chapter by making lists, outlines, charts, and sketches. You can use paper and pencil or word processing software to complete most of the Study Tips.

To work with the Study Tips for this chapter, connect to the **New Perspectives NP8 Web Site.**

www.course.com/np/concepts8/ch12

ONLINE GAMES

Test your comprehension of the concepts introduced in Chapter 12 by playing the NP8 Online Games. At the end of each game, you have three options:

- Print a comprehensive study guide complete with page references
- Print your results to be submitted to your instructor
- Save your results to be submitted to your instructor via e-mail

To work with the Online Games for this chapter, connect to the **New Perspectives NP8 Web Site.**

www.course.com/np/concepts8/ch12

STUDENT EDITION LABS

Extend your knowledge of computer concepts with the Student Edition Labs.

There are currently no Student Edition Labs directly related to the topics covered in Chapter 12, however, you can go to the NP8 New Perspectives Web site to access Student Edition Labs for review and additional exploration.

Go to the NP8 New Perspectives Web site for specific lab topics.

To work with the Student Edition Labs and their corresponding assignments, you can connect to the **New Perspectives NP8 Web Site**.

www.course.com/np/concepts8/ch12

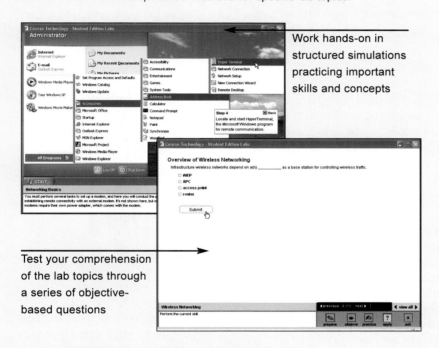

Work hands-on in structured simulations practicing important skills and concepts

Test your comprehension of the lab topics through a series of objective-based questions

Track Your Progress with the Student Edition Labs

- Student Edition Labs test your comprehension of the lab topics through a series of trackable objective-based questions. Your instructor will direct you to either print your results or submit them via e-mail.

- Student Edition Lab Assignments, available on the New Perspectives NP8 Web site, require you to apply the skills learned through the lab in a live environment. Go to the New Perspectives NP8 Web site for detailed instruction on individual Student Edition Lab Assignments.

If you have a SAM user profile, you have access to even more interactive content. Log in to your SAM account and go to your assignments page to see what your instructor has assigned for this chapter.

PREVIEW

Every year, the computer press falls in love with some cool gadget, new technology, great piece of software, or hot Web site. Industry analysts predict great things for these technology darlings. Some of their predictions are correct and innovative products, such as digital music players, become popular. Other products get lots of hype, but seem to go nowhere. TechBuzz takes a look at some of the products that have recently had industry analysts buzzing.

GADGETS

Last year, the iPod made a big splash as a handy audio player and portable backup device. USB continued its move to replace serial, parallel, SCSI, and PS/2 ports. Keychain USB Flash drives increased in popularity as a convenient way to transport data. That's all mainstream news. What else is on the horizon gadget-wise? Here are a few that analysts like.

Tiny, Tiny Hard Disk Drives
In late 2004, Toshiba introduced a hard disk drive with an .85-inch storage surface that's about the size of a nickel. The disk holds 2 GB of data and consumes about half the power of 1.8-inch drives currently used for portable multimedia devices, such as Apple's iPod. Toshiba expects to increase storage capacity to 30 GB before the end of the decade. These drives have potential applications for digital music players, portable movie players, digital cameras, and cell phones.

But how do these drives stack up to solid state storage memory cards? They are currently less expensive per GB of storage, but on the downside, they are somewhat less durable and 2GB is not quite enough for most media applications. Tiny hard drives are likely to fill the bill for some applications, but are an evolutionary, rather than revolutionary, technology.

RFID Lost and Found
The applications of disposable RFID chips keep expanding. Reminiscent of Harry Potter's Maurader's Map that showed the whereabouts of everyone at Hogwarts, families visiting LegoLand in Denmark can rent wristbands containing an RFID tag that can pinpoint a child's location in the park in less than 20 seconds. Wi-Fi signals emitted by the RFID tags are monitored by 38 receiver units within

the park. Parents with lost children can ask for location coordinates simply by sending a text message from their cell phones to the tracking system.

Find That Hotspot
You're all signed up for Wi-Fi service. Now how do you find hotspots? You can check one of the many hotspot maps on the Web, but that assumes you're already connected. Suppose you're toting your Wi-Fi enabled notebook computer on a trip and want to find the nearest hotspot without digging out lots of equipment. A company called Chrysalis thinks it has the answer in a little gadget that fits on your key ring. Just press a button on the Wi-Fi Seeker, and a series of LED lights help you home in on the nearest hotspot. Is this product a very cool idea or just another toy for gadget fans? Let's wait and see if consumers add these devices to their key rings alongside USB flash drives and garage door openers.

New Horizons in Backup

Here's the problem: You've got a home network and you want to back up data from all your computers, but you hesitate to back up everyone's data to your main computer. What if it gets fried? Now Linksys offers an inexpensive server device called a Network Storage Link for USB 2.0 (NSLU2) that you can connect to your network hub. Then attach one USB hard drive for your everyday storage tasks, and when you're ready to back up, connect a second USB hard drive. Built-in utilities let you schedule backups from your computer's hard disk to the USB hard disk and from one USB disk to the other.

This is a very neat solution, but it's still not perfect. Current versions of the Linksys server store data in a different format than the Windows file system. That means you can access data from the disks only when they are attached to the Linksys server. You cannot, for example, connect one of the USB drives directly to your computer and access the data.

High-end Handhelds

Hewlett-Packard's iPaq h6315 pushed the technology envelope by incorporating three connectivity bands: cellular, Wi-Fi, and Bluetooth. For the consumer, these options provide flexibility and cost savings. Wi-Fi service is faster (and often cheaper) than cellular service, so most handheld owners prefer to use it if available. The iPaq switches seamlessly between networks so that users don't have to fiddle with IP addresses and intermittent connections. As with standard handhelds, the multiband iPaq defaults to the cell system's cellular technology. When a Wi-Fi network is nearby, however, the iPaq connects to it in standby mode. At the end of the current HTTP session—for example, after a Web page graphic has been displayed—the iPaq switches to the Wi-Fi network.

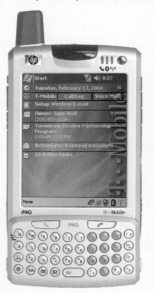

Multiband capability does not come cheap, however. Retail pricing for the iPaq h6315 is about $500 with a 1-year T-Mobile service contract that will set you back almost $80 per month. And yet, this seems to be the future of PDAs and cell phones. Maybe as use increases, prices will come down.

Wi-Fi Boombox

In the past few years, Internet radio has become increasingly popular. Listeners can connect to radio station Web sites anywhere in the world for live audio feeds of music, news, sports, and talk radio. Listeners also tune into their favorite local stations via the Internet when reception is bad. Depending on the station, streaming audio might be available in formats such as Windows Media, Real Audio, or MusicMatch. If your computer doesn't have the right player, most Internet radio sites offer a link for downloading it.

What if you'd like to listen to Internet radio while on the go? Some PDAs include Wi-Fi radios that connect to hotspots using client services, such as Boingo, but the sound quality is not great. For better sound, you need a better box.

Philips offers a high-end stereo system with built-in 802.11b circuitry that streams Internet radio to a pair of powerful woofer-equipped speakers. It includes cool features such as the Info button that e-mails the title of any song you're listening to but can't identify. Unfortunately, the Wi-Fi capabilities are designed for use on a LAN, not as you wander around town from hotspot to hotspot. But you can expect portable Wi-Fi boomboxes to be available soon.

BITTORRENT: SOLUTION TO THE BANDWIDTH BOTTLENECK?

Napster and other music file swap sites, such as Kazaa and eDonkey, turned peer-to-peer networking technology into an overnight sensation. Now the computer press is focused on another peer-to-peer technology called BitTorrent. According to an *InfoWorld* article, BitTorrent has "taken the Internet by storm."

What It Does

A BitTorrent network is designed to reduce the bandwidth bottleneck that occurs when many people attempt to download the same very large file, such as a feature-length film, application software, or an interactive 3-D computer game.

With conventional uploading and downloading technology, simultaneous requests for large files can easily max out a central server's capacity. This bottleneck has made nationwide movie distribution over the Internet impractical. Imagine the server capacity needed to handle simultaneous download requests on the release date of big box office hits. Many industry analysts expect BitTorrent technology to kick-start the online movie download business, making film fans less reliant on trips to their local video stores.

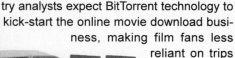

How It Works

BitTorrent reduces download bottlenecks by using computers that download a file to also upload that file to other computers.

Suppose that 100 computers request the film *Robots* at about the same time. A server breaks the movie file into pieces and begins to download those pieces to the first computer that requested the movie. As more computers request the file, they become part of a "swarm" that uses peer-to-peer technology to exchange file pieces with each other. After the server has downloaded all the file pieces to the swarm, its job is complete and it can service other requests. The swarm continues to exchange file pieces until every computer in the swarm has the entire file.

BitTorrent client software is currently available from several Web sites. After installing the client, you can use it to download from any BitTorrent-enabled site simply by clicking the file you want. The BitTorrent client handles the entire file-swapping procedure. After getting the entire file, good etiquette requires clients to remain connected to the swarm so that they can "seed" (see BitTorrent Lingo box below) file pieces to others.

Where It's Headed

Industry analysts seem to anticipate that BitTorrent will power commercial movie download sites similar to music sites, such as iTunes and MSN Music. BitTorrent technology, however, is currently more like Napster and other music-swapping technologies that ran afoul of the recording industry. Pirates use it to transfer illicit copies of software, music, and movies. Watch for future developments to see if BitTorrent can be tamed to serve commercial interests.

BITTORRENT LINGO

Swarm: A group of computers temporarily networked to download a file.

Tracker: Server software that helps establish a swarm of end-user computers.

Seed or seeder: A computer that has downloaded an entire file and can upload pieces to other clients in a swarm.

Leech or leecher: A computer in the process of obtaining file pieces from a swarm.

Chokers: Clients that don't allow other clients to download file pieces.

SECURITY, BOTNETS, AND ZOMBIES: WHY HAS THE INTERNET BECOME SO DANGEROUS?

In the near future, hackers and their troublesome viruses might seem like a civilized group compared to the organized crime syndicates now emerging as the Internet's newest threat. At a Gartner IT Security Summit, author Bruce Sterling offered a bleak depiction of cybersecurity, saying "We had a digital revolution in the 1990s—now we've slid into digital terror." He went on to add "Today's Internet is a dirty mess—it's revolution failed."

To support his criticism, Sterling points out that many of the most recent "innovations" on the Internet include spam, phishing, mass-mailing worms, and viruses that can activate even before an e-mail message is opened.

JPEG of Death

Sterling neglected to mention one of the latest hacker exploits: the JPEG of Death. A critical flaw in Windows XP allows hackers to hide malicious code in JPEG images, which are indistinguishable from uncorrupted images. Typically, corrupted images are posted on porn sites that attract lots of download traffic. When a corrupted image is opened, malicious code turns the infected computer into a "zombie."

Zombies

A "zombie" is a computer that can be remotely controlled by a hacker. In addition to the JPEG of Death, viruses, worms, and e-mail attachments can also harbor code that creates zombies.

Botnets

Getting control of one computer is just a start. Hackers create hundreds or even thousands of zombie computers and link them into temporary peer-to-peer or grid systems called "botnets." In one highly publicized investigation, a botnet of more than 10,000 zombies was discovered and dismantled. Rogue botnets run by hackers can launch denial-of-service attacks or send spam that bypasses IP address blacklists and is difficult to trace. Although some botnets are harmless pranks launched by teenagers, many botnets are highly profitable criminal enterprises that are leased to spammers and used to extort money from owners of sites targeted for denial-of-service attacks.

Law enforcement officials and IT security experts are becoming increasingly worried about terrorist use of botnets. One participant in a *comp.security.UNIX* chast forum draws this disturbing picture: "If you were to execute the world's largest Internet terrorist attack, the best way to go about it would be via a massive botnet. With a large enough botnet, you could bring down the entire Internet." Botnet attacks could disable power grids, banking systems, and communications networks.

Computer owners can take steps to prevent their computers from being used for criminal or terrorist activity by activating firewall software, using antivirus software, and keeping operating system patches up-to-date.

WI-FI GETS SERIOUS

Wireless networks remain in the tech news headlines. Most people today are familiar with popular Wi-Fi technology used for college LANs and Starbuck's hotspots. The basic 802.11b Wi-Fi standard uses the 2.4 GHz band and transmits at 2 Mbps. The follow-up 802.11g Wi-Fi technology also uses the 2.4 GHz band, but transmits at a much faster 54 Mbps. Wi-Fi's major advantage is its unlicensed spectrum that allows anyone to set up a wireless network and offer wireless hotspots. The drawback of Wi-Fi is its limited coverage area, which maxes out at about 300 feet. Directional antennas can increase Wi-Fi's range to a few miles, but that distance limits service to LANs and small hotspots in airports or coffeehouses. Technologies such as WiMax, Mobile-Fi, Wi-Media, and ZigBee might extend Wi-Fi's reach and open new possibilities.

WiMAX

A technology called WiMAX (or Broadband Wireless) has the potential to overcome Wi-Fi's range and data transmission rate limitations. Based on the 802.16 standard, WiMAX has a range of 30 miles and data transmission rates of 70 Mbps. In addition to citywide coverage, WiMAX is being hailed as the ideal technology to provide broadband Internet access in rural areas where DSL and cable Internet service are not available.

Some analysts predict that 100 million people will be using WiMAX by 2006. More conservative industry watchers estimate that widespread WiMAX deployment won't occur for another decade. WiMAX availability might be curtailed by contention among variations of the technology. Some versions of WiMAX use licensed spectrums and seem to be the focus of commercial service providers who'd like to operate local monopolies similar to cable TV and Internet services. Other versions of WiMAX use the unlicensed spectrum and offer opportunities for local service providers or community governments.

Mobile-Fi

Another wireless standard, known as Mobile-Fi, lets people access the Internet while traveling by train, bus, bike, or car. The Mobile-Fi 802.20 standard offers speeds up to 16 Mbps within a range of several miles. It operates in a licensed part of the spectrum, presumably to allow service providers to establish comprehensive networks that hand off signals to neighboring transmitters as users travel along. As with most technologies in the licensed spectrum, Mobile-Fi requires customers to pay for access.

Wi-Media

Another wireless technology called Wi-Media is also in the pipeline. The goal is for Wi-Media to move massive files quickly (up to 500 Mbps) over short distances (100 meters). Its main application is to transfer files between devices within a PAN (personal area network). For example, Wi-Media enabled devices might be used to wirelessly transfer a feature-length film download from a PC to a TV or transfer video footage from a camera to a PC. As this book went to press, work was progressing on an 802.15.3 Wi-Media standard. However, it offers transmission rates of only 55 Mbps on the 2.4 GHz unlicensed band. That's not optimal for real-time media transfers. Clearly, Wi-Media has not yet hit is stride.

Zigbee

In 2003, a ZDNet reporter wrote "Look out for Zigbee, the low power, low speed technology promises to be cheaper than Bluetooth and to run for months on ordinary batteries." ZigBee technology is based on the 802.15.4 standard with the potential to transmit data at 250 Kbps over a 2.4 GHz band in a range of a few hundred feet. Currently, it is used mainly for monitoring and automating utility and alarm systems in homes and offices. In the future, you might find it in home security systems and medical monitoring equipment. Cute name, but not the kind of application that's likely to wow consumers.

Wi-Fi is definitely on the move as technology innovations increase its speed and bandwidth. Some futurists envision a wireless environment where Internet access to data, voice, movies, and music is everywhere!

VOICE OVER IP: IS IT FINALLY READY FOR PRIME TIME?

VoIP (Voice over IP) has languished in the technology doldrums since its lackluster introduction in 1995. Its early promise of free voice calling over the Internet was sabotaged by slow dial-up connections that produced easily dropped and static-filled conversations. Every few years, the computer press got on the VoIP bandwagon, touted its advantages, and predicted a bold new world without monthly telephone bills. That just didn't happen, but recent developments, such as increased broadband use and support from communications companies, might give VoIP the boost it needs to finally gain widespread popularity.

How VoIP Works

In general, there are two ways to use VoIP. Originally, the technology required VoIP client software, such as Microsoft NetMeeting, Skype, or Internet Phone, and a headset connected to your computer. You can still use this technology and it's free. However, you and the person you're calling must have the same software client.

The second VoIP technology is more versatile, but requires you to pay for a service provider's VoIP plan. After connecting an adapter to your computer and telephone, you can dial as usual. Your calls are routed through your VoIP provider, and then to the telephone of the person you're calling.

As 2004 came to a close, AT&T and Vonage were two of the biggest VoIP service providers. Both offer monthly service plans under $30 with unlimited local and domestic long-distance calling, plus extras such as call forwarding. Other telcos and cable companies are evaluating the VoIP market, however, and service plan prices are expected to fall.

VoWLAN and VoWi-Fi

Following close on the heels of VoIP are VoWLAN (Voice over Wireless LAN) and VoWi-Fi (Voice over Wi-Fi). Whereas VoIP has the potential to replace standard wired telephone service, VoWLAN and VoWi-Fi have the potential to replace cellular phone service. In a perfect world of wireless voice technology, callers could stroll down the street connecting seamlessly to local Wi-Fi hotspots to place free voice calls to anyone in the world via the Internet. Unfortunately, wireless voice technologies have been plagued by technical problems that result in poor quality of service. Most Wi-Fi access points have bandwidth to handle fewer than 10 simultaneous calls.

Current adopters of VoIP and VoWLAN tend to be businesses. Individuals who examine the pros and cons of VoIP might decide to stick with their land and cellular service just a little longer.

VOIP PROS

- Unlike cell phones, no per-minute charges

- Can be free or less expensive than standard or cellular monthly service plans

- Allows callers to share data during calls

- Conference calls are as simple as two-party calls

- A single phone number travels with you, wherever you take your VoIP-enabled computer

VOIP CONS

- Audio quality might not be as high as with a wired telephone

- Requires a broadband Internet connection

- Calls to standard handsets require monthly service contracts

- No phone service during a power outage unless your equipment runs on battery backup

WIKI

A Wiki is a collaborative Web site that allows anyone to edit, modify, or delete elements displayed on Wiki-enabled Web pages. In some ways, Wikis are similar to blogs. Both are accessible with a browser and allow anyone to add comments. Wikis, however, allow participants to alter the original posting and even delete postings made by other participants.

Community Portal link. Make sure you read through the instructions, policy guidelines, and style manual so that your contribution conforms to the Wikipedia style. You wouldn't want to waste your time making substandard edits, only to have them deleted by another contributor who is more familiar with Wikipedia style.

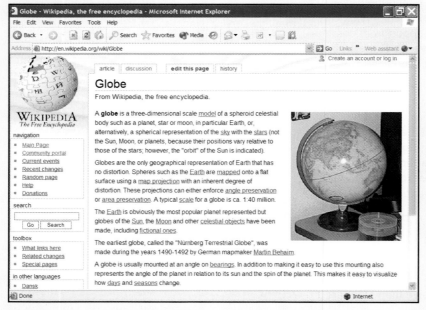

Participants can also create new Wiki pages simply by adding a link to an existing Wiki. All changes are stored in a history file, so participants can trace the evolution of a page and see when changes were made and who made them.

Editing Wiki pages is easy. Simply click the "edit page" link. You can add, modify, or delete the text and graphics displayed on the page. Some Wikis require participants to log in before making changes, presumably to reduce the number of spurious, malicious, and erroneous postings. A list of Wikis can be found by connecting to Internet sites such as *www.worldwidewiki.net/wiki/SwitchWiki*.

Wikipedia

One of the most extensive Wikis is an encyclopedia called Wikipedia located at *www.wikipedia.org*. Connect to Wikipedia and you'll find word definitions, articles about news and events, and extensive entries about a wide range of topics. It's a great source for technical information, with definitions and articles provided by well-known experts.

Wikipedia encourages everyone to contribute to the knowledge base by writing articles, checking facts, adjusting page format, and copyediting. To find a current list of tasks, connect to Wikipedia and click the

Wiki Apps

Small standalone Wikis are being tried for collaborative business projects as an alternative to expensive groupware. It might turn out, however, that Wikipedia becomes the cornerstone of the Wiki world and serves as the core body of information to which contributor-sponsored links and pages can be added.

For anyone who is disillusioned by the runaway commercialization, hacking, defacement, disinformation, and just plain rudeness on today's Web, Wikipedia offers the promise of a serious community of scholars dedicated to open and logical discussion. Once again a technology has appeared with the potential to encourage every voice to speak, but within a process of natural selection that essentially weeds out erroneous information. Whether active vigilance and editing on the part of contributors can fend off hackers and grandstanders is yet to be seen.

WIKI GLOSSARY

Wikitext: User editable source code, which the Wiki server converts into HTML.

Wiki Markup Standard: The syntax used to create and edit Wiki pages; similar to HTML tags used to mark up HTML pages.

CamelCase: A style for generating links on Wiki pages, recognizable because spaces are removed from the words for links, as in ClickToSeeLargePhoto.

WikiGnome: A contributor who makes helpful edits to Wiki pages without much fanfare.

WikiGremlin: A vandal or hacker who defaces or makes malicious edits to Wiki pages.

Wikify: Standardize the format for a Wiki page.

GAMES GONE RETRO: KINGDOM OF LOATHING

3-D computer games have become more sophisticated, with stunning graphics, extensive playing environments, surround sound effects, online access, and multiplayer interaction. Massively multiplayer online games (MMOGs) attract thousands of new players daily. EverQuest remains one of the most popular online games for U.S. players. Another all-time favorite, Doom, is now in its third major revision and attracts scads of devoted followers. These big-budget megahits keep gamers on a steady hardware upgrade path for faster processors and graphics cards.

Stick Figures in a 2-D World

In the pack of online games vying for recognition, the Kingdom of Loathing offers a unique and quirky gaming experience that appeals to a remarkably wide audience. Like popular favorites EverQuest and Doom, Kingdom of Loathing players select characters and guide them on a quest where they fight monsters, solve riddles, gain treasure, and accumulate skills. But Kingdom of Loathing eschews fancy graphics and surround sound for crude stick drawings that give the game a retro quality and appeal similar to text-based adventure-game classics, such as Zork and Colossal Cave.

Pastamancers and Sorcerers

As with conventional role-playing games, characters are categorized as fighters, magic users, or thieves. But in the wacky Kingdom of Loathing, sorcerers are saucepan-wielding "Sorcerers" and spaghetti-tossing "pastamancers." Accordion Thieves, Disco Bandits, Turtle Tamers, and Seal Clubbers round out the character choices.

Characters venture through sites, such as the Misspelled Cemetary and the Orchish Frat House, where they might encounter a ferocious Sabre-toothed Lime, Stone Mariachis, the Fickle Finger of F8, or a Beer Batter.

Players can band together to share useful items, battle monsters, or fend off rival bands of online players. A community of Kingdom fans has its own chat sites, forums, and an online magazine. Chat participants swap strategies, attempt to solve tricky riddles, and barter for loot such as the meatloaf helmet.

Players get a limited number of turns per day—about an hour's worth of play time—and that seems to be just about enough to keep gamers coming back for more.

Built Like a Classic

Classic games, such as Zork and Colossal Cave, were written by a single programmer or small team and released as freeware or shareware on university networks and the ARPANet. Originally designed for mainframe computers without graphics capability, these games were text-based. Gamers read a description of a scene and then used a command-line interface to type their next move. User input like "go straight" or "pickup sword" was interpreted by a noun-verb parser—a sophisticated technology at the time. The games were simple yet challenging, and that was their appeal.

In the style of classic adventure games, the Kingdom of Loathing was created by a single programmer, Zack Johnson, and his "idea man," Josh Nite. A CNET article describes their efforts as "one of the brightest—and weirdest—lights of the independent game development world," then goes on to say that projects with shoestring budgets can still flourish, even though professional game development has become mired in multibillion-dollar budgets and strings of sequels.

Playing Kingdom of Loathing is free. Gamers can support the site by purchasing "An Adventurer is Me!" T-shirts, coffee cups, and mousepads.

QUICK CHECK ANSWERS

ORIENTATION

QuickCheck A
1. unit
2. Start
3. mouse
4. False
5. Backspace

QuickCheck B
1. Start
2. save
3. File
4. Glossary
5. Help

QuickCheck C
1. Internet
2. Web
3. browser
4. search

QuickCheck D
1. @
2. mailbox
3. Inbox
4. delete, erase, remove

QuickCheck E
1. False
2. security
3. Spyware
4. spam

CHAPTER 1

QuickCheck A
1. output
2. False
3. notebook
4. False
5. bits
6. compatible

QuickCheck B
1. backbone
2. IP
3. downloading
4. blog, Web log
5. voiceband
6. False
7. DSL
8. service
9. case
10. password

QuickCheck C
1. hypertext
2. URL
3. HTML
4. search
5. query, key words, search term.
6. operators
7. language

QuickCheck D
1. @
2. MIME
3. spam
4. forward
5. SMTP;
   POP

QuickCheck TechTalk
1. operating
2. POST, power-on self-test
3. Safe
4. True

CHAPTER 2

QuickCheck A
1. digital
2. binary
3. ASCII
4. character;
   binary
5. gigabyte
6. integrated
7. system

QuickCheck B
1. registers
2. control
3. instruction
4. clock
5. processor
6. volatile
7. virtual
8. CMOS

QuickCheck C
1. head
2. lands
3. access
4. random;
   sequential
5. density
6. crashes
7. True
8. double layer

QuickCheck D
1. pointing
2. refresh, vertical scan
3. resolution
4. duplex
5. slots
6. USB
7. device

QuickCheck TechTalk
1. Machine
2. op, operation
3. pointer
4. accumulator, register

CHAPTER 3

QuickCheck A
1. executable
2. source
3. high
4. interpreter
5. application

QuickCheck B
1. resources
2. RAM, memory
3. user
4. bootstrap
5. kernel
6. True
7. False

QuickCheck C
1. document
2. False
3. spreadsheet
4. Database
5. ripper
6. DVD

QuickCheck D
1. requirements
2. installation
3. setup
4. zipped, compressed, consolidated
5. uninstall, remove, delete.
6. open
7. public

QuickCheck TechTalk
1. True
2. Windows
3. HKEY
4. setup

CHAPTER 4

QuickCheck A
1. conventions
2. True
3. native
4. C
5. subdirectories
6. folders
7. size

QuickCheck B
1. Save
2. metaphor, model
3. Explorer
4. tracks;
   sectors
5. shredder

QuickCheck C
1. True
2. backdoor
3. spoofed
4. engineering
5. signature
6. polymorphic

QuickCheck D
1. Registry
2. folder
3. external
4. incremental
5. recovery

QuickCheck TechTalk
1. header
2. support
3. native
4. conversion, import, export

CHAPTER 5

QuickCheck A
1. resources
2. LANs, local area networks
3. hub, router, switch
4. packet;
   circuit

QuickCheck B
1. Ethernet
2. Wi-Fi
3. Bluetooth
4. PNA;
   PLC

QuickCheck C
1. service
2. Ping, Packet Internet Groper
3. TCP;
   IP
4. static, permanent
5. domain

QuickCheck D
1. downstream;
   upstream
2. Always-on
3. DSL, digital subscriber line
4. False
5. hotspots

QuickCheck TechTalk
1. False
2. firewall
3. virtual

CHAPTER 6

QuickCheck A
1. link
2. HTTP, browser
3. XHTML, extensible HTML
4. browser
5. player, plug-in, helper application
6. stateless
7. cookie

QuickCheck B
1. ASCII
2. authoring
3. head
4. style, cascading style
5. JPEG
6. Flash
7. mailto
8. hotspots
9. True
10. post

QuickCheck C
1. XML, Extensible Markup
   Language
2. scripts
3. Java
4. ActiveX
5. certificate

QuickCheck D
1. False
2. GIF
3. SSL
4. sniffer
5. wallets

QuickCheck TechTalk
1. plaintext, cleartext;
   ciphertext
2. Symmetric, Secret, Conventional
3. Asymmetric, Public
4. PGP, Pretty Good Privacy

CHAPTER 7

QuickCheck A
1. USB, USB-2, USB-1
2. resolution
3. dependent
4. grayscale
5. TIFF, Tag Image File Format
6. GIF, Graphics Interchange Format

QuickCheck B
1. True
2. drawing
3. wireframe
4. tracing
5. rasterization, rasterizing
6. Flash

QuickCheck C
1. desktop
2. capture
3. frame
4. False
5. False
6. Streaming
7. VOB, video object

QuickCheck D
1. MIDI, Musical Instrument Digital Interface; waveform
2. sampling
3. AAC
4. playlist
5. recognition

QuickCheck TechTalk
1. ratio
2. algorithm
3. lossless
4. lossy

CHAPTER 8

QuickCheck A
1. manual
2. Babbage
3. prototypes
4. vacuum; transistors
5. integrated; microprocessor

QuickCheck B
1. sectors
2. Silicon
3. offshoring
4. dot
5. retirement
6. vaporware
7. channels, outlets

QuickCheck C
1. False
2. security
3. telecommuting
4. ergonomic
5. information
6. certification

QuickCheck D
1. formats
2. database, job bank
3. portfolio
4. agent
5. metasearch
6. False

QuickCheck TechTalk
1. Moore's
2. molecular
3. DNA
4. qubits, quantum bits, atomic particles

CHAPTER 9

QuickCheck A
1. mission
2. tactical; strategic
3. structured
4. batch; online
5. MIS, management information system
6. decision, what-if
7. expert, knowledge-based

QuickCheck B
1. management
2. Development
3. joint
4. opportunities
5. waterfall
6. requirements, system requirements
7. CASE, computer-aided software engineering

QuickCheck C
1. solutions
2. distributed
3. application
4. RFP, request for proposal
5. specifications

QuickCheck D
1. implementation
2. customized
3. unit; integration
4. system
5. procedure
6. direct
7. acceptance
8. maintenance

QuickCheck TechTalk
1. DFD, Data Flow Diagram
2. data
3. UML
4. use
5. class

CHAPTER 10

QuickCheck A
1. format
2. record
3. occurrences
4. flat
5. hierarchical
6. relational

QuickCheck B
1. ASCII, American Standard Code
   for Information Interchange
2. False
3. independence
4. dynamic
5. False

QuickCheck C
1. key
2. types
3. True
4. sensitive
5. validation
6. redundancy
7. template

QuickCheck D
1. Keywords
2. True
3. Boolean
4. False
5. SELECT
6. UPDATE
7. False

QuickCheck TechTalk
1. OLAP, Online Analytical
   Processing
2. analysis, mining
3. cube
4. warehouse
5. True

CHAPTER 11

QuickCheck A
1. True
2. engineers
3. paradigms
4. third
5. visual
6. debugger

QuickCheck B
1. False
2. procedural
3. flowcharts
4. decision, selection, branch;
   sequence
5. True
6. loop

QuickCheck C
1. object-oriented
2. True
3. UML
4. inheritance
5. messages;
   method

QuickCheck D
1. problem;
   solution
2. decision
3. arguments;
   predicate
4. constant;
   variable
5. instantiation
6. rule, statement, program

QuickCheck TechTalk
1. compiler;
   machine
2. intermediate
3. components
4. API, application program interface

CHAPTER 12

QuickCheck A
1. False
2. out
3. integration
4. virtual
5. performance
6. intensive
7. FLOPS

QuickCheck B
1. False
2. RAID;
   area
3. OCR, optical character recognition
4. attached
5. parallel
6. middleware

QuickCheck C
1. terminals
2. distributed;
   tiered
3. grid
4. fault;
   failover
5. flash

QuickCheck D
1. False
2. throughput;
   metric, technique
3. downtime
4. risk
5. countermeasures
6. False

QuickCheck TechTalk
1. Hierarchical
2. migration, relocation
3. stub, placeholder
4. cost, expense

CREDITS

Cover ©PhotoDisc/Getty Images

Figure 1-2 Courtesy of Fujitsu Ltd. And Microsoft Corp.

Figure 1-3 Courtesy of Handspring

Figure 1-4 Courtesy of Sun Microsystems

Figure 1-5 Courtesy of Microsoft Corp.

Figure 1-6 Courtesy of IBM Corporation

Figure 1-7a Courtesy of Alienware

Figure 1-7b Courtesy of Apple Computer, Inc.

Figure 1-7c Courtesy of IBM Corporation

Figure 1-7d Courtesy of Sony Electronics, Inc.

Figure 1-7e Courtesy of Acer Inc. and Microsoft Corp.

Figure 1-7f Courtesy of Apple Computer, Inc. Apple IMAC 17"

Figure 1-10a Courtesy of Epson America, Inc.

Figure 1-10b Courtesy of Olympus

Figure 1-10c Courtesy of Epson America, Inc.

Figure 1-10d Courtesy of Wacom Tech Corp.

Figure 1-16 Courtesy of Linksys

Issue-1a ©Ron Chapple/Getty Images

Issue-1b ©Dennis MacDonald/Photoedit

CinC-1a Courtesy of the Department of Homeland Security

CinC-1b Courtesy of the Department of Homeland Security

Figure 2-11 Courtesy of Intel Corporation

Figure 2-23 Courtesy of IBM Research

Figure 2-24 Courtesy of Intel Corporation

Figure 2-34a Courtesy of Sony Electronics, Inc.

Figure 2-34b Courtesy of Kingston Technology

Figure 2-34c Courtesy of SanDisk Corp.

Figure 2-34d Courtesy of SanDisk Corp.

Figure 2-34e Courtesy of Kingston Technology

Figure 2-35a Courtesy of Logitech Inc.

Figure 2-35b Courtesy of Microsoft Corp.

Figure 2-35c Courtesy of Think Outside Inc. and Palm Inc.

Figure 2-35d Courtesy of Research in Motion

Figure 2-37a Courtesy of IBM Corporation

Figure 2-37b Courtesy of Kensington Technology Group

Figure 2-37c Courtesy of X-Gaming Inc.

Figure 2-38a Courtesy of Sony Electronics, Inc.

Figure 2-38b Couresy of Sony Electronics, Inc.

Figure 2-38c Courtesy of ViewSonic

Figure 2-41 Courtesy of ATI Technologies, Inc.

Figure 2-42 Courtesy of Epson America, Inc.

Issue-2a ©Gabe Palmer/CORBIS

Issue-2b Courtesy of Lexmark International

CinC-2a ©Computer History Museum

CinC-2b ©Courtesy of Business Wire and Lages & Assoc.

Figure 3-20a Courtesy of Handspring

Figure 3-20b Courtesy of Microsoft Corp.

Figure 3-21 Courtesy of Microsoft Corp.

Figure 3-22a Courtesy of Microsoft Corp.

Figure 3-22b Reprint with permission of Quark Inc., and its affiliates

Figure 3-22c Courtesy of Macromedia, Inc.

Figure 3-31a Courtesy of Wolfram Research

Figure 3-31b ©Julie Cooke, *www.lightdrawing.com*

Figure 3-41a Courtesy of Microsoft Corporation

Figure 3-41b Courtesy of Symantec Corp.

Figure 3-41c Courtesy of Adobe Systems Inc.

Issue-3a Courtesy of Software and Information Industry Association

CinC-3a ©Eli Reed/ MAGNUM Photos

CinC-3b ©Ashley GILBERTSON/AURORA

Figure 4-14a Courtesy of Dell, Inc.

Figure 4-14b Courtesy of Intel Corporation

Figure 4-14c Courtesy of Microsoft Corporation

Figure 4-14d ©AP/Wide World Photos

Figure 4-14e ©AP/Wide World Photos

Figure 4-31 Courtesy of Maxtor Corporation ©2003

Issue-4a ©Dennis O'Clair/ Getty Images

CinC-4a ©A. Ramey/PhotoEdit

CinC-4b ©PETER MACDIARMID/Reuters/Corbis

Figure 5-1 Courtesy of Bob Metcalfe

Figure 5-2 ©Steve Chenn/Corbis

Figure 5-10a Courtesy of Linksys

Figure 5-10b Courtesy of Linksys

Figure 5-16 Courtesy of Motorola, Inc.

Figure 5-22a Courtesy of D-Link Systems

Figure 5-22a Courtesy of D-Link Systems

Figure 5-23 Courtesy of Linksys

Figure 5-25a Courtesy of Nokia

Figure 5-25c Courtesy of NETGEAR, Inc

Figure 5-26 Courtesy of Dell

Figure 5-27 Courtesy of Microsoft Corp.

Figure 5-31 ©Computer History Museum

Figure 5-44 Courtesy of Zoom Telephonics, Inc.

Figure 5-53 ©Royalty-Free/CORBIS

Figure 5-54 Courtesy of Motorola Inc.

Figure 5-55 Courtesy of Hewlett Packard

Issue-5a Courtesy of Ken Paul and the Stone Creek Coffee Company

Issue-5b Courtesy of Rob Flickenger

CinC-5a University of Illinois @Urbana-Champaign Archives

CinC-5b ©John Henley/CORBIS

Figure 6-12 Courtesy of Fujitsu Siemens Computer

Figure 6-42 ©Nicholas DeVore/Getty Images

Figure 6-52 ©A. Ramey/Photo Edit

Issue-6a ©Swim Ink/CORBIS

Issue-6b ©Rudi Von Briel/Photo Edit

CinC-6a Courtesy of ArahWeave *www.arahne.si* and fabric courtesy of MTT Maribor

CinC-6b Courtesy of Scott Jordan of SCOTT EVEST

Figure 7-01 ©Archivo Iconografico, S.A./CORBIS

Figure 7-4b Courtesy of Sony Electronics, Inc.

Figure 7-4d Courtesy of Lexar Media, Inc.

Figure 7-4e Courtesy of IBM Corporation

Figure 7-19 Courtesy of Numonics Corporation

Figure 7-27 Courtesy of id Software

Figure 7-31b Courtesy of Sony Electronics

Figure 7-31c ©Ted Horowitz/CORBIS

Figure 7-31d ©PhotoDisc/Getty images

GLOSSARY

.NET framework A set of programming tools, developed by Microsoft, for building, deploying, and running software applications. 620

24-bit bitmap A True Color graphic, which requires 24 bits for each pixel, used for photographic-quality images that can include any of 16.7 million colors. 351

32-bit bitmap A True Color graphic, which requires 32 bits for each pixel, used for photographic-quality images that can include any of 16.7 million colors. 351

3-D graphics A type of digital graphics format that displays a three dimensional image on a two dimensional space. 362

3-D graphics software The software used to create three-dimensional wireframe objects, then render them into images. 145

AAC (Advanced Audio Compression) A file format that provides highly compressed audio files with very little loss of sound quality and is promoted by Apple on its iTunes Web site. 3378

Abacus A manual calculator that consists of beads mounted on sticks inside a frame with each bead representing a specific quantity. 402

Absolute reference In a worksheet formula, cell references (usually preceded by a $ symbol) that cannot change as a result of a move or copy operation. 140

Acceptance testing The final phase of testing for a new information system, in which the system's new owner determines whether the system performs as required. 492

Access time The estimated time for a storage device to locate data on a disk, usually measured in milliseconds. 81

Accounting software A category of software that includes accounting, money management, and tax preparation software. 151

Active-active cluster A computer cluster (see cluster) in which all nodes are active at the same time. 666

Active-passive cluster A computer cluster (see cluster) that contains at least one active node, and additional nodes, which become active only in case of failover. 667

ActiveX control A set of commands and components that can be used by programmers to add interactive features to Web pages. 315

Actors Object-oriented jargon for people who use an information system. 499

Ad hoc report Also called "demand report," a customized report generated according to supplied specific information not available in scheduled reports. 467

Ada A high-level programming language developed by the Department of Defense and originally intended for military applications. 575

Ad-blocking software A type of software that prevents ads from appearing on your computer screen. 320

Ad-serving cookie A cookie installed by a marketing firm to track user activities on Web sites containing their ads. 323

AES (Advanced Encryption Standard) An encryption standard that uses three separate key sizes and is based on the Rajndael encryption algorithm. 331

AGP Short for accelerated graphics port, an AGP is a type of interface, or slot, that provides a high-speed pathway for advanced graphics. 97

Algorithm An abstract or general procedure for solving a problem, typically expressed as pseudocode, structured English, or a flowchart. 584

Alpha test One of the first phases of software testing, usually conducted by the software publisher's in-house testing team. 420

ALU (arithmetic logic unit) The part of the CPU that performs arithmetic and logical operations on the numbers stored in its registers. 68

Always-on connection A permanent connection, as opposed to a connection that is established and dropped as needed. 19, 259

Analog device A device that operates on continuously varying data, such as a dimmer switch or a watch with a sweep second hand. 60

Analog video camera A device used to collect, store and process video in an analog format on a magnetic tape. 378

Analysis phase Tasks performed by the project team whose goal is to produce a list of requirements for a new or revised information system. 478

Analytical Engine A mechanical calculator designed by Charles Babbage that included memory and a programmable processor and is widely regarded as the most important ancestor to modern computer design. 404

Animated GIF A type of GIF image that displays a sequence of frames to create the appearance of continuous motion. 304

Antivirus software A computer program used to scan a computer's memory and disks to identify, isolate, and eliminate viruses. 196

API (Application Program(ing) Interface) A set of application programs or operating system functions that can be utilized by a program. 622

APL The acronym for A Programming Language, a high-level scientific programming language used to manipulate tables of numbers. 575

Apple I An unassembled computer kit released in 1977 by Apple Computer Corp. for computer hobbyists. 411

Apple II A complete microcomputer system developed by Apple Computer Corp. introduced in 1978 that helped broaden the personal computer market beyond hobbyists. 411

Apple Lisa A personal computer system developed and manufactured by Apple Computer Corp. that featured one of the first graphical user interfaces. 411

Apple Macintosh First released in 1984, it was one of the first commercially successful personal computers sold with graphical user interface software. 412

Application development tool Software, such as 4GLs, expert system shells, and component objects that can be assembled into the applications software for an information system. 484

Application linking A process that allows one or more software applications to exchange data. 640

Application software Computer programs that help you perform a specific task such as word processing. Also called application programs, applications, or programs. 12, 121

Application specifications A detailed description of the way that the software for an information system should interface with the user, store data, process data, and format reports. 487

Application testing The process of testing newly developed application software by running unit tests, integration tests, and system tests. 490

ARCnet (Attached Resource Computer network) One of the oldest, simplest, and least expensive LAN technologies. 238

Argument In the context of Prolog programming, an argument describes a predicate and is enclosed in parentheses in a Prolog fact. 609

ASCII (American Standard Code for Information Interchange) A code that represents characters as a series of 1s and 0s. Most computers use ASCII code to represent text, making it possible to transfer data between computers. 61

ASP (Active Server Page) An HTML document which includes scripts that are processed by a Microsoft Web server before sending a response back to the user. 307

Assembly language A low-level computer programming language that uses simple commands and is translated into machine language by an assembler. 573

Assumption In the context of programming, a condition that you accept to be true, which often places limits on the scope of the programming problem. 576

Asynchronous protocol A data transmission method in which the sender and receiver are not synchronized by a clock signal and must use start and stop bits to control the beginning and ending of transmissions. 236

Atanasoff-Berry Computer (ABC) An early electronic computer prototype that incorporated the use of vacuum tubes for data processing instead of mechanical switches. 405

Attribute In a database, the columns in a table that are equivalent to fields. In object-oriented databases it is a data element that is stored as part of an object. 520

Audio editing software A program that enables users to create and edit digital voice and music recordings. 147

Audio encoding software A computer program designed to convert sound files into a digital sound format, such as MP3 or AAC. 147

AIFF (.aif) Audio Interchange File Format developed by Apple that is a popular cross-platform for storing digital music 378

Automated system recovery A set of recovery disks that users are able to create using the Windows XP Backup utility. 207

Automatic recalculation A feature found in spreadsheet software that automatically recalculates every formula after a user makes a change to any cell. 140

AVI (Audio Video Interleave) A video file format, developed by Microsoft, that is the most common format for desktop video on the PC. 371

B2B (Business-To-Business) An e-commerce exchange of products, services, or information between businesses. 319

B2C (Business-To-Consumer) An e-commerce exchange of products, services, or information between businesses and consumers. 319

B2G (Business-To-Government) An e-commerce exchange of products, services, or information between businesses and governments. 319

Backdoor In the context of computer security, a backdoor is a method of bypassing normal procedures to gain access to a computer system. Some backdoors, such as a hidden password, are inadvertently or intentionally left open, whereas others are opened by viruses and worms. 193

Backtracking In the context of Prolog programming, backtracking is the process of evaluating all combinations of facts and rules. 613

Backup A backup is a duplicate copy of a file, disk, or tape. Also refers to a Windows utility that allows you to create and restore backups. 199

Backup software A set of utility programs that performs a variety of backup related tasks, such as helping users select files for backup. 204

Bandwidth The data transmission capacity of a communications channel. Digital signals are measured in bits per second, analog signals in Hertz. 234

Banner ad A type of advertisement typically embedded at the top of a Web page. 320

BASIC (Beginners All-purpose Symbolic Instruction Code) A simple high-level programming language that was popularized by Microsoft in the 1970s. 575

Batch processing A processing system that involves holding a group of transactions for processing until the end of a specified period of time. 466

Baud rate The number of times per second that a signal in a communications channel varies. 257

Beep code A series of audible beeps used to announce diagnostic test results during the boot process. 45

Benchmarks A set of tests used to measure computer hardware or software performance. 71

Beowulf cluster Several off-the-shelf computers that are interconnected and configured as a cluster to perform high-performance computing tasks. 667

Beta test A testing phase near the end of the software development process in which a software product is tested in real-world computer environments, often by end-users. 420

Binary digits Series of 1s and 0s representing data. 60

Binary number system A method for representing numbers using only two digits, 0 and 1. Contrast to the decimal number system, which uses ten digits: 0, 1, 2, 3, 4, 5, 6, 7, 8, and 9. 60

Biological computing The use of DNA molecules to perform computing tasks. 447

Bit The smallest unit of information handled by a computer. A bit is one of two values, either a 0 or a 1. Eight bits comprise a byte, which can represent a letter or number. 11

Bitmap graphic An image, such as a digital photo, that is stored as a grid work of colored dots. 344

Blade server A modular circuit board in a pizza-box sized housing that contains one or more processors and may include storage. Often mounted in a rack with other similar devices and used as servers. 645

Blended threat A combination of more than one type of malicious program. 193

BLOB (Binary Large OBject) A collection of binary data that is stored in a single field of a database. 535

Blog (WeB LOG) A publicly-accessible personal journal posted on the Web. Blogs often reflect the personality of the author and are typically updated daily. 17

Bluetooth A wireless technology used in conjunction with standard Ethernet networks that allows data transfer rates between 200 and 700 Kbps up to a maximum range of 35 feet. 243

BMP The native bitmap graphic file format of the Microsoft Windows OS. 353

Body section A part of a Web page that begins with the <BODY> tag and contains the text, graphics, and links. 301

Boolean operators A set of search operators such as AND, OR, and NOT that help form complex queries. 549

Boot disk A floppy disk or CD that contains the files needed for the boot process. 206

Boot process The sequence of events that occurs within a computer system between the time the user starts the computer and the time it is ready to process commands. 44

Boot sector virus A computer virus that infects the sectors on a disk that contain the data a computer uses during the boot process. The virus spreads every time the infected disk is in the computer when it boots. 192

Bootstrap program A program stored in ROM that loads and initializes the operating system on a computer. 125

BPR (Business Process Redesign) A technique for improving a business by making radical changes to existing business procedures or organizational structure. 476

Bridge A device that connects two similar networks by simply transferring data without regard to the network format. 231

Broadband A term used to refer to communications channels that have high bandwidth. 234

Broken link A non-functioning Web link. 306

Browser A program that communicates with a Web server and displays Web pages. 28

Brute force method A method of breaking encryption code by trying all possible encryption keys, usually employing supercomputers. 329

Bus topology A network arranged on a common backbone that connects all the network devices. If the backbone fails the network becomes unusable. 230

Business An organization that seeks profit by providing goods and services. 462

Byte An 8-bit unit of information that represents a single character. 11

Bytecode A compiled Java applet that is executed by Java Virtual Machine. 313, 620

C A compiled procedural language that provides both high-level commands and low-level access to hardware. 575

C# A derivative of C++ programming language developed by Microsoft. 575

C++ An object-oriented version of the C programming language. 575

C2C (Consumer-To-Consumer) An e-commerce exchange of products, services, or information between consumers. 319

Cable modem A communications device that can be used to connect a computer to the Internet via the cable TV infrastructure 19, 259

Cache Special high-speed memory that gives the CPU rapid access to data that would otherwise be accessed from disk. Also called RAM cache or cache memory. 70

CAD software (Computer-Aided Design software) A program designed to draw 3-D graphics for architecture and engineering tasks. 146

Capacitors Electronic circuit components that store an electrical charge; in RAM, a charged capacitor represents an "on" bit, and a discharged one represents an "off" bit. 73

Card reader A device that can be used to read and record data on a solid stage storage device. 80

Cardinality A description of the numeric relationship (one-to-one, one-to-many, or many-to-many) that exists between two record types. 517

Cascading style sheet (CSS) A template that can be set to control the layout and design of Web pages. 302

Case sensitive A condition in which uppercase letters are not equivalent to their lowercase counterparts. 22

Case sensitive database A database in which uppercase letters are not equivalent to their lowercase counterparts. 536

CASE tool (Computer-Aided Software Engineering) Software that is used to summarize system requirements, diagram current and proposed information systems, schedule development tasks, prepare documentation, and develop computer programs. 479

CD (Compact disc) An optical storage medium used to store digital information. CD-ROMs are read only. CD-R and CD-RWs can be used to record data. 86

CD drive An optical drive that can work with one or more CD formats, such as CD-ROM, CD-R, or CD-RW. 10

CD ripper software Software that converts the music on an audio CD to a WAV file. 147

CD-R An acronym for compact disc-recordable. CD-R is a type of optical disk technology that allows the user to create CD-ROMs and audio CDs. 87

CD-RW An acronym for compact disc-rewritable. CD-RW is a type of optical disk technology that allows the user to write data onto a CD, then change that data much like on a floppy or hard disk. 87

Cell In spreadsheet terminology, the intersection of a column and a row. In cellular communications, a limited geographical area surrounding a cellular phone tower. 138

Cell references The column letter and row number that designate the location of a worksheet cell. For example, the cell reference C5 refers to a cell in column C, row 5. 139

Central Processing Unit (CPU) The main processing unit in a computer, consisting of circuitry that executes instructions to process data. 4

Centralized computing system A hierarchical arrangement of computers in which a central computer (usually a mainframe host) processes data for a collection of terminals. 657

Centralized processing An information system design in which data is processed on a centrally located computer, usually a mainframe. 493

Certificate authority A company that issues digital certificates and verifies the correct identity of the recipient. 316

Certificate of completion A certification offered to students who successfully complete one or more courses on a specific topic. 434

Certification exam An objective test that verifies your level of knowledge about a particular technology or subject. 434

CGI (Common Gateway Interface) An interface that allows a user to access a Web-based database from a Web browser. 307

Change requests A formal, written request to add, delete, or change the features of an information system. 488

Channel conflict Refers to sales from one channel being pirated by other vendors from within the same channel. 424

Character data Letters, symbols, or numerals that will not be used in arithmetic operations (name, social security number, etc.). 61

Chat group A discussion in which a group of people communicates online simultaneously. 17

Checksum A value, calculated by combining all the bytes in a file, that is used by virus detection programs to identify whether any bytes have been altered. 196

Chief information officer (CIO) The highest-ranking executive responsible for information systems. 427

Child node In a hierarchical database, a record type connected to a record type higher up in the hierarchy. 519

Chipmakers Companies that design and manufacture computer chips used in a wide variety of computer related applications. 414

Ciphertext An encrypted message. 328

Circuit switching The method used by the telephone network to temporarily connect one telephone with another for the duration of a call. 235

CISC A general-purpose microprocessor chip designed to handle a wider array of instructions than a RISC chip. CISC stands for complex instruction set computer. 70

Class In object-oriented terminology, a group with specific characteristics to which an object belongs. 597

Class attribute In the context of object-oriented programming, a class attribute defines a characteristic for the members of a class. Similar to a field in a database. 598

Class diagram A diagram that provides the name of each object, a list of the object's attributes, a list of methods, and an indication of the cardinality between objects. 500

Class hierarchy Like a hierarchical diagram, a class hierarchy is a set of related superclasses and subclasses defined within the object-oriented paradigm. 599

Clear GIF A small graphic on a Web page that installs cookies designed to track your online activities. Also known as a Web bug. 323

Click-through rate The number of times Web site visitors click an ad to connect to an advertiser's site. 320

Client A computer or software that requests information from another computer or server. 9

Client/server network A network where processing is split between workstations (clients) and the server. 229

Client-side script Scripting statements embedded in an HTML document that are executed by a client's browser. 312

Clip art Graphics designed to be inserted into documents, Web pages, and worksheets; available in CD-ROM or Web-based collections. 137

CLR (Common Language Runtime) A client-side utility that converts MSIL into platform specific machine language at run time. 621

Cluster 1) A group of sectors on a storage medium that, when accessed as a group, speeds up data access. 2) A group of two or more devices connected together to share processing, storage, input, or output tasks. 187, 665

Cluster failover The process of transferring the workload from a malfunctioning computer to a working computer within a computer cluster. 666

Cluster node A connection point within a computer cluster—used to refer to a computer in a cluster. 665

CMOS memory A type of battery-powered integrated circuit that holds semi-permanent configuration data (acronym for complementary metal oxide semiconductor). 75

Coaxial cable A type of cable constructed of a center wire surrounded by a grounded shield of braided wire. Used for cable TV and to connect nodes on a network (also called coax cable). 232

COBOL (COmmon Business-Oriented Language) A high-level programming language used for transaction processing on mainframe computers. 575

Code In the context of computer programming, code can be used as a noun to refer to the set of instructions that form a program, or as a verb that refers to the process of writing a program. 570

Codec Derived from the terms COmpressor and DECompressor. A hardware or software routine that compresses and decompresses digital graphics, sound, and video files. 372

Color depth The number of bits that determines the range of possible colors that can be assigned to each pixel. For example, an 8-bit color depth can create 256 colors. 93, 350

Color palette The selection of colors used in graphics software. 351

COLOSSUS An early electronic computer prototype that used binary data representation and was used during WWII to decode messages encrypted by ENIGMA. 406

Command-line interface A style of user interface which requires users to type commands, rather than use a mouse to manipulate graphics. 124

Commercial software Copyrighted computer applications sold to consumers for profit. 158

Commit The act of permanently updating database records only if every step of the transaction can be successfully processed. 466

Common virtual system An advanced form of enterprise application integration in which all computer components are linked and appear to be one unified system. 640

Communications channel Any pathway between the sender and receiver; channel may refer to a physical medium or a frequency. 231

Communications protocol A set of rules that ensures the orderly and accurate transmission and reception of data. 235

Communications satellites Satellites used to send and receive data to and from ground stations. 233

Compact Privacy Policy A header that defines a standard set of security tags that become part of the HTTP header for cookies. 296

CompactFlash (CF) A solid state storage card designed for digital cameras with a built in controller about the size of a matchbook that provides high storage capacity and access speed. 89

Compiler Software that translates a program written in a high-level language into low-level instructions before the program is executed. 119, 620

Component Prewritten objects or modules that programmers can customize and add to their own programs. 622

Compression algorithm The steps that are required to shrink data in a file and reconstitute it to its original state. 384

Compression ratio A measurement of the amount of shrinkage that occurs when data is compressed. 384

Computed field A calculation that a DBMS performs during processing and then temporarily stores in a memory location. 535

Compute-intensive Refers to any task, problem, or product that is able to handle massive amounts of data and complex mathematical calculations. 642

Computer A device that accepts input, processes data, stores data, and produces output. 4

Computer engineer A computer professional who focuses on the design and development of computer hardware and peripheral devices. 428

Computer engineering A career that focuses on the design and development of computer hardware and peripheral devices. 432

Computer industry The corporations and individuals that supply goods and services to people and organizations that use computers. 413

Computer network A collection of computers and related devices, connected in a way that allows them to share data, hardware, and software. 8

Computer operator A computer professional who works directly with and maintains mainframe computers. 428

Computer professional Any person whose primary occupation involves one or more aspects of computer technology. 426

Computer program A detailed set of instructions that tells a computer how to solve a problem or carry out a task. 4

Computer programmer A person who designs, codes, and tests computer programs. 118, 427

Computer programming The process of designing, coding, and testing computer programs. 571

Computer retail store A store that typically sells several brands of computers from a store-front location, such as a mall or shopping center. 422

Computer salesperson A computer professional who sells computers and computer-related products. Also called a sales rep. 428

Computer science A career field that focuses on developing fast and efficient computers, from their construction, to their programming and operating systems. 432

Computer virus A program designed to attach itself to a file, reproduce, and spread from one file to another, destroying data, displaying an irritating message, or otherwise disrupting computer operations. 191

Computer-aided music software Software used to generate unique musical compositions with a simplified set of tools, such as tempo, key, and style. 147

Concurrent-user license Legal permission for an organization to use a certain number of copies of a software program at the same time. 157

Constant In the context of programming, a constant represents an unchanging value. In contrast the data held in a variable can change. 611

Context diagram A simple overview of an information system. 497

Contract worker Computer professionals who do not work directly for one company and often are paid by the job instead of a salary. 430

Control In the context of graphical user interfaces, a control is a screen-based object whose behavior can be specified by a programmer. 579

Control structures Instructions that specify the sequence in which a program is to be executed: sequence, selection, and repetition controls. 590

Control unit The part of the ALU that directs and coordinates processing. 68

Controller A circuit board in a hard drive that positions the disk and read-write heads to locate data. 83

Conversion routine A program that converts data from its current format into a format that can be automatically incorporated into the new database. 544

Cookie A message sent from a Web server to a browser and stored on a user's hard disk, usually containing information about the user. 295

Copyright A form of legal protection that grants certain exclusive rights to the author of a program or the owner of the copyright. 157

Copyright notice A line such as "Copyright 2002 by ACME CO" that identifies a copyright holder. 157

CPL (Combined Programming Language) A programming language developed in the 1960s for scientific and commercial applications. 575

CRM (Customer Relationship Management) A technique for increasing profitability by improving the relationship between a company and its customers. 476

Cropping The process of selecting and removing part of an image. 349

CRT (cathode ray tube) A display technology that uses a large vacuum tube, similar to that used in television sets. 92

Cryptographic algorithm A specific procedure for encrypting and decrypting data. 328

Cryptographic key A specific word, number, or phrase that must be used to encrypt or decrypt data. 328

CSMA/CD (Carrier Sense Multiple Access with Collision Detection) A method of responding to an attempt by two devices to use a data channel simultaneously. Used by Ethernet networks. 240

Cyclic redundancy check An error-checking protocol used by networks to ensure accurate delivery of data. 237

Data In the context of computing and data management, data refers to the symbols that a computer uses to represent facts and ideas. 4

Data analysis The process of interpreting existing information to discover trends and patterns. 554

Data bus An electronic pathway or circuit that connects the electronic components (such as the processor and RAM) on a computer's motherboard. 97

Data center A specialized facility designed to house and protect computer systems and data. 674

Data compression The process of condensing data so that it requires fewer bytes of storage space. 384

Data cube A three-dimensional model of OLAP data. 555

Data dependence The undesirable situation in which data and program modules become so interrelated that modifications become difficult. 524

Data dictionary A tool used by systems analysts to document detailed descriptions of the data that flows through an information system and the data that is stored by that system. 498

Data file A file containing words, numbers, and/or pictures that the user can view, edit, save, send, and/or print. 11

Data flow On a DFD, a line with an arrow on the end, which indicates the direction in which data flows. 496

Data flow diagram (DFD) A diagram that illustrates how data moves through an information system. 496

Data independence The separation of data from the programs that manipulate the data. 524

Data mining Analyzing data to discover patterns and relationships that are important to decision making. 555

Data redundancy Repetition of data within a database. 537

Data representation The use of electronic signals, marks, or binary digits to represent character, numeric, visual, or audio data. 60

Data store A filing cabinet, disk, or tape that holds data. On a DFD, usually represented by an open-ended rectangle. 496

Data transfer rate The amount of data that a storage device can move from a storage medium to computer memory in one second. 81

Data type Used to specify the type of data that can be entered into a field in a data file; data types include character, numeric, date, logical, and memo. 534

Data warehouse A collection of information organized for analysis. 556

Data warehousing The process of collecting historic data so that it can be analyzed to reveal and predict trends. 640

Database A collection of information that might be stored in more than one file or in more than one record type. 142, 514

Database administrator A person who supervises database design, development, testing, and maintenance. 427

Database client software Software that allows any remote computer or network workstation to access data in a database. 526

Database index An index in a database that contains a list of keys, each providing a pointer to the record that contains the rest of the fields related to that key. 539

Database linking In the context of enterprise computing, a process that allows databases to share or replicate information. 640

Database server software Software that is designed to manage a large number of records and perform many simultaneous transactions. 526

Database software The software designed for entering, finding, organizing, updating, and reporting information stored in a database. 142

Database structure The arrangement of the fields, tables, and relationships in a database. 533

Date data type A numeric data type used for fields that contain dates in a format that allows them to be manipulated. 534

DBMS (DataBase Management System) Application software that assists the user in manipulating, storing, and maintaining database files. 525

Debugger A programming utility that helps programmers test and correct a computer program. 581

DEC PDP-8 A computer built by Digital Equipment Corp. and introduced in 1965, it was the first commercially successful minicomputer. 409

Decision model A numerical representation of a realistic situation, such as a cash flow model of a business. 468

Decision query A question or set of instructions that describes the data that needs to be gathered to make a decision. 468

Decision support system (DSS) A computer system that allows decision makers to manipulate data directly, to incorporate data from external sources, and to create data models or "what-if" scenarios. 468

Decision support worksheet A tool used by a project team to evaluate the criteria for each solution by assigning a score and a weight to each criteria which are then compared in a table. 485

Decision table A tabular method for listing rules and specifying the outcomes for various combinations of rules. 609

Declarative paradigm An approach to the programming process in which a programmer writes a program by specifying a set of statements and rules that define the conditions for solving a problem. 608

deColmar's Arithmometer The first commercially successful, mass-produced mechanical calculator. 403

Decryption The process of converting ciphertext into plaintext. 328

Defragmentation utility A software tool used to rearrange the files on a disk so that they are stored in contiguous clusters. 189

DELETE An SQL keyword that removes a record from a table. 547

Demodulation The process of changing a received signal back to its original state (for example, when a modem changes an audio signal back to a digital pulse). 256

Denial of Service attacks An attack designed to overwhelm a network's processing capabilities, shutting it down. 193

DES (Data Encryption Standard) An encryption method based on an algorithm developed by IBM and the National Security Agency that uses 56-bit symmetric key encryption. 330

Design phase The process a project team uses for figuring out how to implement a new system. This phase is undertaken after the analysis phase is complete. 482

Desktop computers Computers small enough to fit on a desk and built around a single microprocessor chip. 6

Desktop operating system An operating system specifically designed for use on personal computers, such as Windows Me or Mac OSX. 126

Desktop publishing software The software used to create high-quality output suitable for commercial printing. DTP software provides precise control over layout. 133

Desktop video Videos stored in digital format on a PC's hard disk or CD. 365

Detail reports Organized lists generated by a management information system (for example, an inventory list). 466

Device driver The software that provides the computer with the means to control a peripheral device. 98

DHTML (dynamic HTML) A variation of the HTML format that allows elements of Web pages to be changed while they are being viewed. 310

Dial-up connection A connection that uses a phone line to establish a temporary Internet connection. 18

Dictionary-based compression A data compression scheme that uses a code word to represent common sequences of characters. 385

Difference Engine A mechanical calculator design created by Charles Babbage that was to use steam power for fully automatic operation. It was never built. 404

Differential backup A copy of all the files that changed since the last full backup of a disk. 205

Digital Any system that works with discrete data, such as 0s and 1s, in contrast to analog. 11

Digital camera A camera that takes and stores a digital image instead of recording onto film. 345

Digital certificate A security method that identifies the author of an ActiveX control. A computer programmer can "sign" a digital certificate after being approved. 316

Digital device A device that works with discrete (distinct or separate) numbers or digits. 60

Digital signal processor Circuitry that is used to process, record, and playback audio files. 378

Digital video A series of still frames stored sequentially in digital format by assigning values to each pixel in a frame. 365

Digital video camera A device used to collect, store and process video in a digital format. 367

Digitize To convert non-digital information or media to a digital format through the use of a scanner, sampler, or other input device. 62

Digitizing tablet A device that provides a flat surface for a paper-based drawing, and a "pen" used to create hand-drawn vector drawings. 358

DIMMs (dual in-line memory modules) A DIMM is a small circuit board that holds RAM chips. A DIMM has a 64-bit path to the memory chips. 65

DIPs (dual in-line package) A chip configuration characterized by a rectangular body with numerous plugs along its edge. 65

Direct conversion The simultaneous deactivation of an old computer system and activation of a new one. 492

Direct satellite service (DSS) A service that uses a geosynchronous or low-earth orbit satellite to send television, voice, or computer data directly to satellite dishes owned by individuals. 263

Directory A list of files contained on a computer storage device. 178

Disaster recovery plan A step-by-step plan that describes the methods used to secure equipment and data against disasters, and how to recover from disasters. 675

Disk density The closeness of the particles on a disk surface. As density increases, the particles are packed more tightly together and are usually smaller. 82

Distributed computer system A collection of connected computers in which processing, data, and application software are dispersed among more than one physical computer. 659

Distributed database A database that is stored on different computers, on different networks, or in different locations. 526

Distributed processing An information system design in which data is processed on multiple workstations or servers. 483

Distribution media One or more floppy disks or CDs that contain programs and data, which can be installed to a hard disk drive. 152

Dithering A means of reducing the size of a graphics file by reducing the number of colors. Dithering uses patterns composed of two or more colors to produce the illusion of additional colors and shading. 352

DMA (direct memory access) DMA refers to specialized circuitry that transfers data between drives and RAM, bypassing the CPU. 84

DOCSIS (Data Over Cable Services Interface Specification) A security technology used for filtering packets to certain ports. 260

Document production software Computer programs that assist the user in composing, editing, designing, and printing documents. 133

Domain name Short for "fully qualified domain name;" an identifying name by which host computers on the Internet are familiarly known (for example, "cocacola.com"). 251

Domain name servers Computers that host the domain name system database. 252

Domain name system A large database of unique IP addresses that correspond with domain names. 252

DOS (Disk Operating System) The operating system software shipped with the first IBM PCs, then used on millions of computers until the introduction of Microsoft Windows. 130

Dot matrix printer A printer that creates characters and graphics by striking an inked ribbon with small wires called "pins," generating a fine pattern of dots. 94

Dot pitch The diagonal distance between colored dots on a display screen. Measured in millimeters, dot pitch helps to determine the quality of an image displayed on a monitor. 92

Double layer DVD A DVD that essentially stacks data in two different layers on the disk surface to store 8.5 GB, twice the capacity of a standard DVD. 86

Downloading The process of transferring a copy of a file from a remote computer to local computer's disk drive. 16

Downstream In direct satellite service terminology, the direction in which DirecPC satellites transmit, from the satellite to the user. 258

Drawing software Programs that are used to create images with lines, shapes, and colors, such as logos or diagrams. 145, 358

Drive bays Areas within a computer system unit that can accommodate additional storage devices. 80

Drive mapping A process of assigning a drive letter to a storage device located on a different network workstation. 245

DSL (Digital Subscriber Line) A high-speed Internet connection that uses existing telephone lines, requiring close proximity to a switching station. 20, 260

DSL modem A device that sends and receives digital data to and from computers over telephone lines. 262

DSLAM (DSL Access Multiplexer) Special equipment used to interpret, separate, and route digital data in telephone lines for DSL providers. 261

DSS (Digital Satellite System) A type of Internet connection that uses a network of satellites to transmit data. 20

DTD files (Document Type Definition files) A type of file that defines how markup tags are interpreted by a browser. 311

Duty cycle A measurement of how many pages a printer is able to produce per day or month. 95

DVD (Digital Video Disc) An optical storage medium similar in appearance and technology to a CD-ROM but with higher storage capacity. The acronym stands for "digital video disc" or "digital versatile disc." 86

DVD drive An optical storage device that reads data from CD-ROM and DVD disks. 10

DVD+RW A DVD technology that allows users to record and change data on DVD disks. 87

DVD-ROM A DVD disk that contains data that has been permanently stamped on the disk surface. 87

DVD video Often refers to commercial videos stored on commercial DVDs. 365

DVD-Video A DVD format used for commercial movies shipped on DVDs. 87

Dye sublimation printer An expensive, color precise printer that heats ribbons containing color to produce consistent, photograph-quality images. 95

Dynamic IP address A temporarily assigned IP address usually provided by an ISP. 250

Dynamic Web publishing A way of displaying data from a database as customized Web pages, which are generated as the page is sent to the browser. 528

EAI (Enterprise Application Integration) The use of networked software and databases for providing unrestricted sharing of data in an organization. 476

Ear training software Software used by musicians to develop tuning skills, recognize keys, and develop musical skills. 147

EBCDIC (Extended Binary-Coded Decimal Interchange Code) A method by which digital computers, usually mainframes, represent character data. 61

E-commerce Short for electronic commerce, it is the business of buying and selling products online. 17, 319

EDI (Electronic Data Interchange) The ability to transfer data between different companies using networks which enable companies to buy, sell, and trade information. 476

Educational software Software used to develop and practice skills. 149

Eiffel An object-oriented programming language with syntax similar to C. 575

Electronic wallet Software that stores and processes customer information needed for an e-commerce transaction. 326

E-mail Messages that are transmitted between computers over a communications network. Short for electronic mail. 17

E-mail account A service that provides users with an e-mail address and a mailbox. 36

E-mail attachment A separate file that is transmitted along with an e-mail message. 37

E-mail client software Software that is installed on a client computer and has access to e-mail servers on a network. This software is used to compose, send, and read e-mail messages. 41

E-mail message A computer file containing a letter or memo that is transmitted electronically via a communications network. 36

E-mail servers A computer that uses special software to store and send e-mail messages over the Internet. 40

E-mail system The collection of computers and software that works together to provide e-mail services. 40

Encapsulation An object-oriented technique in which the internal details of an object are "hidden" in order to simplify their use and reuse. 607

Encryption The process of scrambling or hiding information so that it cannot be understood without the key necessary to change it back into its original form. 328

ENIAC (Electronic Numerical Integrator and Computer) An early electronic computer prototype that was designed for the U.S. Army for calculating trajectories and was completed in 1945. 406

Enterprise application integration (EAI) The process of configuring software applications so that they can exchange data. 639

Enterprise computing The use of one or more information systems that share data and typically provide information to hundreds or thousands of users who may be located in diverse locations. 636

Enterprise hardware integration The process of using specialized hardware and software to connect diverse types of hardware enabling them to exchange data. 639

Enterprise system integration The process of connecting two or more information systems in a way that allows scalability and data sharing. 638

Entity-relationship diagram (ERD) A diagram that graphically depicts relationships between record types. 518

Equipment manufacturers The companies that design and manufacture computer hardware and communication products. 414

Ergonomics The science of designing safe, comfortable, efficient machines and tools for human use. 431

ERP (Enterprise Resource Planning) A system of business management that integrates all resources of a business, including planning, manufacturing, sales, and marketing. 476

Ethernet A type of network in which network nodes are connected by coaxial cable or twisted-pair wire; the most popular network architecture, it typically transmits data at 10 or 100 megabits per second. 239

Ethernet card A type of network interface card designed to support Ethernet protocols. 240

Event In the context of programming, an action or change in state, such as a mouse click, that requires a response from the computer. 580

Event-driven paradigm An approach to programming in which a programmer creates programs that continually check for, and respond to, program events, such as mouse clicks. 581

Event-handling code The program segment that instructs the computer how to react to events, such as mouse clicks. 580

Exception report A report generated by a management information system, listing information that is outside normal or acceptable ranges, such as a reorder report showing low-stock inventory items. 467

Executable file A file, usually with an .exe extension, containing instructions that tell a computer how to perform a specific task. 11

Executive information system (EIS) A special type of a decision support system that is designed to provide senior managers with information relevant to strategic management activities. 468

Expansion bus The segment of the data bus that transports data between RAM and peripheral devices. 97

Expansion card A circuit board that is plugged into a slot on a PC motherboard to add extra functions, devices, or ports. 97

Expansion port A socket into which the user plugs a cable from a peripheral device, allowing data to pass between the computer and the peripheral device. 98

Expansion slot A socket or "slot" on a PC motherboard designed to hold a circuit board called an expansion card. 97

Expert system A computer system incorporating knowledge from human experts, and designed to analyze data and produce a recommendation or decision (also called knowledge-based system). 470

Expert system shell A software tool used for developing expert system applications. 471

Extended ASCII Similar to ASCII but with 8-bit character representation instead of 7-bit, allowing for an additional 128 characters. 61

External entity A person, organization, or device that exists outside an information system, but provides it with input or receives output. On a DFD, usually represented by a square. 496

External information Information obtained by organizations from outside sources. 465

External link A hyperlink that links to a location outside the Web site. 305

External style sheet A template that contains formatting specifications for a group of Web pages. 302

Extranet A network similar to a private internet that also allows outside users access as well. 249

Fact In the context of Prolog programming, a fact is a statement incorporated into a program that provides basic information for solving a problem. 608

FAT32 A file system used by Microsoft Windows 95, 98, and Me operating systems to keep track of the name and location of files on a hard disk. 187

Fault tolerance Refers to a computer system's ability to react gracefully to unexpected software or hardware failures. 666

FDDI (Fiber Distributed Data Interconnect) A high-speed network that uses fiber-optic cables to link workstations. 239

Feature creep An undesirable occurrence during information system development when users, customers, or designers attempt to add features after final specifications have been approved. 488

Fiber-optic cable A bundle of thin tubes of glass used to transmit data as pulses of light. 232

Field The smallest meaningful unit of information contained in a data file. 142, 514

Field format A specification for the way that data is displayed on the screen and printouts, usually using a series of Xs to indicate characters and 9s to indicate numbers. 536

Field name A name that identifies the contents of a field. 514

Field validation rule A specification that a database designer sets up to filter the data entered into a particular field. 536

Fifth-generation languages Either declarative languages, such as Prolog, or programming languages that allow programmers to use graphical or visual tools to construct programs. 574

File A named collection of data (such as a computer program, document, or graphic) that exists on a storage medium, such as a hard disk, floppy disk, or CD-ROM. 11

File allocation table (FAT) A special file that is used by some operating systems to store the physical location of all the files on a storage medium, such as a hard disk or floppy disk. 187

File compression utility A type of data compression software that shrinks one or more files into a single file that occupies less storage space than the files did separately. 388

File date The date that a file was created or last modified. 179

File extension A set of letters and/or numbers added to the end of a filename that helps to identify the file contents or file type. 11

File format The method of organization used to encode and store data in a computer. Text formats include DOC and TXT. Graphics formats include BMP, TIFF, GIF, and PCX. 177

File header Hidden information inserted at the beginning of a file to identify its properties, such as the software that can open it. 63

File management utilities Software, such as Windows Explorer, that helps users locate, rename, move, copy, and delete files. 182

File name A series of letters and characters used to identify a file stored on a computer. 11

File-naming conventions A set of rules, established by the operating system, that must be followed to create a valid filename. 176

File shredder software Software designed to overwrite sectors of a disk with a random series of 1s and 0s to ensure deletion of data. 188

File size The physical size of a file on a storage medium, usually measured in kilobytes (KB). 179

File specification A combination of the drive letter, subdirectory, filename, and extension that identifies a file (for example, A:\word\filename.doc). Also called a "path." 178

File system A system that is used by an operating system to keep files organized. 187

File virus A computer virus that infects executable files, such as programs with .exe filename extensions. 192

First-generation computers A reference to a group of early computers that used vacuum tubes to process and store data such as UNIVAC. 407

First-generation languages Machine languages that were available for programming the earliest computers. 573

Fixed-length field A field in a data file that has a predetermined number of characters. 514

Flash A file format developed by Macromedia that has become popular for animations on Web pages. 361

Flash animation A popular proprietary animation format developed by Macromedia and frequently used on the Web. 304

Flat file A single file that is the electronic version of a box of index cards, in which all records use the same record format. 517

Floppy disk A removable magnetic storage medium, typically 3.5" in size, with a capacity of 1.44 MB. 81

Floppy disk adapter A device that contains a slot for a flash memory module that, when inserted into a floppy disk drive, enables users to transfer data to their PCs. 347

Floppy disk drive A storage device that writes data on, and reads data from, floppy disks. 10

FLOPS (Floating-Point Operations Per Second) A measurement used to describe the speed at which a computer system can process calculations involving floating-point numbers—often used in the context of HPC systems. 642

Flowchart In software engineering, a graphical representation of the way a computer should progress from one instruction to the next when it performs a task. 587

Folders The subdirectories, or subdivisions of a directory, that can contain files or other folders. 178

Font A typeface or style of lettering, such as Arial, Times New Roman, and Gothic. 135

Footer Text that appears in the bottom margin of each page of a document. 136

Form design grid A visual programming tool that allows programmers to drag and drop controls to form the user interface for a program. 579

Format Specified properties for setting a document's appearance. 135

Formatting The process of dividing a disk into sectors so that it can be used to store information. 186

Formatting tags HTML code that is used to change the appearance of text. 289

Formatting utilities Software usually included in an operating system that assists with formatting disks. 187

Formula In spreadsheet terminology, a combination of numbers and symbols that tells the computer how to use the contents of cells in calculations. 139

FORTRAN (FORmula TRANslator) The oldest high-level computer programming language still in use, still used for scientific, mathematical, and engineering programs. 575

Fourth-generation computers A reference to computers that use a general purpose microprocessor for data processing, allowing for faster, smaller, and cheaper computers to be designed and built. 410

Fourth-generation languages A classification of programming and query languages, such as SQL and RPG, that more closely resemble human languages than did third-generation languages. 574

Fragmented files Files stored in scattered, noncontiguous clusters on a disk. 189

Frame rate Refers to the number of frames displayed per second in a video or film. 369

Frames An outline or boundary, frequently defining a box. For document production software, a pre-defined area into which text or graphics may be placed. 137

Freeware Copyrighted software that is given away by the author or owner. 159

Full backup A copy of all the files for a specified backup job. 205

Full duplex A system that allows messages to be sent and received simultaneously. 237

Full-system backup A backup, or copy, of all of the files stored on a computer. 200

Fully justified The horizontal alignment of text where the text terminates exactly at both margins of the document. 136

Function In worksheets, a built-in formula for making a calculation. In programming, a section of code that manipulates data, but is not included in the main sequential execution path of a program. 139, 591

Functional paradigm An approach to programming that emphasizes the use of expressions called "functions." 608

Fuzzy logic A technique used by an expert system to deal with imprecise data by incorporating the probability that the input information is correct. 471

Gateway A device or software code used to join two dissimilar networks by converting data sent from one network into a format compatible to the receiving network. 231

Generic text editor A simple application, such as NotePad, used for entering and editing text and program code. (Also called a "text editor.") 577

GIF (Graphics Interchange Format) A bitmap graphics file format, popularized by CompuServe, for use on the Web. 354

Gigabit (Gb or Gbit) Approximately one billion bits, exactly 1,024 megabits. 63

Gigabyte (GB) Approximately one billion bytes; exactly 1,024 megabytes (1,073,741,842 bytes). 63

Gigahertz (GHz) A measure of frequency equivalent to one billion cycles per second. 69

Global update The changing of data in more than one record at a time. 551

Goal In the context of Prolog programming, a goal is a query that searches for an answer based on a set of Prolog facts and rules. 610

Gradient A smooth blending of shades of different colors, from light to dark. 360

Grammar checker A feature of word processing software that coaches the user on correct sentence structure and word usage. 135

Graphical user interface (GUI) A type of user interface that features on-screen objects, such as menus and icons, manipulated by a mouse. Abbreviated GUI (pronounced "gooey"). 124

Graphics Any picture, photograph, or image that can be manipulated or viewed on a computer. 145

Graphics card A circuit board inserted into a computer to handle the display of text, graphics, animation, and videos. Also called a "video card." 93

Graphics software Computer programs for creating, editing, and manipulating images. 145

Grayscale palette Digital images that are displayed in shades of gray, black and white. 352

Grid client software Client-side software that enables computers to become part of a grid computing system. 662

Grid computing system A network of diverse computers in which each computer is treated as a generic and equal processing resource. 662

Grid management software Software that distributes processing tasks to grid client computers and collects results. 662

Groupware Software that enables multiple users to collaborate on a project, usually through a pool of data that can be shared by members of the workgroup. 151

Half duplex A communications technique that allows the user to alternately send and receive transmissions. 237

Handheld computer A small, pocket-sized computer that is designed to run on its own power supply and provide users with basic applications. 7

Handshaking A process where a protocol helps two network devices communicate. 236

Hard disk drive A computer storage device that contains a large-capacity "hard disk" sealed inside the drive case. A hard disk is NOT the same as a 3.5" floppy disk that has a rigid plastic case. 10

Hard disk platter The component of the hard disk drive on which data is stored. It is a flat, rigid disk made of aluminum or glass and coated with a magnetic oxide. 83

Harvard Mark I An early computer prototype also known as the ASCC (automatic sequence controlled calculator), developed by IBM that used decimal data representation rather than binary. 406

Haskell A functional programming language. (See functional paradigm.) 575

Head crash A collision between the read-write head and the surface of the hard disk platter, resulting in damage to some of the data on the disk. 84

Head section A part of a Web page that begins with the <HEAD> tag and contains information about global properties of the document. 301

Head-end A satellite dish "farm" at which television broadcasts are received and retransmitted. 258

Header Text that is placed in the top margin of each page of a document. 136

Help desk Part of the IS department designated to assist users experiencing problems with their computers or applications. 494

Helper application A program that understands how to work with a specific file format. 291

Hierarchical database A database model in which record types are arranged as a hierarchy, or tree, of child nodes that can have only one parent node. 519

Hierarchical storage management (HSM) The practice of moving infrequently accessed data to a succession of increasingly inexpensive storage devices. 677

High-level language A programming language that allows a programmer to write instructions using human-like language. 119, 572

High-performance computing (HPC) A branch of computer science that focuses on ways to optimize the processing capabilities of computers to better handle compute-intensive tasks. 641

Hollerith Tabulating Machine A mechanical calculator first used in 1890 by the U.S. Census Bureau that used punch cards to store data and led to the creation of IBM. 404

Home page (1) A document that is the starting, or entry, page at a Web site. (2) The Web page that a browser displays each time it is started. 29

HomePLC network A network that uses a building's existing power line cables to connect nodes. 243

HomePNA network A network that uses a building's existing phone lines to connect nodes. 243

Horizontal market software Any computer program that can be used by many different kinds of businesses (for example, an accounting program). 151

Host computer A computer that serves as the main connection point for other computers or terminals. In the context of centralized computing, a mainframe to which terminals are connected. 658

Hot spot An area on a Web page that is designated as a hyperlink. (Also see Wi-Fi hotspot.) 305

HTML (Hypertext Markup Language) A standardized format used to specify the layout for Web page documents. 27

HTML document A plain text or ASCII document with embedded HTML tags that dictate formatting and are interpreted by a browser. 285

HTML form An HTML document containing blank boxes that prompt users to enter information that can be sent to a Web server. Commonly used for e-commerce transactions. 306

HTML frame Part of a Web page that scrolls independently of other parts of the Web page. 307

HTML tags A set of instructions, such as <b>, inserted into an HTML document to provide formatting and display information to a Web browser. 30

HTTP (Hypertext Transfer Protocol) The communications system used to transmit Web pages. HTTP:// is an identifier that appears at the beginning of each Web page URL (for example, http://www.fooyong.com). 26

HTTP status code A code used by Web servers to report the status of a browser's request. 293

Hub A network device that connects several nodes of a local area network. 230

Hyperlink data type A data type assigned to fields that store URLs used to link directly to a Web page. 535

Hypertext A way of organizing an information database by linking information through the use of text and multimedia. Helped the development of the Web. 284

Hypertext link Also called "link," an underlined word or phrase that when clicked, takes you to its designated URL. 285

IBM 360 An early third generation computer that is widely regarded as the first general purpose mainframe. 409

IBM AS/400 A minicomputer manufactured by IBM and is one of the few remaining minicomputers on the market. 409

IBM PC An early, commercially successful personal computer system that featured a 4.77 MHz Intel 8088 processor, 64 KB RAM, and a floppy disk drive. 411

IBM PC XT An early, commercially successful personal computer system that included a hard disk drive. 411

ICANN (Internet Corporation for Assigned Names and Numbers) A global organization that coordinates the management of the Internet's domain name system, IP addresses, and protocol parameters. 252

IDE (Integrated Development Environment) A set of programming tools, typically including editor, compiler, and debugger, packaged into an application for creating programs. 623

Image map An area on a Web page consisting of a single graphic image containing multiple hot spots. 305

IMAP (Internet Messaging Access Protocol) A protocol similar to POP that is used to retrieve e-mail messages from an e-mail server, but offers additional features, such as choosing which e-mails to download from the server. 40

Implementation phase A set of tasks performed with the supervision of the project team where the new information system is constructed. 489

Incremental backup A copy of the files that changed since the last backup. 205

Inference engine Software that can analyze and manipulate a knowledge base that is stored in a computer file. 470

Information The words, numbers, and graphics used as the basis for human actions and decisions. 11

Information engineering methodology A method of developing an information system that focuses on data the information system collects before finding ways to process that data. 478

Information system Refers to a computer system that collects, stores, and processes information, usually within the context of an organization. 462

Information systems (IS or CIS) The career field or academic major that focuses on developing computer systems and networks for businesses. (See information system.) 433

Information systems department The part of a business or organization responsible for developing and maintaining the computers, data, and programs for an information system. 427

Information technology industry (IT industry) Refers to companies involved in the development, production, sales, and support of computers and software. 413

Infrared light A transmission technology that uses a frequency range just below the visible light spectrum to transport data. 233

Inheritance In object-oriented terminology, how objects inherit attributes and methods from a class. 599

Ink jet printer A non-impact printer that creates characters or graphics by spraying liquid ink onto paper or other media. 94

Input As a noun, "input" means the information that is conveyed to a computer. As a verb, "input" means to enter data into a computer. 4

INSERT An SQL keyword that adds a record to a table. 548

Install The process by which programs and data are copied to the hard disk of a computer system and otherwise prepared for access and use. 153

Installation agreement A version of the license agreement that appears on the computer screen when software is being installed and prompts the user to accept or decline. 157

Instant messaging A private chat in which users can communicate with each other in real time using electronically transmitted text messages. 17

Instantiation A programming term that refers to the process of assigning a value to a variable. 612

Instruction cycle The steps followed by a computer to process a single instruction; fetch, interpret, execute, then increment the instruction pointer. 101

Instruction set The collection of instructions that a CPU is designed to process. 69

Integer data type A numeric data type used for fields that contain whole numbers. 534

Integrated circuit (IC) A thin slice of silicon crystal containing microscopic circuit elements such as transistors, wires, capacitors, and resistors; also called chips and microchips. 64

Integration testing The testing of the completed modules of an application, to ensure that they operate together correctly. 490

Intermediate language A set of low-level instructions that can be easily and quickly recompiled into machine language. 620

Internal information Information obtained by an organization from its own resources, such as the accounting or personnel departments. 465

Internal link A hyperlink that links to a location within the same Web site. 305

Internet The worldwide communication infrastructure that links computer networks using TCP/IP protocol. 15

Internet backbone The major communications links that form the core of the Internet. 15

Internet telephony A set of hardware and software that allows users to make phone-style calls over the Internet, usually without a long-distance charge. 17

Interpreter A program that converts high-level instructions in a computer program into machine language instructions, one instruction at a time. 119, 621

Intranet A LAN that uses TCP/IP communications protocols, typically for communications services within a business or organization. 249

Intrapage link A hyperlink that links to a different location on the same Web page. 305

IP (Internet Protocol) One of the main protocols of TCP/IP that is responsible for addressing packets for routing to their destinations. 249

IP addresses Unique identifying numbers assigned to each computer connected to the Internet. 250

ISA (Industry Standard Architecture) A standard for moving data on the expansion bus. Can refer to a type of slot, a bus, or a peripheral device. An older technology, it is rapidly being replaced by PCI architecture. 97

ISDN (Integrated Services Digital Network) A telephone company service that transports data digitally over dial-up or dedicated lines. 20, 262

ISDN terminal adapter A device that connects a computer to a telephone jack and translates the data into a signal that can travel over an ISDN connection. 262

ISP A company that provides Internet access to businesses, organizations, and individuals. 20

Iterative SDLC A series of phases that outlines the development process of an information system where each phase is allowed to repeat as needed in the development process. 477

Java A platform-independent, object-oriented, high-level programming language based on C++, typically used to produce interactive Web applications. 575

Java applets Small programs that add processing and interactive capabilities to Web pages. 313

Java Virtual Machine (JVM) A component found in most browsers that executes Java applets. 313, 620

JavaScript A scripting language, based on Java, that is used to design interactive Web sites. 312

JIT (Just In Time) A manufacturing system in which the parts needed to construct a product are received at the assembly site only as needed. 476

Job search agent An automated program that searches one or more databases and notifies you when it finds a lead on a specific job type. 442

JOIN An SQL command that allows the temporary joining and simultaneous accessing of data from more than one table. 552

Joining tables In SQL terminology, the act of creating a relationship between tables. 552

Joint application design (JAD) A widely accepted design technique that is based on the idea that the best information systems are designed when end-users and systems analysts work together on a project as equal partners. 474

Joystick An input device that looks like a small version of a car's stick shift. Popular with gamers, moving the stick moves objects on the screen. 91

JPEG (Joint Photographic Experts Group) A format that uses lossy compression to store bitmap images. JPEG files have a .jpg extension. 353

Kernel The core module of an operating system that typically manages memory, processes, tasks and disks. 125

Key frame Frames at equal intervals in a digital video clip that contain all data for that frame. The rest of the frames in the video contain only the information that is different from the preceding key frame. 387

Keyword 1) A word or term used as the basis for a Web page search. 2) A command word provided by a programming language. 32, 572

Kilobit (Kbit or Kb) 1024 bits. 63

Kilobyte (KB) Approximately one thousand bytes; exactly 1,024 bytes. 63

Knowledge base The collection of facts and rules obtained from experts that forms the information base of an expert system. 470

Knowledge engineering The process of designing, entering rules into, and testing rules in an expert system. 470

Known information In a problem statement, information supplied to the computer to help it solve a problem. 577

Label In the context of spreadsheets, any text used to describe data. 138

LAN (Local Area Network) An interconnected group of computers and peripherals located within a relatively limited area, such as a building or campus. 8, 229

Lands Non-pitted surface areas on a CD that represent digital data. (See also Pits.) 79

Laser printer A printer that uses laser-based technology, similar to that used by photocopiers, to produce text and graphics. 94

Latency The elapsed time it takes for a packet of data to arrive at its destination. 248

LCD (liquid crystal display) A type of flat panel computer screen, typically found on notebook computers. 92

LCD screen (liquid crystal display) A type of flat panel computer screen, typically found on notebook computers. (See LCD.) 10

Leading Also called line spacing, the vertical spacing between lines of text. 136

Legacy system A computer system that has become outdated due to technology advances or changing organizational requirements. 645

Leibniz Calculator A mechanical calculator capable of performing the four arithmetic functions and helped develop the technology for the first commercially successful calculator. 403

Level 1 cache (L1 cache) Cache memory built into a microprocessor chip. L1 cache typically can be read in one clock cycle. 70

Level 2 cache (L2 cache) Cache memory that is located in a chip separate from the microprocessor chip. 70

Line printer A printer which produces an entire line of text (as opposed to a single character) in one operation. 649

Line spacing Also called leading, the vertical spacing between lines of text. (See leading.) 136

Linear editing A video editing technique involving recording segments of video from one tape to another. 370

Link tags HTML code that is used to designate text as a hyperlink in a document. 289

Links Underlined areas of text that allow users to jump between Web pages. 26

Linux A server operating system that is a derivative of UNIX and available as freeware. 129

LISP (LISt Processor) A declarative programming language that excels at handling complex data structures, artificial intelligence research, and very complex programs. 575

Load balancing The process of distributing processing and storage tasks among the nodes of a cluster in a way that optimizes the performance of the entire system. 666

Local Area Network (LAN) An interconnected group of computers and peripherals located within a relatively limited area, such as a building or campus. 581

Logic error A run-time error in the logic or design of a computer program. 581

Logical data type A data type specifying that a field in a data file is used to store true/false or yes/no data. 534

Logical storage models Also referred to as metaphors, are any visual aid that helps a computer user visualize a file system. 183

Lookup routine A validation process used by database designers to prevent data entry errors by searching for the entry in a file or database table. 537

Loop The section of program code that is repeated because of a repetition control structure. 593

Lossless compression A compression technique that provides the means to reconstitute all of the data in the original file, hence "lossless" means that this compression technique does not lose data. 386

Lossy compression Any data compression technique in which some of the data is sacrificed to obtain more compression. 386

Low-level language A programming language that requires a programmer to write instructions for specific hardware elements such as the computer processor, registers, and RAM locations. 572

Mac OS The operating system software designed for use on Apple Macintosh and iMac computers. 128

Machine code Program instructions written in binary code that the computer can execute directly. 100

Machine language A low-level language written in binary code that the computer can execute directly. 119, 573

Macro virus A computer virus that infects the macros that are attached to documents and spreadsheets. (See macro.) 192

Macs (Macintosh computers) A personal computer designed and manufactured by Apple Computers. 13

Magnetic storage The recording of data onto disks or tape by magnetizing particles of an oxide-based surface coating. 79

Mail merge A feature of document production software that automates the process of producing customized documents, such as letters and advertising flyers. 137

Mail order A type of retailing where a merchant takes orders by telephone or from an Internet site, then ships orders by mail or other courier service. 423

Mailing list server Any computer and software that maintains a list of people who are interested in a topic, and facilitates message exchanges among all members of the list. 17

Mailto link A link in a Web page that automatically opens a pre-addressed e-mail form. 305

Mainframe computer A large, fast, and expensive computer generally used by businesses or government agencies to provide centralized storage processing and management for large amounts of data. 8

Maintenance phase The day-to-day operation of an information system, including making modifications and correcting problems to insure correct operation. 493

Malicious code Any program or set of program instructions, such as a virus, worm, or Trojan horse, designed to surreptitiously enter a computer and disrupt its normal operations. 191

MAN (Metropolitan Area Network) A public, high-speed network that can transmit voice and data within a range of 50 miles. 229

Management information system (MIS) A type of information system that manipulates the data collected by a transaction processing system to generate reports that managers can use to make business decisions. 467

Managers People who make decisions about how an organization carries out its activities. 463

Manual calculator A device that helps solve mathematical calculations and does not contain any algorithms. 402

Manufacturer direct The selling of products by hardware manufacturers directly to consumers, by means of a sales force or mail order. 423

Manufacturing technician A computer professional who participates in the fabrication of computer chips, systems, and devices. 428

Many-to-many relationship A relationship in which one record in a particular record type can be related to more than one record in another record type, and vice versa. 517

Mark-8 A microprocessor based computer system developed by Jonathan A. Titus in 1974 that helped lead to the development of personal computers. 410

Market share A company's share, or percentage, of the total market. 420

Market tiers Categories of computer companies that separate these companies by size, longevity, and market share. 421

Marketing channels Marketing outlets such as retail stores or mail order for computer-related products. 422

Markup language A language that provides text and graphics formatting through the use of tags. Examples of markup languages include HTML, XML, SGML. 286

Mass mailing worm A worm that sends itself to every e-mail address in the address book of an infected computer. 193

Massively parallel processing (MPP) The process of linking multiple processors, each with its own bus, memory, and operating system. 652

Master File Table An index file used in NTFS systems used to maintain a list of clusters and keep track of their contents. 187

Mathematical modeling software Software for visualizing and solving a wide range of math, science, and engineering problems. 141

Mathematical operators Symbols such as + - / * that represent specific mathematical functions in a formula. 139

Mean time between failures (MTBF) A statistic that indicates the average length of time that a device is expected to operate without malfunctioning. 672

Mechanical calculator A machine capable of implementing algorithms used to solve mathematical calculations. 403

Media tags HTML code that specifies how to display media elements in a document. 289

Megabit (Mb or Mbit) 1,048,576 bits. 63

Megabyte (MB) Approximately one million bytes; exactly 1,048,576 bytes. 63

Megahertz (MHz) A measure of frequency equivalent to 1 million cycles per second. 69

Megapixels Millions of pixels, expresses the resolution and quality of an image. 347

Member In a network database model, a record type related to another record type higher up in the network model. 519

Memo data type A data type that specifies that a field in a data file can contain variable-length text comments (also called memo field). 534

Memory The computer circuitry that holds data waiting to be processed. 5

Mesh topology A network arranged in such a way that each device is connected to many other devices. Data traveling on a mesh network can take any of several possible paths. 230

Message In the context of object-oriented programming, input that is collected and sent to an object. 601

Message header The section of an e-mail document that contains the address, subject, and file attachment information. 36

Metafiles Graphics files that contain both vector and bitmap data. 360

Metasearch tool A program that performs broad-based Web searches, such as searching more than one job database at a time. 442

Method The actions that an object can perform. 600

MICR (Magnetic Ink Character Recognition) The use of specialized inks and fonts (such as check routing numbers) to allow printed material to be read by machines. 648

Microcomputer A category of computer that is built around a single microprocessor chip. The computers typically used in homes and small businesses (also called a personal computer). 6

Microprocessor An integrated circuit that contains the circuitry for processing data. It is a single-chip version of the central processing unit (CPU) found in all computers. 6, 68

Microprocessor clock A device on the motherboard of a computer responsible for setting the pace of executing instructions. 69

Microsoft Windows An operating system, developed by Microsoft Corporation, that provides a graphical interface. Versions include Windows 3.1, Windows 95, Windows 98, Windows Me, Windows NT, Windows 2000, and Windows XP. 126

Microwaves Electromagnetic waves with a frequency of at least 1 gigahertz. 233

Middleware A type of software that acts as an intermediary between two other software packages. 654

MIDI (Musical Instrument Digital Interface) A standardized way in which sound and music are encoded and transmitted between devices that play music. 380

MIDI sequence Digitally encoded music stored on a computer. Usually is a file with a .mid, .cmf, or .rol file extension. 380

MIDI sequencing software Software that uses a standardized way of transmitting encoded music or sounds for controlling musical devices, such as a keyboard or sound card. 147

Migration In the context of hierarchical storage management (HSM), the process of moving data from one storage tier to another. Also called relocation. 677

MIME (Multi-purpose Internet Mail Extensions) A conversion process used for formatting non-ASCII messages so that they can be sent over the Internet. 37

MIPS (Millions of Instructions Per Second) A measure of the speed at which a computer executes instructions of any kind. (As opposed to FLOPS, a measure of floating point execution speed.) 642

Mirroring A technique for creating a real-time "mirror image" of a storage medium, such as a hard disk. 647

Mission An organization's goal or plan, and reflected by the organization's activities. 462

Mission statement The written expression of an organization's goals and how those goals will be accomplished. 462

MITS Altair The first commercial microcomputer. It was based on the Intel 8080 processor and sold primarily to computer hobbyists. 410

Modem A device that sends and receives data to and from computers. (See voice band modem and cable modem.) 10

Modified waterfall SDLC A series of phases that outlines the development process of an information system where each phase can overlap and be repeated as necessary in the development process. 477

Modulation The process of changing the characteristics of a signal (for example, when a modem changes a digital pulse into an analog signal). 256

Molecular computing The use of individual molecules to build components that perform functions similar to transistors and other components of microchips. 446

Money management software Software used to track monetary transactions and investments. 141

Monitor A display device that forms an image by converting electrical signals from the computer into points of colored light on the screen. 10

Monochrome bitmap A bitmap image that contains only the colors black and white. 350

Motherboard (See system borad.)

Mouse An input device that allows the user to manipulate objects on the screen by clicking, dragging, and dropping. 10

MP3 A file format that provides highly compressed audio files with very little loss of sound quality. 378

MPEG (Moving Pictures Expert Group) A highly compressed file format for digital videos. Files in this format have a .mpg extension. 366

MRP (Manufacturing Resource Planning) A system of business management where an optimum manufacturing plan is generated based on a wide variety of data. 476

MSIL (Microsoft Intermediate Language) An intermediate language that is the result of compiling code from the .NET framework. MSIL must be further compiled at runtime. 620

MSRP (manufacturer's suggested retail price) The suggested price of a product that is set by the manufacturers, usually higher than the street price. 419

Multidimensional database A database that provides built-in methods to display and store data in a multidimensional structure. 557

Multimedia card (MMC) A solid state storage card about the size of a stamp with a built in controller used in mobile phones, pagers, MP3 players and some digital cameras. 89

Multiparadigm language A programming language that supports more than one paradigm, such as object-oriented and procedural paradigms. 575

Multi-partite viruses A computer virus that is able to infect many types of targets by hiding itself in numerous locations on a computer. 197

Multiple-user license Legal permission for more than one person to use a particular software package. 157

Multiprocessor architecture A type of computer design that incorporates more than one microprocessor to increase processing capacity. 651

Multitasking operating system An operating system that runs two or more programs at the same time. 126

Multiuser operating system An operating system that allows a single computer to deal with simultaneous processing requests from multiple users. 126

NAN Neighborhood area network with a range of a few blocks, such as a Wi-Fi hotspot offered by a coffee shop or neighborhood Free Wi-Fi organization. 229

Nanoseconds Units of time representing 1 billionth of a second. 74

Napier's Bones A manual calculator created by John Napier that could be used to perform mathematical calculations by manipulating numbered rods. 403

Narrowband A term that refers to communications channels that have low bandwidth. 234

Native file format A file format that is unique to a program or group of programs and has a unique file extension. 177

Natural language query A query using language spoken by human beings, as opposed to an artificially constructed language such as machine language. 144

Netiquette Internet etiquette or a set of guidelines for posting messages and e-mails in a civil, concise way. 39

Network access points (NAPs) Access points that link together different network service providers so that data can be transferred from one service provider to the other. 247

Network address translation (NAT) An Internet standard that allows a LAN to use one type of IP address for LAN data and another type of address for data to and from the Internet. 271

Network attached storage (NAS) Storage devices that are designed to be attached directly to a network, rather than to a workstation or server. 648

Network card An expansion board mounted inside a computer to allow access to a local area network. Also called a network interface card (NIC). 9

Network database A collection of physically linked records, in a one-to-many relationship, in which a member (child) can have more than one owner (parent). 519

Network operating system Programs designed to control the flow of data, maintain security, and keep track of accounts on a network. 126

Network service providers (NSP) Companies that maintain a series of nationwide Internet links. 247

Network set Related record types containing an owner and members. 519

Network specialist/administrator A computer professional who plans, installs, and maintains one or more local area networks. 428

Neural network A type of expert system that uses computer circuitry to simulate the way in which the brain processes information, learns, and remembers. 471

Newsgroups An online discussion group that focuses on a specific topic. 17

Node In a network, a connection point; in a hierarchical database, a segment or record type. 230, 519

Non-executing zip files A type of file that has to be unzipped manually to extract the file or files contained within it. 156

Non-linear editing A digital video editing technique that requires a PC and video editing software. 370

Nonprofit organizations Organizations with political, social, or charitable goals that are not intended to generate a profit. 462

Normalization The process of analyzing data to create the most efficient database structure. 537

Notation software Software used to help musicians compose, edit, and print their compositions. 147

Notebook computers Small, lightweight, portable computers that usually run on batteries. Sometimes called laptops. 6

NTFS (New Technology File System) A file system used by Microsoft Windows NT, 2000, and XP operating systems to keep track of the name and location of files on a hard disk. 187

N-tier system A distributed computing system that is divided into some number (n) of tiers. 661

Numeric data Numbers that represent quantities and can be used in arithmetic operations. 60

Object In an object-oriented database or programming language, a discrete piece of code describing a person, place, thing, event, or type of information. 597

Object code The low-level instructions that result from compiling source code. 119, 620

Object-oriented database A database model that organizes data into classes of objects that can be manipulated by programmer-defined methods. 521

Object-oriented methodology A method of developing an information system that treats an information system as a collection of objects that interact with each other to accomplish tasks. 478

Object-oriented paradigm A popular approach to programming that focuses on the manipulation of objects rather than on the generation of procedure-based code. 597

OCR (Optical Character Recognition) A technique for converting printed documents into digital data, usually through the use of a scanning device and character-recognition software. 649

Octet One of four sections of an IP address. 250

Offshoring The corporate practice of relocating production, manufacturing, or customer service to lower-cost, overseas locations. 416

OLAP (Online analytical processing) A system that consists of computer hardware, database software, and analytical tools that are optimized for analyzing and manipulating data. 555

OLTP systems (Online Transaction Processing Systems) Interactive online transaction processing methods that use a "commit or rollback" strategy to ensure accurate transaction processing. 466

One-time-use credit card A number or code distributed by credit card companies that allows consumers to make purchases while keeping their actual credit card number hidden. 325

One-to-many relationship A relationship in which one record in a particular type may be related to more than one record of another record type. 517

One-to-one relationship An association between database entities in which one record type is related to one record of another type. 518

Online job bank An online database of job opening announcements that spans many industries or just one specific industry. 441

Online processing An interactive method in which each transaction is processed as it is entered. 466

Online shopping cart An e-commerce cookie that stores information about items selected and collected for purchase. 322

OODBMS (Object oriented database management system) Database management software used to construct an object-oriented database. 525

Op code Short for operation code, an op code is an assembly language command word that designates an operation, such as add (ADD), compare (CMP), or jump (JMP). 100

Open source software Software that includes its source code, allowing programmers to modify and improve it. 159

Operands The part of an instruction that specifies the data, or the address of the data, on which the operation is to be performed. 100

Operating system The software that controls the computer's use of its hardware resources, such as memory and disk storage space. Also called OS. 12

Operational planning The scheduling and monitoring of workers and processes. 463

Operational tags HTML code used to specify the basic setup and database integration for Web pages. 289

Optical storage A means of recording data as light and dark spots on a CD, DVD, or other optical media. 79

Organization A group of people working together to accomplish a goal. 462

Organizational chart An organizational structure used to coordinate the activities of the people in the organization such as a hierarchy of employees. 463

Output The results produced by a computer (for example, reports, graphs, and music). 5

Outsourcing The use of independent contractors to perform specific jobs, tasks, or projects. 415

Owner In a network database model, a record type that has relationships with other record types at lower levels of the network. 519

P3P (Platform for Privacy Preferences Project) A specification that allows Web browsers to automatically detect a Web site's privacy policies. 296

Packet sniffer A program that monitors data as it travels over networks. 324

Packet switching A technology used by data communications networks, such as the Internet, where a message is divided into smaller units called "packets" for transmission. 235

Packets A small unit of data transmitted over a network or the Internet. 235

Page layout The physical positions of elements on a document page such as headers, footers, page numbering, and graphics positioning. 136

Paint software The software required to create and manipulate bitmap graphics. 145, 344

Palm OS A popular type of operating system produced by PalmSource specifically for handheld computers. 130

PAN (personal area network) An interconnected group of personal digital devices located within a range of about 30 feet. 229

Paragraph alignment The horizontal position (left, right, justified, centered, for example) of the text in a document. 136

Paragraph style A specification for the format of a paragraph, which includes the alignment of text within the margins and line spacing. 136

Parallel conversion A type of system conversion in which the old computer system remains in service while some or all of the new system is activated. 492

Parallel processing The simultaneous use of more than one processor to execute a program. 70, 651

Parameter A delimiting variable used to modify a command, i.e., /ON modifies the DIR command so it displays files in order by name. 548, 572

Parent node In a hierarchical database, a record type that has paths to other record types lower in the hierarchy. 519

Pascal A high-level, procedural programming language developed to help computer programming students learn the structured approach to programming. 575

Pascaline An early mechanical calculator capable of performing addition, subtraction, division, and multiplication. 403

Password A special set of symbols used to restrict access to a user's computer or network. 22

Path A file's location in a file structure. (See File specification.) 178

Payload The action taken by a virus, ranging from displaying annoying message to corrupting the data on a computer's hard disk. 191

Payroll Software A type of horizontal market software used to maintain payroll records. 151

PC card (PCMCIA card) A credit card-sized circuit board used to connect a modem, memory, network card, or storage device to a notebook computer. 98

PCI (Peripheral Component Interconnect) A method for transporting data on the expansion bus. Can refer to type of data bus, expansion slot, or transport method used by a peripheral device. 97

PCMCIA slot A PCMCIA (Personal Computer Memory Card International Association) slot is an external expansion slot typically found on notebook computers. 97

PCs (Derived from the term Personal Computers) Microcomputers that use Windows software and contain Intel-compatible microprocessors. 13

PCX The PC Paintbrush file format that incorporates a compression algorithm. 353

PDA (personal digital assistant) A computer that is smaller and more portable than a notebook computer (also called a palm-top or handheld computer). 7

PDA video Digital video formatted for viewing on a PDA or other handheld device. 365

Peer-to-peer The process by which one workstation/server shares resources with another. Refers to the capability of a network computer to act as both a file server and workstation. 16

Peer-to-peer network A network where workstations act as both file servers and clients. 229

Peripheral device A component or equipment that expands a computer's input, output, and storage capabilities, such as a printer or scanner. 11

Personal computer A microcomputer designed for use by an individual user for applications such as Internet browsing and word processing. 6

Personal finance software Software geared toward individual finances that helps track bank account balances, credit card payments, investments, and bills. 141

Person-to-person payment An e-commerce method of payment that bypasses credit cards and instead, uses an automatic electronic payment service. 327

PGAs A pin-grid array is a common chip design used for microprocessors. 65

PGP (Pretty Good Privacy) A popular program used to encrypt and decrypt e-mail messages. 331

Phased conversion A type of information system conversion in which one module of a new information system is activated at a time. 492

Phonemes Units of sound that are basic components of words, and are produced by speech synthesizers. 382

Photo editing software The software used to edit, enhance, retouch, and manipulate digital photographs. 145

Physical storage model A representation of data as it is physically stored. 186

Physical topology The actual layout of network devices, wires, and cables. 230

PIECES framework A concept developed by James Wetherbe, to help identify problems in an information system. Each letter of PIECES stands for a potential problem such as Performance, Information, Economics, Control, Efficiency, and Service. 476

Pilot conversion A type of system conversion in which a new information system is first activated at one branch of a multi-branch company. 492

Ping (Packet INternet Groper) A command on a TCP/IP network that sends a test packet to a specified IP address and waits for a reply. 248

Pipelining A technology that allows a processor to begin executing an instruction before completing the previous instruction. 70

Pits Spots on a CD that are "burned," representing digital data. 79

Pixel interpolation A process that is used by graphics software that averages the color of adjacent pixels in an image. 349

Pixelated Describes the effect of increasing the size and thus decreasing the quality of an image. 349

Pixels Short for picture element, a pixel is the smallest unit in a graphic image. Computer display devices use a matrix of pixels to display text and graphics. 92

PL/1 (Programming Language 1) A business and scientific programming language developed by IBM in 1964. 575

Plaintext An original, un-encrypted message. 328

Planning phase The first phase of an information system project with the goal of creating a Project Development Plan. 473

Plasma screen A compact, lightweight, flat panel computer screen that displays the pixels of an image using a technology similar to that of neon lights. 92

Platform A "family" or category of computers based on the same underlying software and hardware of a computer. 13

Player Standalone software, helper applications, and plug-ins, that work with one or more file formats, such as MP3, MIDI, or AAC. 296

Plug and Play The ability of a computer to automatically recognize and adjust the system configuration for a newly added device. 98

Plug-in A software module that adds a specific feature to a system. In the context of browsers, a plug-in adds the ability to play files referenced from the EMBED tag. 291

PNG (Portable Network Graphics) A type of graphics file format similar to but newer than GIF or JPEG. 354

Point size A unit of measure (1/72 of an inch) used to describe the height of characters. 135

Pointing device An input device such as a mouse, trackball, pointing stick, or trackpad, that allows users to manipulate an on-screen pointer and other screen-based graphical controls. 91

Pointing stick A mouse-substitute input device that looks like the tip of an eraser embedded in the keyboard of a notebook computer. 91

Polymorphic viruses Viruses that can escape detection from antivirus software by changing their signatures. 196

Polymorphism In the context of object-oriented programming, the ability to redefine a method for a subclass. Also called overloading. 602

POP The Post Office Protocol (POP) is used to retrieve e-mail messages from an e-mail server. 40

POP server A computer that receives and stores e-mail data until retrieved by the e-mail account holder. 41

Popup ad A type of advertisement that usually appears in a separate window when you enter a Web site. 320

Portable audio player A small, lightweight, battery-powered device designed to store and play audio files stored in formats such as MP3 and AAC. 379

PostScript A printer language, developed by Adobe Systems, which uses a special set of commands to control page layout, fonts, and graphics. 96

POTS An acronym for "plain old telephone service." 255

Power-on self-test (POST) A diagnostic process that runs during startup to check components of the computer, such as the graphics card, RAM, keyboard, and disk drives. 44

Predicate In a Prolog fact, the predicate, such as likes, describes the relationship between the arguments in parentheses, such as (John, Mary). 609

Presentation software Software that provides tools to combine text, graphics, graphs, animation, and sound into a series of electronic "slides" that can be output on a projector, or as overhead transparencies, paper copies, or 35-millimeter slides. 146

Primary key A field in a database that contains data that is unique to a record, such as a social security number. 534

Printer Control Language (PCL) PCL is the unofficial standard language used to send page formatting instructions from a PC to a laser or ink jet printer. 96

Printer server A device that controls a cluster of printers by distributing jobs that arrive in its print queue—a list of documents that require printing. 649

Private attribute An attribute for an object, class, or record that can be accessed only from the program routine in which is defined. 598

Private IP addresses IP addresses that cannot be routed over the Internet. 271

Problem statement In an organization, a one-sentence statement that identifies what needs to be improved or fixed; in software engineering, a definition of elements that must be manipulated in order to achieve a result or goal. 576

Procedural language Programming languages used to create programs composed of a series of statements that tell the computer how to perform a specific task. 584

Procedural paradigm An approach to programming in which a programmer defines the steps for solving a problem. 584

Procedure A section of code that performs activities but is not included in the main sequential execution path of a program. 591

Procedure handbook Step-by-step instructions for performing a specific job or task. 491

Process A systematic series of actions that a computer performs to manipulate data; typically represented on a DFD by a rounded rectangle. 496

Process specifications Written explanations of what happens to data within a process. 498

Processing The manipulation of data using a systematic series of actions. 4

Program editor A programming tool, similar to a word processor, but that provides specialized editing and formatting features to streamline the programming process. 578

Programming language A set of keywords and grammar (syntax) that allows a programmer to write instructions that a computer can execute. 119, 572

Programming paradigm Refers to a programming methodology or approach, as in the object-oriented paradigm. 575

Project development plan A planning document that is the final result of a planning phase, which is reviewed and approved by management. 473

Project management software Software specifically designed as a tool for planning, scheduling, and tracking projects and their costs. 151

Prolog A declarative programming language used to develop expert systems modeled after human thinking. 575

Properties The characteristics of an object in a program. 118, 579

Proprietary services Services specific to or offered by one company. 21

Prototype An experimental or trial version of a device or system. 405

Pseudocode A notational system for algorithms that combines English and a programming language. 587

Public attribute An attribute for an object, class, or record that can be accessed from any routine in a program. 598

Public domain software Software that is available for public use without restriction except that it cannot be copyrighted. 159

Public key encryption (PKE) An encryption method that uses a pair of keys, a public key (known to everyone) that encrypts the message, and a private key (known only to the recipient) that decrypts it. 330

Quality assurance specialist A computer professional who participates in alpha and beta test cycles of software. Also refers to a person who examines and tests computer chips and devices. 428

Quality of service (QoS) The level of performance that is provided by a computer system and measured by factors such as response time, downtime, and capacity. 669

Quality-of-service metric A technique for measuring a particular quality-of-service characteristic, such as response time. 670

Quantum computing The application of quantum mechanics to computer systems. 449

Qubit A quantum bit. 449

Query A search specification that prompts the computer to look for particular records in a file. 32

Query by example (QBE) A type of database interface in which the user fills in a field with an example of the type of information that she is seeking. 144

Query language A set of command words that can be used to direct the computer to create databases, locate information, sort records, and change the data in those records. 144

QuickTime A video and animation file format developed by Apple Computer that can also be run on PCs. QuickTime files have a .mov extension. 371

RAID (Acronym for Redundant Array of Independent Disks) Storage devices in which many disk platters are used to provide data redundancy for faster data access and increased protection from media failure. 646

RAM Random access memory is a type of computer memory circuit that holds data, program instructions, and the operating system while the computer is on. 72

Random access The ability of a storage device (such as a disk drive) to go directly to a specific storage location without having to search sequentially from a beginning location. 81

Rapid application development (RAD) A method of developing an information system that focuses on the project team creating prototypes that users can evaluate. 478

Rasterization The process of superimposing a grid over a vector image and determining the color depth for each pixel. 360

Ray tracing A technique by which light and shadow are added to a 3-D image. 362

RCA Spectra 70 An early third generation computer that was among the first to use integrated circuits for data processing. 409

RDBMS (Relational database management system) Database management software used to create, update, and administer a relational database. 525

RDRAM Rambus dynamic RAM is a fast (up to 600 MHz) type of memory used in newer personal computers. 74

Readability formula A feature found in some word processing software that can estimate the reading level of a written document. 135

Read-write head The mechanism in a disk drive that magnetizes particles on the storage disk surface to write data, or senses the bits that are present to read data. 79

Real data type A numeric data type used for fields that contain numbers with decimal places. 534

RealAudio (.ra) An audio file format, developed by Real Networks, created especially for streaming audio data over the Web. 378

RealMedia A video file format, developed by Real Networks, that is popular for streaming Web videos. 371

Recall In the context of hierarchical storage management, the process of locating and retrieving data from the storage hierarchy. 678

Record In the context of database management, a record is the fields of data that pertain to a single entity in a database. 142, 515

Record occurrence A record that has been filled with data for a particular entity. 516

Record type The structure of a record, including the names, length, and data types for each field. 516

Recordable technology (R) A technique of writing data permanently on CD and DVD disks, the data cannot be changed once it has been recorded. 86

Recovery CD A CD that contains all the operating system files and application software files necessary to restore a computer to its original state. 207

Reference software Software that contains a large database of information with tools for sorting, viewing, and accessing specific topics. 149

Refresh rate The speed at which a computer monitor is rewritten, measured in Hertz. Faster refresh rates reduce flickering. 92

Registers A sort of "scratch pad" area of the ALU and control unit into which data or instructions are moved so that they can be processed. 68

Relational database A database structure that incorporates the use of tables that can establish relationships with other, similar tables. 520

Relationship In the context of databases, an association between entities that can be used to link records in more than one file. 517

Relative reference In a worksheet, cell references that can change if cells change position as a result of a move or copy operation. 140

Remarks Explanatory comments inserted into lines of code in a computer program. 582

Rendering In graphics software, the process of creating a 3-D solid image by covering a wireframe drawing and applying computer-generated highlights and shadows. 362

Repeater A network device that receives and retransmits amplified signals so that they can retain the necessary strength to reach their destination. 230

Repetition control structure A component of a computer program that repeats one or more instructions until a certain condition is met (also called loop or iteration). 593

Report generator The component of a data management environment that provides a user with the ability to design reports. 542

Report template A predesigned pattern that provides the outline or general specifications for a report. 542

Request for proposal (RFP) A document sent by an organization to vendors to solicit proposals; it specifies the problem that needs to be solved and the requirements that must be met. 486

Request for quotation (RFQ) A document sent by an organization to vendors requesting a formal price quotation on a list of hardware and/or software. 486

Reserved words Special words used as commands in some operating systems that may not be used in filenames. 177

Resolution The density of the grid used to display or print text and graphics. The greater the horizontal and vertical density, the higher the resolution. 93

Resolution dependent Graphics, such as bitmap, where the quality of the image is dependent on the number of pixels comprising the image. 349

Resource A component, either hardware or software, that is available for use by a computer's processor. 123

Response time The time required to fulfill a request. Time is measured beginning when a user initiates a request for information and ends when the request is filled. 670

Restore The act of moving data from a backup storage medium to a hard disk in the event original data has been lost. 200

Retailers Also called resellers, companies that sell computer-related products. 414

Retro viruses Viruses designed to corrupt antivirus software. 196

Rewritable technology (RW) A technique of writing data on CD and DVD disks that is rewritable. The data can be changed, or deleted after being recorded. 86

RF signals (Radio Frequency Signals) Used to transmit data on wireless networks. 233

Ring topology A network in which all devices are connected in a circle with each device having exactly two neighbors. 230

RISC (Reduced Instruction Set Computer) Refers to a microprocessor chip designed for rapid and efficient processing of a small set of simple instructions. 70

Risk management The process of identifying potential threats to computer equipment and data, implementing plans to avoid threats, and developing plans to recover from unavoidable threats. 671

Rollback The act of returning database records back to their original states if one or more steps of the transaction cannot be successfully processed. 466

ROM (Read-Only Memory) Refers to one or more integrated circuits that contain permanent instructions that the computer uses during the boot process. 74

ROM BIOS A small set of basic input/output system instructions stored in ROM, which causes the computer system to load critical operating files when the user turns on the computer. 74

Root directory The main directory of a disk. 178

Root node In a hierarchical database, the topmost node in the hierarchy. 519

Router A network device that examines the IP address of incoming data, and forwards the data towards its destination. 231

RPG (Report Program Generator) A programming language used to generate business reports. 575

RSA A commonly used public key encryption algorithm developed by Rivest, Shamir and Adelman. 330

Rule In the context of Prolog programming, a rule is a general statement about the relationship between facts. 608

Run-length encoding A graphics file compression technique that looks for patterns of bytes and replaces them with messages that describe the patterns. 386

Runtime error An error that occurs when a computer program is run. 581

Safe Mode A menu option that appears when Windows is unable to complete the boot sequence. By entering Safe Mode, a user can gracefully shut down the computer, then try to reboot it. 46

Sampling rate The number of times per second a sound is measured during the recording process. 377

Scalability The ability of a computer system to shrink or grow as requirements change. 638

Scaling out Adding more computers to increase the overall size of an information system. 638

Scaling up Increasing the performance of an information system by replacing a less powerful computer with a more powerful one, or by upgrading a computer in the system. 638

Scanner A device that converts a printed image into a bitmap graphic. 345

Scheduled reports Reports such as monthly sales summaries that follow a fixed format and are produced according to a preset time table. 467

Scheme A dialect of LISP, used for computer research and teaching. 575

Schickard's Calculator An early mechanical calculator consisting of a series of gears and spokes representing numerical values. 403

Script A program that contains a list of commands that are automatically executed as needed. 312

Scripting error An error that occurs when a browser or server cannot execute a statement in a script. 313

SDK (Software Development Kit) A collection of language-specific programming tools. 623

SDLC (System Development Life Cycle) The series of phases that outlines the development process of an information system. 477

SDRAM Short for synchronous dynamic RAM, it is a type of RAM that synchronizes itself with the CPU, thus enabling it to run at much higher clock speeds than conventional RAM. 74

Search and Replace A feature of document production software that allows the user to automatically locate all instances of a particular word or phrase and substitute another word or phrase. 135

Search engine A program that uses keywords to find information on the Internet and returns a list of relevant documents. 31

Search operator A word or symbol that has a specific function within a search, such as "AND or +". 32

SEC cartridges A single edge contact is a common, cassette-like chip design for microprocessors. 65

Second-generation computers A classification of computers that use transistors for data processing and storage instead of vacuum tubes. 408

Second-generation languages A classification for assembly languages that followed machine languages. 573

Sectors Subdivisions of the tracks on a storage medium that provide a storage area for data. 186

Secure connection An internet connection that encrypts data transmitted between your computer and a Web site. 324

SecureDigital (SD) A solid state storage card based on MultiMedia card technology, but features significantly faster data transfer rates and cryptographic security protection. Usually used for MP3 storage. 89

Security specialist A computer professional who analyzes security threats, implements solutions, and develops policies and procedures to protect computer equipment and data. 427

SELECT An SQL keyword that queries for a particular record or group of records from a table. 549

Selection control structure A component of a computer program that tells a computer what to do, depending on whether a condition is true or false (also called decision structure or branch). 592

Self-closing tag An HTML tag that includes a closing symbol in the opening tag, and therefore does not require a separate closing tag. 287

Self-executing zip files A type of file that can be run to unzip the file or files contained within it. 156

Self-installing executable file A program that automatically unzips and then initiates and runs its setup program. 156

Semiconducting materials (semiconductors) Substances, such as silicon or germanium, that can act either as a conductor or insulator. Used in the manufacture of computer chips. 64

Semi-structured problem A problem for which a general procedure has been established, but which require some degree of discretionary judgment to arrive at a solution. 464

Sequence control structure A programming construct which alters the order in which instructions are executed. 590

Sequence diagram A tool used by a project team that depicts the detailed interactions that take place within an information system. 499

Sequential access A form of data storage, usually on computer tape, that requires a device to read or write data one record after another, starting at the beginning of the medium. 81

Sequential execution The computer execution of program instructions performed in the sequence established by a programmer. 590

Serial processing Processing of data one instruction at a time, completing one instruction before beginning another. 70

Server A computer or software on a network that supplies the network with data and storage. 9

Server farm A group of multiple Web servers used to handle large volumes of requests. 294

Server-side program A program or scripting statement that resides on a Web server and acts as an intermediary between a user's browser and a DBMS. 528

Server-side script Scripting statements that are executed by a Web server in response to client data. 312

Service companies Companies that provide computer-related services such as consulting or support. 414

Service pack A collection of patches designed to correct bugs and/or add features to an existing software program. 158

SET (Secure Electronic Transaction) A system that ensures the security of financial transactions on the Web. 326

Setup program A program module supplied with a software package for the purpose of installing the software. 154

Shared resources On a network, resources such as hardware, software, and data, made available for authorized users to share. 226

Shareware Copyrighted software marketed under a license that allows users to use the software for a trial period and then send in a registration fee if they wish to continue to use it. 158

Shrink-wrap license A legal agreement printed on computer software packaging, which becomes binding when the package is opened. 157

S-HTTP (Secure HTTP) A method of encrypting data transmitted between a computer and a Web server by encrypting individual packets of data as they are transmitted. 324

Simplex A communications technique that allows communication in only one direction. 237

SIMULA (SIMUlation LAnguage) Believed to be the first object-oriented programming language. 575

Single-user license Legal permission for one person to use a particular software package. 157

Single-user operating system A type of operating system that is designed for one user at a time with one set of input devices. 126

Site license Legal permission for software to be used on any and all computers at a specific location (for example, within a corporate building or on a university campus). 157

Slide rule A manual calculator invented by William Oughtred that uses John Napier's logarithms to solve complex engineering and scientific calculations. 403

Smalltalk A classic object-oriented programming language. 575

SmartMedia The least durable portable solid state storage medium that does not include a built-in controller. 89

Smileys Text-based symbols used to express emotion. 39

SMTP server (Simple Mail Transfer Protocol Server) A computer used to send e-mail across a network or the Internet. 412 **SOAP** (Simple Object Access Protocol) A protocol standard that allows a program running on one operating system to communicate with a program running on a different operating system. 655

Socket A communication path over a network between two remote programs. 292

Software The instructions that direct a computer to perform a task, interact with a user, or process data. 4

Software customization The process of modifying a commercially available software application to meet the needs of a specific user. 490

Software engineering The process of developing software using systematic mathematical, engineering, and management techniques. 571

Software license A legal contract that defines the ways in which a user may use a computer program. 157

Software patch A section of software code designed to modify an existing program to fix a specific error or add a feature. 156

Software publishers Companies that produce computer software. 118, 414

Software suite A collection of individual applications sold as one package. 148

Solid ink printer A printer that melts a stick of solid ink and sprays it onto paper where it is fused to produce photograph-quality images without the use of special paper. 95

Solid state storage A technology that records data and stores it in a microscopic grid of cells on a non-volatile, erasable, low-power chip. 80

Sort key A field used to arrange records in order. 539

Sort order In a database table, the order in which records are stored on disk. 539

Sound card A circuit board that gives the computer the ability to accept audio input from a microphone, play sound files stored on disks and CD-ROMs, and produce audio output through speakers or headphones. 10, 378

Source code Computer instructions written in a high-level language. 119, 620

Spam Unsolicited e-mail typically sent as a bulk or mass-mailing and used for fraudulent of deceptive marketing. 40

Spam filter Software that identifies unsolicited and unwanted e-mail messages and blocks them from the recipient's inbox. 40

Spatial compression A data compression scheme that replaces patterns of bytes with code that describes the patterns. 386

Speech recognition The process by which computers recognize voice patterns and words, then convert them to digital data. 382

Speech recognition software The software that analyzes voice sounds and converts them into phonemes. 382

Speech synthesis The process by which computers produce sound that resembles spoken words. 382

Spelling checker A feature of document production software that checks each word in a document against an electronic dictionary of correctly spelled words, then presents a list of alternatives for possible misspellings. 134

Spelling dictionary A data module that is used by a spelling checker as a list of correctly spelled words. 134

Spoofed address A fake return address on an e-mail message designed to hide the address of the real sender. 193

Spreadsheet A numerical model or representation of a real situation, presented in the form of a table. 138

Spreadsheet software Software for creating electronic worksheets that hold data in cells and perform calculations based on that data. 138

Spyware Any software that covertly gathers user information without the user's knowledge, usually for advertising purposes. 323

SQL A popular query language used by mainframes and microcomputers. 546

SQL keywords A collection of special command words that issue instructions to an SQL database. 547

SQL query A query created by SQL database client software that collects user input which can operate directly on a database to carry out a user's instructions. 546

SSL (Secure Sockets Layer) A security protocol that uses encryption to establish a secure connection between a computer and a Web server. 324

Star topology A network configured with a central connection point or hub for all workstations and peripherals. 230

Stateless protocol A protocol, such as HTTP, that allows one request and response per session. 293

Static IP address A permanently assigned and unique IP address, used by hosts or servers. 250

Static Web publishing A simple way to display the data in a database by converting a database report into an HTML document. 527

Statistical compression A data compression scheme that uses an algorithm that recodes frequently used data as short bit patterns. 385

Statistical software Software for analyzing large sets of data to discover patterns and relationships within them. 141

Stealth viruses Viruses that can escape detection from antivirus software by removing their signatures and hiding in memory. 197

Storage The area in a computer where data is retained on a permanent basis. 5

Storage area network (SAN) A network of storage devices and data servers configured to function as a single node on a wider network. 647

Storage device A mechanical apparatus that records data to and retrieves data from a storage medium. 78

Storage hierarchy The collection of storage devices in a hierarchical storage system, typically arranged from high-cost, fast media at the top, to low-cost, slower media at the bottom. 677

Storage management services A collection of software- and hardware-based data storage services, such as the ability to automatically store multiple copies of a file. 647

Storage medium The physical material used to store computer data, such as a floppy disk, a hard disk, or a CD-ROM. 78

Storage metaphor A likeness or analogy that helps people visualize the way that computers store files. 183

Store-and-forward technology A technology used by communications networks in which an e-mail message is temporarily held in storage on a server until it is requested by a client computer. 40

Stored program A set of instructions that resides on a storage device, such as a hard drive, and can be loaded into memory and executed. 5

Strategic planning The process of developing long-range goals and plans for an organization. 463

Streaming video An Internet video technology that sends a small segment of a video file to a user's computer and begins to play it while the next segment is being sent. 372

Street price The average discounted price of a product. 419

Strong encryption Encryption that is difficult to decrypt without the encryption key. 329

Structured English Vocabulary and syntax used by systems analysts to concisely and unambiguously explain the logic of a process. It is limited to words defined in a data dictionary and to specific logical terms such as "if…then,". 587

Structured file A file that consists of a collection of data organized as a set of records. 514

Structured methodology A method of developing an information system that focuses on the processes that take place within the information system. 478

Structured problem A problem for which there exists a well-established procedure for obtaining the best solution. 464

Stub A type of placeholder. In the context of hierarchical storage management, a stub holds the place for a file that has migrated to archival storage. 678

Style A feature in many desktop publishing and word processing programs that allows the user to apply numerous format settings in a single command. 136

Subclass In object-oriented programming, a subclass is derived from a superclass and inherits its attributes and methods. 599

Subdirectory A directory found under the root directory. 178

Subroutine A section of code that performs activities or manipulates data but is not included in the main sequential execution path of a program. 591

Success factors System requirements that also serve as an evaluation checklist at the end of a development project. 479

Summary report A report generated by a management information system that combines or groups data and usually provides totals, such as a report of total annual sales for the past five years. 467

Superclass In object-oriented programming, a superclass can provide attributes and methods for subclasses. 599

Supercomputer The fastest and most expensive type of computer, capable of processing more than 1 trillion instructions per second. 8

SVG (Scalable Vector Graphics) A graphics format designed specifically for Web display that automatically resizes when displayed on different screens. 361

SVGA (Super Video Graphics Array) SVGA typically refers to 800 x 600 resolution. 93

SXGA (Super eXtended Graphics Array) A screen resolution of 1280 x 1024. 93

Symmetric key encryption An encryption key that is used for both encryption and decryption of messages. 330

Symmetric multiprocessing (SMP) A type of parallel processing in which a single operating system controls multiple processors sharing a common bus and memory. 651

Synchronous protocol A method of serial communication in which the transmission of data occurs at regular intervals synchronized by the computer's internal clock (for example, used for the communication that takes place on the main circuit board of a computer). 236

Syntax In the context of programming languages, syntax refers to the grammar rules that create valid program statements. 572

Syntax error An error that results when an instruction does not follow the syntax rules, or grammar, of the programming language. 581

Synthesized sound Artificially created sound, usually found in MIDI music or synthesized speech. 380

System board The main circuit board in a computer which houses chips and other electronic components. 65

System conversion The process of deactivating an old information system and activating a new one. 492

System development life cycle (SDLC) The series of phases that outlines the development process of an information system. 477

System documentation Descriptions of the features, hardware architecture, and programming of an information system written for programmers, designers, and analysts who maintain the system. 491

System operator The person responsible for the day-to-day operation of a computer—usually a mainframe or supercomputer. 493

System palette A selection of colors that are used by an operating system to display graphic elements. 352

System requirements 1) The specifications for the operating system and hardware configuration necessary for a software product to work correctly. 2) The criteria that must be met for a new computer system or software product to be a success. 152, 479

System Requirements Report A report generated at the conclusion of the analysis phase by a project team that has studied a system and determined the system requirements. 480

System software Computer programs that help the computer carry out essential operating tasks. 12, 121

System testing The process of testing an information system to ensure that all the hardware and software components work together. 490

System unit The case or box that contains the computer's power supply, storage devices, main circuit board, processor, and memory. 10

Systems analysis and design The process of planning and building an information system. 473

Systems analyst A computer professional responsible for analyzing requirements, designing information systems, and supervising the implementation of new information systems. 427

Systems programmer The person responsible for installing, modifying, and troubleshooting the operating system of a mainframe or supercomputer. 493

T1 A high-bandwidth telephone line that can also transmit text and images. T-1 service is often used by organizations to connect to the Internet. 262

T3 A type of ISDN service that uses fiber-optic cable to provide dedicated service with a capacity of 45 megabits per second. 262

Table An arrangement of data in a grid of rows and columns. In a relational database, a collection of record types with their data. 137, 520

Tablet computer A small, portable computer with a touch-sensitive screen that can be used as a writing or drawing pad. 7

Tactical planning Short- or near-term decisions and goals that deploy the human, financial, and natural resources necessary to meet strategic goals. 463

Tape backup A copy of data from a computer's hard disk, stored on magnetic tape and used to restore lost data. 85

Tax preparation software Personal finance software that is specifically designed to assist with tax preparation. 141

TCP (Transmission Control Protocol) One of the main protocols of TCP/IP that is responsible for establishing a data connection between two hosts and breaking data into packets. 249

TCP/IP Acronym for Transmission Control Protocol/Internet Protocol. A standard set of communication rules used by every computer that connects to the Internet. 15

Technical support specialist A computer professional who provides phone or online help to customers of computer companies and software publishers. 428

Technical writer A person who specializes in writing explanations of technical concepts and procedures. 428

Telecommuting The act of using available technology to work from home or another off-site location. 430

Temporal compression A data compression scheme that, when applied to video or audio data, eliminates unnecessary data between video frames or audio samples. 387

Terminal An input/output device that features a keyboard and screen, but has no storage capacity and very limited processing capability. 658

Terminal emulation software A type of utility software that allows a personal computer to emulate a terminal. 658

Test area A portion of a computer system where software testing can occur without disrupting an organization's regular information system. 490

Text data type A data type used for fixed-length fields that hold character data such as people's names or CD titles. 534

Text editor A program similar to a word processor that is used to create plain, unformatted ASCII text. 299

Text-to-speech software Software that generates speech, based on written text, that is played back through a computer's sound card. 382

Thermal transfer printer An expensive, color-precise printer that uses wax containing color to produce numerous dots of color on plain paper. 95

Thesaurus A feature of documentation software that provides synonyms. 135

Third-generation computers A classification of computers characterized by their use of integrated circuits instead of transistors or vacuum tubes for data processing. 409

Third-generation languages A classification of programming languages, such as FORTRAN, BASIC, and COBOL, that followed assembly languages and provided English-like keywords. 573

Tier In the context of distributed computing system, a group or layer of computers that performs a specific task. 661

Tiered computer system A computer system that is configured into layers, with each layer assigned a specific task. 661

TIFF (Tag Image File Format) A file format (.tif extension) for bitmap images that automatically compresses the file data. 353

Token Ring network A type of network in which the nodes are sequentially connected in the form of a ring; the second most popular network architecture. 238

Topic directory A list of topics and subtopics arranged in a hierarchy from general to specific. 33

Top-level domain The major domain categories into which groups of computers on the Internet are divided: com, edu, gov, int, mil, net, and org. 251

TQM (Total Quality Management) The process by which an organization analyzes and implements ways to improve the quality of its products and/or services. 476

Trace feature In the context of Prolog programming, a tool that allows programmers to follow the execution path through the rules contained in a program. 618

Traceroute A network utility that records a packet's path, number of hops, and the time it takes for the packet to make each hop. 248

Tracing software Software that locates the edges of objects in a bitmap graphic and converts the resulting shape into a vector graphic. 360

Trackball An input device that looks like an upside down mouse. The user rolls the ball to move the on-screen pointer. 91

Trackpad A touch-sensitive surface on which you slide your fingers to move the on-screen pointer. 91

Tracks A series of concentric or spiral storage areas created on a storage medium during the formatting process. 186

Transaction An exchange between two parties that can be recorded and stored in a computer system. 465

Transaction processing system (TPS) A system that keeps track of transactions for an organization by providing ways to collect, display, modify, and cancel transactions. 465

Transceiver A combination of a transmitter and a receiver used to send and receive data in the form of radio frequencies. 233

Transistors A computer processing technology that was created by Bell Laboratories in 1947, characterizing second generation computers, which replaced vacuum tubes for data processing. 408

Transponder A device on a telecommunications satellite that receives a signal on one frequency, amplifies the signal, and then retransmits the signal on a different frequency. 233

Tree topology Multiple star networks connected into a bus configuration by a backbone. 231

Trigger event An event that activates a task, often associated with a computer virus. 191

Trojan horse A computer program that appears to perform one function while actually doing something else, such as inserting a virus into a computer system or stealing a password. 192

True Color bitmap A color image with a color depth of 24 bits or 32 bits. Each pixel in a true color image can be displayed using any of 16.7 million different colors. 351

Tuple In a relational database, a row in a table, which is equivalent to a record. 520

Turnkey system A complete information system that consists of both hardware and commercial software. 484

Twisted-pair cable A type of cable, with RJ-45 connectors on both ends, where two separate strands of wire are twisted together. Used to connect nodes on a network. 232

UML (Unified Modeling Language) A tool for diagramming a set of object classes. 499, 598

Unicode A 16-bit character-representation code that can represent more than 65,000 characters. 61

Uninstall routine A program that removes software files, references, and registry entries from a computer's hard disk. 156

Unit testing The process of testing a completed application module, to make sure that it operates reliably and correctly. 490

UNIVAC The first commercially successful digital computer. 407

UNIX A multi-user, multitasking server operating system developed by AT&&T's Bell Laboratories in 1969. 129

Unstructured problem A problem for which there is no established procedure for arriving at a solution. 464

Unzipped Refers to files that have been uncompressed. 155

UPDATE An SQL keyword used to alter the values in a database record. 551

Uplink port A connection port on a router to which additional hubs can be attached. 241

Uploading The process of sending a copy of a file from a local computer to a remote computer. 16

Upstream The process of transmitting data from your home computer to the Internet. 258

URL A Uniform Resource Locator is the address of a Web page. 27

USB flash drive A portable solid state storage device nicknamed "pen drive" or "keychain drive" that plugs directly into a computer's USB port. 88

Use case Tasks performed by an actor in an information system. 499

Use case diagram Documentation of the users and their functions of an information system. 499

Usenet A worldwide Internet bulletin board system of newsgroups that share common topics. 17

User documentation Descriptions of how to interact with an information system or program, including instructions on use, features, and troubleshooting. 491

User ID A combination of letters and numbers that serves as a user's "call sign" or identification. Also referred to as a user name. 22

User interface The software and hardware that enable people to interact with computers. 124

Utilities A subcategory of system software designed to augment the operating system by providing ways for a computer user to control the allocation and use of hardware resources. 125

UXGA (Ultra eXtended Graphics Array) A screen resolution of 1600 x 1200. 93

V.44 A voice-band modem standard introduced in 2001 that implements a compression protocol that increases the speed at which data is transmitted. 257

V.90 A standard used by all modems since 1998 that provides a maximum speed of 56 Kbps. 257

V.92 A voice band modem standard that has the potential to provide uplink speeds of 48 Kbps (in contrast to V.90 speeds of 32 Kbps). 257

Vacuum tube An electronic device that controls the flow of electrons in a vacuum and represents binary data. 407

Value A number used in a calculation. 138

Vaporware Software or other products that are announced, but never produced. 419

VAR (Value-Added Reseller) A company that combines one product with additional hardware, software, and/or services to create a system designed to meet the needs of specific customers or industries. 424

Variable A named storage location that is capable of holding data, which can be modified during program execution. 611

Variable-length field A field in a data file that can accept any number of characters up to a maximum limit. 514

VBScript A scripting language, based on Visual Basic, that is used to design interactive Web sites. 312

VDE (Visual Development Environment) Programming tools that allow programmers to build substantial parts of computer programs by pointing and clicking, rather than entering code. 579

Vector graphic An image generated from descriptions that specify the position, length, and direction in which lines and shapes are drawn. 356

Vertical market software Computer programs designed to meet the needs of a specific market segment or industry, such as medical record-keeping software for use in hospitals. 151

VGA (Video Graphics Array) A screen resolution of 640 x 480. 93

Video capture The process of converting analog video signals into digital data stored on a hard drive. 367

Video capture software Software used to control the capture process of digital and analog video data. 368

Video editing software Software that provides tools for capturing and editing video from a camcorder. 148

Videoconferencing camera (Also called a Web camera.) An inexpensive digital camera that attaches directly to a computer and creates a video by capturing a series of still images. 366

Videogame console A computer specifically designed for playing games using a television screen and game controllers. 8

Viewable image size (vis) A measurement of the maximum image size that can be displayed on a monitor screen. 92

Viewing angle width The angle at which you can still clearly see the screen image from the side. 92

Virtual memory A computer's use of hard disk storage to simulate RAM. 73

Virtual private network (VPN) A network connection that typically carries encrypted data over the Internet to and from a remote access server. 271

Virus hoax A message, usually e-mail, that makes claims about a virus problem that doesn't actually exist. 197

Virus signature The unique computer code contained in a virus that helps with its identification. Antivirus software searches for known virus signatures to identify a virus. 197

VisiCalc First released on the Apple II, VisiCalc was the first electronic spreadsheet. 411

Visual Basic An event-driven programming environment where the programmer designs forms graphically and codes procedures in BASIC which responds to all form options. 575

Voice band modem The type of modem that would typically be used to connect a computer to a telephone line. (See modem.) 18

Voice over IP (VOIP) A technology that allows computer users with Internet access to send and receive both data and voice simultaneously. 257

Volatile A term that describes data (usually in RAM), which can exist only with a constant supply of power. 73

Walkthrough In the context of programming, a method of verifying that an algorithm functions properly when using realistic test data. 589

WAN (Wide Area Network) An interconnected group of computers and peripherals that covers a large geographical area, such as multiple branches of a corporation. 229

WAP (Wireless Access Protocol) A communications protocol that provides Internet access for handheld devices. 264

War driving The use of a Wi-Fi equipped notebook computer to covertly search for Wi-Fi signals coming from home and corporate Wi-Fi networks. Also known as LAN-jacking. 242

Waterfall SDLC A series of phases that outlines the development process of an information system where each phase is a discrete step in the development process. 477

Wave (.wav) An audio file format created as Windows "native" sound format. 378

Waveform audio A digital representation of sound, in which a sound wave is represented by a series of samples taken of the wave height. 376

Wavetable A set of pre-recorded musical instrument sounds in MIDI format. 380

Weak encryption Encryption that is relatively easy or simple to decrypt without the encryption key. 329

Web Short for World Wide Web. An Internet service that links documents and information from computers located worldwide, using the HTTP protocol. 26

Web authoring software Computer programs for designing and developing customized Web pages that can be published electronically on the Internet. 133, 300

Web-based video Digital video designed to be stored and played on a computer. 365

Web page header Also called "header," a subtitle that appears at the beginning of a Web page. 301

Web page table A grid of cells that are used as layout tools, for elements such as text and graphics placement in a Web page. 306

Web pages Documents on the World Wide Web that consist of a specially coded HTML file with associated text, audio, video, and graphics files. A Web page often contains links to other Web pages. 26

Web palette A standard selection of colors that all Internet browsers can display. 352

Web portfolio A hypertext version of a resume containing links to Web sites of former employers or schools. 439

Web servers Computers that use special software to transmit Web pages over the Internet. 27

Web site Usually a group of Web pages identified by a common domain name, such as www.cnn.com. 27

Web site designer A computer professional who creates, tests, posts, and modifies Web pages. 428

Web-based e-mail An e-mail system that allows users to access e-mail messages using a browser. 40

WEP (Wired Equivalent Privacy) An encryption algorithm used to transmit data on Wi-Fi networks so that the data is useless to hackers. 242

What-if analysis The process of setting up a model in a spreadsheet and experimenting to see what happens when different values are entered. 138

Wi-Fi A nickname for wireless networks that use 802.11b protocol. 241

Wi-Fi card A type of network interface card that includes a transmitter to send data and plus a receiver and an antenna to transmit signals using Wi-Fi protocols. 242

Wi-Fi hotspot The geographical area in which you can connect to a Wi-Fi signal, such as a Wi-Fi equipped campus or coffeehouse. 264

Windows Explorer A file management utility included with most Windows operating systems that helps users manage their files. 184

Windows Mobile OS An operating system designed by Microsoft for hand-held computers. 130

Windows Registry A crucial set of data files maintained by the operating system that contains the settings needed by a computer to correctly use any hardware and software that has been installed. 161

Wired network A network that uses cables or wires to transmit data form one network device to another. 231

Wireframe A representation of a 3-D object using separate lines, which resemble wire, to create a model. 362

Wireless access point A network device that connects several devices of a local area network by broadcasting signals to any device with compatible Wi-Fi cards. 242

Wireless network Networks that use radio or infrared signals (instead of cables) to transmit data from one network device to another. 231

WISP (Wireless ISP) A wireless internet service provider that maintains a public Wi-Fi network. 264

WMA (Windows Media Audio) A file format that provides highly compressed audio files with very little loss of sound quality and is promoted by Microsoft. 378

WMV Windows Media or Windows Media Video is format for storing digital video. 371

Word processing software Computer programs that assist the user in producing documents, such as reports, letters, papers, and manuscripts. 133

Word size The number of bits that a CPU can manipulate at one time, which is dependent on the size of the registers in the CPU, and the number of data lines in the bus. 70

Workers People who perform the tasks necessary to carry out an organization's mission. 463

Worksheet A computerized, or electronic, spreadsheet. 138

Workstation (1) A computer connected to a local area network. (2) A powerful desktop computer designed for specific tasks. 8

World Wide Web Consortium (W3C) An international consortium of companies involved with the Internet and with the purpose of developing open standards. 286

Worm A software program designed to enter a computer system, usually a network, through security "holes" and then replicate itself. 193

Write-protect window A small hole and sliding cover on a floppy disk that restricts writing to the disk. 82

Xerox Alto An early personal computer prototype developed by Xerox Corp. that featured, among other things, a graphical user interface that became influential in the development of the Apple Macintosh. 411

XForms A database technology that provides an alternative to HTML forms by providing more flexibility and an interface to XML documents. 529

XGA Extended Graphics Array or XGA usually refers to 1024 x 768 resolution. 93

XHTML The follow-up version to HTML 4. 286

XML (eXtensible Markup Language) A document format similar to HTML, but that allows the Web page developer to define customized tags, generally for the purpose of creating more interactivity. 311

XML DBMS An XML DBMS is a database management system that provides authoring and query tools for designing and managing collections of XML documents. 525

XML parser A tool in most browsers used for reading XML documents. 311

XSL (eXtensible Stylesheet Language) A technology that is similar to XML, and is used to create customized tags for displaying data in an XML document. 311

Z3 An early electronic computer prototype designed by Konrad Zuse that was the first to incorporate the use of binary numbers for data representation. 405

Zipped Refers to one or more files that have been compressed. 155

INDEX

* (asterisk), 32
@ (at symbol), 36
\ (backslash), 178
: (colon), 176, 177, 178
" (double quotes), 32
/ (forward slash), 28

A
AAC (Advanced Audio
    Compression) format, 147,
    378, 379, 380
abacus, 402
absolute references, 140
acceptance testing, 492
access time, 81
Access (Microsoft), 149, 525,
    544
accounting software, 151
Accredited Domain Registrar
    Web site, 253
Acrobat (Adobe), 149, 212, 291
ActiveX components
    (Microsoft), 291, 315–318
actors, 499
acts of war, 673
ad hoc reports, 467
ad-blocking software, 320, 323
ad-serving cookies, 323
Ada, 575, 606–607
Add/Remove Programs con-
    sole, 156
Address box, 28, 30, 31
ADR (advanced digital record-
    ing), 85
ADSL (Asynchronous Digital
    Subscriber Line), 20, 260
AES (Advanced Encryption
    Standard), 331
AFIS (Automated Fingerprint
    Identification System),
    216–217
AGP (Accelerated Graphics
    Port) slots, 93, 97
agriculture, 626–627
AI format, 177
AIFF (Audio Interchange
    Format), 378, 380
ALGOL, 595
algorithms, 584–589
ALP (A Programming
    Language), 575

alpha testing, 420
ALU (arithmetic logic unit),
    68–69, 70, 101–102
always-on connections, 19–20,
    259, 325
Amazon.com, 294, 321, 415,
    649
AMD (Advanced Micro
    Devices), 71
AMPS (advanced mobile
    phone service), 266
analog
    devices, 60, 366
    signals, 233–234
    video cameras, 366
analysis phase, 478
Analytical Engine, 404
AND operator, 32, 550
animation, 211, 303–304, 362,
    392–393
antivirus software, 196–197.
    See also viruses
AOL (American Online), 20,
    308
API (application program inter-
    face), 622–623
Apple Computer, first comput-
    ers developed by, 411–412.
    See also Macintosh
AppleTalk, 235, 639
applets, 313–314
application(s). *See also*
    programs; *specific*
        applications
    -based file management,
        180–181
    creating, 489–490
    development toolkits, 484
    linking, 640
    software, overview of,
        12–13, 120–121, 133–151
    specifications, 487
    testing, 490
architecture
    centralized, 657–659
    distributed, 659–660
    enterprise, 657–667
    grid, 662–665, 668
    information systems and,
        504–505
    tiered, 661

ARCnet (Attached Resource
    Computer network), 238
arguments, 609
ARPA (Advanced Research
    Projects Agency), 106, 107,
    214
ARPANET, 107, 214, 246, 249
ASCII (American Standard
    Code for Information
    Interchange), 37–38,
    62–63, 131
    compression and, 385
    databases and, 523
    encryption and, 328
    HTML and, 285
    versions of resumes, 437
Ask Jeeves Web site, 34
ASP (Microsoft Active Server
    Pages), 306, 529–530
assembly language, 573
assumptions, 576–577
asterisk (*), 32
at symbol (@), 36
AT&T (American Telephone &
    Telegraph), 15, 20, 129,
    247, 262
    Bell Labs, 234, 408, 595
    Wireless, 264
    WorldNet, 308
Atanasoff-Berry Computer
    (ABC), 405, 406
Athlon processors, 71
attributes, 520
audio. *See also* music
    digital rights management
        and, 390–391
    editing software, 147
    encoding software, 147
    file formats, 211
    overview of, 376–383
    players, 88, 99, 179, 212,
        379–380
    software, 379
    waveform, 376–379
    Web authoring and, 303
AutoCAD, 146, 362, 434
automatic recalculation, 140
Automated System Recovery
    disks, 206
Automatic Updates, 156, 269
availability, 669–671